Please quote number and last date stamped
if you wish to renew by post or telephone

D1334565

Mark H. McCormack's
The World of
Professional Golf 1992

Photographs by Lawrence Levy

CHAPMANS

Chapmans Publishers
141-143 Drury Lane
London WC2

First published 1992
© IMG Operations, Inc. 1992

Designed and produced by Davis Design

ISBN 1-85592-628-8

Printed and bound in the United States of America.

Contents

APPENDIXES

1. The Sony Ranking

You can pinpoint the time when the Sony Ranking really came of age. It was the week of the 1991 Masters Tournament. Because of a quirk in scheduling (the Masters was played one week later than in 1990), with the adjustment of Sony Ranking points, Nick Faldo lost his No. 1 world ranking as he was about to play for an unprecedented third consecutive Masters title. Ian Woosnam was ranked No. 1, and Jose Maria Olazabal was ranked No. 2.

In some of the press, there was a little skepticism of the Sony Ranking early in the week when the new ranking was announced. But Woosnam was at Augusta National Golf Club, agreeing that he was the No. 1 golfer in the world, and eager to achieve his one unfulfilled ambition, to win a major championship.

Then Woosnam won the Masters, Olazabal placed second and, as *Golfweek* stated in its lead paragraph, "Believe those Sony Rankings!"

Of course, the Sony Ranking was no more or less valid then than it would have been if Woosnam and Olazabal had been completely out of contention. But Woosnam's strong endorsement of the system, and the results of the Masters, focused more favorable attention on the Sony Ranking than ever before.

Woosnam remained No. 1 through 1991, while Olazabal and Faldo bounced between the No. 2 and No. 3 positions, with Faldo finally securing the No. 2 position at the year's end. Meanwhile, Seve Ballesteros made a strong charge to No. 4, and Greg Norman lost his top ranking and slipped to No. 5.

The Sony Ranking was launched during the Masters week in 1986, and so it is now five years since the Sony Corporation first announced this specially-developed computerized method of evaluating the relative performances of the world's leading players. The Sony Ranking is sanctioned by the Championship Committee of the Royal and Ancient Golf Club, and is endorsed by the major professional tours.

In the early days, some golfers and members of the press tended to dismiss the Sony Ranking. Now, while they may not always agree with the standings, they accept the Sony Ranking as the one truly international measurement of professional golf. In other words, if golfers are now not ranked as high as they think they should be, they do not just ignore the Sony Ranking, they want to know why.

Some of the most respected people in golf worldwide bring their opinions to bear on the workings of the system. The Sony Ranking Advisory Committee meets at St. Andrews each October, and its recommendations are passed on to the R&A for approval. In addition to myself, the Sony Ranking Advisory Committee consists of:

Brenda Blumberg (advisor to South African PGA), Peter Dobereiner (Association of Golf Writers), Tim Finchem (U.S. PGA Tour), Taizo Kawata (Japan Golf Association), Colin Maclaine (past captain and chairman of the Championship Committee of the R&A), Colin Phillips (Australian Golf Union), Richard Rahusen (European Golf Association), Pat Rielly (PGA of America), Ken Schofield (PGA European Tour), Frank Tatum (past president, United States Golf Association) and Peter Townsend (PGA European Tour Policy Board).

All tournaments from the world's golf tours are taken into account and points are awarded according to the quality of the players participating in each event. The number of points distributed to each golfer is dependent upon his finishing position.

The four major championships (Masters Tournament, U.S. Open, British Open and PGA Championship) and the flagship events of the major tours (The Players Championship (U.S.), Volvo PGA Championship (Europe), Japan Open and Australian Open) are weighted separately to reflect the greater prestige of the events and the strong fields participating.

The Sony Ranking is based on a three-year "rolling" average, weighted in favor of more recent results, and a divisor is used to take into account the number of tournaments played by each golfer. Points accumulated over the current 52-week period are multiplied by four, points earned over the previous 52-week period are multiplied by two, and points from the first 52-week period are simply added to the total.

Each golfer is then ranked according to his point average, which is determined by dividing his total number of points by the number of starts he has made over the three-year period. A golfer must, however, have a minimum divisor of at least 20 tournaments in each 52-week period, and a minimum divisor of at least 60 tournaments over the three-year period.

For example, if a golfer played in eight tournaments in the first 52-week period, played in 15 tournaments in the second 52-week period, and played in 32 tournaments in the most recent 52-week period, his divisor would be 72 (20 plus 20 plus 32). A golfer who played in 32 tournaments in each of the three 52-week periods would have a divisor of 96 (32 plus 32 plus 32).

Fifty points are awarded to the winner of a major championship, then 30 points for second place, 20 for third, 15 for fourth, 12 for fifth and down to at least one point for every golfer completing the final round. In The Players Championship, 40 points are awarded to the winner, then down to one point for 50th place.

In the Volvo PGA Championship, there is a minimum points level of 32 points for the winner, then down to one point for 41st place. The Australian Open and Japan Open are both assigned minimum points levels of 16 points for the winner, then down to one point for 21st place.

Minimum points levels for the winners of official tour events have been set at six points for events in Asia and South Africa, eight points in Japan, Australia and New Zealand, and 10 points in the United States and Europe. Points are reduced proportionately for events cut from 72 holes to 54 or 36 holes because of weather or other reasons.

Points to be awarded above the minimum levels for these events are determined by the strength of field. This is determined by the number and ranking position of players in the tournaments who are among the top-100 golfers on the Sony Ranking. Each player ranked in the top 100 of the Sony Ranking is assigned "rating points" ranging from 60 points for the No. 1 player, then down to two points each for those ranked 76th to 100th.

The total of the rating points is then applied to the table at the end of this chapter to adjust the Sony Ranking points to reflect the quality of the field.

As a by-product, the Sony Ranking system is able to identify the strongest tournaments in the world, as well as the best golfers. The entire list of tournaments is not publicized because the purpose of the system is to rank golfers, not tournaments, but I will share with you the list of the 20 strongest tournaments in the world last year:

1991 Sony Rating Points Leaders

Event	Points	Event	Points
1. U.S. Open	722	11. Bell's Scottish Open	371
2. British Open	719	12. Lancome Trophy	368
3. PGA Championship	714	13. Benson & Hedges Int'l.	322
4. The Players Championship	685	14. Buick Open	320
5. Masters Tournament	677	15. GA European Open	319
6. The Nestle Invitational	561	15. AT&T Pebble Beach Pro-Am	319
7. Johnnie Walker World Ch.	460	17. Infiniti Tourn. of Champions	313
8. Buick Classic	453	18. MCI Heritage Classic	309
9. Doral Ryder Open	396	19. NEC World Series of Golf	308
10. Memorial Tournament	379	20. Volvo Masters	303

The leaders of the Sony Ranking as of December 31, 1991 are outlined on the following pages, so here I will simply note some of the trends that are reflected in the standings, such as the rapid advancement of Rodger Davis, which has been largely unrecognized in the press. At the end of 1989, Davis was ranked No. 43, then he advanced in 1990 to No. 23, and last year cracked the top 10 of the Sony Ranking in the No. 10 position. At age 40, Davis could still accomplish the crowning achievement of his career and win a major championship.

Similarly, Davis Love III has made a relatively quiet progression up the world rankings, from No. 65 at the end of 1989 to No. 44 in 1990 and No. 23 in 1991. Love will be age 28 in 1992, and the time has come to expect more of him in the major events. His best last year was a tie for 11th place in the U.S. Open.

Those on a downward curve in the past two years include Curtis Strange, who was No. 4 in the world in 1989, following his second consecutive U.S. Open title. Strange fell to No. 12 at the end of 1990, and to No. 25 last year. Tom Kite, who battled Strange in the 1989 U.S. Open, was No. 6 that year, but has since drifted off to No. 8 after 1990 and No. 16 after 1991. In the three years, Mark McCumber has gone from No. 18 to No. 40 to No. 97. Ben Crenshaw's decline has been from No. 17 to No. 28 to No. 52.

Significant changes during 1991 were the strengthening of their high-ranking positions by Ballesteros (No. 7 to No. 4), Fred Couples (No. 11 to No. 6) and Bernhard Langer (No. 11 to No. 7). On the other hand, Norman fell within the top-10 players of the world from No. 1 to No. 5.

Leading a parade of golfers into the top 50 of the Sony Ranking were Steven Richardson (No. 130 to No. 32), John Daly (No. 223 to No. 47), Corey Pavin (No. 56 to No. 18), Billy Andrade (No. 136 to No. 49) and Colin Montgomerie (No. 81 to No. 36).

Others making significant advances were Andrew Magee (No. 151 to No. 62), Nolan Henke (No. 145 to No. 58), Jay Don Blake (No. 175 to No. 74), Russ Cochran (No. 170 to No. 80) and Rocco Mediate (No. 139 to No. 59). On the downside were such golfers as John Mahaffey (No. 71 to No. 142), Mike Donald (No. 83 to No. 150), and Joey Sindelar (No. 68 to No. 131).

The Sony Ranking

(As of December 31, 1991)

POS.	PLAYER, CIRCUIT	POINTS AVERAGE	POS.	PLAYER, CIRCUIT	POINTS AVERAGE
1	Ian Woosnam, Eur 1	17.11	47	John Daly, USA 27	4.71
2	Nick Faldo, Eur 2	15.34	48	Sandy Lyle, Eur 11	4.66
3	Jose Maria Olazabal, Eur 3	15.32	49	Billy Andrade, USA 28	4.63
4	Seve Ballesteros, Eur 4	13.70	50	Peter Jacobsen, USA 29	4.61
5	Greg Norman, ANZ 1	13.11	51	Wayne Grady, ANZ 7	4.57
6	Fred Couples, USA 1	12.78	52T	Ben Crenshaw, USA 30T	4.50
7	Bernhard Langer, Eur 5	12.59	52T	Scott Simpson, USA 30T	4.50
8	Payne Stewart, USA 2	11.83	54	Frank Nobilo, ANZ 8	4.49
9	Paul Azinger, USA 3	10.88	55	Sam Torrance, Eur 12	4.44
10	Rodger Davis, ANZ 2	8.90	56	Steve Jones, USA 32	4.32
11	Ian Baker-Finch, ANZ 3	8.70	57	Gil Morgan, USA 33	4.31
12	Mark McNulty, Afr 1	8.68	58	Nolan Henke, USA 34	4.30
13	Hale Irwin, USA 4	8.31	59	Rocco Mediate, USA 35	4.30
14	Mark O'Meara, USA 5	7.86	60	Mike Hulbert, USA 36	4.25
15	Lanny Wadkins, USA 6	7.61	61	Peter Senior, ANZ 9	4.21
16	Tom Kite, USA 7	7.60	62	Andrew Magee, USA 37	4.17
17	Craig Parry, ANZ 4	7.32	63	Bob Tway, USA 38	4.13
18	Corey Pavin, USA 8	7.29	64	Jeff Sluman, USA 39	4.13
19	Bruce Lietzke, USA 9	7.22	65	John Bland, Afr 3	4.09
20	Mark Calcavecchia, USA 10	7.12	66	Mark Brooks, USA 40	4.08
21	Craig Stadler, USA 11	7.04	67	Blaine McCallister, USA 41	4.04
22	Chip Beck, USA 12	6.94	68	Jim Gallagher, Jr., USA 42	4.04
23	Davis Love III, USA 13	6.89	69	Tony Johnstone, Afr 4	3.99
24	Nick Price, Afr 2	6.60	70	Eamonn Darcy, Eur 13	3.97
25	Curtis Strange, USA 14	6.39	71	Roger Mackay, ANZ 10	3.96
26	Mike Harwood, ANZ 5	6.38	72	John Huston, USA 43	3.92
27	Steve Pate, USA 15	6.34	73	Naomichi Ozaki, Jpn 2	3.88
28	Eduardo Romero, SAm 1	6.05	74	Jay Don Blake, USA 44	3.87
29	Tom Purtzer, USA 16	6.00	75	Kenny Perry, USA 45	3.86
30	Masashi Ozaki, Jpn 1	5.90	76	Tsuneyuki Nakajima, Jpn 3	3.85
31	Larry Mize, USA 17	5.84	77	Vijay Singh, Asa 1	3.84
32	Steven Richardson, Eur 6	5.77	78	Gene Sauers, USA 46	3.82
33	Tom Watson, USA 18	5.62	79	D.A. Weibring, USA 47	3.80
34	Fuzzy Zoeller, USA 19	5.53	80	Russ Cochran, USA 48	3.69
35	Larry Nelson, USA 20	5.48	81	Mike Reid, USA 49	3.61
36	Colin Montgomerie, Eur 7	5.40	82	David Frost, Afr 5	3.52
37	Mark James, Eur 8	5.28	83	Robert Gamez, USA 50	3.51
38	Raymond Floyd, USA 21	5.19	84	Brett Ogle, ANZ 11	3.44
39	Wayne Levi, USA 22	5.16	85	Jose Rivero, Eur 14	3.39
40	Jodie Mudd, USA 23	5.11	86	David Edwards, USA 51	3.35
41	Scott Hoch, USA 24	5.11	87	Peter Fowler, ANZ 12	3.30
42	David Feherty, Eur 9	5.04	88	Loren Roberts, USA 52	3.27
43	Ronan Rafferty, Eur 10	5.02	89	David Gilford, Eur 15	3.17
44	Steve Elkington, ANZ 6	4.94	90	David Peoples, USA 53	3.11
45	John Cook, USA 25	4.92	91	Brad Faxon, USA 54	3.10
46	Tim Simpson, USA 26	4.88	92	Gordon Brand, Jr., Eur 16	3.09

POS.	PLAYER, CIRCUIT	POINTS AVERAGE	POS.	PLAYER, CIRCUIT	POINTS AVERAGE
93	Hal Sutton, USA 55	3.06	147	Phil Mickelson (A), USA 81	1.70
94	Isao Aoki, Jpn 4	3.03	148	Peter Mitchell, Eur 33	1.68
95	Ted Schulz, USA 56	3.03	149	Brian Jones, ANZ 16	1.67
96	John Morse, USA 57	3.01	150	Mike Donald, USA 82	1.67
97	Mark McCumber, USA 58	3.00	151	Dave Rummells, USA 83	1.65
98	Billy Ray Brown, USA 59	2.98	152	David Ishii, USA 84	1.61
99	Paul Broadhurst, Eur 17	2.84	153	Brian Tennyson, USA 85	1.59
100	Ken Green, USA 60	2.78	154	Miguel Angel Jimenez, Eur 34	1.59
101	Fulton Allem, Afr 6	2.72	155	Saburo Fujiki, Jpn 8	1.57
102	Kenny Knox, USA 61	2.63	156	Mark Lye, USA 86	1.56
103	Miguel Angel Martin, Eur 18	2.60	157T	Wayne Riley, ANZ 17	1.56
104	Bob Lohr, USA 62	2.57	157T	Fred Funk, USA 87	1.56
105	Peter O'Malley, ANZ 13	2.56	159	Bill Glasson, USA 88	1.54
106	Per-Ulrik Johansson, Eur 19	2.56	160	Brad Bryant, USA 89	1.54
107	Bob Gilder, USA 63	2.51	161	Jesper Parnevik, Eur 35	1.53
108	Greg Turner, ANZ 14	2.51	162	Howard Clark, Eur 36	1.53
109	Michael McLean, Eur 20	2.48	163	Howard Twitty, USA 90	1.50
110	Andy Bean, USA 64	2.48	164	Tommy Armour, USA 91	1.49
111	Bill Britton, USA 65	2.45	165	Hideki Kase, Jpn 9	1.47
112	Costantino Rocca, Eur 21	2.38	166	Danny Mijovic, Can 2	1.46
113	James Spence, Eur 22	2.38	167	Hiroshi Makino, Jpn 10	1.45
114	Mats Lanner, Eur 23	2.33	168	Koichi Suzuki, Jpn 11	1.44
115	Philip Walton, Eur 24	2.28	169	Carl Mason, Eur 37	1.43
116	Billy Mayfair, USA 66	2.24	170	Doug Tewell, USA 92	1.42
117	Dan Forsman, USA 67	2.24	171	Keith Clearwater, USA 93	1.42
118	Tom Sieckmann, USA 68	2.21	172	Johan Rystrom, Eur 38	1.41
119	Vicente Fernandez, SAm 2	2.19	173	Ed Dougherty, USA 94	1.40
120	Brian Claar, USA 69	2.15	174	Jean Van de Velde, Eur 39	1.39
121	Gary Hallberg, USA 70	2.14	175	Dave Barr, Can 3	1.39
122	Jeff Hawkes, Afr 7	2.14	176	Noboru Sugai, Jpn 12	1.39
123	Jack Nicklaus, USA 71	2.13	177	Bobby Wadkins, USA 95	1.38
124	Anders Forsbrand, Eur 25	2.10	178	Richard Boxall, Eur 40	1.36
125	Rick Fehr, USA 72	2.09	179	Teruo Sugihara, Jpn 13	1.35
126	Graham Marsh, ANZ 15	2.06	180	Stephen McAllister, Eur 41	1.35
127	Donnie Hammond, USA 73	2.05	181	Mike Clayton, ANZ 18	1.34
128	Christy O'Connor, Jr., Eur 26	2.00	182	Tateo Ozaki, Jpn 14	1.33
129	Barry Lane, Eur 27	1.99	183	Lee Janzen, USA 96	1.33
130	Jim Hallet, USA 74	1.96	184	Chris Perry, USA 97	1.32
131	Joey Sindelar, USA 75	1.94	185	Nobuo Serizawa, Jpn 15	1.31
132	Chen Tze Chung, Asa 2	1.93	186	Dan Pohl, USA 98	1.28
133	Phil Blackmar, USA 76	1.92	187	Peter Teravainen, USA 99	1.28
134	Jeff Maggert, USA 77	1.90	188	Des Smyth, Eur 42	1.26
135	Ryoken Kawagishi, Jpn 5	1.90	189	Dillard Pruitt, USA 100	1.26
136	Malcolm Mackenzie, Eur 28	1.88	190	Jay Delsing, USA 101	1.25
137	Roger Chapman, Eur 29	1.88	191	Tsukasa Watanabe, Jpn 16	1.25
138	Russell Claydon, Eur 30	1.86	192	Kirk Triplett, USA 102	1.23
139	Jay Haas, USA 78	1.85	193	Gavin Levenson, Afr 8	1.22
140	Yoshinori Kaneko, Jpn 6	1.84	194	David Williams, Eur 43	1.21
141	Don Pooley, USA 79	1.83	195	Bill Sander, USA 103	1.21
142	John Mahaffey, USA 80	1.82	196	Buddy Gardner, USA 104	1.18
143	Jose Maria Canizares, Eur 31	1.81	197	Glen Day, USA 105	1.17
144	Mark Roe, Eur 32	1.76	198	Peter Lonard, ANZ 19	1.17
145	Masahiro Kuramoto, Jpn 7	1.75	199T	Peter Persons, USA 106T	1.16
146	Rick Gibson, Can 1	1.71	199T	Duffy Waldorf, USA 106T	1.16

Detailed Structure For Allocation of Sony Ranking Points

TOTAL RATING POINTS	1st	2nd	3rd	4th	5th	6th	7th	8th	9th	10th	11th	12th	13th	14th	15th	16th	17th	18th	19th
MAJOR CHAMPIONSHIPS	50	30	20	15	12	10	9	8	7	7	6	6	5	5	5	4	4	4	4
Players Championship	40	24	16	12	10	9	8	7	6	6	6	6	5	5	5	4	4	4	3
776-825	40	24	16	12	10	9	8	7	6	6	6	6	5	5	5	4	4	4	3
726-775	39	23	16	12	11	9	8	8	6	6	6	5	5	5	4	4	4	3	3
676-725	38	23	15	11	9	8	7	7	6	6	5	5	5	4	4	4	3	3	3
626-675	37	22	15	11	9	7	7	6	6	5	5	5	4	4	4	3	3	3	3
576-625	36	22	14	11	9	7	7	6	6	5	5	5	4	4	4	3	3	3	3
526-575	35	21	14	11	9	7	7	6	6	5	5	4	4	4	3	3	3	3	3
501-525	34	20	14	10	8	7	6	6	5	5	5	4	4	4	3	3	3	3	2
476-500	33	20	13	10	8	7	6	5	5	5	4	4	4	3	3	3	3	2	2
451-475 Europe PGA Champ. Minimum	32	19	13	10	8	6	6	5	5	5	4	4	4	3	3	3	3	2	2
426-450	31	19	12	9	8	6	6	5	5	5	4	3	3	3	3	3	2	2	2
401-425	30	18	12	9	7	6	5	5	4	4	4	3	3	3	3	3	2	2	2
376-400	29	17	12	9	7	6	5	5	4	4	4	3	3	3	3	2	2	2	2
351-375	28	17	11	8	7	6	5	4	4	4	3	3	3	3	2	2	2	2	2
326-350	27	16	11	8	8	6	5	5	4	4	4	3	3	3	3	2	2	2	2
301-325	26	16	10	8	6	5	5	4	4	4	3	3	3	3	2	2	2	2	2
276-300	25	15	10	8	6	6	5	4	4	4	3	3	3	3	2	2	2	2	2
251-275	24	14	10	7	6	6	5	4	4	3	3	3	3	2	2	2	2	2	2
226-250	23	14	9	7	6	5	5	4	3	3	3	3	3	2	2	2	2	2	2
201-225	22	13	9	7	5	5	4	4	3	3	3	3	3	2	2	2	2	2	2
176-200	21	13	8	6	5	4	4	3	3	3	3	2	2	2	2	2	2	2	2
151-175	20	12	8	6	5	4	3	3	3	3	3	2	2	2	2	2	2	2	1
126-150	19	11	8	5	4	3	3	3	3	2	2	2	2	2	2	1	1	1	1
116-125	18	11	7	5	4	3	3	3	2	2	2	2	2	2	1	1	1	1	1
106-115	17	10	7	5	4	3	3	3	2	2	2	2	2	1	1	1	1	1	1
96-105 Austr & Japan Opens Minimum	16	9	6	5	4	3	3	3	2	2	2	2	2	1	1	1	1	1	1
86-95	15	9	6	5	4	3	3	2	2	2	2	2	2	1	1	1	1	1	1
76-85	14	8	6	4	3	3	3	2	2	2	2	2	2	1	1	1	1	1	
66-75	13	8	5	4	3	3	2	2	2	2	2	1	1	1	1	1			
56-65	12	7	5	4	3	2	2	2	2	2	1	1	1	1	1				
46-55	11	7	4	3	3	2	2	2	2	2	1	1	1	1	1				
36-45 Eur & USA Minimum	10	6	4	3	2	2	2	2	2	1	1	1	1						
26-35	9	5	4	3	2	2	2	2	1	1	1	1							
16-25 Austr/NZ & Japan Minimum	8	5	3	2	2	2	2	2	1	1	1	1	1						
6-15	7	4	3	2	2	2	1	1	1	1	1								
5 Asia & SAT Minimum	6	4	2	2	2	1	1	1	1	1									
4	5	3	2	1	1	1	1												
3	4	2	1	1	1	1													
2	3	2	1	1	1														
0	2	1	1	1															

Pos.

RATING POINTS

Current Rank of Players	Rating Points
1st	60
2nd to 4th	3 x 45
5th to 7th	3 x 35
8th to 10th	3 x 25
11th to 15th	5 x 15
16th to 25th	10 x 10
26th to 50th	25 x 6
51st to 75th	25 x 3
76th to 100th	25 x 2
Total Available	825

51st plus all making 36-hole cut in major championships

1991 Sony Ranking Review

Major Movements Within Top 50

	Upward				Downward		
	Net Points	Position			Net Points	Position	
Name	Gained	1990	1991	Name	Lost	1990	1991
Seve Ballesteros	290	7	4	Greg Norman	443	1	5
Bernhard Langer	274	14	7	Nick Faldo	345	2	2
Ian Baker-Finch	265	36	11	Mark Calcavecchia	314	10	20
Fred Couples	224	11	6	Curtis Strange	297	12	25
Craig Parry	204	37	17	Tim Simpson	279	18	46
Davis Love III	183	44	23	Ronan Rafferty	275	19	43
Steve Pate	149	49	27	Larry Mize	250	13	31
Rodger Davis	132	23	10	Tom Kite	218	8	16
Nick Price	122	38	24	Masashi Ozaki	217	17	30
Craig Stadler	113	34	21	Jodie Mudd	193	25	40
Bruce Lietzke	100	42	19	Wayne Levi	177	20	39

Major Movements Into Top 50   Major Movements Out of Top 50

	Net Points	Position			Net Points	Position	
Name	Gained	1990	1991	Name	Lost	1990	1991
Steven Richardson	370	130	32	David Frost	304	24	82
John Daly	298	223	47	Mike Reid	180	33	81
Corey Pavin	295	56	18	Mark McCumber	172	40	97
Billy Andrade	262	136	49	Ben Crenshaw	169	28	52
Colin Montgomerie	240	81	36	Wayne Grady	154	27	51
Tom Purtzer	230	70	29	Steve Jones	144	30	56
John Cook	156	98	45	Gil Morgan	134	26	57
Steve Elkington	112	62	44	Peter Senior	43	45	61
Fuzzy Zoeller	110	64	34	Sam Torrance	+29	50	55

Other Major Movements

	Upward				Downward		
	Net Points	Position			Net Points	Position	
Name	Gained	1990	1991	Name	Lost	1990	1991
Andrew Magee	249	151	62	John Mahaffey	154	71	142
Nolan Henke	244	145	58	Mike Donald	152	83	150
Jay Don Blake	219	175	74	Joey Sindelar	142	68	131
Russ Cochran	210	170	80	Bill Glasson	129	85	159
Rocco Mediate	208	139	59	David Ishii	127	89	152
David Gilford	196	287	89	Don Pooley	120	75	141
Mike Hulbert	190	107	60	Ken Green	120	57	89
Frank Nobilo	186	101	54	Tommy Armour III	102	102	164
Per-Ulrik Johansson	164	813	106	Donnie Hammond	102	80	127
Mark Brooks	156	96	66	Richard Boxall	96	110	178
Michael McLean	140	270	109	Brian Jones	96	92	149
D.A. Weibring	139	134	79	Brian Tennyson	89	100	153
Roger Mackay	128	103	71	Howard Clark	88	99	162
Costantino Rocca	122	263	112	Des Smyth	85	105	188
Jim Gallagher, Jr.	121	74	68	Graham Marsh	85	73	126
Paul Broadhurst	120	174	99	Jose Maria Canizares	83	77	143

2. The Year In Retrospect

A six-foot putt that passed just right of the hole—Michael Bonallack, secretary of the Royal and Ancient Golf Club, called it "the greatest pressure putt in the history of golf"—made an indelible impression on the year of professional golf in 1991. By that margin, the United States won back the Ryder Cup from Europe for the first time since 1983.

Bernhard Langer missed the putt, and Hale Irwin earned the one-half point America needed for the victory. "It was a chance a golfer only gets once in a lifetime, to hole a putt for the Ryder Cup," Langer said. "I did my best, but in the end it was just not good enough. I know I will never forget it." But neither the burden nor the praise was theirs alone.

Lanny Wadkins, Raymond Floyd, Fred Couples, Paul Azinger, Chip Beck and Corey Pavin were among America's stars. Wadkins and Couples led the U.S. effort, each with 3-1-1 records, while Azinger and Beck laid the foundation for victory on the final afternoon by, respectively, defeating Jose Maria Olazabal and Ian Woosnam.

No player's reputation was enhanced more than Couples', who was left in tears after losing on the final hole to Christy O'Connor, Jr., two years ago. Nick Faldo congratulated Couples after the match by saying, "You really went ape on us, Freddy."

But Mark Calcavecchia will forever remember that he squandered a four-hole lead with four to play. He finished triple bogey, bogey, triple bogey, bogey—including one of the worst shots ever seen from a top-rank professional, when he skulled his tee shot on the par-three No. 17 into the water halfway to the hole. "It got to the point where obviously for me it was too much," Calcavecchia said. "I don't know if golf was meant to be this way, to have this much pressure. When I got done, I didn't want to be part of this competition anymore. I felt enough tension this week to last a lifetime."

Least-known fact of the Ryder Cup: Calcavecchia had a 2-1-1 record; only Wadkins and Couples were better on the American side. Calcavecchia was a top-10 money winner from 1987-90, and I fully expect that his Ryder Cup experience will only be a temporary setback.

Seve Ballesteros (4-0-1) and Olazabal (3-1-1) were Europe's leaders, but Faldo and Woosnam won just one point each, and lost both matches when they were paired on the first day. The supposedly weak lower half of the European team—including Steven Richardson, Colin Montgomerie, David Feherty and Paul Broadhurst—helped carry the Ryder Cup to the final match of Irwin versus Langer.

The score then was United States 14, Europe 13. As the holder, Europe would retain the cup with a tie if Langer won, and the Americans needed one-half point from Irwin to win. Irwin was two up after 14 holes, but lost the 15th with a bogey and the 17th with three putts from 40 feet, as Langer holed a five-footer for par. "I kept hearing that "U.S.A.! U.S.A.!," said Irwin, whose medal score for the last nine would have been 41. "I couldn't breathe. I couldn't swallow."

A wayward drive and a three-wood shot left Irwin short and right of the

18th green, 70 feet from the hole. Langer was on the right fringe in two, about 45 feet away. Irwin chipped very poorly, 30 feet short. "My disappointment with that chip shot was so great no one could imagine it," he said. Then Langer putted six feet past the hole.

"I really thought I had hit a good first putt, which almost went in, and I was surprised just how fast it went and how far it went by the hole," Langer said. "I was putting into the grain and into the wind, but for some reason it was pretty fast. Then he missed his, and I gave him a one-and-half-foot putt for his bogey.

"Now it was down to me.

"I had a six-foot putt. I looked at the putt from both sides, and I had two spike marks on the line I was going to hit it, which was on the left edge. I asked my caddie what he thought, and he agreed that left edge was probably what it would be, but he pointed out that there were two big spike marks there. I said, 'I know, but what can I do?' He said, 'You should probably hit it straight and it should finish inside left, maybe left of center, so you miss the spike marks; just hit it firmly.' I thought, maybe he's right, maybe I miss the spike marks and hit it a little harder. I hit a fairly good putt and it just turned to the right and went over the right edge."

Agony was etched in Langer's face as the result sent thousands of spectators into a prolonged cheer, chants of "U.S.A.! U.S.A.!" and flag waving. In the midst of it, Irwin hugged Langer. "There is no way I would ever, ever wish on anyone what I felt on that last hole," Irwin said. "No one will ever know the shock and exhilaration I felt when everything turned around 180 degrees over the simple matter of a six-foot putt. I feel very sorry for Bernhard Langer."

Langer later said, "At first, I was hard on myself. But then I thought, 'Well, it should have been won earlier, anyway.' It's all too late now. I know I don't need an excuse because I had come back to play myself into position to keep the Ryder Cup for Europe. It's a team game, after all. One guy shouldn't shoulder the blame."

He did not think that nerves played a part in the missed putt. "I must say I was actually more under control over those last few holes and I played much better golf than earlier in the match or even earlier in the week," Langer said. "I was probably shaking more when I started off than I was over the last few holes, for some reason. What threw me was those spike marks."

This Ryder Cup was a far different event from that the United States had last won in 1983 by an identical 14-1/2 to 13-1/2 score in Palm Beach Gardens, Florida. Americans didn't care much for the Ryder Cup then, there was no real passion among the players and there were few spectators. America had an 18-3-1 record in the Ryder Cup before the competition was expanded from Britain and Ireland to include all of Europe in 1979, and the United States won the first three matches after that. But Europe won in 1985 at The Belfry in Sutton Coldfield, England, won again for the first time on American soil in 1987 at Muirfield Village in Dublin, Ohio, and retained the cup with a tie in 1989 at The Belfry.

Meanwhile, the Sony Ranking revealed that there were no Americans among the top-five golfers in the world. Americans had won only three of the last nine Masters Tournaments and one of the last eight British Open Championships. Now there was nothing in golf that Americans wanted more than the Ryder Cup; 25,000 tickets were quickly sold out in advance, and television geared for a massive 21-1/2 hours of coverage on Pete Dye's new Ocean Course at Kiawah Island, South Carolina.

The Ryder Cup was everything it promised to be. Unfortunately, however, some of the press, players and spectators got carried away, as U.S. captain Dave Stockton said later, "I would like to get rid of this 'War by the Shore' nonsense. This is not World War III, and it does not prove that the U.S. is No. 1 or Europe is No. 1. It just showcases 24 awfully good golfers trying their damndest."

With distance lending some perspective to the view, Stockton reflected on the Ryder Cup. "I have had hardened professionals coming up to me with tears in their eyes, thanking me for getting the cup back," Stockton said. "The response to our victory was phenomenal, and it has been a glorious experience. Even if Bernhard had holed that last putt, I think all our team would have felt that they had been a part of something special that week. I do not think the American public will sleep through another Ryder Cup."

Bob Verdi put it very well in the *Chicago Tribune* on the Monday after the matches.

"By one inch America's stars of golf regained their stripes on Sunday," he wrote. "The confounded game was invented in Scotland, a British seed merchant conceived the event, a German missed the putt, so the Spaniards cried while the Yankees bathed in bubbles on the beach. Golf, which is flog spelled backwards, makes no sense and never will. But on this windy afternoon at the Ocean Course, golf made for sensational theater."

The Ryder Cup meant that this would be no ordinary year in professional golf, and what an exceptional year it was. Player of the Year? We could instead have a dozen Players of the Month, and leave it at that, but my overall choice would be Ian Woosnam followed by Fred Couples, Seve Ballesteros, Bernhard Langer and Ian Baker-Finch, in that order. Readers will be quick to note that my short list does not include the winners of two major championships or the leading money winners of the American, Australian and Japanese Tours.

It was that kind of year, one in which Greg Norman and Curtis Strange did not win a tournament, Nick Faldo had just one victory, and the ninth alternate, someone by the name of John Daly, won the PGA Championship while becoming an immediate sensation by crushing 320-yard drives. With the briefest of acknowledgements to the others—Payne Stewart for winning the U.S. Open and money-list leaders Corey Pavin in the United States, Rodger Davis in Australia and Naomichi (Joe) Ozaki in Japan—let's first consider the performances of the five most dominant players in international golf for 1991, then we will review the significant events and world tours.

IAN WOOSNAM

Event	Position
Fujitsu Mediterranean Open	1
The Nestle Invitational	T-7
USF&G Classic	1

The Players Championship	T-15
Masters Tournament	1
Benson & Hedges International	MC
Lancia-Martini Italian Open	2
Volvo PGA Championship	12
Dunhill British Masters	T-9
Murphy's Cup	T-12
U.S. Open Championship	T-55
Torras Monte Carlo Open	1
Bell's Scottish Open	10
British Open Championship	T-17
Scandinavian Masters	T-3
PGA Championship	T-48
Maruman Open	T-5
GA European Open	T-21
Lancome Trophy	T-20
Dunhill Cup (Team)	4
Toyota World Match Play Championship	T-5
World Cup (Individual)	1
PGA Grand Slam of Golf	1
Sun City Challenge	7
Johnnie Walker World Championship	T-14

Ian Woosnam had three goals for 1991, and accomplished all three in his first five tournaments. He wanted to win in America, to be No. 1 in the world on the Sony Ranking, and to win a major championship. After starting the year with a victory in the Fujitsu Mediterranean Open, Woosnam was off to America for four events, of which he won two, the USF&G Classic and Masters Tournament. He won three more events later in the year, the Torras Monte Carlo Open, World Cup (individual title) and PGA Grand Slam of Golf. He was third on the World Money List with $1,763,159.

He set his ambitions for the year in early January after a round at home with friends at the 6,200-yard Oswestry Golf Club. He shot 57, 13 under par, and he thought it should have been lower. "If I could do that, it was time to believe in myself," he said. "Before I had never been convinced of my ability. I said to myself, 'I'll come out here and show them how I can play.' I knew I could be good."

The week of the Masters, the small, stocky (5 feet, 4-1/2 inches, 162 pounds) Welshman whom everyone calls "Woosie" realized his dreams. On Monday, the Sony Ranking proclaimed Woosnam was No. 1, and Sunday evening, he was wearing the green jacket as the Masters champion.

As usual with Woosnam, it was a matter of putting. "When Woosie starts holing putts," says David Feherty, "we might as well all go home and leave him to put the lights out."

He started the Masters with an unpromising 72 then, as he is prone to do, switched putters, from a Zebra to a heavier Maxfli. He shot 66 in the second round and 67 in the third, and entered the last day leading by one stroke over Tom Watson and by two over Jose Maria Olazabal and Lanny Wadkins.

It was a typical Masters final round—with everything still to be determined as the players began the last nine holes. The crowd was pro-Watson, as one might expect, but there was an added twist when Woosnam drove into trouble left off the 13th tee, and some in the crowd cheered. Earlier, on the 10th hole, someone had reminded Woosnam that he was not playing a links course, but Augusta National. Watson could have ignored it all, but instead his reaction, true to his character, was to calm Woosnam with an anecdote about how Don January used to respond with a phrase that sounded like, "Thank you."

The few unruly spectators certainly were not doing any favor for Watson. Woosnam had the experience to play anywhere and, he noted, "I was furious, but I play better when I'm aggressive. It makes me more determined."

The Masters was decided on the 18th hole between Watson, Olazabal and Woosnam. Wadkins tied for third place, two strokes behind, and everyone remembered that he had four-putted the ninth hole in the second round, including a missed backhanded stab, yet another example of why a man of Wadkins' talent—and temperament—has won only one major championship by age 41.

Olazabal, the 25-year-old Spaniard who entered the week as No. 2 on the Sony Ranking, ahead of defending Masters champion Nick Faldo, was in contention despite a quadruple bogey Friday on the par-three sixth hole. On Sunday, Olazabal bogeyed three consecutive holes starting at No. 8 to fall four strokes off the pace, but birdied three in a row from No. 13 to briefly take the lead. At the 18th, Olazabal drove into the left-side bunker, hit his second shot into the left greenside bunker, and two-putted for bogey from 40 feet to fall one stroke behind.

Watson had pulled into a tie with Woosnam and Olazabal by scoring eagle threes on the 13th and 15th holes. In the final pairing with Woosnam, the two-time Masters champion hit off the tee into the trees right of the 18th hole. "I went with a three wood," he said. "I was trying to fade it down the right side. I did nothing but shove it, opened the face, and it went into the trees."

What Woosnam did next was a stroke of genius—or madness, depending on your point of view at the time. He took his driver on the tee and hit far, far left, on to what is the members' practice fairway. "My plan was to hit it as far as I could, take all the trouble out of play," he said. "The bunker was 260 yards, so I aimed at it. I knew I could carry it and even if I hooked it, I would be all right."

Watson's second shot was with a three iron. He had 160 yards to the front of the green, but his shot found the same bunker as Olazabal's second. "I had a bad lie and couldn't cut it," he said. "I tried to cut it around, and run it up on the green. Maybe I should have just punched out in front of the green." Watson almost holed his bunker shot on the fly, his ball went 30 feet past and he three-putted from there for a double bogey to tie for third place with Wadkins, Ben Crenshaw and Steve Pate.

While Watson struggled from rough to bunker, Woosnam was plotting to negotiate his second shot, helping the marshalls to move as many as possible of the thousands of people in his line to the hole. Those who had been seated by the green since the morning were not about to move for the ghost of Clifford Roberts, much less Ian Woosnam.

When Woosnam realized that no more could or, rather, would be done, he had the composure not to resist further, and proceeded to try to play a blind second shot over the crowd with an eight iron. He did not know, until told about two hours later while dressing for the champion's dinner, whether his second shot had stopped in the fringe or been drawn there by backspin. It had been the latter.

His first putt was from 45 feet, and Woosnam was left with an eight-footer for the title. "It was left-to-right, and I just aimed at the right lip," he said. "I've spent enough time on practice greens, so I said this was the time for me to go to work. When it was three feet away, I knew it was in." Woosnam crouched, drew his right fist and punched the air, then received a crushing hug as caddie Phil (Wobbly) Morbey lifted him off the ground.

"You dream all your life about making a putt to win the Masters," Woosnam told the press later.

At age 33, Woosnam now has 30 career victories since starting on the European Tour 13 years ago. During his first four years on the circuit, before winning his first tournament in the 1982 Swiss Open, Woosnam lived in a van, ate baked beans and slept in his rainsuit on cold nights. This year, he bought an aircraft to ease the travel burdens to and from his home in Wales.

It has been said that Woosnam has a healthy regard for money and will not be extravagant ("I remember when I didn't have any.") and that he keeps his goals big and simple ("All I want to be is the best player I can be."). His tastes are basic ("I just want to be the best and do it in my own little way. Drink a few beers and a have fun."). He is frank about his ability ("Tee to green, there is no one who can touch me... All I've got to do is keep my putter going.").

His sights are now firmly on the major championships. "Maybe not all in one year, but sooner or later," he says.

FRED COUPLES

Event	Position
Infiniti Tournament of Champions	T-3
Northern Telecom Open	T-29
Phoenix Open	MC
Bob Hope Chrysler Classic	5
Shearson Lehman Brothers Open	T-33
Nissan Los Angeles Open	T-12
Honda Classic	T-41
The Nestle Invitational	T-50
The Players Championship	T-23
Masters Tournament	T-35
MCI Heritage Classic	T-49
GTE Byron Nelson Classic	T-33
Buick Classic	T-10
U.S. Open	T-3
Family House Invitational	T-6
Federal Express St. Jude Classic	1
Centel Western Open	3
British Open	T-3
Heineken Dutch Open	T-6
Scandinavian Masters	T-6

PGA Championship	T-27
Fred Meyer Challenge (Team)	T-2
NEC World Series of Golf	T-4
Canadian Open	T-3
B.C. Open	1
Dunhill Cup (Team)	T-9
Toyota World Match Play Championship	T-5
Tour Championship	T-16
Four Tours (Team)	4
Shark Shootout (Team)	6
Visa Taiheiyo Masters	6
Sun City Challenge	T-5
Johnnie Walker World Championship	1

No one had a better record from the U.S. Open in June through the end of the year than Fred Couples, who gets the nod over Seve Ballesteros as the second-best player in international golf for 1991. In addition to starring in the Ryder Cup matches, Couples won twice on the U.S. PGA Tour—for the first time in his career—and capped the year with an impressive last day and victory in the inaugural Johnnie Walker World Championship in Jamaica.

His worldwide earnings were $1,835,721 for second place, and he rose from No. 11 to No. 6 on the Sony Ranking, calculated on a rolling three-year basis, as the top-ranking American player.

In his first 13 starts, Couples missed the cut only once, but he was not a frequent contender either, having just three top-10 finishes. In his next 19 tournaments, Couples was out of the top-six finishers just twice—tied for 27th place in the PGA Championship and for 16th place in the Tour Championship—while winning the Federal Express St. Jude Classic in Memphis and the B.C. Open in Endicott, New York.

Equally impressive was Couples' record in the major championships. His overall performance was the best among the players who completed 72 holes in all four Grand Slam events. He tied for third place in both the U.S. Open and British Open, and tied for 35th place in the Masters, along with that tie for 27th place in the PGA Championship.

The story behind Couples' second-half surge was a week in May that Couples and his wife, Deborah, spent in Kansas City with Tom and Linda Watson. They played golf, watched several baseball games and talked about sports. "Right after that I started playing really well," Couples said. "When I came back, I did some good things and it snowballed. Tom probably didn't feel he helped me, but he did."

In the process, Couples rid himself of a reputation for being lackadaisical and a poor player in the clutch. That was expressed most notably by Tom Weiskopf in a *Golf Digest* interview published in March. Weiskopf described Couples as "Great talent. No goals in life. Not one. You can see the pressure gets to him. He has great touch and power, but if he had Jack's (Nicklaus) goals..."

Among other comments, Couples responded, "I don't think Tom Weiskopf is any Jack Nicklaus, so it goes in one ear and out the other."

Some other players, including Greg Norman, defended Couples. Norman told *Sports Illustrated,* "What Weiskopf said was way out of line. Freddy does get flustered and irritated, but he doesn't show it the way we show it. So he gets this tag on him that he's lackadaisical. I'll defend Freddy to the day I die, because I've played with Freddy, I know what he's like. Freddy's got just as much fire burning inside him as anybody else."

Couples, age 32, now has seven career victories plus two in team events, the Sazale Classic, with Mike Donald, and the Shark Shootout, with Raymond Floyd.

It was the play of Couples and Floyd in the latter event that inspired captain Dave Stockton to pair them in the Ryder Cup. Couples entered the Ryder Cup with a string of 10 consecutive rounds in the 60s and on the heels of his B.C. Open victory.

The first day, Couples and Floyd won twice, defeating Bernhard Langer and Mark James in foursomes, then Nick Faldo and Ian Woosnam in fourballs. The second day, they faced Europe's top pair, Seve Ballesteros and Jose Maria Olazabal, and lost in foursomes, but Couples teamed with Payne Stewart in the fourballs to gain a half with the Spaniards. In the final-day singles, Couples defeated Sam Torrance.

Couples was second to Corey Pavin on the U.S. PGA Tour money list with $791,479, while leading the scoring statistics with a 69.59 average and, as usual, was high among the leaders in driving distance, placing third behind John Daly and Norman with a 280.7-yard average. On the strength of his PGA Tour and Ryder Cup play, Couples was chosen Player of the Year by the players on the PGA Tour and the Golf Writers Association of America.

He achieved one final accolade the week before Christmas in the Johnnie Walker World Championship. United Distillers and our International Management Group conceived this event to bring together—for one of the few times of the year—the leading players of the world.

The qualifiers were the winners of the 28 most prominent events, as selected by our International Advisory Committee. Anticipating duplicate winners, a 26-player field was planned (to be expanded to 28 players, if necessary). Because of duplicate winners and a few unavailable players, the Committee was left to choose four players to complete the field, and one of the selections was Couples.

"I hadn't qualified, and I wasn't even thinking about it, and then I got the invitation," Couples said. "Not even being in the tournament, and then winning it, it's an incredible feeling."

There was a $2,550,000 purse—the largest ever offered—including $525,000 for the champion. With an international press contingent, and television coverage being beamed to over 40 countries, probably the foremost question was how the Tryall Resort course in Jamaica would hold up against this quality of players.

Normally 6,407 yards, Tryall had played to 6,202 yards in January for an LPGA event, and the winning score was six under par. Scores of even 58 or 59 were among the early-year predictions for the Johnnie Walker World Championship.

In preparation for the event, Tryall was expanded to 6,849 yards and the rough was grown to appropriately narrow the fairways. Then came the wind, gusting over 40 miles an hour in the second and third rounds, and with 18 holes to play, Langer and Paul Azinger were tied for the lead at 214, one over par.

No event in the world had produced an over-par winner since the 1990 Volvo Masters in Europe and not since the 1981 (that's right, over 10 years ago) Byron Nelson Classic in the United States.

In the relative calm of the final round, Couples shot five-under-par 66 to win by four strokes over Langer with a nearly flawless performance. His three-under-par 281 was the only below-par total for the championship. He birdied the first two holes, then took command at the par-five No. 5, where he ripped a three-iron shot 215 yards to within three feet of the flag, and tapped in for the eagle.

"This was the best round I ever had to win," Couples said. "It got a little tense today, but I was thinking of Memphis and the B.C. Open and the Ryder Cup. I just tried to think about all the good things that have happened recently, not my screw-ups.

"The money is great, but the best thing is you look around to see who you beat and it's Azinger and Langer and Faldo and Ballesteros and Norman and Purtzer. There's only 26 guys here, but they're the best and that makes it really special."

SEVE BALLESTEROS

Event	Position
Doral Ryder Open	MC
Open de Baleares	T-33
Open Catalonia	MC
The Players Championship	T-63
Masters Tournament	T-22
Dunlop International Open	3
Chunichi Crowns	1
Peugeot Spanish Open	2
Volvo PGA Championship	1
Dunhill British Masters	1
Buick Classic	T-5
U.S. Open	MC
Torras Monte Carlo Open	T-10
Bell's Scottish Open	T-8
British Open	T-9
Scandinavian Masters	2
PGA Championship	T-23
NM English Open	T-3
GA European Open	T-3
European Masters/Swiss Open	2
Lancome Trophy	T-18
Mercedes German Masters	T-20
Toyota World Match Play Championship	1
Volvo Masters	T-4
World Cup (Individual)	T-4
Dunlop Phoenix	T-2
Johnnie Walker World Championship	T-6

Guess who's back?

That theme resounded through the world of golf in late spring as Seve Ballesteros served notice that speculation about his demise was premature, at best. Ballesteros had gone through 1990 with only one victory on the European Tour, then he missed the 36-hole cut in two of his first three events. At the time of the Masters, a tie for 22nd place there was his best finish of the year.

At age 34, after 60 victories including five major titles, it certainly appeared that Ballesteros' star was fading. Once unquestionably the best golfer in the world, the person who most inspired Europe's international success, Ballesteros was now slipping fast from even the top 10 of the Sony Ranking.

Suddenly, Ballesteros found his game, renewed confidence and hope. Starting with a two-event swing through Japan and continuing in Europe, Ballesteros was 61 under par in his next five tournaments, winning three times, losing once in a playoff and placing third in the other. In his last 22 events for the year, after that sluggish start, Ballesteros was out of the top 10 only four times. He totalled four victories, was second four times and a top-five finisher 14 times.

He led the European Tour with £545,353, finished fourth with worldwide earnings of $1,691,958, and was No. 4 on the Sony Ranking. "If the Sony Ranking was done over one year, I would be No. 1," Ballesteros said. "I am very happy to be No. 1 again in Europe, and maybe this is the best one because it proves that all the people who said I was finished were wrong. I think last year made me harder. I learned a bit more how to suffer and to be patient."

Ballesteros would look back on a 20-foot birdie putt to win the Chunichi Crowns in Japan as the stroke which sparked his revival. "It gave me confidence," he said. "I had not made a putt like that in an important situation in a long time."

It was as if Ballesteros had found the old magic. He was struggling at the time against Australia's Roger Mackay, winner of the Dunlop Open the previous week, when Ballesteros finished third. Ballesteros hit a poor tee shot on No. 18, into the trees on the left, but the ball rebounded into the rough, from where he had a seven-iron shot to the green and then the winning putt.

Perhaps no coincidence, Ballesteros had switched putters on the trip, from a Ping which he had used for 15 years, to a Maxfli model (as did Woosnam at the Masters).

Back in Europe the next week, Argentina's Eduardo Romero deprived Ballesteros of a victory in the Peugeot Spanish Open, when Romero holed a 25-foot putt on the 18th green to gain a tie, and won a marathon seven-hole playoff. Then came the Volvo PGA Championship at Wentworth and Ballesteros was the playoff winner against Colin Montgomerie with a shot to rival any in his career.

Winners usually need a bit of luck, and this time Ballesteros was fortunate on the first playoff hole when his low, hooked tee shot bounced off a golf cart, back into the light semi-rough. He had a five-iron shot into a cross wind, with 220 yards to the hole. The shot was almost perfect, stopping three feet left of the flagstick. "Given the situation," he said, "I think that is one of the best shots I ever hit."

The following week, Ballesteros won again, by three strokes in the Dunhill British Masters, and recorded his fourth victory of the year back at Wentworth in the autumn in the Toyota World Match Play Championship, where he defeated Nick Price in the final, 3 and 2. It was Ballesteros' fifth World Match Play title, equalling the record of Gary Player.

"I never really questioned if I could come back and win again," Ballesteros said. "It was a question of when. But it came a little quicker than I expected."

If Ballesteros' 1991 record was suspect in any way, it was in the major championships. In addition to his tie for 22nd in the Masters, he missed the 36-hole cut in the U.S. Open and tied for 23rd in the PGA Championship. He made his strongest challenge in the British Open. He led after the first round and was well-placed after 54 holes, two strokes off the lead. He sounded like a winner that Saturday night, saying of the four men ahead of him, "They may not be afraid of me, but they may be of the trophy.... I don't think I have to attack from here."

He did not count on Ian Baker-Finch shooting 29 for the first nine holes, and a final-round 66, and his uninspired 71 left him tied for ninth place.

BERNHARD LANGER

Event	Position
Hong Kong Open	1
Doral Ryder Open	T-18
Honda Classic	T-37
The Nestle Invitational	T-7
The Players Championship	T-6
Masters Tournament	T-32
Benson & Hedges International	1
Peugeot Spanish Open	T-4
Lancia-Martini Italian Open	WD
Volvo PGA Championship	4
U.S. Open	MC
Carrolls Irish Open	T-16
Torras Monte Carlo Open	T-35
Bell's Scottish Open	T-21
British Open	T-9
Heineken Dutch Open	T-2
PGA Championship	MC
Volvo German Open	T-22
Lancome Trophy	T-25
ANA Sapporo Open	T-7
Mercedes German Open	1
BMW International Open	T-15
Volvo Masters	3
World Cup (Individual)	2
Hassan II Trophy	T-8
Sun City Challenge	1
Johnnie Walker World Championship	2

It's probably true that Bernhard Langer struck two of the three most significant putts of 1991, the other being Ian Woosnam's eight-foot putt to win the Masters. Most important, of course, was the six-footer that Langer missed, handing the Ryder Cup to the United States. Langer's second crucial putt came exactly one week after his miss in the Ryder Cup. This time Langer made a 12-footer to win the Mercedes German Masters.

I daresay it was one of the most popular victories of the year because, as much as America wanted to win the Ryder Cup, there had been no delight in watching Langer miss that putt. There had been tremendous joy in winning the Ryder Cup, yes, but also sympathy for Langer.

As Lanny Wadkins said then, "We all feel real bad for Bernhard, because we all know him and he's a great person. But we also know if one of us had missed that putt, the European players would have been standing on top of the clubhouse spraying champagne. We've caught that act before, and we didn't want it to happen again."

The fear was expressed that the putt might continue to haunt Langer, and perhaps even ruin his career. Langer is much too strong of character for that to have happened, but nevertheless there was a sense of relief when the news came from Stuttgart the following Sunday. Perhaps the only person who didn't share it was Langer's playoff victim, Rodger Davis, but certainly he understood. (Three weeks later, it was Davis' turn. He won the Volvo Masters, after entering the last round tied with Langer.)

"After what happened at Kiawah, when I was in tears like so many other European players at the finish, I didn't know how I would react the next time I came under pressure," Langer said.

"I prayed even harder when I faced up to that putt at the last, having dropped a stroke with a four at the short 15th. I just forced myself to shut out all thoughts of what happened in America and concentrate on the line and speed, and putting a good solid stroke on the putt. This time it went straight in the hole."

Langer had battled all week with a heavy cold and throat infection. He felt that he could not withdraw from the tournament, since he was playing before the home fans in Germany in an event co-promoted with his brother, Erwin. "The people here expect me to win," Langer said. "It is very difficult. I didn't want to let them down, and I feel proud of the way I fought over the last few holes."

The year that Langer lost the Ryder Cup was soon to be the year that Langer became the first golfer ever to win over $2 million in prize money. He won $2,186,700—$1,295,000 of that coming in his last two starts, a $1,000,000 victory in the Sun City Challenge in Bophuthatswana and $295,000 for second place in the Johnnie Walker World Championship.

What made Langer's performance one of the year's best was not just the money, but four victories, three second-place finishes and a total of 15 top-10 placings in 27 events. Like Seve Ballesteros, Langer contended in just one major championship, sharing ninth place with the Spaniard in the British Open. He tied for 32nd place in the Masters, and missed the 36-hole cut in both the U.S. Open and PGA Championship.

In addition to the two late-season victories, Langer won twice in his first seven starts, taking the Hong Kong Open and Benson & Hedges International. He tied for second place in the Heineken Dutch Open, World Cup (individual) and the year-ending Johnnie Walker event. Ranked No. 7 in the world, the 34-year-old Langer now has 33 career victories.

IAN BAKER-FINCH

Event	Position
Daikyo Palm Meadows Cup	MC
Sanctuary Cove Classic	T-3
Vines Classic	T-36
Australian Masters	T-5
Nissan Los Angeles Open	T-24
Doral Ryder Open	T-23
The Nestle Invitational	T-57
USF&G Classic	T-17
The Players Championship	T-41
Masters Tournament	T-7
MCI Heritage Classic	2
BellSouth Atlanta Classic	T-11
Memorial Tournament	T-6
Southwestern Bell Colonial	T-7
Kemper Open	T-51
U.S. Open	T-44
Anheuser-Busch Classic	T-3
Family House Invitational	1
New England Classic	2
British Open	1
Canon Greater Hartford Open	T-73
PGA Championship	MC
The International	T-2
Fred Meyer Challenge (Team)	12
NEC World Series of Golf	T-16
Canadian Open	T-10
Lancome Trophy	T-2
Toyota World Match Play Championship	T-5
Independent Insurance Agent Open	MC
Tour Championship	T-10
Four Tours (Team)	2
Australian Open	T-21
Johnnie Walker Australian Classic	MC
Johnnie Walker World Championship	24

Of 1991's four major championship winners, only Ian Woosnam and Ian Baker-Finch backed up their titles with outstanding years overall, hence my choice of Baker-Finch to round out the top-five international golfers of the past 12 months.

Not only did Baker-Finch win the British Open—the most important championship a non-American, or perhaps anyone, can win—he also was second four times, third another time, and had a total of 14 top-10 placings in his 32 starts. He was fifth in worldwide earnings with $1,495,550, and improved his Sony Ranking position from No. 36 to No. 11 in the world.

The personable, 31-year-old Australian, who now makes his home in Florida as a member of the U.S. PGA Tour, took all the suspense out of the British Open with 29 on the first nine holes after entering the final round tied with Mark O'Meara, his Orlando neighbor and another of golf's truly nice people.

It was the lowest nine-hole score ever in the final round of a major event, and Baker-Finch's closing rounds of 64-66—130 equalled the British Open record set by Tom Watson in his epic duel with Jack Nicklaus in 1977 at Turnberry. Baker-Finch had the luxury of a bogey at the 18th hole for a two-stroke victory over another Aussie, Mike Harwood, while O'Meara tied for third place with Fred Couples, three strokes behind.

It was fitting that Baker-Finch's first major title be the British Open because it was in that championship in 1984 at St. Andrews that Baker-Finch first made himself known on the world stage. The leader after three rounds, Baker-Finch shot 79 on the last day to tie for ninth place. In 1990, again at St. Andrews, he joined Nick Faldo in the final pairing, but shot 73 and tied for sixth place.

Baker-Finch admitted after winning the British Open that the only time he had a negative thought was after he had taken a five-stroke lead with that 29. "I was thinking to myself that I had better not stuff it from here, because you will really cop it," he said.

It was Baker-Finch's 14th career victory, including one in America in the 1989 Southwestern Bell Colonial. He joined the American circuit that year, having proven to himself that he was ready, with 12 wins including three in 1988, when he also was third in the NEC World Series of Golf.

Starting the year with four events in Australia, where he was a top-five finisher twice, Baker-Finch played very consistently throughout, peaking around the times of the Masters and the British Open. He tied for seventh place at the Masters, three strokes behind, and was second to Davis Love III the following week at the MCI Heritage Classic.

Approaching the British Open, Baker-Finch tied for third place in the Anheuser-Busch Classic, then won the Westinghouse-Family House Invitational, a 36-hole affair at Oakmont Country Club in Pittsburgh. "That gave me confidence," he said. "It told me I was playing well enough to win and could handle the pressure. It was only two days, but there was some pressure after I led the first day, and I played well. That was good for me."

He reinforced his confidence in the New England Classic before flying out from Boston to Britain, even if the result was less than desired, a seven-hole playoff loss to surprising Bruce Fleisher, a club pro on the minor Ben Hogan Tour.

A 71-71 start to the British Open put Baker-Finch in position to threaten the leaders, then he came through in the third round with 64, one stroke off the championship record, and proceeded to wipe away the opposition on the last day. "I am sure everyone who wins a major championship thinks it is going to be the first of many," Baker-Finch told the press at Royal Birkdale, and later he expanded on his thoughts.

"Now I will be going into majors knowing I can win, rather than hoping to win, or wondering whether I can win," he said. "I'll just keep playing in all the majors and see if I can give myself another chance."

1991 World Money List

Bernhard Langer was the leading money winner in professional golf worldwide for 1991 with $2,186,700, which broke the record of $1,793,268 set by Ian Woosnam in 1987. Fred Couples was second with $1,835,721, and was followed by Woosnam with $1,763,159. Eight golfers won $1 million or more in 1991—six fewer than in 1990. The $1 million mark has now been broken 38 times, first by Greg Norman in 1986. The complete 1991 World Money List appears in the Appendixes of this annual.

The leading money winners of 1991 were:

Pos.	Name	Money	Pos.	Name	Money
1	Bernhard Langer	$2,186,700	11	Paul Azinger	952,353
2	Fred Couples	1,835,721	12	Steven Richardson	952,115
3	Ian Woosnam	1,763,159	13	Jose Maria Olazabal	951,272
4	Seve Ballesteros	1,691,598	14	Craig Stadler	930,890
5	Ian Baker-Finch	1,495,550	15	Rodger Davis	916,283
6	Corey Pavin	1,077,209	16	Roger Mackay	908,373
7	Tom Purtzer	1,050,618	17	Andrew Magee	896,257
8	Nick Faldo	1,012,673	18	John Daly	895,810
9	Payne Stewart	994,665	19	Tsuneyuki Nakajima	862,107
10	Naomichi Ozaki	958,094	20	Craig Parry	860,076

Honorable mentions for the top five in international golf for 1991 could go to Payne Stewart, the U.S. Open champion, and to Corey Pavin, who won two tournaments and led the U.S. PGA Tour money list with $979,430 ($1,077,209 worldwide for sixth place).

Stewart's year was especially remarkable when you consider that he was out of competition, wearing a neck brace, for 10 weeks because of a herniated disk.

"You can't imagine the relief," Stewart said after he came back from the layoff. "I was afraid my career was over, but in the long run, I think it helped me. I'm not as uptight; I've learned to relax more."

He tried to return for the Masters but was unable, but tied for fourth place the next week at the MCI Heritage Classic. That was one of only four top-10 finishes for Stewart, compared to Ian Baker-Finch's 14. Stewart played six events in Europe and his other two top-10 placings were there, a victory in the Heineken Dutch Open and a tie for third place in the European Open.

At age 34, ranked No. 8 in the world, Stewart now has 12 career victories. And this is the man whom the caddies once called "Avis" for his large number of second-place finishes, but inability to win. Between 1984 and 1989, he finished second 12 times and had 58 top-10 finishes, but only three victories on the PGA Tour (plus three earlier overseas). "I'm as good as I thought I was going to be," Stewart said, after the U.S. Open. "I thought I was good enough to win majors."

Indeed. Stewart now has two major titles—this and the 1989 PGA Championship. He has had a benefit in the majors that Greg Norman, for one, has found lacking: a little help from his competitors.

True, Stewart birdied four of the last five holes in the PGA Championship, but he would not have won, had Mike Reid not dropped three strokes on the 16th and 17th holes. In the U.S. Open, Scott Simpson led by two strokes with three holes to play in both the fourth round and the playoff, and finished with five bogeys and one par. The playoff scores, 75 to 77, were the highest since 1927, when Tommy Armour shot 76 to Harry Cooper's 79.

But Stewart won this U.S. Open. He held or shared the lead after every round, trailed first by Nolan Henke after two rounds, then tied by Simpson in the third and fourth rounds. While Simpson struggled to finish, Stewart saved his best golf for the last three holes, and combined that with patience and determination.

There was a long putt on the 16th green on Sunday afternoon, an eight iron that flew over a 50-foot-high ash tree and was followed by an 18-foot putt that bolted into the cup on the 16th hole of the playoff, and a five iron that never wavered from its target on the 17th hole that were four of the best. Perhaps the best of all was the six iron that Stewart played from a bunker on the 18th in the playoff, a shot that could have been ruined had he taken even a bit of sand.

Corey Pavin returned to the upper echelon of the American circuit last year for the first time since 1987, when he won twice, was 15th on the money list, and No. 5 on the Sony Ranking. Two years before that, Pavin was sixth on the money list, but his placings in the past three years were 50th, 82nd and 26th, and his victory total had been stuck on 10 worldwide since the 1988 Texas Open.

Last year, however, Pavin was Player of the Year according to the points system of the PGA of America, and advanced from No. 56 to No. 18 on the Sony Ranking.

Why the turnaround? Pavin credited his longtime teacher, Bruce Hamilton of Camarillo, California, with whom he lost touch after moving to Florida in 1987. They began working together again at the start of 1990. "I didn't have any confidence in my swing," Pavin said. "I thought I could do it on my own, and I couldn't."

In a 30-tournament schedule, including 25 official PGA Tour events, Pavin was a top-10 finisher 10 times, including six placings in the top three. He won the Bob Hope Chrysler Classic, chipping in on the first playoff hole to beat Mark O'Meara, after both had broken the 90-hole scoring record, and the BellSouth Atlanta Classic, with a par on the second playoff hole against Steve Pate.

Pavin would also list the Memorial Tournament, where he finished third, among his highlights. "The Memorial was my best tournament of the year," he said. "That's a big course where you need to make a lot of tough shots. The Hope pretty much is a putting contest, and everybody hits the greens there. At Atlanta, I played well for 62 holes, but I didn't make a birdie down the stretch. I was shocked when I won."

He later lost a playoff to Billy Ray Brown in the Canon Greater Hartford Open, and that virtually was his year. He tied for 10th in the Tour Championship, winning $54,000 to secure the money title, and went over the million-dollar mark worldwide with small earnings from two Japanese events and $58,000 for 17th place in the Johnnie Walker World Championship.

Readers may have assumed by now that I was less than enthralled by John Daly's performance in the PGA Championship, which is not true. At the time, I was as thrilled as the next fellow, but I have since adopted a wait-and-see attitude.

This is due partly to the question of whether Daly will ever again catch lightning in a bottle. He did little else in 1991, except tie for third place in the Tour Championship and for fourth place in the Honda Classic, and he missed the 36-hole cut 12 times in 35 starts worldwide.

Secondly, I want to know whether Daly has the character that we have come to expect of our golf champions. Whether Daly never wins again, or wins dozens of titles, he will be expected to follow the examples in behavior of such people as Arnold Palmer, Jack Nicklaus and Gary Player—and not what might be tolerated in professional boxing and some other sports.

Rumors of erratic behavior have circulated about Daly since the PGA Championship, right up to the year-ending Johnnie Walker World Championship, where he shot an 87 in the second round and was disqualified for signing an incorrect scorecard under suspicious circumstances.

This was finally reported during the ABC telecast of the Johnnie Walker event, and I agree with commentator Roger Twibell, that Daly needs to decide what kind of champion he is going to be in 1992.

What a waste it will be, if Daly does not measure up to what is expected of him. No one created as much excitement in golf as Daly since the whirlwind of Nancy Lopez (no one could have handled it better) and her five consecutive victories in 1978, which rated equal or better coverage than the U.S. Open that same weekend.

The week after the PGA Championship, Daly knocked George Bush off the cover of *Sports Illustrated*, a feature about the President at play.

Daly did not even know if he would play in the PGA Championship until the morning of the first round. He had driven the previous night from his home in Memphis to the Indianapolis suburb of Carmel, where the championship was to be played at Crooked Stick Golf Club. The ninth alternate, Daly got a spot in the tournament when Nick Price withdrew, staying home to await the birth of his first child.

He shot 69 in the first round on a course he had never seen, but did not attract much attention, then he took the lead on Friday morning and never relinquished it. He scored 21 birdies and one eagle in a 12-under-par 276 performance to win by three strokes over Bruce Lietzke. He led the field by as many as five strokes. "The first two or three drives he hit, I wasn't able to see," Lietzke said, "because the ball was coming off the clubhead faster than I was used to."

He has an extremely long backswing, then just crushes the ball (a record 288.9-yard average) with his high-tech equipment, a Cobra driver with a titanium shaft and Kevlar (a material used in bulletproof vests) head.

Asked by CBS to comment on Daly's swing, Nicklaus looked at a slow-motion replay and said, "Goodness gracious, what a coil, what an unleashing of power. I don't know who he reminds me of. I haven't seen anybody who can hit the ball that far."

"I watched a few of his swings Saturday," said Raymond Floyd, "and I went home with a bad back."

"I loved John Daly's attitude at the PGA," said Greg Norman. "He went out there with a flair, a flamboyant attitude, 'Let's go, let's just rip it! Wherever it lands, I'll hit it again and go.' That's what people want to see. They don't want to see this plop, plop, chip, putt stuff. They want to see a guy who hits it 300 yards.

"Hey, I even sat down to watch him when I finished playing, and I don't even watch golf on television. So you know he caught the imagination of everybody, from golfer to hacker."

There were seven two-time winners on the 1991 U.S. PGA Tour—Fred Couples, Corey Pavin, Billy Andrade, Andrew Magee, Mark Brooks, Nick Price and Tom Purtzer—and notable performances from many others, including Chip Beck, who tied the all-time scoring record with 59 at Las Vegas; amateur Phil Mickelson, who won the Northern Telecom Open in Tucson, and Craig Stadler who ended a seven-year winless streak in America (he had won overseas) with a victory in the Tour Championship to place second behind Pavin on the money list with $827,628 ($930,890 world-wide).

But neither Greg Norman nor Curtis Strange, dominant players of the 1980s, won a tournament.

Couples and Pavin aside, Andrade, Purtzer and Magee attracted the most attention among the two-time winners. Andrade won the Kemper Open and Buick Classic on consecutive weeks before the U.S. Open, underlining the potential of this 27-year-old Wake Forest product, whose best finish since joining the Tour in 1988 was a tie for second place in the 1989 Buick Open. He advanced from No. 149 to No. 49 on the Sony Ranking.

The man with perhaps the most-envied swing on the PGA Tour, Purtzer scored a pair of high-quality victories in the Southwestern Bell Colonial and NEC World Series of Golf, and also won Norman's late-season extravaganza, the Shark Shootout, with Lanny Wadkins. Purtzer entered 1991 with three career victories at age 39, and he had never finished better than 27th on the money list. Last year, he was fourth with $750,568 ($1,050,618 worldwide) and improved his world ranking 31 positions to No. 29.

Ten years Purtzer's junior, Magee was being hailed as the top American golfer under age 30, following his two triumphs. He won against a strong international field in the rain-shortened Nestle Invitational, and set a 90-hole scoring record while winning in a playoff at the Las Vegas Invitational. Magee was $486 behind Purtzer on the money list and earned $896,257 worldwide, after having one victory and $838,900 in his six previous seasons. His Sony Ranking position went from No. 151 to No. 62.

The left-handed Mickelson, the former U.S. Amateur champion who would also be low amateur in the 1991 Masters and U.S. Open, stirred golf followers everywhere with the manner of his Tucson victory. He triple-bogeyed the par-five 14th hole to fall out of the lead, then clawed his way back with two birdies on the last three holes to overtake Purtzer and Bob Tway. He will graduate from Arizona State in 1992 before joining the professional ranks.

Mickelson's triumph was sandwiched between victories by two golfers of the over-40 generation, Tom Kite in the Infiniti Tournament of Champions and Wadkins in the United Airlines Hawaiian Open. Kite then experienced his most discouraging year, placing 39th on the money list, his worst showing since he was 56th in 1973, his first year on the Tour. Wadkins had eight top-10 finishes in his first 11 events before tailing off, but that was enough to put him on the Ryder Cup team. His seven-under-par 65 in wind-whipped Hawaii, to come from six strokes behind to win by four, was one of the year's best rounds.

Paul Azinger won the AT&T Pebble Beach Pro-Am in a run-away and, despite a cancer scare, maintained his place among the world's 10 best golfers in the No. 9 position on the Sony Ranking. He was struggling with his swing in the Johnnie Walker World Championship, but nearly pulled out a victory before placing third and finishing with $952,353 in worldwide earnings.

Steve Pate, who had five top-three finishes including a tie for third at the Masters, scored a victory in the Honda Classic and placed sixth on the money list with $727,997 ($856,778 worldwide). Australia's Steve Elkington produced a three-iron shot from a divot on the 18th fairway to within 12 feet of the hole to win the prestigious Players Championship.

The leading U.S. player in the first four months, however, was Rocco Mediate, a personable 29-year-old from Greensburg in Arnold Palmer's region of Western Pennsylvania. Mediate placed in the top 10 in six of his first seven tournaments, and had a three-birdie finish while defeating Strange in a playoff at the Doral Ryder Open for his first victory. His best after that were ties for ninth in The International and the Johnnie Walker event, but he earned $751,621 worldwide and went from No. 139 to No. 59 on the Sony Ranking.

Just after the Masters, some of the highlights were victories by Davis Love III in the MCI Heritage Classic, and by Brooks at Greensboro (he would later win at Milwaukee) and Price at the GTE Byron Nelson Classic (he would later win the Canadian Open). Kenny Perry, who had never before won a tournament, shot a course-record 63, nine under par, in the second round of the Memorial, then won a playoff against two-time champion Hale Irwin.

If not for John Daly, the surprise of the summer months would have been Bruce Fleisher, a former U.S. Amateur champion and hot Tour prospect who never realized his ambitions 20 years ago. Now age 42 and a club pro, Fleisher was invited to the New England Classic, and won a seven-hole playoff over Ian Baker-Finch.

No surprise was the performance of Jose Maria Olazabal, who last year breezed through Akron to win the World Series by 12 strokes. This summer, the brilliant young Spaniard stopped by to win The International in Denver.

While the Ryder Cup dominated the autumn, the PGA Tour continued on the path to Pinehurst for the Tour Championship in November. Worthy of note were D.A. Weibring's victory at the Hardee's Classic, after Weibring had shot 75 to tie for fifth place in the Canadian Open, where he had held a three-stroke lead, and Mark O'Meara's come-from-behind win in the Walt Disney World-Oldsmobile Classic, also after a hard-luck year.

And yes, of course, Beck's 59 at the par-72, 6,914-yard Sunrise Golf Club in the Las Vegas Invitational, which matched the previous record score by Al Geiberger at Memphis in 1977. The record came in the third round of the 90-hole event, and Beck later tied for third place, two strokes behind.

Turning to the downside, this was a year described in a *Golf World* headline as "The Crash of '91" as Wayne Levi went from No. 1 to No. 87 on the money list; Norman, from No. 2 to No. 53; Jodie Mudd, from No. 5 to No. 102; Mark Calcavecchia, from No. 7 to No. 50, and Tim Simpson, from No. 8 to No. 85.

And there was Scott Verplank, of whom so much was expected after he won on the PGA Tour as an amateur in 1985. Verplank won $3,195 in his last event to avoid going zero-for-1991. He had surgery on an injured right arm, and did not try to re-qualify for the Tour.

Most of the attention, however, was focused on Strange and Norman. The press was inquisitive, but supportive of Strange, while Norman was criticized severely.

Strange has not won since taking his second consecutive U.S. Open title in 1989. He was 53rd on the money list in 1990 and 48th last year, after having won the money title three times in the previous five years. In his first five starts, Strange had a tie for second at Phoenix and the playoff loss at Doral, but his best after that was a tie for sixth place in The Players Championship. He had no other top-10 finishes.

His problem was a mysterious, energy-sapping ailment that sometimes left him almost dizzy. Even the Mayo Clinic could find nothing wrong with him. "It's been a frustrating thing for me," Strange said. "I can do most anything I want to do except play golf, because of the hand-eye coordination involved. I didn't know this would take three months to get over. It comes and goes. I'm still not feeling too great.

"At this point, I'm not as worried about my golf game as I am concerned about getting healthy."

Norman has been a larger-than-life character since he emerged in the 1980s, which has helped make him extremely popular and a very wealthy man. After a while, however, the jealousy of some players became evident, and the press began to view him more critically.

While Norman was totalling 61 career victories, a theme frequently heard was that, at age 36, he had won only one major championship, the 1986 British Open. In other words, you are no Jack Nicklaus or Tom Watson, they were saying. Maybe not, but Norman's play was at a significant plateau above anyone else in the world until last year, when he simply played as everyone else plays most of the time.

His record for 1990 was, at worst, typical of Norman through the better part of his career. He entered 23 tournaments, won three, was in the top five 11 times and in the top 10 four other times. He was a title contender more often than not and rarely, once or twice a year, would miss 36-hole cuts. Others—even the highest-ranking players in the world—could not match that standard, and if their games fell off even for months, it was hardly noticed or reported in the press.

Was Norman's record so terrible in 1991? He played 25 events, and 11 times he was in the top-10 finishers, including second-place finishes in the Daikyo Palm Meadows Cup, Australian Masters and Centel Western Open.

However, for the first time in his career, Norman went an entire year without a victory—and he should have won twice. He struggled over the last nine holes of the Australian Masters, and lost in the Centel Western Open, after holding a five-stroke lead with nine holes to play and bogeying four of the last six holes.

As much as anything, after driving himself to be the best golfer in the world, Norman found in 1991 that he needed to get away from the game, which indeed he did after missing the 36-hole cut at the Masters, although he never fully got back into the groove last year. He went from No. 1 to No. 5 on the world rankings.

While in Australia in December for the Johnnie Walker Classic, Norman received some unexpected support from a former PGA Tour player, Mac O'Grady, who has a forthcoming book in which he is rumored to criticize some of the game's biggest names. The comments he had about Norman were controversial, if only because he was supportive.

In an interview with the *Melbourne Age*, O'Grady said, "He (Norman) makes the wheels of golf turn—forwards, not backwards. Each kid age eight to 80 who sashays down the fairways with him will learn from watching him. Not only about golf, but about the human spirit. If people have any kind of real compassion, sensitivity, feel for the spirit of the game, for life, for Australia, they should praise him for his achievements."

O'Grady said Norman has all the ingredients for success except one: Lady Luck in the major championships. "He has been assassinated by her," O'Grady said. "Maybe that's his destiny, his fate, his karma. Whatever it is, I believe he has handled the loss of these major championships with the nobility of a saint."

"I read the article four times," Norman said. "I was touched. No one has ever done that for me before. I'm looking forward to seeing him to thank him in person."

Norman believes his problems in 1991 were mostly on the greens, that his putting left a lot to be desired. "When I was the best player in the world in 1986," he said, "I never missed from six feet in. I was that confident, no matter how much pressure I had on myself." He has switched back to a blade putter, like the one he used that year.

In last year's annual, the first five pages of this chapter were devoted to what had become known simply as "Shoal Creek," or the integration of private golf clubs resulting from the protests that led Shoal Creek Country Club in Alabama to admit its first black member before the 1990 PGA Championship was played there. It was the most publicized off-course event in golf's history.

All the major golf organizations in America drafted new policies that required the clubs that hosted their tournaments to move towards integration. Eleven clubs out of 123 dropped out as hosts of tournaments, and in 1991 there were only about 10 clubs that either had no minority members or refused to comment on the subject. The total included 55 tournament hosts that were either public or resort courses.

David Fay, executive director of the United States Golf Association, told *The New York Times*, "I think that on the balance the golf world has surprised me with how aggressively they have gone after change since Shoal Creek. Some might say we are not doing it quick enough, but I think there is proof across the board that important changes are continuing to be made." This included the election of the first black member to the USGA's executive committee.

However, critics continued to charge that the changes were made only for financial expediency, and that little had been done to integrate the nearly 6,000 private clubs that do not host tournaments. "There has been a beginning, but I think it has all been token," said the Rev. Joseph Lowery, president of the Southern Christian Leadership Conference, which had brought national attention to the issue by threatening to picket in 1990 at Shoal Creek.

One issue that the USGA did not have to deal with in 1991 was that of U-grooved irons, following its settlement in January of 1990 with Karsten Manufacturing Corporation, maker of the Ping Eye-2 irons. Two years later, as the U.S. PGA Tour continued that legal battle, USGA officials (and particularly the organization's former president, William C. Battle) appeared all the wiser for what had been a controversial decision to settle.

Karsten has a $100 million lawsuit against the PGA Tour, which may go to trial late in 1992. Karsten claims that the Tournament Policy Board deliberately amended its by-laws in order to ban square-grooved clubs, and has obtained a temporary restraining order to prevent the ban. The Tour and three of its members have filed a counterclaim alleging that Karsten "knowingly and intentionally" manufactured irons that did not conform to USGA rules and, therefore, did not conform to the Tour's regulations.

The Tour and the PGA of America were in the midst of making a new agreement. Among the changes were reported to be the PGA giving 20 percent of future Ryder Cup television income to the Tour's Players Retirement Fund; a phasing out of the PGA/PGA Tour Properties, Inc., marketing venture; entry by the PGA into the endorsement of softgoods; the Tour taking full ownership of the World Series of Golf; the PGA assuming the right to stage such competitions as the Grand Slam of Golf, and a reduction of PGA representatives from three to one on the Tour's Tournament Policy Board.

Meanwhile, the Tour was concerned when the Internal Revenue Service ruled that the Cotton Bowl college football game must pay 34 percent tax on fees from its title sponsor, Mobil, because the fees were a form of paid advertising, not a charitable contribution. "We're monitoring the situation," said Ed Moorhouse, the Tour counsel. "If the way it has gone in Dallas is any precedent, professional golf could face a serious situation."

In the time of a recession, some tournaments were already facing financial problems. The Boston-area event was played in 1991 without a sponsor, and several tournaments were scrambling to find sponsors for 1992.

The Federal Trade Commission launched an investigation into the PGA Tour for potential anti-trust violations, restraint-of-trade and other unfair competitive practices. The FTC is interested in the distribution of Tour purses, and rules regarding appearance fees, eligibility of non-Tour members, conflicting events and television releases. In a letter to the players, Commissioner Deane Beman stated his confidence that the regulations were appropriate, and encouraged the players to cooperate in the investigation.

Finally, the Tour's rules officials formed a union to try and negotiate better wage and compensation packages.

Instant television replay had a quick—and deserving—death on the PGA Tour. It began when Paul Azinger was disqualified from the Doral Ryder Open. The next day, a viewer alerted officials that Azinger had unwittingly kicked away some pebbles in a water hazard to improve his stance. Something similar had happened in 1987, when Craig Stadler was disqualified for "building a stance" when he knelt on a towel to protect his pants while hitting a ball from under a tree.

The Tour decided to have an official watch the telecasts, so that penalties for rules infractions could be applied before players signed their scorecards, thus preventing disqualifications for players signing for scores lower than they actually shot.

At the GTE Byron Nelson Classic, Tom Kite hit a shot that went into a lateral water hazard. Kite took a drop where he and Phil Blackmar, with whom he was playing, believed the ball had crossed land into the hazard. An official watching television overruled them, said that Kite's ball had never crossed land and, therefore, Kite should hit again from the tee.

Soon after that, the Tournament Policy Board voted unanimously to discontinue the monitoring of television broadcasts. "In the final analysis, players have traditionally been solely responsible for their actions and their scores," Beman said. "They are willing to accept that. That is very consistent with the spirit in which the game has always been played."

The 1991 European Tour featured seven of the top-12 golfers in the world, according to the Sony Ranking—Ian Woosnam, Nick Faldo, Jose Maria Olazabal, Seve Ballesteros, Bernhard Langer, Rodger Davis and Mark McNulty. Furthermore, the circuit could claim bragging rights to Craig Parry, Mike Harwood, Eduardo Romero, Steven Richardson, Colin Montgomerie, Mark James, David Feherty, Ronan Rafferty and Sandy Lyle. All were among the Sony Ranking's top-50 players.

It mattered little—except when it came to picking a Ryder Cup team—that Davis, Parry and Harwood were from Australia; McNulty, from Zimbabwe, or Romero, from Argentina. These were regular players on the European Tour, a circuit which has never been bound by the geography of Europe.

Ballesteros led the money list with £545,353, and Langer was third with £372,703. Richardson and Montgomerie, both reaching to achieve stardom, were second and fourth, respectively, with £393,155 and £343,575. Most of the familiar names filled the top portion of the list, in contrast to the flux of the American money standings.

Along with the money title, Ballesteros took the honor with the most European Tour victories, three, while two-event winners were Woosnam, Langer, Olazabal, Richardson, Parry and Romero.

There was no "crash" on the European Tour. The closest to it was the play of Faldo, who still maintained the No. 2 position on the Sony Ranking. He was 10th on the money list with £245,892 ($1,012,673 worldwide), and his only victory was the Carrolls Irish Open, the 26th of his career at age 34.

Faldo finished in the top 10 in half of his 22 starts—but none of those finishes were in the major championships. Yet, even in an "off" year, Faldo was consistent. He tied for 12th in the Masters, for 16th in the U.S. Open, for 17th in the British Open and for 16th in the PGA Championship.

Olazabal added three victories to his total, including The International in America, making it 15 triumphs at the age of 25. He won the Open Catalonia and Epson Grand Prix in Europe, and had 12 top-10 finishes in 26 events, including second place at the Masters. He won $951,272 worldwide, and kept third place on the Sony Ranking.

Richardson and Montgomerie made the most progress. In his second year on the Tour, Richardson scored his first victories in the Girona Open and Portuguese Open, both in the first five weeks, and sprinkled 11 top-10 finishes over 26 European starts. Venturing on the American circuit for the first time, he tied for fifth place in the PGA Championship. His Sony Ranking soared 98 positions to No. 32, and he won $952,115 worldwide.

Winner only of the 1989 Portuguese Open, Montgomerie was a top-10 money winner for the first time in his five years, and won the Scandinavian Masters. He lost a playoff when Ballesteros hit that brilliant approach shot in the Volvo PGA Championship, and also was second to Faldo in the Carrolls Irish Open. In 27 European starts, Montgomerie placed 10 times in the top 10, won $827,938 worldwide, and improved 45 positions to No. 36 in the world rankings.

Parry won the Lancia Martini Italian Open and Bell's Scottish Open, while Romero was champion of the Peugeot Spanish and French Opens. Other victories of particular note included Davis' title in the Volvo Masters, to go along with his two Australian triumphs, and Lyle's comeback in the BMW International.

Lyle had not won since 1988, when he took the Masters and four other titles. "After all the hard work I've put into my game over the last two or three years and the frustrations of things not working out," Lyle said, "this is icing on the cake."

In international team events other than the Ryder Cup, Sweden was the big winner, taking the Dunhill Cup at St. Andrews and later, the World Cup in Rome. Sweden's Dunhill Cup team consisted of Per-Ulrik Johansson, Anders Forsbrand and Mats Lanner. Johansson and Forsbrand went on to win the World Cup.

The Dunhill Cup marked the return of South Africa, captained by Gary Player, to international golf competition after having been banned for 11 years before the lifting of South Africa's apartheid laws. "This has been a very exciting week," Player said. "It feels good to know we're back in the world arena of sports. I think this will be a great boost for other sports in the country."

The inspired South African team gained the final against an equally-motivated Swedish trio, two of whom had already recorded 1991 European Tour victories, Johansson in the Belgian Open and Forsbrand in the Volvo Open di Firenze. The outcome was decided in a playoff between Player and Lanner, who holed an eight-foot birdie putt to win.

"This is by far the greatest thing that has happened to Swedish golf," Lanner said.

"This is just as big as the Davis Cup (in tennis)," Forsbrand said. "Sweden has won that a couple of times, and I hope we will be credited just as much."

The African Tours—Safari Tour in the black nations and Sunshine Tour in South Africa—have traditionally been off-season haunts of the players, especially those in the lower echelon. This trend should only grow stronger, now that South Africa has been re-admitted to the international community.

Last year's Million Dollar Challenge in Sun City, Bophuthatswana, and the Hassan II Trophy in Morocco both attracted outstanding fields including such players as Bernhard Langer, Nick Faldo, Payne Stewart and John Daly. Langer dominated the Sun City event, with its $1 million first prize, winning by eight strokes over Mark McNulty, while Fiji's Vijay Singh defeated Stewart in a playoff at the Hassan II Trophy, which was being played for the first time in six years.

South Africa's Fulton Allem won the early-year ICL International and got another victory in America in November at Houston in the Independent Insurance Agent Open. But the dominant players in South Africa did not win elsewhere. John Bland had three victories, and Wayne Westner, two.

McNulty, of Zimbabwe, remained Africa's top golfer in international play, although he slipped from No. 9 to No. 12 on the Sony Ranking in a year in which he won only the Volvo German Open. Nick Price of Zimbabwe, advancing from No. 38 to No. 24 on the Sony Ranking, won twice in America and lost in the final of the World Match Play.

The Australians have grown accustomed to outstanding years worldwide, and this was yet another one, as evidenced by the seven Aussies—plus New Zealander Frank Nobilo—in the Johnnie Walker World Championship. Ian Baker-Finch won the British Open just ahead of Mike Harwood; Craig Parry won twice in Europe, while Harwood and Rodger Davis each won once; Steve Elkington won The Players Championship in the United States and, as you will read shortly, Roger Mackay was a force in Japan. And, of course, there was Greg Norman.

In the early-year events, Davis won the SXL Sanctuary Cove Classic and AMP New Zealand Open, then added Europe's season-ending Volvo Masters to his victory total, which is now 19. The 40-year-old Davis moved from No. 23 to No. 10 on the Sony Ranking while winning $916,283 worldwide.

Parry advanced 20 places to No. 17 on the Sony Ranking and had world-wide earnings of $860,076. Age 25, Parry has seven career victories.

Peter Senior did not win outside Australia, falling from No. 45 to No. 61 on the world rankings, but Senior did win two significant events at home, the Pyramid Australian Masters and Johnnie Walker Australian Classic. Wayne Riley was the surprise winner of the Australian Open, finishing ahead of an even bigger surprise, amateur Robert Allenby, who has the promise to join the other top Aussies in overseas play.

Celebrity came to last year's Asian Tour in the person of Bernhard Langer, who won the Hong Kong Open. He shot eight-under-par 63 for a seven-stroke victory, his first in a tremendous year. At the time it was more of a tonic, after Langer had double-bogeyed the last hole in a storm in Singapore in a Dunhill Cup qualifying tournament, preventing Germany from advancing to the 16-team championship at St. Andrews.

There were two primary themes in the other nine Asian tournaments, victories by young North Americans and favorite sons. First, Dennis Paulson won the San Miguel Philippine Open, Jack Kay, Jr., won the Epson Singapore Open, and Rick Gibson won the Benson & Hedges Malaysian Open. Gibson finished as the Asian Tour's leading money winner with $90,650.

The circuit then went to the Indonesian Open, won by Taiwan's Chen Liang Hsi, who was runner-up to Gibson in Malaysia, for his first victory in four years.

Three of the next four tournaments were won by favorite sons, with only American veteran John Jacobs interrupting the string with his victory in the Sanyang Republic of China Open. Ali Sher, age 26, became the first Indian to win an international golf event when he captured the Wills Indian Open; Suthep Meesamasdi became the first Thai citizen to win the Thai International Thailand Open, and Choi Sang Ho completed a lifelong dream at age 36 when he won the Maekyung Korea Open.

Japan's Dunlop Open, the sixth tournament on the domestic circuit, was also the final event of the Asian Tour. Australia's Roger Mackay, who had pulled out of the previous week's Bridgestone Open because of a sore back, persevered to win by two strokes over Teruo Sugihara and by three over Seve Ballesteros, who was playing the first of two events in Japan.

The following week, Ballesteros holed a 20-foot birdie on the final hole—the putt which he later said helped to restore his confidence—to defeat Mackay for the Chunichi Crowns title.

Mackay was in the running all the way for the Japan Tour's money title, but the race was slow in developing. It took 20 weeks before the eventual winner, Naomichi (Joe) Ozaki, won his first tournament. Ozaki was a contender in the second week, but double-bogeyed the last hole to allow Yutaka Hagawa to win, the first of two in a row. Ozaki finally won at the Nikkei Cup, in a playoff over Eiichi Itai. By that time, Mackay had a second victory in the Mizuno Open.

Their duel became intense in the last five weeks, when most of Japan's big-money events are traditionally held, attracting a number of overseas stars. The first of these was the Visa Taiheiyo Club Masters, and Jose Maria Olazabal was there, aiming for his third consecutive Taiheiyo title. He would finish fourth, five strokes behind.

Mackay registered the Taiheiyo as his third title of the year and became the first overseas player to win more than 100 million yen. He shot 68 in the final round to win by two strokes over Yoshinori Kaneko and by three over Tsuneyuki (Tommy) Nakajima, the 54-hole leader, who made this sad comment, "My driving was poor, I sat on my glasses last night, and I didn't invite my wife to the tournament."

The victory lifted Mackay to the top of the money list and qualified him for the Johnnie Walker World Championship in Jamaica, but he declined the invitation to continue competing for the money title and to rest for the 1992 season.

The next week, Larry Nelson won the Dunlop Phoenix event, with a two-putt par on the fourth extra hole against Ballesteros, Isao Aoki and Jay Don Blake.

Ozaki then won the next two tournaments—Casio World Open and Japan Series—to raise his victory total to four and overtake Mackay in the money standings. He was only the second Japanese winner of the Casio event in 11 years, following Aoki in 1989. He shot 64 in the third round and held on, easing to a two-stroke win over Hajime Meshiai after Nelson double-bogeyed the 17th hole to fall three strokes behind.

On the day before the Japan Series, Ozaki's father, Minora, died at age 76. The other brothers in Japan's most prominent golfing family—Masashi (Jumbo) and Tateo (Jet)—withdrew from the tournament, which featured only the top-20 money leaders. Joe remained, and shot rounds of 71-65-66-

66—268, winning by eight strokes over Nakajima. "Winning is the best dedication to my father," he said.

The final event, the Daikyo Open, was won by Yutaka Makino, and did not change the money standings. Joe Ozaki finished with ¥119,507,474 ($958,094 worldwide), then came Mackay with ¥113,137,135 ($908,373 worldwide). Nakajima was third with ¥111,639,213 ($862,107 worldwide) and Jumbo Ozaki took fourth with ¥99,060,539 ($749,547 worldwide).

Aside from Joe Ozaki and Mackay, there were six two-event winners in Japan: Jumbo Ozaki, Hagawa, Itai, Nakajima, Saburo Fujiki and Harumitsu Hamano. Nakajima won the Japan Open, Jumbo Ozaki won the Japan PGA Championship, and Aoki scored his only victory in the Bridgestone Open.

Other winners of note were young star Ryoken Kawagishi in the Pocari Sweat Open, Raymond Floyd in the Daiwa KBC Augusta Open, and Asian Tour leader Rick Gibson in the Sapporo Kokusai Open, for his second victory of the year.

It is a sad commentary, but there is virtually nothing to report about the Japanese in tournaments outside their country. Sad, because it seems the Japanese are reluctant to compete on the worldwide stage. What other conclusion could one draw when the British Open, the most international of all tournaments, had only Kawagishi and Masahiro Kuramoto in the starting field, and Aoki was there only as a television commentator?

It was such a short time ago that Aoki was winning in Europe and America, and challenging Jack Nicklaus in the U.S. Open, that Jumbo Ozaki was threatening Curtis Strange in the U.S. Open, and that Nakajima was on Greg Norman's trail in the British Open. And many more Japanese players were out there competing.

No wonder that there now are just four Japanese players among the top 100 on the Sony Ranking, and only one (No. 30 Jumbo Ozaki) in the top 50. There is no reason why the Japanese cannot be as successful as, for example, the Australians. But, like the Australians, they must be willing to play worldwide, and in large numbers.

On to the Senior PGA Tour, where sometimes the question arises of what those players would be doing if the over-50 circuit did not exist. This was frequently asked when the Tour was just getting underway in the early 1980s, before it became an accepted, or expected, extension of their careers.

Then last year, Mike Hill reminded everyone of their good fortune. About the time Seniors golf was taking off 11 years ago, Hill quit the regular PGA Tour, totally frustrated after a 13-year career that had yielded three victories. He took up farming, labored on a nine-hole golf course and even chopped wood for $35 a load. "We had some really tough times," he said.

Finally, in January of 1989, Hill could join his more successful, older brother Dave on the Senior Tour.

"Now, when I get down," said the 52-year-old Hill, "I say to myself, 'Hey, Bud, you've made more money in the last three years than you made in your whole life, than your father made in his whole life, and if it wasn't for the Senior Tour, you would be back out there.'"

Hill, who had career earnings of $573,724 on the regular PGA Tour, earned $1,307,782 in his first two years of Senior golf while winning five tournaments. Then, in 1991, Hill had a season beyond his dreams. He had five victories, plus the unofficial Legends of Golf, and won $1,065,657.

He was the first Senior PGA Tour money leader who had not also been a big winner on the regular Tour.

In addition to the five victories—Doug Sanders Kingwood Celebrity Classic, Ameritech Open, GTE Northwest Classic, Nationwide Championship and New York Life Champions—Hill finished second or third in eight other events and was among the top-10 finishers in 21 of his 32 starts.

George Archer, also age 52, who won the Masters and 11 other tournaments on the regular Tour, was just a step behind Hill with earnings of $963,453. Archer, who now has eight Senior titles, did not record his first 1991 victory until August in the Northville Long Island Classic.

He won the GTE North Classic at the first of September, added the Raley's Senior Gold Rush in October, and did not place outside the top-four finishers in his last nine starts. He led the money list entering the season-ending New York Life Champions, and tied for fourth place while Hill won to secure the money title.

Senior PGA Tour rookie Jim Colbert, who reached age 50 in March, also won three tournaments—the rich Vantage Championship plus the Southwest Bell Classic and First Development Kaanapali Classic—and was third on the money list with $880,749. This was more than half as much as Colbert earned in 22 years on the regular Tour, where he had eight victories.

While those players finished with late rushes, Chi Chi Rodriguez won four titles by the middle of May, but nothing else, and placed fourth on the money list with $794,013. Lee Trevino, a million-dollar winner in his rookie year of 1990, had to settle for three victories (plus the Legends of Golf with Hill) and earnings of $723,163.

Jack Nicklaus again played a very limited and highly successful Senior schedule. He entered five tournaments and won three, two of them major titles, the U.S. Senior Open and PGA Seniors Championship, and collected $343,734 to be 17th on the money list.

Club pro Jim Albus provided the surprise of the year by winning a major title, the Senior Players Championship.

After floundering for a year under Bill Blue, the LPGA Tour appeared to be on a steady course in 1991 with new commissioner Charles Mechem at the helm. The 1992 schedule will have 40 events, an increase of three, including the return of the LPGA Skins Game. By December, 22 tournaments had announced increases in prize money.

"We are absolutely delighted with the schedule," said Mechem, the former chairman of Taft Broadcasting Co. "The response we have received from our sponsors further reinforces that the LPGA Tour has the opportunity to make the 1990s a milestone decade for women's professional golf."

It was an outstanding year for the LPGA in most, if not all, respects, led by Pat Bradley and Meg Mallon. Bradley won four tournaments to reach the 30-victory plateau that put her in the LPGA Hall of Fame, while Mallon emerged as the Tour's newest star in her fifth season—never having won a tournament before—with four victories, including major titles in the Mazda LPGA Championship and U.S. Women's Open.

Furthermore, Bradley, Mallon and such players as Beth Daniel, Patty Sheehan, Betsy King, Dottie Mochrie, Deb Richard, Jane Geddes and Amy Alcott created a "power elite," as *The New York Times* described it, along with Nancy Lopez, who had one victory before taking maternity leave.

Richard won three times, and Geddes, Daniel and King had two victories each. Alcott won a major title, the Nabisco Dinah Shore, for her 29th career victory, one shy of Hall-of-Fame status.

Bradley, age 40, dominated nearly all the LPGA's statistical categories. She won $763,118, while Mallon was second with $633,802, and her 70.66 scoring average was .28 better than that of Daniel, the runner-up. In 26 tournaments, she was a top-10 finisher 21 times, including 16 of her last 17 starts.

She birdied three of the last five holes to win the Centel Classic, and won the Rail Charity Classic with a 54-hole scoring record of 19-under-par 197. Then came the victories that put her in the Hall of Fame, back-to-back titles in the Safeco Classic and MBS Classic. It was the first time in her career that she had won two consecutive tournaments.

In the Safeco Classic, Bradley birdied the final hole to force a playoff against Rosie Jones, then sank an 18-foot birdie putt to win on the second extra hole. With many of the other top players waiting at the 18th green to congratulate her, Bradley came through in the MBS Classic by one stroke over Michelle Estill.

Mallon, age 28, scored her first career victory in the second event of the year, the Oldsmobile Classic, then won both the Mazda LPGA Championship and U.S. Women's Open in mid-summer in a three-week period. Both times, Bradley was the runner-up, although sharing second place with Ayako Okamoto in the LPGA. Mallon's fourth win came in Australia in the late-season Daikyo World Championship.

The U.S. Women's Open was the most talked-about event of the year, played in searing heat at the fabled Colonial Country Club in Fort Worth, Texas. As John Garrity wrote in *Sports Illustrated*, "This Open was what an Open is supposed to be: a tense, harrowing four-day test of skill, nerve and resourcefulness."

"I just hung in there," Mallon said. "No one was taking off with it." She trailed Bradley and Joan Pitcock by two strokes after three rounds, and took the lead for the first time with an 18-foot birdie putt on the 14th hole. She sank a 20-footer for birdie on the next hole, to go one under par for the championship and two strokes ahead of Bradley and Alcott. She won by those two strokes and, at one-under-par 283, was the only person below par.

Before turning to the 1991 season in detail, we recall the passing of ... Joe Dey, 83, former executive director of the United States Golf Association and commissioner of the PGA Tour, member of the World Golf Hall of Fame, past captain of the Royal and Ancient Golf Club ... P.J. Boatwright, 63, executive director of rules and competitions for the USGA ... Clyde Mangum, 67, former deputy commissioner of the PGA Tour ... Danny Thomas, 79, television actor and comedian, honorary chairman of the PGA Tour's Memphis event in fund-raising for the St. Jude Children's Research Hospital ... Bill Davis, 68, founder and editor-in-chief emeritus of *Golf Digest* ... George Lanning, 58, Senior PGA Tour player ... Johnny Revolta, 79, winner of 18 tournaments including the 1935 PGA Championship ... Joe Turnesa, 90, member of the first two U.S. Ryder Cup teams.

3. Masters Tournament

What is it about Augusta National that by 1991 had become so inviting to overseas golfers? Something must have grown so attractive that they had an advantage, because with Ian Woosnam's victory, non-Americans had won six of the nine Masters Tournaments since Craig Stadler, in 1982. If you want to go back further, they had won seven of the 12 since Fuzzy Zoeller won in 1979.

As he approached the 1991 Masters, Woosnam had been among the leading players on the European Tour and indeed had been pushing both Greg Norman and Nick Faldo in the Sony Ranking. When the tournament ended, there were no lingering doubts that he belonged among the game's elite, not only because he had won, but because he had stood up to intense challenge from the greatest players not only of his day but of days past. Woosnam won by playing his best when it mattered most, while others failed in the tensest moments. He won by making a par four on the 72nd hole with an enormous drive that carried the fairway bunkers bordering the left side of the wide fairway, then holing a 10-foot putt for his four while Tom Watson drove into the trees along the right, and was left with no shot to the green and double-bogeyed.

Woosnam won with a score of 277, 11 strokes under Augusta National's par, one stroke better than the Spaniard Jose Maria Olazabal, and two better than Watson, Ben Crenshaw, Steve Pate, and Lanny Wadkins. It was the third tournament he had won this year; he would win one more, taking the Monte Carlo Open, in July. He threatened in only one other, placing third in the Scandinavian Masters the first week in August. Strangely enough, Woosnam played dismally in his other two appearances in the United States, other than the Ryder Cup Match, in late September, placing 55th in the U.S. Open, in June, and 48th in the PGA Championship, in August. He did climb to a tie for 17th place in the British Open, in July, but his game seemed to lose its crispness. In two matches in the Ryder Cup, he and Faldo, a formidable combination the last three meetings, didn't win a point, and Woosnam lost his singles match to Chip Beck (he did, however, team with Paul Broadhurst and beat Hale Irwin and Paul Azinger in a four-ball match).

The proposition that European golfers were indeed somehow superior to Americans simmered throughout the year. The premise was based primarily on developments in the Ryder Cup, the British Open, and the Masters within the previous decade. Except for 1989, when no European golfer was involved in the final stages, no American had won the British Open since Watson, in 1983, Europe had won both the 1985 and 1987 Ryder Cup Matches (the 1989 Match was halved), and, as I've said, Europeans had won six of the previous nine Masters; Larry Mize had been the last American winner, in 1987, and even then he had to beat Ballesteros and Norman in a playoff. Since then it had been won by Sandy Lyle, in 1988, and Faldo in both 1989 and 1990.

Faldo, and a somewhat gloating British press corps, had reveled in this apparent European dominance, even though no such trend was noticeable in either the U.S. Open or the PGA, and Faldo had stirred passions further when, on the eve of the Masters, he questioned the resolve of American golfers and their commitment to winning, implying they had been spoiled by relatively soft living.

"On the European Tour of the early 1980s," he said, "we didn't play for a lot of money. We always played just to win—all of us. We played purely to beat each other. We had Norman playing over there then. We have different characters, now, but we're all of similar age. We all started together and have gone through the last 10 years together, and we are all fiercely competitive."

Faldo implied further that the American golfer seemed more concerned with his paycheck than with the glory of winning.

"Every tournament I go to," Faldo said, "I haven't got a clue what the prize money is. I just want to win. We've grown up playing in rough and difficult conditions, and it hasn't done any of us any harm. Here," he said, speaking of the United States, "if the conditions are no good or if the course in is bad shape, some players will say, 'To hell with that,' and not play.

"Some guys will say winning $700,000 means you've had a great year, but you can win that much money without winning a tournament. Some guys are happy with that, but I think you've got to play to beat each other. You've got to win. They (the Americans) are not prepared to sacrifice, and they're not of the belief that going backward is to go forward."

Faldo's remarks may not have inflamed Americans' passions, but they did draw one indifferent response. Rocco Mediate, who had played exceptionally well through the early months of the year, and at the time stood atop the PGA Tour's money list, asked, "How does he know what we think?"

No matter Faldo's opinion at the time, it was fact that only three Americans ranked among the leading 10 players worldwide in the Sony Ranking. Woosnam ranked first, and only Payne Stewart, who was to win the U.S. Open within two months, stood fifth, Azinger, a stronger match player than stroke player, ranked sixth, and Tom Kite 10th.

Believe what you like, but I tend to agree with Faldo's assessment, and I've often said as much. The PGA Tour player can live quite comfortably placing 20th week after week. Twentieth place in a $1 million Tour tournament returns $13,000. Multiply that by say 20 tournaments a year, and it's worth $260,000. It won't lead the money list (actually, Jeff Sluman placed 56th in 1990 with $264,012 in winnings), but not many who work for a living earn that much money in one year.

Faldo's mildly inflammatory comments aside, he still looked like the man to beat when the Masters opened. He had won the previous two tournaments, both in playoffs, first over Scott Hoch and then over Raymond Floyd. He had had an exceptional year in 1990. In addition to the Masters, Faldo had also won the British Open at St. Andrews, and came quite close to winning or at least tying Irwin and Mike Donald in the U.S. Open, but he three-putted the 16th hole, lipped out a 15-footer on the 18th, and missed by a stroke.

Winning any tournament three years running is not easy, and Faldo faced heavy statistical odds going into the Masters. In its 54 playings, no one had ever won it three years running, and as a matter of fact, only he and Jack Nicklaus had won it twice in succession. For that matter, no one had won three consecutive major competitions since Peter Thomson took the 1954, 1955 and 1956 British Opens. Some had come close, though. With one round to go, in 1990 Curtis Strange had been in position to win three consecutive U.S. Opens, but he stumbled through the early holes of the fourth round, shot 75, and fell into a tie for 21st place.

If anyone had the game to do it, though, Faldo seemed to be the man. He had won two British Opens and two Masters within the previous four years, along with two near misses in the U.S. Open. Before his close finish in the 1990 U.S. Open, he had tied Strange at The Country Club in 1988, but lost the 18-hole playoff. Furthermore, few men had ever played the game as he had in 1990. His victory in the British Open had been almost surgical in its precision, and although he had had help in winning the Masters (Floyd first three-putted the 17th hole of the last round, allowing Faldo to tie him, and then pulled his approach to the second playoff hole into the pond bordering the 11th green), he had put the pressure on Floyd, which might have forced him into making those errors. Had he played a better approach into the 16th hole at Medinah during the last round of the 1990 U.S. Open instead of leaving his ball perhaps 80 feet left of the cup, he might have won there as well. Only Ben Hogan, in 1953, had won those three events in the same year.

Speaking on the day before the Masters' first round, Faldo said he approached the tournament just as he had in 1990. It's a very similar feeling," he said. "I'm not thinking of defending or repeating or whatever. Obviously I want to win, but the priority is to treat this as the 1991 Masters and get on with it."

Faldo's record notwithstanding, and common sense aside, a poll of fans conducted by the *Augusta Chronicle* showed Faldo second to Nicklaus as the choice to win the 1991 Masters, with Crenshaw third and Norman fourth. Woosnam, who had climbed over Faldo in the Sony Ranking before play began, came in ninth.

"Woosie's No. 1, is he?" Faldo said when he was told of the revised standings. "Well, good. He always said so."

An aggressive golfer, Woosnam goes for the flag every chance he has. Immensely strong, even though he stands only five-foot-four-and-a-half, he hits high, long shots. He grew up as a farmer's son in Wales spending long summer days at hard labor in the fields, which built up his upper body strength.

Asked if his short height hindered his golf, Woosnam bristled and snapped, "What do you think? I think I'm hitting the ball pretty bloody far." Indeed he was.

Olazabal, another pre-tournament choice, said, "He's a very strong man. Even with his size, he can hit the ball a long way. That alone should tell you something. The man is strong."

Against him, however, stood his record in the United States. He simply had never played well in American tournaments. In one of his early appearances, he shot 86 in the first round of the 1987 PGA Championship, at Palm Beach. Among other things, it indicated he didn't take either American golf seriously, or else his ability to cope with it. He often complained about the rough and the speed of greens; he prefers them slower than they are normally set for the important American competitions.

Woosnam and Faldo are much the same age, born within seven months of one another, Faldo in July of 1957 and Woosnam in February of 1958. And, while Faldo had commanded most of the attention with his victories in both the Masters and British Opens of 1990, Woosnam actually won more often. Faldo had won only those two tournaments, plus another in Hong Kong. Playing 17 tournaments through 10 countries, Woosnam won five, among them the Bell's Scottish Open and the World Match Play, his second in that significant event, and placed second in four others.

Then he opened 1991 by winning the Mediterranean Open in early March, then crossing the Atlantic and winning the New Orleans Open later in the month, his first victory in the United States.

Woosnam's improving record along with the success of other foreign golfers in recent years focused more attention on the perceived reluctance of those who run the Masters to invite overseas golfers. Only a few are asked to Augusta each April. Woosnam, for example, had played only twice before, even though he had won five tournaments in 1987 and had been the European Tour's leading money winner. He was invited only after winning the European PGA, the Irish Open, and the European Open of 1988.

We should not forget, either, that while Faldo had been close in two U.S. Opens, Woosnam finished only a stroke behind Strange in 1989, when Curtis won his second consecutive championship. (The finish was not that close, really, for Strange came to the last hole leading by two strokes and three-putted the final green, taking a safe bogey rather than risking worse with a foolish first putt.)

While he hadn't threatened to win in either of his previous two Masters appearances, he didn't embarrass himself as he had in the PGA. He shot 290 in 1989, seven strokes behind Faldo and Hoch, which was good enough to place him in a tie for 14th place alongside Watson, Azinger and Don Pooley, and he followed with 293 in 1990, much farther behind Faldo and Floyd.

With the Masters among the four most significant competitions of each year, those close to European golf would like to see more of their own in Augusta each spring, and wonder why the field cannot be expanded to more than the normal 80 or so to accommodate them. Certainly there is enough daylight in Augusta in April for a field larger than the 87 who played in 1991. The first pair left the tee Thursday, the first day, at 8:45, a most civilized hour for big-time golf. Starting times certainly could have been advanced by 45 minutes at the least and still allowed sufficient warm-up time for the early starters, and since the field goes off at eight-minute intervals, the number of players could have been expanded by nine or even 11 players (with an odd-numbered field in 1991, three men played in the last grouping, rather than the normal two-man pairing).

Masters officials insist, however, that their field is as big as they want it to be, and that's the end of it.

One final preliminary. Early arrivals at Augusta National strolled down the long grade from the 10th tee to the lowest reaches of the golf course to gaze with some wonder at this corner of the course. A violent storm had dumped twelve and a half inches of rain on Augusta the previous October and caused enormous damage. The creek that flows down the left side of the 11th fairway, then curls across the front of the 12th green and 13th tee, spilled over its banks and rampaged through the lower reaches of the course. Debris collected in the creek, causing the water to rise high enough to cover both the Hogan and Nelson bridges that normally rise five feet above the stream. That wasn't the worst. A vortex caused by the rushing flood acted like a giant auger, boring into the 11th green and chewing it away, and at the same time destroying the pond that acts as a water hazard against the green's left side, where Floyd had misplayed his approach in the 1990 playoff. It was as if the gods, angered at that awful shot, showed their frustration that another foreigner had won the Masters and set out to cleanse their souls by banishing the site from view.

While that was the worst, it wasn't all the damage. At the height of the flood, the 12th green lay under water, along with the forward tee of the 13th. (The Masters tee stood above the rising tide.) When the rains ended and the floodwater drained off, the 11th green was gone and a front bunker of the 12th green had been swept away.

The club faced a massive rebuilding project, but Augusta National has a way of dealing with emergencies of this order. Rebuilding began as soon as the floodwaters had drained. All of the work was handled by the Augusta National grounds crew, led by Marsh Benson, the course superintendent. Restoration involved rebuilding the 11th green's sub-structure, particularly its drainage system, beginning with a base of coarse and fine gravel, and tons of sand and peat moss, interlaced with tiles and plastic pipes. Then the surface had to be restored to its original contours. Here the club had a break. A decade earlier, when the greens had been converted from bermuda to bent grass, engineers had drawn detailed contour maps in two-foot grids; restoration would be no great problem, especially since the crew would be using a laser theodolite, an instrument that measures elevation (one was used to calculate the height of Mount Everest). Then the green was covered by a three-eighths inch layer of bent grass trucked down from Pennsylvania.

The 12th green had suffered no great damage and needed nothing more than some re-sodding. Compared to the monumental work of restoring the 11th green, replacing the lost bunker on the 12th and rebuilding the members' tee on the 13th were easy. Benson and his crew completed the massive job in eight weeks, a model of coordination and organization. At the same time the crew replaced a number of old trees that had been washed away— Southern magnolias, ligustrums, hollies, dogwoods and azalea bushes. By springtime you couldn't tell the new green from the old, and the old course looked as it had always looked.

The Masters this year must rank among the most satisfying and at the same time nerve-tingling we have seen in recent memory. It began with a touch of nostalgia as some of the old favorites rose to the top, reached one climax in the second round that left spectators smiling and talking to one another about how great it was to see Watson and Nicklaus playing so well again, tailed off a bit on Saturday, but then rose to its usual crescendo of excitement on Sunday when so many men had their opportunities to win. Finally, the drama rose to its climax on the final hole, with Watson, Olazabal, and Woosnam even and the result hinging on every shot.

The Masters began with delightful weather—bright, clear skies, mild temperatures and low humidity. The ground lay soft from rains early in the week, and the greens receptive. The scores reflected the conditions. As the first round began, it seemed as if the calendar had turned back and we were living in an earlier time. Wadkins, the first man off the tee, had sped around in 67, and later Watson and Nicklaus stormed in with 68s.

Both Jim Gallagher and Mark McCumber, who, incidentally, was hitting the ball a very long way, matched Wadkins' 67, and a maturing Fred Couples, Jumbo Ozaki, and Olazabal equaled Watson and Nicklaus, at 68. When the day ended, 12 men had broke 70, another 18 finished under par 72—30 men under par.

Since Wadkins had gone out first and Gallagher had played not far behind him, the fans were left wondering throughout the day if their scores would hold up, and if they would see even lower numbers as more of the field made a run at them. As it developed, although others had their opportunities, only McCumber, playing in the next-to-last pairing, could match them. For a time Faldo looked as if he might join the leaders and put pressure on them from the start. Even par after 12 holes with one birdie and a bogey, Nick eagled the 13th and dropped to two under par, but right away he bogeyed the 14th, failed to birdie the 15th, the other par-five hole on the second nine, and dropped another stroke at the 18th. He was in with 72, even par, which left him five strokes behind the leaders, but better off than he had been a year earlier when he opened with 71 and lay seven strokes behind Donald, whose 64 came within a stroke of the course record (Donald, by the way shot 73 and 75 in 1991 and missed the 36-hole cut). His round over, Faldo marched to the putting green. He had bogeyed the 18th by missing a four-foot putt.

While most of the attention centered around the leaders, back at the other end of the scale, Norman and Lyle were practically out of it already, and Seve Ballesteros was struggling. Lyle had disappeared from the world's leaderboards after he won the 1988 Masters, and he was a long way from this one after shooting a first-round 77, but even so, he finished a stroke ahead of Norman, who stumbled in with 78. Both men would miss the 36-hole cut. Ballesteros, on the other hand, would recover his game, play the last 54 holes in seven under par, and finish seven strokes behind Woosnam.

As the first man off the tee, Wadkins was in the position he liked. He had no one ahead of him except Gene Sarazen and Sam Snead, who had teed off 45 minutes earlier and had played their ceremonial nine holes in an hour and a half. Wadkins could play as fast as he liked, and he liked to play fast. He and Jodie Mudd turned the first nine in 90 minutes, and played the 18 holes in three hours and 25 minutes.

As they raced around the course, Leroy Schultz, Lanny's caddie, kept saying, "You gotta be patient, you gotta be patient."

"Dammit, Leroy," Wadkins snapped, "I am patient."

Wadkins had finished the 1990 Masters with a round of 68, the best of the day, and he opened 1991 with 67, once again the best of the day. He built this round with seven birdies, all of them the result of above-average iron play. He holed only one putt as long as 15 feet, after a four iron into the fifth green. He had two bogeys, the first on the eighth, a par five, where he drove into a fairway bunker and his attempt at a long recovery with a five iron didn't work, and on the 11th, where his six-iron approach slipped off to the right of the green. He also three-putted the 13th after playing a 220-yard four wood 40 feet past the hole.

Gallagher started less than an hour behind Wadkins and played the course without a bogey, although he struggled throughout the round. He started by driving into the trees from the first tee and having nothing more than a safe pitch back to the fairway for his second, but he lofted another pitch within six feet and holed the putt to save his par. Another missed green at the fourth, the very difficult 205-yard par three, and another saved par, but he birdied both the seventh and eighth with nice pitches inside 10 feet.

Out in 34, Gallagher continued to struggle, but he refused to yield. He had three birdies coming in, and saved his pars on three other holes, twice from bunkers, and once after overshooting the 15th green.

Gallagher had dreamed of playing in the Masters almost from the time he was three years old and his father, a golf pro, had put a club in his hand. And then, unable to sleep the Wednesday night before the first round, he flipped on a cable network and watched *The Ben Hogan Story*. His assessment: "Hogan was a tough customer."

Gallagher had an interesting background. Not only was he the son of a golf pro, he had a brother, Joe, on the Ben Hogan Tour, a sister, Jackie, on the women's Futures Tour, and his wife, Cissye, was a member of the LPGA. Furthermore, his father-in-law had won the 1970 Mississippi Amateur championship. His family had come to Augusta at the beginning of the week, and after his great start, his in-laws started on their way from Mississippi. Unfortunately, he couldn't keep up that level of play, and fell behind the leaders.

McCumber, who had been close to winning an important championship at least twice in the past (the 1987 PGA and the 1989 U.S. Open), had come into the Masters a new father. Before he teed off on Thursday, he received an express package at his hotel. Inside he found two pictures of his son, Mark Tyler, a pair of golf shoes, and a message: "When you make a bogey (underlined three times), think of this face."

McCumber had to think of it only once, when he missed the eighth green with a sand wedge, and took three strokes to hole out.

By then, though, he stood three under par, and immediately after dropping the stroke on the eighth, he came back with a birdie on the ninth, drilling a six iron within 12 feet of the cup. Out in 33, McCumber swung into Amen Corner, the heart of Augusta National. He played through superbly. After solid pars on the 10th and 11th, the two devilishly difficult par fours, McCumber played an eight iron onto the 12th green, the testing, 155-yard par three with the shallow green that is so difficult to hit, and rolled in a 20-footer for one birdie, then reached the 13th green with a four-iron second to 30 feet for another.

Now he had fallen to five under par, with the 15th, another birdie hole, coming up. Meantime, it was late in the day and play had slowed down. After a routine par four on the 14th, McCumber drove well down the 15th fairway and saw he would have a long wait while George Archer and Pooley, playing ahead of him, holed out. McCumber sat on the ground, lay back with his head resting on his golf bag, pulled the bill of his baseball-type cap over his eyes, and rested.

The green ahead finally clear, he pushed his four iron into the right greenside bunker, blasted out to perhaps 15 feet, and two-putted for a par five. A birdie chance gone, but three more pars would tie for the lead. He made a routine three on the 16th and a four on the 17th, and then came to the 18th needing a birdie three to move in front. With the lead within reach, he pushed his drive into the trees lining the right side of the fairway, and saw only a narrow opening between two pines that might give him a chance to save par at least. Taking his time, he rifled the shot between the tree trunks to within 15 feet of the cup. Now for the birdie.

In a relaxed mood, Mark chatted briefly with the gallery before stepping up to the ball. He tapped it smartly, and the crowd groaned as it slipped past the right lip. He tapped in from about a foot for the par. Back in 34, he had his 67.

Earlier in the day, Watson had come to the 18th needing a birdie to tie Wadkins and Gallagher, but he pulled his five-iron approach left of the green. Heading for trouble, it bounded into the gallery, caromed off a woman's ankle back toward the green. After pitching on and saving his par by holing a six-foot putt, Watson handed the woman the ball, and then kissed her.

First-round scores:

Lanny Wadkins	67
Jim Gallagher	67
Mark McCumber	67
Fred Couples	68
Tom Watson	68
Jack Nicklaus	68
Fred Ozaki	68
Wayne Levi	69
Mark Brooks	69
Phil Mickelson	69
Scott Simpson	69

Other scores of interest:

Nick Faldo	72
Ian Woosnam	72
Seve Ballesteros	75
Sandy Lyle	77
Greg Norman	78
Arnold Palmer	78

The gallery had applauded when Watson kissed the woman spectator he had hit with his ball. They were still applauding him the next day when he sped around Augusta National with another 68 and raced to the front of the pack. This was a special day at Augusta, filled with good feeling, with camaraderie among the spectators and among the players as well. Laughing and smiling, friends and strangers clustered around the big scoreboard by the first hole and told each other what they had both seen, about Watson's fine round, about Wadkins stumbling through the first nine in 39, backhanding a short putt on the ninth and missing, for a six, then, angered, racing home in 32; about the powerful Woosnam hitting the ball great distances, even par at the beginning of the day but roaring into second place with a strong 66; about Mark Calcavecchia, two under at the beginning of the day, playing the first nine in 33 to go five under, and after an up-and-down second nine laying a seven iron within 12 feet on the 18th and catching Woosnam; and above all about Watson playing as he had 10 years earlier, once again paired with Nicklaus, as they had played so many times in the past, friendly rivals fighting to determine who is best on this day, this week. It was a day worth remembering; familiar names, familiar setting, like living life over again. It was fun while it lasted, but it had a brief life.

It also had its bizarre moments:

- Applying body English as McCumber's putt for a birdie on the 16th skimmed past the hole, Chico Hernanadez, his caddie, bent over backwards, lost his balance, and tumbled into a bunker.
- For the first time in his 31 years in the Masters, Nicklaus went four over par on one hole, dropping two balls into the water on the 12th and making seven.
- Olazabal also made seven on the sixth, another par-three hole.
- Nicklaus holed a long, twisting putt for a birdie on the 16th, and then Watson, from a nearly similar position, rolled one in on top of it.

Unlike the Open, the British Open, or the PGA, the Masters re-pairs the golfers each round. Watson and Nicklaus went off third from last, followed by McCumber and Couples, with Wadkins and Gallagher the last men off.

Neither Watson nor Nicklaus started well. Jack had opened the first round by birdieing the first two holes and starting with 33 on the first nine. He opened the second with bogeys on both the third and fourth, then birdied the seventh and ninth.

Watson, meantime, had played the first four holes in two birdies and two bogeys, making his first par at the fifth. Both out in even-par 36, neither man seemed headed for anything special. A birdie on the 10th helped Watson, but not by very much, and then they approached the tantalizing 12th. Up first, Watson played a nice eight iron onto the green. Nicklaus next.

The pin was set on the right, behind the frontal bunker that had been washed away by the storm. Over the years Nicklaus has schooled himself not to play over the bunker when the hole is on the right. In the heat of the moment Jack either forgot or ignored the old lesson. Drawing his eight iron, he went for the flag. The ball drifted slightly right, landed short, slammed into the bank, then rolled back down into the water.

The gallery was stunned. The spectators groaned, and then a low murmur spread through the crowd. They couldn't believe Nicklaus had made such a mistake. Worse was coming. Dropping another ball in the drop zone, Jack played a timid sand wedge that again fell short of the green and tumbled back into the water. Again the gallery turned to one another in wonder; the greatest player of his age was looking like a 15-handicapper on a bad day.

Nicklaus was no less shocked than his fans. "What am I going to make here?" he asked himself. "A 9? 11? 13? I better get out of here." No more cute shots. Jack made sure he cleared the water with his next, hit the ball long, and watched it settle on the back fringe. After he crossed the pond, Nicklaus heard Watson say, "Get it up and down." He did, using his putter and laying his ball within a couple of inches of the cup, then tapping it in. A seven.

Four over par now, Nicklaus seemed headed for the discard heap, but we must never forget that Jack had been the most dangerous player of his time. As quickly as he had thrown four strokes away, he won them back. He talked to himself on the 13th tee, reminding himself, "Okay, dummy, you're only six strokes behind and there are some good birdie holes up ahead. Play some golf and see if you can get back in it."

A booming drive turned the corner, and then a three iron put him on the 13th green. Two putts and he had picked up one stroke. Another big drive on the 14th, followed by a four iron that left his son Jackie, his caddie, in awe. It never left the flag, and braked itself two feet from the cup. Jackie said it was the greatest shot he had ever seen. Another stroke won back.

Another huge drive on the 15th that left him only a six iron to the green set up a third consecutive birdie. Jack claimed it was the second shortest club he had ever hit into the 15th green. Back in 1965 he had driven so far he flew his approach over the green with an eight iron.

Three strokes won back now, then that breaking 30-footer dropped on the 16th, and he had made up for his mistakes of the 12th. The putt took a huge break and prompted Nicklaus to say later, "It was a 30-footer that traveled 50 feet." When it jumped into the hole, the gallery roared, and Jack threw up his hands and covered his head.

A routine par at the 17th, and then he almost lost a stroke on the 18th when he overshot the green, but his ball hit a spectator's foot and caromed back onto the green.

While Nicklaus made up his lost strokes, Watson came to life as well. He threw away a birdie opportunity at the 12th, missing from six feet, but that wasn't new; Watson hasn't been the putter he was in years. Pars at the 13th, another missed opportunity, and the 14th, brought him to the 15th still one stroke under par. There he lashed into a drive and nailed a four iron 15 feet from the cup. A good putt and he would eagle, pick up two strokes with one blow, and drop to three under par for the round. He tapped the ball firmly, and it rolled into the middle of the hole.

Three under for the round, Watson stood seven under par for the 33 holes he had played.

An eight iron left him 35 feet from the hole on the 16th, and then he stood by while Nicklaus holed his improbable putt. Watson's turn now. His ball didn't figure to break as much as Jack's, but it was still a difficult putt to read. Satisfied, he stepped up to his ball, and after a moment's hesitation, rapped it toward the hole. The ball took the slight break, ran to the edge of the cup, hung for an instant, then dropped.

The gallery broke into a cheer that rang throughout the course. The two great heroes of an earlier time were playing at the peak of their games, and it was fun again. Now Watson had fallen to four under par for the day, eight under for 34 holes, and had only the 17th and 18th to play.

Safely through the 17th, and on the 18th with their approaches, the two old warriors climbed the grade to the home green together, smiling and talking to one another.

"This is fun," Watson said to Nicklaus. "I hope we do it again on Sunday, and I'm going to try to beat your buns." Nicklaus grinned and answered, "And I'm going to try to beat yours." Both men made their pars, Watson shooting 68 and taking the lead at 136, and Nicklaus shooting 72, which placed him at 140, four under par and just four behind Watson.

Later, when the cheering had died and he had time to reflect, Watson said of Nicklaus, "Jack has fun playing. When you're in the heat of competition and you're having fun, that's what it's all about."

While Watson and Nicklaus were taking us back into the past, Woosnam was bringing us back to the present. It was on this day that he thrust himself into the thick of the struggle by shooting 66, the second-best round of the day, climbed into second place, at 138, just two strokes behind Watson and in a tie with Wadkins, McCumber, and Calcavecchia, who had come to life briefly with 68. Following at 139 came Billy Ray Brown, whose 65 turned out to be the day's best score, Floyd, Bernhard Langer, and Olazabal.

Olazabal should have been better. His round was ruined by a slightly off-line tee shot into the sixth, a 180-yard par three with the pin set on the upper right shelf. Four under par as the round began, Olazabal had picked up another stroke by the sixth, then missed the green to the right, leaving himself a delicate pitch over rising ground from soft ground spectators had churned to mud. Trying to play too fine a shot, Olazabal nearly reached the top twice, but each time his ball rolled back past his feet. A third, bolder shot with a sand iron ran to the far side of the green, and he three-putted. A seven; back to one under par. Out in 39, Olazabal made up every one of the lost strokes by birdieing four of the last six holes, came back in 32, and shot 71.

Woosnam had no such trouble, especially with the par-five holes. He played them in four under par, with birdies on both the second and 15th, and an eagle on the 13th. After his opening 72, he had begun the second round worried he might miss the cut. Since his putting hadn't been sharp, he changed putters for the second round. Within six holes he had lost his fear of being eliminated. A Promethean drive that ran to the base of the hill on the second hole, a 555-yard par five, left him only a five iron to the green and set up his first birdie. A four iron to seven feet on the difficult par-three fourth and a six iron to eight feet on the sixth dropped him to three under. A momentary lapse at the ninth, where his six iron backed off the green, cost him one stroke, but he took it back with another stunning iron to 10 feet on the 11th.

Three under par once again, Woosnam two-putted from 25 feet on the 12th, and followed up with another massive drive that turned the corner on the 13th and left him another five-iron approach to a par five. His ball settled 10 feet from the cup, and he holed it for an eagle. Five under now, he missed a 15-footer on the 14th that might have fallen, and then hit another of those huge drives on the 15th that left him but a six iron for his second, the same club Nicklaus played. Woosnam missed the green, though, leaving his ball short and right, but he chipped to four feet and holed for the birdie four. Six under par now, he played routine pars over the three remaining holes without ever looking like making another birdie, and came home in 32 for his 66.

While Watson, Nicklaus, Woosnam, and some others may have enjoyed their games, others weren't having much fun. After an opening 72, Faldo followed with 73 and fell nine strokes behind Watson, and at the end of the day trailed 42 other golfers. With 36 holes still to play, he had the time to make up the strokes, but he didn't look to have the game. Faldo had put on 17 pounds over the winter, attempting to build up his strength, but the added weight didn't look good on him, and it seemed to tighten his swing. He didn't look like the golfer he had been in 1990.

Even so, he was better off than Norman. Greg shot 69, the lowest second round he had ever had at Augusta, but it turned out to be one stroke too many. Combined with his opening 78, he shot 147 and missed the 36-hole cut; scores of 146 or better survived.

Other prominent golfers who missed included Lyle, who hadn't survived the cut since he won the 1988 Masters; Gary Player, who is past the age when he might realistically compete; Arnold Palmer, who still draws lively galleries who want so desperately for him to play well again; and more contemporary golfers having bad times, like Robert Gamez, Tim Simpson, Wayne Grady, who only five months earlier had won the PGA Championship; Donald, loser to Irwin in the Open playoff the previous June and who also had opened with 1990 Masers with 64, and Ronan Rafferty, the Northern Irishman who was among the leaders of the 1990 European Order of Merit.

Second-round scores:

Tom Watson	136
Ian Woosnam	138
Mark Calcavecchia	138
Mark McCumber	138
Lanny Wadkins	138
Billy Ray Brown	139
Raymond Floyd	139
Bernhard Langer	139
Jose Maria Olazabal	139

Other scores of interest:

Jack Nicklaus	140
Phil Mickelson	142
Nick Faldo	145
Seve Ballesteros	145
Curtis Strange	146
Tom Kite	146

Under overcast, dull gray skies, rain threatened throughout the third round, and developments lacked the emotional impact of Friday. The day saw Woosnam rush to the front, Nicklaus begin his fall from contention, and Faldo and Mize show flashes of climbing among the leaders. Calcavecchia collapsed, hitting into the water on both the 12th and 15th holes and shooting 77, and McCumber could get nothing going after his 67 on Thursday.

The day had its controversy as well, involving Woosnam and Watson and a misunderstood conversation on the 15th green.

Even with a smaller field, cut to 58 players, Augusta continued to give up low scores. Where 30 men had broken par in the first round and 34 in the second, 32 broke par in the third. Mize had the best of them all.

Larry hadn't won a tournament since he beat Norman by holing his pitch-and-run on the second hole of the 1987 playoff, and although he was playing reasonably well, with 72 and 71 in the first two rounds, he shot an unexpected 66 in the third, built on six birdies. Suddenly he had climbed among the leaders.

His round began with the usual frustrations; three good birdie chances from inside 10 feet on the first three holes slipped past the cup, but his bad luck turned around at the fourth. His three-iron tee shot caught the right greenside bunker, leaving him about 30 yards from the cup, but his recovery from the sand flew hole-high, stopped, backed up, and toppled into the hole. A birdie where a bogey seemed likely.

Mize added a birdie at the seventh, where he lofted a superb nine-iron pitch inside two feet, and then broke loose with four birdies over the six holes from the 10th through the 15th. His three on the 14th ranked among the more spectacular. A loose five iron left him perhaps 50 feet from the cup. Facing a putt with an impossible break of maybe 20 feet, he rapped the ball on a ridiculous path to the right. Nearing the hole, it made a U-turn, and while the gallery gasped, the ball tumbled into the cup. Five under now, he played a much better shot into the 15th, a four-wood second within 15 feet, missed the putt for an eagle, but made his sixth birdie of the round. Routine pars on the last three holes, and he had his 66.

Mize had played well into the first nine before Nicklaus teed off on the first, and from the way Jack started, nobody was paying much attention to anyone else. Birdies on three of the first eight holes dropped him to seven under par for the 44 holes, but like Pickett's Charge at Gettysburg, that was the high-water mark of Jack's Masters. Suddenly he couldn't make a putt. He bogeyed the ninth, then hit a poor second into the 10th that carried over the green and landed in a woman's chair behind the right greenside bunker. Startled, the woman leaped from her chair and knocked the ball free. It trickled down the slope toward the bunker and stopped three feet before it tumbled into the sand. A pitch left Jack eight feet from the cup, and he missed the putt. From seven under par after eight holes, he stood four under after 10, bogeyed the 17th, came back in 38, and shot another 72. At day's end, his 212 left him seven strokes off the lead. Reminded he had come back from five strokes down in the Tradition, a senior tournament played the previous week, Jack agreed he had, but, he added, "We weren't playing the Masters last week."

While Nicklaus was stumbling, Woosnam was playing another sensational round, a 67 to go with his 66 of Friday—133 for 36 holes—and leaped ahead of Watson into the 54-hole lead.

Playing precise, error-free golf, Woosnam went out in 34, picking up one stroke on Watson, who shot 35. Since he had begun the round two strokes back, Woosnam had cut his deficit in half. He passed Watson on the 12th, where he holed a 25-footer after pitching an eight iron onto the green while Watson bogeyed.

Meantime, a few minutes earlier, Olazabal had climbed into contention once again. Three strokes behind at the beginning of the round, he dropped another when he bogeyed the fifth, but he suddenly began holing every putt he looked at and ran off six birdies over the next seven holes, mainly through good iron play. He did hole two 18-footers, on the 10th and 11th, but on the previous three holes he had faced nothing longer than 12-footers, and played a nine-iron pitch to three feet on the seventh and a six iron to six feet on the ninth.

After five consecutive birdies, Olazabal dropped a stroke on the 12th, where he overshot the green, but he came back with another birdie at the

13th, his sixth. Four under par now with another birdie hole coming up, his three iron to the 15th plugged in the right greenside bunker and he could play his recovery no closer than 40 feet—three-putt range. He made six, and shot 69, giving him 208 for the 54 holes.

Behind him, Woosnam's two at the 12th started him on a string of four consecutive birdies, one with a superbly played shot into the 13th green. His drive had drifted into the trees along the right, about 245 yards from the green, but he had a good enough lie, and after a slight hesitation, thinking first he'd go for the green, then no, he'd better simply punch the ball out, he changed his mind once again, went for it, and threaded a gorgeous two iron through the trees, and drew it onto the green. Two putts from 35 feet and he had his second birdie. An eight iron to 15 feet on the 14th and he had his third straight, and then a five iron rolled to the back fringe of the 15th green. Here Woosnam rolled a superb putt that ran true to the hole, slowed its approach as it drew close, but hung on the lip.

As Woosnam began his long walk to the hole and waited momentarily to see if the ball would drop, Watson told him he should mark his ball and be careful that he didn't touch it when he pulled the flagstick from the cup. Speaking on the telecast, Tom Weiskopf misinterpreted Watson's advice. Nevertheless, instead of marking his ball (he said later his ball sat so close to the hole he didn't think he could put it back if he had marked it), Woosnam pulled the flagstick and tapped his ball into the hole. Another birdie.

At the same time, Watson had matched birdies with Woosnam on the 13th, and his approach to the 15th, an outstanding three iron played from a downhill lie, settled on the back of the green slightly closer to the hole than Woosnam's, but where Ian had got down in two, Watson took three putts, dropping another stroke to the Welshman.

They both made routine par threes on the 16th and 17th, and then Woosnam, with another 66 in his hands, bogeyed the 18th.

Watson finished with 70, a score that might have been better except for some loose putting—he had missed a three-footer for a birdie at the second, three-putted the third from 25 feet, and missed eight-footers for birdies on the fourth and sixth before missing the four-footer at the 12th.

As the day ended, Woosnam held a one-stroke lead over Watson, 205 to 206, with Olazabal and Wadkins, who shot 70, two strokes farther back, at 208. Even with his 67, signaling a return to his 1990 form for at least one round, Faldo still had too much ground to make up. He and Nicklaus tied with eight others for 14th place, seven strokes behind Woosnam.

Third-round scores:

Ian Woosnam	205
Tom Watson	206
Jose Maria Olazabal	208
Lanny Wadkins	208
Larry Mize	209
Andrew Magee	210
Ian Baker-Finch	210
Raymond Floyd	210

Other scores of interest:

Nick Faldo	212
Jack Nicklaus	212
Seve Ballesteros	214
Mark Calcavecchia	215
Phil Mickelson	216
Curtis Strange	218

Looking over the situation, Wadkins made a prophesy: "It could be wild and woolly on that back nine tomorrow."

Indeed it was. Before the day ended, Faldo had decided to go for everything in this last round. "I'd better," he said, "I've got to take all the gambles possible today. There're more guys bunched together in front of me than last year." He made a little headway by closing with 70, but not nearly enough and tied for 12th place. Nicklaus had his worst day of the week, shooting 76, and dropping into a tie for 35th place, his worst finish since he withdrew after one round in 1983, and his worst score since he shot 77 in 1982. Wadkins roared into contention briefly, but made no headway on the home nine, and his threat meant nothing. Once again the Masters gave us all a series of heart-stopping moments.

While it was not so evident at first, in the end the tournament evolved into a race among Woosnam, Watson, and Olazabal, and in fact came down to the last hole with all three men tied for first place.

Woosnam began the day at 11 under, paired with Watson, 10 under, with Olazabal and Wadkins, both eight under, one hole ahead of them. After one hole, the situation had changed. Olazabal holed an 18-footer for a birdie three, dropping to nine under, Watson three-putted from 35 feet, and Woosnam parred after his drive drifted a little bit right, nicked a tree branch, and still left him a pitch of less than 100 yards. Now Watson and Olazabal were tied at nine under, two strokes behind Woosnam.

Their positions seemed to change after every hole. Olazabal made a routine five at the second, but both Woosnam and Watson birdied, and then Woosnam missed the fourth green, chipped poorly, and missed a saving 10-footer, while both Watson and Olazabal parred.

Woosnam was playing shaky golf just then. He had overshot the third green with his pitching wedge and had to hole a four-footer to save his par, and after his bogey on the fourth came back with a birdie on the fifth after an eight-iron pitch to 15 feet. Right away he threw away a stroke by three-putting the sixth when his six iron left him 35 feet from the cup, then overshot the seventh and holed an eight-footer for another nervous par. He had played five holes in one over par and might have been worse.

Woosnam came out of this streak of loose golf still 11 under par, just where he had begun the day, but by then he was sharing first place with Olazabal, who had played the first seven holes in three under par. Watson by then had fallen two strokes behind.

The leaderboard changed with nearly every stroke. Where his game had been razor sharp through the early holes, Olazabal suddenly lost control, missing three straight greens and losing a stroke on each of them. One of the lost strokes probably could have been saved by more conservative thinking. After driving into the fairway bunker off the eighth tee, Olazabal could have played a medium iron, say a five through a seven, perhaps reached the crest of the hill, which would have left him not only within range of the green, but also within sight, but he would have had a longer shot into the green than he normally would have played. Instead, he chose to choke down on a one iron and try to play his second shot closer to the green. He played a terrible shot. The ball swerved off to the left, leaving Olazabal no chance to reach the green with his third. He bogeyed, followed up by bunkering his approach to the ninth and missing from seven feet, and then overshot the 10th green for his third straight bogey. Eight under par now, back where he had begun the day.

Woosnam, meantime, had made his five on the eighth, missing an eight-foot birdie opportunity, holed a 15-footer at the ninth, and right away lost the stroke by bogeying the 10th, missing from only four feet. Since Watson had birdied the 10th, he had dropped to 10 under, a stroke behind Woosnam. So had Wadkins, who overcame a double-bogey six on the fifth hole with birdies on the seventh and eighth.

At about that time, playing two hours ahead, Pate had raced around with five birdies, an eagle, and a 45-foot putt for a par on the 18th. He shot 65, and abruptly turned himself into a major player. He was in with 279, nine under par; let the others try to match it. The 1991 Masters was turning into one of the wildest and most unpredictable tournaments within memory, and it would only become more frenzied with each passing hole. At times it grew stormy.

Wadkins didn't make another move throughout the day and eventually tied Pate at 279, and as suddenly as Watson climbed back within a stroke of Woosnam, he gave three more away. A pushed approach missed the 11th green, costing him one stroke, but even more costly, he mishit his seven iron from the 12th tee and watched in frustration as it fell short and into the pond. A double-bogey five and back to seven under par.

A reversal of that scope might have ruined a player with less resolve, but Watson would be back. The gallery had been pulling for him throughout the day, cheering his good shots and dying a little with his errors. He was the last American with any chance of holding back the foreign tide, and he had just lost it. While Woosnam wasn't exactly tearing Augusta National apart, his mistakes seemed small compared to Watson's blunder on the 12th.

No less than Watson, the crowd felt frustrated as well. All at once Woosnam gave them hope. He stood at the 13th tee a stroke ahead of Wadkins and only two ahead of Olazabal now, for the Spaniard had birdied the 13th, and four ahead of Watson.

The pressure had been building with every stroke, for we were now at the heart of Augusta National, the stretch of holes where so many Masters had been won and lost. No one could stand there in the heat of the competition and not feel nervous tension. Normally a reliable driver, Woosnam hooked his tee shot, drawing it low and left, too close to the corner where the fairway turns for its long run to the green, lying just behind the stream. where it knifes across the fairway. Woosnam's ball crashed through the trees, dropped on the far side of the creek, where it parallels the fairway, then rolled onto the bank of the stream.

In an unforgivable breach of etiquette, the gallery cheered. Through the years Americans have been the least jingoistic over their sports heroes of any nation. They have cheered for Player, and rooted for Tony Jacklin, Lyle, Langer, and Olazabal, and they adore Ballesteros. You won't find that attitude in other countries. I've seen British galleries behave especially poorly. I was standing near the 15th green at Hoylake during a match involving an American and a British golfer some years ago and listened to one Englishman calling for the American's tee shot to land in a bunker. "Get in there," he urged, but the ball hit short and bounded onto the green.

Perhaps the best known incident involved David Graham at Sandwich during the 1985 British Open. Graham had a chance to catch Lyle as he played to the 72nd hole. The last man to play his approach, his ball was still rising when the gallery broke loose and swarmed across in front of him, blocking his view of the green, but he heard a loud cheer as it landed. Believing he had played his shot stiff to the pin, he was especially puzzled when be broke through the crowd and saw the green empty of balls. As he wandered around looking for his ball, a loud voice rose from the grandstand calling, "It's in the bunker."

Until the Woosnam incident, I can't recall an episode like this in the United States. Unfortunately, the scene at Augusta grew worse. Woosie was lucky to find an opening back to the fairway from his lie, then punched a low shot to safety, laid up short of the creek with his third, and bogeyed.

Watson, meantime, had had a chat with himself on the tee, telling himself, "Let's eagle 13 and 15." He did, lashing a 195-yard five iron onto the 13th and holing from 15 feet. In one hole he had picked up three strokes on Woosnam, and now stood only one stroke behind. On to the 14th.

As they stood on the tee, someone in the gallery yelled, "Hey, Woosnam. This isn't some links course; you're at Augusta now." Again, sportsmanship at its lowest level.

While Watson and Woosnam waited to drive from the tee, up ahead Olazabal made another move, playing a seven iron inside 10 feet and holing another birdie putt. Ten under now, he had climbed within one stroke of Woosnam.

Both Woosnam and Watson made their pars on the 14th, and when they reached their drives on the 15th, they looked down the long grade and saw Olazabal score his third consecutive birdie, chipping close after his three-iron second had run over. Now Olazabal had passed Woosnam. He stood at 11 under par with his birdie, while Woosnam had fallen to 10 under after his bogey, and Watson stood at nine under. Two strokes separated the three men with only a few holes left to play.

Away, Woosnam played a four iron to the back of the 15th green, and Watson, from 205 yards out, hit another stunning five iron within eight feet of the cup. Now the great crowd exploded into cheers. Minutes later, after Woosnam had lagged close to the hole and tapped in, Watson holed his putt. A second eagle three, and now Watson, Woosnam, and Olazabal had tied one another, all three men at 11 under par. Once again the gallery broke into cheers, and raced ahead, some heading for the 16th, the par three over water, others rushing to find places near the 17th or 18th, for once again the Masters would be decided at the finish.

All three men made their pars on the 16th and 17th, and they came to the 18th hole even with one another, still at 11 under par.

Olazabal arrived first. Drawing his driver, he aimed for the two fairway bunkers that flank the left side of the fairway, put there some years ago to prevent players from driving into the wide open area and avoiding the trees along the right. The hole had been designed to force a risky drive up the right. Asked how to play the hole, Hogan responded once, "You just shave the trees." In his younger years, Nicklaus simply blew his drive left, took the trees out of play, and hit the ball so far, he could reach the green with a comfortable iron.

Now, with those bunkers in place, the players had to avoid them, and at the same time, take care not to drive right into the tall pines on the other side.

Olazabal aimed for the bunkers planning to fade the ball back into the fairway. The fade didn't take; his ball caught the first bunker and lay too close to the high front wall, he couldn't play enough club to clear the bunker's face and still reach the green. Instead of a seven iron, he played an eight and found another bunker at the green's edge.

Climbing down into the sand, he heard Wadkins say, "Get it up and down." He didn't. The hole was set to the rear of the green, on the upper level, but his ball didn't quite make it up the slope, stopped for an instant, and then rolled back down. He made five, shot 70 and finished at 279.

All three men had been under enormous pressure over those last few holes, Olazabal, at 25, with the best part of his career still ahead of him but still straining to win his first important tournament; Woosnam, at 33, at the peak of his game, the leader of the Sony Ranking, like Olazabal striving to win on a big occasion; and Watson, 41 now, his best days behind him, but still with an unbeatable will, fighting for that one last great moment.

Standing on the tee, Woosnam and Watson had watched Olazabal go from bunker to bunker, and now it was their turn. With the honor, Watson played first, and decided to take the bunkers out of play. He drew a three wood, like Olazabal, planning to fade the ball and leave himself in mid fairway with a straight shot to the flagstick. Instead he came into the ball with an open clubface and pushed it. His ball flew into the trees and left him with no chance to reach the green.

Now it was Woosnam's turn. He had seen two wonderful players attempt to play finesse shots that would have put them in position to go for the green with their seconds, and he had seen both of them fail. No finesse for him; Woosie would go with power.

He knew the left fairway bunkers lay 260 yards in the distance, but he also knew that if he met the ball solidly, he could carry them. He had been hitting solid shots all day except for the hook on the 13th, but a hook wouldn't do much damage here. He made his decision. Woosnam is an amazing man. Only five-foot-four-and-a-half-inches tall and weighing, he claims, little more than 160 pounds, he can hit a golf ball farther than only a handful of golfers, and he's a better player than anyone who can outdrive him. Playing the 18th hole at Oak Hill in the final round of the 1989 U.S. Open, Woosnam *carried* his drive 290 yards.

Here he rifled his drive straight at the bunkers, the ball kept climbing, and just when you thought it would start falling back to earth, it climbed a little more, cleared the bunkers, and rolled within 140 yards of the green. Still, he faced a blind approach, since the green sat high above the level where his ball lay, and he would have to be careful of the greenside bunker.

Before Woosnam played, Watson would have to work out his problem. He had very few options, and chose to gamble on reaching the back of the green with a three iron. The shot didn't work; his ball streaked out of the trees, failed to take the fade, and settled into the same bunker that had caught Olazabal. Now Woosnam.

His ball lay at such an unusual angle to the green, the gallery blocked his line, and so he had to wait while marshals cleared a path. Both Watson and Woosnam were under extreme tension, but that is part of this game; the victory would be won by the man who could play at his best when it mattered most.

Woosnam chose an eight iron and hit a timid-looking shot that pulled up just short of the left side of the green, leaving him about 50 feet from the hole. Watson then blasted out of the bunker about 20 feet past the cup. Woosnam would have to putt first.

After studying his line, Woosnam rapped his ball about eight feet past the hole; it wasn't over quite yet. If Watson could hole his putt, he would save his par and at worst force a playoff. Going for the four, he played a bold putt that eased past the cup and rolled four feet beyond.

He still had hope if Woosnam would miss, but Ian rolled his ball dead into the middle of the cup for his par four, a score of 72, and 277 for the 72 holes. The Masters had been won, and we had another international winner. Watson then missed his second putt and fell to third place, behind Olazabal, tied, at 279, with Wadkins, Pate, and Crenshaw, who finished the tournament with two 68s.

So once again we had a European winner of the Masters, and once again we in the United States were left wondering when indeed will we breed a player who can rise at least to this big occasion. Of the last two American winners of the Masters, Nicklaus was 46 when he won in 1986. Furthermore, both Watson and Wadkins had reached 41 in 1991, and Crenshaw was 39. Pate, the other American who had tied for third place, was a month away from his 30th birthday; Mudd, who tied with Andrew Magee and Ian Baker-Finch for seventh place, had reached 30; and Magee was still a year away. Irwin who tied for 10th, was 46.

While Americans had taken seven of the first 11 places, none of them would strike fear in many hearts; the days of Watson, Wadkins and Irwin are over, Crenshaw's moment was brief, indeed, and none of the others have ever amounted to much in the important championships, although Mudd would make a run at the British Open later in the season.

We are bombarded perpetually with propaganda claiming we have more great players on the PGA Tour than ever before. From their showings in both the Masters and the British Open lately, they seem to be at their greatest finishing somewhere other than first.

4. U.S. Open Championship

Twenty-one years had passed since Tony Jacklin had become the first Englishman in 50 years to win the U.S. Open. It had been a difficult 21 years for the Hazeltine National Golf Club, where that 1970 championship had been played. The club had smarted from the comments by nearly every player in the field. Some of those comments had been vicious, particularly the nasty remarks by Dave Hill, who finished second to Jacklin. Among the milder remarks, Hill said the members ruined a good farm when they built the course.

Then, in one June week of 1991, all those painful memories faded, for in many terms, the 1991 Open ranked among the most successful we had ever seen. Not only did Hazeltine set records for attendance—more than 40,000 a day—but the golf course, revised since those days, was universally praised as well; not one player whined the course was unplayable, a record of itself. Furthermore, in Payne Stewart the game had a national champion who deserved the title. Stewart beat Scott Simpson in an 18-hole playoff after they had tied at 282 over 72 holes.

At the same time the 1991 Open stands out as one of the most tragic of any championship ever played. A spectator was killed by lightning during the opening round. Looking for shelter from the pouring rain, William Fadell and five other men huddled under a young willow tree. Lightning struck the tree at 1:07 p.m., knocking every one of them to the ground. The others recovered; Fadell died of cardiac arrest.

Still, not even the fatal storm dampened the enthusiasm of the gallery for very long. They thronged to Hazeltine in record numbers, and endured long and inconvenient delays while busses shuttled them to and from hard-surfaced parking lots miles away that had to be used because rain early in the week turned the surrounding farm fields to mud. Some fans walked a mile or more when those lots filled. No inconvenience mattered. Starved for big-time golf, Minnesotans turned out principally to watch the great players of the day, but also as a matter or pride; they had been hurt by the biting remarks of 21 years earlier, and they came hoping for approval from the players and from out-of-town spectators.

Hazeltine had been a young club then, built in 1962, and like Bellerive five years earlier, rushed into an Open before it should have been. The golf course hadn't been tested enough, even though it had held the 1966 Women's Open and the 1967 Minnesota Classic. The 1970 Open uncovered its flaws. It had plenty. The holes had so many doglegs, Bob Rosburg wondered if it had been laid out in a kennel.

No golf course within living memory had been so maligned, vilified, condemned, defamed, reviled, denounced and slandered. Its most publicized denunciation came from Hill, a competent enough golfer, although he hadn't ever played well enough to scare anybody on a big occasion. Even though he finished second to Jacklin, Hill despised Hazeltine. He had opened with 75, which might sound bad now, but at the time it was one of the best of the day.

Hazeltine sits on the flat Minnesota prairie near the village of Chaska, about 20 miles southwest of Minneapolis, with nothing between it and the north pole except fence posts and telephone poles. A cold wind howled out of the north on opening day, racing across Hazeltine at about 40 miles an hour, ripping tents and nearly uprooting the mammoth scoreboard anchored by a series of six-by-six-inch pilings driven four feet into the ground.

In these conditions the ball couldn't be controlled. Jack Nicklaus went out in 43 and shot 81. Gary Player shot 80, and Arnold Palmer, still a force in the Open, shot 79.

Hill shot 75; only seven men turned in better scores. Jacklin was among them, leading the pack at 71. Under more benign conditions the next day, Jacklin shot 70, and Hill climbed into second place by shooting 69, the third best score of the day. Somebody named Randy Wolff shot 67 and then disappeared from the leaderboard, and Bunky Henry, a former Georgia Tech placekicker, shot 68. Did the 69 make Hill happy? Not that anyone noticed.

Asked to visit the press when he stepped out of the scorer's tent, Hill said he would rather have lunch, then strode off to the clubhouse. His hunger calmed and his thirst slaked with what he later described as a few drinks, Hill presented himself to the ink-stained wretches whose accounts we all awaited breathlessly.

Seating himself at a table overlooking the sea of reporters, Hill sucked on a cigarette and grinned. He had made some harsh but forgotten comments about Hazeltine the previous day, and so someone asked, "Do you like the course better now?"

"No, sir," he answered. "If I had to play this course every day for fun, I'd find me another game." Everyone laughed.

"What does it lack?"

"About 80 acres of corn and a few cows. They ruined a good farm when they built this course." More laughter.

The session had become bizarre. Sensing a bit of comic relief to write about for the next day's editions, the reporters led Hill on, and he responded with the most outrageous charges he could think of. With everybody laughing, Hill acted more like a comedian playing to an audience, and once he started, he didn't seem able to stop. At one point he referred to Trent Jones, who had designed Hazeltine, as an idiot.

Then someone asked Hill, "What do you recommend they do with it?"

Hill answered, "Plow it up and start over. The man who designed this course had the blueprints upside down. All the greens slope away from the shot. My two boys could have done as well designing the eighth hole (a par three with a shallow green on the far side of a pond). If I didn't have some friends with me I probably would have left Tuesday, but we sit around and have some drinks and laugh and cut up."

"Will you win?"

"Oh, I'll win, but I don't like it. It discourages great golfers like Palmer and Nicklaus."

"Why doesn't it discourage you?"

"I'm not smart enough. I just hit the ball and go find it."

Hill followed up with some nasty comments about Britain, saying he'd never go over there again unless he died and his body was shipped to the wrong place.

Outraged, Leonard Crawley, a former Walker Cup golfer who was then covering golf for London's *Daily Telegraph*, wrote, "We are delighted to learn the only way he will visit us again is in a box."

Word of Hill's comments had reached the locker room before him, and when he walked through the doors, a number of players applauded. One called, "If they fine you, we'll pay it."

He was fined (Joe Dey, then the commissioner of the Tour, fined him $150), but of course the others didn't pay.

The press conference had other repercussions. Walking into the press tent the next day, Jones said, "I feel as if I'd been hit by a wedge."

Perhaps, but a great many players felt Hill spoke for them. It was indeed true that landing zones couldn't be seen from many tees, and that nearly every par-four or par-five hole swung either right or left. Neither the first fairway or green could be seen from the tee, and drives from the 18th tee had to be aimed at the chimney of a house. They had a better target there than they had had on the first, where they aimed toward a car in the parking lot, or a passing cloud.

While most Minnesotans bristled, others quietly agreed with the criticism. Hazeltine was dull, and if the club wanted another Open, it would have to revise the golf course.

Given one taste of the national championship, Hazeltine did indeed want more, and quietly set about turning the course into one the USGA would approve. In spite of what it considered an unsatisfactory course, the USGA did, however, take the 1977 Women's Open to Hazeltine. Some minor adjustments had been made to the greens by then, but the major flaws remained. At that time the governing body outlined the type of changes it felt were necessary. For example, P.J. Boatwright, who died in April of 1991 after running the Open for 21 years, hated the 17th, a short par four of 344 yards. Because the players found it prudent to drive with three and four irons, then pitch to a green set among a grove of trees behind a stream, Boatwright felt it would play better as a par three. Neither did he think highly of the 16th, a long par three of slightly more than 200 yards with a kidney-shaped green and a billowing tree that could block the green's left corner. Some players mocked it as the game's only doglegged par three.

Convinced they wanted another Open, and they would get it only after extensive changes, the members brought Jones back for a thorough overhaul. He made some alterations in 1978, the club added some of their own, and by the time they were finished they had a new Hazeltine. Five holes were entirely new, particularly the troublesome first and 18th, and in the most sweeping changes of all, both of Boatwright's nightmares had been eliminated. The 16th had metamorphosed into a short but troublesome par four skirting Lake Hazeltine, which gives the club its name, and the 17th was reborn into the par three Boatwright had suggested. The change in the 16th turned out to be the most significant of all; it became the key hole of the Open.

The revisions completed, the USGA offered the 1983 Senior Open as a test. Billy Casper beat Rod Funseth in a playoff. The USGA liked the course, and after deep discussions, awarded the 1991 Open.

While the USGA might have been pleased, Hazeltine's members felt the course needed more work, and so they brought in Rees Jones, the younger of Trent's two sons, both of whom are in the business of golf course design.

An architect who believes in working within the concept of the original architect's intention, Rees had done impressive work refining The Country Club, in Brookline, Massachusetts, for the 1988 Open. While some of his modifications can be spotted easily, he maintained Hazeltine's character and and the style of architecture popular at the time when his father created the original design. He did extensive work on eight holes and revised the teeing grounds of nine, raising some to bring the landing areas within sight, relocating others, and enlarging some.

He took out bunkers on some holes, added them on others, and softened doglegs, most notably on the seventh, where under the original design the fairway bent nearly 90 degrees.

The first hole gives us a good example of the changes. Where once it had been a dogleg left, it stretched 440 straightaway yards. Players had complained back in 1970 that they couldn't see the fairway because of a rise to the left of the tee. No dummy, Trent knew the hill blocked sight of the landing area and said it would have to be leveled. Here, though, he faced one of the difficulties course architects run into—the powerful member who wants it done his way.

Totton Peavy Heffelfinger, whose family owned and ran the Peavy Company, a big grain dealer in Minneapolis, had been one of the club's founders. He had been president of the USGA in 1952 and 1953, and carried a considerable amount of weight not only in Hazeltine matters but also within the USGA. Without his prodding, it doesn't seem likely the Open would have gone to Hazeltine the first time.

Heffelfinger didn't want the hill cut down, so it stayed where it was. With the revisions, it was cut down.

Heffelfinger had had other influence on the design. The Walker Cup, a match between amateur golfers from the United States on one side and Great Britain and Ireland on the other, is a great occasion for USGA types. Heffelfinger had been out of office for six years at the time of the 1959 match, but he came to meet with old friends and to be a part of a significant occasion in international golf. (To digress, the 1959 American team ranks among the strongest ever assembled and could probably have given the American Ryder Cup teams of the late 1980s and early 1990s all they could handle. It was composed of Jack Nicklaus, Harvie Ward, Deane Beman, Bill Hyndman, Frank Taylor, Billy Joe Patton, Tommy Aaron, Charlie Coe, and Ward Wettlaufer. The United States wiped out the British, 9-3.)

The match had been played at Muirfield, in Scotland, and Heffelfinger had stayed at the Marine Hotel, in North Berwick, only a mile or so away. The hotel overlooks the North Berwick golf course, not a particularly imposing course but one that has had profound influence on the design of holes. Its 15th, the distinct par three known as the redan, has been copied all over the world. The green of its 16th is distinguished by a deep depression that more or less carves it into two greens. Charles B. Macdonald copied the design for the ninth hole at the Yale golf course, in New Haven, Connecticut.

North Berwick is distinguished further by its children's course, a nine hole layout designed for the young golfer, with short holes and no hazards. Adults can play only if they are invited by a child.

Heffelfinger felt this was a great idea, and he insisted Hazeltine have its own children's course. He further insisted it sit just in front of the clubhouse, the area normally reserved for the closing holes of the main course. Trent would have to work around it. Consequently, the ninth and 18th holes turned out fairly pedestrian, both of them uphill par fours that bent around the children's course.

With the revisions, and without interference from Heffelfinger (he had died some years earlier), the children's course was eliminated, except for three holes, and the ninth and 18th straightened and turned into strong tests of 432 and 452 yards, both playing uphill. When the wind blew during the third round, Stewart, one of the longer drivers in the game, had to play a second driver from the fairway in order to reach the green of the 18th.

With all the modifications, the 16th remained Hazeltine's *piece de resistance* or its *bete noire* depending on whom you ask. Unlike most holes designed by committee, this one worked. During the original stages of the reworking, Bob Fischer, Warren Rebholz, the executive director of the Minnesota Golf Association, who was also a Hazeltine member, and Reed Mackenzie, a lawyer who became general chairman of Hazeltine's Open committees, wandered around the 16th looking for enough land to create a par four. It was a painful exercise for Fischer. With all its quirks, he loved that old 16th.

On a brisk afternoon, Mackenzie broke through brush behind the 15th green and skidded down a steep bank to the lake's shore. He found an area of relatively flat land that easily could be converted into a teeing ground about 350 yards from the old green.

Rebholz and Fischer agreed, but they went further, discarded the old green and dreamed of an entirely new hole that skirted the lake shore. They outlined their concept to Trent Jones, and Jones sketched the new hole on a cocktail napkin. The new hole was built during the early revisions, and was in place for the 1983 Senior Open.

When Rees Jones arrived to work his wonders, he noticed what looked like a drainage ditch running along the fairway's left flank. Deciding this wouldn't do, he expanded the ditch into a narrow creek.

This new creation became Hazeltine's most difficult hole. With the creek on the left, Lake Hazeltine on the right, and a big shade tree poking into the fairway from the right, it was without question Hazeltine's most difficult driving target, so narrow the players seldom used their drivers, preferring instead to play safe with a long iron or, in some cases, a fairway wood, first of all to avoid the water on both sides, and second, to position themselves left of the tree for a clear shot into the green, now resting on a short peninsula. It was a difficult hole to play under ideal conditions; with the wind up, it was treacherous.

Nevertheless, where once players had moaned about the course, joked about it, and ridiculed it, now they praised it. After his first practice round, Lanny Wadkins, one of the early arrivals, slumped into a chair in the locker room and said, "There's not a bad hole out there. It's a fair course, the way an Open course is supposed to be. I think it will be a hell of a tournament. I don't think I've seen a better conditioned course."

Greg Norman agreed, saying, "I don't think there'll be many complaints this time. I think it's fabulous. I haven't found a weak hole; it's one of the best golf courses I've played in the U.S. Open."

Curtis Strange called Hazeltine "A very good golf course. The setup is exactly what you'd expect for an Open course. It's fair now, but I think everybody will have a different opinion when the wind blows."

When golfers call a course fair, look out; translated, it usually means they think it's easy. Evidently with relatives in the region, Mark Calcavecchia had played Hazeltine more than anyone in the field.

"I'd be surprised if anyone shoots less than 67 or 68," Calcavecchia said, "and I don't think there will be many of those, either. All you'll want to do is get under par the first day, and then try to stay there."

Larry Mize liked what he saw as well.

"It's a very straightforward course," he said, "You know what you have to do; you know where you have to hit the ball. There are no tricks. I didn't have a blind shot to any green."

They all seemed to agree with Rees Jones' assessment.

"What you see is what you get. It's not going to be a tricky golf course."

Nevertheless it was a long and demanding course, measuring 7,149 yards. Compared to the 1970 Hazeltine, it was better as well. Even Hill became a fan.

Speaking after he had been invited back, Hill said. "The first thing that catches your eye on the first tee isn't a silo. You look down there and see a nicely bunkered green. It's grown into a lovely course. It's definitely a fun golf course and a demanding golf course. I'm sure you'll have a great Open."

As it is with any golf tournament, how great it was can be a matter of opinion. Certainly it had the ingredients—a superb golf course in pristine condition and the strongest field of the year, based on the Sony Ranking. Ian Woosnam, the game's leading player, according to the figures, had come over once again, along with Nick Faldo, whom Woosnam had replaced in the Ranking, and Bernhard Langer, Norman, Ian Baker-Finch, who was to win the British Open a month later, along with the leading American players. All of them had their problems, though.

Woosnam hadn't played much tournament golf since he had won the Masters, in April. Returning to Europe, he had missed the cut in the Benson & Hedges, placed second in the Italian Open, 12th in the Volvo PGA, ninth in the Dunhill British Masters, and finally 12th in the Murphy's Cup only a week before the U.S. Open was to begin. Some players said they were surprised that Woosnam had stayed so late in Europe.

Faldo said, "I'm very surprised he did it. I'd have thought he'd come over and acclimate himself to the time difference. His decision shouldn't be based on money. The U.S. Open is the next major championship, and the best way to prepare, in my opinion, is to come over here."

Woosnam brushed the whole issue aside. He said, "I looked at my schedule and saw I had a commitment to play in the Murphy's Cup. I was just honoring the contract." Then, implying early arrival didn't mean as much as others believed, he reminded his critics, "I played in Europe before the 1989 Open and wound up finishing second. It didn't seem to bother me much then, and I don't think it's bothering me now. I'm just going about things my own way."

He did admit, though, that his game had lost its edge since the Masters.

"I'm not playing very well, and I'm not thinking of winning at the moment. I've got a lot of things to work on before the tournament starts. I'm hoping to get off to a steady start, and then maybe play myself into contention as the week goes on."

He did indeed have work to do. He sprayed his shots all over the place in his practice round Tuesday, uncharacteristic of Woosnam at his best. He's usually among the game's straightest drivers.

While Woosnam had to stand at the top of anyone's rankings, and therefore among those expected to win the Open, Europeans haven't done nearly so well as they have in the Masters and British Opens of the last decade. While they had won six of the previous seven British Opens and seven of the previous 12 Masters Tournaments, including each of the previous four, no European had won the U.S. Open since Jacklin, in 1970. They had threatened, though. Faldo had lost a playoff to Strange in 1988, and Woosnam had tied for second behind Strange the following year. Other overseas golfers had done well, too. They had won one and placed second in four other U.S. Opens since 1979. Player tied for second behind Hale Irwin in 1979; Isao Aoki was runner-up to Nicklaus in 1980; David Graham won the 1981 championship; Norman lost a playoff to Fuzzy Zoeller in 1984; and finally Denis Watson, a South African, Dave Barr, a Canadian, and Tze Chung Chen, from Taiwan, tied for second behind Andy North in 1985. We shouldn't forget, either, that Seve Ballesteros finished third in 1987, behind Simpson, who won, and Tom Watson, the runner-up, and with a bit more luck Faldo could have won in 1990.

Adding further to the case for their strength, while they had played in only a limited number of events, overseas golfers had won 24 PGA Tour tournaments over five years. In addition, overseas players held the top-four positions, and six of the first 10 in the Sony Rankings.

Why this turnaround? Watson said, "They're better. Golf is an international game. The United States didn't invent the game and doesn't own the game. I don't know why the European golfers are doing so well. You'd have to look inside each of them, but right now they're a slight cut above the rest of the world."

Certainly no one could question that Woosnam and Faldo ranked as the two-leading players. Nick had been awesome in 1990, winning not only the Masters but the British Open as well, and coming perilously close to taking the U.S. Open. A loose approach to Medinah's 16th that left him at least 80 feet from the cup led to a three-putt bogey, and even so he missed tying Irwin and Mike Donald by the barest margin. His putt for a birdie on the 18th caught the lip of the cup, but spun out.

While they stood atop the game, the differences between Woosnam and Faldo were almost comic—Woosnam short and blocky, and earthy; Faldo tall, lean, and elegant; Woosnam with a simple, uncomplicated, natural take-it-back-and-swing-it-through motion, like a six-cylinder Ford; Faldo with the more manufactured movement that called for constant fine tuning, like a 12-cylinder Jaguar.

As the Open approached, Faldo must have been looking at his warranty. In three European Tour tournaments, he had placed fifth in the PGA, but fallen to 47th in the Benson & Hedges and, worse, missed the cut in the Spanish Open. He had done little better in four PGA Tour events—seventh at Bay Hill, 57th in The Players Championship, 12th in the Masters, and 50th at Westchester the week before the Open was to begin.

Having won both the Masters and the British Open twice each, he would, of course, have liked to add the U.S. Open.

Speaking shortly after he arrived from New York, Faldo said, "This is a championship I have been close to winning a couple of times, and I would like to win it. My game hasn't been great so far, but I have been working very hard on this for the last four weeks."

We were roughly halfway through the season by then, and Faldo had played in only those seven tournaments. It left most of us wondering if he had played enough to keep his game tournament sharp.

By contrast, Jose Maria Olazabal had been slightly more active, playing eight of the 18 tournaments in Europe, and three in the United States. While he hadn't placed among the leaders with any consistency, he had had his moments. Remember he had come to the 72nd hole at Augusta with a chance to win the Masters, but had bogeyed and finished second to Woosnam. That, of course, had been the highlight of his season, even though he had won the Catalonia Open earlier in the year. Nearly winning the Masters not only made up for other disappointments, it turned his third-place finishes in the Mediterranean and Balearic Open into nearly forgettable experiences.

At the same time, his near-miss in the Masters affected how he played the next few weeks.

"After the Masters," Olazabal explained, "I wasn't mentally prepared to play golf for a couple of weeks. I was obviously disappointed that I gave away a chance to win," he went on. "I haven't played well the last four or five weeks, but I've started to hit it better. I've been struggling with the long shots, both from the tee and to the greens. I've been all over the place—right and left."

Assessing Hazeltine, Olazabal saw trouble.

"All the U.S. Open courses seem to set up the same—long with high rough and fast greens. There aren't a lot of opportunities here to hit a one iron off the tee. You sacrifice too much distance trying to keep the ball in the fairway. If you do that you end up hitting long shots to the green. To do well here you have to hit your driver off the tee, and you have to hit it straight.

"U.S. Open courses aren't anything like we play in Europe. We play in sun and wind and rain and cold. We're not used to conditions as good as they are here. Winning one of the major tournaments is one of my targets, something very important to me."

Of course we couldn't overlook Ballesteros who, with Norman, ranks as one of the game's most exciting players. When he is on his game Ballesteros is a joy to watch, particularly with those little chips and pitches from around the greens. While he has played exceptionally well at Augusta—he won three Masters Tournaments—he has never seemed comfortable in the Open. Some suspect his temperament is no help. He gives the impression he wants so desperately to beat Americans, he becomes so frustrated when he drives into the rough, he loses control of his emotions and throws strokes away.

Seve had played in 13 previous U.S. Opens, and had been in position to win three of them, first in 1983 when Watson threw a 31 at him on the first nine of the last round, and again in 1985, when he played the last few holes badly and slumped to fifth when North won his second Open. Even though he finished third in 1987 he didn't have much chance. He was ruined by a second round of 75 and finished five strokes behind Simpson. He hadn't placed higher than 32nd in the three Opens since then.

Still, he could not be dismissed that easily, particularly since he had been playing so well throughout the year. He had won three of his last four events, one in Japan, two in Europe, including the Volvo PGA Championship, played three weeks earlier at the difficult Wentworth Golf Club. He beat young Colin Montgomerie on the first hole of a playoff, rifling a 220-yard five-iron shot within three feet of the cup. Sensational shots like that make him so much fun to watch. He finished fifth at Westchester, and seemed primed to make another serious run at the Open. Like Norman, though, Ballesteros did not play his best golf at Hazeltine and missed the cut.

Those were the principal European threats. We could predict another from Australia, although Norman had not been playing at his best. Nor had his Open record inspired confidence. Since he lost a playoff to Zoeller in 1984, Norman hadn't placed higher than 12th until 1990, when he tied for fifth behind Irwin. In the previous three, though, he had finished 51st in 1987, and 33rd in 1989. He hurt his wrist playing a shot from the ninth fairway during the second round in 1988 and withdrew.

Furthermore, he had placed lower than 10th only twice in nine 1991 Tour events, and most unsettling of all, had missed the cut in the Masters. Distressed, he pulled out of the Heritage Classic a week later and went home to Australia. Abandoning golf for a few weeks, he and some friends fled to the outback, where they spent their time "mud-crabbing and drinking beer from morning till dark."

His appetite and thirst satisfied, Norman zipped off to Mexico's Yucatan Peninsula to skin-dive and fish.

"Caught 69 sailfish in six days," he beamed.

He also seemed to have refreshed himself. Placing fourth in the Kemper Open, and 10th at Westchester, he was playing his best golf of the year after his return.

He was indeed having fun again, and he came into the Open projecting confidence. He was driving the ball long and straight early in the week. Playing the 15th hole in a practice round on Tuesday, a par five of 590 yards, he hit a mammoth drive, and then teed up his ball in the fairway and rocketed a shot into a greenside bunker, about 300 yards away.

A spectacular shot, though, doesn't mean much.

"I need to get into contention this week," he said.

Norman was never a threat, however. Once again he had to withdraw with an injury.

When those overseas golfers were compared to the best of the Americans, on the face of it the United States didn't have as much to offer. Billy Andrade had been the best of them over the previous few weeks. A 27-year-old Rhode Islander who had never come close to winning in three years on the PGA Tour, Andrade came into the Open behind consecutive victories in the Kemper Open, in Washington, and the Buick Classic, in Westchester, New York. Two strokes behind Jeff Sluman with three holes to play in the Kemper, Andrade birdied both the 16th and 17th, recovered from two bunkers and saved his par on the 18th, then won the playoff by birdieing the 17th, the first playoff hole, drilling a six iron within eight feet of the cup.

The next day he shot 69 and 65, cutting 10 strokes off par in the 36-hole qualifying round for the Open, then headed for Westchester. With nine holes to play, Andrade and Irwin were tied for the lead, one stroke ahead of

Ballesteros and Nolan Henke, but only Andrade played the last nine under par, and he won again.

By then Billy had played 11 consecutive rounds in the 60s, 43 under par for 181 holes, but the string had drained him emotionally and physically.

Looking at the turnaround in his career, Andrade said, "This year I felt like I really wanted to win. I could taste it. I had been on the Tour for three years, and I thought I was ready."

Whether he was ready for the Open is another matter. Those tournaments he had won weren't played under Open conditions, nor did they carry the title of the national championship.

"Jay Haas told me the best time to win your second tournament is the week after you win your first," Andrade quipped. "Who knows? The best time to win my third may be the week after I won my second."

No matter that Andrade had been the hottest of the Americans, his hopes looked as thin as a trail of smoke, and truthfully so did those of Strange, who in 1988 and 1989 had become the first man to win consecutive Opens since Ben Hogan, in 1950 and 1951.

In the two years since he had won his last Open, Strange had lost his touch. In winning those two championships, he had holed every five- and six-foot putt he looked at, but now those putts weren't falling. He hadn't won a tournament since his last Open championship, and 1990 had been one of his worst years. Just how bad can be reflected by his money-winning record. After leading the Tour's money winners three times in the previous six years, he had fallen to 53rd, he wasn't doing much better in 1991, and he gave himself no hope of winning at Hazeltine.

"The Open is the farthest thing from my mind right now," he said shortly after he arrived. "I'm scoring terrible, and I'm putting terrible. I haven't made a putt in six months. I'm fed up with the way I'm playing. I'm in a terrible mood, but I earned it. I played my way there."

He was right; he didn't have a chance.

Again in contrast to the Europeans, who were mostly in their 30s, two of the more reliable Americans had reached their 40s. Watson was 41, and Irwin 46. Remember that Watson had lost the Masters on the 72nd hole by pushing a drive into the woods. This was his best finish in one of the four major tournaments since he had placed second to Simpson in the 1987 Open. He had suffered through hard times since losing the 1984 British Open to Ballesteros, but he had been playing better recently, and had finished among the top 10 in five of the 12 tournaments he had entered.

He said he'd had a hard time focusing his mind on golf, and perhaps more importantly, a hard time seeing the line of a putt. Perhaps that is a matter of concentration, but as Watson said, "When you've been dodging bullets for 20 years, your nerves get plenty frayed."

Nevertheless, his high finishes had buoyed his confidence.

"I've felt I've been on the verge of winning all year," he said. "It's been enjoyable but frustrating. It's like I'm trying to win for the first time all over again."

Watson said he was looking forward to testing himself.

"I'm at peace with myself, but the Open has been known to cause wars."

Although he was five years older than Watson, Irwin had much more of the public's confidence after he had shocked the world by winning the Open at Medinah, near Chicago, a year earlier.

Like Watson, Irwin had played in 12 tournaments so far, and had placed among the low 10 in six of them, but unlike Watson, he was playing his best as the Open approached. He had finished no worse than fourth in his last four, and no worse than third in his last three. He had come to the last nine at Westchester tied for the lead, and eventually finished third, and had placed second to Kenny Perry in the Memorial.

Nevertheless, his play over the last nine holes at Westchester left him disappointed.

"On a scale of one to 10," he said, "my execution was about a three. On the same scale, my management was 10. I'm not hitting the ball close to as well as I need to be."

As the defending champion, Irwin was given a preferred starting time for the first round, and by tradition grouped with Faldo, the 1990 British Open champion, and Phil Mickelson, the tall and lean 20-year-old 1990 U.S. Amateur champion. They left the first tee at 9:30 in threatening weather.

The day had begun under unsettling conditions. Great shards of lightning had rent the dawn sky, and drenching rains had soaked the drying ground. The downpour had stopped by seven o'clock, when the first group left the tee, but the threat lingered. It was a day no one could forget.

Except for the rain, the round began normally enough. Fans began streaming through the gates well before Terry Dear, Jeb Stuart, and Brad Sherfy were scheduled to tee off, and by 6:30 some of them had climbed into the grandstand behind the 18th green, finding good spots for themselves, even though they would have to wait at least four hours for the first group to arrive. Others found seats in the stands behind the first tee, where they could see the entire hole. Still more wandered to the 16th. They had put themselves at risk.

Hazeltine was turning out to be tough. Of the first 24 men who finished, three had matched par, but Andrade had shown that the course could be had. Andrade had birdied five of the first eight holes, and stood at four under par through the 11th. There he ran into more trouble than he'd seen in some time, including an unplayable lie for a ball lodged among tree roots. He staggered off the green with an eight, three over par.

At about that time, Henke had just teed off. The wind had come up by then, and the skies were turning black. Somewhere within the trailer that served as USGA headquarters, someone was tracking the growing storm, watching for signs of lightning. Henke drove into the fairway, but with the wind acting as it was, he couldn't decide which club to play for his approach. Finally settling on a six iron, he lashed into the shot and holed it. He had begun the Open with an eagle two.

As he picked his ball from the hole, Henke was told play had been suspended. An electrical storm had moved in more quickly than anyone predicted, and lightning had been spotted close by.

The warning had been spread throughout the course by hand-held radio, and sirens had been sounded calling off play. Marshals patrolled along gallery ropes warning the spectators the storm was on its way, and warning them to look for shelter.

At 12:49 Mark Stevens, a marshal, approached the 16th tee and heard a cracking over the air and told the growing group of spectators gathering in the vicinity, "Play is suspended."

"Shucks," a woman cried, "Lee Trevino is next."

Now it was 12:53. Craig Parry, an Australian; Corey Pavin, an American, and Ronan Rafferty, an Irishman, marked their positions on the fairway and rushed to one of the yellow school busses positioned around the course to evacuate the players.

In spite of the warnings, not many spectators left. Some headed for their cars, but most either sat where they were, huddled under the steel-framed grandstand alongside the green, or under trees nearby. Still seated in the bus, Parry looked toward the southeast. Lightning flashed across the sky.

"It looks nasty over there," he said. It was just one o'clock.

Rain pounded down, first in big drops, then in sheets. As the storm grew, more and more spectators crowded under the grandstand and the trees. Six men squeezed under a small willow standing about 100 feet from the 11th tee, on the side closest to the 16th fairway. A few of them had dashed over from other trees close by, believing the shorter tree would be less likely to attract lightning. They crowded together as close to the trunk as they could. They seemed to be in the safest spot. They were at the lowest spot on the course, and their tree stood only about 30 feet high, the shortest of any around them. In a moment of black humor, one man joked that it would be just their luck for lighting to strike here. It was 1:07.

Suddenly lightning flashed. Once. Twice. Some say a third time. One spectator said he heard what sounded like gunshots.

The bolt knifed through the sky, flashed past the tall trees, missed the steel-framed grandstand, and ripped into the little willow. It tore the bark from a long narrow patch a little over head high. The air around it smelled of smoke. Six men dropped to the ground.

"They fell like spokes of a wheel," one man said. Another said, "I heard it, I felt it. I saw everyone down. It took about 15 seconds to realize what had happened. When I walked up to two of them, they looked stone cold dead."

Now the crowd was beginning to react. They saw the men sprawled on the ground. None of them moved. Frantic now, they screamed, "Doctor. Doctor. Somebody get a doctor."

A doctor from St. Paul was there. He sped to what looked like the worst case and gave cardiopulmonary resuscitation to William Fadell. Two other doctors ran to the tree. By a stroke of luck, a medical station stood about 50 to 75 yards away, set up for the Open. Paramedics raced across the open ground and within minutes began treating those lying on the ground. One man cried he had no feeling in his legs. Another, his hands still in his pockets, lay across the legs of still another victim.

One of the stricken men, Scott Aune, yelled Fadell's name. No answer. A paramedic tried to attend to him, but Aune said, "I'm okay now. I just want you to take care of my friend."

Doctors inserted a needle into Fadell's arm and tried to revive him with intravenous solutions. They didn't work. Two paramedics hooked up a defibrilator, a machine that gives mild electric shocks intended to restart the heart. They attached it to Fadell's chest. No response. They tried again. Still no response.

Within a few more minutes an ambulance arrived. The crew lifted Fadell inside and sped to St. Francis hospital close by. They tried the defibrilator again. Again no response.

Not even a golf fan, Fadell had been given tickets by his father, Mike Fadell, a gallery marshal for the week. Word reached him that his son had been among those hit by the lightning bolt and taken to St. Francis. He was rushed to his car, and then raced off toward the hospital. Along the way his car phone buzzed. It was the hospital. His son had died. He pulled his car off the road. He couldn't drive any longer. A policeman took him to the hospital, where a priest was waiting.

All the other victims recovered.

As far as anyone knows, this was the first time a spectator had been killed by lightning at a golf tournament. It was the third death at a USGA competition, though. Robert Grant, one of the players, had been stricken by a heart attack and died during the 1983 Senior Open, also at Hazeltine, incidentally. The most bizarre had happened many years earlier. As two players struck their approach shots to one of the late holes during the 1922 Amateur Public Links Championship, a pistol shot sounded toward the rear of the gallery. A thoroughly uninterested spectator had chosen that moment to commit suicide.

Meanwhile, back at the golf course, players milled around in the locker room. Some hadn't started, others waited for the signal to resume. The signal sounded a few minutes before three o'clock. Play had been suspended for two hours and 40 minutes.

Andrade started again at the 14th hole. He had been so exhausted, he had napped during the delay. Whether the suspension had caused it can't be said for certain, but he wasn't the same player. A bogey on the 13th, at 204 yards, the longest of the four par-three holes, just as the storm struck had effectively ended his Open. Within three holes he had fallen from four under par to even. Worse was coming.

Billy snapped back with a nice birdie on the 14th, hitting a useful drive into the fairway, and then playing a nifty pitch within 10 feet. That was the end. He was back to one under par, but threw that stroke away with a bogey on the 15th, the hole where Norman had played two shots to the greenside bunker. Then he came to the 16th, which was to cause so many so much trouble.

Andrade was worn out from his hectic schedule, he had been further drained by the storm delay. When he's fatigued, his drives drift right. You can't allow that on the 16th, where Lake Hazeltine beckons the fading shot. Billy drove into the water. Still, his ball was playable. He punched a six iron back to the fairway, but then misjudged his pitch and overshot the green. Into the lake once more. A drop, another pitch, and then three putts. Andrade had another eight.

Pars on the two closing holes helped, but still Andrade had played the home nine in 43, and shot 76.

Reflecting on the round, Andrade said, "I think I hit a wall." Still, he looked at the round positively, saying that two bad holes in six weeks wasn't bad.

"I had seven birdies, so that's a positive. We've still got three days left. If I get some rest and play the way I played today, except for those two bad shots, I can get right back into this thing." It was a good thought, but he couldn't make it work. A 40 on the second nine the next day, and Billy shot 75. He missed the cut.

The day obviously would not belong to Andrade. It belonged instead to 26-year-old Henke, playing in his second Open, and to Stewart, playing in his eighth.

The storm seemed to have no effect on Henke. Starting over again on the second, he worked out his par there, and then birdied three more holes going out, turning for home in 32 after a saving bogey on the eighth, where he got down in two strokes after pushing his tee shot into the pond.

Four under beginning the second nine, he holed a curling downhill 35-footer on the 10th to dip five under par, then parred his way home. He shot 67. Let someone try to catch him. Within a few holes, it seemed obvious Stewart very well might.

Hazeltine wasn't the same once the storm ended. The rain had soaked the greens, turning them into soft and easy targets, and the gusting wind had died; club selection wasn't so much a guessing game. Stewart had been scheduled to tee off at 1:30, but with the delay he began at four o'clock, then birdied three of the first four holes. A drive and an eight iron settled within 15 feet on the first hole, a nine iron to 12 feet on the third, and a five iron to 15 feet on the fourth, the first of the par threes, and Stewart was off to a fast start.

From there on he played flawless golf. He missed only one fairway, birdied both par fives on the home nine, ran off 12 more pars, didn't bogey a hole, and matched Henke's 67. No one caught them. When the round ended they stood one stroke ahead of Tom Byrum, an obscure 30-year-old from South Dakota who had won only one tournament in six years (strangely enough, he and his older brother, Curt, both scored their only victories in 1989). After a solid 35 on the first nine, Byrum raced home in 33, birdieing the dangerous 16th.

Nicklaus revived old memories by shaving two strokes from Hazeltine's par and shooting 70. He completed the round in sixth place, tied with Simpson, Fred Couples, and six others. They, in turn, placed behind Scott Hoch and Brian Kamm.

Expected to be a severe test of the game, Hazeltine had been a soft touch. In addition to the five men in the 60s, nine shot 70, eight others shot 71, and 15 more matched par 72. Irwin stood among those at 71. He had begun the defense of his title by playing an erratic round. He played the last seven holes in even par, with two birdies, two bogeys and three pars.

Faldo was among those at 72, and Woosnam opened with 73. Donald had had no luck since 1990 had ended. He had rushed to prominence the previous year by shooting 64 in the opening round of the Masters, and then nearly winning the Open, losing to Irwin on the 19th hole of the playoff. He began the 1991 Open with 74 and eventually missed the cut. Stewart had holed his last putt in dying light at 9:05; he had barely been able to see. Play was suspended for the day with 33 men still on the course, some of them among the premier players of the time—Ballesteros was on the 17th hole, Larry Nelson, Sandy Lyle, Craig Stadler, Graham, and Tim Simpson were strung out behind him. They returned at eight o'clock the next morning and finished.

First-round leaders:

Nolan Henke	67	Davis Love III	70
Payne Stewart	67	Scott Simpson	70
Tom Byrum	68	Keith Clearwater	70
Brian Kamm	69	Jim Gallagher	70
Scott Hoch	69	Jack Nicklaus	70
Mark Calcavecchia	69	Fred Couples	70
Craig Parry	70		

As far as we can determine, no one had ever gone 10 under par in an Open. Hogan had reached nine under midway through the last round of the 1948 championship, and Nicklaus had matched him in 1980. Judging from the 1990 and 1991 Opens, that record is bound to fall some day. Both Tim and Scott Simpson toyed with 10 under in 1990, although neither made it, and Stewart made a serious run at Hazeltine.

Payne had played the first round without a bogey, and opened the second with three birdies over the first seven holes. He stood at eight under par then; two more and he would make it. With his game so sharp, it seemed conceivable. He didn't make it though. At 166 yards, the eighth is the shortest of Hazeltine's par-three holes. Payne had not missed a green so far, and had birdied both the second and the seventh, the two par fives on the first nine. His eight-iron tee shot fell short, he misjudged his chip, rolling it five feet past, then missed the putt. His string of bogeyless holes had ended at 25.

No one had known what to expect from Stewart. One of the smoothest swingers in the game (some believe his swing is too loose and relaxed to hold up under severe tension), at the same time he was among the more fragile of men. Pain from a herniated disk in his lower back had grown so severe early in the season, he had laid off for 10 weeks. He had tried to come back in the Masters, but he withdrew before the tournament began. He played the following week in the Heritage Classic, his first event since the last round of the Bob Hope Desert Classic back in early February. He came in fourth at the Heritage, his best tournament of the year. He had placed no higher than 17th in others, and he had missed the cut in the Colonial.

The disk had caused him to lose strength in his left arm. An exercise program corrected the problem, although he still wore a collar to bed every night and a back brace when he played. He also liked a firm bed. His two-year-old son, Aaron, lay sound asleep Thursday night when Payne crept into his bedroom, Stuart lifted the boy and took him to another room. Aaron's bed had a firmer mattress; Payne wanted it.

"He'll sleep in that other bed again tonight," Stewart joked later.

The affliction had also caused him to play a little more cautiously.

"Playing from the rough for a long time is not good for my back," he said. Then, in a lighter mood, he added, "Or for my brain."

Stewart had had trouble with his back since 1989.

"I discovered I had three degenerative disks in my lower lumbar. Then earlier this year I had problems with a herniated disk in my neck. That was the reason why I took 10 weeks off. When I saw my doctor, he told me this was not a career-ending condition. Right then I heaved a sigh of relief."

If Stewart seemed an unlikely leader, consider Henke. He felt so uncomfortable sharing the lead, he said, "I hope somebody passes me so I don't have to worry about it." A strange sort of attitude, but as someone quipped,

"He's not exactly a Type-A personality," a reference to psychological pigeon-holing that means he's not the aggressive type.

Henke added, "I've never had a lot of attention. I've never needed it, never wanted it."

He admitted he was a little shocked on Wednesday when a woman fan approached him asking for an autograph.

"Is your name Fred Funk?" she asked.

"No," he answered, "I'm Nolan Henke."

It didn't stop her.

"That's even better than Fred Funk," she said.

Henke approached blasphemy talking about himself. He admitted he likes fishing if not better than golf, at least as much.

"I wasn't in a very good frame of mind coming in here," he said, "I'm going on a fishing trip next week, and I can't wait to get there."

Since he had won the B.C. Open in 1990, and so earned a place among the exempt players, Henke was in position to pick and choose where he wanted to play for the first time in his career. Until he won, he had struggled to win enough money to keep his playing privileges.

"It used to be I could only play when I could get into a tournament," he explained. "Now I can choose, and there were some courses and tournaments I could never play before that I want to play now. I think I've burned myself out."

Henke was among the early starters in the second round. He teed off at 8:10 over a course still softened by rain, but he didn't play as well as he had in the first round, hitting the ball, as he described it, "all over the place." Once again, though, he mastered the first hole, playing a six iron once again, but within 10 feet of the cup, not directly into the hole. He birdied, but lost that stroke by pushing his drive into the trees and bogeying the second. He went out in 36, even par. Three birdies coming in, including a holed bunker shot at the 13th, and a bogey on the 12th, where he missed another fairway, had him two under par after 17 holes, but he three-putted the 18th hole, came back in 35, and shot 71. His 138 wasn't good enough to hold the lead, but it had kept him within range.

Asked if he was surprised to be among the leaders, and if he thought he could win, Henke drew a deep breath and said, "Yes, I am, and no, I can't. This is a learning experience for me. I guess I could win, provided everybody else broke a leg."

By the time we were midway through the second round, the events of Thursday hadn't exactly dimmed, but they were put behind us. Then a grandstand boardwalk collapsed, and two more spectators, a lawyer and his wife, insisted on being taken to a hospital. The injuries were minor and they were discharged. In spite of a sign warning fans not to stand on the walk, it had been jammed by fans waiting for seats to open in the grandstand.

Softened by the rain, Hazeltine continued to give up low scores. Where 23 men had broken par in the first round, 33 shot under 72 in the second, the second highest in Open history. The record had been set at 47 a year earlier at Medinah.

Pavin, the Tour's leading money winner, led the assault against par, blistering the first nine in 31, and shooting 67. But the day held more bizarre turns. Ken Green, who often makes you wonder, had shot 81 in the first round and didn't bother to show up for the second. Rafferty, one of seven overseas golfers to be given a special exemption into the championship (he had led the 1989 European Order of Merit), walked off the course after the ninth, telling his group he had to visit the locker room. He had opened with 79 and was shooting 40 on the first nine of the second round, watching Pavin shoot 31. He was seen in the Minneapolis airport later in the afternoon, heading home. The European Tour fined him about $8,000 for improper conduct. They felt his walking off could jeopardize the future of those special exemptions.

Then Norman withdrew after the ninth hole. He walked up to Stewart, who was paired with him and Woosnam, and said, "Mate, I have to withdraw."

Norman explained that he had been up half the night with back spasms, and that he had hurt his hip playing his second shot to the third hole.

"It popped out, and we couldn't get it back in."

Norman walked to the fitness trailer that follows the important tournaments, and had his hip examined. Explaining why Norman withdrew, Brett Fisher, a physical therapist, said, "He just decided it was not worth the risk. It just got worse as time went on." He said as well that he had advised Norman not play the second round at all, but Greg had insisted.

Still, the championship went on, and at the end of the day Stewart still stood at the front, with Pavin, Henke, and Simpson close behind.

One of the late starters in the first round, Stewart had played early in the second. He dipped to eight under par quickly, bogeyed the eighth, and then parred every hole coming in. He stood within birdie range after good approach shots to three holes, but he missed all the putts, one from six feet after an exceptional seven iron from the rough, from 10 feet on the 13th following a five-iron tee shot, and from six feet again at the 17th after a four iron that covered the flag all the way. He one-putted only the 18th, where his eight-iron approach settled on the green's collar.

Stewart finished with 70, which, coupled with his opening 67, gave him 137 for 36 holes.

Payne had played well into the second nine before Pavin teed off, at one o'clock, with Parry and Rafferty. He hadn't hit the ball particularly well in the opening round, even though he shot 71, and he still looked shaky as he began the second. After a routine par four on the first, he pulled his drive well to the left of the second fairway, into the five-inch rough. He had missed the fairway so badly, though, his ball lay where the gallery had mashed the grass down, and so he had a better lie than he deserved. A nine-iron second left him still short of the green, about 30 feet from the cup. He chipped it in. A birdie.

"That was a good omen," he said. Indeed it was. Right away he lofted an eight iron to 20 feet on the third and holed it for his second birdie, then in quick order birdied three more holes on the outward nine. When another 20-footer fell on the 10th, Pavin had birdied six of the first 10 holes. The course record stood at 67, set originally by Bob Verwey, a brother-in-law of Player, during the 1967 Minnesota Classic, and matched four times since then, including twice the previous day. Judging from how Pavin was playing, the record would surely fall. He stood at six under par, and needed only to match par over the last eight holes to shoot 66.

It wasn't to be, though. Just as Hazeltine seemed most vulnerable, it refused to yield further. Pavin played solid tee-to-green golf the rest of the way, but he couldn't pick up any further strokes, and came to the 17th still six under. He lost his shot at the record there. A four iron from the tee left him 30 feet short of the hole, and his first putt ran four feet past, leaving him a difficult downhiller. He missed. A bogey four, and now he stood at five under par. A four at the 18th left him with 67 and 138, tied with Henke.

Scott Simpson had been among the later starters, but he had advanced into the second nine at the time Pavin had finished. A man who always plays well in the Open, he had won in 1987, and had hung close in 1990. He had been in position to win after opening with 66, but he was ruined by taking a triple-bogey six in the second round on Medinah's 17th hole. He shot 73, followed with two more 73s, and dropped to a tie for 14th place, five strokes behind Irwin and Donald.

Now he was making another move. Playing superb approach shots, he shot 33 on the first nine, running off four birdies, his longest from 15 feet, but he lost one stroke by three-putting the sixth from 40 feet following a loosely played iron. Rolling now, he birdied the 11th after a seven iron left him within 12 feet of the cup, but then ran into trouble on the 12th, a 432-yard, nearly straightaway par four over fairly flat land. Here he hit his worst drive of the day, hooking into the left rough. He chopped his ball out, pitched an eight iron to 25 feet, and then holed it. A simple par. Four under now, Simpson nearly knocked the flagstick from the hole on the 15th, pitching an eight iron within a foot of the cup. Down to five under, within reach of the course record.

Once again Hazeltine refused to give anything away. After a par four on the 16th, Simpson pushed his three iron into the right greenside bunker of the 17th and left it in with his second shot. His third settled eight feet from the cup, and he holed it for a four.

"If there is such a thing," Simpson said later, "That was a pretty good bogey."

There would be no course record, but a par at the 18th earned him a 68 and lifted him into a tie with Henke and Pavin for second place. They stood one stroke behind Stewart and two strokes ahead of Hoch, Couples, with two 70s, and Stadler, who added a 69 to his opening 71. Hoch shocked even himself with his 71. He had hit only seven of the 14 fairways on driving holes, and just one green on the second nine.

Woosnam showed some signs of life by following up his 73 with 68, and even Lyle, practically moribund since winning the 1988 Masters, seemed to be among the living once more, adding 70 to his opening 72.

At the other end of the scale, the cut fell at 147, which eliminated Byrum, who followed his opening 68 with 80, and such noteworthy players as Paul Azinger, Mark McCumber, Langer, Ballesteros (he shot a grim 77 in the second round), Donald, Andrade, and Strange, whose second-round 74 wasn't nearly good enough to make up for his first-round 77.

Nicklaus had made the cut, but his 76 had dropped him far behind the leaders. He would play no more part in the battle for the championship.

Second-round leaders:

Payne Stewart	137	Fred Couples	140
Nolan Henke	138	Craig Stadler	140
Corey Pavin	138	Ian Woosnam	141
Scott Simpson	138	Jodie Mudd	141
Scott Hoch	140		

The field was down to 65 players by then, and the first starting time had been moved back nearly an hour, from seven o'clock until 7:53. It was fortunate. Saturday, the day of the third round, dawned under threat from the weather once again. Dull gray clouds hung low over Hazeltine, and a light rain fell in early morning. Parking their cars in vacant fields, spectators walked to the course under open umbrellas and found places in the grandstands. At about seven o'clock, nearly an hour before the first pair was scheduled to tee off, everyone was ordered off the course and told to go to the clubhouse. Another severe storm was moving in. The storm didn't hit; instead it skirted the Minneapolis area, but the danger had lasted long enough to delay play for an hour. When the round eventually got underway, at close to nine o'clock, Hazeltine played as the USGA had hoped. Strong winds, gusting to 25 miles an hour or so, not only helped dry the ground and bring back the firm character of the greens, it blew golf balls off course. Where 56 men had broken par over the first two rounds, only Irwin, with 70, and Nick Price, with 71, broke it in the third. Price worked himself into contention with 214 for 54 holes, but at 216, Irwin had fallen too far back.

Simpson matched par 72 and climbed into a tie for the lead with Stewart, who slipped to 73, and at the same time, Scott showed us what was to come.

Playing immediately ahead of Stewart, Simpson went out in 35, clipping a stroke from par with a birdie on the third, and moved into first place when Stewart double-bogeyed the fifth, a 412-yard dogleg par four that swung right in the drive zone to a long, narrow, tightly bunkered green. Payne had played remarkably steady golf. Through the first two rounds he had hit 33 of 36 greens. He followed by hitting four of the first five, including the third, the 580-yard par five, where a drive and three wood left him just short. A chip to eight feet, and a solid putt earned him a birdie four. With that birdie, he dipped to eight under par once again, clearly in the lead. His solid golf ended at the fifth, though.

After driving with his one iron, Stewart hit a dreadful seven iron that scooted under a scoreboard. After taking a penalty-free drop, he played a poor chip that left him still short of the green, and he took three more strokes to get down. This was his second over-par hole in 41 holes of golf and the game's most demanding competition.

Meanwhile, Simpson was playing flawless golf. A birdie on the 10th dropped him to eight under par for 46 holes, but that was as far as he could go. He dropped one stroke on the 12th, where he bunkered his approach and missed a saving eight-foot putt, then won it back again at the 13th by holing a 30-footer, his third birdie of the day.

Two more pars brought him to the 16th, the hole that would cost him so much in this Open. Driving with a three wood, Simpson lofted a high shot that caught in the wind and drifted left into heavy rough. Choosing a wedge, Simpson chopped out to the fairway, lobbed a third shot onto the green 25 feet from the hole, then two-putted. That was bad enough, but he compounded that mistake by three-putting the 17th after dropping a five iron within 30 feet and running his first putt six feet past the hole. From two under par after 15 holes, he had fallen to even par.

Just behind him, Stewart had played 15 holes in one over par, although things looked rocky for a time. His double bogey on the fifth had been only his second over-par hole, but he looked as if he would drop another stroke on the very next hole. Until the revisions, Hazeltine's sixth was the best hole on the course. A 405-yard par four, it plays through an avenue of trees, swings left at the drive zone, and calls for a moderate iron to a peanut-shaped green hugging a pond on the left. It is best to drive to the right, since the green opens up from there. Aiming to the right, Stewart drove with a three wood, but he pushed his ball slightly into the rough. His five iron stopped short, and his chip pulled up 15 feet from the cup. Stewart holed it, saving his par.

Five routine pars brought him to the 11th, a 556-yard par four with two right-hand turns. Stewart had used his driver on only three holes, but he used it here, and followed with a three iron that left him 20 yards short of the green. He nearly holed his pitch; it braked only a foot from the cup, giving him his second birdie of the round, both on par-five holes.

With the birdie, Payne had made up both strokes he had lost on the fifth. He stood at seven under par once again. It didn't last long. Three-putting the 13th from 30 feet, he fell back to six under, two strokes behind Simpson, who had birdied the 13th, picking up two strokes.

They were still two strokes apart after 15 holes, but then Simpson bogeyed the 16th. Moments later, Stewart came to the 16th and nearly threw it all away. The wind swept in from left to right, blowing toward the lake. Using his driver for the first time here, he aimed left, expecting the wind to swing the ball back to the fairway, but it bored through the wind and settled in the heavy rough only an inch or so from the red line marking the boundary of the lateral hazard. Thinking of it later, Stewart said, "It wasn't a particularly desirable place to be."

He slashed at the ball with a five iron and advanced it to within 20 yards of the green, still in the rough, though, and his pitch rolled 35 or 40 feet from the cup. Now he was in serious trouble, facing another double bogey, for he could easily three-putt from there. His putt would have to run up and over a gentle rise in the green, then take a slight right-hand turn toward the cup. Stewart played the shot perfectly. It rolled up the gentle slope, took the break, and tumbled into the cup. He had saved a par where worse seemed inevitable.

When the putt fell, Stewart raised his right leg and pumped his fist.

"That was huge," he said. "I hadn't made a putt all day long. Making that one motivated me."

At about the time Stewart was making his par at the 16th, Simpson was bogeying the 17th. Now they were even with one another again, both at six under par, and that is how they finished. Stewart shooting 73 for 210, and Simpson 72 for the same 54-hole score. They shared the lead, for no one else had kept up with them.

Hoch, meantime, had moved into a tie for third place, even though he had shot 74 and fallen a further stroke off the lead. Where he had trailed Stewart by three strokes after 36 holes, he stood four strokes back after 54. Others ahead of him had scored worse.

The day also saw the end of several other threats. Even though he had played the first 36 holes in six under par, Henke had dropped out of the race by shooting 77. After the rain had softened Hazeltine for the second round, Pavin had complained that Hazeltine wasn't playing as an Open course should. Well, it played like an Open course in the third round, and Pavin shot 79, dropping him well out of the hunt. He was in good company. Woosnam shot 79 as well, and Mickelson shot 80 after opening with 72 and 73. After 54 holes, then, barring utter collapse by both Stewart and Simpson, the 1991 Open had become a two-man race. They stood four strokes ahead of Hoch and Price, who were tied at 214, With Henke, Kamm, and Couples a further stroke behind. Making as spirited a defense of his championship as anyone expected, Irwin had matched par 216.

With the fourth round coming up, the standing looked like this:

Payne Stewart	210	Nolan Henke	215
Scott Simpson	210	Hale Irwin	216
Scott Hoch	214	Rick Fehr	216
Nick Price	214	Craig Parry	216
Brian Kamm	215	Sandy Lyle	216
Fred Couples	215		

By Sunday the weather had improved and the skies were clear and cloudless. A ground fog lay over the Minnesota cornfields in early morning, covering the young sprouts in a misty blanket. The fields where spectators parked their cars had dried out, but the galleries seemed to be arriving later.

Stewart and Simpson were scheduled to tee off at 12:37, but before they began, Nelson made a run at them.

A rather quiet man, Nelson can be a dangerous player. A determined competitor, he had won two PGA Championships, and back in 1983, when the Open looked like a duel between Watson and Ballesteros, Nelson had taken it away from both of them by playing the last 36 holes in 65 and 67. His 132 broke the record that had stood since Gene Sarazen closed with 136 in 1932. By 1991, though, Nelson was 43 years old, and he hadn't placed above 23rd in a tournament that year. He did seem to play his best in Opens, though. He had threatened in 1989, going into the last round four strokes behind Tom Kite, the leader, and he had trailed Donald and Billy Ray Brown, the co-leaders, by only one stroke going into the last round in 1990. Weak closing rounds of 75 had ruined him in both. He would play no weak round on this day, but he had quite a lot of ground to make up.

Playing about 40 minutes ahead of the leaders, Nelson made his first birdie on the fourth, the first of the par threes, holing a 20-foot downhill putt from the back of the green. With that putt he had pulled back to even par, still six strokes behind the leaders, but who could guess what the day might bring.

A seven iron to four feet on the sixth, and then a sand wedge again to four feet on the seventh earned him two more birdies and dropped him to within four strokes of the lead. Three more pars, and then a 30-footer fell on the 13th. Five under for the day now. When the putt rolled into the hole, Nelson felt for the first time that he had a chance.

Just as they glowed brightest, though, his hopes burned out. His drive settled into a bad lie in the 14th fairway and trying to hit a nine iron too hard, he pulled it left of the green and bogeyed. He could pick up no more momentum, and finished the round with 68, giving him 285 for the 72 holes.

Meantime, Zoeller had shot 67, but again that wasn't enough. Nor was Couples' 70. Among those who began the day five strokes behind, Fred birdied both the third and the seventh, the two par fives, to drop to four under par, but he threw both strokes away with bogeys on the eighth and 10th. Two more birdies on the home nine were of little help. The Open would be decided between Stewart and Simpson.

For a good portion of the day, the championship seemed to belong to Simpson, for Stewart was playing some shoddy golf. He drove into a fairway bunker on the first, hit into a greenside bunker at the second, another fairway bunker on the fifth, and another greenside bunker on the sixth. Even so he didn't lose a stroke, and indeed moved ahead by birdieing the third. He looked as if he might pick up another stroke on the 194-yard fourth, for Simpson pushed his tee shot into the right greenside bunker, then bladed his ball all the way over and into the rough. Facing the loss of at least one stroke, Scott saved himself by chipping an eight iron into the cup for his par three.

Still one stroke ahead, Stewart lost his edge by missing the sixth green again after driving into the right rough. Where he had saved his par by holing a good putt a day earlier, he missed a 12-footer that could have saved him again. Now they were even.

Not for long, for Simpson began pulling away. A nine iron to 10 feet and Simpson birdied the seventh. One stroke ahead now. Two pars and then an eight iron to 10 feet for another birdie on the 10th. Now Simpson had moved two strokes ahead.

As Simpson made his move, Stewart could get nothing going. He hadn't played especially well until a few holes into the home nine, but he had played the shots he had to play to keep in the chase—a pitch from just off the green to save par on the 12th, and a 12-footer to save another par at the 14th after hitting his approach fat, then compounding the mistake with a weak chip. He had also missed a number of makeable birdie putts, but his frustration reached its peak at the 15th. A sand wedge left him only four feet from the cup, but his ball nicked a spike mark and veered off line just enough to ease past the cup. On to the 16th.

Trent Jones had said before the Open had begun that if a man wanted to win the Open he would have to play the 16th in even par. So far Stewart had made his par in every round, but Simpson had bogeyed in the first. Now Scott stood on the 16th two strokes ahead with only three holes to play. If he wanted to win, he would have to par in.

Simpson hadn't bogeyed a hole all day. He stood at two under par and held the Open in his hand, but Scott simply could not play the 16th. Driving with a one iron, he pulled the shot into the left rough once again, about 150 yards short of the green in grass so deep and dense he couldn't reach it with a seven iron. He left his ball 60 yards short and still in the rough.

With Simpson in trouble, Stewart split the fairway with his two iron, then lofted a nine iron within 25 feet. Now Simpson had to play a precise pitch to save par. His wedge settled nowhere near the hole; when it stopped rolling it sat on the fringe of the green about 45 feet from the cup. His first putt pulled up four feet from the hole, and he made it for a bogey five. Stewart, meantime, got down in two. Now Simpson's lead was down to one stroke.

Both men parred the 17th, Simpson coaxing a chip from the back of the green close enough to save his three, and Stewart again barely missed his birdie from perhaps five feet. On to the the 18th, with Simpson still a stroke ahead.

Up first, Stewart drove into the fairway, but Simpson pulled his drive once again. His ball rolled only inches into the left rough, but his ball lay so badly he couldn't reach the green. He played a nine iron out, then another nine iron 30 feet from the hole.

Stewart followed his solid drive with a five iron that covered the flag but rolled a foot or so over the green. Simpson missed his putt and bogeyed, but Stewart still had work to do. He had rolled his first putt five feet past the hole, and he needed this to tie Simpson. He holed it. Both men shot 72 for the round, even par, and had matching 72-hole scores of 282, six strokes under Hazeltine's par, and well clear of the rest of the field. They would meet in a playoff the next day.

Final scores:

Payne Stewart	282
Scott Simpson	282
Larry Nelson	285
Fred Couples	285
Fuzzy Zoeller	286
Scott Hoch	287
Nolan Henke	288

The galleries had been enormous throughout the week. Although Hazeltine's committees had no way to determine exactly how many spectators turned out, they estimated the crowds reached at least 40,000 each day. While these were the largest galleries ever to have seen an Open, at the same time they were the best behaved. They stood in absolute stillness when a golfer played his shot, moved from hole to hole with no fuss, and generally added to the atmosphere of the championship.

With the playoff set for a Monday afternoon, a working day, no one knew what size crowd to expect, and so some guessed attendance would be light. They were wrong. Perhaps 25,000 turned out on a bright, cloudless spring day to see two men play for the national championship.

Hazeltine had dried out by then, and the greens had grown quite firm. Only a well struck shot had much chance of holding close to the flagstick. Simpson saw the problem both men would face on the first hole. His two-iron second skidded over the green and into a bunker. He bogeyed and fell a stroke behind right away, for Stewart had saved his par four with a deft chip to three feet after his approach, too, had rolled over.

Simpson looked beaten as early as the second hole. He drilled a perfect three wood down the middle of the second fairway and a nine iron within 30 feet. Then he ruined two good shots by three-putting. After only two holes he stood two strokes behind, for once again Stewart made his par, getting down in two from 40 feet.

Scott was playing sloppy golf. He zig-zagged back and forth across the third fairway, hitting from one rough to the other, but saved par by holing a six-footer. He missed the fourth green once again, but saved another par with a reasonable chip to four feet.

Stewart, meantime, hadn't made a mistake since his four iron had rolled over the first green, and still held a two-stroke lead. With his game unraveling, Simpson pulled himself together and rattled the flagstick on the fifth hole with a six iron to three feet. Meantime, Stewart yanked his six iron left of the green, dumped a tentative recovery into the bunker, and was lucky to save a bogey.

When Scott holed his birdie, he had made up both strokes he had given away and had climbed back even with Stewart. This was the first of three two-stroke swings that day.

On and on they struggled, Simpson moving ahead and Stewart catching up and eventually pulling ahead after the 13th. Payne had moved into the lead only through Scott's errors, for he was making no birdies of his own. Now, with Stewart sensing he could win the Open, we had the second two-stroke swing of the day. Simpson birdied the 14th and Stewart bogeyed. Now Simpson had gone ahead once again by a stroke. Then, when Stewart three-putted the 15th from nearly 60 feet, Simpson held what looked like a safe two-stroke lead with only three holes to play.

Those three holes, however, had cost Scott dearly throughout the week. Compounded with his history of weak finishes in the Open, he had left the issue still in doubt. Had Scott played the last 18 holes in even par, he would have won both the 1988 and 1989 Opens, and had he played the last 21 holes in par, he would have been playing for his fifth Open at Hazeltine. But he didn't.

Both men drove with irons. Simpson's ball settled in excellent position to the left, Stewart's on the right edge of the fairway, his direct line to the flag blocked by a spreading tree. With the hole cut to the rear of the green, Simpson played a weak seven iron that pulled up on the front. Stewart then lofted an eight iron over the tree and onto the green about 20 feet right and short of the flag. After Simpson ran his first putt well past the hole, Stewart stroked his ball.

Payne hadn't birdied since the third hole of the fourth round, but now he rolled the putt home, his first birdie in 31 holes. When Simpson missed and bogeyed, we had the third of those two-stroke swings, and once again the two men stood level. On to the 17th.

Quickly, though, Stewart went ahead. After Payne had played a lovely five iron that flew over the flagstick and settled less than 20 feet from the hole, Simpson stepped up to his ball. What happened then is difficult to understand. Simpson hadn't played the 17th well throughout the championship. He had made his pars in both the first and fourth rounds, but he had bogeyed it twice. Here he played a four iron, but somehow turned the shot well left of the green. The ball slammed into the side of a steep bank leading downward toward a pond, and dove into the water. Simpson dropped his club and bent over, clutched his knees, and stared at the ground. He knew he was finished. With that stroke he had thrown the Open away once again.

In his favor, he played a superb recovery from a high ridge on the far side of the pond and holed his putt for a bogey four where worse looked certain.

Still, he had fallen a stroke behind, for Stewart had made his three and walked to the 18th tee one stroke in front.

The Open wasn't over just yet, though. Neither man drove well. Stewart's ball settled in a fairway bunker and Simpson's ball ran through the same bunker onto a downhill lie in heavy rough. From lies like this, anything might happen.

The first to play, Stewart stepped up to his ball, but then backed away. He had heard one of the grounds crewmen telling another to replace the flagstick on the first hole, because it looked as if the playoff would go to sudden death. Payne didn't like that thought. Composing himself, he stepped into the bunker once again and played a wonderful six iron that carried to the green and ran onto the collar.

Seeing Stewart's shot and knowing he would have to birdie to force extra holes, Simpson played a seven iron, but his ball ran off the back of the green. His chip rolled past the cup, and when Stewart made his par, he had won the Open.

Stewart had shot 75 and Simpson 77. While their scores weren't impressive, and indeed might seem rather shabby, we must take Hazeltine's difficulty into account. It had become tougher each day since the rains had stopped, and a good wind added further trouble. The course had turned out to be a thorough examination of the game.

In Stewart the Open had a sound champion. He often plays his best on the great occasions, and while he had missed the cut in three of the previous seven Opens, he had also placed fifth, sixth, 10th, and 13th. He had indeed been in position to win the 1986 championship with six holes to play, but he stumbled over the closing holes at Shinnecock Hills and dropped to sixth. He was younger then, though, and he admitted he had been intimidated by Raymond Floyd, his playing partner.

He had also placed second to Faldo in the 1990 British Open, giving him a good run until losing a few strokes toward the end, and to Lyle in the 1985 British Open. Stewart had won the 1989 PGA Championship, and while it has to be said that Mike Reid threw it away with some nervous golf over the last few holes, we must remember that Stewart birdied four of the last five to take advantage of Reid's collapse.

He had a sound record, and should his health allow it, he showed indications he could become an even bigger winner.

5. British Open Championship

The late Leo Durocher, a legendary figure in American baseball, once handed down a commandment that will echo as long as competitive sports shall live.

"Nice guys," Durocher said, "finish last."

Durocher's dictum doesn't translate quite that harshly into golf. Given the complexities of the exercise, the number of competitors, and the breaks of the game, nice-guy golfers are not necessarily doomed to finish last. But adherents to the Durocher philosophy will tell you, they simply don't win. And that's what they had been saying about Ian Baker-Finch, the tall, easy-going Australian. He was too nice to win.

Observers will point first to his crash in the 1984 British Open at St. Andrews, even though it was only his first real exposure to the world outside of Australian golf. He was tied for the lead going into the final round. Then a series of pressure-induced problems swept him away. Now, he was at Royal Birkdale for the 1991 Open, and he explained the collapse of 1984. "I was just a 23-year-old kid with stars in my eyes," he said.

But there had been other near-misses, most recently just the week before this Open, when Bruce Fleisher, a 42-year-old club pro re-trying his wings, beat him in a playoff in the New England Classic on the American PGA Tour. Baker-Finch, now 30, had come to Royal Birkdale with a record of 11 victories on the Australian and Japanese Tours, but in the fastest company of all, the American Tour, he had just one victory in four years. So the label stuck—too nice to win.

Speaking of "nice," there is another expression, not confined to sports, and that is—"It couldn't happen to a nicer guy." And that was the refrain that echoed through Royal Birkdale early in the evening of Sunday, July 21, when Baker-Finch—a Mr. Nice Guy if there ever was one—ran off with the 120th Open Championship. He certainly wasn't among the pre-Open favorites, not even close. He didn't even surface until the third round. But he broke away with a torrid start in the fourth round, and became one of the most decisive Open champions in years—the two-stroke margin was wider than it looked—and also one of the most welcomed.

When it came to handicapping this British Open, Baker-Finch was among the longest of long shots. If the prognosticators were right, an Open at Birkdale would finally be won by a European. In the six previous Opens there, Peter Thompson of Australia won twice, in 1954 and 1965, and the others were Americans—Arnold Palmer, 1961; Lee Trevino, 1971; Johnny Miller, 1976, and Tom Watson, 1983. Not only was history on the European side, so was the talent. "I think you've got to give the Europeans the advantage," Watson said, repeating the truism of the day. "They've proved themselves to be the top players in the world in the major championships."

How you ranked them depended on which measure you preferred. The bookmakers made Nick Faldo a 13-2 favorite to win his second consecutive Open, followed by Ian Woosnam, 8-1; Seve Ballesteros, 11-1, and Jose Maria Olazabal and Payne Stewart, both at 14-1. But off current form, it had to be Woosnam, who had won four times already—the Masters and the USF&G Classic in the United States, and the Mediterranean Open and Monte

Carlo Open in Europe. Ballesteros was no worse than a close second. He had come rocketing back from a long slump, and in one stretch in the spring, won three times and finished second in four starts. Olazabal won the Catalan Open early in the season, then went into a slide. "I have always been in control of the game," he said, "but right now the game is in control of me."

Stewart, the U.S. Open champion, was the only American the bookies mentioned in the same breath with these four. He was no stranger to British Open pressure. He was runner-up in 1985 and 1990, and had five other top-10 finishes.

This Open was also a grand reunion, and how time had left its mark. Three of the five who won at Birkdale had returned. Trevino, who won the first of his two Opens at Birkdale in 1971, was 51 now, and a big star on the American Senior PGA Tour. He not only made the 36-hole cut, his closing three-under-par 67 was one of a precious few bogey-free rounds, and he finished at one-over-par 281, tied for 17th with, by the way, Faldo and Woosnam. Miller, the 1976 champion, was 44 now and best known as a television commentator. He would not make the cut. Watson, who won the last of his five Opens at Birkdale in 1983, was 41 now, and his game was in decline. But he not only made the cut this time, he was on the leaderboard for a while. He finished tied for 26th, at 282.

And a great star was born at Birkdale—a fiery Spanish teenager who thrilled the world with his boldness and his skill. Ballesteros didn't win at Birkdale in 1976, but that is where he challenged the world and almost pulled it off before finishing second to Miller. He was 34 now, and married, and had a son not quite a year old.

Allowing for a bit of oversimplification, one can say that generally speaking, this Open would be the story of the Tiger and the Pussycat. Every course has its strong holes and its weak ones, but few have them so sharply defined as Royal Birkdale's. This Open would depend a lot on how well a man could handle the Tiger (No. 6) and the Pussycat (No. 17). They played within a fraction of a stroke of each other, No. 6 at an average of 4.59 strokes, No. 17 at 4.22. The catch is, No. 6 is a par four, and played more than a half-stroke over par, the hardest hole on the course. But No. 17 is a par five, and played nearly a full stroke under par, the easiest. Here's another way to compare them—No. 6 gave up no eagles, No. 17, 38; birdies, 18-357; pars 235-128; bogeys, 243-11; double bogeys, 41-2.

No. 6 is 473 yards long (a par four for members), a dogleg right with a dangerous cross-bunker at the right side of the elbow. "You are never sure what to do," Ballesteros said. "You don't want to hit the driver because you probably won't get over the bunker, but if you play short, you won't get on in two." No. 17 is 525 yards long, fairly straight away. With a favorable breeze, almost anybody could reach it in two.

There were some interesting performances. For instance: Olazabal, Mark McNulty and John Oates played them in perfect symmetry. They bogeyed No. 6 and birdied No. 17 in all four rounds. That seems like a wash, but in effect, they lost ground by not gaining ground. Alastair Webster got hit the worst at No. 6—a triple bogey and three singles, for a six-over-par total. What really counted, on balance, was the combined performance at the two, and five men did the best, playing them in an aggregate of five under par. One of those men was Baker-Finch, en route to the Open title.

Baker-Finch gave no indication in the first round that he would be a factor in this Open. Certainly nothing like he did in the 1984 Open, his coming-out party, where he started with 68, one stroke off the first-round lead, and so immediately became 1984's "no-name." This time he attracted no attention at all. A 71 doesn't capture many imaginations, even one marked by a lifesaving finish. He went out in even par, with a bogey at No. 2 and a birdie at No. 9. Then came a real struggle—bogeys at Nos. 12, 13 and 15. He hauled himself out of that mess by birdieing the last two holes.

And so he was just another smiling face at the end of the day. At 71, he was five strokes and 19 players behind the leader. But he had passed his first big test. He parred No. 6. Some couldn't make that happy claim. Wayne Grady, Mark James and Jack Nicklaus were making double bogeys there, and Peter Jacobsen, seven. For contrast and maybe comic relief, two figures, so distant as to be invisible, were handling No. 6 and No. 17 with impunity.

Thus the 1991 Open began, and a Spaniard was whipping up the course. It seemed like 1976 all over again. Except this Spaniard wasn't named Ballesteros. He wasn't even named Olazabal. He was Santiago Luna.

The Spaniard named Olazabal, by the way, introduces a bizarre episode into this Open, through no fault of his own. It was shortly after he teed off at 2:50 p.m., that a teenage girl decided this was a good time and place to make a statement. So she took off her clothes on the spot, and nude, she raced down the first fairway to a baffled Olazabal, and hugged him and gave him a kiss on the cheek. It was generally agreed that, as statements go, at least this one beat the vandalism at the sixth green in 1983, when a group was protesting for some prisoner. It also beat the male streaker in the 1985 Open at Royal St. George's.

If a proper Open needs a streaker, it also needs an unknown to take the lead at some point. It makes for a romantic backdrop, a Cinderella flavor. Baker-Finch in 1984, for example. But this Open had two—Martin Gates, an Englishman nearing his 27th birthday, and the Spaniard, Luna, 28. They don't come much more unknown than these two.

Gates was the son of a banker, he honed his game in American college golf (the University of Oklahoma), and he was an obscure rookie on the European Tour. Luna was the son of a golf club electrician, he came up as a caddie, and he had spent about seven unrewarding years on the Tour, his best finish a tie for seventh.

Both had to qualify to get into the Open, and Luna did it the hard way. He was part of the longest playoff in Open qualifying history. He was one of 10 men tied at 148 and playing for three Open berths. Luna finally won his at the eighth extra hole. The playoff ran out of daylight, and was finished the next morning when Spain's Yago Beamonte took the last spot from Ireland's Jimmy Heggarty. All told, the playoff lasted 10 hours and 16 holes. (And ironically, Heggarty, as first alternate, got in anyway when Ronan Rafferty was forced to withdraw because of a shoulder injury.) Luna and Gates would finish the first round tied for second place at 67, but for a while, they shared the lead. What were the odds against two unknowns taking the lead? Or second place, for that matter?

Luna, Gates, and the veteran Chip Beck shared the lead at 67—for a while. But Ballesteros, as he had done so many times, erupted late in the day to take the top spot with a 66. Still, it was quite a day for Gates. Playing in the second group, off at 7:25 a.m., he wasted no time. He chipped in at No. 1 for the first of his five birdies. He had seven one-putt greens. Four were for birdies, including an eight-footer at No. 17. And just as important, he one-putted No. 6 from six feet for a par.

He played the last five holes in three birdies and two pars, and only a rookie error cost him a tie with Ballesteros. At No. 9, some television cables lay between his ball and the green. He opted to chip over them. He hit them instead. The error cost him one of his two bogeys, and, as it turned out, a share of the lead. Live and learn. Next time, he said, he'll have someone hold them up and he'll chip under them. At any rate, he was comfortably in the clubhouse with the early lead. "Apart from being thrilled, it was a tough day," Gates said. "I didn't realize I was leading. I never looked at a scoreboard."

Beck, playing more than two hours behind him, shook off two early bogeys and played the last 14 holes in five under par for his 67. "I play in streaks," Beck said. "And I think you play your streaks out. You play with momentum, and when it runs out, you have to go back to the drawing board."

Luna came along later. He teed off at 12:25 p.m., and he also wasted no time—getting into trouble. He two-putted No. 1 from five feet for a bogey, thus launching one of the most hair-raising rounds of the Open. All told, his wild, up-and-down 67 included four bogeys, five birdies, and an eagle. He got past No. 6 with a par, though, but bogeyed the easy par-three seventh, missing from two feet. He bogeyed the par-five fifteenth, then came back with a birdie at No. 16, and then an eagle at No. 17, where he put an eight-iron second stiff. "Like that," he said, holding his hands about 18 inches apart. Then at No. 18, he three-putted from 40 feet and bogeyed. Before that, he had put on a pretty good putting show. He had 10 one-putt greens—four to save par, five for birdies, the longest from 33 feet, and one for the eagle. After a day like this, what would he think about at night? "I don't want to think nuthin'," he said, struggling with English. "I just want to play golf." Are you nervous? "No," he said. "I am dreaming."

Faldo, who turned 34 on this day, July 18, also was dreaming—of a repeat championship. He ended up in a good position with a 68, but things had looked chancy for a while. Then things brightened at the par-three 14th hole, where he smoothly got a 15-footer down for a birdie. "That turned around a day that was hard work," Faldo said. "I'd been swinging well, but just failing to reward myself. I'm putting myself under pressure, because if I hit a bad shot, I'm struggling to scramble." He even bopped himself on the head with his putter at No. 10, then he missed a birdie chance, one of seven missed birdies. The birdie at No. 14 eased the pain, and then birdies at No. 16, from eight feet, and No. 17, on two putts from 40, brought him home smiling with that 68.

Watson, now 41, was another dreamer—dreaming of 1983, at Birkdale, when he won his fifth and last British Open, and dreaming of 1987, when he won his last tournament of any kind, the Nabisco Championship on the American Tour. His problem? "Age," he replied, with that warm, toothy grin. "I don't get the club back quite so far, and then I get ahead of the ball." Watson turned back the calendar a bit when he shook off two early bogeys and went on to join the leaderboard with a 69.

Woosnam, the man with 1991's Grand Slam monkey on his back, posted a par 70 and pronounced himself pleased. "I didn't play my best today," he said. "Before I started off, I would have been happy with a par round, so I can't complain."

Stewart (72) spent the day getting to the fringe, but then couldn't get down. "I hit the ball well, but I wasted shots from the fringe," he said. He could make 15-footers, all right. Four of them for birdies, in fact. But he also made four of his six bogeys using his putter from the fringe.

Nicklaus also started with a 70, but he had to fight to salvage it. First, he was an early victim of No. 6. He caught that nasty cross bunker off the tee, blasted out, then hit a three iron to 35 feet, and three-putted for a double-bogey six. A great finish saved him. Fighting the wind, he made three birdies over the last six holes, the last of them a two putt from 20 feet at No. 17. "I told you on Tuesday I was playing as badly as I could," Nicklaus said. "But I got hold of it a little bit better yesterday. I didn't do a lot with the putter, but it's the best tempo I've had in a long time."

Jamie Spence, the man who burst into the spotlight in the 1990 Open with a 65 in the second round, was about to upstage himself this time—until the crash. Spence was out in four-under-par 30 and was three under coming to the final hole. He bunkered his approach, had to come out sideways, then chipped poorly, and three-putted from five feet for a triple-bogey seven and a round of 70. "My dad will be here tomorrow," Spence said. "It will probably give him a heart attack when he sees what happened at No. 18."

Elsewhere in the supporting cast: Mike Harwood, the stringbean Aussie, finished at 68, but flirted with much less. He missed a birdie from three feet at No. 1, for example, and then he bogeyed No. 6 when he needed two to get out of a bunker. Costantino Rocca turned in the day's only bogey-free round, a 68, and fretted over his putting. He holed from 25 feet and 12 inches for his two birdies, but missed once from four feet, three times from nine, twice from 10, and once from 13. "I just wasn't hitting the putts well," he said.

But other golfers—among them Nicklaus and Greg Norman (74)—said the greens were "spongy" and slow. Nicklaus, speaking as a golf course architect this time, offered the notion that Birkdale sits down in something of a topographical "bowl," and so the greens are shielded from winds that would dry them out and make them firm and fast.

Luna, the obscure Spaniard, had practically no chance to enjoy his new-found fame. Ballesteros had teed off over an hour after Luna. And about the time Luna was describing his eagle at No. 17, the scoreboard flashed the news that Ballesteros had just eagled No. 17 to go to three under. "You're tied with Seve," someone said. Luna grinned. "*Muy bien*," he said. But the tie wouldn't last long. Ballesteros was on one of his tears.

Ballesteros battled through a long afternoon of cutting winds and chill temperatures for a four-under-par 66 and a one-stroke lead. It took folks back 15 years, to the 1976 Open, when a young Spaniard nobody ever heard of suddenly set Birkdale on fire. But there was a big difference between that 19-year-old kid and this 34-year-old seasoned warrior. The Ballesteros who brought Birkdale to heel this time was disciplined. He didn't try to beat the course into submission.

What was that Miller said back in the 1976 Open? "If Seve had left his driver in the bag," Miller said, "he would have won." Was this an echo? In one of those wonderfully coincidental R&A pairings, Ballesteros and Miller were united again at Birkdale. And Ballesteros left his driver in the bag this time. He used it only four times, getting three pars and an eagle. He teed off with long irons the rest of the way, the better to keep the ball in play. He was out in a solid one-under 33, and coming home, two birdies were offset by two bogeys, setting the stage for a spectacular finish. At No. 17, with the wind behind him, he used his driver and bombed a drive some 375 yards, flipped a nine iron to about four feet, and holed the putt for an eagle.

It was about this time, back in the press tent, that Luna was informed Ballesteros had just tied for the lead. Moments later, Ballesteros took the lead alone with a birdie at No. 18, dropping a 40-foot putt that seemed to roll forever. Oddly enough, he had teed off with a four iron—a four iron on a 472-yard hole. "Why a four iron?" a writer asked. "Why?" Ballesteros retorted. "You think I play the hole the wrong way?" At all events, it seemed that Ballesteros was back. Or as a BBC commentator put it, "It's nice to hear Seve smiling again."

The first-round leaderboard:

Seve Ballesteros	66	Mike Harwood	68
Martin Gates	67	Graham Marsh	69
Chip Beck	67	Wayne Grady	69
Santiago Luna	67	Tom Watson	69
Gary Hallberg	68	Tony Johnstone	69
Mike Reid	68	Carl Sunesson	69
Barry Lane	68	Nick Price	69
Nick Faldo	68	Ian Woosnam	70
Costantino Rocca	68	Eduardo Romero	70
Mark Mouland	68	Fulton Allem	70

The second round was a strange one. It was a round seen in a funhouse mirror, all distorted and making little sense. Harmony definitely did not prevail on Friday, July 19.

To begin with, the day dawned as one of those typical Open days, with harsh winds and driving rain. Sensible people dive back into their toasty beds. At Birkdale, the early reports were not encouraging. Sandy Stephen, six-year veteran of the European Tour, was hanging by a thread after an opening 75, and now he was in the first group off. He arrived at the course at 6 a.m., went to the practice tee, and got soaked and frustrated for his trouble. "The wind was blowing so hard, I couldn't hit a five iron past the 120-yard marker," he said. His group went off at 7:15 a.m. Stephen did well to post 79, but he would need a lot less than that to make the 36-hole cut.

The weather was at its worst early in the day, and moderated later, which means there should have been a very definite profile to the day's play. But there was only a faint pattern. Statistics buffs could note that by the end of the day, there were 16 men on the leaderboard, with only two strokes separating the top from the bottom. Only three of them teed off before 10 a.m., and only two others before noon, which meant that 11 played under somewhat more agreeable conditions. That's understandable, but how to explain the rest of the card? For example: Some men you would ordinarily think would play well didn't, and some you'd think wouldn't, did. As plots go, this one was out of Agatha Christie.

Ballesteros, the first-round leader and a man who begs for foul weather, stepped right into the teeth of it and slipped back with a 73. He had teed off at 8:20 a.m. Bob Tway, who prefers the baking heat and sun of Oklahoma, teed off 10 minutes after Ballesteros. He returned a 66. At 8:50, Harwood, who shakes easily in a stiff breeze, he's so reedy, shot his way into a share of the lead with 70. But he was upstaged by his playing partner, the heralded American amateur Phil Mickelson, low amateur in the Masters and the U.S. Open, who was a newcomer to the British Open and British Open weather. Mickelson improved by fully 10 strokes, to a 67.

And what could be expected from Andrew Oldcorn, a man so sick so recently that it was a minor miracle he was even playing golf. Yet he came through late in the day with a 67 to tie for the lead with Harwood and Gary Hallberg (70) at 138. The big guns are supposed to do these things, but the big guns were whispering. Stewart and Woosnam returned 72s, and Faldo's chances of winning a second consecutive Open slipped farther astern when he put up a 75. Then Mark O'Meara, with a back so painful he almost didn't enter, put on an incredible finish, taking the last three holes in birdie, eagle, birdie for a 68—139, one stroke off the lead.

As the bookies might observe, things weren't going according to form. For anybody trying to get a grip on this Open, what it all added up to was confusion.

Oh, there was one thing that did go according to form. The honeymoon ended abruptly for the two overnight celebrities. Gates started the second round with two bogeys, and struggled to 75 for a 142 total. "Realistically, I had two goals," Gates said. "The first was the make the cut, and the second was to finish in the top 25, and be exempt from qualifying for the 1992 Open." The first dream came true, the second one didn't. Gates finished at eight-over-par 288, tied for 73rd.

Luna was in the third group off, at 7:35 a.m., right in the face of the foul weather. His hopes died fast. At No. 1, he hit his approach out of bounds, and made a triple-bogey seven. Then he double-bogeyed the 11th, and ballooned by 10 strokes over his first round, to a 77 and a 144 total. The weather and nerves were not the cause, he said, pointing out that he had hit only two bad shots and that they had cost him five strokes. But he did make the cut. And there was another plus. "I need to experience the pressure of leading in a big tournament like this," he said. He would finish at nine-over 289, tied for 80th.

So the dream was over. But there was one precious thing they would take with them. Gates might have been speaking for both of them. "I still have the memories," he said. "To think that for one of the four days, I was in the limelight."

And they had the supreme satisfaction of making the 36-hole cut, which was good work even by this Open's generous standards. The low 70 players plus ties, plus anyone within 10 strokes of the lead would qualify for the last two rounds. The cut came in at eight-over-par 148, and thanks in part to Oldcorn, a record 113 players made it. (The previous known record was 94, in 1982 at Royal Troon, the R&A announced.) Oldcorn instantly became a hero to 15 players about 8:40 p.m. Friday when his bunker shot at No. 18 ran over the edge of the hole but didn't drop. Had it fallen in for the birdie three, he would have had a 66 and a two-round total of 137. Under the 10-stroke rule, that would have knocked out 15 players who were already in at 148. Among the grateful survivors: 1973 Open champion Tom Weiskopf (74-74), Tom Kite (77-71), Magnus Persson (77-71), Craig Stadler (77-71), and Sam Torrance (72-76).

Ballesteros was the man to watch at first, and he wasted no time falling from grace. He stuck to his prudent game plan, but it didn't help. He used a two iron off the first tee in that bleak, cold, rainy morning, and pulled the shot into a fairway bunker. That cost him a bogey. He three-putted No. 2 from 35 feet for another bogey. At No. 6, he weighed his strategy again: Use the driver and risk the cross bunker, or use an iron and risk not getting home in two. He opted for the one iron, failed to get home with the two iron, and finally got on with a wedge. Then he two-putted from 10 feet for another bogey.

No Ballesteros round is complete without an adventure, and the adventure of this day came at the 414-yard, par-four 16th, a dogleg right. He chanced the driver this time, and it promptly put him far to the left of the fairway, into a bush in Birkdale's stunted white willows. He had to take a penalty drop on a spectator path, but first he had to deal with the crush of spectators. The wry Ballesteros humor bubbled to the surface. "Where are all the marshalls?" he asked the sky. "Having their lunch or something?"

So he had to work the crowd control himself. They wouldn't budge. "Do you want me to stay here all day?" he said. "Yes," came the timid reply from two middle-aged women. Finally, the gallery adjusted itself. Ballesteros surveyed his position. He was about 170 yards from the green, and in a real fix. He was looking at a double bogey, at least, possibly a triple bogey. I see bushes and trouble and photographers and people—everything but the green," he said. "I don't think I want to go back there again." It was a typical Ballesteros escape. He hit a four iron just short of a green he couldn't see, pitched on to three feet, and holed the bogey. "A great five," Ballesteros said. The only other thing he could smile about this day was his lone birdie, a three-foot putt at No. 9.

He didn't win any prizes for fashion, either. He was wearing two hats, a tweed cap and a rain hat on top of that. From a distance, he looked like a character out of Greek statuary, with the helmet tipped back. Someone wondered about this. "Why was I wearing two hats?" Ballesteros said. "To keep my head warm." And so he left the field with a three-over-par 73 and 139, a stroke off the 36-hole lead. "I don't like to be leading the tournament so early," he said. "It is always difficult to hold on, leading the first round. I like to be leading on the last day."

Golf is so peculiar. Note that the weather was really battering the early morning brigade, even Ballesteros, the storm-lover. Then there was this: In the 8:30 threesome right behind him, Heggarty, the man who got in when Rafferty pulled out, was piling up a 76, and Masahiro Kuramoto an 80, and both would miss the cut by a mile. At the same time, their partner, Tway, must have been playing in a vacuum. He had a 66. This was a jewel that had to be viewed in its setting.

First, Tway was in the eighth threesome, thus among the first 24 players that morning. And not only was he the only one of them under par, he was five strokes better than the next best, McNulty (71). And he was more than nine strokes better than the average for the other 23, namely 75.43. One other thing—Tway's 66 included a double bogey. "When I set out, my thoughts were on making the cut," said Tway, who had posted 75 in the first round. "But after making six at the second hole, I didn't know where my thoughts were." It brightened his spirits at No. 3 when he dropped a 15-footer for a birdie. And after three uneventful holes, he exploded. He birdied the par-three seventh from 20 feet, then holed a 190-yard seven iron for an eagle two at No. 8. "It hit about 20 feet short of the hole, took one bounce, and somehow went in," Tway said. Two more birdies brought him home in 66—141, three off the lead.

Tway thrilled the big galleries early (his 66 would stand as the low round of the day, tied by Roger Chapman, who played later), and what few fans were left late in the day went home with a new hero. Oldcorn became everybody's sentimental favorite for this Open. He had come from nowhere, almost literally, to take a share of the lead. First, he had to qualify to get into the Open. And to do that, he had to overcome some heavy obstacles. Oldcorn, 31, an Englishman who lives near Edinburgh, was supposed to be a cinch to succeed on the European Tour, so impressive were his amateur credentials. He had won the English Amateur in 1982, and in 1983 became the first Englishman to win all four of his matches in the Walker Cup. But about the time he was learning his craft on the Tour, he contracted the "yuppie flu," a debilitating disease with the formidable medical name of myalgic encephalomyelitis.

"Two years ago, I was a total wreck," Oldcorn said. "I could hardly walk, let alone play golf. I thought I may never play again. The worst part is not having the energy to read a newspaper or watch TV or walk 50 yards from the house." But he fought his way back. His greatest accomplishment was just being able to play in the Open, and so tying for the lead was fairy tale stuff. His moment of triumph came in the deepening dusk and almost in seclusion. Playing in the next-to-last group, he finished about 8:40 p.m., long after the television cameras had been turned off, and with only a few spectators scattered in the stands at No. 18 to see the bunker shot that nearly wiped out 15 hopefuls. Oldcorn then holed what was left, about 30 inches, and had 67 and a share of the lead on 138 with Hallberg and Harwood.

Oldcorn, who opened with 71, didn't seem to be a threat at first. He ran off six consecutive pars to start his round, and got to one under for the day with a birdie at No. 7, on a 25-foot putt. He gave the stroke back with a bogey four at No. 12, two-putting from five feet. "I felt a bit tired there," he said. "But No. 14 got me going again." He chipped in from 40 feet for a birdie, then dropped an eight-footer at No. 16, and two-putted from 12 feet at No. 17. Only the near-miss at No. 18 keep him from the outright lead. "I think what has pleased me more is that I haven't backed off, and I've played solid golf," he said. "I haven't thought about my illness or anything. Just gone out and played."

Oldcorn's co-leaders also had to overcome problems. Nothing on the order of his illness, to be sure, but obstacles nonetheless. With Harwood, it was two things—a broken rib, the result of a fall while jogging (it knocked him out of action for nearly two months), and "lazy legs." That meant simply not getting enough leg action into his shots.

Time and rest healed the former, and a visit to a guru the latter. He returned a balanced three-birdie, three-bogey 70. The last birdie would send him into the third round in a good frame of mind. It was a clutch eight-foot putt at No. 17 that got him back to even par for the day. "I struggled a bit over the last few holes," he said. "The ball wasn't running as far as it was yesterday, and I found I was coming up short of where I wanted to be on the fairway." Harwood started at 8:50, in harsh weather that was no small consideration for a stringbean who stands 6-feet-4 and weighs only 170 pounds. "Never mind me being tall," he said. "The wind today was strong enough to rock everyone."

A chance meeting is what lifted Hallberg's spirits and his game. "I never wanted to see a sports psychologist," he said. "People think there's something wrong with you." But he bumped into one at a tournament in the spring, made a few visits, and hadn't missed a cut since. He kept the explanation simple. "I used to be a mechanical player," he said. "Now I play by feel."

Here's what that means on the golf course, he said: On the practice range in the morning, he decided he would have to hit a low ball to get under the wind. Good strategy, bad feel. It left him with 40- and 50-foot putts. It also helped cost him a bogey at No. 9 and a double-bogey five at No. 12, where he missed the green. "After that, I decided that instead of hitting low, blocked punch shots, I'd just go ahead and hit it," he said. The result: At No. 14, he hooked a four iron to eight feet and made it for a birdie. At No. 17, he missed the green, chipped to four feet, and made that for another birdie. And at No. 18, a two iron, six iron combination put him 30 feet from the flag, and he made that, too. Three birdies in five holes, and he was back to par.

Elsewhere around Birkdale, the labors of the stars served to underline the strangeness of the day:

• Woosnam (72—142) was one under through the turn, then crashed. He missed the green at No. 11, and bogeyed. At No. 13, he shanked a seven iron into the trees. "After that, I just lost it," he said. He doubled-bogeyed there, and then hooked his tee shot at the par-three 14th and bogeyed. And at No. 15, a 543-yard par five, trying for the green on his second shot, he pulled a weekender's special—he topped a fairway wood. Then he did the only thing left to do. He started to laugh.

• Faldo (75—143) was tormented by his putting. "There was no feel, no nothing," he said. "Good mixture—I didn't read the putts right, and then I didn't hit them where I meant to, anyway." Someone noted that he still was only five strokes off the lead. Faldo just sat there, chin in hand. "Yeah," he said.

• Stewart (72—144) saw his chances leak away, not just in score but in an erratic game as well. "I got into trouble off the fairways too often," he said. At No. 2, he pulled his drive and double-bogeyed. Coming home, he missed the fairway once, the green three times.

There seemed to be no end of oddities. For the two most notable victims, take two ex-Open champions—Sandy Lyle (1985) and Mark Calcavecchia (1989).

Lyle, still mired in his slump, hit rock-bottom this time. Spectators were reminded of the time in the 1989 Nestle Invitational in Florida, that he hit a shot in the water at the final hole of the second round. He just gave up and walked in. Not that completing the round would have mattered. He had no chance of making the cut. He had no chance this time, either. A 79 in the first round left him muttering about "my most disgusting golf ever." Now he came to No. 18 tee in the second round, two over par for the day and 11 over for the Open, and with nothing in front of him but hungry fans crammed into the stands around the green.

He had heard those fans roaring before, and he wanted to hear them again. "I stood on the tee and I thought, 'To hell with it,' and I gambled with the driver," he said. "I knew that if I hit it well, I could have a wedge to the green, and that I might even hole that one and go out in a blaze of glory." This fairy tale had a sour ending. Lyle watched his ball heading out of bounds, then felt it had come down safely. He began the long march up the fairway, and then discovered the ball had gone out. "I decided to call it a day," he said. There was no point in going back to the tee, and just holding up the Open. Sympathetic R&A officials agreed, and so in the scores, Lyle's name carries an "NR"—No Return. It was a poignant moment in Open history. Had a former champion ever walked off in disgust before?

Calcavecchia, who posted 79, probably made some history, too. Had a former champion ever given his clubs away before? Like Lyle, Calcavecchia was also in a slump, but not nearly as deep and desperate. His game had come unglued after he won the 1989 Open, and this Open did nothing to revive it. Now he was having a wild ride across Birkdale. He had an epic outward half, a 43 that included two bogeys, three double bogeys, one triple bogey and an eagle two. In the press tent, a bunch of writers sat transfixed as the numbers went up relentlessly beside his name. One writer, a poker fan, noted that part of Calcavecchia's card, in numerical order, read 2-3-5-6-7. "Calc," the poker fan observed drily, "needs a '4' to fill his inside straight." Calcavecchia got the four. He even managed a chuckle when someone told him about his poker hand.

Something stranger than that had occupied the fans at No. 18 moments earlier. Calcavecchia had hit his approach to the green, then calmly lifted his irons from his bag and carried them off to the right rough, and handed them to a man holding a rake. The man was the bunker raker for the threesome. He also was a club pro whose clubs had been stolen, and now he was one stunned fellow. He tried to talk Calcavecchia out of giving him those clubs. "I told him, 'Oh, you can't do that here!' And he said, 'Sure I can. Here—take 'em.'" Calcavecchia explained why he gave the clubs away. "Because I hate 'em, basically," he said. Then someone said, but what will you use tomorrow? "The airplane," Calcavecchia said. "I've missed the cut."

Others would be sticking to their clubs. Among them:

At 139: Steve Elkington (68), another of the rising Australians, eagled No. 17 but just missed a share of the lead when he missed a two-foot birdie putt at No. 18. David Gilford (67), runner-up in the Dunhill British Masters, made the cut for the first time in five Opens. Grady (70), co-runner-up in the 1989 Open, started with a double bogey at No. 1, where he hit himself on the knee, swinging from an awkward stance in the bunker, and he bogeyed Nos. 11, 12 and 13, but offset it all with five birdies.

And at 141, after some adventures: Fred Couples eagled No. 17 from three feet, but had to make a 10-footer for a par at No. 18 for his 69. Resurgent Watson needed only a par at No. 18 to come in one stroke off the pace, but his tee shot ended up against a fence and cost him a double bogey and a

72. And Olazabal, none the worse for wear after the streaker's visit the day before ("It was a naked woman, that was all"), closed with some phenomenal putting. He parred No. 15 from nine feet, then birdied the last three from 18, 18, and 30 feet for a 67.

All told, of the 156 starters, some 130 of them had drawn little attention except from family and friends. Among these was a tall, easy-smiling Australian, Baker-Finch. For a man about to win the Open, he gave no sign whatever. He teed off at 8:40 a.m., catching the brunt of the bad weather, and bogeyed the second, fourth, and sixth holes. A birdie at No. 9 sent him through the turn at two-over-par 36. He came home steadily, but without fireworks. He birdied No. 17, parred the rest, and put up his second one-over-par 71. In the 1984 Open at St. Andrews, he had 66 in the second round and was at 10-under-par 134 and leading by three. He was at two-over-par 142, trailing by four and in 27th place.

The second-round leaderboard:

Mike Harwood	138	Mark O'Meara	139
Gary Hallberg	138	Howard Clark	140
Andy Oldcorn	138	Mark James	140
Seve Ballesteros	139	Roger Chapman	140
Mike Reid	139	Richard Boxall	140
David Gilford	139	Colin Montgomerie	140
Wayne Grady	139	Barry Lane	140
Steve Elkington	139	Vijay Singh	140

The third round had a theme running through it, something on the order of "One man's meat is another man's poison." Or even, "One man's meat is also his poison." They were talking about Royal Birkdale's greens. Open week had begun with a chorus of complaints. "Spongy" was the kindest word heard about them. The campaign broke out again in the third round. "If they want consistent greens here," said Stewart, "they should dig them up and put in new ones." Woosnam, who turned 66 into 69, was steaming. "The short putts are all over the place," he said. "I don't know what the trouble with the greens is. They may have cut them down too late. When they go all white like that, it's because of the soil underneath." Kite likened them to sponge cake. Said Nicklaus, "You watch your partner's putt break one way, then yours breaks the other." He said he had offered the expertise of his golf course architecture company. "I sent my guy over," he said, "but I don't think they paid a whole lot of attention." And Ballesteros chipped in with a little barb. "The greens?" he said. "They are perfect. Fantastic." And even Baker-Finch, who handled the greens beautifully in this round, and in fact soared into a share of the lead on them, said they looked like the courts at Wimbledon.

So much for the poison. Now for the meat: Certainly the complaints had at least some validity, but how does one explain this?—That out of 112 starters (there had been 113, but one player had to quit), 30 of them broke par in the third round? Take the start of the Open—out of 156, 17 were under par in the first round, and 19 in the second. Well, for better or for worse, that was the flap of the day, and it was a loud one. But there was golf's redeeming factor: Good greens or poor greens, everybody had to play the same ones.

There was another episode in the third round, and it was hard to believe. How can a man break his leg swinging at a golf ball? But that's exactly what happened to Richard Boxall. No, he didn't hit himself with the club. The leg simply broke as he was hitting. "Richard was complaining of a pain in his leg walking up six and seven," said Colin Montgomerie, his playing partner. "On the ninth tee, he came through the ball, and there was a loud crack, and he collapsed on his left side." He was rushed to a nearby hospital, and the report was that his left tibia—the shinbone—had snapped. Golf seemed unimportant at the moment, but it should be noted that the misfortune ruined a good chance for Boxall. He was at 71-69—140 for the first two rounds, and was one over par and two strokes off the lead at the time of the accident.

The Open that dangled just out of Faldo's reach continued to taunt him. It remained so close, yet so far away. Putting was still his problem, he said. He had been threatening to retire the putter that was offending him, and this time he did. He went back to the putter that had helped him win three of his four majors. It worked beautifully—for a while. He birdied the second hole from 15 feet and the third from three. An errant drive sent him to a bogey at No. 6, but he was still in good shape, until he was on his way home.

"Twelve and fourteen were ridiculous," he snapped. "I hit good shots, but I just didn't reward myself." The two holes were more than ridiculous, they were almost eerie. Both are par threes of 184 and 199 yards, respectively. He hit a five iron to 20 feet at each, and three-putted each for a bogey. He struggled to 70 and a three-over 213 total. He had improved by five strokes, but he was losing ground fast. He slipped from five to seven strokes off the lead. "Mentally, I'm having a difficult time," Faldo said. "I'm not doing anything right. Nothing is going for me." Not that Faldo had written off his chances for a repeat championship, but he could read the scoreboard—and the cards—as well as anybody.

The issue was a lot clearer for U.S. Open champion Stewart. An entire army of players would have to collapse for him to have a chance. He returned a bumpy 71 for a 215 total, losing three more strokes to the field. He would stand nine off the lead going into the final round.

Of the "big three," only Masters champion Woosnam seemed to have a prayer. A 69—211 left him five out of the lead going into the final round. But Woosnam was fairly seething at the thought of what might have been. "I've made some single putts," he said, "but these greens are not very good for a major tournament." Whatever the cause, Woosnam would have been at least three strokes closer but for his putting. He missed from three feet at No. 10, from 30 inches at No. 11, and from 16 inches at No. 15, turning all three into bogeys. But he had five birdies, a two putt at No. 17, and three one putts of 12, 14, and 14 feet, and a pitch-in from 40. "From 20 feet, you really couldn't go for it," Woosnam said. But come the final round—"I'm really going to go for it."

The three-way tie for the lead coming into the third round didn't last long. The Tiger and the Pussycat had had their say. Some golfers got past the Tiger and not the Pussycat, and most got past the Pussycat and not the Tiger, but when both the Tiger and the Pussycat got you, you're simply not having a good day. Thus did Oldcorn exit from the hopeful few for this Open. He double-bogeyed No. 6, then bogeyed four of the last five holes, making one of the four bogeys made at No. 17 all day. The damage added up to a 77, and a 215 total, which dropped him from the lead to nine strokes behind going into the fourth round. Oldcorn would rebound and finish at 72—287, tied for 64th, which was quite a performance for a man who was lucky to be playing at all.

Another of the second-round triumvirate, Hallberg, just seemed to sink out of sight. He returned a nondescript 73 that included four bogeys, one of them at No. 6, and one birdie, that at No. 17. (He would finish tied for 32nd.)

The third co-leader, Harwood, on the other hand, had to be the only man in the field to get scolded by his wife. Things had looked encouraging. He got one of the day's six birdies at No. 6 (a three wood to 15 feet), and was just one over through the turn. Then he started to fold. He bogeyed the ninth and 11th holes, and when he bogeyed the 12th as well, two-putting from five feet, Lynda Harwood had had enough. "She had words with me," Harwood said. "She said, 'You've forgotten to eat.'" He remembered the bananas he had in his golf bag, the better to keep that lanky furnace stoked. Then he practically sprinted home. He birdied four of the last six holes, and his irons were deadly. He holed from five feet at No. 13, two at No. 14, 15 at No. 16, and he two-putted from 20 feet at No. 17. His 69 put him at three-under-par 207, one stroke off the lead.

Harwood had tied Eamonn Darcy, who had finished about an hour and a half earlier, and who was surprised to find himself deep in the hunt. "I've never been as close as this in an Open at this stage," the pleasant Irishman said. (His previous best was 11th at Royal St. George's in 1985.) "I played very solid, and I was comfortable with my game, but I don't feel really confident on the greens from four or five feet. They are really difficult." Even so, he suffered only two bogeys, the first at No. 9, ending a hot outward half. He chipped in from 30 feet for a birdie at No. 1, holed from 12 and six feet at the fifth and sixth, and then from six at the eighth to go to four under. Two inward birdies bracketed a bogey, and he was in with 66. "I'll probably be thinking about it overnight," he said. "I'll be glad to get going tomorrow."

There were other notable accomplishments, or oddities, if you prefer. There were, for example, Nolan Henke, an American in his first Open, and another Australian, Brett Ogle. Both just made the cut at 148, they were paired together for the third round, teeing off at 8:20 a.m., and both returned 66s, matching Ballesteros' record for the slightly revised course. The together-ness would end in the fourth round, though, Henke finishing 70—284, tied for 38th, and Ogle 74—288, tied for 73rd. Their claim to a record didn't last long. They were matched by Darcy's afternoon 66, but by that time, Baker-Finch had already put up 64.

Then there was Davis Love III, the amiable American. Where Oldcorn's chances just drained away, Love's went sky-high on one hole. He moved into contention with an outward 30, and blew it all at No. 10. He pulled his three-iron tee shot into a bush. He chipped out, but was still in the rough, meaning grass would get between his clubface and the ball—a "flyer." His six iron then flew into the shaggy hillside behind the green. "The crowd heard the ball, but no one saw it," he said. He went back and played another, put that on the hillside, chopped it to the green, and two-putted for a qua-druple-bogey eight. A beautiful round had just gone up in smoke. Love managed another birdie, and put up 69—212, six strokes off the lead going into the last round.

Ballesteros was playing well, but he couldn't recapture the electricity of that first-round 66. He shook off two early bogeys and settled down into what he termed "steady and solid" golf, which translated into three birdies the rest of the way. He holed a 15-foot putt at No. 8, a three-footer at No. 12, and took two putts from 25 feet at No. 17. That gave him a 69 and a 208 total. He was two strokes off the lead going into the final round, and that didn't bother him. In fact, he was so comfortable that he touched off a flap just talking about it.

"My position is where I want to be," he said. "I don't think I have to attack. I have to wait for them to fall."

That message went crackling through Birkdale. How do you read it? People chose up sides. The general view was that Ballesteros was saying that with him in pursuit, the leaders would choke and fall back. This was the ultimate in arrogance, or at least a tasteless stroke of gamesmanship. Others decided it was the best Ballesteros could do in English to say that the pressure of the Open would ultimately take its toll, and that he wouldn't have to take any reckless gambles. "You have to play solid," Ballesteros said, trying to defuse the situation. "You have to be patient, and be a little lucky. And it isn't only how good you are playing, but how good you control yourself and your emotions." There, did that get him off the hook?

Baker-Finch's two 71s were ideal scores for the first two rounds—not bad enough to leave him too far behind, and not good enough to thrust him into the heat and pressure of the lead. So he had gone unnoticed for two rounds. Then he came crashing out of the underbrush in the third round, with three birdies in the first five holes. He dropped a 20-foot putt at No. 2, and then a 20-footer at No. 3, and that's when a veil lifted. "The greens are difficult to read, and patchy, like Wimbledon," he said later. "But the birdie at No. 3—that's when I really started to realize it was possible to hole putts."

He was on his way. He holed another 20-footer at No. 5 to go to three under par, and he even sneaked past No. 6 with a par, which is almost like gaining another stroke. He three-putted from 40 feet and bogeyed the par-three seventh, and that paid a kind of left-handed dividend. "My caddie reminded me to be patient," Baker-Finch said, "and he also reminded me that everyone was having the same troubles on the greens.

Now he was warming up. He came through the turn at two under, and promptly went to three with a birdie at No. 10, after slashing a five iron to eight feet. He holed a two-footer at No. 13, then suffered another three-putt bogey at a par-three, No. 14. Then he closed with a bang. At No. 17, he hit a five iron 195 yards to 20 feet, and dropped the putt for his first and only eagle of the Open. At No. 18, he hit a five iron more than 180 yards out of a fairway divot hole to six feet, and made that for a birdie.

Suddenly, there he was, with a course-record six-under-par 64, a 208 total, and the lead in the Open. He would get company about an hour later, when the sore-backed O'Meara came charging home. But for now, he was all alone. He was familiar with the feeling, and not all that happy about it. He remembered 1984, at St. Andrews, folding in the final round, how it hurt.

And he remembered 1990, also at St. Andrews, playing in the final round with runaway winner Faldo, how cool he was. "I was letting things bother me," Baker-Finch said. "But Nick was focused on his job. He knew what he was doing, and he did it well."

O'Meara had teed off at 2:28 p.m., more than an hour after Baker-Finch, and the thing was, he was lucky to be walking, much less playing in the Open. Golfers are celebrated sore-back victims, and O'Meara had an especially vicious one going. He had played only three competitive rounds since the U.S. Open in mid-June. Treatment eased the pain for a short while, but when it came time to catch the plane for England, he almost changed his mind. "The muscle spasms were terrible," he said. "But I took some anti-inflammatory medication, and it started to get better, so we flew over." About the time he was finishing his first-round 71, he was wondering if he'd made a mistake. "When I walked off No. 18, I didn't know whether I was going to play anymore," he said. Medication got his back through the second round, and what got his spirit through was that birdie-eagle-birdie finish.

Maybe they can call Birkdale's finishing holes "O'Meara's Alley," because here he came again in the third round, and almost more so. He started his run with a birdie at No. 15, but a weekender's error cooled him down at No. 16. He was trying a delicate pitch over a bunker. "And I chunked it about eight feet," he said. "I felt like a 16-handicapper." But he picked himself up and made his second consecutive eagle-birdie finish—a five-foot putt at No. 17 for the eagle, and a 20-foot putt at No. 18, the end of a 27-putt day.

And so the third round ended, and the longest wait of all began. If there were any way to read what the coming finale held, maybe the principal characters revealed it themselves, in their parting words:

Darcy: "I'm a streaky type of player, and I've never been fired up the week of the Open."

Harwood: "I'm not one of the great players, but if nobody wants to win it, then I'll be hanging around, ready."

Ballesteros: "I don't think any player is afraid of me. The thing is, they are afraid of the trophy more than me. The trophy means so much."

O'Meara: "I'm going to play tomorrow if I have to crawl out."

Baker-Finch: "I will remember the pain of '84 and the experience of '90, and do it."

The third-round leaderboard:

Ian Baker-Finch	206	Mike Reid	209
Mark O'Meara	206	Martin Poxon	210
Eamonn Darcy	207	Mark Mouland	210
Mike Harwood	207	Craig Parry	210
Seve Ballesteros	208	Mark James	210
Vijay Singh	209		

The 1991 Open came to the final round, and picking a winner would be easy. Just pull a name out of the hat. Baker-Finch and O'Meara were tied at four under par, Darcy and Harwood were one stroke behind, and the intimidating Ballesteros one stroke further back. In all, there were nine men within three strokes of the lead. And only one of them, Ballesteros, knew what it was like to survive and win a major. Two others knew what it was like not to survive. One was Baker-Finch, who crashed in the final round of the 1984 Open (he called this "the pain"), and who felt so futile playing alongside Faldo in the 1990 Open (he called this "the experience"). The other non-survivor was Mike Reid, who stumbled over the closing holes of the the 1989 American PGA Championship. Another stroke or two back were winners of majors—current Masters champion Woosnam; Grady, American PGA; Bernhard Langer, Masters, and Strange, U.S. Open.

But it never happened. This Open was over early. It was about 3 p.m. that warm and sunny Sunday, on the fourth hole, when Baker-Finch rolled in a six-foot putt for his third consecutive birdie. He led by three strokes over Darcy, and by four strokes over his playing partner, O'Meara. All he had to do was hold himself together. At No. 18, Baker-Finch almost got knocked down in the ceremonial stampede of the fans. That was the only scare he had all day.

There were some interesting diversions, however, before he could lift the old wine jug. For example, Jodie Mudd, the journeyman American pro who seems to save his best for the majors. In his two previous Opens, he finished fifth in 1989, a joint fourth in 1990. Now he was the early leader in the clubhouse, if only by definition. Mudd, who started at four over par and eight strokes off the lead, came roaring in with a seven-under-par 63. It was a course record and also a final-round record for the Open. "That was maybe the greatest round of golf I've ever played," Mudd said. He finished at 277, tied for fifth.

Then big-hitting Couples put up 64—275, tied for third, his best in seven Opens. Couples was another of the walking wounded. He had a bad back. One newspaper story said he had to sleep in his hotel room bathtub because the bed was too soft. "Not true," Couples said. "I slept on the floor."

Faldo, whose dreams of a repeat Open title had died much earlier, finished at 68—281, tied for 17th, and departed with a sharp shot. "It will be nice to get on some good greens," he said, "because then I can know where I am." Ballesteros didn't feel much better. He finished tied for ninth on 71—279, and said, "I played well enough to shoot 66, but I lost my confidence on the greens." Nicklaus (71—285, tied for 44th) joined the chorus. "I couldn't read the break from one green to another," he said, adding that he wasn't finding fault. His playing partner was in a better mood. That was Jim Payne, 21, former British Youths champion, who took the amateur silver medal with 70—284, and in the process blocked American Mickelson's try for an amateur "grand slam" in the majors. Mickelson, who won the amateur medal in the Masters and the U.S. Open, finished tied for 73rd on 71—288.

As the final round worked itself out, only three men had the most remote chance against the rampaging Baker-Finch.

Darcy hoped to become the first Irishman since Fred Daly, in 1947, to win the Open. He got a glimmer of hope when he birdied No. 4. But it went out when he bogeyed No. 6, after hooking his drive. But he wouldn't give up. "Even though I was three behind, I felt I could win," he said, "until the fourteenth." He hooked his tee shot and bogeyed, then double-bogeyed the par-five No. 15 after bunkering his drive. He finished at 70—277, tied for fifth. And he had one parting salute to Birkdale's greens: "Those horrible three-footers—I made all of them!"

O'Meara had the best chance of all, starting tied for the lead, and also the best view, playing with Baker-Finch. "I just didn't make any putts," he said. "I was just watching Ian make birdie after birdie." O'Meara closed with a 69—275, tying Couples for third, and it was the bogeys at No. 4 and No. 8 that ended his hopes. He lost six strokes to Baker-Finch by the turn. If he didn't feel low enough already, the stampede of the fans at No. 18 did the rest. Baker-Finch got bounced, but O'Meara got knocked to the ground and almost trampled. But he regained his feet and his poise and parred the hole.

In the end, it was Harwood who had the best chance, the man who said if no one wants it, I'll take it. Unfortunately for him, Baker-Finch wanted it. "Ian blew us away in the first nine holes," Harwood said. "We never had a chance." But Harwood, playing just in front of Baker-Finch, gave it a try. He shook off a bogey at No. 6, played the rest of the round in four birdies and eight pars, and finished at 67—274, six under par. A disaster would have to hit Baker-Finch for that to be good. The closest thing to a disaster Baker-Finch could provide was a bogey at the final hole. All it did was cut his winning margin over Harwood to two strokes.

"The Open Championship is the most special event of my life," Baker-Finch said. "Just to play in it is a great thrill, but to win it is a dream. I'm in a dream world right now."

Actually, he was in a dream world at 2:20 p.m., when he was at No. 1 tee, ready to start this final round. If he permitted himself the thought, he could go back to the same instant seven years ago, to the 1984 Open at St. Andrews. He stood on the first tee of the final round tied for the lead then, too. "I was just a 23-year-old kid with stars in my eyes," he said. And a thumping heart in his chest. When that approach shot hit the first green, then drew backward into Swilcan Burn, the collapse was on. He hit the green this time, too, and the ball stuck. He two-putted from 20 feet for a routine par, and was still tied with O'Meara. Then he parted company with him and everybody else. It was the new Ian Baker-Finch the rest of the way.

He ran off three consecutive birdies, from 12 feet at No. 2, then 10 and six feet. He conquered the mighty sixth with a drive, seven iron, and six-foot putt, and holed from 15 feet for another birdie at the par-three seventh, and then played for two conservative pars. He was through the turn in five-under-par 29. The Open was over. Except in his mind.

There was a sobering episode at No. 10. "Once I hit that tee shot into the bunker, that's when I quit playing cautiously," he said. "That reminded me that I still had some golf to play." Cautious or bold, he played the six holes in two-putt pars, ranging from 10 to 30 feet. He added a stroke to his lead at No. 17, two-putting from 50 feet for his third birdie there (to go with one eagle), completing a five-under-par week at that hole. At No. 18, things were scary for a moment, when the crowd ran wild and bumped him and knocked O'Meara down. Rattled, he hit a poor drive, and it cost him a closing bogey, not exactly the way a champion likes to finish. "I hate to make excuses for hitting bad shots," Baker-Finch said, "but I felt like I was being stampeded."

And thus ended the barbs and questions from others, and the awful self-doubts. "When I got to four or five ahead," he said, "I thought, boy, you'd better not stuff up now, or you'll really cop it."

6. PGA Championship

Nothing in golf creates more excitement than a long driver hitting the ball straight. John Daly gave us that in the 1991 PGA Championship at Crooked Stick Golf Club, near Indianapolis, Indiana. His massive drives averaged slightly more than 300 yards on the two test holes, reducing what could have been an unplayable course to one that, if it wasn't brought to its knees, at least had them bent. As the old saying goes, the woods are full of long hitters. For one week, though, Daly hit the ball straight, confounding even himself. When the championship ended and the totals tallied, Daly had hit 35 of the 56 fairways on driving holes, and 54 of the 72 greens. He putted exceptionally well, too. Back in 1959, Billy Casper had created a sensation by using only 115 putts in winning the U.S. Open. Daly needed only 112, a remarkable figure under the circumstances.

Putting and iron play aside, his long game caught everyone's attention. He had the galleries gasping and laughing to one another as they watched him pound his drives over the trouble that had been so carefully built into the design. Not only the galleries, but the players as well shook their heads and even smiled watching him. Bruce Lietzke, who finished second, and Craig Stadler, who came in seventh, played immediately ahead of Daly during the last round. After playing their approaches to the 14th, a strong par four of 468 yards with a right-to-left dogleg of nearly 90 degrees, they hurried toward the green. To carry the corner, a drive must *carry* about 265 yards to clear a creek and a belt of rough. Daly had carried the corner in every round, and Lietzke and Stadler wanted to move out of his range. Once again he carried the corner. When they saw where the ball landed, they turned to one another and smiled.

I bring up the 14th because it had been lengthened especially to prevent cutting the dogleg. Designer Pete Dye figured the approach shot would have to be played from 200 yards out. After moving the tee 20 yards or so back, Dye felt even Greg Norman and Fred Couples, the longest drivers among the leading players, couldn't carry the bend. Daly could, though. Where the rest of the field was left playing 190- to 200-yard approaches, Daly played from 140 to 150 yards, not much of a shot for him. For example, playing the eighth hole in the third round, he overshot the green, 143 yards away, with a sand wedge.

Consider his extraordinary length. Coming into the PGA Championship, he led the PGA Tour's statistics in driving distance averaging 286 yards. Of course he drove farther in the PGA. He also estimated he hits his three iron 245 yards, his five iron 210 yards, his seven iron 190 to 195 yards, and his nine iron from 150 to 165 yards.

He hits the ball so hard, he had to give up drivers made with ordinary materials. He caves in the faces of metal woods and wears out the faces of real wooden clubs. Instead, he uses a driver whose head is made of kevlar, the compound used for the modern battle helmet worn by the American military. Kevlar is also used in bulletproof vests, but Daly claims the compound isn't really bulletproof. He had a friend shoot a kevlar head with a

.357 Magnum pistol. The head shattered.

He's tough on golf balls as well. Brian Alexander, a club pro from Memphis, said he had caddied for Daly on days when John used a dozen golf balls over 18 holes.

"He may play one hole and it's gone. It's just not round any more. You hold it up and see it's oblong. Big time."

Daly saved a tournament that had the proper ingredients to make it very dull. Consider that the setting, Crooked Stick Golf Club, had been stretched out to 7,289 yards, the second-longest course where one of the game's glamour events had ever been played. Columbine Golf Club, in Denver, had measured 7,436 yards for the 1967 PGA, but at an elevation of more than 5,000 feet, a ball travels an estimated eight percent farther than at sea level. While Columbine measured more than 7,400 yards, it played to less than 6,900 yards.

On a course as long as Crooked Stick, the PGA could have developed into nothing more than a slugging contest, with long carries to greens, followed by long putts. We could have been in for a dreary week. With Daly we had instead a championship of surpassing interest.

Daly was born in Sacramento, the son of a nuclear engineer. His family moved to Arkansas when he was four years old, and he began playing golf when he was six. His unconventional swing—he has the longest overswing since the young Ben Hogan—traces back to his father. Jim Daly gave his son a sawn-off set of men's clubs whose heads felt so heavy to the young boy, and tugged his arms so far around at the top of the backswing, that the shaft pointed nearly straight down toward the ground.

Daly's game improved, he eventually attended the University of Arkansas, where he was selected to the All-America golf team twice but then he quit after three years, saying school wasn't for him. He couldn't see playing golf without being paid.

Logically, Daly had no business playing in the PGA Championship. Other than leading in driving distance, Daly had not made much of an impression in this, his first year on the PGA Tour. He stood 72nd in money winnings, and he had missed the cut in 11 of the 24 tournaments he had played. Still, he had won $160,000, and his prospects looked better than they had a year earlier. He had reached the lowest point of his career in the New England Classic, on the Ben Hogan Tour. He shot 91 and missed the cut. In a moment of despair, he told a Tour official, "I'm almost broke. I don't know how much longer I can hang on out here."

Daly did hang on, though, and began the long climb up. After touching bottom in New England, he placed second in consecutive weeks, and then won the Utah Classic. From almost quitting, he had risen to ninth in Ben Hogan Tour winnings, earning $64,692, and moved on to the big time for 1991.

While he had failed to qualify for the last 36 holes in 11 events, he had had some promising finishes. Daly placed fourth in the Honda Classic in Fort Lauderdale, hurt by a 76 in the third round, and third in the Chattanooga Classic, played while the leading golfers were busy at the British Open.

He had other promising finishes as well—20th at Pebble Beach, 17th at New Orleans, 16th in the Kemper Open, 15th in the Western Open, and 11th at New England. With $166,590 in earnings, he seemed to be on his way. Still, he hadn't arrived just yet.

Not exempt into the PGA Championship, he had to win a place through sectional qualifying. He failed, and wound up as the ninth alternate. For him to play, eight others would have to withdraw. Some did. Bill Sander pulled out, Mark Lye and Brad Bryant followed, and other alternates turned down their places. Suddenly first alternate, Daly decided to take a chance. Climbing into the new BMW he had bought for his fiancée, he drove seven and a half hours, from his home in Dardanelle, Arkansas, about 60 miles from the Oklahoma border, to Indianapolis. By chance, Nick Price pulled out at the last minute; his wife was about to have their baby, and he wanted to be with her.

When Daly walked into his hotel room shortly after midnight, he saw the red "message" light blinking on his telephone. He was in, and he would play at 1:58 the next day, paired with Bob Lohr and Billy Andrade. He hadn't even seen the course. Evidently that didn't matter, for Daly was about to take a good bit of the sting out of what some players called the hardest course they had ever seen.

Crooked Stick was the creation of Pete Dye, one of the game's most celebrated golf course architects. It was his first high-budget course. A native of Indiana who had won the state's Amateur championship, Dye had given up selling insurance in the late 1950s and laid out two minor courses. Crooked Stick gave him his first opportunity to do something memorable. He took advantage of it. Indeed, he organized the entire effort.

Searching for a suitable location, Dye came across a 400-acre tract of flat, featureless land north of the city available at a reasonable price he thought he could turn into a first-class golf course. Using the sales techniques he had learned in the insurance business, he sold four friends on the idea. They formed the 106th Street Ditch Association and brought together enough others to raise money to begin work.

Building Crooked Stick turned out to be a long-term project. While the original group raised enough money for Pete to begin the job in 1964, there wasn't enough for him to finish. After building the first nine, the second on the finished routing, Dye went off to build The Golf Club, in New Albany, Indiana, then came back and completed Crooked Stick in 1967.

In the process, Dye shoved dirt around and converted what had been flat cornfields into rolling, undulating ground ideal for golf. In moving ground from one area to another, he created deep pits, then filled them with water to create ponds. Three of them became principal features of four holes. The green of the sixth, the second of the par threes, sits behind a small pond; the drive on the eighth, a 438-yard par four, crosses another bigger body of water, then runs alongside for a distance; the fairway of the 10th shaves the side of another lake; both the fairway and the green of the 18th flirt with the other side of the same lake; and the green of the 16th sits alongside another small pond.

The pond at the 16th wasn't supposed to be there. It had been a pond at first, then it was changed into a sand bunker. The change came about during a revision. Topsoil had been excavated around a new grouping of tees near the fourth hole, leaving a deep pit. The question of what to do with the hole came before the Crooked Stick board of governors, along with the sand bunker beside the 16th green. The board voted to fill the hole at the fourth and cover it with grass, and leave the bunker at the 16th. The board met on Tuesday. Wednesday Dye filled both holes with water.

Defending himself, Dye laughed, "I'm not charging much, so I should do what I want some of the time."

When he had finished with his revisions for the PGA, Dye had created a course he felt made up for the added distance of the modern golf ball. Pete believes the ball flies at least 20 yards farther than it did when Hogan was at his best. In setting up Crooked Stick for the PGA and stretching it to the distance he had, Dye wanted to create a course as testing as those Hogan faced.

"I think a strong course needs some par fours that call for long-iron approach shots," Dye said. "I keep reading you can't build a course long enough for these young guys. I think it's just that these guys aren't used to hitting two, three and four irons into par-four holes, but I believe it should be part of the game." Bobby Jones once hit his two iron from the fairway on 13 holes in one round at the British Open. What about the famous one iron Hogan hit to the 18th at Merion, in 1950? That was a par-four hole. Being forced to hit those shots is just going to bring out the best in the best players."

While Dye's arguments seemed logical, not everyone agreed a course set up as he had prepared Crooked Stick would assure that the PGA would be won by the game's best players. Fuzzy Zoeller hoped PGA officials wouldn't play the far back tees, even though he is a fairly long hitter.

"It will favor one type of golfer," he said, "the one who hits it high and long. They'll eliminate three-quarters of the field."

When Dye completed Crooked Stick, it did indeed ask for long iron approaches. Eight of its 10 par-four holes measured more than 430 yards, four of those more than 450 yards, and both the 14th and 16th came within a yard or so of 470. Its par threes ranged from 180 to 212 yards, and the fifth, the first of the four par fives, stretched 600 yards. Of all the par fives, only the fifth couldn't be reached with the second shot, and it was threatened. The others ranged from the 533 yards of the 11th to the 507 yards of the 15th.

Actually, Crooked Stick has never been completed. This was where Dye played his golf, and like Donald Ross and Pinehurst No. 2, he tinkered endlessly. Originally, for example, Dye had laid out the 14th at 447 yards to force a long shot to the green, but that wasn't long enough for the modern golfer. Preparing for the PGA, Dye moved the tee 20 yards back.

There were more changes. After he had designed Harbour Town, in Hilton Head Island, South Carolina, some years earlier, Dye stood alongside the 16th hole watching how it was being played. He had laid out one of those long stretches of sand he calls a waste bunker, and since the fairway bends left around that bunker before beginning its run to the green, he expected to see drives drawn into the sand. When group after group played shots that drew nicely around the corner, Dye realized a big tree in front of the bunker helped the players shape their shots. The tree came down.

A day or so later, an upset Harbour Town member scolded Dye, crying, "Dammit, man, it took God 200 years to grow that tree, and you knocked it down in 10 minutes."

Not at all intimidated, Pete snapped, "Wrong. It took me 25 minutes. It was a healthy sonofabitch."

Pete ran into the same situation on Crooked Stick's second hole, a 432-yard par four that swings around a big bunker. Once again a tree helped the golfer visualize the shot, and once again Pete had the tree taken down.

Not all of his adjustments had been so dramatic. The course had matured over the 24 years since it had opened. It had been adjusted, greens altered, and bunkers and lakes added and expanded. The result seemed intimidating.

Indianapolis had gone through a period of dry weather in the weeks leading up to the championship, and the fairways had become firm and fast. Attempting to save the grass, Crooked Stick watered the fairways, draining the wells nearby and upsetting the neighbors. Then the weather changed on Tuesday; heavy rain fell throughout the day, and the course became so soft, Tom Kite claimed that during a practice round he played a number of wooden clubs for his second shots into par-four holes.

Walking off the course, Tom Kite made no news by saying, "This is the longest course we've played all year. The fairways were so soft my shots were backing up."

"It's the longest course I've ever played," Ian Woosnam added.

Not everyone seemed upset, though. One of the game's longest hitters, Davis Love III suggested, "The big hitters definitely have the edge, but only if they hit the ball straight. The guy who hits it in the rough five times will be in big trouble here."

Defending his championship at Crooked Stick, Wayne Grady said, "I think I'll leave my seven, eight and nine irons out of my bag and load up on woods."

Jack Nicklaus agreed, saying, "This is the toughest course I've ever seen. I don't know how many times you have to hit three, four and five irons into these greens. Never mind, you never get to hit a five iron."

With a course that long, Couples seemed like a logical contender. Aside from Daly, no one hit the ball farther than Couples. Furthermore, he had been a contender not only in the 1990 PGA, where he led after the 12th hole of the final round, but he had also played well in the U.S. Open two months earlier, and in the British Open, in July, tying for third place in both.

Strangely enough, even though he had the length to cope with Crooked Stick, Couples was never a factor. He opened with 74, rallied with 67 in the second round, then blew himself out of the championship with 76 in the third round. At the end he finished 12 strokes behind Daly.

None of obvious choices did well. Neither Woosnam, who had won the Masters, nor Payne Stewart, the U.S. Open champion, nor Ian Baker-Finch, who had won the British Open a month earlier, stood anywhere near the lead at the end.

Baker-Finch walked off the golf course after three holes of his practice round on Tuesday complaining of pain in his lower back. After an examination by a chiropractor, he said he would withdraw if he hadn't recovered by the time of the opening round.

Baker-Finch had been struck by back pains during the Hartford Open, two weeks earlier. After finishing with 77 and 73, he had returned to his Orlando home. He said he couldn't move the Wednesday and Thursday before the PGA was to begin after he was awakened both nights by muscle spasms that didn't relax for three or four hours.

It was a bitter blow to Baker-Finch. After making two runs at the British Open, first in 1984, when he led going into the last round, and in 1990, when once again he went into the last round in position to win, he had finally come through in July, blistering Royal Birkdale's first nine with 29, and closing with 66. Now his career seemed in danger.

His condition evidently improved enough for him to play, but he shot indifferent golf for two rounds and missed the cut.

Baker-Finch at least made it. Paul Azinger withdrew on Tuesday, saying he wasn't ready for competition just yet. He hadn't recovered sufficiently from surgery on his shoulder seven weeks earlier. He was one of those whose withdrawal led to Daly's entrance into the championship.

Daly was a hit from the start. He opened with 69, but he wasn't taken seriously at first. Fans reacted to his score by telling one another, "Isn't it nice that young alternate had played so well?" At the same time, they didn't expect to hear of him again. Surely he would find the level of his game and drop from sight. His opening round was most likely an aberration.

By the time Daly went off a few minutes before two o'clock, Woosnam had already finished his round in 67, but once again, as it had at Hazeltine in the U.S. Open, the golf seemed unimportant. A thunderstorm moved in during the afternoon, causing suspension of play, and players and spectators fled to shelter from the driving rain. Some huddled inside hospitality tents, most rushed to their cars.

Thomas Weaver, a 39-year-old man who lived within six miles of Crooked Stick, hurried to his car, parked in a field near the 15th fairway. Sheltered by his open umbrella, Weaver had closed within 100 yards of his car when lightning flashed. Weaver fell to the ground. Seeing the bolt strike, several doctors and a nurse in the lot sped to him. They treated him until emergency personnel arrived.

An ambulance reached him within minutes. Rescue Squad members worked to revive him before he was taken to a hospital within two miles of Crooked Stick. Nothing worked; he was pronounced dead at 3:42 p.m.

Weaver's death stunned the gallery and tournament officials as well. We had never heard of a spectator being killed by lightning until this year, and now we had had two deaths within two months.

Those incidents had made clear that nothing can be done to provide total protection from lightning. An emergency warning had been posted at 1:15, about an hour before play was suspended, giving spectators sufficient time to reach shelter.

They had also shown how unpredictable lightning can be. The bolt at Crooked Stick had knocked the umbrella from the hands of a friend next to Weaver, but he wasn't hurt.

Meantime, the players had found Crooked Stick a little milder for the opening round than it had been during practice. The markers had been moved ahead on most holes, shortening the course by an estimated 200 yards. Of the 124 men who completed play the first day, 48 either matched or bettered par. Twenty-seven players were still on the course, their starting times delayed by an hour and 46 minutes because of the storm.

Back at the clubhouse, Woosnam said, "The course played at least two shots easier. The tees were up 20 yards on some holes. If you drive it straight, you have a chance at a good score. It all depends on how you drive.

I drove well."

Woosnam shared first place with Kenny Knox. Both men shot 67 and stood one stroke ahead of Stadler, Sandy Lyle, Ken Green, and Lietzke, while with his 69, Daly tied with Jim Hallet, Tom Purtzer, Billy Ray Brown, and Raymond Floyd.

Of that group lingering around the top, only Woosnam and Floyd might have been expected to hang on; all the rest were expected to fade over the next three days. The projections turned out to be correct with three exceptions—Stadler, Lietzke and Daly.

Woosnam went off at 9:19, with Baker-Finch and Stewart. It seemed to be a dream pairing, but only Woosnam lived up to his reputation. While Woosnam played as he was expected to play, the others didn't. They each shot 74, and had no impact at all on the championship.

Meantime, the big hitters who were expected to take charge found Crooked Stick more than just a long course. Norman shot 70, shaving two strokes from par, Love matched par 72, and Couples slipped to 74, two over par. At the same time, Nick Faldo, Mark Calcavecchia and Hale Irwin stood within three strokes of the lead, with 70s; Nicklaus, Lanny Wadkins, and Seve Ballesteros lurked only a further stroke behind, at 71, and Grady held at even-par 72. Nicklaus had a better round going, but he double-bogeyed the 18th. Farther off the mark, needing substantial improvement to make an impact, Andrade, the sensation of the springtime, had 73, Tom Watson 74, and Jose Maria Olazabal was all but eliminated after opening with 77.

At the same time the big hitters were struggling, Knox, one of the game's shorter players, was having a fine round. Knox claimed he had hit the ball barely long enough to reach the fairways, but even so he owned a short game nearly every other golfer envied.

"I'm not known for distance or accuracy off the tee," Knox admitted, "but I feel I can chip and putt with anyone in the world. When I hear someone call, 'One-putt,' I look around to see who wants me."

Far from one of golf's glamour players, Knox describes himself as a grinder, one who turns out whenever there is a tournament to be played. By the time of the PGA, he had played in 23 of the PGA Tour's 32 tournaments, and had finished among the five leaders in three of them. He had a rather grim record in past PGA Championships though. He had played in four, and had missed the cut in three. In the one he actually completed, he placed ninth at Oak Tree, in 1988. Oak Tree, of course, is another Dye design.

Knox was among the early starters. Off at 8:34 with Love and Jay Don Blake, 45 minutes ahead of Woosnam, he built his score around two eagles. He holed a sand wedge from 45 yards out on the ninth, and a full five iron from 168 yards on the 12th, at 395 yards one of only two par fours under 430 yards (the first measured 343).

"The last time I had two eagles in a round," Knox joked later, "I was playing in a gangsome at the Capital City Country Club, in Tallahassee, back in 1977. I won $36."

He stood to win considerably more here if he could hold onto his position.

Knox began as if he might not make the cut. He missed three of the first four greens, dropping two strokes to par, and saved himself from still another bogey by holing a testing 10-footer on the eighth. Then, in one stroke, he brought himself back to even par. He had driven well on the ninth, then laid a four wood into a narrow neck of fairway just short of the green. Planning his next shot, he said to his caddie, "I have to hit this either absolutely perfect or have a great deal of luck." A flick of his sand iron, and the ball hopped twice and dove into the hole.

That shot, along with the 10-footer that fell on the eighth, restored his confidence, and he began playing with more assurance. A solid drive on the 10th left him 235 yards from the hole, no place to think of birdies. Drawing his four wood, he told his caddie, "We'll just play for par."

He hit a gorgeous shot. The ball carried to the green and rolled within 12 feet of the cup. The putt fell, and Knox dipped one under par. It was the longest putt he holed all day. Two holes later he drilled the five iron to the 12th and watched his ball hit eight feet short of the hole, then trickle into the cup as if he had putted.

Three under par now, he lost one of his strokes at the 14th, the sharp right-to-left dogleg, where he pulled his drive into the rough and couldn't reach the green. Back to two under, Knox rushed to the front with three consecutive birdies, making a four at the 15th where two woods left him only a chip shot, a three at the 16th after a terrific seven iron just short of the cup, and then a two at the 17th, perhaps the hardest of the par threes, where he played a four iron to the middle of the green, just eight feet from the cup.

A par at the 18th and he had his 67, five under par.

Knox had hit only 13 greens, but he made up for it with his envious short game and the unlikely effect of the two eagles. He had also driven exceptionally well, hitting 11 of the 14 fairways on driving holes.

Even though he stood at the head of the field, Kenny did not exactly brim with confidence. "My chances of winning the golf tournament are very shaky," he said. "Nobody is worrying about Kenny Knox."

He was right. They were much more concerned with Woosnam. While Knox was working his miracles, Woosnam was playing a steadier round, built around six birdies and a single bogey. At the start, however, Woosnam looked as if he were off his game. He drove into fairway bunkers on both the first and second holes, but came out of it one under par. A superb approach played from the sand settled only three feet from the cup on the first hole, and another on the second pulled up within 25 feet.

Woosnam made his single bogey of the day on the fourth, where once again he drove into the rough. This mistake cost him one stroke, but from there on he played first-class golf, hitting 12 of the remaining 13 greens, and reeling off five more birdies. He might have had two more, but he missed opportunities on both the ninth and the 15th, two par-five holes.

After an eight-footer fell on the eighth, Woosnam drove into another fairway bunker on the ninth, but reached the green with his third, and lay only 15 feet from the cup. A bold player, Woosie knocked his birdie attempt well past the cup, then saved a potential bogey by holing out from eight feet.

Out in 35, one stroke under par, Woosnam birdied the 11th after a pitch to seven feet, and followed with a run of three birdies in the four holes from the 13th through the 16th. He holed his longest putt on the 13th, rolling it in from 20 feet, and made 15-footers on both the 14th and 16th.

One of the longest hitters in the game, even though at five-foot-four-and-a-half-inches he is quite the shortest, Woosnam played nothing longer than a five iron into the greens of the par-four holes, but at the same time he failed to reach any of the par fives with his seconds, even though at least two of them were eminently reachable. It seemed likely that to stay at the top, he would have to do better on the par fives.

At least he would have the chance. Curtis Strange wouldn't. Once one of the most dangerous players in the game, Strange had become a non-factor over the last year. Playing the loosest kind of golf, Curtis played the first nine with three bogeys and two double bogeys—both on the par-five holes—shot 43, steadied somewhat on the second nine, came back in 38, and shot 81. His round reached the absurd when he botched a short approach to the 11th, a hole a player of his caliber should think of as an automatic birdie. Frustrated, he flung his wedge at his golf bag. The club boomeranged, ricocheted back at him and cracked him on his head. At the end of the round, Strange signed his scorecard and withdrew. So did Ben Crenshaw, another 81-shooter.

First-round leaders:

Ian Woosnam	67	Jim Hallet	69
Kenny Knox	67	Tom Purtzer	69
Craig Stadler	68	Billy Ray Brown	69
Sandy Lyle	68	Raymond Floyd	69
Ken Green	68	Andrew Magee	69
Bruce Lietzke	68	John Daly	69

As he stepped off the 18th green after completing his first round, Daly confronted only one reporter. John was, after all, the most obscure player in the field. A day later he faced the full press corps, for he had suddenly rushed to the front of the pack. He shot 67, a remarkable score considering it included one bogey and a double bogey. It also included an eagle on the ninth, and seven birdies.

Combined with his opening 69, Daly had a 36-hole score of 136, and stood one stroke ahead of Lietzke, another unlikely leader. Knox hung close at 138 following a round of 71, while Faldo, Stadler and Woosnam followed, with 139. Woosnam shot 72, the first step toward his decline.

At this stage Faldo seemed to be the most dangerous threat. He had played steady golf over the first 36 holes, shooting 70 in the first round and 69 in the second, but this was all illusion. He made no serious move the rest of the way and, like Woosnam, gradually fell back.

When the day ended, 77 players had survived the 36-hole cut, which fell at 147, three strokes over par. Caught were Watson and Bernhard Langer, at 149, Baker-Finch and Olazabal, with 150, and Scott Simpson, with 151.

The 18th continued to bedevil the field. Both Woosnam and Faldo bogeyed, and Nicklaus double-bogeyed once again. None of them matched Gary Hallberg, though. Two under par with three holes to play, Hallberg double-bogeyed the 16th and bogeyed the 17th. Even now, he played a perfect drive into the center of the 18th fairway, then went for the green with a four iron. His shot slid right and splashed into the water. He dropped another, and hit another four iron into the water. Determined, Hallberg hit two more into the lake, finally played one on, and made 12. He was not around for the last two rounds.

The three leaders were indeed surprising—Daly and Knox for the obvious reasons, and Lietzke because of his schedule. The owner of an elegant swing but also a putting disorder, Lietzke hadn't played golf in a month. Going back even further, he had played in only two tournaments since May, missing the cut at Westchester the week before the Open, and tying for 15th place in the Western Open, which ended July 7. He said he hadn't touched a club from the end of the Western until his first practice round at Crooked Stick three days before the PGA began.

Lietzke seldom plays tournament golf during the summer. He prefers instead to spend those months at home with his family.

"Since my children are out of school for the summer," he explained, "my idea of a vacation is not taking them to a golf tournament. They might have fun, but I would be out there working. That's why I take time off during the summer." He had turned 40 a month earlier. "Until I was 29," he continued, "golf was No. 1 with me. Now my priorities, in order, are my wife, my kids, my cars, golf and fishing. Golf is not a strong fourth. My wife and kids are more important than anything."

Walking off the course after a solid round of 69, Lietzke admitted he was a bit tired. "I'm a little hungry, too, and my back is beginning to get stiff." He was also a little astonished. "Having all aspects of my game come together at this point is surprising because of my schedule. Coming off a layoff, you usually leave part of your game at home—either your driving, your iron play, or your putting—but for the last two days I haven't had any real weaknesses. I've hit a lot of greens (nine in the first round, 14 in the second), and I'm happy with the way I'm playing right now."

Lietzke was among the late starters, teeing off just before 3:30 on a cloudy afternoon. By the time he began, Daly had been in for nearly two hours.

No one paid much attention to Daly when he began his round in mid-morning. Not many spectators, or anyone close to the game believed he had any chance at all of continuing to play reasonably well, and there were some who speculated he might not even make the cut. With no pressure at all, then, Daly drew back and let it fly. The result was an outstanding round of golf.

Driving enormous distances, he flew his ball over the hazards Dye had placed so carefully over the years, and he continued to play first-class irons. Hitting 13 greens in the second round, in two days he had reached 27 greens in the regulation number of strokes. He had also putted rather well, with only 25 in the second round. While it wasn't exactly shaky, his driving could have been more accurate. He had been in the fairways of 19 of the 28 driving holes in the first two rounds, but at the same time, when he missed, he was usually long enough to reach the greens. He had also been in nearly total control of the par fives. In two rounds he had either birdied or eagled six of the eight he had played.

Daly played some erratic golf at the beginning of the second round. After routine pars on the first three holes, he birdied the fourth and fifth, but then threw both strokes away with a misplayed tee shot to the sixth, the first of the par threes. A six iron dropped into the water guarding the front and right, and he double-bogeyed. Even par now, he birdied the seventh, then dropped another stroke at the eighth, where his wedge approach dropped into a greenside bunker.

Angry, Daly told his caddie he would "kill" his drive on the ninth. Indeed he did; he crushed it and flew the ball 320 yards, leaving himself just under 200 yards to the green of a 525-yard hole. A stunning six iron pulled up nine feet from the hole, and he ran the putt home for the eagle three. Back to two under once again.

He picked up another stroke on the 11th, then put himself in position to add another with a fine eight iron to 10 feet on the 13th. He threw it away instead by three-putting, taking a bogey where he might reasonably have expected a birdie. Instead of four under, he fell back to two under. Better things lay ahead.

Stepping to the 14th tee, he crushed another drive that carried the corner of the dogleg and left him only a seven iron to the green. Woosnam, remember, had needed a five iron a day earlier, and Knox would play a four iron. A 20-footer fell, and then another at the 15th. Another, fine 285-yard drive into a crosswind on the 18th, and a seven iron that flew 165 yards and dropped within eight feet of the cup set up still another birdie. Back in 33, he had his 67.

Lietzke had no thought of catching Daly, considering how little he had played, but he didn't show it. Instead, he played a round that had only one flaw, a mishit drive on the 18th drifted into the lake, costing him a bogey five. He had stood four under par through 17 holes, with two birdies and an eagle. He made his first birdie on the sixth with an exquisite five iron to two feet, and added another at the ninth. A driver and a three iron left him 12 feet from the cup, in position for an eagle that would have matched Daly's, but his first putt slipped a foot past the cup.

He made his eagle at the 15th, the shortest of the par fives, reaching the green with a drive and 236-yard two iron inside 20 feet. The putt rolled down a gentle slope, caught the right lip of the hole, and tumbled into the cup. He came back in 35 after going out in 34, and had his 69.

Knox had finished by then, still in the thick of the race. He had, in fact, caught Daly at eight under par when he birdied the 13th hole. After going out in 35, he played two woods and a nine iron to 15 feet and birdied the 11th, then drilled a six iron onto the 13th green and holed another 15-footer.

By then the field had backed up, causing Knox to wait about half an hour on the 14th tee. When he finally drove, his ball smacked into the soft ground and picked up a glob of mud. He had a shot of 228 yards to the front of the green, but he missed the green. His ball settled on a divot that had been replaced upside down. A chip to 25 feet and his putt for a par lipped out. Back to two under for the round, seven under for the distance.

Another bogey at the dangerous 16th, and Knox finished with 71, only two strokes from the lead.

Second-round leaders:

John Daly	136
Bruce Lietzke	137
Kenny Knox	138
Nick Faldo	139
Craig Stadler	139
Ian Woosnam	139

The third round began with at least half a dozen men in position to win.

When it ended, the championship was Daly's, if he could hold on. It began with the expectation that Daly's game would collapse and he would sink into the crowd. Instead, it ended with him grabbing a three-stroke lead by playing his third consecutive round in the 60s.

Daly shot 69, and while his 205 for 54 holes had opened a gap between him and those closest behind him, he couldn't feel comfortable just yet. Knox had hung on even though so many of Crooked Stick's holes played at the extreme end of his range, and Stadler had played his best golf in years. Both men had 208, Knox after shooting 70 in the third round, Stadler after a 69. Behind them lurked Lietzke, at 209, followed by Faldo, Andrew Magee, and Bob Gilder, at 210.

It was an exciting day for Daly, and it almost turned into a deflating experience. His caddie stood the flagstick on the 11th green in a position some felt pointed out the line to the hole, a violation of the Rules of Golf that could have cost Daly a two-stroke penalty. PGA rules officials studied video tape of the incident and decided Daly's caddie had committed no sin. No penalty.

Daly had never experienced a day like this. The gallery cheered him and urged him on at every hole.

"I had 12 or 13 holes where chills just ran up and down my body," Daly said. "I have never seen people react to me like they have this week. I want to play golf for them, and I want to win this for the fans."

Strangely enough, the other players seemed as enthusiastic about this refreshing young man as the fans.

"He had some Arnold Palmer-type receptions today," Lietzke said.

Stadler grinned after the experience of playing behind Daly.

"It's great to see. He's like every 15- and 16-year-old kid. He just rears back and hits it as far as he can, and if he can find it, he's okay."

Paired with Daly in the third round, Lietzke said, "After playing with him, he showed me he can win the tournament."

Gilder, who shot 67, the best round of the day, said, "If I was Daly I'd be ripping it off the tee and ripping it at the hole, too. The kid has nothing to lose."

Daly did indeed rip it throughout the third round. More than that, he played some wonderful pitches into Crooked Stick's greens. Of course, he didn't play an approach on any of the par-four holes with more than a seven iron, and he reached the 15th, the last par five, with a five iron. On the 16th, for example, at 469 yards the longest par four in pure yardage, Daly's Brobdingnagian drive left him only a wedge. Cutting the corner of the dogleg 14th left him just an eight iron.

His length, combined with what was for him unusual accuracy, gave him a distinct advantage over every other man in the field. He hit 10 fairways once again, reached 15 of the 18 greens in the proper number of strokes, and once again putted well.

Shrugging off any thought that his game might fall apart under increasing tension, Daly reeled off three consecutive birdies beginning with the fourth hole, where he lofted a lovely eight iron within a foot of the hole. When the ball braked so close, a roar thundered from the gallery. Daly smiled, then holed the putt. He won more cheers on the fifth, the 600-yard par five, when he rocketed his drive, then reached into his bag for his three wood; he would go for the green with his second. His ball pulled up just short, and he chipped to within a foot and a half of the hole. Two under par. After another birdie at the sixth, he had opened a lead of four strokes.

Daly had the crowd with him now. They left the other golfers and rushed ahead, straining for a good spot to see this amazing display of golf from a totally unknown player who was standing up to the challenge far better than other, better known, and, in truth, better-equipped golfers.

On to the seventh, and another sand wedge to a hole that measured 441 yards. His ball settled 15 feet away. No birdie, but a safe par. Now to the eighth, a 438-yard hole that skirts a pond. Once again Daly threaded the fairway and reached for a sand wedge. A very quick player, he wasted no time setting himself for the shot. He had about 145 yards to the hole. A waggle or two, and he moved into the ball. He miscalculated. The ball shot off slightly left and long, then plunged into the water. Imagine, a sand wedge that carried 150 yards or more. He double-bogeyed, wasting two of his birdies.

No matter; he won one stroke back with a birdie on the ninth, reducing a par five of 525 yards to little more than a medium-length par four with another mammoth drive and a five iron into a greenside bunker. He came out to eight feet, and holed the putt. Out in 35, Daly turned for home by scrambling for his par at the 10th, where his sand wedge missed the green, and he had to hole from eight feet for the four.

Now to the 11th, a 533-yard par five where he looked as if he might have run afoul of the law. Daly drew wild cheers from the enthusiastic gallery by rifling another huge drive, then ripping into a one iron. His ball bounced onto the green and settled about 35 feet from the cup. A chance for an eagle three.

Daly and his caddie studied the line. and his caddie took the flagstick from the hole. While he and Daly talked to one another, the caddie stood the flagstick on the ground a foot or so to the right of the cup. They spoke again, the caddie lifted the flagstick and stepped aside, and Daly putted the ball. He had aimed left of the hole, though, the other side of the cup from the spot his caddie had set the flagstick. That would become the critical point of the discussion.

Almost immediately television viewers began calling the PGA, claiming Daly had violated the rules. Officials said nothing to Daly at the time, allowing him to finish the round without alarming him.

He missed the putt, but even so he had birdied, and now he stood two under par for the day, 10 under for the 47 holes he had played. Three more pars brought him to the 15th, another par five, but of only 507 yards. A series of bunkers lined the left side of the fairway in position to catch the pulled drive. To clear the bunkers a drive would have to carry 285 yards. Daly carried them. His drive covered 320 yards and once again he had only a five iron into a par-five hole. His ball settled 30 feet away, and he birdied.

Three under now, he lost a birdie chance at the 16th, missing from seven feet, then lost a stroke at the 17th, a hard par three with a table-like green set above deep bunkers on both sides. Daly missed the green and did well to save a bogey.

Another massive drive into the center of the 18th fairway left him only an eight iron and set up still another birdie. Back in 34, he had shot 69.

As he stepped into the trailer set up to check scores, Daly was told not to sign his card; there was a question about the 11th hole. Led to the CBS compound, Daly, his caddie, and Lietzke watched the video tape and convinced PGA rules officials no infraction had taken place. Daly's line lay well left of the spot where his caddie had held the flagstick. His 69 stood.

Even though he played steady, reliable golf, with two birdies and two bogeys, Lietzke constantly fell behind, dropping to fourth place. Meantime, Stadler was playing the most consistent golf of anyone. Through the first 36 holes, he had gone over par on only the 16th hole of the second round. Once again he played a bogey-free round in the third, going out in 34 and coming back in 35. With 69, he climbed over Faldo, Woosnam and Lietzke and claimed a share of second place.

Stadler seemed to have absolute command of Crooked Stick's opening hole. He had birdied the first hole in the first round, made his par four in the second, and birdied once again in the third, dropping a wedge within seven feet. Seven consecutive pars, and then another wedge pitch to six feet set up his second birdie, on the ninth.

Reaching the 15th still two under par for the day and seven under for the distance, Stadler looked as if he had made a mistake. He pushed his drive into the deep rough, dug it out with a four iron, then played a loose pitch perhaps 30 from the hole. He holed it, his third birdie of the day. Par in and he had his third sub-par round.

After holing those birdie putts, and a few more for pars, Stadler said he felt confidence in his putting for the first time in a long while.

Aside from his three birdies, Stadler had saved pars after missing the greens of six holes.

"That makes a difference," he claimed. "It helps to know you're not automatically going to make a bogey when you miss a green. When you're playing two and three irons into the par fours, it's pretty decent if you get your shot within 25 feet."

For a time during the early 1980s, Stadler had ranked among the game's leading players. He had won the Masters, the highlight of his career, along with three other tournaments in 1982, but his game had gone into steady decline. He had won nothing since the 1984 Byron Nelson Classic. He had not ranked among the Tour's 20 leading money winners since 1985. His apparent revival in the PGA surprised us all.

His game, though, did seem to fit the requirements of Crooked Stick. Stadler stood among the top-eight percent of Tour players in driving distance, averaging a bit more than 270 yards. He shrugged it off.

"I can hit the ball," he admitted, "but compared to Daly, you can't call me long. He put the ball in places I haven't ever seen. Some of his tee shots were unbelievable. We've got guys out here like Calcavecchia and Couples who can hit the ball, but they're not within 40 yards of this guy."

Stadler also admitted he had played some unusual golf.

"If you've seen me play," he joked, "you know bogey-free golf is not exactly my forte."

Third-round leaders:

John Daly	205
Kenny Knox	208

Craig Stadler	208
Bruce Lietzke	209
Nick Faldo	210
Bob Gilder	210
Andrew Magee	210

Back at Dardanelle, Arkansas, signs had sprung up all over town. "Go, John, Go," one cried. "Good Luck, John," another said. Out at the nine-hole Bay Ridge Golf Course, where Daly had taught himself to play, patrons crowded into the golf shop to watch the telecast. The course had run a scramble, but most patrons preferred to watch the PGA and cheer on their friend.

Debbie Slusher, the shop manager, admitted sportsmanship might have suffered. "We see one of those other players hit a ball into the deep stuff, or have a putt lip out, and we cheer," she smiled. "There are lots of nice people in this town, but I've never seen everybody come together like this."

Nobody cheered, though, after the first hole.

Daly had gone into the last round with a three-stroke edge over Knox and Stadler, but he came away from the first hole leading by only two. He drove into the woods, bladed his second into a bunker, and bogeyed. Meantime, up ahead, Lietzke had birdied.

Daly bounced right back with a birdie on the second, and when he birdied the fifth for the third consecutive day, he had built his lead to four strokes once again. Only Lietzke mattered by then, for Stadler had double-bogeyed the first and bogeyed the third on his way to 38, and Knox had hit his tee shot into the water and double-bogeyed the sixth, falling six strokes behind Daly. Minutes earlier, Lietzke had helped Daly's cause by three-putting the sixth.

When John turned for home in 35, only his total collapse could make a difference. Playing an hour ahead of him, Jim Gallagher was on his way to 67, but he had begun nine strokes behind and had far too much ground to make up.

Nevertheless, the tension continued to build. Could Daly hang on? Would he fall apart under the growing pressure? He stood 10 under par after the first nine, but his lead had been cut to three strokes once again, for Lietzke had birdied the ninth while Daly had managed only a par, missing a holeable 12-footer.

Stadler steadied himself on the home nine, but it was too late. With four bogeys and a double, he shot 76. Magee, only five strokes behind going into the round, shot 75, Faldo faded to 76, Woosnam shot a second consecutive 76, and Grady dropped out with 77.

Daly held the PGA in his hands. Lietzke couldn't catch up without a lapse by Daly, and John gave Bruce hope only once, far too late in the round.

For a time Daly indeed hinted he might throw it away, but he recovered each time. A pulled drive on the 10th left him a shot over trees to reach the green, but he pulled it off and saved his par, and then he pulled another drive on the 11th. His ball jumped into a high-faced fairway bunker, cutting off any chance of reaching the green, but he played out safely with a six iron, then pitched on 20 feet from the hole and made his par.

Another par at the 12th, and then Daly played a nice eight iron within 25 feet on the 13th, the 180-yard par three played to a green protected on the right front and side by a running brook. He holed the putt. Lietzke had parred moments before, and now Daly led by five strokes.

Still the anxiety grew. Daly had reached the dangerous 14th now, and the gallery wondered if he would try to make the long carry across the corner or play percentage golf, fly his drive straight out and take his chances on reaching the green with a longer iron. He didn't hesitate. While Stadler and Lietzke looked back over their shoulders, Daly lashed into another powerful drive and cleared the corner easily. The two men up ahead watched the ball clear the creek and the wide band of rough beyond, shook their heads, and smiled to one another.

Daly had left himself only a nine iron. He made his par, then ripped a five iron over the 15th green. A chip to a foot, and he had still another birdie, his fourth of the round.

Daly stood 12 under par then, and Lietzke had just about given up hope. Talking about it later, Bruce said he didn't think he could get to 12 under. "I thought I could get to 10 under, but I felt he would have to drop back for me to have a chance."

The tension reached its climax on the 17th. Another huge drive left Daly only a nine iron to the 16th. He made his par, then strode to the 17th tee. There, for the first time, Daly looked as if he might give it away.

For the second straight day he missed the 17th green, but where he had left himself in position to play a decent recovery shot on Saturday, here he pulled his ball into the left greenside bunker. The sand lay about 12 feet below the level of the green. Daly couldn't see the green, of course, and he had to be sure to reach it and give himself a chance to save par. John hit the ball a little too hard. It hit the green but skipped over into the rough. He needed three more strokes to get down. A double-bogey five, and he was back to 10 under par.

Lietzke, meantime, hadn't made it to 10 under, but with Daly's shaky 17th, Bruce might have put more pressure on him by birdieing the 18th. Instead, he dropped his approach into a greenside bunker and had to hole a 35-footer to save par. He shot 70, and finished at 279, nine under par.

Only the dangers of the 18th stood between Daly and the championship now. Still the gallery wondered if he could make it. A loose drive could land in the water, and who could guess what might happen then. Even after Daly played a safe drive onto the left side of the fairway no one felt he was safe. The water still lurked off to the right, and anything could happen.

Nothing did. Daly played an eight iron onto the green, and the crowd stood and cheered. It was over. Twelve under par, he could four-putt and still win. Daly knew it, too. Walking toward the green, he waved his hand above his head, wringing even more cheers from the fans. They quieted down enough for him to make his par, holing his second from five feet or so, then erupted again. Daly had shot 71, his fourth sub-par round, and posted a 72-hole score of 276.

Lietzke claimed second place, at 279, and Gallagher climbed over 15 men to claim third place, at 281. With 74, Knox dropped to fourth place, and Stadler tied for seventh.

"It feels wonderful," Daly said. "It just feels so wonderful it's hard to put into words. It's a dream come true."

7. Ryder Cup Matches

The transformation of the Ryder Cup began in 1983. Up to then the matches had been a one-sided contest of little interest in the United States. Since then, the competition has become so competitive and successful that this year's event was one of the greatest sporting occasions of the past 25 years.

Each Ryder Cup since 1981 has stood for something special. In 1983 there was the sight of Jack Nicklaus kissing Lanny Wadkins' divot after Wadkins had played the match-winning pitch. The U.S. had just lost the America's Cup; Wadkins' pitch made sure they didn't lose the Ryder Cup, as well. Europe's victory in 1985 was the first for nearly 30 years, and the best thing that could have happened to the competition. The 1987 match was unforgettable because Europe had never before won away from home; nor had the U.S. ever lost two matches in a row. And the events at The Belfry two years ago take their place in golfing history by being only the second tie since the matches began in 1927.

There has been no more than eight points between the two teams in the matches since 1981, which gives you some idea of how close it has been. Europe has won 72½ points, America 67½.

I heard more excited talk about the Ryder Cup this year than ever before, and this renewed interest was confirmed by ticket sales, which were limited to 25,000 each day and were sold out long before the event started. "See you at Kiawah" was said to me so often I became rather tired of hearing it. Yet it was an accurate reflection of the upsurge in interest in the matches. So too was the huge television coverage by the USA Network and NBC— 16 cameras, 12 tape machines, 50 microphones all linked by more than 32 miles of cable to provide 21½ hours of television in all, 13 hours on USA Network on Friday and Saturday morning and eight and a half on NBC on Saturday afternoon and Sunday. These two networks provided more television coverage of the Ryder Cup matches than any other three-day sports event in history. There were also more than a thousand media personnel at Kiawah Island.

The American and European teams seemed more even than any before. In its Ryder Cup preview, *Golf Digest* polled a number of American and European luminaries and reported that 12 were predicting the U.S. would win, and eight, Europe, and four hedged their bets.

Here are the comments of some past captains:

Raymond Floyd, 1989 captain: "The U.S. should win because it has a far more experienced team than we had in 1989 when we had five rookies and three others playing for the second time." In a prophetical remark he added: "Nobody on the outside understands the value of experience, the intense pressure the players are under..."

Dave Marr, 1981 captain: "The U.S. will win. Our players have taken enough grief and gotten enough battle scars from the last three matches. From them they learned that the other guys don't fall over on the first tee just because they're playing against Americans."

Nicklaus, 1983 and 1987 captain: "We'll have our best players in there and they should be good enough to win. What worries me is that Europe is no longer a four- or five-man team. Their other players are good now, too. But one of (U.S.) captain Dave Stockton's major elements of preparation was stressing match play. He's had his boys thinking match play most of the summer."

Lee Trevino, 1985 captain: "We've got a high mountain to climb. Europe has the top-three players in the world and the site is a links-type golf course. They should have moved the matches to Harbour Town right after Hugo hit. The European players don't like tight courses."

I said: "It's a tie. The teams are very close, Europe stronger in the first six spots and the U.S. better in the bottom six."

The interest in the 29th Ryder Cup matches focused on a number of issues. The chief one was Pete Dye's new course on Kiawah Island, a 10,000-acre barrier island 20 miles from Charleston.

The Ocean course was laid out on the southeastern tip of the 10-mile long and 1.5-mile wide island. It was a last-minute replacement for PGA West in La Quinta, California, when it was realized that play would not finish on the west coast in time for television to beam it back to Europe. As Landmark Land Co., the owners of PGA West, also owned Kiawah, the switch of venues was made. It wasn't without criticism. Moving this historic event to an unbuilt course on a small island with only one narrow two-lane road on it did not seem to be a very good idea, but it is fair to say that the course was as exciting a venue as could have been chosen.

It was lucky that Hurricane Hugo was not about. Hugo, you remember, ravaged this part of the eastern seaboard at about this time in 1989. Winds of 184 mph and a 20-foot tidal surge were recorded and more than $25 million of damage was done. "It looked like a nuclear holocaust," said Terry Florence, director of golf at Wild Dunes resort, 40 miles up the coast from Kiawah. "The scene was one of total devastation. There were no birds singing, no crickets chirping, nothing. Trees were reduced to stubs. It was so overwhelming everyone cried."

When Dye, one of America's most inventive golf course architects, first saw the land he was being given to work on, he rubbed his eyes and said: "If this doesn't turn out to be a good golf course, I should be shot. Everything is here. It's the finest piece of ground I've ever had to work with. The golf course has 18 holes with the same perspective: the ocean on one side, the marsh on the other. When you're playing 10 of the holes you look east and the next thing you see is Madrid."

The course Dye created is a links-type, true oceanfront course, one of the very few to have been built in the U.S. in recent years. He installed a complete internal drainage system that recycles irrigation water while protecting adjacent wetland from runoff. Each day 300,000 gallons of fresh water are recycled.

Dye raised the level of the course by six feet so the sea was visible from more holes and created many of the sandhills that look as though they've been there for years.

He gave it wide fairways, used some of the wonderful old trees that were on the site (just look at the short par-four third) and built raised greens. In short, it is like no other newly built course in the U.S. and to some it looked too European and would thus give the visitors an advantage. Dye has long felt that many courses have become too short and he wanted to bring the long-iron second shot back into golf. He did this at the Ocean course, a 7,240-yard, par-72 test that could be lengthened to nearly 7,800 yards and could contain nine par fives.

There are 18 subspecies of mammals on Kiawah, including white-tailed deer, bobcats and river otter. Signs warn of alligators. All around the course you could see species of these wild life: an alligator basking in a lagoon, a heron rising majestically to the sky, a fawn breaking from the forest in the shadowy light of twilight.

The Americans brought an experienced team to Kiawah with only three men new to Ryder Cup play—Corey Pavin, the leading money winner on the Tour, Steve Pate and Wayne Levi, the 1990 PGA Tour Player of the Year. U.S. team captain Stockton had picked Chip Beck and Floyd as his two wild-card selections, the former on the say-so of the players and the latter for his toughness. Floyd's record in recent Ryder Cup matches is poor: seven victories and 13 defeats and, in the past two matches, two victories and six defeats.

European captain Bernard Gallacher had five rookies—Paul Broadhurst, David Feherty, David Gilford, Colin Montgomerie and Steven Richardson. Gallacher's selections were Nick Faldo, Jose Maria Olazabal and Mark James.

It struck me that the Americans might lack an on-course leader if Floyd wasn't playing well. There were doubts about his ability at age 49 to cope with the physical demands of such a tiring course. Furthermore, he could be facing men half his age—four of the Europeans were less than 26. What Floyd, who had won two PGA Tour events before Olazabal and Richardson were born, lacked in fitness he made up for in experience, however. Thanks partly to him, the American team had won as many major championships as the Europeans. The totals of Floyd (four), Hale Irwin (three), Payne Stewart (two) and one each for Wadkins and Mark Calcavecchia were matched by Seve Ballesteros (five), Faldo (four) and Ian Woosnam and Bernhard Langer one each for the Europeans.

According to the Sony Ranking, the visitors had the edge. Woosnam, Olazabal, Faldo, Ballesteros and Langer were among the top 10, as were Stewart, Couples and Azinger. On the other hand, James, Feherty, Broadhurst, Sam Torrance and Gilford were all outside the top 40.

In the months preceding the Ryder Cup, Stockton did a wonderful job of raising the event's profile travelling all over the U.S. talking to whomever would listen about its history and how important it was for American golf to retrieve the trophy that had not been on this side of the Atlantic for six years. His thoroughness was such that he encouraged those likely members of his team to go to Kiawah all through the summer and play a round there. "I've had one philosophy from the start," said Stockton. "I want these 12 guys knowing the course and liking it. I think coming out here and playing together has brought our team closer together mentally. If we handle it, then we'll be sitting here victorious Sunday night."

Of the two captains I felt that Gallacher had the harder job. Gallacher, a doughty, 42-year-old Scot who was born near Edinburgh, had to follow the extraordinarily successful Tony Jacklin, whose teams had only lost one of the four matches they played under his leadership. Gallacher had played more Ryder Cup matches than Jacklin (eight from 1969 to 1983 compared with Jacklin's seven from 1967 to 1979) and won more points than Jacklin. There were, nevertheless, slight mutterings about his ability to do the job as well as his predecessor. "If Bernie's team wins it will be hailed as a success for the team that Jacko built," said Brian Barnes, Gallacher's teammate from the Ryder Cup of the 70s. "If they lose he will get the blame, which is unfair."

"Bernard is in a no-win situation," said Stockton, piling a little pressure on his rival. "If Europe wins then it's no more than expected and he will not get the praise he would deserve. But if he loses, then..."

In a quiet moment at the Wentworth Club where he is head professional, Gallacher admitted before he left for Kiawah: "All the hype has made me careful. I have made a big effort to protect my family but there are still times when I'm caught out by it all.

"Tony broke the mold but he did all the things I would have done. He bred a great team spirit, enabled players to relax by keeping them apart, and demanded the best. The Americans used to have first-class treatment while we flew out at the back of the airplane. They made more money, even had better shoes. Tony felt it was wrong but, in some ways, it made me play all the harder."

A press conference was called for Tuesday morning, and as soon as he appeared, it was clear that Gallacher was edgy. He wanted to get something off his chest. "I'm offended that anyone would think we're underprepared," he said. "We got here on Monday, the tournament starts on Friday and that's one more day to learn the golf course than we usually have. It gives us three days and with dedicated professionals that's enough.

"I was only invited here once and that was after we had played four events in Europe. The letter said I could bring my team here if I wanted. I felt like writing back and asking what my team was going to be because at that time any 12 out of 100 players could have made it.

"No one seems to have given any thought to the logistical impossibility of coming here when you live 5,000 miles away. As for coming after the Masters or the U.S. Open, the players are concentrating on those events, not thinking about the Ryder Cup. And what if you come to Kiawah and play a round in the total calm? Where's the benefit of that? Anyway, I don't remember the Americans coming over and playing The Belfry."

Stockton wanted to get something off his chest, too. He had read that Faldo and Woosnam were claiming that Europe led the world in golf. "I can't believe they're saying these things," said the American captain. "I think we just have to shut up, bring the course to its knees and the Europeans along with it. I've read some brilliant comments they've made about how quickly they can learn this course. Well, since they're the best in the world, I guess so—but we'll see on Sunday."

In those days before the event started there was an air of a phoney war about it all. The players were edgy and so were the two captains. The massive contingent of journalists wanted stories. A lot of time was spent pulling the competition to pieces.

One subject that kept coming up was the different methods of team selection. The Europeans picked the top nine from their 1991 money list and allowed Gallacher to select a further three players. The Americans selected the top-10 points winners at events between January 7, 1990, through the

1991 PGA Championship. In addition, Stockton picked two wild cards.

"Are we talking about the same match here?" asked Steve Hershey in *USA Today*. "One team is picked on '91 performances; the other goes back 21 months. One gets three wild-card picks, the other two. Makes no sense."

"The Europeans have an advantage," said Paul Azinger in this same article. "They pick their team strictly on how they perform this year, so they are more likely to have guys who are hot."

Levi was a case in point. He had got into the U.S. team because of an outstanding 1990 when he won four events, was second on the money list with a little over $1 million and was voted PGA Tour Player of the Year. So far this year he had had three top-10 finishes (and only one since March), missed 12 cuts in 22 starts and was 79th on the money list.

Azinger suggested that selection should be done over a one-year period, or that points for the first year should only count half.

Other aspects of the format came in for criticism. "Why go through this agony to pick 12 guys. Then for days only eight get to play," said Hershey. "Eight fine players get to twiddle their thumbs Friday and Saturday." Stockton said he had asked to play five pairs on each of the first two days but that he hadn't even got a reply. "Why should four of my players have to sit out? We could increase the golf by 20 percent, which would have been better for television."

The Europeans' answer to that is simple. They feel their strength lies in their top-half-dozen players and to have to play two more men in each series on the first two days would expose their weaker players. "Why mess with a successful formula?" says Tony Jacklin. "It's obviously working very well. Why change it."

Then, on Wednesday night, as the two teams were heading into Charleston to the official banquet, the car carrying Pate and two other vehicles in the 15-car cavalcade crashed into one another. Pate was thrown forward and injured his ribs and left hip. Sharron Pavin, wife of Corey, suffered a bruised elbow as well. Pate went to a hospital but was later allowed out.

This was a blow Stockton could have done without. Pate had played himself into the U.S. team with a gutsy performance in the PGA, the last event in which U.S. players could qualify, and had been impressive in practice. "I had him penciled in to play five matches," said Stockton. "I simply don't know what I'm going to do now. It could be that he will be available for Sunday's singles matches but I probably won't know until then."

The Ryder Cup rules permitted Stockton to draft in a replacement up to the opening ceremonies. Tim Simpson was the next available player on the Ryder Cup points list and the man Pate bumped from the top 10 by his performance in the PGA. Stockton chose to wait and see how Pate recovered. "By the time Tim gets here, he won't have time to practice," said Stockton.

The format for this year's matches was the same as before; that is, two days of foursomes before lunch and four balls after lunch, with 12 singles being held on the third day. The big surprise of the opening foursomes was Gallacher's selection of two rookies, Montgomerie and Gilford. This bore the stamp of a last-minute decision because the two of them hadn't been paired together in practice. "Rookie is a word that's in the dictionary, not in golf," said Gallacher. "Both of them have impressed me immeasurably with the way they've been playing this week."

The rookies were drawn to play Wadkins and Irwin, who between them had played in 10 Ryder Cups. Stockton said Irwin was a replacement for Pate. "Pate is a fighter and he's going to be playing before this is all over," said Stockton. "But Irwin has impressed me a lot these past two days."

Other than Montgomerie and Gilford, Gallacher's pairings were much as expected. He led off with Ballesteros and Olazabal, which was no surprise since the two of them had won 6½ points out of eight together, followed by Langer and James. The fourth pairing was as predictable as the first: Woosnam and Faldo, who had lost only one of their eight previous matches together.

An odd statistic: Europe had not won an opening foursomes series in a Ryder Cup for 18 years. This time they were nearly whitewashed. Ballesteros and Olazabal led off at a snail's pace, taking 55 minutes for the first three holes against Azinger and Beck. After nine holes Azinger and Beck were three up when the match was interrupted by controversy. Ballesteros noticed that on the seventh tee Beck had changed from a 100 compression ball to a 90 compression ball, thereby breaking a Ryder Cup rule which says that a player must use the same compression ball throughout the match.

Ballesteros did not call in the referee immediately. Instead, Gallacher was summoned and spoke to officials on the 10th tee. There was an unpleasant hiatus, and Azinger and Beck admitted the ball had been changed without realizing they were violating a rule. "We made a mistake, but we certainly aren't cheating," Azinger said.

"We don't say that, Paul," said Ballesteros. "It has nothing to do with cheating. Cheating and breaking the rules are two different things."

Had the Europeans complained on the eighth tee, they would have been awarded the hole because the Americans broke a rule. But officials ruled that the incident had to be reported before the hole was concluded or on the tee of the next hole.

This incident was just the latest in the continuing series of incidents that happen whenever Ballesteros and Azinger are in opposition. They had clashed twice in the previous Ryder Cup, once when Seve wanted to change his ball on the second green because it was damaged and Azinger wouldn't let him, and then again on the 18th, when Azinger drove into the water and got a drop in a position that Ballesteros felt was incorrect. "There's always light-ning around when these guys meet," said Stockton.

It galvanized the Europeans, who recovered from their three-hole deficit to win the match 2 and 1. Ballesteros holed a 10-foot putt for a birdie on the 17th to close out Azinger and Beck.

This match dominated the morning's play, which ended 3-1 in favor of the U.S. Floyd and Couples were four up after eleven holes and had to endure a spirited fight back by Langer and James before they beat the Europeans 2 and 1. "I finally won a Ryder Cup match," said Couples, who was 0-2 in Ryder Cup matches before this one.

Irwin was in brilliant form when paired with Wadkins and they raced away from Montgomerie and Gilford. One up after the first hole, two up after the third, three up after the fifth, four up after the sixth. "Hale's shots were God-like," said Montgomerie. "We played steady enough golf, but under that kind of fire there isn't much you can do."

Stewart and Calcavecchia overcame Gallacher's bankers, Woosnam and

Faldo, the two most recent Masters champions, in the bottom match. The Americans' short game never let them down (Calcavecchia chipped in on the 16th), and they were never behind though they frightened themselves on the 17th.

Dormie two up, Stewart drove into the water, a portent of the trouble he and his teammates were to have all week on that chilling short hole. Woosnam's four iron found the green. Then Calcavecchia missed the green from the drop area, and so the Americans conceded the hole. A half in four on the 18th was good enough to give them a one-hole victory.

For the afternoon's four balls Stockton stayed with Azinger and Beck, who were drawn against Ballesteros and Olazabal again, and with Floyd and Couples. But he rested Irwin and brought in O'Meara to partner Wadkins and Pavin to partner Calcavecchia. Gallacher's reaction to his teams' poor performance in the morning was to drop the rookies Montgomerie and Gilford and break up the James and Langer partnership by bringing in Richardson to play with James.

Wadkins and O'Meara and Torrance and Feherty halved their match. Although Wadkins and O'Meara were three up after 10 holes and two up after 13, they were let off on both the 16th and 17th hole. On the 16th Feherty missed a putt that would have squared the match, and on the next Torrance nearly holed for an ace. O'Meara sank a five-foot putt to halve the hole. Feherty sank an eight-foot putt on the last green to snatch the half.

Just as they had in the morning, Azinger and Beck found the Spaniards were too good for them in a tense and exciting match. There was never more than one hole in it. The Europeans were one up on the 17th tee, Ballesteros having birdied the 14th. Olazabal and Ballesteros played first. Olazabal's tee shot finished in the sand dunes and Ballesteros' 15 feet from the flag. The Americans capitulated weakly, first Azinger and then Beck driving into the water. Europe won 2 and 1.

Pavin and Calcavecchia were up against a partnership that worked well together in Richardson, a rookie, and James who was playing in his fifth Ryder Cup. James birdied the first two holes; Richardson sank a 20-foot putt for a birdie on the sixth and holed from a bunker on the seventh for an eagle three. Europe was four up. There was no coming back for the Americans after that.

If the Spaniards were the Europeans' strongmen, then Couples and Floyd were just as unbeatable for the Americans. Before the match started, Floyd had said he was playing as well as at any time in his life, and there was no denying it on this afternoon's form. Couples set the Americans off by holing a putt from off the green on the first after Floyd had lost his tee shot. Floyd and Couples were handed the second hole when their pars beat the Europeans' bogeys. It was all square at the ninth. That was the signal for the Americans to raise their game.

Floyd holed from 15 feet for a birdie on the 10th and from five feet for a birdie on the 11th. They won both holes, although they shouldn't have won the 11th. Woosnam missed a three-foot putt for a birdie and Faldo stubbed a chip. All four men were putting for birdies on the 12th. When Couples coaxed in his downhill five-footer, the U.S. was three up and eventually won by 4 and 3.

If you thought you saw Rocco Mediate at this match, you were correct.

Mediate, 12th on the money list, was wearing a stars-and-stripes hat and purple-and-white sneakers. He was carrying equipment for a photographer.

Saturday was another absorbing day, windy, sunny and thrilling as the Americans fought to maintain their 4½ to 3½ overnight lead. Once again the dominant figure was Ballesteros, not only for what he did but also for what he said.

Play followed Friday's pattern. The U.S. won three of the morning foursomes. Azinger and O'Meara were far too good for Faldo and Gilford, who looked an unhappy pair and hardly spoke a word to one another. Perhaps Gallacher thought that Gilford's good putting and Faldo's tee-to-green steadiness would blend together. If so, he was let down. Azinger and O'Meara won 7 and 6. Wadkins and Irwin, the same partnership that had been so good on the first morning, rose to the occasion once again. This time they defeated Feherty and Torrance 4 and 2.

Then Calcavecchia and Stewart won as well, just as they had 24 hours earlier. They defeated Europe's fancied pair, James and Richardson, on the last hole. Richardson experienced the full, potent force of Ryder Cup pressure. He faced a two-foot putt on the 18th to win the hole and halve the match. He missed it.

It was left to the Spaniards to save the day as they had in the first day's foursomes. Three up at the turn, they defeated the formerly invincible pairing of Couples and Floyd by 3 and 2. The U.S. now led by 7½ to 4½ and the Americans were on target for overall victory, sensing that their greater strength in depth would be crucial in the next day's singles. Europe had never won a series of singles matches in the U.S.

Ballesteros was worried and spoke out. "I was happy with our performance, but I am a little disappointed with some of my teammates' play," he said at lunch, and it had the desired effect. In this Ryder Cup, Ballesteros was like a man transformed. He was so clearly relishing every minute of it that he became an inspirational figure to his teammates. Truth to tell, he wasn't always at his best. But his charisma, magnetism and character was such that he dominated the European team.

Admonished by Ballesteros, the Europeans rallied strongly in the afternoon and in the rising wind they played impressive golf. Woosnam, who had been dropped from the morning foursomes, came in and partnered Broadhurst. Faldo was dropped and went off to practice under the eye of his coach, David Leadbetter. Gallacher persisted with James and Richardson, who had played so well together and paired Langer with Montgomerie.

Every tactical ploy that Gallacher tried paid off. Woosie and the rookie Broadhurst blended as well as James and Richardson, and their success highlighted Gallacher's mistake in not playing Broadhurst earlier.

The young Englishman, who had finished tied for ninth in the B.C. Open behind Couples the previous Sunday, his first tournament in the U.S., holed a 30-foot birdie putt on the 10th to put Europe level and one of 10 feet at the 13th to take the lead. If he was feeling the pressure, he didn't show it. Azinger and Irwin were unable to make any impression over the closing holes and were one down on the 17th tee. Europe played first, and once again made sure that they cleared the water. Woosnam's ball was in sand by the side of the green, Broadhurst's over the back.

The American team's failing on this hole was demonstrated once more.

Irwin's shot came down short of the green, hit a stanchion supporting the putting surface and rebounded into the lake. Azinger went way out to the right. Azinger could only reach the green in three and missed his bogey putt. Woosnam played a brilliant bunker shot to three feet and made the putt to win the hole and the match.

Pate and Pavin, a new partnership, did not win a hole against Montgomerie and Langer, another new partnership, in a match that took five hours and 10 minutes for 17 holes. Pate was playing, said Stockton, to give him a game before Sunday. As early as the fourth hole Pate required attention from team therapist Brett Fischer.

The 13th was one key hole, the 15th another. On the 13th Pavin hit his second shot to three inches; Montgomerie followed to three feet and then holed for a half. On the 15th Pate sank a 15-yard putt from off the green for a birdie. Moments later Montgomerie matched this by sinking a testing 18-foot downhill putt.

Wadkins and Levi found themselves facing some good scoring by Richardson and James. Richardson, in particular, hadn't cooled down after missing that short putt on the 18th green before lunch and, helped by the Americans bogeying two of the first three holes, he and James were three up after three holes. Wadkins birdied the 16th to pull the Europeans back to two up but then both Wadkins and Levi missed the green of the 17th while the Europeans both hit it and the Americans conceded.

Stewart and Couples halved with Ballesteros and Olazabal in the last match of the day, the first match the Spaniards had not won. Couples was the star for the Americans, Olazabal for the Europeans. Couples and Stewart were two up after the 12th, Ballesteros birdied the 13th and the 15th to level the match. They halved the 16th, halved the 17th when Olazabal missed from five feet, and halved the 18th—but only after Olazabal sank a six-foot putt for a par.

Europe, having been undefeated in the afternoon's fourballs, levelled the score at 8 to 8. They were tied, with all to play for on Sunday. It seemed about right.

The Americans' misfortune in losing Pate was matched by the Europeans' disappointment at the poor form of Woosnam and Faldo, who had won one point from six matches by Saturday evening.

Gallacher's technique was to summon Faldo and announce to him that he was playing first in the singles. Faldo faced Floyd. Stockton tried to guess where Gallacher would play Ballesteros to avoid another confrontation between the Spaniard and Azinger. He succeeded. Ballesteros drew Pate in the seventh of the 12 singles and Azinger found Olazabal instead.

Soon after breakfast on Sunday morning, it was announced that Pate could not play because of his injury. This meant that the envelope rule was enforced. That morning the two captains had each named one of their players to sit down in the event of the opposition being unable to play. Gallacher nominated Gilford. He withdrew from his match against Levi, who dropped down the order to face Ballesteros, who would have played Pate. Both teams claimed a half point.

So the score became U.S. 8½, Europe 8½.

The Americans then got off to the worst possible start when Floyd was defeated by Faldo by two holes and Stewart lost to Feherty.

Europe 10½, U.S. 8½.

Calcavecchia looked as though he would provide the Americans with their first point of the day. He was five up after the ninth and four up with four holes to play. Then in one of the most spectacular collapses in the history of golf, Calcavecchia went 7, 6, 6, 5—triple bogey, bogey, triple bogey, bogey against a par of four, five, three, four—and Montgomerie gratefully took all four holes. The 17th was the most remarkable. Montgomerie drove into the water and then Calcavecchia followed him in. Both men hit the green from the drop zone. Montgomerie two-putted, Calcavecchia three-putted.

Europe 11, U.S. 9.

If there was one match that was pivotal to the outcome of the day then it was the next one, Azinger against Olazabal. The Spaniard had endured a dull season after the disappointment of finishing second to Woosnam at the Masters, and it wasn't until the week before the Ryder Cup that he snapped out of his slump with victory in the Epson Grand Prix.

Like Ballesteros, he was an invigorated man at Kiawah and, if the truth be told, he was the stronger partner in the all-Spain alliance. But Azinger's feistiness won out. They pushed each other to the limits and, in the end, Azinger's victory inspired his teammates in the way that a triumph by Olazabal would have inspired his.

Only four of the 17 holes were halved and it all came down to the 17th hole, which the Americans had played so badly throughout. The previous afternoon, for example, 18 attempts were made to reach the green of the 200-yard hole. Only seven reached the putting surface, and of those seven, only two were Americans—Pavin and Couples. The successful Europeans were Montgomerie, Langer, James, Richardson and Olazabal.

But if Azinger failed on Saturday, he succeeded on Sunday. He hit a two iron and it landed 50 feet from the hole. "I absolutely killed it," said Azinger. "If I missed it the slightest bit I would have been in the water on the line I took." A three there quelled Olazabal and a par on the 18th was enough to give Azinger victory by two holes.

Europe 11, U.S. 10. Europe needed 2½ points to retain the cup.

Pavin out-chipped and out-putted Richardson to make it 11 to 11, but then Ballesteros defeated Levi.

Europe 12, U.S. 11.

Beck was too steady for Woosnam, who has yet to win a singles match after five attempts in the Ryder Cup. He won two of the first three holes and then when Woosnam pulled back to level, Beck holed a wedge for an eagle on the 11th.

Europe 12, U.S. 12.

O'Meara couldn't match Broadhurst's steadiness. O'Meara lost three of his first five holes. Broadhurst had two birdies all day, the second one coming on the 17th which gave him victory by 3 and 1. It had been some Ryder Cup for him. Played two, won two. He contributed as many points as Faldo and Woosnam together.

Europe 13, U.S. 12.

Couples was never in danger against Torrance. He was five up after 12 holes and won 3 and 2. This victory went some way towards redeeming his performance in the 1989 match when he missed the 18th green at The Belfry and lost his match against Christy O'Connor, Jr. Couples' 1991 record was 3-1-1.

Now the score was tied again: Europe 13, U.S. 13.

Wadkins, in the penultimate match, had little difficulty in beating James. He was four up after nine holes, winning the ninth with a bogey. James got two holes back when Wadkins bogeyed the 10th, 13th and 15th but Wadkins closed him out on the 16th with a par. The emotion was such that Wadkins was close to tears at the end and unable to speak to an interviewer. "That's only happened to me once before, and that was at the 1983 Ryder Cup," said Wadkins, whose Ryder Cup record was now 18-10-2. "I'm a pretty vocal guy, so talking isn't usually a problem. That just shows you how much this means to everybody on this team."

U.S. 14, Europe 13.

And so it all came down to the last pair, Irwin, a three-time U.S. Open champion, and Langer, the 1985 Masters champion. Irwin was two up after 14 holes but lost the 15th with a bogey. Langer halved the 16th by getting up and down from a bunker. Now Irwin only led by one hole. That lead disappeared when Irwin three-putted from 40 feet on the 17th for a bogey and Langer bravely holed a five-footer for a winning par.

Every one of the 25,000 spectators was around the green or lining the fairway back to the tee, seemingly, as the players approached the last green. Irwin's drive had gone way left but rebounded towards the fairway from where he hit a three wood to the side of the green. His 25-yard chip with a sand wedge was poor. It pulled up 30 feet short of the hole. Langer putted to six feet. Irwin's first putt stopped 2½ feet from the hole. He had taken 41 strokes to play the back nine.

Langer conceded Irwin's putt and got down to the business of concentrating on his own. If he holed it he would win his match and that point would be sufficient for Europe to retain the trophy they had held since 1985. Irwin went to the greenside and crouched down.

As Langer lined up the putt there wasn't a sound from the spectators. In a minute Jacklin would say, "No man should have to bear this pressure." But for a moment one did, Langer did, and every eye was focused on him.

The roar that went up as Langer's putt slid by the hole told the story. Langer had missed. The U.S. had regained the Ryder Cup 14½ to 13½. Amid the exultation Irwin walked slowly towards Langer. Irwin had an idea of the mental torment Langer was in. He had suffered a little of it himself after throwing away that two-hole lead with four holes remaining and then chipping weakly on the 18th. He embraced Langer warmly, a gesture that spoke volumes for their mutual respect and sportsmanship.

"No one in the world could have holed that putt," said Ballesteros later. "Jack Nicklaus wouldn't have holed it, nor would Tony Jacklin. And I certainly wouldn't have holed it." Michael Bonallack, the secretary of the R&A, later described it as "the greatest pressure putt in the history of golf."

That was pressure such as Langer has never known before. Nor have any of the Americans. And that is what makes the Ryder Cup so special. "All of a sudden it's 12 guys, a team and a captain and the U.S. and that's pressure," said Floyd. "There's a difference in playing with a team. It's something we're not accustomed to."

8. Dunhill Cup

Just as all good things come to an end sooner or later, so do the bad. A case in point was the Dunhill Cup at St. Andrews, which marked the return of South Africa to the world of international golf. Not since 1981 had they been allowed to share the stage with other nations. The change in the political climate as the barriers of apartheid were slowly broken down gave the International Advisory Committee the opportunity to offer the hand of friendship. When it became clear that Japan would be unable to enter a worthwhile team for the Dunhill Cup because of a conflict with the Japan Open, the invitation was instead extended to South Africa.

It was a significant moment in sports history. The world gymnastics championships had been held a few months before in Indianapolis, when South Africa was also allowed to enter a team. But golf has much more media attention; the event was being played at St. Andrews, historically the greatest venue of them all since it was the cradle of the game; and it featured in Gary Player a man who, more than any other, had had to endure the insults and criticism of a country to which he always remained loyal.

Certainly Player was a man who opposed apartheid but because of his nationality he was held, in some eyes, to be as guilty as a slave trader. By his deportment and his pride in personal performance, Player survived it all and it was only right that, at the advanced age of 55, when no one could argue but that he was past his best, he should captain his country on so momentous an occasion.

There was criticism of his appointment from golfers who thought they should have been there instead. But his choice was the right one and when South Africa went on to the reach the final, beaten though they then were by Sweden, it was still more a triumph than a failure.

This was not then quite a fairy-tale return. If it had been, Player would have been there leading his country triumphantly home when all depended on him. He was there with the final tied at one game each, and Mats Lanner and Player were tied after 18 holes, all depending on them. It was then that the script had its twist. It was not Player who won, but Lanner, with a birdie three at the first extra hole.

All week a grey curtain of fog had hung over the Old Grey Toon and it dropped again as Player's shoulders also drooped in defeat while beside him the Swedes—Lanner, Anders Forsbrand and Per-Ulrik Johansson—celebrated the first meaningful victory for Sweden in professional golf. Each had had their moments as individuals, but now they were triumphant as a team, completing a double since the previous year Sweden had also won the Eisenhower Trophy, another team event for amateurs, in New Zealand.

In time this may be seen as one of golf's turning points, when the old gave way to the new, but for four days anyway it was South Africa that caught all the headlines, beating Switzerland, the United States and then Scotland before falling at the very last hurdle.

To have competed was nevertheless enough, a point Player made on the eve of the tournament as he rejoiced not only at being back, but back at St.

Andrews, where, in 1955, he had played in his first British Open. Twenty-six years later, it was forgivable for him to reminisce, even if fantasy occasionally got in the way of fact.

He recalled that year of his first trip to Britain, his first tournament at Moor Park, north of London; how he caught a train to Leuchars and then a bus to St. Andrews where, with what must have been a near-empty wallet, he claimed to have slept in the dunes until a kindly hotelier took pity on him and gave him shelter.

It was a tallish story, but no one was too particular, any more than they were when Player said he had played in trousers with one leg black and the other white. Those with memories long enough knew that it was much later that such a sartorial touch had come in Player's career.

What they did accept was Player's first impression of St. Andrews. "I said they had spoiled a good marsh," he recalled. "I did not like the course, and Bobby Jones did not like it either. Many people have not enjoyed it the first time, but he and I and others find you come to enjoy it and appreciate it. The more you play it, the more you appreciate it. It is steeped in history, and St. Andrews is now one of my best places to play golf."

It was a particularly good place to have played on that opening day of the Dunhill Cup; South Africa's first appearance as a team since the World Cup of 1981 in Colombia. That was before the days of the Dunhill Cup, the Davis Cup of golf, and the intervening years had seen many changes. Ten years ago Switzerland, their opponents in the first round, would hardly have dared to share the same locker room.

Now they not only did but very nearly won; so nearly that David Frost, who with Player and John Bland formed the South African team, admitted how lucky they were to have got through. Frost himself had done his bit, 69 to beat Andre Bossert by four strokes. He was to win his every game, just proof of his standing in the current world of golf.

However, if this always looked a certain point, it was at the same time hard to see where the other one was going to come from. Behind him Bland was three shots down to Paolo Quirici playing the 14th hole while, behind them, Player was two strokes down to Karim Baradie as they went up the 13th.

What turned it all around was Bland's birdie-four at the 14th when Quirici took three putts, a two-stroke swing for South Africa. The next three holes were halved, which meant that Quirici was still one stroke ahead with one hole to play. The four that would have won Switzerland the match was beyond him, however, and three putts for equal rounds of 74 sent him and Bland into extra holes.

There was further hope for South Africa in the last game as Player, with typical tenacity, drew level with Baradie at the 17th. Neither were very near the flag at the last. Player putted first from some 60 feet and just missed and then Baradie, from 40 feet, holed for a three. It was a cruel blow for South Africa and with one game apiece now, everything depended on Bland against Quirici.

At the first extra hole, the Swiss mishit his second shot short of the burn, chipped on and holed from 15 feet for the half. At the second extra hole, Bland drove into a bunker, seemed certain to lose and then sank a putt of 35 feet for the half. Player, watching anxiously from the side of the green, could not believe his eyes. It was a telling moment for at the third extra hole, Quirici went through the green and Switzerland was beaten.

If that was one cliffhanger of a finish, soon there was to be another. Scotland was in disarray against Italy, Costantino Rocca continuing a fine season with his defeat of Sam Torrance with 72 against 74. This was balanced by Colin Montgomerie, who had performed well in his first Ryder Cup match a fortnight earlier, beating Giuseppe Cali with 67 to 71, and that left everything on the middle game between Gordon Brand, Jr., of Scotland, and Alberto Binaghi.

They tied for 18 holes with rounds of 74, Brand having come back from three shots down with eight holes to play. He had to hole from eight feet at the last to stay alive, and the five extra holes it took him to win equalled the Dunhill Cup record.

Defeat had stared Brand even more strongly in the face at the second extra hole. He hooked into the rough and was so badly bunkered with his second shot that he had to play out away from the hole. It left him with a putt of nearly 40 feet for the half, since Binaghi was right beside the hole in three. In it went, and three holes later, at the fifth or 23rd hole, Brand prevailed with a birdie four.

The surprise of the day was Canada's 2-1 defeat of Australia, which had been seeded to meet the United States in the final. It was the second consecutive year that Australia had lost in the first round. Danny Mijovic got the Canadians away to a good start, his 71 being two strokes too good for Mike Harwood. The nine-foot putt he sank for a half at the 17th was as important as any, particularly in the knowledge that Dan Halldorson was being well beaten by Craig Parry (70 against 75).

That left everything riding on Dave Barr, three strokes down to Wayne Grady as they played the 15th hole. Both had putts for birdies, but Grady missed and Barr, on much the same line, holed. Next Grady found the Principal's Nose bunker at the 16th, took five and had his lead wiped out, since Barr managed a second birdie. With another dropped shot at the 17th, Australia had lost the advantage and, as it turned out, interest in the competition. Canada went into the second round.

Also gaining the second round was the United States, which a year ago had received a shock when France won in the first round. This time, it was again far from plain sailing when Curtis Strange, who has not had the best of years, lost the middle game to Choi Sang Ho, who had 72 and won by two shots. Strange's drive over the wall and out of bounds at the 14th let Choi get past him.

America's Steve Pate, now recovered from the badly bruised side he had suffered in a car crash on the eve of the Ryder Cup which forced him out of the singles play, played strongly and drew first blood with 71 to Park Nam Sin's 70. That left no margin for error, Nam Sin keeping close right to the end, thanks to a big putt to save par at the 16th and then a fine up-and-down at the 17th. This was the key game, for at the end Fred Couples was always in command, beating Lee Kang Su by five strokes with 71 to 76.

Wales also won by the odd match, 2-1 against a Spanish team not at its strongest. It all hinged on Ian Woosnam's victory in extra holes against Santiago Luna. Woosnam had been in charge for some time, but Luna caught him at the 13th and every hole from then on was halved until the Welshman broke the deadlock with a birdie at the 20th hole.

Behind Woosnam, Philip Parkin's 74 was fairly comfortably beaten by Jose Rivero's 71 but Phillip Price, the anchorman, just held on to beat Miguel Martin with 73 to 74, his two putts from 50 feet at the last being a real tester under pressure.

The most consistent golf of the day came from England, 3-0 winners over Thailand and very impressively so since Paul Broadhurst (70), Nick Faldo (69) and Steve Richardson (71) were all under par. No other team could match that, though the low round of the day belonged to Colin Montgomerie of Scotland with that 67.

Broadhurst, one of the successes of the European Ryder Cup team, led England off with 70 and coasted home by seven shots over Sukree Oncham. If there was a key hole it was probably the 11th, where Broadhurst had a two and Oncham a five, going over the back of the green and then three putts.

It was around here that Faldo got away from Thaworn Wiratchant, who never looked at home in the lingering fog, the first green being out of sight from the clubhouse. Faldo's 69 was good enough to win by six, and that was the difference as well between Richardson and Boonchu Ruangkit. It looked like being more, but Richardson took seven at the 17th.

Ireland, twice winners of the Dunhill Cup in recent years, also got off to an impressive-looking start, beating Paraguay 3-0. An analysis of their scoring was less impressive than that of England, Ronan Rafferty alone beating par with 70 even though, as he said afterwards, "It seemed I was hitting it in every bunker I could find on the back nine." He got away with it, however, and finished four strokes clear of Carlos Franco.

David Feherty had so much difficulty in judging his shots in the fog that he deliberately played short from the tee so that he could hit first to the green and put pressure on Pedro Martinez. It worked well enough, 77 to 75 being the same margin as that by which Eamonn Darcy defeated Angel Franco. Early on, Darcy was two strokes down but a two-shot swing at the fifth, where Darcy had a birdie-four and Franco a six, turned the game around.

Finally came Sweden, 2-1 winners over the Chinese Taipei team, Mats Lanner, 73 to Chung Chun Hsing's 77, and Anders Forsbrand (72 to Yu Chin Han's 82) making up for Per-Ulrik's defeat by Wang Ter Chang, who had 72 for a two-stroke victory.

Through its still relatively short life, the Dunhill Cup had been lucky in that, despite the apparent gamble of the fairly late date in the calendar, and also as far north as Scotland, it had almost unfailingly been blessed with good weather; often indeed idyllic with the Old Course playing much more hospitably than during, say, the British Open month of July when there is more bounce in the course. This year, however, the gremlins moved in. While Thursday had been a bit of a "blind man's bluff" in the persistent North Sea haar, on Friday it became a veritable fog, as had happened just once before, in 1988, when it rolled in with the dusk and delayed an Ireland victory over England until the following morning.

This time not a ball was hit all day, the start being delayed, delayed again and then finally aborted altogether with the first green seemingly permanently lost from view from the clubhouse. Disappointed spectators were consoled by the fact that their tickets were made valid for either the following day or the Sunday and in the end the tournament was able to make up for the lost time with the minimum of inconvenience. Two rounds, the quarter and semi-finals, were played on the Saturday and the only change to the original plan was that Sunday's final was reduced to 18 holes.

Straightaway South Africa again stole the headlines. In the first round they had landed a pretty small fish in Switzerland, but on this still misty, grey morning they now hauled in a much bigger one in the United States, by a 2-1 margin. Again it was Bland and Frost who were responsible for the victory. Player, placing himself as anchor man, met more than his match, going down by seven strokes to Couples, who was round in 67. His only bogey came at the 17th hole, where he was short of the green in two strokes, took his putter but did not get close enough to sink the next putt. Two birdies in his first three holes had given Couples the advantage and it was a gap Player never looked like closing.

Bland's match with Strange was a real cracker, the second, third and fifth holes all being halved in birdies and Strange drawing ahead with a fourth birdie at the sixth hole. The American was out in 32 but Bland caught him at the 10th hole, where Strange three-putted, and then Bland moved ahead at the 12th as his pitch with an eight iron stopped not more than a yard from the hole. Strange squared their game again at the 15th hole with a most unlikely three as he holed from 45 feet, and it was the 17th hole which proved to be decisive.

Bland played a finely judged "all hands" low pitch to eight feet and holed the putt whereas Strange, from long grass short and right of the green, could not get much control on the ball, came up 25 feet short and missed the putt. With another four at the last, Bland was round in 68 and won by one stroke.

Immediately behind them, Frost and Pate were also locked in a fine battle, both out in 34 and, with exchanges at the 13th and 14th, still level when they came to the 17th. Frost had a bit of luck because his drive was not far from being out of bounds by the hotel. He got a free drop from some temporary railings, which gave him a clear swing, and from there he was able to hit the green with his second shot with a three iron. Pate went through onto the dreaded road and though he got his third shot, with his putter, closer to the flag, it was still Frost who holed for the four. It gave the South African a one-stroke lead, and with a round of 70 he won by one.

Scotland swept over Ireland, the defending champions, winning 3-0 in the next of the quarter-finals. It lined Scotland up against South Africa in the afternoon for a place in the final. Torrance got off on the right foot with three birdies in his first five holes and, with an outward half of 33, was still three strokes clear at the turn. It became a five-stroke lead with more birdies at the 11th and 12th holes, and from then on Torrance was able to coast easily home with 68 to Rafferty's 72.

Brand took more time to establish himself against Darcy, the Irishman being ahead after nine holes, which he completed in 35. But birdies by Brand at the 10th and 11th revived him, and Darcy then lost his grip with bogeys at the 15th, which he three-putted, and 17th. This left him two strokes behind and a birdie at the last was too late, Brand coming in ahead by a stroke with 71.

It was of no consequence that Montgomerie did the sweeping-up operation, though this was a rather untidy match, 73 still being good enough to take care of Feherty. "I never got into the game," said Feherty afterwards. "I had two three putts and very few singles. I never seemed to get the lie to play the right shot. I was in eight divots, but there have been divots here for 200 years and there is no reason to stop them now." Though Feherty had two birdies in his first three holes, he still took 37 to the turn to trail by two strokes and took another 37 coming back. Even though Montgomerie took one more, it was no sort of recovery.

Having played the best golf of the day on Thursday, England's 2-0 defeat (one game was halved) at the hands of Sweden was very much a surprise. The Swedes certainly had to play to do it, their task nonetheless being made all the easier by another lackluster performance by Faldo, who took 74 and lost by a stroke to Johansson, who subsequently became the European Tour's Rookie of the Year.

Faldo's whole season seemed to be one of indifferent putting and so it continued. Out in a very presentable 35, which Johansson matched, Faldo proceeded to three-putt the 10th, 12th and 15th holes, and though he had what he felt were good chances of birdies at the 16th and 18th, he could not make them and Johansson took the victory.

Lanner was given much more of a fright by Broadhurst, whom he trailed by two strokes with three holes to play. Broadhurst dropped shots at both the 16th and 17th, first with three putts and then with another three with his putter from off the green at the Road Hole. Broadhurst could have lost when Lanner made a birdie at the last hole. However, he followed with a matching three and that would have meant extra holes, except that they were not needed. Behind them, Forsbrand was just too good for Richardson with 69 against 70.

Forsbrand had an outward half of 33 to lead by three strokes and, with further birdies at the 12th and 16th holes, was five under par with two to play and still in a very commanding position. However, Forsbrand made a mess of the 17th. He drove into the rough on the left, got an awful lie and, after extricating himself, hit his third shot with a nine iron into the Road bunker. His six made the difference between them only one stroke and there it stayed, though Richardson could have drawn even, only to miss a putt of a little more than two yards at the last hole. "If we Swedes play well," said Forsbrand, "it will be hard to beat us. I was lucky today. I holed a few putts and Steve did not hole any. He played solid but could not really get the ball close on the first 12 holes, which is where you make your score."

Though Woosnam can be in a class of his own, not too many expected Wales to last long for, with due respect, there had to be question marks against Parkin and Price, neither being front-ranking players. All the more credit to them, therefore, for their defeat of Canada, which had earlier removed Australia, by 2-1. How well they all played, each of them round in under 70, with Woosnam's 67 the best.

Woosnam's was the decisive match against Halldorson, but a place in the semi-finals would not have been possible without Price, who just got the better of Mijovic with 69 against 70. Hot stuff it was, too, both of them three under par for the first seven holes and Price, with another birdie at the ninth, out in 32. Both drove the 10th green, but Mijovic three-putted from 45 feet, and when the Canadian then took six at the 13th via a bunker and another three putts, Price was five strokes clear.

There was brief anxiety when Price took six at the long 14th, Mijovic further punishing him with a birdie four, but that was as close as the Canadian got, his three at the last hole making the result look closer than in fact it was.

This was just what was needed, because at the back of the field, Woosnam was always in control against Halldorson, his breakthrough coming at the ninth hole where he holed his second shot with a sand wedge for an eagle-two. This put him out in 32, two shots to the good, and when he then drove the 10th green there was just a faint chance of a second consecutive eagle. However, a putt of 60 feet was rather too tall an order. A birdie had to suffice, and with next a two at the 11th, Woosnam was four strokes clear. Although Halldorson played the last nine holes in even par, it made no difference.

Parkin's defeat at the hands of Barr in the middle match was of no significance. Even so, Parkin put up a stern fight, one stroke down at the turn with 33 against Barr's 32. Parkin took the lead with birdies at the 10th and 13th holes, but his seven at the 14th, a three-shot swing, upset his progress. He got one stroke back at the 16th, but he could not quite close the gap.

Having come up trumps in the morning, Scotland hardly knew what hit them in the afternoon. South Africa was in inspired form as they made their way into the final with a decisive 3-0 victory. It is safe to say that it was the first three holes that settled matters. Frost began birdie, birdie, birdie against Torrance, Player began birdie, birdie against Brand, and Bland began birdie, birdie, birdie against Montgomerie. Straightaway Scotland was three, two and three strokes behind, and there was nothing they could do about it.

Frost was very much the star, with 64 to beat Torrance by six strokes. Bland had 69 to defeat Montgomerie by three and Player's 70 left him with four strokes to spare over Brand. "David and John played such wonderful golf today," said Player. "To see them getting those red numbers on the board was an inspiration, and I was proud to do the same. To be accepted back at St. Andrews means a lot to all of us. The ovation coming up No. 18, beating Scotland here at the Home of Golf, was something we really appreciated."

The other semi-final was a much more fraught affair and indeed was not concluded, dusk falling with Wales one game to the good against Sweden and the other two all square. Almost inevitably, it was Woosnam who put Wales within reach of the final, playing his finest golf with 65 to Johansson's 68 in a game of the highest quality.

Both were out in 33 but it was Woosnam's burst of three, two, three from the 10th hole that established his grip. Though Johansson also had birdies at the 11th and 12th holes, he took five at the 10th with three putts. Even so the Swede hung on, closed the gap to one stroke again at the 15th with a birdie and was still in with a chance. However, Woosnam's answer to that was threes at the 16th and 18th and his 132 strokes for the day (67, 65) over the Old Course was something of which he could be very proud.

Parkin and Forsbrand tied at 68 apiece and both also had fours at the first extra hole before they were called in because of darkness. Here was some more splendid golf on both sides, both out in 33, Forsbrand drawing ahead with a birdie at the 10th, Parkin catching him with a par at the 12th, leading with a birdie at the 14th, caught by a birdie at the 15th, falling behind at the 17th but drawing level once again with a three at the last. Behind all that was the wonderful putt of 12 feet Parkin holed at the 17th to avoid a six after having been on the road, and then another of the best part of five yards for a birdie at the 18th.

This was heroic stuff and there was more of the same from Price, who was one stroke down to Lanner at the turn (35 to the Swede's 34) and two behind when Lanner also made a birdie at the 10th. However, Price hit a great five iron to the 11th, sank a short putt for his two and was level again, as Lanner three-putted from not very far. And there they remained, halving each of the last seven holes, six of them in par and the other, the 17th, in five. There was no time for extra holes, but Wales was a third of the way into the final, needing only one of these two games for victory, whereas Sweden required both.

The odds were consequently stacked against Sweden but, stacked or not, they came through at first light the following morning. Forsbrand beat Parkin at the third extra hole, sinking a putt for a birdie at the first (only the first and 18th holes were used) after the Welshman had hit his second shot into the burn, dropped out and sunk his next for a four. All, therefore, rested on Lanner and Price, and again it was the Swede who prevailed, though only at the fifth extra hole, again with a birdie.

Having come so far on their return to the international arena, the romantic ending would have been for South Africa to win the Dunhill Cup. But it was not to be. Sweden, which already held the Eisenhower Trophy in amateur golf, completed the double with a 2-1 victory in the final. However, it was desperately close, all being decided when Lanner edged out Player at the first extra hole.

Because of the delayed finish to Sweden's semifinal with Wales, there was not sufficient time to play the final over the projected 36 holes. This was probably to South Africa's advantage, with Player well into his 50s and Bland just as far advanced into his 40s, but in the end it did not make any difference. Still, even to reach the final was an outstanding achievement.

This was also quite a landmark for Sweden, and Forsbrand and Johansson were also later to win the World Cup, a unique double or even triple if you count the Eisenhower event at the end of 1990. They have so often promised much without quite coming up with the goods, noticeably in Ryder Cup terms, as they have not yet provided a player to the European team.

Having taken what appeared to be a firm grip in the Dunhill Cup final, they very nearly let South Africa off the hook. In the top match, for instance, Forsbrand, having gone out in 33 to Bland's 34, held a two-shot lead after he had made a birdie three at the 13th. Needing only a seven iron for his second shot to the 17th, as compared to Bland's four iron, Forsbrand still could not get a four and the margin between them was back to one stroke.

Swedish hearts were even further in their mouths at the last hole, for here Bland hit a glorious wedge to six inches, indeed briefly thinking that the ball was going to go in for a two. A birdie was, therefore, a formality, but Forsbrand, having also played a fine shot to six feet, holed the putt and with 68 to the South African's 69, he had got a point on the board.

The lead was, nevertheless, short-lived. Behind him, Johansson, having held Frost to the turn with 35 apiece, suddenly went hopelessly awry at the 13th, 14th and 15th, where he dropped three strokes, Frost consequently finding himself four strokes ahead and then six ahead as he made birdies at the 15th and 16th. Frost's 68 against a 74 gave him a comprehensive victory.

Not that it seemed likely to make much difference, for Lanner, finding Player some way below his best, led by two strokes at the turn, even though he was no better than 37 for the first nine holes. This became three at the 10th, where the Swede pitched to a yard. Player got one back at the 11th, where Lanner three-putted, and another at the 14th as this time he holed a putt of 25 feet. Now it was a game again, as they halved the next three holes in par.

It looked as if Lanner had passed his crisis, but at the last hole he hit his second shot none too close to the hole, three-putted and there they were all square, both round in 74 and extra holes were needed to decide it all. It did not last long. At the 19th Lanner was closer to the hole after two shots and, after Player had missed for his birdie, the Swede calmly sank his for a birdie and the Dunhill Cup was Sweden's.

Forsbrand, Johansson and Lanner each received checks for £100,000 and a place in the Swedish record books. "This will mean a hell of a lot to us," said Forsbrand. "It is just like winning the Davis Cup. We have 300,000 golfers and only 200 courses and up north in the winter there is only 30 minutes of daylight." St. Andrews 1991 marked for them a day of high summer.

9. Toyota World Match Play

Of all the courses around the world on which Seve Ballesteros has paraded his talents, the West Course at Wentworth, near London, must be among his favorites. He has played 25 tournaments over the demanding Burma Road and won seven, including this year's World Match Play Championship, the sponsorship of which had this year been taken over by Toyota. Thus his success rate is a victory in every fourth event at Wentworth.

Ballesteros loves the World Match Play Championship, not least because of its venue, which he has come to know so well. "I know this course as good as my course back home in Pedrena. I know where to go, all the shots, all the breaks on the greens and I play it so many times and in so many rounds this really is an advantage."

His appearance in this year's World Match Play was his 16th in succession, the most by any player. With this victory he became one of only two men to win the World Match Play on five occasions. Gary Player is the other. Ballesteros has won 27 of his 35 matches and in one five-year spell in the 1980s he won the title four times.

Player's victories came between 1965 and 1973. As Ballesteros won his first in 1981, his span of victories is already longer than Player's and it would be a brave man who said it was over. Who would dare to say, remarkable man that Ballesteros is, that he won't outdo Player and record a sixth or seventh victory in his third decade of competing?

The £150,000 that Ballesteros won made him the world's leading money winner this year with a total of $1.3 million—and there were still several events left.

Coming just three weeks after his inspiring performance for Europe in the Ryder Cup, when he won 4-1/2 points out of a possible five, Ballesteros confirmed with this victory that at match play he is a man apart. He relishes the cut and thrust of this type of play, the opportunity it gives him to outmaneuver his opponents. And he knows that match play requires one characteristic in particular, and it is one that he is not short of—courage.

"The perfect round does not exist. I think the key to success in golf is consistency, to make the putts and to be good under pressure. When you are able to do these things then you win golf tournaments. At match play it is more important to have a big heart than a good game. There are many good strikers of the ball who do not have the heart."

The final victory by 3 & 2 over Nick Price was something of a reprise. In the British Open three years ago, Price led by two strokes going into the fourth round. He did as much as he could have expected, shooting a two-under-par 69, and had every right to expect to win his first Open. But that day Ballesteros played the round of his life, 65, and snatched the title from Price.

In this year's final Ballesteros went round in 65 in the morning and had taken 59 strokes for 16 holes when he defeated Price on the 16th green in the afternoon. Ballesteros played 34 holes without a bogey, equalling Player's record set against Jack Nicklaus in the 1971 final. An indication of the high quality of their golf was that they had 14 birdies between them in the morning—eight by Ballesteros and six by Price.

At first Price was by far the stronger of the two men. He birdied the second, third and fourth holes while Ballesteros was missing the first, second and third greens. "It did not look very good for me," said Ballesteros. "I was watching him and I thought he looked very confident. He was certainly playing very well."

Price won the seventh by one-putting from just inside Ballesteros, perhaps 12 feet. Out in 34, one under par, Ballesteros was three down. Price had gone out in 31. Ballesteros set about his opponent on No. 10 when he holed from six feet, on the 11th from 30 feet and on the 14th from nine feet. This birdie on the short 14th was his third on the four short holes. When Price missed the 15th green with his five-iron second shot, Ballesteros stepped in again and won this hole, too. The two long finishing holes were covered in birdies, neither man conceding an inch. After his slow start, Ballesteros had come back in 31 for 65 and was tied with Price who had gone round in 66.

There was a noticeably friendly atmosphere about this match. Price is one of the most popular men in golf, and no one would wish to do him a bad turn. On the 13th hole there had been an example of the friendliness of the match. As Price took his club back to play his second shot, Ballesteros, who was standing nearby, choked on a piece of cake. Price's shot ended in a bunker. Ballesteros asked the referee if Price could play it again but this was refused, as Ballesteros surely knew it would be. When they reached the green, Ballesteros offered Price a half. Price refused. "Let's play golf. It didn't bother me. It was a bad swing."

Thirty-six hole matches are often won by the man who gets away quicker after lunch—and so it proved. Ballesteros, who had started so sluggishly in the morning, was at his best in the afternoon. A steady par was good enough for Ballesteros to win the second hole when Price bunkered his eight-iron tee shot. "That was a bad hole for me," Price admitted later. "I fell asleep." Ballesteros took the third as well with another par. Price again missed the green.

Ballesteros struck two more quick blows: On the fifth hole his five iron ended less than one foot from the hole, and on the ninth Ballesteros was on in two while Price drove into the trees, had to wedge out and then reached the green with a five iron. Ballesteros two-putted to go back to three up. Every hole coming was halved. Price wasn't giving up the chase but found it hard to sink any putts and Ballesteros was determined not to let him in. There was no hint of a mistake.

"The key today was my play on the par threes," said Seve. "I made three birdies. My putting also was good. I felt as good as in the Ryder Cup. In golf, no matter how good you play, if you don't make the putts then it is hard to win. I would say of my rounds today this is the best final I have played in."

No World Match Play event is complete without its controversy just as this form of golf is rarely uneventful. Last year it was why Ballesteros was not seeded. This year it was why Jose Maria Olazabal was not invited. The answer is simple. He was not playing well enough at the time the invitations went out.

The field was not as strong as last year's when all four winners of the major championships were present. Even so, Ian Woosnam, the Masters champion and defending champion, and Ian Baker-Finch, the British Open champion, were at Wentworth and seeded first and second, respectively, and Nick Faldo was the third seed, and Ballesteros, the fourth seed. John Daly, the U.S. PGA champion, and Payne Stewart, the U.S. Open champion, cited previous commitments and declined invitations, as did Corey Pavin, the leading money winner on the U.S. Tour.

Since 1973 the World Match Play Championship has carried on a tradition of inviting an outstanding young player each year to the event. Among those who have gone on to make their names are Lanny Wadkins (1973), Ballesteros (1976), Faldo (1977), Bill Rogers (1979), the first and only player to win the event the first time he played, and Olazabal (1988).

This year two such men where invited. The first was Steven Richardson, 25, the sensation who had won two tournaments on the European Tour and was second on the European money list when the event started. The second was Billy Andrade, 27, who received an Arnold Palmer scholarship to Wake Forest University, where he graduated in sociology in 1987, and joined the U.S. Tour the following year. In June of this year he had won his first tournament, the Kemper Open with the then lowest total of the season, 25 under par, and the following week he took the Buick Classic at Westchester, New York.

The match that immediately caught the eye when the draw was announced was between Mark Calcavecchia, the 1988 British Open champion, and Colin Montgomerie. The pairing of these two men was a repeat of their extraordinary singles match in the Ryder Cup the previous month. At Kiawah Island, Calcavecchia was four up with four holes to play (and had been five up after nine) and then finished double bogey, double bogey, triple bogey, bogey allowing Montgomerie to snatch a half point.

"I predicted this when I saw who was playing," said Calcavecchia. "I said I would play Colin in the first round. But I don't have any thoughts of revenge. I just know I will have to go out there and play well to beat him on this course."

The first day was a typically autumn day: Windy, overcast and thoroughly wintry. Montgomerie struck immediately, reaching the green of the opening hole with a three wood and two-putting from 60 feet to go one up. Calcavecchia pulled Montgomerie back to even on the second with a birdie, on the fourth with another birdie and on the 10th with a par.

The 17th hole was pivotal. Both failed to find the green with their second shots but Calcavecchia chipped to five feet and looked certain to birdie the hole. Montgomerie, meanwhile, chose to putt from well off the green and left his ball 15 feet short. When he sank that putt for a birdie he felt relieved to remain one up.

At the 18th, so much depends on the accuracy of the drive. Go too far right and the green is out of sight. Go too far left and the green is unreachable in two. Calcavecchia had the honor and played left and safe. Montgomerie hit a screamer with a three wood and, helped by the following wind, needed only a four iron to reach the green and duly got his birdie. Calcavecchia's second shot rolled into a bunker and, though he exploded to five feet, he missed the putt. Montgomerie was now two up when he might have been even.

After lunch, Montgomerie moved quickly to five up after the fifth hole. At the seventh Calcavecchia put his third shot 30 feet from the flag and two-putted while Montgomerie chipped to nine feet and sank the putt. On the eighth Calcavecchia took three shots to reach the green, which cost him the hole, and then hit a wild second shot to the ninth, a three wood that soared away into the trees. It went so far off line he didn't even bother to look for it. "It could have gone 40 yards right or left," said Montgomerie, "and that was me eight up. His head went down then. He was a long way from home, it was cold and windy. It was understandable."

Calcavecchia delayed his defeat by winning three holes in a row but when they halved the short 14th with solid pars Montgomerie won 5 & 4. "I was glad to finish it off," said Montgomerie. "I told myself it was just a matter of time. But there was also the thought that with that sort of lead there was only one way to go and that was down." Montgomerie's level-par golf represented good playing on such a windy day. "The moment I went six down I knew I was history," said Calcavecchia. "I'm not sure I deserved to be here on my record this year. My driving and my putting were horrible."

Fred Couples, who was in such dazzling form at home in the United States that he had finished in the top 10 in all but one of his past 11 tournaments, faced Naomichi (Joe) Ozaki, the second-best of the famous brothers from Japan. Couples arrived with a sore throat and dressed as if he was on the ski slopes, wearing a rain suit, wool hat, thick gloves and several sweaters. Though he might not have felt at his best, he was relishing his first appearance at Wentworth.

"In weather like this there are not going to be too many birdies," he said. "We'll be winning holes with pars. Your game changes when you play in weather like this. Your swing changes a bit, too. I know I am not going to play two great rounds in weather like this, but I hope to be consistent."

Couples was on the American team in the previous week's Dunhill Cup and his wife, Debbie, had carried his bag around St. Andrews. "She likes to caddie for me but she won't be caddieing here," he said. "Two rounds a day is too much. She is good for me. She gives me a pat on the back now and then and doesn't ask stupid questions. And when the game's over and we go out to dinner the last thing we want to talk about is golf."

Couples was four up after six holes, having gone birdie, eagle, birdie from the third to the fifth. He was five up after nine. Ozaki was floundering in his wake but to his credit won the 12th, 13th and 14th. He birdied the 12th by chipping to one foot. He hit an enormous drive on the 13th, wedged to nine feet and two-putted while Couples sent his nine-iron second shot into a bunker and took three more to get down. And on the short hole Ozaki two-putted from 20 yards and Couples three-putted from even further away. At lunch Couples remained two up.

Both men played raggedly in the afternoon. Couples, who had gone out in 32 in the morning, was five strokes worse after lunch and Ozaki's 39 was two strokes more than his score before lunch. Ozaki saved himself on the 10th when he missed the green but chipped to five feet and one-putted. On the 11th Couples moved to four up by holing from 40 feet for a birdie. The end came for Ozaki on the 15th. Couples' seven iron ended seven feet away and he holed the putt for victory by 4 & 3.

The difficulty for Andrade was that he and Tom Purtzer are close friends.

"It's hard to play against a friend," said Andrade. "But my first victory came in a playoff against Jeff Sluman, my closest friend on tour."

Andrade was never more than two up over the first 18 holes, which he covered in level-par 72 against Purtzer's 74, but the evenness of their morning round was not repeated in the afternoon. Purtzer fell away badly. His outward half contained two double bogeys and four bogeys. It took him three strokes to reach the green of the short fifth and four strokes to find the putting surface on the eighth. At these moments he didn't resemble the man who was enjoying an Indian summer on the U.S. Tour and had finished fourth in the BMW International in Munich four days earlier.

Meanwhile, Andrade had to do little more than keep his ball in play, which he did. He was seven up with eight holes remaining and then three-putted the 13th, 14th and 15th to lose them all before holing from 40 feet on the 16th to make sure of victory by 3 & 2.

"It was tough out there today," said Price after defeating Richardson by 5 & 3. Which only goes to show how well he had played. He had only two bogeys in 33 holes and, if Purtzer looked a shadow of the man who had been so successful on the U.S. Tour this year then, Price didn't. In his best year to date, Price had won both the Canadian Open and Byron Nelson Classic events and, frankly, it showed.

"Since the U.S. Open my game has reached a new level," said Price. "I've got more control of my swing and my putting is better than ever." He said this was a result of returning to the style he had used as an amateur. "I've widened my stance and put more weight on my left side and this has enabled me to hit through the ball. It has given me confidence and this technique is beginning to feel natural."

Price, out in 35, was three up and was still three up after 18 holes. He pulled away quickly against the burly Englishman, who looked a little jaded, and though they halved seven successive holes in the afternoon, Price parred the 15th, which Richardson bogeyed by missing the green with a seven iron, to win.

"This is my 14th season as a pro and it is so fulfilling to play golf as I am at the moment," said Price. It is very hard to take time off because it is going so well. I hit a driver and a one iron on the ninth this afternoon and I couldn't have hit two shots any better."

There was no obvious reason why Woosnam should have collapsed so spectacularly against Andrade in the quarter-finals. He had played well at St. Andrews the previous week, winning three of his four matches in the Dunhill Cup and Wentworth was one of his favorite courses. "I like this course because you are playing different shots with different clubs all the time. I enjoy playing on it and that is a boost to my confidence."

Woosnam's troubles were mainly on the greens. He had spent two days practicing his putting only to three-putt the first green and lose the hole. "If you've been working for days to get the putting right, and then you three-putt immediately, you wonder what you've been doing, wasting your time," said a disconsolate Woosnam.

Woosnam's length did him no favors on the fourth hole. He hit a one iron that sent his ball bounding down the slope and then a six iron. Andrade used a driver from the tee and a five iron for his second shot. The difference was that Andrade's second shot finished seven feet from the flag, and Woosnam's, off the edge of the green. Woosnam's chip only got to within 15 feet of the flag and he two-putted. To rub it in, Andrade holed his putt for an eagle. This was just one demonstration of Woosnam's poor chipping and putting. In all, he chipped eight times and only once got up and down.

Woosnam made only one birdie and won only one hole all afternoon and capitulated on the 12th. A drive and a one iron got him within chipping distance of the green, but the way he was chipping he would rather have been 50 yards away. Sure enough, he hit a poor chip. As Andrade was on the green in two, Woosnam decided to end the agony and walked over to congratulate him. He had lost by 7 & 6, a dog license as they say in England, which in pre-decimalization days was how much it cost to buy a dog license. Andrade was seven under par for holes played throughout the day.

"I think I need to get right away from it," said Woosnam. "I haven't had a holiday without my golf clubs for years. I'm not over-golfed because I've only played 22 tournaments so far this year. It's my putting. (He had taken 58 in 30 holes.) Over the putts I am thinking of a method all the time and it is just mind-boggling. I can't put a stroke on it. I need to hole putts and when I don't I get down.

"It was the right result. I don't deserve more than that. He played well. I was just off, inconsistent. When you are putting badly you try to hit it close and I was putting too much pressure on myself. I couldn't even pitch it close. Disgraceful."

The two sick men of the tournament sniffed and limped their way around. It was questionable as to who was the more ill. "I'm struggling," said Ballesteros. "I can't walk, I can't swing. I am having trouble following through." Couples was taking vitamin tablets and throat lozenges for his sore throat.

Couples won the first hole when he sank a 30-foot putt. Ballesteros drew level on the second by holing from 20 feet. They were still tied at the turn, and then Ballesteros began to pull away. At the 10th he hit a six iron to 40 feet and holed the putt. Ballesteros three-putted the 11th to hand the hole to Couples but then won three of the next four holes.

The long 12th was well within range of two such long hitters, but only Ballesteros reached it—with a drive and a two iron. Couples drove into the trees on the left, back-handed a six iron out, hit the same club to the green and then two-putted. When Couples bunkered his six-iron approach to the 13th green he went three down and when he missed the 14th, this time with a five iron, it didn't matter that Ballesteros birdied the uphill short hole with a good 10-foot putt. Couples lost it anyway.

It was Ballesteros' turn to miss a green on the 15th. He played for position on this very difficult driving hole, using a three wood, but then hit a poor four iron, chipped and two-putted. So Couples, who had also used a three wood from the tee and reached the green with a six iron, was back to three down and remained so as they halved the three closing holes. He was round in 71, Ballesteros in 68.

By the turn in the afternoon, three holes had changed hands. Couples won two of them and was back to two down only to lose the 10th when he hit his seven iron into a ditch and had to take a penalty drop to get out. The 11th was halved but it took a breathtaking shot by Couples to save himself from losing another hole. He hit his second shot too far and it ended on the 12th tee, 50 yards from the flag. "He had no shot," said Ballesteros and when Ballesteros says something like that, then you know he has no shot. Somehow, Couples squeezed the ball off the tee to within five feet of the hole and sank the putt. Even Ballesteros was impressed. "A miracle shot," he said.

That was a key moment, Ballesteros said. He could have been four up (he was expecting to be) but not only did Couples snatch this miraculous half but he won the 12th when Ballesteros drove into the trees. Couples got back to one down when Ballesteros drove into the trees again, this time on the 15th.

At this point Ballesteros seemed to give himself a talking to. He birdied the 16th, playing a one iron from the tee and a nine iron to nine feet, and then was sitting pretty on the 17th green, 18 feet from the hole after a drive and a three wood. Couples chose to play a three wood off the tee, thus sacrificing considerable distance, hit a four iron and then a wedge to reach the green. He attempted a token putt before accepting defeat.

"I played the right shots when I needed to," said Ballesteros. "The second shot on the 16th and the putt and the three wood on the 17th. Fred was playing very good. He was striking the ball fantastic. From tee to green he was better than me but I beat him on the greens."

The significance of this match was that Couples was removed as one of the favorites and Ballesteros' star rose correspondingly. It rather overshadowed the remaining two matches between Faldo and Montgomerie and Baker-Finch and Price.

Only once and then for only one hole was there more than one hole between Montgomerie and Faldo, and after 18 holes they were tied. Faldo moved ahead after lunch when Montgomerie took six on the first hole and a four on the second, but by the sixth they were level again. Faldo's golf was better from tee to green but he was let down, as so often happens, by a baulky putter.

They then halved the next 10 holes, approaching the steadiness shown by Nicklaus and Player, who halved the first 11 holes in the 1971 final before Player went on to win 5 & 4. Montgomerie had the honor on the 17th but pulled his drive out of bounds. Faldo saw his chance. He took a two iron for safety and successfully steered his way onto the green in three to win the hole.

One up on the 18th tee, Faldo was determined to avoid hitting his drive too far to the right. He successfully did this. Instead he hit it too far left and couldn't reach the green in two. Montgomerie's second shot ended in a bunker from where he got out to six feet. With Faldo down in five, Montgomerie had to hole his tricky putt to force a playoff.

He did so, and off they went down the first hole, which they halved. At the second Montgomerie hit an eight iron, which landed on the green but rolled back down the slope at the front of the green. It was just about the worst place to be on this hole, if you are going to miss this green. The second is one of the many greens at Wentworth that slope down from back to front. The third, seventh and 14th are others. It is always better to be long than to be short on these greens. To make matters worse, his first chip pulled up short of the flag as well. Seeing the way Montgomerie's ball rolled back, Faldo selected one club more, a seven iron, and hit it to 15 feet from where he two-putted for victory when Montgomerie's 13-foot putt missed its target.

Price was never behind against the British Open champion, whose mind may well have been on Laura Jane, his newly born daughter (and their second child) back home in Australia's Gold Coast. Price was two up after three holes. He holed from 12 feet on the second and from 15 feet on the third. The third was playing every inch of its 452 yards, and Price had to hit a good two iron to reach the green. Price was still two up at lunch time.

Price's five iron ended five feet from the flag on the fifth for a birdie that put him three up. He became four up when Baker-Finch three-putted from 40 feet on the sixth green.

Baker-Finch was not going to recover from that position against someone playing as well and as steadily as Price. He did win the 10th with a good two, only to lose the 12th to a birdie four, and he won the 13th with a three, thanks to a putt of 45 feet. But time was running out for him, and he went back to four down when he couldn't match Price's par on the short 14th. Two holes later, a half in four gave Price victory by 3 & 2.

For Andrade to defeat Woosnam so comfortably and win through to face Ballesteros was almost a dream come true. "Seve to me is like a Nicklaus in world golf," said the personable American, whose relaxed manner, openness and friendliness won him many admirers. "I am really looking forward to facing him."

The reason for Andrade's obvious contentment was that he was completely at ease at Wentworth. "I feel comfortable and enjoy playing here. The fans are wonderful. Here they are the best spectators you can have. They are well educated. In America it's more of a party and people come for the corporate thing rather than to watch golf."

Ballesteros has not been beaten by any American in this competition since losing to Peter Jacobsen in 1981. After a second injection for the soreness in his right foot, which the doctor said was caused by uric acid inflaming the tendon, Ballesteros set about extending that run of success.

Andrade, though, struck first with a three on the opening hole. He made it look easy, yet it was only the second birdie of the week on this hole: good drive, a three wood into the heart of the green and a putt from 30 feet.

Andrade should have gone further ahead at the third and fourth. Ballesteros missed both greens but when presented with chances to win, the American three-putted both. This proved costly. If there is one thing you don't do when playing Ballesteros, it is to let him off the hook. He is likely to bounce back fiercely. He did so now. He birdied the fifth by holing from 12 feet and hit a wedge to within three feet of the flag on the sixth for a second consecutive birdie. Then he birdied the seventh as well—a one iron and nine iron and an 11-foot putt.

Andrade was learning one match-play lesson from the maestro: take every chance offered. Instead of being three up, as he might have been, he was two down. On the 10th he made another mistake. After watching Ballesteros slice his tee shot down a bank, Andrade followed him and they halved the hole.

On the 16th Ballesteros drove into a bunker. Andrade, again playing second, hooked his drive much further left. Now he was three down and that is how they went in to lunch, Ballesteros having gone round in 68, Andrade in 73.

Andrade began well after lunch, knowing that not to do so, or not to be able to do so, would probably be fatal. He gathered a safe par on the second after Ballesteros' tee shot drifted short and left and fell into that bunker that awaits just such a shot.

As he was to do in the final the next day, Ballesteros played the short holes well—the second being the exception. On the fifth his six iron ended 11 feet from the flag and Ballesteros holed the putt to go three up. Andrade won the 12th to get back to two down, when Ballesteros hooked wildly off the tee, not for the first time, only to lose the 14th and with it the match.

"It was an experience I will never forget," said Andrade. "If you'd said a couple of months ago that I'd be in this position I'd have said you were crazy. I tested my game against the best and if I had not let him off the hook early on, the result could have been different."

Price said he was tired after his match against Baker-Finch and he needed to get a good night's sleep to be at his best to face Faldo. "I was late coming over here, having played the five-round Las Vegas Invitational and did not get here until Tuesday, and that would have allowed me to get over the eight-hour time change. Ideally, it would have been better to have arrived on Sunday. Still," he said cheerfully and optimistically, "a good night's rest will see me OK."

What would see Faldo OK would be a hotter putter. From tee to green he was playing well, if not quite as imperiously as the previous year, but whether he had a good round or not depended on how well he putted. "I hit the lip of the hole about 10 times and they all stayed out," he remarked after beating Montgomerie. "If I can hole some putts I can do anything."

It wasn't his putting that let him down at first against Price. Faldo missed the third, seventh and eighth greens, the seventh and eighth with a nine iron and seven iron, respectively. Such poor iron play got the reward it deserved; Price was four up at the turn and five up after the 10th, which he birdied.

Faldo won the 16th when Price three-putted and the 18th by hitting a wonderful iron to within a few feet for an eagle. He was two down at lunch and struggling and he couldn't cope with Price's burst after lunch.

Price covered the outward nine in 31 and was five up. Faldo chipped closer than Price and one-putted to win the 13th, only to drive into a ditch on the 15th and concede the hole. Price won by 5 & 3.

"Nick's putting is not as it normally is," said Price. "It's frustrating and demoralizing when you play good and do not hole putts, and I can relate to Nick because I have suffered that for two years. If anything, Nick's stroke looked a little quicker than normal, but that happens when you get apprehensive and doubts creep in.

"Everyone is going to expect Seve to win tomorrow," Price continued. "I'm probably the only one who doesn't. I think I have a good chance. I have played some really good golf this week and if I can keep it going for another day I could do it."

It wasn't so much that Price failed to play well as that Ballesteros was memorable in the final, which was a highlight of the best year Ballesteros has ever had in financial terms. He won nearly $400,000 at Wentworth this year alone from the Toyota World Match Play Championship and the Volvo PGA Championship. No wonder he likes the course. No wonder he says it suits his game.

10. Johnnie Walker World Championship

Golf, one of the most universal sports, had not had a world champion until the Johnnie Walker World Championship made its debut last December at the Tryall Club in Jamaica, bringing together the world's top players for the purpose of finding out who was the best. The winner was Fred Couples, the popular, big-hitting American, with a dramatic finish that ended one of the most testing weeks any golfer would ever face.

Against this field, on this golf course under very windy conditions, the winner had every right to claim the title of world champion. Soft tropical nights and steel drum serenades aside, this was no stroll in paradise.

The first Johnnie Walker World Championship went better than anyone might have expected. The field was extraordinary. Except for Jose Maria Olazabal, all of the world's leading players were at Tryall. The purse was $2,550,000, the richest in golf history. The winner received $525,000, and the last-place finisher (there was no cut), $50,000. The World Championship also received the widest television coverage of any golf event in the world. It was carried, either live or tape-delayed, in 34 countries.

The field was to be made up of 26 players who qualified by winning one of 28 designated tournaments worldwide. Because of duplicate winners, and a few golfers who were not able to play, the International Advisory Committee chose four players to round out the field. Among the Committee's selections was Couples, who was completing his best year ever. He had already won twice, tied for third place in two of the major championships, and was outstanding in the Ryder Cup. Greg Norman, Paul Azinger, and Corey Pavin were also Committee selections.

Johnnie Walker already had a huge presence in golf. By 1991, the commitment had grown to about $18 million, including sponsorship of tournaments in Australia and Asia, and the European Ryder Cup team. And now the World Championship. So the press was asking whether Johnnie Walker was sowing the seeds of a world tour.

"No, not really," said Paul Antrobus, of United Distillers, maker of Johnnie Walker whisky. "It's worth considering—let's put it that way. But a world tour is not our objective at the moment. We're in the business of promoting excellence in golf. Right now, we have to be sure that this event works perfectly."

Said Johnnie Walker spokesman Wyn Fanshawe, "We look to add value to the world of golf. We're not in competition with the tours. We have a close relationship with the tours. We help them, they help us. These are opportunities. Nobody's looking for conflict."

It has been acknowledged that our International Management Group—which conducted the Johnnie Walker World Championship for United Distillers—could produce a world tour, if we so desired. We do not want to do it, because there could be political uproar and lawsuits that would be detrimental to the sport. But the fact is, golf is now a worldwide sport and, however slowly, that is going to get through to the public and things will start happening accordingly. It is just a matter of time.

The real significance of the Johnnie Walker World Championship, perhaps obscured by speculation about a world tour, was that for one of just a handful of occasions in 1991, nearly all the top golfers were competing against one another. Golf was starving for this calibre of competition, and this week in Jamaica was extra special for that reason.

"You could feel it," Norman said. "I don't get to play with Woosie or Faldo or Seve that often. We all—the players and the fans—get up for it when we do. This is what golf needs."

As Jaime Diaz pointed out in *Golf World*, "Golf has things backwards. As it got bigger, it got more provincial. The (U.S.) PGA Tour is the world's strongest tour, but it no longer has the strongest players, in part because they generally don't like to—nor does their commissioner want them to—play anywhere else.

"At the same time, the increasing strength of the European Tour, while adding international depth, actually has created less international competition. Promising European players no longer come to America to build their games and make money. They can now do the same thing at home."

For the moment, however, Tryall was the golfers' problem. It didn't take them long to discover that Tryall wasn't going to offer a day at the beach. "I was expecting a resort-type course," said Craig Parry. "I wasn't expecting a course this tough."

Tryall had been stretched from 6,407 to 6,849 yards, with the unusual par of 34-37—71, and tailored for some serious golf. You could see the frustrations as the golfers played their practice rounds. Take Wednesday, for example. It was a hot, sunny day. A light breeze was coming off the sea. It was refreshing, unless you were trying to hit a ribbon of fairway about 270 yards out. Every shot was either crosswind, downwind, or into a headwind.

Tryall is an inland-type course set in seacoast conditions. With the bunkering, gullies, and elevated greens, the wind-cheating bump-and-run shot was out of the question. It was practically an all-carry course.

The test was stiffened when the rough was allowed to grow in, narrowing fairways to only 25 yards in some places. ("These fairways are about as tight as I've ever seen," Paul Azinger said.) The first cut of rough was fairly forgiving, only about two inches deep. Beyond that, it was a foot high. A golfer would be lucky to advance the ball 30 yards. "I lost about 12 balls in two practice rounds," Bernhard Langer said. "I can't remember ever losing that many in practice." And one other thing: The greens were small and fast.

So it was clear from the start that the Johnnie Walker World Championship would be an exercise in course management and patience. Tryall showed its teeth in the first round. Rain had softened the course, making it play easier, and Thursday was sunny and hot, with just a gentle breeze. It was about as benign as it could be. Even so, only seven of the 26 golfers broke the par of 71, and only another five matched it.

"The course is very, very demanding," said Frank Nobilo, the bearded New Zealander, the early leader with a bogey-free 69. "You've only got to visit the rough once or twice, and it's an instant bogey." Nobilo was a study in steadiness, with 13 consecutive pars, then two birdies, then three more pars. The birdies came at No. 14, where he chipped in from 20 feet for his two, and at No. 15, where he two-putted from 40 feet for his four.

Someone asked Nobilo to pick a favorite. "The odds favor a guy who's used to playing for big money," Nobilo answered. "But more than that," he added, "a guy who can find the fairway."

Nobilo's lead lasted only as long as it took the second group of the day to finish. The new leader was Parry, the muscular little Australian, with 68 and a one-stroke lead. While others were using various irons off the tees trying to sneak past the menacing rough, Parry challenged it. "I figure if I'm going to hit it into the rough, I might as well do it a long way down," he said. So Parry used his driver as much as possible. In fact, he used it nine times. He missed only three fairways. On two misses, he was in short rough, and on the other he was in deep rough, but recovered for his par. He and Nobilo were the only players to escape without a bogey.

Andrew Magee came within a whisker of tying Parry for the early lead. Magee shot 69 in what he called three different rounds—seven good holes, six fair holes, and five poor ones. The five poor ones included bogeys at the eighth, 10th, and 12th holes, all after driving into the rough. "I never played in rough like this—ever," Magee said. He moved back into contention with three birdies over the last six holes. At the par-five 17th, his chip shot missed being an eagle by just two inches. He tapped in for his birdie and a share of second place.

Seve Ballesteros got off to a tentative start and shot 70. He got a shock at the par-three fourth hole. "I was nervous," he said. "I can't remember needing three putts from such a short distance." He had smacked an eight iron to five feet, then proceeded to three-putt for a bogey. "I didn't play that badly, but that three-putt—I lost my confidence," he said.

Ballesteros got his confidence back in time to run off three consecutive birdies from No. 15, including a morale-builder at No. 16. "I hit one of the best shots of my career," he said. "A sand wedge, 130 yards. I had to go between two trees, and draw the ball to the left. It came out perfect." To five feet, in fact.

Azinger was shaky on the first nine, taking bogeys at the eighth and ninth holes, but regrouped for three birdies coming in for 69. He birdied the 12th and 13th holes, using a two iron off both tees, and at the par-five 17th, he flipped a wedge to 18 inches for another birdie. But he wasn't impressed with his handiwork. "I'm lucky to shoot what I shot," he said. "I haven't played a competitive round since October, so I'm a bit rusty."

For Norman, this was his final chance of the year to keep his record alive. He had won at least one tournament each year since becoming a Tour pro in 1976. But time was fast running out on 1991. The 15-year streak could well come to an end in a few days. The question was blunt: How does it play on your mind? The answer was blunt, too. "It doesn't play on my mind at all," Norman said sharply. "If I don't win here, it won't be the end of my career. I'm not going to give up the game."

Norman was off to a running start this time. He was one over par on the first nine, then barrelled home in a four-under-par 33 for 68, one stroke off the lead. He had plotted the course well in his practice session. He used a one iron off the tee at the 12th hole, a three iron at the 13th, and birdied both with medium-range putts. Then he used the driver at both par fives coming in, and birdied both. He pitched to three feet at No. 15, and he two-putted the 17th from 45 feet.

Couples didn't draw much attention in the first round. He was steady, but not especially productive. He birdied No. 4 and bogeyed No. 14 in a round of 71, four strokes off the lead and in a five-way tie for eighth place that included Ballesteros and Steve Elkington. There were some very big names further back: Masters champion Ian Woosnam, 72; British Open champion Ian Baker-Finch and Nick Faldo, 75, and U.S. Open champion Payne Stewart and rookie sensation John Daly, the U.S. PGA champion, both at 77.

The day had progressed almost like a script, building to a climax at the end. In fact, millions of television viewers around the world were treated to the spectacle of Langer wrapping up the day on the final hole with a dramatic 55-foot putt that gave him the lead at four-under-par 67. When the ball dropped, Langer gave a little smile and raised his hand in triumph. "A nice way to finish," he said.

Langer was out in one over par, and came home in five birdies, no bogeys, for 32. Only once was he in trouble. He tried to hook his tee shot around the dogleg at the par-five 15th hole, and ended up in the deep rough. But he managed to chop the ball out and save his par. The birdies came easier. Langer started at No. 10, with a 10-foot putt. Like so many, he birdied the 12th and 13th holes, both from medium range. Then safely past the 15th, he closed with two surprise birdies. At the 17th, he chipped 15 feet past, but made it coming back. And at the 18th came the cross-country putt.

Someone asked Langer to predict the winning score. "Maybe 10 under, or even 12," he said. That prediction wouldn't last another day.

First-round leaders:

Bernhard Langer	67
Craig Parry	68
Greg Norman	68
Andrew Magee	69
Frank Nobilo	69
Paul Azinger	69

The second round was going to be something else. The golfers knew what they were in for, long before they got to the golf course. Friday dawned gray and overcast, and to the roar of heavy winds, 35 to 45 miles an hour, bending the palm trees. This wouldn't be a day for low scoring. The course would play to an average of 76.5—5.5 strokes over par. This was a day for surviving. And one prominent golfer didn't.

Daly's adventures in a first-round 77 paled in comparison to those in the second round. He shot 87 but signed for 86, and the electrifying rookie of 1991, in the final outing of his triumphant year, came to an ignominious end. He was disqualified.

He was out in a two-over-par 36, a reasonably good score in the battering wind. The inward trip, however, was a dark comedy of errors. He ended up having to putt with his driver, then his one iron, and finally his three iron. Daly was still in good shape through the 10th hole, but at No. 11, the wind carried his one-iron tee shot out of bounds. Then he three-putted for a quadruple-bogey eight. And his putter suddenly was out of commission.

"Broken?" someone asked.

"No, just bent a little," Daly said, chuckling.

"Hit a tree or something?"

"No—My foot got in the way."

Daly made nine at the par-four 12th, putting with his one iron. "I four-putted, or something," he said. And so it went.

Daly's caddie discovered the scoring error. The caddie was in the press tent, scanning the scoreboard, when he noticed that Daly was credited with a five at the 18th hole. He knew Daly had made six. The caddie informed an official, and Daly was disqualified. Earlier, in the interview room, Daly had been almost prophetic. "This is the time of year I should be home with my family," he said. "I'm tired, burned out."

Daly had been the first out in the second round, with Russ Cochran at 10:20 a.m., and so they were the first to discover that a monster had been let out on the course. The wind had aroused it, and the wind didn't let up all day. The monster was the 11th hole, running parallel to the shore, a par four of 433 yards, with a narrow fairway and an elevated green sitting behind a rocky gully. The drive and the all-carry second shot were at the mercy of the left-to-right winds off the sea to the left. You could read the wind in the scores. The hole played to an average of 4.3 on the first day, then 5.7 on the second, 4.5 on the third, and 4.5 on the fourth.

In the second round, there was only one birdie at No. 11. Rocco Mediate hit a two iron out of light rough to about four feet. There were three pars, 10 bogeys, three sixes and six sevens. There were also two eights. Daly had one. Nobilo had the other, and rocketed 10 strokes above his opening score to 79—148. Stewart suffered the worst score, nine.

The 11th helped change the face of the leaderboard. Four challengers bogeyed the hole: Langer (77) and Norman (76) were tied at 144, and Parry (77) and Ballesteros (75) were tied at 145.

Magee was among the victims of the 11th hole, but a strange one. "I hit a great four-iron shot to eight feet—and I had no putt," Magee said. His ball sat above the hole on the fast, sloping green. He tapped it, just to get it rolling. "I was just hoping it would hit the hole," Magee said. "It went 15 feet past." Two more putts got him a bogey, his fourth of the day against one birdie, for 74 and a share of second place at 143.

Faldo had a wild round, with six birdies and five bogeys for a two-under-par 69, the only sub-par score of the day. That put him at 144, three strokes behind. "In weather like this, you know that if you keep saving par, you're gaining," Faldo said. "It's hard work, but if you hit the ball solidly, you can play in this wind."

You can also play if your putting touch returns. Three of Faldo's birdies came from about 30 feet. He was so delighted, he even saw a silver lining. "The wind gives you a chance to get back into the tournament," he said. "If it blows again the next two days, par might win."

Couples agreed. "When you're hitting the ball well, you want the conditions to be as tough as they can be," he said. "But it's not so much the wind, it's the rough. You're going to miss fairways in this wind. Then you're lucky to advance the ball 30 yards." He shot 72 and tied for second with Magee at 143.

If Faldo had a wild round, Couples had an unreal back nine. It was the stuff of which championships are made. He shot 33 on the first nine, with birdies at the first and sixth holes, both from 10 feet. "After No. 7, the course opens up," he said, "and the wind was just howling." It dropped him short of the green at No. 8, and he bogeyed.

Coming home, Couples shot a 39 that tested his patience. He had only one par, and that was at No. 18.

He birdied No. 10 with a putt from 10 feet. Then, two under par, he blew it all on one hole, the 11th. "Steve Elkington and I both made triple bogey—after perfect drives," Couples said. The wind took their second shots out of bounds. Couples bounced right back for a birdie three at the 12th, on a nine iron to six feet. At No. 13, he shanked his two-iron tee shot out of bounds and double-bogeyed. Then came a pair of three-putt bogeys, from 40 feet at the 14th and 30 feet at the 15th. In the span of five holes, he had gone from two under par to four over.

"On a day like this," Couples said, shrugging, "the best thing is to just walk along and enjoy it." Then he finished with a flash. He birdied the 16th from 20 feet, eagled the 17th with a drive, seven iron and 10-foot putt, and then parred the 18th.

Couples was tied for second place, just two strokes behind, but it was too early to get excited. "Sunday," he said, echoing Nobilo's sentiments, "the guy who hits a lot of fairways—no matter how well he putts—will be the one to watch."

For the moment, the one to watch was Azinger, a skeptical leader. He birdied two of the first six holes and was four under par for the tournament, but he knew he couldn't keep it up, not in that wind. "This is the hardest wind I've ever played in," said Azinger, famed for breezing through Muirfield's winds when he almost won the 1987 British Open.

Here Azinger was again, at home in the wind. "It paid off that I can hit it as low as I do," he said. While Langer was slipping, Azinger built his lead with birdies on two of the par-three holes on the first nine.

The first sign of trouble came at No. 8, where Azinger had a three-putt bogey. He birdied the 10th and was leading at four under par, and then the problems started. Four holes later he had only one stroke of his lead left.

At the 11th, the wind carried Azinger's approach shot out of bounds. He bogeyed. At the 12th, he missed the fairway and the green, and bogeyed again. At the par-three 14th, he missed a tap-in for his par. "The shortest putt I ever missed," he said. He finished the day leading by a stroke, and he wasn't sure why. "I happen to be leading now, but I sure don't feel like a leader," he said. "I'm not a very confident leader right now."

Second-round leaders:

Paul Azinger	141	Greg Norman	144
Fred Couples	143	Bernhard Langer	144
Andrew Magee	143	Craig Parry	145
Steve Elkington	144	Seve Ballesteros	145
Nick Faldo	144		

The wind let up on Saturday, but not much. The golfers were still dragging themselves off the course. It was like a heavyweight bout for some. "You feel like you've gone 15 rounds with Mike Tyson out there," Norman said.

Azinger felt the same. "It's like you just got the tar beat out of you for 11 rounds, and you still have a round to go," he said.

Couples shot another 72 and was just a stroke behind the leaders—Azinger, who was sagging, and Langer, who had rallied. "Every shot, you think something is going to go wrong," Couples said.

Said Langer: "I don't think the course was set up for this kind of wind. But it's the same for everyone, so it doesn't matter." The course did play a little easier. "The big difference is the rough," Parry said. "It was wet yesterday, and you couldn't move the ball. Today the rough dried out, and you could at least advance it."

The course did play easier, the average score dropping from Friday's 76.5 to 74.2. Even No. 11 played easier—from 5.7 on Friday to 4.5. It should be remembered that No. 11 is a par four. There was only one horror story this time. Baker-Finch took a triple-bogey seven without going out of bounds. He used his strokes to chop his way out of the rough.

Langer, who seemed out of contention after that 77 the day before, suddenly was right back with 70 for a one-over-par 214 total to catch Azinger. He started with birdies on the first two holes, No. 1 on almost a tap-in and No. 2 from 20 feet. He had a rocky second nine, and it would have been worse except for some brilliant chipping. He had back-to-back bogeys, a three-putt at the 11th and a missed green at the 12th. He missed the green at the 13th, too, but chipped in from 70 feet for a birdie. The 15th hole hurt him again. "Yesterday I hit a six iron and it ballooned into a bunker, short," Langer said, exasperated. "Today I hit a five iron, and it went 10 yards over the green." He bogeyed again. And at the 18th, he got his second chip-in birdie, this one from 15 feet.

The way things were developing, chances were very good that Langer's 214 might hold up for the lead. He was in the fourth group from the last, and the men playing behind him were laboring. "Someone suggested you could shoot 59 here," Norman said. "I'd like to shoot 69." Norman's round started with a buried lie in a bunker. He finished with five bogeys, a double bogey, and five birdies—three of them over the last four holes—for 73—217. In the next group, Faldo sputtered at the start and went out in 37. He would finish with 73—217.

Magee, tied for second place at the start of the day, blew to 42 on the second nine for 76—219. Suddenly there were only two players who could catch Langer—Couples and Azinger.

Azinger was struggling. "Playing in this wind," he said, "no matter how well you're playing, you're always trying to manufacture something." He was out in 38 with four bogeys. He bogeyed once more on the second nine and was four over par for the tournament coming to the final three holes. Suddenly, something clicked. He birdied the 16th from eight feet, and eagled the 17th with a drive, three iron and 40-foot putt. A par at the 18th gave him 73—214 and a tie for the lead with Langer.

Right behind was Couples, still amazingly steady. He shot another 72, and now was at 215, two over par and one stroke off the lead. He double-bogeyed No. 3 after he pull-hooked an iron into deep rough. At No. 5, a chip shot took him by surprise and scooted 15 feet past the cup.

The greens, dried out by the raw wind, had got faster. "First the tall rough and the strong wind," Couples said, "and now the greens are very fast." He birdied No. 7 from 12 feet, but he bogeyed again at No. 11. Then he birdied the 12th and 16th holes on 10-foot putts.

"I have a chance to win!" Couples said.

Third-round leaders:

Paul Azinger	214	Nick Faldo	217
Bernhard Langer	214	Greg Norman	217
Fred Couples	215	Seve Ballesteros	218
Craig Parry	216	Tom Purtzer	218

That Sunday, Jamaica was a tropical paradise—hot, sunny, the sky almost clear, and no more hammering winds. The wrap-up of the tournament can be told in a few words: Azinger stumbled, Langer stood still, and Couples charged. He took the lead for good with a dramatic eagle at No. 5, and rode a nice cushion the rest of the way, and won by four strokes over Langer. His only bogey of the day was at No. 18.

Couples shot five-under-par 66, the lowest round of the tournament. His winning total of 281 was three under par, the only sub-par total. Langer's prediction that 10 or 12 under par might win was wiped out when the wind arrived in the second round. Langer was second at 285, one over par.

The final round had started as a three-man race. "I struggled all week," Azinger said. The last round was no exception. He was pretty much out of contention when he bogeyed the third and fifth holes, but he rallied on the second nine.

"I finally found a swing key around the eighth or ninth," Azinger said. He birdied three of four holes from No. 12 to get within three strokes of Couples. His chances were gone when he pulled an iron shot at the 16th and double-bogeyed. He finished third with 72—286, two over par and five strokes behind Couples.

Azinger and Langer were the final twosome, and Couples was just ahead of them. It was a Couples-Langer battle from early in the round, and not a long battle, at that. Couples jumped into a one-stroke lead with birdies on the first two holes, a 10-foot putt at No. 1, a two-footer at No. 2, against pars by Azinger and Langer.

Azinger began slipping with the bogey at No. 3. Langer birdied it from 30 feet to tie Couples, then went a stroke ahead with a 12-foot birdie at No. 4. He held the lead for as long as it took the big-hitting Couples up ahead to fire a three iron 215 yards to within three feet at No. 5 and drop the putt for an eagle three. It was his second eagle of the tournament and gave him a one-stroke lead.

His lead grew to two when Langer drove into the rocks at No. 9 and bogeyed. Moments later, Couples birdied the 10th hole on a 10-footer and led by three (and by six over Azinger). Langer slipped two more strokes behind with bogeys at the 11th (a hooked drive) and the 14th (a bunkered tee shot). He had one birdie left, a 20-foot putt at the 16th.

In contrast, Couples was steady and relentless. He parred all the way through the treacherous back stretch to the 17th, where a fine bunker shot set up a tap-in birdie. At the 18th, he lost a bit of the sparkle off his performance. He drove into the left rough behind a palm tree, and bogeyed. It cost him 65. But 66 looked awfully good to the first world champion.

11. U.S. Tour

Let's get the bad news out of the way first.

On the U.S. PGA Tour, some of the game's biggest names all but disappeared in 1991, giving way to less than show-stoppers. No golfer won more than twice, and the list of seven who did win twice hardly reads like golf's who's who—Billy Andrade, Mark Brooks, Nick Price, Andrew Magee, Tom Purtzer, Fred Couples and Corey Pavin.

There were 13 first-time winners and only one player, Paul Azinger, can be said to have any kind of streak going. He has now won a tournament for five consecutive years, the longest such streak on the Tour.

Adding to the Tour's depression were Curtis Strange and Greg Norman, who finished 48th and 53rd, respectively, on the money list, didn't win a tournament and had only nine top-10 finishes between them in 45 tournaments.

Strange suffered from an on-again, off-again, energy-sapping ailment that at times left him dizzy and disoriented. He finished with $336,333, but $225,000 of that came before March with a tie for second in Phoenix and a second at Doral, where he lost in a playoff to Rocco Mediate.

Norman never got it going often enough, and when he did, he became disoriented in the final round. After leading the money list with $1,165,477 and winning the Vardon Trophy with a 69.10 stroke average in 1990, Norman won only $320,196 last year and his stroke average was 70.35.

Others who disappeared in 1991:

Wayne Levi, the 1990 PGA Tour Player of the Year with four victories and $1,024,647, second to Norman, cracked the top 10 only three times and finished 87th on the money list with $195,861. Levi performed so poorly during the year that U.S. Ryder Cup captain Dave Stockton played him only twice against the Europeans, once in foursomes to let him get the feel of the course in competition and the second time in the final singles.

Jodie Mudd, winner of the 1990 Players Championship and Nabisco Championship, was in the money in 19 of 23 tournaments in 1990 and won $911,746. In 1991, he slipped to $148,453, had three top 10s and no wins, no places, no shows.

And here's one more for the book of bizarre tales of 1991. Scott Verplank, of whom greatness was predicted after he won the 1985 Western Open as an amateur, missed 24 consecutive cuts, and only a $3,100 check in the Las Vegas Invitational in October kept him from going zero-for-1991.

And now, the good news:

• The United States won the Ryder Cup, more with grit than ability.

• Pavin has never had a bad year, but this time he had a great one. He won the PGA of America's Player-of-the-Year award; was No. 1 on the money list with $979,430; won twice, both in playoffs at the Bob Hope Classic and BellSouth Atlanta Classic; had 10 top-10 finishes and 16 top 20s; missed only one cut; and finished just .04 behind Couples in the Vardon Trophy standings.

• Couples finally exploded from his own shadow and became the force long expected of him. He was the star of the Ryder Cup, purging himself of the "choke" label from the 1989 matches. He also set career highs in tournaments won, with two; earnings with $791,749; top-10 finishes with nine; cuts made, 20 in 21 events; scoring average, 69.59 to win the Vardon Trophy.

• Chip Beck put his name in golf's record book, shooting 59 in the Las Vegas Invitational, joining Al Geiberger as the only players to break 60 in PGA Tour competition. He did it with a flourish, birdieing the last three holes.

• John Daly was the last player added to the PGA Championship field and, without the benefit of a practice round, shot 69-67-69-71—276 to win by three strokes over Bruce Lietzke. He held nothing back from the tee, bashing 300-yard-plus drives, much to the delight of the galleries and CBS, which had record ratings for the event. Daly became only the third rookie to earn his first PGA Tour victory in a major championship, joining Jack Nicklaus (1962 U.S. Open) and Jerry Pate (1976 U.S. Open).

• Pinehurst No. 2, Donald Ross' gem in the North Carolina sandhills, was the venue of the Tour Championship, as the PGA Tour returned to the classic setting. Craig Stadler, whose last Tour victory came in 1984, won in a playoff over Russ Cochran.

Other notable accomplishments:

Payne Stewart's victory in the U.S. Open. He was two strokes down with three holes to play on Sunday and forced a playoff against Scott Simpson, where he again was two down with three holes to play and won, 75-77.

Ian Woosnam beat Jim Hallet in a playoff to win his first U S. event, the USF&G Classic in New Orleans, and two weeks later fought off Tom Watson with a final-hole, six-foot par putt to win the Masters for his first major title.

Bruce Fleisher joined the PGA Tour in 1972 and never finished higher than 64th on the money list in 12 years. After seven years as a club pro, he entered the New England Classic as an alternate, then won the tournament.

Infiniti Tournament of Champions—$800,000
Winner: Tom Kite

Tom Kite delivered an early message as the 1991 U.S. PGA Tour season began with the Infiniti Tournament of Champions at LaCosta Resort.

In effect, Kite said, "What you saw in 1990 is not what you're going to see in 1991." The meaning was that slipping from No. 1 on the money list in 1989 to No. 15 in 1990 got his attention. The second part of his message was, "The fact that I'm over 40 shouldn't be taken that I'm on the downside of my career."

Kite delivered that two-prong memo emphatically. He shot four sub-par rounds—68-67-68-69—272—and won the $800,000 tournament by one stroke over Lanny Wadkins. In doing so, Kite also struck a blow for cross-handed putters everywhere. He had gone back and forth in 1990, conventional one round, unconventional the next. The result was disastrous. After Kite failed to make the cut in the British Open, he made the decision to go cross-handed all the way.

"That's one of the problems I had last year, switching back and forth. No way that does my game any justice. Everyone associates it with bad putters. There's some reasonable evidence that it's a decent way to putt," said Kite, after averaging 26.5 putts per round in the Tournament of Champions.

This was a two-man tournament almost from the beginning. Wadkins took the first-round lead with 65, three strokes in front of Kite and Chip Beck. After two rounds, Wadkins still led Kite by three strokes, but he slumped to 73 on Saturday and Kite moved up with 68, two shots ahead of Wadkins and Fred Couples, who shot 71.

"For two days I can't miss anything and today I couldn't make anything," Wadkins said of his third-round putting.

At one point in the final round Kite led by three strokes, then almost as quickly trailed by one. Wadkins birdied Nos. 12, 13 and 14 to tie, and took the lead when Kite bogeyed No. 14. Kite drew even with a birdie at No. 16, and the tournament fell in his lap on the par-five 17th, where Wadkins three-putted from 18 feet for a bogey.

Wadkins knew he needed to make that putt, figuring that Kite would birdie it. He looked across the pond at the big electronic scoreboard and saw that Kite had just made another birdie, a 20-footer at No. 16, to tie.

Always an aggressive player, Wadkins tried to jam it into the hole. Instead, he rolled it through the break, running it almost four feet past the hole. "The only bad putts I hit all day were on 17," he said. "I had in the back of my mind the putt at 15, where I left it dead in the hole. I wanted to make this putt and put the heat back on him. All I did was take the heat off him."

That was the end of the spirited battle. Ahead by one stroke, Kite easily parred the last two holes. In fact, he missed six-foot birdie putts on both holes. "I wish Tom had made that putt at 18," Wadkins said. "I probably would feel a little better."

Beck, Couples and Player-of-the-Year Wayne Levi tied for third place, four strokes behind Kite.

It was like old times for Kite, who won this tournament in 1985. It wasn't so much that he won, but how he won, with typically consistent, steady play, the kind of thing he lacked the year before.

"Consistent, round after round," Kite said of his play. "I think last year I lost sight of what it takes to play well out here. Maybe I got lazy. I got swing-conscious and I wasn't thinking about scoring. As a result, my short game went to pot. I didn't chip or putt well all year. Maybe you need a kick in the rear to force you to go back and take care of business. It's a heck of a lot harder to stay on top than it is to get there."

Northern Telecom Tucson Open—$1,000,000
Winner: Phil Mickelson

Golf has been longing for someone to come out of the amateur ranks and stand the sport on its ear. That person may have been found in the first full-field event of 1991.

His name is Phil Mickelson, a bright-eyed and fearless junior from Arizona State University. Playing left-handed, this 21-year-old Californian didn't blink after making a triple-bogey eight on the par-five 14th hole to lose the lead. He birdied two of the last three holes and climbed over Tom Purtzer and Bob Tway to win the Northern Telecom Tucson Open.

It's not like Mickelson came unknown into the sudden glare of this improbable pictorial. He had won the U.S. Amateur and NCAA championship in 1990—only Jack Nicklaus before him had turned that trick in the same year—and he was the low amateur in the U.S. Open, shooting even-par 288 at Medinah. Even Nicklaus didn't win a professional tournament as an amateur. Others had, however; Gene Littler in the 1954 San Diego Open, Doug Sanders in the 1956 Canadian Open, and Scott Verplank in the 1985 Western Open.

Mickelson shot 65-71-65-71—272 and won by one stroke over Purtzer and Tway. Being an amateur, he couldn't accept the $180,000 prize that goes to the winner, but the qualifying exemption that goes to Tour winners will be there when he graduates in 1992. He said he would finish school before turning pro. "I want to defend my Amateur and NCAA titles and play on the Walker Cup team," he said. "Money is no problem right now. I'm on scholarship. There's no pressure on me."

This was Mickelson's home turf, as it was the year before when Robert Gamez won here in his rookie season. He was never far from the lead—one stroke behind Tway and Hal Sutton after the first round, three strokes behind Tway, Craig Stadler, Brian Tennyson, Scott Hoch and Corey Pavin after two rounds. He led after three rounds by two strokes over Pavin and David Peoples.

Mickelson might have faded into the desert sun on Sunday except that Purtzer, Peoples and Tway faded from sight ahead of him. Peoples bogeyed five of the last seven holes. Purtzer had it won until he tried a delicate nine-iron shot over a deep bunker at No. 18 when he didn't need to, and came up short. He then left his bunker shot in the sand and made double bogey. Tway then had the lead, but he bogeyed the 17th.

Mickelson seemed to be out of contention when he took an eight at No. 14. The 506-yard par five is a birdie hole, reachable in two shots by the long hitters, of which Mickelson is one. To the dismay of his huge following, Mickelson hit his tee shot to the left, deep in the desert. After a drop and stroke penalty, he hit a three iron to the right into another unplayable lie. Another drop, another penalty stroke. Then, his nine-iron approach went left and into a bunker, from where he blasted to eight feet and two-putted.

Surely, Mickelson would need to birdie three of the last four holes to have a chance. But with the pros playing like amateurs, Mickelson birdied No. 16 for a tie and made an eight-footer at No. 18 for the victory. "He's just on a different level," Tway said. "You have to give him credit. That was just great golf. You have to go out and do it, and he was able to."

Mickelson birdied the 16th by hitting a sand wedge within a foot, safely got his par at No. 17, then hit a soft nine iron from 149 yards to set up the winning putt. "I stood behind the putt and I knew the break," Mickelson said. "It was just a matter of rolling it. About a foot from the hole I knew it was in."

Purtzer and Tway each collected $144,000 for finishing second. "You'd have to go back to Nicklaus to find an amateur like Phil," Purtzer said. "Guys like Phil and Nicklaus and Tom Watson don't come down the pike too often."

United Airlines Hawaiian Open—$1,100,000
Winner: Lanny Wadkins

Whatever it is about turning 40 that makes a golfer realize that his time is limited was at work again this week in the United Airlines Hawaiian Open. Two weeks after 41-year-old Tom Kite waltzed in at the Infiniti Tournament of Champions, Lanny Wadkins stepped into victory circle at Waialea Country Club in Honolulu.

Wadkins, who was second to Kite at the Tournament of Champions, shot 65 in a gusty wind to come from six strokes off the third-round lead held by John Cook and won by four shots over Cook, who finished with 75. Wadkins, who had rounds of 69, 67, 69 before his 65, took a $198,000 winner's share of the $1.1 million purse.

Before Wadkins turned 40 the previous year, he felt like he had forever to make his mark. "But suddenly I realized there's only a limited amount of time left. You know you don't have 15 years left, not like you had thought before." Fired by that urgency and Cook's collapse, Wadkins played what he called "one of the four or five best rounds I've ever played, especially considering the conditions."

It was Wadkins' 20th career victory, and it put him on track for a seventh Ryder Cup appearance. "Seven Ryder Cups. Not many guys have done that," he said. "It's a pretty good barometer of your career."

The week's early noise was made by Scott Simpson, who opened with a 10-under-par 62 to lead by one stroke over Ben-Hogan-Tour-graduate Ed Humenik. Cook shot 64 and was tied for third place with Larry Mize. At the halfway point, Cook and Simpson were tied at 14-under 130, two strokes ahead of Humenik, Chip Beck and Gil Morgan. Cook added a third-round 69 and was alone at the top by one stroke over Morgan.

Then the winds came howling off the ocean and through the hills, and Cook was blown away by his own errors and Wadkins' daring and tenacity. Cook bogeyed three holes starting out to fall three strokes behind, got back to within one stroke with an eagle three at No. 15, then butchered the par-three 17th with a double bogey.

"I'm still learning," Cook said. "I hope I can use this as a stepping stone. I feel real bad, but it's just one of those things you have to overcome out here. Lanny shooting 65 out there was about as good as you can play. But he's one of the all-time greats. He's always a threat to win, even five or six back like today."

Wadkins did a lot of good things in the final round, and the wind coming up as it did was the break he needed. It was like throwing B'rer Rabbit in the briarpatch. Look it up. Wadkins came from behind to win at windy Colonial in 1988, at Doral in 1987, and in the nearly unplayable final round of the 1979 Players Championship. "I can't remember when I had a better ball-striking round than today," Wadkins said after his final 65. "I only missed three greens, incredible under these conditions. The ball bored through the wind. Even the crosswinds didn't affect it. I had makeable putts all over the course."

Phoenix Open—$1,000,000
Winner: Nolan Henke

A funny thing happened to Nolan Henke on the final day of the Phoenix Open. He went out with a four-stroke lead, lost it and fully expected Curtis Strange to win. But Strange, who shot 67, three-putted the 72nd hole for a bogey, and Henke stepped through with an 18-foot birdie putt for the victory.

It was Henke's second win in less than a year. His first came late in 1990 at the B.C. Open. He finished with an even-par round of 71 over the TPC of Scottsdale course for a 16-under 268 total, earned $180,000, more than half of what he made in all of 1990.

By making birdie on the final hole, Henke avoided a four-way playoff with Strange, Gil Morgan and Tom Watson. Morgan and Watson came out of nowhere to get so close. Morgan shot 66 and Watson, putting like the Watson of old, birdied five of the last six holes for 65.

Steve Jones shot 63 to take the first-round lead by one stroke over Strange. Henke was two back. At the halfway point, Henke and Strange were tied at 131. It was Henke's tournament to lose after 54 holes, when his 66 left him four strokes in front of Robert Wrenn and five ahead of Strange. After 54 holes, only three of the 80 players who made the cut were over par.

Henke continued to ride a hot streak since last September. In 29 straight rounds, since the first round of the B.C. Open, his six worst scores had been even par and his stroke average was 68.17. "I'm on a pretty good streak," Henke said before teeing off in the final round. "I just hope I don't do anything stupid." But he did. He almost lost it, seeming to pay more attention to the scoreboard showing Strange, who was two groups in front, moving up with four birdies on the first nine and two more at Nos. 12 and 13. From a three-shot lead after 10 holes, Henke fell into a tie with a bogey at No. 13 and momentarily dropped one behind with another bogey at No. 15, where he got too aggressive off the tee and hit his drive into the lake that runs down the left side of the fairway.

Strange was keeping things interesting. It had been awhile since he had been in contention on Sunday and it showed. After tying Henke at No. 13, he bogeyed No. 14, then left a birdie putt short at No. 15 and had to save par from a deep bunker at No. 16. "They actually weren't bad shots," Strange said of those three holes.

Strange got himself into the battle by whittling Henke's lead to two shots at the turn and went to the 18th hole with a one-shot lead. And Henke knew it. "I kept thinking Curtis was going to win, the way he was making birdies and I was making bogeys," Henke said. "I was real fortunate. He had won so many times. I don't know what happened to Curtis."

What happened was this. Strange missed a 10-footer for birdie at No. 17 and went to No. 18 thinking he was one stroke behind when he was one ahead. "It shocked me," Strange said. "I'm going to 18 thinking I've got to make three and then find out I'm leading." After hitting what he thought was a perfect tee shot, Strange found his ball in a divot and had to chop down on a nine iron rather than hitting the eight iron he wanted. His shot came up 80 feet short of the pin. His first putt rolled six feet past and he missed coming back for bogey. "It's still mechanical," said Strange of his putting, which contributed heavily to his being shut out in 1990. "The killers were

17 and 18. I just didn't trust my stroke."

Henke still thought there would be a playoff when he hit his approach to 18 feet on No. 18. He didn't think he could make it. When he did, pure shock registered on his face, followed by a big smile. "I can't believe it went in," said Henke, who now hasn't had a score over par in his last 29 rounds, dating back to the first round of the B.C. Open in September. "The way I was putting today, I thought I'd have to hit it within a foot to make it."

AT&T Pebble Beach National Pro-Am—$1,100,000
Winner: Paul Azinger

As love-hate relationships go, the one Paul Azinger had with the Pebble Beach Golf Links ranked up there with any of them. He couldn't stand the place until it was time to go back there, then he couldn't stand not being there.

But no more. Not after Azinger shot second- and fourth-round 67s over this majestic paradise by the sea and won the AT&T Pebble Beach National Pro-Am. He had another 67 at Spyglass Hill, 73 at Poppy Hills for a 14-under-par 274 total, four shots better than Corey Pavin and Brian Claar, who tied for second place. Defending champion Mark O'Meara, going for his third straight victory at Pebble Beach, did not make the cut.

John Cook and his amateur partner, actor Jack Wagner of "General Hospital" fame, won the pro-am when Cook birdied the final hole. And again, Jack Lemon, playing with Peter Jacobsen, didn't make the cut.

Poppy Hills became one of the venues after Cypress Point fell victim to the new PGA Tour policy that called for the pursuit of minority membership at all participating clubs. Cypress Point would not change its membership policy in order to speed up that process. Poppy Hills did not open to rave reviews. It could have been because it was following Cypress Point, which is impossible, or because of the severity of the greens and the number of blind shots. More than likely, it was a combination of the two.

Few players complained openly, however, fearing fines from PGA Tour Commissioner Deane Beman, who issued a gag order on criticism. "I'll just say the best hole on the course is the 19th hole and leave it at that," Azinger said.

To Azinger, those other courses are mere distractions anyway. He would rather play four rounds at Pebble Beach and take his chances. It's his favorite, but until this year he had not played well there. "I've never been able to break 70 here," he said. "It's tough for your favorite course to be one you can't play worth a darn. Every time I play here, I always say I'm never coming back. But I always do."

After his bogey, double bogey start at Poppy Hills, Azinger couldn't wait to get back to Pebble Beach. In the past, he had been frustrated by an inability to read the greens, where the breaks are determined by the pull of the ocean. Azinger had no trouble with them this year. No bogeys, either. "It's like Augusta. You have to get to know them," Azinger said of the greens. "I have an idea now how much the ocean will pull a putt. I didn't have to guess as much."

Azinger was never far from the lead. He was two shots behind Ben-

Hogan-Tour-graduate Mike Standly after a first-round 67 at Spyglass, two strokes ahead through 36 holes after shooting another 67, this time at Pebble Beach, and two strokes behind following his 73 at Poppy Hills. On Sunday, he turned spectacular Pebble Beach into his best new friend.

Rocco Mediate was ahead when the final round began. Mediate was four strokes behind after an opening 69 at Pebble Beach, but leap-frogged his way into second place after 36 holes with a spectacular 67 at Poppy Hills, which included a hole-in-one at No. 15, then took the lead with 69 at Spyglass.

Mediate's good fortune ran out on Sunday and Azinger's got a late start. Starting two strokes behind Mediate, Azinger got even with an eagle three at No. 2, took the lead with a 45-foot birdie at the fourth, made a clutch 15-footer for par at the ninth, and secured the victory with a five-iron shot to within two feet at No. 17.

Mediate and Davis Love III, playing in the final group, both bogeyed No. 9 and were heard from no more. Cook, playing with Azinger, also bogeyed No. 9 and followed it with a double bogey at No. 10. No one challenged Azinger after that. "After 13, I wasn't even nervous," Azinger said. "I can't imagine how thrilled Mark O'Meara must be to have won three of these things. It's such a prestigious place, so much history. What a great golf course this is."

Bob Hope Chrysler Classic—$1,100,000
Winner: Corey Pavin

When Corey Pavin chipped in from 40 feet on the first hole of a playoff to win the Bob Hope Chrysler Classic, Mark O'Meara stood there stunned and disbelieving.

O'Meara was on the 17th green, 18 feet from the hole, and Pavin was short of the green, in rough so heavy you could see only the top of the ball. The worst that O'Meara could expect was to halve the hole and go on. Pavin's shot landed softly, 20 feet from the pin, and rolled straight into the hole. Visibly shaken, O'Meara missed badly on his birdie attempt that would have tied Pavin.

It was some week. Pavin's winning score of 29-under-par 331 (65, 69, 66, 66, 65) broke Lanny Wadkins' tournament record by two strokes. It was Pavin's second Hope victory in four years and his first anywhere since the 1988 Texas Open. And the $198,000 winner's share of the purse moved him atop the PGA Tour money list. O'Meara also broke the record, as did Tim Simpson, who finished a stroke out of the playoff, and Raymond Floyd tied the record and got only fourth place.

"I make three bogeys in 90 holes, make 32 birdies, break the tournament record, and lose," O'Meara said. "I'm not very happy. Who would be?"

This was a shootout from the beginning. With perfect weather and the four courses—LaQuinta, Bermuda Dunes, Indian Wells and PGA West Palmer—were equally as good. Robert Gamez shot 64 to lead the first round; Simpson had 64 and O'Meara, 65, to share the second-round lead; they were still tied after 54 holes, but O'Meara had the lead alone—by one stroke over Simpson and two over Pavin—as they headed into Sunday.

After O'Meara birdied Nos. 2 and 5, Pavin trailed by four strokes. That was as far as Pavin had been from the lead all week, and it was a turning point. After a scrambling par at No. 5, Pavin ran off four straight birdies to pull even with O'Meara. As the three leaders weaved their way between the palms on the second nine, Simpson's comments from Saturday on the key to victory seemed accurate. "Dominate the par fives, get past 10 and 11 and see what happens," he said.

Pavin and O'Meara birdied the last three par fives; Simpson, only two of them. O'Meara and Pavin both parred the 10th and 11th; Simpson birdied and bogeyed. Pavin and O'Meara both birdied No. 14, but at No. 15, Pavin hit what he called "probably the best shot I've hit in a long time." It was a 170-yard seven iron that rolled to within eight inches of the hole for a birdie and a tie at 28 under par.

Both players matched stroke for stroke coming in. Simpson had a chance to make it a three-way playoff a couple of times. His putt for a birdie at No. 17, which looked good a foot from the hole, rolled over the edge, and he hit his approach into No. 18 into the back bunker. "Just wasn't supposed to win," Simpson said. "I play five great rounds and don't get a sniff. These other guys just played a shot better."

O'Meara could have kept the playoff going even after Pavin's chip-in. He faced the same putt at the 17th in regulation and that one stayed mostly straight. On a similar line in the playoff, it slid away. "Any time you play well it's satisfying," Pavin said. "But playing that well when you need to win is what it's all about. Competition is what I've always loved about golf."

Pavin has almost always had O'Meara's number. When they were college adversaries, Pavin at UCLA and O'Meara at Long Beach State, Pavin won four of the six events in which they competed. His triumph over O'Meara in the Hope was turnabout fair play as professionals. O'Meara had beaten him in a playoff in 1985 at Kapalua.

"He's a tough little competitor," O'Meara said of Pavin. "He's not as long off the tee, but has a wonderful short game. I thought he would get up and down on the playoff hole, but I didn't expect him to make it. I was somewhat shocked when it went in."

Shearson Lehman Brothers Open—$1,000,000
Winner: Jay Don Blake

Jay Don Blake finally crossed that fine line that separates the winners from the losers on the PGA Tour, and what better place for a first-time winner than the Shearson-Lehman Brothers Open at Torrey Pines, where three of the last six champions walked into the victory circle for the first time.

Blake, a former NCAA champion and All-American from Utah State, shot his second consecutive 67 over the South Course and came from two strokes behind third-round leader Steve Pate to beat Bill Sander by two shots and defending champion Dan Forsman by three. "I always thought my game was good enough to win, but you wonder when it's going to happen," said the 32-year-old Blake.

Blake's journey to his first victory had been a long and frustrating one. Although he beat Hal Sutton in a four-hole playoff for the 1980 NCAA title at Ohio State's Scarlet Course and then was named a first team All-American, he did not join the PGA Tour until 1987. That was after six trips through the qualifying tournament.

During those frustrating years, Blake made occasional stops on the mini-tour circuit, but spent most of his time working at a club in his St. George, Utah, hometown and in the local hardware store. Once Blake got on the Tour, it was still a struggle. In the first four years, he had but six top-10 finishes. His best was a tie for third place in the 1989 Atlanta Classic, and his highest finish on the money list was 71st. Last year, he was 106th after missing 14 of 30 cuts.

Unlike many first-time winners who stumble their way to victory, Blake could afford no missteps. It wasn't until he rolled in a 15-footer for a birdie at No. 17 that he could relax.

Through the tournament, Blake was no more than four shots off the lead at the end of any round. Ben Crenshaw opened with 65 and Blake had 69. After 36 holes, he trailed Pate and Forsman by two strokes, and heading to Sunday, he was two back of Pate.

Blake was comfortable throughout. For one thing, he had started the AT&T Pebble Beach Pro-Am with a triple bogey and the Hope with a double bogey. His first two holes Thursday and Friday were only bogeys, and for another, he was hitting greens, 59 out of 72, and making birdie putts when he had them.

He did blaze his trail to victory in an odd way, however. The normal way to win at Torrey Pines is to dominate the par fives. Blake, though, birdied only nine of the 16 and only four of eight on the weekend. On the plus side, 10 of his 14 weekend birdies came from 10 feet or less.

Blake's Sunday game plan was to par the tough 453-yard first hole, which plays into the wind, then take it from there. He birdied the second hole to close to within one stroke, and tied Pate with a birdie at No. 4. Pate played himself out of contention before reaching the turn. Gambling with a one iron from a fairway bunker on No. 7, he slashed it into a canyon and wound up with a triple-bogey seven. Brad Faxon also was in the running at that point, but made double bogey on No. 7. "That knocked the steam out of both of us," Faxon said.

Blake took over the lead at that point and clung to it. He got a little breathing room with an 18-foot birdie putt at No. 15, then could exhale for the first time when he birdied the 17th. "I'm glad that's over with," Blake said after accepting the $180,000 winner's share of the purse. "They say this is supposed to be fun, winning a tournament. But I think it's pretty nerve-racking."

Nissan Los Angeles Open—$1,000,000
Winner: Ted Schulz

Ted Schulz became the hero of range-ball pickers everywhere by winning the Nissan Los Angeles Open at Riviera Country Club.

Schulz, a 31-year-old native of Louisville, Kentucky, had his best week ever, shooting rounds of 69-66-69-68—272, then had to sweat out a slick five-footer that Jeff Sluman missed for a tie. Bruce Lietzke was in third place, two strokes back after three-putting the final hole. "I just prayed I'd play my best and accept whatever happened," Schulz said. "The thing was, I putted so well and that's what has been holding me back. I feel like now I have something I can fall back on."

Schulz had taken a curious route to his finest moment. In 1983, he worked for eight months as the range-ball picker at Bermuda Dunes in Palm Springs, California. He also spent a year on the Asian Tour and took five trips through the qualifying tournament. Until Sunday, his victory total numbered one, the 1989 Southern Open in Columbus, Georgia. "It has been a slow process, but worth it," Schulz said. "It's something most of the guys out here go through."

Schulz was on nobody's list of favorites when the week began. He had been putting so poorly that he had missed the cut in his first four tournaments this year. It was so bad, he skipped the San Diego stop, went to Palm Springs where his in-laws live, and back to Bermuda Dunes. This time, he picked up a putting lesson from an old friend, Till Tindall, the golf coach at the University of Washington. He arrived at Riviera confident, not so much that he would win, but that he wouldn't miss those three-footers.

While Schulz was on center stage Sunday afternoon, he was merely a bit player for most of the tournament.

Andrew Magee got everyone's attention in the first round when he set sail with a seven-under-par 28 at the turn before he succumbed to 38 coming in. The 66 left him one stroke behind Wayne Grady and Larry Nelson. Magee felt pretty good until he got to the 10th tee. Then someone in the gallery yelled, "28-30," Magee said. "I thought, 'that's 58, not 59,' and then hit my first bad shot of the day. I started thinking. After that bad shot, I got careful. I was unconscious until then."

The second round belonged to Lietzke, his 52-inch putter and an eight-under-par 63, just one stroke off the course record, which left him two in front of four other players, including Schulz and Sluman. Entering the final round, Lietzke and Sluman were at 10-under-par 203, but Schulz was only one stroke behind.

On Sunday, Schulz moved into a tie with a birdie at No. 11, then parred in, while Sluman made a couple of bogeys and only one birdie, then missed the tying putt at No. 18.

Schulz held a one-shot lead when his approach shot at No. 18 came up short, 50 feet from the pin. His putt was as long as the green, but he lagged to within a foot, of which he said, "I can make most of those." Then he had to sweat out Sluman and Lietzke. Lietzke's approach stopped 30 feet short, while Sluman nailed a three iron to within five feet above the hole. Lietzke missed, then missed again from four feet, his putt sliding by the right edge, which had an effect on what Sluman did next.

Having seen Lietzke's line, Sluman played his putt inside the right edge of the hole and watched it break sharply to the left. Schulz was the winner. "I didn't know what to think about Jeff's putt," said Schulz, who watched from the scorer's tent. "He's a good putter, but it was no gimme. I was prepared to do whatever I had to do, but I held my breath and didn't exhale until it broke off."

Doral Ryder Open—$1,400,000
Winner: Rocco Mediate

Once upon a time, the long putter was considered only by those over-50 guys, who found it was the perfect fix for frayed nerves as they faced two-footers on the Senior PGA Tour. But no longer. Not after 28-year-old Rocco Mediate pressed the handle against his chest and putted his way to victory in the Doral Ryder Open against one of the best fields of the season.

Mediate won his first PGA Tour event in rather spectacular style. Going out on Monday to the 11th hole to complete Sunday's washed-out final round, he birdied No. 12 from six feet, No. 17 from 10 feet, No. 18 from eight feet to tie Curtis Strange, then made a five-footer on the first playoff hole.

Strange looked like a winner when he completed a final-round 67 with birdies at Nos. 16 and 17, but he couldn't make his 10-footer in the playoff. Mediate had rounds of 66-70-68-72—276, and Strange, 69-68-72-67—276. Andy Bean and Russ Cochran finished one stroke behind.

Mediate and the long putter became friends after he played a round with Senior PGA Tour player Jim Ferree during Thanksgiving and watched him make everything. "He holed a lot of putts and Jim never was a good putter," Mediate said. "I felt that a younger guy, with better eyes and feel, it might help him. And it has."

It had already been a strange week even before Mediate worked his magic.

First there was the case of Paul Azinger and the long-distance disqualification. On Thursday, Azinger kicked away some rocks while standing in a hazard, on the edge of the lake at No. 18. He got a par for 69, and the next day shot 65. A television camera caught him kicking those rocks, which calls for a two-shot penalty, and a club pro watching in Denver noticed the infraction and alerted officials, who had no choice but to disqualify Azinger.

Azinger accepted the PGA Tour's decision that he'd broken a rule, but he didn't like suffering what amounted to a citizen's arrest. "I think the decision is correct," Azinger said. "It's just hard for me to swallow. What I did was an infraction. It also was a trivial thing. It had nothing to do with the shot."

Secondly, there was Jack Nicklaus, who will not go quietly into his senior years. After a respectable 71 on Thursday, Nicklaus moved up the leaderboard like a blue-chip stock. He shot 63 and missed two putts inside eight feet, but again, he made almost everything else. The near course-record-tying round left Nicklaus one stroke from the lead held by Kenny Perry, who had an unnoticed 64. "Of course, I surprised myself, and everybody in the field, too," Nicklaus said. "It surprised my wife, too."

Reality returned for Nicklaus on Saturday, however. After taking the lead early in the round, he bogeyed No. 13, double-bogeyed No. 14 and bogeyed No. 17 for 75. A closing 70 left him tied for fifth place at 279 with Davis Love III. "Those two holes early on the back nine just killed me on Saturday," Nicklaus said.

With Nicklaus gone, Cochran and Bean moved into the spotlight. Bean has been winless since taking the last of his three Doral titles in 1986. He shot 67 Saturday to move into a one-stroke lead over Cochran, but they finished 74 and 73, respectively, on Monday, turning things over to Mediate and Strange.

Mediate made more birdies Monday than any of the others. He had three in eight holes, plus another in the playoff. Strange had two. "My improved play is more than just the putter," said Mediate, who had been one of the most consistent players coming in, with ninth-place finishes at Tucson and Phoenix, fourth at Pebble Beach, sixth at Los Angeles and 13th at the Hope. "I feel better with the putter. With the short putter, my back would tighten up when I practiced. And if you don't practice, you're not going to be that good, especially in this league."

Mediate's victory was the first on the PGA Tour for a player using the long putter. It also was worth $225,000, which pushed him over $1 million in career earnings in his sixth season. "I don't remember much of the play-off," Mediate said. "I was in a daze, but I was calm. Walking to the first tee for the playoff, I caught myself saying, 'Pretty good, you birdied the last two holes to tie. That's good enough.' But when Curtis missed his birdie putt, I knew I'd make mine."

Honda Classic—$1,000,000
Winner: Steve Pate

There will be a Honda Classic in 1992, but not at Eagle Trace, not after a few of the game's biggest names—and only a few play here anymore—decided there were better things to do this second week in March than being blown away like Dorothy in Kansas.

Steve Pate isn't in that group, however. He took his beating on the way to a nine-under-par 279 total and a three-shot victory over Paul Azinger and Dan Halldorson. "Maybe I hate myself, but I like playing here," Pate said after his fourth career victory. "I've gotten used to it. I play well here a lot, maybe because I just try to survive. It's definitely survival."

Pate was about the only player to offer even a back-handed compliment. Greg Norman let his feelings be known on Saturday, six holes into the third round. "Now you guys know why nobody comes here," Norman said, walking up the sixth fairway. "This is a joke." That comment came before he made a quadruple bogey with two shots in the water on the seventh hole on the way to a 77. "You won't see me back here next year," Norman told a marshall before completing his round. "I don't need to be playing carnival golf."

Even Azinger, who at one point shared the lead on Sunday, expressed disdain for the Arthur Hills layout that can be a pussycat in calm conditions, but a tiger in the wind. I'm not in love with this place," he said. "I'll tell you, it's not often you can finish second and say you're definitely not coming back."

The wind blew harder the previous week at Doral and there were few complaints. Why? "Because Doral was designed to be played in the wind," Norman said. "You can't bounce balls into these greens. At Doral, you can hit it low. You can't here. This course wasn't designed to be played in extremely windy conditions."

How bad was it? The first two rounds were played in relatively calm conditions and 54 scores of 70 or less were posted and the cut was even-par 144. The last two rounds were played in 40-mile-an-hour winds and three players broke 70, Davis Love III and Ted Schulz on Saturday and Billy Andrade on Sunday. Ten didn't break 80, including Curtis Strange, who had 86 on Sunday.

Pate was 10 under par after 36 holes, and won at nine under par. "My theory here is just to avoid the big numbers," he said. "It's not a very satisfying way to play golf, but it seems to work here, I just feel like a wimp, bailing out all the time."

Pate got his first victory in three years because he got up and down for pars all week. He chipped well, putted better, and suffered only one double bogey all week. At the halfway point, Pate shared the lead with Dan Halldorson and John Huston, just one stroke ahead of Norman, Azinger and Mike Sullivan. After three rounds, Pate led by five strokes with a 70 that felt more like 60. Norman was gone with 77, and Halldorson, with 78. Only Azinger, who shot 75, was able to recover.

Pate's five-shot lead lasted only for nine holes Sunday. He bogeyed the sixth, made a double bogey at No. 7 and three-putted No. 9 for another bogey. Meanwhile, Azinger caught him after 10 holes, thanks in part to an eagle three on No. 5. The drama was short-lived. Azinger three-putted No. 13 for a bogey, missed a short putt for a birdie at No. 14, bogeyed No. 15 and double-bogeyed No. 16.

From there, Pate's only anxious moment came at No. 18, where he hit his approach shot over the green and into the deep rough. Pate couldn't find his ball. Not for four minutes, 45 seconds, or 15 seconds before it would be declared lost. Once it was found, Pate hacked it out and onto the green and two-putted for bogey and his three-shot victory.

"I put the pressure on him, but he never leaked," Azinger said. "It's a great course to have the lead at. In the wind, everybody has to play safe and when you don't, it's going to get you eventually."

The Nestle Invitational—$1,000,000
Winner: Andrew Magee

That adage on the PGA Tour that says "When it's your turn to win, you win," was at work again in The Nestle Invitational at Bay Hill. That's as good a reason as any in explaining how Andrew Magee, who had won only once in his career, beat a world-class field which included Nick Faldo, Greg Norman, Ian Woosnam, Curtis Strange, Tom Watson, Tom Kite and other such luminaries.

"It's the highlight of my career," Magee understated.

Maybe we should have seen it coming. In Phoenix, Magee cost himself a chance to win by three-putting the final hole. He shot 28 on the first nine at Riviera in the Los Angeles Open. He was knocking on the door at Doral until he blew away with 77 in the final-round gale. He was ninth at the Honda Classic. Fourteen of his last 16 rounds were under par. He had three top-10 finishes in six events. He was due to win.

He had a tough act to follow—Robert Gamez's seven iron to beat Greg Norman the year before. There was no such drama this time, only anxiety. Magee had to wait three hours on Sunday before the last groups could finish the rain-delayed tournament, which was shortened to 54 holes.

Magee shot rounds of 68-69-66—203, two strokes better than Tom Sieckmann, and his finish was the only time he led at the end of a round. Mark Calcavecchia and Donnie Hammond shared the first-round lead with 66s and Don Pooley, at 134, was the second-round leader. At this point, Magee was three strokes back.

Magee's finish wasn't dull, however. In the third round, he birdied Nos. 14 and 15 to get to 11 under par for the tournament before play was suspended until Sunday because of rain. He picked up Sunday morning where he left off, making a 30-foot putt for eagle at No. 16, which moved him into the lead, then parred in. Almost as soon as he had signed his scorecard, play was stopped again and just over two hours later, officials declared it a 54-hole tournament.

When that eagle putt went in, I thought, 'Hey, I'm leading by one, and this could be a 54-hole tournament,'" Magee said. "I still had some nervous time left, however. There were a couple of guys out there who could still tie, unlikely as it was.

One was Calcavecchia, who had to hole out from the fairway at No. 18. This was no Gamez seven-iron shot, however. He had a 205-yard two iron into a cross wind, and all he could hit with it was the left bunker.

The other was Sieckmann, who had to birdie the last two holes after making a bogey at the par-five 16th, where his second shot hit the bank fronting the green and rolled back into the lake. The best Sieckmann could do was two pars.

"I'm disappointed we couldn't play a fourth round," Calcavecchia said. "I was hitting it great and putting it great, and I didn't get a chance to win the tournament. I'm not happy settling for third."

"It was strange winning it while in the locker room," Magee said. "You don't want to be too elated in there in front of all the guys. You make it like, 'It's no big deal. It's an everyday deal.' But it's not. I've played 30 tournaments a year for seven years. That's 210 tournaments and I had won once before now. The odds weren't exactly in my favor. It's a special feeling."

USF&G Classic—$1,000,000
Winner: Ian Woosnam

After trailing behind Nick Faldo, Greg Norman and Jose Maria Olazabal in the race for golf's No. 1 ranking, Ian Woosnam finally found his moment to declare that he, not those others, was the world's best player.

He said so after beating Jim Hallet in two playoff holes to win the USF&G Classic at English Turn near New Orleans. It was his first PGA Tour victory, and when asked to name the world's best player, Woosnam said, "I am."

That proclamation came despite the Sony Ranking, which then considered Faldo as No. 1 in the world. But after rounds of 73-67-68-67—275, and then two extra holes, Woosnam wasn't about to let the moment go.

"I don't think that's so at all," Woosnam said. "I won five tournaments last year and I'm two-for-three already this year. He's won two majors and a Hong Kong tournament. I just don't get the recognition he does. I feel I've been underestimated."

The Sony Ranking would soon declare him No. 1, but Woosnam wasn't even No. 1 in New Orleans until midway of the final round. The early attention focused on Jack Nicklaus and Tom Watson, two undisputed No. 1s in their days. Watson was in a fivesome leading at 67 with Billy Mayfair, Craig Rudolph, Dillard Pruitt and Phil Blackmar after the first round. Nicklaus was only one stroke behind.

Nicklaus stepped out front on Friday with 68, two strokes ahead of Watson and Tom Sieckmann, which set up a dream pairing for Saturday, Nicklaus and Watson. It was their first pairing in the final group since the 1977 British Open at Turnberry, but not nearly as exciting. Nicklaus putted like a 51-year-old and shot 74, while the 41-year-old Watson missed one four-footer after another in a round of 73. The parade passed them by. As Ronnie Black, who moved into second place with 66 said, "They were the guys I pulled for when I was growing up. I tried not to look at their names as I went passed them."

Woosnam shot 68 and moved into a second-place tie with Black and Mayfair, three strokes behind Hallet, who shot 65. Hallet's lead was short-lived. He bogeyed four of the first six holes, while Woosnam birdied three of the first seven. When Woosnam birdied Nos. 11 and 12, he led the faltering field by four strokes. Sieckmann made a run with birdies at Nos. 16 and 17, then just as he had done the week before when he got close, he found the water and made double bogey.

Woosnam bogeyed the 18th and began the wait for his only pursuer, Hallet, who suddenly discovered on the second nine what had deserted him on the first nine. He made four straight birdies and just missed a fifth, a short one at No. 16. After a par at No. 17, Hallet drilled a four iron to within four feet at No. 18 and made the tying putt.

Hallet had no more heroics left. After both players parred the first extra hole, Hallet could not make a par from the bunker at the second hole, and Woosnam two-putted for a winning par.

"To be the best in the world, they say you have to win in America and you have to win a major," Woosnam said. "I won in America this week. Now, let's see what we can do about the other in two weeks."

That would be the Masters, where Woosnam explained his previous downfalls there this way: "The trouble has been I've let myself down because I've got to play too aggressive and kept trying to force a score. If I can only rely on myself two-putting from 40 feet I'll be more relaxed about it.

"If I don't win a major in the next three or four years, I don't know that I'll ever win one. But I think I have a chance at the Masters. You never know."

The Players Championship—$1,600,000
Winner: Steve Elkington

The Players Championship may never be the fifth major event that PGA Tour Commissioner Deane Beman envisioned, but that's okay with Steve Elkington. It was major enough for him to beat the best field ever assembled at the TPC, earn $288,000, a 10-year exemption and finally make him a household name in his native Australia, albeit somewhere below one Greg Norman. "Greg's the big shark and I'm a little fish," Elkington admitted.

"But I'm a bigger fish now than I was yesterday."

If there was any doubt that Elkington played first-class golf, you need only look at his final nine which he played in 33 strokes in gusty winds and thick pressure.

The players had always loved this tournament, but not the Tournament Players Club course, until this year. Dubbed the Marriott Muny last year for its sorry condition, the course could not have been better this time. "Just perfect," said Paul Azinger. "It's the first time we've been able to stand over a putt and have a reasonable chance of making it. Maybe they've got it right. I hope they remember what they did."

There was abundant praise for the field, too. It would have included the entire top 20 of the Sony Ranking if Payne Stewart hadn't withdrawn because of injury. Most of the top Europeans were there, courtesy of the PGA Tour's decision to give special invitations.

This event, however, was an All-American show, if you include Elkington, who, though a native of Australia, played college golf at the University of Houston and lives in that city. Bob Tway led the first round with 65, one stroke better than Elkington, while Azinger was close with 67 and Tom Watson, with 68. It was a benign day where even par was in 80th place. It never had been this easy.

It wasn't on Friday, when strong, gusty winds began to separate the best from the rest. Azinger birdied the last four holes for 68 to lead by one over Elkington, Fuzzy Zoeller and Ian Baker-Finch. Only 28 players broke par and Elkington was one of the lucky ones who played in the morning and missed the brunt of the wind. Curtis Strange moved into contention with 68.

The potential was there Saturday for a two-man race as Azinger and Zoeller shot 69s and pulled away. Elkington had 72 and slipped four strokes behind. But not for long. Sunday, when Azinger and Zoeller couldn't get putts to drop, the pack of pursuers caught up. Elkington was among them, thanks to back-to-back birdies at Nos. 10 and 11 and another at No. 15, which moved him into a share of the lead.

Phil Blackmar birdied Nos. 15 and 16 to tie Elkington, but ended his chances by dunking one in the water at No. 18, a shot he called a mental mistake, adding, "I wasn't prepared to be in the lead here. Maybe I should have thought about it more."

In the end, it came down to Elkington and Zoeller, who made a slick downhiller at No. 13 to go 11 under par. Elkington seemed to have things under control even after missing a short birdie putt at the par-five 16th. But he bogeyed the 17th, three-putting from 50 feet or so. The three-putt may have helped him. It made him mad, and he was thinking only of a birdie as he went to the 18th tee. He got it, too.

"Bet you thought I couldn't birdie the last, did you?" Elkington asked playfully.

It was unlikely at best after he three-putted the 17th to fall into a tie with Zoeller, and seemed improbable when his drive at the 18th came to rest in a sand-filled divot almost 200 yards from the green.

Elkington got everybody's attention, however, when he drew a three-iron shot short of the green and then watched as it ran up to within 12 feet of the pin. When he calmly stroked the putt into the center of the hole he looked to all the world like the champion, which he was moments later.

Zoeller came there also needing a birdie to tie. He drove perfectly, then hit a four-iron approach pin-high, 15 feet away, but his putt raced past the left edge of the hole. He later said, "It tricked me. It broke left."

"It's great to finish second, but I wanted my name on that trophy," Zoeller said. "I wanted the history."

Instead it went to Elkington, who hasn't played much in his home country in recent years. He was too busy trying to make it on this Tour. "Up until I won at Greensboro (1990), I didn't feel I was a good enough player to zoom over to Australia and play," he said. "This gives me more freedom to do that. I'll probably play more over there now."

Deposit Guaranty Classic—$300,000
Winner: Larry Silveria

If the Deposit Guaranty Classic is a coming out party for the up-and-coming of the PGA Tour, then Larry Silveria came out in style on the week the great ones were in the Masters. Trailing by five shots entering the final round, Silveria birdied himself into a three-way playoff with 63, then won on the first playoff hole, defeating Russ Cochran and Mike Nicolette.

"Maybe," said Silveria, who calls himself The Kid, "this is the start of something big for The Kid. Sure, this will boost my confidence. Knowing that with some pressure on me, I can play like I did today. That's important."

The Deposit Guaranty Classic doesn't give its winner a green jacket or exemptions to big events. What it mostly gives is confidence and hope. And Silveria looks the part of a future star. He was a two-time All-American at Arizona, where he played ahead of Robert Gamez, and won the 1988 Arizona Open. But before this week, Silveria's results on the PGA Tour hadn't matched his potential. "Mostly mental," Silveria said in explaining why in three years his largest check was $20,250 for finishing 12th in the 1990 St. Jude Classic. "I've had trouble staying focused."

As usual, this tournament was a shootout. The Hattiesburg Country Club course was playing easier than normal, and not surprisingly, low scores were the rule. Grant Waite's 63 led after the first round. Nicolette took over the second and third rounds with 65 and 68.

After shooting 66s Thursday and Friday, Silveria was only two strokes off the lead, but he appeared to shoot himself out of things with a 71 on Saturday to drop five strokes behind. "But I was hitting the ball so good, just not making any putts," Silveria said. "I really believed if I made any putts Sunday I had a chance to win."

Silveria didn't have to make any long ones. Seven of his eight birdies came from eight feet or less. His shakiest moment came at No. 18, where he left a 30-foot birdie putt four feet short. He made it for 63 and a 14-under-par 266 total, and was tied with Cochran, who also had 63. Together they waited on Nicolette.

In 1983, Cochran shot a final-round 63 to come from far back to win by two shots. "What I didn't count on was someone else shooting 63 this time," Cochran said.

Nicolette wasn't counting on anybody shooting 63. At 12 under par, he knew he was beating all those who started close to him Sunday. He made a couple of birdies, then put his game on cruise control, unaware that Silveria and Cochran, playing several groups in front, were making moves. "I didn't look at the leaderboard until No. 16, and that's when I saw Larry and Russ were in at 14 under," Nicolette said. "I needed a birdie. I didn't get it. I didn't count on anyone shooting 63 and two of them did it."

In the playoff, Nicolette and Cochran had 25- and 30-foot putts for birdies and missed. Silveria made an eight-footer, and just like that, his bank account was increased by $54,000. "I knew I was going to make that putt," Silveria said. "Ever since I've been on tour I've dreamed of having just that type putt to win a tournament. I knew it was going in."

MCI Heritage Classic—$1,000,000
Winner: Davis Love III

In 1987, Davis Love III was standing near the scorer's tent, hard by Calibogue Sound, when his first PGA Tour victory, the MCI Heritage Classic, was gift-wrapped by Steve Jones' double bogey on the final hole. Four years later in the same place, Love won it the hard way. He earned it.

Love won in spite of a triple bogey at No. 8 that erased all but one of a four-shot lead, and he won in spite of losing that margin with a bogey at No. 11. He won because he is a better player than he was in 1987, when he was in his second year on the PGA Tour, and thought he could win with his awesome power rather than finesse.

He was never more than one shot out of the lead all week. He opened with 65 to tie Kirk Triplett for first place. He shot 68 Friday and was second by one stroke to Chip Beck, who with 64 was at 132. He regained the lead Saturday with another 68, and shot 70 Sunday for a 13-under-par 271 total to beat Ian Baker-Finch by one stroke.

Lanny Wadkins finished in third place, one stroke in front of Payne Stewart, who was seeking a third consecutive Heritage title but playing for the first time in two months due to a neck injury. He surprised everyone with his play, which was questionable in the beginning.

Also questionable was the strength of field, depleted by the exodus of the Europeans in general after the Masters, and of Ian Woosnam in particular. Tom Watson begged off after coming so close in Augusta, and Tuesday, Greg Norman and Curtis Strange sent their regrets.

What was left wasn't bad. There were 15 of the top-20 money winners, the first 16 in the U.S. Ryder Cup standings, and eight of the first 10 Americans in the Sony Ranking. But much of the sparkle was missing. But not for long. Those who did come put on quite a show.

Love reached both front-side par fives in two strokes for birdies Thursday, made his third birdie at No. 11, eagled the long 15th, holing a wedge shot from 105 yards, and capped off his round with a birdie at No. 17. Triplett struggled, but the result was the same, a bogey-free 65.

Storm clouds rolled in Friday, and heavy rains caused a three-hour delay in play, but when the day was done, Beck had shot 64 and moved to the front, one stroke in front of Love. Baker-Finch also had 64, moving from a tie for 97th into a tie for 12th place. Baker-Finch kept the heat on Saturday. He birdied four of the first six holes, and four more later, to shoot 65 and overtake all ahead of him except Love, whose 68 provided him with a three-shot lead.

On a sunny and breezy Sunday, Love stretched his lead to four strokes through seven holes, but it was only one a hole later when he made triple-bogey seven at No. 8. Baker-Finch tied him with a birdie at No. 9, and led after another birdie at No. 11.

Things happened rapidly after that. Love regained the lead with a birdie at No. 13, after Baker-Finch had three-putted for bogey. It was tied again after Baker-Finch birdied the 15th and Love didn't, the first time he hadn't birdied a par-five hole all week.

The tournament turned at No. 16, where Baker-Finch made a routine birdie and Love a spectacular one. From behind the tree at the corner, Love had to play a 30-yard hook and pulled it off, leaving himself a 10-foot birdie putt, which he made. "It was one of the best golf shots I've ever seen anywhere," Baker-Finch said. "He was dead. There was no way to get it close, but Davis did it. I thought I'd have at least a one-shot lead going to No. 17."

As it was, Love took a one-shot lead to the 18th. Both players missed the green at the 197-yard 17th. Baker-Finch couldn't get up and down from the back bunker, and Love did from the thick rough on the bunker's bank. Love routinely parred the 18th and Baker-Finch's bogey was meaningless.

"I'm just happy to get my name on the trophy a second time," said Love. "A lot of people said I backed into the first one, and I guess they might say I did again. But I went out and won today."

Kmart Greater Greensboro Open—$1,250,000
Winner: Mark Brooks

Before play began in the Kmart Greater Greensboro Open, Mark Brooks didn't need to be told why he had been struggling for the better part of the first four months of 1991. Reminded that his Sunday scoring average was a lofty 73.56, he nodded and said, "You don't have to tell me. I've lived it." Then Brooks went out and did something about it. In spectacular fashion, he won the tournament, beating Gene Sauers on the third playoff hole.

With his 64, Brooks bettered by nearly 10 shots his fourth-round scoring average, and along the way equaled the PGA Tour's longest streak of birdies for the year, six in a row.

That run broke Brooks' Sunday trend and temporarily ended a losing battle with obscurity. "My Sunday scoring average wasn't much better last year, but most of that was playing the last hole badly when I had a chance to win and took chances. Before today, it's been the entire round. My goal today was to break that trend," said Brooks, who won $225,000.

Until Sunday, however, Brooks was playing in obscurity. He opened with 71 and trailed Bob Wolcott by four strokes. A second-round 70 left him seven behind Sauers and Lanny Wadkins, who were tied at 134, and he was still seven strokes back after Saturday's third round, this time chasing Wolcott and Duffy Waldorf, who shot a course-record-tying 63 made up of eight birdies, one eagle and one bogey.

"Nothing happened for three days and frankly there was no indication it was going to get any better Sunday either. It was par, par, par for seven holes. Boring stuff until No. 8," Brooks said. "I was just treading water, then everything started going in."

His six-birdie string began with a 45-footer at No. 8, followed by putts of five feet, 18 feet, 15 feet, a 35-foot bunker shot and finally from 30 inches at No. 13. He was now three shots from the lead, and following a bogey at No. 14, he birdied three of the last four holes. That left him at 13 under par in the clubhouse, where he waited to see if anyone beat him.

Sauers came close. He had a three-foot birdie putt at No. 13 and missed it. Then missed his par putt. "I knew that I hadn't blown the tournament there," Sauers said. "But I knew it wasn't going to be good." It wasn't. He couldn't get that lost stroke back.

Brooks and Sauers parred the first two playoff holes, Nos. 17 and 18. Back to No. 17. Brooks found the left bunker, Sauers the right bunker. Sauers didn't make a 20-foot par putt. Brooks made his from five feet.

"My friends back home have always asked me what it's like to have a five-footer to win and I never could tell them," said Brooks, who is from Fort Worth, Texas. "Now I can. And what I'll tell them is, 'It's scary.'"

Though it was a twosome at the end, it had been a gangsome at other times Sunday. After nine holes, Wolcott led by one over Sauers, Waldorf and Sluman. Sluman was first to go with bogeys at Nos. 10 and 12. Waldorf, who had shot 63 in Saturday's third round, stumbled all the way to an incoming 40 and a closing-round 75. And Wolcott bogeyed two of the last five holes.

"Same old song for me," Wolcott said. "My trouble is putting four rounds together."

That's a song Brooks no longer has to sing.

GTE Byron Nelson Classic—$1,100,000
Winner: Nick Price

Nick Price hadn't won a golf tournament in so long he wasn't sure if he wasn't good enough to win, was afraid to win, or didn't have the desire to win. Once he decided all three were incorrect, he laid them all to rest by winning the GTE Byron Nelson Classic.

Price last had won in the 1983 World Series of Golf, shooting 10 under par and whipping the field by four shots. He shot 10-under at the TPC at Las Colinas, too, but it was no walk in the park, only a stroke better than Craig Stadler, who barely missed a tying birdie on the 72nd hole.

"I was so nervous playing the last two holes," said Price, who had rounds of 68-64-70-68 and won $198,000. "When you haven't won in so long, you begin to wonder if you'll ever win again. I kept questioning myself. Fortunately, I laid all that to rest this week."

Price's seven-year itch was caused by either a balky putter or, when it cooperated, someone played better. He led the 1989 British Open at Royal Lytham by two strokes after 54 holes and shot 69 in the final round. Only problem was Severiano Ballesteros shot 65. Price beat everyone else by four strokes, but lost by two.

He also finished second to Tom Watson at the 1982 British Open at Royal

Troon, and began this week chasing Watson again.

Watson led the first round, putting a 65 on the board and let the cold, windy, rainy weather protect it. He was one stroke in front of Lanny Wadkins, Mark Wiebe and Emlyn Aubrey.

Watson added a scrambling 69 Friday, but his 134 total fell two strokes shy of the lead, which Price assumed with a dream round of 64, leaving him at 132. It was a dream round because the likeable native of Zimbabwe took only 27 putts, which he said was about nine less than normal.

It was Tom Kite's turn at the top Saturday as the 41-year-old added his second straight 66 after an opening 68 and stood at 10-under-par 200, two strokes ahead of Price, Stan Utley, Mike Sullivan, Phil Blackmar and Bruce Lietzke. Price reached 11 under par through the first seven holes, but slipped on the back side and returned to the field.

"The lead is nothing," Kite said. "When I get in this position, I'm usually optimistic. But there's far too many people with a chance to win for me to feel comfortable. What have we got, 22 within five shots?"

Though Kite didn't know it at the time, he would be the focus of Sunday's final round, long before Price took his victory walk up the 18th fairway, needing only a par to win. Kite became the PGA Tour's first victim of instant replay, which left his face flushed.

Kite already had fallen behind Price by three strokes and was on his way to a closing 75 when he hit his drive at the par-four 11th hole. He and his playing partner, Blackmar, agreed that the ball crossed the hazard line before it hit water, meaning he could take a drop on the other side of the hazard. But George Boutell, the PGA Tour's rules official and designated monitor watcher, decided otherwise, determining it had not crossed the hazard line. That meant Kite had to play again from the tee.

The ruling resulted in a double bogey and one mad Mr. Kite. "I don't think TV has any business doing what it is doing," Kite said, furious that his judgement was questioned and overruled. "Putting an official in the TV trailer is a cop-out."

Bogey or double bogey, Kite wasn't going to catch Price, who made the turn in 10 under par after birdies at the eighth and ninth holes. He gave a stroke back at No. 10, made five straight pars, then birdied the 16th, breaking a tie with Stadler. He played to the middle of the greens on the last two holes and made routine pars to complete a tournament that in his eyes was anything but routine. He won it.

"Over the last few years, my wife kept telling me to hang in there," Price said. "My caddie kept telling me to hang in there. My teacher (David Leadbetter) kept telling me to hang in there. I was tired of hanging in there. I wanted to win!"

BellSouth Atlanta Classic—$1,000,000
Winner: Corey Pavin

Ever notice that each time Corey Pavin seems to get lost in the shadows cast by the giants of the PGA Tour, he does something that makes you wonder, "Now, where did he come from?"

It happened at this year's Bob Hope Classic where he was sure to lose in a playoff to Mark O'Meara. What does he do? He chips in for birdie from the rough in front of the green, and it's O'Meara who's left with a look of disbelief.

And it happened again in the BellSouth Atlanta Classic, also known as the Rain Suspended Open. For most of the final 36 holes, legendary Tom Kite and rising star Mike Springer bullied their way in and out of the lead, while Pavin seemed to plod along. So what happened? Pavin won it all. In a playoff again, on the second extra hole over friend and former UCLA team-mate Steve Pate, leaving Kite and Springer to wonder what went wrong.

Pavin never led at Atlanta Country Club until he won with a two-putt at the second playoff hole for par, after Pate couldn't get up and down from a buried lie in a bunker. When it was over, Pavin had shot 68-67-67-70— 272, 16 under par, he had won for the second time in 1991 and, with the $180,000 winner's share of the purse, climbed to No. 1 on the money list with a career-best $634,092.

"It was a strange day," Pavin said. "I didn't make a birdie for the last 10 holes and came away with the victory. My pars were good enough. I was the last one standing, I guess."

Strange, indeed.

For three rounds, the Atlanta Classic was golf's version of basketball's fast break, birdies coming with the ease of lay-ups. Then with the tournament on the line, the leaders went into their delay offense until Pavin broke loose to win it.

It easily could have been a foursome in the playoff, but third-round leader Kite and Springer, the midway leader, came apart on the closing holes. Kite shot 74 and Springer, 73, to tie for third place at 273 with Hale Irwin, who closed with 66.

Heavy rains, more than five inches the week before, left an already waterlogged Atlanta Country Club course like a bog. All four rounds were played under the lift, clean and place rule, which to golfers is like hunters shooting doves in a baited field. You can't miss.

Former Maryland golf coach Fred Funk shot an opening-round 62 to lead by two strokes over Kite. Pavin shot 68 and hardly anyone noticed. Springer came to the front Saturday with 63 and, at 131, led Kite by one stroke. Pavin had 67 and quietly moved into a tie for third place with Andrew Magee and Mike Standly at 135.

The third round was aborted at 2:35 p.m., when more than an inch of rain fell in a 10-minute period, making lakes in the bunkers and waterfalls from the hills. Only 19 golfers completed their rounds and 22 had played less than nine holes. Sunday's play began at 7 a.m. to conclude the third round. Kite finished in 67 for a 199 total to take a one-shot lead over Springer, who had 69. Pavin also had 67 and was at 202.

Twelve hours later, the birdie barrage was over. Kite and Springer made five between them. Pavin had two. After a birdie at No. 8, Pavin hit fairways and greens, but made no birdies and never trailed by more than two strokes.

Kite could have forced the issue, but did not. He had a two-shot lead over Springer after a birdie at No. 8, then began to unravel. He bogeyed Nos. 9 and 10 to hand Springer the lead, got a share of it back with a birdie at No. 14, then fell with three-putt bogeys at Nos. 16 and 17.

"I could have and should have won this tournament," Kite said later.

"There's no excuse for the way I played coming in."

Springer handled the lead like it was a hot poker. He made a double-bogey six at No. 15. Pate moved into a tie with Pavin with a birdie at No. 18, and the two headed for the playoff, beginning at No. 10, after Pavin failed to birdie the 18th.

It was over quickly. After both got up and down for par at No. 10, Pate drove into the left bunker at No. 16 and came up with a plugged lie. He gouged it out, but over the green, then left his chip 20 feet short. "I never considered not winning the tournament until I had a 20-foot putt for bogey in the playoff," Pate said. "Then reality set in."

Though the round began with Kite leading at 17 under par, it took only 16 under par to win. "If they had told me I could take 16 under and not play today, I wouldn't have taken it," Pavin said. "The way everybody was making birdies for three rounds, I thought it would take 20, 21 under to win. I'm surprised it didn't."

Memorial Tournament—$1,200,000
Winner: Kenny Perry

Common sense dictates that your average PGA Tour professional can't win one of the most prestigious events on one of the most difficult courses against one of the best fields assembled.

How then to explain that 30-year-old Kenny Perry, who hadn't won any-thing since he played the Space Coast mini-tour in 1986, won the Memorial Tournament at Muirfield Village Golf Club in sudden death over Hale Irwin, who just happens to be one of the greatest players of all time, not to mention the reigning U.S. Open champion?

"I always knew it was in me," Perry said of his improbable victory. "Before this week, I just kept getting in my own way. It was really neat. Winning is everything out here."

Perry did little in the first round to indicate that this would be his week. He opened with 70 and was tied for 17th place, four strokes behind Corey Pavin. He caught lightening in a bottle on Friday with a course-record 63 that propelled him to a three-shot lead over Chip Beck, then added rounds of 69 and 71 on the weekend and birdied the first playoff hole.

"Rounds like that 63 just happen," Perry said. "I've never seen so many balls go in the hole. The ball must have had a magnet in it. You can't say you'll go out and shoot 63. You can't say you'll go out and shoot 69. I didn't even know how many under par I was."

Tournament host Jack Nicklaus might have had something to say about who won this thing if he had putted well Friday. He hit 17 greens in regu-lation, but shot only 68 and was more than a little irritated at being six strokes behind Perry, rather than one or two. "I had one of those rounds where you feel like you turned 62 into 68," Nicklaus said. "It's one thing to have a chance to shoot a really low round, it's another thing to do it. Kenny did it. As well as he played today, I'm a little surprised he hasn't won out here."

Not only had Perry not won on the PGA Tour, he hadn't been close too often. But not this time. The challengers all tested Perry and he had survived long before he two-putted for birdie at No. 15, the playoff hole, to beat Irwin. "During five years of hard work, sometimes you don't feel like it will ever pay off," Perry said. "I showed myself I could finally do it."

Perry missed only nine fairways all week and used only 25 putts during each of the second and third rounds, and he made a hole-in-one at No. 16, which happens to be one of the hardest par-three holes around.

If there was any doubt that Perry wouldn't make the grade, it was erased Sunday afternoon. He didn't fold, even after hitting one into the lake at No. 9 and making double bogey, wiping out most of a three-shot lead. He answered another test when he came to the final hole tied with Irwin and needing a par. He responded with a perfect drive and a solid five-iron approach to 20 feet and almost made it.

There were a couple of other shots that were too good not to mention. Like the wedge shot to No. 11 that spun back for a two-foot birdie and the three-iron shot to No. 16—again—that resulted in a four-foot birdie. He bogeyed the 17th to fall back into a tie with Irwin, but that three-iron shot to No. 16 is not the kind of shot non-winners are supposed to hit down the stretch.

Any remaining doubt was erased by Perry's second shot on the playoff hole. With Irwin struggling, Perry boldly went for the green in two shots and left himself 30 feet past the hole. Once Irwin missed the green with his third shot, Perry lagged his eagle putt to two feet and that was that.

"I've always wondered what it would feel like to be able to two-putt from two feet and win. It was unbelievable," said Perry, who never won a tournament while playing golf at Western Kentucky. "It's a nice way to win, beating the U.S. Open champion. And what a great place to win your first tournament."

Perry credited his sudden good play—he had no top-10 finishes, three top 20s and missed four cuts this year—to putting. He changed everything, putter, grip and stance. The results spoke for themselves. He ranked 179th in putts per round before the Memorial, then averaged only 27 putts per round.

Southwestern Bell Colonial—$1,200,000
Winner: Tom Purtzer

If Ben Hogan had happened upon Tom Purtzer as he played the 13th hole Sunday at Colonial Country Club, he would have been impressed. For surely, what Purtzer manufactured would have given Hogan hope that this new breed can indeed come up with the improbable.

Seemingly with no shot from the bunker, Purtzer pulled out his putter, and from the downslope stroked it, then watched as it hopped over the lip, onto the green and rolled into the hole for a birdie-two. Five holes later, he was the Southwestern Bell Colonial winner.

"I couldn't do that again if I put another thousand balls in there," said Purtzer, who shot rounds of 70-66-67-64—267 and won by three strokes over Bob Lohr, Scott Hoch and David Edwards. "It was one for the books."

It was a shot worth seeing, and will be the one memory from this tournament that will linger. Purtzer's charge with a final-round 64 may be forgotten, along with the final-round fade by the 14 golfers who were ahead of Purtzer when the day began. Only one of them, Lohr, shot under par, and as a group, they compiled a cumulative Sunday total of 25 over par.

Purtzer had taken the lead from Lohr with four straight birdies beginning at No. 6, had added another at No. 11 and the miracle birdie at No. 13 put him two strokes ahead. He tried to give it away coming in with a bogey at No. 16 and some poor putting for pars at the others, but Lohr didn't make a birdie the last day after the seventh hole and bogeyed the 13th and 14th.

Lohr shot 63 Saturday to take the lead, but bogeyed the third hole and made no birdies on the back side when he needed birdies to keep pace with the flying Purtzer.

Gene Sauers, who fought a hook all week, began one shot back, but bogeyed four times during a seven-hole stretch, beginning at No. 9.

Mark Calcavecchia, Fred Funk, Stan Utley, Chris Perry and Keith Clearwater were two strokes back, but none threatened.

Calcavecchia, who shared the first-round lead with Funk and Peter Persons, was at first awful, with three consecutive bogeys early, then brilliant with birdies at Nos. 12, 13, 14 and 17. He was two strokes back playing No. 18, but sailed his approach over the green and into the water, made double bogey and lost $84,000. That was the difference between a sole second-place finish, which is what a par would have done, and his tie for fifth.

"I'm a mental basket case," Calcavecchia said. "I have the mind of a 12 year old, a total waste of space. Disgusting, absolutely disgusting. I don't even think I could win a Hogan event now. I would find some way to screw it up. It's disheartening. I've got the yips on my putts and the yips on my chips. I was just trying to hit the thing at the pin, an eight iron, for crying out loud, from the middle of the fairway, and I hit a 125-yard duck hook. Hell, I wasn't trying to win. I was just trying to hit the green."

Tom Watson was three strokes behind Purtzer, his playing partner, but hit his tee shot at No. 13 into the lake and made triple bogey.

That everyone backed up didn't really surprise Purtzer. He still remembered the double-bogey six he took on the final hole in Tucson, and handed the title to Phil Mickelson. "It's difficult being in the lead," he said, "especially after a round like Bob had Saturday. It puts a lot of pressure on you.

"You don't know if you'll ever win again. I had a great chance at Tucson and in a way, I gave it away. Tucson was the best I've ever hit the ball, and to come up empty, was kind of a letdown. I know how the guys here felt today."

Purtzer hopes this victory takes that pressure off. Either way, he will savor it a long time. "The shot at 13, I'll never forget," he said. "And it's a fantastic win. This is one of the places everybody wants to win. Everybody wants their name up on that wall."

Kemper Open—$1,000,000
Winner: Billy Andrade

Destiny rode again on the PGA Tour, this time with Billy Andrade in the saddle. Andrade returned sterling rounds of 68-64-64-67—263 around the TPC at Avenel in Potomac, Maryland, then beat his friend Jeff Sluman on the first playoff hole for his first Tour victory.

So, what's so special about that, you say. It happens all the time on the Tour, you say. Yes, but you haven't heard the rest of the story.

Consider: Andrade wasn't going to play in the Kemper Open, until he forgot to enter last week's Byron Nelson Classic.

Consider: In Sunday's final round, he hit a drive at No. 6, a par-five hole that the field had devoured all week, that was headed off the golf course before it bounced off a tree and hopped across a creek. He could have made a big number, but instead made a ho-hum birdie.

Consider: It took a spectator's casual remark ("Good showing anyway this week") after he missed a makeable birdie at No. 15 to start a birdie-birdie-par finish to tie Sluman, who could have won it outright had he not missed an eight-footer for birdie at No. 18.

Consider: Before the final round began, Sluman walked up to Andrade on the putting green and said, "C'mon, babe, you and me today."

Consider: An acknowledged poor long bunker player, he made par from not one, but two bunkers at No. 18 to stay alive.

Having taken advantage of all these elements for 72 holes, Andrade took it from there in the playoff. He nailed a six iron to within seven feet of the pin at No. 16 that put all kinds of pressure on Sluman, whose shot came up short and bounced off the bank and into the pond. "That's when I knew I had won the golf tournament," Andrade said. "I felt really bad for Jeff. I couldn't believe he went in the water. It's very difficult when you have to beat your best friend in a playoff."

For a while Sunday, it looked like Greg Norman and Hal Sutton would be the leading players. They had played together Saturday and shot matching 64s, and when the final round began Sutton was one ahead of Norman and Andrade. Sutton never got anything going and shot 71. Norman destructed on the back nine. He bogeyed the par-three 11th, didn't birdie the par-five 13th and hit his drive—a lay-up with a three iron—into the creek at No. 14 and made another bogey. He and Sutton tied for fourth place, one stroke behind Bill Britton. "Another disappointment, but it was a bittersweet week for me," said Norman. "I shot 17 under and could have won, but those other guys did what you have to do, and I congratulate them."

Prior to the Kemper, Andrade's only professional victory came in the 1987 Rhode Island Open, where he made all of $2,000. "I felt totally in control of things this week, but the thing that got me going was that spectator saying, 'Good showing, anyway,' after I didn't birdie 15," Andrade said. "It ticked me off. I felt I still had a chance to win. I won as a junior and as an amateur, but I really hadn't won where it counts, out here. Until you win here, you aren't fully respected by your peers. I wanted to become a winner and I worked toward that. Until you win, you don't know what it's like. Now I do."

Buick Classic—$1,000,000
Winner: Billy Andrade

Encore. Encore. It took Billy Andrade three years to win his first PGA Tour event and only a week to win his second. Once he got the hang of it, he realized it wasn't all that difficult after all.

Rising star? You could say that. Hardly anyone wins back-to-back events anymore. Hale Irwin did it in 1990—the U.S. Open and Buick—and Tom Kite the year before won The Nestle Invitational and Tournament Players Championship. But those are veterans. Andrade's only been out here for three years or so.

You want more. Consider this. The day after he won the Kemper Open playoff, Andrade played 36 holes in qualifying for the U.S. Open and shot 10 under par. He then played two five-hour pro-ams on Tuesday and Wednesday. A little advice from Jay Haas helped Andrade on the eve of the Buick Classic's opening round. "I know you're tired," Haas said, "but you should hang in there. The best time to win your second one is right after your first."

And so Andrade did. He opened with 68, two off the pace of Paul Azinger, Fulton Allem, Brad Bryant and Chris Perry. Another 68 left him two strokes behind Azinger, Perry and Dennis Watson, and a third-round 69 put him three strokes behind Irwin. "I was just holding on and not really concerned with winning like at the Kemper," Andrade said. "But I was hitting the ball solid and putting well. Then on the back nine Sunday, things just fell into place for me."

Andrade came to the back nine Sunday wrestling for the lead with Irwin, Bryant and Seve Ballesteros, and let them make the mistakes. Irwin was tied for the lead going to the final nine and was quickly joined by Nolan Henke, who eagled the ninth and birdied the 10th. Ballesteros joined the fray with a birdie at No. 10, and when Andrade also birdied No. 10, he had a one-shot lead.

The pursuers fell back, one by one. Ballesteros was first. He drove into the rough at No. 12 and bogeyed it for the fourth straight day, then hit three greenside bunkers on his way in. Irwin was next. He also bogeyed the 12th and later three-putted the 15th for another bogey and slipped back. Henke bogeyed Nos. 13 and 14. Only Bryant held on, but he left a couple of short putts short and finally dropped from the lead with a three-putt bogey at No. 15.

Andrade played solid golf coming in. He did make a bogey at No. 12, but regained the lead with a birdie at No. 15 and widened it to two strokes when Bryant bogeyed it. Andrade probably won the tournament at No. 16, where he made only a bogey from double-bogey range when he made a remarkable recovery from a downhill lie in the greenside bunker. "One of the scariest shots I've ever had," Andrade said later. "I could have made a big number."

From there, Andrade parred the 17th and had only a tap-in birdie at the short par-five 18th for a three-under 68. It was a clutch performance compared to the other 10 leading contenders going into the final round. Henke, who shot 70, fired the only other sub-par round, while as a group, the 10 shot 16 over par. "I'm exhausted. I'm about ready to drop," Andrade said. "I haven't had a day off in two weeks or slept a whole lot."

Looking at the last two weeks, you find that Andrade was rolling. He was 21 under par at the Kemper Open and birdied the first playoff hole to beat Jeff Sluman. He shot 10 under par in the U.S. Open qualifying and was 11 under par in the Buick Classic. That's 181 holes in 43 under par.

"Before last Sunday, there was doubt if my swing could hold up under pressure, could my putting hold up, could I hold up," Andrade said. "Until you win, you don't know. Kemper convinced me I could do all those things."

He held up two weeks in a row, won $360,000 and moved into seventh place on the money list and had the hot hand at the right time, with the U.S. Open next. Andrade missed the cut at The Country Club in 1988 in his only other U.S. Open appearance.

"The best time to win your third is right after you win your second," Andrade said. "Only joking, but if I can get a little rest, I'll go the Open thinking anything can happen."

Anheuser-Busch Classic—$1,000,000
Winner: Mike Hulbert

You could call Mike Hulbert's victory in the Anheuser-Busch Classic a shot in the dark and it would have nothing to do with his chances of winning and everything to do with reality. For it was a four-foot putt he made under near-dark conditions on the first hole of a playoff that did it.

It was past 8 p.m. when Hulbert made the putt that broke the heart of Kenny Knox, who didn't want to start the playoff under those conditions and felt in losing that he was more the victim of circumstances than anything else.

Both players, especially Knox, had only themselves to blame to still be out there at such a late hour. Playing a group ahead, Hulbert came to the final hole tied with Knox and made bogey when he missed the green and left his 12-foot par putt short. Then came Knox, who left his approach shot short of the green and failed to get up and down. "I wasn't enthusiastic about going back out for a playoff," Knox said. "I wanted to come back and finish Monday morning, but the tournament officials said we had time to get one hole in."

But Hulbert was ready to go. "I didn't want to come back. I was glad we went out."

Attitude isn't everything, but maybe it made the difference this time. After Hulbert drove in the middle of the fairway, Knox pushed his tee shot close to a cart path. He got a drop, but couldn't see several twigs. His ball hit one of them and caromed into deep grass on a severe downhill lie. "I guess that's what happens when you're in the woods at eight o'clock at night," said Knox, who missed the green short and then left his pitch 19 feet short.

Hulbert hit the green with a seven iron, 15 feet from the hole. Knox narrowly missed his long par putt. Hulbert thought he had made it. So did Knox. "I hit the ultimate putt," Knox said. Hulbert ran his first putt four feet past the hole, but made it coming back for the victory.

"Neither one of us had any momentum going to the playoff, so I thought whoever executed better on the first hole had a good shot at winning," Hulbert said.

"I was a victim of circumstances," Knox said. "But it could have worked out the other way just as easily."

Several other players had a chance to win Sunday, but couldn't pull it off. Fuzzy Zoeller and Ian Baker-Finch came closest, finishing tied for third place, one back. Zoeller made the strongest bid. He started the last round six shots off the pace and pulled within one with a birdie at No. 17. But like Hulbert and Knox, Zoeller couldn't close the deal. He drove wild right and came up short on his approach. His bold chip shot hit the hole and spun out, going five feet past. Zoeller missed the come-backer for 65, the day's best round but one stroke short. Dan Pohl, coming off major surgery on his back that kept him off the Tour for more than a year, faltered in the final round. After scoring a tournament-record 17-under-par 196 total for a two-shot lead after 54 holes, Pohl drifted back to a tie for eighth place with a closing 77.

Hulbert jumped into the fray with an eagle at No. 7 and a birdie at No. 9 to get to four under par on his round, then made eight straight pars until the 18th. Looking back, Knox could see past No. 18 and find where he lost it—a three-putt at No. 11 from 12 feet for a double bogey.

They finished at 266, 18 under par, tying the tournament record set by Lanny Wadkins in 1990. Due to the soft conditions, the course was like a shooting gallery. Baker-Finch shot 62 in the opening round to tie the course record and Knox and Brian Claar duplicated it in the third round.

For Hulbert, the victory was the end of a long, long day. He was one of 14 golfers who had to be at the course at 8 a.m. to complete the third round. Then came a two-hour rain delay and finally the playoff. Still, it was worth the wait. Two years ago he had three-putted No. 16 and bogeyed the 18th to miss a playoff. "I felt I gave it away then. Today I was more patient," Hulbert said of his third career victory.

Westinghouse-Family House Invitational—$700,000
Winner: Ian Baker-Finch

Ian Baker-Finch had never seen revered Oakmont Golf Club until he arrived in Pittsburgh for the $700,000 Westinghouse-Family House Invitational. After two days there, Baker-Finch was not likely to forget it.

In shooting rounds of 65 and 69 for a 134 total, Baker-Finch had one bogey on the first hole the first day, nine birdies and 26 pars. He missed only three fairways, one by 10 yards, the other two by inches. And he beat a field that included Raymond Floyd, Bob Tway, Fred Couples, Curtis Strange, Tom Kite and Fuzzy Zoeller. His margin of victory was three shots over Mike Donald.

Baker-Finch felt a little heat only in the first round, when Scott Hoch ravaged the front nine in seven-under-par 29, which included an eagle two and a hole-in-one. But he cooled to 37 coming in, then went into the deep freeze with 73 in the second round.

Even if the event was only a two-day benefit outing, Baker-Finch was no less inspired. "To win on Oakmont, to play so well on a great course is uplifting. It has to boost my confidence," said Baker-Finch, who won $140,000.

Federal Express St. Jude Classic—$1,000,000
Winner: Fred Couples

They've always said of Fred Couples that no matter how he's playing, he always looks calm, cool and collected. Well, two out of three wasn't bad at the St. Jude Classic, where Couples was playing very, very well in his normal calm and collected way. But cool? No way, not on the almost shadeless

Tournament Players Club at Southwind, not when the temperature is straining to reach 100 degrees.

"The only thing that bothered me was the heat. It was tiring," said Couples after he tacked a final-round 68 onto earlier rounds of 68-67-66 for a 15-under-par 269 total and an easy three-shot victory over Rich Fehr.

Everything else was a walk in the park, as Couples won his second tournament of the year and for the fifth time in his career, collecting $180,000 in the process. His final round wasn't flashy. There were no streaks of brilliance, no moments of high drama. He didn't have the best round any of the four days, but no one else recorded four sub-70 rounds.

If the tournament was won by consistency, it was overrun by inconsistency. Jim Thorpe tied Rich Fehr for the first-round lead with 64, then finished with three rounds over par. Jim Woodward tied the course record with a second-round 62, but he also had a pair of 77s and tied for 69th.

"I had a lot of pars on the first 11 holes," Couples said of his 11 straight pars to begin Sunday's round. Then he mixed in three birdies—no bogeys—over the final seven holes, the first coming at No. 12, where he made a 20-foot putt after a 130-yard fairway bunker shot. "Biggest shot I hit all day," Couples said.

During Couples' streak of pars, Peter Persons went from one stroke behind to one ahead. He took over with a birdie at No. 4 and held on through No. 8, but from there nothing went right as the third-year pro played the next 10 in six over par for 74 and a tie for 10th place.

Persons' demise was typical of the day. Second-round co-leader Fuzzy Zoeller began three strokes back and got within two strokes before his game collapsed with two double bogeys midway through the back nine. He shot 74 and tied for 17th place.

Hal Sutton, who started the round tied with Persons one behind Couples, had made enough birdies, 19, the first three rounds to run away with the lead, but didn't because of eight bogeys. He continued his erratic play sans birdies and shot 75, tied for 13th place.

Those who did play well Sunday had too much ground to make up. Jay Haas and David Canipe shot 67s and were only two strokes behind Couples when they finished, but Couples was only at No. 14. When the two co-leaders in the clubhouse heard a roar from that direction, Canipe said, "It's his tournament to lose." Haas was more to the point. "It's hard to see him making any bogeys the rest of the way. I'd like to be in his shoes, with his swing, with his nerves."

The only major development down the stretch was Rich Fehr finishing with 67 to take second place. "I played great, but never gave a thought to Freddie collapsing," Fehr said. "He's too solid."

Add to that relaxed and unruffled, two things his critics hold against him. "They say I don't practice very hard, that I play early in the year and take the rest of the year off. They say I don't want to win," Couples said. "But I know how much of myself I give out there. I just try to stay as relaxed as I can."

Centel Western Open—$1,000,000

Winner: Russ Cochran

At first glance, Russ Cochran looked out of place when play began in the final round of the Centel Western Open. There he was, a nine-year veteran who had never finished higher than 51st on the money list, tied for the lead in one of the PGA Tour's oldest tournaments with two of the game's golden boys, Greg Norman and Fred Couples.

"I was in a position where no matter what I did, I couldn't lose," Cochran said. "If I choked nobody would notice. There was no pressure on me. Nobody was picking me. And all that probably made it a little easier on me."

No question about it, being overshadowed by his playing partners' considerable reputations allowed Cochran to hide in the background, and when Norman and Couples fell away down the stretch, the 32-year-old Kentuckian was there to pick up the pieces as well as his first victory.

Couples gradually fell behind early and never clawed his way more than halfway back, while Norman self-destructed when it appeared there was no way he could lose. In the end, Couples shot 72 for 278; Norman, 71 for 277, and Cochran a workman-like 69 for 275 and a $180,000 check, the largest of his career.

Both losers were gracious in defeat. "Give Russ credit, he was there the whole day, didn't make any mistakes," Norman said. "I'm happy for Russ. He outplayed us both all day," Couples said.

Cochran had been where they've been. "I've blown a couple in my days and had a few stolen," he said. "I've learned the hard way that to win out here, the best thing you can do is just hit good, solid shots down the stretch."

This Western Open was significant in another way. The tournament had been forced from its home of 17 years, Butler National, when that all-male club refused to immediately conform to the PGA Tour's new anti-discriminatory policy. Officials relocated to Cog Hill, a 72-hole daily fee facility, and set up shop at the 7,040-yard Dubsdread Course, one of the finest, public or private, in Illinois.

Cog Hill was a big hit from the beginning, especially when Norman became a late entry, playing for the first time since an injury caused him to withdraw from the U.S. Open. It took him only two rounds to stir up the galleries. After an opening 69, which left Norman three strokes back of the 66-shooting Cochran, Mark Lye, Mike Sullivan and Raymond Floyd, Norman posted a sparkling, no-bogey, six-birdie 66 to take the lead by two strokes over Lye. Cochran and Couples were within three shots.

Norman slipped a little Saturday, shooting 71 as sunny, windswept Dubsdread grew firm and dryer. He was at 10-under-par 206, but had company from Cochran and Couples, whose reputation had taken a beating earlier in the year.

After a fast start to the season, Couples had a stretch of seven tournaments in which he finished no higher than 12th place and his stroke average jumped from 68.8 to 70.4. Plus, he was criticized severely by Tom Weiskopf and Tony Jacklin in a couple of monthly golf publications. But he quieted some critics with his victory last week in Memphis.

Cochran was the pest in the group, like one of those flies that won't go away. But he sounded less than enthusiastic about his chances. "I haven't won and they've won a bunch," he said. "I don't have any of that experience to draw off of."

The way Norman started Sunday, it didn't seem to matter who he was playing. He birdied the first two holes, made an eagle two at the fourth and birdied the fifth to go 15 under par for the tournament. By the 11th tee, he was 16 under and ahead by five strokes.

"The way Greg was playing, I didn't see any way either of us could win," Cochran said of himself and Couples. "He was pretty amazing. Then all of a sudden, he lost it. Just like that, he didn't know where it was going."

After Cochran picked up a shot with a birdie at No. 12, Norman began to lose it. At No. 13, Norman found the hazard, made bogey and Cochran pulled to within three shots. Both bogeyed No. 14, but Cochran cut off two more strokes at the par-five 15th, where he made an up-and-down birdie and Norman's adventure among the bushes and rocks cost him a bogey.

Norman's misery reached its zenith at the 16th, where from the right rough he hit a flier over the green, through a bunker, up a hill and under a woman's purse, leading to a fourth straight bogey. Cochran became the leader when he coaxed home a 35-foot birdie.

Norman had now thrown away a five-shot lead in six holes, and Cochran's two steady pars coming in were good enough to seal the victory.

And what of Couples? After being trampled by Norman's early rush, he was never able to close the gap between himself and the leader to less than two strokes. Ugly approach shots to the 13th and 16th did him in.

"I always thought I could win out here," Cochran said. "But to be honest when Greg got off to such a great start, I didn't think it would be this week. But I kept plugging, and here I am."

New England Classic—$1,000,000
Winner: Bruce Fleisher

We all know that life begins at 50 on the Senior PGA Tour, but when was the last time life began at 42 for someone on the PGA Tour? Until Bruce Fleisher, the answer is never.

Remember Fleisher? He was a rising young star back in 1968 when he won the U.S. Amateur, but a bust for the next 12 years as a member of the PGA Tour. But after spending the last seven years as a club pro, he's back at 42, courtesy of a most improbable victory—his first—in the New England Classic.

"This is crazy," Fleisher said after surviving a zany seven-hole playoff against Ian Baker-Finch. "Today is a real dream come true. This is a fairy tale."

The finish was unbelievable. After starring defeat in the eye time and time again, Fleisher made a 50-foot putt that appeared to miss but at the last instant dropped into the back of the cup. "It was huge, a great effort by Bruce," said Baker-Finch, who before the week had only heard Fleisher's name, but couldn't remember where or when. "He looked like he was losing it a couple of times. It's a fantastic victory for him. It gives him a new start on a career."

As a tournament winner, Fleisher has two years of PGA Tour exemptions.

It got him into the World Series of Golf, where he made his last Tour check, $8,000, as the reigning PGA Club Pro champion. It gets him into the Masters for the first time since 1969, then as the U.S. Amateur champion. And he qualified for the Tournament of Champions.

But most of all, it got Fleisher off the Ben Hogan Tour, where he was hoping to finish among the top-20 money winners and into the final portion of the PGA Tour qualifying tournament. Fleisher had hoped to work his way back to the Tour slowly, to prepare for the Senior Tour. But he didn't expect to get there so soon, if at all. "I'd be stupid to say I'm not going to play the Tour now," he said. "I can't sit here and say, 'Hey, I don't have it yet.' I showed myself I do have it, although I'm aware I have some weaknesses in my game."

Fleisher would find it difficult to say that he climbed back onto the Tour over the backs of the game's best players. They weren't here this week, the week before the British Open. Only four of the top-25 money winners showed up. Only four of the top-50 players in the Sony Ranking came by, and none of the top 24. Not many in the field knew who Fleisher was, even after an opening 64 gave him a one-shot lead over such luminaries as Ted Schulz, Blaine McCallister, Ernie Gonzalez and Dennis Watson.

The most recent additions to Fleisher's portfolio were as defending champion of the Bahama, Jamaican and Brazilian Opens. Before that, he was the PGA National Club Pro champion in 1989. He tied for third place in the last two Hogan events and ranked 39th on its money list. His closest brush with PGA Tour fame came in the 1974 Quad Cities Open, where he three-putted the final green and lost by one stroke to Dave Stockton. The $180,000 he won here this week was more than a third as much as his career total.

And to think, he almost didn't make the field. He was the last alternate to get in, courtesy of Bobby Cole's withdrawal Tuesday afternoon. Still, early Sunday, it appeared all Fleisher would get was an "atta boy, good playing, anyway." Gene Sauers appeared to have his name ready to go on the winner's check, holding a two-shot lead heading to the back nine. But as Sauers has proven before this year, he can't always close the deal.

Fleisher caught Sauers with three birdies, the last one a clutch six-footer at No. 18, just as Sauers and Baker-Finch bogeyed the 16th. Baker-Finch forced the playoff with a two-putt birdie at No. 18, while Sauers missed a 30-foot birdie try.

That Fleisher won in the playoff is even more amazing. He got up and down from a bunker at No. 10, while Baker-Finch missed a 10-foot birdie putt. He two-putted from 70 feet on the second hole, making a five-footer for par, and Baker-Finch barely missed from 12 feet for birdie. He made another saving four-footer at the third to stay alive. On the fourth hole, he nearly dunked his eight-iron second shot after Baker-Finch drove deep into the right woods. He made bogey and let Baker-Finch off the hook. Back at No. 10, again, his second shot narrowly avoided careening down a huge, wooded hill and he got up and down, making another four-footer, while Baker-Finch left his eight-foot birdie putt hanging on the lip. Finally, at the last hole, Fleisher made his 50-footer, a no-brainer if ever there was one, leaving the winner jumping in the air. "God, that was a good putt," the winner said.

"Look where he made fours from," Baker-Finch said, almost in disbelief.

"At No. 10, I thought it was over there. I felt great. Then on the 50-footer, it's going six feet past. I didn't think it had a chance. I don't think Bruce did either. I hit a lot of good putts. I was just unlucky."

Chattanooga Classic—$700,000
Winner: Dillard Pruitt

Say what you will about the competitive nature of the players on the PGA Tour, it doesn't keep them from helping their fellow pros work out problems in their games. Take Dillard Pruitt, for example. Before coming to the Chattanooga Classic, Pruitt was in a slump that saw him miss two consecutive cuts. Tips from Billy Ray Brown and brother-in-law Jay Haas helped Pruitt to shoot a tournament-record-tying 260 total, 20 under par, on rounds of 66-65-65-64 to win the tournament.

As usual, this was a shootout over the 6,641-yard Valleybrook Country Club course. Marco Dawson shot a course-record 61 to lead the first round by two strokes over Ted Schulz, Steve Lowery and Lee Janzen. Lennie Clements took over at the halfway mark, adding 62 to his opening 65 for 13-under-par 127, and predicted that it might take 20-under to be in the lead going to Sunday.

There's something about the weekend that brings caution to the field and Lance Ten Broeck took the 54-hole lead at only 15-under 195, one stroke ahead of Pruitt, who shot his second consecutive 65. "I really didn't think the scores would be so low this year," said Pruitt before Sunday's final round. "There's more rough and the golf course is playing longer. It just goes to show you what these guys can do."

Pruitt wasted no time Sunday in showing what he could do. His key to victory came early—birdie, birdie, birdie, birdie. Only one of those putts was from inside 15 feet. "That start took a lot of pressure off me," Pruitt said. "It wasn't like I had a cushion, but when you start the final round with four birdies, it gives you a lot of confidence. I needed it because Lance came back to within one at No. 15, but I held on."

Pruitt never lost the lead after his birdie binge start, but Ten Broeck remained uncomfortably close with birdies at Nos. 2 and 5, and Brad Fabel made it a threesome when he got to 16 under par at No. 12. He was gone two holes later, however, courtesy of a double bogey. Ten Broeck made the mistake he couldn't afford with a bogey at No. 11, leaving him two strokes behind. He came back to birdie No. 15 and close within one, but bogeyed the 18th as Pruitt easily two-putted for the victory.

Pruitt credited Brown and Haas for his play. "Billy Ray watched me hack it around last week and suggested I move the ball back in my stance," Pruitt said. "I'd been going pretty good up until Memphis, but awful since then. With Billy Ray's tip, I go from missing two cuts to playing it 20 under. And Jay noticed I was moving my head when I putted. I didn't putt great this week, but it was a whole lot better than before I got here."

Canon Greater Hartford Open—$1,000,000
Winner: Billy Ray Brown

Better golfers than Billy Ray Brown have gone nuts trying to figure out this crazy game of golf, so he wasn't even going to try after winning the Greater Hartford Open. The 28-year-old former NCAA champion came here ranked 172nd out of 175 on the PGA Tour in putting. What did he do but make a clutch 10-footer for par on the last hole to tie Rick Fehr and Corey Pavin, and followed with a 25-footer on the first playoff hole to win.

"You figure it out. I can't," said Brown, who shot rounds of 67-72-65-67—271 over the par-70 TPC at River Highlands in Cromwell, Connecticut. "I've been struggling for four years to win a tournament and then the weakest part of my game becomes my strength when I needed it and I win. It's a crazy game."

It couldn't have come at a better time. The Greater Hartford Open was the last tournament in which to qualify for the PGA Championship. The top-70 players on the money list were eligible and Brown needed to make $50,000 to qualify. He made it with $130,000 to spare. It wasn't that easy. At one point Sunday, there was a seven-way tie for first place.

Billy Andrade made an early charge and drove the short par-four 15th hole, but then three-putted for par and lipped out a 15-footer for birdie at No. 18 to finish one shot out of the playoff.

Jim Gallagher, Jr., looked like a winner when he holed out for eagle at No. 14 to take the lead at 10 under par. But, he finished a shot behind after making bogey at the easy 15th hole then missed a short par putt at No. 18.

Scott Hoch disappeared with a pair of triple bogeys at Nos. 10 and 13. Dan Pohl was tied for the lead after he birdied No. 16, then finished bogey, bogey. Ken Green, a Connecticut native, charged to within one shot of the lead through No. 15, but bogeyed Nos. 16 and 18.

The course may have had something to do with these disasters. Of the 11 leading contenders going into Sunday, only four shot under par, and as a group, they played six over par. Brown's 67 was low round of the day.

Brown was lurking, but that's about all until Sunday. Jim Hallet shot 64 to lead the first round by one stroke over Pavin, Hoch, Dillard Pruitt and Mark Calcavecchia. Pavin took over the lead on Friday with 67 for 132, one stroke ahead of Billy Mayfair, Gallagher and Hoch. Then it was Fehr's turn. A 66 left him at nine-under 201, ahead by one shot over Pavin. Brown was three strokes back.

Fehr could have won at No. 18, but his 10-footer just slid by the hole. Pavin got in the playoff with a clutch 30-footer at No. 18. On the playoff hole, Fehr was first to miss, from 30 feet. After Brown watched his 25-footer curl around the hole and fall, he held his breath until Pavin's 20-footer drifted right of the cup. "It felt incredible," Brown said. "When you're 172nd of 175 in putting, that's not good. That means I'm only better than three guys, but I made the key putts this week."

With his victory, Brown was finally able to bury his 1990 U.S. Open memories. He missed a 10-footer for birdie on the 72nd hole that left him one shot out of the playoff with Mike Donald and eventual winner Hale Irwin. "I thought about that putt every day for probably eight months," Brown said. "Now, I have one to take its place, a much sweeter one."

Buick Open—$1,000,000
Winner: Brad Faxon

If a player is measured not by winning a tournament but by whom he beat to get there, then Brad Faxon has moved up a rung on the ladder of respect. He won the Buick Open, shooting a six-under-par 66 in the final round to come from five shots behind and beat Chip Beck in a playoff and the rest of the field that included Greg Norman and Nick Faldo.

Faldo, coming off clutch birdies at Nos. 16 and 17 and needing a birdie at No. 18 to join the playoff, hit a terrible drive and made bogey instead. Norman led after 36 holes, but went into a weekend slide with a pair of 71s and tied for 10th place.

Faldo was here preparing his game for next week's PGA Championship and despite his last-hole collapse was upbeat about his chances in the season's final major. "I managed to sort out a lot of things on the back nine," he said. "I putted 100 percent better than I did in the British Open. It was a good productive week and I look forward to the PGA Championship. This was a little tweak of fine-tuning before a major and I'm optimistic I'll play well."

Norman's presence was a boost to attendance, but he did little to boost his game. His Saturday's round was marked by a par on the easy 13th hole and a bogey on the 322-yard 14th hole, the shortest par four on the course. Attempting to drive the green, he drove it the only place you can't hit it— right, behind a large cottonwood tree—and wasn't in contention again.

Beck, trying to become the first back-to-back Buick Open champion since Tony Lema in 1964-65, birdied the last hole to shoot 271, one stroke better than he did in winning last year and it got him only into a playoff.

Still, Beck was probably the favorite to win the playoff, and he looked good when he drove it perfectly on the playoff hole and Faxon found the left rough. After Faxon flew an eight-iron approach shot within 30 feet of the hole, Beck hit a poor nine-iron shot, barely making the green, 60 feet from the hole. Faxon two-putted, and Beck three-putted.

It was the Buick Open's first playoff since 1981, when Hale Irwin defeated Peter Jacobsen, Bobby Clampett and Gil Morgan, and was a fitting climax to one of the best Buick Opens ever.

For Faxon, victory meant entry into the World Series of Golf, the Tournament of Champions, the Masters and a lot of other perks that go to tournament winners. "I got good breaks all week," Faxon said. "I shot 29 when I was sick, I started birdie, birdie Sunday, and after a bogey at No. 4, I birdied Nos. 6 and 8, and there aren't many birdies made there, and I holed a wedge shot for eagle at No. 14. I guess that's how you win tournaments."

Faxon was three strokes behind Scott Hoch's 63 on Thursday, and two behind on Friday, with Norman leading by one stroke over Hoch. He was five shots back after Saturday, as Marco Dawson fought his way to the top with 64. "When you're that far back, all you can do is let it fly," Faxon said. "I birdied the first two holes and never hit many bad shots, and when I did I got away with them. But with so many good players between me and the lead, well, you don't really think about winning."

Faxon put himself in position to win on the second nine. He saved par at No. 12 with a 10-foot putt, birdied the 13th, made an eagle at No. 14 and birdied No. 16, remembering a putt he made there in the 1983 Buick Open.

He closed out the round with a six-foot par putt, and waited.

For Faxon, who was 73rd on the money list, it was like winning a major championship. He had been hearing a lot of questions from New Englanders who wondered why Faxon, three years older than his pal and fellow Rhode Islander Billy Andrade, wasn't winning. "I couldn't find my shadow this year," Faxon said. "Winning is how people get measured. Everyone back home wondered why I wasn't winning. But that's golf. The first one was hard and a long time coming. Maybe it'll be easier from now on."

The International—$1,100,000
Winner: Jose Maria Olazabal

It is said that the one thing that separates the best European golfers from the best Americans is their ability to create shots. "Nothing bothers them," Jack Nicklaus has said. "They have more imagination than we do. It's something our guys should learn to do."

After the shot Jose Maria Olazabal played on the 17th hole in the final round of The International, maybe more Americans will sit up and take notice. Olazabal came to the vulnerable 492-yard, par-five 17th tied for the lead with Ian Baker-Finch, who just a couple of weeks earlier won the British Open. Fighting his driver all week, the Spaniard hit his tee shot into the left rough, 213 yards from the green. There seemingly was no way for Olazabal to work his second shot around the hill that stood in his way.

Many players would have conceded the chance to make a birdie and simply pitched back into the fairway. But Olazabal would not take the easy way out. If he couldn't go around the hill, maybe he could go over it.

So Olazabal climbed the hill—rattlesnakes be damned—and took a view. He saw that if he hit a six iron just right, it should clear the hill, miss the pines on the left and land somewhere close to the green. And it did.

"It wasn't the only shot I had, but it was the best I had if I wanted to win the tournament," Olazabal said. "I had a good lie. The ball was like on a tee."

His shot was short of the green, but any man who has enough imagination to get it there should be able to get down in two strokes, which Olazabal did for his birdie. That, combined with Baker-Finch's bogey at No. 16, was good enough for the victory.

"It was the key shot in the tournament," Olazabal said. "Last year I came to this hole with a chance to win and hit it right and had no chance. I made double bogey. Today, I stood on the tee and said, 'Don't miss it right.' I missed it left." It hardly mattered. Olazabal's 10 points was the lowest winning total in the six-year history of the tournament and his margin of victory was three points over Baker-Finch, Bob Lohr and Scott Gump.

Under the modified Stableford system of scoring, a par was worth nothing; a birdie, two points, and an eagle, five points. One point was deducted for bogey and three for any score worse than bogey. There were cuts after 36 holes and after 54 holes, then the 24 survivors started even for the final 18 holes.

Considering what had gone before, a shootout was expected. In the first round, Keith Clearwater had a record 18 points, and Ricky Kawagishi had

16 points on Thursday. Bobby Clampett led after 54 holes with 29 points, but all it got him was a late tee time for the final round.

Olazabal put his 10 points on the board early and retired to the locker room, certain that the best he could hope for was a playoff. There was no way, he thought, that 10 points would win, not with Baker-Finch behind him with eight points and the 17th hole to play.

It was enough, however. Baker-Finch bogeyed No. 16 to drop to seven points, then managed only a par and no points at No. 17 after he drove into the left rough and made par, which was followed by another par at No. 18.

"I didn't think it was that hard out there," Baker-Finch said. "The scores should have been lower. I suppose I should be happy with second place, but I'm disappointed with the way I finished. A par-birdie-par finish isn't that difficult to do."

Others had their chances, too. Tom Watson, Larry Mize, Ted Schulz and Clampett to name four, but they frittered it away before getting to the final three.

"To win in the States is great," said Olazabal, who last year put a hurting on the world's best in the World Series of Golf, winning by 12 strokes. "I'd like to play a year over here because it doesn't matter what tournament you play, the field is strong every week."

Fred Meyer Challenge—$700,000
Winners: Paul Azinger/Ben Crenshaw

It says in the PGA Tour book that Ben Crenshaw never has won a sudden-death playoff. Zero-for-seven. Those numbers are still the same in the PGA Tour book, but the way Crenshaw sees it, he's now one-for-eight after a 35-foot birdie putt on the second extra hole enabled him and Paul Azinger to beat Fred Couples and Raymond Floyd in the Fred Meyer Challenge.

Peter Jacobsen's annual best-ball tournament at Portland Golf Club in Portland, Oregon, finished in a three-way tie at 19 under par. Mark Calcavecchia and Bob Gilder, who led most of the final round, were eliminated on the first extra hole.

Floyd and Couples, the defending champions, had a chance to win in regulation after Floyd hit a three-wood second shot to within 10 feet on the par-five 18th hole. But Floyd missed the putt.

"When Raymond hits a shot like that, he usually finishes it off," said Crenshaw, whose three-footer a moment later gave him and Azinger a share of the lead. "He played a gorgeous shot in, but he didn't have that usual look in his eye when he was over the putt. Maybe that's why he missed it."

Then Floyd and Couples had a chance to win on the first playoff hole, but both missed almost identical 10-foot birdie putts.

Crenshaw didn't miss anything. He birdied five of the last seven holes, including the 35-footer that won it. "My partner was unbelievable, just to get us a tie in regulation," Azinger said. "Then he made that little bitty guy on No. 17 (second playoff hole) to win it. Nobody, but nobody, can putt like my man Ben."

It was the kind of putt that Crenshaw loves. "It went up over a little bit of a hill and then went a little bit down," he said. "I had a good feel today for the most part. I saw it go out about halfway and thought it looked pretty good, and about three-quarters of the way, it looked better."

This was one of the more competitive Fred Meyer Challenge events. Couples and Floyd shot 62 to lead the first round, one stroke in front of Azinger and Crenshaw, Calcavecchia and Gilder, Chip Beck and Tim Simpson, and Wayne Levi and Gil Morgan.

It quickly became a three-team race early in the second round. Calcavecchia and Gilder held a two-shot lead early on the back nine but leveled off, and were caught at No. 18 by the birdies of Crenshaw and Floyd.

NEC World Series of Golf—$1,200,000
Winner: Tom Purtzer

Now we know just how great a performance Spain's Jose Maria Olazabal put on in last year's NEC World Series of Golf, with rounds of 61-67-67-67 for an 18-under-par 262 total.

This year, Tom Purtzer won at one under par, shooting 72-69-67-71—279. Then Purtzer defeated Davis Love III and Jim Gallagher, Jr. on the second playoff hole.

"Jose's score will never be matched," Purtzer said. "It'll never happen again. Never, ever. Not in my lifetime. What he did astounds me. I was reading about it last year and thinking they must have changed the golf course."

Purtzer played four solid rounds of golf. He didn't have one of those magical weeks with his putter, but he hit 53 of 72 greens in regulation.

This time Olazabal shot 11-over-par 291, 29 strokes higher than before.

A case can be made that the World Series isn't what it used to be. International stars Nick Faldo, Severiano Ballesteros and Ian Woosnam skipped the event, and several U.S. stars such as Curtis Strange, Mark Calcavecchia and Hale Irwin didn't qualify.

The World Series, however, does offer a 10-year PGA Tour exemption, which in 39-year-old Purtzer's case will carry him until he's ready for the Senior Tour. Also, there was a $1.2 million purse, of which the winner got $216,000. So what if the Firestone South course is one of the most difficult anywhere. You should have to work hard for those kinds of rewards. "This might be the hardest course we play all year," Purtzer said.

Fred Couples argued that, "It's hard to shoot four good rounds here. I remember Tom Watson once shot three 65s here and a 75, and I couldn't believe the 65s." But not this week. Only Purtzer, Love and Gallagher broke par for four days, and Mark Brooks and Couples matched par to finish one stroke out of the playoff.

Disasters abounded. PGA Champion John Daly hit a lot of big drives in the first round and a lot of fairways, but not the ones for which he was aiming, and shot 80. Nolan Henke led the first round with a 66, then shot 75 and 80, and tied for 40th place. Lanny Wadkins was in good shape after three rounds, but began the final round with a triple bogey. Joey Sindelar had almost one of everything to start the last round—bogey, eagle, par, triple bogey.

Dillard Pruitt, who carried a three-shot lead over Purtzer into the last round, played his first six holes in four over par. Even Purtzer wasn't immune. After birdies at Nos. 2 and 3 to pressure Pruitt, Purtzer missed short birdie putts at Nos. 10 and 11, then three-putted No. 12 for bogey and bogeyed No. 17 to drop into a tie with Love and Gallagher.

Love and Gallagher made determined finishes, Love with birdies at Nos. 16 and 17 for 69, and Gallagher with birdies at Nos. 15 and 16 for 69. But their momentum was short-lived. All three players parred the first playoff hole, No. 10, then moved to No. 18, where Purtzer's tee shot found the middle of the fairway. Gallagher hit his shot right, Love hit his left, and neither had a shot at the green. Purtzer made a par and won.

It was Purtzer's second victory of the year, the first coming at Colonial in May, but it was only his fifth in a 17-year career, far below expectations. "I never had the confidence that I should have," Purtzer said. "Maybe if I had more success early in my career, a lack of confidence wouldn't be the case. I was my own worst enemy and got in my own way. But winning at Colonial reinforced that I could win again. And this week proved it."

Greater Milwaukee Open—$1,000,000
Winner: Mark Brooks

Mark Brooks has a reputation of having one of the great short games in all of golf. If there's a way to get up and down, the pundits insist, then Brooks will find it. A case in point was the Greater Milwaukee Open, where the 30-year-old Texan turned bogeys into pars and double bogeys into bogeys and made more than his share of birdies to shoot 18-under-par 270 and break the heart of Robert Gamez.

When Brooks wasn't leading, he was never far from it. The first round belonged to Gamez and his 61, but Brooks had 63. Gamez added a 66 on Friday, but Brooks hung close with 67. He jumped ahead with a third-round 70 and held on down the stretch for his second victory of the year and his third in three years. "I'm happy to win but I'm disappointed I didn't do this a month earlier. Maybe it would have gotten me on the Ryder Cup," said Brooks who had four top-10 finishes in the last two months. "Right now, I'm really playing well."

Despite Brooks' steady play, the tournament had a Gamez look to it from the first day, when he lipped out a seven-foot birdie putt on the last hole for a 61, 11 under par. Starting on the back nine, Gamez made the turn in four under par, but so did six other players, and the round seemed to flatten out when he failed to birdie the par-five second hole.

Then Gamez broke loose: No. 3, 15-foot birdie; No. 4, 15-foot birdie; No. 5, 20-foot birdie; No. 6, eagle from out of the bunker; No. 7, six-foot birdie; No. 8, three-foot birdie. And his seven-foot putt at No. 9 had birdie written all over it before spinning out.

"I sure never thought I would shoot 61 after I was only four under par at the turn," Gamez said. "It's the best score I've ever shot."

It also was the best score his playing partner, Jim Gallagher, Jr., had ever seen. "I knew Ken Green had shot 61 here, but I never could see how he did it. Now, I know. Funny thing is, at No. 9 I told my caddie when Robert's nine-iron shot was in the air, 'That's going in. That's a 59.' It was all over the flag."

When Gamez followed the 61 with 66, he looked ready to bury the field, but had an off-day with his putter and shot 74, allowing Brooks, who holed a 56-yard wedge for eagle at No. 16, to take a one-stroke lead over Gamez and Jeff Maggert into the final round. "The way Robert played the first two days, it looked like his week," Brooks said. "But I guess that's why we play 72 (holes)."

Sunday's round quickly turned into a two-man race. Brooks, playing with Maggert, birdied four of the first six holes, but Gamez, a group ahead, stayed close with a birdie and another eagle at No. 6.

A turning point came at No. 11. After missing the green, Brooks bladed his chip shot over the green, down an embankment and into the gallery. Then, facing a much more difficult up-and-then-downhill shot, Brooks pitched it within two feet and tapped in for his bogey. It dropped him into a tie with Gamez, but it could have been much worse.

"I was walking down No. 12 and saw what Mark had and told my caddie, 'I've got him now,'" Gamez said. "No way he gets it up and down from there."

The second turning point came at No. 16, an easy par five. Gamez went for the green in two shots, but came up short in a bunker, 35 yards from the green. He didn't carry his next shot over the far end of the bunker, then hit his next within eight feet, but missed the putt. A probable birdie became a costly bogey. "The par fives on the back side killed me this week," said Gamez, who played them in even par. "They cost me the tournament."

Indeed. Brooks played them in five under par, but it was an up-and-down par there Sunday that put him one ahead. Mr. "Chips" also got it up and down from the bunker at No. 17. He bogeyed No. 18, but it didn't matter. So did Gamez. "It wasn't a pretty way to finish, but I got the job done," Brooks said. "My short game saved me all week."

Canadian Open—$1,000,000

Winner: Nick Price

Nick Price always showed the promise of being one of the best to play the game, but did not have the victories to prove it. He came into 1991 with a series of disappointing finishes, but then charged to victory in the Canadian Open.

"I feel my game has moved up a step this year," said the 34-year-old Price. "Now, I hope to go on to the next step—winning major championships."

While that remains to be seen, Price certainly proved in the Canadian Open that he has that kind of game. He was far enough back that he wasn't thinking about winning when he came to the 11th tee to play "The Hole," the players' name for the five holes that run along the floor of a 100-foot-deep gorge.

But after he birdied all five holes and parred the final three holes for a closing 66, he had to change his thinking, especially when the leaders began to crumble.

D.A. Weibring was the first to go. He had started the round one stroke ahead of Ken Green and had played solidly all week, including a second-round 64 and a hole-in-one at No. 7 on Saturday. But with a four-shot lead with 12 holes to play, Weibring began to fade at No. 7, where he flew the green and made double bogey. Double bogeys at the 10th and 11th holes erased his chances. He shot 75 and tied for fifth place. "I played some good golf this week," Weibring said. "Today was very disappointing. I just hit some bad shots over that stretch of holes. Double bogeys will kill you out here. But I'll be back. I'll get over it and be ready to go next week."

Green appeared to have the best chance when he birdied No. 16 to pull within one shot. But he bogeyed the 17th, missing a three-foot putt, and erased any chance he had of an eagle at No. 18 by driving into the right rough. He tied for third place with Fred Couples.

David Edwards made almost as good a charge as Price. He chipped in for eagle at No. 16 and finished birdie, birdie to take second place, one stroke behind Price. "Great finish, but not much happened before those last three holes," said Edwards, who shot 68.

Price said his birdie surge was the result of hard work on the practice green. His five consecutive birdie putts came from 20, six, 15, 12 and 20 feet. It was his best putting round in almost five months, since the Byron Nelson Classic. "Last year, I played well here, but I couldn't make any putts," Price said. "I couldn't see the light at the end of the tunnel. But at the Nelson, I started putting better, then got away from what I was doing for a while, but it's coming back. It's been three months of good, solid putting."

The result was a good, solid year. The $180,000 first prize lifted his season's earnings to over $600,000 and assured him a spot in the season-ending Tour Championship at Pinehurst. "This is very, very special to me," Price said. "I've been close in a couple of British Opens and learned from those experiences. Winning a national championship of this stature is important to me. It gives me more confidence than I've had before."

Hardee's Classic—$1,000,000
Winner: D.A. Weibring

Only minutes after D.A. Weibring had destructed in the final round of the Canadian Open, he gathered himself together, remembering something he had always told his son Matt and daughters Katey and Allison. "You have a choice when something disappointing happens to you," he said. "You can feel sorry for yourself, which is the easy way out, or you can go back to work. I pride myself on being a guy who goes back to work."

Weibring went back to work and proved his point. He won the Hardee's Classic just a week after one of the biggest disappointments of his life. Weibring fought back from his Canadian Open disaster with rounds of 68-67-68-64—267, 13 under par at Oakwood Country Club in Coal Valley, Illinois. In doing so, Weibring made good on his promise to Matt that he would win a tournament in 1991.

"People can be pretty frank sometimes, and my wife and children had heard things in the gallery, like my inability to be a force on the PGA Tour," Weibring said. "I put a little pressure on myself by making that promise. That's part of what happened to me last Sunday."

One Sunday later, however, Weibring had the day he knew was in him, passing a number of PGA Tour stars to win his third career victory, and first since the 1987 Western Open. "I've always prided myself on being able to come back from disappointments," said Weibring of his victory on the course where 12 years earlier he had won his first tournament, the Quad Cities Open.

To win his second title here, Weibring rallied from four shots behind third-round leader David Edwards and passed the likes of Paul Azinger, Peter Jacobsen and the newly confident Greg Norman. Both Azinger and Jacobsen barely missed birdie putts on the 18th hole that would have produced a playoff and tied for second place, while Norman and Scott Hoch tied for fourth.

Weibring was a long time getting to the front, however. He was four strokes out after Norman opened with 64, and he trailed Leonard Thompson, who shot 62 on Friday, by six strokes at the halfway point. Edwards led him by four strokes going into the last round.

Then, he was just one in a pack of pursuers. As the final twosome of Edwards and Azinger made the turn, five players were tied for the lead. Weibring birdied three of the first six holes coming in and was the first to reach 13 under par, which eliminated Jacobsen, who was in at 12 under par.

Soon no one but Azinger was left. His 45-foot birdie-tying putt was dead-on, but banged the right side and rolled a couple of feet past. "If it's a foot softer, it's going in," said Azinger, who declared himself physically fit and ready to go in the Ryder Cup matches. "I got robbed so many times. I putted great all week. It's not often that I hit it the way I did and putt the way I did and don't win."

In the next instant, however, Azinger was paying tribute to Weibring. "I want to commend D.A.," he said. "He suffered a heartbreaker last week, and that's not easy to recover from. Sometimes things like that are devastating to a guy."

But not to Weibring. Not when he has promises to keep.

B.C. Open—$800,000
Winner: Fred Couples

Fred Couples came to the B.C. Open with two goals. One was to prepare his game for next week's Ryder Cup matches, and the other was to win the tournament. He left Endicott, New York, and En Joie Country Club, having succeeded in both.

After posting four rounds in the 60s, Couples declared himself ready for the European invasion of Kiawah Island. The fact that he had won for the second time in a year—the first time he had done that in his career—was an added bonus. Quite a bonus it was, too. His $144,000 share of the $800,000 purse moved him to No. 2 on the money list behind Corey Pavin and pushed his career earnings over $4 million.

"I came here to play expecting to prepare for the Ryder Cup," said Couples, who shot rounds of 66-67-68-68—269. "But it was a relaxing week, because if I didn't play well, I'd fly back to Houston and practice for the Ryder Cup. But competing was part of it, too. I don't think anyone who believes he's a good player just goes out to play and walk around."

Maybe the best Ryder Cup preparation for Couples was having to fight for the victory. It was no stroll. Though he won by three strokes over Peter Jacobsen, who finished second for the second consecutive week, it wasn't until third-round leader Brad Faxon double-bogeyed No. 17 that he could relax.

Faxon began with a one-shot lead over Couples. It became two strokes when Couples bogeyed No. 1, and Faxon stretched it to three with a birdie at No. 2. It was the wake-up call that Couples needed. He birdied the next three holes. Couples eventually took the lead with a par at No. 11 and held that margin until No. 17, where Faxon came over the top on a four-iron shot to the 198-yard hole and missed the green. His ball came to rest against a fence and the resulting double bogey was all the cushion Couples would need. "I was hanging in there until I made a horrible swing at 17," Faxon said. "But I had a good week. I played well."

Faxon opened with 65, one stroke behind Blaine McCallister, took the lead with a second-round 64 in which he made nine birdies. At this point, Couples was four strokes back. Faxon slipped to 71 on Saturday, one stroke up on Couples and four ahead of Jacobsen. "I started driving the ball poorly on Saturday and didn't give myself the chance to make birdies," Faxon said. "When you shoot 13 under the first two rounds and two over on the weekend, you're not going to win."

Jacobsen was six strokes behind at one point in the final round, but fought back and when he rolled in a 30-footer for birdie at No. 18, he was three shots back. He had no illusions of grandeur, however. Missed birdie chances at Nos. 14 and 15 made him a realist. "I had a chance to win, but when I missed those putts at Nos. 14 and 15, that was it," Jacobsen said. "After that, I needed a total collapse from Freddie and I knew that wasn't going to happen. Not the way he was playing."

With his four sub-70 rounds, Couples ran his streak of rounds in the 60s to 10. "This is great for me, a real confidence builder going to next week," Couples said. "It was good for me to have to play hard today in order to win. My concentration was a little off early, but when Brad birdied the second hole to go three ahead, it was the jolt I needed."

Buick Southern Open—$700,000
Winner: David Peoples

David Peoples is the exception to the rule that says if you don't think you can win, you won't win. Standing on the first tee in the final round of the Buick Southern Open, three shots behind Larry Nelson and Robert Gamez, Peoples had conceded victory. His reason was that both Nelson and Gamez had accomplished what he had not, winning on the PGA Tour.

"I wasn't thinking about winning," Peoples said. "I was just thinking about doing my best."

His best was a course-record-tying 66, six under par over the 7,050 Mountain View course at Callaway Gardens, Georgia, a 72-hole total of 12-under-par 276 and a one-shot victory over Gamez.

He also found a new attitude and the knowledge he could win. "That knowledge, along with the chance to play in next year's Masters means everything to me," said Peoples, who earned $126,000.

Peoples started the final round with a birdie, then made three more birdies over the next five holes to get to 10 under par and take the lead. Following a birdie at No. 4, it dawned on Peoples that maybe he could win. It was more than his nerves could handle.

Standing on the fifth tee with his playing partner, Brandt Jobe, and the twosome in front, Scott Gump and John Huston, Peoples' nerves got the best of him and he headed for a nearby Port-A-John.

"The waiting is what did it," he said. "I'm not like Fuzzy Zoeller and some other guys. I'm not able to laugh and slap my knee when I'm going around out there. I needed to get off by myself. I had to go somewhere and collect myself. In this case, it was the Port-A-John."

One of the things he pondered was how could he be playing so well on such a difficult golf course with the wind swirling through the tall pines, on a golf course he had never played until this week.

The fact was, few players in the field had played it. There had been a change in courses after 21 years at Green Island in Columbus, and the tournament moved down the road to Callaway Gardens, which allowed for more parking, easier access and hopefully a better field and more spectators.

The course more than held its own. With two-inch Bermuda rough and fast Bermuda greens, attacking the course was out of the question. "This is one of the best we play," Gamez said. "If they narrowed the fairways a little bit, made the pins a little tougher, you could hold a major here. You're going to see more guys playing here in the future."

Scores were three or four shots higher than at Green Island, where 62s and 63s were common. People, Neal Lancaster and Dave Sutherland shot 67s to lead the first round. Jobe took over on Friday at 135, two strokes ahead of Nelson and Lee Janzen. Nelson and Gamez shared the third-round lead at 207.

Nelson hadn't won since the 1988 Atlanta Classic, but figured to be the man to beat in Sunday's final round. "You never know which one is going to be your last," said Nelson. "But the way I'm putting, this may not be it either. It may be someone else's turn."

Nelson was never a factor on Sunday, shooting 72 to tie for third place with Sutherland. Gamez gave it a run early with a couple of birdies, but made none coming in and shot 70 to finish second.

Peoples, however, held on. After calming his nerves at No. 4, Peoples picked up another birdie at No. 10 to get to 11 under par, then dropped an eight-footer on No. 17. The clincher came at No. 18, where he had to make a 10-footer for par.

"To shoot a 66 in the final round when you have a chance to win is the ultimate rush," Peoples said. "Last year, I was tied for the lead at Green Island and couldn't handle it. I finished fourth. I've never had the confidence that I could win. Winning this week is just unbelievable."

H.E.B. Texas Open—$900,000
Winner: Blaine McCallister

Deep in the heart of Texas is where Blaine McCallister has longed to win a golf tournament. It's where he lives and where his father lives, and McCallister has always wanted to win one in front of the home folks.

Who could blame McCallister for getting a little choked up after he defeated Gary Hallberg on the second playoff hole to win the H.E.B. Texas Open in San Antonio. "This one is for my dad," McCallister said. "My goal has always been to win with my father watching. And I pulled it off. He's always been there for me."

The special moment didn't come easy. McCallister was two strokes behind with three holes to play, and only a questionable decision by Hallberg opened the door.

McCallister held the second- and third-round leads, and was holding on by one stroke until he bogeyed the 13th hole and Hallberg birdied it. Hallberg went two shots up with another birdie at No. 14 and, after a safe par at No. 15, decided the tournament was his. "All week, I had been aggressive and it had paid off," said Hallberg, who put together back-to-back 65s in the middle two rounds. "But when I got to No. 16, I thought I had the tournament won and got too conservative."

Rather than hitting his driver on the uphill 16th, Hallberg went with a three iron and left himself an uphill 170-yard shot to the green. He hooked it into a bunker and made bogey. McCallister made a 12-foot birdie putt to tie Hallberg. They remained tied after McCallister saved par from a bunker for par at No. 18 and Hallberg sank a five-footer for his par.

"I've always believed you have to seize the moment," McCallister said. "I did it when Gary bogeyed No. 17, and there was no way I was going to let this one get away. I was going to do whatever I had to do to win it." What he had to do was birdie two playoff holes. After both made birdies on the par-five 10th, they moved to the par-four 17th, where McCallister sank a 25-footer and Hallberg missed from 20 feet.

"That's two years in a row I had a chance to win here," said Hallberg, who three-putted the last hole in 1990 and lost by one stroke to Mark O'Meara. "Last year, I gave it away. This time, though, Blaine won it."

The victory was McCallister's third overall and first since the 1989 Bank of Boston Classic. Financially, it was worth $162,000. Emotionally, it was worth much more. "There was a lot of pressure out there," said McCallister. "I didn't want to blow it. When I made that 25-footer in the playoff, I looked over at Dad, and I think we both had tears in our eyes."

Las Vegas Invitational—$1,500,000
Winner: Andrew Magee

Years from now, maybe sooner, Andrew Magee will be the answer to a trivia question: When Chip Beck shot 59 in the 1991 Las Vegas Invitational, who won the tournament?

Already, he's being called Anticlimactic Magee. First, there was his other victory this year, The Nestle Invitational. Magee was sitting in the locker room when the final round was rained out and he was declared the winner. In Las Vegas, Magee had the tournament of his life, shot 31-under-par 329 in the 90-hole event, then had to play two more holes before beating D.A. Weibring in a playoff.

First things first, Beck's 59, which tied one of golf's best known and most elusive records. Only one other player had done it in competition, Al Geiberger in the 1977 Danny Thomas Memphis Classic. "At least nobody broke it," said Geiberger, who was playing in a Senior Tour event when he heard the news. "I suppose I'm a little disappointed."

When Geiberger shot his 59, nobody expected it. When Beck turned the trick, it was still a big deal, but not totally unexpected. Robert Gamez predicted it on Tuesday after a practice round on the Sunrise Golf Club course, one of three used in the tournament. "I think we could see a 59," Gamez said Tuesday. "It's too easy. It's too short. There's no trouble on it. My brother broke 80 on it, and that's all I need to know."

Sunrise was listed at 6,914 yards, but played much shorter in the desert air. There were no trees. The fairways were firm and the greens were perfect.

But you still have to make all the shots and sink all the putts to shoot 59. Beck did it in dramatic fashion with birdies on the final three holes. Playing the back nine first, he birdied No. 10, parred No. 11, birdied the next six holes and parred No. 18 for 29. On the front nine, he birdied Nos. 1, 2 and 4, saved par after missing the green at No. 6, then birdied the last three holes.

He won a $1 million bonus offered this year by Hilton Hotels to anyone breaking 60, with half going to Beck and half to charity.

"I knew it was going to happen someday," Beck said. "I'm surprised it hasn't happened sooner. I'm just happy it happened to me. And I don't care what they say about the course. The way I hit it today, I could have shot 59 a lot of places."

Unlike Geiberger, however, Beck didn't win the tournament. His 59 came in the middle of 65-72 and 68-67 for a 331 total and a tie for third place.

Magee didn't become a contender in this event until a fourth-round 62 placed him in a tie for the lead with Craig Stadler, Bruce Lietzke and Weibring. Stadler and Lietzke were out of contention at the turn, giving way to Weibring, who had moved into a two-shot lead over Brooks.

Brooks got one stroke back at No. 14, and came to the 18th trailing by one. Now it was time for a little extra drama. After driving into the left rough on a knoll, Brooks faced a 216-yard carry over water and if he made it, a certain birdie. Or, he could lay up as Weibring did, and hope to win a putting contest.

Brooks chose the bold play. He pulled out a three iron, caught it flush and his ball landed 25 feet above the hole for a potential eagle. Luckily for Weibring, who made a routine par, Magee missed the putt that would have given him the victory outright. His birdie, however, forced a playoff. "I played the percentage shot by laying up," Weibring said. "I wanted to force Mark to play a great shot, and he did."

After such a dramatic finish in regulation, the playoff was anticlimactic. Brooks saved par from a bunker to halve the first playoff hole, No. 12, and Weibring couldn't do the same from the bunker at No. 16, and Brooks won with par.

"I'm overwhelmed," Brooks said. "I had missed three cuts before I got here and can't believe I shot 31 under par. I haven't won many, this is only the third, but it means more than the others."

Chip Beck's 59 at Sunrise Golf Club

No. 10, 460 yards, par 4—Driver to right rough, seven iron to front of green, 40-foot putt, birdie.

No. 11, 466 yards, par 4—Driver down left side of fairway, five iron to green, two putts from 25 feet, par.

No. 12, 164 yards, par 3—Five iron to four feet below hole, one putt, birdie.

No. 13, 616 yards, par 5—Driver into fairway bunker, two iron short of green, wedge to six feet, one putt, birdie.

No. 14, 334 yards, par 4—Three wood off the tee, sand wedge from 80 yards to 16 feet, one putt, birdie.

No. 15, 187 yards, par 3—Five iron to 20 feet right of hole, one putt, birdie.

No. 16, 546 yards, par 5—Driver to fairway, three wood to green, two putts from 25 feet, birdie.

No. 17, 366 yards, par 4—Three wood off tee, wedge from 101 yards to 10 feet, one putt, birdie.

No. 18, 443 yards, par 4—Driver to fairway, six iron from 173 yards to 35 feet, two putts, par.

No. 1, 460 yards, par 4—Driver to fairway, nine iron from 139 yards to four feet, one putt, birdie.

No. 2, 331 yards, par 4—Four iron off tee, wedge from 111 yards to 10 feet, one putt, birdie.

No. 3, 439 yards, par 4—Driver to fairway, six iron from 172 yards to 20 feet, two putts, par.

No. 4, 524 yards, par 5—Driver to fairway, three wood short of green, chip to two feet, one putt, birdie.

No. 5, 361 yards, par 4—Three wood to fairway, wedge from 90 yards to 10 feet, two putts, par.

No. 6, 157 yards, par 3—Seven iron to fringe, two putts from 20 feet, par.

No. 7, 498 yards, par 5—Driver to fairway, two iron from 210 yards to 25 feet, two putts, birdie.

No. 8, 191 yards, par 3—Five iron off tee to six feet, one putt, birdie.

No. 9, 408 yards, par 4—Driver to fairway, eight iron from 157 yards to three feet, one putt, birdie.

Walt Disney World-Oldsmobile Classic—$1,000,000
Winner: Mark O'Meara

There's something about PGA Tour events with a pro-am theme that bring out the best in Mark O'Meara. In 1985, he won the Bing Crosby Pro-Am at Pebble Beach, and in 1989 and 1990, back at Pebble Beach, he won twice more, in the AT&T Pebble Beach Pro-Am.

Most recently, O'Meara won the Walt Disney World-Oldsmobile Classic at Walt Disney World Resort near Orlando, just a 15-minute ride from his home. He has now won seven times on the Tour and four victories have been in the company of amateur partners.

O'Meara was never far from the lead all week. He should have led the first round, but missed three putts inside six feet and fell a shot shy of Larry Nelson, Corey Pavin and Steve Elkington. "I turned a 63 into an easy 66 and it's aggravating," O'Meara said. "If I ever get my putting straightened out, I could have a good week."

Another 66 on Thursday—the tournament began on Wednesday and ended Saturday—brought him a two-shot lead over Ben Hogan Tour graduate Jeff Maggert, with Nelson lurking at 135 and Pavin, at 136.

In the third round, however, O'Meara had another one of "those putting days" and limped in with 71, while Paul Azinger assumed the lead with his second straight 65. O'Meara was one back.

Azinger might have been in a runaway position if not for an opening-round 72 that saw him play the first 14 holes in five under par and the last four in five over par.

"I'm going along, playing great, hitting it great, putting great and all of a sudden I can't hit my driver in the fairway," said Azinger, who drove into the water each time. "I should have a six-shot lead. Now, I'm in a real fight."

The last-round lead seesawed almost frantically, with six players either leading or sharing the lead. John Cook grabbed the lead with a front-nine 30. Then Azinger, David Peoples, Davis Love III, Ken Green and Scott Gump all make a run at the victory. O'Meara finally latched onto it when he holed out a five-iron shot from 178 yards for eagle on No. 9.

It came down to a five-foot par putt on the 72nd hole. It was the kind of putt that O'Meara routinely missed most of the summer, but not this time.

"Golf is definitely a battle," said O'Meara, whose final-round 64 edged Peoples by one shot and Azinger by two. "It's a battle against yourself, a battle against your emotions, a battle against the golf course and a battle against all the other players.

"You have to beat all those things to win and today I did that."

Independent Insurance Agent Open—$800,000
Winner: Fulton Allem

It took more than six months, but the Independent Insurance Agent Open finally had a happy ending and the happiest of all was tournament winner Fulton Allem.

During the scheduled tournament week in April, it rained so much the tournament was postponed until the open week in November before the season-ending Tour Championship. The original date served as a lead-in to the Masters and drew an all-star cast—Seve Ballesteros, Nick Faldo, Jose Maria Olazabal and other international stars. The new date had a different, if still solid, look. The Europeans didn't come back, but U.S. Open champion Payne Stewart did, as did British Open champion Ian Baker-Finch, PGA champion John Daly and Players Championship winner Steve Elkington, as well as Greg Norman and Tom Kite.

Allem was facing a return to the PGA Tour qualifying tournament before he shot 15-under-par 273 on rounds of 71-69-67-66 for a one-stroke victory and a $144,000 payday. "I came in here 143rd on the money list," Allem said. "My livelihood was at stake. I'd never been to qualifying school and I didn't want to go now. I've heard horror stories and was not looking forward to it."

Allem can thank his lucky stars that Billy Ray Brown, the hometown favorite who won the NCAA Championship while playing at the University of Houston, couldn't finish what looked to be an almost-certain victory. Brown had the lead at 16 under par through 11 holes, but double-bogeyed No. 12 and bogeyed No. 13, then couldn't convert a 15-foot birdie putt at No. 18 to force a playoff.

Kite finished in a tie for second with Brown and Mike Hulbert, and also could have won. Kite missed a six-foot birdie putt at No. 17, then knocked the pin down at No. 18, the ball stopping 10 feet away. He missed that putt, also. "If the ball doesn't hit the pin, it's a three-footer," Kite said. Allem had one more bullet to dodge. Hulbert, playing in the last group, had a 25-foot putt to tie, but left it 18 inches short.

Another fellow who could have won was Jeff Maggert. He shot 65-65 to set a 36-hole tournament record of 130, and had a four-stroke lead over Duffy Waldorf and Brown. A third-round 70 left him three strokes in front of Donnie Hammond, Mike Reid, Brown and Hulbert. Then came disaster. He started the final round with a bogey at No. 2, hit into the water at Nos. 3 and 4 and closed it all out with a triple bogey at No. 18 for 80.

Allem wasn't gloating in victory, realizing the misfortune of others were contributing factors. But he surely was happy. "I played good golf this week, got a break when some of the other fellows didn't finish well and here I am," Allem said. "Golf is such an incredible game."

Tour Championship—$2,000,000
Winner: Craig Stadler

Golf is a never-ending game of surprises. How else to explain Craig Stadler winning the Tour Championship... in a playoff against Russ Cochran?

Nothing wrong with Stadler or Cochran. Both are good players. But the leading men in this final act were the U.S. Ryder Cup players—Corey Pavin, Lanny Wadkins, Payne Stewart, Paul Azinger, Chip Beck and Fred Couples. And the British Open champion, Ian Baker-Finch, and PGA Champion John Daly.

"To tell you the truth, I am more shell-shocked than anything, or anybody else right now," said Stadler, who won $360,000. "It will take awhile to sink in that you've finally done what you were trying to accomplish."

Stadler was referring to the fact he hadn't won in America since the 1984 Byron Nelson Classic. Always a good striker of the ball, Stadler had been close any number of times, but his putter seemed to always let him down.

Maybe it was the change of scenery that did it. When this tournament flew the banner of Nabisco, it made the rounds of courses often visited by the PGA Tour—Pebble Beach, Harbor Town, Colonial. Seeking something different, if not new, the Tour settled on Pinehurst's No. 2 course, in the sandhills of North Carolina. Everybody knew the course and everybody loved it. But few of the touring pros had ever played it before.

"Where has this been all my life?" asked Baker-Finch. "You could play a U.S. Open here, without rough, without doing anything. I haven't been this pumped up to play since the British Open."

Said Azinger, "It's a lot like Augusta National in that you have to play here a bunch to know where all the dips and bumps are. It's not normal to have an eight or nine iron in your hand and aim 15 feet right of the pin. Normally, you would shoot at it. This week, you'll make bogeys and double bogeys with those clubs."

The PGA Tour seemed to like it, too. It's coming back in 1992, and may make Pinehurst the permanent home of the championship.

Stadler felt at home immediately. He was tied for the first-round lead at 68 with Cochran, Daly and Baker-Finch, by one stroke over Stewart, Nolan Henke, Scott Hoch, Steve Elkington and Jay Don Blake. A second 68 on Friday left Stadler alone at the top, one stroke in front of Cochran, Azinger and Nick Price. By Saturday afternoon, Stadler and Cochran were tied at 208, three strokes ahead of Couples. Azinger had disappeared with 78 and shot another 78 Sunday.

After the first few holes of the final round, only Daly was within striking distance of the leaders. He birdied No. 2 to pull within three strokes, but was never to get any closer. Couples made three bogeys and a double bogey in the first five holes early on the way to 78.

The finish was suitably tense, dramatic and well played, with both Stadler and Cochran shooting final-round 71s. Stadler forced the playoff when he made a five-foot par putt, this after missing one from three feet at No. 15 that would have given him the lead. "I made a good putt at No. 18, and that was more surprising than anything," Stadler said. "Making that putt when I needed to make one gave me a lot of confidence going to the playoff."

Both players made routine birdies at the par-five 16th hole. At the 190-yard 17th, Stadler faded a high five-iron shot to within six feet. Cochran, spooked by a spectator jumping around in the bleachers behind the tee, came up short with a six iron. He chipped to four feet, but Stadler then made his winning birdie.

"That person's timing was pretty good," Cochran said sarcastically. "We'd just played the hole 20 minutes earlier and I knew exactly what club to hit. Then the noise startled me."

Nothing bothered Stadler. For once, his patience held up. "I can't say I knew it would happen, but the way I was playing this year, I felt I'd put four good rounds together sooner or later," he said.

The Tour Championship was a case of the rich getting only modestly richer. Of the players who ranked in the top 10 on the money list coming in, only Pavin and Price finished in the top half of the 30-player field. Seven of the top 10 finished 19th or worse. Among the top-four finishers—Stadler, Cochran, Daly and Bruce Lietzke—none came in ranked better than 25th.

Pavin's tie for 10th place earned him $54,000 and enabled him to hold onto the money lead and win the Arnold Palmer Award. He won the PGA of America's Player-of-the-Year Award with the help of Stadler, who vaulted past Couples into second place on the money list. Pavin and Couples were tied going into the final event. Couples did win the Vardon Trophy, though, edging out Pavin 69.59 to 69.63.

Amoco Centel Championship—$750,000
Winner: Jim Thorpe

Before teeing off in the first round of the Amoco Centel Championship, Jim Thorpe told his brother and caddie for the week, Chester, "There's no cut and we're guaranteed $10,000, so let's go out and try to make some birdies."

And make some birdies Thorpe did. There were eight on Thursday in a round of 64, then eight more in the next two rounds of 68 and 68 for a 54-hole 200 total. That was good enough for a five-stroke victory over Don Pooley and Mark McCumber in this first-ever tournament for the 40-Something gang at Hilton Head National Golf Club in South Carolina.

This $750,000 tournament was the idea of Jack Frazee, CEO of Centel Corporation, which sponsors the Centel Western Open, as well as events on the LPGA and Ben Hogan Tours. Frazee brought his idea to IMG and we agreed that together we could make it happen. Frazee then recruited as a co-sponsor Centel's corporate neighbor in Chicago, Amoco Oil Company. "It seemed to me that with the regular PGA Tour, Senior Tour and Ben Hogan Tour, this was the only thing missing," Frazee said.

The field of 32 players loved it. There was no 36-hole cut and every player was guaranteed $10,000. "I would like to see more of these," Thorpe said. "Hopefully, next year we'll play three or four."

Thorpe was the individual star of the first Amoco Centel Championship, removing any drama with his dominating play. His opening 64 gave him a three-stroke lead over Bobby Wadkins. He was still three ahead of Wadkins after 68 on Friday and, after Saturday's play was rained out, breezed in Sunday with another 68, five strokes ahead of Pooley and Mark McCumber. "This is the best I've played in quite some time," Thorpe said. "For one reason or another, it hasn't been a good year, so this helps."

He has been bothered in recent years with wrist injuries and had a pin removed from his wrist last spring. As a result, he made the cut in only 13 of 27 events, finished 179th on the 1991 money list, lost his PGA Tour exemption and will have to play his way back.

Mexican Open—$600,000
Winner: Jay Haas

As the PGA Tour hit the halfway point of the season, Jay Haas kept thinking he would win. It didn't happen. But the 38-year-old former Wake Forest star finally made it happen in the Mexican Open. Haas used a pair of 15-foot birdie putts, one on the last hole of regulation to catch Ed Fiori and the other on the third hole of a playoff to win for the first time since the 1988 Houston Open. He earned $100,000 for the victory in a field dominated by Americans. Twelve of the top 13 were from the United States.

Haas and Fiori tied with 11-under-par 277 totals at the 7,135-yard Chapultepec Golf Club outside Mexico City. Kenny Knox finished in third place and Lennie Clements was fourth.

"I really played well the last five or six months this season and about halfway through it, I thought I would win one, but it didn't happen," Haas said. "Although the field here wasn't as deep as we usually find on our Tour, I'm delighted with the victory."

Haas was steady all week. He opened with two 69s and trailed Clements, who had rounds of 67 and 69, by two strokes at the halfway point. A third-round 70 gave Haas a one-shot lead over Nolan Henke, as Clements slumped to 74.

Fiori came on with a rush in the last round, after seemingly having played himself out of contention early in the week. He shot 70 and 74, but rallied with 68 in the third round and caught Haas with 66 on Sunday. He was in the clubhouse with a one-stroke lead when Haas came to the 382-yard 18th hole. A good drive and excellent eight iron to 15 feet set up the tying birdie and the playoff.

After each parred the first two holes, Haas hit a pitching wedge to 15 feet and made his birdie after Fiori missed from 20 feet. "I played too good today to lose," Fiori said. "But I take my hat off to Jay. He made a big putt at No. 18 to get a tie and a good putt on the third hole to win. It was his day."

PGA Grand Slam of Golf—$1,000,000
Winner: Ian Woosnam

The PGA of America finally came up with the right formula to lure the four major championship winners to its Grand Slam of Golf: Offer a $1 million purse, take the show to Hawaii and televise it.

Except for agonizing delays dictated by WTBS' insistence that every shot be shown, it was a good show. There was plenty of good golf and drama, too, as Masters champion Ian Woosnam birdied four consecutive holes to catch and pass British Open champion Ian Baker-Finch and win the $400,000 first-place check.

Woosnam shot 69-66—135 over the Kauai Lagoons Kiele course. Baker-Finch had 68-71—139, while U.S. Open champion Payne Stewart finished at 70-71—141, and PGA champion John Daly shot 73-70—143.

Patience was the key in this two-day event as the television production people kept slowing down the players so each day's round would last the full four hours. Woosnam, one of the fastest players in the world, coped with it, but Daly did not. "The pace of play was just too slow for me," said Daly, who never got into a rhythm. "I just couldn't get into it."

Despite the pace, the Grand Slam had its moments, especially over the final five holes. Woosnam was two strokes behind Baker-Finch when they stood on the 14th tee the last day.

It was then that Woosnam began his charge and Baker-Finch suddenly couldn't make a putt. Woosnam cut Baker-Finch's lead to one with a birdie at No. 14, and got a tie with a two-putt for birdie at the par-five 15th after Baker-Finch's putt lipped out. "That's where the momentum switched," Woosnam said. "I could see he was down after missing his putt and I told myself this was the chance to win it."

Woosnam went on to win in style. He holed a 30-footer for birdie at No. 16, and Baker-Finch, who missed eight birdie putts in the final round, saw another opportunity just slip by the hole from 12 feet. Woosnam pulled away with a 15-foot birdie on the difficult par-three 17th and took a two-shot lead to No. 18.

"No. 16 was the killer for me," Baker-Finch said. "I had missed about eight in a row and he makes a long one and mine just slipped by. When he birdied No. 17 to go two ahead, there wasn't much hope left."

There was no hope left after Baker-Finch drove into a depression in the left rough at No. 18, then tried to hit a four iron out, 180 yards over water. It never had a chance.

"Under any other situation, I probably wouldn't attempt that shot, but the situation dictated I try," said Baker-Finch, who made double bogey. "Woosnam was fantastic. Four birdies in a row under pressure like that was tremendous. That's what you have to do, that's the game. It's hard to be upset when you win $250,000, but I am." Baker-Finch birdied the first three holes but never made another one.

"You have to make the putts when it counts and I did," Woosnam said. "The first day I missed about three or four greens and didn't give myself much of a chance. Today I hit the greens and made the putts."

Woosnam didn't get off without paying, however. The four players had agreed that the winner would buy dinner for the others. "I'm sure they'll make it a very expensive dinner," he said.

Ping Kapalua International—$750,000
Winner: Mike Hulbert

Mike Hulbert proved once again that patience means as much to winning a golf tournament as 300-yard drives and 60-foot birdie putts. Following one disaster with another on the 12th hole at the Plantation Course, Hulbert rebounded to beat Davis Love III on the first playoff hole and win the $150,000 first-place check in the Ping Kapalua International.

The road to victory was not easy. First Hulbert had to survive one of those television rules incidents that in earlier times had afflicted Craig Stadler, Paul Azinger and Tom Kite.

In Friday's third round, Hulbert was about to hit his second shot from just off the fairway on No. 12, when he picked up and tossed aside a long, dry piece of grass from behind his ball. The problem was, Hulbert didn't notice the grass was still rooted and therefore was not a loose impediment.

This time, however, it didn't take a long distance call from a viewer to alert PGA Tour rules officials. Announcer Johnny Miller raised the question on the air and officials advised Hulbert not to sign his card until he had a chance to review the videotape with them. One look, and Hulbert knew. "I couldn't believe my eyes," he said. "I knew I had moved the grass, but didn't realize it was attached. I had to penalize myself." The two-stroke penalty turned Hulbert's 70 into 72 and put him four strokes behind third-round leaders Love and Jim Hallet.

There was more. In Saturday's final round, Hulbert had dug himself out of the hole and was within one stroke of Love when disaster struck again at No. 12. He drove into the deep grass and stepped on his ball while looking for it. That meant a one-shot penalty for moving his ball, then another stroke for taking an unplayable lie. A double bogey was the result.

Luckily for Hulbert, however, Love bogeyed the hole, so Hulbert was only two strokes down. He got one back on No. 13 and the other one at No. 17, where Love three-putted. Both players birdied No. 18 to force the playoff. Hulbert completed his turnaround with a birdie on the first playoff hole, No. 18 again, to win. "To win is always gratifying, but to have to overcome so many obstacles to win makes it special," he said.

Hulbert had been around the lead all week. He was one stroke behind Mark Calcavecchia, who shot 66 in the first round. A second-round 69 left Hulbert one stroke ahead of Steve Pate, and only the two-stroke penalty in the third round put him behind going to Sunday.

This was the third time in five years that Love finished second in this event. The first was 1986, when he three-putted three times in the final round and finished two strokes behind Andy Bean. He was second to David Peoples last year despite a final-round 63.

"I feel like I'm due to win this thing one year," said Love, who put himself into position to win this time with a third-round 66 that included five birdies on the final seven holes. "My putter got me in position to win, but I couldn't make the putts when I needed to in the last round. But give Mike credit. He hung in there."

Shark Shootout—$1,000,000
Winners: Tom Purtzer/Lanny Wadkins

Pair one of the PGA Tour's sweetest swingers with one known for dogged determination and the chances are that this duo will be hard to beat. Their names are Tom Purtzer and Lanny Wadkins, and win they did in Greg Norman's Shark Shootout at Sherwood Country Club in Thousand Oaks, California.

The Purtzer-Wadkins team blitzed the field with rounds of 61, 65 and 63 for a 189 total, four strokes ahead of host Norman and Jack Nicklaus, who rallied with a final-round 59. Defending champions Raymond Floyd and Fred Couples finished in sixth place.

If there can be a turning point in such a victory, it came at No. 16 for Purtzer and Wadkins. Purtzer hit his second shot at the 537-yard par-five hole into a greenside bunker, and holed it from there for an eagle. "It shouldn't have been close," Wadkins said of the victory. "We missed some short putts the first few holes that gave Norman and Nicklaus a shot at us. But we started to make some putts and the eagle at No. 16 iced it."

Norman and Nicklaus started the final round tied for third place, eight strokes behind Purtzer and Wadkins. They closed ground quickly with three eagles, a Shark Shootout record, but they had left themselves in a deep hole with a first-round 68. "We stubbed our toe right out of the box," Nicklaus said. "We played the four par fives in one over par. You would expect us to be at least four under par, maybe five, on those holes. We just had too much ground to make up."

The 10-team tournament had a different format each day, but it didn't matter to Purtzer and Wadkins. They opened with 61 under the better-ball format, shot 65 while playing alternate shots, then had 63 in the closing scramble round. "It was fun," Purtzer said, "especially the scramble part. A lot of guys got it way under par in that format."

Indeed. Ben Crenshaw and Bruce Lietzke finished last, but shot 59 in the last round. Chi Chi Rodriguez and Chip Beck also had 59 and were next-to-last.

JCPenney Classic—$1,100,000
Winners: Billy Andrade and Kris Tschetter

In every relationship, one partner at times is called on to provide a calming influence on the other when things get tough. It's true in marriage, in business, even in golf. In this case, it was the JCPenney Classic, a mixed-team affair featuring players from the PGA and LPGA Tours.

With his partner Kris Tschetter a bundle of nerves, it fell to Billy Andrade to get them over the rough spots. He did it with a series of dandy approach shots and a rah-rah attitude which resulted in a playoff victory over the team of Ed Humenik and Elaine Crosby. "It was great to do this with Billy out there," Tschetter said. "He's a great cheerleader. He really kept me calm out there. When you haven't won and you're playing with someone who has, you're afraid of messing up."

The title, though unofficial, was Tschetter's first in her four years on the LPGA Tour. The pair not only survived the playoff, they also overtook the favored but faltering defending champions Davis Love III and Beth Daniel.

"I really expected they were the team to beat," said Crosby, whose team began the final round tied with Daniel and Love, one behind Andrade and Tschetter and Gene Sauers and Hollis Stacy. "I thought Kris might get a little nervous. She played well the beginning of the year, but not so good lately. I think Billy pumped her up and gave her a lot of confidence."

Andrade could relate to that not-having-won syndrome until he did it back-to-back at the Kemper Open and Buick Classic earlier this year. All he did in the Penney was relate it to Tschetter. "I know how she felt," Andrade said. "I was trying to help by putting positive thoughts in her mind that she is good. And she is good. You're going to hear a lot from Kris."

12. U.S. Senior Tour

Over its 11-year history, the Senior PGA Tour has had an array of talents finish the seasons as the leading money winner and No. 1 player. Don January and Miller Barber passed the distinction back and forth the first five years, followed by Australian great Peter Thomson, fellow Aussie Bruce Crampton, Chi Chi Rodriguez, Bob Charles back to back and, in 1990, Lee Trevino. Yet, that potpourri has one thing in common. All were big and frequent winners in their younger days. Which makes the emergence of Mike Hill as the No. 1 senior of 1991 so singular and impressive. In his nearly 15 seasons as a full-time player on the PGA Tour, Hill managed just three victories and always seemed to be in the shadow of his older brother... Dave Hill's younger brother, they would say. After 1991, it's the other way around.

Mike was impressive from the start after joining the Senior PGA Tour in early 1989. He won more than $400,000 that season, then five tournaments and second-ranking $895,678 in 1990. He duplicated the victory total in 1991, but increased his earnings to $1,065,657, the second year in a row that the Senior Tour's leading money winner topped the $1 million mark and out-earned the No. 1 man on the regular PGA Tour. Hill played in 32 individual events in 1991 and, besides the five wins (and an unofficial sixth as Trevino's partner in the Legends of Golf), he was second or third in eight other events and was out of the top 10 just 11 times in his rigorous season.

George Archer was just a step behind Hill at season's end. He led the money list going into the season-ending New York Life Champions tournament in mid-December, had three victories and was closing the season in a rush. Starting with his second victory in early September, Archer finished: Nationwide—tied for fourth; Bank One—tied for third; Vantage Championship—tied for second; Raley's Gold Rush—victory; Transamerica Championship—tied for fourth; Security Pacific—tied for second; Kaanapali—third, and New York Life—tied for fourth. He wound up the season just over $100,000 behind Hill.

Almost as impressive as Archer in the final months was Jim Colbert, the Senior Tour newcomer, who gave up the television tower and turned his main attention away from his golf businesses in favor of a return to competitive golf in his 50th year. Colbert also won three times, all in the final six months of the year and got the big boost toward his $880,749 winnings and third-place position on the money list with his $202,500 collection for winning the Vantage Championship. No other rookie seniors were even close.

The season of Rodriguez went the other route. Rodriguez had won four titles by the middle of May and was running toward a second money-winner title, then flattened out in the late season, finishing fourth. Trevino failed to match his brilliant debut season of 1990 when he led the money list and won seven times, although three victories (plus the Legends of Golf) and more than $700,000 could hardly be considered anything but a fine season. Of the year's six first-time winners, the most surprising was Jim Albus, a club professional from Long Island, who set all of the game's fine players aside and won the prestigious Senior Players Championship in Detroit in early

June. Besides Albus and Colbert with his three wins, the rookie victors were Rocky Thompson with two, DeWitt Weaver, Larry Ziegler and John Brodie.

Then there was the impact player... Jack Nicklaus. Jack played in only five tournaments and won three of them—the important U.S. Senior Open and PGA Seniors, along with the rich Tradition in Arizona.

The season began at La Costa with...

Infiniti Senior Tournament of Champions—$350,000
Winner: Bruce Crampton

Bruce Crampton was the best of the surviving dozen in the Senior PGA Tour's version of the Infiniti Tournament of Champions, mastering the small field with a nine-under-par 279 and a four-stroke victory, the 18th of his six years on the over-50 circuit with at least one in all six full seasons. Sixteen seniors qualified for the annual tournament at La Costa Country Club in Southern California with 1990 victories, but the potentially banner field lost much of its luster when Jack Nicklaus, Gary Player and Bob Charles declined invitations and Lee Trevino exited early with a back injury.

The 56-year-old Crampton, who won 14 times in two decades on the regular PGA Tour, took control in the second round and outfought Frank Beard, his only serious challenger, the rest of the way. Beard shook off the effects of a triple bogey on the third hole and mustered 69 to take the opening-round lead by one stroke over the Australian. Trevino looked like the probable leader when he moved to four under at the 12th hole, but a pulled muscle in his back contributed to an ultimate 71 and he withdrew the next day when treatments failed to remedy the problem.

With 69, Crampton surged into a five-stroke lead Friday as Beard slumped to 75, at one point suffering five straight bogeys. Beard made up one shot Saturday, but took a double bogey on the par-five second hole on the way to his 68 to Crampton's second consecutive 69. It gave him a four-stroke lead, which dwindled to one after eight holes Sunday before Beard missed a two-foot par putt at No. 10 and makeable birdie putts on the next three holes. Crampton increased his edge to three when he birdied the par-five 12th and saved pars from the sand on the next two holes to preserve the margin. The two men ultimately shot 71s as Crampton posted the 279 and his four-shot victory. George Archer and Mike Hill finished another four back in a third-place deadlock.

Royal Caribbean Classic—$450,000
Winner: Gary Player

It was classic Gary Player. Playing the final hole of the Royal Caribbean Classic at the Links at Key Biscayne in south Florida, nervously nursing a two-stroke margin, Player put his approach in a greenside bunker. But the game's premier wizard of the sand clicked off a routine par for 68, a 200 total and a two-stroke victory over the powerful triumvirate of Lee Trevino, Chi Chi Rodriguez and Bob Charles. It was Player's first Senior PGA Tour win in almost a year, but the 16th in little more than five years on the circuit and the 141st in his remarkable career.

The opening event of the Florida swing on the excellent public Key Biscayne course drew a strong field, missing only Jack Nicklaus and Arnold Palmer, who were playing in the concurrent AT&T Pebble Beach Pro-Am tournament on the regular Tour. Two of the best—Bruce Crampton, the Tournament of Champions winner in January, and Rodriguez—led the first day with five-under-par 66s on the 6,715-yard course, Crampton with a solid, five-birdie round and Rodriguez with seven birdies and two bogeys. Player took charge Saturday, firing a 65 that set a tournament record at 132 and gave him a two-shot lead over Rodriguez, three over Al Geiberger and four over Crampton (70) and four others. His 1961-vintage putter produced seven birdies, including one from 35 feet, a poor tee shot at the fifth hole costing him his only bogey.

Player made three birdies on the first five holes Sunday, but Charles came on even stronger and caught Gary when Player drove into a hazard and took a bogey at No. 9 and Charles birdied the 10th and 11th. But Player followed with a birdie himself at No. 11 and never trailed after that. He had uneasy moments watching Trevino make a move with birdies at the 14th, 15th and 16th, but Gary's birdie at the 14th kept him enough ahead that a bungled chip shot and bogey at the 15th did little damage other than increase the tension over the final three holes, which he parred for the 68. Charles and Trevino closed with 66s and Rodriguez with 68 to forge the three-way runner-up tie at 202.

GTE Suncoast Classic—$450,000
Winner: Bob Charles

The GTE Suncoast Classic moves to the TPC of Tampa course in 1992, not exactly good news for Bob Charles. So far as Charles is concerned, the tournament should stay put at Tampa Palms, its site for its first four years. For good reason. The New Zealand southpaw won there twice, following up his playoff victory of 1989 with a four-stroke victory in 1991 that was not as easy as the margin indicates.

Charles didn't spring clear of the final threat to his victory until the 53rd hole Sunday. He and Lee Trevino, playing in the final grouping, were tied for the lead at five under par as they came to the 17th, a pivotal hole in Charles' 1989 win. Just as Dave Hill did that year, Trevino butchered the hole, starting with a sliced drive into marshy oblivion and ending with an approach into the water and an ultimate eight. Charles made a routine par five and birdied the 18th for a closing 70 and a six-under-par 280. With 73, Trevino fell back into a second-place deadlock with George Archer at 214.

Opening with 68, Charles never trailed en route to his 16th victory on the Senior PGA Tour (and four other unofficial seniors wins.) Troubled for a while in early 1990 by the rules-forced change of his putter grip, Charles felt that, by the latter part of the season, he had come to terms with the feel of the club. He won twice in the latter half of the year and attributed his good start in Tampa to the greens weapon. He had no bogeys, holed a 12-foot par putt at the 15th and closed with a 27-footer for birdie at No. 18 Friday. Frank Beard and Bob Brue shared the first-day lead. A par 72 Saturday for 140 set Charles a stroke in front of Trevino and two ahead of Bobby Nichols, as Archer had the day's only round in the 60s—68—after an opening 76 to get back into contention.

In the run-up to Trevino's disaster at the 17th Sunday, Charles mustered three birdies, but three-putted for his second bogey at the 16th to fall back into the tie with Lee, who had four birdies and two bogeys up to that point. His admittedly unwise choice of a driver on the 17th tee cast the final die.

Aetna Challenge—$450,000
Winner: Lee Trevino

The mark of a great player. He can kick away a tournament, wipe the disappointment and anger from his mind and bounce back the next time out. Case in point: Lee Trevino in the Aetna Challenge, fourth stop on the 1991 Senior PGA Tour at The Vineyards at Naples, Florida, in mid-February.

Up the road at Tampa the previous Sunday, Trevino had blown his chance for an early 1991 victory with a triple bogey at the 71st hole in the GTE Suncoast Classic and had to settle for a second straight runner-up finish in Florida. Enough is enough, he apparently decided when he arrived in Naples. For two days, he rode closely on the heels of Dale Douglass, then nipped him in an exciting duel over the final holes Sunday with a 10-foot birdie putt on the 18th green. It gave Lee a six-under-par 66 for 205 and a one-stroke victory over Douglass, whose steady 68—four birdies, no bogeys—probably would have beaten any other close pursuer.

Douglass, a seven-time winner on the senior circuit, was the only man able to cope well with the windy weather in Friday's opening round. A low-ball hitter, he shot 67 with seven birdies and two bogeys and jumped off with a four-stroke lead over Trevino and six other players. It turned cold Saturday, the thermometer dipping into the 40s through the day, and Dale's game chilled as well. He shot 71 for 138 and held the lead, but Trevino surged to within a stroke with a 68 and South African Simon Hobday and J.C. Snead, both senior circuit freshmen, and Jimmy Powell finished just two back at 140.

Trevino and Douglass gave the gallery a great show on the final nine Sunday. Lee birdied the par-five 10th to draw even with Dale. Between them, they then made seven birdies coming in and they were both playing so well that only one of the putts was longer than 12 feet. Twice they topped each other on the par threes, the second time at the 17th, where Douglass made a difficult 30-footer only to have Trevino drop in his 12-footer to maintain the deadlock, then win his first 1991 title and eighth in little more than two years on the Senior PGA Tour with the birdie on the 18th green.

Chrysler Cup—$600,000
Winner: United States

Lack of depth continues to plague the International team in the annual Chrysler Cup matches at the TPC at Prestancia in Sarasota, Florida. The United States team, captained for the first time by Miller Barber, broke from a second-day tie to win five of the eight singles matches in the final round for a 58-1/2-to-41-1/2 victory, the Americans' fifth victory in the six-year history of the competition.

The U.S. team, infused with two or three of the hottest current players each year while captain Gary Player has to try to manipulate mostly the same men year after year, won its fourth straight and should continue to dominate, since no strong foreign players, aside from Japan's Isao Aoki (1992), are on the verge of turning 50.

As if the team didn't have the depth-shortage handicap to begin with, the Internationals started in the hole Friday in the modified Chapman alternate-shot competition. Bob Charles, who had never played this form of alternate-shot game, hit his own ball for the second shot instead of Player's nearby ball as required under the format. No one realized the error until Player did as they approached their tee shots on the next hole. Player then called the infraction and it meant disqualification.

That gave the Al Geiberger-Mike Hill team five points, the ultimate first-round margin after Harold Henning and Simon Hobday beat Chi Chi Rodriguez and Charles Coody, 66-67; Lee Trevino and Jim Dent defeated Bruce Devlin and Roberto De Vicenzo, 68-72, and Barber and George Archer tied at 68-68 with Bruce Crampton and Brian Waites.

The Americans maintained their five-point lead Saturday, splitting the four better-ball, stroke-play matches with Trevino/ Geiberger and Hill/Dent winning for the U.S., Crampton/Waites and Player/Charles for the Internationals, the latter team making up for the first-round goof with a 61-67 rout of Barber and Rodriguez. The issue seemed to be in doubt Sunday with the early singles matches, in which Internationals Waites, Charles and Player and Americans Hill and Coody (with 63) won. However, the strongest U.S. players—Rodriguez and Trevino—had their matches well in hand from the start and Archer tripped Crampton to establish the decisive margin of victory.

GTE West Classic—$450,000
Winner: Chi Chi Rodriguez

Not too often does a pro golfer welcome a rainstorm. One who did at the end of February was Chi Chi Rodriguez, fighting off a case of flu on the eve of the GTE West Classic at Ojai Valley Inn and Country Club. "If the tournament had not been rained out Friday, I would have had to withdraw," Chi Chi revealed after he posted a 132 total in the abbreviated tournament and won by a stroke over Bruce Crampton.

With the extra day of rest, Rodriguez deserted the sick bed Saturday and positioned himself nicely with a four-under-par 66 on the 6,190-yard course, joining Gary Player, Walt Zembriski, Dick Rhyan and Dick Hendrickson a shot off the first-day pace of Bruce Crampton. The Australian, winner of the season-opening Tournament of Champions not far to the south in California, flashed strong approach play in racking up six birdies, only one putt from outside seven feet, in scoring his 65. While the other 66 shooters had five birdies and bogey in their rounds, Rodriguez reached his 66 with four birdies, two bogeys and a 45-foot chip-in at the par-five ninth.

The field remained bunched at the top after nine holes Sunday with at least six of the players carrying good victory bids onto the back nine. In fact, when Crampton bogeyed the 13th hole, it created a five-way tie for first place. But, the contenders immediately began to fall by the wayside. Crampton and Zembriski bogeyed and Rhyan headed for a back-nine 40 and 29th place with a double bogey.

Only Rodriguez among the contenders avoided the bogeyman on the way in. As the others faltered, Chi Chi hit a five iron to seven feet and pitched to eight inches on the last two greens for the birdies, then produced another 66 and the victory. Player also birdied the 18th from a bunker, but his 67 left him a stroke behind and Crampton closed a short time later with a birdie at the 18th to tie Gary for second at 133. The victory was the 17th on the Senior PGA Tour for the recuperated Rodriguez in his five seasons-plus and his first of 1991.

Vantage at the Dominion—$350,000
Winner: Lee Trevino

When the ball rocketed from the face of Rocky Thompson's driver on the last hole of the rain-shortened Vantage at the Dominion tournament, it seemed that, at age 51, he was finally about to win his first tour tournament ever. Thompson had just seized a one-shot lead with a birdie at the 17th hole and the tee shot at No. 18 looked perfect, long and straight down the middle of the fairway. But, a winner he was not to be. When the ball landed, it bounded crazily into the left rough and almost flush against a tree. Rocky could only pitch out sideways and, shaken by the cruel turn of luck, wound up taking a bogey six.

You can't open the door like that to a player with the experience and ability of Lee Trevino, a man who had been out of the top 10 in just three of his 32 starts as a senior. Trevino, one of the three players a shot behind Thompson, jumped on a five-wood shot that hooked around a tree and carried the water in front of the green, carrying 255 yards to within eight feet of the hole. After Thompson had taken his six and Charles Coody a par for 73s and 139s, Lee rolled in the eagle putt for 70 and 137, notching his second 1991 victory and ninth Senior PGA Tour title since joining the circuit in December of 1989. Mike Hill finished ahead of them with 71, joining Thompson and Coody in a second-place deadlock.

The tournament nearly didn't get off the wet ground. Heavy, cold rains hit San Antonio shortly after the start of play Friday, making the course unplayable in little more than an hour. It was still bad Saturday morning, but play finally began four hours behind schedule and they managed to squeeze in the first round as darkness enveloped the Dominion Country Club.

Coody and Thompson, who was winless after some 600 tries on the regular and senior Tours over the years since 1964, took the lead with 66s, Trevino was one back and J.C. Snead, Ken Still and Hill trailed by two. Little changed on the front nine Sunday, Trevino and Coody turning at six under, a stroke ahead of Thompson. Coody double-bogeyed the 12th and Trevino bogeyed the 13th to create a three-way tie. It stayed that way until Thompson made his seven-footer at the 17th to take his ill-fated lead.

Vintage Arco Invitational—$500,000
Winner: Chi Chi Rodriguez

Chi Chi Rodriguez continued a late-winter pattern of taking turns with Lee Trevino when he won the classy Vintage Arco Invitational at Indian Wells, California. His one-stroke victory at The Vintage Club followed Trevino's win at Naples, his own in the GTE West at Ojai and Lee's triumph at San Antonio and it nipped him into first place on the Senior PGA Tour's money list after seven official events.

Rodriguez holed a severely breaking 15-foot birdie putt on the 18th green Sunday for a 69 and a 10-under-par 206, avoiding a playoff with Mike Hill and 61-year-old Don January, who were already in with 207s. The $75,000 paycheck for his 18th Senior Tour title jumped Chi Chi's 1991 earnings to $229,169 before the end of March.

Jimmy Powell got away fast on the Vintage Club's testing Mountain course with a 66 in Friday's opening round, running off seven birdies after a bogey at the third hole. It gave him a two-stroke lead over John Brodie, Bobby Nichols and Walt Zembriski as Trevino started with 69 and Rodriguez with 70. Lee never got going, but Chi Chi moved into a three-way tie for the lead with Powell and Terry Dill Saturday, when he shot 67 for 137 and still complained about missed birdie putts. Dill shot 68 and Powell 71.

The drama focused on the final holes Sunday. Rodriguez birdied the fourth hole to go eight under, then ran off 10 straight pars before nailing a 10-foot birdie putt at the par-five 15th. Meanwhile, January, the king of the "super (over 60) seniors" but a non-winner since 1987, had jumped into contention with an outgoing 31, but made nine straight pars on the back nine, missing a four-foot birdie putt at the 17th and leaving a 13-footer on the lip at the 18th.

Hill, constantly a threat, lost his chance with bogeys at the 16th and 17th holes before canning a 12-foot birdie putt at the 18th to catch January. Trailing them in, Rodriguez executed a brilliant sand shot from the back bunker to save par at the short 17th before holing the decisive putt on the 18th, one he "knew" because "I made the same putt earlier in the week."

Fuji Electric Grand Slam—$360,000
Winner: Miller Barber

Miller Barber rectified a 1990 oversight. For the first time since joining the Senior PGA Tour in 1981, Barber had failed to score at least one victory. He made up for that on his 60th birthday far, far from his Sherman, Texas, home when he rolled to a four-stroke victory in the Fuji Electric Grand Slam tournament, an annual event that attracts a strong American field to Japan. Miller fashioned a sparkling 14-under-par 202 at the Glen Oaks Country Club under gray, wet skies at the end of March to win the Grand Slam for a second time.

With six birdies and a bogey in miserable weather, Barber grabbed the first-round lead over Lee Trevino, Ichio Sato and Hideyo Sugimoto, who played briefly in America in the 1960s. The two Americans then reversed scores Saturday and wound up in a first-place tie at 135 entering the final round. They led Billy Casper and Seiichi Kanai by three, Jimmy Powell by four.

Barber prevailed easily in the head-to-head duel with Trevino Sunday. He ran off six birdies and took a lone bogey for his closing 67, duplicating his opening-round statistics. Trevino was no match for the 60-year-old, but his 71 and 206 slid him easily into the runner-up slot as Casper also shot 71, Kanai and Powell 75s. Bob Charles, who had won the Fuji Electric Grand Slam the three previous seasons, tied Kanai and Harold Henning for fourth at 213.

The Tradition at Desert Mountain—$800,000
Winner: Jack Nicklaus

Age and an occasional ache and pain are having absolutely no deleterious effects on the remarkable game of Jack Nicklaus, even though he has cut his playing schedule drastically in recent years. He proved it in his 50th year with two wins, a second and a third on the Senior PGA Tour, tuned up for the 51st by caging the big money in the Senior Skins and, a couple of months later, made the greatest tournament comeback of his brilliant career to claim the important Tradition at Desert Mountain title for the second year in a row.

For two days, it appeared that the Nicklaus' game in his first Senior Tour start of the year had acquired too much rust. When Phil Rodgers opened the tournament, one of the few four-rounders in senior golf, with a 65 and took a three-stroke lead, Nicklaus was six back at 71. Rodgers' eight-birdie round put him three in front of Don January and Bob Brue. When the rotund Rodgers doubled his margin with a 67 for 132, holing a 40-foot chip shot for his sixth and last birdie, Nicklaus found himself 12 strokes off the pace in 30th place after a 73. A hopeless situation for most players. Not Nicklaus.

With Saturday's best round—66—Nicklaus jumped into a tie for fifth place with John Paul Cain at 210 and was only five behind when Rodgers, winless on the tours since the 1966 Buick Open, struggled to a 73 and 205. Phil birdied all four par fives, but had four bogeys and a double bogey on the first 11 holes as he dropped into a first-place tie with Senior Tour rookie Jim Colbert, who shot a "good, solid" 67.

Although Rodgers and Colbert managed only 73s and Jim Dent started too late en route to his 69, Nicklaus applied the pressure, particularly when, after a six-foot birdie putt at No. 3, he watched in astonishment as a measured 94-foot putt at the next hole fell in the cup for an eagle. Two birdies and a bogey later at the turn, Nicklaus trailed only Colbert... by two. Though only one under on the back nine for 67, Jack was ahead by two before Colbert, Dent and Rodgers reached the par-five 18th. They all birdied the hole, as had Nicklaus, missing the eagles they needed to force a playoff. Nicklaus collected a $120,000 chunk of the $800,000 purse.

PGA Seniors Championship—$550,000
Winner: Jack Nicklaus

When last seen on the Senior PGA Tour, Jack Nicklaus was completing a remarkable rally and winning the Tradition again in Arizona. Next up on the limited senior circuit menu of Nicklaus was the Senior PGA Championship in his backyard at Palm Beach Gardens, Florida, and he had no desire to go through that again. Instead, he completely turned the tables, led from the start and ambled to a six-stroke victory, his fourth in six appearances on the Senior PGA Tour. Nobody besides runner-up Bruce Crampton was within 11 shots of the top at the finish.

It went like this on the 6,630-yard Champion course at PGA National Golf Club, a layout that had Nicklaus leaving his driver in the bag much of the time:

First Round—Jack finished with two birdies, seven in all, for 66 and a one-stroke lead over club pro Tom Joyce from Old Westbury, New York. George Archer was at 68; Phil Rodgers, Dick Hendrickson and Rolf Deming at 69. Expected contenders such as Lee Trevino, Mike Hill, Chi Chi Rodriguez, Bob Charles and defending champion Gary Player were no closer than par 72.

Second Round—Nicklaus eagled the 10th hole with a 65-yard pitch as he repeated his opening 66 and moved five strokes ahead of the field. Jim Dent advanced to the runner-up slot with a 66 of his own, Joyce hung on with 71 for 138 and Crampton entered the picture with 67 for 139.

Third Round—The Nicklaus margin went to eight strokes, a Senior Tour record, even though Jack shot just 69 and got off to such a slow start that Dent climbed to within a stroke at the eighth hole. Both birdied the ninth hole just before a thunderstorm forced a two-hour delay. It was a different story when play resumed. Nicklaus played the back nine in 32 while Dent was stumbling to a 42 and giving up second place to Crampton, who shot 70 for 209.

Fourth Round—Crampton gave Nicklaus a bit of a battle until he three-putted the ninth green. When Bruce three-putted again at the 11th, Nicklaus led by 10 strokes and he breezed home with a back-nine 36, Crampton's four birdies coming in merely reducing the final margin.

Doug Sanders Kingwood Celebrity Classic—$300,000
Winner: Mike Hill

Mike Hill, a five-time winner in 1990 and frequent contender in the early months of 1991, got onto the victory list in the Doug Sanders Kingwood Celebrity Classic in late April, thanks to an unexpected turn of events at the final green of the Deerwood Club. Hill was losing a tournament-long duel with George Archer as the two played the last hole, apparently needing a birdie just to catch big George and bring about a playoff. Hill got an easy birdie when he stiffed his approach—two feet—and got the win when Archer uncharacteristically three-putted from 25 feet.

Hill had the upper hand on Archer after Friday's first round. He shot 66 and shared the lead with Jimmy Powell, who started the day by holing a wedge shot for birdie from a difficult position 20 yards behind the green. Archer positioned himself close at 68 with five others, including Gary Player, Bob Charles and hometowner John Paul Cain, the sometimes stock broker.

Hill repeated the 66 Saturday, this time without taking a bogey, but saw Archer overtake him with a course-record 64, George birdied five of the first seven holes, three-putted the eighth and nailed four more birdies on the back nine. The two men had moved three shots ahead of the field, Bobby Nichols the closest at 135.

Lee Trevino made a run at the leaders Sunday, forging a three-way tie when he birdied the seventh hole, but he was then fresh out of that commodity and wound up in a tie for third with Gibby Gilbert at 207 after a 71. Archer also birdied the seventh to regain the lead, but Hill surged two in front with birdies at the ninth and 10th and Archer's bogey at the 12th. Mike bogeyed the 14th and George leap-frogged in front when he knocked a four-iron second shot four feet from the hole at the par-five 16th, setting up the tense finish. Hill was trying to get his pitching-wedge approach within 10 feet and, when it wound up just 24 inches from the cup, "there was some luck involved." It paid off with a $45,000 check and moved his 1991 earnings over $200,000.

Las Vegas Classic—$450,000
Winner: Chi Chi Rodriguez

It should have surprised nobody when Chi Chi Rodriguez won the Las Vegas Classic. He was in a great frame of mind going into the tournament, calling it "one of my favorite events." For good reason. He was the defending champion, had finished second in two earlier years and fifth in his first appearance in 1986.

Rodriguez trailed by a stroke going into the final round, then put together a six-under-par 66 that created a three-stroke margin of victory at Las Vegas' venerable Desert Inn Country Club course behind one of the gambling city's pioneer casinos. It was the year's second successful title defense—Nicklaus at the Tradition the other—and made him the season's first three-time winner.

Chi Chi lingered just off the pace for two days. Bruce Crampton and Ken Still were the first-round leaders on a storm-interrupted day with 67s, Still the more surprising. He birdied all four par fives. Gary Player moved in front Saturday with his 69-68—137, a stroke in front of Rodriguez (70-68), Bob Charles (71-67) and Crampton, who shot 71 Saturday. Still skied to 76. Player was four under on the par fives, chipping in at the 10th for an eagle.

Player held onto the lead Sunday until Chi Chi tied him with a six-foot birdie putt at the sixth hole, where Gary bogeyed. Player regained first place and held it until he three-putted the 14th green as Rodriguez was firing an eight-iron approach two feet from the hole. Player three-putted from the fringe at the 15th to fall two back and eventually shot 71 for 208, placing third.

Walt Zembriski made a strong charge on the back nine with birdies on the 10th, 12th and 15th holes, but he missed an eight-footer for another at the 16th and settled for 68 as Chi Chi birdied the 18th for 66 and his 12-under-par 204, three ahead of Zembriski. The $67,500 check pushed his Tour-leading total to $335,703, almost $100,000 more than that of runner-up Lee Trevino, who did not play at Las Vegas.

Murata Reunion Pro-Am—$400,000
Winner: Chi Chi Rodriguez

When he and Jim Colbert finished the Murata Reunion Pro-Am's regulation 54 holes in a tie, Chi Chi Rodriguez was not pleased. "I don't like playoffs," he said. "It's like match play and I don't like match play." What he didn't mention was that he was 0-4 in playoffs on the Senior PGA Tour, said he didn't realize it. "Just goes to show you. I forget my failures."

No failure this time at Stonebriar Country Club in suburban Dallas, although it took Rodriguez four extra holes on a steamy Texas afternoon that left him physically drained. He dropped a 15-foot birdie putt before Colbert, gunning for his initial Senior Tour victory in his freshman season, missed from 10 feet in the season's first playoff. Chi Chi's triumph, coming a week after his win at Las Vegas, was his fourth of the season and 20th during his six years on the circuit. He trails only Miller Barber and Don January in that category.

The playoff capped a wild final round in which five different pros had pieces of the lead on the back nine and Lee Trevino unexpectedly faded from contention, eventually shooting 75 after putting shots in the water and taking double bogeys at the 11th and 12th holes.

Rodriguez, who had entered the final round with 71-70, two strokes behind Trevino, the leader through the first two rounds—67-72—despite two double bogeys, began with a bang. He birdied the first three holes, twice from 30 feet, and had the figurative lead before Lee had even teed off at No. 1. Chi Chi nailed two more birdies on the front nine for a two-stroke lead, then struggled through the back nine.

Colbert, who began the day at 71-69—140, prevailed over the other contenders. His nine-iron approach to four inches at the 15th put him a shot in front but Chi Chi sank a 15-footer at the 17th and both parred the 18th, Rodriguez for 67—208 and Colbert for 68-208. Chi Chi missed a three-footer on the third extra hole before ending the long day with the 15-footer on the next hole.

Liberty Mutual Legends of Golf—$770,000
Winners: Lee Trevino and Mike Hill

When tournament director Fred Raphael, the founder of the Legends of Golf in the late 1970s, spliced Lee Trevino and Mike Hill as a team for the 1991 tournament, he created an instant favorite. How could one bet against a twosome with 15 victories between them in the previous 16 months? If one did, one shouldn't have. The Hill/Trevino tandem took charge of Liberty Mutual's unique event at Austin's Barton Creek Country Club in the second round with a 13-under-par 59 and never relinquished the lead after that. The two wound up at 252 with a two-stroke victory.

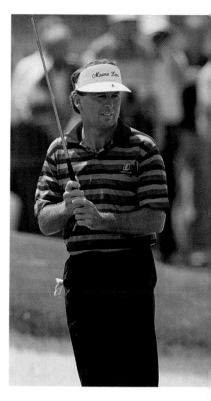

Tom Watson (above right) dueled Ian
Woosnam, while Lanny Wadkins shared third
place after a careless missed putt.

Woosnam played far left of the 18th fairway, then took two strokes from the
fringe for the victory.

In a playoff at Hazeltine, Payne Stewart secured his second major championship.

Larry Nelson (above) and Fred Couples (below) tied for third place, three strokes behind.

Scott Simpson faded on the closing holes of the fourth round and the playoff.

British Open

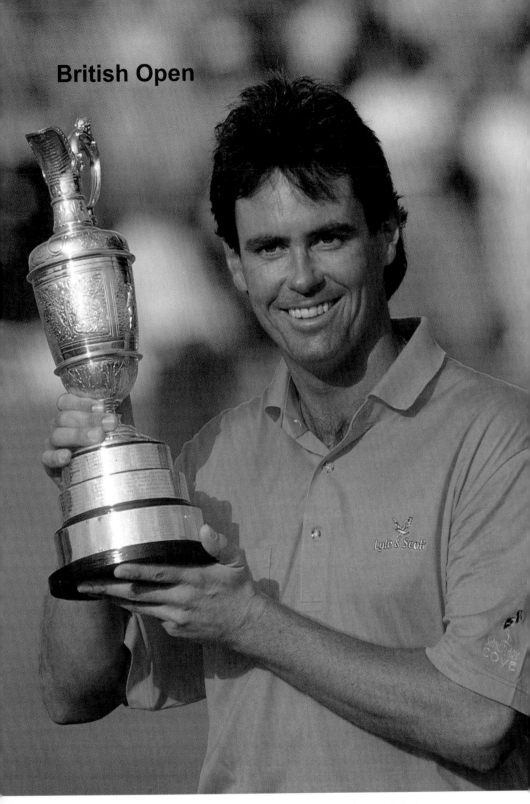

The third time was a charm for Ian Baker-Finch in the British Open.

Aussie Mike Harwood was second.

Fred Couples (right) charged to a share of third place with Mark O'Meara (above), who was tied for first place entering the last round.

"Long John" Daly left with the PGA title and a nickname.

While Daly amazed
the galleries, Bruce
Lietzke (left) and
Kenny Knox (below)
were frustrated in
their attempts to
catch him.

Ryder Cup

The margin was one-half point—or less than an inch—but the Stars and Stripes waved over the Ryder Cup.

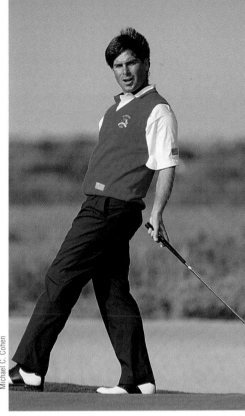

Michael C. Cohen

Europe was led by Spain's Seve Ballesteros and Jose Maria Olazabal (left) while Fred Couples (right) was among America's stars.

One photograph that typifies a familiar phrase—the thrill of victory, the agony of defeat.

Toyota World Match Play

Under the banner of a new sponsor, the World Match Play was won by Seve Ballesteros for the fifth time.

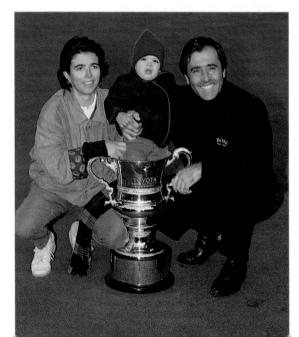

Wife Carmen and son Baldomero celebrate Ballesteros' triumph.

Runner-up to Ballesteros in
the 1988 British Open, Nick
Price lost in the World
Match Play final, 3 and 2.

Young American star Billy Andrade (left) thrashed Ian Woosnam, 7 and 6, in
the second round.

Johnnie Walker World Championship

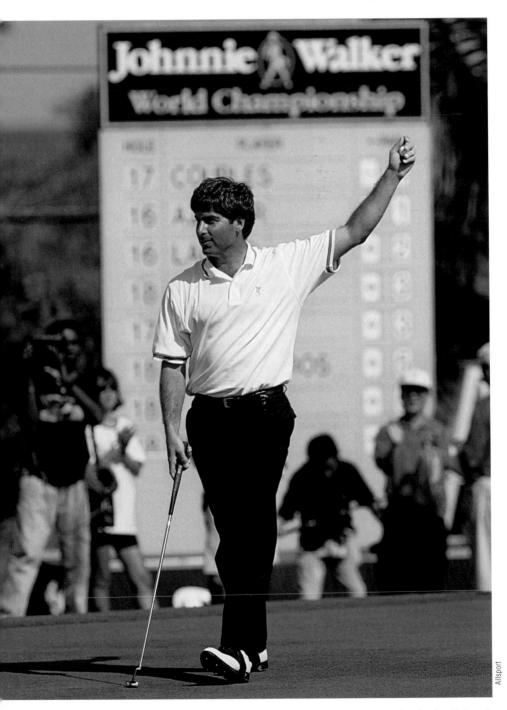

Fred Couples shot five-under-par 66 to walk off with the trophy in the Johnnie Walker World Championship. His four-stroke victory was worth $525,000.

Bernhard Langer placed second to go over $2 million for the year.

Paul Azinger was third after getting in trouble late in the final round.

Winds gusting over 40 miles an hour tested the skill and patience of the world's best golfers.

Dunhill Cup

The Swedish team recorded its first significant victory in international golf.

South Africa returned to competition, led by Gary Player (above right), and advanced to the final.

But for a rain delay of more than two hours the first day, Trevino and Hill might have led from start to finish. Mike holed the team's seventh birdie putt from five feet for 29 as the storm halted play. Afterward, they managed just 35 for 64. George Archer and Don Bies, also out in 29, came back in 32 to seize first place by two strokes with 61. On Friday, both Trevino and Hill had birdie putts on 17 of the 18 holes. Lee made nine of his and Mike the rest in racking up the 59 and moving into a three-stroke lead over Archer/ Bies.

They stretched the margin to five strokes Saturday, although they led Bies and Archer by just a shot at the turn. They gained breathing room when Trevino holed a 25-foot birdie putt from 10 feet off the green and the Archer/ Bies duo absorbed a bogey. Trevino eagled the 18th for 63.

Innocuously positioned behind the leaders' 186 were Al Geiberger and Harold Henning, yet they provided the winners with their strongest challenge Sunday. Jim Colbert and Tommy Aaron made a run from five back with birdies at six of the first seven holes to close to within a stroke, but they lost steam and eventually finished in a third-place tie at 256 with Chi Chi Rodriguez and Dave Hill.

Then came Henning and Geiberger. Henning birdied seven of the first nine holes for 29, birdied again at the 10th, then Geiberger sank eagle putts of 18 and 25 feet at the par-five 12th and 15th. When Henning followed with two more birdies, the team was 34 under and in the lead by a shot. Hill and Trevino had just bogeyed the 14th, but they bounced back with birdies at the next two holes and won by two with a final birdie at the 18th for 66 and the 252.

Bell Atlantic Classic—$550,000
Winner: Jim Ferree

At the PGA Senior Tour level, the age range is narrower and more decisive than on the regular Tour. After the first five or six years, the Senior Tour's victory column was dominated by players in their early-to-mid 50s. The pattern continued during the first five months of the 1991 campaign until the circuit reached Philadelphia and the Bell Atlantic Classic.

There, Jim Ferree, the jaunty Carolinian with a spotty playing record over the years, commanded the field from start to finish and scored a two-stroke victory just two weeks shy of his 60th birthday. It was just his second win in 10 years on the Senior Tour—Grand Rapids in 1986 was the other. He won only once on the regular circuit—in 1958 at Vancouver, British Columbia—along with three victories on the short-lived Caribbean Tour in the 1960s.

Ferree, the dapper dresser who was one of the early converts to the long putter, had the only bogey-free round the first day as he shot 67 at the 6,674-yard White Manor Country Club, the new home for the Bell Atlantic Classic in suburban Malvern. He led Babe Hiskey by one shot, Lee Trevino and Mike Hill by two and remarked: "If I keep shooting 67s, I might win."

He shot no more 67s, but still won. Chipping had been a big help in avoiding bogeys Friday. The long putter was the decisive weapon Saturday for Ferree after he made a spectacular par save at the first hole. A 69-foot putt dropped for an eagle at the 15th and a 35-footer for a birdie at the 18th as Jim posted a 69 and, at 136, he was one shot ahead of Jim Colbert, who shot 66 in mounting another strong bid for his first senior win, and three in front of Trevino.

Neither of the two could muster a challenge Sunday, enabling Ferree to grab the triumph with a par-72 finish for 208. They had the chance as Jim ran through 10 straight pars at the start of the round. "The birdie at No. 11 was critical... my first one putt of the day (from 12 feet)," he noted later. That was to be his only birdie of the day, but it gave him a cushion to handle a drive into the trees and an ultimate bogey on the final hole. Colbert shot 73 and Trevino 71 to tie for second place at 210. Harold Henning finished at 212 and Hill in a tie with Larry Ziegler at 213.

NYNEX Commemorative—$400,000
Winner: Charles Coody

Coming off a banner year in which he finished third on the Senior PGA Tour's money list with more than a quarter-million dollars in prize money, Charles Coody had been struggling in the early months of 1991. Things went from bad to worse when the death of his 81-year-old father early in the year had a profound effect on him. Finally, it all turned around in resounding fashion in the NYNEX Commemorative at Westchester County's Sleepy Hollow Country Club. With rounds of 66-62-65, Coody tied the Senior Tour's 54-hole tournament record, his 193 matching the score Bob Charles shot two years earlier over the 6,545 yards of the Sleepy Hollow course.

Sleepy Hollow, a pleasant members' course, always yields striking scores by the senior pros, so the opening-round 64s of Charles, a two-time Commemorative winner, and Rocky Thompson were not at all surprising. Thirty-eight others broke par 70, with Coody and defending champion Lee Trevino among nine at 66. Coody made his move Saturday as both he and Don Bies shot 62s and finished the day one-two in the standings at 128 and 129. Charles had seven birdies, an eagle and a bogey as he took the lead, reaching the 457-yard sixth hole with a two iron and holing a 12-foot putt for the eagle.

Coody had a "comfortable" round Sunday as he held off a challenge by fellow Texan Don Massengale, who started the day five strokes off the lead and finished in second place at 196 after a closing 63. The key to the round may have come early when, after a shaky start, Coody ran in a 45-foot birdie putt at the second hole. He followed with an 18-footer for another birdie at the third hole and was never seriously threatened after that. He also birdied the fifth hole, and turned in 32. He was a bit erratic coming in with four birdies and two bogeys, the second one at the 16th preventing him from setting a new 54-hole record on the circuit. Defender Trevino, who had made a fast round trip in a private jet to Dallas to attend high school graduation of daughter Troy on the eve of the tournament, shot the opening 66 on just a few hours of sleep and followed with two more to finish third at 198. The victory for Coody, the 1971 Masters champion, was his third on the Senior Tour.

Mazda Senior Players Championship—$1,000,000
Winner: Jim Albus

Because of the magnitude of the tournament, John Daly's victory in the PGA Championship was almost universally recognized as 1991's surprise of the year in golfing circles. By comparison, though, it doesn't seem to belong in the same league with what happened in the Senior PGA Tour's prestigious Mazda Senior Players Championship, the second-richest event on that circuit. Though little known to the average golf fan, Daly had established a bit of an inner-circle reputation with some overseas success and the tremendous length of his game. On the other hand, Jim Albus teed off in the Senior Players Championship at the TPC of Michigan a virtual unknown beyond the Metropolitan New York area in which he worked and played as the club pro at the Piping Rock Club on Long Island and won a bundle of sectional events.

Four days later, Albus was the talk of the Senior Tour after overcoming one of the year's strongest fields, attracted to the TPC of Michigan by the important title and million-dollar purse, with a come-from-behind victory in the final round. His closing, two-under-par 70 brought him from three strokes off the pace to a three-shot victory at 279. The joint runners-up at 282 were Bob Charles, Dave Hill and Charles Coody, but the major victim was Lee Trevino, Albus' playing partner on Sunday. Trevino, whom Albus had never met until that day, had led after the second and third rounds with scores of 70-67-69 for 206, but came apart Sunday. He never made a birdie and bogeyed three of the last four holes for 78, dropping into a tie for eighth place.

Albus was a late addition to the Players Championship's exclusive, 78-player field when his high finish the previous week gave him enough prize money to qualify. He proved he belonged with an opening 66 that gave him a two-stroke lead, but slipped three behind Trevino with a 74 Friday. Jim matched Lee's 69 Saturday to position himself in second place for the final run. He went three over par on the first two holes, but got them back with three birdies before the turn. Hill had the lead by three, but a triple bogey at the 11th crippled Dave. Albus took the lead for good with a 25-foot birdie putt at the 15th and the margin grew to three as he parred in and the other challengers self-destructed.

MONY Syracuse Classic—$400,000
Winner: Rocky Thompson

Talk about persistence. In 27 years of competition on the regular and Senior PGA Tours, Texan Rocky Thompson had been close a few times, but had never won, even though he had amassed 57 titles in junior, adult amateur and off-tour pro events over the years. By his own count, he was 0-for-611 on the tours when he teed off in the MONY Syracuse Classic at Lafayette Country Club in mid-June. Finally, it happened. Thompson opened with a sensational 62 and led all the way to a one-stroke victory over hard-charging Jim Dent, who had won the Syracuse Classic the two previous years.

The 62 gave Thompson a four-stroke lead and the way the round began, Rocky knew he had a shot at the 50s. He birdied the first five holes, all putts dead center and three from 20 feet or longer, and he hadn't even come to the first of Lafayette's five reachable par fives. He birdied four of them and the par-four 14th for the tournament-record 62. Five players shot 66 and Dent was among five others at 67.

Thompson's game turned erratic Saturday, but he still managed to maintain all but a stroke of his big lead with 68 for 130. He holed a sand wedge approach at No. 10 and a nine-foot putt at the par-five 16th for eagles to offset three bogeys amid afternoon thunderstorms that twice interrupted play. Dent fashioned a solid 66 to move into second place at 133, a stroke ahead of Mike Hill and J.C. Snead, who was later disqualified when he failed to turn in a signed scorecard when he finished.

The final round became a Thompson-Dent duel with Jim getting in first licks with a birdie on the opening hole. However, Rocky, the unanimously elected mayor of Toco, Texas (Population: 138), maintained his poise and led by three after 14 holes. Dent then launched a powerful bid for the victory. He birdied the 15th and 16th and eagled the par-five 17th with a 30-footer to draw even with Thompson, who two-putted for birdie there. Dent drove into the fairway, Thompson into the left rough on the final hole. Rocky hooked his approach onto the green, but Jim put his onto the back fringe. His downhill putt rolled six feet past the cup and he missed coming back before Thompson tapped in his at-long-last winning putt.

PaineWebber Invitational—$450,000
Winner: Orville Moody

Things had soured a good bit in the 1990s for Orville Moody. In the three previous seasons, he had won almost $1.5 million and seven titles, including the prestigious Senior TPC and U.S. Senior Open in 1989. Not a lot of good happened in 1990 nor in the early months of 1991. In fact, Moody left his clubs in the bag for three weeks to rest an aching back just before teeing it up in the PaineWebber Invitational at Charlotte's TPC at Piper Glen as one of the PGA Senior Tour's founding events moved into June dates for the first time.

Victory was Moody's reward for taking the time off as he nipped Dick Hendrickson in the 11th edition of the North Carolina event. Starting the final round a shot behind leader Mike Hill, Orville shot 70 for 207, nearly blowing the lead on the final hole with a bogey to Hendrickson's closing birdie for 71 and 208, his best finish and biggest check ($40,000) ever. Moody came to the watery, par-five 18th with a two-stroke lead, but pushed his drive into some trees. He pitched out, then bounced his approach off the rocks into the lake. However, he salvaged a bogey and the win with a 15-foot bogey putt.

Hill, with two 1991 wins already in the books, had command of the tournament the first two days. His opening 66 gave him the lead, but he had to share the accolades Friday with 61-year-old Arnold Palmer, the tournament host and Charlotte favorite, who emerged from a lengthy slump with a 67 on the strength of a holed 60-yard wedge shot at the par-five sixth. Just as he did the first day, Hill played the final three holes in three under Saturday to maintain his one-stroke lead. He eagled the par-five 16th with a 35-foot putt en route to the 70 and 136. Palmer fell back with 73 as Moody (68), Hendrickson and George Archer (66s) moved into second place, a shot off the lead.

Hendrickson, a club pro most of his life, grabbed the lead early Sunday with an eagle at the second hole, but yielded to Moody and his birdies at the seventh, ninth and 10th. Hill crippled his chances when he drove into the water and double-bogeyed the 14th and blew his last hope with another wet drive at the 18th. He tied for third with Bruce Crampton, the defending champion, at 209.

Southwestern Bell Classic—$450,000
Winner: Jim Colbert

Jim Colbert grew up in Kansas City, where he was the second-string golf hero behind a fellow named Tom Watson. So, when he came back to Kansas City in his rookie season on the Senior PGA Tour, Colbert had a big following as the Southwestern Bell Classic set up shop for the first time in the Missouri city. Which can be bad or good. It's bad so often because the player just tries too hard and it affects his game. This seems to happen more often than not in pro golf. It's good when the player feeds off the enthusiasm and elevates his game a notch or two.

This was the case for Colbert, as he scored his first senior victory in his fourth month on the circuit after giving up his role as an ESPN golf analyst and cutting back on his responsibilities with his company in Las Vegas. After sharing the lead for two days, Jim broke to a three-stroke victory with a nine-under-par 201 at Loch Lloyd Country Club, his first title since he scored his eighth win on the PGA Tour in the 1983 Texas Open.

It had appeared that it was just a matter of time through Colbert's first nine starts. He finished second three times, once to Jack Nicklaus in the Tradition and another time losing a playoff to Chi Chi Rodriguez. With a big gallery of support, he opened the Southwestern Bell with 66 and tied for the lead with Larry Laoretti and Jack Kiefer, describing the round as "the best I've played" even though it included a double bogey. He followed with 67 Saturday, a bogey on the final hole dropping him into a tie with Al Geiberger (68-65) as Laoretti slipped three strokes behind in a third-place tie with Don January and Rodriguez.

After five holes Sunday, Geiberger led by two, but three straight birdies, starting at No. 8 and ending with a 30-footer at No. 10, jumped Colbert into a two-stroke lead. Birdies were hard to come by in the winds that raked the back nine, Colbert getting the only one among the two contenders at the par-five 13th. Jim clinched the victory at the 17th, where he saved par from the rough with a chip to two feet as Al was taking a bogey. Colbert finished with a 68, Geiberger with 71 for 204, dropping into a runner-up tie with Laoretti.

Kroger Classic—$600,000
Winner: Al Geiberger

Al Geiberger just had to wait an extra week before ending a modest victory drought on the Senior PGA Tour. Jim Colbert outplayed Geiberger in the final round of the Southwestern Bell Classic the Sunday before Geiberger bypassed Dale Douglass and nipped Larry Laoretti to win the Kroger Classic at Kings Island, Ohio, near Cincinnati, picking up his sixth senior title and first since the GTE Northwest Classic in August of 1989. He came from two strokes off the lead on the Grizzly course at the Jack Nicklaus Sports Center with a final-round 68 for 203 and a one-stroke victory over Laoretti.

Geiberger's 66 start and those of co-leaders Dudley Wysong, Terry Dill and Douglass were obscured a bit by the day's feature attraction—the first-ever grouping of Arnold Palmer, Lee Trevino and Nicklaus. It packed the house. For the record, Trevino shot 68, Nicklaus 71 and Palmer 76, and none of them really got into serious contention. Among the leaders, Douglass ran off six birdies in a row in the middle of the round, one coming on a 90-foot putt at the par-three eighth, and Dill joined the group with a 10-foot eagle putt at the par-five 18th.

Though big crowds continued, things settled into more normal conditions Saturday as Douglass assumed a two-stroke lead over Geiberger, Wysong and Bob Charles. Dale shot a four-under-par 67 despite a double-bogey six when he drove out of bounds at No. 6. He was at 133 and Nicklaus made his presence felt with a 66 to move within four strokes of the lead. It stirred memories of his huge comeback in the Tradition earlier in the season.

However, the final round turned into a duel between Geiberger and Douglass and a sneak attack by Laoretti at the end. After 14 holes, they were even at 10 under. Geiberger bogeyed the 14th from the sand but reforged the tie when he chipped in at the 15th. That seemed to unnerve Douglass, who three-putted the 16th and drove into a creek at the 18th for another bogey. Meanwhile, Laoretti had birdied the last two holes for 67 and nine-under 204, requiring Geiberger to par the 18th to clinch the victory. Which he did. Douglass tied for third at 205 with Miller Barber and Harold Henning.

Seniors British Open—£150,000
Winner: Bob Verwey

Bob Verwey kept it in the family in an unlikely finish to the fifth Seniors British Open, succeeding brother-in-law Gary Player, the defender and only two-time winner of the tournament. Always very much in the shadow of the family's Hall-of-Famer in his native South Africa and on his forays to Europe and America in his prime years, Verwey stood up to the pressure of the final holes to score a one-stroke victory. The rookie senior closed with 70 for a one-over-par 285 in the championship's first staging at England's Royal Lytham and St. Annes, a frequent British Open venue as is Turnberry, the Senior Open's locale in Scotland the first four years. The winning score was the highest in the event's brief history, five strokes more than Player posted after surviving the raging, final-day weather in 1990. The 1991 tournament was the first under the auspices of the Royal and Ancient Golf Club.

Royal Lytham was difficult from the start. Bob Charles, the 1989 champion, shared the first-round lead with Englishmen Peter Butler and Tommy Horton, both former Ryder Cuppers, at two-under-par 69. Ironically, Verwey and Player opened with 70s and Bernard Hunt, the former British Ryder Cup captain, and Canadian Bob Rose shot 71s. Heavy weather came up Friday and Player managed to take over first place with a 73 for 143. Verwey had 74 to tie for second with Butler at 144, a stroke in front of Charles, Rose and Horton. The eventual winner, who had just turned 50 in January, nosed in front Saturday, matching par for a 215 total. Player, Butler and Horton were at 216, then it was three strokes back to the next group—Charles, Rose, Brian Waites and amateur Charles Green.

Charles turned out to be Verwey's most vigorous pursuer Sunday. He shot the week's best score—67—with a solid playing round and a hot putter on the front nine. He and Horton, with a closing 70, were on the board with 286s when Verwey drove into a fairway bunker at the par-four finishing hole, needing a par to avoid a playoff. He played out safely from the sand, pitched six feet from the cup and rolled in the winning putt for the £25,000 first prize, the biggest check of his career.

Newport Cup—$325,000
Winner: Larry Ziegler

Meanwhile, at the same time back in the United States, another first-time winner in senior golf was being crowned at the Newport Cup, the Senior PGA Tour's regular stop opposite the Seniors British Open. Larry Ziegler, whose first full season on the over-50 circuit was curtailed because of a wrist injury, scored his first tournament victory in 15 years at historic Newport Country Club and did it in tournament-record fashion with a 17-under-par 199, a stroke better than Miller Barber shot in 1983 in the tournament which has been played in several forms since 1980 when Sam Snead won a 36-hole event there.

Ziegler has always been a bit of a free spirit who makes light of the fact that his first win on the PGA Tour in 1969 was in a fly-by-night affair called the Michigan Golf Classic that defaulted on the purse, forcing the Tour to come up with his $20,000 check. He won twice more during his long career on the PGA Tour, the most recent at New Orleans in 1976. The 52-year-old St. Louis native, one of 14 children, had no particular hope of ending the drought at Newport, though encouraged by a strong finishing round the previous week at Cincinnati. In fact, he had arrived so late that he had only played the front nine before teeing off in the first round Friday. Still, he shot 66, including 33 on the unexplored back side, and, with Jim Dent, the 1989 winner, trailed leader George Archer by a shot.

Larry repeated his 66 Saturday and moved into the lead, two shots ahead of Tom Shaw and Dent, as Archer fell back with 72 for 137. Perhaps the best indication Sunday that it was going to be his day came when, after both playing partners Shaw and Dent birdied the first hole, he came back by nearly holing his approach at the par-four second and restoring the two-stroke lead. Nobody got closer than that the rest of the day. He led by four at the turn after holing a 12-foot par putt at the ninth. Shaw made a run at him on the back nine with consecutive birdies on the first three holes, but that final threat disappeared when Shaw took a triple bogey at the 16th hole. Ziegler breezed home with a 67 for the 199 and a six-stroke victory over Archer, Dent and Shaw.

Ameritech Open—$500,000
Winner: Mike Hill

For two months, the players who had been dominating the Senior PGA Tour had been giving way to first-time winners and men who had been out of the winners' circle for extended periods of time. The pattern changed in mid-July at the Ameritech Open in suburban Chicago, where Mike Hill, the No. 2 money winner in 1990, moved up to that position on the 1991 standings with a hard-fought victory. Winning his second title of the year and seventh in 30 months on the Senior Tour, Hill compiled a 16-under-par 200 total at Stonebridge Country Club in Aurora, Illinois, finishing two strokes in front of Bob Charles.

Hill maneuvered himself into good position the first two days. He opened with 67, positioning himself comfortably two strokes off the lead of Al Geiberger, who had won two weeks earlier in Cincinnati. Like Hill, Geiberger had his son by his side as his caddie and said that it's a booster. He ran off seven birdies. Hill had six after three-putting the first green, the 67 tying him with Orville Moody and George Archer. Bruce Crampton shot 66.

Hill seized a three-stroke lead Saturday with a 66 that included just one par on the back nine. He had nine birdies and three bogeys on the windy day that Mike hoped would repeat itself Sunday. He plays well in the wind and "it's harder for the rest of the guys to shoot low numbers."

It calmed down Sunday and, as Hill feared, trouble emerged in the form of Charles, who started the day five strokes off the lead and carried the battle to the final hole, shooting the week's lowest round—64. The left-hander worked out a near-perfect round, hitting every green and canning eight birdie putts. The last one was at the 16th, where Hill missed his first green but dropped the five-foot par putt. Bob had a six-footer for a ninth birdie on the final green, a chance to put the squeeze on the leader, but he pushed it off line. Moments later, Hill dropped a five-footer there for 67 and the final, two-stroke margin over Charles. Geiberger got going too late and his four birdies in a five-hole stretch on the back nine merely assured his third-place finish—68 for 204.

U.S. Senior Open—$600,000
Winner: Jack Nicklaus

An interesting parallel surfaced as Jack Nicklaus won his third tournament in five 1991 starts on the Senior PGA Tour—the coveted U.S. Senior Open Championship. The victory, which gave Nicklaus a quickly attained sweep of the circuit's three most important titles, came in a playoff at Oakland Hills, the first club to host a second Senior Open. Thus, he became the second man to have won the U.S. Amateur, the U.S. Open and the U.S.

Senior Open. The first? Arnold Palmer, who also completed that triad with a playoff victory at Oakland Hills in 1981.

Chi Chi Rodriguez locked horns with Nicklaus in the extra round at Oakland Hills that Monday. Rodriguez responded with a good 69 on the demanding course in suburban Detroit, at which the two men finished in the deadlock with scores of two-over-par 282. But Nicklaus was at the top of his game and shot 65. He birdied five of the first eight holes, including a 40-foot chip-in at No. 7 after Rodriguez had pulled within a stroke with a 35-foot birdie putt at the sixth. Jack was three in front at the turn and finished comfortably after Chi Chi missed a six-foot birdie putt at the 16th and he almost aced the par-three 17th.

The week's play at Oakland Hills focused down to the final holes Sunday and the playoff. Mike Hill, coming off his victory in the Ameritech Open in Chicago the previous Sunday, led the first day with 68, then fell back. It was J.C. Snead's turn in front Friday with his 71-69—140, a shot in front of Nicklaus (72-69), Rodriguez (73-68) and Al Geiberger (71-70). Lee Trevino took his turn on top Saturday with 68 for 210 with Snead (71) and Nicklaus and Rodriguez (70s) at 211. The issue was still undecided as Nicklaus and Trevino, the last twosome, reached the tee of the rugged, par-three 17th. They were part of a four-way tie for the lead with Rodriguez and Geiberger at three over par. Nicklaus struck a magnificent five iron five feet from the hole and birdied while Trevino ended his chances with a bogey. Ahead, Rodriguez played a brilliant approach over a bunker at the 18th that rolled two feet from the cup. He made it, Nicklaus parred moments later for his 71 and Monday overtime was ordained.

Northville Long Island Classic—$450,000
Winner: George Archer

It was only a matter of time. George Archer had been flirting with victory all season—second three times, seventh or better in nine of his 20 starts prior to his defense of the Northville Long Island Classic championship he had won among his four 1990 triumphs. He had collected more than $300,000 without winning. Victory time came up again at the Meadow Brook Club for Archer, who had scored a rare mid-summer victory there last year. He won by one in 1990, by two in 1991 with rounds of 68, 67 and 69 for 204, 12 under par. The final-round 69 broke him away from a 36-hole tie with Larry Laoretti, the former club pro on Long Island who never played on the PGA Tour, and held off the challenge of Jim Colbert.

At 68 Friday, Archer trailed Colbert, Laoretti and Homero Blancas by a stroke. The cigar-smoking Laoretti had some luck going for him as he chipped in for an eagle at the par-five 10th and dropped an 85-foot birdie putt on the next green. He had no bogeys, nor did Colbert, who had been nursing a touchy back for weeks. Blancas birdied the last four holes, mostly from close range, for his 67.

The logjam opened up Saturday as Archer, with his 67, and Laoretti, with 68, established a three-stroke lead on the field at 135. Big George racked up seven birdies, starting fast with two of them at the early par-five first and third holes and making two confidence-building par putts at the second and fourth. Laoretti started even more strongly with an 18-foot eagle putt at the first and a birdie at the third. Colbert was among five players at 138.

For most of the day Sunday, it was Archer vs Laoretti with nobody else in sight and George was getting the better of it. He was never in serious trouble after he eagled the third hole with a 15-foot putt, but didn't go in front to stay until Laoretti bogeyed the ninth hole. Larry fell two back with another bogey at No. 11 and did not seriously threaten after that. Instead, Colbert made his run on the back nine, out in 37, Jim birdied the first six holes after the turn, parred Nos. 16 and 17, but put his sand-iron tee shot at the 18th in the right bunker and failed to rescue par. Archer methodically put up eight pars amid all that to score the victory.

Showdown Classic—$350,000
Winner: Dale Douglass

Talk about gifts. Nobody was more surprised than Dale Douglass when he found himself the winner of the Showdown Classic at Salt Lake City's suburban Jeremy Ranch Golf Club. He was the beneficiary of a monumental collapse of his friend, Charles Coody, on the last two holes of the early-August tournament. Virtually all players of consequence in tournament golf have frittered away a victory in one way or another, but few have had it happen so suddenly and devastatingly as the disaster that befell Coody that Sunday afternoon.

The 1971 Masters champion had led the tournament from the start. He opened with a seven-under-par 65, registering three birdies and an eagle on the par-five holes, and took a one-stroke lead over Bobby Nichols and Bob Wynn. Then, on Saturday, he opened a four-stroke lead with 69 for 134, recovering from a double bogey at the par-five third, where he hooked his second shot out of bounds. He made six birdies and nine pars the rest of the way. Douglass joined Nichols and Wynn in the runner-up spot with the day's best round—a 67—even though he bogeyed the last two holes with over-powered approaches.

Coody gave some earlier signs of trouble Sunday when he bogeyed one par-five hole and double-bogeyed the other one—to a Douglass eagle—on the front nine, but he appeared to have things in hand after birdies on the back nine's two par fives, the latter at the 16th where it gave him a three-stroke lead. Playing partner Douglass, with whom he won the 1990 Legends of Golf, was more concerned then about second place with Archer and Don Bies heading toward 210s and him at seven under. The Coody debacle started at the par-three 17th, where he came up short of the green, stubbed his first chip and was long with his second, taking a double bogey and leading then only by one. Shaken, Charley hit a rare bad tee shot at No. 18 and the ball hooked into a bush, almost unplayable. He chopped it out to get a shot, but put the ball into the front bunker. His weak sand shot remained on the lower level of the green, 45 feet from the cup, and he three-putted, not only handing the victory to Douglass, who made a good par from just over the green for 71 and 209, but falling below Archer and Bies as well with his 77 and 211.

GTE Northwest Classic—$400,000
Winner: Mike Hill

Mike Hill's superb season continued in Seattle, where he accepted a winner's check for a fourth time in 1991 with his victory in the GTE Northwest Classic. In the previous 11 starts on his busy playing schedule, Hill was out of the top 10 just once and won the Ameritech Open and the Legends of Golf with Lee Trevino. Earlier, he won the Doug Sanders Celebrity Classic and had a pair of second-place finishes. And the victory at Seattle's Inglewood Country Club exemplified the calibre of the golf the 52-year-old pro from Michigan had been flashing on the Senior PGA Tour. He came from four strokes off the lead with a final-round, eight-under-par 64 to snatch the title away from Chi Chi Rodriguez with his 18-under-par 198.

With four 1991 victories already in the bag, Rodriguez appeared likely to pad his record and his No. 1 position on the circuit's money list when he came out of the starting gate Friday with a nine-under 63. Yet, he had only a two-stroke lead over Jim Ferree, who started and finished his round with eagles for his 65. Gibby Gilbert, a first-year senior, had 66 and the rest of the field was spread back from 68. Rodriguez finished off the 63 with a 30-foot putt for birdie, his fourth on the last five holes. He missed a four-footer for his only bogey at the 13th.

Rodriguez doubled his margin Saturday when he followed with 67 for 130, building the entire margin on the last four holes. He holed a 25-footer for an eagle at the par-five 15th, then birdied the last three holes to open his four-stroke margin over Hill, DeWitt Weaver, Dick Hendrickson, Bruce Crampton and 65-year-old Joe Jimenez, who shot a remarkable 63 for his 134. Hill holed three long birdie putts in shooting 66 to stay in the hunt. Mike picked up two strokes on the front nine Sunday and overtook Rodriguez when he birdied the 10th and 11th. Both birdied the 13th, but Chi Chi regained the lead with a 12-footer at the 14th. Mike finally went in front to stay when he holed a 20-footer for eagle at the 15th and got some padding when Rodriguez bogeyed the par-three 16th. They both birdied the 18th, Hill for 64 and his 198, Rodriguez for 70 and 200. Hendrickson finished third at 202 with a closing 68.

Sunwest Bank/Charley Pride Classic—$350,000
Winner: Lee Trevino

Chi Chi Rodriguez, coming off a strong runner-up finish in Seattle into his defending champion's role in the Sunwest Bank/Charley Pride Classic in Albuquerque, shot a 204 at Four Hills Country Club, a stroke better than the score that brought him the title in 1990. "The only trouble," he quipped afterward, "was that Trevino showed up." Lee didn't just show up, either. Playing for the first time in three weeks on the Senior PGA Tour and nursing a thumb he blistered in a club-repair accident, Trevino put together three rounds in the 60s and rolled to a four-stroke victory. It was his third individual title of the season (plus the Legends of Golf with Mike Hill), impressive by most standards but well behind his 1990 pace when he had six victories in the first seven months.

Trevino opened strongly with 66 in the late-August event, but trailed Babe Hiskey and Don Bies by two strokes at day's end. Rodriguez birdied four of the last seven holes for 67. Trevino birdied four of the last six, but three-putted the 18th. Lee seized the lead Saturday with a nicely paced 65 for 131 and a two-stroke lead over 61-year-old Don January, one of the early major stars on the Senior PGA Tour. Lee bogeyed the ninth hole, then shot the back nine in five-under 31, holing lengthy putts at the 14th, 15th and 18th. January, who won the over-60 Vantage Classics competition by six shots and was bidding to become the first Vantage Classics winner to take the tournament title as well, also shot 31 on the back nine. It was three strokes back to the next players—Hiskey, Jack Kiefer and Don Massengale—and Rodriguez was at 137.

Trevino couldn't buy a birdie in the early going Sunday as Chi Chi charged with a four-birdie string, starting at No. 4. He bogeyed the ninth, but came back with birdies at the next two holes to stand just a stroke off the lead. Trevino finally got his first birdie at the 11th with a 20-footer moments later and was never in trouble thereafter. Rodriguez had pars on his last seven holes, while Trevino moved to his final margin with three birdies and a bogey coming in for 69 and 200, breaking Gene Littler's 1986 tournament record. Jim O'Hern, with 65, tied Rodriguez for second at 204.

GTE North Classic—$450,000
Winner: George Archer

Something good is bound to happen when you keep throwing sub-par rounds at the field. It paid off for George Archer the first week of August when he won his first 1991 title at Northville. He kept posting those under-par scores through the next four tournaments and, presto, he had victory No. 2 of the year. It came in the GTE North Classic at Broadmoor Country Club in Indianapolis, where his rounds of 66, 66 and 67 held off the hot pursuit of Dale Douglass and gave him a one-stroke victory with the 17-under-par 199.

Larry Mowry, who had suffered an inner-ear problem and missed most of the summer schedule, played his first full tournament in four months and got off with a bang, making eight birdies, no bogeys and shooting 64, an 18-hole tournament record. Archer and Douglass shared the runner-up spot at 66 with Dick Rhyan. Eight others were at 67.

Harold Henning entered the picture Saturday. Spurred on by an eagle at the ninth hole, the South African shot the back nine in 32 for 65 to share the lead at 132 with Archer and did it with a set of clubs, minus two broken ones, that arrived in the mail that morning. Archer had three birdies and a bogey on the last five holes for his 66. Douglass was at 133 after his 67.

Archer quickly moved in front Sunday with a six-foot birdie putt at the first hole and was never really headed. He birdied the seventh and ninth and was out in 32, two ahead of Henning, four in front of Douglass. The South African pulled within a stroke with a birdie at the 10th, but bogeyed the 11th and dropped out of contention with a double bogey at the par-five 12th, where he left a shot in the sand and missed a three-foot putt. Douglass took up the chase and birdied five of the last seven holes for 67. Not enough, as Archer birdied the par-five 13th and 17th, the latter giving him a two-shot cushion to cover Dale's final birdie at the 18th. Henning wound up with 72, tying Chi Chi Rodriguez for third. Archer's 199 set a tournament record and was the third-lowest score of the season to that point. It was his seventh victory in less than two years on the Senior PGA Tour.

First of America Classic—$350,000
Winner: Harold Henning

The week before in Indianapolis, Harold Henning had put himself in position to win and, as had been happening too often during the last three years, let the chance escape. He had begun to think he "had run out of bullets," that there might not be another victory in the cards for him. So, when he turned around the Indianapolis finish that he had called "absolute rubbish" and won the First of America Classic in Grand Rapids, Michigan, he particularly savored the tough triumph that came on the first hole of a playoff against Gibby Gilbert, a 1991 newcomer on the Senior PGA Tour. Other than his team victory with Al Geiberger in the 1989 Legends of Golf, Harold had not won on the Senior PGA Tour since the GTE Classic in early 1988.

For the first two days, the lead was in the hands of Syracuse winner Rocky Thompson. He opened with 66 after some serious practice on his putting. He one-putted nine times, six for birdies on the par-71 Highlands course at Grand Rapids as he took a one-stroke lead over Larry Laoretti and 61-year-old Gene Littler. Henning had a one-over 72 and received an "inspirational" pairing with Arnold Palmer Friday. Palmer, beginning a late-season spurt of good performances on the circuit, stirred his immense gallery when he birdied two of the first three holes and Henning "joined the party." In a 10-hole stretch in the middle of the round, Harold ran off five birdies and an eagle for 64. It jumped him into a four-way tie for second with Littler, Lee Trevino and Bob Reith, a stroke behind Thompson, who had 69 for 135. Palmer shot 69.

Henning and Gilbert emerged from one of the most exciting blanket finishes Sunday. At the turn, just two strokes separated the top seven contenders, but Henning felt he wasn't in the race until things began to happen on the back nine. He birdied the 11th, 14th, 15th and 17th holes and missed a 25-footer for another and the outright win at the last hole, finishing with 66 and 202. Meanwhile, Gilbert was producing a near-flawless 64, hitting every green in regulation or better and racking up seven birdies. Both men played from greenside bunkers at the par-five 10th, the first playoff hole, and Henning ended it with a 12-foot birdie putt after Gibby missed his from 15 feet.

Digital Classic—$400,000
Winner: Rocky Thompson

Rocky Thompson's average is getting better. Carrying an ignominious .000 victory record into the MONY Syracuse Classic in June, Thompson finally scored his first win in 612 starts in tournaments on the PGA and Senior PGA Tours over the past 27 years. Twelve events later, when the Senior PGA Tour arrived at Nashawtuc Country Club in Concord, Massachusetts, for the Digital

Classic, Rocky scored another first, making it two for 624, still not a great percentage but a lot better than the many thousands who have tried the Tours and never won. He shot a final-round 70 for a 205 total, holding off Bruce Crampton by one stroke.

Thompson positioned himself well in Friday's first round. He birdied three of the last four holes (seven in all) for 66, just one shot off the 65s of co-leaders Lee Trevino and Jim Colbert. Both eagled the par-five 10th, Trevino making six birdies and taking a bogey while Colbert bogeyed twice but had five consecutive birdies on the front nine. Thompson moved into the lead Saturday, offsetting two bogeys with five birdies, including one from 25 feet at the 18th, for 69 and 135. Trevino remained close, shooting 71 for 136 to share second place with Al Geiberger. Crampton was next at 138.

Sunday's finale pitted Thompson against Trevino and the charging Crampton. Rocky struggled a bit on the front nine, hitting only three of the greens in regulation, and, when he bogeyed the ninth, he found himself tied with Trevino at 10 under par. Although birdies remained hard to come by on the rainy afternoon, Thompson was hitting the greens and holding his own against Trevino, who missed important putts at the 11th and 13th, the latter for bogey, and dropped into a tie for third when his tee shot at the par-three 17th trickled into the water. Meanwhile, Crampton had gotten to 10 under when he holed a 14-foot birdie putt at the same hole, tying the leader. However, after laying up from the rough at the par-five finishing hole, Thompson pitched to eight feet and made "the real easy putt" to clinch the victory. Mike Hill matched Crampton's closing 68 to tie Trevino for third at 208. Bob Charles, who had won the last two Digital Classics, was never in contention and finished eight shots back at 213.

Nationwide Championship—$700,000
Winner: Mike Hill

Atlanta returned to the Senior PGA Tour after a two-year absence with one of the year's biggest purses—$700,000—and the Georgia fans saw Mike Hill, the season's most successful player, score his fourth victory and take over first place on the circuit's money list. Hill eased somewhat shakily into the winner's chair, settling for bogeys on the last two holes and the 71 that he knew was all that he needed to finish a stroke in front of Tom Shaw, who was already in with 69—213. Hill's 212 was the highest winning score of the season.

"It's more fun out here than it was on the regular Tour because I don't have the same pressure... but I'm glad this one is over. I feel like I was the survivor," Hill remarked Sunday. "My nerves were a little jumpy all day." Hill had started the round two strokes behind leader Charles Coody and three-putted two of the first three holes. However, he birdied the second and fourth and took the lead as Coody bogeyed three of the first four holes en route to a 78 and a seventh-place finish. Hill birdied again at the fifth hole and built his cushion for the flat finish with two more birdies at the ninth and 15th holes.

Meanwhile, Shaw, a Senior Tour winner at Salt Lake City in his rookie 1989 season, had come racing into contention. Six over par after 27 holes,

Tom had a five-birdie string Saturday to get back into contention with par 144. He shot 69 on the 6,677-yard Country Club of the South course in Alpharetta Sunday and his score surprised Hill in the final going. The electronic scoreboards had malfunctioned and Hill thought he had a five-stroke lead when he reached the 17th tee. After he bogeyed from a bunker there, he learned his margin was just two. After driving into the rough at the 18th, he played a safe lay-up, pitched on and two-putted for the victory, noting afterward that "they don't give you any more money if you win by one or three." His early rounds were 70 and 71 before the closing 71. At 70 Friday, he trailed leader Jim Dent by four. Just as Coody faded from the lead Sunday, Dent drifted back with 76 Saturday, enabling Coody to move in front, even though he played the last 14 holes in three over par after three birdies on the first four. Hill was tied for second at 141 with big Dick Hendrickson, who also was a non-factor Sunday.

Bank One Classic—$300,000
Winner: DeWitt Weaver

In 1971, winless playing partner DeWitt Weaver was little more than an onlooker as J.C. Snead prevailed in the 36-hole finish of the Tucson Open, scoring his first victory on the PGA Tour. Twenty years later, Weaver and Snead found themselves winless again, this time on the Senior PGA Tour, and head to head in a playoff for the Bank One Classic title in Lexington, Kentucky. It was Weaver's turn. DeWitt, who "whopped my first golf ball" when he was two years old and living in nearby Danville, matched birdies with Snead on the first playoff hole, then dropped a six-footer for another to win his first senior title.

The two men emerged from a group of contenders in the stretch Sunday to forge the 54-hole tie at 207 and bring about the playoff, Weaver by holing six-foot birdie putts at the 16th and 17th and two-putting the par-five 18th for another birdie and a 65, Snead by dropping an eight-footer at No. 17 and also two-putting the last hole for 68. George Archer missed a 10-footer for birdie and Larry Laoretti a 25-footer for eagle, either of which would have put them in a playoff. Chi Chi Rodriguez, winner of four 1991 tournaments but none since May, was on the way to No. 5 until he ran into the three-putts over the last 11 holes and finished at 209 with Walt Zembriski.

The 52-year-old Weaver, who won twice on the PGA Tour, the second and last time in 1972 in the Southern Open, gave a hint of things to come the week before when he tied for third in the rich Nationwide Championship and won $50,000, ironically $5,000 more than his first-place check at Lexington. DeWitt, who earned full-time playing status on the Senior PGA Tour with his fifth-place finish in the qualifying tournament, thanks to a closing 62, trailed leader Rodriguez by three with his opening 70 at the Kearney Hills Links. Snead was at 68.

When he followed with 72 Saturday, Weaver disappeared into the ranks of the overlooked at 142, seven strokes off the lead of Rodriguez and Gibby Gilbert. Snead, however, was just two off the pace with his 68-71—139; Archer one back at 138. Weaver played almost flawlessly Sunday, never missed a green, three-putting for his only bogey before registering birdies on three of the last five holes to set up the playoff and victory.

Vantage Championship—$1,500,000
Winner: Jim Colbert

A relieved Jim Colbert called his narrow victory in the Vantage Championship "the most meaningful of my career" after holding off an array of challengers in the stretch and scoring a one-stroke win with his 11-under-par 205 at Tanglewood Park's Championship course outside of Winston-Salem in early October. "Just think, $202,500," he remarked when he received the winner's check in the richest tournament on the Senior PGA Tour. "I've been building up to this tournament for a month. It's like winning 3⅓ tournaments on our tour." It was the second of the season for the Senior PGA Tour rookie, who left the ESPN tower and joined the circuit when he turned 50 in March.

The decision was in doubt until the final shots Sunday. Colbert started the day at 138 (68-70), three strokes behind leader George Archer and projected himself into contention with a solid 32 on the front nine and followed with two more birdies at Nos. 10 and 11 to take a two-stroke lead. Those were his last birdies and he scrambled skillfully the rest of the way, finding sand on five of the last seven holes, yet giving up just one bogey as he finished with 67 and the 205. In the process, he was fending off five other contenders on the back nine and almost had to deal with Arnold Palmer, who had one of his best finishes of the year—eighth—after getting within two shots of the lead on the front nine before falling back.

Archer, who had seized the lead Saturday with a front-nine 29 and ultimate 64, didn't have the same luck on the greens Sunday. He missed "five makeable putts on the last nine holes, particularly at 16 and 17" and just missed a chip for a tie at the 18th. Jim Dent, who shared the first-round lead with Al Kelley (67s), a shot ahead of Colbert, Bob Charles and Ben Smith, rallied from four shots back Sunday and was 11 under par until he dumped his approach at No. 18 into the front bunker and bogeyed. Dale Douglass and Simon Hobday also had tastes of first place briefly in the closing battle; and Gibby Gilbert, playing with Colbert, lipped out a chip from behind the 18th green for a tying birdie before Jim chipped close and sank his winning putt. Gilbert, Dent and Archer each picked up $100,000 for their second-place finishes.

Raley's Senior Gold Rush—$400,000
Winner: George Archer

It was certainly no foregone conclusion, but George Archer's victory in Raley's Senior Gold Rush at Sacramento should not have come as any great surprise. Archer clearly was ready to win his third title of the year on the Senior PGA Tour. He had good shots at winning each of the last three tournaments in which he played on the circuit, finishing a stroke behind the victor the two previous Sundays. Besides, he was the defending champion at Rancho Murieta and he had already repeated victories in two other events (one non-tour) earlier in the year.

But, it was close. Archer posted a 206, just enough to offset the charging finish of South African Simon Hobday and to take advantage of Butch Baird's collapse on the closing holes. They emerged from a cavalry charge of players in the late going Sunday. At one point, Bob Charles led at eight under par and eight others were at seven under. This was after Baird and Lee Trevino started the final round at 137, a stroke in front of Charles and Archer, who, in turn, had shared the first-round lead with Trevino and Bruce Crampton.

Baird broke from the pack and built a two-stroke lead through 15 holes. He was 11 under par when disaster struck at the 164-yard 16th. He hooked his six-iron tee shot and the ball landed on hardpan and bounced out of bounds. The double bogey there dropped him into a three-way tie with Archer and Hobday, who was already in the clubhouse with his nine-under 207 on the strength of a closing 65. Archer, playing ahead of Baird, a two-time winner on the PGA Senior Tour, birdied the 18th for 68 and the 10-under 206. Baird followed with three-putt bogeys on the last two holes for 72, dropping into a tie for fourth with Charles, Crampton, Dale Douglass and Jim O'Hern at 209 as Mike Hill jumped into third place at 208 with a final 66. Trevino, who also knocked a tee shot out of bounds at the 16th, managed just a 73 and tied for ninth at 210. A disconsolate Baird likened his finish to "throwing away money with a fan... through a window... from 10 stories up." With his $65,500, Archer moved into second place on the Senior Tour money list behind Hill, who collected $32,500.

Transamerica Championship—$500,000
Winner: Charles Coody

Charles Coody picked up some wind insurance and it paid off with a record-setting victory in the Transamerica Championship, enabling him to carry a big lead to a rather close win against the pressure of Lee Trevino on the closing holes. Scoring his second victory of the 1991 season on the Senior PGA Tour, Coody managed a closing 71 on a hot, windy Sunday afternoon at Silverado Country Club in Napa, California, for 204, two strokes ahead of Trevino and one shot better than the Silverado record score posted by Trevino in his 1990 victory in the Transamerica. Coody had teed off with a two-stroke lead and the comforting feeling that "it would be difficult for somebody to shoot 65 or 66." He was right, as the winds, which fanned the nearby Oakland fire disaster, prevented anybody from shooting better than the 68s of third-place finisher Tommy Aaron and Bobby Nichols.

Coody, a four-time winner in senior golf, had his game grooved the first two days. On Friday, he birdied three of the four par fives and three other holes with sizeable putts, taking a lone bogey for 67. Trevino was even more solid with his matching 67 off five birdies as he made some putting adjustments after a poor putting finish at the Gold Rush the previous Sunday. Coody came back Saturday with 66—six birdies—to open a two-stroke lead on Jim Colbert and four or more on the rest of the field. Dale Douglass shot 63 for 137, joining Trevino (70), Simon Hobday (69-68) and Mike Hill (70-67).

Nobody took advantage of Coody's slow start Sunday. He marked up seven pars and a bogey on the first eight holes, then put himself out of reach with birdies at Nos. 9, 11 and 12 to go 13 under par. Colbert had been in solid contention to that point, but he faded to 75 after taking a triple bogey at the 12th hole. Then in second place three back, DeWitt Weaver double-bogeyed the 12th and Coody led by five. Arnold Palmer had closed to one with a birdie at the 10th, but he couldn't maintain the move and finished in a fourth-place tie at 208.

Trevino made the only real challenge on the back nine. He birdied Nos. 14 and 15 and when he birdied again at the 17th and Coody followed with a bogey, the margin dwindled to the final two as both men parred the last hole.

Security Pacific Classic—$500,000
Winner: John Brodie

John Brodie knew which side of his bread to butter back in 1960 when he turned pro in golf early in his career as quarterback of the San Francisco 49ers. He stuck with football and became one of the game's finest at the position, regained his amateur status in golf and never expected to have an opportunity to play professionally. Even when his football-playing career ended in 1973, Brodie went into sportscasting rather than professional golf. Then along came the Senior PGA Tour in the early 1980s and he couldn't resist. He joined the Senior Tour when he turned 50 in 1985 and, over the next six seasons, sometimes as an exempt player, other times as an invitee, competed in 157 tournaments with a couple of first-and-goals but no touchdowns.

Finally, it happened in his home state in rather unlikely fashion. He defeated two of the circuit's major players—Chi Chi Rodriguez and George Archer—in a playoff in the Security Pacific Classic at the storied, municipal Rancho Park course in Los Angeles. Brodie left a 12-foot birdie putt inches short on the final regulation hole Sunday, scored 68 and entered the playoff against Rodriguez and Archer, who had both closed with 66s for their 13-under 200s, Rodriguez canning a 12-footer for his par there. No doubt considered the underdog in the playoff, Brodie saw his approach on the first extra hole bounce onto the green and roll to a stop four inches from the hole. He tapped in for the long-awaited victory after his two opponents missed their birdie attempts.

Brodie was never out of the lead at Rancho. He opened with 66 and shared first place with Rodriguez, Miller Barber and Dan Morgan, then duplicated the score Saturday and found himself tied with Larry Laoretti at 132, a shot ahead of Dick Rhyan and two in front of Rodriguez, Archer, DeWitt Weaver, Lee Trevino and Ben Smith. He would have had the lead to himself, but drew a one-stroke penalty for an improper drop off a temporary green. Brodie was in and out of the lead during the final round. He was one behind Rodriguez and Archer until he hit a five iron a foot from the hole and birdied the par-three 17th to forge the final deadlock.

Du Pont Cup—$550,000
Winner: United States

Although their juniors are giving way or being seriously challenged most of the time these days by their international peers, the leading players on the PGA Senior Tour continue to dominate the special events in which they are pitted against overseas senior stars.

In the late-season Du Pont Cup Matches, in which a select team of American seniors traveled to Japan to face a like team of Japanese pros, the men of the U.S. breezed to a 24-8 victory at Sawara Springs Country Club in mid-November, winning for a third straight year.

The U.S. jumped off to a 6-2 lead in the opening round of alternate-shot matches with the teams of Al Geiberger/Jim Dent, Charles Coody/Dale Douglass and George Archer/Rocky Thompson scoring victories and Miller Barber/Mike Hill losing to Hiroshi Ishii and Shigeru Uchida, 66-70, in the final match. Geiberger and Dent nipped Shozo Miyamoto and Ryosuke Ohta, 73-74; Douglass and Coody won handily, 69-72, over Hisashi and Teruo Suzumura, and Archer and Thompson held off Hideo Jibiki and Yoshimasa Fujii, 73-75.

The next day, when better-ball competition was the format, the Americans built a 13-3 lead with three wins and a Douglass/Coody tie with Ishii/Uchida at 66. Hill and Barber rebounded from their alternate-shot defeat to crush the Suzumuras, 62-73. Geiberger and Dent defeated Miyamoto and Ohta again, this time 67-73, and Archer and Thompson whipped Jibiki and Fujii, 66-69.

The Americans won five of the eight singles matches and tied another Sunday. Geiberger and Dent completed perfect records, victimizing the Suzumuras again—Geiberger over Teruo, 69-71, and Dent over Hisashi, 71-76. Hill, Douglass and Coody were the other winners, Hill over Uchida, 72-76; Douglass over Miyamoto, 69-73, and Coody over Ishii, 71-75. Archer tied Jibiki, 72-72; Ohta beat Thompson, 71-77, and Fujii fumbled to a 79-81 victory over Barber in the other pairings.

Each American player received $45,000; each Japanese pro, $18,750.

First Development Kaanapali Classic—$600,000
Winner: Jim Colbert

Any possible doubt had long since disappeared when Jim Colbert wrapped up "Rookie-of-the-Year" honors on the Senior PGA Tour with his impressive victory in the First Development Kaanapali Classic in Hawaii the first week of December. No other first-season player on the circuit won a single title, while Kaanapali was Colbert's third of the year, putting him within reach of the top spot on the 1991 money list. Low scores were the order of the week amid the five-year-old tournament's best-ever weather, so Colbert's winning score of 195, just two off the Senior PGA Tour's 54-hole record, gave him only a two-stroke victory and five other players were under 200.

Dale Douglass got the low scoring underway Friday with his seven-under-par 63 on Kaanapali Golf Club's 6,439-yard North course, but he led the tournament by just one stroke over Jim Dent, two over George Archer and three ahead of a four-man group at 66 that included Colbert. Dale birdied five of the first six holes, four of them virtual tap-ins. With a 65 and 128 Saturday, Douglass figured to widen his lead.

Instead, he yielded it to Colbert and his record-tying 61 for 127, also record-tying on the circuit. Dent birdied the first six holes, turned in 29 and added four birdies on the back nine. Defending champion Bob Charles joined Dent and Archer at 131 by shooting 63 and Lee Trevino shot the same score for 132.

The scoring was not quite as incendiary Sunday, so Colbert's start of eight straight pars didn't cost him. In fact, when he birdied finally at the ninth, when he wedged to two feet, and Douglass took his second bogey to go one over par on the front nine, Colbert led by three. The margin went to five with Douglass' bogey at No. 11 and his 25-foot birdie putt at No. 12, then things turned around when Colbert hit a poor drive into the rough and put his second unplayable against a tree, eventually taking a double bogey. Douglass made it a three-shot swing with a 25-foot birdie putt there and narrowed the gap to one with another birdie at the par-five 15th. Archer entered the picture with a birdie at the par-three 17th, but Douglass and Colbert matched that when they reached the hole and Jim widened the final gap to two when he birdied the last hole for 68 and the 195.

New York Life Champions—$1,000,000
Winner: Mike Hill

Mike Hill fit the tournament title like a glove when he climaxed by far the finest season of his career with his triumph in the year-ending New York Life Champions on the East course of the Hyatt Dorado Beach in Puerto Rico.

The victory, with its attendant bonus money, made him the leading official money winner in American golf with $1,065,657. The victory was his fifth of the season, more than any other player in American golf. And the victory came the way a champion should win, with a spurt of birdies in the closing run against one of the challengers to his place on the throne of the Senior Tour.

Mike moved into the lead Saturday following the surprising first-day showing of 62-year-old Don January, who shot 67 and took a one-stroke lead over Orville Moody and Walt Zembriski. Hill started the exclusive tournament with 70, then bombarded the field with birdies the second day. He birdied the first three holes and made nine in all in shooting 65 and taking a two-shot lead over Bob Charles.

George Archer, the top-money winner going in, and Jim Colbert, the two players with a chance to deprive Hill of the No. 1 spot, were within range at 138. Colbert tried. As Hill was running off 11 pars and a birdie, Colbert was ringing up five birdies and taking a one-stroke lead after the 12th hole. They both birdied the par-five 13th, but Hill kept it going with two more on the next two holes to regain the lead and he iced the marvelous season at the final hole when he deposited his nine-iron approach just inches from the cup.

13. European Tour

History will have to prove it, of course, but even the most jaded observer would have to agree that 1991 was very probably a benchmark year on the PGA European Tour. Never mind the loss of the Ryder Cup. The strength of the game being what it is on both sides of the Atlantic, the Americans were bound to win it back, sooner or later. No, what will make 1991 a historic year—begging history's indulgence in advance, of course—is the return of two of the game's greats, the rise of two young stars, and the emergence of a bright young prospect.

The two greats came back with a vengeance—Seve Ballesteros and Sandy Lyle. You could practically hear the fans cheer when these two found their way back.

The new muscle? First, Steven Richardson, previously little-known Englishman, age 25. What he did, in only his second year on the Tour, was to win twice, finish second to Ballesteros on the money list, and gain a berth on the Ryder Cup team. With him came Colin Montgomerie, 28, who fulfilled the promise he showed as the 1988 Rookie of the Year with a victory, two seconds, and a flock of other top-10 finishes. He was fourth on the money list, and also won a berth on the Ryder Cup team.

And one newcomer may force Ryder Cup observers to change their minds. When they were saying a Swede was sure to make the team soon, they were talking about Ove Sellberg, Anders Forsbrand and Mats Lanner. Another Swede was waiting in the wings, but no one knew it because that was a long way off—in Arizona, in fact. His name is Per-Ulrik Johansson, 25, and like many young European hopefuls, he had taken his game to be forged in the hot competition of American collegiate golf. He played at Arizona State University, and he remained largely obscure because of a teammate. The No. 1 man on that team was the brilliant American left-hander, Phil Mickelson. With his college days over, Johansson returned home, turned pro, and came flying through the qualifying tournament late in 1990. Then leaving nothing undone, he joined the Tour at the start of 1991, scored his breakthrough victory in the Renault Belgian Open, and he led the entire Swedish contingent at 23rd on the money list.

The regulars were still being heard from. Ian Woosnam won twice, the Fujitsu Mediterranean Open and Torras Monte Carlo Open, and Bernhard Langer also won twice, the Benson & Hedges International and Mercedes Germans Masters. Others winning twice: Eduardo Romero, the Peugeot Spanish Open and Peugeot French Open, and Jose Maria Olazabal, the Open Catalonia and the Epson Grand Prix. Olazabal, however, labored much of the year, and so did Nick Faldo. Faldo won the Carrolls Irish Open, but for the most part his putter was a stranger to him all season.

The 1991 season actually had become a part of history even before it started. It was scarred by the Persian Gulf War, in which Britain, the United States, Saudi Arabia, and other allies united to drive invading Iraqi forces out of Kuwait. The troop buildup had begun months earlier, and tensions increased gradually and inexorably, and then the warfare broke out early in

January. The European Tour canceled the Dubai Desert Classic, which is played in the Gulf region. Also canceled, but for business reasons, was the El Bosque Open in Spain. Added were the Volvo German Open, in August (won by Mark McNulty), and the Scandinavian Masters (won by Montgomerie), which combined the Scandinavian Enterprise Open and the PLM Open. The European Tour picture was changing, but most of all, it was tense.

"These are indeed difficult and uncertain times," executive director Ken Schofield wrote to the players. "Economic recession is prevalent in much of our marketplace. The war in the Gulf is adding extreme concern to business life. Many non-European businesses with whom we have sponsorship arrangements are presently reluctant to travel." Even so, the Tour was left with a schedule of 35 events worth some £20 million in prize money, an increase of £3 million over 1990.

The Tour opened late in February with the Girona Open in Spain, and Richardson, who just missed out on Rookie-of-the-Year honors in 1990, staked his claim in 1991 with his first victory. He also had the purists scratching their heads.

The game has seen its share of oddities on the putting green, from Arnold Palmer's knocked-knee stance to Sam Snead's sidesaddle to the new broom-like putters. Richardson added something else. "I cut the ball at the cup," he said. That puzzled a lot of people. Even his father told him it probably wouldn't work for long. "But I think for the time being I'll be sticking with it," Richardson said. As he soon proved, that made very good sense. Just four weeks later, shortly after he finished second in the Open de Baleares, he scored his second victory, taking the Portuguese Open.

"This boy is the next great hope of European golf, without a shadow of a doubt," said the veteran Brian Barnes, who was paired with Richardson in the final round.

This was in March, just five weeks into the season, long before Barnes or anyone else could realize that Johansson might enjoy a share of that "next great hope" label. Johansson drew considerable attention by finishing fourth at Girona, his Tour debut. He continued to have some good finishes, and then broke through early in June, taking the Renault Belgian Open in a playoff against Paul Broadhurst. This was the 16th week of the Tour. "I'm surprised to have won so soon," Johansson said. He wasn't alone.

The fans and the press might have made more of Johansson's dramatic emergence except for one thing—Ballesteros suddenly was dominating the headlines.

Ballesteros won the 1990 Open de Baleares in March, then he went into an eclipse. It seemed nothing would go right. The doomsayers decided his time had already passed, his star had gone out. Then early in March, 1991, he won the Chunichi Crowns in Japan. It wasn't only that Ballesteros had won, but how he had won. He came through in the clutch. He needed a 20-foot putt for a birdie on the last hole. He got it. And that set off a stunning streak. The following week, he was in the Peugeot Spanish Open, and this time a long putt was his undoing. Romero holed a 25-footer on the final hole to tie him, and then beat him in a playoff—on the seventh extra hole.

"Many people were thinking that Seve would not come back," Ballesteros said. "Today, I proved them wrong." If there were still any doubters, he would soon convince them. Two weeks later he won the Volvo PGA Championship, beating Montgomerie in a playoff. And then the following week, he ran away with the Dunhill British Masters. In that one, he was leading by seven strokes in the final round. Seve was back.

Later, he revealed a secret he had kept hidden for four years. He had just about lost his confidence on the greens. The problem dated to the 1987 Masters. That was the Masters of Larry Mize's long chip shot that beat Greg Norman on the second extra hole of a playoff. Ballesteros was also in that playoff, but he bowed out on the first extra hole when he missed a putt of only five feet. After that, he said, he was never sure he could make short putts, not the way he used to. Now it was like old times again. Ballesteros underscored the point by winning the Toyota World Match Play Championship in October, and ending up No. 1 on the money list with £545,353, more than £150,000 ahead of Richardson.

Back to Montgomerie. His runner-up finish in the Volvo PGA Championship wasn't due to any letdown by him. He birdied the last two holes for 67, and he had all but won it until Ballesteros made a miracle birdie at the final hole to tie him. Ballesteros then birdied the first hole of the playoff to win. Except for the playoff, the positions were reversed some 10 weeks later, in the Scandinavian Masters. This time Ballesteros shot 64 in the final round, but Montgomerie withstood the Spaniard's intimidating pressure, posted a 67 of his own, and beat him by one stroke, at 18 under par. "I'm proud I could come from behind and win under pressure," Montgomerie said. He decided he'd finally proved himself, noting that in his breakthrough victory in the 1989 Portuguese Open, he suffered no pressure whatever. He won by 11 strokes.

The year was almost complete, but not quite because Lyle was still without a victory. Back in 1988, he won the Masters and two other tournaments in the United States, and he won twice in Europe. And then the slump set in, and nothing he could do would make it lift. For three years he was a forlorn man. Then suddenly, late in 1991, the good single rounds started to come faster.

Lyle hit the first peak late in the summer, when he finished second to Mike Harwood in the GA European Open. Six weeks later, he raced away with the BMW International, winning by three strokes. Perhaps what he said after that win were the words he would live by in 1992. "When you've had a three-year dry spell," Lyle said, "fear is always around the corner."

Girona Open—£250,000
Winner: Steven Richardson

His father told him he'd never make a living putting like that. "I cut the ball at the cup, and Dad feels that, long-term, it's an unreliable method," Steven Richardson said. "But I think for the time being I'll be sticking with it."

Good thinking. For despite his odd putting method—or perhaps because of it—Richardson, 24-year-old Englishman entering his second year on the Tour, gave the new season a brand-new winner. The 1991 European Tour season opened in the last week of February with the Girona Open, and Richardson, who just missed Rookie-of-the-Year honors in 1990, made it the stage for his first victory. He shot the 6,736-yard, par-72 Pals course at

Barcelona in 71-64-67-70, for a 16-under-par 272. He won by two strokes over Spain's Miguel Angel Jimenez, whose only sin was that the best he could do in the second round was a 66. Jimenez matched Richardson digit for digit in the other three rounds—71-67-70, but the 66 in the second round did him in. Because Richardson shot 64. And critics of his odd putting style should note: "I had only 26 putts in both the second and third rounds," Richardson said.

Only one of the big guns had come out, Jose Maria Olazabal, and he was the top-heavy favorite. But his putter let him down. He suffered a three-putt and a four-putt, both for double-bogey sixes, and shot 75 in the first round. He had to work to get back to a tie for 11th. Mark Mouland, who hadn't swung a club in three months, took the first-round lead with a 67 that included an eagle two from 95 yards out at his 11th hole, and a near eagle at the 12th. The rust showed up in a pair of 73s the next two days. Then there was the veteran Peter Mitchell, who went to a kung-fu guru for help with his concentration. The guru had him put on a headset and listen to blaring punk rock music while reading a book. Mitchell opened with a 68, one stroke off the lead. If there was magic, it left the next day. A 76 sent him on his way to 55th. And then there was Sweden's Per-Ulrik Johansson, a product of American college golf. Johansson played No. 2 to the brilliant American amateur, Phil Mickelson, on the Arizona State University team. Johansson qualified for the Tour at the 1990 qualifying tournament, then opened his bid for Rookie-of-the-Year honors with 70-68-71-68—277, good for fourth place in the Girona.

Richardson took command with that 64 in the second round, and in the third round put on a show with his odd putting style. He made four birdies coming home, holing from 25 feet at the 12th and 30 feet at the 16th and 18th. Jimenez didn't lack for putting fireworks, holing birdies from 42 feet at No. 11 and 25 feet at No. 16, keeping pace with Richardson's 67 to stay two strokes behind. The chase continued in the final round.

"Miguel kept pushing me, so I could never really relax," Richardson said. Nor could Jimenez. Richardson birdied the first hole from 10 feet to take a three-stroke lead, and both birdied No. 2 from 15 feet. It was a classic duel, and it was decided on the greens. From No. 9 through No. 12, Jimenez missed four birdie putts from 13 feet or less. "That was the key to my whole round," Jimenez said. "I should have holed at least one."

Richardson had no such problem. "When I birdied the 16th," he said, "I finally thought I had it."

Fujitsu Mediterranean Open—£400,000
Winner: Ian Woosnam

On March 2, Ian Woosnam turned 33. On March 3, he won the Fujitsu Mediterranean Open. But it was not his idea of a birthday gift.

"I'm just a little bit despondent," Woosnam said. "It has to be the least satisfying of all my victories." He had 19 European Tour victories now, but he didn't win this one so much as have it thrust upon him. Michael McLean was leading by four strokes with three holes to play. Then he crashed to a bogey-bogey-double-bogey finish. Woosnam, with a cool birdie at the 17th, picked off his first victory of the season in his first outing of the season.

McLean was nearing a birthday, too. He would turn 28 on March 6. But he was in no mood to celebrate.

"I've just got to try to bounce back," McLean said. "I'm a worrier and an analyst. It's going to take a bit of getting over."

Said Woosnam: "I can only hope he'll bounce back. It's a terrible thing to happen, and I feel sorry for him."

Woosnam, who wasn't really in the hunt until late, shot 70-71-71-67—279, five under par at the 6,476-yard, par-71 Golf d'Esterel Latitudes on France's Cote d'Azur. But he was just tagging along till the end. He trailed by four strokes in the first round, five in the second, and three in the third. The doomed McLean shared the first-round lead, and led outright by two through the middle two rounds. He shot 66-70-73-71—280, and lost by a stroke.

"I don't feel that I choked," McLean said. "I don't think my nerve went. It was a technical problem that crept in under pressure." McLean had one victory in his 10-year career, the 1990 Portuguese Open-Tournament Players Championship. He came from nowhere to win that one, and later admitted that he was a little rattled. "I get a bit twitchy on the course in the final stages ...," he had said. This time, it was fatal.

The tournament actually went beyond Woosnam's dreams, even his expectations, despite his confidence. "I never stopped believing I could win," Woosnam said, "but I felt I needed to finish with three birdies." The reason: McLean had birdied the 12th, 13th and 14th holes to dip to eight under par.

Then, just as success was beckoning, disaster ambushed him. At the 16th, he hooked his approach shot from the middle of the fairway. That cost him a bogey. At the 17th, he hooked his drive and ended up in a bush and had to come out sideways. That cost him another bogey. At the 18th, his tee shot ended up in the scrub to the right. "I could have come out sideways again, and concentrated on getting into a playoff," McLean said. "But I wanted to win." He found a gap in the greenery. If he could thread it, he might make the green. But he failed to get the ball out of the trees. And his next shot ended up in a bunker. Standing with one foot in the sand and one out, he made a strong recovery shot, to six feet. He needed that putt to tie. But he missed it. Woosnam was the champion.

Maybe McLean will never forget this tournament, but for all of his suffering, it will probably be remembered for something else—six holes-in-one. It was like a shooting gallery. Eamonn Darcy got two himself, both at the 139-yard 15th, but from different tees—a nine iron in the first round, and an eight iron in the third. The other four got theirs on the 133-yard No. 2: Vijay Singh, nine iron in the first round; Glen Day, seven iron in the second; Jean Van de Velde, eight iron in the second, and Olazabal, a wedge in the fourth.

Open de Baleares—£275,000
Winner: Gavin Levenson

It may be hard to believe, but one of the highlights in Gavin Levenson's career wasn't even a victory. It was a 25th place in the 1990 Portuguese

Open-TPC, the last open of the season. It was his last chance to win enough money to keep his European Tour playing card. If not—off to the qualifying tournament. But 25th place saved him. Then early in March, 1991, despite winds that brought in sand from the Sahara, he enjoyed another highlight— a victory in the Open de Baleares. Levenson, coming from behind, birdied three of the last seven holes and beat Steven Richardson by a stroke. It was Levenson's second European victory—he won the Belgian Open in 1979, the year he joined the Tour—and it even made a bit of geopolitical history.

This was the first time South African golfers could play in Spain since 1987, when they and all South African athletes were banned in a protest against their country's apartheid policy. "I couldn't wait to come back," Levenson said. "I've always played well in Spain." Ernie Els was the only other South African in the field. He tied for 59th.

This outing was an exercise in faith and self-confidence for Levenson. He had no real reason to think he could win this one. He was four strokes off the lead in the first round, six off in the second, and two behind going into the final round.

"I seemed to come from nowhere," Levenson conceded, "because it looked like I hadn't really been in contention." He shot 72-74-67-69—282, six under par at Santa Ponsa, on the island of Majorca. Richardson, who broke through to win the season-opening Girona Open two weeks earlier, shot 71-69-72-71—283. And if it looked like a two-man battle, that was another illusion because fully six men were separated by one stroke before Levenson pulled away. Also in his wake: Jose Maria Olazabal, a solo third at 73—284, and Miguel Martin (74), Stephen Bennett (74), and Costantino Rocca (70), tied for fourth at 285.

And if Levenson was the star of the show, then Santa Ponsa's 10th hole, a par five of 650 yards, was the center of attention. Consider the especially stiff winds in the second round. "When you need a driver, a one iron, and then a four iron just to reach the green," Olazabal said, "then you know you're in trouble." He bogeyed the hole which wasn't a bad score. Only six players birdied it that round. In the third round, it gave up only two birdies, and it played to an aggregate of 42 over par.

Olazabal, the pre-tournament favorite, led the first round outright, shared the lead through the next two rounds, then faltered in the final round. But aside from saying he tired fast coming in, he declined to blame the flu that had bothered him all week. He blamed his putting, instead. Richardson blamed poor play on the par threes in the final round. "I blew a great chance by taking four at two short holes," he said. He hooked his tee shot at No. 12, then missed a four-foot par putt, and at No. 15, he was short off the tee and three-putted.

The six-man scramble had shrunk to two men, and the decisive moment arrived at No. 17. Levenson lobbed a wedge shot to within three feet of the flag. Then he turned it into his fifth birdie of the day—and his first European victory in 12 years.

"I'm just overwhelmed," Levenson said. "If I could use only one word about my feelings, it would be—unbelievable!"

Open Catalonia—£300,000
Winner: Jose Maria Olazabal

There were perhaps two uncertain moments for Jose Maria Olazabal in the Open Catalonia—if a one-stroke deficit in the first round and a three-stroke lead in the fourth can be considered uncertain.

Otherwise, Olazabal was a runaway winner, scoring his first victory of the season and the 10th of his career by six strokes over David Feherty, who rocketed into contention with a course-record, 11-under-par 61 in the third round. Olazabal shot 66-68-64-73—271, 17 under par at the 7,050-yard Club de Golf Bonmont Terres Noves at Tarragona, Spain, making its debut on the European Tour. Feherty shot 71-73-61-72—277.

Even Mike McLean's prayer couldn't stop Olazabal. Said McLean, who was tied for second with Feherty, seven strokes after going into the final round: "We need a gale to blow tomorrow, and for him to be blown away." The mid-March weather obliged. Bonmont had been defenseless without wind in the first three rounds. Then came the howlers, blowing down tree limbs and battering the field. Out of 68 finishers, only seven broke par the last day. There were 39 rounds from 75 through 79, and five rounds of 80 or more. It was not an easy day to win a golf tournament, but after some shaky moments, Olazabal squared himself and won it.

The first round was the only one that wasn't Olazabal's. It belonged to Justin Hobday, who took the first-round lead with 65 after turning a near-disaster into a small miracle at the 572-yard 17th hole. He drove into a deep ravine, took a penalty drop, then slashed a four wood to the edge of the green and rolled in a 30-foot putt. Instead of suffering a bogey or worse, he birdied. Olazabal eagled the hole—a three iron to 12 feet—and briefly tied Hobday. He settled for 66 and a share of second.

The second round was notable principally for four things: 1. Hobday skidded to a 74 that included a small nightmare. At the second hole, he hit out of bounds over the green, made a triple-bogey seven, and then was threatened with a fine for delaying play by asking for second and third opinions from tournament officials. (He was on his way to finishing 51st.) 2. McLean shot a crazy 69 that included nine birdies, a double bogey, and a triple bogey. 3. The struggling Seve Ballesteros, who hadn't won in over a year, shot 77 and missed the 36-hole cut. 4. Olazabal went into the lead for good.

Olazabal birdied four of his first five holes, shot 68 and led by three strokes after 36 holes. He boosted that to seven in the third round with as obscure a 64 as you'll find. At the same time, Feherty was busy creating a masterpiece 61. He made 11 birdies, matching the European record he himself had already shared. "I've shot 62 five times," Feherty said, "but never 61."

"I don't remember ever losing from seven shots clear," Olazabal said, going into the final round. "Touch wood." Before long, he would be reaching for every good luck charm he could find. "There were moments when I thought I could lose," Olazabal was to confess after his victory. "Especially over the front nine..." He bogeyed the first, third and sixth, and Feherty birdied No. 2. Olazabal's lead was down to three strokes after he bogeyed No. 9, going out in 40, while Feherty was making a birdie. Olazabal restored order and a five-stroke lead at the 10th, sinking a 25-foot downhill putt for a birdie while Feherty was making bogey from the fringe.

"I thought for a while that it was slipping away, especially on the front nine," Olazabal said. "With such a big lead, you can't play your own game. But when I holed the long putt at the 10th, I think that was the turning point."

Portuguese Open—£275,000
Winner: Steven Richardson

Steven Richardson, 24, had just won the Portuguese Open. It was his second victory of the young season, and also the second of his two-year career. His first was five weeks earlier, in the season-opening Girona Open. Most golfers would settle for that as a year's work. But now a new ambition was talking.

"I want to win a British event with all the big boys in the field," said Richardson. Why? Because he still had something to prove. The European stars hadn't come out yet. They were in the United States getting ready for the Masters.

One man didn't need convincing—the venerable Brian Barnes, age 45, back on the Tour after taking six years off to build and promote his own golf course. A closing 74 dropped him out of contention and into a tie for fourth.

"This boy is the next great hope of European golf, without a shadow of a doubt," said Barnes. He was paired with Richardson in the final round. He liked what he saw—Richardson outrunning one challenger and holding off another. Richardson was three strokes off the lead in the first round, behind Des Smyth (68), then charged to the front and stayed there the rest of the way. He shot 71-67-71-74—283, five under par on the 6,701-yard Estela course, outside Oporto. He won by three strokes over fast-closing Vicente Fernandez (67—286).

"His victory was the easiest I've ever seen," Barnes said.

Richardson went the first 36 holes without a bogey. He took the lead in the second round with a 67, and at 138 he was two strokes up on the Swedish rookie, Per-Ulrik Johansson, who kept the pressure on with a 69. Johansson made a real fight of this one, shooting 71-69-70. He trailed Richardson by just a stroke going into the final round. Then the heavy winds got to him, and a double bogey at the par-three second sent him reeling to a 79—289 and seventh place. Fernandez, however, solved the winds with a deadly short game. He made seven birdies from eight feet and less to clinch second place with his closing 67.

With Johansson fading and Fernandez charging, Richardson all but assured himself of the win by escaping disaster at No. 5. He had hit a bunker shot over the green and into a lie so bad that he was facing a double bogey or worse. But he somehow got to the ball and flicked it gently to within 10 feet of the hole.

"Fantastic shot," Barnes said. Richardson then sank the putt, limiting the damage to a bogey. His closing 74 in heavy winds was only his second over-par round in 20 rounds, and it wrapped up a heady start to his year. Playing in all five tournaments, he finished first, 19th, second, fourth, and now first again.

Even Richardson was surprised. "I never expected to do so well," he said. But he hoped to do better. First, to win against the big boys, especially Nick Faldo, "because he's the best in the world." And to play in the British Open—"I think I can count on being exempt now"—and beat his dad's best showing, 13th at St. Andrews in 1970. And then make the Ryder Cup team.

"There's still a bit to go yet," Richardson warned himself, "but I have to admit I can nearly see over the fence now."

Volvo Open di Firenze—£200,000
Winner: Anders Forsbrand

It was as though Anders Forsbrand wanted to give the European Tour a good nudge in the ribs and say, "Hey, don't forget what Tony said!" Tony Jacklin, then European Ryder Cup captain, had predicted a Swede would soon make the team. Here it was, another Ryder Cup year, and here was Forsbrand—whose game had been a wreck—charging out of the pack to take the Volvo Open di Firenze.

In the sunny chill of late March, the pros found Florence's short but tricky Uglino course—6,280 yards, par 72—much to their liking. Note that 18 broke 70 in the first round, 16 in the second round. But Forsbrand wasn't one of them. He started 71-72 and was eight strokes off the lead. He was five behind going into the final round. But he powered his way to a 66-65 finish for a 14-under-par 274, edging Barry Lane by one stroke. Lane, after posting 68-69-67, closed with nothing more sinful than a 71.

It had been a long time between celebrations. Forsbrand's only other European victory was in the 1987 European Masters-Swiss Open, and if he didn't look like a champion this time, nobody else did, either. The way things started out, it seemed Switzerland might ring up a winner, with Andre Bossert taking the first-round lead with a 65. Then he shot 75 in the second round, and a Swede went atop the leaderboard. Two of them, in fact, and one of them was named Forsbrand. It wasn't Anders, age 30. It was his younger brother, Vilhelm, 21, shooting 68 to join countryman Mats Lanner (65) at nine-under-par 135, one stroke up on the field.

Vilhelm, a 21-year-old rookie, unfortunately was having a tough time adjusting to life on the Tour. He was fined £250 for slow play in the Open de Baleares, then was disqualified for taking an illegal drop in the Catalan Open. This time a serious question was raised about whether he was testing the sand in a bunker, or merely shuffling his foot in taking an awkward stance. Tournament officials opted for the latter. He tied for 24th place with 67-68-73-77—285, three under par.

"I'm trying to help Vilhelm," said Anders. Not long ago, it was Anders who needed the help. It had gotten to the point where he couldn't break an egg, as the saying goes. In 1989, he won only £28,564, plunging from 22nd to 114th on the Order of Merit. He sought out guru David Leadbetter. "Like Nick Faldo," he said, "I've changed absolutely everything. My swing is different from top to bottom." It paid off in Florence.

He charged into contention in the third round with a birdie-birdie-eagle finish for a 66 that lifted him to within five strokes of third-round leader Barry Lane. Lane's edge evaporated fast. He started the final round by dropping three strokes in the first two holes. He rallied for four birdies, but tripped at the 16th hole. His drive strayed just a bit, hit the last of a line of trees, and dropped into a bunker. He bogeyed the hole. Forsbrand, meanwhile, was tearing up Ugolino for eight birdies and the 65 that got him home. Whereupon he got a big hug from his brother.

Said big brother Anders: "I really wanted him to win. I'd have been happy to be second. But I'm glad a Forsbrand won."

Jersey European Airways Open—£200,000
Winner: Sam Torrance

For some spooky irony, tune in the Jersey European Airways Open. Four years earlier, a little man played the 1987 Jersey Open half in anger, half in tears. No slight intended, but Ian Woosnam made no secret of it—he would much rather have been playing in the Masters that week. He insisted that he had the credentials to be there. But he hadn't been invited. Now come forward: A man playing the 1991 Jersey Open was crying the same sad song. But this was a different man.

This was Sam Torrance. He wasn't as angry as Woosnam was four years earlier, but he felt just as slighted and just as determined. So much so that he went out and won the Jersey Open, as Woosnam had done before him. And to complete this irony, while Torrance was winning at La Moye, Woosnam was over in America winning the Masters, his first major championship.

Torrance had to break free of Mats Lanner coming down the final stretch, which was no cakewalk in the 40-mile-an-hour winds that lashed the 6,817-yard, par-72 La Moye course. After rounds of 68, 69 and 69, Torrance fought through the gale for a 73 and a 279 total, nine under par. He won by a stroke over Mark Davis, the young Englishman, whose 71 was one of only three sub-par rounds on the brutal final day.

Torrance gave much of the credit for his win to the persuasive abilities of his caddie, Malcolm Mason. Thanks to Mason, Torrance made two crucial birdies, both at par threes playing downwind in the gale. A man has to swallow hard to hit the clubs he hit. The first birdie came at the 163-yard 12th. "I wanted to hit a nine iron, but Malcolm made me switch to the wedge," Torrance said, "and I holed from 15 feet for a two." The next was the 14th hole, 190 yards. Torrance decided it was a seven-iron shot. Mason held out for the eight iron. "He was right again," Torrance said. His tee shot was 20 feet from the cup. He rolled it in and was on his way. Not that the force of the wind surprised him. At the 165-yard first hole, he flew the green with a wedge. At the 522-yard No. 2, he reached the green with a three wood and a wedge.

Earlier, Torrance was back in the pack. Peter McWhinney led the first round with a 66 (followed by a crippling 77). Jeff Hawkes and Craig Parry matched tournament-low 65s in the second round to share the 36-hole lead at nine-under-par 135. Torrance, never more than two strokes off the lead, moved to the top with a 69 in the third round, and he led by one over Anders Sorensen going into the final round. He held that lead through No. 9, then turned things into a shootout when he bogeyed the 10th. Lanner took the lead with a brilliant eagle three at the 502-yard 11th. He hit driver-driver to the fringe, and holed from 25 feet. Torrance fired back with the birdies at the 12th and 14th, and locked up his 15th European Tour victory. Then the pique over the Masters surfaced.

"I've been on winning Ryder Cup sides here and in America," Torrance said. "And if that isn't a major achievement, I don't know what is. I believe all current Ryder Cup players ought to earn automatic invites to all four majors." The Masters, of course, doesn't see it that way. Torrance played in the 1985 Masters, and just missed the top-24 finishers and the automatic return invitation. And at age 37, time was running out.

"I'll just have to win the [British] Open," Torrance said, "and then they can't ignore me." The moral of this story: Watch future Jersey Opens for ironic results.

Benson & Hedges International Open—£400,000
Winner: Bernhard Langer

The 1991 Benson & Hedges International Open may go down in history better known for what didn't happen than what did.

What did happen is that Bernhard Langer finally broke his jinx there. Something was always popping up to vex him. In 1981 at Fulford, for the most notable example, he had to climb a big tree to chip his ball off a limb. So the B&H International was forever dancing just off his fingertips. He finally caught it, but it took a burst of five birdies over the last 11 holes. He shot 73-68-75-70, two-under-par 286—the only man under par for all four rounds—and won by two strokes over Vijay Singh.

St. Mellion, 7,054 yards and par 72, the B&H International venue for the second year, is a test under the best of conditions. But this mid-April week in England, it was a dragon. It was cold, and the wind was harsh and icy. Frost delayed the start of play all four days. Only seven players broke 70 all week, and nobody did it in the first round. The 36-hole cut came at 156, 12 over par. This was seven strokes higher than the cut in 1990, and the highest on the Tour since the 1978 Italian Open and the 1983 Portuguese Open.

Now, as to what didn't happen: Two of the world's best golfers didn't figure.

First, Ian Woosnam, who won the Masters the week before, and rated No. 1 in the world on the Sony Ranking, opened with an 82. "I can't remember the last time when I had a score like that," he said. Then he shot another one and missed the cut for the first time in almost three years. "I just can't hit the ball," he said. "It's unbelievable."

Nick Faldo did better, but not by much. He shared the first-round lead with a 70, then shot an 80 in the icy winds in the second, and an 82 in the third. "I don't think I've played this badly since I was a teenager," Faldo said. Here's what he meant: After seven holes of the second round, he was eight strokes ahead of his playing partner, Steven Richardson, but he finished two strokes behind him. "At least the crowd enjoyed it," Faldo cracked. "They're getting to see me hit more shots." He closed with a 73 for 305, 19 strokes behind Langer.

While the labors of Woosnam and Faldo occupied center stage, it was Jose

Rivero who solved St. Mellion in the blustery weather of the third round. He shot a tournament-best 67 for a 212 total and a three-stroke lead on Gordon Brand, Jr. (69—215). Langer (75—216) was four strokes off the pace. A wobbly start in the fourth round dropped him five strokes behind. But he refused to count himself out.

"For some reason, I still felt confident that I would be there at the end," Langer said. "I just told myself to hang in there, because other players were having the same problems."

Especially Rivero. He struggled much of the way, then crashed to a triple-bogey seven at the 404-yard, uphill 13th. He skied to a 77, and tied for third place at 289.

So the heat came from Singh, who had moved into contention with a 69 in the third round. In the fourth round, a clutch 15-foot putt at No. 16 got him back to even par for the tournament. And then a birdie at the 18th might tie Langer, who was playing behind him. But he didn't get it, and he settled for second with 70—288.

Anyway, Langer was equal to Singh's pressure. He matched Singh's birdie at the 16th, then locked up the title with a birdie at the 18th—a perfect drive, a pinpoint approach to three feet, and one putt.

"I went up and down the leaderboard like a yo-yo all week," Langer said. "And when I was five shots behind after four holes in the last round, things didn't look too bright. But I still felt comfortable. I still believed I would be there in the end."

Madrid Open—£275,000
Winner: Andrew Sherborne

It wasn't long ago that Steven Richardson was saying his main ambition was "...to win a British event with all the big boys in the field." Now here came Andrew Sherborne, saying he wanted to be like Richardson. It suddenly had become the season for proving oneself on the European Tour. It was a question of pride.

A word of background: Richardson scored his career-first victory in the Girona Open at the start of the season, then added the Portuguese Open. It wasn't enough. He wanted to prove he could win against the best. Sherborne, 30, hadn't reached that stage yet. He plucked the Madrid Open for the first victory of his seven years on the European Tour. Now he wanted to be like Richardson. "I want to win again," he said, "to prove it wasn't a fluke."

It wasn't a fluke, but there was some irony to his victory. His victim was the diminutive Spaniard, Miguel Angel Martin, who also was looking for his first victory. What a time: Martin was just days from his 29th birthday, in his 10th year on tour, and he was the favorite of the home spectators at the 6,941-yard, par-72 Puerta de Hierro course. Martin was just about home free. Then Sherborne rushed up with a 66 to snatch the victory away by a stroke. Sherborne's good news: His first prize, almost £46,000, was more than he had won in all of his best previous year, 1989.

Sherborne, who trailed until the final round, shot 70-67-69-66—272, 16 under par. Martin, the leader through the middle rounds, shot 69-67-67-70—273. Mark James closed with a tournament-low 65 and took third place with

275, but he was a serious threat for a while. He was out with six birdies for a six-under-par 30, and his seventh birdie, at No. 11, tied Sherborne at 13 under par for the tournament. But he missed a pair of three-foot putts for pars, and he was done. The real battle ended where it began, between Sherborne and Martin.

Martin started the final round at 13 under par and leading Sherborne by three strokes. And almost instantly, Martin's lead was down to one stroke, when Sherborne birdied No. 2 and Martin three-putted for a bogey. The tug-of-war was on. At the par-three 11th, Martin thrilled the home crowd by firing his tee shot to within two feet of the cup. Sherborne upstaged him by holing his 30-footer for a birdie. He birdied the 12th after narrowly missing an eagle. His approach hit the flagstick.

Martin was nothing if not a fighter. He'd proved that by winning his U.S. PGA Tour card in the qualifying tournament in 1988. He battled back with birdies at the 13th and the 16th holes—the latter from 30 feet—to pull within a stroke of Sherborne. A 20-footer at the 18th would have forced a playoff. But he missed, and settled for second place and his fourth top-seven finish of the year.

Sherborne said he owed his success to Paul Curry, fellow golfer and sharp-eyed friend. In the Benson & Hedges International the week before, at windy St. Mellion, Curry noticed that Sherborne was lining up wrong. "Probably because of all the wind we were playing in," Sherborne said. Once he got straightened out, the pull-hooks disappeared. Then it was a matter of learning to win, as the veteran winners say.

"I know I can handle the pressure," said Sherborne, whose best previous finish was third in the 1987 Portuguese Open. "I didn't drop a stroke in the final round."

In fact, he dropped only three strokes in all four rounds.

Credit Lyonnais Cannes Open—£350,000
Winner: David Feherty

This could be called the Tale of the Reluctant Champion. David Feherty, the personable Irishman, would rather sing opera than play golf. In fact, he once trained for the opera. The heart was willing but the voice wasn't quite enough, and when the opportunity presented itself, opera's loss was golf's gain. In the Credit Lyonnais Cannes Open, in the first week of May, there arose another opportunity, and Feherty came from behind for his first European Tour victory since the 1989 BMW International, and the fourth of his 13 years on the circuit.

"This was easily my most satisfying victory," Feherty said. He was speaking principally of the distractions of a restless French gallery. At all events, Feherty shot 69-68-69-69—275, 13 under par at Cannes Mougins. A dazzling if unneeded birdie at the last hole gave him a three-stroke victory over Craig Parry (72-71-67-68—278). Mark McNulty, co-leader with Feherty coming into the last round, slipped to a 73 and finished third at 279.

It was pretty much a Feherty-McNulty finale. McNulty had taken the 36-hole lead with a 66—136, and Feherty shot 68 and was a stroke behind. Going into the final round, they were tied for the lead at 10 under par, two strokes up on the field. McNulty was in trouble immediately. His game started acting up. A hooked tee shot cost him a bogey at No. 1. Always the tough campaigner, he bounced back and birdied the third, fourth and fifth holes. McNulty dropped another shot at No. 7, when his ball ended up against a tree. Feherty was rock-solid going out, with a birdie at No. 3 and the rest pars. They made the turn still tied, but now leading the field by three strokes.

Feherty inched ahead with a birdie at the 10th, after a wedge to three feet. He bogeyed the 11th, where the shuffling gallery made him back away five times, but he got that back at the 12th with a birdie from 30 feet. The 15th hole was the decisive one. McNulty's balky game turned fatal here. His tee shot ended up in the water, costing him a double-bogey five and dropping him three strokes behind.

With McNulty safely out of the way, and nobody else making a move, all Feherty had to do was find his way safely home. But he didn't turn conservative. He went after the par-five 16th in two shots. It paid off in a birdie on two putts from 35 feet. It was a comfortable cushion, because at the 17th, a poor lie cost him a bogey. Still not content to tiptoe home, he fired away at the 18th, and went at the cup from 110 yards out. A brilliant wedge left him two feet from the hole. He tapped in for the three-stroke victory.

Denis Durnian and David Williams shared the first-round lead at 66, then slipped into the 70s. Per-Ulrik Johansson, the Swedish rookie, continued to show early strength. He opened with a 67, one stroke off the lead, then also drifted into the 70s. And what of Steven Richardson, the Order-of-Merit leader who was setting the Tour on fire? Well, he never really threatened, but he gave it a good chase and finished fourth, five strokes off at 72—280, adding to a phenomenal record. Through the first 10 weeks of the Tour, he had six top-10 finishes, two of them victories.

Peugeot Spanish Open—£350,000
Winner: Eduardo Romero

Maybe Eduardo Romero would like the picture engraved on his trophy. It's a picture of sheer joy. He's on the green, stretching up and back, like a man doing a swan dive heavenward. He has just holed a 25-foot putt on the last green to tie the resurgent Seve Ballesteros in the Peugeot Spanish Open. He would feel the same thrill an eternity later, when he beat Ballesteros in a grinding playoff that went seven holes.

Theater demanded a playoff. They had turned the early-May tournament into a two-man battle from the start, leapfrogging each other all the way. Ballesteros opened with a course-record 63. Romero matched it in the second round. Ballesteros reclaimed the lead in the third round. Then Ballesteros' shaky fourth round left them tied at 13-under-par 275 at the 6,966-yard, par-72 Club de Campo in Madrid. Romero shot 68-63-72-72, and Ballesteros 63-70-67-75. Vijay Singh was a distant third at 280, five strokes back, for his third top-10 finish in four outings.

Young sensation Steven Richardson (284) finished seventh, which gave him two victories and five other top 10s in 11 events. Ronan Rafferty (75-76) missed the 36-hole cut, and that ended his bid to tie Neil Coles' European Tour record of making 56 consecutive cuts. Nick Faldo's string of consecutive cuts ended at 46, on 73-75.

The loss stung Ballesteros, but there were good signs. Just the week before, he ended a 14-month drought by winning the Chunichi Crowns in Japan. His putting touch had returned. He said he had lost his confidence when he missed that five-foot putt on the first playoff hole of the 1987 Masters, the one in which Larry Mize sank the long chip shot to beat Greg Norman on the second hole. This was the original Ballesteros. In his opening 63 he missed three fairways and five greens, but needed only 24 putts. He eagled the 541-yard No. 7 with a 20-foot putt, and sank a 25-footer at No. 18. "This was the best I've felt in a long time," he said.

The ink was barely dry on his 63 when Romero tied it the next day, scorching the course with eight birdies in a 10-hole stretch. Ballesteros shot 70, and went from five ahead to two behind.

Romero was playing inspired golf, and he credited the man he was trying to beat, Ballesteros, his idol. "But I still consider Seve the greatest player in the world," he said.

It was Ballesteros' turn in the third round. He missed only one fairway and managed a 67—only three men broke 70—despite the stiff winds. He actually fell three strokes behind Romero when he bogeyed No. 1 after a bunkered approach. He rebounded beautifully, and went four strokes ahead when he eagled the 12th hole from 18 feet. Romero shot 72. "The difference," he said, "was the putting. He holed them and I didn't."

After all that brilliance, they came around nearly 180 degrees in the fourth round. Ballesteros made seven bogeys in 16 holes and shot 75. Romero could have won outright, but bogeyed three of the last six holes for a 72. His 72nd stroke was the 25-foot birdie putt for the tie. Then the fireworks began.

At the third playoff hole (No. 18), Ballesteros went from trees to a car to TV cables (free drop) and then into spectators at the green. Then he nearly holed his 60-yard chip shot. Romero rescued himself at the fifth extra hole, firing boldly out of a fairway bunker to the front of the green. And on they went. The playoff record, nine holes, was on the horizon. But Romero ended things abruptly with a birdie from five feet at the seventh hole.

This was his third victory in eight years on the European Tour. But it was a bittersweet one.

"I had joy and sorrow today," he said. "Joy, because I won an important tournament. And sorrow, because I've beaten my friend and idol."

Lancia Martini Italian Open—£325,400
Winner: Craig Parry

There's a lot to be said for playing golf with tunnel vision, as Craig Parry will tell you. Fellow-Australian Graham Marsh had given him an important tip: Leaderboards are often wrong, so don't watch them. The advice served Parry beautifully in the Lancia Martini Italian Open.

"I never bothered checking what Woosnam was doing, but just played my own game," Parry said. In the battle of the big-little men, the five-foot-six Parry fought off the five-foot-four-and-a-half Ian Woosnam and won by a stroke for the third European Tour victory of his career, and his first in two years.

Parry hadn't won since 1989—ironically, Woosnam was one of his victims back then, too—and now he was practically a rebuilt golfer. He had changed his putter, his driver and his swing. "It seems to be coming together," Parry said. You would get no argument from Woosnam. Parry had lost the lead to the hard-charging Woosnam, then reclaimed it down the final stretch and held on. Parry shot four sub-par rounds—71-71-67-70—279, nine under par at the 6,852-yard, par-72 Castelconturbia Club, near Milan. Woosnam carded 69-71-73-67—280.

Woosnam had won the Mediterranean Open early in March and the Masters in mid-April, and now in mid-May he was clearly the pre-tournament favorite in this Italian Open. It looked like his tournament from the opening gun. He was a stroke off the lead in the first round, and he shared a one-stroke lead through 36 holes with a 71—140 in the second round. Parry trailed him by two strokes in the first round and two again in the second. Then came a case of the stumbles in the third round. "Ridiculous," Woosnam said, chastising himself. He bogeyed four of the first six holes, bogeyed two more coming in, then rallied for two birdies and a hole-in-one. The ace, his ninth overall and fourth in tournament competition, came on a five iron at the 189-yard 17th. "The perfect solution to my putting problems," Woosie said with a big grin. It all added up to a one-over-par 73, and a three-under-par 213 total. This left him tied for third, and he was four strokes off the lead when Parry tied the course record and took the lead with a 67 for a 209 total. England's David Gilford, a former Walker Cup player was second at 71—211.

For Parry, the final round had a familiar feel to it. It felt like match play, and this let a little irony into the tournament. In his previous (and only) two European Tour victories, both in 1989, he had to go to playoffs to win. One victim was Mark James, in the German Open. The other was Woosnam, in the Wang Four Stars Pro-Celebrity Classic.

Parry wouldn't look at the leaderboard, but it was as if he was reading minds. "I had a feeling Woosie had birdied No. 14 to go in front," Parry said. Then came another message. It was the silence that spoke to him. "There were no cheers when Woosie walked off the 15th," Parry said, "so I guessed he had bogeyed. And I was right."

In fact, Woosnam had regained a one-stroke lead, then let it slip when he three-putted the par-three 15th. Then he saw three birdie chances go up in smoke. He missed from four feet at the 16th, from 12 feet at the 17th and from 15 feet at the 18th. Parry, meantime, took the lead with a birdie at the 16th, then kept the frustrated Woosnam at bay with pars at the last two holes.

Said Woosnam: "It was frustrating, because after putting like an idiot in the third round, I got it together. I should have won after getting in front."

Said Parry: "It's great to win again."

Volvo PGA Championship—£500,000
Winner: Seve Ballesteros

It was just like the good old days—a spot of trouble here, a near-disaster there, and then the great escape and the victory. Seve Ballesteros was back. For now, anyway.

Ballesteros, who practically ruled the game in Europe through the late 1980s, tailed off badly in 1990. He won just once. In the Volvo PGA Championship, he not only won, he was his flamboyant old self. He grabbed the lead in the third round, squandered a two-stroke edge with three holes to play, made a semi-miracle birdie on the 72nd hole to tie Colin Montgomerie, then beat him with a spectacular birdie on the first playoff hole.

"Many people were thinking that Seve would not come back," Ballesteros said. "Today, I proved them wrong." It was a great May. He won the Chunichi Crowns in Japan the first week, ending a 14-month drought. The next week he was runner-up in the Spanish Open, losing in a playoff to Eduardo Romero. Now the victory in the last week. It was his first European win since the Balearic Open in March, 1990; his second PGA Championship, 47th European win, and 62nd worldwide. Ballesteros toured Wentworth Golf Club's West Course (his sixth victory there) in 67-69-65-70. Montgomerie, coming within a whisker of the second victory of his five-year career, shot 69-66-69-67. ("Amazing," he said. "I usually blow it in the third round.") They tied at 17-under-par 271.

Montgomerie birdied the last two holes for 67, and had all but won when Ballesteros answered them with back-to-back bogeys. At the 16th, he drove into the gallery, then missed the green. At the 17th, he drove with an iron for accuracy but pushed it behind a tree to the right. Now Ballesteros needed a birdie at the par-five 18th to tie. That seemed doubtful. His approach was short and left of the green. It seemed more doubtful when his delicate chip ended up eight feet from the flag. Then he holed the putt.

The playoff was vintage Ballesteros. At the 471-yard first hole, Montgomerie missed the green with his second shot. Ballesteros reached it and then some— a five iron over 200 yards, to within three feet. Montgomerie chipped to within six inches. Ballesteros sank his birdie and picked up the win.

It was a fitting finish to a fiery return. Ballesteros bolted into the lead in the third round with a dazzling putting display. He had been hovering just to the rear, trailing by four in the first round and by two after the second. He sank a 30-foot putt for an eagle three at the 12th, a 20-footer for a birdie at the 15th, and a pair of 25-footers for birdies at the 17th and 18th. "It's been a long time since I holed a lot of long putts," he said.

It looked like anything but Ballesteros' time when the tournament started. Wayne Riley opened with a course-record 63, nine under par, for a three-stroke lead. That included eagles at No. 4 and No. 12. He missed another eagle, from five feet. "A 63 is good enough," he said. "Why get upset about not making 62?"

He followed with a 71 and shared the second-round lead with Bernhard Langer (67) at 10-under 134, and then both would drift back. Langer finished fourth, and Riley tied for 15th. Other European stars played well, but never really threatened. Nick Faldo tied for fifth place on 274, three strokes out of the playoff; Sandy Lyle tied for eighth at 277, his best finish in a year;

Ian Woosnam was a solo 12th on 278, and Jose Maria Olazabal was a distant 45th on par 288. It was an old story. They were all chasing Ballesteros.

"When I went to the playoff hole, I was thinking I could not always lose," Ballesteros said. "I told myself I had to win sometime, and I did."

Dunhill British Masters—£450,000
Winner: Seve Ballesteros

It was one of the hottest free-for-alls in years—Tony Johnstone, Eamonn Darcy, Sam Torrance, David Gilford and Keith Waters, five men all within three strokes of each other coming into the final round of the Dunhill British Masters. It would be a shame if anybody lost, so nobody did. They all birdied the last hole, and Johnstone shot 68; Gilford, Waters and Torrance 69, and Darcy 71. They all tied at 278, 10 under par at Woburn Golf and Country Club. But that was for second place. It was the only game in town.

Seve Ballesteros had made a shambles of the tournament. The closest anyone got to him was a tie for the lead in the first round, on 66. That was Colin Montgomerie. In fact, if Ballesteros hadn't grown bored in the last round, nobody would have got within shouting distance of him. He finished with a 75, and that at least made things believable. He won by three strokes. Before that, his margin was absurd.

"With a seven-stroke lead, it's always difficult to play," he said, "because automatically, you start to play conservatively. But I did play well today. I didn't make any putts, but I did have a slow start. That was the reason I shot 75. But for me, the main thing was to win the tournament, so that was my target, and I won, and I'm very pleased."

Ballesteros, the man who had been written off, was becoming a caricature of himself. This not only was his second victory in six days, it gave him a dreamland four-tournament stretch through the first week of June: A win in the Chunichi Crowns in Japan, a playoff second in the Spanish Open, a playoff victory in the Volvo PGA Championship, and now a rampage win in the Dunhill British Masters on 66-66-68-75—275, 13 under par. That 14-month drought seemed such a long way off.

"A year ago, for me to go to the golf course was like a pain in the head," Ballesteros said. "Now I get up in the morning, and I look forward to coming to the course. I've played the past month nearly as good as I can."

Only one man could make this tournament interesting, and that was Ballesteros himself. He did his best. As he had said, a seven-stroke lead can be too cushy. You tend to get soft. He got through the first hole smoothly enough, with a par. Then the trouble started. At the 134-yard No. 2, he flew the green with his wedge tee shot. It cost him a bogey. Then he double-bogeyed the par-four third after an errant approach left him with an unplayable lie in the bushes. His lead was down to four.

"It was difficult to play from there on," he said. But he kept things in hand. He got two strokes back with birdies at Nos. 4 and 10, and even though he bogeyed the 14th and 16th, he was in such good shape that when he reached the par-five 18th, he could have made a double-bogey seven and still won. But he didn't. He parred the hole for a 75 and won by three.

"I can't shoot 66 every time," he said. "I'm not God, you know."

Murphy's Cup—£350,000
Winner: Tony Johnstone

In the Murphy's Cup, scoring is more a matter of bookkeeping than simple arithmetic. The tournament, the European version of The International on the American tour, is played under the Stableford scoring system. Rather than adding up the strokes, you add up points—six for a double eagle, four for an eagle, and two for a birdie. And zero for a par, minus one for a bogey, minus two for a double bogey or worse. Tony Johnstone, the diminutive Zimbabwean, is getting to be an expert at it. He arrived at Fulford the first week in June with two top-10 finishes but no victories to show for his seven outings, and he walked away with his second consecutive Murphy's Cup, beating Eamonn Darcy in a playoff. It was his third victory in 12 years on the European Tour.

They said it was a case of lightning striking twice, maybe thrice, but this time they were more correct than Johnstone would have preferred. One strike—he repeated as champion. The second strike—he eagled the 18th twice in the same day, once to force the playoff, the second to win it. The third lightning was the real thing, and Johnstone was a frightened man.

A thunderstorm rolled in during the final round. "I'm not afraid to admit that I have a phobia about thunder and lightning," he said. "My knees were knocking, and I putted off the green at No. 5." He also bogeyed No. 6, then headed for shelter. "I just wanted to get the hell out of it," he said, recalling the time he saw two Africans who had been killed by lightning on a golf course in Zimbabwe. "The sight has stuck in my head," he admitted.

Johnstone laid out a little lightning of his own, but not until the final round. Wayne Westner and Jose Rivero led the first round with 16 points each. Stephen Field, a young Englishman and an assistant club pro, was third with 15 points. Harwood took the lead in the second round with 28 points. Johnstone had yet to surface.

In the third round, things were looking grim for Field. He was out with one-over-par 37, and at the par-five 11th, he smacked his drive into the trees at the left. He managed to chop it out sideways to the fairway, and with 205 yards left to the hole, he hit a four iron. Things improved immediately. "I couldn't believe my eyes," he said, "when the ball went straight into the hole for an eagle three." That helped get him a tie for third place with Australian Peter O'Malley, and was worth enough to earn him his European Tour card.

In Stableford competition, boldness is rewarded—if the golfer brings the shots off. Johnstone was a pirate in the 1990 tournament, shooting a 61 and a 65. It was time to be bold again. Johnstone was at No. 14, coming down the final stretch, and saw that O'Malley was already in with 38 points. "I knew I had to shoot four under over the remaining holes," he said. That's four under par over the last four holes—and that's what he did. He dropped 15-foot putts for birdie threes at the 16th and 17th, then holed a 20-footer for an eagle at No. 18 for 40 points. Darcy birdied the last two holes to tie him and force the playoff.

The second playoff hole was No. 18, which Johnstone had eagled from 20 feet earlier. Now he faced a 25-footer for another eagle. And down it went for the title.

Renault Belgian Open—£250,000
Winner: Per-Ulrik Johansson

The folks out in the cruel heat of Arizona, in the American Southwest, would tell you it was only a question of time before the cool Swede hit it big. But even they would have to admit they didn't mean in his first year.

This was Per-Ulrik Johansson, who cut his golf teeth on the Arizona State University golf team, a teammate of the heralded American amateur, Phil Mickelson. Johansson helped Arizona State win the American collegiate championship in 1990. His college days over, Johansson headed straight for the European Tour qualifying tournament in November, 1990. In his first outing, the season-opening Girona Open late in February, he finished fourth. To complete this little fairy tale, the only thing left for him to do was to win. That may be asking a bit much, but that's what Johansson obligingly did in the Renault Belgian Open in mid-June. And in a playoff, in only his 10th start as a pro. It all seemed so pat, as though sketched out by some ambitious script-writer. He was upstaged only by the U.S. Open, going on the same week at Hazeltine, in Minnesota.

"I'm surprised to have won so soon," said the 24-year-old Johansson. "But playing college golf in America certainly helped me." Which speaks volumes about American collegiate golf, increasingly a powerful learning ground for overseas and American youths hoping to hit the pro tours.

Johansson's breakthrough was theater all the way. He had a running battle through four rounds with an opponent from the past.

English pro Paul Broadhurst, 25, a fourth-year pro, was hot on the trail of his third victory. He was in the lead all the way, sharing it with Paul Way in the first round, then Johansson, then Robert Karlsson, another Swedish rookie.

Down the final stretch, Johansson was chasing Chris Williams, 32, an Englishman living in South Africa, in his second year on the Tour. Williams had finished with a 64 and a course-record 277 total. Johansson broke that record moments later. He eagled the par-five 17th hole from 40 feet and inched into the lead at 12-under-par 276, shooting 68-70-70-68 at the par-72 Royal Waterloo. A short while later, along came Broadhurst, more than equal to the dramatic moment. Broadhurst (67-71-69-69) caught Johansson with a birdie-birdie-eagle finish. Johansson was sitting in the grandstand, watching Broadhurst bang home a 30-foot eagle putt at the 18th to force the playoff.

"I wasn't surprised," said Johansson, who had lost to Broadhurst in the European Championships five years earlier. "I know how good he is under pressure."

The playoff began and ended at the par-five 17th. Broadhurst drove down the middle, but hit his two-iron approach into a greenside bunker. He bladed his blast across the green and under a bush. He had to chop it out, and then nearly holed his chip for a par. But he settled for a bogey. Johansson, who had driven into the right rough, got his third shot on and two-putted for the par and the victory. That kept the Belgian Open crown in Sweden. Ove Sellberg, who missed the cut, was the defending champion. Another bit of irony: Johansson became the Tour's first rookie winner since the Cannes Open in 1989. The rookie champ then? Paul Broadhurst.

Carrolls Irish Open—£365,800
Winner: Nick Faldo

It didn't look like much, that 70. It was just two under par.

The author: Nick Faldo, a man with something to prove. He had been coming up empty. He won the Johnnie Walker Classic in Hong Kong in December, but aside from that he hadn't won since the 1990 British Open. Now it was late in June, 1991, nearly a whole year later, and he had practically nothing to show for his reputation as one of the best in the world. Now he was at Carrolls Irish Open, at Killarney, the first time since 1975 that it was held outside Dublin.

Back to that so-so 70: Put it into context, and it starts to look like what it really was—the pivotal point in the Irish Open. Faldo shot it in the third round. You search through the 74 players and find only one other 70, and there's only one score better, a 69. Heavy weather had hit the 7,061-yard, par-72 inland course, and Faldo was one of the few to ride it out. It got him back into the lead and set him up for that elusive victory.

"I've been working hard on my game the last two months," Faldo said, after posting 68-75-70-70, a five-under-par total of 283 and a three-stroke victory over Colin Montgomerie (68-72-76-70—286). "It's finally paid off. I've finally been able to make it click when I wanted to."

Things started to work in the first round. "I only missed one green," Faldo said. "So I know there's nothing basically wrong with my game. It's just got to click, that's all." Which it did, in spades. Faldo eagled the par-five fifth hole from 15 feet and eagled the par-five 11th from five feet en route to a four-under-par 68 and a share of the first-day lead with Montgomerie. U.S. Open champion Payne Stewart—he had won the week before—tied for third place at 69 with four birdies coming in. "It wasn't a bad effort for the first time that I played the course," he said.

Things went clunk instead of click for Faldo in the second round. He shot 75 in the swirling winds and slipped three strokes off the lead, shared at 140 by Montgomerie (72) and Stewart (71). The third round, battered by gales and heavy rain, made the difference. "The weather was as bad as I can remember," Faldo said. "There was always another black cloud coming over the mountains. I just tried to cut the ball and hold it in the wind, rather than trying to draw it the way I did in the second round." And there was his 70, a jewel in a setting of other scores: Montgomerie, 76; Stewart, 77; Jose Maria Olazabal, 75; Mark Calcavecchia, 78. And there were seven players in the 80s.

So Faldo went into the final round and its balmy weather with a three-stroke lead over Montgomerie, Olazabal, Frank Nobilo and Russell Claydon. He had no trouble keeping them at bay. He birdied No. 2, and the par fives, Nos. 5, 11 and 16. Only two bogeys marred his card. At No. 15, he chipped poorly from the rough behind the green, and at No. 18, he drove into a fairway bunker. So it was just a stroll in the shadows of the Macgillycuddy Reeks.

"The conditions really favored Nick," said Montgomerie, who was content to hold his ground. "I was really just trying to get into second on my own. My hands were sweating, and I was thinking about the Ryder Cup all the way around." He took his second place with 70—286, a stroke ahead of Carl

Mason (69) and Frank Nobilo (71). Olazabal tied for fifth on 72—288, and Stewart plunged to a tie for 16th on 76—293.

"It's a relief to win again," Faldo said. "Now I just need to get my putter hot for the British Open next month."

Peugeot French Open—£400,000
Winner: Eduardo Romero

Eduardo Romero was homing in on his second victory of the year with such ease that it was going to take a disaster to head him off. And that's almost what he got before he pulled out of his spin.

"I don't know what happened," the pleasant Argentinian said. He led by four strokes going into the final round of the Peugeot French Open, on a sunny, breezy day at the end of June. Actually, he was leading by six strokes with six holes to play. Then came the crash dive. He pulled out just in time to get that second win of the year and the fourth in his eight years on the European Tour. Romero shot 69-69-67-76—281, seven under par at the par-72 National Golf Club at Paris. He won by two over Jose Maria Olazabal (74-67-68-74) and Sam Torrance (72-70-72-69), who tied at 283.

And it was a scary two-stroke victory. Romero's lead had dropped to one stroke with one hole to play.

Maybe he has a thirst for drama. He had plenty in winning the Spanish Open in May. He frittered away his chances down the stretch and had to go seven extra holes to beat Seve Ballesteros.

"I lost my concentration on No. 13," Romero said, trying to explain this one. "I can't hit a driver. I can't putt. It was strange. Maybe it was because I was so far ahead." Ballesteros said the same thing in the Dunhill British Masters a month earlier. He led by seven strokes going into the last round, shot 76, won by three, and explained that big leads make a man too conservative.

Wind, chill and rain greeted the start of the tournament, and the man everyone was watching, Nick Faldo, winner of the Irish Open the week before, could manage no better than a 73. "It was bloody tough out there," Faldo said. Only 10 men broke 72, and only two broke 70. Romero and Frank Nobilo shot 69s and shared a one-stroke lead. They shot 69s in the second round, too, for 138 totals, and opened a two-stroke lead on Paul Broadhurst (68) and Vijay Singh (70). Olazabal made his move with a 67 that included two eagles, and pulled to within three at 141.

Romero and Nobilo parted company in the third round. They had started the day tied, and ended it 11 strokes apart. Romero spun a 67 and Nobilo rocketed to a 78. So Romero entered the last round four strokes ahead of Olazabal and a huge nine ahead of Torrance.

In the fourth round, it was all over by the second hole—or so it seemed. Olazabal, playing with Romero, had watered his four-iron approach. Romero's lead was up to six strokes. He was still six ahead with six holes to play, and then the skid began. He bogeyed No. 13, and led by five strokes with five to play. After saving par out of heavy rough at the 14th, he bogeyed the 15th. Suddenly, Torrance's prospects brightened. He was already in the clubhouse with his 69—283, and Romero was backing up fast.

Romero and Olazabal salvaged par at the par-three 16th, and then who could blame Torrance if he relished the thought of the par-four 17th. "A bloody difficult hole," he called it. A tee shot either left or right could easily end up as a double bogey. And, as if on cue, that's exactly what Romero got. He started with a hook off the tee and a penalty drop from jungle rough, and ended by missing a three-foot bogey putt. His lead was one stroke over Torrance with one hole to play. He needed a talking-to.

"I said to myself, 'Well, you've got to make a birdie on the 18th,'" Romero said. The 18th, a 511-yard par five, was playing downwind. Romero, one of the longest hitters, reached it with a perfect drive and a pitching wedge to the water-ringed green. He got his birdie and his two-stroke win. Olazabal eagled it for his 74 to tie Torrance for second.

Torras Monte Carlo Open—£400,000
Winner: Ian Woosnam

Before the Torras Monte Carlo Open could run its course, Ian Woosnam had reduced the tournament to an exercise in small talk. Let's see: Woosie had joined the jet-setting golfers and bought his own airplane, so they talked about that. U.S. Open champion Payne Stewart, minus the signature knickers (plus-twos to the British), upset some folks at the Monte Carlo Beach Club by playing his compact disk player too loud. The biggest pro-am prize in European golf was sitting there for the taking—a £120,000 boat for a hole-in-one. And so it went. Once Woosie's game clicked in, there was little else left to do but chat.

Mont Agel perches on a mountain high above the luxurious Cote d'Azur, and as golf courses go—at 6,198 yards and par 69—it's no secret that it is not one of the brutes of the European Tour. Even so, a 61 is a remarkable accomplishment, and that's what Woosnam authored in the third round. He hurtled from a six-stroke deficit to a three-stroke lead, and he rolled on from there to win by four strokes over Anders Forsbrand.

It was Woosnam's fourth victory of the year. He had won twice in the United States—the USF&G Classic and the first major of his career, the Masters. This was not only Woosnam's second win in Europe, it was his second successful title defense. It seems he has an affinity for the Cote d'Azur. Back in March, just up the coast at Golf de L'Esterel, he won his second consecutive Mediterranean Open. Someone noted that in 1990, he won at Monte Carlo and then won the Scottish Open the following week. Could he do that again now? Woosnam stopped short of a prediction, but he didn't downplay the idea, either. "I've got such a good putting stroke going," he said, "that I must have every chance of doing that double again."

So it would seem. He shot Mont Agel in 67-66-61-67—261, 15 under par, running away from Forsbrand (72-62-66-65—265). The four-way tie for third place at 10-under 266 showed how thoroughly Mont Agel had got shot up. Vijay Singh and Rodger Davis each had a 62, Mats Lanner a 63 and Peter Mitchell had nothing higher than a 67. Peter McWhinney shot all four rounds in the 60s and tied for 35th place. Par for the course, 276, was only good for 51st place.

Fully 50 of the 143 starters broke par in the first round. Seve Ballesteros, who had two victories and a second in his last three European outings, led the onslaught with a seven-under-par 62. It included eight threes on his second nine, starting with an eagle three off a one iron to 10 feet at the 10th hole. "I can't play every day like that," he explained the next day, when he returned a par 69 for a 131 total that dropped him to a tie for third. The new leader in the second round was a little-known Scot named Sandy Stephen, who had missed the cut in 12 of his 14 European tournaments. This time Stephen, 37, matched Ballesteros' 62 for 127 and a three-stroke lead on Rodger Davis (62—130).

The third round found Mont Agel under hot, calm conditions, and Woosnam with a hot hand. "I wasn't happy with my game yesterday," he said. "But today, after a slight change in my grip, it all clicked back into place. I was interested in winning again." He streaked to that 61 with nine birdies overall and five over the last six holes. He started the last round with birdies on the first three holes, and left the guys talking to themselves.

Bell's Scottish Open—£500,000
Winner: Craig Parry

It was a vignette out of Greek mythology, where the hero has to overcome obstacles in order to gain the prize. In this case, the prize was the Bell's Scottish Open, and Craig Parry overcame one obstacle after another—there weren't any dragons—until there was just one left. All he had to do was birdie the last hole.

He didn't know this, though. He's a student of Graham Marsh, and if there's one thing Marsh teaches, it's to forget the leaderboards. "He told me never to try to find out what the others were doing, but just to concentrate on my own game," Parry said. He slipped only once, and did risk a peek at the leaderboard. Even Marsh would forgive him this one, though. He was on the final hole, with just a tap-in for the victory.

But wait. True to the story line, even with victory that close, it wasn't certain. A rejuvenated Mark McNulty lay just some eight feet from the hole, putting for an eagle. If he would make it, Parry would have no better than a tie. But the fates relented. McNulty's eagle putt grazed the hole and stayed out, and Parry got his birdie, and his victory. He shot the par-70 Gleneagles King's course in 65-67-69-67—268, 12 under par. McNulty, making his first appearance after six weeks off for knee surgery, seemed his old self with 65-68-70-66—269. This was Parry's second European Tour victory of the season—he won the Italian Open in May—and his fourth in five years. And it came at a crucial time, the week before the British Open.

"I feel I'm playing well enough to have a great chance in the Open," Parry said. The awkward thing about this burst of confidence, however, was that Parry was still two rounds from winning the Scottish Open. He was saying this at the halfway point, before he had even smelled the lead. His opening 65 left him two behind Mark Roe and the dangerous Seve Ballesteros. He shot 67 in the second round, but fell back a stroke, three strokes behind Canadian Danny Mijovic, who was leading on 64-66—130, 10 under par. It was when the heavy weather hit that Parry really sparkled.

Play was suspended for almost two hours in the third round because of a torrential rain storm, which was driven by strong winds. Scores rose accordingly. Of the 67 finishers, 28 shot 74 or more, and three shot 80. Only three players could manage the par of 70, and only seven could break it, and Parry was one of them. His 69 was enough to lift him into a one-stroke lead (nine-under-par 201) over Ballesteros (71—202). McNulty (70) and Mijovic (73) were two off the lead. Then came the challenges.

With Ballesteros fading in the wind and rain of the final round (he finished with 73 for 275), Mijovic became a real threat. He got to 10 under par when he holed a 30-foot birdie putt at the 14th hole. But he three-putted the 15th, 17th and 18th, and that would drop him to fourth place at 272. Mats Lanner came within close range, but a double bogey at the 16th knocked him out. David Gilford closed with a 65, the best round of the day, but it wasn't enough to overhaul the leaders, and he fell three strokes short, finishing third on 271. That left McNulty. His charge started at No. 1, where he birdied from 30 feet. It ended at No. 18, where the eagle putt just missed. The week was hardly a waste, though—a strong second place and a good test for a repaired knee heading into the British Open. It was even better for Parry. "This week," he said, "had a great feel to it." Would that feel last for just one more?

Heineken Dutch Open—£500,000
Winner: Payne Stewart

Payne Stewart came to the Heineken Dutch Open in July as man of triumph and disappointment. He had won the U.S. Open just over a month ago, but the week before coming to the Netherlands, he finished a distant 32nd in the British Open. He was a man with something to prove. If crushing a golf tournament proves anything, Stewart proved it. He reduced the field and the 6,826-yard, par-72 Noordwijkse course to rubble with his 67-68-62-70—267. That's 21 under par and a victory by nine strokes, the biggest victory margin on the European Tour to date in 1991. Then he felt the need to apologize.

"The golf wasn't pretty in the final round," he said. "In fact, it was downright boring. The main thing I had to do was focus on not beating myself. It's not my nature to play conservatively, but nobody threatened me, and I just got the job done."

The co-runners-up at 276 were Bernhard Langer, the leader in the first two rounds (63-71-69-73), and Swedish rookie Per-Ulrik Johansson, the Belgian Open winner, who made an astounding recovery after a disastrous start (78-67-62-69). And those were not paper tigers back in the field. Also crushed by Stewart were British Open runner-up Mike Harwood, and Fred Couples, who tied for third, and David Feherty and Mark James, among others.

The victory was Stewart's first in Europe, and completed his global grand slam. "I've won on all the main tours now," he said. "It's filled a void in my career. If you want to be known as a world-class golfer, you've got to win all over the world." He has won eight times in the United States (including two majors, the U.S. Open and the PGA Championship), twice in Asia, and once in Australia. Twice he almost made the British Open his first European victory. He was runner-up in 1985 and in 1990.

Aside from Stewart, Johansson was the story of the week. After that opening 78, he checked out of his hotel and booked a flight home. But the flight was delayed when he closed the second round with birdies at the 17th (from 12 feet) and the 18th (from 15 feet) for a 67 that just made the cut at 145. He was still in poor shape, 11 strokes behind co-leaders Langer and Danny Mijovic. Then came the 10-birdie 62 in the third round, matching Stewart for the course record.

Stewart's 62—his 11 birdies tied the European Tour record—gave him the luxury of a six-stroke cushion going into the final round. "I've never had a lead that big before," Stewart said later. "It was a strange feeling." Complacency was his only opponent. And he was far from complacent, as he showed down the final stretch. At the par-five 14th, he boldly went at the flag, firing a two iron to within a foot to set up an eagle three. Then he birdied the 15th and 17th en route to his closing two-under 70.

Golf writers wondered whether this powerful exhibition was a sign for the approaching Ryder Cup matches. "The Ryder Cup is a team event and it's two months away," Stewart said. "I don't know how I'll be playing by then, or how anyone else will be playing." But he did reveal an ambition that surprised no one: "I've played on a losing side and a side that tied, and I'd love to be on a winning team. Hopefully at Kiawah Island."

Scandinavian Masters—£600,000
Winner: Colin Montgomerie

Beating Seve Ballesteros in the Scandinavian Masters may not have been a case of pure revenge for Colin Montgomerie, but it was the next best thing. It was also a case of learning how to win.

Back in the Volvo PGA Championship in May, Ballesteros had caught him with a birdie on the final hole, then beat him on the first extra hole. History seemed ready to repeat itself here in the inaugural Scandinavian Masters. But this time the curly-haired Scot passed Ian Woosnam, took the lead down the stretch, and simply refused to let the hard-charging Spaniard catch him.

Montgomerie, after rounds of 68-65-70, closed with a five-under-par 67 for an 18-under-par 270 to beat Ballesteros (70-64-73-64—271) by a stroke. It was his second victory in five years on the Tour, and the more rewarding by far. Montgomerie not only became the first winner of a £100,000 check in an official European Tour event, he also locked up his first Ryder Cup team berth.

"I'm proud I could come from behind and win under pressure," Montgomerie said. "There was no pressure on me when I won by 11 strokes in Portugal two years ago." That was the 1989 Portuguese Open-TPC. A golfer is hardly tested in a runaway, so even though Montgomerie had eight top-10 finishes this season, there was a question whether he could stand up under heat.

"I was surprised that Woosie didn't put more pressure on me," Montgomerie said. "But he'd had his great round the day before." Woosnam had shot 63 in the third round. He held a two-stroke lead going into the final round, and was four up on Montgomerie. Then his putter cooled—"I'm the worst putter in the world," he insisted—and he slumped to a 73. But Ballesteros took up the chase, and it was a hot hand he was chasing.

Montgomerie charged into the lead with birdies on six of the first 12 holes. Woosnam was out of the way, but now Ballesteros was the threat. He finished with a 64 that included an eagle and six birdies, three of them over the last three holes. "It was one day too much," he was to lament, looking back at the triple-bogey seven the day before. Still, he was in at 271, waiting. The question was whether Montgomerie could hold himself together. And that Montgomerie did, wrapping up a tournament that was a free-for-all from the start.

Consider the case of big-hitting Fred Couples. He tamed the 6,747-yard, par-72 Drottningholms course with his power but couldn't solve its greens at first. He five-putted one hole (for a triple-bogey six), and four-putted two others, and shot a 74 that was much worse than it looked. Of the four-round players, 75 was the highest opening score.

Couples, who would tie for sixth, erased it in the second round with a stunning 11-under-par 61, tying the course record. He birdied 14 of his first 16 holes and ended up with a European-Tour-record 12 birdies overall. "I certainly didn't expect what I shot today," he said.

It was the kind of thing that kept Montgomerie almost in the shadows. His opening 68 left him three strokes out of the lead, behind fast-improving Paul Broadhurst and Derrick Cooper, who had missed three consecutive cuts. A 65 in the second gave him a share of the lead on 11-under-par 133 with Mark Roe (64) and David James (65), who had missed the cut in 16 of his 18 European starts. A third-round 70 dropped him four strokes behind Woosnam, and then came the thrilling finish.

"Some people have doubted my ability to withstand pressure," Montgomerie said. "I think I proved today that I've got what it takes. I think I can handle the different kinds of pressure I'll come under in the Ryder Cup."

European Pro-Celebrity—£250,000
Winner: Paul Broadhurst

Whoever said figures don't lie wasn't watching Paul Broadhurst's performance in the European Pro-Celebrity.

The figures say that Broadhurst trailed in the first round, shared the lead in the second, and pulled away by himself in the last two rounds, shooting 67-70-69-66, for a 16-under-par total of 272 at Royal Liverpool. He led by three strokes going into the final round. The figures also show that Ronan Rafferty shot 68-72-69-70—279. Which means that Broadhurst won by a staggering seven strokes.

Well, that might be enough to satisfy an accountant. But what the figures don't show—that is, where the figures lie—is that there was nothing really luxurious about this victory. It was nothing like the nine-stroke romp Payne Stewart enjoyed in the Dutch Open. This one was as tense and dramatic as any on the Tour this season. The fact is, Broadhurst had squandered his three-stroke lead, and then he proceeded to go on a rampage of nine birdies in 10 holes.

"I just ripped the back nine—tore it to pieces," Broadhurst said. Just in time, too. He had started the final round at 10-under-par 207, leading Rafferty and Christy O'Connor, Jr. by three strokes. But he wasted most of that lead with a double-bogey seven at No. 3, and before he knew it, the rest of the lead was gone as well. The tournament—and the prospects for a happy 26th birthday in three days, on August 14—had taken a turn for the worse. Then something kicked in. Starting at No. 8, he birdied nine of the next 10 holes, and six of them in succession from the 12th. And only one birdie putt was longer than 10 feet. The charge killed the hopes of Rafferty (70), O'Connor (71), and Keith Waters (69) who tied O'Connor for third on 280.

The performance didn't surprise Broadhurst watchers. He was stamped as a man to watch from the moment he turned pro in 1988. He justified the enthusiasm of his backers by winning the Cannes Open along with Rookie-of-the-Year honors in 1989. He came back from wrist surgery to win the Motorola Classic in 1990. He seemed to be a prime talent in the formative stage, as evidenced by periodic flashes of brilliance. Take, for example, his third round in the 1990 British Open at St. Andrews. He birdied eight of the first 10 holes and shot 63, setting the Open record for the Old Course and tying the record for the Open overall. In the Belgian Open in June, he lost to Per-Ulrik Johansson in a playoff, but he had eagled the final hole to catch him.

Rafferty was a surprise runner-up. He was just coming back from the shoulder injury that knocked him out of the British Open a month earlier. "I'm hitting the ball a lot better," he said. "I'm very encouraged by what's happened this week."

Broadhurst, with his victory, was on the verge of taking a Ryder Cup berth. And the Ryder Cup was the furthest thing from his mind. "I went into the final round thinking more about getting into the England Dunhill Cup side," he said. "But now I must have a chance at the Ryder Cup, if I keep playing the way I am."

It's just a question of figures. Nine birdies in 10 holes? Now, there's a set of figures that don't lie.

NM English Open—£450,000
Winner: David Gilford

Little-known Englishman David Gilford all but locked up a Ryder Cup berth with his maiden victory in the NM English Open. And veteran Sandy Lyle all but shut himself out. Lyle shot 77 in the first round and pronounced himself dead for a sixth Ryder Cup appearance, despite the encouragement of European captain Bernard Gallacher. If that didn't do it, a 76 in the second round did. Lyle had missed the 36-hole cut for the third consecutive time.

Gilford, outlasting Roger Chapman, Steven Richardson, and Seve Ballesteros, shot 70-71-67-70—278, 10 under par at The Belfry. "I've been close two or three times before this year, so this is most satisfying," Gilford said. "Things have started to snowball, and I'm playing with a lot more confidence." Gilford, 25, in his sixth season on the European Tour, tied for second in the Dunhill British Masters, tied for fourth in the Italian Open, and was a solo third in the Scottish Open.

Gilford won by two strokes over Chapman, whose late collapse cost him a chance at his first victory in 11 years on the Tour. Chapman led by a stroke after two rounds, and had a chance to tie Gilford but bogeyed the final two holes. He shot 69-66-74-71—280. "I haven't played well the last two days, but I hung in there till the 17th," said Chapman, who has been working with a sports psychologist. "You live and learn."

Two others in the hunt also faded at the end. Mark James, bidding for a third consecutive English Open title, led the first round with a 66, was one stroke behind at the halfway point, and two behind after three rounds. But he crashed coming home. Hitting bunkers and water, he double-bogeyed the 17th. Then he bogeyed the 18th for 76—286, and tied for eighth place. Per-Ulrik Johansson, another Ryder Cup hopeful, was three strokes off the lead going into the final round, and closed with a 73 to tie for fifth on 284.

The tournament really started, as they say, on the final nine. Gilford and Chapman were tied at eight under par through the turn. Then the seesawing began. Gilford had the lead handed to him when Chapman, playing in the group ahead, hit his approach shot into the water and bogeyed the par-four 10th hole. He shook it off, however, and went on a tear. He birdied the 11th from 35 feet, the 15th from three feet, and the 16th from 10 feet, and he led Gilford by one stroke. Gilford also birdied the 11th, holing from 30 feet, but a three-putt par was the best he could do at the 15th. He caught Chapman at the 16th, rolling in a 10-foot putt for a birdie. Now the tournament came down to two holes—and disaster for Chapman.

At the par-five 17th, he put his one-iron second shot into a fairway bunker about 100 yards from the green. He came out short, pitched to about 10 feet, and two-putted for the bogey. At the 18th, his five-iron approach ended up near No. 9 green. A great pitch shot put him four feet from the cup, but he missed the putt and suffered his second consecutive bogey for a 71. It meant his fifth runner-up finish in 11 years on the Tour.

The door was open to Gilford, and he marched through with a steady hand and clear head. He two-putted from 45 feet to save par at the 17th, and at the 18th he chipped to a foot and tapped in for his first championship and a possible Ryder Cup berth. He put it all down to experience. "I've learned that the more you play with the top players, the more you realize how many bad shots they hit," he said. "They're only human, too."

Volvo German Open—£525,000
Winner: Mark McNulty

There was a lot more than the tournament title at stake in the Volvo German Open. This was late August, the last chance to make the European Ryder Cup team, a fact that rated no worse than equal billing with the German Open. Fully 14 players arrived at the Hubbelrath Club at Dusseldorf with either a chance to win a berth outright, or else with hopes of getting in on a wild-card selection. All of which gave rise to a peculiar coincidence: Paul Broadhurst became a loser and a winner at the same time.

Mark McNulty (he's Zimbabwean, remember, and not eligible for the European team) beat Broadhurst in a playoff for his fourth German Open and second in succession. And Broadhurst, runner-up in the Belgian Open and winner of the recent European Pro-Celebrity, locked up a Ryder Cup berth on point standings.

"I'm a bit disappointed," Broadhurst said. "I lost a playoff to Per-Ulrik Johansson in Belgium, and I don't want to get the reputation of always doing that."

There were a lot of disappointments. Chris Williams, the Englishman who lives in South Africa, led the first round (66) and was a stroke behind after the second round. Then a 74-75 finish knocked him back to a tie for 39th place. Gordon Brand, Jr., a stroke off the lead going into the final round, shot 76. Sam Torrance, who made the Ryder Cup team for the sixth time, led by a stroke going into the final round, and was still leading with nine holes to play. Then a bogey six at the 12th and a double-bogey seven at the 17th dropped him to a tie for third. The sharpest pain of all was left for the long-suffering Sandy Lyle, who hadn't won in 34 months. A 67-69 start put him just a stroke off the 36-hole lead. Hope had dawned. But it was just a taunt. He finished 74-76—286 and plummeted to 43rd.

The two finalists took separate paths to the playoff. McNulty led after 36 holes and was two strokes behind going into the last round. Broadhurst came from a long way off. He trailed by seven strokes in the first round, five in the second, and three in the third. McNulty shot 68-67-72-66—273, Broadhurst 73-67-68-65, and they tied at 15-under-par 273.

The tournament came down to the final nine holes, with Torrance leading but about to get run over. At the par-five 12th, Broadhurst fired a nine-iron approach to about 12 feet, and holed the putt for his second eagle of the day and a one-stroke lead on McNulty. He saved par out of a bunker at No. 13, and parred the 14th as well. McNulty, playing behind him, birdied the 12th then eagled the par-four 13th with a 147-yard seven iron. McNulty was leading by two. Broadhurst had four holes in which to catch him.

Then only two, after pars at the 15th and 16th. It was no time to be timid. At the par-five 17th, he hit his driver off the fairway. His hopes for an eagle died when he missed the green, but he pitched on to 10 feet and made the birdie. Then at No. 18, he fired his second to 15 feet and holed that for another birdie. He had caught McNulty.

And with that, Broadhurst's magic had run out. At the first playoff hole, he was short with his second shot, and so short with his chip that the ball came rolling back down the slope to him. He made six, and McNulty was an easy winner with a par four.

"I think he lost his concentration after getting on the Ryder Cup team," McNulty said.

Broadhurst wasn't happy about that stumble in the playoff hole. But there was that silver lining.

"I've made the Ryder Cup team," he said, knowing the thrill of all Ryder Cuppers. "I have no idea where Kiawah Island is. And I've never even been to America."

GA European Open—£500,000
Winner: Mike Harwood

It was at the British Open some six weeks earlier that tall, spindly Mike Harwood noted, "I'm not one of the great players, but if nobody wants to win it, then I'll be hanging around, ready." On the subject of greatness, who wants to can take him at his word. But "hanging around" wasn't something he was content to do at the GA European Open at Walton Heath.

The tournament ended on September 1, and Harwood welcomed the new month by coming from three strokes off the lead, and outrunning the likes of Seve Ballesteros, Payne Stewart and Sandy Lyle for his first European Tour victory of the year and the fifth of his career. Harwood, runner-up to fellow Aussie Ian Baker-Finch in the British Open in July, tore through the famed, 7,163-yard course for a seven-under-par 65 and a two-stroke victory over the slumping Lyle, who—if seeing could be believing—was showing signs of his former life. Lyle, winless for three years, finished second on 74-69-69-67—279. It was his best 72-hole European showing since a tie for second in the 1988 Scottish Open. But it still was Harwood's week. He shot 70-72-70-65—277, 11 under par.

"I played unbelievably," Harwood said. "I played so well, I could have shot anything. I play well on good courses. I like them long." He also likes strong fields. This one was loaded. Of the European Ryder Cup team, only Bernhard Langer and Jose Maria Olazabal were missing. Harwood, barely noticed in the first three rounds, made his move in the final round. He went out in four-under 32, with two birdies and an eagle. Then he turned for home and vaulted into the lead with two early birdies—two-putting at the par-five 11th, and firing an eight iron to within a foot at the 12th. That put him six under par for the round and 10 under for the tournament. He suffered his only bogey at the 14th and lost the lead briefly to Ballesteros. He got it back at the 15th, flipping a wedge to within six inches. He also birdied the 475-yard, par-four 16th, holing a 15-foot putt for a three-stoke lead. Two closing pars gave him 65.

The European Open began as an all-Australian show. Peter Fowler and Ken Trimble led off, tying South African John Bland for the first-round lead on 69. Then Trimble slipped, but Fowler, a four-time European Tour runner-up, took the 36-hole lead with 69—138. Up jumped another Aussie, Craig Parry, winner of the Italian and Scottish Opens, to tie for second at 69—139. Then Italy's Costantino Rocca interrupted the Down-Under party with a third-round 69—209 for a one-stroke lead on Parry, Fowler and Ballesteros going into the final round.

It was Ballesteros' tournament to win or lose late in the fourth round. He took a one-stroke lead when he birdied the 13th while Harwood was bogey-ing the 14th up ahead. Then Ballesteros fell back with two bogeys, missing the green at the 14th and bunkering his tee shot at the 15th. "That's been my problem," Ballesteros would say. "Last-day blues." He tied for third at 280 with Bland (67) and Payne Stewart (68), who had to play in a brace to shore up his aching back.

Harwood certainly wasn't hanging around. He got the birdies at the 15th and 16th to go three ahead, then finished with two pars, the last on an excellent escape from a greenside bunker. Then he sat back to wait. He didn't have to wait long.

Actually, there were two winners. The other, of course, was the long-suffering Lyle, the runner-up. "This is the week I've been looking for, for quite a while," he said. "It felt like a win to me."

Canon European Masters-Swiss Open—£444,015
Winner: Jeff Hawkes

Going into the final round of the Canon European Masters-Swiss Open, Seve Ballesteros had it figured just about right. "I thought 65 would be good enough to win," he said. He went two better, in typical Ballesteros fireworks. He birdied the last six holes for a 63. Even that wasn't enough.

Jeff Hawkes, 38-year-old South African and a four-time runner-up since joining the European Tour in 1976 but never a winner, had taken the lead with a 65 in the third round. In the fourth, he shook under the Ballesteros pressure but refused to crack. He shot 66 and beat Ballesteros by one stroke.

"Now I can retire!" Hawkes said. It was a narrow escape. One moment, he was leading by five strokes. The next, Ballesteros had pulled to within two. "Boy," Hawkes said, "was my heart racing." Hawkes, who trailed by four strokes in the first and second rounds, shot 68-69-65-66—268, 20 under par. Ballesteros (69-67-70-63—269), who had won twice already this season, was runner-up for the third time.

There was another show going on, by the way. The comeback of Sandy Lyle, runner-up the week before in the European Open, was still gathering steam. After an opening 68, he stumbled on middle rounds of 73-74, then closed with a stunning 62 for a tie for 27th place on 277. The round included eight birdies and an eagle. And he mourned the ones that got away. "I could have had a 59," Lyle said.

The 6,745-yard, par-72 Crans-Sur-Sierre course high in the Alps took a beating from the start, and Hawkes and Ballesteros were not exactly threats. Gordon Brand, Jr., who hadn't won since 1989, got some encouragement with an opening 64. He led by one stroke over Manuel Pinero and Glenn Ralph. Hawkes was four strokes behind, Ballesteros, five. In the second round, Eduardo Romero (65—133) took a two-stroke lead over a small traffic jam. Ballesteros (67) improved and was three behind, and Hawkes (69) stayed at four behind. The cast changed again for the third round, with Hawkes shooting 65—202 for a one-stroke edge over Peter Teravainen (64) and Romero (70). Ballesteros (70—206) was four behind. That set up a finale that had a taste of re-match to it. Hawkes had had a thrilling brush with victory in the 1987 Epson Grand Prix Match Play. In the semifinals, he shocked everybody, including himself, by beating Ballesteros, 4 and 3. He lost in the final, but he had beaten Ballesteros head-to-head, which is more than most golfers can say. And so here they were again.

Hawkes started strong in the fourth round. He birdied two of the first three holes, then three in succession from No. 7. On he went—birdies at the 10th and 12th got him to 21 under par. Then came trouble. At No. 13, he glanced at the leaderboard and discovered that despite his hot pace, Ballesteros had closed the gap from five strokes to two. "I was suddenly shaky," Hawkes admitted. He watered a lay-up at the par-five 14th and bogeyed. At the 16th, tree trouble cost him another bogey. Now the question was, could he hold together for two more holes? The answer came in the form of a gentle scolding from his caddie, a teenage girl named Bettina. Said Hawkes: "She said, 'OK, you're back down to earth. Now let's play some golf.'"

Just in time, too. Ballesteros had birdied Nos. 5, 7 and 9, on nothing longer than a 10-foot putt, and he was just warming up. He birdied his way home from No. 13—six in succession. Hawkes shook it off. At the par-four 17th, he flicked a pitch from 81 yards that stopped on the edge of the hole. The tap-in birdie all but wrapped it up.

Lancome Trophy—£450,000
Winner: Frank Nobilo

The defending champion was trying to regain his wounded spirit. Another man was suffering from poor drives and worse irons. Another found the answer to the greens—hundreds of short practice putts, and yet another dreaded seeing his name up in lights. It was an odd mix that was challenging for the Lancome Trophy, so maybe it was poetic justice that an unlikely fellow with the real secret to golf came on to win it.

In the select field of 66 golfers who gathered at St. Nom La Breteche, near Paris, this was one of the unlikeliest of all—New Zealander Frank Nobilo—and his secret was simple, foolproof and tongue-in-cheek.

Said the man who finished second three times in the past 12 months and who, though only 31, was wondering whether the game was all over for him: "The best way to win is to finish a shot clear of second. And that's what I did."

That's not the sort of secret that will sell well out of the pro shop, but it did translate easily on the scoreboard. Nobilo shot the par-70 St. Nom La Breteche course in 65-68-69-65 for a 13-under-par 267. He had to sweat out a small pack of hounds. But the mixed foursome had to settle for a tie for second—Ryder-Cup-bound David Gilford, little-known James Spence, and two Australians, Peter Fowler and British Open champion Ian Baker-Finch.

It was Nobilo's second victory in Europe, and his first since the 1988 PLM Open, and for a while it seemed it might not come so easily. Nobilo, who shared the 36-hole lead, started the final round two strokes off the pace. He finished early with his 65—267, then had to wait beside the 18th green as one golfer after another took a shot at him. Fowler birdied the 17th to tie him, but bogeyed the 18th after bunkering his tee shot. He shot 67, tying for second at 268 with Spence (68), Baker-Finch (67), and Gilford (65).

Nobilo, who had won four times back home, indeed was an unlikely winner given the strong field. The defending champion was Jose Maria Olazabal and his spirits had been flagging because of that final-hole bogey that cost him a chance at the Masters back in April. "After that, I just didn't have the will to play golf," he said. Of course he pulled himself together enough to win The International on the American tour in mid-August. He challenged only briefly this time.

The man with the poor drives and worse irons was American star Mark Calcavecchia. He was trying hard to get his game going. "This hasn't been a good season for me," he said. "Now I need a good tournament before the Ryder Cup." But it wouldn't be this one.

The man of a thousand putts was Colin Montgomerie, who took the first-round lead with a 64 and thanked his old American college coach. Montgomerie, now a Ryder Cupper for the first time, played under Dave Mannen at the University of Houston. "Dave insisted we make 200 two-foot putts every night before leaving the course," he said. Montgomerie went back to that teaching, and spent three hours on short putts two days before the Lancome began.

Spence was the reluctant star. He shot 64 in the third round, to take a one-stroke lead into the final round, and he promptly revealed a personal quirk. "I get too excited when I see my name on the leaderboard," Spence said. "I've been in contention a few times this year, but I've lost my concentration every time." He must not have been watching the scoreboard in the third round. He made five birdies in six holes on the outward nine, and had seven overall. His only bogey was a missed 10-footer at the 18th.

Spence kept his head down in the final round. But it wasn't enough. Nothing was—not for him or any one else, except Nobilo.

Epson Grand Prix of Europe—£450,000
Winner: Jose Maria Olazabal

Golfers have always struggled to explain what turned their games sour. Leave it to a Spaniard to come up with probably the most cogent answer, and certainly the most succinct. Jose Maria Olazabal had started out strong, won the Catalan Open in March, and then his game mysteriously went into a slide. About mid-summer, he had the answer. "I used to be in control of the game," he said, "and now it is in control of me."

Now it was mid-September, and the European Tour had reached Chepstow, Wales, for the Epson Grand Prix. Maybe it was the good Welsh air. Maybe the inspiration of the Ryder Cup matches coming up in South Carolina. Whatever it was, there was no doubt of who controlled what this time. Olazabal posted a wire-to-wire victory, shooting the 6,922-yard, par-71 St. Pierre course in 64-68-67-66—265, 19 under par, and winning by nine strokes. The distant second place belonged to Ryder Cup teammate Mark James, who shot 70-64-70-70—274.

"My game and my confidence are back to 100 percent," said Olazabal, a man completely different from the crestfallen, moody man of a few weeks ago. "And," he added, with an eye on the Ryder Cup now, "it's encouraging that Mark is playing well, too." It was Olazabal's second win of the season and the 11th of his six years on the European Tour.

For sheer dominance of the field and the course, this performance was reminiscent of the 1990 World Series of Golf, in which Olazabal ran rampant, going from an opening 61 to a 12-stroke victory. Ollie, as he has come to be known, opened the Epson with a seven-under-par 64 that included an eagle and six birdies. He suffered his only bogey at the par-three 13th. He got that back and more by playing the last five holes in four under par, starting with an eagle at the 521-yard 14th, on a 20-foot putt. At the 454-yard 16th, he fired a one iron to a foot and birdied. And at the 17th, he pitched to three feet and birdied again. It was a dazzling performance, but all it got him was a one-stroke lead on Mediterranean Open runner-up Mike McLean (65). He led by two over Ryder Cupper Colin Montgomerie and Rodger Davis, who tied at 66.

Olazabal's head didn't rest comfortably, however. In the second round, he shot a 68—he birdied the 16th again, this time from 45 feet—and gained a stroke on the field. McLean slipped with a 73, but James moved up to second, within two strokes, on 64—134. Montgomerie stayed close with 69—135. And then it was all over. Olazabal took leave of his companions with a third-round 67 that carried him five strokes clear of James (70—204). It wasn't enough to start him celebrating, yet, not even in the corners of his mind.

"Five is not an impossible gap," Olazabal said. "I have got to play well tomorrow to win."

Which, of course, he did, once James turned up the heat. Olazabal complained that he wasn't aggressive enough on the first several holes. But he got aggressive when James got three consecutive birdies from the sixth. So Olazabal, who lost a stroke of his lead despite going out in two-under-par 33, turned up his own heat coming in. He birdied the 10th, 12th, and 15th to go to 19 under par for the nine-stroke victory. Then it was on to the United States, for the Ryder Cup. He would catch up with Ian Woosnam, Nick Faldo and Seve Ballesteros there. They sat out the Epson to get ready for the Ryder Cup.

Mitsubishi Austrian Open—£250,000
Winner: Mark Davis

The final week of September, 1991, will go down in golf history as the time of one of the most exciting Ryder Cup matches ever. Forgive Mark Davis, though. It will mean something entirely different to him. That's when he won the Mitsubishi Austrian Open. There was something very special about it.

"It's a great feeling to win," Davis said, with a sigh and a huge grin. "But I'm really relieved to get my first victory out of the way. It takes a lot of the pressure off me."

The pressure came from a bright amateur career highlighted by the English Amateur Stroke Play Championship in 1984. He turned professional in 1986, joined the European Tour in 1987, and then nothing much happened. Until now.

Davis, 27-year-old Englishman, didn't merely win the Austrian Open, he crushed it. He even defied the script. It is written: A player looking for his first win, and leading going into the final round, will collapse under the pressure. Davis not only didn't collapse, he picked up speed. He took a two-stroke lead in the second round, led by three after the third, then won by five, shooting a 66 in the final round—his third 66 of the week. Which was all the more remarkable when one considers that after four previous years of frustration on the Tour, his 1991 season to date was marked by a runner-up finish in the Jersey Open in April, his career-best, and then by eight missed cuts in his last 10 tournaments. But there was no stopping him this time.

The Gut Altentann course (6,806 yards, par 72) at Salzburg was no match for him. He shot 66-66-71-66, a 19-under-par total of 269, for a runaway win over Michael McLean (71-68-71-64—274), himself one of the heroes of the piece. McLean started the final day seven strokes off Davis' lead, and put on a great charge. He just had too much ground to make up. It would have worked if Davis had folded the way he was supposed to.

"The young man's game really held up, all the way around," said McLean, also runner-up in the Mediterranean Open in March. "Not many guys can hold a three-shot lead overnight, and then go out and shoot 66 in the last round."

Students of the game might detect a fine Spanish hand in these proceedings. Davis was quick to credit Seve Ballesteros, who gave him some tips during the Swiss Open early in September. "He told me I was playing too quickly," Davis said. "He said that I should slow down, especially around the greens. So now I'm concentrating more." The advice finally took hold, but it wasn't noticeable at first. Davis opened with a 66, but Stephen McAllister overshadowed everybody with a 64. Then McAllister zoomed to an awesome 80 in the second round, and Davis—who would have 12 birdies and an eagle in the first two rounds—posted another 66, and was ahead by two and in the lead to stay.

Davis led by three going into the final round, and a big test was about to come. McLean launched his charge, that eight-birdie 64, and at one point closed to within two strokes. Davis might have folded here. Instead, he scored another eagle, his second of the day, and widened the gap again. He simply wouldn't be denied.

Mercedes German Masters—£500,000
Winner: Bernhard Langer

The Mercedes German Masters was the story of two putts, a week apart. The first almost destroyed Bernhard Langer. The second resurrected him.

The stage for this drama was set in the Ryder Cup matches at Kiawah Island in South Carolina, in the last week of September. While the world watched, Langer, on the final hole of the final match against Hale Irwin, faced a six-foot putt for the tie that would keep the cup in Europe. Then the world saw a man in real anguish as the putt just missed. Moments later, he was sobbing. He had let his team down.

The fates quickly gave Langer another chance. Just a week later, in the Mercedes German Masters, it came down to the final hole of the final round again. This time, Langer faced a 12-foot putt for a birdie to tie Rodger Davis. You couldn't read the turmoil inside the man. He looked as calm and deliberative as ever. He studied the putt, stepped up, and rolled it home.

Then on the first playoff hole, Davis pulled his drive behind some trees. Langer made a routine par four for his second victory of the year, the 25th of his European Tour career. Both had come from behind and tied at 13-under-par 275 at the par-72 Stuttgarter Club. Langer shot 68-72-67-68, and Davis 73-72-65-65. Nick Faldo led by two strokes going into the final round. But some putting difficulties plus a double bogey out of the trees at the 16th did him in. He shot 72 and finished a solo third at 277. Langer started the final round two strokes behind, tied with three others. Mike Harwood, who shot a dazzling 62 in the third round, tied for fourth on 71—278, matching Jose Maria Olazabal, and Steven Richardson slipped to a 74 and dropped to a tie for 11th on 281.

Davis had stolen the show. The 73-72 start left him 10 strokes back after 36 holes. Then he rocketed to the top with a pair of 65s. He blitzed the inward half on Sunday for a 31, getting five birdies in the span of six holes. But it was the six-footer at the 18th that cost him the victory. He had made all kinds of putts for birdies and pars—four feet, 10, 12, 25, even 35. Now he lay just six feet from victory. "The hole looked as big as a bucket," he said. "I don't know how I missed that putt." But he did. Langer needed a birdie from 12 feet to tie him.

It was a tribute to Langer's determination that he had even got that far. True, he felt obliged to play because he and his brother, Erwin, were staging the tournament. But he was fighting a cold, a throat infection, and a 102-degree fever, and he was playing against his doctor's advice. Maybe he wondered why he had bothered. He bogeyed the first hole. But then he birdied three of the next four, and caught Faldo at the turn. He birdied No. 10 from 20 feet to inch into the lead, then birdied the 13th. But he bogeyed the par-three 15th, where a shot from an awkward lie trickled back into a bunker. Now he had only three holes left in which to catch Davis. It came down to the final hole, and the 12-foot putt—his second crucial putt in two weeks.

"After what happened at Kiawah, when I was in tears like so many other European players," Langer said, "I didn't know how I'd react the next time I came under pressure. I prayed even harder when I faced up to that putt. I just forced myself to shut out all thoughts of what happened in America, and concentrate on the line and the speed, and putting a good, solid stroke on the putt. This time, it went straight into the hole."

BMW International Open—£400,000
Winner: Sandy Lyle

One of modern golf's most baffling mysteries came to a happy end in the BMW International Open. Or, as time might prove, at least it had taken a holiday. Sandy Lyle wasn't quibbling. He had finally won again. It was his first victory in three years, almost to the day. From mid-October, 1988, to mid-October, 1991. All the self-doubts, all the pain, all the maddening questions—it was all over.

"After all the hard work I've put into my game over the last two or three years, and the frustration of things not working out," Lyle said, "this is icing on the cake." In retrospect, maybe you could see this coming. Lyle was runner-up in the European Open six weeks earlier. A week later he was strong in the European Masters, closing with a 62. Were those signs that his once-mighty game was stirring again? It seems they were.

Lyle's case was weird. There was nothing gradual about his decline. It was as though a door had slammed. One minute he was beating the world, the next he couldn't break an egg. It came right after he had his best year. It was 1988. He started with three victories on the American tour—the Phoenix Open in January, the Greater Greensboro Open in the spring, and then the following week, the crowning accomplishment, the Masters. He returned to Europe and won the Dunhill British Masters the first week of June. Then in mid-October, he won the World Match Play.

There was nothing weak or flukish about Lyle's BMW International victory. He went wire-to-wire on a challenging course, the 6,910-yard, par-72

Golfplatz Munchen, Nord-Eichenried at Munich; and against a strong field that included such American stars as Paul Azinger, the defending champion, and U.S. Open champion Payne Stewart and World Series of Golf winner Tom Purtzer, and Bernhard Langer, who won the German Masters the previous week. Against all this, Lyle shot 65-65-71-67—268, 20 under par, for a three-stroke victory over Tony Johnstone (67-70-67-67—271).

Lyle opened with a seven-under-par 65 and shared the first-round lead with Azinger and Sweden's Magnus Sunesson. He was all alone after that. Another 65 put him at 130 after 36 holes, four ahead of D.J. Russell (68). And a 71 in the third round, for a 201 total, kept him a stroke ahead of Azinger, who charged back from a second-round 73 with an eight-birdie 64. That set up a heated finish.

Lyle opened the final round with a birdie, putting a little more cushion between him and Azinger. But Azinger wasn't the only threat. Peter Fowler, who started out four strokes off the pace, and Mark Mouland, who was five, began to pile up birdies. Fowler even caught up with Lyle at 16 under par. But a bogey at the par-three 17th knocked him out. Then Azinger got cracking again. At No. 15, he pitched to 18 inches for one birdie, and he holed a 15-foot putt at No. 16 for another. The situation was tense. Then Lyle followed him in with a 10-footer. It was decided at the 17th. Azinger bogeyed (as Johnstone had), and Lyle holed a 35-footer from off the green. Lyle's long exile had ended.

If Lyle had a secret, maybe it was that piece of paper in his pocket. He had scribbled some notes to himself. "One was to remember to look happy today, even though I might lose," he said. "Calmness was another. That was the key. When you've had a three-year dry spell, fear is always around the corner." Lyle had just turned that corner.

Volvo Masters—£600,000
Winner: Rodger Davis

Who would have thought that Rodger Davis could win the Volvo Masters? He was playing tennis. There was a sharp pain in his leg. What odds would a bookmaker quote on a golfer on crutches? For that matter, what chance would the golfer give himself? Davis reasoned that if you could barely walk, there was little sense in trying to play golf. So he decided not to play. But then, decided, it's the last event of the European season. He might as well try.

He was still on crutches when he arrived at Sotogrande, on Spain's Costa del Sol, that last week of October. Come time to play, he was easy to spot. He was the one limping around the course, no mean feat at Valderrama, a 6,951-yard par 71 that many players call possibly the toughest test of the year. Add to that a field that was probably the strongest since the British Open, and you had a hopeless situation for a golfer with a sore leg. So, of course, the thing that no bookie or sensible golfer would dream of, came true—Davis won the Volvo Masters.

Davis had to hold off a charging Nick Faldo to lock up the one-stroke victory. Davis shot 68-73-68-71—280, four under par, second-highest only to Bernhard Langer's two-under total at the Benson & Hedges in April.

Faldo shot 72-70-71-68—281. Langer finished third, three behind Davis; Seve Ballesteros tied for fourth, four off the lead; the rejuvenated Sandy Lyle tied for ninth, eight back; and Jose Maria Olazabal tied for 12th, nine behind.

Ballesteros, another rejuvenated golfer, was favored to win his second consecutive start (he had won the World Match Play the week before), but two closing bogeys for a first-round 72 put him into a hole he couldn't get out of. He was five strokes off Mark James' pace-setting 67. James led by one over Davis and Steven Richardson, the early season sensation. Rain battered the tournament in Friday's second round, forcing some to finish on Saturday, but when it was all straightened out, Richardson, after a 70, held the 36-hole lead on four-under-par 138. Davis was three behind on 73—141, and it wasn't until the third round, with a 68, that he took the lead for the first time, sharing it with Langer (70) at four-under 209. So the season finale would end with a re-match. It was just three weeks earlier that Langer beat Davis in a playoff for the German Masters.

The re-match misfired when Langer ran into difficulties. While he was shooting a 74, the threat came from Faldo, charging from four strokes off the pace to come within a whisker. Davis nearly ruined his chances with two early bogeys, but he recovered in time, got those strokes back for a par 71 and his sixth European victory. It was another jewel for the man who, now 40, just gets better with age. Davis joined the European Tour in 1977, at the age of 26. It took him five years (1981) to win his first tournament. He went through four more lean years, and then, starting in 1986, he won five more. And he's got to be the only champion who ever showed up on crutches. It had been a fine year.

World Cup—$1,100,000
Winner: Sweden/Ian Woosnam

The World Cup was held in Rome, with 32 two-man teams for four days of competition, and it all came down to a lapse in concentration. Ian Woosnam forgot to mark his ball, suffered a one-stroke penalty, and Sweden had its second team championship in a month, a bookend to match the Dunhill Cup won at St. Andrews. To be sure, it wasn't quite that simple. The Swedes— Anders Forsbrand and Per-Ulrik Johansson—had to be playing very well just to be that close in the first place.

"We finished well in round three, and got off to a great start today (in the fourth)," Forsbrand said. "We blended really well together. Like our effort at St. Andrews, it was, above all, a team effort. It's a shame Mats Lanner couldn't be with us this time." (Lanner played in the Dunhill Cup, which has three-man teams.)

The decisive moment came in the final round, at the 15th green, when Woosnam, who was teamed with Philip Price for Wales, picked up his ball and repaired his ball mark. "Then I suddenly realized I'd forgotten to put a marker behind it first," Woosnam said. He was assessed a one-stroke penalty, and that was the margin of victory.

The Swedes shot 563 to 564 for Wales. Scotland was a distant third at 567, and England and defending champion Germany even more distant, tied for fourth at 570. If the Swedes were the surprise for winning, the Americans and Australians were the disappointments. They tied for 12th with Italy at 578.

"Winning cups is getting to be a very nice habit," Forsbrand said. "This is a fantastic double for Swedish golf." Johansson decided the answer lay in compatibility. "We played very well together because we are very similar players and personalities," said Johansson. "We're both emotional. When we're down, we fret for a few seconds, and then it's forgotten. But when we play good, the adrenaline really starts to pump."

The third round was pivotal. Spain, with Seve Ballesteros and Jose Rivero, led by three strokes after 36 holes. Then in the third round, Ballesteros shot 71, carding only one birdie, and Rivero, 72. Two other challengers also slipped. Torsten Giedeon shot 78, offsetting teammate Bernhard Langer's 71, leaving Germany at 431. England's tone was set early, when Steven Richardson made a triple-bogey eight at the first hole. He and Nick Faldo went on to a matching pair of 74s. It was a tough eight. Richardson was addressing his ball for his third shot when it moved about an inch. He called the penalty on himself.

The Swedes, meanwhile, got a tournament-low 65 from Forsbrand and 69 from Johansson, while Woosnam had 67 and Price 72 for Wales. The stage was set for a shootout in the final round, but it ended up a misfire on Woosnam's error. But he was mollified somewhat by winning individual honors with 70-69-67-67—273. Langer was second with 276, and Forsbrand, third with 279. Johansson tied for eighth with 284.

14. African Tours

Golf has been an international game ever since the Scots and the British began taking it with them wherever they went. Hence the courses at pre-Mao Shanghai, Royal Montreal, Royal Calcutta, Royal Melbourne, and other points. By a kind of cross-pollination, places such as Wack-Wack in the Philippines, and Golfklubbur Islands, or the Golf Club of Iceland, sprang up all over the globe.

Having the playing grounds is one thing, having quality players is another. When it comes to quality players, there's a new dimension to the notion of internationalism. And that's what the world saw, if in a modest way, in 1991 in Africa—practically a United Nations of golf.

One, James Lebbie, ran away with the Nigerian Open. He is from Sri Lanka. Another, Michel Besanceney, won the Ivory Coast Open. He is from France, which is starting to flex its golf muscles. These men aren't on the level of Nick Faldo and Seve Ballesteros, but the fact that they plunged into international competition and came out with the victory says something about the rising level of the game. Add to them Fiji's Vijay Singh, a fixture on the European Tour since he won the 1989 Volvo Open and the 1990 El Bosque Open. He beat U.S. Open champion Payne Stewart in a playoff to win the revived and rich Hassan II Trophy in Morocco. Then, in addition to the regular assortment of British and South Africans winning on the Sunshine and Safari Tours, we had a German, Bernhard Langer, taking the resurrected Million Dollar Challenge.

We almost had a Swede to add to our list. But for a nose-dive into a flower bed, European Tour veteran Anders Forsbrand might have beaten De Wet Basson in the Fancourt Hall of Fame Championship. (The Fancourt event and the Bell's Cup were new events on the Sunshine circuit in 1991.)

Internationalism in golf was marked in another way in 1991. This was the return of South Africa to the community of nations, and hence to the world of sports. Long shunned by other countries, South Africa was changing its apartheid laws and becoming accepted again. In golf, this allowed for the resumption of the Million Dollar Challenge with the top players in the world (it was threatened with extinction after the 1990 playing), and it also opened the way for South African golfers to play elsewhere in the world.

Aside from these "geo-athletic" considerations, it was pretty much business as usual out on the golf course. On the Sunshine Tour, that meant that John Bland, 46-year-old South African, continued to dominate. He kicked off 1991 by winning the first event, the Palabora Classic, early in January. It was the first Palabora victory of his career, just the thing for a man who has won just about everything else. Six weeks later, he won the Bell's Cup by one stroke, and the following week he ran away with the Trust Bank Tournament of Champions, which he started with a 10-under-par 62.

Wayne Westner was the only other multiple winner on the Sunshine circuit. In the South African Open, he was 16 under par and won by four strokes, thanks in part to two key shots. One was a miracle recovery from under some trees, and the other was a carom off a spectator's head. The following week, he left the trees and spectators unscathed, and went 15 under par to win the AECI Charity Classic by three strokes. These were his second and third South African victories in four years.

Westner wasn't the lone author of the carom shot. Mark James had one in a playoff for the Lexington PGA Championship. He banked it off a woman, and back into the fairway. But that was the end of his luck. Roger Wessels beat him on the second extra hole. American Hugh Royer was the heroic story of the circuit. He had to borrow $12,000 to fund his South African foray. He paid off his debt and then some with a four-stroke victory in the Hollard Swazi Spa Sun Classic, plus two second-place finishes.

If Langer was still suffering from that missed putt in the Ryder Cup, it wasn't showing. Not only had he snapped right back to take the Mercedes German Masters, but he came to Sun City, set a few records, and walked off with $1 million in the Million Dollar Challenge. Even he was surprised. "Amazing golf...," he said.

On the Safari Tour, it was all-British in the early-1991 segment, but it wasn't all easy. Keith Waters had to go five extra holes to win the Zimbabwe Open, and David R. Jones took the Zambia Open by one stroke. On the other hand, Jeremy Robinson practically had a stroll in the park at the Standard Chartered Kenya Open. A 62 will give a man a lot of breathing room.

The rest of the United Nations checked in later in the year—Singh winning in Morocco in November, then France's Besanceney making a miracle recovery shot to set up his playoff victory in the Ivory Coast Open, and Sri Lanka's Lebbie running rampant in the Nigerian Open for a four-stroke victory that wasn't nearly that close.

There was one other thing that stamped 1991 in the history books—a shot in the Bell's Cup, sponsored by the Scotch whisky maker. This was a hole-in-one by South African Ben Fouchee. It had to be the richest ace of the year. When the ball dropped, Fouchee won a boatload of Bell's Scotch whisky.

Zimbabwe Open—£48,750
Winner: Keith Waters

Keith Waters had waited 11 long years for this one, and the fates and the weather were going to make him cool his heels just a tad longer. The Zimbabwe Open, kicking off the 1991 Safari Tour, started with a rain delay, and ended with a long, grueling playoff. But to the 32-year-old Englishman, it was worth the wait.

The tournament started on January 10 and was greeted quickly by torrential rains whipping at the 7,173-yard, par-72 Chapman Golf Club at Harare. Only 48 of the 108 starters were able to complete their rounds before play was suspended in mid-afternoon. The rest returned early the next day, Friday, and they knew what they were shooting at. Native son Nick Price, a veteran of the American tour, and England's Grant Turner, the defending champion, had posted two-under-par 70s before the suspension. They didn't hold up long. Peter Harrison wrapped up a six-under-par 66 in the morning for a two-stroke lead on Wayne Henry (68).

Harrison also led through 36 holes, but it took until the next day for everybody to find out, thanks to the domino effect of Thursday's storm delay. Harrison, one of more than 60 players who had to complete the second round on Saturday morning, was five under par with five holes to play when the round was suspended. He came back out on Saturday, finished off a 73 for a 139 total and a one-stroke lead on Turner (78—140). Then a third-round 78 knocked Harrison out of the running.

Meanwhile, nothing had been seen yet of Waters. He was five strokes off the lead in the first round, then four behind after the second. In fact, neither he nor any one else was in the hunt until the final nine holes. That's when Price's game started to unravel.

Price began the final round with a two-stroke lead, and was up by five with nine holes to play. Then his fortunes went into reverse. He dropped three strokes through the 14th and his lead was down to two with four to play. Then that promptly disappeared. He bogeyed the 15th and double-bogeyed the par-three 16th, and he had to birdie the par-five 18th for a final-round 74 and a place in the playoff. He bowed out at the first hole, when Turner and Waters birdied. On the fifth extra hole, Waters dropped a 10-foot putt for the birdie and the win, his second as a pro, after the 1980 News of the World Under-23 Match Play Championship.

Waters, who made up six strokes on Price in the last round, shot 71-72-71-68. Turner returned a 70-70-74-68, and Price 70-72-66-74, the trio tying at six-under-par 282.

"I've been trying for such a long time to win," Waters said, "that I didn't think I was ever going to see a trophy."

Zambia Open—£75,000
Winner: David Jones

The Lusaka Golf Club course, stretching 7,252 yards and carrying a par of 73, is enough to daunt the most ambitious of golfers. If nothing else, it's a pressure-packed march of over four miles each day. But David R. Jones, former England Youths International team member and now all of 23, found it just to his taste. In fact, the sweet taste of victory is exactly what he had in mind when he turned pro four years earlier, at age 19, and here was his first.

(The middle initial "R." by the way, distinguishes him from David Jones, the Northern Ireland golfer.)

The first round set the tone for the entire tournament, a Jones-Paul Carrigill shootout. Carrigill, the 1987 Zambia Open champion, opened with a three-under-par 70, a one-stroke lead over Philip Golding, Chris Platts, Tim Price, Ian Spencer and Jeremy Robinson, all at 71. Jones was two behind at 72.

Jones took the lead in the second round with a four-under-par 69, one of only seven rounds in the 60s for the entire tournament. Carrigill slipped a stroke behind with a 72, but rebounded in the third with a 71 that tied him with Jones at six-under-par 213 going into the final round.

Jones, who tied for 48th in the Zimbabwe Open the week before, set up his victory with an excellent six-iron approach up over the trees at the dogleg 17th. That left him only an eight-foot putt. When he dropped it, that all but locked up the win.

He wrapped up his sub-par week and the championship with a final-round

72 for a one-stroke victory over Carrigill and Golding. Jones was under par for all four rounds with 72-69-72-72, a seven-under-par total of 285. Golding, the only other man with four under-par rounds, missed a chance for the title when he bogeyed the final hole. He finished second for the second consecutive year on 71-72-71-72—286, tying with Carrigill (70-72-71-73).

And statistics buffs might find this interesting. Lusaka yielded only seven rounds under 70—six 69s, including Jones', and the tournament-low 68 by Sweden's Daniel Westermark in the fourth round. After rounds of 76-78-75, that got him a tie for 28th place at 297, five over par.

Standard Chartered Kenya Open—£66,639
Winner: Jeremy Robinson

You couldn't say you really saw it coming, but there was at least a hint that England's Jeremy Robinson was ready to break through. It came a week earlier, in the Zambia Open. The long and punishing par-73 Lusaka Golf Club course had given up just seven rounds under 70—one 68 and six 69s. Robinson shot one of the 69s, in the last round. He had to be looking back, then, at his 79 in the second round. Anyway, the 69 boosted him to a one-over-par 293 and a tie for 11th place.

Robinson had known his share of disappointments. He turned professional after the 1987 Walker Cup, and he had won three times on the Challenge Tour. The bad news, however, is that he failed in four attempts at gaining his European Tour card, and he even lost his sponsor at the end of the 1990 season. So here he was, late in January, the week of his 25th birthday, with little more than stubborn hope at his disposal.

It was a perfect time for a man to win, and he did that with a flourish. He bashed the 6,765-yard, par-71 Muthaiga Golf Club for a course-record, nine-under-par 62 in the second round, and ran off with a five-stroke victory. His 68-62-69-70 gave him another mark, a four-round total of 15-under-par 269, beating the old course record by two strokes.

The second-round 62—including eight birdies and an eagle—was the key, of course. There are a couple of ways to look at the impact of such a performance. The first thing was an abrupt change in leaders. Steven Richardson led the first round with a 65, and Robinson was at 68. So the 62 rocketed Robinson from a three-stroke deficit to a four-stroke lead. Tied for second at 134 were Philip Golding (68) and Alan Saddington (65). Richardson had slipped to 70 and was five off the lead.

For a long-term impact, consider the frustrations of Sandy Stephen. He shot all four rounds in the 60s and could do no better than tie for second place, five whopping strokes behind. Stephen carded 69-69-69-67, tying at 10-under 274 with Paul Affleck (70-67-71-66) and Golding (66-68-72-68), a joint runner-up for the second consecutive week.

Richardson was threatening to make a dogfight of it in the final round, but three three-putt greens in the first six holes cooled him off. They also comforted the jittery Robinson.

"Steve's putting problems gave me the leeway I needed when I was nervous," Robinson said. "And when I was five ahead with five holes to play, I knew it was in the bag."

Palabora Classic—R280,000
Winner: John Bland

"Conditions were really tough out there," John Bland was saying, after the final round. "With that strong, gusty wind blowing, I found it difficult to get the ball near the hole. Club selection kept me guessing."

This was at the Palabora Classic, kicking off the New Year in South Africa, and the prevailing opinion was that if the 45-year-old South African really was guessing, he must have guessed right a lot. He guessed himself right into the first Palabora title of his career. Bland shot the Hans Merensky Golf Club at Phalaborwa in 70-69-68-71—278, 10 under par, outrunning countryman Mark Wiltshire, who fell just short at 72-70-67-70—279.

Bland had to survive a host of challenges to get there.

First was Hugh Baiocchi, another veteran. He started the final round tied with Bland at nine under par. Then he hit a rocky road. He bogeyed the third and fourth holes, birdied the fifth, bogeyed the eighth and birdied the ninth. That came to an erratic 37 going out. He came home considerably steadier. A birdie at No. 11 got him back to even par, then he bogeyed the 15th and had to settle for a one-over-par 73 and third place at eight-under-par 280, two strokes behind Bland.

Another challenge came from Fulton Allem, another native son but one spending most of his time on the American tour. A burst of three birdies from No. 3, then two more birdies at the 11th and 12th put him nine under par. Then his hopes were chilled by a rash of bogeys at the 14th, 15th, and 17th. A birdie at No. 18 gave him a 71 and a tie for fifth at 282 with American Don Robertson (69) and South African Ernie Els, who slipped to a 74 after starting the day a stroke off the lead.

The real threat came from Wiltshire. It nearly materialized a number of times, but he just couldn't get a grip on his round. Wiltshire picked up ground with a birdie at the par-five fifth, then backslid with bogeys at the par-four sixth and the par-three eighth. Then came another birdie, this a three at No. 9. Down the stretch, he breathed right down Bland's neck with one last, desperate triumph. That was an eagle three at the 16th, which put him nine under, just a stroke behind Bland. And that was as close as he would get.

ICL International—R280,000
Winner: Fulton Allem

Fulton Allem wasn't all that happy with his game in the tight final round. He would concede this much—his driving was more or less acceptable. Aside from that, he said, he hadn't played very well. OK, then how do you explain that final score? Numbers don't lie—a glance at the final figures says that protests aside, he played well enough to beat a good field by two strokes in the ICL International.

Allem, a native South African and also a member of the American tour, shot the par-72 Zwartkops Country Club course in 69-67-64-71—271, 17 under par. Tony Johnstone put on a strong finish but could only make up enough ground to take second on 69-66-70-68—273. Three men tied for third at 274, and therein lies a tale. The three were defending champion Gavin Levenson, Wayne Westner and Ashley Roestoff, a promising youngster. Roestoff led after 36 holes on 68-64—132. He posted a strong 68 in the third round, and Allem caught him with a 64. They were tied at 16-under-par 200 going into the finale.

Roestoff went head-to-head against the seasoned veteran, and was holding his own nicely until they came to No. 11. Roestoff hit his approach into a greenside bunker, and found himself with an awful lie. Trying to coax it out, he blasted across the green and into another bunker. When he finally got down, he had a double-bogey six, and there went his hopes. Roestoff bogeyed No. 14, got the stroke back with a birdie at the 15th, but then let a short putt get away from him at the 18th. But not surprisingly, it was the double bogey at the 11th that set the course of the final holes.

"I thought I needed a 68 to win," Allem said. "But when Ashley made that six at the 11th, I had a three-shot lead."

Allem could hardly allow himself the luxury of coasting in, but with the pressure eased, he wasn't pushed. Nor was he impressed with his work. "A 71 was really two over par on this course," Allem said. "But I did the job. I'm thrilled, and I'm looking ahead to the next two weeks."

He meant the two biggest weeks on the Sunshine Circuit—the Lexington PGA Championship, followed by the South African Open.

Lexington PGA Championship—R350,000
Winner: Roger Wessels

Fulton Allem can tell you what it feels like to play a bank shot off the gallery. It might bring a silly smile to your face—and an ache to the spectator—but it can save your hide. It's probably only a coincidence, but given the Mark James episode in this tournament, the Lexington PGA Championship may soon be regarded as something of a shooting gallery. Allem won the 1990 PGA with a big boost from a woman spectator at the green of the par-three 15th in the final round. His tee shot was headed for trouble when it was brought to an abrupt and safe stop by a collision with a woman spectator's backside.

Fate handed James, the British veteran, a similar opportunity this time, in a playoff against Roger Wessels, 29-year-old South African. But he wasn't able to capitalize on it. There was no second chance. Wessels quickly plucked the first big title of his career.

Actually, it was a three-man playoff. Wessels (68-66-68-69), James (67-68-67-69), and American Hugh Royer (63-69-67-72) had tied at 271, nine under par at the par-70 Wanderers Country Club, Johannesburg. The playoff began at the par-three 17th. Royer was knocked out by a bogey when his tee shot went through the green, and he chipped back to eight feet and two-putted. Wessels and James made their par threes. And now two bad shots on one hole would knock James out at the second playoff hole, the par-four 18th.

Bad Shot No. 1—He sliced his drive into the right rough, under some trees. He fired away the best he could, and his approach seemed headed for more trouble, but it hit a woman spectator and caromed back safely into the fairway. Bad Shot No. 2—He chipped strong, over the green. From there, it took him three to get down, for a double-bogey six. Wessels, meantime, had driven into the fairway, fired his approach to the green, about 40 feet from the cup. James was away on his second and third putts, and when he finally got down for the six, Wessels had only a tap-in left for his par four and the championship.

Royer, who had opened with the 63, saw his hopes for an outright win die with a double bogey on No. 10. His final-round 72 included two birdies and two bogeys. David Feherty made a run at it with a outward 33, but a clutch of bogeys coming home left him with a 68 and a stroke out of the playoff, at 272.

Wessels didn't look much like a winner when he bogeyed No. 1. But three outward birdies put him in the lead at 10 under par—a 12-foot putt at No. 2, two putts at No. 5, and a one-footer at No. 6. He cooled off coming in. He drove into the trees at the 10th and 16th, and bogeyed both, and he needed a birdie at the 18th to tie Royer and James. He got it off an eight iron to three feet. The victory got him the biggest payday of his career, and a berth in the rich World Series of Golf in Akron, Ohio, in August.

Protea Assurance South African Open—R400,000
Winner: Wayne Westner

You could see the jokes coming—something about knowing how to get "a head" in the world, or something on that theme. Wayne Westner wouldn't object. His bank account was fatter and his future brighter after his win in the Protea Assurance South African Open at Durban Country Club.

There were three key elements to his victory: A fine-tuning of his putting stance, a miracle shot from under the trees and a bank shot off some poor spectator's head. It was the second consecutive week that hitting a spectator figured prominently in the outcome. Mark James conked a spectator in the Lexington PGA Championship the week before, but he couldn't cash it in and so he settled for joint second. James was also part of this episode, but as a victim, not beneficiary.

First came the miracle shot. "One of the best shots of my life," Westner said. His drive at No. 11 ended up in the trees. He had to bend over low to swing, and somehow he cut an exquisite four iron to within 28 feet of the flag and saved his par.

Durban's par-three 12th, with its domed green, is known as the "Prince of Wales" hole, in recognition of Edward VII's adventure there. He once batted his ball up and down the hill 10 times en route to a 12. For a while, it seemed James was bent on duplicating that performance. His tee shot went over the green and down the slope. His first attempt to reach the green came rolling back down to him, and so did the second. He managed to limit his damage to a double-bogey five, but that ended his challenge.

Westner, playing with James, watched aghast as his own tee shot was rocketing off to a similar fate. Then bop!—the ball hit a spectator in the head and caromed back onto the green, toward the flag, and he saved his par. He also parred the 13th and 14th, but he was getting frustrated. "I just couldn't get any putts to drop," he said. "Then I began trying too hard on the greens."

A change was in order. He made a slight adjustment in his putting stance, and immediately ran off four consecutive birdies. He dropped a 30-footer at the 15th, an 18-footer at the 16th, a 12-footer at the 17th and he two-putted after driving to the back fringe of the short 18th with a one iron.

That gave him his second South African Open title in four years in a runaway win, and a berth in the World Series of Golf at Akron, Ohio, in August. Westner shot 65-70-69-68—272, 16 under par, breaking the tournament-record 273 set 22 years earlier by Gary Player, also at Durban. James shot 70-66-69-71 and tied at 276 with Tony Johnstone (68-68-72-68).

AECI Charity Classic—R280,000
Winner: Wayne Westner

As they were saying on the Sunshine Tour, the Rand Park course, near Johannesburg, was again host to the AECI Charity Classic, but there wasn't anything charitable about the course anymore. "Gone are the days of 23 under par," said Bobby Lincoln, after a pre-tournament visit to the revamped course. "This is a tough layout now."

Lincoln would know. He shot a then-record 63 in the final round when he won the AECI event in 1988. Rand Park is a long course, at some 7,300 yards, but had few teeth in it, as the big-hitting American youth, John Daly, showed in the 1990 AECI. He shot 70-67-62-65, for the 23-under-par 265 Lincoln was talking about. Still, it was a fight to the finish. Daly beat the faltering David Feherty with a birdie on the final hole. That 10-under-par 62 in the third round, by the way, merely tied the course record set by Feherty in the first round. (Daly was on a tear at the time. Two weeks later, he beat John Bland for the Swazi Sun Classic title.)

Rand Park was practically new from stem to stern. All 18 greens had been rebuilt and replanted with bent grass, water hazards were extended, and 35 new bunkers had been added.

It all was very much to the liking of Wayne Westner. Just the week before, at Durban Country Club, Westner had won his second South African Open title in four years. Now he tacked on the AECI for good measure. Lincoln was right for now. There was no 23-under this time. But Westner's 15-under-par 273 total was a pretty robust outing. He closed with a final-round 65 to beat American Tom Tolles by three strokes.

Hollard Insurance Swazi Spa Sun Classic—R280,000
Winner: Hugh Royer

It was the best $12,000 Hugh Royer ever spent, even if he did have to borrow it.

Royer, a 27-year-old American from Aiken, South Carolina, wanted to test his wings on the Sunshine Tour. But first, there was the question of capital. Once he settled that by borrowing the $12,000, he was on his way—to both the Sunshine circuit and to success. He was co-runner-up in the Lexington PGA Championship, where Roger Wessels beat him and Mark James with a par on the second hole of their playoff. This time, in the Hollard Insurance

Swazi Spa Sun Classic, it wasn't even close when the leaders made the final turn.

Royer shot the Royal Swazi Spa and Country Club in 64-66-67-68 for a 265 total and a four-stroke victory over Robin Freeman, a fellow American from Palm Springs, California, and Des Terblanche, who tied at 269. Terblanche wasn't really in the chase. It was a Royer-Freeman duel most of the way.

Royer led by a stroke after the first round, his 64 to Freeman's 65. They were tied after 36 holes, Royer shooting 66, Freeman another 65, for 130 totals. A new challenger stepped forward in the third round—Wayne Player, son of Gary. Player trailed by three through the second round, but bulled his way into the chase with a 64 for a 197 total to tie Royer (67) in the third round. Then came two disasters that decided the outcome.

The tournament was settled over the last nine holes. In fact, at the 16th hole, a par three guarded by water. Royer found the green and birdied it, and Freeman found the water. "Disastrous," Freeman said, posting the 71 that knocked him back into a tie with Terblanche. If that was a disaster, what was Player's finish? He finished with a 77 and a 274 total. He was tied for the lead at the start of the round, and nine strokes behind at the end.

The entrepreneurial Royer's investment in himself nearly tripled in value. The victory lifted him to No. 8 on the Order of Merit, with about $32,000 to his credit.

Bell's Cup Players Championship—R280,000
Winner: John Bland

This was the debut of the Bell's Cup Players Championship, and no pun intended, but if the name has a familiar ring to it, that's because it's a direct descendant of Bell's Scottish Open. Bell's Scotch Whisky was looking for a marketing avenue in South Africa, and what would be more fitting for a Scottish company than golf? So the Bell's Cup made its debut on the Sunshine Tour late in February at Mowbray Golf Club, Cape Town.

If Bell's was hoping for instant impact, they certainly got it with their hole-in-one prize. The hole-in-one prize is fairly common at tournaments. A car is the usual offering. But at a tournament sponsored by a producer of Scotch whiskey, what would be more appropriate than the product? The hole was the 151-yard 16th, and the prize was—well... Ben Fouchee, former South African amateur struggling to make it on the Tour, had birdied the 16th all week. Then in the final round came his magical moment. He aced it. His prize: A ship's container of Bell's Scotch. That amounted to about 1,000 cases of it, worth £350,000, or nearly $600,000.

Almost lost in the commotion of that moment was the fact that old faithful, John Bland, was the man over the long haul. Bland rang up his second victory in seven 1991 tournaments with a card of 68-67-71-71—277, 11 under par, for a one-stroke victory over Des Terblanche (71-70-67-70), co-runner-up for the second consecutive week; Tony Johnstone (70-71-65-72), a three-time runner-up, and rookie Retief Goosen (72-68-73-65).

Goosen, bearing down fast on Rookie-of-the-Year honors, was the leader in the clubhouse after that closing 65. But it would be an hour of tense waiting before he would know whether he had won. He had to sweat out the veterans, Bland and Johnstone.

His wait all but ended when Bland sank a 15-foot putt for a birdie at No. 17. Then it was all over when Bland negotiated the final hole in par.

Trust Bank Tournament of Champions—R280,000
Winner: John Bland

Someone who just happened to drop in on the game of golf would get the impression that this John Bland fellow can't play a lick. The authority for this belief would be none other than John Bland himself. Note Bland's observation after the Trust Bank Tournament of Champions. "I'm just a little fat guy who hasn't got a great swing," Bland said. "And I can't even hit the ball very far."

So much for self-evaluation. Happily, there is another and more objective way of measuring Bland, and that is his performance. Back to the Tournament of Champions. What a made-in-Hollywood episode—a runaway finish to a runaway New Year on the Sunshine Tour. Bland simply raced off with his second victory in succession and his third in the eight-tournament segment that ended early in March. He led off with the Palabora Classic in January, and added the Bell's Cup the week before taking this finale.

Bland went wire-to-wire, going from a brilliant start to a flashing finish for a crushing seven-stroke victory. Bland shot the Kensington Golf Club in 62-71-70-66 for a 269 total, a huge 19 under par. Justin Hobday, who gave him a tussle for a while, was the distant runner-up on 276 (67-66-71-72).

For a while, things were tighter than they looked. Hobday had made up five strokes in the second round with a 66, catching Bland (71) at 133. Then came the finale.

"I was a bit worried going into the last round," Bland said. And he stayed a bit worried for 13 holes. "Then when Justin bogeyed the 14th, that took the pressure off me," Bland said. "That relaxed me completely."

He expressed his relief by dropping a 15-foot putt for a birdie at No. 15, and then ended the day by firing his approach at No. 18 to within a foot.

By the way, he did admit that though he was fat and didn't have a swing and couldn't hit the ball very far, there were a couple of reasons why he kept winning.

"I do my homework and I've got a lot of heart, and that," Bland said, "makes all the difference."

Million Dollar Challenge—US$2,500,000
Winner: Bernhard Langer

Nick Faldo was contemplating his situation in the Million Dollar Challenge: He had just shot a 68 in the third round, a very good day's work on the 7,665-yard, par-72 Gary Player Country Club course at Sun City, Bophuthatswana. That put him at seven-under-par 209, and in third place. But he wasn't impressed. "I could shoot 62 tomorrow," he said, with a little smile, "and still lose."

That's how thoroughly Bernhard Langer was dominating the 10-man field.

Mark McNulty was second, eight strokes behind, and Faldo third, nine behind. Langer was at 200, 16 under par. Mark Calcavecchia said Langer couldn't lose. "Unless he goes off in the bushes," he said. "Which he won't."

And he didn't. McNulty led the first round with 66, and then Langer took over and kept on climbing. The closest thing to a threat was Calcavecchia's closing 67. And that merely cut Langer's margin from eight to five strokes, Langer shot 68-65-67-72—272, 16 under par, against Calcavecchia's 72-67-71-67—277, 11 under. McNulty was third at 282, and Faldo fourth at 285.

Langer set two tournament records, 200 total for 54 holes, and 272 final total. He tied two others—133 for 36 holes, and the single-round low, 65 in the second.

"It's nice to go into the record book," Langer had observed after the third round, "but you can't buy anything with it." Just 18 holes later, the buying could begin.

The Challenge had its strongest field in years, thanks to reforms in South Africa's apartheid policies, which began to return many aspects of the country to international acceptance. The field included No. 1-ranked Ian Woosnam, and No. 2 Faldo, and American PGA champion John Daly. McNulty led the first round with 66, and he credited it to playing with Daly. "All you can do is watch and grin, because you know you can't hit it anything like the same distance," McNulty said. That way, you play your own game. He led Steve Elkington by one, and Langer by two. Daly shot 72, and was never a threat. He finished eighth on six-over-par 294.

In the second round, seven of the 10 players players broke par on the hot, early December day, but it was Langer's party—a flawless, seven-birdie 65 that gave him a four-stroke lead. "It really could have been a 62," he said. "I left a few putts just short, or on the side."

Still, his putting was hot. In the third round, he knocked in a 20-footer for a birdie at No. 1, birdied No. 2, and at the par-five ninth, hit a three-wood second 240 yards to the island green, setting up another birdie. He suffered only one bogey, at the 12th, then birdied the next two, and was a happy man. "This," said Langer, troubled for years by the yips, "was by far my best putting in a long time—maybe the best in four or five years."

Langer closed with his worst score of the tournament, 72, and still no one could get close. McNulty, with 74, and Faldo, with 76, took themselves out of the hunt. What little heat there was came from Calcavecchia, who had started 10 strokes off. He pulled to within four with a birdie at the 16th, but a bogey at the 18th gave him a 277 total, runner-up by five strokes. And five strokes ahead of the third-place McNulty.

Some other challenges never materialized. Elkington, after an opening 67, crashed to 74-79-78. Frost finished last on 300. Woosnam closed with 78-74—293, seventh place, and noted, "You can't play well every week."

Langer had the last word. "I surprised myself," he said. "That's pretty amazing golf."

Fancourt Hall of Fame Championship—R450,000
Winner: De Wet Basson

Walter Hagen cautioned us to be sure and take time to smell the flowers. That advice might not sit too well with Anders Forsbrand. He had enough of the flowers in the Fancourt Hall of Fame Championship, the next-to-last event on the Sunshine Tour for 1991. Forsbrand, veteran European Tour campaigner, stopped at the flowers all right, but not to smell them. And there went opportunity, dead among the posies.

As to Hagen's advice—on the other hand, De Wet Basson may tell you that one man's poison is another man's honey. When Forsbrand stepped into the flowers, Basson stepped into the winner's circle.

Basson earned the Fancourt victory, of course. He was tied for the lead with John Bland going into the final round, and he held on against all comers, particularly Forsbrand, who had started out one stroke behind him. The issue was still very much in doubt until Forsbrand came to the 17th hole. It's a tough par three of nearly 200 yards, but a pretty one, with a lush bed of flowers behind the green. It was in that flower bed that Forsbrand hit his tee shot. He called for a ruling, hoping for a free drop. But the rules official pronounced the awful verdict: The flower bed was part of the golf course. Forsbrand now had two options. He could play the ball as it lay, or he could declare it unplayable and take a penalty drop.

Since the penalty drop would mean at least a bogey, Forsbrand opted to take his chance among the flowers. He wasn't happy with the result. His shot came up short in the fringe, and it took him two to get down from there. The bogey four gave Basson a little more breathing room, but he was already earning the win on his own. He closed with a five-under-par 67 to Forsbrand's 68, and won by two strokes. The final figures: Basson shot 71-70-68-67—276, 12 under par. Forsbrand posted 69-72-69-68—278.

Basson climbed fast to reach the top of this tournament. He started out four strokes off the lead, his 71 trailing Justin Hobday and Chris Williams, first-round co-leaders at 67. Forsbrand was in a trio at 69, and veterans Tony Johnstone and David Frost were in a group at 70. Williams skied to 77 in the second round, en route to a tie for ninth place, and Hobday took the solo lead after 36 holes with 72—139. He was one stroke up on Johnstone, who was in a rut that many would find pleasant, but one that was frustrating to him. With four consecutive 70s, Johnstone couldn't budge a soul ahead of him, but he couldn't be budged, either. He finished third at 280, two strokes behind Forsbrand and three ahead of Bland.

Basson, sitting third after the second round, rose to the top in the third with a 68—208 that tied him with Bland (66). Then things sorted themselves out in the fourth round. Bland, who ruled the Sunshine Tour with three victories earlier in the year, limped in with 74 and closed his season with a fourth at 283. Forsbrand visited the flowers, and Basson, the man who stuck to the straight and narrow, picked up the spoils.

Goodyear Classic—R300,000
Winner: Justin Hobday

If a golfer learns nothing else, he learns that good play is not necessarily rewarded by success. But few get this lesson burned into them the way Justin Hobday did early in the season. It was in the Trust Bank Tournament of Champions, a jewel on the Sunshine Tour. He shot a 276 total, 12 under par at Kensington. That's usually enough to win. But this time it was only good enough for a distant second, seven strokes behind runaway winner John Bland.

Now it was the week before Christmas. The Tour had come to the Goodyear Classic at Humewood Golf Club, a touchy 6,454-yard, par-72 course at Port Elizabeth. And now Hobday was enjoying the fruits of another of golf's teachings—be patient and persevere. Hobday did both, and came from behind to take a four-stroke victory on 71-71-69-69—280, eight under par. It was an encouraging week for the 28-year-old who had been laboring since he turned pro in 1985. He also had been trying to hammer out a place for himself on the European Tour, where the 1991 season ended in disappointment. He won £35,913, and finished 100th on the Volvo Order of Merit.

The Goodyear Classic was all the sweeter because it came against a field that included the three men who had dominated the first half of the year. Of the eight tournaments in that segment, Bland won three, the Palabora Classic, Bell's Cup and Trust Bank; Wayne Westner won two, the South African Open and AECI, and Hugh Royer won the Hollard Swazi Sun Classic and was a playoff runner-up in the Lexington PGA Championship.

So things didn't look all that promising for Hobday when the Goodyear Classic opened. He had a lot of ground to make up against stiff competition. Westner and Jack Ferenz shared the first-round lead at five-under-par 67. Royer was a tight second, along with Michael Du Toit, at 68. Three others were tied at 69, and six at 70. Hobday, meanwhile, was one of eight at 71. That's a long way from the lead—four strokes and 11 men behind.

Then came the sudden shift. The leaders crumbled in the second round. Westner suffered a 76, Ferenz 77, Royer 76 and Du Toit 76. Hobday, with a second 71, zoomed to second place, a stroke behind Malcolm McKenzie (70-71—141). A 69 in the third round lifted him into the lead, three strokes ahead of Royer, and another 69 gave him the win. Royer finished second at 70—284, and Westner was fourth at 70—287. Ferenz was shot down by middle rounds of 77-78, and tied for 16th place. Du Toit, with 76-83 middle rounds, plunged to a tie for 43rd place. Bland, though never a real threat, was a solid sixth place at one-over-par 289.

Hassan II Trophy—$500,000
Winner: Vijay Singh

The Hassan II Trophy was established by King Hassan II of Morocco, to promote tourism in that country. This was the 20th playing overall, and the first in six years.

The victory and $100,000 first prize were that much the sweeter for Fiji's Vijay Singh, because he not only outdistanced Nick Faldo by two strokes and Bernhard Langer by seven, he beat reigning U.S. Open champion Payne Stewart in a playoff. It was his first win since the European Tour's El Bosque Open in April, 1990, ending a dry spell of about 19 months.

"Having beaten three major champions," Singh said, "it was well worth waiting for." Not that it was a lark on the demanding Royal Dar-Es-Salam course, a par-73 brute of 7,035 yards.

Singh led most of the way. Stewart charged and caught him in the final round, and Faldo had caught Stewart for a while. Singh shot 70-73-71-71— 285, seven under par. Stewart shook off a rocky start and shot 76-70-70-69 to tie him. Faldo finished third with 287, and Brian Marchbank and Brian Claar tied for fourth on 288. Langer couldn't get any steam up and tied for eighth at par 292.

Singh, who had played very little since the Volvo Masters three weeks earlier, showed mid-season form in the first round, shooting a three-under-par 70. That was good for a one-stroke lead, a margin he would hold through the next two rounds.

Stewart started his fourth-round charge with a birdie at No. 3. Then came three birdies in succession from the sixth for 34 on the first nine. Coming home, he birdied the 10th, 12th and 13th, en route to his 69 and 285 total. His strategy was simple. Since the course had no scoreboards to guide him, "... it was a question of shooting as low as possible, and hoping," he said. Faldo also was hoping. He chipped in for an eagle at the par-five 10th and tied Stewart at five under par, then he bogeyed the 11th. So Faldo needed an eagle at the par-five 18th to catch Stewart. But his chance died when he put his second shot into the trees.

Singh, Faldo's playing partner, was the only one left with a chance to catch Stewart. A one-over-par 37 on the front nine cost him the lead. He got a stroke back with a birdie at No. 10. "I thought I'd blown it," Singh said. He was two strokes behind with two holes to play. He narrowed things with a birdie from four feet at the par-three 17th.

"I knew I had to birdie the last, and almost managed to mess it up," Singh said. His approach was 60 feet short, and in the rough. Then his chip was weak. He faced a 10-foot putt for the birdie he needed to stay alive. "I didn't take too long over the putt," he said. "I just got over it, and hit it, and thought, 'Don't miss.'" And he didn't.

At the first playoff hole, the par-four 16th, Stewart put his approach 18 feet from the hole. Singh, getting a free drop after someone apparently tramped on his drive, hit a seven iron to six feet. Then Stewart missed, but Singh didn't.

Ivory Coast Open—£81,697
Winner: Michel Besanceney

First the Swedes, and now who—the French?

Michel Besanceney, with four strong rounds and a Ballesteros-like recovery shot in a playoff, joined the hopefuls who seem bent on adding France to the emerging powers on the European Tour. With his victory in the Ivory Coast Open, Besanceney joined such rising Frenchmen as Jean Van de Velde, Marc Farry, and Marc Pendaries.

Besanceney's career to now had been a struggle. He tied for 153rd in the 1990 European Tour qualifying tournament, 103 spots away from qualifying for his playing card. He spent some of 1990 on the Challenge Tour, and won the Open Vittel in France, and finished 19th on the Challenge Order of Merit with £15,279. He was still looking for the key that first week of December at the 6,677-yard, par-72 President Golf Club at Yamoussoukro. But it didn't seem he was about to find it.

Paul Carman, 25-year-old English rookie, took the first-round lead with the authority of a veteran, shooting a seven-under-par 65. He led by a stroke over Wayne Stephens. Besanceney was back in the pack, at 68. It was in the second round that the door opened to Besanceney, even though he was nowhere near it. That's when Carman ballooned to a 76, which ultimately cost him the tournament. Jeff Pinsent vaulted into the 36-hole lead with 68— 137. Unfazed, Carman climbed back to the top with a third-round 66 for a 207 total, and led Stephens by two strokes going into the finale.

Until now, Besanceney was just another face in the background. He was three strokes out of the lead in the first round, four strokes in the second, and five huge strokes out going into the last. And suddenly he caught fire, and set the stage for a theatrical finish. Besanceney closed with a 67, Carman with a 72, and they tied at nine-under-par 279 (Besanceney, 68-73-71-67; Carman, 65-76-66-72). That set up a battle between 1990 qualifying tournament rivals—Carman, who passed (he won his card with a 45th-place finish) against Besanceney, who failed.

Besanceney was about to fail again. He drove into the trees at the first playoff hole. Carman hit down the middle, then on the green, just 15 feet from the hole. Besanceney needed a miracle, and he created one, a low shot that bounced onto the green, hit the flagstick, and stopped a foot from the hole. Carman three-putted for a bogey five. Now Besanceney, playing last, could have two-putted from a foot and still won with a par. But he didn't. He got the birdie.

Nigerian Open—£105,027
Winner: James Lebbie

On paper, James Lebbie beat Paul Eales by four strokes to win the Nigerian Open. Actually, the closest they ever were to each other was in the Kenya Open back in January, when both missed the cut at 146. In this Nigerian Open, in mid-December, neither Eales nor anybody else got anywhere near Lebbie, a 33-year-old from Sri Lanka.

It was to Eales' credit that he was the only one who could narrow the gap that much. Lebbie simply made the Ikoyi Club at Lagos his personal property, shooting the 6,389-yard, par-71 course in an untroubled 67-66-66-71, for a 14-under-par total of 270. He held a one-stroke lead in the first round (over Gordon J. Brand and Paul Lyons); a five-stroke lead in the second (over Brand and Garry Harvey), and five-stroke lead going into the final round (over David Llewellyn).

15. Australasian Tour

The list of stars on the 1991 Australasian golf circuit had a strange look about it. There was no Greg Norman, no Ian Baker-Finch, and not a mention of Craig Parry or Mike Harwood. Instead, there were Rodger Davis and Peter Senior, who each won twice, while Wayne Grady and Wayne Riley had one victory each.

Riley won the Australian Open at Royal Melbourne in style. Where most other players were throwing away shots, Riley birdied the final three holes. The Australian Open needed a shot in the arm. The weather was gloomy for the most part, and the greens and pin positions attracted criticism.

Norman's putting problems left him without a win on the circuit, and that was a disappointment to his many fans in Australia. He has been the catalyst for the boom in Australian golf, his victories and his charismatic approach captivating all who wanted to see Australia's name emblazoned throughout the sports world.

His long-time coach, Charlie Earp, said when he watched him in Australia that his swing was in excellent shape and he was hitting the ball superbly, but his putting was letting him down.

Another of the reasons that no single Australian or New Zealander dominated the scene in 1991 was that there were a lot of very good golfers teeing it up in the 14 events, and there were many good young players coming along to pressure the established performers.

Greg Turner started it by winning the Daikyo Palm Meadows Cup, then Davis won at Sanctuary Cove, but American Blaine McCallister got past everyone at the Vines the following week. After that, another American, Chris Patton, won the Mercedes-Benz Match Play at Kingston Heath. The 1990 Australian Open champion, American John Morse, had a horrendous year in 1991 but suddenly found his touch and won the Air New Zealand Shell Open and was a threat in the Johnnie Walker Classic. Peter Teravainen survived a nail-biting last afternoon for a victory in Singapore, and Europe thrashed Australia, who played without a New Zealand representative in the Asahi Glass Four Tours event at Royal Adelaide.

One of the stalwarts of the Australasian Tour, Stewart Ginn, won in Malaysia, signalling a change of direction where they now start the second half of the circuit with three events in Asia. Of even more significance than Ginn's win was the victory a week later by Tod Power in the Perak Masters. Power is a very promising young golfer, one of a number of rookies who could do well in future years.

Robert Allenby is another who, at age 20, has enormous potential. He turned professional immediately after finishing second in the Australian Open at Royal Melbourne. He is a cool player and a good one.

Australians did well at the end of the circuit. Brett Ogle, Grady and Riley won the South Australian Open, Australian PGA and Australian Open, respectively. In the final event of the year, the Johnnie Walker Classic at the Lakes in Sydney, Senior made it back to the winner's circle with a 10-under-par victory in difficult, windy conditions.

For Rodger Davis, it was a mixed finish. His second place at the Lakes lifted him to No. 1 on the money list, but Davis blew a four-stroke lead on the last afternoon. It was an out-of-character performance from the gritty Australian and, following his collapse at Royal Melbourne the previous week, where he had seemed on the last afternoon to have the Open in his grasp, it was not the manner in which he would have wanted to end the year.

Daikyo Palm Meadows Cup—A$1,200,000
Winner: Greg Turner

Greg Turner, with another outstanding victory on the Australasian Tour, provided a further boost for David Leadbetters's teaching methods, winning by four shots in the Daikyo Palm Meadows Cup. The 27-year-old New Zealander was eight shots behind Greg Norman's 66 after the first round, had caught him by the end of the second, breezed into a one-shot lead on the third day from Brad Faxon and Chris Patton, and held off Norman's charge with a 68 to Norman's 69 over the final 18 holes. Turner's 271 total, 18 under par, produced a four-stroke margin.

Norman provided a sensation in this tournament in 1990 when he disqualified himself after shooting 66 and 63. He took relief incorrectly on the 10th hole in the opening round and, on the morning of the third round, after television replays had been consulted, he announced his withdrawal from the event and spent the remaining two days as a television commentator. In 1991, when he took three drops on the 15th hole after a line-of-sight ruling concerning a television tower, the Palm Meadows switchboard lit up again, but this time there were no problems because of the rules. His opening rounds of 66, 70 and 70 gave him the chance to start the last day only three strokes behind Turner.

Two shots ahead of Norman as the final round began, on 204, was Faxon whose entry for the following week's event at Sanctuary Cove had been arranged by Ian Baker-Finch. It was an interesting experience for the 29-year-old American, because he had to pre-qualify at Redlands, a nearby course, had no time to measure the fairway distances, the flags on the green were only half the height he is used to, and Baker-Finch's father caddied for him. He made it through the qualifying round with a 72, and then, after shooting a third-round 65, was tied for second place coming into the last round. Even though Faxon shot 75, he still made $26,700. By contrast, Baker-Finch failed to make the cut.

For Turner, this was a magnificent victory. He followed up his late 1990 Johnnie Walker Classic win with steady and, at times, spectacular golf which featured faultless play around the greens, particularly in his second-round 62. The Palm Meadows course is an exacting 6,973 yards with plenty of water hazards, and a prevailing afternoon breeze can make things difficult for late starters.

Turner's confidence had been built up through the teaching of Leadbetter, Mitchell Spearman and Dennis Pugh, and the fact that his golf had become far more consistent in the previous year. The real test for Turner was in the last round when Norman, playing in front of him, set the target of 275 which meant Turner, if able to combat the pressure, could win by shooting a one-under-par 71.

Any nerves present were well concealed, and Turner played steadily for 68, with his short game once again very much under control. At Turner's press conference, he made it clear the two victories and $396,000 were equally welcome, because of the financial pressures which had come in his two years without a victory.

There were heartening performances from some of the younger Australian players, Terry Price and Peter Lonard finishing only one shot behind Norman's 275, and Glenn Joyner's 279 earned him the same prize money as Faxon. Johan Rystrom, the first-round leader with an eight-under-par 64, followed with 71, 72, 75, a fine performance from the Swedish player.

SXL Sanctuary Cove Classic—A$700,000
Winner: Rodger Davis

There is no better golfer in Australia than Rodger Davis when the going is tough, and Davis came through over wind, storms and lightening to win the Sanctuary Cove Classic by one stroke over New Zealander Frank Nobilo. Ian Baker-Finch was desperately unlucky, starting the final round nine shots behind the leader, Nobilo, and then producing a string of birdies as the storm clouds began to gather. Baker-Finch, after hitting a perfect drive into the 50 miles-an-hour wind at the 512-yard 18th hole, was still so far from the green he couldn't hit another driver over the water and had to lay up with a four iron. Had Baker-Finch played the hole 20 minutes later, after the storm and a switch in the wind, he would have used a seven iron. His 67 and 280 total left him tied for third place with Mike Ferguson, two strokes behind Davis.

It all made for a dramatic afternoon on a course rated by the professionals as one of the most difficult in Australia, although there were some murmurings early on that the Arnold Palmer-designed layout was not as awkward as made out by its pre-tournament publicity. Three days of calm led them into the trap. At 7,308 yards, Sanctuary Cove required Davis' 10-under-par 278 to take first prize. Five players had 69 or better in the opening round and then failed to break par for the 72 holes. One of those was Hiromichi Namiki who, with Craig Parry, led the field with 67s on the first day by one shot over Peter Senior. Parry was still there after the third round, just two shots behind Nobilo, and Tod Power had moved to one shot behind the New Zealander.

Power, based on the Gold Coast only a few miles from the course, is one of Australia's most promising young golfers who used the Asian Tour in 1990 as a springboard for further success. He set up his chance of victory in the third round, an action-packed day when he matched Davis with 67 and moved to within one shot of Nobilo, with Davis hovering two strokes further back.

Hometown advantage was shared between Power, who is coached by Sanctuary Pines' resident teacher, Bob Weir; Baker-Finch, who is the touring professional; and Davis, who is the touring professional just down the road at Coolum.

In the final round Nobilo had birdies at the first and second holes, but then bogeyed three times to start the back nine at one over par for the day. Power drifted out of contention with four bogeys, but still won $29,120, while Baker-Finch, despite his brilliance, had his chance destroyed by the change of weather.

When it hit the course, the fierce electrical storm blacked out 8,000 homes in an adjoining suburb and the rain was so heavy it was impossible to see the greens from the tees.

Nobilo still had his chance when it came down to the final putt, but his 15-footer slid by the hole to give Davis the title.

The Vines Classic—A$700,000
Winner: Blaine McCallister

When American Blaine McCallister flew into Perth, Western Australia, his mission was to win The Vines Classic and he said he had not made the trip for fun; victory was his intention and he produced a betting slip for a wager with a Darwin bookmaker showing he had taken 33-to-1 about his chances and bet $500 on himself.

On the final day of the tournament, McCallister was faced with 245 yards to the pin on the 18th hole, pulled out a two iron and hit the ball 10 feet from the pin. He sank the putt for birdie and a one-shot win over Wayne Grady and Greg Turner, plus the winnings from the Darwin bookie. Tied for fourth place was Graham Marsh, the designer of the course.

McCallister took the title but, for much of the time, he was closely pressed by another American, 24-year-old Michael Bradley, who is based in Florida. Bradley led with 66 in the opening round and shared the lead with McCallister in the second and third rounds.

When the final day began, Bradley and McCallister, at eight under par, were one stroke ahead of Turner, Grady and Danny Mijovic, the Canadian player. The least experienced of the five were Bradley and Mijovic, and their games fell away with 74 and 76, respectively, although Bradley's $27,104 check was easily the biggest of his career.

Bradley was right with the leaders until the 15th hole, where he double-bogeyed, and then he had bogeys on the 16th and 17th as well. The 17th and 18th holes proved the undoing of Turner and Grady, but McCallister relished the challenge.

On the 17th, McCallister was in trouble and hit a splendid two iron close to the pin to save par and then, on the 18th, after his yardage was confirmed at 245, he hit what he later described as the best two iron of his life. The spectacular shot flew the water hazard at the front of the green and then the putt went in the center of the hole for a victory worth $126,000, plus $16,500 from the bookmaker.

Mercedes-Benz Australian Match Play—A$200,000
Winner: Chris Patton

Match play is a great leveller in golf, and a change of pace for the professionals from the 72-hole stroke tournaments which make up the majority of competitive events. It also brings some shocking results, as evidenced by the demise of Greg Turner and Peter Fowler in the opening round of the Mercedes-Benz Australian Match Play Championship at Kingston Heath.

The Match Play was extended for the first time to 64 players instead of 32. Apart from Turner and Fowler, other prominent names to disappear on the first morning were Peter O'Malley, Ian Stanley, Roger Mackay, Mike Clayton, Jeff Woodland and Lyndsay Stephen, who was slaughtered 8 and 6 by Bob Shearer. Shearer then went out at the 24th hole to Peter McWhinney, in a match characterized by a display of nerves from both.

The winner, and much sought after by the media, was former U.S. Amateur champion Chris Patton, who had been the recent subject of an article concerning him being overweight and questioning whether the word "athlete" should be used about a man weighing 280 pounds. Patton said he had booked himself into a weight-loss program in a few weeks and, meanwhile, intended to try to win this event. He proceeded to do just that.

It was a triumph of skill and deft touch, long driving and sound putting, excellent temperament and a determination to show those who had written about him that being an athlete was not simply a case of bulging muscles and no finesse. An indication of how popular Patton was with the hometown crowds was that he was cheered through the last day when he played Australian Ken Dukes. He said later the crowds were really appreciative of his play and kept encouraging him throughout the 33 holes they played.

Pyramid Australian Masters—A$500,000
Winner: Peter Senior

Australia has a no-more-determined golfer than Peter Senior, who has overcome putting yips, chipping yips and driving yips. When putting yips returned, he waved them away again with an extra long putter. Only 12 months earlier, driving from the tee in the Scottish Open, Senior found himself unable to take the club away from the ball and had to take a step back. Understandably, Senior found this disconcerting and, after his win in the Pyramid Australian Masters, confessed that at the time he wondered if he would be able to continue in the game.

Seven months later, having hit a perfect drive, Senior was walking down the center of the 72nd hole of this tournament at Huntingdale, while Greg Norman trudged off to the practice fairway to the left, in order to play his second shot into the green. They were paired on the fourth day after Senior's 69 in the third round tied him with Norman at the top of the leaderboard, both at 11 under par.

Norman profited from a slice of luck on the seventh hole, measuring 515 yards. Norman hit two massive shots to the front of the green, and Senior had a putt for birdie. Just as Norman was playing his 30-yard chip shot, a spectator clicked a camera, the ball was thinned, and Norman swung around and berated the offender. However, while he was turned away, the ball hit the flagstick and fell into the hole for an eagle. Senior missed his putt, parred the hole and Norman had gone two strokes ahead. Then Norman had problems on the 12th and 14th holes, where Senior sank good putts, and they were neck-and-neck from there to the 72nd hole.

Norman, having hooked his drive onto the practice fairway, chose to play a five iron an estimated 179 yards to the pin, over the hospitality stand in front of him. If the ball then went over the green and into the greenside hospitality tents, he would have a free drop. But the ball bounced on top of a roof behind the green, and rocketed back into a greenside bunker. With Senior only 15 feet away, facing a birdie putt, Norman then needed to hole the sand-wedge shot to have a chance of forcing a playoff.

Senior was three feet short with his first putt and there was still the chance of a playoff, but his second putt went safely into the hole, and he beat Norman by one stroke.

Mike Clayton, who led the first day with 67, finished two strokes behind Norman with a final-round 69, along with Peter O'Malley, who had 70 and then raced for a flight to London in a bid to qualify for a European Tour card which he achieved.

Tasmanian Open—A$80,000
Winner: Chris Gray

The 1990 Australian Amateur champion, Chris Gray, became the youngest player ever to win the Tasmanian Open, which dates back to 1913, when the 22-year-old from Perth shot a two-under-par 70 in the final round to win by two strokes at Royal Hobart Golf Club. Gray had rounds of 68, 71, 71 and the closing 70 for a 280 aggregate, eight under par, to defeat Brad Hughes, Jon Evans and Robert Stephens.

Gray turned professional after the World Amateur Team Championship in November, 1990, in Christchurch, New Zealand. Collecting the A$15,300 check, Gray said, "This is the best feeling I've had in golf since I started playing when I was a kid."

Birdies on the 11th, 12th and 13th holes in the final round gave Gray the edge he needed. Evans needed a par on the final hole to tie him, but Evans hit his tee shot right of the fairway, underneath a tree. He had an unplayable lie. Hughes needed a birdie to tie, but hit his approach shot into a bunker.

AMP New Zealand Open—NZ$200,000
Winner: Rodger Davis

Frank Nobilo was earning a reputation for being a bridesmaid, with five second-place finishes in 18 months, two of those occurring in six weeks, when he finished second behind Rodger Davis both times. The first was at Sanctuary Cove, and then in this AMP New Zealand Open, Davis beat him by two shots despite Nobilo's last-round 68. The outcome was a combination of Davis' aggression and Nobilo having bogeys at crucial times in the last round.

On the 71-par Paraparamu Beach Golf Club near Wellington, Nobilo led the first day, but then Davis took over. Davis led by two strokes after the second round, by one stroke after the third round, and then Nobilo seemingly had the tournament in his hands when he eagled the 12th hole on the last day. Nobilo was still in the lead when he stepped on the 16th tee, but a pushed stroke finished in an awkward position and, in trying to chip out, he ended up in the rough. At the 17th his tee shot brought groans from his New Zealand fans and another bogey gave Davis his chance.

Davis said later he decided to gamble on attacking the pin on the 16th and 17th holes, and two great shots gave the opportunities for birdie putts. Davis' birdie at the 17th left Nobilo to count the cost of his two errant holes. His solid par at the 18th gave the New Zealander no chance of a playoff.

There was no lack of sympathy from Davis towards Nobilo, because Davis himself had a similar experience over 18 months starting in February 1979. He was second 14 times in that period but, when he started to win, there was no stopping him. On the final day the leaderboard was dominated by Davis and Nobilo, although both American John Morse and Glenn Joyner, the young Australian professional, were challenging at different times.

Rothmans Malaysian Masters—A$291,000
Winner: Stewart Ginn

Stewart Ginn's career was in doubt as he won the Rothmans Malaysian Masters by three shots over Nandasena Perera on the Royal Selangor Golf Club course in Kuala Lumpur. Ginn arrived in Malaysia after receiving warnings about the possibility of finishing in a wheelchair if he continued to play golf, following knee surgery. He was told not to play golf again. "I told myself I still had plenty of golf left in me, and I was right," he said. "The last-round 68 took away the pain."

Ginn's course management was a contributing factor in his win, not surprising in the light of his previous victories in Malaysian Opens on the same course, in 1977 and 1986. This time his consistency saw him shoot 70, 70, 70 in the first three rounds but, even so, he was still one stroke behind Tony Maloney and Anthony Painter when the final day began.

Maloney had a disastrous last-round 76 and, although Painter managed a one-over-par 73, it was not good enough once Ginn got to work with his chipping and putting, and finished with 68 and a 278 total. Ginn gave credit to fellow Australian Lyndsay Stephen for the improvement in his putting, saying that a few months earlier in Seoul, Stephen persuaded him to change to the overlapping grip from the conventional one. It made all the difference to his short game, with three putts becoming a thing of the past.

Ginn had only the one birdie on the first nine on the final day, but played scorching golf on the way back with birdies at the 12th, 14th and 15th holes, before playing a loose tee shot on the par-three 16th. "I was fired up with the way things were going and hit a six iron to the left of the pin which is definitely three-putt territory," he said. "As it turned out, it didn't matter all that much because I hit a great iron into the 17th and sank the putt to pick up another shot."

Perera, of Sri Lanka, was the surprise of the tournament. Perera, 36 years old, has been a professional for only one year and was runner-up in the golf championship at the Asian Games, beaten in a playoff. He was disconsolate at the end at Royal Selangor, having missed birdie putts between two and 15 feet on seven holes, four of them on the back nine when he was trying to make a charge at Ginn.

Perak Masters—A$150,000
Winner: Tod Power

Tod Power broke through for his first professional victory in the Perak Masters at Ipoh, but not before he was involved in the disqualification of a competitor in his group. Power was storming home for a final-round 67, with Singapore's Samson Gimson and new Zealander Simon Owen, when his and Owen's attention was caught by Gimson, who had been having a trying time on the greens.

Nothing would drop, so on the 15th hole, after he had missed relatively easy birdie attempts on the previous two greens, Gimson tried what everyone thinks of doing at some stage, to snap his putter in two. After the round, Gimson was disqualified, losing seventh place, which cost him $4,000.

Gimson had shared the lead going into the final round with Owen and Australians Peter Lonard and Power. Lonard was responsible for an astonishing display of golf in the second round where he had a dream start to the day. He eagled the 517-yard first hole, birdied the second, and scored a hole-in-one on the 168-yard third. Five under par after three holes started him on his way to an outward 29, but then he took 37 back, missing several birdie chances with a balky putter. This was Lonard's first hole-in-one and it won him a Peugeot car.

Power's third-round 66 brought him into contention in the tournament. Then, over the first nine holes on the last day, he concentrated on playing steady golf while both Owen and Gimson fell away with bogeys. On the back nine his superb iron play set up several birdie chances which were converted in a hot putting streak, allowing him to come home in a blistering 31 shots, for 67 and a 275 total, 13 under par, to win by five strokes over Americans Scott Taylor and Louis Brown. Taylor, Brown and Jim Empey all finished strongly with 68, 69 and 67, respectively.

Power was quick to pay tribute to Stewart Ginn's advice before he started the last round. "Stewart is very experienced and won the Rothmans Malaysian Masters a week ago in similar circumstances," he said. "He told me to set a realistic target and then go and concentrate on playing good golf. I set myself 68, which was what he shot to win last week, I then had 67 and concentrated on my golf rather than the leaderboard. It was great advice."

Pioneer Singapore PGA Championship—A$150,000
Winner: Peter Teravainen

Peter Teravainen hung on to halt an Australian charge on the Sime Course at the Singapore Island Country Club, edging out Tony Maloney by one shot in a great last-day battle in the Pioneer Singapore PGA Championship.

It was no easy task for Teravainen who, at one stage, looked as if he would throw away the title. Later, Teravainen gave credit for the victory to Seve Ballesteros, not for any tips the Spanish golfer passed on, but for the experience he gained in playing with him at the Swiss Open.

"I had the good fortune to be paired with him in that event and just to see how he went about the job did wonders for my temperament," Teravainen said. "I made a poor start on the opening nine and I needed to pull myself together. It was a question of temperament and making certain I didn't panic despite those opening holes. There's no doubt watching Seve in a similar situation was a great help."

Teravainen had a final-round 71 and 274 total. 14 under par.

It was one of those tournaments where different players were making a charge at the leaders throughout the four days, and 43 of those who made the cut at even-par 144 then finished under par for the tournament. Nandasena Perera of Sri Lanka finished tied for third to continue his good play, shooting a last-round 68, and four of the top-13 players shot 67s over the last 18 holes.

Samson Gimson, the Singapore professional disqualified the previous week for trying to snap his putter in half, was one of those with 67 and that gave him a share of sixth place and $5,000.

Early on the final day, it looked as though Maloney had the measure of Teravainen when he had birdies at the 10th and 11th, while the leader was having three bogeys and two birdies in a nervous display.

Teravainen has a Singapore-born wife and a two-week-old child, and so the local fans were cheering for him. He had birdies at the 15th and 16th holes and then pars on the last two holes. Maloney couldn't match that, and Teravainen was able to celebrate.

Air New Zealand Shell Open—NZ$250,000

Winner: John Morse

Some golfers attract publicity. They are eye-catching off the tee with 280-yard drives, they jump out of the pack and provide the clenched-fist salute on the 72nd hole when the final putt drops. Others, like John Morse, have a textbook swing and appear almost apologetic as they collect the first-place check.

Morse walked away with the Air New Zealand Shell Open in just that fashion, despite appalling late afternoon last-day conditions, where strong winds and heavy showers put a premium on the players' will as well as their skill. Morse finished with a three-over-par 73 and 273 total, winning by three strokes.

Morse said that in all his career he had never played on a day quite like the last one at Titirangi. "There was rain and hail, wind and sunshine and then bitter cold and, when we were playing the eighth hole, it seemed that we encountered all of them from the tee to the green," he said. By the time Morse reached the 18th hole with his three-shot lead intact, the torrential rain had halted play and water had to be swept from the green before the last group could putt out.

It was just the kind of day when physiotherapists come into their own. Morse, when playing the European Tour earlier in the year, had serious back problems and was in so much pain that he needed constant treatment. "I even developed a twitch in my right eye from the back problem and I can assure you that did nothing for my putting," he said. In Auckland, however, a New Zealand physiotherapist, Ace Neame, dramatically eased Morse's back and neck problems and the 1990 Australian Open winner never really looked like losing at Titirangi.

In second place was Nandasena Perera, the 36-year-old Sri Lankan golfer who, earlier had finished second to Stewart Ginn in the Malaysian Masters and also played well in Singapore. His short game was excellent in the awful conditions and he shot 66. He uses a baseball grip and claims one of the reasons he is straight off the tee is that as a child if he lost a ball, he couldn't play again until he found another ball in the jungle bordering the course where he was a caddie.

Asahi Glass Four Tours Championship—A$1,150,000
Winner: Europe

Europe recorded its first victory in six years of the Asahi Glass Four Tours Championship at the Royal Adelaide Golf Club, defeating Australasia 8-4 in the final. Because of the format of the competition, stroke/match play, it was a closer contest than appeared in the results, although there was no doubting the superiority of the European team, which was without Seve Ballesteros, Nick Faldo, Ian Woosnam and Jose Maria Olazabal.

The Four Tours concept brings together teams from Europe, the United States, Australasia and Japan, each team with six players, and the format is stroke play, with each player playing a match on all four days. Before even a ball was struck in Adelaide, the American team claimed the Australasians had little to celebrate from victory in 1990 which had come about, they said, because of a technicality. This involved a last day wash-out in Tokyo, at which point the fact that Wayne Levi had not posted a first-round card became relevant. The Americans lost all points for that day.

It was ironic that this year Australasia kept the United States out of the final. The two teams were tied with 19 points each, and the Australasians went on because of having beaten the Americans 7-5 on the second day.

The Australasia-Japan match on the third day found the Americans in front of the clubhouse cheering Japan, when it looked as though Hiroshi Makino would defeat Roger Mackay and thus give the United States team the final berth against Europe. On the 17th, Makino was 35 feet from the flag, putting for eagle, and Mackay hit his second shot to six feet, bringing applause from the pro-Australian gallery. That was muted when the Japanese player sank his putt, but Mackay made his putt as well, and then parred the 18th for a one-shot victory. The United States was knocked out.

The final between Europe and Australasia was highlighted by Ronan Rafferty's brilliant golf, as he shot 65, 12 strokes better than his opening 77 against Japan. His round included one duffed tee shot, one where he left a ball in a bunker, eight birdies and only 21 putts. It was a performance which brought roars from the gallery, even though he was beating Australia's Rodger Davis, who shot 70.

With Paul Broadhurst easily beating Ian Baker-Finch, the two key games involved Graham Marsh and Craig Parry and they were beaten by Ryder Cup players David Feherty and Sam Torrance, respectively. For Torrance, the European captain, they even had the massed pipe band marching down the 18th fairway, a nice Scottish touch to end the event.

West End South Australian Open—A$200,000
Winner: Brett Ogle

Brett Ogle has been one of the most exciting young golfers in Australia and, until his win in the West End South Australian Open, he was also one of the unluckiest. "It's been a private hell," he said of the past year, when two injuries kept him off the course for four months. His 13-under-par 279 was a brilliant performance and the gallery at the 18th hole gave him a standing ovation, in part for his two-stroke win but also in recognition of his fight back from near disaster.

At the 1990 Australian Open, he was in contention when, on the 71st hole, he smashed a two-iron shot from under a bush and the ball rebounded back to his kneecap. The injury sidelined him for several weeks. Then, in Portugal, he was injured after being hit by a pro-am player and was out for 10 weeks. When he played his first round after the injury he found he had shaking hands and feared "the yips."

At the Royal Adelaide course, Ogle began with a two-under-par 71 and followed that with 70 and a pair of 69s. He didn't have things his own way, though, because after the opening day, when a gale allowed only 12 players to better par, Mike Harwood chased Ogle and was still in with a chance with three holes to play.

"He's a tough man that Harwood," Ogle said after he parred the last hole. "He keeps coming at you and never gives up for a moment. It's difficult to express just what the victory means to me after all the bad luck and being out of the game, and I'm glad I managed it by playing good golf. It means a lot to me not to lose from that position."

Harwood turned in a wonderful effort. The 1991 British Open runner-up reduced the deficit to one shot when he birdied the 15th hole, but Ogle remained in command with Harwood forced to try for birdies on the remaining three holes. On the 18th Ogle deliberately hit well down the left side of the rough to the hospitality tents and played his second shot from the dropping zone, making a safe par after Harwood's 45-foot birdie putt stayed short.

Colin Field, a 21 year old, became the latest young Australian to hit the headlines when he shot 70, 66 in the last two rounds to finish third and collect the biggest check of his short career as a professional.

Ford Australian PGA Championship—A$250,000
Winner: Wayne Grady

There was more to Wayne Grady's victory in the Australian PGA Championship than stepping forward to take the winner's check. It was also, he said, the first time he has ever broken 70 in all four rounds of an event of any importance in the 13 years he had been a professional golfer. That gave him nearly as much pleasure as winning by three shots over Brett Ogle with a 271 total, 12 under par.

England's Steven Richardson tied for third place at 277 with 25-year-old Australian Neil Kerry. Kerry said there was no doubt that the experience was priceless. "One thing I'll know about next time is allowing my concentration to slip," he said. "I birdied the third, fourth and fifth holes on the final day and then made the mistake of looking for a leaderboard to see how I was doing. I was within two strokes of Wayne, and started getting caught up in the atmosphere of the occasion, instead of concentrating on striking the ball and thinking about each separate shot."

Grady's saddest day was not winning the playoff for the 1989 British Open at Royal Troon, and the highlight was the 1990 U.S. PGA Championship. His first win was the West Lakes Classic in 1978 in Adelaide, two years after Greg Norman won the same event for his first victory. As an Australian, he will always be compared with the Great White Shark, but Grady freely admits he is a grinder rather than a star.

"I played really well here at Concord this week," Grady said at the prize-giving. "I struck the ball well off the tee, my irons were good and I have started to putt very solidly. In the end though it was like Shoal Creek, where I started to 'leak a little oil' over the last few holes. It was good to win again because although I don't class myself as a world-beater, I know I can play well and I was particularly happy to break 70 in each round for the first time."

Ogle gave him no respite, with two closing rounds of 67 and 67, but every time the slim challenger picked up shots, Grady knuckled down and matched him. Ogle said later, "When I holed for an eagle at the 14th, I reckoned I was only one behind, but when I stepped onto the next tee the leaderboard said I was four back. I thought Wayne must have skipped a couple of holes."

Australian Open Championship—A$700,000
Winner: Wayne Riley

Occasionally a free spirit will burst through to win a golf tournament, and no one better fits that description than Wayne Riley, who birdied the last three holes to snatch the 1991 Australian Open Championship. It was a wonderful performance from a 29-year-old who has had more nicknames than victories on the Australasian and European Tours since he first turned professional nine years ago.

At one stage on the European Tour he was known as the "Wild Colonial Boy," and then, when he settled down a little, was tagged "Radar." There have been other sobriquets, and he is a character. He is also a very good golfer, as he has shown on many occasions. The head-shaking at some of his extrovert behaviors has been tinged with genuine pleasure at his successes, and he is well liked around the golfing world.

At Royal Melbourne on the last afternoon, when he might have let the tournament slip away, as his fellow professionals were doing, he added birdies on each of the last three holes, a wonderful performance. When he came to the 18th, having just sunk the putts on the par-three 16th and the par-five 17th, he knew he had to make birdie to beat amateur Robert Allenby, who was sitting in the clubhouse at 286, two under par, after a sensational last-round 68.

Allenby seemed to have lost his chance when, in horrendous conditions on the second day, he shot 78 and was eight strokes off the pace. He fought back, though, in the manner of a potential champion, and a two-under-par

70 and then his 68 on the last day had him in good shape to become the first amateur winner since Bruce Devlin in 1960. There is little doubt about Allenby's future, and it was merely a question of when, not if, he would be turning professional.

Riley's tee shot on the 18th was good, but he knew that if his putter were to work for a third time in three holes, he had to keep the ball under the hole on a green which had posed problems for anyone too strong with their approach shots. Riley hit his long-iron approach well enough, but the ball finished 25 feet below the hole, and he was faced with a putt that had to be hit at perfect speed, allowing for a slight right-to-left break. Not much had gone in the side of any hole during the four days, but this putt did, just as spectators thought it was about to slide over the edge, and Riley was the leader in the clubhouse.

He wasn't the winner at this stage because Rodger Davis and Steven Richardson were still on the course and had the winning of the tournament in their own hands. Neither was able to hold his game together when it mattered, and each required a birdie-birdie finish to tie Riley, a task which in the end proved beyond them, though Davis birdied the 72nd hole to snatch third place from Richardson, Brett Ogle and Jamie Spence. The latter at one stage was in the running for a check of $75,000, but a bogey, and then Davis' birdie, reduced that by $37,000, an expensive twist for the young Englishman.

Davis, with his experience and knowledge of Royal Melbourne, looked to have the tournament in his grasp at the start of the final day, but he began so badly that he all but slipped from contention in the first six holes. Birdie opportunities were thrown away on the second and third holes, and then he failed to take advantage of a lucky break on the seventh hole, where only the pin stopped a bunker shot from finding the sand again. He then missed a four-footer for birdie on the 12th, and took three to get down from 40 feet on the 13th for a double bogey. Any chance he may have retained was gone when a good tee shot on the par-three 16th rolled gently to the left and found sand, from where he bogeyed. It was the end for Davis, and his playing partner, Richardson, had almost as many problems in his final-round 76.

They weren't the only players to find trouble over the four days where, for the first 54 holes, a combination of strong winds, chilly temperatures and lightning-fast greens made the game a misery for the competitors. It was a tournament where the big names were unable to threaten for any length of time, hitting the leaderboard and then suddenly disappearing and being overtaken by lesser-known names.

Greg Norman looked likely to miss the cut, but then fought back to finish tied for 16th. Ben Crenshaw was one who did not make the halfway cut, after two days of being unable to come to grips with the greens, and there were other well-known names who joined him outside a very high cut of 152.

Johnnie Walker Classic—A$1,000,000

Winner: Peter Senior

Only a month earlier, Peter Senior had been wondering from where his next decent round of golf would come, without concerning himself about actually winning a tournament. The week before the Johnnie Walker Classic, he confided that his game was starting to recover, and the recovery was completed with a splendid one-stroke win over Rodger Davis and Frank Nobilo, in conditions which required great skill and temperament.

The Lake course in Sydney is a testing layout and, when the stiff northeasterly breeze blows, it provides a stern examination for the best professionals. Nobilo became the firm favorite on the final day, after shooting a six-under-par 67, and was leader in the clubhouse at nine under par. His round included an eagle and six birdies and, as conditions grew tougher, Nobilo had every right to feel confident. Senior and Davis, with eight holes still to play, knew they needed to shoot par rounds if they were to win.

Davis was in the best shape of the challengers and, for a short while, was 12 under par and four strokes clear of the field. Senior, with two bogeys on the opening nine, wasn't living up to his hopes of the previous evening, after tieing Davis for the lead.

But Senior pulled his game together, had a solid string of pars and birdied the 14th and 17th holes just when something special was needed. It was the 17th which produced the swing that dropped Davis out of the lead and left him tied with Nobilo at nine under par. Davis hit his second shot on the 488-yard par five much too far to the left, had to play his third from the lake, without a shoe or sock on his right foot, and yet still made a brilliant recovery for par. Senior's wonderfully executed chip left him a tap-in putt for birdie and then a solid par at the par-three 18th gave him the trophy and the $180,000 winner's check.

John Morse's double-bogey five on the 18th cost him $9,000 and outright fourth place, but there were excellent performances from two of Australia's younger players, Peter Lonard and Richard Backwell, who were six and five under par, respectively. Norman finished at two under par, without sinking a putt of any consequence over the four days, and Wayne Grady shot a fine 69, after indifferent rounds on the second and third days saw him drop three shots to par.

Senior's return of confidence was underlined by his first-round seven-under-par 66, which allowed him to share the lead with Hank Baran.

Baran had a magnificent run of seven consecutive threes from the fourth hole, and had some good fortune on the last two holes. On the 17th, he pulled his second shot and a lucky bounce kept the ball out of the lake down the left-hand side of the hole. Then, on the 18th, a 95-foot putt scuttled into the hole to have him join Senior in the lead. Senior remained at or near the top of the leaderboard throughout the first three days, a second-round 71 keeping him tied for second place.

Defending champion Greg Turner had a disappointing tournament, after an opening-round 67 had him just one shot off the pace, and he surrendered his money list lead to Davis, whose second-place finish took him $38,000 ahead of the New Zealander.

16. Asia/Japan Tours

It was a year of national pride and pathos in Asia, a year of new names and big money, a year in which the dominant pros of the recent past made their presences felt but were not as overwhelming as usual. In short, 1991 was unpredictable as golf flowed through the 30-year-old Asia Circuit, with its cast of hopefuls and meager money, into the younger but healthy and wealthy, year-long Japan Tour and its rather reclusive star players, who battle each other through most of the season and never seem to be quite the match for the top golfers from abroad who come in for a handful of the rich events.

The Japan Tour has fattened its purses in recent years to the point that its total money is now quite respectable compared to that of the PGA Tour in America. In 1991, total prize money on the Japan Tour exceeded $26 million, compared to the PGA Tour's $46.5 million. Three players in Japan—Naomichi Ozaki, Roger Mackay and Tsuneyuki Nakajima—topped the ¥100 million mark. Converted at the average 1991 rate of 135 yen to the U.S. dollar, those figures place Ozaki, Mackay and Nakajima above $750,000 in earnings. Only the top five on the PGA Tour finished in the same vicinity.

The money race on the Japan Tour attracted more than the usual attention in 1991. It came down to the wire with an unexpected contender and a new first-place finisher for whom the position will carry bittersweet memories. Naomichi (Joe) Ozaki, the youngest of the three standout brothers on the Japan Tour, stepped in as the oldest, Masashi (Jumbo) Ozaki, relinquished the money crown.

It was still very much up in the air when Naomichi had to play the critical, next-to-last tournament—the Japan Series—burdened by the jolting awareness of the sudden death of his father that very week. Ozaki responded in admirable fashion by running away with that tournament for his fourth 1991 victory, clinching the money title and finishing the year with ¥119,507,974 ($885,224). His closest challenger was Australia's Roger Mackay, who won three times in his third season as a Japan Tour regular and was the first non-Japanese player to exceed ¥100 million with his ¥113,137,135. Nakajima, a top-level star in Japan for years, won twice, one victory his fourth Japan Open, and earned ¥111,639,213. Jumbo Ozaki fell less than ¥1 million short of the nine-figure mark and counted his Japan PGA Championships as one of his two 1991 triumphs. Isao Aoki, now 49 and contemplating his future with Senior Tour eligibility in Japan and elsewhere looming, won just once, picking up his 58th victory in the rain-abbreviated Bridgestone event in the fall.

Only four other players scored multiple victories, all in pairs. Two of them—Harumitsu Hamano and Eiichi Itai—had never won before. Saburo Fujiki scored his two wins early in the season, but the second, long after Yutaka Hagawa, the comeback player of the season in Japan, posted the year's only back-to-back victories in the Imperial and Shizuoka tournaments in March. Left-hander Hagawa, in the early 1980s considered by most to be the next Bob Charles, then virtually disappeared from contention, was a frequent contender through the season and finished eighth on the final money list with ¥62,590,240.

As usual, overseas players made a mark on the Japan Tour. Besides Mackay, Americans Raymond Floyd and Larry Nelson, Spain's Seve Ballesteros and Taiwan's Chen Tze Chung scored victories. Nelson and Ballesteros made particularly strong showings, Nelson finishing second in the Casio World Open after winning the Dunlop Phoenix, the richest event in Japan, and Ballesteros losing in the Dunlop Phoenix playoff and finishing third in the Dunlop Open besides his triumph in the Chunichi Crowns, the gem of the early season.

Canadian Rick Gibson also won in Japan—the Sapporo Tokyu—and had that opportunity because he led the Asia Circuit money list, which allowed him a place on the Japan Tour. The 29-year-old Gibson, in his sixth season in the Far East, landed the Benson & Hedges Malaysian Open and had enough high finishes in other of the circuit's 10 events to take the No. 1 position well in front of Taiwan's Chen Liang Hsi, who won in Indonesia.

What was most notable about the Asia Circuit were the victories by native sons at three of the events—Ali Sher, who just a few years earlier was a caddie at Delhi Golf Club where he won the India Open; Suthep Meesamasdi, a lightly regarded Thailand pro who won the Thai International Thailand Open, and veteran pro Choi Sang Ho, who fulfilled a lifetime ambition to win his country's national championship, the Maekyung (Korea) Open. The other winners were two Americans—Dennis Paulson in a playoff over Chen Tze Ming in the San Miguel Philippine Open and John Jacobs, the 1984 Asia Circuit champion, the Republic of China Open for a second time, also in a playoff against Filipino Antolin Fernando—as well as Canadian Jack Kay, Jr. at Singapore; Mackay, who does not play the Asia Circuit, in the tour-merged Dunlop Open; and the circuit's only 1991 marquee player, Bernhard Langer, who launched his most lucrative season with victory in the Hutchison Telecom Hong Kong Open.

The Asia Circuit staged its first four tournaments before the Japan Tour swung into action with the Daiichi Fudosan Cup. The two seasons went like this:

Hutchison Telecom Hong Kong Open—US$200,000
Winner: Bernhard Langer

The Asia Circuit put another marquee name into its winners' log when Bernhard Langer launched his lucrative 1991 season with a resounding victory in the Hutchison Telecom Hong Kong Open in mid-February, the opening event of the 10-tournament season in the Far East. On the verge of a pre-tournament withdrawal because of back trouble, Langer created agony for the rest of the field with a splendid, eight-under-par 63 the final day at Royal Hong Kong Golf Club that produced a 269 total and a seven-stroke win.

Langer remained close to the top the first two days. The 33-year-old German star was one behind the 64 of Craig McClellan Thursday, then two behind Mike Cunning's 135 when he took a 72 Friday.

He moved a stroke in front of Taiwan's Chen Tze Chung with a 69—206 Saturday and shifted his game into high gear Sunday. After Chen triple-bogeyed the first hole, Langer birdied seven of the next 10 holes and played in conservatively, making his eighth birdie on the final hole to finish seven ahead of Korean Cho Sang Ho and Lu Wen Ter of Taiwan. Over its long history, the Hong Kong Open has had the likes of Greg Norman, Ian Woosnam, Peter Thomson and Orville Moody among its winners.

San Miguel Philippine Open—US$150,000
Winner: Dennis Paulson

That 1991 was to be a year of the big hitter might have been tipped off at the San Miguel Philippine Open. Californian Dennis Paulson, a former U.S. long-driving champion, became just the fifth American winner in the long history of Asia's oldest event when he prevailed in a playoff against the experienced Chen Tze Chung (T.C. Chen when he played in America) at Manila's Valley Golf Club. Paulson needed only a par on the first extra hole for the win as Chen drove into trees and took four the reach the green. It was a bitter disappointment for the Taiwan star, who had been a strong contender the week before in Hong Kong, and forced the playoff at Valley with a fine 66 in the final round after trailing Paulson and Rick Gibson by five after 54 holes. Paulson and Chen finished with seven-under-par 281s.

Gibson and American Tim Fleming led the first day with 70s, then yielded first place to Paulson (71-68) and Chen (72-67) Friday. Gibson shot 71, Fleming 72. Chen appeared to let his chances escape Saturday when he took a 76 as Paulson was shooting 71 and Gibson 69 for their leading 210s. The Canadian, who was to go on to a fine campaign on the Asia Circuit, missed the playoff by two when he bogeyed the last two holes for 73, finishing alone in third place at 283.

Epson Singapore Open—US$400,000
Winner: Jack Kay, Jr.

Jack Kay, Jr. has to like Singapore. The Canadian tied for fourth in the 1990 Singapore Open and came back to pick up all the marbles in 1991. They were valuable marbles, too, worth $66,640 of the Epson Singapore Open's big $400,000 purse. Kay shot a final-round 69 to edge Australian Wayne Riley by two strokes with his 280. Chen Tze Chung endured a third near-miss in a row on the Asia Circuit, finishing third at 283.

Kay and fellow Canadian Rick Gibson finished one-two the first day at Tanah Merah Country Club, Kay opening with a five-under-par 67 and Rick posting 68. The frustrated Chen, playoff loser to Dennis Paulson the previous Sunday, began at Singapore with 69 and took the second-round lead when he duplicated it to go a stroke in front of Kay (72), Gibson (71) and Riley (69).

Riley seized first place with a 71 for 210 Saturday as Chen hurt his chances with 75. Kay shot 72 for 211 and Gibson 73 for 212, where he was tied by American Jim Strickland. In Sunday's finale, Kay took the lead with a birdie at No. 2 and held off the contenders with four more birdies and two bogeys. Riley, plagued by erratic putting, managed just a par round. Chen came back with 70 to finish third at 283 as Gibson shot 75 and slipped to 10th place.

Benson & Hedges Malaysian Open—US$200,000
Winner: Rick Gibson

The door finally opened for Rick Gibson. A solid contender at the two previous Asia Circuit stops, Gibson battled several contenders down the stretch and birdied the last two holes to score a one-stroke victory over Taiwan's Chen Liang Hsi in the Benson & Hedges Malaysian Open at Royal Subang Golf Club at Kuala Lumpur. He birdied from five feet at the 17th and from 18 feet at the 18th for 70 and 277, 11 under par for the distance.

Fellow Canadian Remi Bouchard, the 1989 India Open champion, grabbed the first-round lead with 67 as 15 other players broke 70, Gibson's first-round score. Little-known Kim Jong Duk of Korea, with a pair of 68s, moved in front the second day, but Gibson closed in with 67 and 137. Rick took over Saturday with 70 for 207, but had to share first place with American Gerry Norquist, who shot 67. Another Yankee, Tray Tyner, trailed by only a stroke and, with five holes to play Sunday, led by a stroke. However, he bogeyed three times and dropped to sixth place. Chen shot 68-69-69 the last three rounds to pick off second place at 278, a stroke in front of Norquist, John Morse, the surprise American winner of the 1990 Australian Open, and Park Nam Sin, who closed with 65, the week's low round.

Indonesian Open—US$150,000
Winner: Chen Liang Hsi

Chen Liang Hsi, who came up one stroke short the previous weekend in Malaysia, made sure that it didn't happen again when the Asia Circuit visited Indonesia in early March. The 32-year-old Chen grabbed a three-stroke lead with a six-under-par 66 in the third round of the Indonesian Open and eased home Sunday with a par 72 for a two-shot victory at 277. It was the first win on the circuit for the Taiwanese pro since the 1987 Korea Open.

For two days, the attention fell on one of Chen's prominent countrymen—52-year-old Kuo Chi Hsiung—who won his first two of nine Asia Circuit titles in 1974. Kuo built a four-stroke lead during the first two rounds as he opened with 66 and followed with 69 on the Halim II course at Jakarta. In the runner-up slot at 139 were Americans Jim Strickland and Edward Kirby, Li Wen Sheng and Chen, who had rounds of 69 and 70. However, the senior veteran Kuo was unable to maintain the pace and yielded to Chen's 66 Saturday as he shot 74 and slipped back into a three-way tie for third with Li and Frankie Minoza, the defending champion, at 209, a shot behind Wang Ter Chang. Nobody seriously threatened Chen Sunday, Minoza shooting 70 to take second place at 279 in the first strong showing of 1991 for the 1990 circuit king. Kuo, Li, Wang and American David Toms tied for third.

Wills India Open—US$150,000
Winner: Ali Sher

Circuit history was made and national pride soared as Ali Sher, a former caddie at Delhi Golf Club, sank a birdie putt on Delhi's 18th green that he knows so well, to win the 1991 Wills India Open. No Indian had ever won on the Asia Circuit, nor had any Indian professional ever captured the India Open. Major P.S. Sethi, the redoubtable amateur, won in 1965 before the India Open became a part of the Asia Circuit. So delighted was the club that Ali Sher was immediately given an honorary membership.

The 26-year-old Sher, who had missed the cut in his two previous India Open appearances since turning pro in 1988, made his presence felt Friday, when he made a $5,000 hole-in-one at No. 7 en route to a five-under-par 67 and 138, taking a one-stroke lead over Americans Mark Aebli, a former Asia Circuit winner, and David Tentis and Rigoberto Valasquez of Colombia. Gregory Lesher, the first-round leader with 66, shot his first of three 74s Friday. Heavy overnight rains seemed to stiffen the course Saturday. Ali Sher managed only a 74 and, with K. Nandasena Perera of Sri Lanka, slipped a stroke behind Todd Hamilton of the U.S. and Wang Ter Chang of Taiwan, who had one of the day's best rounds (68) for his 212.

Playing steadily Sunday, Sher caught leader Wang at the 14th and secured the victory when he played two strokes to just off the edge of the green at the par-five 18th, used his putter and almost sank the 60-foot effort. He watched then as Hamilton and Wang played the 18th behind him. Hamilton, needing an eagle to tie, went for the green and put his second in a bunker, while Wang, needing a birdie to tie, laid up with his second and pitched 20 feet short of the hole. He missed and Hamilton got up and down from the sand to share second place at 284 with their 73s.

Thai International Thailand Open—US$150,000
Winner: Suthep Meesamasdi

It was almost as though somebody had scripted the India Open and sent it over to Thailand for a rerun the following week. In an incredible similarity of circumstances and results, Suthep Meesamasdi captured the Thai International Thailand Open.

As it was with Ali Sher at New Delhi, Meesamasdi was the first native Thai professional ever to win his country's national championship or any tournament on the Asia Circuit or elsewhere in the world. As Ali Sher did, Meesamasdi won by a single stroke by making a clutch birdie on the 72nd hole. Suthep faced the birdie-putt pressure on the last hole because Robert Pactolerin, the 1990 Philippine Open winner, had shattered the course record by shooting 62 ahead of him after starting the final round nine strokes off the pace. The birdie gave Meesamasdi a 70 and 272 to Pactolerin's 273.

Meesamasdi's third-round 65 set up the victory. It moved him a stroke into the lead at 202 after his previous rounds of 67 and 70. His closest pursuers then were Tony Maloney of Australia, the second-round leader at 66-67—133, and American Mark Aebli, a three-time winner in Asia in the 1980s, who was in front the first day with 64 and wound up seventh when he closed with 74. Maloney finished third with 71—274.

Sanyang Republic of China Open—US$300,000
Winner: John Jacobs

Seven years after John Jacobs won the China and Dunlop Opens on his way to the tour's overall championship, the rangy American, now 46 and pretty much out of the public eye in recent years, returned to the Taiwan Golf and Country Club at Taipei and won again, giving the big U.S. contingent on the Asia Circuit just its second victory in eight events. This time, Jacobs and Antolin Fernando of the Philippines wound up in a deadlock and Jacobs won on the second extra hole, a par three, when he put his tee shot a foot from the hole. In tough conditions, Jacobs shot 75 and Fernando 74 Sunday for 285s, the highest winning score of the season but usual for the China Open.

Fernando shared the first-round lead at 68 with little-known Yeh Chang Ming of Taiwan, as Jacobs began with 73. However, Jacobs jumped into the lead with a 67 Friday, his 140 putting him two in front of Fernando and three ahead of Tom Pernice. Fernando chipped a shot off the American's lead Saturday with a 69 to Jacobs' 70. The nearest other contenders were three strokes behind Fernando and were not factors Sunday, even with the high scores posted by the playoff participants. Veteran Kuo Chi Hsiung, a three-time winner of the tournament at the end of the 1970s, closed with two par rounds on the weekend to take third place at 288, a stroke ahead of Aaron Meeks.

Maekyung (Korea) Open—US$300,000
Winner: Choi Sang Ho

The year of home country winners continued at the ninth stop on the Asia Circuit when Choi Sang Ho, a frequent contender but never a winner on the tour, finally captured his nation's national championship at Nam Seoul Country Club. Thus, he followed in the footsteps of India's Ali Sher and Thailand's Suthep Meesamasdi, who also won the national titles of their countries earlier in the season.

Choi had a tough fight on his hands in the person of China's Hsieh Chin Hsing in Sunday's final round. The 36-year-old Korean had started the tournament five behind leader Park Jung Woong's 69, then closed in on first place Friday with 67—141, placing himself just a stroke behind countryman Park Nam Sin (71-69—140). With 69 Saturday, Choi advanced a stroke in front of Park and three ahead of Hsieh, the 1990 runner-up in Seoul. The Taiwanese pro took the lead with birdies at the 14th and 15th holes Sunday, but Choi climbed back into a tie when he eagled the par-five 16th. That seemed to jolt Hsieh, who bogeyed the last two holes as Choi parred in to the long-awaited win. Rick Gibson, the points leader for the circuit title, added to his total with a 10th-place finish.

Daiichi Fudosan Cup—¥100,000,000
Winner: Saburo Fujiki

The second edition of the Daiichi Fudosan Cup as the opening official tournament on the Japan Tour almost became a duplicate of the inaugural as Australian Brian Jones made a strong run at a repeat victory in the well-endowed event that drew a top-flight field. However, Jones could not cope with the splendid 65 mustered by Saburo Fujiki Sunday and yielded the title to him by a stroke at the Hibiscus Golf Club at Sadoharacho. Fujiki finished with a 17-under-par 271, Jones with a closing 68 at 272. It was a six-stroke gap to Roger Mackay and Toru Nakamura in third place.

Jones took the lead Friday from Harumitsu Hamano, who was in front of five other players with his opening 67, the product of a bogey at the second hole and six subsequent birdies. Jones and Fujiki were among the 68 shooters. Jones, a regular and frequent winner on the Japan Tour over the years, moved ahead by a stroke Friday but bogeyed the last two holes for his 68. Mackay and Kiyoshi Murota were second at 137. Fujiki advanced into the runner-up slot Saturday as Jones widened his margin to two with his third straight 68 for 204. Saburo had a 67, the day's best score. He continued to roll from the start when he made his first of seven birdies at No. 1, caught Jones at the 12th and made his final birdie at the 18th to nail the victory.

Imperial Tournament—¥65,000,000
Winner: Yutaka Hagawa

It had been so long, one could understand the trouble Yutaka Hagawa had in finishing off his victory in the Imperial Tournament. Left-hander Hagawa, who was being touted as the next Bob Charles in the early 1980s, particularly after he won the 1981 Japan Open, had not won since 1983 and only occasionally had even been in contention. Hence, he came up with a shaky final round after shooting a third-round 66 to share first place at 208 with Naomichi Ozaki, one of the leading pros in Japan.

Fortunately for Hagawa, Ozaki also had Sunday problems and nobody else started the day close enough to cause trouble. Hagawa shot 74, two over par at the Seve Ballesteros Golf Club at Sakuragawamura, and Ozaki 75 and still finished well ahead of third-place finisher Tsukasa Watanabe, even though he had a 67. Ozaki, a three-time winner in 1990 with 14 titles overall on his record, and Hagawa were the main figures in the tournament from the start. Both opened with 70s to lead, then Ozaki moved into a three-stroke lead Friday with 68—138 as Yutaka shot 72 and slipped to third place at 142, a stroke behind Kiyoshi Murota. The third-round tie was forged when Hagawa came up with his 66 and Ozaki had 70.

Daido Shizuoka Open—¥80,000,000
Winner: Yutaka Hagawa

Yutaka Hagawa didn't wait as long as he had before winning the 1991 Imperial Tournament. After going eight years without a victory prior to the Imperial triumph, Hagawa came back the following week with a decisive win in the Daido Shizuoka Open, the 20-year-old event at Shizuoka Country Club that has an impressive roster of champions. The 34-year-old Hagawa came from a stroke off the lead with a final-round 67 and his 278 was just enough to edge Noboru Sugai, who soared from 19th place to second with a blazing 63 for 279.

Hideki Kase commanded the field the first two days. He opened with 66 to lead Tsuneyuki Nakajima by a stroke and followed with 73 to remain on top at 139, a shot ahead of Britain's Paul Hoad, as Nakajima fell back with a 76. Hagawa, with a 70-72 start, was just three back and he moved closer Saturday as veteran Isao Aoki, with 69, and Hiroshi Makino, with 68, claimed the lead at 210. Hagawa's 69 put him at 211 and Pete Izumikawa advanced to 212 with 66, the day's best score. Aoki and Makino spun their wheels with 72s Sunday and dropped to eighth place as Hagawa landed his fifth Japan Tour title.

Taylormade KSB Open—¥60,000,000
Winner: Masanobu Kimura

After going more than three years without a victory, Masanobu Kimura might be expected to be conservative as a contender in the Taylormade KSB Open with the holes running out. Instead, Kimura made sure of the win by going after birdies and getting them on the last three holes. That strong finish gave him a 69, a 15-under-par 273 and a three-stroke victory over the amazing senior, Teruo Sugihara, and Nobuo Serizawa at Shido Country Club in Shidocho. Kimura had scored the only previous victory of his nine-year career on the Japan Tour in the 1987 Kansai Open.

The winner carried a two-stroke lead into the final day after rounds of 69, 66 and 69 for 204, at which point he led Serizawa by two, Yoshinori Mizumaki by three and Sugihara by four. The 53-year-old Sugihara, who has compiled an astonishing 59 victories during his long career, opened the tournament with an eight-under-par 64 for a two-stroke lead over Serizawa, who duplicated his 66 Friday and went three shots in front of Kimura and Noboru Sugai. Sugihara's par 72 left him four back. Kimura moved up Saturday and set up his strong finish during the early going Sunday.

Pocari Sweat Open—¥45,000,000
Winner: Ryoken Kawagishi

They could have been father and son teeing off in the final round as co-leaders of the Pocari Sweat Open at Daiwacho's Hakuryuko Country Club— 24-year-old Ryoken Kawagishi, the highly touted young pro, and 53-year-old Teruo Sugihara, the enduring veteran in another promising bid for his

60th victory on the Japan Tour. Sugihara was not up to the challenge that Sunday as Kawagishi, a three-time winner in his rookie 1990 season, turned the final round into a runaway. He fired a five-under-par 66 for 199 and a four-stroke victory over Hiroshi Makino. Sugihara shot 71 and dropped into a tie for third at 204 with Tsukasa Watanabe, Tomohiro Maruyama, Brian Jones and Kiyoshi Murota.

Kawagishi was never out of the lead at Hakuryuko. He launched his successful victory bid with a 67 Thursday, sharing the lead with Yoshinori Kaneko and Maruyama. Sugihara produced his second 64 in two weeks to overtake Kawagishi Friday at 133. Kawagishi had a 66. Heavy rains came to the Hiroshima area Saturday, washing out the round and shortening the tournament to 54 holes. Kawagishi ran off six birdies and took a lone bogey at the final hole.

Bridgestone Aso Open—¥50,000,000
Winner: Kiyoshi Murota

Kiyoshi Murota's victory in the Bridgestone Aso Open hardly could be considered unlikely. Murota had been operating in the higher strata of competition throughout the early season in Japan and was coming off a tie for third in the previous week's Pocari Sweat Open when he scored his first tour victory at Aso Golf Club with a six-under-par 208 in the rain-abbreviated tournament. He won by two over Taisei Inagaki, another non-winner.

Murota was one of seven pros who blanketed first place with 68s when the tournament finally got underway Friday after rainy weather, which also shortened the Pocari Sweat Open the previous week, wiped out the scheduled Thursday start at Aso. Sharing the lead with him were David Ishii, Tomohiro Maruyama, Seiki Okuda, Kinpachi Yoshimura, Hiroshi Gouda and Shigeru Namiki. Things thinned out Saturday as Okuda shot 69 to lead at 137, a shot ahead of Yoshinori Kaneko and Yoshimura and two in front of Murota and Isamu Sugita. Murota got his opening when Okuda couldn't keep up the pace and eventually shot 74. Murota matched his opening-round 68 for the 208. Inagaki shot 69 for his 210 and Okuda dropped into a tie for third with Sugita and Noboru Sugai at 211.

Dunlop Open—¥100,000,000
Winner: Roger Mackay

The Dunlop Open, as usual, produced two winners. Australian Roger Mackay, bad back and all, shot the week's best score at Ibaraki Golf Club in the seventh stop on the Japan Tour and captured his third title in Nippon. Meanwhile, Canadian Rick Gibson was posting a 10th-best score, but it made him the other winner as the champion of the Asia Circuit for 1991.

Mackay, playing the Japan Tour as a regular, held off the challenge of the venerable Teruo Sugihara to score a two-stroke victory with his 16-under-par 272 total. The Dunlop Open is also the concluding event on the 10-tournament Asia Circuit and Gibson clinched that season's No. 1 spot, needing only to play 72 holes at Ibaraki to do so because of the big lead he carried into the event, since Taiwan's Chen Liang Hsi, in second place, had to win the Dunlop to have a shot at the title, its $37,500 cash prize and exemptions for the British Open and Memorial Tournament in the U.S.

Mackay, who had pulled out of the previous week's Bridgestone Aso Open because of an aching back, nearly had to do so again after the second round of the Dunlop, even though he had just tied Naomichi Ozaki and Hideto Shigenobu for the lead at 136. However, successful treatment after the round kept him going and, in a rare circumstance, he, Ozaki and Shigenobu all shot 68s Saturday to maintain their positions atop the standings going into the final round.

Mackay had chipped in at the final green for his 68 and he repeated the feat there Sunday to secure his victory. Ozaki and Shigenobu fell back in the early going and Mackay moved three strokes in front with a birdie at the 14th hole. However, he bogeyed the 15th and 17th holes before holing his 45-foot chip, knowing he needed a par to avoid a playoff with Sugihara, already in with 274 after a 65 he fashioned with 23 putts, holing at least 10 from long range. Seve Ballesteros, in Japan for two weeks, finished third with a final 66 and 274.

Chunichi Crowns—¥120,000,000
Winner: Seve Ballesteros

Seve Ballesteros had a plane to catch, so he went boldly for the cup with his 20-foot birdie putt at the conclusion of the rich Chunichi Crowns tournament at Nagoya Golf Club. In it went and Ballesteros edged Roger Mackay by that stroke to post his sixth career victory in Japan, and his first since the Pacific Masters in 1988. It gave him a 69 and 275, cutting off Mackay's bid for two consecutive wins on the Japan Tour. Mackay, winner of the previous week's Dunlop Open, fired a closing 65 and was in the clubhouse with 276 before Ballesteros reached the final green and holed the clutch putt for his 61st career victory and first in more than a year.

In typical fashion, Ballesteros had been hot and cold in the earlier rounds. After opening with 67, trailing only Yoshimi Niizeki, the Spanish great skied to 75 Friday and fell four shots off the pace of Isao Aoki, who had the likes of Naomichi Ozaki, Tsuneyuki Nakajima and Australia's Mike Harwood right behind. However, Ballesteros rebounded Saturday with a six-under-par 64 for 206 and jumped a stroke ahead of Yoshikazu Yokoshima, two in front of Nakajima. At that point, Mackay was five back at 211. He became Ballesteros' challenger Sunday and watched helplessly as the Spaniard's birdie putt dropped at the 18th. Tatsuya Shiraishi also shot 65 Sunday and finished third at 278.

Fuji Sankei Classic—¥87,500,000
Winner: Saburo Fujiki

The season's first playoff decided the Fuji Sankei Classic winner and it was a bizarre one, to say the least. In the first place, it involved four players— Saburo Fujiki, Isao Aoki, Hideki Kase and Brian Jones. In the second place, all four men bogeyed the first playoff hole—the par-four 18th. Finally, as

Fujiki won it for his second 1991 victory with a masterful tee shot a foot from the hole, the great Aoki was taking another bogey and the other two surrendered without reaching the green after two tries each.

Australian Jones had the lead for two days. He opened with 65, one-putting 11 greens at the resort Kawana Hotel Golf Club's Fuji seaside links, then followed with 71 Friday to share the top spot with Koichi Suzuki, who shot 70-66 for his 136 and got a big boost with an eagle chip-in at No. 4. Fujiki was a stroke behind after rounds of 69 and 68. Scoring soared Saturday and Suzuki opened a two-stroke lead with his one-over-par 72. Jones slipped to 74 and Suzuki, with his 72, moved into second place, offsetting three early birdies with four bogeys later in the round. Another 72 Sunday did Suzuki in and Fujiki's 70 was just enough to put him in the playoff as Jones came back with 69, Kase shot 67 and Aoki a brilliant 64 to match his 279.

Japan Match Play Championship—¥50,000,000
Winner: Satoshi Higashi

Just about everything favored Tsuneyuki Nakajima in the final of the Japan Match Play Championship. He is a major star on the Japan Tour with 44 victories on his record, had won the Match Play in 1983 and 1986 and was coming off an 8-and-7 rout of Hideki Kase in the semi-finals. Satoshi Higashi, on the other hand, was playing in the Match Play for the first time, had just two victories to his credit and had a far tougher time beating Tsukasa Watanabe in the other semi-final clash. So, of course, Higashi won the championship, scoring a 2-up victory in the 36-hole title match at the Shinyo Country Club.

Nakajima, a three-time winner in 1990 but winless to that point in 1991, led most of the way against Higashi after chipping in at the second hole for an eagle to go one up. He retained that margin through the first 18 holes, and went two up on the first hole after lunch. Satoshi got a hole back at No. 2 with an almost-identical, chip-in birdie to that of Nakajima at the same hole in the morning and evened the match at the 30th hole. He finally gained the lead with a birdie at the 33rd and made it a 2-up victory with a conceded birdie at the final hole.

Higashi's advance to the semi-finals included victories over Seiichi Kanai, 1 up; Naomichi Ozaki, 3 and 2, and Nobuo Serizawa, 4 and 3. Nakajima's wins leading up to that point were over Tsuyoshi Yoneyama, 1 up at the 19th hole; Shigeru Kawamata, 5 and 3, and Masanobu Kimura, 3 and 1.

Pepsi Ube Kosan—¥80,000,000
Winner: Chen Tze Chung

Even though the only player from Taiwan ever to win on the U.S. PGA Tour, Chen Tze Chung had never compiled a particularly impressive record in Asia—three victories dating back 10 years, the last one in the Dunlop Open in 1985. Still, he was a frequent contender over the seasons and earlier in 1991 had two near-misses on the Asia Circuit. Finally, Chen landed his first championship since his American victory at Los Angeles in 1987, coming from six strokes off the pace in the final round of the Pepsi Ube to register a two-shot victory with a 10-under-par 274.

Par took a beating in the opening round over the West course at Ube Country Club as 34 players shot 70 or better on the par-71 course, Tadami Ueno and Kiyoshi Maita showing the way with 65s. Hiroshi Makino had 66 Friday and took the lead with his 135, two strokes ahead of Naomichi Ozaki, David Ishii, Masahiro Shiota and Ueno. Enter Saburo Fujiki, already a two-time winner in 1991, with a record-shattering 61 to take a three-stroke lead at 203. Fujiki ran off 11 birdies and took his lone bogey at the 14th after racking up five birdies in a row. Chen shot 66 and rested in fifth place behind Makino (206), Shiota (207) and Hikaru Emoto (208) before his big move Sunday, when he shot a one-bogey 65 for 274, whipping past Fujiki, who faltered with 73 and dropped into second place at 276.

Mitsubishi Galant—¥85,000,000
Winner: Koichi Suzuki

Isao Aoki charged, Tsuneyuki Nakajima spun his wheels and Koichi Suzuki outplayed his two more successful compatriots in the stretch to win the Mitsubishi Galant the first weekend of June. Suzuki shrugged off the shock of a three-putt double bogey and slipped in a stroke in front of Nakajima and Aoki to scored his seventh victory in 16 years of campaigning on the Japan Tour. He followed the jolt at the 12th with three birdies on the last five holes for 68 and an eight-under-par 280 at Noto Country Club in Oshimizumachi as Aoki raced home with 65 and Nakajima managed just 70 for a pair of 281s. It was the second time in three weeks that Nakajima came up just short in his bid for a 1991 victory.

Takeru Shibata had his moment in the sun Thursday when he opened the Mitsubishi Galant with 68 for the lead, a shot in front of Tateo Ozaki, Rick Gibson, Hiroshi Makino, Joji Furuki and Takumi Horiuchi. With 72-67—139, Nakajima vaulted into the lead Friday, a stroke ahead of Gibson, the Asia Circuit champion. Makino and Yoshinori Mizumaki joined Nakajima on top at 211 Saturday, Makino shooting 67, the day's best, and Mizumaki sporting an eagle in his 68. Koichi and Katsunari Takahashi were at 212 and Aoki was a distant 216 before launching his sizzling bid Sunday that reached 65 when he eagled the 18th.

JCB Sendai Classic—¥70,000,000
Winner: Tadami Ueno

Because Tadami Ueno's record is deceptive on its surface, the 42-year-old pro's victory in the JCB Sendai Classic in early June was particularly gratifying for him. Before the Sendai Classic, Ueno had registered five victories, more than most players achieve in a career, but the catch is that all five came in the Chushikoku Open, one of the six regional tournaments played during a single week in late summer, obviously with diluted fields. With his one-stroke victory in the Sendai at Zao Kokusai Golf Club at Shibatamachi, he finally captured a title after 19 years in a tournament in which he was competing against a normal, full Japan Tour field.

Ueno's success overshadowed another disappointing finish for Tsuneyuki Nakajima, who had come up short at the end of two of the three previous circuit tournaments. Nakajima had entered the final round at 203, the leader by a stroke over Ueno, Yutaka Hagawa, Graham Marsh and Hiroshi Makino, and remained in front through the first 14 holes. But, bogeys at the 15th and 18th holes for 71 dropped him into an eventual tie for fourth at 274. Ueno had started badly with bogeys at the first and third holes, then gathered himself together and got back into contention with birdies on the next three holes. Three more on the back nine produced a 67 and 271, just enough to edge Marsh, the 47-year-old Australian who has 25 Japanese victories on his record. Hagawa, with 69—273, finished third and Koichi Suzuki, with 69, tied Nakajima for fourth, while Makino, who had shares of the lead the first two days, finished sixth with 71—275.

Sapporo Tokyu Open—¥60,000,000
Winner: Rick Gibson

In normal circumstances, Rick Gibson would have been competing on the low-key national tour in his native Canada at the time of the Sapporo Tokyu Open in Japan. But, 1991 was not a normal year for the 29-year-old pro from Vancouver. As the champion of the 1991 Asia Circuit via its point system, Gibson was eligible to play on the Japan Tour. The Sapporo Tokyu was his fourth start and he won it in a three-way playoff against veteran Japanese pros Masahiro Kuramoto and Shinsaku Maeda with an eight-foot birdie putt on the first extra hole. The win complemented his March victory in the Benson & Hedges Malaysian Open.

Gibson, Kuramoto and Maeda emerged from a large group of contenders led into the final round on the Shimamtsu course at Sapporo Kokusai Country Club by Chen Tze Ming, the Taiwanese veteran and seven-time winner in Japan, who built a one-stroke, 54-hole lead with rounds of 70-69-68 and missed the playoff by the same single-shot margin Sunday. Among those contenders was Tadami Ueno, who came off his victory the previous Sunday in the JCB Sendai Classic with a first-round 68 and a share of the first-round lead at Sapporo with Yoshimi Niizeki and Shinji Ikeuchi. Niizeki led after 36 holes with 138 and trailed Chen by a stroke going into the final round. Gibson, with a four-birdie 70, and Kuramoto and Maeda, with 71s, passed them both Sunday and forged the playoff for the par-five 18th hole. Maeda parred and Kuramoto bogeyed before Gibson rolled in his winning putt.

Yomiuri Sapporo Beer Open—¥80,000,000
Winner: Tsuneyuki Nakajima

Tsuneyuki Nakajima found a way to get his first 1991 victory into the books after several failed attempts in previous weeks of late spring. He shot himself so far in front over the first 54 holes that even a lapse or two in steady rain in Sunday's final round of the Yomiuri Sapporo Beer Open did little serious harm. He won by three strokes over Rick Gibson, the Canadian winner of the previous week's Sapporo Tokyu event, with a 16-under-par 272 on the Yomiuri Country Club's Member Course at Nishinomiya. His second Yomiuri Sapporo Beer victory gave the Japanese star No. 35 for his victory log.

Nakajima was never out of the lead at Yomiuri. His opening 65 put him in a first-place tie with Katsuji Hasegawa. Then, when he repeated the 65 Friday, he spurted six strokes into the lead over Naomichi Ozaki, Shigeru Namiki and Hasegawa, who slipped to 71 for his 136. Nakajima gave up a stroke of his lead when he shot 71 Saturday, Ozaki and Toru Nakamura moving into the runner-up slot and Gibson moving up to 207. Nakajima was on his way to a major rout Sunday when he birdied the first, second and eighth holes to go 18 under par. However, he became a bit erratic on the back nine, bogeyed the 12th and double-bogeyed the 15th, enabling Gibson to move within two strokes of him. Tsuneyuki then iced it with a final birdie at the par-three 17th from 10 feet for 71 again and the 272 total. Gibson shot 68 for 275 and nobody else was closer than 278.

Mizuno Open—¥52,500,000
Winner: Roger Mackay

Roger Mackay kept the Mizuno Open title "in the family" when he added it to his earlier victory of the Japan Tour season in the Dunlop Open. Mackay succeeded fellow Australian Brian Jones as the Mizuno champion, winning the rain-shortened tournament on the first hole of a playoff against Satoshi Higashi at Tokinodai Country Club at Hakui. The two had tied at the end of the final round (54 holes) Sunday with nine-under-par 207s, then Mackay won with a par on the first extra hole as Higashi bunkered his approach at the par-four 18th and missed a 12-foot par putt.

The finish was anything but routine. Mackay, carrying a one-stroke lead, double-bogeyed the par-three 17th when he hooked his tee shot into trouble, then regained a tie at the 18th with a 24-foot birdie putt. The Australian led the tournament from the start, opening with a six-under-par 66 and a three-shot advantage over six players at 69. Even though he bogeyed the last two holes Friday, he remained in front with 70 for 136. Little-known Nichito Hashimoto shot 67 for 138 and second place, a stroke in front of Isao Aoki, Masahiro Kuramoto and Higashi, the reigning Match Play champion. Higashi was the only serious challenger to Mackay Sunday, shooting 68 to Roger's 71 to achieve the deadlock and get the playoff chance.

Takeda Cup—¥100,000,000
Winner: Harumitsu Hamano

Harumitsu Hamano picked an excellent time to score his first victory on the Japan Tour after nine years of trying. His win came in the new Takeda Cup, a new event on the circuit and, with its ¥100,000,000 purse, the richest since the Chunichi Crowns in early May. Hamano faced off the pressure of Masashi (Jumbo) Ozaki and posted a four-stroke victory at Gurenmoa Country Club at Sakaemachi, Chiba Prefecture.

The 33-year-old Hamano, who began the tournament Thursday with 65, a shot behind leader Seiji Ebihara, went in front to stay Friday with 67—132, jumping four strokes ahead of Ebihara and Yoshinori Kaneko in the runner-up position. His margin dwindled to two when he shot 70 Saturday. Yoshiyuki Isomura gained second place with his 204 and Ozaki moved into third place with 67—205. With an adventurous front nine—five birdies, two bogeys, two pars—of 33, Ozaki grabbed a one-stroke lead, but Hamano fought back, regained first place with a birdie at the 13th and gained his big final margin unexpectedly when Ozaki triple-bogeyed the last hole for 72 at 277. Hamano shot 71 for his 273 and the long-sought victory. Isomura faded to 75, but still finished third at 279.

Yonex Open Hiroshima—¥70,000,000
Winner: Eiichi Itai

Eiichi Itai must have liked what happened in the Takeda Cup tournament the previous week—a first-time victory for Harumitsu Hamano. Himself a non-winner on the Japan Tour at age 40, Itai took inspiration from Hamano's win and finally broke the ice in the Yonex Open Hiroshima, finishing with a blistering, six-under-par 65 to stake himself to a two-stroke victory with his 272.

Itai was close all week at Hiroshima Country Club but never had the lead until the final round was well underway. Yukio Noguchi shot a 29 on the back nine Thursday en route to 65 and the first-round lead, by two over Itai, Ikuo Shirahama and Satoshi Higashi. Noguchi followed with 68 Friday and remained in front, by one over Yoshinori Mizumaki and two over Itai and Tsuyoshi Yoneyama. Noguchi tumbled to 74 and out of contention Saturday, opening the way for Mizumaki to claim the lead with his 69—203. Yoneyama was second at 205, Shinsaku Maeda third at 206 and Itai four back with Noguchi at 207. In his victory surge Sunday, Itai had an eagle, five birdies and a bogey on the 6,635-yard Hiroshima course. Mizumaki and Yoneyama tied for second at 274.

Nikkei Cup—¥80,000,000
Winner: Naomichi Ozaki

Eiichi Itai made a strong bid to make it two in a row the week after his maiden victory in the Yonex Open at Hiroshima. Instead he was a faltering playoff victim in the late July Nikkei Cup tournament as Naomichi Ozaki finally shifted into the right gear and began the run that would bring him the money-winning championship of the 1991 Japan Tour. With some unintended help from Itai, Ozaki gained a tie Sunday in the rain-shortened tournament at Yasu Kogen Country Club at Yasu and won the playoff on the first extra hole.

Itai had a second victory within reach Sunday, but he double-bogeyed the final hole and wound up in the deadlock at 203 when Ozaki followed with a bogey there. That sent them into the playoff and Itai promptly ruined his chances when he drove into the woods and wound up with another double bogey, enabling the 35-year-old Ozaki to take the win with a bogey. Yoshitaka Yamamoto was very much in the picture the first two rounds. He opened with 64 and the lead Thursday and shared first place Friday with Ozaki at 133. He had 69 and Ozaki followed an opening 67 with 66. Itai, who had begun with 70, tacked on a fine 65 Friday and went into the final round two strokes off the pace. Yamamoto lost his game Sunday and Itai made up the two shots with a 68 to Ozaki's 70.

NST Niigata Open—¥60,000,000
Winner: Akihito Yokoyama

For the third time in four tournaments on the Japan Tour, a stranger to victory spoils enjoyed them as Akihito Yokoyama scored a two-stroke victory in the NST Niigata Open at Jyoetu Kokusai Country Club at Tokamachi. Unlike Harumitsu Hamano (Takeda Cup) and Eiichi Itai (Yonex Hiroshima), Akihito Yokoyama had won before, but it had been three years earlier and the victory came in the Kanto Open during the week in late summer when the circuit splinters six ways for regional events.

Yokoyama gave no hint of victory in the opening round. He shot 73 and was six strokes off the pace of Koichi Suzuki and Yukio Noguchi. Then on Friday, he shot 67 and moved into contention at 138, two strokes behind leaders Seiji Ebihara, Hideki Kase and Katsuji Hasegawa. Suzuki regained the lead Saturday with 68 for 207 as Yokoyama remained two back with five others, including the three Friday leaders, Pete Izumikawa and Hideto Shigenobu. When Suzuki slipped to 73 Sunday, Yokoyama took advantage, carding four birdies and a bogey for 69 and a 10-under-par total of 278. Suzuki tied for second with Hideki Kase.

Japan PGA Championship—¥100,000,000
Winner: Masashi Ozaki

Perhaps it was the prestige of the Japan PGA Championship that inspired Masashi (Jumbo) Ozaki to his long-overdue first victory of the 1991 Japan Tour season following three years as No. 1 on the money list and winner of 17 tournaments or the desire to keep up with younger brother Naomichi, who had just won his first 1991 title two weeks earlier. Whatever, Ozaki showed why he has been the country's leading player since 1988 by destroying the opposition with a final-round, 11-under-par 61 (equalling the year's and tour's best) that gave him a six-stroke victory at, ironically, Prestige Country Club at Azusamachi. It was his fourth Japan PGA Championship dating back 20 years and the 69th victory of his brilliant career.

For three days at Prestige, attention focused on, first, brother Naomichi and lightly regarded Shigenori Mori. The younger Ozaki opened with 67, leading Chen Tze Chung and Yoshikazu Yokoshima by a stroke. Then, Mori roared from 67th place to the top Friday with 63, one of the few other low scores of the week. The 33-year-old pro, winless in seven seasons on the circuit, wedged in for an eagle and had seven birdies for his 137 and one-shot lead over Yokoshima. He barely hung on to first place Saturday with his par 72, at 209 one in front of Naomichi Ozaki, Yokoshima and Tsukasa Watanabe. Meanwhile, Jumbo Ozaki had moved into contention with 68 after his mediocre 71-73 start and played "perfect golf" on Sunday, running up nine birdies before capping the great round with a 20-foot eagle putt. He won so decisively that, besides runner-up Watanabe at 279, nobody was closer than nine back—six men at 282.

Maruman Open—¥100,000,000
Winner: Tetsu Nishikawa

A monstrous birdie putt three holes into a playoff prevented Tateo (Jet) Ozaki from joining his two brothers in the 1991 Japan Tour winners' circle within a four-week span in late summer. The putt, described in news reports as being 103 feet long, gave the Maruman Open title to Tetsu Nishikawa, an undistinguished fourth-year pro better known as the son of famous Japanese singer Midori Satsuki than for his golf. The victory at Hatoyama Country Club made him just the fourth first-time winner of the 1991 season in Japan.

   The Maruman moved up a step in class in 1991 with the entry of Ian Woosnam, the Sony Ranking's No. 1 player in the world and a member of the Maruman golf staff. The Welshman showed the fans a bit of his skill when he produced a second-round 66 and shared the lead at 137 with Yoshinori Kaneko, Hiroya Kamide and Toshiaki Nakagawa, who led the first day with 67. Woosnam shot 71 Saturday on his way to a fifth-place finish as Nishikawa bolted in front with 66 for 204, a shot ahead of Kaneko and two in front of Tateo Ozaki, who also had a 66. Tateo followed with 68 Sunday to overtake Nishikawa, who shot 70 for his 14-under-par 274 and the tie. Tetsu ended the playoff three holes later with the startling putt from another continent.

Daiwa KBC Augusta Open—¥100,000,000
Winner: Raymond Floyd

The home country forces had things pretty much to themselves all summer on the Japan Tour. That ended, at least briefly, when American star Raymond Floyd, the Ryder Cup player and former captain, came over for the Daiwa KBC Augusta Open at the end of August and scored his first-ever victory in Japan and only win of the year.

   Floyd, who has four U.S. majors among his 27 career victories, started strongly with 66 at Kyushu Shima Country Club which gave him a share of first place with Frankie Minoza of the Philippines, another visitor for the tournament. On Friday, Raymond shot his first of three 69s for 135 and retained a piece of the lead, then with Canadian Brent Franklin, who opened with 68-67. Minoza, with 70, slipped a stroke behind, where he was joined by Dan Forsman, the other U.S. Tour winner in the field.

   Floyd inched a shot in front with his second 69 Saturday. Forsman matched it to take over second place, two ahead of Minoza. Although not making enough birdies to break it open, Floyd played bogey-less golf Sunday and his 69 for a 15-under-par 273 was just enough to edge Minoza, the 1990 Asia Circuit champion, who closed with a 67 for 274. Forsman managed just a par round Sunday for 277, two better than the total of Japanese great Isao Aoki, who turned 49 during the tournament. Franklin, Jumbo Ozaki and ageless Teruo Sugihara were among the 280 shooters.

Kansai Open—¥20,000,000
Winner: Toshikazu Sugihara

Kanto Open—¥22,500,000
Winner:Yoshinori Kaneko

Chubu Open—¥20,000,000
Winner: Teruo Nakamura

Hokkaido Open—¥10,000,000
Winner: Katsunari Takahashi

Chusikoku Open—¥20,000,000
Winner: Kosei Miyata

Kyushu Open—¥20,000,000
Winner: Kinpachi Yoshimura

The Japan Tour took its usual one-week break from national competition the first weekend of September with many of the circuit regulars playing in the six regional events.

Toshikazu Sugihara edged namesake Teruo Sugihara, the defending champion and 10-time winner, by a stroke with his 283 in the Kansai (Western Japan) Open, while Yoshinori Kaneko shot a final-round 64 for 202 to win the rain-shortened Kanto (Eastern Japan) Open by five strokes over Yonex Open Hiroshima winner Eiichi Itai. Teruo Nakamura shot 279 and won the Chubu Open by seven; Katsunari Takahashi won his fourth Hokkaido Open with 281, a three-stroke victory; Kosei Miyata took the Chushikoku Open by three strokes with 284 despite a closing 77, and Kinpachi Yoshimura had only one sub-par round in capturing the Kyushu Open with 290.

Suntory Open—¥100,000,000
Winner: Naomichi Ozaki

Naomichi (Joe) Ozaki added another achievement to the list of his family's feats when he won the Suntory Open in mid-September. All three Ozaki brothers have now won the Suntory, Masashi back in 1974 and Tateo twice in the 1980s. In the thick of things from the start, Naomichi birdied two of the last four holes at Inzai's Narashino Country Club for 68 and a two-stroke win with his 12-under-par 276. It was the second of the season and 19th career victory for the 35-year-old pro, youngest of the three brothers.

Naomichi was one back the first day when he shot 67 as Yoshinori Mizumaki, Akiyoshi Omachi and Hiromichi Namiki posted 66s. A 69 Friday moved Ozaki into a first-place tie with American Larry Nelson, the 1989 Suntory winner, who shot a pair of 68s. Mizumaki slipped into second place at 137 with Chen Tze Chung, the Pepsi Ube victor in May.

Chen and Canadian Brent Franklin were the new leaders after Saturday's round, Franklin shooting 69 and Chen 70 for their 207. Ozaki, with 72, trailed by a stroke. By the turn Sunday, the issue was down to three players. After the 14th hole, Ozaki and Chen were tied for the lead with Franklin just a stroke back. Then, Naomichi made sizeable birdie putts at the next two holes to seize the lead for keeps. Chen shot 71 for 278 and Franklin 73 for

280 and third place. Interestingly, Jumbo and Jet Ozaki tied for seventh. Nelson faded badly in the last two rounds, his 75-77 dropping him into a 10-way tie for 15th place.

All Nippon Airways Open—¥100,000,000
Winner: Akiyoshi Omachi

Akiyoshi Omachi ended a two-year victory drought, holding off a strong field of international players, including Bernhard Langer and Mark O'Meara, to score a two-stroke victory with his closing 71 and total of 282, six under par on the Wattsu course at Sapporo Golf Club. Akiyoshi, who took an unsuccessful run at the U.S. Tour several years earlier, had last won in Japan in the 1989 Japan Series.

Omachi, 32, joined an impressive array atop the scoreboard at the end of the first round when he shot 68, as did Tsuneyuki Nakajima, Teruo Sugihara, Ryoken Kawagishi and Masahiro Shioda, with Joe and Jumbo Ozaki among seven 69 shooters. The scoring rose noticeably Friday as journeyman Pete Izumikawa shot one of the day's two rounds in the 60s—68—and took the lead at 138, a shot in front of Omachi (71—139) and two ahead of Satoshi Higashi, the other 68 shooter.

Omachi was the man the rest of the way. His par 72 on a rugged Saturday, when scores went even higher than Friday, was enough to give him a two-stroke lead over Kawagishi and Izumikawa, who took a 75. Omachi never let his margin slip Sunday as both he and Kawagishi shot 71s for a one-two finish, Akiyoshi at 282, Ryoken at 284. Nakajima was third at 286, the only other player to break par. O'Meara and Langer tied for seventh at 289.

Jun Classic—¥110,000,000
Winner: Masashi Ozaki

Ryoken (Ricky) Kawagishi had to figure the odds were stacked against him as he battled Masashi (Jumbo) Ozaki for the Jun Classic title; that is, if he had any knowledge of the history of the 15-year-old tournament. Except for one interruption in 1988, the Jun crown had wound up in the hands of an Ozaki every year since 1986 and there was Kawagishi toward the end of the day coming from nine strokes off the lead and overtaking Jumbo Ozaki with a blazing 64 finish. The 24-year-old might have known that Ozaki would beat him in the subsequent playoff, which he did with an eight-foot par on the first extra hole. Now, the record book on the Jun Classic shows Jumbo Ozaki with four wins, Jet and Joe with one apiece.

For three days, Yutaka Hagawa seemed the likely winner. Hagawa shared the first-round lead at 67 with Chen Tze Chung and Roger Mackay and improved his position each of the next two rounds. He shot 68 for 135 Friday, moving a stroke in front of Taisei Inagaki and two ahead of Ozaki. He widened the margin to three Saturday with 69 for 204, but his closest pursuer, ominously, was Ozaki. Kawagishi was out of sight at 213. As Hagawa was plunging to a 75, Ozaki was producing an up-and-down round of 70 with six birdies, two bogeys and a double bogey, while Kawagishi was running off nine birdies and a bogey for his 64 to force the playoff. His loss in overtime made him a runner-up for the second week in a row.

Tokai Classic—¥100,000,000
Winner: Eiichi Itai

Eiichi Itai, who got his first taste of victory on the Japan Tour in July, liked it so much that he sampled it again in early October in the Tokai Classic, this time as a front-runner winning going away. Itai seized the lead with a second-round 65 at Miyoshi Country Club to take a three-stroke lead and was never really threatened after that. He finished with a nine-under-par 279 and won by four strokes, picking up the biggest check of his career—¥18,000,000.

Naomichi (Joe) Ozaki, seeking his third victory of the year, took the lead the first day with 68, a shot ahead of brother Tateo and Australian veteran Graham Marsh, a frequent winner in Japan over the years and twice the Tokai champion. Then came Itai's 65 which propelled him to a fourth-place tie at 70 to 135 and a three-stroke lead over Yuji Takagi, a non-winner in 13 years of campaigning. The 40-year-old Itai had eight birdies and a bogey in the round. Holding steady in the rain Saturday, Itai shot a par round with a birdie and a bogey and that was good enough to widen his margin to five strokes over Jet Ozaki, Nobumitsu Yuhara and Yoshitaka Yamamoto, whose 67 for his 212 was the day's best score.

Conditions remained difficult Sunday, so Eiichi's second straight 72 carried him to the four-stroke triumph over Yuhara. Yamamoto and Nobuo Serizawa were next at 284, American Larry Mize and Ozaki at 285. Only three rounds Sunday were in the 60s, but one of them was a 63 by Yoshinori Kaneko, hoisting him from 56th to 13th place.

Japan Open—¥100,000,000
Winner: Tsuneyuki Nakajima

Though not as dominant as he once was on the Japan Tour, Tsuneyuki Nakajima still has the ability that he always seems to have had to shift his game up an extra notch or two when the country's prestige tournaments come up on the schedule. He illustrated this once again in October of 1991 when just his second victory of the season was his fourth in the Japan Open... to go with three Japan PGA Championships, two Japan Match Play Championships and one Japan Series Championship. These and 26 other victories grace the outstanding record of the 36-year-old star in his home country.

The fourth Open title came the hard way—in a playoff against the surprising Noboru Sugai, from whom little had been heard since his second-place finish at the start of the season at Shizuoka. In fact, Nakajima had to shrug off disaster just to make the playoff Sunday at Shimonoseki Golf Club in Toyoura. He absorbed a quadruple-bogey eight at the seventh hole to fall well off the pace, but remarkably bounced back immediately with two birdies. He lost a stroke at the 11th, parred the next six and reached the 18th knowing he needed a birdie to tie Sugai, who was already in with 70 and a two-over-par 290. He got it with a 20-foot birdie putt and won the playoff much more easily with a par as Sugai missed the green at the par-three 17th and bogeyed.

Although the likes of Isao Aoki and Jumbo Ozaki were close by, lesser lights had the upper hands early. Amateur Kazuyoshi Yonekura shared the first-round lead at 70 with Kiyoshi Murota, Seiji Ebihara and Masaji Kusakabe. Murota moved two strokes in front of Hiroshi Makino with his 140 Friday, then skidded back into a tie with Eiji Mizoguchi and Makino Saturday when he shot 76 for 216. Nakajima was then in position at 217 after rounds of 72, 74 and 71. Sugai was three shots farther back with his 74-70-76. Aoki fell a stroke short with his closing 69, tying for second with Tetsu Nishikawa, the Maruman Open winner, and Ozaki could do no better than 73.

Asahi Beer Golf Digest—¥120,000,000
Winner: Harumitsu Hamano

When the opening came in the final round of the Asahi Beer Golf Digest tournament, Harumitsu Hamano employed his new-found confidence to take advantage of it and capture his second victory of the Japan Tour season after nine years as an also-ran. Nobumitsu Yuhara, who had built a three-stroke margin after 54 holes with middle rounds of 65 and 66 for 202, blew the lead Sunday, but the nearest contenders failed to capitalize as well as Hamano did. He fired a 66, with a four-under-par 32 on the front nine, clinching the victory with a 12-foot birdie chip-in at the 17th hole. Masashi Ozaki, in the middle of the year's money-winnings race, came up a stroke short a short time after Hamano posted his 273. Ozaki finished with 69 and 274 at Tomei Country Club.

The lead changed hands after each of the first three rounds. Akihito Yokoyama opened with 65 for a two-stroke lead over Ozaki and five others, then gave way Friday to Hideki Kase and his 68-67—135. Yuhara's 65 that day moved him into second place and the 66 Saturday gave him the three-shot margin over Jumbo Ozaki, five over Jet Ozaki, Haruo Yasuda and Kase. Hamano started his move Sunday with an eagle on the first hole and even had a bogey in his 65. Greg Norman and Hale Irwin came in for the event, but were never in contention, tying for 20th.

Bridgestone Open—¥60,000,000
Winner: Isao Aoki

Isao Aoki, who has his name on virtually every long-standing tournament's winners' list, finally found a way to bag one of the few that had escaped him—shoot 63, take the lead Saturday and accept the plaudits as the winner when the final round is rained out. That's how the 49-year-old veteran finally captured the Bridgestone Open at the end of October, his 58th win on the Japan Tour and first since the Mitsubishi Galant in May of 1990.

Actually, the Sunday rain-out at Sodegaura Golf Club in Chiba was the second of the week, causing the Bridgestone to be shortened to a rare 36-hole event. Saburo Fujiki, the defending champion and a two-time winner earlier in 1991, launched his quest for a repeat Thursday with a 67 and shared first place with Akiyoshi Omachi and Tsutomu Higa as Aoki began with 71 and was tied for 23rd at that point.

The first of the two rain cancellations occurred Friday. Aoki equalled his all-time best tournament score with the 63 Saturday, creating it with an eagle, nine birdies—four on the last four holes—and two bogeys on the par-72 course. At 134, he was a stroke in front of Tsuyoshi Yoneyama, who had 63 Saturday.

Lark Cup—¥190,000,000
Winner: Yoshikazu Yokoshima

Yoshikazu Yokoshima, a veteran with five victories scattered over his 19-year career on the Japan Tour, picked an excellent time to add No. 6 to his record. The first of the big-money events—the ¥190 million Lark Cup—came up on the schedule as Yokoshima's game came together at the ABC Golf Club in Tojocho. He posted four steady but unspectacular rounds for a 280 total and a two-stroke victory over Roger Mackay, the money-crown contender from Australia.

Yutaka Hagawa, continuing his fine comeback season, seized the first-round lead with 66, a stroke ahead of Hideki Kase and Shigenori Mori as Yokoshima opened with a two-under 70. Australian standout Peter Senior shot 68 Friday and edged into a one-stroke lead over Hagawa, who slipped to 74, and Mori, who had a 73. With 71, Yokoshima moved within two of the top. Yet another new leader emerged Saturday in the person of England's Barry Lane, who scored a 68 for 209 and led Yokoshima (69), Kase (69) and Mori (70) by one, Mackay (68) by two. Yoshikazu maintained his tournament-long pace with another 70 Sunday, which nobody could challenge, and collected the healthy ¥34,200,000 first prize. Mackay had 71 for his 282, the runner-up check of ¥19 million boosted his bid for the money title.

Acom International—¥75,000,000
Winner: Masahiro Kuramoto

Masahiro Kuramoto, one of Japan's better-known players in world circles and winner of 26 tournaments at home, had not really fared well since 1988 when he won five times and was fourth on the money list. He had picked up just one of those 26 titles since then—the Setonaikai in early 1990—so his November victory in the off-beat Acom International, a variation on the International in America, was particularly welcome to him.

Kuramoto won decisively in the Stableford-style event at Narita Springs Country Club at Yamadacho that was shortened to 54 holes because of fog and rain Friday. Picking up the bulk of his points in Sunday's final round, Masahiro registered a 10-point victory over Toru Nakamura, Yoshinori Mizumaki and Canadian Brent Franklin with his 32 total. Mizumaki started with a bang, jumping off to a six-point lead Thursday with 18, then lost a point when play resumed Saturday, yielding the lead to Tomohiro Maruyama, who compiled 23 points in the first two rounds. Meanwhile, Kuramoto had posted seven points Thursday and again on Saturday and was tied for sixth entering the final round. Nine birdies produced 18 points Sunday and carried Masahiro to his 10-point win. Bob Gilder, the defender from the U.S., finished with eight points.

Visa Taiheiyo Club Masters—¥150,000,000
Winner: Roger Mackay

Most of Australia's international players over the years have chosen either the American or European Tours for their primary overseas campaigning. A few—for example, Graham Marsh and Brian Jones—preferred Japan and did very well by it. The latest, and perhaps biggest success story, is that of Roger Mackay, who chose Japan because "it's only a 10-hour flight from Perth (his home)." When Mackay scored his biggest of three 1991 wins on the Japan Tour—the Visa Taiheiyo Club Masters—he not only vaulted to the top of the circuit's money list but also became the first foreigner ever to win more than ¥100 million in a single season.

Although close behind from the start, the 35-year-old Mackay rode into serious contention on his putter Saturday, when he had eight birdies and shot 65 to move within a stroke of Tsuneyuki (Tommy) Nakajima, then the current money leader and a former Taiheiyo Masters winner. They proved to be the only real contenders Sunday, although Yoshinori Kaneko, the first-round leader (68), slipped into second place ahead of Nakajima with a birdie at the last hole for 68 and 274.

Nakajima had led from the second round on—70-65—135, then 68—203—before Mackay caught up with a birdie at the first hole Sunday. The deadlock remained until Roger birdied the 11th and 12th. When Tommy missed a three-footer at the 13th for bogey, Mackay breezed home, matching pars with Nakajima the rest of the way, shooting 68 for his 16-under-par 272 on the Taiheiyo Club's Gotemba course at the foot of famed Mount Fujiyama. Nakajima, hampered by damaged glasses which he had sat on the night before, finished with 72 and 275.

Dunlop Phoenix—¥200,000,000
Winner: Larry Nelson

With business interests occupying much of his time, Larry Nelson played in only 16 tournaments on the U.S. Tour in 1991 before heading for Japan in late November for the Dunlop Phoenix, the richest event on the Japan Tour. He had accumulated a modest $160,543 and no victories for the third year in a row. Considering what happened, perhaps Nelson should consider moving his base of operations to Japan. The soft-spoken but gritty 44-year-old Georgian prevailed in a classic four-man playoff at Miyazaki's Phoenix Country Club and received a check for ¥36,000,000, far more than his total U.S. earnings for 1991.

As is the case in many of the tournaments and many sports events of all kinds, the Dunlop Phoenix drama focused on the finishing stretch Sunday. Almost forgotten was the front-running performance of American Mark Brooks the first three days. Brooks, who had won in Milwaukee in September, took the first-round lead with a six-under-par 66, one ahead of fellow Yank Nolan Henke; widened the margin to two over Katsuji Hasegawa with 68—134 Friday and birdied the 18th hole Saturday for 71—205 to remain a stroke in front, then over Roger Mackay and Seve Ballesteros, the Dunlop Phoenix winner in 1977 and 1981.

The finish was virtually a cavalry charge. With nine holes left, six players, not including Nelson or Brooks, were tied for the lead. Three of them—Henke, Mike Reid and Craig Stadler—fell by the wayside on the back nine; the others—Ballesteros, Jay Don Blake and Isao Aoki—finished in the four-way deadlock at 276 with Nelson, who surged into contention with birdies at Nos. 12, 13 and 15. All had birdie chances at the par-five 18th. Aoki, who closed with 66, then Nelson two-putted from considerable distance. Blake missed from 12 feet and finally Ballesteros did likewise from 10 feet, activating the playoff.

Blake went out at the first extra hole with a six. At the third, Nelson holed a 35-footer for birdie with Aoki sitting six feet away in two. Isao, looking for his 59th career win and first Dunlop Phoenix title, sank his putt, eliminating Ballesteros, but lost to Nelson's two-putt par at the next hole when he put his tee shot on the par three in heavy rough and didn't get close.

Casio World Open—¥140,000,000
Winner: Naomichi Ozaki

Naomichi (Joe) Ozaki's accomplishments in the Casio World Open, last of the big-money events on the 1991 Japan Tour schedule, were fourfold. With his two-stroke victory in a hard-fought closing duel against American star Larry Nelson, the 35-year-old Ozaki (1) matched Roger Mackay's season-leading total of three wins, (2) exceeded the ¥100 million mark and closed in on money leader Mackay, (3) kept one of the titles of the three premier year-end events in Japan and (4) became just the second Japanese winner in the 11-year history of the Casio World Open.

Hot individual rounds determined the Casio leaders each of the first three days before Ozaki and Nelson went at it head to head in the final round. Masahiro Kuramoto, the Acom International winner earlier in the month, opened with 65 to lead Taisei Inagaki by a shot, the rest by at least three. Nelson, coming off his exciting victory in the Dunlop Phoenix the previous Sunday, fired a flawless eight-under-par 64 Friday and rose into a two-stroke lead at 134 over Masashi (Jumbo) Ozaki, Hajime Meshiai and Kuramoto. Enter Ozaki Saturday. He matched Nelson's 64 for 202 and inched a stroke ahead of Nelson.

The two virtually matched stroke for stroke through most of the final round. Both birdied the third. Nelson birdied the fourth and fifth to go a stroke ahead. Both three-putted the 10th. Ozaki preserved his position when he holed a putt from the fringe to match a Nelson birdie at the 11th. Naomichi regained a tie when he birdied the 16th, then Nelson cracked at the par-three 17th when wind drifted his tee shot into a pond after Ozaki had put his safely on the green. That made Naomichi's closing birdie for 68 (for 270) unnecessary. With the double bogey at the 17th, Nelson finished with 273 and lost the runner-up position to Meshiai and his closing 66.

Japan Series Hitachi Cup—¥60,000,000
Winner: Naomichi Ozaki

Naomichi Ozaki was a man on a sad mission in the Japan Series Hitachi Cup. On the eve of the special, limited-field event that brings together the winners and leading players of the year at the end of the Japan Tour season, he and brothers Masashi and Tateo got word that their 76-year-old father, Minora, had died of a heart attack. The other two withdrew from the tournament but convinced Naomichi, who was the defending champion and was locked in a battle with Roger Mackay and Tsuneyuki Nakajima to top Japan's Order of Merit, that he should stay and compete. He did, shot a first-round 71, then made a six-hour round trip to southern Japan for his father's funeral. Obviously drawing great resolve from the circumstances, Ozaki was virtually unbeatable upon his return to Tokyo's Yomiuri Country Club for the balance of the tournament.

Masahiro Kuramoto and Kinpachi Yoshimura, the latter making his first appearance in the Series, had led the first day with 66s. Shaking off the trauma of the events, Ozaki ran off seven birdies for a 65 Friday that elevated him into a first-place tie at 136 with Yoshikazu Yokoshima and Nobumitsu Yuhara. Finally getting a little rest overnight, Naomichi came back Saturday with an eagle, six birdies and a 66 that shot him to 202, three shots in front of Yuhara. Nakajima moved into third place at 206 and Mackay had a 207 total to remain in the race for No. 1. They were all but out of it a day later after Ozaki shot 66 again for 268, 20 under par, and won by eight strokes, the biggest margin of the season. "I think my father is pleased now," said Ozaki after it was over.

Daikyo Open—¥120,000,000
Winner: Yutaka Makino

The season-ending Daikyo Open at Okinawa had an anti-climactic air to it after the excitement and tragedy of the immediately preceding events, particularly when, after the early action, it became apparently that the results weren't going to affect Naomichi Ozaki's position as the money leader. Of course, though, it wasn't anti-climactic for Yutaka Makino, who had won just one time in his 11 years on the Japan Tour. Makino picked up the second with a closing one-under-par 70 for 276 at Daikyo Country Club, nipping Brent Franklin, the third-round co-leader, and Seiki Okuda by a stroke. Okuda finished with a 70, Franklin with a 71.

Koichi Suzuki led the Daikyo for two rounds, starting with a five-under-par 66 and adding 69 in his bid for a second 1991 victory to go with his win in the Mitsubishi Galant in June. However, he fell back with 75 Saturday, opening the way for the Canadian, Franklin, and Makino to move into the lead at 206, Brent shooting 70 and Makino 67. Okuda was just a stroke back. Makino had three birdies and two bogeys Sunday.

17. Women's Tours

Years from now, golf experts in one of their bull sessions will look back on 1991 as the year of do-or-die for the LPGA, and come to the conclusion that it was a do.

It was the year that Charles Mechem stepped out of retirement as a television executive to succeed William Blue as commissioner and righted most of the wrongs his predecessor created. Mechem went to every LPGA event, soothed frayed feelings of tournament sponsors, led cheers for his players and created a positive atmosphere overall.

The product was a good one and a competitive one. There was a nice blend of the old, who continued to shine, and the young, who proved they are ready to make the transition a smooth one.

It was a year in which Nancy Lopez proved to be as good a mother as she is a golfer, giving birth to her third child.

It was a year in which dogged Pat Bradley at the age of 40 won her final two tournaments of the year, Nos. 29 and 30 of her career, and kicked down the door of the LPGA Hall of Fame, becoming only its 12th member. Ironically, it was the first time in her career she had won two straight. Bradley won three times in all, was the Rolex Player of the Year and leading money winner.

It was a year when Amy Alcott won the Nabisco Dinah Shore to move within one victory of the Hall of Fame, but did not win again.

It was a year that will be remembered as where a changing of the guard began, where the dynasty of Bradley, Pat Daniel, Patty Sheehan, Alcott and Betsy King started to wind down.

It was a year when four players in their 20s managed to crack the LPGA's top 10—Meg Mallon and Deb Richard, both 28, and Dottie Mochrie and Danielle Ammaccapane, both 26—while a fifth, Jane Geddes, was only 31.

Other than Bradley's heroic entry into the Hall of Fame, Mallon was the story of the year.

Her first career victory came in the Oldsmobile Classic in late January, but that was only a spark compared to the explosion she created later. She won the Mazda LPGA Championship in early July and three weeks later shocked the world again by winning the U.S. Women's Open. She became the first player since Sandra Haynie in 1974 to win the Open and LPGA in the same year.

In all, Mallon won four times, more than $600,000 and with her easy smile and personality may be the player the LPGA can hang its hat on for years to come.

The LPGA's other major, the Du Maurier Classic, was won by 30-year-old Nancy Scranton.

The next dynasty, however, may not happen. The year 1991 was one of unprecedented parity where 15 different players won the first 15 events, and 24 different players won overall. Quality of play was at an all-time high. Since 1980, the average 36-hole-cut score has dropped more than six shots.

"Our goal is to make the LPGA the No. 1 women's sports organization in the world," Mechem said. "We are blessed with both talented veterans and younger players and the years to come should be our best. I suspect there are exciting days ahead."

Jamaica Classic—$500,000
Winner: Jane Geddes

Sometimes it's the simple things that turn the ridiculous into the sublime as it relates to the distance and direction a golf ball will fly.

Take the case of Jane Geddes, who for 42 holes in the season-opening Jamaica Classic was hitting everything short and right, and quickly losing sight of leader Patty Sheehan. Standing on the seventh tee on Sunday, three strokes behind Sheehan, Geddes mentally began going through her check list, when out of the blue it came to her. She was standing too close to the ball. She moved back a bit, began ripping it, played the final 12 holes in seven under par, including a couple of eagles at Nos. 15 and 17, and won going away.

Geddes' final-round 64, low for the week by four shots, gave her a three-stroke victory over Sheehan, who bogeyed the final two holes, Ok Hee Ku and Dottie Mochrie, who early in the final round led by one stroke. "I saw what Sheehan and the others were doing early and knew if I didn't get my act together, I could forget it," Geddes said. "It was a simple thing, just standing too close to the ball. Once I moved back, wow, I began hitting it solid and long."

The eagle at No. 15 drew Geddes even with Sheehan, but Sheehan pulled two in front with birdies at Nos. 15 and 16. Geddes again applied the pressure by hitting the green on the 517-yard 17th hole in two shots and made her 35-foot eagle putt. "When somebody goes eagle-par-eagle-birdie, and they're not far from the lead, chances are they're going to win," Sheehan said of Geddes' hot finish. "I had a little lapse at 17 and it cost me."

Sheehan knew going to the 17th tee that Geddes had finished under par, and knew what she had to do. She had to go for it. She put a little too much oomph in her tee shot and pulled it off the fairway and under a tree. "One of those beginning-of-the-year lapses," she called it. With her ball under the high palm branch, Sheehan's only play was a punch out onto the fairway. She then left her third shot short of the green, chipped to 20 feet and missed her putt for par. Needing an eagle on the 18th, Sheehan hit her second shot to the back of the green and three-putted for a meaningless bogey.

Geddes' victory was her first on the LPGA Tour since she won five events in 1987. But she hadn't gone winless over that stretch. Two years ago, she won the Ladies British Open and, late last year, won the Australian Masters by making birdie on the first playoff hole to beat Kristal Parker. "I'm usually kind of like that, a streak player," she said. "It certainly was that way in 1987, but after winning in Australia last month, I came here with confidence in my game, even though I struggled the first two days."

Considering the purse, $500,000, and that it was the season-opener, some players didn't come at all. The field was rather lame. Only three of the top-10 money winners played—Sheehan, Cathy Gerring and Cindy Rarick. Player-of-the-Year Beth Daniel had shoulder problems, Betsy King was tired, Nancy Lopez was skiing, and Pat Bradley wasn't ready. But Geddes was.

Oldsmobile Classic—$400,000
Winner: Meg Mallon

Four years on the LPGA Tour is experience enough for anyone to win her first tournament, but the way Meg Mallon did it in the Oldsmobile Classic made it more than just your average newspaper headline. First, she had to baby-sit her caddie four rounds; secondly, she had to fight off such experienced winners as Betsy King and Pat Bradley. And, last, but hardly least, she had to birdie the final two holes to avoid a playoff with 23-year-old rookie Dana Lofland, who was playing her first LPGA event. Mallon put together rounds of 66-70-69-71 for a 12-under 276 total and picked up the largest paycheck of her career, $60,000.

Mallon's week started with *Sports Illustrated* writer Sonja Steptoe carrying her bag. Steptoe was doing a first-person story on caddieing on the LPGA Tour, and Mallon agreed to be her guinea pig. Mallon had to teach her everything, but it worked in a positive way, as she became more focused, more prepared. She carried her own yardage book, made club selection on her own and read every putt. "There wasn't time to think about distractions," Mallon said. "That's the most focused I've been for four rounds in my life."

After taking a two-stroke lead over King and a three-stroke lead over Dottie Mochrie and Bradley into the final round, Mallon had to endure an overnight weather postponement with 11 holes to play. No problem. She came out Monday morning and parred the first eight holes, while Mochrie bogeyed two of her last three, King three-putted the last two and Bradley double-bogeyed the 18th.

Lofland, however, wouldn't go away. She sneaked past the big names with three birdies on the back nine and moved into a tie after Mallon bogeyed No. 16. I was fuming for letting everyone back into the tournament," Mallon said. "It got my attention."

Mallon hit a five-wood shot over a lake to four feet at No. 17 and made birdie to reclaim the lead. At No. 18, she sealed the victory, hitting a three iron across another lake to four feet and made it. "I can't figure out what made me hit those shots," Mallon said. "I guess it had been so long since I'd made a birdie, I was just thinking about hitting solid shots. This is a great feeling. Obviously, I'd like to feel it again sometime."

Phar-Mor at Inverrary—$500,000
Winner: Beth Daniel

There was some not-so-good news for the LPGA when Beth Daniel won the Phar-Mor at Inverrary tournament. It was Daniel's first tournament of the year, and all she was trying to do was to see how her ailing shoulder and collarbone would hold up. Winning was totally unexpected. Daniel's 67-73-69—209 was good for a victory by two strokes over Nancy Lopez and by three over Laura Baugh, and $75,000 of the $500,000 purse.

In December, doctors discovered tendinitis in Daniel's right shoulder. When that cleared up, her right collarbone became hyper mobile. She couldn't practice until the last weekend in January, and had to watch the Jamaica and Oldsmobile tournaments from the sidelines.

Despite the layoff, Daniel was still Daniel. In three days, she missed just six greens and was over par on only five holes. Her putting was only average, but she still made her share of the 10- and 15-footers that winners must make. And on Sunday, when first Colleen Walker and then Lopez passed her on the front side, Daniel put her game into overdrive on the final nine. She hit every fairway, every green and made three birdies that clinched the victory.

Daniel wore a smile on her face and an ice bag on her shoulder to the post-tournament press conference, while Lopez mockingly played a phantom violin. "I came here with no expectations," Daniel said. "I just wanted to test the shoulder and get back into competition. But if I said the shoulder hurt, the other players would probably start throwing things at me in the lockerroom."

The victory was Daniel's 12th in the last 18 months on the LPGA Tour, dating back to the 1989 Greater Washington Open. She also continued a nice streak in Florida. In October of 1990, she won the Centel Classic; in November, she was the only player on either side to win all three points in the Solheim Cup, and in December, she teamed with Davis Love III to win the JCPenney Classic.

Daniel opened the Phar-Mor tournament with three birdies on her first four holes, made two more coming in and her 67 was one stroke better than Walker and Hiromi Kobayashi. Saturday, the wind blew and the scores went up. Daniel soared to 73 and, at 140, led Kobayashi again by one, with Lopez and Walker at 142.

Walker and Lopez moved one stroke ahead in the final round when Daniel bogeyed No. 9. But not for long. Walker was the first to fall. She three-putted Nos. 11 and 12 and eventually tied for sixth. Lopez bogeyed No. 12 and lost the lead to Daniel's birdie, then at No. 13 Lopez missed a two-footer for par and never recovered.

With the victory, Daniel became eligible for the $1 million annuity bonus offered by Phar-Mor to any player who wins both the Inverrary event and the companion Phar-Mor in Youngstown later in the year. "I wouldn't bet against her," Lopez said. "She's at the peak of her career and is capable of doing almost anything. I think she's going to stay on this high for quite a while."

Orix Hawaiian Open—$350,000
Winner: Patty Sheehan

Patty Sheehan and Beth Daniel didn't bring their best games to Honolulu for the Orix Hawaiian Open, but often less than their best is good enough. This time, Sheehan got away with being merely average. Despite an erratic streak with her driver and a confession that she wasn't hitting the ball solidly, Sheehan managed rounds of 68-69-70—207, nine under par over the 6,241-yard Ko Olina Golf Club on Oahu, and defeated runner-up Daniel by three shots.

It was another three shots back to third-place finisher Pat Bradley, and only five other players managed to break par of 216. The victory was Sheehan's first of the season, but her sixth since the beginning of 1990. In that same span, Daniel had won eight events including seven in 1990 when she and

Sheehan battled to the wire for Player-of-the-Year honors.

They have been sharing center stage so long, they are experts on each other. "Patty was vulnerable this week, and I could have won the tournament if I'd just gotten any putts to fall," Daniel said. "Beth didn't play as well as she's capable," Sheehan noted. "Any victory means a lot, but they mean more when you beat the people who are playing well."

In the beginning, it was relatively unknown Jennifer Wyatt who set the pace with a six-under-par 66, two strokes in front of Sheehan and three better than Daniel and Ok Hee Ku. Wyatt was almost apologetic for taking the lead—"I didn't expect to shoot 66," she said—and prophetic about the rest of the week, adding, "So I can't expect too much tomorrow."

Wyatt didn't get much, either, a 79, and turned the tournament over to those who did expect better things. Sheehan shot 69 with a string of four straight birdies from Nos. 12 to 15, while Daniel had 70 and didn't make any putts. Still, only two shots separated them going to Sunday's finale.

Only the veteran Bradley made a run at the leaders on Sunday. Starting five strokes behind Sheehan, Bradley birdied five of the first 14 holes and was within one shot, but she triple-bogeyed the short 350-yard 15th hole and faded. Daniel didn't help herself by missing short birdie putts at Nos. 4 and 5, one for par at No. 6, and a six-footer at No. 16 that would have pulled her to within one stroke. Then she stubbed another six-foot par putt at No. 17 and that was it.

There was one bright spot for Daniel, however. With her runner-up check of $32,375, she moved over $3 million in career earnings, joining Bradley, Betsy King and Nancy Lopez. Next could be Sheehan, who won $52,500 to increase her career earnings to $2,943,213.

Women's Kemper Open—$500,000
Winner: Deb Richard

As sure things go, Cindy Rarick figured to be one when the LPGA Tour moved to Wailea, Hawaii, for the Women's Kemper Open. For openers, Rarick loves Hawaii, went to college there, won her first LPGA event there, met her husband there, and for the first three days and most of the fourth was on top of her game and the leaderboard. So how did it happen that Deb Richard won? Simply stated, because Rarick proved to be a poor closer.

Holding a four-shot lead with six holes to play, Rarick played those holes in three over par, then bogeyed the second hole of a playoff. "I lost it more than Deb won it," Rarick said. "She played steady golf, but I gave it away." Richard was there to take the second victory of her six-year career, and her first since the 1987 Rochester International. She toured Wailea Golf Club in nine-under-par 275, with consistent rounds of 68-70-67-70, while Rarick ruined a great start of 66-68-69 with a closing 72. Next closest was Dawn Coe, two shots behind at 277.

In the middle of all this, Beth Daniel and Jane Geddes both made runs at the title. Daniel was only two strokes out at the halfway mark, but a triple-bogey seven at No. 8 in the third round sent Daniel reeling to 76 and an eventual tie for 28th place, 11 strokes back. Geddes was within one shot early on the back nine on Sunday before self-destructing with a bogey at No.

13, a triple bogey at No. 14 and a double bogey at No. 17 to finish with 73 and a tie for eighth place.

Richard didn't succumb to the same pressures as Rarick did. When Rarick's lead was four strokes after both players bogeyed No. 12, Richard told herself, "Ok, Deb, let's get moving." The move began at No. 13, where Richard hit a six iron to 18 feet for birdie and picked up two shots when Rarick bogeyed, her third bogey in the last five holes. Richard closed to within one stroke as Rarick three-putted the 15th and finally caught the leader with a birdie at No. 16. They parred in, setting up the first playoff in each of their careers.

Rarick appeared to have won on the first hole when her 12-foot putt for birdie at No. 18 spun out of the hole. "Honest to God, I thought she had made it," Richard said. "It was a great putt. I don't know how it stayed out." Richard then ended it quickly, making a six-footer for birdie on No. 10, while Rarick didn't give herself a chance, hitting her approach shot over the green.

"I knew the moment I hit my putt, it was in," Richard said. "Before I hit it, I told myself, 'If you don't do it now, you never will.' That was the most solid putt of my life."

Rarick was talking to herself, also, over missed opportunities. "If I hadn't three-putted No. 15, I would have won," she said. "I played great for three days, felt comfortable, but I just didn't handle my nerves very well today. I wasn't a very good closer."

The victory was worth $75,000 to Richard, but more importantly was a big confidence booster. "It's been four long years since my last win, and sometimes you start to wonder when it will happen again," she said. "Let me tell you, this one feels even better than the first one. Maybe, the next one won't take so long."

As we shall see, it didn't.

Inamori Classic—$400,000
Winner: Laura Davies

According to critics, Laura Davies' problem has been in not recognizing that sometimes it's better to keep the head cover on her driver and reign in all that power that many times put her drives in no-man's land.

Finally, it appeared that Davies got the word, at least for a week at StoneRidge Country Club in Ponway, California, where she shot rounds of 70-68-72-67—277 and won the Inamori Classic by an impressive four strokes over Lynn Connelly and Judy Dickinson.

Davies used her driver just three times, from the fairway on the uphill 10th hole, and won for only the fourth time on the LPGA Tour and the first time since the 1989 Lady Keystone Open.

Though she ironed out her problems off the tee, Davies won the tournament with her putter. Davies went into Sunday's final round one shot behind Tina Barrett, then promptly three-putted the first hole from 50 feet and missed a 10-footer for birdie at No. 2. "Those two putts got my attention," Davies said. "I was being too aggressive. It was time to change strategy." She did, and was off and running. She one-putted the next five holes for four birdies and a sand save that brought her from three strokes down to one up. Over that span, Barrett couldn't buy a putt. "We were in a shootout there for a while. But Laura made her putts and I missed mine," Barrett said.

While Davies was missing few putts, she was missing even fewer fairways. She had struggled throughout the 1990 season. After playing in the last group at the Kemper Open last March, Davies played in 18 events, missed eight cuts, had no finish higher than a tie for 26th and had six finishes at 44th or lower. Her confidence was a wreck.

"I found I couldn't make birdies from somebody's garden," Davies said, in explaining her strategy to store the driver for something she could control, trading power for position.

Davies' opening 70 put her two strokes off the lead shared by Martha Foyer, Caroline Keggi and Robin Walton. A 68 Friday gave her a one-shot lead over Barrett, and her 72 Saturday left her only one stroke behind Barrett's 70.

As usual on Sunday, someone came dashing up through the field. This time it was Connelly, who started five strokes out, but shot 67, which included seven threes and four birdies on the last nine from inside eight feet. In at seven under par for the tournament, Connelly thought she had a chance to win, but only if Davies stumbled. Playing for pars, Davies birdied the 16th hole from 60 feet and the par-five 17th from four feet. Normally, Davies would go for the 448-yard uphill 17th in two shots, but this time she hit a four iron, six iron and sand wedge. "I felt like a chicken," Davies said. "I hate playing like this, but I like scoring like this."

The money wasn't bad, either. The winner's share of the $400,000 purse was $60,000, her biggest payday in over a year. "The driver has been driving me to the poor house," Davies said. "Maybe I'll use it again, but at least I think now I know when I should and when I shouldn't."

Desert Inn International—$400,000
Winner: Penny Hammel

Given her choice of trying to win a golf tournament paired with Beth Daniel or with just about anyone else, Penny Hammel will choose the latter every time. It's not that Hammel dislikes Daniel. She's just intimidated by her.

So it came to pass in the Desert Inn International that Hammel breathed a sigh of relief when, in the second round, Daniel clipped her by three shots, dropping her two behind Daniel and out of Sunday's featured pairing.

Able to play her own game, which is considerably shorter than Daniel's, Hammel played along with Sally Little and Cathy Johnson, shot a six-under-par 66 and won for only the third time in her career. Hammel finished at 211, five under par, one stroke in front of Daniel, who had 69, and picked up the $60,000 winner's share of the purse.

"That was probably good for me, not having to play with Beth," Hammel said. "Beth's a long-ball hitter and I'm not. She can be intimidating and it affects my game. It shouldn't but it does."

More intimidating, for the entire field, was the weather for Friday's opening round. It was cold and rainy. The temperature at noon was 39 degrees, the wind-chill factor was in the low 20s, and snow was falling in the mountains.

Thirty-two players didn't break 80 and that led to the highest 36-hole cut score—nine-over-par 153—and highest winning score on the Tour this season.

Hammel was the only player to break par, her 71 leading eight others, including Daniel and Patty Sheehan, by one stroke. "It felt like a 65 on a normal day," Hammel said. "I was so cold I couldn't feel my hands or my feet. It was brutal."

Daniel took the lead by one stroke over Sheehan with 71 Saturday, but it could have been better, much better. She was four under par after 11 holes before hooking her drive at No. 12 and made double bogey, then hooked an eight-iron shot and bogeyed the 13th.

For the most part, it was all Daniel and Hammel Sunday. Daniel birdied the first hole to move three strokes ahead, but Hammel came back with three birdies of her own at Nos. 2, 3 and 5 to tie, and she was never out of the lead thereafter. Hammel missed only one fairway, holed a 15-yard bunker shot and only one of her six birdies came from outside six feet. That was a 20-footer downhill at No. 17 that proved to be the winner.

Rosie Jones, playing three groups ahead of Hammel, briefly tied for the lead at No. 13. She shot 66 and passed 30 players to finish third.

From early on, however, it was going to be Daniel or Hammel. Daniel had her chances. She missed makeable birdie putts at Nos. 12 and 13, then birdied Nos. 14 and 15 for a tie, but Hammel broke the tie with her gutsy 20-footer at the 17th. Daniel had chances with 18-footers at both Nos. 17 and 18 to tie, but failed to make the putts.

Daniel was asked Sunday night if she was a little miffed after being four under par after 25 holes earlier, and a total of five under par won. "I never thought about it," Daniel said. "I wanted to win and had some opportunities. I gave it a good fight. That's about all I can do."

The victory was a tonic for whatever questions Hammel had about her game. Mostly it was self-induced pressure after winning the 1989 Jamie Farr Classic. "I kept trying to fix what wasn't broken," Hammel said. "I learned today I can win. I can play well on the last day against Beth Daniel. I can make birdie putts when I need to."

Standard Register Ping—$550,000
Winner: Danielle Ammaccapane

Every so often a player comes along with can't-miss tags hanging all over her. Then, it seems, those tags change to can't-win. Danielle Ammaccapane was one of them until she shot four-under-par 69 to hold off Meg Mallon and Barb Bunkowsky to win the Standard Register Ping event at Moon Valley Country Club in Phoenix.

"It's tough out there," Ammaccapane said. "No one understands what's going on inside me. You start playing for money instead of trophies, and golf becomes a job. It's just different."

It was Ammaccapane's first victory since she joined the Tour in 1988 following a sterling amateur career, which included an NCAA championship and a USGA Public Links title. In three-plus years as a professional, she had hardly been a flop. In 1990, she was second twice and won $300,000. But she had never won.

She was the hometown favorite, playing in front of friends and her 86-year-old grandfather, who was watching his first golf tournament. She played a nearly flawless final round in the glare of being the 54-hole leader.

All this was slow in coming. Bad weather followed the women from Las Vegas to Phoenix and only three players broke par 73 in Thursday's 40-degree temperatures. Cathy Gerring led with 71, followed by Betsy King and Caroline Keggi at 72. Ammaccapane was three strokes back. Bunkowsky moved ahead with a second-round 68 to lead by two strokes over Gerring (74), King (72), and Ammaccapane (70). Bunkowsky was magical, with one-putt greens and eight birdies.

Ammaccapane took control of the tournament on Saturday. The day before, when asked how she liked her position, she said, "I haven't been in this position. I don't know what's going to happen."

What happened was, in the presence of veterans King and Bunkowsky, Ammaccapane had four birdies, one bogey and three times saved par. She took the lead with 70 by one stroke over Colleen Walker (70), Michelle McGann (68) and Bunkowsky (73). "I don't consider a one-shot lead leading," she said. "I don't even want to think about winning yet. I'm tired."

Sunday's final was a free-for-all. Five players—Ammaccapane, Walker, Bunkowsky, King and Mallon—shared the lead at some point. King and Walker were the first to fade. Mallon made six birdies in 11 holes to lead briefly, but made no more and finished two strokes back. Bunkowsky was tied after 14 holes, but her putter went cold. She missed putts between seven and 12 feet over the final four holes.

Ammaccapane broke free with a 15-footer at No. 14 and clinched the victory with another birdie from 18 inches at the 17th.

"The days you win are the days when things are going your way," Ammaccapane said. "That's how it was for me today. I was never in between clubs. I had no bad lies. I was decisive under pressure."

That's not to say it was easy.

"Getting my first victory took a lot longer than it should have," she said. "But I finally did it. This was the longest day of my life. I kept wondering, 'Am I ever going to get to the 18th tee?' It should be a little easier next time."

Nabisco Dinah Shore—$600,000
Winner: Amy Alcott

Just when people began wondering if Amy Alcott was going to win again, the lady in question answered with an exclamation point. She put an end to such nonsense with a record-setting eight-shot victory in the Nabisco Dinah Shore, the LPGA's first major championship of the year.

To prove that she remembered what victory is all about, Alcott and her caddie, Bill Kurre, jumped into the lake beside the green and carried tournament host Dinah Shore with them. "I wanted to accept this trophy with dignity," Alcott said. "But I guess that's just not my style. Two years ago, Dinah told me if I won again, she would jump in with me."

The jump into the lake wasn't artistic, but Alcott's game was. She strung together rounds of 67-70-68-68 and led wire-to-wire. Her 15-under-par 273 total bettered the tournament record by one stroke, a record she set in 1988. It also was the third lowest 72-hole score ever shot in a women's major event, one stroke behind Patty Sheehan's 272 in the 1984 LPGA Championship and that of Jody Rosenthal in the Du Maurier Classic.

Alcott made only four bogeys the entire week, two of them on three putts. Despite beginning the final round with a seven-shot lead, she promised she wouldn't play it safe, then went out and hit 17 greens in regulation. She never had less than a five-stroke lead and the margin of victory over Dottie Mochrie was the biggest in a women's major event since Nancy Lopez finished eight strokes ahead of Alice Miller in the 1985 LPGA Championship.

"I don't remember playing this well in a tournament, much less a major," Alcott said. "I played steady, brilliant golf."

It was Alcott's 29th career victory, leaving her one short of the 30 needed to enter the LPGA Hall of Fame. It was her fifth major championship—three Dinah Shores, a U.S. Open and the Peter Jackson (now Du Maurier) Classic.

When the week began, however, Alcott's wasn't the name on everyone's lips. She hadn't won anywhere since the 1989 Boston Five Classic, more than 20 months ago, the longest drought of her career." In 1990, for the first time in 11 years she won less than $100,000, and finished 42nd on the money list. A larger void, however, was the death of her mother, Lea. "We had a very unique relationship," Alcott said. "I will miss her terribly."

Alcott's golf this week was flawless. She opened with a seven-birdie, two-bogey 67 to lead Ok Hee Ku. Alcott described her round as "Absolutely great. I've been hitting it great for a few weeks now. It was only a matter of time before the scores came around."

That was only the beginning. Playing in the second half of Friday's afternoon draw, she putted for birdie on every hole and received a standing ovation at No. 18 after hitting a 119-yard eight-iron shot from a fairway bunker to within six feet of the pin. She missed the putt, and finished with 70 for a two-shot lead over Shirley Furlong and three over Lauri Merten, Meg Mallon and Ayako Okamoto.

"Disappointed? You bet," said Alcott of her score. "I should have made more than two birdies. I really ought to be nine or 10 under. But the way I'm playing, I could win this tournament by a lot."

That she did win by a lot can be traced to Saturday's round when she extended her lead on the early holes, then refused to crack with a series of sloppy shots near the end. In the first 11 holes, she made four birdies to go 11 under par and was up by six strokes. Then she scrambled over the next seven holes, but still led by seven shots over Sheehan, Mochrie, Tammie Green and Martha Nause.

"Anything can happen," Sheehan said, "but Amy's on a mission this week and someone is going to have to shoot a great round to catch her. That's assuming she doesn't keep playing like she has."

For her part, Alcott promised not to hold anything back on Sunday. She doesn't know how to stand in the fairways and aim at the middle of the greens. "If I do that, I'll make bogeys. I need to try and knock the pins down," she said. Which is what she did. After a routine par at the first hole, a birdie at No. 2 and a bogey at No. 3, she birdied Nos. 5 and 7, played the next five holes in pars and secured the victory with a four-iron shot stiff to the pin at No. 13. With a seven-stroke lead, it was a smooth walk to the winner's circle.

Alcott's comeback from two mediocre years started when she sat down at the beginning of the season and set a few goals. She decided she wanted to win a major event, particularly the LPGA Championship,which she had never won. And the Hall of Fame was very much on her mind.

"When you've had a bad stretch like I have the last two years, it's easy for people to ask, 'What's wrong? Why isn't she winning? Is Amy washed up?'" Alcott said. "I may have lost a little confidence, but never the belief in myself that I could play this well. I feel like I have a lot of victories left in me. I wanted to win this one very badly."

Ping/Welch's Championship—$350,000
Winner: Chris Johnson

After enduring a four-year slump that included only one victory, Chris Johnson cherished her triumph in the Ping/Welch's Championship—warts and all.

Johnson, an 11-year veteran, was brilliant for three rounds over Tucson's Randolph Park North Golf Club course. Scores of 67, 69 and 65 gave her the 54-hole tournament record at 201. More importantly, her three-shot lead was cushion enough to overcome a shaky putting stroke, a final-round 72 and a late charge from Kris Tschetter.

Johnson's 273 total was just one stroke off the tournament record, which she set in 1984 as part of her "Desert Double," when she won the Turquoise Classic in Phoenix a week before. Tschetter finished second, four shots back with a final-round 66.

Those 1984 victories in the desert were Johnson's initial breakthroughs, and by 1986 she had become a top-10 money winner. She won twice in 1987 and made close to $400,000 before the bottom dropped out in 1988. Her stroke average zoomed to 73.35 and her earnings dipped to $46,219. She began to turn it around last year, winning the Atlantic City Classic, a victory she says was the key in her comeback.

"It feels good to win again," Johnson said of her Ping/Welch's victory. "It wasn't pretty, but it beats playing pretty and losing. "I couldn't seem to relax out there, but when you haven't won in so long, it's like starting all over. I believe this will be the springboard to better play."

Johnson's victory left another player on the comeback trail in deep depression. Jan Stephenson entered the final round just three strokes behind and never happier with her game since the January, 1990, mugging that resulted in a mangled ring finger. But she missed two short putts on the first five holes to fall five shots back, eventually shot 75 and finished tied for third place with Betsy King and Kristi Albers. "It's so depressing, just when I was coming back," Stephenson said. "I blew it with my putting. I was too aggressive early. I gave the tournament to her. I'll cry all the way home. It's not like Chris won it. I lost it."

Tschetter was shedding no tears, however. It was the best finish ever for the fourth-year pro, who completed her round with six straight birdies, the longest birdie streak on the LPGA this season.

Johnson and King shared the first-round lead with 67s but Johnson was all alone at 136 at the halfway point, one stroke in front of Joan Pitcock and Michelle McGann. Meg Mallon and Stephenson were three strokes back. Saturday's third round evolved into a duel between Johnson and Stephenson, who was ecstatic about her play. "There was no pain in the finger," she said. "This is the best I've played in a long, long time. It's very encouraging."

After playing the first 12 holes in one under par Saturday, Stephenson unleashed a torrid closing half-dozen holes. She birdied Nos. 12 and 13, 16 and 17 and holed a 22-foot chip for eagle at No. 18 and a round of 65, which pulled her to within one of Johnson, who was playing the 18th hole. Johnson heard the gallery screaming and figured Stephenson had made an eagle. So, she made one of her own.

"What I'm going to have to do now is go out Sunday and make some putts early, get something going and put the pressure on the rest of the field," Johnson said.

She didn't make those putts, but thanks to Stephenson she didn't have to.

Sara Lee Classic—$425,000
Winner: Nancy Lopez

Whenever Nancy Lopez takes time off from being wife and mother to grace wherever the LPGA Tour is stopping, two things happen. In victory or defeat, the 34-year-old Hall-of-Famer shows both her competitive and sensitive side.

And so it was again this week in Nashville, Tennessee, at Hermitage Golf Club, where she led wire-to-wire to win the Sara Lee Classic, the 44th victory of her career, then dedicated it to friend and fellow pro Heather Farr. "I know you're fighting out there and I was fighting here today," Lopez told Farr, who is undergoing treatment for breast cancer which required a bone marrow transplant. "You hang in there. We're all pulling for you and know you'll win."

It was Lopez's first victory since September, 1990. Furthermore, she did it in motherly fashion, as she and her husband Ray Knight are expecting their third child in November. With rounds of 65-70-71—206, Lopez defeated six-year-pro Kris Monaghan by two strokes. Lopez led Monaghan by two shots after the first round, was one in front of Sherri Steinhauer after two holes and then had to rally over the final nine holes on Sunday. That was where the competitiveness of Lopez was never more evident. Following a bogey at No. 9, she trailed Monaghan by three strokes, then played the back nine in two under par while Monaghan, feeling the pressure, bogeyed three holes down the stretch.

"I knew I had to be patient," Lopez said. "The grass was wet and you have to be careful when it's like that. On the back side, things started falling together a little better. I didn't panic after the bogey at No. 9 and saw I was three behind. I knew I had to take care of myself and not worry about what Kris was doing."

Monaghan took the loss in stride. The week had been a great experience. She had been paired with Patty Sheehan on Friday, Lopez on Saturday and Pat Bradley on Sunday. "That's three of the greatest golfers in the game," Monaghan said. "It means a lot just to rub elbows with them. I hit the ball well enough to win, but I got a little nervous when I knew I was leading. I guess I haven't been there enough."

Monaghan's nerves were frayed when she three-putted No. 15 from 30 feet for bogey, leaving her first putt five feet short. She also bogeyed Nos. 17 and 18, saying, "I was feeling the pressure through the whole back nine. I could hear the crowd roaring behind me and knew that Nancy was making birdies. That's hard to ignore."

No one else made a run at Lopez. Fact is, they went in the other direction. JoAnne Carner started only two strokes behind, but didn't make a birdie and shot 75. Steinhauer followed back-to-back 68s with 73.

"It was fun being in front the whole time," Lopez said. "When you're used to winning and haven't in some time, you savor it even more because you have to work so hard to get it."

Crestar Farm-Fresh Classic—$400,000
Winner: Hollis Stacy

To those who have wondered whatever happened to Hollis Stacy who won all those U.S. Opens years ago, plus more than a dozen other LPGA titles, the lady herself provided an answer. "Nothing," said Stacy, after winning the Crestar Farm-Fresh Classic at the Greenbrier Country Club outside Chesapeake, Virginia. "I've been here all along. Just not where anybody noticed."

They noticed this week. Stacy, 37 and winless on the LPGA Tour for more than six years, shot rounds of 70-71-72-69—282 and experienced all the nerves again of a rookie before beating Patty Sheehan, Tammie Green and Elaine Crosby by one shot. The 18-year veteran from Savannah, Georgia, clinched her 18th career victory by stringing together three birdies on the back nine on Sunday while her closest pursuers faded down the stretch.

"I'm very happy," Stacy said. "The drought was very frustrating, but what are you going to do? You're only human. You can only do your best and for the last six years, my best wasn't good enough. But I never lost faith in myself. I never doubted I could win again."

Crestar had been the scene of last year's most dominating performance, a 16-under-par nine-shot romp by Dottie Mochrie. To avoid further embarrassment of both the course and the field, tournament officials lengthened the layout by 150 yards. Scores came down considerably, and Mochrie appeared primed to win again before she injured her forearm Friday and bogeyed seven of her final 10 holes. And after shooting 80 Saturday, she withdrew.

Nina Foust and Jayne Thobois were the first-round leaders with 68s, then gave way to Green by one stroke over Crosby at the end of two rounds. Green and Crosby reversed positions heading into the final round, which saw Stacy bogged down, four shots behind.

As the tournament headed into the final nine holes Sunday, the standings were Crosby, Green, Sheehan and Stacy, in that order. Sheehan was first to fall away. A bogey at No. 13 dropped her behind, and she couldn't make it up. Green was next with a double bogey at No. 13 and a bogey at No. 15. They left the door open for Stacy and Crosby.

Stacy made her move quickly. She birdied three straight holes beginning at No. 16 and led Crosby by one stroke. Stacy bogeyed No. 17, but so did

Crosby, and Stacy won it with a par at No. 18. "When I was walking to the 18th green, a spectator asked me how I felt," Stacy said. "I told her I felt like throwing up. That's what happens when you haven't won in six years and suddenly you're a putt or two away from winning again."

Since her last victory, the 1985 Mazda Classic of Deer Creek, Stacy had fallen on hard times. Her short game, once the envy of all, went sour; she suffered a severe case of whiplash in an automobile accident in 1988 and that set her back a couple of years. And this year, she had missed the cut in two of her last three events.

"It's so competitive out here now, you can't just turn it on and off like you could 10 or 12 years ago," Stacy said. "Oh, you can turn it off, but by the time you get it going again, everyone's left you in their dust. That's why this one is special. I needed to prove I could compete with all these young ones out here now. It was very satisfying."

Centel Classic—$1,100,000
Winner: Pat Bradley

For 13 holes in the final round of the Centel Classic, the richest event in LPGA history, 39-year-old Pat Bradley couldn't buy a putt and could be seen talking to herself with every miss. Determination took over for the next five holes, however, and she birdied three of them to steal a one-shot victory over Ayako Okamoto.

"In 18 years out here, I can't remember putting worse while in contention," Bradley said. "I had to grind it out and I guess that's why it's so satisfying to win."

Bradley had rounds of 70-68-69-71—278, 10 under par for four trips over Killearn Country Club in Tallahassee, Florida. "I didn't really putt very well," she said, "But I guess I have my competitors to thank for this one. They didn't really putt very well, either." Okamoto was the only player in Sunday's final three groups who did putt well. She didn't make a bogey all day, but made only two birdies.

The victory was the 27th of Bradley's career, moving her within three of the required 30 victories she needs to enter the LPGA Hall of Fame. Her first-place check of $165,000 pushed her past Patty Sheehan into first place on the LPGA money list with $264,076. Bradley's triumph also continued the LPGA's current parity trend. The Centel Classic was the 13th tournament of the year and Bradley became the 13th different winner. That was the longest such streak to open a season since the LPGA was chartered in 1950. The previous record was 10 opening the 1985 campaign.

This tournament, however, was unlike the 12 which preceded it. It had a different feel than last year's Centel, which was played in October. The Killearn course was lengthened about 100 yards and played longer, due to recent heavy rains. The weather was unseasonably hot and humid. Then, there were the greens, which proved to be the players' biggest opponent. The LPGA hadn't played on Bermuda greens since the Hawaiian swing nearly three months ago, and most were baffled by the extremely grainy greens.

Through the first three rounds, more than a half-dozen players took turns leading, but none were able to break away. Nearly everyone blamed the greens and heat for the blahs. But none of them expected it to continue. After settling into the 54-hole lead at nine under par, by one stroke over Dickinson, Bradley predicted, "Tomorrow someone's going to get hot." And 24 hours later, she marveled, "I never thought I could shoot 71 and still win."

It was good enough because Patty Sheehan and Laura Davies self-destructed by missing three-foot putts for birdies at No. 5 and equally short ones for pars at No. 6. It was good enough because Dickinson, after making birdies on three of the first five holes to take the lead, couldn't make another birdie. It was good enough because Dottie Mochrie, the only player to sustain a charge all day, began too far back for her 68 to make any difference. She tied for third place with Dickinson, two strokes behind Bradley.

And Bradley's 71 was good enough because she wasn't frustrated by an early stretch of putting that she admitted was pathetic. Like missing an easy 10-footer at No. 2, then nullifying birdies at Nos. 5 and 7 with three-putt bogeys at Nos. 6 and 8. After missing four-foot par putts at both Nos. 10 and 11 to fall two behind Okamoto, she had had enough.

Bradley got the boost she needed on the 11th green, when she overheard her caddie tell someone a playoff would start on the 16th hole. "I decided there wasn't going to be a playoff," Bradley said. From there, she made a 25-footer at No. 14, caught Okamoto with a 12-footer at No. 15 and got the break she needed at the 455-yard uphill par-five 17th. From just off the green, Okamoto left her 30-yard pitch shot short into the fringe, while Bradley ran her pitch to within a foot of the hole for an easy birdie.

"It was a frustrating kind of day, but I never let it get to me," Bradley said. "It's easy to be patient when you're hitting the ball all over the lot and still scrambling for pars. But it's hard to be patient when you're hitting good shots and not making the putts. But I guess I fared pretty well."

Corning Classic—$400,000
Winner: Betsy King

Considering the events of a year ago, it was only right that Betsy King should win this year's Corning Classic.

In 1990, King, Nancy Lopez, JoAnne Carner and Jan Stephenson were invited to play in the LPGA Skins Game the same week. Only King called to seek tournament chairman Lee Robbins' blessing and said if he wasn't happy, she would play in his event. Robbins never forgot the gesture, and it was with extra pleasure that Robbins presented King with the $60,000 winner's check this year.

That tells you what kind of person King is. Her play tells you about the golfer. Seven strokes behind Deb Richard 36 holes into the event, King won by six. After two rounds, King was at two-under-par 142 and struggling. As has been the case most of the year, she couldn't make a putt. But on the weekend, her putter became a lethal weapon in rounds of 65 and 66 that included no bogeys and only 55 putts.

"I made every crucial putt I had the last two days," King said. "Once I got ahead, Deb tried to come back, but I never really gave her the chance."

For two rounds, it appeared no one would get in the way of Richard. She opened with 68 and 67 to lead Ayako Okamoto and Martha Foyer by three strokes. No one was paying much attention to King, who started with 69 before appearing to shoot herself out of contention with 73. She found nothing positive about her play on the greens until Saturday, when she made seven birdies, five on putts of between five and 25 feet, and added two clutch eight-footers for pars. Her 65 moved her to nine-under 207, just three strokes behind Richard, who birdied the last two holes for 69.

Was Richard feeling the pressure? "I know Betsy is capable of making a lot of birdies, but I am too," Richard answered.

But when King gets it going, intimidation usually sets in. Sunday, Richard's three-shot lead turned to one shot on No. 1, with her double bogey. For the next nine holes, the two rivals played flawlessly, with three birdies and six pars to pull away from the rest of the field.

"It was a pretty tough fight," King said. "It was a matter of one of us making the first mistake." Richard did. She missed the green at the 158-yard 11th hole with her tee shot. King knocked hers to 20 feet, and made the putt. Richard bogeyed. When King birdied the 12th hole, she led by two strokes. The breaking point came at No. 15 where King made an easy birdie. Richard three-putted for bogey and was gone, staggering in with a bogey at No. 16 and a double bogey at No. 18.

"I'm not going to tell you I played great because I didn't," Richard said. "Betsy knows how to play on Sundays. I guess I'm still learning. But I'll be back."

King thus became the 14th different winner in as many tournaments, a fact she hardly found surprising. "There could be 20 different winners after 20 weeks," King said. "That's how good the competition has gotten. You see players practicing all the time now. Our Tour has become more serious, more of a business."

Rochester International—$400,000
Winner: Rosie Jones

Just when it appeared the LPGA Tour's string of 14 different winners in its first 14 tournaments was about to end, up stepped Rosie Jones to keep the streak going and in the process ended one of her own.

When Jones came to the Rochester International, she came riding a 32-month absence from the winner's circle, dating back to the 1988 Nestle World Championship. "Yea for me," said Jones, obviously more relieved than jubilant after her two-stroke victory in the $400,000 tournament. "I was the one who stayed focus. I was the one who concentrated well. I'm really proud of how I handled the pressure this week."

Coming off her 1990 performance, it was only a matter of time before Jones would win again. She enjoyed her career-best in top-10 finishes with 15; stroke average, 71.48, and earnings, $353,832. She lost by one shot to Beth Daniel in the Kemper Open; blew a 36-hole lead at the Turquoise Classic, and a poor second round cost her the Red Robin Inamori Classic.

The biggest disappointment, however, came in the LPGA Championship where she led by two strokes after 54 holes, closed with a respectable 72 but lost by one stroke to Daniel, who roared in with 66. "Last year was hard," Jones said. "I just couldn't get the monkey off my back."

She sent the ape packing this week, however, with a dazzling 66 of her own, giving her a 72-hole total of 276 and a two-shot victory over Danielle Ammaccapane, who also had 66, and long-hitting Brandie Burton, who turned a potential 65 into a closing 68.

The real losers were Colleen Walker, Daniel and Pat Bradley. This marquee threesome began the final round first, second and third, but all stumbled badly. Bradley shot two-under 70 and finished fourth, bogeying the 16th and 18th when it appeared she might catch Jones. Daniel and Walker never got that close. They tied for fifth place.

Nobody expected them to fade, throwing the tournament open to anyone who could keep the ball in play on Locust Hill's narrow fairways and putt its slick, multi-tiered greens.

Jones took the job. She went out Sunday trailing by four strokes and took the lead with three consecutive birdies, beginning at No. 2 and played catch-me-if-you-can. Nobody could. The only player to make much of a run at Jones was Burton, who tied for the lead with a birdie at No. 11. But she hit a wild drive at No. 12 and bogeyed, losing two shots when Jones made birdie. It got no better for Burton. At No. 13, she drove 60 yards past Jones, then pulled a pitching wedge into the back bunker. She missed birdie putts of four and nine feet at Nos. 14 and 15, then drove more than 290 yards at No. 16 before hitting her pitch 40 feet past the pin. "I had hands of stone on my tee shots today," Burton said. "Unfortunately, I had them on my second shots and putts as well."

When Jones holed another 20-footer to birdie No. 16, she led by three strokes. A late charge by Ammaccapane came to nothing and, with solid pars at Nos. 17 and 18, Jones had broken her dry spell. "It's about time," Jones said. "When you know you're good enough to win and playing almost good enough to win but not winning, it gets to you. Today, it was my turn."

Atlantic City Classic—$300,000
Winner: Jane Geddes

Some golfers win because they get all the right breaks. But Jane Geddes won the Atlantic City Classic because she got all the right bumps—on the greens that is. The tournament came down to one 20-foot putt on the 53rd hole, one that Geddes had to make. It twisted and tumbled, bobbled and bumbled and finally stumbled into the cup. And that putt, for all intents and purposes, kept the door to the LPGA Hall of Fame closed at least one more week to Amy Alcott.

Alcott, looking for the magic No. 30 to meet LPGA requirements, had her fist ready to knock down the door when she birdied four of the last six holes to catch Geddes, only to see Geddes make her crucial putt and Alcott miss one of five feet on the same green. Alcott eventually finished at four-under 209 with Cindy Schreyer, a third-year pro from Peachtree City, Georgia. "I felt I played very well," Alcott said. "I just wish I could have gotten a few more putts to drop. It just didn't happen here."

Nobody was making many putts on these greens of burned-out Poa ana that were asphalt hard and wash-board bumpy. And, knowing they were going to be that way at Greate Bay Country Club, players stayed away in droves. Only 121 of them played, including one of the top-10 money winners, and only five of the 15 tournament winners from 1991. But Geddes was one of them and thus became the first player to win twice.

Another one was Alcott, who predicted before the tournament started, "No one will run away with this one because no one's going to hole a lot of putts. The greens will be the big equalizer." For two rounds, it was Alcott who holed the putts. Her opening 69 put her one back of leader Jenny Lidback, and her second-round 68 moved her past Lidback and into the lead by one stroke. Two shots behind, and all by herself in third, was Geddes, who was coming off two weeks vacation.

Geddes began the final round by making short work of the deficit. Alcott gave her an assist with a three-putt bogey at No. 3, then she took it from there with consecutive birdies at Nos. 6, 7 and 8. When she added an eight-footer at No. 12, she led Judy Dickinson by two strokes and Alcott by four.

The momentum shifted quickly. Geddes double-bogeyed No. 13, Alcott birdied. Three-shot swing. Then Alcott made a 40-footer at the next hole, and the two were tied. Then the momentum shifted again. Until No. 17, Alcott had managed to avoid thinking about the Hall of Fame. But on the tee, a fan repeatedly yelled, "Two more birdies and you're in."

"It wasn't that pleasant," Alcott said. "I was trying to approach this as just another tournament. I didn't need to be reminded that it wasn't."

After both players missed the green with their approach shots, Geddes chipped to 20 feet, Alcott to five. Geddes made her putt. Alcott didn't. "That ball went left, right, left, right and into the hole," Geddes said.

"The putt on 17 was the whole tournament," Alcott said.

"My feelings are mixed," Geddes said. "I knew that Amy was under a lot of pressure, and a part of me was very respectful of what she was trying to do. But I wanted it badly, too." And got it.

Lady Keystone Open—$400,000
Winner: Colleen Walker

While watching 15 different players win in the first 16 tournaments, Colleen Walker kept wondering, "Why not me?"

And with reason. Over one 12-round stretch, she was in the 60s seven times. At Rochester, she led by two strokes on Sunday and gave it away, and overall, she had nine top-10s in 12 starts.

Until the LPGA moved to Hershey, Pennsylvania, and the Lady Keystone Open, Walker had done everything but win. She took care of that in rather dramatic fashion—eagle at No. 16, birdie at No. 17 for a final-round 67 to charge past Kris Tschetter and Beth Daniel and win by two strokes. Walker shot 70-70-67—207 to finish nine under par. And the eagle at 16th meant the world. "I looked at the leaderboard coming off the 14th tee and saw Beth was seven under and knew I needed to make at least two birdies coming in because I knew Beth was going to make one—the 16th is so short," Walker said.

After a par at No. 15, Walker drove it 292 yards on No. 16, then hit a six iron eight feet from the pin and made the putt for eagle, and birdied the 17th from 18 feet. Now at nine under par, all she could do was wait for Daniel and hope. Daniel's finish was disappointing. She did birdie No. 16, but bogeyed No. 18 to fall into a tie with Tschetter, who finished strong with 68. "I was right in the hunt and that's all I can ask for," Daniel said. "Golf has been hard work lately. It hasn't been much fun."

Walker earned $60,000, moving her into fifth place on the money list. "I knew if I kept finishing in the top 10 every week, eventually something good was bound to happen," Walker said. "I'm not a quitter. I thought I'd have to shoot 65 or 66 to have a chance to win."

Walker began the day at four under par after consecutive 70s and trailed co-leaders Jody Anschutz and Barb Mucha by three strokes. But Anschutz struggled early on the way to 74, while Mucha got to eight under par early before making three back-nine bogeys for 73.

At different points in the final round, Walker, Daniel and Michelle Estill had the lead, and anyone of eight players could have won. Walker was the most consistent. She chipped in from 30 feet on the first hole for birdie and made no bogeys, the only contender to avoid them. "At Rochester, I gave it away on Sunday," Walker said. "So, I took a week off, thought about it and came here with a positive attitude. This is kind of a payback."

McDonald's Championship—$750,000
Winner: Beth Daniel

Just a week ago, Beth Daniel was saying that golf had been hard work lately and really hadn't been much fun. That was after finishing second to Colleen Walker. Daniel was singing a different tune this week after blowing away the field with a final-round 67 for a four-stroke victory over Pat Bradley and Sally Little in the McDonald's Championship in Wilmington, Delaware.

"I was a little bit nervous the first couple of holes because I knew the course was going to play tough and I had to play well," Daniel said. "I really, really wanted to win today."

Daniel figured it might be her day when she woke up, looked out her window and saw it was raining, adding to an already soggy course that was playing longer than its 6,378 yards. The conditions played into the hands of Daniel. "I hit the ball high and I carry it a long way," Daniel said. "On a dry course, I don't get a lot of roll, so I love it when it rains. I knew those who depend on a lot of roll would be at a disadvantage today."

Daniel not only hit it long, but also straight. On the rainy and oft-times breezy afternoon, she hit 11 fairways and 17 greens, made four birdies and only one bogey, a three putt from 60 feet at No. 10.

Little, seeking her first victory since the 1988 Du Maurier Classic, finished with 74 after three straight sub-70 rounds. Bradley couldn't mount any kind of charge and shot 71 to get a share of second place. Daniel's four-shot margin put a damper on the excitement created by a reunion of sorts—Daniel, Little and Bradley in the final group—involving three players with a collective 68 victories.

While only Daniel had her way with the Du Pont Country Club on Sunday, just about everyone did on Thursday as 42 players broke par, led by Tammie Green's 64 which broke the tournament record shared by Ayako Okamoto and Betsy King. Green's round included four birdies right out of the box, seven overall and only one on the three par fives. She needed only 26 putts in taking a three-shot lead over Daniel, Little, Deb Richard and Mary Beth Zimmerman.

The magic was gone the next day for Green, but her 71 was good enough for a share of the lead with Okamoto, who birdied six of the last nine holes for 65. They were one stroke in front of Little, Bradley and Michelle McGann, who had 66. Daniel was only three strokes back.

Little came to the front on Saturday with 67 for a 54-hole total of 203, two shots in front of Daniel (67) and three up on Bradley (70). Green and Okamoto faded with 72 and 73, respectively. It was the first time Little had led this far into an event since the 1988 Du Maurier Classic, and it left her both satisfied with her game and appreciative of being able to play. "I'm basically in the ultimate position for me as a player," said Little, who owns 15 titles, but only one since 1982. "Golf is my passion and to play it well is the ultimate."

Daniel was far less in love with her game, despite a round that included seven birdies. She complained about her short game, her putting, too many swing thoughts and said she wouldn't bet on her chances of coming out of this sane. "I think I need a psychiatrist," she said.

What Daniel got was some good advice from her caddie Greg Sheridan, who convinced his player to replace about four swing thoughts with one simple concept and go with it. She took it to the practice range Sunday morning, found it worked and went to work on winning the tournament.

With a clear mind and the damp conditions, Daniel moved early toward the lead. She gained a shot when Little bogeyed No. 2, pulled even with a birdie at No. 4 and took the lead for good with a 15-foot birdie putt at No. 12. Bradley bogeyed the 14th to fall back and Little doubled the 15th.

"My brain can handle one thought, not three or four, and I was able to get one good one starting out today and hit the ball very, very well," said Daniel, who became the Tour's second straight double winner. "Maybe this game is starting to be fun again for me."

Mazda LPGA Championship—$1,000,000
Winner: Meg Mallon

Just when an expectant Nancy Lopez has left the LPGA Tour and future Hall-of-Famers Amy Alcott, Beth Daniel, Betsy King, Pat Bradley and Patty Sheehan are beginning to talk of winding down their careers, up jumped a 20-something bundle of charisma to give Commissioner Charles Mecham's circuit just what it needed.

What better way to introduce Meg Mallon to those who thought the LPGA would forever be mired as a third-rate Tour badly in need of a transfusion of youth, exuberance and plain old-fashioned guts.

And what better place to do it than in the Mazda LPGA Championship at Bethesda (Maryland) Country Club, on national television with a spine-tingling, pressure-packed, 15-foot birdie putt on the 72nd hole. With that putt Mallon won the championship and went from being the Tour's friend-liest member to one of its best players. She had been around for four years and was into her fifth before she posted her first victory in this year's Oldsmobile Classic.

Mallon had a total of 10-under-par 274 on one of the Tour's tightest and most demanding layouts, including a last-round 67 produced in 98-degree heat which added to the tense atmosphere of a major championship. The final putt, a downhill, left-to-right breaker, gave her a one-shot victory over the more experienced Ayako Okamoto and Bradley, who had left putts hanging on the lip. When Mallon's putt fell, the gallery exploded and the first ones to reach the new champion were the greats she may one day replace. King yelled. Alcott cried. Daniel extolled, "No big deal, right Meg? I mean, it was only for the LPGA Championship." And Bradley gave her a great big bear hug.

Mallon was the only one seemingly in control, oblivious to the pressure and now the importance of what she had done. "Seriously, I tried not to get caught up in all the hype of this being a major and all," she said. "It's the media's job to make it bigger than it is. My job was to take things one shot at a time."

Like most majors, it took awhile for the most likely to succeed to get on track. Deborah McHaffie shot 66, then was gone with a second-round 81 as Okamoto moved in front with a course-record-tying 64 and a two-stroke lead over Bradley (68) and Mallon (68). Okamoto's 64 was one of 26 sub-70 rounds the first two days, two more than in all of last year's championship, when just Daniel and Rosie Jones broke par for 72 holes. The lower scores were credited to course familiarity and softer greens, but the players also predicted they would go up on the weekend.

They went up as much because of the heat as the pressure of a major. The mercury soared to 96 degrees and the humidity went up with it. Players hid in the shade or under silver-lined umbrellas between shots, but still their legs cramped, their faces drooped and the pace of play slowed dramatically. Only eight players broke par while Bradley and Mallon matched it for three-day totals of 207, and when Okamoto three-putted Nos. 17 and 18, they found themselves in a three-way tie for the lead. Barb Bunkowsky was one back and Deb Richard was at 209 with Daniel, who birdied the last five holes for an incoming 30 and a round of 68.

There would be no such charge on Sunday, however. Daniel made enough birdies, six, but had four bogeys, shot 69 and finished fourth. The battle was waged in the final pairing of Okamoto, Bradley and Mallon, with the emphasis on the latter two. Tee-to-green, Okamoto had played the best of the trio over the final 36 holes, but her putter kept aborting. After her 64 Friday, Okamoto went 27 holes without a birdie, despite 14 chances inside 10 feet. "If she burned the edge once, she burned it 20 times," Bradley would say sympathetically.

When Okamoto did make one, a 10-footer at No. 10, she was already three strokes behind Mallon, who turned in 32. Things tightened up at No. 10, where Mallon bogeyed to fall back into a tie with Bradley and Okamoto's birdie moved her to within one stroke. Back and forth they went, Mallon leading after birdies at Nos. 12 and 13, and Bradley and Okamoto catching up at No. 15. Bradley bogeyed No. 16. Mallon bogeyed No. 17. The three of them went to No. 18 tied at nine under par. "The pressure was as thick as the humidity," Bradley said. "It was like we were the only three players on the golf course. That's how hard we were concentrating."

Mallon showed her grit at No. 18 after both Bradley and Okamoto had driven into the middle of the fairway, 20 yards ahead of her drive. Undaunted, Mallon pulled out a five iron and hit it 15 feet from the pin. In retrospect, such a shot under such pressure shouldn't have surprised anyone. At the Oldsmobile Classic, Mallon won by hitting tremendous approach shots to the final two holes—a five wood at the 17th and a three iron at the 18th, each over water and into the wind to within six feet. Bradley and Okamoto followed with respectable approaches, both about 20 feet, Bradley below the hole, Okamoto to the right of it. Bradley was first to putt. It was dead in the hole, but came up three turns short. Okamoto's was more heartbreaking, defying the break of the green and hanging on the right edge by a whisker, which is as close as she's ever come to winning a major title.

Now Mallon. She looked at the putt from all sides, then kind of smiled like she knew she was going to make it. "I was glad it was downhill. I knew all I had to do was hit it on line," she said. She did, looked up and knew it was in before it was in. "It was something you dream about," she said, "making a putt on the last green to win a major championship."

The defeat only meant added frustration for the Japanese star. She is 40 years old, in her 10th season and her 16 career victories and 1987 Rolex Player of the Year Award made her one of the most successful foreign golfers ever to play in the U.S. But she's never won a major title, a fact the Japanese press will not let her forget. "There is a lot of pressure on me to win a major and today I came close," she said. "I thought I had made the putt, but not so. I am happy for Meg. She was a pleasure to play with. We enjoyed each other's company."

Mallon's victory was a popular one. As Bradley said, "Today was a tough loss for me, but Meg is a delightful person, very likeable. When people like her win, you can't help but be happy for them." While obviously glowing in victory, Mallon wasn't ready to take a place among the game's greats. "Not yet," she said. "I have a long way to go before I'm anything close to a Beth Daniel or a Patty Sheehan. I'm a slow learner and I've spent a long time observing. I hope it will make for a longer career. I don't want to be a flash in the pan."

Jamie Farr Toledo Classic—$350,000
Winner: Alice Miller

If you think it's difficult to play your way into victory circle the first time, try getting back there after a slump as long as Alice Miller's. Since winning four times in 1985, finishing third on the money list and setting records for the fastest player to earn $200,000 and $300,000 (17 events), Miller seemed to have disappeared without a trace. In the next five years, she had only one top-10 finish, her stroke average jumped from 71.55 to 76.42, and her total earnings were less than $65,000.

It had gotten to the point this year where Miller gauged success by the number of cuts made. The streak had reached nine when she came to the Jamie Farr Toledo Classic and made it all the way back to the top, beating Deb Richard on the third hole of a playoff. "I think she reverted to the Alice of old, the Alice who was a winner," Richard said. "She handled everything well, like, 'Hey, I've been here before. I can do this.'"

In the mid-1980s, Miller was a rival of Betsy King and Beth Daniel, playing right along with them. But they continued to climb and Miller fell off the face of the earth. "I'm not back in the sense that I'm a top-10 player," Miller said, "but to win in 1991 with so many good players out here is not easy."

Not to put a damper on Miller's victory, but there weren't so many good players here this week. Sandwiched between the LPGA Championship and the U.S. Women's Open, plus fighting the July 4th weekend, only six of the top 25 money winners showed up. Miller could have cared less. Meg Mallon was there and didn't win. Richard was a winner and Miller beat her, and King was here and didn't finish in the top 30. "My goal lately has been just to beat somebody," Miller said. "The 66 I had in the second round was my first since 1985 and I've had only three rounds below 70 all year. I just wanted to play with consistency this week, so I'm ahead of schedule."

Miller was never far off the lead. She opened with 69, two strokes back of Richard, then took the lead with that Saturday 66, which included seven birdies and two bogeys. That also created another first since 1985, a visit to the media center. "I don't even know the LPGA media people," Miller said. "That's how long it's been since I've been asked to the interview room. It's been a very slow process getting my game going again."

Miller shot a closing 70, but was caught by Richard, who birdied the 13th, 14th and 15th holes for a final-round 68. Richard, who won the Women's Kemper Open earlier this year in a playoff with Cindy Rarick, could have won this one if she had figured out a way to play the 18th hole. She bogeyed it the first day with a ball out of bounds, double-bogeyed it Saturday to hand Miller a two-shot lead, then missed a winning six-foot birdie putt Sunday, forcing the playoff.

On the first extra hole, Richard had a 10-footer to win and missed, and Miller came through with a 14-foot birdie putt on the third hole.

Long before the playoff, however, Miller had to survive a couple of shaky moments. She saved par at No. 5 after driving deep into the woods, then hit a three wood 192 yards through the trees and onto the green. And at No. 17, she had to make a 20-footer for par. "The three wood at No. 5 was the best shot I've hit in a long, long time," Miller said.

The victory was the eighth of Miller's career and the $52,500 first-place check was more than she earned in the last four seasons combined. "It's hard to say what this does for my career, but I know what it does for me. It's called confidence," Miller said. "The mental damage that comes with five years of bad play is something you can't imagine."

U.S. Women's Open Championship—$600,000
Winner: Meg Mallon

This U.S. Women's Open was one for the books.

It was the first one ever played in Texas, at storied old Colonial Country Club in Fort Worth.

It was won by Meg Mallon, who became the first player to win the Women's

Open and PGA Championship in the same year since Sandra Haynie in 1974.

It brought two-time defending champion Betsy King to tears over the media's reporting of her complaints that the USGA was trying to embarrass them on national television.

And it brought under questioning the USGA's decision to hold a major championship on bent grass greens at the hottest time of the year on a golf course the members played right through the July 4th weekend.

When all was said and done, however, Debbie Massey, 15-year LPGA veteran and USGA committee member, put things into perspective, saying, "USGA events are about golf for everybody. Sometimes we expect the Women's Open to be just like it is on the LPGA Tour each week, and it's just not going to be like that.

"The champion this week will be someone who works herself 150 percent, and who isn't concerned with how shiny her bag is, or whether her logos are showing. That's what the Women's Open is about. The players who play the course as they find it, who keep in mind that everyone in the field has to battle spike marks, the heat and the slow play, and are able to shrug off the bad breaks and go on to the next hole will be the ones to succeed."

That would be Meg Mallon, who, after posting rounds of 70-75-71-67— 283, one under par, to beat Pat Bradley by one stroke, observed, "I'm patient. I sit back, observe and try and take the positive out of whatever situation I'm in. I think that attitude helps a lot."

It also helped Mallon that she has a solid swing, a putting touch others would kill for and laser-sharp concentration. She doesn't see bad greens, just greens. And complaining about the heat won't make it go away. That kind of attitude has turned the 28-year-old Mallon into the hottest pressure player in golf. She used it three weeks ago to overcome oppressive humidity and a fourth-round pairing of Bradley and Ayako Okamoto and shoot a 67 to win her first major title.

On a course baked by the sun and in a field frazzled by the conditions, Mallon crafted another final-round 67 to pass veterans Bradley and Alcott. "No one's more surprised than I am," Mallon said after her victory.

Not Bradley, who fell a shot shy again. "She's on a roll and riding it to the fullest."

Not Alcott, who led late in the final round and had visions of finally bursting down the LPGA Hall of Fame door before finishing with 71 for 286. "I was ready to buy champagne for everyone," she said. "But Meg went out and won the golf championship."

Alcott then cleared up whatever confusion might be remaining as to Mallon's sudden success. "The key to winning any major championship is consistency," Alcott said. "Meg is consistent, which means she has a complete game. She's been a contender and now she's reached that time in her career when she's supposed to win. Plus, she's a happy person."

Happiness was as absent as a cooling breeze or greens that weren't patchy and loaded with spike marks. Players complained about everything and when some members of the media interpreted it as whining, King countered with, "When we complain about conditions, we're just bitches. But when the men do it, people think, 'Well, it really must be hard.'"

King did not have a good week, at one point offering $1,000 to any USGA official who could hit a shot close to a particularly impossible hole location. She had rounds of 74-78-74 before closing with 68 to finish at 294, tied with Vicki Goetze who missed by a stroke of finishing as low amateur for the third straight year.

While King was fuming, Bradley continued to play as she had all year. She took the first-round lead with a two-under-par 69, one shot in front of Mallon, Laurel Kean and Joan Pitcock. Her 73 on Friday retained a share of the top spot with Pitcock, who celebrated her 24th birthday with 72 and observed, "The greens aren't nearly as bad as everyone thinks they are. But when a few key players say they're bad, it catches on."

Alcott moved into contention with 68, but Mallon fell three strokes back after a 75 and went into a long-distance telephone conversation with her teacher Mike McGetrick, head pro at Cherry Hills. It must have worked. She came back with 71 on Saturday and picked up one on Bradley, Pitcock and Alcott, who had 72s.

"Nobody was taking off," said Mallon, who went into Sunday in a three-way tie for fifth place at 216 with Kris Tschetter and Chris Johnson, behind Bradley and Pitcock at 214 and Brandie Burton at 215. "There were no expectations and no pressure. Everything was low key."

That wasn't the case as the field turned for home Sunday. Pitcock, Burton, Tschetter and Johnson had fallen back, leaving it to Bradley, who after eight holes led Alcott by two strokes, and Mallon, who trailed by three. But Bradley bogeyed Nos. 9 and 10 to drop into a tie with Alcott, and at No. 11, Mallon's putter began to heat up.

Mallon birdied No. 11 from 21 feet to make it a threesome at the top; parred Nos. 12 and 13, then jumped in front with 18- and 25-footers for birdies at Nos. 14 and 15. Alcott got closest with birdies at Nos. 13 and 14, but three-putted No. 16, and Bradley made eight straight pars after her bogeys at Nos. 9 and 10. "It's disappointing, it's tough," Bradley said. "I didn't get these gray hairs for the hell of it. But they haven't seen the last of me yet."

It's likely, however, they haven't seen the last of Mallon, either. "Majors are intense," she said. "But that intensity makes me focus on one shot at a time. I don't know any other way."

JAL Big Apple Classic—$500,000
Winner: Betsy King

You might get Betsy King down, but you don't keep her down. A week after experiencing one frustration after another in the U.S. Women's Open, King couldn't wait to get out of Texas and away from Colonial Country Club. By the time King got to New Rochelle, New York, and friendly Wykagyl Country Club, the Women's Open was just a bad memory. Nothing more. And to prove it, King offset opening and closing 73s with middle rounds of 66 and 67 for a five-under-par 279 and a one-stroke victory over Ayako Okamoto.

King successfully defended the title she won last year in a final-round duel with Beth Daniel. It was her 25th career victory and her second of the year. But in no way did she consider it a pay-back for her performance in the Women's Open. "No," she said. "I didn't think about the Women's Open at all this week. By the time I got to New York, I had put that tournament out of my mind."

While the Women's Open may have been a distant memory, the LPGA season has been anything but a joy ride. Her swing has been erratic, her short game a disaster, and except for a couple of rounds here and there, her putting has been mediocre at best. To make matters worse, she came to the JAL Big Apple Classic off her worst two-week stretch of the year—tied for 31st and 28th places in the Jamie Farr and Women's Open—and still had three tournaments to go in an eight-week stretch. It was time for some drastic change from a player who doesn't resort to them.

What King did was retire the irons she had used since 1983, and in all her 24 previous victories, for another set. The results she sought weren't instant, but they happened. "I had been playing so bad that I figured things couldn't get much worse," King said. "I found the ball flew higher with the new irons and stopped quicker."

After 73 on Thursday, King had made all the adjustments, and a five-under 66 Friday gave her a one-shot lead over Cindy Figg-Currier and Heather Drew. Saturday, she hit 17 greens in regulation, made seven birdies and, even with three three-putt bogeys, shot 67 to extend her lead to three strokes over Figg-Currier.

Figg-Currier, known for her ability to save par from almost any situation, hadn't won but looked like she might after making five up-and-downs Saturday to remain in contention. But she started Sunday's round with four bogeys in five holes, and even playing the last 12 in one under par didn't help. She shot 74 and tied for third place with Caroline Keggi and Elaine Crosby.

Sunday belonged to King and Okamoto, King because she held on to win, and Okamoto because at one time early in the round, she was nine strokes back and lost by only one.

"Maybe I was uncomfortable with the lead," King said. "It seemed like I was playing for the middle of the greens and trying to make pars instead of shooting at the pins and putting for birdies. Ayako almost caught me."

King's slide began at No. 4, with a three-putt bogey from 30 feet. Then she hit a poor tee shot and weak chip to bogey the par-three seventh and later three-putted the 10th hole from 60 feet. Ahead, Okamoto made birdies at Nos. 9, 10 and 12 and was only two strokes behind. She then holed a 60-foot bunker shot for birdie at No. 14 to cut the deficit to one.

King was falling apart, and she knew it. "I don't care how many tournaments a person has won, anyone who says they don't get nervous is crazy," King said. "It was like I'd never been in this position before."

When King needed it, however, she found it. After seeing a leaderboard at No. 15 that showed Okamoto had made another birdie for a tie, King pulled herself together and reclaimed the lead with a two-putt birdie of her own at the par-five hole. Both players parred the final three holes.

"I was too far behind early and even when I began to catch up I wasn't confident I could win," said Okamoto, who played in her final U.S. event before heading home to Japan. "I had a feeling Betsy would make some birdies coming in."

King was more relieved than joyous after her victory. "I just hung on, that's all," she said. "I think I might keep the irons, but I'm definitely looking for another putter."

Bay State Classic—$400,000

Winner: Juli Inkster

Juli Inkster was back—back in the LPGA winner's circle after two years, most of it spent doing what all new mothers do, making sure the family was running smoothly before she went out to play.

It was vintage Inkster at the Bay State Classic in Canton, Massachusetts, where she came from rounds of 70 and 72, and six shots behind at the halfway point, to a one-stroke victory over Caroline Keggi with weekend rounds of 66 and 67.

Inkster did it the only way she knows, aggressively. On the final hole, she ripped a three-wood shot just short of the green and went on to a winning birdie. "A birdie on the final hole to win a tournament. That's what it's all about," said a very satisfied Inkster, who now has 14 victories, but won for the first time since the 1989 Crestar Classic.

Between her 13th and 14th victories, Inkster spent more time with her new daughter, Hayley Carole, now 17 months old, than on her golf game. She returned to the Tour this year, but hadn't been much of a factor until this week.

Deb Richard shot 67 to take the first-round lead by one stroke over Pat Bradley. After two rounds, it was Mitzi Edge at eight-under-par 136, by one stroke over Richard and Nancy Scranton. Inkster was six strokes behind.

Two former collegiate golfing friends, Keggi of New Mexico and Kay Cockerill of UCLA, shot 69s to lead after 54 holes, but Inkster's 66 moved her to within one stroke, joined there by rookie Brandie Burton. Only two shots behind were Meg Mallon, Bradley, Cindy Scholefield, Edge and Scranton.

Saturday night, Juli and her husband, Brian, a teaching pro, talked about how to approach Sunday's final round. "We talked about her trying to go out and have a good round," Brian said. "We had to realize there were eight good players near the top and anything can happen out there, so just play well.

"It had been two years since she had won and there had been some setbacks. At Hershey, Juli was one back going to the final round and I think she got to the first tee thinking, 'Hey I've won here before. I can do it again.' She double-bogeyed the first hole and suddenly the balloon popped. We needed a different approach this time."

Inkster and Keggi traded the lead on the first nine holes, but Inkster took over at No. 11. Mallon, playing a group ahead, got to within one stroke with a birdie at No. 13, but bogeyed the 14th and faded. The stretch run was reduced to Keggi and Inkster when Cockerill bogeyed No. 16. The two came to the 18th hole tied, creating a decision time for both.

"I could have bumped something down the middle and had a full wedge to the green, but I decided to go to my strength," Inkster said. "Besides my caddie would have shot me if I'd pulled out an iron." After Keggi hit a two iron to the middle of the fairway, Inkster pulled out the driver and hit a low draw 235 yards. Keggi hit another iron, leaving her 100 yards from the green. Inkster then hit the three wood just short of the green, 65 feet from the pin. Keggi's approach shot over a bunker stopped 15 feet from the hole; Inkster chipped to two feet. Keggi missed. Inkster didn't.

"I guess I knew deep down I could do it," Inkster said of her victory. "But

I had to get past shooting 75s and 76s. Now I can go back to being Juli Inkster and winning tournaments. Thinking you can win and doing it aren't the same. But at least I remember how."

Phar-Mor in Youngstown—$500,000
Winner: Deb Richard

You had to be a Phar-Mor accountant, or at least someone who religiously follows the LPGA Tour, to explain how Deb Richard did everything right and won the Phar-Mor in Youngstown in a playoff over Jane Geddes, and still wound up with only the third biggest check of the week.

In case you're neither, the bonus pool worked this way. The payoffs were based on how a player finished in this tournament and the drug store chain's earlier event, the Phar-Mor at Inverrary. Danielle Ammaccapane won the most, $223,750, for finishing fourth in both events, and Jane Geddes, who was second in the pool, earned $146,250.

Richard won $83,000—$75,000 for shooting rounds of 70-69-68—207 and making a 15-foot putt in the playoff to beat Geddes. And she was perfectly happy. "I don't mind at all," Richard said. "I got what I came here for. I won the tournament."

It was Richard's second victory of the year—she beat Cindy Rarick in a playoff to win the Women's Kemper Open—and her most satisfying win, considering the way things had gone for the past 11 weeks.

Beginning with the Corning Classic in May, where she finished second to Betsy King, Richard had played in eight events, won once in a playoff, lost once in a playoff, had three other top-10 finishes and a stroke average of 70.07. The $75,000 this week increased her yearly earnings to $317,655 and moved her to fourth place on the 1991 money list.

The reason Richard was overlooked was that Meg Mallon had been spectacular, winning two major championships in three weeks. "It doesn't bother me," Richard said. "Meg deserves it."

Richard wasn't given much respect for most of this week, either. She bided her time the first two days, with rounds of 70 and 69, while Ammaccapane (opening-round 66) and Juli Inkster (second-round 65 for a two-day total of 135) swapped the lead. Inkster began the final round three strokes ahead of Ammaccapane and Pat Bradley, and stretched it to four strokes at the first hole, but fell behind with bogeys at Nos. 5, 8 and 10. When neither Bradley nor Ammaccapane could take control, Richard, Geddes and Tammie Green did. "Being so far behind, all you can do is try to make birdies as fast as you can," Richard said.

Green and Richard shot four-under-par 31s on the front to take the lead, two strokes in front of Geddes. Green dropped out of contention with a bogey at No. 15, and missed an opportunity to make it a three-way playoff by three-putting No. 18. Geddes caught Richard with birdies at Nos. 13 and 15, and both finished regulation play at nine-under-par 207.

The playoff was almost anticlimactic. Because of the bonus pool and the winning share, many spectators and players were more interested in whether Ammaccapane could two-putt the final green to finish fourth for the week and win all the money. Whatever happened to the real purpose of the week:

Who could win?

Richard did on the first playoff hole. After Geddes missed a putt from 18 feet, Richard made hers from 15 feet. "I didn't pay any attention to all that other stuff," Richard said. "They can all go away talking about how much money they won, but I've got the trophy."

Stratton Mountain Classic—$450,000

Winner: Melissa McNamara

Melissa McNamara's past suggested that her star would shine on the LPGA Tour. She was the daughter of Dale McNamara, the Tulsa women's golf coach, and she had won the 1988 NCAA championship and numerous lesser college tournaments. But before the third round of the Stratton Mountain Classic, there was little to indicate she had much of a future. She was 120th on the money list for her rookie year with $18,088, and had only one top-10 finish and a scoring average of 74.97. She was 123rd on this year's money list.

Then out of nowhere, she shot a five-under-par 67 in the third round at Stratton Mountain to tie Patty Sheehan for the lead and on Sunday out-dueled Sheehan and Richard to win the championship. "I can't seem to wipe this silly smile off my face," said McNamara, who managed rounds of 71-70-67-70—278, 10 under par in the cool, windy and often rainy conditions that dominated the week. "I guess this was an upset, huh?"

You bet, considering that she had never contended in an LPGA tournament, and considering that midway through Thursday's first round, she ran off a birdie-eagle-birdie streak, saw her name on the leaderboard and was frightened into a flurry of bogeys. And so, yes, it was surprising that it was Sheehan, one of the LPGA's best players, and Richard, one of the hottest this year, who collapsed on Sunday.

Between them, Sheehan and Richard missed eight putts inside five feet, opening the door for McNamara, who took the lead with a 20-foot birdie at No. 16 and protected it with a veteran-like save for par at No. 18. All the while, McNamara was talking to herself. "I was just trying to stay loose," she said of the one-way conversation down the stretch. "I had to keep whispering to myself, 'I deserve to be here. Not only that, I enjoy being here.'"

Sheehan was convinced. "Melissa played extremely well, like she had been there before," she said.

"My ball-striking was pathetic all last year," McNamara said. "I couldn't hit it over 200 yards. There were par fours I couldn't reach in two shots. I was beginning to wonder if I should find another line of work."

Instead, four months ago, McNamara found a new teacher, Tim Cusick, who diagnosed her problem as one of poor posture, which led to a faulty swing plane which resulted in hitting the ball everywhere but on the middle of the club face. Suddenly, 30 yards returned to her drives.

McNamara remained in the background for the first two rounds. Her opening 71 trailed Richard, Rosie Jones and Laura Baugh by three strokes. After shooting 70 on Friday, she was still three shots back, behind Sheehan, Cathy Gerring and Richard. She moved into a share of the third-round lead when Sheehan bogeyed the 17th, leaving them two strokes in front of Richard and three ahead of Bradley.

"I was so nervous Sunday at breakfast that I couldn't eat," McNamara said. "But once I got to the course, I was fine. I figured nobody thought I could win, so what the heck. Just have fun."

Neither Bradley nor Richard got anything going early, and when Sheehan three-putted No. 2, McNamara had the lead. She went ahead by two strokes with a birdie at No. 4. After a double bogey at No. 5, McNamara showed her grit with birdies from 18 and 25 feet at Nos. 8 and 10 to catch Sheehan.

After McNamara birdied from 20 feet at No. 15, Sheehan missed from 10 feet then compounded the mistake by bogeying No. 16, missing a three-foot par putt. Sheehan's last gasp came at No. 17, where she left a 15-foot birdie putt short, and McNamara was perfect with an eight-foot putt for par.

"There's bound to be a time when the youngsters beat us old-timers," Sheehan said. "I remember the first time I beat (Kathy) Whitworth and (JoAnne) Carner. I'm sure Melissa must be just as thrilled."

Northgate Computer Classic—$400,000
Winner: Cindy Rarick

One round into the Northgate Computer Classic, Cindy Rarick was experiencing the same old feeling. "Oh, no, here we go again," she said to herself following 75, leaving her eight shots behind Brandie Burton and Jane Crafter. She had two missed cuts and had a tie for 34th, 51st, 55th, 58th and 69th in her last seven tournaments. In the last 23 rounds, her best score was 71.

The way Rarick had been playing, she knew it would be difficult to make up eight strokes in a 72-hole event and impossible to do in a 54-hole event. It was all so puzzling. Early in the year, she was just missing, like losing in a playoff to Deb Richard in the Women's Kemper. And although she came here this week 23rd on the money list with $123,337, almost $100,000 of that came in the season's first three months.

Nothing lasts forever, though. Rarick was the best player for the last two days at Edinburgh USA in Brooklyn Park, Minnesota, shooting a pair of 68s—her first rounds in the 60s since early June—to tie Jody Anschutz and Beth Daniel, then beat Daniel on the third playoff hole after Anschutz was eliminated on the first hole.

"In golf, you can never take anything for granted," Rarick said. "I started off the year with a bang, then all of a sudden, I hit the wall. I couldn't sleep at night. I was an absolute mess."

Getting out of it wasn't easy. Chuck Hogan, the sports psychologist, helped her feel good about herself. Johnny Miller, Harvie Ward and Dave Pelz helped her with her game, and the leaders hit walls of their own on Sunday to help her win.

Rarick posted her second straight 68 an hour before the leaders came stumbling in. Burton, who started the final round just one stroke back, made an eight on the par-five 12th hole and shot 78. Terry Jo Myers was only two strokes back, but slumped to 73. Daniel, also two behind, made only one birdie and finished with 71. Anschutz lost a two-stroke lead with a double bogey at No. 17 and shot 73.

"I had made only one bogey all week, then make a double bogey at No.

17," Anschutz said. "I had one bad swing all day and that was it. I was trying to hit a shot to the middle of the green, but I came off it and hit it in the water."

Daniel appeared to have the tournament won when she hit her approach six feet from the pin on No. 18, the first playoff hole, but her birdie putt barely missed. At No. 10, Rarick made a 12-footer for birdie, but Daniel also birdied from 10 feet. It was over at No. 11. Daniel drove poorly, missed the green, chipped to eight feet and made the putt for par, but Rarick birdied from seven feet.

"Boom, it was right in the center," Rarick said. "Oh, what a feeling! Anytime you can be that far out of the lead, then catch up and beat such a veteran player as Beth, it gives you a warm glow and a lot of satisfaction. Not to mention a confidence boost."

Chicago Sun-Times Shoot-Out—$425,000
Winner: Martha Nause

Even the harshest critics of women's golf—those who insist that it's like watching paint dry—would have trouble finding anything to grouse about if they had watched the final round of the Chicago Sun-Times Shoot-Out at Oak Brook Golf Club.

Whatever could they find wrong with this finish?

Martha Nause came to the final four holes four strokes behind Kris Monaghan and played those holes in birdie, birdie, birdie, eagle to shoot seven-under-par 65 and win the tournament by one shot.

Now that's a shootout.

Laurel Kean got rolling with an opening-round 66. Nancy Scranton shot a 66 of her own to lead at the halfway point, and Monaghan went them one better, a course-record 65 on Saturday to take a three-stroke lead into Sunday.

"I've never seen so many low scores in my life," said Pat Bradley. "Everybody out here was shooting lights out for three days. I shoot nine-under on the weekend and finished tied for sixth."

Because of its length, only 6,231 yards, the course eliminated as many as it included. In the words of Betsy King, "It gave everyone a chance. It just brings everybody back into the field. I think that's indicated by the players who are doing well."

And no one was doing it better than Monaghan. She birdied No. 14 to go to 12 under par and, with a four-shot lead, looked unbeatable. What others couldn't see, however, was the fires starting to roar within Nause, who was playing two groups ahead and had missed birdie putts inside 10 feet at Nos. 13 and 14.

"I was hitting the ball so well at that point, but wasn't making any putts," Nause said. "I knew if I could make anything coming in, I could get close to the lead. You always think you can win but, realistically, being four behind with four to play is pretty long odds. But you never give up. I was a little excited, and I think it was affecting my stroke. I knew I had to find a way to relax and suddenly the putts started dropping."

The finish unfolded this way. Nause made a 12-footer at No. 15, a six-footer at No. 16 and closed to within one stroke with a three-foot birdie at the short 310-yard 17th. About this time, Monaghan had moved to the 17th tee and checked a leaderboard for the first time since early on the back nine. Nause's name was all she saw, that and the red number 11 by her name. "I was still one ahead and felt that a birdie at No. 17 might close it out for me," Monaghan said. "But I missed my birdie putt and then I heard the roar."

It was more than a roar, almost an explosion, and it came from the 18th green. After a perfect drive and lay-up, leaving her 107 yards from the pin, Nause hit a wedge that landed 18 inches behind the hole and rolled back into the cup. "I heard the crowd," Monaghan said. "There is a birdie noise and then there is something better. I knew somebody had holed out. Then somebody yelled eagle and that it was Martha. It rattled me a little, but I knew I still had a chance to do the same thing, at least make birdie and tie her."

It didn't happen. Monaghan hit a nine-iron approach to within eight feet of the hole, but her birdie putt stopped at the right edge. "I think I played better because the last month I decided I've been way too hard on myself and that wasn't working," said Nause, whose only previous victory was the 1988 Pat Bradley International. "I don't have to concentrate on golf every waking moment. I know I have the skills."

Monaghan felt more victim than loser in finishing second. "I know I could have won and played well enough to win," she said. "But what are you going to do when somebody plays the last four holes in five under and eagles the last one from the fairway to beat you? That's just great playing."

Rail Charity Classic—$400,000
Winner: Pat Bradley

It was the time of the year when some players began to lose interest, the grind of a long season having taken its toll. But Pat Bradley wasn't one of them. A case in point. On a stormy weekend in Springfield, Illinois, Bradley came back on the Tuesday after Labor Day's final round was suspended and birdied her first two holes to put the finishing touches on a seven-under-par 65 and a six-shot victory over Danielle Ammaccapane in the Rail Charity Classic.

Bradley, whose $60,000 first prize pushed her earnings to a personal-high $616,040, finished with an LPGA 54-hole record 19-under-par 197 total, eclipsing the old mark of 18-under 198 shot by Jan Stephenson in the 1981 Mary Kay Classic. It also was Bradley's 28th career victory, leaving her two short of qualifying for the LPGA Hall of Fame.

"At this stage of my career, anytime I enter the record book, it's great," Bradley said. "Plus, it gets me one step closer to the ultimate goal, the Hall of Fame."

Beginning the final round on Labor Day tied with Britain's Laura Davies, Bradley jumped to a four-shot lead over Davies and Meg Mallon with consecutive birdies at Nos. 11, 12 and 13. Then play was suspended until Tuesday, when she picked up where she left off, making birdies at Nos. 14 and 15, giving her five straight.

"I don't think I've made this many birdies since my banner year in 1986,"

Bradley said. "But in Saturday's first round, it didn't matter how many birdies I made. It was second best."

Bradley was referring to Davies, who played the Rail Golf Club course for the first time in competition and dismantled the 6,403-yard layout with a record-setting 10-under-par 62. The 62 tied the all-time LPGA mark shared by Mickey Wright in the 1964 Tall City Open and Vicki Fergon in the 1984 San Jose Classic.

"I've never played here because it also conflicted with a tournament in Europe," Davies said. "But I'll be back. It lets me use my driver, but you have to make the putts, also." The 62 included eight birdies and an eagle, that coming on a 70-foot putt at the 485-yard par-five sixth hole.

Bradley, who played with Davies all three days, was philosophical about Davies' start. "It's one of those days of good news, bad news," she said. "The good news is I shot a great round of five under. The bad news is I'm five shots behind. I was very impressed with Laura's play."

It didn't help Bradley when Davies opened the second round with a birdie on the first hole to go 11 under par, but Bradley had some ammunition of her own. "I needed to do something in a hurry. It was getting away from me."

Bradley hurried her way to a birdie-birdie-eagle-birdie burst from No. 3 through No. 6 to pull within one shot. She got a share of the lead with a birdie at No. 10, fell one stroke behind after Davies' birdie at No. 12, then regained a tie with a short birdie at No. 18.

Before Monday's suspension of play, Bradley moved to a three-shot lead with her three birdies, while Davies leveled off, eventually shooting 72 to tie for third place with Meg Mallon. Ammaccapane, one of 18 players who had to finish Tuesday, posted a 66 to finish second.

Ping-Cellular One Championship—$400,000
Winner: Michelle Estill

Nearly everyone associated with the LPGA Tour figured that Brandie Burton would be Rookie of the Year. Among those in Burton's corner was Michelle Estill, a rookie herself and a teammate of Burton for the one year Burton attended Arizona State University.

That was before the Ping-Cellular One Championship at Columbia Edgewater Country Club in Portland, Oregon. That was before Estill, not Burton, who tied for 22nd place, became the first rookie to win since Tina Barrett in 1989. Now, all bets were off.

"This is the greatest thing that's ever happened to me," Estill said. "Until today, the greatest thing was my college graduation on December 22, 1989. I still think Brandie will be tough to beat, but I'm in the chase."

With her victory, Estill's season earnings jumped to $131,794, about $9,000 ahead of Burton.

What's unusual about all this is Estill's age. She is 28. And her golf background. She quit golf at age seven and didn't play again until she was 22, in 1985, the year she entered Arizona State. The next year, Estill finished second in the NCAA Championship.

"Basketball was my sport all those years," Estill said. "After I got out of high school, I worked three years for a mortgage company before I went to college. I actually started hitting golf balls at ASU as an outlet. I had no intention of making the game a career."

The more balls she hit, however, the more she wanted to play. She made the Arizona State team, and in 1988 and 1989 was a medalist and semifinalist in the USGA National Public Links Championships. She turned pro in 1990, but didn't qualify for the LPGA, and spent the year playing on the European Women's Tour.

"It's been tough this year," Estill said. "During one stretch, I missed nine cuts in 11 tournaments and wondered if I had made a good decision," she said. "Now, I know I did."

Estill opened the tournament with 69, one stroke behind Missie Berteotti, Danielle Ammaccapane and Vicki Fergon. She took the lead with a second-round 69 and followed it with 70, barely holding off Rosie Jones for a one-stroke victory.

Du Maurier Ltd. Classic—$700,000
Winner: Nancy Scranton

The Du Maurier Ltd. Classic, the fourth and final major on the LPGA Tour, is fast getting the reputation as a haven for the up-and-comers, a place to win for the first time. The trend started in 1989, when Tammie Green made this championship her first victory. Then came Cathy Johnston a year ago. And now, we have Nancy Scranton, who with seven holes to play was hoping to hang on and finish third. She wound up first, thanks to "the most magnificent seven holes I've ever seen played," said Debbie Massey, her playing partner and the tournament leader since the opening round.

Coming off bogeys at Nos. 10 and 11, Scranton trailed Massey by four shots. Then she caught lightening in a bottle—birdie, eagle, birdie, par, par, birdie, birdie. It left Massey in second place by three shots.

"For the longest time I would hear people talk about me and say 'the potential is there,'" said Scranton, whose best previous finish was second place in the 1989 Ocean State Open. "For me, any win would be wonderful. But to make your first win a major, against a strong field and on a golf course like this, well, it's doubly great."

Her final-round 68 gave her a 72-hole total of 279 and $105,000 from the $700,000 purse.

Victory was as sweet for Scranton as the champagne she sipped afterwards. The 30-year-old blonde joined the LPGA Tour in 1985 and had been a steady money winner until this year, when her five-year marriage to Gary Brown, once her caddie, ended in divorce. The stress left her game in a shambles, so much so that she almost gave up on the season. "I was just hoping to make $100,000," said Scranton, who had made well over that the last two years. "When I finished 10th a couple of weeks ago, I began to look for a fast finish."

Scranton's idea of a fast finish, however, didn't include winning a major championship, especially after opening rounds of 72 and 75 allowed her to survive the cut by only three shots. But Saturday, she broke Sally Little's course record with an eight-under-par 64, thanks to a hot putter that resulted in eight birdies, including three in a row from 30 feet, beginning at No. 2.

"I've never made three putts like that in the same week, never mind in succession," said Scranton, who jumped from 65th place and 10 shots out of the lead into second place, two behind Massey.

Massey was never out of the lead until Scranton's tornado swept everything and everyone out of the way. She opened with 67 to share the lead with Laura Rinker and Trish Johnson, moved one shot in front of Johnson and Dottie Mochrie with a second-round 70, and took a one-shot lead over Pam Wright into Sunday's finale. Scranton, Johnson and Rosie Jones were two strokes back.

"I was leading, but I wasn't comfortable. I was missing too many putts," Massey said. "Still, with seven holes to go, I thought I was in pretty good shape. Nobody was doing much. Then wham! It was amazing."

Scranton's iron play was deadly. Over the final seven holes, she made two birdie putts from six feet, another from five feet, one from 10 feet, missed a couple from seven feet and holed a wedge from 109 yards for her eagle at No. 13. "All I did when I shot 64 was make birdie putts, all from 15 feet or longer. I didn't hit my irons that well," Scranton said. "But today, well, I can't remember the last time I've hit my irons that well."

Massey couldn't remember when she putted so poorly. "I said before the round started I would have to shoot under par today to win, and I didn't," she said. "I had 36 putts and you don't win tournaments with 36 putts. But, really, I don't feel I lost. I was beaten."

Three players from Britain finished third at 284—Johnson, Wright and Laura Davies—while another, Caroline Pierce, tied for sixth place.

Scranton had a good feeling about the week. The Du Maurier Classic is one of her favorite tournaments. She was seventh in 1989 at Beaconsfield Golf Club in Pointe Claire, and in 1988 tied for fourth place over this same Vancouver Golf Club course. "Coming in, I had a lot of fond memories of this course," she said. "It plays long and sets up nicely with my game. But I wasn't so sure the first part of the week. On Friday, I was just battling to make the cut, and after I bogeyed Nos. 10 and 11 on Sunday, all I was trying to do was hang on and finish as high as I could."

Safeco Classic—$400,000
Winner: Pat Bradley

Sometimes Pat Bradley wonders if all the pressure involved in chasing the elusive membership into the LPGA Hall of Fame is worth it. Other times, she knows it is. The most recent of those times came in the Safeco Classic.

She turned what looked to be a walk-in-the-park victory into anything but before finally winning for the third time this year and the 29th time in her career, just one shy of the 30 victories needed for inclusion in the Hall of Fame.

"When I do make it, and I will make it, I'll probably look back on this one as an example of what it takes to get there," Bradley said. "It wasn't easy, just as getting into the Hall of Fame isn't easy."

With the victory at Meridian Valley Country Club in Kent, Washington, Bradley pushed her all-time earnings over the $4 million mark, to the unprecedented height of $4,040,074, best in LPGA history.

"I had a chance to widen my margin (of victory), but no, I had to let it go right down to the wire," Bradley said. After leading much of the four-day tournament with rounds of 69-67-72, the 40-year-old Bradley lost her advantage on the final nine to hard-charging Rosie Jones. When Jones ran into putting problems down the stretch, Bradley forced a playoff with a birdie on the final hole. Then it took her two holes before a birdie decided things.

Jones could have extended Bradley's Hall-of-Fame anxiety. She began the final round three strokes back, then ran off four birdies in five holes, beginning at No. 8, to take a one-shot lead. Chances are, Jones would have won except for putting disasters at Nos. 14 and 15. She four-putted the 14th for double bogey, missing a three-foot par putt and 18-inch bogey putt. She compounded the problem by three-putting No. 15.

At this point, Bradley was one stroke ahead, but Jones fought back with birdies at Nos. 17 and 18 and led until Bradley forged a tie with a birdie at No. 18.

"Yeah, I know I should have won," Jones said. "But I was prouder of the birdies at Nos. 17 and 18 that dug me out of a hole than the ones at Nos. 8 and 9 that got me started."

Both were shaky on the first playoff hole. Bradley sliced her drive into the creek and had to make an 18-footer for par, while Jones flew the green and made a six-footer to tie. Bradley figured enough was enough and won it on the next hole. "Twenty-nine down, one to go," Bradley said. "The waiting is killing me, but it's been worth it. My day will come, if not next week, then the next. If not this year, then next year."

MBS Classic—$350,000
Winner: Pat Bradley

Everybody knew Pat Bradley wouldn't wait until next year. Not the way she relentlessly pursued this milestone in her career. Nothing says it better than the way she finally kicked down the door of the LPGA Hall of Fame and stormed in, becoming only the 12th member.

Bradley won No. 29 last week. She won No. 30 this week. Never before in her career had she won back-to-back tournaments.

Last week, she wouldn't let Rosie Jones beat her. This week, she wouldn't let anybody beat her. Last week, she won on the second playoff hole. This week, she shot a final-round 68 and won by making the most pressurized three-foot bogey putt of her career to avoid a playoff with Michelle Estill.

"I'm thrilled. I'm happy. I'm also relieved," Bradley said after an impromptu, informal induction ceremony and champagne dousing. "And to think, I did it by winning two straight for the first time. What a great day."

Bradley was wary of her chances this week, considering her lack of success the week following a victory. And she was playing in her sixth consecutive tournament in a late-season flurry to gain the Hall of Fame before the season ended.

"That's highly unusual for me," Bradley said. "But I had to take advantage of this opportunity. The Hall of Fame is not available to everyone. And I'm glad I had to fight so hard this week to win. Nobody backed off and gave me anything."

Bradley was correct there. She opened with rounds of 72-70 at Los Coyotes Country Club, and was six strokes behind Lisa Walters, who shot a second-round course-record-tying 65. Walters, winless in eight LPGA seasons, likely was no major threat to Bradley, but between the two of them were some who could have been, such as Meg Mallon, Betsy King, Hollis Stacy and Colleen Walker. "It's never the number of strokes you are behind that worries you, it's how many players do you have to pass to get there," Bradley said. "Everybody's not going to drop back."

Bradley made her move Saturday with 67 and trailed Walters by two strokes, but only Mallon and Judy Dickinson were between her and the leader. Mallon and Dickinson faded Sunday with 73s. Walters held on for nine holes before she was swept aside by a Bradley streak of four birdies in six holes.

By the time Bradley made a 20-footer at No. 17 go five under par for the day, Walters had collapsed and would finish with 77 and tied for 11th place. Bradley's only nemesis now was the pressure. She was 12 under par, and Estill was in the clubhouse at 10 under par.

Bradley drove into a fairway bunker on the 474-yard par-five hole. "Before I went into the bunker, I asked my caddie where I stood," Bradley said of the final hole. "He told me I had a two-shot lead. All I wanted to do was get to the green with a putt for par." It wasn't that simple. Bradley pitched into the fairway and hit her approach within wedge distance of the green, but her fourth shot hung up in the fringe. She chipped weakly, leaving her with a three-footer for bogey and the victory. "I'd come too far to screw it up now," Bradley said. "I gave it a good look, but I didn't want to overdo it."

She didn't.

Daikyo World Championship—$325,000
Winner: Meg Mallon

Meg Mallon, the U.S. Women's Open and LPGA Championship winner, scored another impressive victory when she won the relocated $325,000 Daikyo World Championship of Women's Golf by five strokes over Dottie Mochrie.

Mallon was the only player in the elite 16-woman field to match or better par all three days over the windy and difficult 6,358-yard par-73 Paradise Palms Country Club in Cairns, Australia. Her rounds were 73, 72 and 71.

If anything negative can be said about Mallon's victory it's that all the best players weren't there. Missing were Pat Bradley, Beth Daniel, Patty Sheehan, Nancy Lopez, Nancy Scranton, Colleen Walker and Cindy Rarick. Some declined invitations, and others withdrew. Part of the reason was the late switch from France to Australia.

Whether any of them could have beaten Mallon this week is debatable at best. As it was, she had to contend with the likes of Deb Richard, Danielle Ammaccapane, Amy Alcott, Betsy King, Juli Inkster, Jane Geddes and international stars Laura Davies and Ayako Okamoto.

"I wish everybody had been here," Mallon said.

The real obstacle was the Paradise Palms course, which perplexed the field with its length, blustery conditions and difficult pin locations. "It was very, very demanding," said Mallon, who won $100,000. "At one point in the final round I had a six-shot lead and I still didn't feel comfortable."

How difficult was it? Alcott broke 80 only in the final round, and King and defending champion Cathy Gerring shot 81s the first day. And only Ammaccapane had a round in the 60s, an opening four-under-par 69, good for a three-shot lead. The next day, she blew to 78, helped by three bogeys and two double bogeys.

"One day I had a solid ball-striking round and got what I deserved," Ammaccapane said. "The rest of the week I didn't hit it well at all and got what I deserved. This was a killer course."

After taking a one-shot lead with her second-round 72, Mallon played cautiously, a catch-me-if-you-can style, and nobody could.

It had been a storybook season for the five-year veteran. Winless coming in, she finished with four victories, which matched Bradley's total. Her earnings of $607,677 more than tripled her previous best. And to top it off, the Women's Sports Foundation named Mallon its professional athlete of the year.

"Winning my first tournament early in the year made me believe I could compete with the top players, and things snowballed from there," Mallon said. "I've had an unbelievable year. Does it have to end?"

Nichirei International—$350,000
Winner: United States

There might have been plenty of new American faces at the Nichirei International, but the results were devastatingly familiar to the Japanese. The team of U.S. LPGA players defeated its Japanese counterpart 21½ to 10½.

It was the seventh straight victory for the American team, and their 11th overall in a series that dates to 1979. The Japanese have won only twice, the most recent coming in 1984. Each member of the U.S. team won $14,000, while each Japanese collected $7,875. The most valuable player was Deb Richard, one of the five Americans to go undefeated and untied through the three-day competition.

Whatever drama was anticipated disappeared the first day when the U.S. won seven of the eight better-ball, medal play matches, including the first six. In that string, only the team of Cindy Rarick and Elaine Crosby failed to break 70 on the 6,286-yard, par-72 Tsubuka Country Club course. Leading the way was Colleen Walker and Sherri Steinhauer with a seven-under-par 65. Ai Yu Tu and Yueh Chyn Huang was the only Japanese pair to break 70 in defeating Jane Geddes and Barb Bunkowsky, 69-71.

The Japanese girls hoped to get back into the match Saturday, but those hopes were dashed early as Richard and Dottie Mochrie easily defeated Aiko Takasu and Hiromi Takamura 67-72 in the opening match. Miki Oda and Mayumi Hirase managed to halve with Tammie Green and Ayako Okamoto, who curiously played for the U.S. rather than for Japan, but then were swept away by Walker-Steinhauer (66), Rarick-Crosby (64) and Laura Davies-Meg

Mallon (65). That made it 11½ to 1½ and though the Japanese won the final three matches of the day, the damage was done.

"The Japanese have some nice players, but they are not yet the calibre of our players," Walker said. "Our entire team played well the first two days and that made Sunday a formality." Indeed. The U.S. won nine of 16 singles on Sunday and halved two others. Green was the only player to break 70, shooting 68 in the cool, windy conditions. The Americans' winning margin of 11 points made it the most one-sided result in the series since 1985 when the U.S. won 32-16. The U.S. won the 1989 edition, contested at stroke play, by 81 shots.

Mazda Japan Classic—$550,000
Winner: Liselotte Neumann

There wasn't the usual bit of drama in this year's Mazda Japan Classic that signals the end of the official LPGA Tour season. Pat Bradley already had locked up Rolex Player-of-the-Year and Vare Trophy honors. But don't tell Sweden's Liselotte Neumann this one wasn't special. She came to the Seta Golf Club in Shiga, Japan, winless since 1988 and had no great expectations of winning here.

But when Neumann fought off Bradley and Meg Mallon with a final-round 69 to win by two strokes over Caroline Keggi and Dottie Mochrie, nothing could have been more special. "I can't believe I won. It's been so long," said Neumann, whose only previous LPGA Tour victory was the 1988 U.S. Women's Open. "When the tournament started, I had absolutely no expectations for myself. I was just trying to take it easy and have some fun. I wound up playing as well as I have in a long, long time."

Three years ago at the Mazda Japan Classic, Neumann appeared to have LPGA stardom in her hip pocket. With her U.S. Women's Open victory and Rookie-of-the-Year award, she wasn't all that disappointed when she lost the tournament to Patty Sheehan in a playoff. "I thought my career was just beginning. It had been a great year," Neumann said. "I had no idea I would be gone this long."

Neumann would have been gone longer, had not another player withdrawn, allowing her to make the field. She made the most of her opportunity, using her 69 to vault past 36-hole co-leaders Mallon and Tatsuko Ohsako. It was the only sub-70 round of the day and just one of four recorded all week on the 6,524-yard course.

She showed in the first round that this could be her week, opening with 70 to share the lead with Colleen Walker and Ohsako. Then Mallon took the spotlight with a career-best 65, leaving her tied with Ohsako and one in front of Neumann, Bradley, Mochrie, Elaine Crosby and Aki Nakano. She hit 18 greens and had only 29 putts in her bogey-free round. Only an opening 76 kept her from being in a runaway position to win for the fifth time.

"My concentration was so poor yesterday I could hear a pin drop," Mallon said. "All I wanted to do today was come out and think a little better. That 76 was a killer."

The final round looked to be a battle between Mallon and Bradley, but both stumbled to 73s, and Neumann, with four birdies in the first 16 holes, coasted to victory and won $82,500, her biggest paycheck ever.

Since her playoff loss to Sheehan in 1988, Neumann's career had stalled. Her U.S. earnings dropped to $119,915 in 1989, and even further the following year, to $82,232. Never did she come close to winning. Critics cited her lack of length. Neumann cited the competition. "I haven't played that badly," she said. "The other players have just improved so much every year that I became kind of lost."

JBP Cup Match Play Championship—$500,000
Winner: Deb Richard

Kris Tschetter was having a JCPenney Classic-kind-of-week at the JBP Cup Match Play Championship until she ran into Hawaii's newest favorite Deb Richard, who wishes the entire LPGA schedule was played there. "The islands have been awfully good to me the last 12 months," said Richard after defeating Tschetter, 2 and 1, in the 18-hole final.

The 28-year-old Richard was the defending runner-up in the event, having lost to Betsy King a year earlier. Three months later she was back and won the Women's Kemper Open, setting the stage for her best year ever—three victories and almost $500,000 in prize money. "I think I'll ask the commissioner if we can have at least a 20-week Hawaiian schedule," said Richard upon accepting the trophy and winner's check for $100,000. "Hawaii has been very, very good to me."

Richard more or less breezed to the final. She beat Jennifer Sevil, 5 and 4; Laura Davies, 3 and 1; Kristi Albers, 3 and 2, and Michelle Estill, 2 and 1, to reach the final. Her only disappointment—or was it relief—was that King wasn't there for a re-match. Tschetter took care of that in the semis, upsetting the defending champion 3 and 1.

Tschetter shouldn't have been there at all, but when Japan's Yuko Moriguchi was injured in an automobile accident, she got the call as the first alternate. And turned giant-killer. Tschetter dispatched Meg Mallon, 3 and 2, romped over Elaine Crosby, 4 and 3, survived against Martha Nause, 1 up, then beat King, 3 and 1. Her run ended on a series of missed short putts—Where was Andrade when she needed him again?—leaving her four down at the turn. She won the 14th and 16th to cut it in half, but Richard closed her out with a par at No. 17.

Tschetter's $70,000 second-place check eased the disappointment. "I'm going to write Yuko and tell her I hope she's recovering well and that I owe her a steak dinner," Tschetter said.

The $100,000 that went to Richard capped off a splendid season and set her up, she hopes, for an even better 1992. "In 1991, I wanted to build a golf swing that would allow me to hit the ball solid one shot after another," she said. "In 1992, my goal is to win a major."

Women's European Tour

Valextra Classic—£80,000
Winner: Laura Davies

Maintaining the winning form she had shown in America earlier in the season, Laura Davies won the opening event of the WPG European Tour, the Valextra Classic, in Rome. Her closing 69 for a total of seven-under-par 281 gave her the victory by four strokes.

Dale Reid, Alicia Dibos and Sarah Nicklin took the first-round lead with 69s, while Davies shot 71. Davies, the former U.S. Open champion, made her move in the second round, when she added another 71 to move within one shot of the lead held by Reid and Dibos.

A third-round 70—despite suffering from food poisoning—gave Davies the lead at 212, one stroke ahead of Reid. Davies produced an impressive performance over the closing round for her third title on Italian soil. Tania Abitbol was her nearest challenger, moving through the field with a final-round 68.

AGF Ladies Open de Paris—FF151,000
Winner: Suzanne Strudwick

England's Suzanne Strudwick gained her second victory on the European Tour when she won the AGF Ladies Open de Paris at La Boulie, France, by three strokes over England's Laura Davies and Scotland's Cathy Panton-Lewis.

Xonia Wunsch-Ruiz of Spain set the pace on the opening day with 67 while Strudwick had 70. Strudwick made her move in the second round with 67 for a 137 total, and she never relinquished the lead. She led by one shot over Trish Johnson going into the third round, then opened a three-stroke advantage by shooting 70 for a 207 total.

She played solidly through most of the final round, and not even a disappointing finish, with two sixes, allowed her rivals a sniff of the title.

Ford Ladies' Classic—£65,000
Winner: Dale Reid

Dale Reid became the European Tour's first honorary member by capturing her 20th victory at the Ford Ladies' Classic at Woburn. Any player winning 20 or more titles is awarded the honor and Reid qualified as the first when she beat Alison Nicholas by one shot to collect the £9,750 first prize.

She could have picked no finer place for her achievement than the Tour's longest running event, which was celebrating its 10th anniversary. She did it in style, leading from start to finish and holding off a tremendous challenge from Nicholas.

Reid opened with 68 to share the lead with Nicholas. She added 70, while Nicholas slipped to 74, to produce a four-shot gap. Nicholas shot 68 in the third round while Reid could only manage 71. It was an epic last round but Nicholas, having tied for the lead at the 15th, faltered at the 71st hole, where she failed to make par and fell one stroke behind. Reid's 71 and 280 total was 21 shots better than Jenny Lee Smith's winning score in 1982.

BMW European Masters—£130,000
Winner: Corinne Dibnah

Australia continued to dominate the BMW European Masters in Brussels, when Corinne Dibnah provided Australia's third victory in the event in four years.

Sweden's Catrin Nilsmark led on the first day with 69, and Dibnah was one shot behind. She took the lead with a second-round 71, one stroke ahead of Nilsmark and two ahead of Florence Descampe and Helen Alfredsson. A third-round 71—although Alfredsson was tied for the lead at one point—opened the gap to three shots.

Alfredsson never made a move on the final day and a last-round 72 by Dibnah meant her three-shot lead became a three-shot victory with a total of 284. Dibnah collected a check for £19,500, one of the top prizes in women's European golf.

La Manga Classic—£70,000
Winner: Corinne Dibnah

Corinne Dibnah won her second successive event on the WPG European Tour, the La Manga Classic in Spain. She beat South Africa's Laurette Maritz-Atkins at the first hole of a playoff to take the title. Both finished tied at six-under-par 286, two strokes ahead of Dale Reid.

Dibnah opened with 72 and was five shots behind the leaders. A disastrous second-round 77 would have meant the end for most professionals. The Australian kept her cool, however, to come back with a 69 and haul herself into contention.

She was still five shots off the pace when the final round began, but three birdies in the opening nine holes moved her one shot behind the leader, Belgium's Florence Descampe. A last-round 68 from Dibnah left Maritz-Atkins needing a par at the last to tie her. However, her success was short-lived, as Dibnah made a birdie at the first playoff hole to take the £10,500 first prize.

Hennessy Ladies' Cup—£100,000
Winner: Helen Alfredsson

Helen Alfredsson maintained her challenge for the No. 1 spot in Europe when she won the £100,000 Hennessy Ladies' Cup, which was held outside of France for the first time in its history. The Swede halted Corinne Dibnah's run of successive wins when she beat her and Marie Laure de Lorenzi in a playoff in Cologne, Germany.

Peru's Alicia Dibos set the pace with 67, but Alfredsson, Dibnah and De Lorenzi were just behind. The Australian shot 67 on the second day to move into the lead, two strokes ahead of De Lorenzi and one ahead of Alfredsson. A 71 on the third day saw her lead grow to three shots.

Alfredsson and De Lorenzi were clearly not giving up without a fight, and fired rounds of 68 and 67 to set an eight-under-par target of 280. Dibnah could do no better than a closing 71 and found herself in a three-way play-off.

All three scored birdies at the first extra hole, but De Lorenzi was eliminated at the second when she failed to match the birdies of the other two. Alfredsson scooped the £15,000 first prize with yet another birdie at the third hole. Her win moved her into second place on the money list, £14,000 behind Dibnah.

Trophee Coconut Skol—£100,000
Winner: Helen Alfredsson

Helen Alfredsson closed the gap on leader Corinne Dibnah with her second successive win in the £100,000 Trophee Coconut Skol in Paris. Alfredsson followed her triumph in the Hennessy Ladies' Cup in Germany to collect another £15,000 check for her 12-under-par total of 276.

Dibnah set the early pace with 69, but Alfredsson soon found herself in her winning stride. A second-round 68 followed by a third-round 66—equalling the course record—earned her a five-stroke lead.

At this point, Dale Reid made her move in spectacular fashion. She had begun the final round nine strokes behind Alfredsson, but hit back with two birdies in the opening three holes. She continued the onslaught on her way to a course-record 65, which would haul her into second place. But even that did not deter the Swede, whose final-round 71 was enough to secure her the title by three shots. It was not enough to dislodge Dibnah from the top of the money list, but left her only £1,100 behind.

Bloor Homes Eastleigh Classic—£70,000
Winner: Dale Reid

A final-round 58 on a par-65, 4,456-yard course enabled Scotland's Dale Reid to win the Bloor Homes Eastleigh Classic title at Fleming Park in Hampshire, England. It was her 21st European victory and took her career earnings to £300,000 since 1979.

Another Scot, Jane Connachan, set the opening lead with another 58 over the short but still testing Fleming Park course. Reid opened with 63 and then shot 64, while Connachan slipped to 70, to put her one stroke off the half-way lead held by Xonia Wunsch-Ruiz of Spain.

A third-round 64 put Reid two shots ahead of four players. She showed no mercy in the opening holes and was five under par after five, thanks to three birdies and an eagle, and was well on her way to the 58. No one could catch her, and she eventually finished at 249, eight strokes ahead of her nearest rival, Diane Barnard.

Lufthansa Ladies' German Open—£100,000
Winner: Florence Descampe

A reputation with the crowds as an exciting player was enhanced when Florence Descampe stormed through on the final day of the Lufthansa Ladies' German Open to take her first title of the season. The 22-year-old has a maturity on the golf course which belies her age, as a closing course-record 64 clearly demonstrated.

She showed signs of her form in the opening round, when she shot 66 to tie America's Jane Geddes, with defending champion Ayako Okamoto only one shot behind. A 71 in the second round saw her slip slightly, and Australia's Mardi Lunn took over at the top of the leaderboard, one stroke ahead of Descampe and three other players. Another 71 in the third round did not help the Belgian's claim on her first title, and she was three shots off the lead now held by Dale Reid.

The scoring on the final day was described as unbelievable and rightly so. Liselotte Neumann, Ayako Okamoto and Descampe were three players who made the most of it. Descampe shot 64, which included nine birdies, while Okamoto had 65 to move into third place, and Neumann, a 66 to finish second to Descampe.

Weetabix Women's British Open—£150,000
Winner: Penny Grice-Whittaker

England's Penny Grice-Whittaker came back in spectacular fashion when she won her first tournament since 1986, the Weetabix Women's British Open at Woburn. She beat a top-class field and demonstrated that one who had been regarded as one of the most talented players was back. The Yorkshire professional had taken a year off to have a baby, and her previous best finish of the season had been 11th place.

She started with 69 to be one stroke off the lead held by rookie Helen Wadsworth of England. Another 69 in the second round enabled her to take over the lead by three strokes over Kelly Markette, while Wadsworth slipped out of the picture with 75. Grice-Whittaker faltered on the third day when her 77 allowed Wadsworth to catch her. They went into the final round tied at four-under-par 215. Laura Davies and Diane Barnard were only one shot further back.

Grice-Whittaker played superbly under the pressure of having this elite pack chasing her, and finally moved a stroke ahead with a birdie at the 11th hole. It was the start of an impressive closing stretch in which she finished with 69 and a total of 284, three strokes ahead of Diane Barnard and Helen Alfredsson, while Wadsworth had to be content with sixth place.

IBM Ladies Open—£80,000
Winner: Liselotte Neumann

Huge crowds cheered Liselotte Neumann on her way to her first victory in three years at the £80,000 IBM Ladies Open at Haninge, Sweden. It was an impressive victory by the 25-year-old Swede who, since winning the 1988 U.S. Open, had not won in either Europe or America, where she now spends most of her time. Her opening three rounds, which included two 69s, earned her a five-stroke lead over rookie Lisa Hackney beginning the final day. Not even Neumann's 74 left the way open for her rivals, as Hackney slipped to 75.

Marie Laure de Lorenzi shot a record-equalling 68 in the final round to move through the leaderboard, along with Laura Davies, who shot 69, but it was not good enough to catch the Swede. It earned her valuable points in the table to decide the European Solheim Cup team for 1992. The IBM Ladies Open was the first counting event to decide the seven automatic places and set the Swede off to an impressive start to clinch her place.

BMW Italian Ladies Open—£100,000
Winner: Corinne Dibnah

Corinne Dibnah regained her place at the top of the money list with her third victory of the season in the BMW Italian Ladies Open at Albarella. With just three events remaining, there was now less than £1,500 separating Dibnah from second-place Helen Alfredsson.

She opened disappointingly with 71 but 65 in the second round moved her into contention, four shots off a blistering pace set by Marie Laure de Lorenzi at 132. A third-round 69 saw her settle in just one shot behind the new leader, Siobhan Keogh of Ireland, who was having the tournament of her career. She had only made the halfway cut three times this year and could feel the pressure mounting up as she led going into the final round.

The Australian's experience finally showed with a run of birdies which put her two strokes ahead and on her way to a three-shot victory over Florence Descampe.

English Open—£75,000
Winner: Kitrina Douglas

A new name was placed on the season's winners list as Kitrina Douglas captured the English Open title at the Tytherington Club in Cheshire. She beat Evelyn Orley at the third hole of a playoff and ended two years on the European Tour without a victory.

Laura Davies led the play on the opening day with 68, but Orley and Corinne Dibnah moved into the lead at the halfway stage at 141, with Douglas two shots behind. Davies lost touch with the leaders following a second-round 77 and Dibnah followed suit in the third round with 78. Orley was left in charge, two strokes ahead of Julie Forbes. Douglas was three strokes back going into the final round.

The par-five holes destroyed Orley's chances of outright victory, while Douglas battled to a last-round 70. They tied at 285. The Bristol professional had a chance to win at the second extra hole when a three-foot putt slipped away, but made up for it at the third, when Orley failed to save par from a bunker.

Woolmark Ladies Match Play Championship—£80,000
Winner: Federica Dassu

Italy's Federica Dassu ended six years on the European Tour without a victory at the Woolmark Ladies Match Play Championship, and she could not have picked a better place to do it. The event was held in Dassu's home town of Milan, and she did not let the home fans down when she beat Scotland's Dale Reid by a convincing margin of 5 and 4 in the final.

Match play always makes for some exciting golf, and the results in this year's championship were no exception. Laura Davies, Alison Nicholas, Diane Barnard, Marie Laure de Lorenzi and British Open champion Penny Grice-Whittaker all lost on the opening day. Then it was Dassu's turn for some "giant killing," and she beat Corinne Dibnah in the second round. The most memorable match of the day was between Gillian Stewart and Helen Wadsworth, which had to be resumed the following day after darkness closed in. Wadsworth won at the 26th hole.

Dassu eventually found herself with a tough semi-final against Trish Johnson while Reid was up against Pam Wright, who was enjoying a three-event spell on the European Tour, her first since turning professional. It turned out to be a tough match for both competitors, with Dassu finally beating Johnson by two holes and Reid eliminating Wright on the last green. In the final, four birdies in seven holes put Dassu two up and she went further ahead as Reid bogeyed three holes in a row.

Longines Classic—£110,000
Winner: Penny Grice-Whittaker

The £110,000 Longines Classic, one of the richest events on the European Tour, finally decided the 1991 money race following a season-long battle between Corinne Dibnah and Helen Alfredsson, with less than £2,000 separating them at the start of the tournament.

Penny Grice-Whittaker completed a marvellous year by winning the event, but a superb performance by Dibnah saw her finish second to snatch the money title from Alfredsson. Dibnah led with £77,508, and Alfredsson had £67,900. Dale Reid was third with £59,994.

Laura Davies led on the first day with 68. A second-round 63 by Grice-Whittaker moved her into a share of the halfway lead with Davies at 134. Dibnah made her move in the third round with 66, but Davies kept command with 69 for a total of 203, two shots ahead of Grice-Whittaker.

The final round was a grand finale to the 1991 season, with Dibnah climbing into a share of second place with a closing-round 69 and Grice-Whittaker clinching her second title with a birdie on the final hole for a total of 277.

APPENDIXES

World Money List

This listing of the 200 leading money winners in the world of professional golf in 1991 was compiled from the results of all tournaments carried in the Appendixes of this edition, along with other non-tour and international events for which accurate figures could be obtained and in which the players competed for prize money provided by someone other than the players themselves. Skins games and shootouts are not included.

In the 26 years during which World Money Lists have been compiled, the earnings of the player in the 200th position have risen from a total of $3,326 in 1966 to $174,876 in 1991. The top-200 players in 1966 earned a total of $4,680,287. In 1991, the comparable total was $91,827,807.

Because of fluctuating values of money throughout the world, it was necessary to determine an average value of non-American currency to U.S. money to prepare this listing. The conversion rates used for 1991 were: British pound = US$1.70; 135 Japanese yen = US$1; South African rand = US38¢; Australian dollar = US78¢.

POS.	PLAYER, COUNTRY	TOTAL MONEY
1	Bernhard Langer, Germany	$2,186,700
2	Fred Couples, U.S.	1,835,721
3	Ian Woosnam, Wales	1,763,159
4	Severiano Ballesteros, Spain	1,691,958
5	Ian Baker-Finch, Australia	1,495,550
6	Corey Pavin, U.S.	1,077,209
7	Tom Purtzer, U.S.	1,050,618
8	Nick Faldo, England	1,012,673
9	Payne Stewart, U.S.	994,665
10	Naomichi Ozaki, Japan	958,094
11	Paul Azinger, U.S.	952,353
12	Steven Richardson, England	952,115
13	Jose Maria Olazabal, Spain	951,272
14	Craig Stadler, U.S.	930,890
15	Rodger Davis, Australia	916,283
16	Roger Mackay, Australia	908,373
17	Andrew Magee, U.S.	896,257
18	John Daly, U.S.	895,810
19	Tsuneyuki Nakajima, Japan	862,107
20	Craig Parry, Australia	860,076
21	Steve Pate, U.S.	856,778
22	Davis Love III, U.S.	854,226
23	Lanny Wadkins, U.S.	853,229
24	Billy Andrade, U.S.	839,890
25	Colin Montgomerie, Scotland	827,938
26	Steve Elkington, Australia	798,069
27	Mark Calcavecchia, U.S.	769,263
28	Mark O'Meara, U.S.	759,454
29	Greg Norman, Australia	753,092
30	Rocco Mediate, U.S.	751,621

POS.	PLAYER, COUNTRY	TOTAL MONEY
31	Masashi Ozaki, Japan	749,547
32	Mike Hulbert, U.S.	749,390
33	Nick Price, Zimbabwe	746,875
34	Russ Cochran, U.S.	742,701
35	Mark Brooks, U.S.	714,622
36	Chip Beck, U.S.	678,920
37	Mark McNulty, Zimbabwe	675,425
38	Anders Forsbrand, Sweden	659,587
39	Jay Don Blake, U.S.	649,789
40	Per-Ulrik Johansson, Sweden	618,476
41	Bruce Lietzke, U.S.	610,522
42	Scott Hoch, U.S.	605,967
43	Jim Gallagher, Jr., U.S.	605,627
44	Jeff Sluman, U.S.	603,794
45	Larry Nelson, U.S.	596,934
46	John Cook, U.S.	583,566
47	Nolan Henke, U.S.	559,682
48	D.A. Weibring, U.S.	558,648
49	Sam Torrance, Scotland	552,539
50	Isao Aoki, Japan	549,910
51	Ted Schulz, U.S.	542,724
52	Hiroshi Makino, Japan	540,505
53	Raymond Floyd, U.S.	536,396
54	Frank Nobilo, New Zealand	532,699
55	Yoshinori Kaneko, Japan	527,409
56	David Feherty, Northern Ireland	523,722
57	Mike Harwood, Australia	522,121
58	Blaine McCallister, U.S.	519,204
59	Hale Irwin, U.S.	517,452
60	Tom Kite, U.S.	510,154
61	Paul Broadhurst, England	509,852
62	Vijay Singh, Fiji	495,358
63	Kenny Knox, U.S.	488,570
64	Chen Tze Chung, Taiwan	469,656
65	Yutaka Hagawa, Japan	463,631
66	Bob Tway, U.S.	457,680
67	Koichi Suzuki, Japan	457,373
68	Saburo Fujiki, Japan	456,580
69	Curtis Strange, U.S.	453,330
70	Brad Faxon, U.S.	452,187
71	Yoshikazu Yokoshima, Japan	447,237
72	Kenny Perry, U.S.	440,060
73	John Bland, South Africa	435,049
74	David Peoples, U.S.	431,846
75	Tsukasa Watanabe, Japan	426,904
76	David Gilford, England	423,709
77	Eduardo Romero, Argentina	422,795
78	Fuzzy Zoeller, U.S.	422,489
79	Eiichi Itai, Japan	421,390
80	Sandy Lyle, Scotland	421,371
81	Nobumitsu Yuhara, Japan	420,954
82	John Huston, U.S.	420,823
83	Mats Lanner, Sweden	420,634
84	Gene Sauers, U.S.	417,835
85	Bob Lohr, U.S.	416,609
86	Masahiro Kuramoto, Japan	410,662

POS.	PLAYER, COUNTRY	TOTAL MONEY
87	David Edwards, U.S.	402,295
88	Hideki Kase, Japan	398,796
89	Tony Johnstone, Zimbabwe	387,688
90	Ryoken Kawagishi, Japan	386,686
91	Peter Senior, Australia	386,682
92	Hal Sutton, U.S.	384,658
93	Wayne Grady, Australia	380,715
94	Yoshinori Mizumaki, Japan	376,992
95	Tom Watson, U.S.	373,159
96	David Frost, South Africa	370,334
97	Eamonn Darcy, Ireland	368,842
98	Jim Hallet, U.S.	363,335
99	Harumitsu Hamano, Japan	360,931
100	Scott Simpson, U.S.	358,141
101	Phillip Price, Wales	355,798
102	Robert Gamez, U.S.	355,688
103	Billy Ray Brown, U.S.	353,282
104	Bob Gilder, U.S.	352,827
105	Noboru Sugai, Japan	350,420
106	Peter Jacobsen, U.S.	344,155
107	Ronan Rafferty, Northern Ireland	343,273
108	Rick Gibson, Canada	342,558
109	Graham Marsh, Australia	336,838
110	Michael McLean, England	329,630
111	Steve Jones, U.S.	326,694
112	Greg J. Turner, New Zealand	324,338
113	Gary Hallberg, U.S.	323,738
114	Mark James, England	321,817
115	Ben Crenshaw, U.S.	321,538
116	Larry Mize, U.S.	320,720
117	Tateo Ozaki, Japan	320,449
118	Gil Morgan, U.S.	318,027
119	Brian Jones, Australia	315,198
120	Jay Haas, U.S.	310,087
121	Rick Fehr, U.S.	306,196
122	Ken Green, U.S.	304,165
123	Gordon Brand, Jr., Scotland	301,673
124	Tom Sieckmann, U.S.	297,236
125	Barry Lane, England	295,683
126	Teruo Sugihara, Japan	293,196
127	Brent Franklin, Canada	291,195
128	Jose Rivero, Spain	288,022
129	Bill Britton, U.S.	286,744
130	Brian Claar, U.S.	286,409
131	Akiyoshi Omachi, Japan	283,242
132	Loren Roberts, U.S.	281,174
133	Fulton Allem, South Africa	281,132
134	James Spence, England	279,588
135	Nubuo Serizawa, Japan	277,882
136	Satoshi Higashi, Japan	277,484
137	Dillard Pruitt, U.S.	276,861
138	Tetsu Nishikawa, Japan	276,027
139	Dan Forsman, U.S.	275,995
140	Wayne Riley, Australia	274,407
141	Miguel Angel Martin, Spain	273,224
142	Keith Clearwater, U.S.	272,429
143	Bruce Fleisher, U.S.	271,598

POS.	PLAYER, COUNTRY	TOTAL MONEY
144	Jeff Maggert, U.S.	265,712
145	Toru Nakamura, Japan	264,740
146	Yoshitaka Yamamoto, Japan	262,100
147	Buddy Gardner, U.S.	259,602
148	Costantino Rocca, Italy	259,015
149	Bobby Wadkins, U.S.	257,622
150	Peter Fowler, Australia	255,872
151	Katsunari Takahashi, Japan	254,270
152	Kiyoshi Murota, Japan	254,143
153	Howard Twitty, U.S.	253,795
154	Wayne Levi, U.S.	250,777
155	Peter Mitchell, England	243,420
156	Tim Simpson, U.S.	241,667
157	Fred Funk, U.S.	238,815
158	Billy Mayfair, U.S.	238,093
159	Mark McCumber, U.S.	237,702
160	Andy Bean, U.S.	237,376
161	Brett Ogle, Australia	236,230
162	Chen Tze Ming, Taiwan	235,421
163	Tadami Ueno, Japan	234,186
164	Lee Janzen, U.S.	232,742
165	Akihito Yokoyama, Japan	227,725
166	Frankie Minoza, Philippines	227,270
167	Jeff Hawkes, South Africa	226,983
168	Phil Blackmar, U.S.	223,938
169	Dave Rummells, U.S.	223,090
170	Seiki Okuda, Japan	219,931
171	Tsuyoshi Yoneyama, Japan	216,493
172	Joey Sindelar, U.S.	212,665
173	Hajime Meshiai, Japan	211,736
174	Peter Teravainen, U.S.	210,427
175	Scott Gump, U.S.	210,384
176	Ed Dougherty, U.S.	210,108
177	Hideyuki Sato, Japan	209,163
178	David Ishii, U.S.	208,568
179	Masanobu Kimura, Japan	207,824
180	Jodie Mudd, U.S.	206,536
181	Philip Walton, Ireland	206,350
182	Mike Reid, U.S.	205,204
183	Peter O'Malley, Australia	204,753
184	Duffy Waldorf, U.S.	198,581
185	Dan Halldorson, Canada	193,909
186	Malcolm Mackenzie, England	193,807
187	Kinpachi Yoshimura, Japan	193,005
188	Ed Humenik, U.S.	192,497
189	Mike Donald, U.S.	192,373
190	Jean Van de Velde, France	192,274
191	Vicente Fernandez, Argentina	191,603
192	Roger Chapman, England	191,314
193	Danny Mijovic, Canada	191,198
194	Mike Springer, U.S.	183,337
195	Neal Lancaster, U.S.	182,987
196	Dave Barr, Canada	179,555
197	Tomohiro Maruyama, Japan	178,051
198	Andrew Sherborne, England	177,445
199	Ed Fiori, U.S.	175,722
200	Dan Pohl, U.S.	174,876

The Sony Ranking
(As of December 31, 1991)

Pos.	Player	Circuit	Points Average	Total Points	No. of Events	88/90 Total	88/90 Minus	1991 Plus
1 (4)	Ian Woosnam	Eur 1	17.11	1249	73	1207	-662	704
2 (2)	Nick Faldo	Eur 2	15.34	1120	73	1465	-833	488
3 (3)	Jose Maria Olazabal	Eur 3	15.32	1226	80	1343	-729	612
4 (7)	Seve Ballesteros	Eur 4	13.70	1041	76	751	-494	784
5 (1)	Greg Norman	ANZ 1	13.11	957	73	1402	-797	352
6 (11)	Fred Couples	USA 1	12.78	1086	85	862	-492	716
7 (14)	Bernhard Langer	Eur 5	12.59	1020	81	746	-402	676
8 (5)	Payne Stewart	USA 2	11.83	982	83	1109	-599	472
9 (6)	Paul Azinger	USA 3	10.88	838	77	954	-540	424
10 (23)	Rodger Davis	ANZ 2	8.90	783	88	651	-360	492
11 (36)	Ian Baker-Finch	ANZ 3	8.70	853	98	588	-331	596
12 (9)	Mark McNulty	Afr 1	8.68	634	73	805	-443	272
13 (16)	Hale Irwin	USA 4	8.31	540	65	585	-313	268
14 (22)	Mark O'Meara	USA 5	7.86	668	85	658	-370	380
15 (21)	Lanny Wadkins	USA 6	7.61	586	77	569	-339	356
16 (8)	Tom Kite	USA 7	7.60	570	75	788	-454	236
17 (37)	Craig Parry	ANZ 4	7.32	739	101	535	-296	500
18 (56)	Corey Pavin	USA 8	7.29	656	90	361	-201	496
19 (42)	Bruce Lietzke	USA 9	7.22	433	60	333	-204	304
20 (10)	Mark Calcavecchia	USA 10	7.12	662	93	976	-562	248
21 (34)	Craig Stadler	USA 11	7.04	549	78	436	-251	364
22 (15)	Chip Beck	USA 12	6.94	576	83	695	-419	300
23 (44)	Davis Love III	USA 13	6.89	620	90	437	-229	412
24 (38)	Nick Price	Afr 2	6.60	581	88	459	-266	388
25 (12)	Curtis Strange	USA 14	6.39	460	72	757	-469	172
26 (32)	Mike Harwood	ANZ 5	6.38	619	97	594	-307	332
27 (49)	Steve Pate	USA 15	6.34	602	95	453	-279	428
28 (35)	Eduardo Romero	SAm 1	6.05	502	83	428	-218	292
29 (70)	Tom Purtzer	USA 16	6.00	492	82	262	-150	380
30 (17)	Masashi Ozaki	Jpn 1	5.90	460	78	677	-401	184
31 (13)	Larry Mize	USA 17	5.84	485	83	735	-394	144
32 (130)	Steven Richardson	Eur 6	5.77	502	87	132	-66	436
33 (43)	Tom Watson	USA 18	5.62	337	60	307	-182	212
34 (64)	Fuzzy Zoeller	USA 19	5.53	332	60	222	-130	240
35 (47)	Larry Nelson	USA 20	5.48	340	62	295	-187	232
36 (81)	Colin Montgomerie	Eur 7	5.40	529	98	289	-148	388
37 (31)	Mark James	Eur 8	5.28	412	78	478	-274	208
38 (48)	Raymond Floyd	USA 21	5.19	327	63	292	-165	200
39 (20)	Wayne Levi	USA 22	5.16	392	76	569	-297	120
40 (25)	Jodie Mudd	USA 23	5.11	378	74	571	-313	120
41 (39)	Scott Hoch	USA 24	5.11	475	93	487	-272	260
42 (46)	David Feherty	Eur 9	5.04	469	93	446	-233	256
43 (19)	Ronan Rafferty	Eur 10	5.02	457	91	732	-395	120
44 (62)	Steve Elkington	ANZ 6	4.94	459	93	347	-184	296

( ) : Figures in brackets indicate 1988/90 positions.

Pos.	Player	Circuit	Points Average	Total Points	No. of Events	88/90 Total	88/90 Minus	1991 Plus
45 (98)	John Cook	USA 25	4.92	359	73	203	-112	268
46 (18)	Tim Simpson	USA 26	4.88	429	88	708	-367	88
47 (223T)	John Daly	USA 27	4.71	358	76	60	-30	328
48 (41)	Sandy Lyle	Eur 11	4.66	401	86	456	-343	288
49 (136)	Billy Andrade	USA 28	4.63	435	94	173	-90	352
50 (29)	Peter Jacobsen	USA 29	4.61	350	76	483	-273	140
51 (27)	Wayne Grady	ANZ 7	4.57	434	95	588	-314	160
52T (28)	Ben Crenshaw	USA 30T	4.50	324	72	493	-313	144
52T (54)	Scott Simpson	USA 30T	4.50	360	80	342	-198	216
54 (101)	Frank Nobilo	ANZ 8	4.49	418	93	232	-126	312
55 (50)	Sam Torrance	Eur 12	4.44	386	87	357	-183	212
56 (30)	Steve Jones	USA 32	4.32	363	84	507	-276	132
57 (26)	Gil Morgan	USA 33	4.31	323	75	457	-254	120
58 (145)	Nolan Henke	USA 34	4.30	370	86	126	-64	308
59 (139)	Rocco Mediate	USA 35	4.30	361	84	153	-84	292
60 (107)	Mike Hulbert	USA 36	4.25	433	102	243	-130	320
61 (45)	Peter Senior	ANZ 9	4.21	450	107	495	-277	232
62 (151)	Andrew Magee	USA 37	4.17	409	98	160	-103	352
63 (51)	Bob Tway	USA 38	4.13	359	87	411	-236	184
64 (69)	Jeff Sluman	USA 39	4.13	396	96	334	-218	280
65 (55)	John Bland	Afr 3	4.09	331	81	345	-186	172
66 (95)	Mark Brooks	USA 40	4.08	412	101	256	-148	304
67 (84)	Blaine McCallister	USA 41	4.04	384	95	306	-166	244
68 (74)	Jim Gallagher, Jr.	USA 42	4.04	416	103	295	-151	272
69 (86)	Tony Johnstone	Afr 4	3.99	351	88	259	-148	240
70 (82)	Eamonn Darcy	Eur 13	3.97	302	76	243	-137	196
71 (103)	Roger Mackay	ANZ 10	3.96	309	78	181	-104	232
72 (65)	John Huston	USA 43	3.92	337	86	312	-167	192
73 (58)	Naomichi Ozaki	Jpn 2	3.88	365	94	379	-218	204
74 (175)	Jay Don Blake	USA 44	3.87	348	90	129	-73	292
75 (90)	Kenny Perry	USA 45	3.86	297	77	224	-119	192
76 (66)	Tsuneyuki Nakajima	Jpn 3	3.85	358	93	314	-188	232
77 (76)	Vijay Singh	Asa 1	3.84	411	107	302	-155	264
78 (61)	Gene Sauers	USA 46	3.82	294	77	314	-176	156
79 (134)	D.A. Weibring	USA 47	3.80	270	71	131	-85	224
80 (170)	Russ Cochran	USA 48	3.69	347	94	137	-78	288
81 (33)	Mike Reid	USA 49	3.61	267	74	447	-268	88
82 (24)	David Frost	Afr 5	3.52	327	93	631	-388	84
83 (53)	Robert Gamez	USA 50	3.51	298	85	308	-154	144
84 (52)	Brett Ogle	ANZ 11	3.44	323	94	384	-205	144
85 (79)	Jose Rivero	Eur 14	3.39	244	72	213	-129	160
86 (111)	David Edwards	USA 51	3.35	261	78	166	-93	188
87 (60)	Peter Fowler	ANZ 12	3.30	327	99	395	-212	144
88 (59)	Loren Roberts	USA 52	3.27	294	90	359	-189	124
89 (287)	David Gilford	Eur 15	3.17	247	78	51	-28	224
90 (119)	David Peoples	USA 53	3.11	258	83	187	-97	168
91 (120)	Brad Faxon	USA 54	3.10	279	90	188	-109	200
92 (78)	Gordon Brand, Jr.	Eur 16	3.09	272	88	294	-170	148
93 (97)	Hal Sutton	USA 55	3.06	269	88	219	-118	168
94 (63)	Isao Aoki	Jpn 4	3.03	270	89	330	-196	136
95 (115)	Ted Schulz	USA 56	3.03	309	102	195	-98	212
96 (72)	John Morse	USA 57	3.01	214	71	196	-98	116
97 (40)	Mark McCumber	USA 58	3.00	213	71	383	-242	72

( ) : Figures in brackets indicate 1988/90 positions.

Pos.	Player	Circuit	Points Average	Total Points	No. of Events	88/90 Total	88/90 Minus	1991 Plus
98 (93T)	Billy Ray Brown	USA 59	2.98	265	89	237	-120	148
99 (174)	Paul Broadhurst	Eur 17	2.84	224	79	104	-52	172
100 (57)	Ken Green	USA 60	2.78	264	95	384	-260	140
101 (96)	Fulton Allem	Afr 6	2.72	242	89	229	-135	148
102 (157)	Kenny Knox	USA 61	2.63	263	100	164	-93	192
103 (108)	Miguel Angel Martin	Eur 18	2.60	226	87	186	-104	144
104 (172)	Bob Lohr	USA 62	2.57	226	88	138	-92	180
105 (91)	Peter O'Malley	ANZ 13	2.56	218	85	194	-100	124
106 (813T)	Per-Ulrik Johansson	Eur 19	2.56	164	64	0	0	164
107 (117)	Bob Gilder	USA 63	2.51	216	86	194	-118	140
108 (127)	Greg Turner	ANZ 14	2.51	198	79	134	-68	132
109 (270T)	Michael McLean	Eur 20	2.48	196	79	56	-28	168
110 (113)	Andy Bean	USA 64	2.48	186	75	161	-87	112
111 (114)	Bill Britton	USA 65	2.45	223	91	198	-103	128
112 (263)	Costantino Rocca	Eur 21	2.38	174	73	52	-26	148
113 (219T)	James Spence	Eur 22	2.38	188	79	72	-36	152
114 (124)	Mats Lanner	Eur 23	2.33	205	88	151	-82	136
115 (88)	Philip Walton	Eur 24	2.28	203	89	233	-126	96
116 (67)	Billy Mayfair	USA 66	2.24	226	101	302	-152	76
117 (104)	Dan Forsman	USA 67	2.24	190	85	220	-126	96
118 (177)	Tom Sieckmann	USA 68	2.21	188	85	121	-77	144
119 (138)	Vicente Fernandez	SAm 2	2.19	162	74	124	-62	100
120 (141)	Brian Claar	USA 69	2.15	176	82	120	-60	116
121 (205)	Gary Hallberg	USA 70	2.14	182	85	93	-47	136
122 (150)	Jeff Hawkes	Afr 7	2.14	171	80	124	-73	120
123 (140)	Jack Nicklaus	USA 71	2.13	128	60	104	-56	80
124 (206)	Anders Forsbrand	Eur 25	2.10	191	91	104	-69	156
125 (222)	Rick Fehr	USA 72	2.09	159	76	78	-43	124
126 (73)	Graham Marsh	ANZ 15	2.06	163	79	248	-141	56
127 (80)	Donnie Hammond	USA 73	2.05	166	81	268	-150	48
128 (87)	Christy O'Connor, Jr.	Eur 26	2.00	138	69	199	-113	52
129 (147)	Barry Lane	Eur 27	1.99	197	99	159	-98	136
130 (202)	Jim Hallet	USA 74	1.96	200	102	122	-74	152
131 (68)	Joey Sindelar	USA 75	1.94	165	85	307	-218	76
132 (146)	Chen Tze Chung	Asa 2	1.93	164	85	134	-82	112
133 (171)	Phil Blackmar	USA 76	1.92	163	85	125	-66	104
134 (162)	Jeff Maggert	USA 77	1.90	139	73	94	-47	92
135 (116)	Ryoken Kawagishi	Jpn 5	1.90	167	88	166	-83	84
136 (143)	Malcolm Mackenzie	Eur 28	1.88	171	91	157	-82	96
137 (109)	Roger Chapman	Eur 29	1.88	169	90	207	-122	84
138 (121)	Russell Claydon	Eur 30	1.86	147	79	150	-75	72
139 (93T)	Jay Haas	USA 78	1.85	163	88	237	-154	80
140 (156)	Yoshinori Kaneko	Jpn 6	1.84	186	101	137	-71	120
141 (75)	Don Pooley	USA 79	1.83	132	72	252	-156	36
142 (71)	John Mahaffey	USA 80	1.82	151	83	305	-178	24
143 (77)	Jose Maria Canizares	Eur 31	1.81	114	63	197	-107	24
144 (159)	Mark Roe	Eur 32	1.76	150	85	141	-75	84
145 (128)	Masahiro Kuramoto	Jpn 7	1.75	168	96	184	-120	104
146 (280)	Rick Gibson	Can 1	1.71	116	68	44	-24	96
147 (465T)	Phil Mickelson (A)	USA 81	1.70	102	60	12	-6	96
148 (305)	Peter Mitchell	Eur 33	1.68	141	84	44	-23	120
149 (92)	Brian Jones	ANZ 16	1.67	159	95	255	-152	56
150 (83)	Mike Donald	USA 82	1.67	179	107	331	-172	20

( ) : Figures in brackets indicate 1988/90 positions.

Pos.	Player	Circuit	Points Average	Total Points	No. of Events	88/90 Total	88/90 Minus	1991 Plus
151 (125)	Dave Rummells	USA 83	1.65	157	95	189	-116	84
152 (89)	David Ishii	USA 84	1.61	135	84	262	-167	40
153 (100)	Brian Tennyson	USA 85	1.59	156	98	245	-129	40
154 (231)	Miguel Angel Jimenez	Eur 34	1.59	116	73	64	-32	84
155 (132)	Saburo Fujiki	Jpn 8	1.57	163	104	180	-97	80
156 (131)	Mark Lye	USA 86	1.56	136	87	163	-87	60
157T (229)	Wayne Riley	ANZ 17	1.56	168	108	102	-62	128
157T (238)	Fred Funk	USA 87	1.56	140	90	72	-36	104
159 (85)	Bill Glasson	USA 88	1.54	111	72	240	-141	12
160 (188)	Brad Bryant	USA 89	1.54	140	91	110	-58	88
161 (219T)	Jesper Parnevik	Eur 35	1.53	112	73	72	-36	76
162 (99)	Howard Clark	Eur 36	1.53	121	79	209	-124	36
163 (261)	Howard Twitty	USA 90	1.50	132	88	72	-40	100
164 (102)	Tommy Armour	USA 91	1.49	149	100	251	-138	36
165 (152)	Hideki Kase	Jpn 9	1.47	135	92	127	-64	72
166 (192)	Danny Mijovic	Can 2	1.46	104	71	80	-40	64
167 (212)	Hiroshi Makino	Jpn 10	1.45	152	105	110	-62	104
168 (211)	Koichi Suzuki	Jpn 11	1.44	125	87	92	-55	88
169 (200)	Carl Mason	Eur 37	1.43	119	83	98	-59	80
170 (169)	Doug Tewell	USA 92	1.42	105	74	120	-79	64
171 (254)	Keith Clearwater	USA 93	1.42	129	91	78	-45	96
172 (209)	Johan Rystrom	Eur 38	1.41	114	81	78	-40	76
173 (279)	Ed Dougherty	USA 94	1.40	118	84	61	-31	88
174 (278)	Jean Van de Velde	Eur 39	1.39	124	89	56	-28	96
175 (123)	Dave Barr	Can 3	1.39	110	79	167	-109	52
176 (142)	Noboru Sugai	Jpn 12	1.39	142	102	164	-86	64
177 (176)	Bobby Wadkins	USA 95	1.38	130	94	134	-80	76
178 (110)	Richard Boxall	Eur 40	1.36	109	80	205	-112	16
179 (158)	Teruo Sugihara	Jpn 13	1.35	119	88	133	-70	56
180 (129)	Stephen McAllister	Eur 41	1.35	123	91	153	-78	44
181 (122)	Mike Clayton	ANZ 18	1.34	146	109	223	-121	48
182 (155)	Tateo Ozaki	Jpn 14	1.33	129	97	152	-103	80
183 (299)	Lee Janzen	USA 96	1.33	110	83	44	-22	88
184 (133)	Chris Perry	USA 97	1.32	127	96	178	-91	40
185 (153)	Nobuo Serizawa	Jpn 15	1.31	131	100	161	-90	60
186 (135)	Dan Pohl	USA 98	1.28	78	61	122	-92	48
187 (361)	Peter Teravainen	USA 99	1.28	115	90	32	-17	100
188 (105)	Des Smyth	Eur 42	1.26	101	80	186	-125	40
189 (338)	Dillard Pruitt	USA 100	1.26	98	78	38	-20	80
190 (191)	Jay Delsing	USA 101	1.25	104	83	101	-53	56
191 (204)	Tsukasa Watanabe	Jpn 16	1.25	125	100	108	-63	80
192 (166)	Kirk Triplett	USA 102	1.23	92	75	102	-54	44
193 (298)	Gavin Levenson	Afr 8	1.22	113	93	56	-31	88
194 (198)	David Williams	Eur 43	1.21	115	95	117	-66	64
195 (187)	Bill Sander	USA 103	1.21	99	82	118	-67	48
196 (242T)	Buddy Gardner	USA 104	1.18	112	95	90	-54	76
197 (385T)	Glen Day	USA 105	1.17	74	63	20	-10	64
198 (268)	Peter Lonard	ANZ 19	1.17	75	64	46	-23	52
199T (216T)	Peter Persons	USA 106T	1.16	100	86	80	-40	60
199T (307)	Duffy Waldorf	USA 106T	1.16	100	86	51	-27	76

( ) : Figures in brackets indicate 1988/90 positions.

World's Winners of 1991

U.S. TOUR

Infiniti Tournament of Champions	Tom Kite
Northern Telecom Tucson Open	Phil Mickelson
United Airlines Hawaiian Open	Lanny Wadkins
Phoenix Open	Nolan Henke
AT&T Pebble Beach National Pro-Am	Paul Azinger
Bob Hope Chrysler Classic	Corey Pavin
Shearson Lehman Brothers Open	Jay Don Blake
Nissan Los Angeles Open	Ted Schulz
Doral Ryder Open	Rocco Mediate
Honda Classic	Steve Pate
The Nestle Invitational	Andrew Magee
USF&G Classic	Ian Woosnam (2)
The Players Championship	Steve Elkington
Masters Tournament	Ian Woosnam (3)
Deposit Guaranty Classic	Larry Silveira
MCI Heritage Classic	Davis Love III
Kmart Greater Greensboro Open	Mark Brooks
GTE Byron Nelson Classic	Nick Price
BellSouth Atlanta Classic	Corey Pavin (2)
Memorial Tournament	Kenny Perry
Southwestern Bell Colonial	Tom Purtzer
Kemper Open	Billy Andrade
Buick Classic	Billy Andrade (2)
U.S. Open Championship	Payne Stewart
Anheuser-Busch Classic	Mike Hulbert
Westinghouse-Family House Invitational	Ian Baker-Finch
Federal Express St. Jude Classic	Fred Couples
Centel Western Open	Russ Cochran
New England Classic	Bruce Fleisher
Chattanooga Classic	Dillard Pruitt
Canon Greater Hartford Open	Billy Ray Brown
Buick Open	Brad Faxon
PGA Championship	John Daly
The International	Jose Maria Olazabal (2)
Fred Meyer Challenge	Paul Azinger (2)/Ben Crenshaw
NEC World Series of Golf	Tom Purtzer (2)
Greater Milwaukee Open	Mark Brooks (2)
Canadian Open	Nick Price (2)
Hardee's Classic	D.A. Weibring
B.C. Open	Fred Couples (2)
Ryder Cup Matches	United States
Buick Southern Open	David Peoples
H.E.B. Texas Open	Blaine McCallister (2)
Las Vegas Invitational	Andrew Magee (2)
Walt Disney World-Oldsmobile Classic	Mark O'Meara
Independent Insurance Agent Open	Fulton Allem (2)
Tour Championship	Craig Stadler
Amoco Centel Championship	Jim Thorpe
Mexican Open	Jay Haas
PGA Grand Slam of Golf	Ian Woosnam (6)
Ping Kapalua International	Mike Hulbert (2)
Shark Shootout	Tom Purtzer (3)/Lanny Wadkins (2)
JCPenney Classic	Billy Andrade (3)/Kris Tschetter

CANADIAN TOUR

Payless-Pepsi Open	Rick Todd
Alberta Open	Rick Todd (2)

B.C. Open	Guy Boros
Willows Classic	Perry Parker
Manitoba Open	Kelly Gibson
Windsor Charity Classic	John Erickson
Lactantia-Sealtest Quebec Open	Phillip Hatchett
Canadian PGA	Tom Harding
Perrier Atlantic Classic	Robert Meyer
Canadian TPC	Mark Wurtz

SOUTH AMERICAN TOUR

Barquisimeto Open	Lee Porter
Prince of Wales Open	Angel Franco
Los Leones Open	Ramon Franco
Brazil Open	Angel Franco (2)
Argentina Open	Jay Don Blake (2)

U.S. SENIOR TOUR

Infiniti Senior Tournament of Champions	Bruce Crampton
Royal Caribbean Classic	Gary Player
GTE Suncoast Classic	Bob Charles
Aetna Challenge	Lee Trevino
Chrysler Cup	United States
GTE West Classic	Chi Chi Rodriguez
Vantage at the Dominion	Lee Trevino (2)
Vintage Arco Invitational	Chi Chi Rodriguez (2)
Fuji Electric Grand Slam	Miller Barber
The Tradition at Desert Mountain	Jack Nicklaus
PGA Seniors Championship	Jack Nicklaus (2)
Doug Sanders Kingwood Celebrity Classic	Mike Hill
Las Vegas Classic	Chi Chi Rodriguez (3)
Murata Reunion Pro-Am	Chi Chi Rodriguez (4)
Liberty Mutual Legends of Golf	Lee Trevino (3)/Mike Hill (2)
Bell Atlantic Classic	Jim Ferree
NYNEX Commemorative	Charles Coody
Mazda Senior Players Championship	Jim Albus
MONY Syracuse Classic	Rocky Thompson
PaineWebber Invitational	Orville Moody
Southwestern Bell Classic	Jim Colbert
Kroger Classic	Al Geiberger
Seniors British Open	Bob Verwey
Newport Cup	Larry Ziegler
Ameritech Open	Mike Hill (3)
U.S. Senior Open	Jack Nicklaus (3)
Northville Long Island Classic	George Archer
Showdown Classic	Dale Douglass
GTE Northwest Classic	Mike Hill (4)
Sunwest Bank/Charley Pride Classic	Lee Trevino (4)
GTE North Classic	George Archer (2)
First of America Classic	Harold Henning
Digital Classic	Rocky Thompson (2)
Nationwide Championship	Mike Hill (5)
Bank One Classic	DeWitt Weaver
Vantage Championship	Jim Colbert (2)
Raley's Senior Gold Rush	George Archer (3)
Transamerica Championship	Charles Coody (2)
Security Pacific Classic	John Brodie
Du Pont Cup	United States
First Development Kaanapali Classic	Jim Colbert (3)
New York Life Champions	Mike Hill (6)

EUROPEAN TOUR

Girona Open	Steven Richardson
Fujitsu Mediterranean Open	Ian Woosnam
Open de Baleares	Gavin Levenson
Open Catalonia	Jose Maria Olazabal
Portuguese Open	Steven Richardson (2)
Volvo Open di Firenze	Anders Forsbrand
Jersey European Airways Open	Sam Torrance
Benson & Hedges International Open	Bernhard Langer (2)
Madrid Open	Andrew Sherborne
Credit Lyonnais Cannes Open	David Feherty
Peugeot Spanish Open	Eduardo Romero
Lancia Martini Italian Open	Craig Parry
Volvo PGA Championship	Severiano Ballesteros (2)
Dunhill British Masters	Severiano Ballesteros (3)
Murphy's Cup	Tony Johnstone
Renault Belgian Open	Per-Ulrik Johansson
Carrolls Irish Open	Nick Faldo
Peugeot French Open	Eduardo Romero (2)
Torras Monte Carlo Open	Ian Woosnam (4)
Bell's Scottish Open	Craig Parry (2)
British Open Championship	Ian Baker-Finch (2)
Heineken Dutch Open	Payne Stewart (2)
Scandinavian Masters	Colin Montgomerie
European Pro-Celebrity	Paul Broadhurst
NM English Open	David Gilford
Volvo German Open	Mark McNulty
GA European Open	Mike Harwood
Canon European Masters-Swiss Open	Jeff Hawkes
Lancome Trophy	Frank Nobilo
Epson Grand Prix of Europe	Jose Maria Olazabal (3)
Mitsubishi Austrian Open	Mark Davis
Mercedes German Masters	Bernhard Langer (3)
Dunhill Cup	Sweden
BMW International Open	Sandy Lyle
Toyota World Match Play	Severiano Ballesteros (4)
Volvo Masters	Rodger Davis (3)
World Cup	Sweden/Ian Woosnam (5)
Johnnie Walker World Championship	Fred Couples (3)

AFRICAN TOURS

Zimbabwe Open	Keith Waters
Zambia Open	David R. Jones
Standard Chartered Kenya Open	Jeremy Robinson
Palabora Classic	John Bland
ICL International	Fulton Allem
Lexington PGA Championship	Roger Wessels
Protea Assurance South African Open	Wayne Westner
AECI Charity Classic	Wayne Westner (2)
Hollard Insurance Swazi Spa Sun Classic	Hugh Royer
Bell's Cup Players Championship	John Bland (2)
Trust Bank Tournament of Champions	John Bland (3)
Million Dollar Challenge	Bernhard Langer (4)
Fancourt Hall of Fame Championship	De Wet Basson
Goodyear Classic	Justin Hobday
Hassan II Trophy	Vijay Singh
Ivory Coast Open	Michael Besanceney
Nigerian Open	James Lebbie

AUSTRALASIAN TOUR

Daikyo Palm Meadows Cup	Greg Turner
SXL Sanctuary Cove Classic	Rodger Davis
The Vines Classic	Blaine McCallister
Mercedes-Benz Australian Match Play	Chris Patton
Pyramid Australian Masters	Peter Senior
Tasmanian Open	Chris Gray
AMP New Zealand Open	Rodger Davis (2)
Rothmans Malaysian Masters	Stewart Ginn
Perak Masters	Tod Power
Pioneer Singapore PGA Championship	Peter Teravainen
Air New Zealand Shell Open	John Morse
Asahi Glass Four Tours Championship	Europe
West End South Australian Open	Brett Ogle
Ford Australian PGA Championship	Wayne Grady
Australian Open Championship	Wayne Riley
Johnnie Walker Classic	Peter Senior (2)

ASIA/JAPAN TOURS

Hutchison Telecom Hong Kong Open	Bernhard Langer
San Miguel Philippine Open	Dennis Paulson
Epson Singapore Open	Jack Kay, Jr.
Benson & Hedges Malaysian Open	Rick Gibson
Indonesian Open	Chen Liang Hsi
Wills India Open	Ali Sher
Thai International Thailand Open	Suthep Meesamasdi
Sanyang Republic of China Open	John Jacobs
Maekyung (Korea) Open	Choi Sang Ho
Daiichi Fudosan Cup	Saburo Fujiki
Imperial Tournament	Yutaka Hagawa
Daido Shizuoka Open	Yutaka Hagawa (2)
Taylormade KSB Open	Masanobu Kimura
Pocari Sweat Open	Ryoken Kawagishi
Bridgestone Aso Open	Kiyoshi Murota
Dunlop Open	Roger Mackay
Chunichi Crowns	Severiano Ballesteros
Fuji Sankei Classic	Saburo Fujiki (2)
Japan Match Play Championship	Satoshi Higashi
Pepsi Ube Kosan	Chen Tze Chung
Mitsubishi Galant	Koichi Suzuki
JCB Sendai Classic	Tadami Ueno
Sapporo Tokyu Open	Rick Gibson (2)
Yomiuri Sapporo Beer Open	Tsuneyuki Nakajima
Mizuno Open	Roger Mackay (2)
Takeda Cup	Mitsuharu Hamano
Yonex Open Hiroshima	Eiichi Itai
Yokohama Open	Nobuo Serizawa
Nikkei Cup	Naomichi Ozaki
NST Niigata Open	Akihito Yokoyama
Japan PGA Championship	Masashi Ozaki
Maruman Open	Tetsu Nishikawa
Daiwa KBC Augusta Open	Raymond Floyd
Kansai Open	Toshikazu Sugihara
Kanto Open	Yoshinori Kaneko
Chubu Open	Teruo Nakamura
Hokkaido Open	Katsunari Takahashi
Chushikoku Open	Kosei Miyata
Kyushu Open	Kinpachi Yoshimura
Suntory Open	Naomichi Ozaki (2)

All Nippon Airways Open	Akiyoshi Omachi
Jun Classic	Masashi Ozaki (2)
Tokai Classic	Eiichi Itai (2)
Japan Open	Tsuneyuki Nakajima (2)
Asahi Beer Golf Digest	Harumitsu Hamano
Bridgestone Open	Isao Aoki
Lark Cup	Yoshikazu Yokoshima
Acom International	Masahiro Kuramoto
Visa Taiheiyo Club Masters	Roger Mackay (3)
Dunlop Phoenix	Larry Nelson
Casio World Open	Naomichi Ozaki (3)
Japan Series Hitachi Cup	Naomichi Ozaki (4)
Daikyo Open	Yutaka Makino

WOMEN'S TOURS

Jamaica Classic	Jane Geddes
Oldsmobile Classic	Meg Mallon
Phar-Mor at Inverrary	Beth Daniel
Orix Hawaiian Open	Patty Sheehan
Women's Kemper Open	Deb Richard
Inamori Classic	Laura Davies
Desert Inn International	Penny Hammel
Standard Register Ping	Daniel Ammaccapane
Nabisco Dinah Shore	Amy Alcott
Ping/Welch's Championship	Chris Johnson
Sara Lee Classic	Nancy Lopez
Crestar Farm-Fresh Classic	Hollis Stacy
Centel Classic	Pat Bradley
Corning Classic	Betsy King
Rochester International	Rosie Jones
Atlantic City Classic	Jane Geddes (2)
Lady Keystone Open	Colleen Walker
McDonald's Championship	Beth Daniel (2)
Mazda LPGA Championship	Meg Mallon (2)
Jamie Farr Toledo Classic	Alice Miller
U.S. Women's Open Championship	Meg Mallon (3)
JAL Big Apple Classic	Betsy King (2)
Bay State Classic	Juli Inkster (2)
Phar-Mor in Youngstown	Deb Richard (2)
Stratton Mountain Classic	Melissa McNamara
Northgate Computer Classic	Cindy Rarick
Chicago Sun-Times Shoot-Out	Martha Nause
Rail Charity Classic	Pat Bradley (2)
Ping-Cellular One Championship	Michelle Estill
Du Maurier Ltd. Classic	Nancy Scranton
Safeco Classic	Pat Bradley (3)
MBS Classic	Pat Bradley (4)
Daikyo World Championship	Meg Mallon (4)
Nichirei International	United States
Mazda Japan Classic	Liselotte Neumann
JBP Cup Match Play Championship	Deb Richard (3)

WOMEN'S EUROPEAN TOUR

Valextra Classic	Laura Davies (2)
AGF Ladies Open de Paris	Suzanne Strudwick
Ford Ladies' Classic	Dale Reid
BMW European Masters	Corinne Dibnah
La Manga Classic	Corinne Dibnah (2)
Hennessy Ladies' Cup	Helen Alfredsson
Trophee Coconut Skol	Helen Alfredsson (2)

Bloor Homes Eastleigh Classic	Dale Reid (2)
Lufthansa Ladies' German Open	Florence Descampe
Weetabix Women's British Open	Penny Grice-Whittaker
IBM Ladies Open	Liselotte Neumann (2)
BMW Italian Ladies Open	Corinne Dibnah (3)
English Open	Kitrina Douglas
Woolmark Ladies Match Play Championship	Federica Dassu
Longines Classic	Penny Grice-Whittaker (2)
Benson & Hedges Mixed Team Trophy	Anders Forsbrand (2)/Helen Alfredsson (3)

Multiple Winners of 1991

PLAYER	WINS	PLAYER	WINS
Mike Hill	6	Laura Davies	2
Ian Woosnam	6	Anders Forsbrand	2
Severiano Ballesteros	4	Angel Franco	2
Pat Bradley	4	Saburo Fujiki	2
Bernhard Langer	4	Jane Geddes	2
Meg Mallon	4	Rick Gibson	2
Naomichi Ozaki	4	Penny Grice-Whittaker	2
Chi Chi Rodriguez	4	Yutaka Hagawa	2
Lee Trevino	4	Mike Hulbert	2
Helen Alfredsson	3	Eiichi Itai	2
Billy Andrade	3	Betsy King	2
George Archer	3	Andrew Magee	2
John Bland	3	Blaine McCallister	2
Jim Colbert	3	Tsuneyuki Nakajima	2
Fred Couples	3	Liselotte Neumann	2
Rodger Davis	3	Masashi Ozaki	2
Corinne Dibnah	3	Craig Parry	2
Roger Mackay	3	Corey Pavin	2
Jack Nicklaus	3	Nick Price	2
Jose Maria Olazabal	3	Dale Reid	2
Tom Purtzer	3	Steven Richardson	2
Deb Richard	3	Eduardo Romero	2
Fulton Allem	2	Peter Senior	2
Paul Azinger	2	Payne Stewart	2
Ian Baker-Finch	2	Rocky Thompson	2
Jay Don Blake	2	Rick Todd	2
Mark Brooks	2	Lanny Wadkins	2
Charles Coody	2	Wayne Westner	2
Beth Daniel	2		

Career World Money List

The following is a listing of the 50 leading money winners for their careers through the 1991 season. It includes active and inactive players. The World Money List from this and the 25 previous editions of this annual and a table prepared for a companion book, *The Wonderful World of Professional Golf* (Atheneum, 1973), form the basis for this compilation. Additional figures were taken from official records of major golf associations, although the shortcomings in records-keeping in professional golf outside the United States in the 1950s and 1960s and exclusions from U.S. records in a few cases during those years prevent these figures from being completely accurate. Conversions of foreign currency figures to U.S. dollars are based on average values during the particular years involved.

POS.	PLAYER, COUNTRY	TOTAL MONEY
1	Greg Norman, Australia	$8,768,458
2	Severiano Ballesteros, Spain	8,754,571
3	Bernhard Langer, Germany	7,831,788
4	Tom Kite, U.S.	7,768,181
5	Curtis Strange, U.S.	7,513,278
6	Ian Woosnam, Wales	7,283,241
7	Jack Nicklaus, U.S.	7,229,446
8	Lee Trevino, U.S.	7,214,385
9	Lanny Wadkins, U.S.	6,921,911
10	Payne Stewart, U.S.	6,890,521
11	Tom Watson, U.S.	6,802,311
12	Fred Couples, U.S.	6,494,006
13	Masashi Ozaki, Japan	6,445,483
14	Isao Aoki, Japan	6,271,337
15	Gary Player, South Africa	6,195,289
16	Nick Faldo, England	6,137,853
17	Ben Crenshaw, U.S.	6,000,306
18	Raymond Floyd, U.S.	5,954,019
19	Miller Barber, U.S.	5,866,962
20	Hale Irwin, U.S.	5,522,242
21	Tsuneyuki Nakajima, Japan	5,514,995
22	Bob Charles, New Zealand	5,509,944
23	Craig Stadler, U.S.	5,504,986
24	David Frost, South Africa	5,470,333
25	Paul Azinger, U.S.	5,270,808
26	Sandy Lyle, Scotland	5,126,515
27	Chip Beck, U.S.	4,863,960
28	Mark Calcavecchia, U.S.	4,846,192
29	Chi Chi Rodriguez, U.S.	4,844,497
30	Mark O'Meara, U.S.	4,725,247
31	Bruce Crampton, Australia	4,681,244
32	Graham Marsh, Australia	4,658,039
33	Jose Maria Olazabal, Spain	4,591,110
34	Gene Littler, U.S.	4,560,375
35	Andy Bean, U.S.	4,535,846
36	Arnold Palmer, U.S.	4,516,993
37	Scott Hoch, U.S.	4,511,136
38	Billy Casper, U.S.	4,440,835
39	Naomichi Ozaki, Japan	4,375,691
40	Bruce Lietzke, U.S.	4,315,751

POS.	PLAYER, COUNTRY	TOTAL MONEY
41	Larry Nelson, U.S.	4,299,168
42	George Archer, U.S.	4,258,355
43	Don January, U.S.	4,208,510
44	Ian Baker-Finch	4,184,005
45	John Mahaffey, U.S.	4,078,145
46	Mark McNulty, Zimbabwe	4,007,523
47	Al Geiberger, U.S.	3,985,130
48	Rodger Davis, Australia	3,974,240
49	Larry Mize, U.S.	3,959,325
50	Wayne Levi, U.S.	3,915,143

These 50 players have won $275,599,629 in their lifetimes playing professional tournament golf.

World Senior Money List

This list includes official earnings on the Senior PGA Tour, along with other winnings in established unofficial events in the United States and elsewhere when reliable figures could be obtained.

POS.	PLAYER	TOTAL MONEY
1	Mike Hill	$1,230,657
2	George Archer	1,082,044
3	Jim Colbert	909,499
4	Lee Trevino	907,600
5	Chi Chi Rodriguez	904,763
6	Bob Charles	744,978
7	Dale Douglass	656,949
8	Al Geiberger	654,926
9	Jim Dent	645,815
10	Charles Coody	612,915
11	Bruce Crampton	547,009
12	Jack Nicklaus	544,730
13	Harold Henning	495,546
14	Gary Player	486,506
15	Rocky Thompson	480,794
16	Miller Barber	479,151
17	Gibby Gilbert	420,161
18	Simon Hobday	378,654
19	Larry Laoretti	375,090
20	J.C. Snead	307,287
21	Jim Albus	301,406
22	Jim Ferree	284,384
23	Don Massengale	282,835
24	Dick Hendrickson	281,863
25	Dave Hill	280,217
26	Tom Shaw	278,103

POS.	PLAYER	TOTAL MONEY
27	Walter Zembriski	270,951
28	Don January	267,687
29	DeWitt Weaver	264,569
30	Bobby Nichols	257,764
31	Terry Dill	249,490
32	Arnold Palmer	241,016
33	Orville Moody	235,906
34	Don Bies	205,174
35	Butch Baird	194,264
36	Gene Littler	192,231
37	Tommy Aaron	192,126
38	John Brodie	185,444
39	Dick Rhyan	179,486
40	Ben Smith	178,258
41	Bruce Devlin	176,707
42	Larry Ziegler	169,686
43	Jimmy Powell	165,194
44	Babe Hiskey	164,604
45	Al Kelley	163,884
46	John Paul Cain	155,385
47	Frank Beard	149,932
48	Rives McBee	146,995
49	Homero Blancas	139,254
50	Jim O'Hern	137,067

LPGA Money List

This list includes official winnings from the U.S. LPGA Tour, along with earnings from the JCPenney, Nikkei Cup and JBP Cup World Match Play.

POS.	PLAYER	TOTAL MONEY
1	Pat Bradley	$763,118
2	Meg Mallon	653,802
3	Beth Daniel	504,501
4	Dottie Mochrie	496,017
5	Deb Richard	493,140
6	Danielle Ammaccapane	384,425
7	Betsy King	382,785
8	Ayako Okamoto	357,312
9	Patty Sheehan	342,204
10	Jane Geddes	329,240
11	Kris Tschetter	323,532
12	Colleen Walker	313,345
13	Rosie Jones	292,164
14	Elaine Crosby	272,110
15	Amy Alcott	264,269

POS.	PLAYER	TOTAL MONEY
16	Judy Dickinson	260,467
17	Tammie Green	259,748
18	Laura Davies	258,331
19	Caroline Keggi	238,784
20	Nancy Scranton	235,427
21	Michelle Estill	230,275
22	Cindy Rarick	229,092
23	Juli Inkster	226,346
24	Brandie Burton	192,712
25	Sherri Steinhauer	185,568
26	Dawn Coe	175,513
27	Barb Bunkowsky	175,469
28	Sally Little	174,042
29	Martha Nause	165,952
30	Vicki Fergon	165,495
31	Tina Barrett	161,482
32	Kristi Albers	160,932
33	Nancy Lopez	153,772
34	Lynn Connelly	153,010
35	Liselotte Neumann	151,367
36	Kris Monaghan	143,878
37	Chris Johnson	141,416
38	Laurel Kean	136,334
39	Ok Hee Ku	134,771
40	Michelle McGann	131,963
41	Debbie Massey	131,158
42	Missie Berteotti	125,642
43	Cindy Figg-Currier	125,408
44	Hollis Stacy	125,031
45	Jody Anschutz	122,550
46	Alice Miller	118,344
47	Missie McGeorge	113,959
48	JoAnne Carner	106,057
49	Marta Figueras-Dotti	104,896
50	Alice Ritzman	102,576

U.S. Tour

Infiniti Tournament of Champions

La Costa Country Club, Carlsbad, California
Par 36-36—72; 7,022 yards

January 3-6
purse, $800,000

	SCORES				TOTAL	MONEY
Tom Kite	68	67	68	69	272	$144,000
Lanny Wadkins	65	67	73	68	273	86,400
Chip Beck	68	69	70	69	276	41,600
Fred Couples	70	68	67	71	276	41,600
Wayne Levi	70	71	69	66	276	41,600
Tommy Armour	72	71	72	66	281	26,800
Greg Norman	70	71	73	67	281	26,800
Bob Tway	73	67	70	71	281	26,800
Ben Crenshaw	74	70	67	71	282	21,275
Wayne Grady	69	72	72	69	282	21,275
Nolan Henke	72	72	70	68	282	21,275
Mark O'Meara	72	69	70	71	282	21,275
Paul Azinger	74	72	69	68	283	18,000
John Huston	70	67	73	73	283	18,000
Dan Forsman	72	71	71	71	285	16,500
Kenny Knox	71	76	72	66	285	16,500
Jodie Mudd	71	72	71	71	285	16,500
David Ishii	70	72	71	75	288	15,000
Davis Love III	74	72	69	73	288	15,000
Gil Morgan	73	74	70	71	288	15,000
Payne Stewart	74	70	75	71	290	14,000
Jim Gallagher, Jr.	77	72	74	69	292	13,250
Peter Persons	72	73	73	74	292	13,250
Joey Sindelar	76	72	74	70	292	13,250
David Frost	71	74	72	76	293	12,750
Steve Elkington	76	74	72	72	294	12,118.75
Morris Hatalsky	74	74	71	75	294	12,118.75
Hale Irwin	73	74	73	74	294	12,118.75
Peter Jacobsen	71	76	71	76	294	12,118.75
Robert Gamez	75	78	68	76	297	11,500
Tony Sills	76	75	76	74	301	11,250

Northern Telecom Tucson Open

TPC at Starpass
Par 36-36—72; 7,010 yards
Tucson National Golf Resort
Par 36-36—72; 7,305 yards
Tucson, Arizona

January 10-13
purse, $1,000,000

	SCORES				TOTAL	MONEY
*Phil Mickelson	65	71	65	71	272	
Tom Purtzer	70	70	66	67	273	$144,000
Bob Tway	64	70	71	68	273	144,000
Craig Stadler	69	64	72	70	275	68,000

	SCORES				TOTAL	MONEY
John Cook	66	69	75	66	276	39,375
Jeff Maggert	68	69	70	69	276	39,375
David Peoples	70	67	66	73	276	39,375
Brian Tennyson	69	65	73	69	276	39,375
Scott Hoch	68	66	70	73	277	27,000
Neal Lancaster	70	68	72	67	277	27,000
Rocco Mediate	67	69	70	71	277	27,000
Corey Pavin	67	67	69	74	277	27,000
Dave Rummells	71	71	67	68	277	27,000
Greg Bruckner	71	70	66	71	278	18,200
Nolan Henke	66	72	72	68	278	18,200
Kenny Knox	68	73	65	72	278	18,200
Don Pooley	69	72	68	69	278	18,200
Greg Whisman	73	67	72	66	278	18,200
Buddy Gardner	68	71	69	71	279	12,171.43
Hubert Green	69	68	70	72	279	12,171.43
Dan Pohl	70	71	69	69	279	12,171.43
Loren Roberts	70	69	71	69	279	12,171.43
Ted Schulz	70	69	71	69	279	12,171.43
Duffy Waldorf	75	67	65	72	279	12,171.43
Bobby Clampett	71	69	66	73	279	12,171.42
Mark Lye	68	70	72	70	280	8,166.67
Mike Reid	73	68	71	68	280	8,166.67
Morris Hatalsky	66	74	69	71	280	8,166.66
Bill Britton	67	73	73	68	281	6,650
Mark Brooks	74	66	65	76	281	6,650
Fred Couples	68	71	67	75	281	6,650
David Frost	71	71	70	69	281	6,650
Tommy Moore	70	67	69	75	281	6,650
Kirk Triplett	71	69	76	65	281	6,650
Ronnie Black	70	68	73	71	282	5,400
Bobby Wadkins	71	71	71	69	282	5,400
Mark Wiebe	71	70	71	70	282	5,400
Mark Calcavecchia	70	71	68	74	283	4,200
Keith Clearwater	69	73	68	73	283	4,200
Gary Hallberg	66	69	72	76	283	4,200
Dan Halldorson	70	69	72	72	283	4,200
Jim Hallet	66	75	67	75	283	4,200
Bill Sander	70	68	73	72	283	4,200
Larry Silveira	68	74	70	71	283	4,200
Mike Standly	68	71	74	70	283	4,200
Robert Gamez	70	67	73	74	284	2,928
Sean Murphy	72	69	72	71	284	2,928
Ray Stewart	68	68	73	75	284	2,928
Stan Utley	69	72	72	71	284	2,928
Denis Watson	68	71	70	75	284	2,928

United Airlines Hawaiian Open

Waialae Country Club, Honolulu, Hawaii
Par 36-36—72; 6,975 yards

January 17-20
purse, $1,100,000

	SCORES				TOTAL	MONEY
Lanny Wadkins	69	67	69	65	270	$198,000
John Cook	64	66	69	75	274	118,800
Ed Dougherty	70	68	66	71	275	74,800
Chip Beck	66	66	70	74	276	41,470

	SCORES				TOTAL	MONEY
Phil Blackmar	66	70	71	69	276	41,470
Mark Calcavecchia	68	67	72	69	276	41,470
Hale Irwin	66	69	68	73	276	41,470
Gil Morgan	66	66	69	75	276	41,470
Mark Lye	66	70	71	70	277	25,457.15
Craig Stadler	67	73	66	71	277	25,457.15
Bart Bryant	70	66	70	71	277	25,457.14
Fred Funk	69	64	71	73	277	25,457.14
Buddy Gardner	68	65	72	72	277	25,457.14
Larry Mize	64	70	70	73	277	25,457.14
Dave Rummells	67	70	65	75	277	25,457.14
Paul Azinger	67	72	68	71	278	16,500
Tom Kite	68	70	70	70	278	16,500
Corey Pavin	66	71	70	71	278	16,500
Loren Roberts	68	67	71	72	278	16,500
Curtis Strange	70	67	69	72	278	16,500
Jay Don Blake	71	70	67	71	279	9,790
Bill Britton	70	68	72	69	279	9,790
Barry Cheesman	73	65	69	72	279	9,790
Keith Clearwater	68	70	70	71	279	9,790
Ed Fiori	70	67	68	74	279	9,790
Jerry Haas	71	66	73	69	279	9,790
Ed Humenik	63	69	71	76	279	9,790
Lee Janzen	65	68	72	74	279	9,790
Tim Simpson	67	70	70	72	279	9,790
Brian Tennyson	72	68	71	68	279	9,790
Bob Estes	67	72	71	70	280	6,523.40
Scott Hoch	67	74	69	70	280	6,523.40
Steve Pate	72	69	67	72	280	6,523.40
Scott Simpson	62	68	75	75	280	6,523.40
Mike Sullivan	70	67	69	74	280	6,523.40
Brad Fabel	69	68	72	72	281	4,846.63
Jay Haas	67	70	73	71	281	4,846.63
Dan Halldorson	67	69	75	70	281	4,846.63
John Huston	71	66	73	71	281	4,846.63
Ronnie Black	69	68	71	73	281	4,846.62
Mark Brooks	66	69	73	73	281	4,846.62
Russ Cochran	70	70	69	72	281	4,846.62
Gene Sauers	67	69	72	73	281	4,846.62
Scott Gump	70	70	69	73	282	3,630
Billy Mayfair	68	68	71	75	282	3,630
Mike Standly	70	69	72	71	282	3,630
Bob Eastwood	70	67	74	72	283	3,021.34
Mike Hulbert	68	69	73	73	283	3,021.33
Larry Silveira	70	68	72	73	283	3,021.33
Dave Barr	69	72	71	72	284	2,614.86
Andy Bean	72	69	70	73	284	2,614.86
Joel Edwards	71	70	72	71	284	2,614.86
Bob Wolcott	68	73	73	70	284	2,614.86
Robert Wrenn	71	69	72	72	284	2,614.86
David Ishii	68	70	73	73	284	2,614.85
Ken Schall	66	74	71	73	284	2,614.85

Phoenix Open

TPC of Scottsdale, Scottsdale, Arizona
Par 35-36—71; 6,992 yards

January 24-27
purse, $1,000,000

	SCORES				TOTAL	MONEY
Nolan Henke	65	66	66	71	268	$180,000
Gil Morgan	66	67	70	66	269	74,666.67
Tom Watson	68	68	68	65	269	74,666.67
Curtis Strange	64	67	71	67	269	74,666.66
Jay Don Blake	68	66	70	66	270	35,125
Mike Hulbert	68	72	65	65	270	35,125
Bruce Lietzke	67	68	68	67	270	35,125
Andrew Magee	72	65	67	66	270	35,125
Rocco Mediate	70	68	68	65	271	27,000
Gene Sauers	65	69	68	69	271	27,000
Bob Tway	65	69	68	69	271	27,000
Fred Funk	71	65	66	70	272	19,000
Steve Jones	63	70	70	69	272	19,000
Sandy Lyle	65	70	70	67	272	19,000
Mark O'Meara	70	65	70	67	272	19,000
Dan Pohl	68	68	68	68	272	19,000
Robert Wrenn	65	69	67	71	272	19,000
Michael Allen	68	68	71	66	273	12,600
Chip Beck	68	69	69	67	273	12,600
Larry Mize	68	67	69	69	273	12,600
Tom Purtzer	65	70	71	67	273	12,600
Jeff Sluman	69	69	69	66	273	12,600
Mike Standly	69	71	67	66	273	12,600
Billy Ray Brown	70	69	65	70	274	7,737.50
Brian Claar	69	69	68	68	274	7,737.50
Mark Lye	69	64	70	71	274	7,737.50
Steve Pate	69	68	68	69	274	7,737.50
David Peoples	70	67	68	69	274	7,737.50
Tom Sieckmann	69	69	68	68	274	7,737.50
Hal Sutton	69	70	67	68	274	7,737.50
Howard Twitty	70	67	67	70	274	7,737.50
Jay Delsing	69	69	68	69	275	5,414.29
Gary Hallberg	71	69	67	68	275	5,414.29
Scott Hoch	70	68	68	69	275	5,414.29
Davis Love III	66	67	73	69	275	5,414.29
John Adams	68	67	68	72	275	5,414.28
Andy Bean	68	69	67	71	275	5,414.28
David Edwards	68	70	66	71	275	5,414.28
*Phil Mickelson	67	70	68	70	275	
Peter Jacobsen	69	70	67	70	276	4,100
Lee Janzen	68	71	69	68	276	4,100
John Mahaffey	68	68	68	72	276	4,100
Chris Perry	72	68	67	69	276	4,100
Loren Roberts	68	71	67	70	276	4,100
Curt Byrum	68	68	69	72	277	3,108
Tommy Moore	68	70	70	69	277	3,108
Mike Smith	69	70	67	71	277	3,108
Kirk Triplett	67	69	68	73	277	3,108
Bobby Wadkins	71	66	71	69	277	3,108
Phil Blackmar	68	68	71	71	278	2,443.34
Mark Calcavecchia	69	70	68	71	278	2,443.34
Bart Bryant	70	68	72	68	278	2,443.33
David Graham	69	67	74	68	278	2,443.33
Ed Humenik	68	67	72	71	278	2,443.33
Greg Whisman	70	70	72	66	278	2,443.33

AT&T Pebble Beach National Pro-Am

Pebble Beach Golf Links
Par 36-36—72; 6,799 yards
Spyglass Hill Golf Club
Par 36-36—72; 6,810 yards
Poppy Hills Golf Course
Par 36-36—72; 6,865 yards
Pebble Beach, California

January 31-February 3
purse, $1,100,000

	SCORES				TOTAL	MONEY
Paul Azinger	67	67	73	67	274	$198,000
Brian Claar	66	73	71	68	278	96,800
Corey Pavin	71	71	69	67	278	96,800
Rocco Mediate	69	67	69	74	279	45,466.67
Mike Smith	70	73	71	65	279	45,466.67
Davis Love III	67	70	69	73	279	45,466.66
Jay Haas	68	70	74	68	280	34,283.34
John Cook	66	72	69	73	280	34,283.33
Larry Mize	71	66	73	70	280	34,283.33
Mark Calcavecchia	71	72	71	67	281	29,700
Chip Beck	70	70	69	74	283	24,200
John Inman	72	69	72	70	283	24,200
Hal Sutton	71	74	68	70	283	24,200
Bobby Wadkins	73	70	73	67	283	24,200
Bill Britton	69	72	74	69	284	17,600
Brad Faxon	74	67	73	70	284	17,600
Jeff Maggert	67	75	73	69	284	17,600
Kirk Triplett	71	73	69	71	284	17,600
Howard Twitty	70	68	75	71	284	17,600
Billy Ray Brown	72	70	74	69	285	11,471.43
Brandel Chamblee	74	67	72	72	285	11,471.43
John Daly	68	76	73	68	285	11,471.43
Jay Delsing	68	68	76	73	285	11,471.43
Clark Dennis	72	69	72	72	285	11,471.43
David Frost	73	68	70	74	285	11,471.43
Payne Stewart	69	71	74	71	285	11,471.42
Billy Andrade	73	71	72	70	286	7,322.13
Raymond Floyd	71	74	71	70	286	7,322.13
Peter Jacobsen	70	74	69	73	286	7,322.13
Mac O'Grady	74	70	68	74	286	7,322.13
Jim Hallet	74	69	74	69	286	7,322.12
Lee Janzen	70	72	73	71	286	7,322.12
John Joseph	70	74	69	73	286	7,322.12
Dave Sutherland	69	72	72	73	286	7,322.12
Jim Benepe	76	72	67	72	287	5,422.60
Howard Clark	75	71	70	71	287	5,422.60
Danny Edwards	74	71	70	72	287	5,422.60
Ed Fiori	73	72	72	70	287	5,422.60
Tom Watson	72	72	71	72	287	5,422.60
Greg Bruckner	71	71	75	71	288	4,070
Jerry Haas	70	75	71	72	288	4,070
Hale Irwin	69	72	75	72	288	4,070
Sandy Lyle	71	75	70	72	288	4,070
John Mahaffey	70	69	76	73	288	4,070
Mike Standly	65	78	73	72	288	4,070
Dicky Thompson	73	71	72	72	288	4,070
Bob Eastwood	74	70	71	74	289	2,863.67
Johnny Miller	72	73	72	72	289	2,863.67
Doug Tewell	69	72	74	74	289	2,863.67

	SCORES				TOTAL	MONEY
Willie Wood	74	70	72	73	289	2,863.67
Craig Stadler	71	73	72	73	289	2,863.66
Jeff Wilson	72	71	72	74	289	2,863.66

Bob Hope Chrysler Classic

Indian Wells Country Club
Par 36-36—72; 6,478 yards
Bermuda Dunes Country Club
Par 36-36—72; 6,927 yards
LaQuinta Country Club
Par 37-35—72; 6,854 yards
PGA West, Palmer Course
Par 36-36—72; 6,931 yards
Palm Springs Desert Area, California

February 6-10
purse $1,100,000

	SCORES					TOTAL	MONEY
Corey Pavin	65	69	66	66	65	331	$198,000
Mark O'Meara	66	65	66	67	67	331	118,800
(Pavin defeated O'Meara on first extra hole.)							
Tim Simpson	67	64	66	68	67	332	74,800
Raymond Floyd	71	68	66	64	64	333	52,800
Fred Couples	67	69	64	67	67	334	44,000
Blaine McCallister	66	70	63	68	68	335	39,600
Bob Tway	66	68	71	68	64	337	34,283.34
Scott Hoch	72	64	69	63	69	337	34,283.33
Jeff Sluman	71	65	69	67	65	337	34,283.33
Jim Hallet	67	70	70	67	64	338	27,500
Bob Lohr	69	68	68	69	64	338	27,500
Jim McGovern	66	67	69	69	67	338	27,500
Ed Dougherty	70	70	69	66	64	339	18,857.15
Steve Elkington	70	69	70	66	64	339	18,857.15
Ed Fiori	66	69	69	70	65	339	18,857.14
Rocco Mediate	76	63	68	64	68	339	18,857.14
Larry Mize	70	65	69	68	67	339	18,857.14
Steve Pate	70	70	65	64	70	339	18,857.14
Richard Zokol	71	72	64	66	66	339	18,857.14
Bob Gilder	73	69	65	69	64	340	13,273.34
John Cook	72	67	74	63	64	340	13,273.33
Andrew Magee	71	67	69	66	67	340	13,273.33
Robert Gamez	64	70	70	69	68	341	10,560
Nolan Henke	69	71	64	69	68	341	10,560
Mike Sullivan	66	70	71	67	67	341	10,560
Peter Jacobsen	70	71	65	68	68	342	7,486.34
Billy Mayfair	68	71	67	70	66	342	7,486.34
Payne Stewart	68	69	72	66	67	342	7,486.34
Bill Britton	70	68	67	67	70	342	7,486.33
Brad Fabel	69	68	68	69	68	342	7,486.33
Jim Gallagher, Jr.	67	70	67	70	68	342	7,486.33
John Huston	69	72	67	69	65	342	7,486.33
Tom Kite	69	73	66	65	69	342	7,486.33
Fuzzy Zoeller	69	67	70	67	69	342	7,486.33
Lee Janzen	73	66	69	67	68	343	5,080.38
Davis Love III	67	68	67	73	68	343	5,080.38
Nick Price	70	70	67	69	67	343	5,080.38
Robert Wrenn	68	69	69	69	68	343	5,080.38
Jodie Mudd	70	67	67	69	70	343	5,080.37

	SCORES					TOTAL	MONEY
Larry Rinker	68	71	66	65	73	343	5,080.37
Scott Simpson	70	69	68	70	66	343	5,080.37
Mike Springer	66	71	67	72	67	343	5,080.37
Mark Brooks	74	68	68	68	66	344	3,432
Keith Clearwater	71	67	68	69	69	344	3,432
David Edwards	69	65	71	70	69	344	3,432
David Frost	70	69	69	67	69	344	3,432
Buddy Gardner	68	69	73	70	64	344	3,432
Gil Morgan	73	69	66	71	65	344	3,432
David Peoples	71	67	66	71	69	344	3,432
Jay Haas	69	72	70	67	67	345	2,678.50
Morris Hatalsky	67	70	69	68	71	345	2,678.50
John Mahaffey	69	70	69	67	70	345	2,678.50
Tom Purtzer	69	71	68	67	70	345	2,678.50

Shearson Lehman Brothers Open

Torry Pines Golf Club, La Jolla, California
North Course: Par 36-36—72; 7,021 yards
South Course: Par 36-36—72; 6,659 yards

February 14-17
purse, $1,000,000

	SCORES				TOTAL	MONEY
Jay Don Blake	69	65	67	67	268	$180,000
Bill Sander	68	65	71	66	270	108,000
Dan Forsman	68	64	71	68	271	68,000
Ben Crenshaw	65	68	70	69	272	48,000
Jim Hallet	68	69	66	70	273	36,500
Steve Pate	67	65	67	74	273	36,500
Robert Wrenn	68	66	68	71	273	36,500
Brad Faxon	69	64	67	74	274	29,000
Dudley Hart	68	70	71	65	274	29,000
Ed Humenik	69	70	68	67	274	29,000
Corey Pavin	67	68	65	75	275	22,000
Dillard Pruitt	71	68	67	69	275	22,000
Joey Sindelar	70	70	68	67	275	22,000
Kirk Triplett	69	70	67	69	275	22,000
Emlyn Aubrey	70	63	69	74	276	16,000
Tom Byrum	68	70	68	70	276	16,000
Keith Clearwater	68	66	70	72	276	16,000
John Cook	73	67	66	70	276	16,000
Donnie Hammond	70	68	70	68	276	16,000
John Wilson	69	70	69	69	277	10,428.58
Russ Cochran	72	67	67	71	277	10,428.57
Rick Fehr	69	68	70	70	277	10,428.57
Buddy Gardner	67	72	65	73	277	10,428.57
Steve Jones	67	71	67	72	277	10,428.57
Loren Roberts	70	69	69	69	277	10,428.57
Hal Sutton	66	73	69	69	277	10,428.57
Dave Barr	69	70	69	70	278	6,950
Bob Estes	72	68	72	66	278	6,950
Jerry Haas	72	67	68	71	278	6,950
Neal Lancaster	69	68	72	69	278	6,950
Bob Lohr	70	69	71	68	278	6,950
Billy Mayfair	69	71	67	71	278	6,950
Fred Couples	69	69	68	73	279	5,775
Nick Price	67	69	70	73	279	5,775
John Adams	68	70	71	71	280	4,721.43

	SCORES				TOTAL	MONEY
Andy Bean	66	72	69	73	280	4,721.43
Bart Bryant	66	71	72	71	280	4,721.43
Dan Halldorson	71	68	70	71	280	4,721.43
John Huston	70	68	72	70	280	4,721.43
Scott Simpson	67	69	72	72	280	4,721.43
Bill Glasson	71	68	74	67	280	4,721.42
Ronnie Black	68	72	71	70	281	3,217.50
Lennie Clements	70	68	73	70	281	3,217.50
David Frost	70	70	68	73	281	3,217.50
Jeff Maggert	69	71	71	70	281	3,217.50
Blaine McCallister	73	66	70	72	281	3,217.50
Dave Rummells	75	64	70	72	281	3,217.50
Jim Thorpe	71	64	77	69	281	3,217.50
D.A. Weibring	67	71	69	74	281	3,217.50
*Phil Mickelson	66	74	71	70	281	

Nissan Los Angeles Open

Riviera Country Club, Los Angeles, California
Par 35-36—71; 6,946 yards

February 21-24
purse, $1,000,000

	SCORES				TOTAL	MONEY
Ted Schulz	69	66	69	68	272	$180,000
Jeff Sluman	66	69	68	70	273	108,000
Bruce Lietzke	70	63	70	71	274	52,000
Davis Love III	70	65	69	70	274	52,000
Craig Stadler	66	71	71	66	274	52,000
Rocco Mediate	70	69	66	70	275	33,500
Sam Randolph	72	65	69	69	275	33,500
Scott Simpson	71	68	67	69	275	33,500
Rick Fehr	68	69	71	68	276	27,000
Andrew Magee	66	69	70	71	276	27,000
Duffy Waldorf	66	72	72	66	276	27,000
Fred Couples	67	70	68	72	277	19,600
David Frost	67	69	69	72	277	19,600
Bob Gilder	70	72	67	68	277	19,600
Donnie Hammond	71	68	67	71	277	19,600
Tom Kite	70	68	70	69	277	19,600
Ronnie Black	69	71	72	66	278	15,000
Bob Estes	71	71	68	68	278	15,000
Bobby Wadkins	71	71	68	68	278	15,000
Keith Clearwater	72	69	67	71	279	11,650
Steve Jones	72	68	68	71	279	11,650
Mike Springer	70	66	72	71	279	11,650
Bob Wolcott	72	71	67	69	279	11,650
Ian Baker-Finch	68	75	68	69	280	8,100
Mark Calcavecchia	70	69	71	70	280	8,100
Ben Crenshaw	69	68	72	71	280	8,100
Clark Dennis	73	66	70	71	280	8,100
Corey Pavin	69	70	69	72	280	8,100
Jim Woodward	72	70	70	68	280	8,100
Greg Bruckner	71	70	72	68	281	6,075
Wayne Grady	65	75	69	72	281	6,075
Gary Hallberg	68	72	68	73	281	6,075
Mark Lye	70	71	69	71	281	6,075
Gil Morgan	67	71	72	71	281	6,075
Tom Purtzer	69	70	71	71	281	6,075

	SCORES				TOTAL	MONEY
Chip Beck	67	71	70	74	282	4,916.67
John Cook	69	70	70	73	282	4,916.67
Mark Brooks	67	71	69	75	282	4,916.66
Steve Pate	66	74	73	70	283	4,200
Dave Rummells	71	72	70	70	283	4,200
Ray Stewart	71	71	69	72	283	4,200
Lanny Wadkins	71	70	71	71	283	4,200
Jay Don Blake	74	69	71	70	284	2,870.91
Buddy Gardner	72	71	68	73	284	2,870.91
John Inman	71	69	72	72	284	2,870.91
Pat McGowan	69	72	70	73	284	2,870.91
Larry Nelson	65	71	76	72	284	2,870.91
Chris Perry	71	71	71	71	284	2,870.91
Dan Pohl	73	69	71	71	284	2,870.91
Dillard Pruitt	73	69	70	72	284	2,870.91
Mike Reid	70	71	71	72	284	2,870.91
Greg Twiggs	70	71	71	72	284	2,870.91
Brad Bell	70	71	74	69	284	2,870.90

Doral Ryder Open

Doral Resort & Country Club, Blue Course, Miami, Florida
Par 36-36—72; 6,939 yards

February 28-March 3
purse, $1,400,000

	SCORES				TOTAL	MONEY
Rocco Mediate	66	70	68	72	276	$252,000
Curtis Strange	69	68	77	67	276	151,200
(Mediate defeated Strange on first extra hole.)						
Andy Bean	68	68	67	74	277	81,200
Russ Cochran	69	67	68	73	277	81,200
Davis Love III	71	68	68	72	279	53,200
Jack Nicklaus	71	63	75	70	279	53,200
Mark Calcavecchia	68	70	69	73	280	46,900
Lanny Wadkins	71	67	70	73	281	43,400
Wayne Levi	67	70	71	74	282	40,600
Tom Sieckmann	68	72	71	72	283	37,800
Buddy Gardner	72	70	70	72	284	30,800
Mike Hulbert	70	73	67	74	284	30,800
Mark O'Meara	67	69	74	74	284	30,800
Mike Smith	70	72	70	72	284	30,800
Chip Beck	66	71	74	74	285	23,800
Kenny Perry	69	64	75	77	285	23,800
Brian Tennyson	70	70	69	76	285	23,800
Steve Elkington	71	69	72	74	286	18,256
Jim Hallet	66	74	71	75	286	18,256
Nolan Henke	69	70	70	77	286	18,256
Bernhard Langer	69	70	73	74	286	18,256
Andrew Magee	72	67	70	77	286	18,256
Ian Baker-Finch	69	70	72	76	287	14,000
Ted Schulz	72	69	70	76	287	14,000
Ben Crenshaw	68	71	76	73	288	10,686.67
Kenny Knox	73	70	72	73	288	10,686.67
Tom Purtzer	67	72	75	74	288	10,686.67
Scott Simpson	68	73	72	75	288	10,686.67
Brian Claar	71	69	72	76	288	10,686.66
Bruce Lietzke	69	73	71	75	288	10,686.66
John Mahaffey	71	71	72	75	289	8,890

	SCORES				TOTAL	MONEY
Doug Tewell	68	72	72	77	289	8,890
Gil Morgan	68	72	73	77	290	7,910
Paul Trittler	69	74	72	75	290	7,910
Bob Wolcott	68	74	72	76	290	7,910
Jay Don Blake	68	74	73	76	291	6,310
Curt Byrum	74	69	75	73	291	6,310
Mike Donald	72	70	73	76	291	6,310
Bob Estes	70	73	76	72	291	6,310
Tom Eubank	68	73	72	78	291	6,310
Greg Norman	71	71	75	74	291	6,310
Jim Thorpe	69	73	74	75	291	6,310
Hale Irwin	70	69	76	77	292	4,760
Mark Lye	68	73	75	76	292	4,760
Mike Reid	69	68	76	79	292	4,760
Jeff Sluman	72	70	75	75	292	4,760
Billy Andrade	69	72	75	77	293	3,552.50
Tom Byrum	75	67	73	78	293	3,552.50
Keith Clearwater	66	73	76	78	293	3,552.50
Brad Faxon	72	69	76	76	293	3,552.50
Dan Forsman	67	76	71	79	293	3,552.50
Blaine McCallister	71	72	73	77	293	3,552.50
Mike Sullivan	72	70	71	80	293	3,552.50
Bobby Wadkins	71	72	74	76	293	3,552.50

Honda Classic

TPC at Eagle Trace, Coral Springs, Florida
Par 36-36—72; 7,037 yards

March 7-10
purse, $1,000,000

	SCORES				TOTAL	MONEY
Steve Pate	69	65	70	75	279	$180,000
Paul Azinger	68	67	75	72	282	88,000
Dan Halldorson	67	67	78	70	282	88,000
Billy Andrade	68	72	75	68	283	41,333.34
John Daly	68	68	76	71	283	41,333.33
Bruce Lietzke	72	67	70	74	283	41,333.33
Bart Bryant	69	71	72	72	284	33,500
Dave Barr	70	66	74	75	285	31,000
Andy Bean	70	71	73	72	286	26,000
Davis Love III	74	70	68	74	286	26,000
Andrew Magee	70	71	71	74	286	26,000
Blaine McCallister	69	70	73	74	286	26,000
Greg Norman	69	66	77	75	287	21,000
Gary Hallberg	70	68	74	76	288	17,500
Lee Janzen	72	70	71	75	288	17,500
Ted Schulz	71	73	69	75	288	17,500
Kirk Triplett	71	66	72	79	288	17,500
Mark Brooks	70	67	74	78	289	12,171.43
Brad Faxon	68	68	79	74	289	12,171.43
Raymond Floyd	67	71	75	76	289	12,171.43
John Huston	69	65	83	72	289	12,171.43
John Inman	72	67	74	76	289	12,171.43
Doug Tewell	74	69	74	72	289	12,171.43
Dan Forsman	70	68	72	79	289	12,171.42
Fred Funk	71	71	72	76	290	8,166.67
Dillard Pruitt	73	70	75	72	290	8,166.67
Keith Clearwater	70	68	74	78	290	8,166.66

	SCORES				TOTAL	MONEY
Brad Bryant	70	70	78	73	291	6,650
Brandel Chamblee	75	69	72	75	291	6,650
Mike Donald	72	71	71	77	291	6,650
Mark McCumber	72	72	73	74	291	6,650
Kenny Perry	68	70	80	73	291	6,650
Joey Sindelar	72	67	78	74	291	6,650
Carl Cooper	70	70	73	79	292	5,400
Neal Lancaster	72	71	73	76	292	5,400
Jim McGovern	72	72	71	77	292	5,400
Dudley Hart	73	70	73	77	293	4,600
Bernhard Langer	72	69	73	79	293	4,600
Bob Lohr	70	70	78	75	293	4,600
Mike Sullivan	69	66	79	79	293	4,600
Curt Byrum	70	69	78	77	294	3,500
Fred Couples	71	70	74	79	294	3,500
Bob Eastwood	73	69	77	75	294	3,500
Buddy Gardner	70	74	73	77	294	3,500
Gene Sauers	77	67	69	81	294	3,500
Lance Ten Broeck	73	66	75	80	294	3,500
D.A. Weibring	68	75	77	74	294	3,500
Bill Glasson	72	70	77	76	295	2,513.34
Nick Price	75	64	81	75	295	2,513.34
Tommy Armour	73	71	72	79	295	2,513.33
Bob Estes	71	72	76	76	295	2,513.33
Karl Kimball	72	71	76	76	295	2,513.33
Joe Lloyd	67	75	76	77	295	2,513.33

The Nestle Invitational

Bay Hill Club and Lodge, Orlando, Florida
Par 36-36—72; 7,114 yards
(Fourth round cancelled — rain, course unplayable.)

March 14-17
purse, $1,000,000

	SCORES			TOTAL	MONEY
Andrew Magee	68	69	66	203	$180,000
Tom Sieckmann	70	65	70	205	108,000
Mark Calcavecchia	66	69	71	206	58,000
Steve Pate	72	66	68	206	58,000
Mark O'Meara	68	69	70	207	40,000
Jay Don Blake	69	69	70	208	36,000
Bob Tway	70	71	68	209	28,083.34
Ian Woosnam	70	70	69	209	28,083.34
Nick Faldo	67	71	71	209	28,083.33
Scott Hoch	70	66	73	209	28,083.33
Bernhard Langer	70	69	70	209	28,083.33
Rocco Mediate	68	69	72	209	28,083.33
Kenny Knox	69	72	69	210	18,750
Dave Rummells	71	71	68	210	18,750
Jeff Sluman	69	69	72	210	18,750
Fuzzy Zoeller	70	69	71	210	18,750
Buddy Gardner	67	70	74	211	14,000
Blaine McCallister	71	67	73	211	14,000
Don Pooley	68	66	77	211	14,000
Curtis Strange	70	67	74	211	14,000
Tom Watson	72	70	69	211	14,000
Andy Bean	69	74	69	212	10,800
Davis Love III	68	70	74	212	10,800

	SCORES			TOTAL	MONEY
Fulton Allem	72	69	72	213	7,737.50
Paul Azinger	71	72	70	213	7,737.50
Keith Clearwater	71	69	73	213	7,737.50
Donnie Hammond	66	73	74	213	7,737.50
Nolan Henke	68	73	72	213	7,737.50
Peter Jacobsen	71	69	73	213	7,737.50
Arnold Palmer	72	71	70	213	7,737.50
Tom Purtzer	69	73	71	213	7,737.50
Ed Dougherty	73	69	72	214	5,080
Raymond Floyd	70	71	73	214	5,080
Jim Hallet	69	71	74	214	5,080
Mike Hulbert	72	70	72	214	5,080
Tom Kite	70	70	74	214	5,080
Mark McNulty	72	72	70	214	5,080
Kenny Perry	76	68	70	214	5,080
Gene Sauers	71	72	71	214	5,080
Leonard Thompson	68	70	76	214	5,080
Robert Wrenn	70	70	74	214	5,080
Billy Ray Brown	73	72	70	215	3,217.50
David Frost	71	72	72	215	3,217.50
Wayne Grady	73	71	71	215	3,217.50
Gary Koch	73	69	73	215	3,217.50
Greg Norman	70	71	74	215	3,217.50
Craig Parry	71	70	74	215	3,217.50
Corey Pavin	72	70	73	215	3,217.50
Duffy Waldorf	69	71	75	215	3,217.50
Mark Brooks	70	72	74	216	2,460
Fred Couples	70	71	75	216	2,460
Brad Faxon	73	72	71	216	2,460

USF&G Classic

English Turn Golf & Country Club, New Orleans, Louisiana
Par 36-36—72; 7,116 yards

March 21-24
purse, $1,000,000

	SCORES				TOTAL	MONEY
Ian Woosnam	73	67	68	67	275	$180,000
Jim Hallet	69	71	65	70	275	108,000
(Woosnam defeated Hallet on second extra hole.)						
Tom Sieckmann	71	68	70	68	277	68,000
John Huston	72	70	68	68	278	48,000
Ronnie Black	68	74	66	71	279	36,500
Joel Edwards	73	71	64	71	279	36,500
Tim Simpson	71	72	71	65	279	36,500
Curt Byrum	72	72	68	68	280	29,000
Kenny Knox	68	75	66	71	280	29,000
Tom Watson	67	72	73	68	280	29,000
Phil Blackmar	67	77	66	71	281	23,000
Billy Mayfair	67	73	68	73	281	23,000
Mike Smith	73	70	71	67	281	23,000
Bob Lohr	68	74	70	70	282	18,500
Jack Nicklaus	68	69	74	71	282	18,500
Lee Janzen	72	76	67	68	283	17,000
Ian Baker-Finch	71	73	67	73	284	14,500
Lennie Clements	70	71	74	69	284	14,500
John Daly	72	72	68	72	284	14,500
Stan Utley	71	72	68	73	284	14,500

	SCORES				TOTAL	MONEY
Raymond Floyd	77	70	67	71	285	10,800
Scott Hoch	72	72	68	73	285	10,800
Sam Randolph	67	77	72	69	285	10,800
Lance Ten Broeck	71	74	71	69	285	10,800
David Frost	70	77	70	69	286	7,800
Neal Lancaster	76	72	71	67	286	7,800
Mark O'Meara	71	76	68	71	286	7,800
Craig Parry	72	74	73	67	286	7,800
Dave Rummells	74	73	71	68	286	7,800
Brian Claar	71	77	67	72	287	5,812.50
Keith Clearwater	73	76	66	72	287	5,812.50
Ben Crenshaw	71	70	72	74	287	5,812.50
Mike Donald	72	72	70	73	287	5,812.50
Bob Eastwood	71	77	65	74	287	5,812.50
Dillard Pruitt	67	78	71	71	287	5,812.50
Loren Roberts	70	78	71	68	287	5,812.50
Brian Watts	70	77	71	69	287	5,812.50
Bart Bryant	74	72	70	72	288	4,400
Trevor Dodds	77	66	73	72	288	4,400
Craig Stadler	72	74	71	71	288	4,400
Brian Tennyson	72	72	70	74	288	4,400
Marco Dawson	72	72	72	73	289	3,500
Ed Humenik	76	73	71	69	289	3,500
Bill Kratzert	72	72	72	73	289	3,500
Craig Randolph	72	71	73	73	289	3,500
Ken Schall	72	76	71	70	289	3,500
Brandel Chamblee	72	76	71	71	290	2,537.50
Steve Elkington	69	78	71	72	290	2,537.50
Rick Fehr	72	74	70	74	290	2,537.50
Dan Halldorson	72	74	69	75	290	2,537.50
Dudley Hart	71	73	76	70	290	2,537.50
Sandy Lyle	72	73	74	71	290	2,537.50
Peter Persons	72	74	72	72	290	2,537.50
Willie Wood	72	69	72	77	290	2,537.50

The Players Championship

TPC at Sawgrass, Stadium Course, Jacksonville, Florida
Par 36-36—72; 6,896 yards

March 28-31
purse, $1,600,000

	SCORES				TOTAL	MONEY
Steve Elkington	66	70	72	68	276	$288,000
Fuzzy Zoeller	68	68	69	72	277	172,800
Paul Azinger	67	68	69	74	278	83,200
Phil Blackmar	67	72	69	70	278	83,200
John Cook	71	73	69	65	278	83,200
Bernhard Langer	70	70	71	69	280	53,600
Bruce Lietzke	71	72	68	69	280	53,600
Curtis Strange	71	68	70	71	280	53,600
Bob Lohr	68	71	68	74	281	41,600
Nick Price	68	75	67	71	281	41,600
Gene Sauers	68	74	68	71	281	41,600
Bobby Wadkins	68	74	69	70	281	41,600
Jay Delsing	71	71	71	69	282	32,000
Mark McCumber	70	72	69	71	282	32,000
Keith Clearwater	72	72	70	69	283	25,600
John Huston	72	71	70	70	283	25,600

	SCORES				TOTAL	MONEY
Rocco Mediate	69	74	68	72	283	25,600
Craig Parry	70	74	69	70	283	25,600
Ian Woosnam	72	69	70	72	283	25,600
Bob Eastwood	66	74	71	73	284	19,306.67
Neal Lancaster	71	73	69	71	284	19,306.67
Tom Watson	68	74	65	77	284	19,306.66
Fred Couples	70	74	69	72	285	14,720
Blaine McCallister	67	75	70	73	285	14,720
Mark McNulty	70	72	72	71	285	14,720
Larry Nelson	72	72	70	71	285	14,720
Jay Don Blake	67	75	75	69	286	9,394.29
Bill Britton	69	71	74	72	286	9,394.29
Billy Ray Brown	72	73	69	72	286	9,394.29
Ken Green	69	76	71	70	286	9,394.29
Andy North	72	72	70	72	286	9,394.29
Jumbo Ozaki	73	72	72	69	286	9,394.29
Loren Roberts	69	73	71	73	286	9,394.29
Robert Wrenn	70	72	73	71	286	9,394.29
Billy Andrade	68	71	74	73	286	9,394.28
Ed Dougherty	71	70	69	76	286	9,394.28
Hale Irwin	68	74	69	75	286	9,394.28
Steve Pate	69	73	70	74	286	9,394.28
Chris Perry	69	71	71	76	286	9,394.28
Peter Persons	66	75	71	74	286	9,394.28
David Edwards	71	73	70	73	287	5,064.73
David Frost	69	71	72	75	287	5,064.73
Buddy Gardner	70	71	74	72	287	5,064.73
Bill Glasson	72	70	72	73	287	5,064.73
Steve Jones	71	70	71	75	287	5,064.73
Corey Pavin	69	76	71	71	287	5,064.73
Bob Tway	65	77	72	73	287	5,064.73
D.A. Weibring	67	74	72	74	287	5,064.73
Ian Baker-Finch	69	69	71	78	287	5,064.72
Brian Claar	70	69	69	79	287	5,064.72
Joey Sindelar	68	75	67	77	287	5,064.72

Masters Tournament

Augusta National Golf Club, Augusta, Georgia
Par 36-36—72; 6,905 yards

April 11-14
purse, $1,347,700

	SCORES				TOTAL	MONEY
Ian Woosnam	72	66	67	72	277	$243,000
Jose Maria Olazabal	68	71	69	70	278	145,800
Ben Crenshaw	70	73	68	68	279	64,800
Steve Pate	72	73	69	65	279	64,800
Lanny Wadkins	67	71	70	71	279	64,800
Tom Watson	68	68	70	73	279	64,800
Ian Baker-Finch	71	70	69	70	280	42,100
Andrew Magee	70	72	68	70	280	42,100
Jodie Mudd	70	70	71	69	280	42,100
Hale Irwin	70	70	75	66	281	35,150
Tommy Nakajima	74	71	67	69	281	35,150
Mark Calcavecchia	70	68	77	67	282	26,500
Nick Faldo	72	73	67	70	282	26,500
Billy Mayfair	72	72	72	66	282	26,500
Craig Stadler	70	72	71	69	282	26,500

	SCORES				TOTAL	MONEY
Fuzzy Zoeller	70	70	75	67	282	26,500
Raymond Floyd	71	68	71	73	283	18,920
Jim Gallagher, Jr.	67	74	71	71	283	18,920
Peter Jacobsen	73	70	68	72	283	18,920
Mark McCumber	67	71	73	72	283	18,920
Larry Mize	72	71	66	74	283	18,920
Seve Ballesteros	75	70	69	70	284	12,960
Steve Elkington	72	69	74	69	284	12,960
Rocco Mediate	72	69	71	72	284	12,960
Corey Pavin	73	70	69	72	284	12,960
Scott Simpson	69	73	69	73	284	12,960
Jay Don Blake	74	72	68	71	285	10,200
Mark O'Meara	74	68	72	71	285	10,200
Morris Hatalsky	71	72	70	73	286	9,200
John Huston	73	72	71	70	286	9,200
Jeff Sluman	71	71	72	72	286	9,200
David Frost	71	73	71	72	287	8,000
Bernhard Langer	71	68	74	74	287	8,000
Wayne Levi	69	73	70	75	287	8,000
Mark Brooks	69	72	74	73	288	6,371
Fred Couples	68	73	72	75	288	6,371
Ken Green	70	74	71	73	288	6,371
Scott Hoch	72	70	73	73	288	6,371
Mark McNulty	72	74	75	67	288	6,371
Jack Nicklaus	68	72	72	76	288	6,371
Jumbo Ozaki	68	77	69	74	288	6,371
Billy Ray Brown	74	65	77	73	289	4,875
Donnie Hammond	72	73	73	71	289	4,875
Davis Love III	72	71	74	72	289	4,875
Curtis Strange	72	74	72	71	289	4,875
Don Pooley	72	71	69	78	290	4,050
Joey Sindelar	72	70	70	78	290	4,050
*Phil Mickelson	69	73	74	74	290	
Tommy Aaron	70	74	73	74	291	3,533
Nick Price	72	73	72	74	291	3,533
Lee Trevino	71	72	77	71	291	3,533
Paul Azinger	72	73	67	80	292	3,300
Nolan Henke	73	71	72	77	293	3,200
Brian Tennyson	78	67	75	73	293	3,200
Larry Nelson	74	69	76	75	294	3,100
Tom Kite	71	75	78	71	295	3,100
*Manny Zerman	71	71	77	80	299	

Out of Final 36 Holes

Bill Britton	72	75			147	
John Cook	77	70			147	
Greg Norman	78	69			147	
Gary Player	72	75			147	
Billy Casper	77	71			148	
Mike Donald	73	75			148	
Steve Jones	73	75			148	
Tom Sieckmann	72	76			148	
Robert Gamez	72	77			149	
Ronan Rafferty	73	76			149	
Loren Roberts	72	77			149	
Chip Beck	74	76			150	
Wayne Grady	74	76			150	
Bob Tway	75	75			150	
Kenny Knox	72	79			151	

	SCORES	TOTAL
Tim Simpson	73 78	151
Jim Benepe	78 74	152
Gay Brewer	78 74	152
Ted Schulz	74 78	152
Sandy Lyle	77 76	153
Frankie Minoza	78 75	153
Gil Morgan	77 76	153
*James Stuart	81 72	153
Charles Coody	77 77	154
*Michael Combs	81 74	155
John Inman	75 80	155
*Rolf Muntz	80 75	155
Arnold Palmer	78 77	155
George Archer	73 WD	

(Professionals who did not complete 72 holes received $1,500.)

Deposit Guaranty Classic

Hattiesburg Country Club, Hattiesburg, Mississippi   April 11-14
Par 35-35—70; 6,496 yards   purse, $300,000

	SCORES				TOTAL	MONEY
Larry Silveira	66	66	71	63	266	$54,000
Russ Cochran	69	65	69	63	266	26,400
Mike Nicolette	65	65	68	68	266	26,400
(Silveira defeated Cochran and Nicolette on first extra hole.)						
Fred Funk	66	67	68	66	267	14,400
Brandel Chamblee	71	67	64	66	268	11,400
Jerry Haas	66	69	66	67	268	11,400
Frank Conner	65	66	68	70	269	7,818.75
Brad Fabel	70	65	67	67	269	7,818.75
Dan Halldorson	68	68	66	67	269	7,818.75
Greg Ladehoff	70	64	67	68	269	7,818.75
Chris Perry	68	67	67	67	269	7,818.75
Mike Springer	66	70	66	67	269	7,818.75
Grant Waite	63	73	66	67	269	7,818.75
Brian Watts	65	68	69	67	269	7,818.75
Greg Bruckner	66	69	69	66	270	4,950
Brian Kamm	68	70	65	67	270	4,950
Steve Lamontagne	67	72	65	66	270	4,950
Gene Sauers	70	67	68	65	270	4,950
Jerry Anderson	67	68	67	69	271	3,510
Jim Booros	67	70	68	66	271	3,510
Ed Fiori	74	65	67	65	271	3,510
Jim Nelford	66	69	67	69	271	3,510
Ken Schall	67	69	69	66	271	3,510
John Wilson	66	69	68	68	271	3,510
Michael Allen	69	69	66	68	272	2,392.50
Emlyn Aubrey	73	67	70	62	272	2,392.50
Dudley Hart	64	69	68	71	272	2,392.50
Don Shirey, Jr.	64	72	68	68	272	2,392.50
*Steve Summer	67	71	65	69	272	
Trevor Dodds	71	69	67	66	273	1,866.43
Jeff Hart	66	71	69	67	273	1,866.43
Karl Kimball	70	69	69	65	273	1,866.43
Bill Kratzert	67	70	67	69	273	1,866.43

	SCORES				TOTAL	MONEY
Mike Smith	70	64	69	70	273	1,866.43
Billy Tuten	71	66	70	66	273	1,866.43
Dillard Pruitt	69	71	71	62	273	1,866.42
Mitch Adcock	69	69	69	67	274	1,291.67
Ed Dougherty	69	71	67	67	274	1,291.67
Webb Heintzelman	67	70	68	69	274	1,291.67
Barry Jaeckel	67	70	68	69	274	1,291.67
Lee Janzen	71	69	66	68	274	1,291.67
Duffy Waldorf	68	71	66	69	274	1,291.67
Charles Bowles	69	71	64	70	274	1,291.66
Carl Cooper	71	66	66	71	274	1,291.66
Fred Wadsworth	73	66	69	66	274	1,291.66
Brandt Jobe	68	69	71	67	275	858
Neal Lancaster	66	71	67	71	275	858
Gary Rusnak	68	71	67	69	275	858
Sonny Skinner	71	69	69	66	275	858
Paul Trittler	70	67	69	69	275	858
Dennis Trixler	67	71	71	66	275	858

MCI Heritage Classic

Harbour Town Golf Links, Hilton Head Island, South Carolina   April 18-21
Par 36-35—71; 6,912 yards   purse, $1,000,000

	SCORES				TOTAL	MONEY
Davis Love III	65	68	68	70	271	$180,000
Ian Baker-Finch	75	64	65	69	273	108,000
Lanny Wadkins	68	68	70	68	274	68,000
Payne Stewart	68	68	70	69	275	41,333.34
Hale Irwin	70	70	66	69	275	41,333.33
Mark O'Meara	68	69	68	70	275	41,333.33
Fred Funk	69	69	68	71	277	31,166.67
Billy Mayfair	68	72	66	71	277	31,166.67
Chip Beck	68	64	73	72	277	31,166.66
Bobby Clampett	72	66	67	73	278	27,000
Jay Delsing	73	68	68	70	279	24,000
John Huston	69	70	70	70	279	24,000
Don Pooley	70	72	72	66	280	19,333.34
Jay Haas	76	67	68	69	280	19,333.33
Bob Lohr	70	68	69	73	280	19,333.33
Fulton Allem	71	67	70	73	281	15,500
David Canipe	67	69	71	74	281	15,500
Tom Purtzer	72	71	68	70	281	15,500
Mike Sullivan	73	69	66	73	281	15,500
Brad Fabel	75	66	71	70	282	11,650
Nolan Henke	73	70	68	71	282	11,650
Blaine McCallister	69	70	71	72	282	11,650
Corey Pavin	72	70	71	69	282	11,650
Jim Booros	68	73	71	71	283	7,914.29
Bill Britton	71	73	68	71	283	7,914.29
David Edwards	68	74	71	70	283	7,914.29
Dan Forsman	67	73	71	72	283	7,914.29
Mark Brooks	69	70	67	77	283	7,914.28
Loren Roberts	70	70	69	74	283	7,914.28
Hal Sutton	68	73	69	73	283	7,914.28
John Cook	67	73	70	74	284	6,062.50
Steve Pate	70	72	69	73	284	6,062.50

	SCORES				TOTAL	MONEY
Stan Utley	74	67	69	74	284	6,062.50
Willie Wood	72	70	67	75	284	6,062.50
Andy Bean	68	71	77	69	285	4,618.75
Ed Fiori	71	71	67	76	285	4,618.75
Lee Janzen	69	72	72	72	285	4,618.75
Roger Maltbie	77	67	72	69	285	4,618.75
Gil Morgan	71	73	72	69	285	4,618.75
Leonard Thompson	70	74	70	71	285	4,618.75
D.A. Weibring	67	74	67	77	285	4,618.75
Fuzzy Zoeller	69	72	71	73	285	4,618.75
Billy Andrade	73	71	72	70	286	3,206.67
Wayne Grady	70	72	71	73	286	3,206.67
Morris Hatalsky	72	72	69	73	286	3,206.67
Jeff Sluman	70	72	70	74	286	3,206.67
Steve Jones	70	71	71	74	286	3,206.66
Mark McCumber	66	73	70	77	286	3,206.66
Paul Azinger	69	71	69	78	287	2,405
Fred Couples	74	67	72	74	287	2,405
Rick Fehr	71	71	71	74	287	2,405
Jim Hallet	70	72	73	72	287	2,405
Scott Hoch	72	70	68	77	287	2,405
Tom Kite	73	70	70	74	287	2,405
Mark Lye	71	71	73	72	287	2,405
Doug Tewell	71	67	72	77	287	2,405

Kmart Greater Greensboro Open

Forest Oaks Country Club, Greensboro, North Carolina April 25-28
Par 36-36—72; 6,958 yards purse, $1,250,000

	SCORES				TOTAL	MONEY
Mark Brooks	71	70	70	64	275	$225,000
Gene Sauers	70	64	72	69	275	135,000
(Brooks defeated Sauers on third extra hole.)						
John Huston	74	68	69	65	276	72,500
Bob Wolcott	67	69	68	72	276	72,500
Bill Britton	70	70	69	68	277	43,906.25
Mike Hulbert	70	70	69	68	277	43,906.25
Jeff Sluman	69	67	70	71	277	43,906.25
Lanny Wadkins	69	65	72	71	277	43,906.25
Marco Dawson	71	71	69	67	278	33,750
Davis Love III	75	67	67	69	278	33,750
Loren Roberts	71	71	68	68	278	33,750
Jay Delsing	73	71	68	67	279	26,250
Jeff Maggert	71	73	68	67	279	26,250
Duffy Waldorf	71	70	63	75	279	26,250
Bob Eastwood	70	74	68	68	280	21,875
Blaine McCallister	70	71	70	69	280	21,875
Brad Faxon	71	67	74	69	281	17,500
Kenny Perry	73	70	71	67	281	17,500
John Ross	71	67	72	71	281	17,500
Payne Stewart	69	69	70	73	281	17,500
Greg Twiggs	71	68	73	69	281	17,500
Chip Beck	72	69	69	72	282	13,000
Billy Ray Brown	71	70	72	69	282	13,000
David Edwards	74	69	70	69	282	13,000
Jim Booros	72	70	73	68	283	7,891.67

	SCORES				TOTAL	MONEY
Bobby Clampett	73	65	75	70	283	7,891.67
Keith Clearwater	74	69	73	67	283	7,891.67
Mark Lye	72	70	70	71	283	7,891.67
Chris Perry	68	71	75	69	283	7,891.67
Dillard Pruitt	73	69	70	71	283	7,891.67
Bill Sander	72	69	72	70	283	7,891.67
Joey Sindelar	69	74	71	69	283	7,891.67
Dicky Thompson	70	70	73	70	283	7,891.67
Leonard Thompson	71	73	73	66	283	7,891.67
Ed Dougherty	71	69	69	74	283	7,891.66
Brad Fabel	72	71	69	71	283	7,891.66
Robert Gamez	74	66	69	74	283	7,891.66
Dudley Hart	71	70	70	72	283	7,891.66
Rocco Mediate	72	71	69	71	283	7,891.66
Andy Bean	75	68	71	70	284	4,875
Bill Buttner	72	70	71	71	284	4,875
Brian Claar	69	73	71	71	284	4,875
John Inman	70	67	76	71	284	4,875
Willie Wood	70	70	71	73	284	4,875
Jim Gallagher, Jr.	71	71	70	73	285	3,575
Gary Hallberg	70	72	71	72	285	3,575
Dan Halldorson	71	71	72	71	285	3,575
Mark O'Meara	68	72	74	71	285	3,575
Dave Rummells	71	72	70	72	285	3,575
Robert Thompson	70	73	74	68	285	3,575

GTE Byron Nelson Classic

TPC at Las Colinas, Irving, Texas
Par 35-35—70; 6,850 yards

May 2-5
purse, $1,100,000

	SCORES				TOTAL	MONEY
Nick Price	68	64	70	68	270	$198,000
Craig Stadler	68	66	70	67	271	118,800
Raymond Floyd	67	69	67	69	272	52,800
Corey Pavin	68	66	69	69	272	52,800
Scott Simpson	68	68	68	68	272	52,800
Hal Sutton	68	68	67	69	272	52,800
Lanny Wadkins	66	71	68	68	273	36,850
Phil Blackmar	70	66	66	73	275	30,800
Tom Kite	68	66	66	75	275	30,800
Loren Roberts	71	68	66	70	275	30,800
Tom Watson	65	69	70	71	275	30,800
Jay Don Blake	68	69	70	69	276	20,900
Gary Hallberg	72	64	69	71	276	20,900
Kenny Perry	70	66	69	71	276	20,900
Dave Rummells	67	70	70	69	276	20,900
Howard Twitty	68	67	68	73	276	20,900
Richard Zokol	68	70	67	71	276	20,900
Bruce Lietzke	67	67	68	75	277	15,950
Stan Utley	67	66	69	75	277	15,950
Larry Silveira	73	64	72	69	278	13,273.34
Mike Sullivan	69	67	66	76	278	13,273.33
Mark Wiebe	66	73	67	72	278	13,273.33
David Frost	70	68	69	72	279	9,271.43
Jay Haas	69	70	65	75	279	9,271.43
Dudley Hart	67	68	73	71	279	9,271.43

	SCORES			TOTAL	MONEY
Mark Lye	74	68	68	69	279	9,271.43
John Mahaffey	69	67	69	74	279	9,271.43
Mark O'Meara	72	68	70	69	279	9,271.43
Jay Delsing	70	66	68	75	279	9,271.42
Payne Stewart	70	70	65	75	280	7,150
Doug Tewell	67	70	68	75	280	7,150
Willie Wood	70	69	70	71	280	7,150
Ronnie Black	69	70	69	73	281	6,077.50
Bobby Clampett	71	68	72	70	281	6,077.50
Fred Couples	70	70	70	71	281	6,077.50
Mike Springer	70	68	72	71	281	6,077.50
Emlyn Aubrey	66	71	72	73	282	4,840
Jim Booros	70	70	70	72	282	4,840
Jerry Haas	72	69	69	72	282	4,840
Greg Ladehoff	67	69	72	74	282	4,840
Neal Lancaster	74	68	69	71	282	4,840
Lindy Miller	71	69	70	72	282	4,840
Charles Bowles	73	68	69	73	283	3,214.20
Billy Ray Brown	71	71	66	75	283	3,214.20
Curt Byrum	71	71	65	76	283	3,214.20
David Edwards	70	70	68	75	283	3,214.20
Morris Hatalsky	71	71	68	73	283	3,214.20
Roger Maltbie	72	70	69	72	283	3,214.20
Dillard Pruitt	73	66	69	75	283	3,214.20
Tom Purtzer	70	70	71	72	283	3,214.20
Tim Simpson	72	69	68	74	283	3,214.20
Bobby Wadkins	67	74	69	73	283	3,214.20

BellSouth Atlanta Classic

Atlanta Country Club, Atlanta, Georgia
Par 36-36—72; 7,018 yards

May 9-12
purse, $1,000,000

	SCORES			TOTAL	MONEY
Corey Pavin	68	67	67	70	272	$180,000
Steve Pate	68	70	68	66	272	108,000
(Pavin defeated Pate on second extra hole.)						
Hale Irwin	71	69	67	66	273	52,000
Tom Kite	64	68	67	74	273	52,000
Mike Springer	68	63	69	73	273	52,000
David Edwards	70	68	68	68	274	34,750
Fred Funk	62	77	67	68	274	34,750
Jay Don Blake	68	73	68	66	275	29,000
Jodie Mudd	69	69	68	69	275	29,000
Leonard Thompson	70	69	67	69	275	29,000
Ian Baker-Finch	72	68	67	69	276	21,200
Larry Mize	69	68	69	70	276	21,200
Dillard Pruitt	70	72	66	68	276	21,200
Gene Sauers	70	70	66	70	276	21,200
Hal Sutton	68	69	70	69	276	21,200
Chip Beck	71	70	68	68	277	16,000
Nolan Henke	71	67	72	67	277	16,000
Scott Simpson	68	70	70	69	277	16,000
Joel Edwards	71	69	68	70	278	13,500
Larry Rinker	72	67	70	69	278	13,500
Raymond Floyd	68	74	69	68	279	10,800
Gary Hallberg	70	70	71	68	279	10,800

	SCORES				TOTAL	MONEY
Mark McCumber	69	71	67	72	279	10,800
David Peoples	68	69	67	75	279	10,800
Russ Cochran	68	72	69	71	280	7,633.34
Tommy Moore	72	70	68	70	280	7,633.34
Buddy Gardner	69	70	72	69	280	7,633.33
Mike Hulbert	69	72	72	67	280	7,633.33
Kenny Perry	70	68	70	72	280	7,633.33
Doug Tewell	72	70	70	68	280	7,633.33
Lennie Clements	71	71	69	70	281	5,930
Marco Dawson	66	73	69	73	281	5,930
Ed Dougherty	71	70	69	71	281	5,930
Kenny Knox	72	65	73	71	281	5,930
Larry Nelson	71	71	69	70	281	5,930
Ronnie Black	74	68	69	71	282	4,305.56
Phil Blackmar	70	70	70	72	282	4,305.56
Sam Randolph	69	72	70	71	282	4,305.56
Ted Schulz	69	69	71	73	282	4,305.56
Greg Twiggs	69	72	69	72	282	4,305.56
Dave Barr	70	70	72	70	282	4,305.55
Tom Byrum	71	69	71	71	282	4,305.55
Dudley Hart	71	69	71	71	282	4,305.55
Jeff Sluman	69	70	70	73	282	4,305.55
Michael Allen	71	70	69	73	283	2,928
Perry Arthur	65	76	72	70	283	2,928
Rick Fehr	72	70	71	70	283	2,928
Jay Haas	73	68	71	71	283	2,928
Tim Simpson	71	69	69	74	283	2,928
Brad Bryant	74	68	70	72	284	2,460
Neal Lancaster	71	69	69	75	284	2,460
Mark Wiebe	70	69	73	72	284	2,460

Memorial Tournament

Muirfield Village Golf Club, Dublin, Ohio
Par 36-36—72; 7,106 yards

May 16-19
purse, $1,200,000

	SCORES				TOTAL	MONEY
Kenny Perry	70	63	69	71	273	$216,000
Hale Irwin	73	69	65	66	273	129,600
(Perry defeated Irwin on first extra hole.)						
Corey Pavin	66	71	67	71	275	81,600
Mike Hulbert	73	67	72	67	279	52,800
Craig Stadler	71	70	70	68	279	52,800
Ian Baker-Finch	69	73	69	69	280	41,700
Chip Beck	70	66	74	70	280	41,700
Andy Bean	69	69	72	71	281	30,000
Jay Don Blake	69	71	72	69	281	30,000
John Cook	72	72	69	68	281	30,000
David Frost	69	71	73	68	281	30,000
Larry Mize	72	69	73	67	281	30,000
Ted Schulz	69	71	67	74	281	30,000
Doug Tewell	69	69	72	71	281	30,000
Jack Nicklaus	71	68	69	74	282	20,400
Tom Watson	68	73	70	71	282	20,400
Fuzzy Zoeller	68	69	75	70	282	20,400
Billy Andrade	69	71	71	72	283	16,800
Dave Rummells	67	74	68	74	283	16,800

	SCORES				TOTAL	MONEY
Scott Simpson	76	71	71	65	283	16,800
John Huston	74	69	70	71	284	13,920
Steve Pate	69	75	72	68	284	13,920
Paul Azinger	72	71	67	75	285	11,040
Fred Funk	76	68	69	72	285	11,040
Tom Purtzer	71	69	71	74	285	11,040
Bob Tway	69	70	74	72	285	11,040
Greg Norman	71	75	69	71	286	9,060
Lanny Wadkins	72	70	73	71	286	9,060
Nolan Henke	71	72	74	70	287	7,465.72
Scott Hoch	73	71	72	71	287	7,465.72
Hal Sutton	75	69	73	70	287	7,465.72
Brian Claar	73	70	74	70	287	7,465.71
Peter Jacobsen	73	72	72	70	287	7,465.71
Loren Roberts	73	69	73	72	287	7,465.71
Joey Sindelar	73	69	75	70	287	7,465.71
Jim Gallagher, Jr.	69	70	74	75	288	6,030
Payne Stewart	79	68	72	69	288	6,030
Fulton Allem	75	67	72	75	289	4,560
Mark Calcavecchia	73	71	72	73	289	4,560
Jay Delsing	69	76	75	69	289	4,560
Buddy Gardner	73	73	70	73	289	4,560
Kenny Knox	71	71	73	74	289	4,560
Bruce Lietzke	69	74	74	72	289	4,560
Davis Love III	72	74	68	75	289	4,560
Mark McCumber	74	73	71	71	289	4,560
David Peoples	70	73	72	74	289	4,560
Brian Tennyson	70	74	72	73	289	4,560
Robert Gamez	74	72	70	74	290	3,016
Dan Halldorson	75	72	70	73	290	3,016
Chris Perry	71	71	74	74	290	3,016
Peter Persons	76	71	72	71	290	3,016
Bill Sander	74	74	70	72	290	3,016
Curtis Strange	72	71	76	71	290	3,016

Southwestern Bell Colonial

Colonial Country Club, Fort Worth, Texas
Par 35-35—70; 7,010 yards

May 23-26
purse, $1,200,000

	SCORES				TOTAL	MONEY
Tom Purtzer	70	66	67	64	267	$216,000
David Edwards	66	68	68	68	270	89,600
Scott Hoch	67	67	70	66	270	89,600
Bob Lohr	68	68	63	71	270	89,600
Mark Calcavecchia	65	68	68	70	271	45,600
Fred Funk	65	68	68	70	271	45,600
Ian Baker-Finch	70	65	71	66	272	36,150
Wayne Grady	68	67	67	70	272	36,150
Stan Utley	68	64	69	71	272	36,150
Tom Watson	68	66	69	69	272	36,150
Keith Clearwater	68	64	69	72	273	27,600
Jim Hallet	66	72	64	71	273	27,600
Scott Simpson	70	67	67	69	273	27,600
Chip Beck	71	68	69	66	274	21,000
Russ Cochran	71	66	68	69	274	21,000
Jeff Sluman	68	66	68	72	274	21,000

	SCORES				TOTAL	MONEY
Bobby Wadkins	70	67	67	70	274	21,000
Nolan Henke	68	69	65	73	275	15,648
Mike Hulbert	67	70	65	73	275	15,648
Bruce Lietzke	66	69	70	70	275	15,648
Gene Sauers	66	66	68	75	275	15,648
Doug Tewell	70	70	65	70	275	15,648
Clark Dennis	69	70	70	67	276	10,380
Steve Elkington	73	69	62	72	276	10,380
Wayne Levi	67	65	73	71	276	10,380
Blaine McCallister	68	69	68	71	276	10,380
Chris Perry	66	65	70	75	276	10,380
Dan Pohl	71	67	70	68	276	10,380
Ed Dougherty	68	68	70	71	277	7,980
Dan Forsman	71	70	72	64	277	7,980
Peter Persons	65	70	72	70	277	7,980
Loren Roberts	67	66	69	75	277	7,980
Phil Blackmar	69	72	71	66	278	6,205.72
Mike Reid	69	72	68	69	278	6,205.72
Bob Tway	73	69	68	68	278	6,205.72
Dave Barr	68	72	68	70	278	6,205.71
Dan Halldorson	67	69	71	71	278	6,205.71
Corey Pavin	71	66	71	70	278	6,205.71
David Peoples	70	65	69	74	278	6,205.71
Buddy Gardner	73	64	70	72	279	4,800
Larry Mize	67	68	71	73	279	4,800
Steve Pate	68	71	68	72	279	4,800
Curtis Strange	70	70	67	72	279	4,800
Brad Faxon	69	68	70	73	280	3,628
Jim Gallagher, Jr.	68	70	70	72	280	3,628
Robert Gamez	70	68	71	71	280	3,628
John Huston	69	72	66	73	280	3,628
Davis Love III	71	69	70	70	280	3,628
Duffy Waldorf	68	71	71	70	280	3,628
Kirk Triplett	69	70	72	70	281	2,852.58
Ken Green	69	70	70	72	281	2,852.57
Tom Kite	69	71	69	72	281	2,852.57
Kenny Knox	74	65	70	72	281	2,852.57
Billy Mayfair	67	68	72	74	281	2,852.57
Rocco Mediate	75	67	66	73	281	2,852.57
Robert Wrenn	72	67	69	73	281	2,852.57

Kemper Open

TPC at Avenel, Potomac, Maryland
Par 36-35—71; 6,917 yards

May 30-June 2
purse, $1,000,000

	SCORES				TOTAL	MONEY
Billy Andrade	68	64	64	67	263	$180,000
Jeff Sluman	70	64	64	65	263	108,000
(Andrade defeated Sluman on first extra hole.)						
Bill Britton	67	67	66	66	266	68,000
Mark Brooks	67	67	68	65	267	41,333.34
Greg Norman	67	65	64	71	267	41,333.33
Hal Sutton	66	65	64	72	267	41,333.33
Scott Hoch	69	69	65	65	268	33,500
Steve Jones	71	65	65	68	269	30,000
Stan Utley	68	70	64	67	269	30,000

	SCORES				TOTAL	MONEY
David Edwards	68	69	66	67	270	27,000
Jay Don Blake	67	69	65	70	271	21,200
Dan Forsman	69	67	66	69	271	21,200
Morris Hatalsky	69	70	65	67	271	21,200
Howard Twitty	66	68	68	69	271	21,200
Bobby Wadkins	69	66	65	71	271	21,200
Andy Bean	70	67	67	68	272	13,575
Tom Byrum	68	68	69	67	272	13,575
Ben Crenshaw	70	67	65	70	272	13,575
John Daly	69	67	66	70	272	13,575
Bob Gilder	65	68	68	71	272	13,575
Jeff Maggert	69	70	66	67	272	13,575
Larry Mize	69	68	65	70	272	13,575
Mark O'Meara	70	67	67	68	272	13,575
Fulton Allem	69	69	67	68	273	7,566.67
Greg Bruckner	71	68	67	67	273	7,566.67
Clark Dennis	69	68	69	67	273	7,566.67
Jay Haas	70	67	72	64	273	7,566.67
Mike Standly	69	68	67	69	273	7,566.67
Payne Stewart	71	66	67	69	273	7,566.67
Ed Fiori	69	68	66	70	273	7,566.66
Ted Schulz	69	70	63	71	273	7,566.66
Doug Tewell	68	68	65	72	273	7,566.66
Jim Gallagher, Jr.	69	69	64	72	274	5,775
Brian Watts	69	69	69	67	274	5,775
Ronnie Black	67	71	67	70	275	4,721.43
Keith Clearwater	70	70	64	71	275	4,721.43
Buddy Gardner	66	68	69	72	275	4,721.43
Gary Hallberg	69	65	70	71	275	4,721.43
Joey Sindelar	71	66	68	70	275	4,721.43
D.A. Weibring	73	67	68	67	275	4,721.43
Neal Lancaster	66	68	69	72	275	4,721.42
Mike Smith	69	70	72	65	276	3,305.72
Lanny Wadkins	70	67	68	71	276	3,305.72
Greg Whisman	69	71	70	66	276	3,305.72
Perry Arthur	66	69	69	72	276	3,305.71
Trevor Dodds	75	65	65	71	276	3,305.71
Scott Gump	65	70	68	73	276	3,305.71
Lee Janzen	72	68	65	71	276	3,305.71
Brian Tennyson	69	71	68	69	277	2,560
Richard Zokol	70	66	69	72	277	2,560

Buick Classic

Westchester Country Club, Rye, New York
Par 36-35—71; 6,779 yards

June 6-9
purse, $1,000,000

	SCORES				TOTAL	MONEY
Billy Andrade	68	68	69	68	273	$180,000
Brad Bryant	66	70	68	71	275	108,000
Nolan Henke	69	70	67	70	276	58,000
Hale Irwin	67	69	67	73	276	58,000
Seve Ballesteros	70	67	69	71	277	36,500
Wayne Levi	71	72	67	67	277	36,500
Larry Rinker	68	73	65	71	277	36,500
Fulton Allem	66	69	70	73	278	30,000
Raymond Floyd	69	68	69	72	278	30,000

	SCORES				TOTAL	MONEY
Fred Couples	70	65	72	72	279	24,000
Greg Norman	70	68	70	71	279	24,000
Loren Roberts	68	73	67	71	279	24,000
Howard Twitty	70	70	70	69	279	24,000
Paul Azinger	66	68	78	68	280	18,000
Steve Elkington	73	67	69	71	280	18,000
Brandt Jobe	71	68	69	72	280	18,000
Emlyn Aubrey	68	71	72	70	281	13,533.34
Payne Stewart	72	71	69	69	281	13,533.34
Wayne Grady	67	71	72	71	281	13,533.33
Roger Maltbie	67	75	64	75	281	13,533.33
Tom Purtzer	71	69	70	71	281	13,533.33
Duffy Waldorf	71	69	68	73	281	13,533.33
Mark Brooks	68	74	73	67	282	8,225
Bart Bryant	68	69	71	74	282	8,225
Ed Dougherty	74	69	69	70	282	8,225
David Edwards	71	71	70	70	282	8,225
Robert Gamez	70	73	68	71	282	8,225
Buddy Gardner	69	70	69	74	282	8,225
Steve Pate	68	72	70	72	282	8,225
Craig Stadler	68	70	73	71	282	8,225
John Cook	72	67	71	73	283	5,671.43
Brad Faxon	73	70	72	68	283	5,671.43
Jim Hallet	72	69	73	69	283	5,671.43
Mike Hulbert	69	70	75	69	283	5,671.43
Hal Sutton	69	71	72	71	283	5,671.43
D.A. Weibring	71	70	71	71	283	5,671.43
Brett Upper	71	66	69	77	283	5,671.42
Brian Claar	71	72	71	70	284	4,500
Ken Green	68	70	74	72	284	4,500
Peter Persons	68	68	74	74	284	4,500
David Canipe	67	73	73	72	285	3,315.56
Jim Gallagher, Jr.	69	71	74	71	285	3,315.56
Dan Halldorson	73	70	70	72	285	3,315.56
Jose Maria Olazabal	71	70	74	70	235	3,315.56
Jeff Sluman	74	68	74	69	285	3,315.56
Russ Cochran	73	68	71	73	285	3,315.55
Jerry Haas	71	71	69	74	285	3,315.55
Sean Murphy	71	69	72	73	285	3,315.55
Chris Perry	66	68	74	77	285	3,315.55
Charles Bowles	68	74	73	71	286	2,460
Jay Delsing	71	69	74	72	286	2,460
Nick Faldo	72	69	73	72	286	2,460

U.S. Open Championship

Hazeltine National Golf Club, Chaska, Minnesota
Par 36-36—72; 7,149 yards

June 13-16
purse, $1,300,000

	SCORES				TOTAL	MONEY
Payne Stewart	67	70	73	72	282	$235,000
Scott Simpson	70	68	72	72	282	117,500
(Stewart defeated Simpson in playoff, 75-77.)						
Fred Couples	70	70	75	70	285	62,574
Larry Nelson	73	72	72	68	285	62,574
Fuzzy Zoeller	72	73	74	67	286	41,542
Scott Hoch	69	71	74	73	287	36,090

	SCORES				TOTAL	MONEY
Nolan Henke	67	71	77	73	288	32,176
Raymond Floyd	73	72	76	68	289	26,958.34
Jose Maria Olazabal	73	71	75	70	289	26,958.33
Corey Pavin	71	67	79	72	289	26,958.33
Jim Gallagher, Jr.	70	72	75	73	290	20,909.20
Hale Irwin	71	75	70	74	290	20,909.20
Davis Love III	70	76	73	71	290	20,909.20
Craig Parry	70	73	73	74	290	20,909.20
D.A. Weibring	76	71	75	68	290	20,909.20
Nick Faldo	72	74	73	72	291	17,186
Sandy Lyle	72	70	74	75	291	17,186
Tom Watson	73	71	77	70	291	17,186
Billy Ray Brown	73	71	77	71	292	14,166.58
Mark Brooks	73	73	73	73	292	14,166.57
John Cook	76	70	72	74	292	14,166.57
Peter Persons	70	75	75	72	292	14,166.57
Nick Price	74	69	71	78	292	14,166.57
Tom Sieckmann	74	70	74	74	292	14,166.57
Craig Stadler	71	69	77	75	292	14,166.57
Rick Fehr	74	69	73	77	293	11,711.60
Jodie Mudd	71	70	77	75	293	11,711.60
Mike Reid	74	72	74	73	293	11,711.60
Tim Simpson	73	72	76	72	293	11,711.60
Bob Tway	75	69	75	74	293	11,711.60
Ed Humenik	72	70	78	74	294	10,133.17
Peter Jacobsen	72	73	74	75	294	10,133.17
Brian Kamm	69	73	73	79	294	10,133.17
Chris Perry	72	73	75	74	294	10,133.17
Dave Rummells	72	73	77	72	294	10,133.16
Lance Ten Broeck	72	73	74	75	294	10,133.16
Mark Calcavecchia	69	74	78	74	295	8,560.43
Keith Clearwater	70	76	74	75	295	8,560.43
Buddy Gardner	74	72	74	75	295	8,560.43
Tom Kite	71	75	74	75	295	8,560.43
Andy North	71	71	77	76	295	8,560.43
Tom Purtzer	77	68	77	73	295	8,560.43
Billy Mayfair	72	73	76	74	295	8,560.42
Ian Baker-Finch	77	70	75	74	296	7,477.50
Jim Hallet	72	74	73	77	296	7,477.50
Rodger Davis	74	68	81	74	297	6,875.67
Jack Nicklaus	70	76	77	74	297	6,875.67
Blaine McCallister	72	72	76	77	297	6,875.66
Mike Harwood	71	74	77	76	298	6,033.75
Wayne Levi	72	72	76	78	298	6,033.75
Steve Pate	72	75	77	74	298	6,033.75
Loren Roberts	75	70	74	79	298	6,033.75
John Inman	72	72	77	78	299	5,389
Larry Rinker	72	72	77	78	299	5,389
Steve Elkington	77	69	76	78	300	5,164.50
Steve Gotsche	72	75	76	77	300	5,164.50
Larry Mize	73	73	79	75	300	5,164.50
Ian Woosnam	73	68	79	80	300	5,164.50
*Phil Mickelson	73	72	80	75	300	
David Graham	74	71	80	77	302	5,008
Stan Utley	73	71	81	78	303	4,958
John Adams	72	75	78	79	304	4,958
Wayne Grady	73	74	78	80	305	4,958
Terry Snodgrass	74	73	80	78	305	4,958
Lanny Wadkins	76	70	80	79	305	4,958

Out of Final 36 Holes

Paul Azinger	72	76	148
Tom Byrum	68	80	148
Bob Estes	72	76	148
Lee Janzen	74	74	148
Eric Johnson	77	71	148
Jeff Sluman	75	73	148
Mitch Adcock	79	70	149
Fulton Allem	71	78	149
Seve Ballesteros	72	77	149
Jon Chaffee	74	75	149
Jay Delsing	74	75	149
Frank Dobbs	73	76	149
Tom Eubank	75	74	149
David Frost	75	74	149
John Huston	72	77	149
Bernhard Langer	75	74	149
Mark McCumber	76	73	149
Gil Morgan	76	73	149
Mark O'Meara	73	76	149
Timothy Robyn	79	70	149
Lee Trevino	77	72	149
Dave Barr	76	74	150
Jim Benepe	74	76	150
Bob Boyd	75	75	150
Mike Donald	74	76	150
*Allen Doyle	76	74	150
Scott Gump	77	73	150
Robert Meyer	76	74	150
Brad Sherfy	78	72	150
Hal Sutton	77	73	150
Kirk Triplett	75	75	150
John Wilson	78	72	150
Billy Andrade	76	75	151
Bill Britton	73	78	151
Fred Funk	75	76	151
*Chris Gorgone	76	75	151
Dan Halldorson	76	75	151
David Jackson	70	81	151
Rocco Mediate	77	74	151
Rick Price	77	74	151
Curtis Strange	77	74	151
Thomas Tolles	74	77	151
Billy Tuten	75	76	151
Bobby Wadkins	75	76	151
Dennis Zinkon	78	73	151
Chip Beck	75	77	152
Steve Jones	76	76	152
Jumbo Ozaki	77	75	152
Jerry Pate	78	74	152
Rocky Walcher	76	76	152
Phil Blackmar	77	76	153
Jerry Foltz	77	76	153
Jon Hough	76	77	153
Andrew Magee	74	79	153
Ray Stewart	77	76	153
Robert Gamez	76	78	154
Jim McGovern	77	77	154
Rick Osberg	73	81	154
Jay Overton	81	73	154

	SCORES				TOTAL
Dicky Thompson	75	79			154
Bruce Zabriski	83	71			154
Eric Booker	78	77			155
Ed Dougherty	79	76			155
Brad Faxon	79	76			155
Bob Lasken	81	74			155
Bryan Norton	78	77			155
Cary Hungate	77	79			156
John Ross	77	79			156
Brian Tennyson	77	79			156
Jacob Ferenz	75	82			157
Jay Gunning	83	74			157
John Paesani	82	75			157
Jeb Stuart	78	79			157
Scott Beaugureau	81	77			158
*Jeff Lee	80	78			158
Sam Randolph	81	78			159
Rick Vershure	79	80			159
Michael Weeks	79	80			159
James Detrixhe	80	80			160
Louie Garcia	82	78			160
Terry Dear	83	78			161
Darrell Kestner	78	83			161
Clay Devers	81	81			162
Jack Kay, Jr.	79	83			162
Joe Hajduch	88	75			163
Chris Endres	85	80			165
George Daves	82	85			167
Paul Oglesby	86	81			167
Greg Norman	78	WD			
Ronan Rafferty	79	WD			
Ken Green	WD				

(All professionals who did not complete 72 holes received $1,000.)

Anheuser-Busch Classic

Kingsmill Golf Club, Williamsburg, Virginia
Par 36-35—71; 6,776 yards

June 20-23
purse, $1,000,000

	SCORES				TOTAL	MONEY
Mike Hulbert	66	67	65	68	266	$180,000
Kenny Knox	67	69	62	68	266	108,000
(Hulbert defeated Knox on first extra hole.)						
Ian Baker-Finch	62	68	68	69	267	58,000
Fuzzy Zoeller	67	69	66	65	267	58,000
Brian Claar	68	68	62	71	269	38,000
Bob Gilder	63	68	70	68	269	38,000
Brad Fabel	66	67	68	70	271	33,500
Jay Don Blake	67	68	70	68	273	25,000
Bill Britton	69	69	68	67	273	25,000
Keith Clearwater	69	66	69	69	273	25,000
Mike Donald	66	64	68	75	273	25,000
Kenny Perry	67	68	68	70	273	25,000
Dan Pohl	64	67	65	77	273	25,000
Nick Price	67	69	69	68	273	25,000
Tommy Armour	68	69	68	69	274	16,000

	SCORES				TOTAL	MONEY
Tom Purtzer	67	68	68	71	274	16,000
Jeff Sluman	68	71	64	71	274	16,000
Lanny Wadkins	68	64	71	71	274	16,000
Mark Wiebe	69	67	67	71	274	16,000
Ronnie Black	72	65	69	69	275	10,833.34
Sam Randolph	66	68	72	69	275	10,833.34
Jim Hallet	67	68	68	72	275	10,833.33
Lon Hinkle	69	70	66	70	275	10,833.33
Steve Pate	70	68	65	72	275	10,833.33
Bobby Wadkins	68	64	69	74	275	10,833.33
Bill Buttner	67	69	69	71	276	6,950
Jim Gallagher, Jr.	69	71	64	72	276	6,950
Gary Hallberg	73	66	71	66	276	6,950
Davis Love III	67	66	73	70	276	6,950
John Mahaffey	69	70	66	71	276	6,950
Dillard Pruitt	69	70	65	72	276	6,950
Tim Simpson	69	69	67	71	276	6,950
Mike Sullivan	66	67	71	72	276	6,950
Dan Forsman	71	66	70	70	277	5,050
Morris Hatalsky	71	68	64	74	277	5,050
Scott Hoch	66	69	73	69	277	5,050
Dave Rummells	69	71	68	69	277	5,050
Lance Ten Broeck	69	69	69	70	277	5,050
Robert Wrenn	68	67	71	71	277	5,050
Wayne Grady	73	66	67	72	278	3,414
Dan Halldorson	67	68	71	72	278	3,414
Dudley Hart	65	71	68	74	278	3,414
Ed Humenik	70	66	72	70	278	3,414
John Inman	74	65	69	70	278	3,414
Blaine McCallister	65	67	72	74	278	3,414
Chris Perry	66	71	69	72	278	3,414
Mike Springer	70	69	70	69	278	3,414
Ron Streck	70	69	66	73	278	3,414
Hal Sutton	70	68	67	73	278	3,414
Fulton Allem	68	67	67	77	279	2,412
Mike Reid	64	73	69	73	279	2,412
Larry Rinker	68	68	71	72	279	2,412
Tom Sieckmann	70	69	67	73	279	2,412
Curtis Strange	71	67	70	71	279	2,412

Westinghouse-Family House Invitational

Oakmont Country Club, Oakmont, Pennsylvania
Par 36-35—71; 6,972 yards

June 24-25
purse, $700,000

	SCORES		TOTAL	MONEY
Ian Baker-Finch	65	69	134	$140,000
Mike Donald	68	69	137	80,000
Jay Don Blake	71	67	138	41,666
Raymond Floyd	67	71	138	41,666
Bob Tway	66	72	138	41,666
Hal Sutton	70	69	139	21,166
Fred Couples	69	70	139	21,166
Wayne Grady	69	70	139	21,166
Davis Love III	68	71	139	21,166
Wayne Levi	67	72	139	21,166
Scott Hoch	66	73	139	21,166

	SCORES			TOTAL	MONEY
Steve Pate	74	67		141	12,000
David Frost	70	71		141	12,000
Curtis Strange	67	74		141	12,000
Nick Price	71	71		142	12,000
Tom Kite	70	72		142	12,000
Steve Elkington	69	73		142	12,000
Bob Ford	70	73		143	12,000
Rocco Mediate	72	72		144	12,000
Larry Mize	68	76		144	12,000
Roger Maltbie	73	72		145	12,000
Tom Purtzer	72	73		145	12,000
Mike Hulbert	72	74		146	12,000
John Cook	71	75		146	12,000
Andrew Magee	74	73		147	12,000
Fuzzy Zoeller	73	74		147	12,000
John Huston	72	75		147	12,000
Steve Jones	71	77		148	12,000
Brian Tennyson	71	78		149	12,000
Billy Mayfair	77	73		150	12,000

Federal Express St. Jude Classic

TPC at Southwind, Memphis, Tennessee
Par 36-35—71; 7,006 yards

June 27-30
purse, $1,000,000

	SCORES				TOTAL	MONEY
Fred Couples	68	67	66	68	269	$180,000
Rick Fehr	64	70	71	67	272	108,000
David Canipe	69	69	70	65	273	58,000
Jay Haas	70	65	73	65	273	58,000
Russ Cochran	66	67	73	68	274	40,000
Mark Brooks	68	66	69	72	275	32,375
Nick Price	71	65	69	70	275	32,375
Doug Tewell	68	71	66	70	275	32,375
Robert Thompson	67	72	69	67	275	32,375
Bob Gilder	68	74	67	67	276	25,000
Greg Ladehoff	70	71	67	68	276	25,000
Peter Persons	67	70	65	74	276	25,000
David Edwards	70	71	68	68	277	18,750
Scott Gump	67	68	72	70	277	18,750
Scott Hoch	68	69	69	71	277	18,750
Hal Sutton	68	67	67	75	277	18,750
Gary Hallberg	75	63	69	71	278	15,500
Fuzzy Zoeller	69	64	71	74	278	15,500
Tom Kite	74	67	70	68	279	10,522.23
Gil Morgan	70	70	72	67	279	10,522.23
Bill Buttner	70	70	70	69	279	10,522.22
Trevor Dodds	68	69	71	71	279	10,522.22
Donnie Hammond	72	68	68	71	279	10,522.22
Mike Hulbert	68	67	69	75	279	10,522.22
Loren Roberts	71	69	70	69	279	10,522.22
Kirk Triplett	70	70	70	69	279	10,522.22
John Wilson	71	71	69	68	279	10,522.22
Greg Bruckner	67	67	76	70	280	6,950
John Cook	68	71	69	72	280	6,950
Billy Mayfair	66	70	73	71	280	6,950
Dillard Pruitt	71	66	71	72	280	6,950

	SCORES				TOTAL	MONEY
Tommy Armour	69	70	70	72	281	5,414.29
Ben Crenshaw	70	67	74	70	281	5,414.29
John Daly	70	66	75	70	281	5,414.29
Gene Sauers	71	68	71	71	281	5,414.29
Jeff Maggert	68	66	74	73	281	5,414.28
Larry Mize	69	72	67	73	281	5,414.28
Brian Tennyson	66	69	71	75	281	5,414.28
Dave Barr	70	69	72	71	282	4,000
Kenny Knox	69	69	72	72	282	4,000
Jim McGovern	69	70	73	70	282	4,000
Ted Schulz	71	71	70	70	282	4,000
Bobby Wadkins	70	71	72	69	282	4,000
Robert Wrenn	70	69	72	71	282	4,000
Mike Donald	69	72	75	67	283	2,860
Bob Estes	73	66	72	72	283	2,860
Tommy Moore	72	68	74	69	283	2,860
Lanny Wadkins	70	66	74	73	283	2,860
Brian Watts	71	69	74	69	283	2,860
Kim Young	71	68	75	69	283	2,860

Centel Western Open

Cog Hill Golf Club, Dubsdread Course, Lemont, Illinois
Par 36-36—72; 7,040 yards

July 4-7
purse, $1,000,000

	SCORES				TOTAL	MONEY
Russ Cochran	66	72	68	69	275	$180,000
Greg Norman	69	66	71	71	277	108,000
Fred Couples	70	68	68	72	278	68,000
Bob Gilder	70	71	70	70	281	48,000
Dave Barr	70	74	68	70	282	32,750
Gary Hallberg	67	71	70	74	282	32,750
John Huston	72	70	71	69	282	32,750
Kenny Knox	73	69	70	70	282	32,750
Nick Price	71	71	70	70	282	32,750
D.A. Weibring	71	72	73	66	282	32,750
Jim Gallagher, Jr.	76	67	69	71	283	22,000
Lee Janzen	67	71	73	72	283	22,000
Andrew Magee	69	69	70	75	283	22,000
Mike Springer	70	70	68	75	283	22,000
Chip Beck	68	73	72	71	284	17,000
John Daly	69	73	71	71	284	17,000
Bruce Lietzke	71	72	71	70	284	17,000
Billy Andrade	70	74	69	72	285	14,000
Ronnie Black	72	74	65	74	285	14,000
Howard Twitty	70	71	73	71	285	14,000
Jim McGovern	72	74	71	69	286	9,133.34
Scott Simpson	71	73	71	71	286	9,133.34
Richard Zokol	73	73	69	71	286	9,133.34
Tommy Armour	70	70	70	76	286	9,133.33
Keith Clearwater	70	72	72	72	286	9,133.33
Raymond Floyd	66	73	74	73	286	9,133.33
Loren Roberts	71	69	72	74	286	9,133.33
Leonard Thompson	76	70	68	72	286	9,133.33
Kirk Triplett	72	73	69	72	286	9,133.33
Rick Dalpos	67	76	74	70	287	6,075
Hale Irwin	70	76	70	71	287	6,075

	SCORES				TOTAL	MONEY
Steve Jones	70	73	72	72	287	6,075
Mark Lye	66	71	74	76	287	6,075
Mike Sullivan	66	76	70	75	287	6,075
Brian Tennyson	75	71	69	72	287	6,075
Michael Allen	70	76	71	71	288	4,507.15
Lance Ten Broeck	76	70	70	72	288	4,507.15
Mark Calcavecchia	67	77	74	70	288	4,507.14
Brad Fabel	74	68	73	73	288	4,507.14
Tom Kite	73	71	71	73	288	4,507.14
Mike Nicolette	71	72	75	70	288	4,507.14
Tom Watson	74	72	72	70	288	4,507.14
Marco Dawson	75	70	72	72	289	2,870.91
Ed Dougherty	73	72	72	72	289	2,870.91
Steve Elkington	68	75	73	73	289	2,870.91
Rocco Mediate	70	73	75	71	289	2,870.91
Dan Pohl	72	74	73	70	289	2,870.91
Greg Powers	70	74	73	72	289	2,870.91
Tim Simpson	73	73	70	73	289	2,870.91
Joey Sindelar	72	69	72	76	289	2,870.91
Bobby Wadkins	69	72	74	74	289	2,870.91
Brian Watts	74	68	76	71	289	2,870.91
Mark Brooks	74	69	77	69	289	2,870.90

New England Classic

Pleasant Valley Country Club, Sutton, Massachusetts
Par 36-35—71; 7,110 yards

July 11-14
purse, $1,000,000

	SCORES				TOTAL	MONEY
Bruce Fleisher	64	67	73	64	268	$180,000
Ian Baker-Finch	66	68	66	68	268	108,000
(Fleisher defeated Baker-Finch on seventh extra hole.)						
Gene Sauers	67	67	66	69	269	68,000
Ted Schulz	65	69	71	67	272	48,000
Charles Bowles	68	68	71	66	273	35,125
Ed Dougherty	69	67	70	67	273	35,125
Brad Faxon	70	68	65	70	273	35,125
Barry Jaeckel	70	65	68	70	273	35,125
John Adams	69	68	67	70	274	28,000
Lance Ten Broeck	70	66	72	66	274	28,000
Billy Andrade	68	66	71	70	275	20,500
John Daly	69	65	69	72	275	20,500
Fred Funk	68	69	70	68	275	20,500
David Peoples	67	70	73	65	275	20,500
Mike Springer	67	67	70	71	275	20,500
Jeff Woodland	70	70	68	67	275	20,500
Billy Ray Brown	70	69	68	69	276	11,800
Brad Bryant	67	68	69	72	276	11,800
Joel Edwards	68	68	70	70	276	11,800
Buddy Gardner	68	69	70	69	276	11,800
Jim Hallet	69	71	68	68	276	11,800
Lon Hinkle	71	67	68	70	276	11,800
Brian Kamm	66	74	69	67	276	11,800
Steve Lowery	69	68	70	69	276	11,800
Bob Wolcott	70	69	67	70	276	11,800
Robert Wrenn	69	68	68	71	276	11,800
Mike Donald	69	67	70	71	277	7,250

	SCORES				TOTAL	MONEY
Morris Hatalsky	73	64	68	72	277	7,250
Blaine McCallister	65	69	74	69	277	7,250
Joey Sindelar	71	69	71	66	277	7,250
Ronnie Black	73	64	69	72	278	5,550
Marco Dawson	69	68	72	69	278	5,550
Ernie Gonzalez	65	69	71	73	278	5,550
Nolan Henke	69	71	68	70	278	5,550
Kenny Knox	66	70	69	73	278	5,550
Dave Rummells	72	67	67	72	278	5,550
Duffy Waldorf	70	70	66	72	278	5,550
Mark Wiebe	68	72	67	71	278	5,550
Emlyn Aubrey	66	73	70	70	279	3,800
Curt Byrum	71	68	69	71	279	3,800
Neal Lancaster	66	71	74	68	279	3,800
Mike McCullough	70	67	74	68	279	3,800
Bryan Norton	69	71	69	70	279	3,800
Jack Renner	68	68	72	71	279	3,800
Ken Schall	69	66	72	72	279	3,800
Brian Watts	70	69	72	68	279	3,800
Barry Cheesman	71	69	71	69	280	2,568.58
Dave Barr	68	70	71	71	280	2,568.57
Trevor Dodds	65	75	69	71	280	2,568.57
Andy North	74	66	68	72	280	2,568.57
Don Pooley	70	70	71	69	280	2,568.57
Francis Quinn	69	71	70	70	280	2,568.57
Sam Randolph	72	68	70	70	280	2,568.57

Chattanooga Classic

Valleybrook Golf and Country Club, Hixson, Tennessee
Par 35-35—70, 6,641 yards

July 18-21
purse, $700,000

	SCORES				TOTAL	MONEY
Dillard Pruitt	66	65	65	64	260	$126,000
Lance Ten Broeck	64	65	66	67	262	75,600
John Daly	65	66	67	66	264	33,600
Jim Gallagher, Jr.	64	68	65	67	264	33,600
Steve Lowery	63	65	69	67	264	33,600
Dave Rummells	69	66	68	61	264	33,600
Perry Arthur	67	64	67	67	265	21,087.50
Russ Cochran	68	66	67	64	265	21,087.50
Brad Fabel	67	65	66	67	265	21,087.50
Kenny Knox	70	63	67	65	265	21,087.50
Phil Blackmar	67	64	67	68	266	15,400
Scott Hoch	68	68	67	63	266	15,400
Peter Persons	67	65	68	66	266	15,400
Ken Schall	67	64	68	67	266	15,400
Frank Conner	68	66	67	66	267	10,500
Jay Delsing	71	65	65	66	267	10,500
Brad Faxon	67	66	69	65	267	10,500
Ed Fiori	68	67	66	66	267	10,500
Ray Stewart	64	68	65	70	267	10,500
Ron Streck	67	66	68	66	267	10,500
Howard Twitty	64	65	69	69	267	10,500
Mitch Adcock	66	66	68	68	268	6,310
J.C. Anderson	69	66	66	67	268	6,310
Marco Dawson	61	69	69	69	268	6,310

	SCORES				TOTAL	MONEY
Bob Estes	71	61	69	67	268	6,310
Gibby T. Gilbert	64	69	69	66	268	6,310
Scott Gump	67	69	65	67	268	6,310
Don Shirey, Jr.	69	67	67	65	268	6,310
Lon Hinkle	70	67	69	63	269	4,355.15
Stan Utley	68	67	68	66	269	4,355.15
Lennie Clements	65	62	70	72	269	4,355.14
Joel Edwards	69	67	64	69	269	4,355.14
Greg Ladehoff	64	67	68	70	269	4,355.14
Mike Smith	66	70	66	67	269	4,355.14
Harry Taylor	64	70	68	67	269	4,355.14
Emlyn Aubrey	69	68	71	62	270	3,154.86
Buddy Gardner	70	66	69	65	270	3,154.86
Jerry Haas	65	69	69	67	270	3,154.86
Jack Renner	69	63	69	69	270	3,154.86
Sonny Skinner	66	71	69	64	270	3,154.86
Clark Burroughs	67	67	67	69	270	3,154.85
David Peoples	68	67	66	69	270	3,154.85
Jim Benepe	67	68	71	65	271	2,450
Jim Carter	68	64	70	69	271	2,450
Chris Perry	67	70	68	66	271	2,450
Jack Ferenz	68	66	70	68	272	1,984.50
Barry Jaeckel	67	67	72	66	272	1,984.50
Pat McGowan	70	67	68	67	272	1,984.50
Bob Wolcott	69	67	71	65	272	1,984.50
Andy Dillard	70	65	69	69	273	1,644.23
Blaine McCallister	69	68	69	67	273	1,644.23
John Adams	68	69	67	69	273	1,644.22
Brandel Chamblee	67	67	68	71	273	1,644.22
Lee Janzen	63	71	69	70	273	1,644.22
Gary Koch	66	69	69	69	273	1,644.22
Ted Schulz	63	66	69	75	273	1,644.22
Denis Watson	69	64	65	75	273	1,644.22
Willie Wood	70	66	65	72	273	1,644.22

Canon Greater Hartford Open

TPC at River Highlands, Cromwell, Connecticut
Par 35-35—70; 6,820 yards

July 25-28
purse, $1,000,000

	SCORES				TOTAL	MONEY
Billy Ray Brown	67	72	65	67	271	$180,000
Rick Fehr	68	67	66	70	271	88,000
Corey Pavin	65	67	70	69	271	88,000
(Brown defeated Fehr and Pavin on first extra hole.)						
Loren Roberts	68	69	68	67	272	41,333.34
Billy Andrade	72	66	66	68	272	41,333.33
Jim Gallagher, Jr.	68	65	70	69	272	41,333.33
Dan Pohl	70	69	67	67	273	31,166.67
Mike Reid	71	69	68	65	273	31,166.67
Larry Rinker	71	66	66	70	273	31,166.66
Dave Barr	67	69	71	67	274	24,000
Dan Forsman	67	67	71	69	274	24,000
Ken Green	67	69	71	67	274	24,000
Kenny Perry	67	67	70	70	274	24,000
David Edwards	67	69	71	68	275	16,500
Jim Hallet	64	71	68	72	275	16,500

	SCORES				TOTAL	MONEY
Billy Mayfair	68	65	70	72	275	16,500
Mark McCumber	70	69	68	68	275	16,500
Jim McGovern	69	71	67	68	275	16,500
David Peoples	67	71	68	69	275	16,500
Mike Hulbert	67	72	67	70	276	11,650
Joey Sindelar	68	70	68	70	276	11,650
Ray Stewart	69	69	70	68	276	11,650
Howard Twitty	69	72	66	69	276	11,650
Jim Benepe	70	69	69	69	277	8,300
Mark Brooks	71	69	69	68	277	8,300
Brad Faxon	69	70	70	68	277	8,300
Dudley Hart	70	69	70	68	277	8,300
Mike Sullivan	67	68	69	73	277	8,300
John Adams	71	65	72	70	278	5,955.56
Ronnie Black	72	69	68	69	278	5,955.56
Tom Byrum	72	67	70	69	278	5,955.56
Hal Sutton	70	70	70	68	278	5,955.56
D.A. Weibring	71	70	69	68	278	5,955.56
Chip Beck	72	66	69	71	278	5,955.55
Scott Hoch	65	68	70	75	278	5,955.55
John Inman	70	69	67	72	278	5,955.55
Dicky Thompson	73	68	65	72	278	5,955.55
Ed Humenik	69	70	69	71	279	4,400
Jeff Maggert	70	70	68	71	279	4,400
Rocco Mediate	70	67	69	73	279	4,400
Jeff Sluman	69	69	70	71	279	4,400
Jim Booros	72	67	72	69	280	3,072
Clark Burroughs	69	70	70	71	280	3,072
Mark Calcavecchia	65	71	73	71	280	3,072
John Cook	71	70	70	69	280	3,072
Joel Edwards	69	70	71	70	280	3,072
Steve Jones	70	71	68	71	280	3,072
Bill Sander	69	71	73	67	280	3,072
Mike Springer	71	69	71	69	280	3,072
Lance Ten Broeck	69	69	71	71	280	3,072
Robert Wrenn	70	70	69	71	280	3,072

Buick Open

Warwick Hills Golf and Country Club, Grand Blanc, Michigan
Par 36-36—72; 7,014 yards

August 1-4
purse, $1,000,000

	SCORES				TOTAL	MONEY
Brad Faxon	66	68	71	66	271	$180,000
Chip Beck	67	67	68	69	271	108,000
(Faxon defeated Beck on first extra hole.)						
John Cook	68	73	66	65	272	52,000
Scott Hoch	63	70	72	67	272	52,000
Steve Pate	68	69	69	66	272	52,000
Nick Faldo	68	69	65	71	273	32,375
Gene Sauers	67	68	69	69	273	32,375
Hal Sutton	69	69	66	69	273	32,375
Howard Twitty	71	66	66	70	273	32,375
Bill Britton	69	69	65	71	274	23,000
Marco Dawson	66	70	64	74	274	23,000
Wayne Grady	68	66	71	69	274	23,000
Greg Norman	67	65	71	71	274	23,000

	SCORES				TOTAL	MONEY
Tim Simpson	72	68	64	70	274	23,000
Jay Don Blake	74	67	65	69	275	17,000
Lee Janzen	71	65	68	71	275	17,000
Duffy Waldorf	69	68	68	70	275	17,000
Ed Fiori	69	70	70	67	276	14,500
Lanny Wadkins	69	69	67	71	276	14,500
J.C. Anderson	70	69	70	68	277	11,650
Brad Bryant	73	66	66	72	277	11,650
Jay Delsing	68	69	69	71	277	11,650
David Edwards	68	68	71	70	277	11,650
Barry Jaeckel	67	69	71	71	278	8,525
Kenny Knox	69	66	72	71	278	8,525
Gil Morgan	69	66	71	72	278	8,525
Dicky Thompson	70	70	68	70	278	8,525
Billy Andrade	72	66	69	72	279	6,650
Bobby Clampett	70	70	68	71	279	6,650
Ken Green	72	67	71	69	279	6,650
Mark McCumber	70	71	69	69	279	6,650
Bryan Norton	70	70	65	74	279	6,650
Mike Sullivan	70	70	68	71	279	6,650
Steve Lowery	68	69	73	70	280	5,160
Andrew Magee	69	66	72	73	280	5,160
Don Pooley	69	72	70	69	280	5,160
Jim Thorpe	69	71	73	67	280	5,160
Brett Upper	72	68	70	70	280	5,160
Fulton Allem	67	74	70	70	281	3,700
Jim Benepe	69	71	74	67	281	3,700
David Canipe	70	71	70	70	281	3,700
Ben Crenshaw	68	68	74	71	281	3,700
Scott Gump	70	68	75	68	281	3,700
Tommy Moore	67	70	73	71	281	3,700
Mike Smith	69	71	70	71	281	3,700
Dave Sutherland	67	71	71	72	281	3,700
Brian Watts	70	67	72	72	281	3,700
John Inman	70	68	72	72	282	2,580
John Mahaffey	71	69	71	71	282	2,580
Dan Pohl	75	65	69	73	282	2,580
Mike Standly	68	70	71	73	282	2,580

PGA Championship

Crooked Stick Club, Carmel, Indiana
Par 36-36—72; 7,289 yards

August 8-11
purse, $1,350,000

	SCORES				TOTAL	MONEY
John Daly	69	67	69	71	276	$230,000
Bruce Lietzke	68	69	72	70	279	140,000
Jim Gallagher, Jr.	70	72	72	67	281	95,000
Kenny Knox	67	71	70	74	282	75,000
Bob Gilder	73	70	67	73	283	60,000
Steven Richardson	70	72	72	69	283	60,000
David Feherty	71	74	71	68	284	38,000
Raymond Floyd	69	74	72	69	284	38,000
John Huston	70	72	70	72	284	38,000
Steve Pate	70	75	70	69	284	38,000
Craig Stadler	68	71	69	76	284	38,000
Hal Sutton	74	67	72	71	284	38,000

	SCORES				TOTAL	MONEY
Jay Don Blake	75	70	72	68	285	24,000
Andrew Magee	69	73	68	75	285	24,000
Payne Stewart	74	70	71	70	285	24,000
Nick Faldo	70	69	71	76	286	17,000
Ken Green	68	73	71	74	286	17,000
Wayne Levi	73	71	72	70	286	17,000
Sandy Lyle	68	75	71	72	286	17,000
Rocco Mediate	71	71	73	71	286	17,000
Gil Morgan	70	71	74	71	286	17,000
Howard Twitty	70	71	75	70	286	17,000
Seve Ballesteros	71	72	71	73	287	11,500
Chip Beck	73	73	70	71	287	11,500
Mike Hulbert	72	72	73	70	287	11,500
Jack Nicklaus	71	72	73	71	287	11,500
Fred Couples	74	67	76	71	288	8,150
Rick Fehr	70	73	71	74	288	8,150
Jim Hallet	69	74	73	72	288	8,150
Mark McNulty	75	71	69	73	288	8,150
Loren Roberts	72	74	72	70	288	8,150
Billy Andrade	73	74	68	74	289	6,000
Mark Calcavecchia	70	74	73	72	289	6,000
David Edwards	71	75	71	72	289	6,000
Steve Elkington	74	68	74	73	289	6,000
Dan Forsman	73	74	68	74	289	6,000
Davis Love III	72	72	72	73	289	6,000
Jodie Mudd	74	71	74	70	289	6,000
Greg Norman	70	74	72	73	289	6,000
Corey Pavin	72	73	71	73	289	6,000
Tom Purtzer	69	76	71	73	289	6,000
Doug Tewell	75	72	74	68	289	6,000
Ed Dougherty	75	70	69	76	290	4,030
Wayne Grady	72	70	71	77	290	4,030
Scott Hoch	71	75	72	72	290	4,030
Craig Parry	73	70	76	71	290	4,030
Lanny Wadkins	71	74	72	73	290	4,030
Keith Clearwater	72	72	76	71	291	3,175
Brad Faxon	72	71	76	72	291	3,175
David Frost	74	70	75	72	291	3,175
Ian Woosnam	67	72	76	76	291	3,175
David Graham	72	73	73	74	292	2,725
Tom Kite	73	72	75	72	292	2,725
Mark McCumber	74	72	71	75	292	2,725
Eduardo Romero	72	75	73	72	292	2,725
Tom Sieckmann	68	76	74	74	292	2,725
Fred Funk	71	69	72	81	293	2,537.50
Nolan Henke	74	70	75	74	293	2,537.50
Blaine McCallister	71	76	77	69	293	2,537.50
Lindy Miller	72	72	77	72	293	2,537.50
Dave Barr	75	72	76	71	294	2,462.50
Jeff Sluman	73	73	74	74	294	2,462.50
Gene Sauers	75	71	70	79	295	2,400
Joey Sindelar	74	73	71	77	295	2,400
Bob Wolcott	73	71	79	72	295	2,400
Dillard Pruitt	72	75	73	76	296	2,312.50
Bob Tway	73	71	78	74	296	2,312.50
Mark Wiebe	72	73	73	78	296	2,312.50
Scott Williams	70	77	76	73	296	2,312.50
Denny Hepler	71	75	75	76	297	2,225
Lonnie Nielson	74	71	74	78	297	2,225
David Peoples	74	73	75	75	297	2,225

	SCORES				TOTAL	MONEY
Phil Blackmar	73	72	82	71	298	2,137.50
Billy Ray Brown	69	75	79	75	298	2,137.50
Hale Irwin	70	76	74	78	298	2,137.50
Don Pooley	72	74	72	80	298	2,137.50
Kenny Perry	72	73	79	76	300	2,075

Out Of Final 36 Holes

	SCORES		TOTAL
Bill Britton	71	77	148
Mark Brooks	73	75	148
Brian Claar	76	72	148
Russ Cochran	73	75	148
John Cook	74	74	148
Bob Lohr	78	70	148
Tommy Nakajima	72	76	148
Peter Persons	73	75	148
Peter Senior	74	74	148
Dave Stockton	71	77	148
Fuzzy Zoeller	72	76	148
Scott Bentley	75	74	149
Jay Delsing	70	79	149
Terry Florence	75	74	149
Ricky Kawagishi	75	74	149
Bernhard Langer	75	74	149
Larry Mize	72	77	149
Lee Rinker	73	76	149
Ken Schall	74	75	149
Bobby Wadkins	77	72	149
Tom Watson	74	75	149
Ian Baker-Finch	74	76	150
Billy Mayfair	73	77	150
Jose Maria Olazabal	77	73	150
Ted Schulz	75	75	150
Tim Simpson	74	76	150
Hubert Green	73	78	151
Morris Hatalsky	74	77	151
Stu Ingraham	73	78	151
John Mahaffey	77	74	151
Scott Simpson	72	79	151
Greg Farrow	74	78	152
Larry Gilbert	79	73	152
Mike Kallam	74	78	152
Darrell Kestner	74	78	152
Larry Nelson	75	77	152
Sam Torrance	74	78	152
Gary Trivisonno	77	75	152
Jim Masserio	74	79	153
Brett Upper	74	79	153
Bruce Fleisher	76	78	154
Buddy Gardner	74	80	154
Gary Hallberg	72	82	154
Mark O'Meara	75	79	154
Stan Utley	77	77	154
Tom Wargo	76	78	154
Mel Baum	78	77	155
Fran Marrello	75	80	155
Arnold Palmer	77	78	155
Milan Swilor	77	78	155
Tim Thompson	79	76	155
Bob Borowicz	80	76	156

	SCORES		TOTAL
Dave Rummells	77	79	156
Andy Bean	80	77	157
Brent Buckman	79	78	157
Terry Dear	74	83	157
Mike Harwood	73	85	158
Jeff Roth	80	78	158
Brad Sherfy	76	82	158
Bob Lendzion	76	83	159
Brian Tennyson	76	83	159
Brent Veenstra	77	82	159
Robert Wilkin	76	84	160
Tom Woodard	84	76	160
Mike Lawrence	82	79	161
Benny Passons	85	77	162
Steve Veriato	82	80	162
Gregg Wolff	81	81	162
John Hendricks	83	80	163
Shawn McEntee	81	82	163
Jim White	76	87	163
Jim Dickson	83	85	168
Ben Crenshaw	81	WD	
Curtis Strange	81	WD	

(All players who did not complete 72 holes received $1,500.)

The International

Castle Pines Golf Club, Castle Rock, Colorado
Par 36-36—72; 7,559 yards

August 15-18
purse, $1,100,000

FINAL ROUND

	POINTS	MONEY
Jose Maria Olazabal	10	$198,000
Bob Lohr	7	82,133.34
Ian Baker-Finch	7	82,133.33
Scott Gump	7	82,133.33
Tom Watson	6	38,637.50
Larry Mize	6	38,637.50
Bobby Clampett	6	38,637.50
Ted Schulz	6	38,637.50
Rocco Mediate	5	30,800
Keith Clearwater	5	30,800
Ricky Kawagishi	4	27,500
Peter Senior	3	23,100
Craig Stadler	3	23,100
Bob Estes	3	23,100
Duffy Waldorf	2	19,800
Howard Twitty	1	18,150
Ken Green	1	18,150
Dudley Hart	0	15,950
Lee Janzen	0	15,950
Mike Reid	-1	14,300
Lon Hinkle	-2	12,760
Brad Faxon	-2	12,760
Robert Wrenn	-3	11,440
Steve Pate	-4	10,560

IN THE MONEY

	THREE ROUND TOTAL	MONEY
Richard Zokol	15	8,983.34
Jeff Maggert	15	8,983.33
Dillard Pruitt	15	8,983.33
Jim Hallet	14	7,975
Gene Sauers	14	7,975
Perry Arthur	13	6,682.84
Andrew Magee	13	6,682.84
Mark Calcavecchia	13	6,682.83
Dan Forsman	13	6,682.83
Mark Hayes	13	6,682.83
Willie Wood	13	6,682.83
Chip Beck	12	5,407.67
Raymond Floyd	12	5,407.67
Steve Jones	12	5,407.66
Dan Halldorson	11	4,730
Bob Tway	11	4,730
Wayne Westner	11	4,730
Bart Bryant	10	3,454
Jay Haas	10	3,454
Hale Irwin	10	3,454
Greg Ladehoff	10	3,454
Mark Lye	10	3,454
Bryan Norton	10	3,454
Chris Perry	10	3,454
Eduardo Romero	10	3,454
D.A. Weibring	10	3,454

Fred Meyer Challenge

Portland Golf Club, Portland, Oregon
Par 36-36—72; 6,612 yards

August 19-20
purse, $700,000

	SCORES		TOTAL	MONEY (Each)
Paul Azinger/Ben Crenshaw	63	62	125	$50,000
Fred Couples/Raymond Floyd	62	63	125	37,500
Mark Calcavecchia/Bob Gilder	63	62	125	37,500
(Azinger/Crenshaw won playoff on second extra hole.)				
Chip Beck/Tim Simpson	63	63	126	28,750
Wayne Levi/Gil Morgan	63	63	126	28,750
Bobby Wadkins/Lanny Wadkins	66	64	130	25,250
Hale Irwin/Corey Pavin	65	65	130	25,250
Mike Donald/Curtis Strange	66	65	131	24,125
Peter Jacobsen/Arnold Palmer	66	65	131	24,125
Tom Kite/Dave Stockton	66	67	133	23,125
Joey Sindelar/Craig Stadler	65	68	133	23,125
Ian Baker-Finch/Wayne Grady	65	69	134	22,500

NEC World Series of Golf

Firestone Country Club, Akron, Ohio
Par 35-35—70; 7,149 yards

August 22-25
purse, $1,200,000

	SCORES				TOTAL	MONEY
Tom Purtzer	72	69	67	71	279	$216,000
Jim Gallagher, Jr.	72	68	70	69	279	105,600
Davis Love III	72	66	72	69	279	105,600
(Purtzer defeated Gallagher and Love on second extra hole.)						
Mark Brooks	72	64	74	70	280	52,800
Fred Couples	74	70	69	67	280	52,800
Joe Ozaki	72	70	68	72	282	38,850
Nick Price	72	70	71	69	282	38,850
Dillard Pruitt	71	66	68	77	282	38,850
Joey Sindelar	70	68	73	71	282	38,850
Steve Elkington	71	70	71	71	283	30,000
Andrew Magee	73	68	70	72	283	30,000
Corey Pavin	72	68	74	69	283	30,000
Jay Don Blake	71	73	70	70	284	23,200
Bruce Fleisher	68	72	72	72	284	23,200
Mark O'Meara	73	68	71	72	284	23,200
Ian Baker-Finch	72	71	71	71	285	18,600
Brad Faxon	72	68	74	71	285	18,600
Mike Reid	70	68	75	72	285	18,600
Payne Stewart	73	77	68	67	285	18,600
Billy Ray Brown	71	71	71	73	286	13,480
Rocco Mediate	71	74	69	72	286	13,480
Larry Mize	68	71	76	71	286	13,480
Ted Schulz	73	76	71	66	286	13,480
Bob Tway	69	72	71	74	286	13,480
Russ Cochran	73	71	75	68	287	10,175
Brett Ogle	76	71	71	69	287	10,175
Ricky Kawagishi	74	75	66	73	288	9,116.67
Wayne Levi	73	68	74	73	288	9,116.67
John Morse	71	76	69	72	288	9,116.67
Tim Simpson	73	67	77	71	288	9,116.67
Peter Senior	73	68	72	75	288	9,116.66
Lanny Wadkins	73	70	69	76	288	9,116.66
Peter Persons	73	72	72	72	289	8,600
Billy Andrade	77	72	69	72	290	8,350
Satoshi Higashi	75	69	74	72	290	8,350
Kenny Knox	74	68	72	76	290	8,350
Steve Pate	73	71	76	70	290	8,350
Jose Maria Olazabal	70	78	71	72	291	8,050
Brett Upper	75	66	73	77	291	8,050
John Daly	80	72	71	69	292	7,875
Nolan Henke	66	75	80	71	292	7,875
Hideki Kase	74	71	74	73	292	7,875
Jodie Mudd	69	72	74	77	292	7,875
Mike Hulbert	74	70	78	73	295	7,750
Paul Azinger	76	74	71	76	297	7,700
Wayne Westner	69	76	75	78	298	7,650
Kenny Perry	79	72	76	78	305	7,575
Roger Wessels	75	75	72	83	305	7,575

Greater Milwaukee Open

Tuckaway Country Club, Franklin, Wisconsin
Par 36-36—72; 7,030 yards

August 29-September 1
purse, $1,000,000

	SCORES				TOTAL	MONEY
Mark Brooks	63	67	70	70	270	$180,000
Robert Gamez	61	66	74	70	271	108,000
Steve Jones	71	66	69	67	273	68,000
Jeff Maggert	65	65	71	73	274	48,000
John Adams	68	68	72	68	276	38,000
Neal Lancaster	67	66	73	70	276	38,000
Nick Price	72	67	72	66	277	31,166.67
D.A. Weibring	67	67	72	71	277	31,166.67
Hal Sutton	65	66	74	72	277	31,166.66
Ken Green	70	69	70	69	278	23,000
Jay Haas	67	70	70	71	278	23,000
Jodie Mudd	72	68	70	68	278	23,000
Chris Perry	68	68	72	70	278	23,000
Joey Sindelar	66	70	72	70	278	23,000
Rick Fehr	69	70	70	70	279	16,000
Jim Gallagher, Jr.	69	71	71	68	279	16,000
Greg Ladehoff	71	69	68	71	279	16,000
Mark Lye	66	65	73	75	279	16,000
Steve Pate	67	67	74	71	279	16,000
Tom Kite	66	71	74	69	280	12,066.67
Tom Sieckmann	71	66	73	70	280	12,066.67
Dave Barr	69	66	73	72	280	12,066.66
Brad Bell	67	68	76	70	281	8,650
Gary Hallberg	69	66	74	72	281	8,650
Peter Jacobsen	69	69	73	70	281	8,650
Brian Kamm	69	68	74	70	281	8,650
Bill Kratzert	70	67	74	70	281	8,650
Jim Thorpe	70	70	72	69	281	8,650
Bob Estes	67	72	73	70	282	5,955.56
Sean Murphy	69	68	76	69	282	5,955.56
Mike Reid	69	69	74	70	282	5,955.56
Dave Rummells	70	69	73	70	282	5,955.56
Mike Standly	70	70	72	70	282	5,955.56
David Canipe	68	68	72	74	282	5,955.55
Keith Clearwater	68	68	75	71	282	5,955.55
Billy Mayfair	73	67	71	71	282	5,955.55
Ted Schulz	66	70	74	72	282	5,955.55
Tommy Armour	69	70	72	72	283	4,100
Perry Arthur	67	70	74	72	283	4,100
Jay Delsing	67	70	72	74	283	4,100
Brad Fabel	70	70	71	72	283	4,100
Karl Kimball	63	71	74	75	283	4,100
Dan Pohl	69	67	79	68	283	4,100
Loren Roberts	70	69	73	71	283	4,100
Scott Gump	70	68	74	72	284	2,752.50
Jerry Haas	66	72	76	70	284	2,752.50
Dan Halldorson	67	69	76	72	284	2,752.50
Mark Hayes	66	64	74	80	284	2,752.50
Dick Mast	67	68	81	68	284	2,752.50
Dave Miley	68	68	74	74	284	2,752.50
Craig Rudolph	70	68	73	73	284	2,752.50
Howard Twitty	71	66	74	73	284	2,752.50

Canadian Open

Glen Abbey Golf Club, Oakville, Canada
Par 35-37—72; 7,102 yards

September 5-8
purse, $1,000,000

	SCORES				TOTAL	MONEY
Nick Price	71	69	67	66	273	$180,000
David Edwards	69	69	68	68	274	108,000
Fred Couples	69	69	68	69	275	58,000
Ken Green	68	69	68	70	275	58,000
Jeff Sluman	69	72	72	64	277	38,000
D.A. Weibring	69	64	69	75	277	38,000
Jim Benepe	64	67	75	72	278	33,500
Brian Kamm	65	67	74	73	279	30,000
Neal Lancaster	70	70	70	69	279	30,000
Paul Azinger	70	68	70	72	280	24,000
Ian Baker-Finch	68	72	71	69	280	24,000
Bob Lohr	69	69	71	71	280	24,000
Ray Stewart	68	69	70	73	280	24,000
Clark Burroughs	71	69	72	69	281	16,500
Scott Gump	69	71	71	70	281	16,500
Steve Jones	69	68	75	69	281	16,500
Billy Mayfair	70	68	71	72	281	16,500
Blaine McCallister	73	67	72	69	281	16,500
Payne Stewart	73	68	68	72	281	16,500
Lee Janzen	69	75	70	68	282	10,428.58
Jerry Haas	75	69	68	70	282	10,428.57
Dan Halldorson	69	71	73	69	282	10,428.57
Bruce Lietzke	74	69	67	72	282	10,428.57
Mark Lye	73	70	69	70	282	10,428.57
Jim McGovern	67	71	68	76	282	10,428.57
Corey Pavin	69	72	72	69	282	10,428.57
Bill Britton	73	71	71	68	283	6,950
Barry Cheesman	71	72	69	71	283	6,950
Mark McCumber	73	67	72	71	283	6,950
Jack Nicklaus	74	68	74	67	283	6,950
Loren Roberts	67	73	72	71	283	6,950
Greg Whisman	70	73	70	70	283	6,950
Chris Perry	73	67	73	71	284	5,283.34
Craig Stadler	64	70	78	72	284	5,283.34
Rick Fehr	71	68	71	74	284	5,283.33
John Inman	72	68	72	72	284	5,283.33
Rocco Mediate	72	70	70	72	284	5,283.33
Dave Sutherland	70	69	70	75	284	5,283.33
Lennie Clements	72	72	69	72	285	4,000
Wayne Levi	70	68	77	70	285	4,000
Gil Morgan	70	69	73	73	285	4,000
Mark O'Meara	74	65	74	72	285	4,000
Mike Sullivan	69	75	67	74	285	4,000
Bob Tway	71	70	71	73	285	4,000
Michael Allen	72	70	70	74	286	2,752.50
Tom Byrum	74	70	70	72	286	2,752.50
Ed Dougherty	70	72	74	70	286	2,752.50
Brad Faxon	74	70	73	69	286	2,752.50
David Frost	71	66	75	74	286	2,752.50
Greg Norman	70	71	72	73	286	2,752.50
Jim Thorpe	72	72	73	69	286	2,752.50
Howard Twitty	69	73	74	70	286	2,752.50

Hardee's Classic

Oakwood Country Club, Coal Valley, Illinois
Par 35-35—70; 6,606 yards

September 12-15
purse, $1,000,000

	SCORES				TOTAL	MONEY
D.A. Weibring	68	67	68	64	267	$180,000
Paul Azinger	65	65	70	68	268	88,000
Peter Jacobsen	65	66	72	65	268	88,000
Scott Hoch	69	65	69	66	269	41,333.34
Greg Norman	64	67	70	68	269	41,333.33
Leonard Thompson	67	62	73	67	269	41,333.33
Brad Fabel	68	69	67	66	270	31,166.67
Steve Jones	68	69	64	69	270	31,166.67
Steve Lowery	65	66	70	69	270	31,166.66
David Edwards	66	69	64	72	271	24,000
David Frost	66	71	66	68	271	24,000
John Huston	67	71	66	67	271	24,000
Tom Purtzer	68	69	68	66	271	24,000
Carl Cooper	68	66	70	68	272	16,000
Trevor Dodds	69	68	67	68	272	16,000
Bob Estes	67	71	67	67	272	16,000
Dan Forsman	69	69	68	66	272	16,000
Robert Gamez	70	64	68	70	272	16,000
Jeff Maggert	69	66	67	70	272	16,000
Gil Morgan	67	69	68	68	272	16,000
Jay Haas	66	68	70	69	273	9,387.50
Mark Hayes	67	69	70	67	273	9,387.50
Mike Hulbert	68	70	67	68	273	9,387.50
Kenny Knox	69	67	69	68	273	9,387.50
Blaine McCallister	66	66	72	69	273	9,387.50
Dan Pohl	70	68	66	69	273	9,387.50
Loren Roberts	69	67	67	70	273	9,387.50
Larry Silveira	65	68	72	68	273	9,387.50
Fulton Allem	67	67	72	68	274	5,955.56
Lennie Clements	65	68	73	68	274	5,955.56
Marco Dawson	69	68	71	66	274	5,955.56
Neal Lancaster	68	69	72	65	274	5,955.56
Dave Rummells	69	68	69	68	274	5,955.56
Bart Bryant	68	67	69	70	274	5,955.55
Bob Gilder	68	70	66	70	274	5,955.55
Jerry Haas	66	72	67	69	274	5,955.55
Bobby Wadkins	71	67	66	70	274	5,955.55
Dave Barr	71	64	69	71	275	4,000
Ed Fiori	66	69	73	67	275	4,000
Bruce Fleisher	69	66	73	67	275	4,000
Gary Hallberg	69	69	68	69	275	4,000
Donnie Hammond	70	67	70	68	275	4,000
Jim Thorpe	67	67	71	70	275	4,000
Mark Wiebe	67	70	70	68	275	4,000
Robert Wrenn	70	68	67	70	275	4,000
John Adams	70	67	70	69	276	2,520
Michael Allen	65	68	71	72	276	2,520
Perry Arthur	65	68	73	70	276	2,520
Emlyn Aubrey	68	69	71	68	276	2,520
Bill Britton	71	64	71	70	276	2,520
Mike Donald	66	70	71	69	276	2,520
Andrew Magee	69	66	68	73	276	2,520
Billy Mayfair	68	66	72	70	276	2,520
Ted Schulz	71	65	71	69	276	2,520

	SCORES				TOTAL	MONEY
Tom Sieckmann	66	71	69	70	276	2,520
Ray Stewart	65	69	72	70	276	2,520
Dave Sutherland	71	66	72	67	276	2,520

B.C. Open

En-Joie Golf Club, Endicott, New York
Par 37-34—71; 6,966 yards

September 19-22
purse, $800,000

	SCORES				TOTAL	MONEY
Fred Couples	66	67	68	68	269	$144,000
Peter Jacobsen	68	68	68	68	272	86,400
Brad Faxon	65	64	71	73	273	46,400
Blaine McCallister	64	68	72	69	273	46,400
David Peoples	69	70	66	69	274	32,000
Lee Janzen	73	68	65	69	275	28,800
Mark Lye	70	70	70	66	276	25,800
Steve Pate	68	70	68	70	276	25,800
Paul Broadhurst	66	69	71	71	277	20,800
Jerry Haas	70	70	70	67	277	20,800
Mike McCullough	70	70	66	71	277	20,800
Greg Twiggs	71	68	69	69	277	20,800
Billy Andrade	67	70	71	70	278	14,560
Lennie Clements	69	67	71	71	278	14,560
Mike Reid	68	67	71	72	278	14,560
Mark Wiebe	67	68	71	72	278	14,560
Robert Wrenn	69	68	72	69	278	14,560
Emlyn Aubrey	71	70	69	69	279	11,600
Mike Smith	69	70	71	69	279	11,600
Ken Green	72	71	69	68	280	8,992
Tom Kite	70	73	70	67	280	8,992
Billy Mayfair	65	72	71	72	280	8,992
Rocco Mediate	69	71	71	69	280	8,992
Dan Pohl	71	69	70	70	280	8,992
Greg Bruckner	71	71	68	71	281	6,240
Bruce Fleisher	70	72	70	69	281	6,240
Jay Haas	72	68	68	73	281	6,240
Barry Jaeckel	69	66	74	72	281	6,240
Greg Whisman	69	70	66	76	281	6,240
Jim Benepe	70	69	70	73	282	4,754.29
Brad Bryant	73	70	69	70	282	4,754.29
Ed Humenik	67	72	69	74	282	4,754.29
Curtis Strange	68	72	70	72	282	4,754.29
Carl Cooper	73	69	70	70	282	4,754.28
Brian Kamm	70	70	66	76	282	4,754.28
Dicky Thompson	70	70	71	71	282	4,754.28
Brad Bell	74	69	69	71	283	3,200
Phil Blackmar	71	70	71	71	283	3,200
Ed Fiori	67	71	73	72	283	3,200
Steve Lowery	66	72	71	74	283	3,200
Jim McGovern	71	68	71	73	283	3,200
Mac O'Grady	70	65	75	73	283	3,200
Jeff Sluman	67	73	71	72	283	3,200
Mike Sullivan	71	71	71	70	283	3,200
Lance Ten Broeck	66	70	74	73	283	3,200
Howard Twitty	68	73	74	68	283	3,200
Scott Gump	71	71	71	71	284	2,054.86

Corey Pavin led the U.S. money list with $979,430, and won two tournaments.

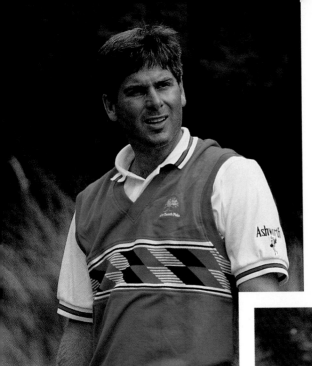

Fred Couples had two U.S. victories, among other accomplishments.

Andrew Magee won at Orlando and Las Vegas and was fifth on the money list.

Victories on consecutive weeks made Billy Andrade an immediate star.

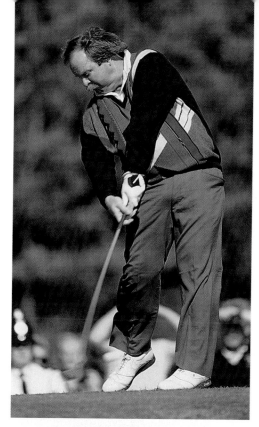

Craig Stadler took the Tour Championship.

Tom Purtzer distinguished himself by winning the Colonial and World Series titles.

Steve Elkington had a big victory—The Players Championship.

Mark Brooks won at Greensboro and Milwaukee.

Buick Open champion Brad Faxon.

Nick Price took the Byron Nelson and Canadian titles.

Heritage winner Davis Love III.

Rocco Mediate out-played Curtis Strange in extra holes at Doral.

Hawaiian champ Lanny Wadkins.

At age 46, Hale Irwin won $422,652.

Amateur Phil Mickelson was the Tucson winner.

Paul Azinger was a four-stroke winner of the Pebble Beach title.

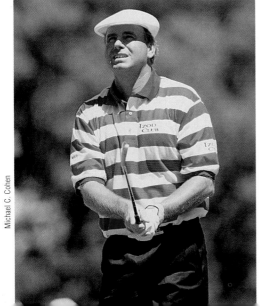

Chip Beck broke the 60 mark with 59 at Las Vegas.

D.A. Weibring won at the Hardee's Classic.

A Year of Ups and Downs

Greg Norman (left) went without a victory while his pal Ian Woosnam posted some Shark numbers.

Also winless, Curtis Strange (shown here with brother Allan at the British Open) struggled with health problems.

Payne Stewart, in a neck brace, tried to amuse himself. In three months, he would be U.S. Open champion.

The sun doesn't always shine, not even on Arnold Palmer, who was impressive nevertheless with his even-par showing in The Nestle Invitational.

Ian Woosnam and Craig Stadler scored impressive wins in 1991, but both were frustrated here in the U.S. Open.

A familiar face, that of Seve Ballesteros, returned to center stage on the European Tour. He had four victories worldwide.

Steven Richardson was No. 2 on the European money list.

Bernhard Langer won twice in Europe.

Colin Montgomerie emerged as a European Tour star.

A strong Aussie presence was led by Craig Parry, with two wins.

David Feherty won at Cannes.

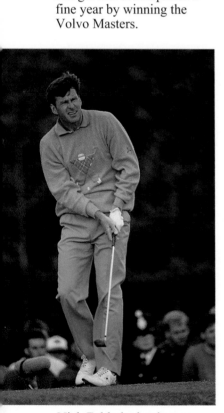

Rodger Davis completed a fine year by winning the Volvo Masters.

David Gilford won the English Open.

Nick Faldo had only one victory, the Irish Open.

Jose Maria Olazabal won twice in Europe, once in America.

Vijay Singh won in Morocco.

Sandy Lyle ended his slump.

Belgian champ Per-Ulrik Johansson.

Eduardo Romero had two victories.

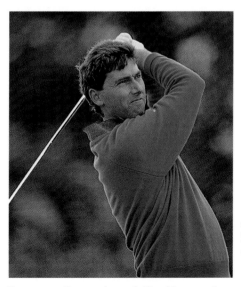
European Open winner Mike Harwood.

Mark McNulty won the German Open.

Danielle Fluer

Senior Tour

Mike Hill climbed to the top of Senior golf with $1,065,657.

George Archer (left) was No. 2 on the money list. Jack Nicklaus (above) scored three wins.

Jim Colbert won the Vantage title.

Chi Chi Rodriguez had four wins.

Jim Albus was the surprise TPC winner.

Lee Trevino won three times.

The Women's Tour

Pat Bradley won three times and entered the LPGA Hall of Fame.

Meg Mallon claimed the LPGA and USGA titles.

Amy Alcott was the Dinah Shore champion.

Michael C. Cohen

Nancy Scranton won the du Maurier.

Michael C. Cohen

Beth Daniel had two victories.

Michael C. Cohen

Michael C. Cohen

Despite pregnancy, Nancy
Lopez (left) won. Betsy King
(above) won twice.

Asia/Japan Tour

Isao Aoki was a British Open commentator, but later won in Japan.

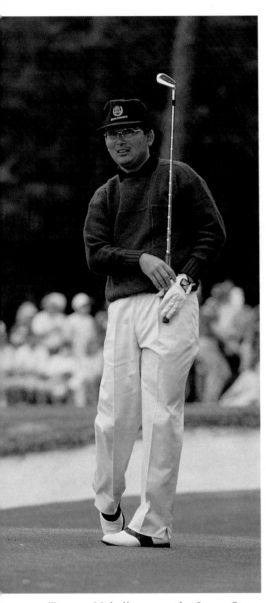

Tommy Nakajima won the Japan Open.

Jumbo Ozaki had two victories, but yielded the money title to brother Joe.

	SCORES				TOTAL	MONEY
Mike Hulbert	68	72	72	72	284	2,054.86
Neal Lancaster	69	70	75	70	284	2,054.86
Loren Roberts	70	71	74	69	284	2,054.86
Ken Schall	71	71	71	71	284	2,054.86
Michael Allen	72	67	72	73	284	2,054.85
Donnie Hammond	69	71	70	74	284	2,054.85

Ryder Cup Matches

Ocean Course, Kiawah Island, South Carolina   September 27-29
Par 454 434 534—36; 454 434 534—36—72; 7,303 yards

FIRST DAY
Morning Foursomes

Seve Ballesteros and Jose Maria Olazabal (Europe) defeated Paul Azinger and Chip Beck (USA), 2 and 1

Ballesteros/Olazabal	4 5 4	6 4 4	5 3 5	40	4 5 3	3 3 4	5 2	
Azinger/Beck	4 4 4	6 3 4	5 3 4	37	5 5 4	4 3 5	5 3	

Raymond Floyd and Fred Couples (USA) defeated Bernhard Langer and Mark James (Europe), 2 and 1

Langer/James	5 5 4	5 3 6	5 3 4	40	5 4 4	3 3 4	6 3	
Floyd/Couples	4 6 4	5 2 4	5 2 4	36	4 4 5	5 5 4	5 3	

Lanny Wadkins and Hale Irwin (USA) defeated David Gilford and Colin Montgomerie (Europe), 4 and 2

Gilford/Montgomerie	5 4 C	5 3 5	W 3 4	X	4 6 4	5 4 5	C	
Wadkins/Irwin	3 4 W	5 2 4	C 2 4	X	4 5 4	5 5 6	W	

Payne Stewart and Mark Calcavecchia (USA) defeated Nick Faldo and Ian Woosnam (Europe), 1 up

Faldo/Woosnam	4 5 4	C 4 4	5 3 4	X	4 4 5	4 3 4	5 W 4	X	X
Stewart/Calcavecchia	4 4 4	W 4 5	5 3 4	X	4 5 4	3 3 4	5 C 4	X	X

Afternoon Fourballs

Sam Torrance and David Feherty (Europe) halved with Lanny Wadkins and Mark O'Meara (USA)

Torrance	4 4	4 3 4	4 4 4	X	4 4 4	4 4 4	5 2 5	36	X
Feherty	4 6 4	4 4 4	4 4 5	39	4 4 5	5 2 4	5 3 4	36	75
Wadkins	4 4	4 3 4	5 3 3	X	4 5 4	4 3 4	5 3 5	37	X
O'Meara	4 4	4 3 4	4 3 3	X	4 5 4	4 3 4	5 2 5	36	X

Seve Ballesteros and Jose Maria Olazabal (Europe) defeated Paul Azinger and Chip Beck (USA), 2 and 1

Ballesteros	4 6 4	4 3 4	4 2 5	36	4 5 5	2 4	5 3	
Olazabal	5 5 4	4 2 4	5 3 4	36	3 4 4	4 3 4	4	
Azinger	4 3	4 3 3	5 3 4	X	3 4	3 3 4	4 5	
Beck	4 5 4	4 3 4	5 3 5	37	4 5 4	4 3 4	4	

Steven Richardson and Mark James (Europe) defeated Corey Pavin and Mark Calcavecchia (USA), 5 and 4

```
Richardson     4 5 4 3  3 3 5  X  4 4 4  4 4
James          4 4 3  4 3       3 5  X  4 5    4 3
Pavin          4 5 4  4 3 4     2 4  X  4 5 5  4 4
Calcavecchia   4 5  4 3 4  4 4     X  4 5     4 4
```

Raymond Floyd and Fred Couples (USA) defeated Nick Faldo and Ian Woosnam (Europe), 5 and 3

```
Faldo     4 6 4  4 3 4  4 2 4  3 5  4 5 4  4 3 4
Woosnam   4 6 3  3 3 4  5 3 4  3 5  4 5 4  4 3 4
Floyd     5 5 4  4 3 3  5 3 4  3 6  3 4 4  5 3 4
Couples   3 5 4  4 4 4  4 3 4  3 5  4 5 3  3 4 3
```

SECOND DAY
Morning Foursomes

Lanny Wadkins and Hale Irwin (USA) defeated David Feherty and Sam Torrance (Europe), 4 and 2

```
Feherty/Torrance   4 6 4  4 3 5  4 4 4  38  4 6 5  4 5 5  C
Wadkins/Irwin      6 5 5  4 3 4  4 3 5  39  3 6 4  5 4 4  W
```

Mark Calcavecchia and Payne Stewart (USA) defeated Mark James and Steven Richardson (Europe), 1 up

```
James/Richardson       4 6 5  4 3 4  4 3 4  37  5 5 5  4 3 4  6 W 5  X  X
Calcavecchia/Stewart   5 5 4  4 4 4  5 2 3  36  4 6 3  4 3 4  6 C 5  X  X
```

Paul Azinger and Mark O'Meara (USA) defeated Nick Faldo and David Gilford (Europe), 7 and 6

```
Faldo/Gilford      5 5 5  5 3 5  C 3 5  X  4 5 C
Azinger/O'Meara    3 5 4  5 2 4  W 3 5  X  3 5 W
```

Seve Ballesteros and Jose Maria Olazabal (Europe) defeated Raymond Floyd and Fred Couples (USA), 3 and 2

```
Ballesteros/Olazabal   5 5 4  4 2 4  4 3 4  35  4 5 4  4 3 5  6
Floyd/Couples          4 5 5  4 3 5  4 3 5  38  4 5 4  4 4 4  6
```

Afternoon Fourballs

Ian Woosnam and Paul Broadhurst (Europe) defeated Paul Azinger and Hale Irwin (USA), 2 and 1

```
Woosnam     4 6     4 3 4   3 5    X  W 5 4  4 4 5  5 3
Broadhurst  4 6 4  4      4 3 C  X  3 6 4  3 3 5
Azinger     5 5 4  4 3 4  5 4 3  37  C 5 4  4 3 6  5 4
Irwin       4 5 4  4      4 4 4  X  C  4  4 4 5  5 C
```

Bernhard Langer and Colin Montgomerie (Europe) defeated Corey Pavin and Steve Pate (USA), 2 and 1

```
Langer       4 5 4  3 3 4  4 4 5  36  4 5 4  4 3 4  5 3
Montgomerie  4 5 4  4 3 5  4 4 5  38  5 5 4  3 6 3  5 3
Pavin        4 5 5  4 3 5  6 4 5  41  5 5 5  3 3 4  5 3
Pate         6 5 4  5 3 4  5 3 4  39  5 6 5  3 4 3  5 3
```

Mark James and Steven Richardson (Europe) defeated Lanny Wadkins and Wayne Levi (USA), 3 and 1

```
James       4 5 4  5 3 4  4 3      X  5  4  4 3 4  C W
Richardson  4 4 3  5 3 4      4   X  4 4   3       3
Wadkins     5 5 4  4 3 4  4 3 4  36  4 4 4  4 3    W C
Levi        5 7 5  4 3 4  5 3   X  4        4
```

Seve Ballesteros and Jose Maria Olazabal (Europe) halved with Payne Stewart and
Fred Couples (USA)

Ballesteros	4 5 4	4 3 4	4 4 4	36	4 5	3 3 3	5 3 5	X	X
Olazabal	4 4 4	4 3 4	3 4	X	4 5 4	4 3 4	5 3 4	36	X
Stewart	4 6 4	5 3 3	5 3 4	37	4 6 4	4 3	5 4	X	X
Couples	4 5 4	4 3 4	3 3 4	34	4 4 4	4 4	5 3 4	X	X

THIRD DAY
Singles

The match between David Gilford (Europe) and Steve Pate (USA) was not played
because of injury to Pate. Gilford and Pate halved.

Nick Faldo (Europe) defeated Raymond Floyd (USA), 2 up

Faldo	4 4 5	4 4 5	3 2 4	35	3 4 5	4 C 5	4 4 4	X	X
Floyd	5 5 6	4 3 4	5 3 4	39	3 5 4	4 W 5	4 3 5	X	X

David Feherty (Europe) defeated Payne Stewart (USA), 2 and 1

Feherty	4 4 4	4 3 5	4 3 4	35	4 5 4	4 3 5	6 3
Stewart	5 6 4	5 3 3	4 3 4	37	4 6 4	5 3 4	5 3

Colin Montgomerie (Europe) halved with Mark Calcavecchia (USA)

Montgomerie	4 6 4	6 4 4	5 4 5	42	3 4 4	4 C 5	5 5 4	X	X
Calcavecchia	3 5 6	4 4 4	4 3 3	36	4 5 4	4 W 7	6 6 5	X	X

Paul Azinger (USA) defeated Jose Maria Olazabal (Europe), 2 up

Olazabal	4 W 3	6 3 4	5 3 5	X	3 C 4	4 3 5	5 4 C	X	X
Azinger	3 C 4	5 3 3	6 3 4	X	4 W 5	3 4 5	5 3 W	X	X

Corey Pavin (USA) defeated Steven Richardson (Europe), 2 and 1

Richardson	3 5 C	5 4 4	5 3 5	X	4 5 4	4 4 4	6 3
Pavin	4 4 W	4 4 5	4 3 5	X	4 6 4	5 3 4	5 3

Seve Ballesteros (Europe) defeated Wayne Levi (USA), 3 and 2

Ballesteros	4 7 3	4 3 4	5 2 3	35	4 W 4	4 3 5	5
Levi	4 8 4	4 3 4	4 4 4	39	4 C 4	3 3 4	6

Chip Beck (USA) defeated Ian Woosnam (Europe), 3 and 1

Woosnam	4 5 5	W 3 4	5 3 4	X	4 4 4	4 4 5	C C
Beck	4 4 4	C 4 4	5 2 5	X	4 3 4	4 4 5	W W

Paul Broadhurst (Europe) defeated Mark O'Meara (USA), 3 and 1

Broadhurst	4 6 4	4 3 4	5 2 4	36	5 5 4	4 3 4	5 2
O'Meara	4 5 5	5 4 4	5 3 4	39	4 6 4	3 3 4	5 C

Fred Couples (USA) defeated Sam Torrance (Europe), 3 and 2

Torrance	5 5 4	4 4 5	5 3 4	39	4 6 5	4 4 5	5
Couples	4 5 4	4 4 4	4 3 4	36	4 5 4	5 5 5	5

Lanny Wadkins (USA) defeated Mark James (Europe), 3 and 2

James	4 C 5	5 3 4	5 4 6	X	4 5 4	4 3 4	6
Wadkins	5 4 4	5 2 4	5 3 5	37	5 5 4	5 2 5	5

Bernhard Langer (Europe) halved with Hale Irwin (USA)

Langer	5 C W	4 4 3	5 4 4	X	4 5 4	4 5 4	5 3 5	39	X
Irwin	4 W C	4 4 4	5 3 3	X	4 6 4	4 4 5	5 4 5	41	X

LEGEND: C—conceded hole to opponent; W—won hole by concession without holing
out; X—no total score.

Buick Southern Open

Calloway Garden Resort, Pine Mountain, Georgia
Par 36-36—72; 7,057 yards

September 26-29
purse, $700,000

	SCORES				TOTAL	MONEY
David Peoples	67	71	72	66	276	$126,000
Robert Gamez	71	70	66	70	277	75,600
Larry Nelson	69	68	70	72	279	40,600
Dave Sutherland	67	71	70	71	279	40,600
Buddy Gardner	73	69	71	69	282	25,550
Dudley Hart	71	72	69	70	282	25,550
Morris Hatalsky	71	70	69	72	282	25,550
David Canipe	73	72	71	67	283	20,300
Scott Hoch	70	72	73	68	283	20,300
Bob Lohr	71	70	71	71	283	20,300
Brandel Chamblee	70	74	73	67	284	14,840
Ed Fiori	69	73	70	72	284	14,840
John Huston	71	69	71	73	284	14,840
Brandt Jobe	68	67	75	74	284	14,840
Steve Jones	71	73	74	66	284	14,840
Louis Brown	72	73	74	66	285	9,820
Bart Bryant	71	74	70	70	285	9,820
Mike Donald	73	71	70	71	285	9,820
Joel Edwards	69	74	70	72	285	9,820
Gary Hallberg	72	70	70	73	285	9,820
Lee Janzen	70	67	74	74	285	9,820
Davis Love III	73	70	72	70	285	9,820
J.C. Anderson	68	72	74	72	286	6,055
Lennie Clements	70	70	76	70	286	6,055
Bob Estes	73	70	74	69	286	6,055
Scott Gump	68	72	71	75	286	6,055
Larry Mize	73	72	68	73	286	6,055
Chris Perry	69	69	73	75	286	6,055
Bobby Clampett	72	70	76	69	287	4,355.15
John Daly	74	68	76	69	287	4,355.15
Mark Brooks	74	67	72	74	287	4,355.14
Bill Buttner	68	73	74	72	287	4,355.14
Mike Reid	71	67	76	73	287	4,355.14
Ray Stewart	70	75	71	71	287	4,355.14
Mark Wiebe	73	70	72	72	287	4,355.14
Charles Bowles	72	72	69	75	288	3,084.25
Brad Fabel	69	73	71	75	288	3,084.25
Jay Haas	74	71	70	73	288	3,084.25
Clarence Rose	71	73	72	72	288	3,084.25
Howard Twitty	69	73	78	68	288	3,084.25
D.A. Weibring	71	72	71	74	288	3,084.25
John Wilson	71	73	72	72	288	3,084.25
Willie Wood	72	72	70	74	288	3,084.25
Perry Arthur	71	72	75	71	289	2,066
Mike Holland	74	69	75	71	289	2,066
Tommy Moore	76	68	72	73	289	2,066
Greg Twiggs	71	71	74	73	289	2,066
Bobby Wadkins	70	71	76	72	289	2,066
Bob Wolcott	72	71	69	77	289	2,066
Jim Woodward	70	71	75	73	289	2,066

H.E.B. Texas Open

Oak Hills Country Club, San Antonio, Texas
Par 35-35—70; 6,576 yards

October 3-6
purse, $900,000

	SCORES				TOTAL	MONEY
Blaine McCallister	66	64	69	70	269	$162,000
Gary Hallberg	70	65	65	69	269	97,200
(McCallister defeated Hallberg on second extra hole.)						
Bill Britton	66	68	68	71	273	43,200
Brian Claar	68	66	72	67	273	43,200
Ben Crenshaw	67	68	68	70	273	43,200
Bob Lohr	68	67	69	69	273	43,200
Mark Calcavecchia	65	71	68	70	274	25,275
John Cook	67	67	66	74	274	25,275
Bob Estes	69	68	67	70	274	25,275
Lee Janzen	71	68	69	66	274	25,275
Jeff Sluman	70	67	68	69	274	25,275
Bobby Wadkins	71	64	70	69	274	25,275
Bob Gilder	66	68	70	71	275	16,380
Scott Hoch	70	67	73	65	275	16,380
John Huston	70	69	68	68	275	16,380
Gil Morgan	68	71	67	69	275	16,380
Corey Pavin	69	69	68	69	275	16,380
Paul Azinger	68	67	73	68	276	12,600
Jim Hallet	70	67	72	67	276	12,600
Kenny Knox	68	67	70	71	276	12,600
Ronnie Black	67	70	71	69	277	9,720
Keith Clearwater	63	72	73	69	277	9,720
Clark Dennis	66	72	69	70	277	9,720
Loren Roberts	68	69	71	69	277	9,720
Mark Hayes	67	69	71	71	278	7,177.50
Steve Jones	67	70	68	73	278	7,177.50
Gene Sauers	68	69	73	68	278	7,177.50
D.A. Weibring	71	65	73	69	278	7,177.50
Jay Don Blake	68	67	71	73	279	6,390
Mark Brooks	72	66	70	72	280	5,231.25
Marco Dawson	69	70	69	72	280	5,231.25
Dan Halldorson	70	71	67	72	280	5,231.25
Greg Ladehoff	71	65	72	72	280	5,231.25
Tommy Moore	70	66	70	74	280	5,231.25
Scott Simpson	66	71	69	74	280	5,231.25
Greg Twiggs	68	72	70	70	280	5,231.25
Mark Wiebe	69	68	68	75	280	5,231.25
Ed Fiori	69	67	75	70	281	3,960
Wayne Grady	66	68	73	74	281	3,960
John Inman	70	68	70	73	281	3,960
Bryan Norton	70	67	73	71	281	3,960
Steve Elkington	68	67	72	75	282	3,150
David Frost	71	69	71	71	282	3,150
Jay Haas	66	73	73	70	282	3,150
Tom Kite	72	68	71	71	282	3,150
Willie Wood	68	73	73	68	282	3,150
David Ogrin	72	69	72	70	283	2,472
Tom Purtzer	71	70	70	72	283	2,472
Ray Stewart	69	70	74	70	283	2,472
Bill Buttner	69	68	70	77	284	2,170.80
Rick Fehr	71	68	72	73	284	2,170.80
John Mahaffey	73	68	71	72	284	2,170.80
Peter Persons	67	72	73	72	284	2,170.80
Larry Silveira	70	70	73	71	284	2,170.80

Las Vegas Invitational

Las Vegas Country Club, 7,162 yards
Desert Inn Country Club, 7,111 yards
Sunrise Golf Club, 6,914 yards
All par 36-36—72
Las Vegas, Nevada

October 9-13
purse, $1,500,000

	SCORES					TOTAL	MONEY
Andrew Magee	69	65	67	62	66	329	$270,000
D.A. Weibring	70	64	65	64	66	329	162,000
(Magee defeated Weibring on second extra hole.)							
Chip Beck	65	72	59	68	67	331	78,000
Jim Gallagher, Jr.	69	65	69	61	67	331	78,000
Ted Schulz	65	68	67	66	65	331	78,000
Bruce Lietzke	68	63	65	67	69	332	54,000
Ed Humenik	66	69	68	64	66	333	48,375
Mark McCumber	69	64	67	66	67	333	48,375
Ken Green	70	65	67	67	65	334	42,000
Dicky Thompson	70	68	68	61	67	334	42,000
Russ Cochran	68	70	66	65	67	336	37,500
Bill Glasson	71	66	64	69	67	337	33,000
Steve Jones	65	69	63	67	73	337	33,000
Jeff Maggert	69	67	68	67	67	338	25,500
Dan Pohl	67	69	67	68	67	338	25,500
Nick Price	67	70	69	68	64	338	25,500
Jeff Sluman	66	68	70	68	66	338	25,500
Craig Stadler	67	64	66	66	75	338	25,500
John Cook	66	69	72	66	66	339	17,550
John Daly	66	63	73	68	69	339	17,550
Kenny Knox	69	66	67	67	70	339	17,550
Davis Love III	71	68	67	67	66	339	17,550
David Peoples	70	69	68	65	67	339	17,550
Greg Whisman	67	71	67	69	65	339	17,550
John Adams	69	70	68	67	66	340	10,968.75
Billy Andrade	69	68	68	66	69	340	10,968.75
Steve Elkington	66	69	69	69	67	340	10,968.75
Mike Hulbert	68	68	69	67	68	340	10,968.75
Gene Sauers	69	70	65	68	68	340	10,968.75
Tom Sieckmann	63	73	69	68	67	340	10,968.75
Hal Sutton	68	64	72	67	69	340	10,968.75
Duffy Waldorf	67	66	71	66	70	340	10,968.75
David Edwards	68	69	68	70	66	341	8,100
Scott Hoch	69	69	69	67	67	341	8,100
Larry Rinker	70	63	74	70	64	341	8,100
Kirk Triplett	64	72	66	71	68	341	8,100
Bobby Wadkins	68	67	68	68	70	341	8,100
Emlyn Aubrey	70	72	65	67	68	342	6,450
Scott Gump	72	66	67	67	70	342	6,450
Lee Janzen	67	72	67	65	71	342	6,450
Roger Maltbie	67	65	73	69	68	342	6,450
Larry Mize	67	69	70	66	70	342	6,450
Tommy Armour	66	71	63	68	75	343	4,383
Andy Bean	65	68	72	66	72	343	4,383
Jay Don Blake	70	68	68	69	68	343	4,383
Jim Booros	69	65	66	72	71	343	4,383
Keith Clearwater	70	68	67	68	70	343	4,383
Bob Estes	65	71	69	69	69	343	4,383
Buddy Gardner	71	68	66	70	68	343	4,383
Jay Haas	69	70	67	69	68	343	4,383

	SCORES					TOTAL	MONEY
Wayne Levi	67	70	67	68	71	343	4,383
Mike Springer	67	74	66	69	67	343	4,383

Walt Disney World-Oldsmobile Classic

Magnolia Course, 7,190 yards
Palm Course, 6,967 yards
Lake Buena Vista Course, 6,706 yards
All par 36-36—72
Orlando, Florida

October 16-19
purse, $1,000,000

	SCORES				TOTAL	MONEY
Mark O'Meara	66	66	71	64	267	$180,000
David Peoples	68	67	68	65	268	108,000
Paul Azinger	72	65	65	67	269	68,000
Steve Elkington	65	71	67	67	270	48,000
John Cook	69	69	68	65	271	36,500
Scott Gump	71	67	66	67	271	36,500
Davis Love III	71	66	66	68	271	36,500
Robert Gamez	68	71	68	65	272	28,000
Ken Green	69	68	67	68	272	28,000
Nolan Henke	67	70	69	66	272	28,000
Larry Nelson	65	70	70	67	272	28,000
Jay Don Blake	67	70	68	68	273	20,250
Jeff Maggert	67	67	73	66	273	20,250
Corey Pavin	65	71	69	68	273	20,250
Mark Wiebe	69	70	68	66	273	20,250
David Frost	70	67	71	66	274	15,500
Wayne Levi	72	68	69	65	274	15,500
Bruce Lietzke	72	67	68	67	274	15,500
Fuzzy Zoeller	68	67	72	67	274	15,500
Russ Cochran	68	69	71	67	275	12,500
Hal Sutton	68	70	69	68	275	12,500
Lee Janzen	69	67	72	68	276	10,000
Dave Rummells	77	68	67	64	276	10,000
Mike Sullivan	70	70	68	68	276	10,000
Duffy Waldorf	66	70	70	70	276	10,000
Tommy Armour	71	67	72	67	277	7,400
Mike Hulbert	69	68	72	68	277	7,400
Pat McGowan	70	69	70	68	277	7,400
Gene Sauers	69	69	70	69	277	7,400
Kirk Triplett	72	68	70	67	277	7,400
Curt Byrum	70	72	70	66	278	5,800
Brandel Chamblee	69	71	68	70	278	5,800
Mark McCumber	71	70	69	68	278	5,800
Leonard Thompson	71	71	67	69	278	5,800
Greg Twiggs	67	69	72	70	278	5,800
Howard Twitty	71	67	69	71	278	5,800
Brian Claar	70	71	69	69	279	4,400
Neal Lancaster	71	66	73	69	279	4,400
Larry Mize	72	72	65	70	279	4,400
Chris Perry	68	69	72	70	279	4,400
Scott Simpson	70	72	67	70	279	4,400
Payne Stewart	70	68	69	72	279	4,400
Andy Bean	73	69	70	68	280	3,206.67
David Canipe	72	69	71	68	280	3,206.67
Scott Hoch	69	70	71	70	280	3,206.67

	SCORES				TOTAL	MONEY
Jim Thorpe	70	72	71	67	280	3,206.67
Bill Britton	71	71	70	68	280	3,206.66
Mike Springer	75	68	67	70	280	3,206.66
Bart Bryant	69	71	71	70	281	2,422.86
Marco Dawson	68	71	71	71	281	2,422.86
Bruce Fleisher	68	69	74	70	281	2,422.86
Billy Mayfair	69	68	71	73	281	2,422.86
Willie Wood	71	74	68	68	281	2,422.86
Kenny Perry	68	70	70	73	281	2,422.85
Robert Wrenn	72	67	73	69	281	2,422.85

Independent Insurance Agent Open

TPC at The Woodlands, The Woodlands, Texas
Par 36-36—72; 7,042 yards

October 23-27
purse, $800,000

	SCORES				TOTAL	MONEY
Fulton Allem	71	69	67	66	273	$144,000
Billy Ray Brown	67	67	69	71	274	59,733.34
Mike Hulbert	68	69	66	71	274	59,733.33
Tom Kite	69	73	64	68	274	59,733.33
Mike Springer	71	70	69	65	275	30,400
Duffy Waldorf	67	67	72	69	275	30,400
Gary Hallberg	68	69	70	69	276	23,280
Donnie Hammond	69	68	66	73	276	23,280
Steve Jones	65	74	70	67	276	23,280
Bryan Norton	70	70	69	67	276	23,280
Mike Reid	67	68	68	73	276	23,280
Bobby Clampett	75	67	69	66	277	15,200
Joel Edwards	68	70	70	69	277	15,200
John Huston	71	71	70	65	277	15,200
John Mahaffey	72	70	66	69	277	15,200
Payne Stewart	69	67	70	71	277	15,200
Kirk Triplett	71	68	68	70	277	15,200
Bob Estes	72	69	70	67	278	9,737.15
Larry Mize	72	69	69	68	278	9,737.15
Ronnie Black	69	71	68	70	278	9,737.14
Scott Gump	72	69	67	70	278	9,737.14
Jerry Haas	70	72	66	70	278	9,737.14
Brad Lardon	70	70	67	71	278	9,737.14
Richard Zokol	68	70	68	72	278	9,737.14
Bart Bryant	70	71	70	68	279	6,106.67
Buddy Gardner	70	71	67	71	279	6,106.67
Billy Mayfair	71	69	69	70	279	6,106.67
Peter Persons	67	71	73	68	279	6,106.67
John Daly	70	72	71	66	279	6,106.66
Jeff Sluman	73	67	66	73	279	6,106.66
Ed Dougherty	70	71	69	70	280	4,256
Dan Forsman	73	66	74	67	280	4,256
Jim Gallagher, Jr.	70	71	69	70	280	4,256
Jay Haas	72	64	73	71	280	4,256
Lee Janzen	68	69	72	71	280	4,256
Jeff Maggert	65	65	70	80	280	4,256
Roger Maltbie	67	75	67	71	280	4,256
Dick Mast	70	71	69	70	280	4,256
Blaine McCallister	69	70	69	72	280	4,256
Brian Tennyson	70	70	70	70	280	4,256

	SCORES				TOTAL	MONEY
Charles Bowles	71	70	69	71	281	2,532.37
Fred Funk	72	70	68	71	281	2,532.37
Dillard Pruitt	72	69	69	71	281	2,532.37
Craig Stadler	67	73	70	71	281	2,532.37
Michael Allen	68	72	71	70	281	2,532.36
Keith Fergus	71	71	70	69	281	2,532.36
Ed Fiori	70	68	70	73	281	2,532.36
Bruce Lietzke	71	68	68	74	281	2,532.36
Bob Wolcott	71	70	68	72	281	2,532.36
Jim Woodward	68	71	72	70	281	2,532.36
Kim Young	67	74	72	68	281	2,532.36

Tour Championship

Pinehurst Country Club, No. 2 Course,
Pinehurst, North Carolina
Par 35-36—71; 7,005 yards

October 31-November 3
purse, $2,000,000

	SCORES				TOTAL	MONEY
Craig Stadler	68	68	72	71	279	$360,000
Russ Cochran	68	69	71	71	279	216,000
(Stadler defeated Cochran on second extra hole.)						
John Daly	68	76	68	70	282	138,000
Bruce Lietzke	71	69	72	71	283	96,000
Chip Beck	72	70	72	71	285	71,000
Jim Gallagher, Jr.	71	74	69	71	285	71,000
Nolan Henke	69	70	74	72	285	71,000
Nick Price	70	67	75	73	285	71,000
Steve Elkington	69	75	71	71	286	60,000
Ian Baker-Finch	68	76	71	72	287	54,000
Corey Pavin	74	69	72	72	287	54,000
Jeff Sluman	74	71	69	73	287	54,000
Jay Don Blake	69	72	74	73	288	46,466.67
Ted Schulz	70	71	75	72	288	46,466.67
Billy Andrade	73	74	68	73	288	46,466.66
Mark O'Meara	72	72	72	73	289	41,066.67
D.A. Weibring	71	73	74	71	289	41,066.67
Fred Couples	72	73	66	78	289	41,066.66
Davis Love III	72	72	75	71	290	38,800
Andrew Magee	74	72	70	74	290	38,800
Scott Hoch	69	75	76	71	291	37,200
Payne Stewart	69	76	75	71	291	37,200
Lanny Wadkins	74	73	72	73	292	36,000
Paul Azinger	69	68	78	78	293	34,800
Mark Brooks	78	72	71	72	293	34,800
Rocco Mediate	73	74	72	75	294	33,400
Steve Pate	75	74	71	74	294	33,400
John Cook	73	71	75	77	296	32,800
Tom Purtzer	73	72	75	77	297	32,400
Mike Hulbert	75	75	73	79	302	32,000

Amoco Centel Championship

Hilton Head National Golf Club, Hilton Head Island, South Carolina   November 7-10
Par 36-36—72; 6,761 yards   purse, $750,000

	SCORES			TOTAL	MONEY
Jim Thorpe	64	68	68	200	$115,000
Don Pooley	68	68	69	205	60,000
Mark McCumber	68	68	69	205	60,000
Gil Morgan	70	71	66	207	40,000
David Graham	70	69	69	208	29,000
Doug Tewell	68	68	72	208	29,000
Bobby Wadkins	67	68	74	209	25,000
Tom Kite	68	72	70	210	23,250
Roger Maltbie	70	69	71	210	23,250
Bruce Fleisher	69	70	72	210	23,250
Hubert Green	70	68	72	210	23,250
Howard Twitty	71	70	70	211	21,500
Leonard Thompson	70	70	71	211	21,500
Gary McCord	72	68	71	211	21,500
Fuzzy Zoeller	75	69	68	212	20,250
Larry Nelson	71	70	71	212	20,250
John Mahaffey	70	71	73	214	14,312.50
Mark Hayes	70	71	73	214	14,312.50
Bob Eastwood	70	72	72	214	14,312.50
Andy North	68	72	74	214	14,312.50
Danny Edwards	68	72	75	215	13,000
Morris Hatalsky	73	73	70	216	12,375
George Burns	74	67	75	216	12,375
Ron Cerrudo	69	72	76	217	12,000
Calvin Peete	74	70	74	218	11,750
Rik Massengale	71	75	76	222	11,500
Mac O'Grady	78	75	70	223	11,250
Dave Eichelberger	79	73	79	231	11,000
Jim Simons	84	75	74	233	10,750
Jerry McGee	78	81	76	235	10,500
Barry Jaeckel	72	70 WD			10,125
Ed Sneed	76	80 WD			10,125

Mexican Open

Chapultepec Golf Club, Mexico City, Mexico   November 7-10
Par 36-36—72; 7,135 yards   purse, $600,000

	SCORES				TOTAL	MONEY
Jay Haas	69	69	70	69	277	$100,000
Ed Fiori	70	73	68	66	277	55,000
(Haas defeated Fiori on third extra hole.)						
Kenny Knox	71	70	69	69	279	36,000
Robert Wrenn	69	73	72	66	280	26,000
Lennie Clements	67	69	74	71	281	23,000
Bob Lohr	71	68	74	69	282	19,250
Danny Mijovic	71	70	72	69	282	19,250
Jaime Gomez	73	72	73	65	283	17,500
Tom Byrum	72	71	70	71	284	16,500
Gary Hallberg	69	74	70	72	285	15,500
John Cook	74	68	70	74	286	14,250
Bruce Lietzke	71	71	75	69	286	14,250

	SCORES				TOTAL	MONEY
Donnie Hammond	71	73	72	71	287	13,500
Scott Verplank	71	71	72	75	289	11,438
Nolan Henke	70	71	71	77	289	11,438
Joey Sindelar	74	74	71	70	289	11,438
Tom Sieckmann	75	72	70	72	289	11,438
Dan Pohl	70	73	73	73	289	11,438
Tom Lehman	70	73	76	70	289	11,438
Juan Brito	71	73	71	74	289	11,438
Carlos Espinosa	72	73	74	70	289	11,438
Bill Glasson	70	76	69	75	290	9,000
Jim Benepe	73	73	72	72	290	9,000
Enrique Serna	73	72	72	73	290	9,000
Oscar Cerda	72	75	72	71	290	9,000
Tommy Armour III	68	76	74	73	291	7,600
Mark Wiebe	68	75	76	72	291	7,600
Rodolfo Cazaubon	74	74	73	70	291	7,600

PGA Grand Slam of Golf

Kauai Lagoons Kiele Course, Lihue, Hawaii
Par 36-36—72; 7,035 yards

November 13-14
purse, $1,000,000

	SCORES		TOTAL	MONEY
Ian Woosnam	69	66	135	$400,000
Ian Baker-Finch	68	71	139	250,000
Payne Stewart	70	71	141	200,000
John Daly	73	70	143	150,000

Ping Kapalua International

Kapalua Resort, Plantation Course, Kapalua, Hawaii
Par 36-36—72; 6,671 yards

November 13-16
purse, $750,000

	SCORES				TOTAL	MONEY
Mike Hulbert	67	69	72	68	276	$150,000
Davis Love III	68	70	66	72	276	89,500
(Hulbert defeated Love on first extra hole.)						
Andy Bean	68	74	72	67	281	43,767
Greg Norman	74	69	69	69	281	43,767
Steve Pate	67	70	72	72	281	43,767
Sandy Lyle	70	72	72	69	283	22,750
Jim Hallet	71	71	66	75	283	22,750
Chip Beck	71	74	71	68	284	16,750
Hale Irwin	70	70	74	70	284	16,750
Peter Jacobsen	71	68	73	73	285	14,500
Ben Crenshaw	73	71	73	69	286	11,875
Mark Calcavecchia	66	73	75	72	286	11,875
John Mahaffey	73	68	71	74	286	11,875
Billy Andrade	71	71	70	74	286	11,875
Bruce Fleisher	72	70	74	71	287	9,463
John Cook	68	71	77	71	287	9,463
Rick Fehr	69	74	73	71	287	9,463
Scott Hoch	70	70	73	74	287	9,463
Lee Trevino	70	72	72	73	287	9,463
Craig Stadler	71	73	70	73	287	9,463

	SCORES				TOTAL	MONEY
Dave Rummells	75	70	68	74	287	9,463
Ken Green	70	72	69	76	287	9,463
Peter Persons	71	74	71	72	288	7,850
Andrew Magee	74	66	75	73	288	7,850
Russ Cochran	70	68	73	77	288	7,850
David Peoples	70	70	78	71	289	7,200
Kenny Knox	70	76	71	72	289	7,200
Keith Clearwater	75	70	76	68	289	7,200
Tom Sieckmann	72	76	67	74	289	7,200
Dan Forsman	70	70	71	78	289	7,200
Ronan Rafferty	74	70	73	73	290	6,750
Billy Mayfair	70	73	75	74	292	6,525
Bob Gilder	73	74	69	76	292	6,525
Blaine McCallister	68	73	78	74	293	6,150
Fred Funk	73	67	74	79	293	6,150
Scott Simpson	71	69	74	79	293	6,150
Nolan Henke	75	72	74	73	294	5,900
Jay Don Blake	72	74	76	73	295	5,800
Bob Lohr	76	71	73	76	296	5,600
Tom Purtzer	77	73	71	75	296	5,600
David Edwards	72	75	76	73	296	5,600
David Ishii	74	72	72	79	297	5,350
Ed Dougherty	74	76	70	77	297	5,350
Billy Ray Brown	74	78	72	74	298	5,200
Brian Claar	77	71	74	80	302	5,150
Phil Blackmar	79	74	73	82	308	5,100
Mark Rolfing	86	78	79	77	320	5,020
Dillard Pruitt	73	74	WD			5,000

Shark Shootout

Sherwood Country Club, Thousand Oaks, California
Par 36-36—72; 7,025 yards

November 22-24
purse, $1,000,000

	SCORES			TOTAL	MONEY
					(Each)
Tom Purtzer/Lanny Wadkins	61	65	63	189	$125,000
Greg Norman/Jack Nicklaus	68	66	59	193	70,000
Tom Kite/Davis Love III	65	69	60	194	48,000
Curtis Strange/Billy Andrade	66	69	60	195	42,750
Mark O'Meara/Steve Elkington	64	69	62	195	42,750
Fred Couples/Raymond Floyd	68	69	60	197	39,000
Steve Pate/Hale Irwin	65	69	64	198	35,250
Arnold Palmer/Peter Jacobsen	68	70	60	198	35,250
Chi Chi Rodriguez/Chip Beck	66	74	59	199	32,000
Ben Crenshaw/Bruce Lietzke	69	72	59	200	30,000

JCPenney Classic

Innisbrook Golf Resort, Tarpon Springs, Florida
Men—Par 71; 7,065 yards
Women—Par 71; 6,394 yards

December 5-8
purse, $1,100,000

	SCORES				TOTAL	MONEY (Each)
Billy Andrade/Kris Tschetter	67	66	66	67	266	$110,000
Ed Humenik/Elaine Crosby	66	67	67	66	266	68,000
(Andrade/Tschetter defeated Humenik/Crosby on second extra hole.)						
Buddy Gardner/Lynn Connelly	67	69	67	65	268	35,000
Mike Hulbert/Laura Davies	64	72	66	66	268	35,000
Davis Love III/Beth Daniel	66	66	68	68	268	35,000
Rocco Mediate/Missie Berteotti	67	67	68	68	270	19,183
Fulton Allem/Sally Little	67	66	69	68	270	19,183
Andy North/JoAnne Carner	67	69	65	69	270	19,183
David Peoples/Barbara Mucha	67	66	69	69	271	10,300
Scott Hoch/Brandie Burton	68	70	65	68	271	10,300
Brad Fabel/Vicki Fergon	69	68	65	69	271	10,300
Tim Simpson/Michelle McGann	69	67	66	69	271	10,300
Gene Sauers/Hollis Stacy	70	65	64	72	271	10,300
Rick Fehr/Caroline Keggi	71	67	67	67	272	7,750
Bob Gilder/Cindy Rarick	69	67	66	70	272	7,750
Ted Schulz/Jane Crafter	64	70	68	71	273	7,000
Kenny Knox/Nancy Scranton	70	70	67	67	274	5,750
Fred Funk/Tina Barrett	69	68	70	67	274	5,750
Tommy Armour III/Lori Garbacz	71	68	68	67	274	5,750
Gary Hallberg/Shirley Furlong	68	71	66	69	274	5,750
Joey Sindelar/Juli Inkster	70	69	69	67	275	4,750
Mike Smith/Martha Nause	68	70	70	67	275	4,750
Mike Springer/Melissa McNamara	68	68	70	69	275	4,750
Ken Green/Barb Bunkowsky	66	67	71	71	275	4,750
Lee Janzen/Colleen Walker	69	69	68	70	276	4,500
Brad Faxon/Jody Anschutz	71	68	69	69	277	4,250
Jay Delsing/Penny Hammel	71	70	68	68	277	4,250
Bob Wolcott/Mitzi Edge	68	70	68	71	277	4,250
Dan Forsman/Dottie Mochrie	71	71	68	67	277	4,250
Mark McCumber/Debbie Massey	68	72	68	70	278	3,850
Bill Britton/Donna White	70	69	70	69	278	3,850
Keith Clearwater/Dale Eggeling	71	68	73	66	278	3,850
Lance Ten Broeck/Cindy Figg-Currier	72	71	69	66	278	3,850

U.S. Senior Tour

Infiniti Senior Tournament of Champions

La Costa Country Club, Carlsbad, California
Par 36-36—72; 6,715 yards

January 3-6
purse, $350,000

		SCORES			TOTAL	MONEY
Bruce Crampton	70	69	69	71	279	$80,000
Frank Beard	69	75	68	71	283	50,000
George Archer	76	71	71	69	287	34,000
Mike Hill	74	73	71	69	287	34,000
Dale Douglass	76	74	72	74	296	22,666.67
Chi Chi Rodriguez	77	77	70	72	296	22,666.67
Jim Dent	76	73	71	76	296	22,666.66
Charles Coody	76	70	75	76	297	18,000
Al Kelley	77	73	74	74	298	15,000
Rives McBee	74	76	73	75	298	15,000
Jimmy Powell	76	75	76	73	300	13,000
Don Massengale	74	77	77	73	301	12,000
Lee Trevino	71	WD				

Royal Caribbean Classic

The Links at Key Biscayne, Key Biscayne, Florida
Par 35-36—71; 6,715 yards

February 1-3
purse, $450,000

		SCORES		TOTAL	MONEY
Gary Player	67	65	68	200	$67,500
Lee Trevino	70	66	66	202	32,833.34
Bob Charles	69	67	66	202	32,833.33
Chi Chi Rodriguez	66	68	68	202	32,833.33
Al Geiberger	70	65	69	204	21,500
Bruce Crampton	66	70	70	206	18,000
Butch Baird	71	68	69	208	13,622.50
Dale Douglass	70	68	70	208	13,622.50
Al Kelley	71	69	68	208	13,622.50
Tom Shaw	71	65	72	208	13,622.50
George Archer	67	70	72	209	9,870
Miller Barber	68	72	69	209	9,870
Charles Coody	73	67	69	209	9,870
Simon Hobday	68	68	74	210	8,300
Rocky Thompson	69	72	69	210	8,300
J.C. Snead	71	69	71	211	7,625
Tommy Aaron	69	70	73	212	7,000
Mike Hill	69	69	74	212	7,000
Don Massengale	69	73	71	213	6,101.67
Walter Zembriski	68	71	74	213	6,101.67
Jim Ferree	70	68	75	213	6,101.66
Jim Dent	74	70	70	214	5,315
Ben Smith	74	70	70	214	5,315
Terry Dill	75	69	71	215	4,642.50
Gibby Gilbert	72	72	71	215	4,642.50

	SCORES			TOTAL	MONEY
Lou Graham	70	71	74	215	4,642.50
Orville Moody	71	74	70	215	4,642.50
Gay Brewer	74	68	74	216	3,857.50
Don January	71	67	78	216	3,857.50
Larry Laoretti	68	74	74	216	3,857.50
Phil Rodgers	71	73	72	216	3,857.50
Frank Beard	73	73	71	217	2,975
Homero Blancas	72	74	71	217	2,975
John Paul Cain	69	71	77	217	2,975
Harold Henning	70	70	77	217	2,975
Bobby Nichols	71	72	74	217	2,975
Jimmy Powell	73	74	70	217	2,975
Babe Hiskey	72	75	71	218	2,243.58
Jim Albus	70	73	75	218	2,243.57
Don Bies	70	72	76	218	2,243.57
Jack Kiefer	73	73	72	218	2,243.57
George Lanning	73	72	73	218	2,243.57
Charles Owens	71	73	74	218	2,243.57
DeWitt Weaver	74	72	72	218	2,243.57

GTE Suncoast Classic

Tampa Palms Golf & Country Club, Tampa, Florida
Par 37-35—72; 6,631 yards

February 8-10
purse, $450,000

	SCORES			TOTAL	MONEY
Bob Charles	68	72	70	210	$67,500
George Archer	76	68	70	214	35,750
Lee Trevino	70	71	73	214	35,750
Dale Douglass	70	75	70	215	20,662.50
Mike Hill	70	74	71	215	20,662.50
Don Massengale	74	72	69	215	20,662.50
Bobby Nichols	69	73	73	215	20,662.50
Harold Henning	71	74	71	216	12,780
Orville Moody	69	75	72	216	12,780
J.C. Snead	72	74	70	216	12,780
Don January	70	73	74	217	10,765
Terry Dill	70	77	71	218	9,123.34
Jim Dent	73	73	72	218	9,123.33
Chi Chi Rodriguez	75	71	72	218	9,123.33
Charles Coody	73	73	73	219	7,425
Ted Hayes	73	72	74	219	7,425
Jack Kiefer	74	72	73	219	7,425
Walter Zembriski	69	74	76	219	7,425
Dave Hill	74	75	71	220	6,101.67
Richard Rhyan	71	76	73	220	6,101.67
Bob Brue	68	75	77	220	6,101.66
Jim Albus	74	74	73	221	4,760.72
Simon Hobday	70	79	72	221	4,760.72
Al Kelley	77	72	72	221	4,760.72
Frank Beard	68	79	74	221	4,760.71
Homero Blancas	76	71	74	221	4,760.71
Bruce Devlin	75	78	68	221	4,760.71
George Lanning	70	75	76	221	4,760.71
Butch Baird	74	74	74	222	3,945
Gay Brewer	74	75	74	223	3,230
Bob Erickson	71	77	75	223	3,230

	SCORES			TOTAL	MONEY
Larry Laoretti	75	73	75	223	3,230
Gary Player	74	75	74	223	3,230
Tom Shaw	74	76	73	223	3,230
Rocky Thompson	73	74	76	223	3,230
Dudley Wysong	76	74	73	223	3,230
Rives McBee	72	75	77	224	2,513.34
Don Bies	77	77	70	224	2,513.33
Charles Owens	70	82	72	224	2,513.33
Bruce Crampton	73	76	76	225	2,198.75
Doug Dalziel	76	78	71	225	2,198.75
Lloyd Moody	70	75	80	225	2,198.75
DeWitt Weaver	71	78	76	225	2,198.75

Aetna Challenge

The Vineyards, Naples, Florida
Par 36-36—72; 6,827 yards

February 15-17
purse, $450,000

	SCORES			TOTAL	MONEY
Lee Trevino	71	68	66	205	$67,500
Dale Douglass	67	71	68	206	39,000
Mike Hill	76	66	68	210	29,750
Gary Player	75	67	68	210	29,750
Terry Dill	71	70	70	211	16,465
Harold Henning	72	69	70	211	16,465
Jimmy Powell	72	68	71	211	16,465
Ben Smith	73	69	69	211	16,465
Rocky Thompson	78	67	66	211	16,465
Bob Charles	71	72	69	212	9,960
Simon Hobday	73	67	72	212	9,960
Joe Jimenez	71	71	70	212	9,960
Bobby Nichols	75	69	68	212	9,960
Chi Chi Rodriguez	78	65	69	212	9,960
Bob Brue	74	72	67	213	7,626.67
Bruce Crampton	75	70	68	213	7,626.67
Larry Mowry	79	65	69	213	7,626.66
Tommy Aaron	75	71	68	214	5,959.17
Al Geiberger	77	69	68	214	5,959.17
Dave Hill	72	71	71	214	5,959.17
George Lanning	71	74	69	214	5,959.17
Quinton Gray	72	70	72	214	5,959.16
J.C. Snead	71	69	74	214	5,959.16
Jim Dent	75	73	67	215	4,867.50
Orville Moody	75	72	68	215	4,867.50
Butch Baird	77	72	67	216	4,135
Charles Coody	76	71	69	216	4,135
Dick Hendrickson	73	73	70	216	4,135
Don January	71	75	70	216	4,135
Arnold Palmer	75	70	71	216	4,135
Robert Gaona	75	73	69	217	3,320
Rives McBee	74	72	71	217	3,320
Charles Owens	75	72	70	217	3,320
DeWitt Weaver	75	72	70	217	3,320
George Archer	77	68	73	218	2,668.75
Gary Cowan	74	73	71	218	2,668.75
Chick Evans	76	72	70	218	2,668.75
Lou Graham	74	73	71	218	2,668.75

	SCORES	TOTAL	MONEY
John Paul Cain	75 72 72	219	2,333.34
Gay Brewer	77 72 70	219	2,333.33
Larry Laoretti	77 67 75	219	2,333.33

Chrysler Cup

TPC at Prestancia, Sarasota, Florida
Par 36-36—72; 6,763 yards

February 22-24
purse, $600,000

Final Result: United States 58.5; International 41.5.

FIRST ROUND
Modified Chapman Alternate Shot

Al Geiberger-Mike Hill (U.S.) defeated Gary Player-Bob Charles, disqualification.
Harold Henning-Simon Hobday (Int.) defeated Chi Chi Rodriguez-Charles Coody, 66-67.
Lee Trevino-Jim Dent (U.S.) defeated Bruce Devlin-Roberto De Vicenzo, 68-72.
Miller Barber-George Archer (U.S.) halved with Bruce Crampton-Brian Waites, 68-68.

Standings: United States 12.5, International 7.5.

SECOND ROUND
Better Ball, Stroke Play

Trevino-Geiberger (U.S.) defeated De Vicenzo-Devlin, 65-66.
Hill-Dent (U.S.) defeated Henning-Hobday, 63-64.
Crampton-Waites (Int.) defeated Archer-Coody, 63-64.
Player-Charles (Int.) defeated Barber-Rodriguez, 61-67.

Standings: United States 28.5, International 23.5.

THIRD ROUND
Individual, Stroke Play

Waites (Int.) defeated Geiberger, 71-72.
Charles (Int.) defeated Barber, 66-70.
Hill (U.S.) defeated Devlin, 67-72.
Coody (U.S.) defeated Henning, 63-69.
Player (Int.) defeated Dent, 66-69.
Archer (U.S.) defeated Crampton, 70-72.
Rodriguez (U.S.) defeated Hobday, 65-71.
Trevino (U.S.) defeated De Vicenzo, 68-77.

Each member of United States team received $50,000; each member of the International team received $25,000.

GTE West Classic

Ojai Valley Inn & Country Club, Ojai, California
Par 35-35—70; 6,190 yards
(First round cancelled - rain, course unplayable.)

March 1-3
purse, $450,000

	SCORES	TOTAL	MONEY
Chi Chi Rodriguez	66 66	132	$67,500
Bruce Crampton	65 68	133	35,750

	SCORES		TOTAL	MONEY
Gary Player	66	67	133	35,750
Terry Dill	68	67	135	19,350
Dick Hendrickson	66	69	135	19,350
Harold Henning	70	65	135	19,350
Don Massengale	69	66	135	19,350
Walter Zembriski	66	69	135	19,350
Miller Barber	69	67	136	10,064.29
Gibby Gilbert	72	64	136	10,064.29
Rives McBee	70	66	136	10,064.29
Orville Moody	69	67	136	10,064.29
Al Geiberger	68	68	136	10,064.28
Al Kelley	68	68	136	10,064.28
Arnold Palmer	67	69	136	10,064.28
George Archer	67	70	137	7,021.25
John Brodie	69	68	137	7,021.25
Don January	73	64	137	7,021.25
DeWitt Weaver	72	65	137	7,021.25
Larry Mowry	72	66	138	5,756.67
Rocky Thompson	70	68	138	5,756.67
Lee Trevino	68	70	138	5,756.66
Bob Betley	70	69	139	4,650
Bob Charles	69	70	139	4,650
Bruce Devlin	68	71	139	4,650
Dale Douglass	71	68	139	4,650
Lee Elder	68	71	139	4,650
Simon Hobday	72	67	139	4,650
Jerry Barber	70	70	140	3,589
Frank Beard	72	68	140	3,589
Quinton Gray	70	70	140	3,589
Jimmy Powell	72	68	140	3,589
Richard Rhyan	66	74	140	3,589
Tommy Aaron	70	71	141	2,494.50
Bob Brue	71	70	141	2,494.50
John Paul Cain	70	71	141	2,494.50
Charles Coody	68	73	141	2,494.50
Joe Jimenez	71	70	141	2,494.50
Jack Kiefer	72	69	141	2,494.50
Gene Littler	69	72	141	2,494.50
Phil Rodgers	70	71	141	2,494.50
Dudley Wysong	69	72	141	2,494.50
Larry Ziegler	68	73	141	2,494.50

Vantage at the Dominion

Dominion Country Club, San Antonio, Texas
Par 36-36—72; 6,814 yards
(First round cancelled - rain, course unplayable.)

March 15-17
purse, $350,000

	SCORES		TOTAL	MONEY
Lee Trevino	67	70	137	$52,500
Mike Hill	68	71	139	25,166.67
Rocky Thompson	66	73	139	25,166.67
Charles Coody	66	73	139	25,166.66
Don January	74	66	140	12,085.84
Chi Chi Rodriguez	71	69	140	12,085.84
Billy Casper	69	71	140	12,085.83
Dale Douglass	69	71	140	12,085.83

	SCORES			TOTAL	MONEY
Jim Ferree	69	71		140	12,085.83
J.C. Snead	68	72		140	12,085.83
J.C. Goosie	69	72		141	7,351.25
Harold Henning	70	71		141	7,351.25
Al Kelley	71	70		141	7,351.25
Larry Ziegler	70	71		141	7,351.25
Jim Colbert	71	71		142	5,576
Lou Graham	71	71		142	5,576
Dick Hendrickson	72	70		142	5,576
Bob Wynn	72	70		142	5,576
Walter Zembriski	73	69		142	5,576
Tommy Aaron	71	72		143	3,870
Homero Blancas	69	74		143	3,870
Jim Dent	72	71		143	3,870
Lee Elder	70	73		143	3,870
Rives McBee	71	72		143	3,870
Bobby Nichols	76	67		143	3,870
Richard Rhyan	72	71		143	3,870
Charles Sifford	71	72		143	3,870
Ken Still	68	75		143	3,870
Jack Kiefer	73	71		144	2,905
Gene Littler	69	75		144	2,905
Ben Smith	73	71		144	2,905
Bill Collins	72	73		145	2,242.15
Dave Hill	71	74		145	2,242.15
John Paul Cain	75	70		145	2,242.14
Gary Cowan	76	69		145	2,242.14
Bruce Devlin	74	71		145	2,242.14
Gibby Gilbert	69	76		145	2,242.14
Orville Moody	70	75		145	2,242.14
Bob Brue	71	75		146	1,455.39
Joe Jimenez	74	72		146	1,455.39
George Lanning	73	73		146	1,455.39
Phil Rodgers	72	74		146	1,455.39
DeWitt Weaver	71	75		146	1,455.39
Bert Yancey	71	75		146	1,455.39
Butch Baird	70	76		146	1,455.38
Gay Brewer	74	72		146	1,455.38
John Brodie	69	77		146	1,455.38
Babe Hiskey	75	71		146	1,455.38
Larry Laoretti	80	66		146	1,455.38
Don Massengale	74	72		146	1,455.38
Charles Owens	75	71		146	1,455.38

Vintage Arco Invitational

The Vintage Club, Indian Wells, California
Par 36-36—72; 6,907 yards

March 22-24
purse, $500,000

	SCORES			TOTAL	MONEY
Chi Chi Rodriguez	70	67	69	206	$75,000
Mike Hill	69	70	68	207	41,000
Don January	70	70	67	207	41,000
Bob Charles	73	66	70	209	21,987
Terry Dill	69	68	72	209	21,987
Gibby Gilbert	70	70	69	209	21,987
Bobby Nichols	68	73	68	209	21,987

	SCORES			TOTAL	MONEY
Jimmy Powell	66	71	72	209	21,987
Charles Coody	72	69	69	210	14,365
Tommy Aaron	71	71	69	211	12,825
Gay Brewer	71	70	70	211	12,825
Tom Shaw	70	74	68	212	10,772.50
Lee Trevino	69	72	71	212	10,772.50
George Archer	73	70	70	213	8,515.84
Bruce Crampton	71	72	70	213	8,515.84
Miller Barber	71	72	70	213	8,515.83
Dale Douglass	72	70	71	213	8,515.83
Dave Hill	70	71	72	213	8,515.83
Walter Zembriski	68	73	72	213	8,515.83
John Brodie	68	72	74	214	6,278
Bob Brue	69	72	73	214	6,278
Jim Colbert	73	72	69	214	6,278
Harold Henning	72	73	69	214	6,278
Joe Jimenez	73	70	71	214	6,278
Billy Casper	71	75	69	215	5,307.50
Al Geiberger	69	73	73	215	5,307.50
Frank Beard	75	71	70	216	4,617.50
Simon Hobday	75	67	74	216	4,617.50
Arnold Palmer	71	73	72	216	4,617.50
J.C. Snead	74	68	74	216	4,617.50
Jim Ferree	74	70	73	217	4,105
Homero Blancas	75	75	68	218	3,591.25
Al Kelley	75	71	72	218	3,591.25
Rives McBee	74	71	73	218	3,591.25
Orville Moody	70	74	74	218	3,591.25
Bruce Devlin	72	77	70	219	2,925
Lou Graham	72	74	73	219	2,925
Larry Mowry	71	77	71	219	2,925
Rocky Thompson	74	72	73	219	2,925
Dick Hendrickson	75	73	72	220	2,615
Charles Sifford	75	73	72	220	2,615

Fuji Electric Grand Slam

Glen Oaks Country Club, Chiba-Ken, Japan
Par 36-36—72, 6,614 yards

March 29-31
purse, $360,000

	SCORES			TOTAL	MONEY
Miller Barber	67	68	67	202	$77,281
Lee Trevino	68	67	71	206	34,347
Billy Casper	71	67	71	209	25,761
Harold Henning	72	72	69	213	15,743
Bob Charles	71	72	70	213	15,743
Seiichi Kanai	70	68	75	213	15,743
Charles Coody	74	71	69	214	9,589
George Archer	69	73	72	214	9,589
Jimmy Powell	70	69	75	214	9,589
Terry Dill	73	70	72	215	7,299
Sadao Ogawa	71	70	74	215	7,299
Hiroshi Ishii	70	72	73	215	7,299
Shozo Miyamoto	77	70	69	216	6,383
Butch Baird	74	72	70	216	6,383
Hideo Jibiki	75	69	72	216	6,383
Ichiro Togawa	76	68	72	216	6,383

	SCORES			TOTAL	MONEY
John Paul Cain	73	70	73	216	6,383
Takaaki Kono	69	71	76	216	6,383
Arnold Palmer	73	73	71	217	5,732
Mitsuo Hirukawa	74	71	72	217	5,732
Jun Nobechi	75	69	73	217	5,732
Hideyo Sugimoto	68	72	77	217	5,732
Teruo Suzumura	75	73	70	218	5,281
Mike Kelly	73	73	72	218	5,281
Chen Chien Chung	79	67	72	218	5,281
Ichio Sato	68	75	76	219	5,067
Hsu Chi San	76	73	71	220	4,938
Hisashi Suzumura	72	73	75	220	4,938
Takao Hara	77	72	72	221	4,508
Masayuki Imai	77	72	72	221	4,508
Billy Dunk	73	75	73	221	4,508
Kouichi Okuno	76	72	73	221	4,508
Jack Kiefer	74	73	74	221	4,508
Shigeru Uchida	73	74	73	221	4,508
Kesahiko Uchida	75	72	74	221	4,508
Ichiro Teramoto	72	74	75	221	4,508
Larry Laoretti	73	74	75	222	3,993
Seiichi Sato	75	72	75	222	3,993
Shiro Matsuda	73	73	76	222	3,993
Akio Toyoda	73	72	77	222	3,993

The Tradition at Desert Mountain

Desert Mountain, Cochise Course, Scottsdale, Arizona
Par 36-36—72; 6,837 yards

April 4-7
purse, $800,000

	SCORES				TOTAL	MONEY
Jack Nicklaus	71	73	66	67	277	$120,000
Jim Colbert	70	68	67	73	278	58,000
Jim Dent	69	69	71	69	278	58,000
Phil Rodgers	65	67	73	73	278	58,000
Dale Douglass	71	72	72	66	281	38,000
Charles Coody	75	68	70	69	282	28,533.34
George Archer	69	69	73	71	282	28,533.33
Chi Chi Rodriguez	69	69	73	71	282	28,533.33
Tom Shaw	74	69	71	69	283	20,643.34
Jim Ferree	72	68	71	72	283	20,643.33
Ben Smith	69	69	71	74	283	20,643.33
Frank Beard	74	70	72	68	284	16,158.34
Tommy Aaron	70	70	71	73	284	16,158.33
Bob Charles	74	66	74	70	284	16,158.33
Dave Hill	70	73	69	73	285	13,510
Babe Hiskey	71	75	71	68	285	13,510
Gary Player	69	71	77	68	285	13,510
Miller Barber	70	73	74	69	286	10,821
Bob Brue	68	75	71	72	286	10,821
Bobby Nichols	71	73	69	73	286	10,821
Jimmy Powell	72	73	69	72	286	10,821
DeWitt Weaver	73	71	72	70	286	10,821
Bruce Crampton	71	71	76	69	287	8,060.72
Bruce Devlin	72	70	79	66	287	8,060.72
J.C. Snead	76	71	71	69	287	8,060.72
Harold Henning	75	72	70	70	287	8,060.71

	SCORES				TOTAL	MONEY
Mike Hill	69	72	74	72	287	8,060.71
Simon Hobday	73	70	73	71	287	8,060.71
Rives McBee	73	68	74	72	287	8,060.71
John Brodie	73	74	72	69	288	6,355
Dick Hendrickson	70	73	72	73	288	6,355
Walter Zembriski	70	70	74	74	288	6,355
John Paul Cain	70	69	71	79	289	5,562.50
Lee Trevino	75	75	69	70	289	5,562.50
Gay Brewer	73	69	74	74	290	4,640
Billy Casper	73	70	72	75	290	4,640
Gibby Gilbert	73	76	71	70	290	4,640
Don January	68	75	71	76	290	4,640
Larry Ziegler	74	72	71	73	290	4,640
Terry Dill	72	70	74	75	291	4,052.50
Orville Moody	76	77	72	66	291	4,052.50

PGA Seniors Championship

PGA National Golf Club, Champion Course, Palm Beach Gardens, Florida April 18-21
Par 36-36—72; 6,630 yards   purse, $550,000

	SCORES				TOTAL	MONEY
Jack Nicklaus	66	66	69	70	271	$85,000
Bruce Crampton	72	67	70	68	277	55,000
Bob Charles	72	71	68	71	282	40,000
Homero Blancas	70	72	70	71	283	30,000
George Archer	68	74	68	74	284	25,000
Jim Dent	71	66	75	73	285	18,725
Rocky Thompson	72	72	72	69	285	18,725
Jim Colbert	73	67	72	74	286	14,150
Orville Moody	72	72	70	72	286	14,150
Gary Player	73	73	68	72	286	14,150
Lee Trevino	72	72	72	71	287	12,000
Larry Laoretti	74	69	69	76	288	10,500
Chi Chi Rodriguez	73	72	70	73	288	10,500
Bruce Devlin	71	71	75	72	289	8,500
Dick Hendrickson	69	71	73	76	289	8,500
Tom Joyce	67	71	75	76	289	8,500
Dave Hill	73	73	70	74	290	7,000
Richard Rhyan	72	73	69	76	290	7,000
Walter Zembriski	71	71	75	73	290	7,000
Miller Barber	71	75	71	74	291	5,200
John Brodie	71	75	72	73	291	5,200
Dale Douglass	72	71	76	72	291	5,200
Jim Ferree	72	76	68	75	291	5,200
Harold Henning	71	71	72	77	291	5,200
Richard Crawford	76	67	72	77	292	3,700
Joe Jimenez	74	76	68	74	292	3,700
George Lanning	74	67	71	80	292	3,700
Jimmy Powell	74	72	73	73	292	3,700
Mike Hill	72	73	71	77	293	3,100
Bobby Nichols	72	74	73	74	293	3,100
Tommy Aaron	73	71	75	75	294	2,700
Butch Baird	76	74	70	74	294	2,700
Simon Hobday	72	76	72	74	294	2,700
Al Kelley	73	70	73	78	294	2,700
Don Massengale	70	78	70	76	294	2,700

	SCORES			TOTAL	MONEY
Bob Brue	73	75	75	72	295	2,300
Terry Dill	72	75	75	73	295	2,300
Don January	75	75	69	76	295	2,300
Gay Brewer	75	74	77	70	296	1,962.50
Jack Kiefer	74	72	70	80	296	1,962.50
Phil Rodgers	69	76	74	77	296	1,962.50
Brian Waites	76	75	71	74	296	1,962.50

Doug Sanders Kingwood Celebrity Classic

Deerwood Club, Kingwood, Texas
Par 36-36—72; 6,594 yards

April 26-28
purse, $300,000

	SCORES			TOTAL	MONEY
Mike Hill	66	66	71	203	$45,000
George Archer	68	64	72	204	27,000
Gibby Gilbert	72	66	69	207	20,160
Lee Trevino	69	67	71	207	20,160
Bobby Nichols	68	67	73	208	14,781
Bob Charles	68	71	70	209	12,312
Jim Dent	69	71	70	210	11,082
John Paul Cain	68	71	72	211	8,418.75
Dick Hendrickson	71	71	69	211	8,418.75
Gene Littler	70	70	71	211	8,418.75
Doug Sanders	74	69	68	211	8,418.75
Larry Laoretti	71	69	72	212	6,771
Orville Moody	70	69	74	213	5,848
J.C. Snead	70	72	71	213	5,848
Walter Zembriski	70	72	71	213	5,848
Bob Brue	74	69	71	214	4,690.80
Dave Hill	76	69	69	214	4,690.80
Simon Hobday	73	69	72	214	4,690.80
Don Massengale	72	69	73	214	4,690.80
Gary Player	68	74	72	214	4,690.80
Bruce Crampton	74	73	68	215	3,662.25
Harold Henning	69	74	72	215	3,662.25
Rives McBee	71	72	72	215	3,662.25
Tom Shaw	73	73	69	215	3,662.25
Miller Barber	72	72	72	216	3,108
Babe Hiskey	71	69	76	216	3,108
Rocky Thompson	70	74	72	216	3,108
Bruce Devlin	70	75	72	217	2,647.50
Jimmy Powell	66	72	79	217	2,647.50
Charles Sifford	73	71	73	217	2,647.50
Bob Toski	73	74	70	217	2,647.50
John Brodie	73	68	77	218	2,216
Charles Coody	73	74	71	218	2,216
Bert Yancey	73	73	72	218	2,216
Homero Blancas	76	70	73	219	1,909.50
Charles Owens	74	72	73	219	1,909.50
Terry Dill	76	72	72	220	1,724
Jack Kiefer	73	74	73	220	1,724
George Lanning	77	71	72	220	1,724
Lee Elder	73	72	76	221	1,508.25
Joe Jimenez	74	75	72	221	1,508.25
Ben Smith	74	75	72	221	1,508.25
DeWitt Weaver	73	76	72	221	1,508.25

Las Vegas Classic

Desert Inn & Country Club, Las Vegas, Nevada
Par 36-36—72; 6,810 yards

May 3-5
purse, $450,000

	SCORES			TOTAL	MONEY
Chi Chi Rodriguez	70	68	66	204	$67,500
Walter Zembriski	69	70	68	207	40,200
Gary Player	69	68	71	208	33,100
Bob Charles	71	67	71	209	24,550
Bobby Nichols	70	70	69	209	24,550
Bruce Crampton	67	71	72	210	18,200
Jim Colbert	68	73	70	211	15,083
Rocky Thompson	68	72	71	211	15,083
Gay Brewer	70	70	72	212	11,978
Charles Coody	71	70	71	212	11,978
Ken Still	67	76	69	212	11,978
Mike Hill	73	70	70	213	9,673
Gene Littler	70	69	74	213	9,673
Tommy Aaron	72	74	68	214	8,293
George Archer	73	69	72	214	8,293
Don January	75	66	73	214	8,293
Miller Barber	72	72	71	215	6,632.20
Jim Dent	70	76	69	215	6,632.20
Gibby Gilbert	75	70	70	215	6,632.20
Dave Hill	72	71	72	215	6,632.20
Joe Jimenez	72	73	70	215	6,632.20
Al Geiberger	73	75	68	216	5,457.50
Larry Ziegler	70	76	70	216	5,457.50
Orville Moody	73	72	72	217	4,997.50
Charles Sifford	70	72	75	217	4,997.50
Bob Brue	78	70	70	218	4,341.50
Phil Rodgers	73	74	71	218	4,341.50
Martin Roesink	76	73	69	218	4,341.50
J.C. Snead	73	71	74	218	4,341.50
Don Bies	73	70	76	219	3,778
Tom Shaw	72	76	71	219	3,778
Homero Blancas	72	78	70	220	3,224.75
Bruce Devlin	75	72	73	220	3,224.75
Al Kelley	74	75	71	220	3,224.75
Bert Yancey	78	73	69	220	3,224.75
Terry Dill	79	71	71	221	2,672.34
Butch Baird	73	75	73	221	2,672.33
Dale Douglass	72	74	75	221	2,672.33
Frank Beard	76	75	71	222	2,303.20
Jim Ferree	75	72	75	222	2,303.20
Bob Goalby	76	74	72	222	2,303.20
Doug Sanders	77	70	75	222	2,303.20
Ben Smith	79	71	72	222	2,303.20

Murata Reunion Pro-Am

Stonebriar Country Club, Frisco, Texas
Par 36-36—72; 7,064 yards

May 10-12
purse, $400,000

	SCORES			TOTAL	MONEY
Chi Chi Rodriguez	71	70	67	208	$60,000
Jim Colbert	71	69	68	208	35,000

(Rodriguez defeated Colbert on fourth extra hole.)

	SCORES			TOTAL	MONEY
Mike Hill	70	72	67	209	26,000
Gene Littler	75	65	69	209	26,000
Tommy Aaron	69	71	71	211	15,446.25
Bob Betley	73	68	70	211	15,446.25
Larry Laoretti	70	71	70	211	15,446.25
Orville Moody	70	75	66	211	15,446.25
Al Kelley	70	71	72	213	10,727.50
Robert Rawlins	73	68	72	213	10,727.50
Ben Smith	72	74	68	214	9,137.50
Lee Trevino	67	72	75	214	9,137.50
Rives McBee	75	71	69	215	7,548.34
Frank Beard	69	73	73	215	7,548.33
Jim Dent	71	73	71	215	7,548.33
DeWitt Weaver	73	74	69	216	6,383.34
Bruce Crampton	72	73	71	216	6,383.33
Jim Ferree	68	73	75	216	6,383.33
Charles Coody	70	73	74	217	5,126
Gibby Gilbert	69	72	76	217	5,126
Babe Hiskey	70	74	73	217	5,126
Tom Shaw	78	74	65	217	5,126
Larry Ziegler	71	74	72	217	5,126
Dale Douglass	70	70	79	219	4,310
Rocky Thompson	71	77	71	219	4,310
Simon Hobday	76	74	70	220	3,912.50
Jack Kiefer	74	74	72	220	3,912.50
Miller Barber	75	77	69	221	3,416.25
Dave Hill	75	72	74	221	3,416.25
Lloyd Moody	72	69	80	221	3,416.25
Walter Zembriski	73	76	72	221	3,416.25
Don Bies	74	71	77	222	2,780
Gary Cowan	71	74	77	222	2,780
Terry Dill	74	75	73	222	2,780
Jack Rule	74	73	75	222	2,780
Gay Brewer	76	73	74	223	2,105.63
Bob Erickson	77	74	72	223	2,105.63
Bob Goalby	74	78	71	223	2,105.63
Charles Owens	72	76	75	223	2,105.63
Al Geiberger	75	69	79	223	2,105.62
Don January	74	69	80	223	2,105.62
Richard Rhyan	72	73	78	223	2,105.62
Phil Rodgers	73	69	81	223	2,105.62

Liberty Mutual Legends of Golf

Barton Creek Country Club, Austin, Texas
Par 36-36—72; 6,769 yards

May 16-19
purse, $770,000
(unofficial)

	SCORES				TOTAL	MONEY (Team)
Lee Trevino-Mike Hill	64	59	63	66	252	$140,000
Al Geiberger-Harold Henning	69	63	64	58	254	80,000
Chi Chi Rodriguez-Dave Hill	64	65	65	62	256	57,500
Tommy Aaron-Jim Colbert	64	64	63	65	256	57,500
Jim Dent-Gibby Gilbert	68	65	66	59	258	43,000
Arnold Palmer-Miller Barber	67	63	65	64	259	35,500
Butch Baird-Gay Brewer	63	64	68	64	259	35,500
George Archer-Don Bies	61	65	65	69	260	28,000

	SCORES				TOTAL	MONEY
						(Team)
Homero Blancas-Don Massengale	65	66	68	62	261	22,000
Bruce Crampton-Orville Moody	65	62	69	66	262	15,000
Bob Charles-Bruce Devlin	64	64	67	67	262	15,000
Don January-Gene Littler	65	67	68	63	263	10,500
Doug Sanders-Rives McBee	68	65	64	66	263	10,500
Dale Douglass-Charles Coody	64	67	69	66	266	10,000
Frank Beard-Larry Mowry	69	64	69	69	271	10,000
Jim Ferree-Tommy Jacobs	71	65	67	69	272	10,000
Peter Thomson-Walt Zembriski	67	67	68	70	272	10,000
Bobby Nichols-J.C. Snead	67	66	70	71	274	10,000
Lee Elder-Ken Still	70	68	69	68	275	10,000
Jackie Burke-Mike Souchak	71	65	70	71	277	10,000

Bell Atlantic Classic

White Manor Country Club, Malvern, Pennsylvania
Par 36-36—72; 6,674 yards

May 24-26
purse, $550,000

	SCORES			TOTAL	MONEY
Jim Ferree	67	69	72	208	$82,500
Jim Colbert	71	66	73	210	44,250
Lee Trevino	69	70	71	210	44,250
Harold Henning	71	71	70	212	33,000
Mike Hill	69	74	70	213	24,250
Larry Ziegler	73	74	66	213	24,250
Babe Hiskey	68	74	73	215	18,600
Rocky Thompson	72	69	74	215	18,600
Miller Barber	72	72	72	216	13,783.75
Bruce Crampton	74	73	69	216	13,783.75
Dale Douglass	72	71	73	216	13,783.75
Charles Owens	75	70	71	216	13,783.75
George Archer	72	72	73	217	9,419.29
Al Kelley	73	73	71	217	9,419.29
Don Massengale	73	72	72	217	9,419.29
Walter Zembriski	76	71	70	217	9,419.29
Gay Brewer	76	68	73	217	9,419.28
Richard Rhyan	70	73	74	217	9,419.28
J.C. Snead	72	71	74	217	9,419.28
Charles Coody	70	71	77	218	6,748
Jim Dent	73	68	77	218	6,748
Simon Hobday	75	72	71	218	6,748
Larry Laoretti	72	73	73	218	6,748
DeWitt Weaver	73	68	77	218	6,748
Butch Baird	70	77	72	219	5,707.50
Don January	73	74	72	219	5,707.50
Agim Bardha	72	77	71	220	4,630
Bob Charles	73	75	72	220	4,630
Terry Dill	73	73	74	220	4,630
Lee Elder	78	72	70	220	4,630
Ted Naff	71	75	74	220	4,630
Chi Chi Rodriguez	72	75	73	220	4,630
Deray Simon	72	74	74	220	4,630
Tommy Aaron	75	69	77	221	3,443.75
Roberto De Vicenzo	75	74	72	221	3,443.75
Joe Jimenez	71	74	76	221	3,443.75
Gene Littler	73	75	73	221	3,443.75
Robert Gaona	75	73	74	222	2,921.25

	SCORES			TOTAL	MONEY
Jim O'Hern	75	74	73	222	2,921.25
Robert Rawlins	73	77	72	222	2,921.25
Tom Shaw	76	71	75	222	2,921.25

NYNEX Commemorative

Sleepy Hollow Country Club, Scarborough, New York
Par 35-35—70; 6,545 yards

May 31-June 2
purse, $400,000

	SCORES			TOTAL	MONEY
Charles Coody	66	62	65	193	$60,000
Don Massengale	67	66	63	196	35,000
Lee Trevino	66	66	66	198	28,000
Miller Barber	68	66	65	199	21,550
Simon Hobday	68	65	66	199	21,550
Don Bies	67	62	71	200	15,105
Bob Charles	64	68	68	200	15,105
Jim Albus	69	68	64	201	10,866.25
Dale Douglass	66	68	67	201	10,866.25
Rocky Thompson	64	69	68	201	10,866.25
Chuck Workman	66	68	67	201	10,866.25
Walter Zembriski	65	67	70	202	8,740
Al Kelley	69	68	66	203	7,350
Gary Player	67	66	70	203	7,350
Chi Chi Rodriguez	65	72	66	203	7,350
Bob Wynn	66	70	67	203	7,350
John Paul Cain	68	68	68	204	6,197.50
Jim Dent	72	68	64	204	6,197.50
Billy Casper	65	68	72	205	5,126
Terry Dill	68	69	68	205	5,126
Gibby Gilbert	68	67	70	205	5,126
Babe Hiskey	70	66	69	205	5,126
Ben Smith	69	69	67	205	5,126
Gay Brewer	69	67	70	206	4,410
Doug Dalziel	69	70	68	207	3,837
Harold Henning	67	72	68	207	3,837
Richard Rhyan	67	72	68	207	3,837
Tom Shaw	66	71	70	207	3,837
Ralph Terry	66	73	68	207	3,837
George Archer	69	71	68	208	3,098.75
Bob Erickson	70	72	66	208	3,098.75
Jack Kiefer	66	76	66	208	3,098.75
Dudley Wysong	70	73	65	208	3,098.75
Gene Borek	72	71	66	209	2,251.12
Bill Garrett	70	72	67	209	2,251.11
Dick Hendrickson	70	70	69	209	2,251.11
Joe Jimenez	71	67	71	209	2,251.11
Tom Joyce	69	69	71	209	2,251.11
Jim O'Hern	71	69	69	209	2,251.11
Bob Reith	69	70	70	209	2,251.11
Deray Simon	71	68	70	209	2,251.11
Steve Spray	69	69	71	209	2,251.11

Mazda Senior Players Championship

TPC of Michigan, Dearborn, Michigan
Par 36-36—72; 6,876 yards

June 6-9
purse, $1,000,000

	SCORES				TOTAL	MONEY
Jim Albus	66	74	69	70	279	$150,000
Bob Charles	69	71	73	69	282	73,333.34
Charles Coody	71	69	70	72	282	73,333.33
Dave Hill	71	68	70	73	282	73,333.33
John Paul Cain	71	73	69	70	283	41,333.34
Don Bies	68	75	66	74	283	41,333.33
Terry Dill	74	69	68	72	283	41,333.33
Jim Colbert	70	71	69	74	284	27,350
Dale Douglass	74	72	67	71	284	27,350
Mike Hill	69	71	72	72	284	27,350
Lee Trevino	70	67	69	78	284	27,350
Bruce Crampton	75	68	70	72	285	22,000
George Archer	72	73	70	71	286	18,500
Miller Barber	76	67	73	70	286	18,500
Al Geiberger	68	73	70	75	286	18,500
Tom Shaw	74	73	69	70	286	18,500
Gay Brewer	68	73	73	73	287	15,200
Simon Hobday	73	69	71	74	287	15,200
J.C. Snead	72	71	69	75	287	15,200
Frank Beard	70	71	73	74	288	13,200
Harold Henning	75	72	71	70	288	13,200
Don Massengale	70	73	71	75	289	11,600
Jack Nicklaus	77	70	69	73	289	11,600
Walter Zembriski	73	73	70	73	289	11,600
Gibby Gilbert	70	79	71	70	290	9,450
Dick Hendrickson	74	71	71	74	290	9,450
Larry Laoretti	76	71	75	68	290	9,450
Bobby Nichols	68	71	74	77	290	9,450
Chi Chi Rodriguez	73	71	68	78	290	9,450
Deray Simon	73	76	72	69	290	9,450
Jack Kiefer	73	68	73	77	291	7,600
Gene Littler	75	69	76	71	291	7,600
Bert Yancey	70	72	73	76	291	7,600
Robert Boldt	75	76	73	68	292	6,120
Rives McBee	76	72	73	71	292	6,120
Charles Sifford	75	72	74	71	292	6,120
Rocky Thompson	77	69	68	78	292	6,120
DeWitt Weaver	79	68	70	75	292	6,120
Butch Baird	75	74	73	71	293	5,100
Bob Betley	78	73	70	72	293	5,100
Joe Jimenez	82	69	71	71	293	5,100
Charles Owens	70	74	72	77	293	5,100

MONY Syracuse Classic

Lafayette Country Club, Jamesville, New York
Par 36-36—72; 6,540 yards

June 14-16
purse, $400,000

	SCORES			TOTAL	MONEY
Rocky Thompson	62	· 68	69	199	$60,000
Jim Dent	67	66	67	200	35,000
Bruce Devlin	66	70	67	203	28,000

	SCORES			TOTAL	MONEY
Babe Hiskey	66	69	70	205	19,666.67
Bobby Nichols	66	71	68	205	19,666.67
Mike Hill	67	67	71	205	19,666.66
George Archer	69	68	70	207	11,555
Jim Ferree	67	70	70	207	11,555
Gibby Gilbert	72	66	69	207	11,555
Jim O'Hern	68	69	70	207	11,555
Walter Zembriski	66	70	71	207	11,555
Terry Dill	70	70	68	208	7,846.25
Robert Gaona	70	69	69	208	7,846.25
Dick Hendrickson	70	70	68	208	7,846.25
Simon Hobday	68	69	71	208	7,846.25
Dudley Wysong	69	66	74	209	6,755
Bob Erickson	72	71	67	210	5,880
Jack Kiefer	69	67	74	210	5,880
Charles Owens	67	70	73	210	5,880
Richard Rhyan	71	70	69	210	5,880
John Paul Cain	73	67	71	211	4,728.75
Quinton Gray	68	71	72	211	4,728.75
David Philo	68	71	72	211	4,728.75
Ken Still	72	69	70	211	4,728.75
Bruce Crampton	72	70	70	212	3,837
Al Kelley	71	73	68	212	3,837
Gene Littler	71	69	72	212	3,837
Rives McBee	70	71	71	212	3,837
Paul Moran	69	74	69	212	3,837
Bob Betley	74	69	70	213	2,860
Denny Felton	72	72	69	213	2,860
Joe Jimenez	66	75	72	213	2,860
George Johnson	71	71	71	213	2,860
Larry Laoretti	69	73	71	213	2,860
Lloyd Moody	71	70	72	213	2,860
DeWitt Weaver	72	70	71	213	2,860
Butch Baird	72	70	72	214	2,145
Bill Garrett	71	72	71	214	2,145
Dan Morgan	73	71	70	214	2,145
Phil Rodgers	72	68	74	214	2,145
Ben Smith	70	74	70	214	2,145

PaineWebber Invitational

TPC at Piper Glen, Charlotte, North Carolina
Par 36-36—72; 6,774 yards

June 21-23
purse, $450,000

	SCORES			TOTAL	MONEY
Orville Moody	69	68	70	207	$67,500
Dick Hendrickson	71	66	71	208	40,000
Bruce Crampton	68	70	71	209	29,750
Mike Hill	66	70	73	209	29,750
George Archer	71	66	73	210	18,550
Al Geiberger	69	72	69	210	18,550
Chi Chi Rodriguez	69	70	71	210	18,550
Richard Rhyan	71	69	71	211	14,000
Larry Ziegler	70	70	71	211	14,000
Butch Baird	72	67	73	212	10,095
Bob Brue	69	72	71	212	10,095
Simon Hobday	72	71	69	212	10,095

	SCORES			TOTAL	MONEY
Don January	75	69	68	212	10,095
Bob Wynn	69	70	73	212	10,095
Doug Dalziel	68	74	71	213	8,075
Jim Colbert	74	69	71	214	6,655
Joe Jimenez	73	68	73	214	6,655
Arnold Palmer	67	73	74	214	6,655
Gary Player	74	71	69	214	6,655
Tom Shaw	70	73	71	214	6,655
Rocky Thompson	72	71	71	214	6,655
Dave Hill	71	70	74	215	5,091.25
Mike Joyce	73	72	70	215	5,091.25
Ken Still	72	75	68	215	5,091.25
DeWitt Weaver	74	73	68	215	5,091.25
Bob Betley	76	70	70	216	4,135
Charles Coody	72	71	73	216	4,135
Gibby Gilbert	71	71	74	216	4,135
Jim O'Hern	73	70	73	216	4,135
J.C. Snead	74	74	68	216	4,135
Miller Barber	74	71	72	217	3,320
John Paul Cain	70	72	75	217	3,320
Larry Laoretti	71	72	74	217	3,320
Bobby Nichols	74	73	70	217	3,320
Don Bies	73	68	77	218	2,780
Robert Gaona	73	74	71	218	2,780
Bob Charles	76	75	68	219	2,513.34
Jim Dent	75	70	74	219	2,513.33
Jack Kiefer	70	77	72	219	2,513.33
Gay Brewer	76	72	72	220	2,243.34
Bruce Devlin	71	73	76	220	2,243.33
Jim Ferree	73	74	73	220	2,243.33

Southwestern Bell Classic

Loch Lloyd Country Club, Belton, Missouri
Par 35-35—70; 6,496 yards

June 28-30
purse, $450,000

	SCORES			TOTAL	MONEY
Jim Colbert	66	67	68	201	$67,500
Al Geiberger	68	65	71	204	35,750
Larry Laoretti	66	70	68	204	35,750
Lee Trevino	72	67	66	205	27,000
Charles Coody	70	69	67	206	19,750
Rocky Thompson	71	66	69	206	19,750
Don Massengale	67	71	69	207	15,125
Richard Rhyan	70	68	69	207	15,125
Gary Player	70	71	67	208	11,668.34
Bob Charles	69	70	69	208	11,668.33
Chi Chi Rodriguez	68	68	72	208	11,668.33
Bob Betley	72	70	67	209	9,422.50
Dave Hill	69	70	70	209	9,422.50
George Archer	68	69	73	210	7,645
Jerry Barber	72	70	68	210	7,645
Don Bies	73	71	66	210	7,645
John Brodie	71	69	70	210	7,645
John Paul Cain	69	70	71	210	7,645
Robert Gaona	70	70	71	211	6,101.67
Phil Rodgers	75	68	68	211	6,101.67

	SCORES			TOTAL	MONEY
Bruce Crampton	72	68	71	211	6,101.66
Ray Beallo	67	72	73	212	4,979
Bruce Devlin	68	73	71	212	4,979
Jim Ferree	70	71	71	212	4,979
Mike Hill	70	73	69	212	4,979
Ken Still	71	70	71	212	4,979
Butch Baird	76	69	68	213	4,036.25
Miller Barber	69	71	73	213	4,036.25
Simon Hobday	71	69	73	213	4,036.25
Walter Zembriski	72	69	72	213	4,036.25
Dale Douglass	73	71	70	214	3,140
J.C. Goosie	75	69	70	214	3,140
Don January	68	68	78	214	3,140
Jack Kiefer	66	73	75	214	3,140
Tom Shaw	73	69	72	214	3,140
Charles Sifford	72	71	71	214	3,140
Homero Blancas	71	72	72	215	2,467.50
Bob Brue	70	72	73	215	2,467.50
Lee Elder	68	72	75	215	2,467.50
Bob Erickson	72	71	72	215	2,467.50

Kroger Classic

Jack Nicklaus Sports Center, Grizzly Course, Kings Island, Ohio   July 5-7
Par 36-35—71; 6,628 yards   purse, $600,000

	SCORES			TOTAL	MONEY
Al Geiberger	66	69	68	203	$90,000
Larry Laoretti	67	70	67	204	51,200
Miller Barber	71	67	67	205	35,083.34
Dale Douglass	66	67	72	205	35,083.33
Harold Henning	68	69	68	205	35,083.33
Bob Charles	68	67	71	206	23,500
Terry Dill	66	71	70	207	17,134
Gibby Gilbert	69	73	65	207	17,134
Mike Hill	70	70	67	207	17,134
Jack Nicklaus	71	66	70	207	17,134
Lee Trevino	68	71	68	207	17,134
Doug Dalziel	70	69	69	208	11,981.67
J.C. Snead	73	67	68	208	11,981.67
DeWitt Weaver	68	69	71	208	11,981.66
Babe Hiskey	69	68	72	209	9,753.75
Chi Chi Rodriguez	68	68	73	209	9,753.75
Rocky Thompson	70	73	66	209	9,753.75
Walter Zembriski	72	68	69	209	9,753.75
Don January	71	71	68	210	8,250
Dudley Wysong	66	69	75	210	8,250
George Archer	68	72	71	211	7,011.25
Charles Coody	71	72	68	211	7,011.25
Jim Dent	70	68	73	211	7,011.25
Gene Littler	72	69	70	211	7,011.25
Bob Brue	71	73	68	212	5,818.75
Jack Kiefer	72	71	69	212	5,818.75
Don Massengale	71	69	72	212	5,818.75
Ben Smith	72	70	70	212	5,818.75
Homero Blancas	71	73	69	213	4,950
Richard Rhyan	69	70	74	213	4,950

	SCORES			TOTAL	MONEY
Larry Ziegler	72	73	68	213	4,950
John Brodie	71	71	72	214	4,240
Bruce Devlin	74	68	72	214	4,240
Joe Jimenez	74	71	69	214	4,240
Frank Beard	73	70	72	215	3,575
Jim Ferree	74	67	74	215	3,575
Bob Reith	72	69	74	215	3,575
Al Kelley	74	72	70	216	3,181.67
Phil Rodgers	70	75	71	216	3,181.67
Bob Wynn	72	69	75	216	3,181.66

Seniors British Open

Royal Lytham and St. Annes, St. Annes, England
Par 36-35—71; 6,673 yards

July 11-14
purse, £150,000

	SCORES				TOTAL	MONEY
Bob Verwey	70	74	71	70	285	£25,000
Bob Charles	69	76	74	67	286	12,775
Tommy Horton	69	76	71	70	286	12,775
*Charles Green	72	75	72	70	289	
Gary Player	70	73	73	74	290	7,350
David Butler	75	75	70	72	292	6,150
Neil Coles	73	75	73	72	293	4,071.25
Arthur Proctor	72	76	72	73	293	4,071.25
Brian Waites	73	74	72	74	293	4,071.25
Hedley Muscroft	74	73	75	71	293	4,071.25
Peter Butler	69	75	72	78	294	2,795
Bernard Hunt	71	76	76	71	294	2,795
Charles Mehok	73	77	72	73	295	2,560
Arnold Palmer	72	77	75	74	298	2,370
Bob Rose	71	74	74	79	298	2,370
Frank Rennie	76	73	75	76	300	2,093.33
Frederick Boobyer	76	81	72	71	300	2,093.33
John Fourie	79	75	71	75	300	2,093.33
Vance Moxom	75	81	73	72	301	1,870
Chick Evans	79	79	73	70	301	1,870
Ross Whitehead	76	81	72	73	302	1,682.50
Hugh Boyle	74	77	76	75	302	1,682.50
Bryan Carter	78	77	74	73	302	1,682.50
David Jimenez	79	74	77	72	302	1,682.50
Art Silvestrone	81	75	74	73	303	1,580
Jimmy D. Wright	79	78	76	71	304	1,500
Anthony Grubb	75	77	78	74	304	1,500
Howell Fraser	73	79	76	76	304	1,500
*Gordon Edwards	75	78	78	73	304	
Joe Carr	82	75	75	73	305	1,380
Rafe Botts	74	78	76	77	305	1,380
Ramon Sota	75	83	74	73	305	1,380
William Hector	79	81	73	73	306	1,280
Terry Squires	79	80	72	75	306	1,280
Jim McAlister	75	81	74	77	307	1,160
Peter Gill	78	81	72	76	307	1,160
Alec Bickerdike	79	80	76	72	307	1,160
Deray Simon	76	78	75	78	307	1,160
Norman Drew	74	82	78	74	308	981
Jack O'Keefe	77	80	76	75	308	981

	SCORES			TOTAL	MONEY
Bill Large	76	81 72	79	308	981
Walter Jones	74	83 75	76	308	981
Roger Fidler	77	78 70	83	308	981

Newport Cup

Newport Country Club, Newport, Rhode Island
Par 36-36—72; 6,566 yards

July 12-14
purse, $325,000

	SCORES			TOTAL	MONEY
Larry Ziegler	66	66	67	199	$48,750
George Archer	65	72	68	205	24,310
Jim Dent	66	68	71	205	24,310
Tom Shaw	68	66	71	205	24,310
Simon Hobday	67	70	69	206	12,956.50
Rives McBee	68	71	67	206	12,956.50
Richard Rhyan	68	72	66	206	12,956.50
J.C. Snead	68	72	66	206	12,956.50
Robert Rawlins	69	67	71	207	9,337
Gary Cowan	68	70	70	208	8,671
Dudley Wysong	73	66	70	209	8,001
Jim Albus	72	70	68	210	6,224.50
Miller Barber	71	72	67	210	6,224.50
Terry Dill	70	70	70	210	6,224.50
Gibby Gilbert	73	70	67	210	6,224.50
Mike Joyce	71	70	69	210	6,224.50
Jim O'Hern	70	72	68	210	6,224.50
Harold Henning	74	69	68	211	4,427.67
Babe Hiskey	75	68	68	211	4,427.67
Larry Laoretti	76	69	66	211	4,427.67
DeWitt Weaver	70	72	69	211	4,427.67
Gay Brewer	70	69	72	211	4,427.66
Rolf Deming	71	70	70	211	4,427.66
Paul Moran	71	74	67	212	3,616.50
Chuck Workman	71	73	68	212	3,616.50
Jack Kiefer	73	71	69	213	3,284
Bob Wynn	72	73	68	213	3,284
Bob Betley	69	74	71	214	2,801.20
Mike Fetchick	69	75	70	214	2,801.20
Don Massengale	70	75	69	214	2,801.20
Phil Rodgers	74	70	70	214	2,801.20
Ken Still	71	72	71	214	2,801.20
Doug Dalziel	71	75	69	215	2,401
George Bruno	72	73	71	216	2,000.50
Bob Erickson	70	76	70	216	2,000.50
Quinton Gray	74	74	68	216	2,000.50
Al Kelley	72	73	71	216	2,000.50
Billy Maxwell	71	66	79	216	2,000.50
Bobby Nichols	72	70	74	216	2,000.50
Jack Fleck	69	75	73	217	1,667
Dick Hendrickson	71	73	73	217	1,667
Dan Morgan	73	73	71	217	1,667

Ameritech Open

Stonebridge Country Club, Aurora, Illinois
Par 36-36—72; 6,905 yards

July 19-21
purse, $500,000

	SCORES			TOTAL	MONEY
Mike Hill	67	66	67	200	$75,000
Bob Charles	69	69	64	202	44,000
Al Geiberger	65	71	68	204	36,000
George Archer	67	71	68	206	30,000
Babe Hiskey	73	66	68	207	20,666.67
Ken Still	70	70	67	207	20,666.67
Don Massengale	70	68	69	207	20,666.66
Tom Shaw	72	67	69	208	14,233.34
Jim Colbert	69	70	69	208	14,233.33
Jim Ferree	68	69	71	208	14,233.33
Bruce Crampton	66	74	69	209	10,300
Jim Dent	72	68	69	209	10,300
Bruce Devlin	74	69	66	209	10,300
Dave Hill	74	68	67	209	10,300
Gene Littler	71	69	69	209	10,300
Butch Baird	71	71	68	210	7,416.67
Richard Rhyan	69	73	68	210	7,416.67
Chi Chi Rodriguez	71	72	67	210	7,416.67
Walter Zembriski	70	71	69	210	7,416.67
Dale Douglass	73	67	70	210	7,416.66
Ted Hayes	71	69	70	210	7,416.66
Billy Casper	71	69	71	211	6,050
Miller Barber	72	71	69	212	5,300
Bob Brue	69	72	71	212	5,300
Gibby Gilbert	70	72	70	212	5,300
Larry Laoretti	73	74	65	212	5,300
Rives McBee	69	72	71	212	5,300
Homero Blancas	72	72	69	213	4,000
John Brodie	70	73	70	213	4,000
Joe Jimenez	72	72	69	213	4,000
Charles Sifford	71	70	72	213	4,000
Ben Smith	74	70	69	213	4,000
J.C. Snead	74	71	68	213	4,000
Larry Ziegler	69	71	73	213	4,000
Bill Collins	73	71	70	214	2,920
Dick Hendrickson	78	64	72	214	2,920
Jack Kiefer	72	71	71	214	2,920
Rocky Thompson	69	76	69	214	2,920
Dudley Wysong	75	68	71	214	2,920
Bob Betley	71	75	69	215	2,450
Don Bies	71	72	72	215	2,450
Charles Coody	74	70	71	215	2,450
Bob Reith	74	72	69	215	2,450

U.S. Senior Open

Oakland Hills Country Club, Birmingham, Michigan
Par 35-35—70; 6,718 yards

July 25-28
purse, $600,000

	SCORES				TOTAL	MONEY
Jack Nicklaus	72	69	70	71	282	$110,000
Chi Chi Rodriguez	73	68	70	71	282	55,000

(Nicklaus won playoff, 65-69.)

	SCORES				TOTAL	MONEY
Al Geiberger	71	70	72	70	283	33,137
Jim Dent	73	72	72	67	284	21,604
Lee Trevino	70	72	68	74	284	21,604
Don Bies	72	69	72	73	286	15,633.50
Charles Coody	78	68	69	71	286	15,633.50
Bob Charles	72	70	73	72	287	12,346.67
Gary Player	69	73	73	72	287	12,346.67
Mike Hill	68	74	71	74	287	12,346.66
Bruce Crampton	75	69	72	73	289	9,813.50
Harold Henning	73	73	70	73	289	9,813.50
Bobby Nichols	71	73	74	71	289	9,813.50
Ken Still	76	71	72	70	289	9,813.50
Babe Hiskey	73	72	71	74	290	8,434.50
J.C. Snead	71	69	71	79	290	8,434.50
Frank Beard	73	74	74	70	291	7,687.50
Jack Kiefer	75	72	69	75	291	7,687.50
Jim Colbert	74	70	74	74	292	6,932.67
Joe Jimenez	77	74	73	68	292	6,932.67
Bruce Devlin	71	73	72	76	292	6,932.66
Chick Evans	75	75	73	70	293	6,360.50
Don Massengale	75	72	75	71	293	6,360.50
Miller Barber	75	77	71	71	294	5,698.60
Dale Douglass	73	70	73	78	294	5,698.60
Gibby Gilbert	73	73	75	73	294	5,698.60
Rocky Thompson	73	76	72	73	294	5,698.60
Brian Waites	75	76	70	73	294	5,698.60
Tommy Aaron	73	73	71	78	295	4,989.50
Jim Albus	75	76	70	74	295	4,989.50
Snell Lancaster	72	74	74	75	295	4,989.50
Richard Rhyan	73	74	76	72	295	4,989.50
Mike Joyce	77	73	74	72	296	4,696
Ben Smith	75	74	74	74	297	4,529.50
Walter Zembriski	76	74	66	81	297	4,529.50
*Jim Patti	78	68	73	78	297	
J.C. Goosie	78	74	74	72	298	4,307.50
Larry Ziegler	79	73	75	71	298	4,307.50
*Dick Siderowf	71	80	72	75	298	
Walter Morgan	77	75	73	74	299	3,865.67
Phil Rodgers	71	77	74	77	299	3,865.67
Tom Shaw	74	73	74	78	299	3,865.67
Steve Spray	76	75	73	75	299	3,865.67
Orville Moody	77	71	70	81	299	3,865.66
Jack Rule	73	76	72	78	299	3,865.66

Northville Long Island Classic

Meadow Brook Club, Jericho, New York
Par 36-36—72; 6,655 yards

July 29-August 4
purse, $450,000

	SCORES			TOTAL	MONEY
George Archer	68	67	69	204	$67,500
Jim Colbert	67	71	68	206	35,750
Larry Laoretti	67	68	71	206	35,750
Bob Charles	68	70	69	207	27,000
Bob Brue	69	72	67	208	19,750
Jim Dent	68	70	70	208	19,750
John Brodie	73	69	67	209	14,275

	SCORES			TOTAL	MONEY
Gary Player	68	72	69	209	14,275
J.C. Snead	69	69	71	209	14,275
Charles Coody	70	69	71	210	10,318.75
Dick Hendrickson	70	68	72	210	10,318.75
Rocky Thompson	72	67	71	210	10,318.75
Lee Trevino	78	66	66	210	10,318.75
Miller Barber	68	71	72	211	7,851.25
Mike Joyce	68	73	70	211	7,851.25
Gene Littler	71	70	70	211	7,851.25
Jim O'Hern	70	70	71	211	7,851.25
Gary Cowan	69	70	73	212	6,460
Jack Kiefer	72	70	70	212	6,460
Chi Chi Rodriguez	70	71	71	212	6,460
Butch Baird	74	70	69	213	5,585
Dale Douglass	69	72	72	213	5,585
Dave Hill	73	71	70	214	4,755
Babe Hiskey	71	72	71	214	4,755
Paul Moran	72	71	71	214	4,755
Dan Morgan	75	71	68	214	4,755
Deray Simon	70	73	71	214	4,755
Al Kelley	70	77	68	215	3,588.58
Homero Blancas	67	76	72	215	3,588.57
John Paul Cain	73	72	70	215	3,588.57
Billy Casper	71	71	73	215	3,588.57
Joe Jimenez	73	72	70	215	3,588.57
Richard Rhyan	72	71	72	215	3,588.57
DeWitt Weaver	72	72	71	215	3,588.57
Don Massengale	71	73	72	216	2,720
Charles Sifford	71	77	68	216	2,720
Larry Ziegler	71	70	75	216	2,720
Fred Hawkins	72	74	71	217	2,378.75
Ken Still	70	73	74	217	2,378.75
Dudley Wysong	72	72	73	217	2,378.75
Bert Yancey	74	74	69	217	2,378.75

Showdown Classic

Jeremy Ranch Golf Club, Park City, Utah
Par 36-36—72; 7,103 yards

August 5-11
purse, $350,000

	SCORES			TOTAL	MONEY
Dale Douglass	71	67	71	209	$52,500
George Archer	70	69	71	210	27,500
Don Bies	75	68	67	210	27,500
Charles Coody	65	69	77	211	18,587.50
Don January	71	73	67	211	18,587.50
Al Geiberger	73	69	70	212	11,711.25
Larry Laoretti	69	71	72	212	11,711.25
Gene Littler	70	73	69	212	11,711.25
Bob Wynn	66	72	74	212	11,711.25
Terry Dill	70	72	71	213	7,680
Mike Hill	69	74	70	213	7,680
Bobby Nichols	66	72	75	213	7,680
Rocky Thompson	71	70	72	213	7,680
DeWitt Weaver	71	72	70	213	7,680
Bob Betley	67	72	75	214	5,880
Paul Moran	70	74	70	214	5,880

	SCORES			TOTAL	MONEY
Jimmy Powell	73	72	69	214	5,880
Homero Blancas	73	73	69	215	5,260
Robert Gaona	73	73	70	216	4,259.29
Don Massengale	75	72	69	216	4,259.29
Orville Moody	72	71	73	216	4,259.29
Walter Morgan	73	71	72	216	4,259.29
Bruce Devlin	72	70	74	216	4,259.28
Lloyd Moody	67	72	77	216	4,259.28
Ben Smith	71	70	75	216	4,259.28
John Brodie	69	74	74	217	2,978.75
Billy Casper	72	70	75	217	2,978.75
Gary Cowan	73	71	73	217	2,978.75
Bruce Crampton	74	72	71	217	2,978.75
Chick Evans	72	76	69	217	2,978.75
Jack Kiefer	71	74	72	217	2,978.75
Jim O'Hern	73	74	70	217	2,978.75
Chi Chi Rodriguez	72	74	71	217	2,978.75
Ray Beallo	70	75	73	218	2,160
Simon Hobday	69	78	71	218	2,160
Phil Rodgers	75	76	67	218	2,160
Bert Yancey	72	76	70	218	2,160
Butch Baird	72	77	70	219	1,833.75
Dick Hendrickson	71	70	78	219	1,833.75
Richard Rhyan	70	76	73	219	1,833.75
Dudley Wysong	74	73	72	219	1,833.75

GTE Northwest Classic

Inglewood Country Club, Kenmore, Washington
Par 37-35—72; 6,501 yards

August 16-18
purse, $400,000

	SCORES			TOTAL	MONEY
Mike Hill	68	66	64	198	$60,000
Chi Chi Rodriguez	63	67	70	200	35,000
Dick Hendrickson	68	66	68	202	28,000
Bruce Crampton	68	66	69	203	21,550
Bob Wynn	71	67	65	203	21,550
Dale Douglass	71	67	68	206	15,900
George Archer	68	70	69	207	11,555
Miller Barber	69	69	69	207	11,555
Gibby Gilbert	66	71	70	207	11,555
Gary Player	72	68	67	207	11,555
DeWitt Weaver	68	66	73	207	11,555
J.C. Snead	72	72	64	208	8,078.34
Al Geiberger	72	66	70	208	8,078.33
Harold Henning	71	67	70	208	8,078.33
Don Bies	71	71	67	209	5,504.55
Terry Dill	71	69	69	209	5,504.55
Jim Ferree	65	74	70	209	5,504.55
Al Kelley	72	72	65	209	5,504.55
Gene Littler	71	69	69	209	5,504.55
Bob Reith	70	70	69	209	5,504.55
Bob Brue	68	70	71	209	5,504.54
Don January	69	70	70	209	5,504.54
Joe Jimenez	71	63	75	209	5,504.54
Jim O'Hern	68	71	70	209	5,504.54
Rocky Thompson	70	69	70	209	5,504.54

	SCORES			TOTAL	MONEY
Deray Simon	70	73	67	210	3,826.67
Bert Yancey	72	70	68	210	3,826.67
Larry Laoretti	69	69	72	210	3,826.66
John Brodie	69	71	71	211	3,178
Simon Hobday	72	73	66	211	3,178
Jack Kiefer	71	70	70	211	3,178
Arnold Palmer	72	69	70	211	3,178
Jimmy Powell	70	71	70	211	3,178
Billy Casper	72	70	70	212	2,541.67
Rives McBee	71	71	70	212	2,541.67
Bruce Devlin	74	68	70	212	2,541.66
Homero Blancas	71	69	73	213	2,225
Robert Gaona	76	68	69	213	2,225
Orville Moody	71	72	70	213	2,225
Chick Evans	75	69	70	214	1,946.25
Howie Johnson	70	74	70	214	1,946.25
Tom Shaw	73	69	72	214	1,946.25
Charles Sifford	70	73	71	214	1,946.25

Sunwest Bank/Charley Pride Classic

Four Hills Country Club, Albuquerque, New Mexico
Par 36-36—72; 6,722 yards

August 23-25
purse, $350,000

	SCORES			TOTAL	MONEY
Lee Trevino	66	65	69	200	$52,500
Jim O'Hern	70	69	65	204	27,500
Chi Chi Rodriguez	67	70	67	204	27,500
Jim Dent	70	67	68	205	18,587.50
Tom Shaw	69	68	68	205	18,587.50
Miller Barber	67	72	67	206	13,840
Don Bies	64	73	70	207	8,351
Billy Casper	67	72	68	207	8,351
Terry Dill	72	66	69	207	8,351
Jim Ferree	72	67	68	207	8,351
Dick Hendrickson	70	71	66	207	8,351
Don January	67	66	74	207	8,351
Jack Kiefer	70	66	71	207	8,351
Larry Laoretti	74	64	69	207	8,351
Don Massengale	69	67	71	207	8,351
Bobby Nichols	68	70	69	207	8,351
Jimmy Powell	68	71	69	208	5,258.34
Jim Colbert	68	71	69	208	5,258.33
Charles Coody	72	66	70	208	5,258.33
Bob Reith	72	69	68	209	4,438.34
Babe Hiskey	64	72	73	209	4,438.33
Gene Littler	68	71	70	209	4,438.33
George Archer	70	71	69	210	3,508.58
Bob Charles	73	66	71	210	3,508.57
Doug Dalziel	70	68	72	210	3,508.57
Gibby Gilbert	66	73	71	210	3,508.57
Harold Henning	70	70	70	210	3,508.57
Richard Rhyan	69	72	69	210	3,508.57
Rocky Thompson	71	67	72	210	3,508.57
Ben Smith	69	74	68	211	2,905
Robert Gaona	72	69	71	212	2,490
Al Geiberger	68	69	75	212	2,490

	SCORES			TOTAL	MONEY
Simon Hobday	72	71	69	212	2,490
Joe Jimenez	71	70	71	212	2,490
Bob Wynn	69	71	72	212	2,490
Orville Moody	72	72	69	213	1,970
Paul Moran	71	74	68	213	1,970
Chuck Workman	72	70	71	213	1,970
Dudley Wysong	75	73	65	213	1,970
Frank Beard	68	74	72	214	1,660
Bob Brue	67	74	73	214	1,660
Chick Evans	71	72	71	214	1,660
Charles Sifford	73	69	72	214	1,660
Ken Still	75	70	69	214	1,660

GTE North Classic

Broadmoor Country Club, Indianapolis, Indiana
Par 35-37—72; 6,670 yards

August 30-September 1
purse, $450,000

	SCORES			TOTAL	MONEY
George Archer	66	66	67	199	$67,500
Dale Douglass	66	67	67	200	39,000
Harold Henning	67	65	72	204	29,750
Chi Chi Rodriguez	68	69	67	204	29,750
Simon Hobday	73	66	67	206	21,500
Gene Littler	71	67	69	207	17,075
Lee Trevino	67	68	72	207	17,075
Jim Ferree	70	70	68	208	12,780
Al Kelley	69	68	71	208	12,780
Larry Mowry	64	72	72	208	12,780
Don Bies	68	69	72	209	9,870
Terry Dill	67	74	68	209	9,870
Mike Hill	69	70	70	209	9,870
Butch Baird	72	67	71	210	7,447.50
Bruce Crampton	71	71	68	210	7,447.50
Jack Kiefer	67	67	76	210	7,447.50
Ben Smith	67	71	72	210	7,447.50
J.C. Snead	69	71	70	210	7,447.50
Rocky Thompson	72	67	71	210	7,447.50
Miller Barber	67	71	73	211	5,922.50
Charles Coody	69	69	73	211	5,922.50
Jim Albus	71	70	71	212	5,091.25
Don January	68	71	73	212	5,091.25
Paul Moran	71	70	71	212	5,091.25
Arnold Palmer	75	66	71	212	5,091.25
Tommy Aaron	70	72	71	213	4,135
Robert Gaona	76	68	69	213	4,135
Dick Hendrickson	67	74	72	213	4,135
Bobby Nichols	71	72	70	213	4,135
Jimmy Powell	71	71	71	213	4,135
Bob Charles	70	72	72	214	3,320
Jim O'Hern	71	71	72	214	3,320
Bob Reith	68	72	74	214	3,320
DeWitt Weaver	70	71	73	214	3,320
Joe Jimenez	73	71	72	216	2,720
Robert Rawlins	73	72	71	216	2,720
Richard Rhyan	66	78	72	216	2,720
Homero Blancas	69	73	75	217	2,153.89

	SCORES			TOTAL	MONEY
El Collins	74	70	73	217	2,153.89
Rolf Deming	70	73	74	217	2,153.89
Mike Fetchick	71	74	72	217	2,153.89
Don Massengale	70	72	75	217	2,153.89
Mal McMullen	69	73	75	217	2,153.89
Tom Shaw	70	75	72	217	2,153.89
Dudley Wysong	73	72	72	217	2,153.89
Dave Hill	73	69	75	217	2,153.88

First of America Classic

The Highlands, Grand Rapids, Michigan
Par 36-35—71; 6,419 yards

September 6-8
purse, $350,000

	SCORES			TOTAL	MONEY
Harold Henning	72	64	66	202	$52,500
Gibby Gilbert	70	68	64	202	30,000
(Henning defeated Gilbert on first extra hole.)					
Jim Ferree	69	68	66	203	22,750
Lee Trevino	68	68	67	203	22,750
Jim Dent	71	68	65	204	14,323.34
Gene Littler	67	69	68	204	14,323.33
Rocky Thompson	66	69	69	204	14,323.33
Jack Kiefer	70	69	66	205	9,848.34
Dick Hendrickson	71	66	68	205	9,848.33
Mike Hill	70	68	67	205	9,848.33
Gary Cowan	70	69	67	206	7,955
Charles Sifford	69	68	69	206	7,955
Arnold Palmer	72	69	66	207	6,573.34
Rives McBee	70	69	68	207	6,573.33
Bob Reith	68	68	71	207	6,573.33
Dale Douglass	69	73	66	208	5,130.84
Simon Hobday	69	72	67	208	5,130.84
Jim Albus	68	70	70	208	5,130.83
Dave Hill	69	71	68	208	5,130.83
Walter Zembriski	68	72	68	208	5,130.83
Larry Ziegler	72	68	68	208	5,130.83
Joe Jimenez	70	68	71	209	4,100
Don Massengale	71	71	67	209	4,100
Larry Laoretti	67	73	70	210	3,666.67
Bobby Nichols	71	69	70	210	3,666.67
Paul Moran	71	67	72	210	3,666.66
John Brodie	69	70	72	211	3,250
Robert Rawlins	68	69	74	211	3,250
Butch Baird	70	73	69	212	2,559.38
Homero Blancas	71	74	67	212	2,559.38
Richard Rhyan	70	73	69	212	2,559.38
Chuck Workman	75	69	68	212	2,559.38
Bobby Breen	74	69	69	212	2,559.37
Jim O'Hern	70	72	70	212	2,559.37
J.C. Snead	70	72	70	212	2,559.37
DeWitt Weaver	73	68	71	212	2,559.37
Bruce Crampton	71	74	68	213	1,967.50
Jimmy Powell	73	73	67	213	1,967.50
Bob Brue	72	71	71	214	1,730
Bruce Devlin	71	73	70	214	1,730
Mike Fetchick	70	73	71	214	1,730

	SCORES			TOTAL	MONEY
Al Kelley	73	71	70	214	1,730
Dudley Wysong	74	71	69	214	1,730

Digital Classic

Nashawtuc Country Club, Concord, Massachusetts
Par 36-36—72; 6,453 yards

September 13-15
purse, $400,000

	SCORES			TOTAL	MONEY
Rocky Thompson	66	69	70	205	$60,000
Bruce Crampton	67	71	68	206	35,000
Mike Hill	68	72	68	208	26,000
Lee Trevino	65	71	72	208	26,000
Jim Colbert	65	74	70	209	17,500
Al Geiberger	67	69	73	209	17,500
Frank Beard	71	68	71	210	14,310
Dick Hendrickson	72	69	70	211	11,800
Jimmy Powell	72	68	71	211	11,800
Doug Dalziel	71	71	70	212	9,535
Harold Henning	75	68	69	212	9,535
Bob Reith	69	70	73	212	9,535
Paul Barkhouse	69	71	73	213	7,151
Bob Betley	69	70	74	213	7,151
Homero Blancas	69	70	74	213	7,151
Bob Charles	70	73	70	213	7,151
Larry Laoretti	73	69	71	213	7,151
Gary Cowan	72	73	69	214	5,721.67
Jim O'Hern	69	73	72	214	5,721.67
John Brodie	68	72	74	214	5,721.66
Miller Barber	72	71	72	215	4,522.50
Joe Carr	72	70	73	215	4,522.50
Jim Dent	73	70	72	215	4,522.50
Jim Ferree	71	71	73	215	4,522.50
Joe Jimenez	73	70	72	215	4,522.50
George Johnson	74	70	71	215	4,522.50
John Paul Cain	71	75	70	216	3,496
Ted Hayes	72	71	73	216	3,496
Simon Hobday	67	74	75	216	3,496
Tom Shaw	69	73	74	216	3,496
Deray Simon	73	71	72	216	3,496
Bob Wynn	73	74	70	217	2,940
Walter Zembriski	71	73	73	217	2,940
Bob Brue	74	73	71	218	2,431
Gordon Jones	73	72	73	218	2,431
Rives McBee	74	70	74	218	2,431
Lloyd Moody	73	71	74	218	2,431
Orville Moody	76	72	70	218	2,431
Robert Gaona	71	77	71	219	1,986
Paul Moran	71	71	77	219	1,986
Dan Morgan	74	71	74	219	1,986
Charles Owens	73	74	72	219	1,986
Robert Rawlins	73	73	73	219	1,986

Nationwide Championship

Country Club of the South, Alpharetta, Georgia

September 20-22

Par 36-36—72; 6,677 yards

purse, $700,000

	SCORES			TOTAL	MONEY
Mike Hill	70	71	71	212	$105,000
Tom Shaw	75	69	69	213	60,800
DeWitt Weaver	71	73	71	215	50,000
George Archer	74	73	69	216	33,733.34
Jim Albus	70	75	71	216	33,733.33
Gibby Gilbert	76	67	73	216	33,733.33
Jim Colbert	69	75	73	217	20,115
Charles Coody	67	72	78	217	20,115
Jim Dent	66	76	75	217	20,115
Dick Hendrickson	72	69	76	217	20,115
Arnold Palmer	71	74	72	217	20,115
Dale Douglass	74	73	71	218	12,917.50
Jim Ferree	73	70	75	218	12,917.50
Al Geiberger	73	69	76	218	12,917.50
Don January	71	72	75	218	12,917.50
Bobby Nichols	73	74	71	218	12,917.50
Ben Smith	71	75	72	218	12,917.50
Larry Laoretti	72	73	74	219	8,573.34
Chi Chi Rodriguez	74	73	72	219	8,573.34
Larry Ziegler	76	71	72	219	8,573.34
Bill Collins	70	73	76	219	8,573.33
Dave Hill	73	72	74	219	8,573.33
Simon Hobday	73	71	75	219	8,573.33
Larry Mowry	71	74	74	219	8,573.33
Gary Player	73	71	75	219	8,573.33
Charles Sifford	73	71	75	219	8,573.33
John Brodie	74	74	72	220	6,505
Orville Moody	75	74	71	220	6,505
Gary Cowan	70	78	73	221	5,396.67
Bruce Devlin	74	72	75	221	5,396.67
Babe Hiskey	70	76	75	221	5,396.67
Richard Rhyan	73	73	75	221	5,396.67
Homero Blancas	76	70	75	221	5,396.66
J.C. Snead	74	70	77	221	5,396.66
Rives McBee	72	76	74	222	4,198.34
Gay Brewer	74	70	78	222	4,198.33
Paul Moran	78	69	75	222	4,198.33
Miller Barber	73	77	73	223	3,666.25
Bruce Crampton	75	77	71	223	3,666.25
Harold Henning	75	72	76	223	3,666.25
Dan Morgan	76	75	72	223	3,666.25

Bank One Classic

Kearney Hill Links, Lexington, Kentucky

September 27-29

Par 36-36—72; 6,744 yards

purse, $300,000

	SCORES			TOTAL	MONEY
DeWitt Weaver	70	72	65	207	$45,000
J.C. Snead	68	71	68	207	26,000
(Weaver defeated Snead on second extra hole.)					
George Archer	71	67	70	208	19,000

	SCORES			TOTAL	MONEY
Larry Laoretti	70	70	68	208	19,000
Chi Chi Rodriguez	67	70	72	209	12,992.50
Walter Zembriski	72	71	66	209	12,992.50
Gay Brewer	71	71	68	210	8,942.50
Jim Colbert	68	73	69	210	8,942.50
Gibby Gilbert	69	68	73	210	8,942.50
Don January	69	73	68	210	8,942.50
Dick Hendrickson	74	71	66	211	6,481.67
Jimmy Powell	75	67	69	211	6,481.67
Gary Player	71	69	71	211	6,481.66
Miller Barber	68	73	71	212	5,156.25
Dave Hill	71	71	70	212	5,156.25
Jim O'Hern	72	70	70	212	5,156.25
Rocky Thompson	70	70	72	212	5,156.25
Paul Moran	69	73	71	213	4,243.34
Rafe Botts	71	69	73	213	4,243.33
Charles Mehok	71	71	71	213	4,243.33
Dudley Wysong	74	73	67	214	3,583.34
Chick Evans	74	72	68	214	3,583.33
Bert Yancey	75	69	70	214	3,583.33
Bob Betley	71	75	69	215	2,982
Simon Hobday	71	71	73	215	2,982
Joe Jimenez	70	73	72	215	2,982
Bob Reith	71	75	69	215	2,982
Bob Wynn	71	72	72	215	2,982
Jim Dent	72	73	71	216	2,415
Mike Hill	75	73	68	216	2,415
Gordon Jones	75	67	74	216	2,415
Al Kelley	72	74	70	216	2,415
Bruce Crampton	70	75	72	217	1,942.50
Bruce Devlin	71	73	73	217	1,942.50
J.C. Goosie	74	72	71	217	1,942.50
Rives McBee	72	75	70	217	1,942.50
Gary Cowan	73	73	72	218	1,591
Doug Dalziel	77	70	71	218	1,591
Babe Hiskey	72	74	72	218	1,591
Tom Shaw	76	73	69	218	1,591
Larry Ziegler	71	73	74	218	1,591

Vantage Championship

Tanglewood Park, Clemmons, North Carolina
Par 36-36—72; 6,680 yards

October 4-6
purse, $1,500,000

	SCORES			TOTAL	MONEY
Jim Colbert	68	70	67	205	$202,500
George Archer	71	64	71	206	100,000
Jim Dent	67	72	67	206	100,000
Gibby Gilbert	70	68	68	206	100,000
Simon Hobday	69	67	71	207	65,500
Dale Douglass	69	67	72	208	51,750
Al Geiberger	71	69	68	208	51,750
Arnold Palmer	70	72	67	209	42,700
Robert Gaona	72	69	69	210	33,995
Larry Laoretti	69	73	68	210	33,995
J.C. Snead	69	72	69	210	33,995
Bob Wynn	69	73	68	210	33,995

	SCORES			TOTAL	MONEY
Bob Charles	68	72	71	211	24,466.80
Mike Hill	70	69	72	211	24,466.80
Gary Player	73	68	70	211	24,466.80
Richard Rhyan	69	73	69	211	24,466.80
Chi Chi Rodriguez	72	68	71	211	24,466.80
Bruce Crampton	71	69	72	212	19,574
Rocky Thompson	71	70	71	212	19,574
Walter Zembriski	73	67	72	212	19,574
Charles Coody	73	70	70	213	15,472.34
Orville Moody	71	72	70	213	15,472.34
John Paul Cain	73	69	71	213	15,472.33
Harold Henning	72	69	72	213	15,472.33
Jimmy Powell	74	68	71	213	15,472.33
Ben Smith	68	71	74	213	15,472.33
Butch Baird	70	76	68	214	11,417.58
Miller Barber	74	69	71	214	11,417.57
Bob Betley	73	68	73	214	11,417.57
Doug Dalziel	69	71	74	214	11,417.57
Dave Hill	72	70	72	214	11,417.57
Gene Littler	72	71	71	214	11,417.57
Larry Mowry	73	72	69	214	11,417.57
Don Bies	72	68	75	215	7,849
Bruce Devlin	71	72	72	215	7,849
Dick Hendrickson	69	74	72	215	7,849
Babe Hiskey	72	71	72	215	7,849
Don January	71	69	75	215	7,849
Lloyd Moody	70	73	72	215	7,849
Robert Rawlins	76	66	73	215	7,849
Lee Trevino	75	67	73	215	7,849

Raley's Senior Gold Rush

Rancho Murieta Country Club, Rancho Murieta, California
Par 36-36—72; 6,701 yards

October 11-13
purse, $400,000

	SCORES			TOTAL	MONEY
George Archer	67	71	68	206	$67,500
Simon Hobday	73	69	65	207	39,000
Mike Hill	72	70	66	208	32,500
Butch Baird	71	66	72	209	19,350
Bob Charles	69	69	71	209	19,350
Bruce Crampton	67	72	70	209	19,350
Dale Douglass	73	68	68	209	19,350
Jim O'Hern	69	72	68	209	19,350
Homero Blancas	68	74	68	210	11,668.34
J.C. Snead	69	70	71	210	11,668.33
Lee Trevino	67	70	73	210	11,668.33
John Paul Cain	71	75	65	211	9,123.34
Charles Coody	69	72	70	211	9,123.33
Don Massengale	70	72	69	211	9,123.33
Gay Brewer	69	72	71	212	6,857.86
Jim Dent	72	73	67	212	6,857.86
Alton Duhon	72	70	70	212	6,857.86
Al Geiberger	69	73	70	212	6,857.86
Kermit Zarley	74	67	71	212	6,857.86
Harold Henning	69	71	72	212	6,857.85
Rocky Thompson	70	69	73	212	6,857.85

	SCORES			TOTAL	MONEY
Al Kelley	74	71	68	213	5,203.34
John Brodie	71	69	73	213	5,203.33
Rives McBee	72	69	72	213	5,203.33
Miller Barber	75	66	73	214	4,332
Gibby Gilbert	74	74	66	214	4,332
Joe Jimenez	76	67	71	214	4,332
Larry Mowry	73	68	73	214	4,332
Bob Reith	69	73	72	214	4,332
Gary Cowan	75	69	71	215	3,410
Dick Hendrickson	73	72	70	215	3,410
Bobby Nichols	73	75	67	215	3,410
Chi Chi Rodriguez	72	74	69	215	3,410
Bob Wynn	76	70	69	215	3,410
Don Bies	71	74	71	216	2,668.75
Billy Casper	69	74	73	216	2,668.75
Robert Gaona	69	75	72	216	2,668.75
Tom Shaw	73	73	70	216	2,668.75
Larry Laoretti	73	72	72	217	2,333.34
Bob Brue	73	71	73	217	2,333.33
Larry Ziegler	71	74	72	217	2,333.33

Transamerica Championship

Silverado Country Club, Napa, California
Par 35-37—72; 6,632 yards

October 18-20
purse, $500,000

	SCORES			TOTAL	MONEY
Charles Coody	67	66	71	204	$75,000
Lee Trevino	67	70	69	206	44,000
Tommy Aaron	69	70	68	207	36,000
George Archer	72	66	70	208	24,666.67
Arnold Palmer	69	69	70	208	24,666.67
Dale Douglass	74	63	72	209	15,900
Butch Baird	70	69	70	209	15,900
J.C. Snead	70	70	69	209	15,900
DeWitt Weaver	69	69	71	209	15,900
Jim Albus	72	67	71	210	12,500
Jim Colbert	70	65	75	210	12,500
Mike Hill	70	67	74	211	11,000
Simon Hobday	69	68	75	212	10,000
Don Bies	74	69	70	213	9,000
Bob Charles	68	71	74	213	9,000
Rives McBee	72	69	72	213	9,000
John Paul Cain	74	67	73	214	7,400
Dave Hill	72	68	74	214	7,400
Don January	70	70	74	214	7,400
Gary Player	69	74	71	214	7,400
Tom Shaw	71	73	71	215	6,083.34
Bruce Crampton	69	72	74	215	6,083.33
Dick Hendrickson	69	72	74	215	6,083.33
Al Kelley	72	73	71	216	4,633.34
Don Massengale	72	72	72	216	4,633.34
Orville Moody	76	67	73	216	4,633.34
Bob Brue	73	70	73	216	4,633.33
Gibby Gilbert	71	69	76	216	4,633.33
Dan Morgan	70	71	75	216	4,633.33
Bobby Nichols	74	74	68	216	4,633.33

	SCORES			TOTAL	MONEY
Bob Rosburg	72	70	74	216	4,633.33
Bert Yancey	72	71	73	216	4,633.33
Al Geiberger	73	70	74	217	3,400
Larry Mowry	74	74	69	217	3,400
Bob Reith	71	72	74	217	3,400
Homero Blancas	77	69	72	218	2,850
Gay Brewer	72	72	74	218	2,850
Jim Dent	71	73	74	218	2,850
Joe Jimenez	70	72	76	218	2,850
Miller Barber	71	74	74	219	2,400
Billy Casper	71	78	70	219	2,400
Babe Hiskey	77	71	71	219	2,400
Larry Laoretti	72	75	72	219	2,400
Bob Wynn	73	71	75	219	2,400

Security Pacific Classic

Rancho Park Golf Course, Los Angeles, California
Par 36-35—71; 6,307 yards

October 25-27
purse, $500,000

	SCORES			TOTAL	MONEY
John Brodie	66	66	68	200	$75,000
George Archer	67	67	66	200	40,000
Chi Chi Rodriguez	66	68	66	200	40,000
(Brodie defeated Archer and Rodriguez on first extra hole.)					
Larry Laoretti	68	64	70	202	27,000
Ben Smith	68	66	68	202	27,000
Richard Rhyan	67	66	70	203	20,000
Dave Hill	70	65	69	204	18,000
Bob Charles	68	69	68	205	14,233.34
Dan Morgan	66	69	70	205	14,233.33
Lee Trevino	68	66	71	205	14,233.33
Jim Albus	73	65	68	206	10,300
Jim Dent	67	68	71	206	10,300
Al Geiberger	68	68	70	206	10,300
Harold Henning	70	66	70	206	10,300
Mike Hill	70	66	70	206	10,300
Miller Barber	66	70	71	207	7,825
Homero Blancas	69	70	68	207	7,825
Charles Coody	69	68	70	207	7,825
Dick Hendrickson	71	66	70	207	7,825
Don January	69	67	72	208	6,120
Jack Kiefer	70	68	70	208	6,120
Phil Rodgers	71	68	69	208	6,120
Tom Shaw	68	69	71	208	6,120
J.C. Snead	67	70	71	208	6,120
Jim Colbert	73	68	68	209	5,175
Gary Cowan	69	68	72	209	5,175
Bruce Devlin	69	67	74	210	4,400
Rives McBee	68	71	71	210	4,400
Arnold Palmer	70	72	68	210	4,400
Gary Player	73	69	68	210	4,400
DeWitt Weaver	71	63	76	210	4,400
Roberto De Vicenzo	70	72	69	211	3,242.86
Joe Jimenez	70	71	70	211	3,242.86
Jim O'Hern	73	72	66	211	3,242.86
Rocky Thompson	71	70	70	211	3,242.86

	SCORES			TOTAL	MONEY
Bob Wynn	70	70	71	211	3,242.86
Babe Hiskey	70	70	71	211	3,242.85
Al Kelley	71	69	71	211	3,242.85
Don Bies	70	69	73	212	2,400
Billy Casper	71	68	73	212	2,400
Lee Elder	70	69	73	212	2,400
Lloyd Moody	69	70	73	212	2,400
Larry Mowry	67	70	75	212	2,400
Bobby Nichols	73	69	70	212	2,400
Walter Zembriski	72	69	71	212	2,400

Du Pont Cup - Japan vs U.S.

Sawara Springs Country Club, Sawara City, Japan
Par 36-36—72; 6,719 yards

November 15-17
purse, $550,000

FINAL RESULT: United States 24, Japan 8

FIRST ROUND
Alternate Shot

Al Geiberger and Jim Dent defeated Shozo Miyamoto and Ryosuke Ohta, 73-74.
Charles Coody and Dale Douglass defeated Hisashi Suzumura and Teruo Suzumura, 69-72.
George Archer and Rocky Thompson defeated Hideo Jibiki and Yoshimasa Fujii, 73-75.
Hiroshi Ishii and Shigeru Uchida defeated Miller Barber and Mike Hill, 66-70.

United States 6, Japan 2.

SECOND ROUND
Better Ball

Hill and Barber defeated Hisashi and Teruo Suzumura, 62-73.
Geiberger and Dent defeated Miyamoto and Ohta, 67-73.
Archer and Thompson defeated Jibiki and Fujii, 66-69.
Douglass and Coody tied with Ishii and Uchida, 66-66.

United States 13, Japan 3.

THIRD ROUND
Singles

Hill defeated Uchida, 72-76.
Dent defeated Hisashi Suzumura, 71-76.
Geiberger defeated Teruo Suzumura, 69-71.
Douglass defeated Miyamoto, 69-73.
Coody defeated Ishii, 71-75.
Ohta defeated Thompson, 71-77.
Fujii defeated Barber, 79-81.
Archer tied with Jibiki, 72-72.

(Each U.S. player received $45,000; each Japanese player received $18,750.)

First Development Kaanapali Classic

Kaanapali Golf Club, North Course, Kaanapali, Maui, Hawaii
Par 34-36—70; 6,439 yards

December 6-8
purse, $600,000

	SCORES			TOTAL	MONEY
Jim Colbert	66	61	68	195	$90,000
Dale Douglass	63	65	69	197	51,200
George Archer	65	66	67	198	42,250
Al Geiberger	67	66	66	199	28,833.34
Lee Trevino	69	63	67	199	28,833.33
Bob Charles	68	63	68	199	28,833.33
Gene Littler	69	64	67	200	21,200
Butch Baird	69	69	63	201	16,775
Jim Albus	69	66	66	201	16,775
Jim Dent	64	67	70	201	16,775
DeWitt Weaver	68	69	65	202	14,145
Dave Stockton	66	69	68	203	12,965
Bob Rawlins	66	70	68	204	11,490
Harold Henning	71	65	68	204	11,490
Bobby Nichols	69	68	68	205	9,500
Don Massengale	70	66	69	205	9,500
Gibby Gilbert	69	66	70	205	9,500
Ben Smith	69	66	70	205	9,500
Charles Coody	66	67	72	205	9,500
Chi Chi Rodriguez	70	71	65	206	7,777.50
Don January	69	66	71	206	7,777.50
Orville Moody	73	67	67	207	6,687.50
Mike Hill	71	70	66	207	6,687.50
Jim O'Hern	69	70	68	207	6,687.50
Tommy Aaron	67	71	69	207	6,687.50
Paul Moran	67	71	70	208	5,553.75
Seiichi Kanai	70	68	70	208	5,553.75
Babe Hiskey	68	68	72	208	5,553.75
Rocky Thompson	67	69	72	208	5,553.75
John Brodie	72	68	69	209	4,832.50
Bob Wynn	68	69	72	209	4,832.50

New York Life Champions

Hyatt Dorado Beach, East Course, Dorado, Puerto Rico
Par 36-36—72; 6,740 yards

December 13-15
purse, $1,000,000

	SCORES			TOTAL	MONEY
Mike Hill	70	65	67	202	$150,000
Jim Colbert	69	69	66	204	110,000
Bob Charles	74	63	68	205	80,000
Al Geiberger	72	68	68	208	54,000
George Archer	71	67	70	208	54,000
Simon Hobday	70	71	68	209	36,000
Don January	67	71	71	209	36,000
Harold Henning	72	67	70	209	36,000
Walter Zembriski	68	72	70	210	27,666.67
Don Massengale	71	70	69	210	27,666.67
Bruce Crampton	70	68	72	210	27,666.66
Gibby Gilbert	70	74	67	211	22,625
Lee Trevino	73	70	68	211	22,625
J.C. Snead	70	72	69	211	22,625

	SCORES			TOTAL	MONEY
Terry Dill	72	67	72	211	22,625
Dave Hill	70	69	73	212	20,250
Jim Dent	70	68	74	212	20,250
Larry Laoretti	75	70	68	213	19,500
Bobby Nichols	71	74	69	214	18,250
Jim Albus	75	70	69	214	18,250
Miller Barber	73	70	71	214	18,250
Jim Ferree	71	69	74	214	18,250
Dale Douglass	71	72	72	215	17,000
Dick Hendrickson	72	71	73	216	16,250
Orville Moody	68	74	74	216	16,250
Chi Chi Rodriguez	75	73	69	217	15,083.34
Charles Coody	70	77	70	217	15,083.33
Tom Shaw	71	73	73	217	15,083.33
DeWitt Weaver	74	75	71	220	14,500
Rocky Thompson	77	73	72	222	14,250

European Tour

Girona Open

Club Golf de Pals, Girona, Spain
Par 36-36—72; 6,736 yards

February 21-24
purse, £250,000

	SCORES				TOTAL	MONEY
Steven Richardson	71	64	67	70	272	£41,660
Miguel Angel Jimenez	71	66	67	70	274	27,770
Jose Rivero	72	64	72	67	275	15,650
Per-Ulrik Johansson	70	68	71	68	277	12,500
Russell Claydon	71	72	67	68	278	10,600
Keith Waters	70	68	70	71	279	8,750
Miguel Angel Martin	75	69	68	68	280	6,087.50
Vijay Singh	72	70	68	70	280	6,087.50
Sam Torrance	70	67	72	71	280	6,087.50
Bill Longmuir	69	68	71	72	280	6,087.50
James Spence	71	68	74	68	281	4,182.50
Eoghan O'Connell	71	72	70	68	281	4,182.50
Paul Way	70	71	71	69	281	4,182.50
Jose Maria Olazabal	75	70	66	70	281	4,182.50
Robert Karlsson	70	72	72	68	282	3,595
Chris Moody	69	74	70	69	282	3,595
Paul Broadhurst	72	68	72	71	283	3,375
Lucien Tinkler	75	69	72	68	284	3,062.50
Paul Hoad	71	68	76	69	284	3,062.50
Giuseppe Cali	71	73	71	69	284	3,062.50
Philip Walton	69	72	67	76	284	3,062.50

	SCORES				TOTAL	MONEY
Emmanuel Dussart	70	74	72	69	285	2,625
Carl Mason	73	72	72	68	285	2,625
Rob Huff	71	72	72	70	285	2,625
Colin Montgomerie	69	67	78	71	285	2,625
Mark Mouland	67	73	73	72	285	2,625
Vicente Fernandez	72	70	70	73	285	2,625
Jose Maria Canizares	71	70	70	74	285	2,625
Des Smyth	75	70	71	70	286	2,093.75
Justin Hobday	71	73	72	70	286	2,093.75
Eamonn Darcy	74	71	74	67	286	2,093.75
Philip Parkin	72	71	72	71	286	2,093.75
Phillip Price	73	71	71	71	286	2,093.75
Ross McFarlane	74	68	72	72	286	2,093.75
Michael McLean	72	72	69	73	286	2,093.75
Darren Clarke	72	70	69	75	286	2,093.75
Donald Stirling	76	68	72	71	287	1,775
Manuel Pinero	74	70	72	71	287	1,775
Paul Carrigill	74	67	73	73	287	1,775
David Williams	73	71	70	73	287	1,775
Christian Hardin	75	70	71	72	288	1,525
Juan Quiros	75	70	73	70	288	1,525
Christy O'Connor, Jr.	74	71	74	69	288	1,525
Mikael Hoegberg	72	66	77	73	288	1,525
Ignacio Feliu	70	73	71	74	288	1,525
Ken Brown	71	70	72	75	288	1,525
Glen Day	76	67	74	72	289	1,300
Richard Boxall	73	72	73	71	289	1,300
Steen Tinning	71	71	71	76	289	1,300
Mark Davis	76	69	72	73	290	1,100
Juan Rosa	70	75	74	71	290	1,100
John Hawksworth	73	68	78	71	290	1,100
Ove Sellberg	69	75	76	70	290	1,100
Jose Rozadilla	76	68	77	69	290	1,100

Fujitsu Mediterranean Open

Golf d'Esterel Latitudes, St. Rafael, France
Par 36-35—71; 6,476 yards

February 28-March 3
purse, £400,000

	SCORES				TOTAL	MONEY
Ian Woosnam	70	71	71	67	279	£66,660
Michael McLean	68	70	73	71	280	44,440
Jose Maria Olazabal	70	75	68	69	282	22,520
Miguel Angel Martin	73	70	68	71	282	22,520
Grant Turner	71	70	71	72	284	16,940
Miguel Angel Jimenez	72	74	71	68	285	10,046.67
Mark James	70	74	72	69	285	10,046.67
Giuseppe Cali	70	70	74	71	285	10,046.67
Chris Moody	71	71	72	71	285	10,046.67
Jean Van de Velde	74	71	69	71	285	10,046.67
Daniel Silva	72	76	63	74	285	10,046.67
Juan Quiros	77	70	69	70	286	6,480
Peter Smith	68	77	70	71	286	6,480
Eoghan O'Connell	69	69	74	74	286	6,480
Paul Broadhurst	68	74	77	68	287	5,520
Steen Tinning	75	74	70	68	287	5,520
Carl Mason	71	71	73	72	287	5,520

	SCORES			TOTAL	MONEY
Peter Mitchell	70	76	68	73	287	5,520
Steven Richardson	71	71	75	71	288	4,565.71
Manuel Pinero	68	76	73	71	288	4,565.71
Barry Lane	73	73	71	71	288	4,565.71
Glenn Ralph	75	73	69	71	288	4,565.71
Derrick Cooper	70	70	76	72	288	4,565.71
Vijay Singh	70	72	73	73	288	4,565.71
Eamonn Darcy	70	77	67	74	288	4,565.71
Jose Davila	71	71	76	71	289	3,960
James Spence	74	73	74	68	289	3,960
Phillip Price	72	77	73	67	289	3,960
Sam Torrance	77	72	71	70	290	3,540
Peter Teravainen	69	75	72	74	290	3,540
Paul Hoad	66	74	78	72	290	3,540
Jay Townsend	72	69	76	73	290	3,540
Ove Sellberg	71	76	74	70	291	3,240
Colin Montgomerie	69	78	71	73	291	3,240
Alberto Binaghi	74	73	73	72	292	3,040
Andrew Murray	77	70	73	72	292	3,040
Mats Lanner	68	78	71	75	292	3,040
Jeremy Bennett	71	76	71	75	293	2,840
Brett Ogle	74	73	74	72	293	2,840
Costantino Rocca	75	74	74	71	294	2,440
David Williams	74	73	74	73	294	2,440
Mike Clayton	66	76	79	73	294	2,440
Paul Carrigill	71	76	75	72	294	2,440
David A. Russell	71	77	74	72	294	2,440
Philip Walton	69	76	73	76	294	2,440
Steven Bottomley	69	76	78	71	294	2,440
Mark Davis	69	71	79	75	294	2,440
Steven Bowman	71	76	75	73	295	1,960
Ronan Rafferty	75	71	76	73	295	1,960
Manuel Moreno	73	74	76	72	295	1,960
Jim Rutledge	73	75	76	71	295	1,960

Open de Baleares

Santa Ponsa Golf Club, Santa Ponsa, Majorca
Par 36-36—72; 7,152 yards

March 7-10
purse, £275,000

	SCORES			TOTAL	MONEY
Gavin Levenson	72	74	67	69	282	£45,825
Steven Richardson	71	69	72	71	283	30,530
Jose Maria Olazabal	68	72	71	73	284	17,215
Costantino Rocca	70	72	73	70	285	11,676.67
Miguel Angel Martin	69	71	71	74	285	11,676.67
Stephen Bennett	73	67	71	74	285	11,676.67
Malcolm Mackenzie	70	70	76	72	288	6,369
Miguel Fernandez	70	76	70	72	288	6,369
Tony Johnstone	72	73	72	71	288	6,369
Miguel Angel Jimenez	75	71	71	71	288	6,369
Johan Rystrom	73	70	72	73	288	6,369
Jose Maria Canizares	75	73	68	73	289	4,453.33
Per-Ulrik Johansson	71	72	76	70	289	4,453.33
Kenneth Trimble	71	74	71	73	289	4,453.33
Philip Walton	73	72	71	74	290	3,957.50
Brett Ogle	71	73	75	71	290	3,957.50

	SCORES				TOTAL	MONEY
Justin Hobday	74	71	74	72	291	3,386.67
David Feherty	70	74	75	72	291	3,386.67
Mark James	72	74	76	69	291	3,386.67
Colin Montgomerie	70	76	74	71	291	3,386.67
Vicente Fernandez	73	70	71	77	291	3,386.67
Glen Day	74	70	71	76	291	3,386.67
Vilhelm Forsbrand	72	76	72	72	292	2,889
Gordon Brand, Jr.	72	73	71	76	292	2,889
Jeremy Bennett	69	74	74	75	292	2,889
Robert Lee	72	75	72	73	292	2,889
Denis Durnian	71	75	73	73	292	2,889
Glenn Ralph	72	74	70	77	293	2,474
Anders Forsbrand	74	72	73	74	293	2,474
Carl Mason	74	69	75	75	293	2,474
Mats Lanner	75	71	72	75	293	2,474
Michael McLean	76	69	74	74	293	2,474
Martin Gates	71	77	74	72	294	2,007.50
Peter Lonard	76	69	73	76	294	2,007.50
Alberto Binaghi	73	72	76	73	294	2,007.50
Manuel Moreno	72	72	78	72	294	2,007.50
Severiano Ballesteros	73	75	78	68	294	2,007.50
Eduardo Romero	71	73	77	73	294	2,007.50
Barry Lane	71	73	76	74	294	2,007.50
Derrick Cooper	74	72	72	76	294	2,007.50
Vijay Singh	71	74	72	77	294	2,007.50
Jesper Parnevik	74	71	75	74	294	2,007.50
Fredrik Lindgren	72	73	74	76	295	1,567.50
Joakim Haeggman	71	73	75	76	295	1,567.50
Juan Anglada	72	74	77	72	295	1,567.50
Christian Hardin	73	75	73	74	295	1,567.50
David A. Russell	75	73	76	71	295	1,567.50
Peter Teravainen	75	73	71	76	295	1,567.50
Jay Townsend	74	72	69	81	296	1,127.50
Per Haugsrud	74	73	70	79	296	1,127.50
Mike Clayton	74	72	73	77	296	1,127.50
Robert Karlsson	75	70	74	77	296	1,127.50
Paul Broadhurst	76	71	76	73	296	1,127.50
Des Smyth	70	77	73	76	296	1,127.50
Steven Bowman	72	75	78	71	296	1,127.50
Stephen Hamill	74	70	76	76	296	1,127.50
Patrick Hall	73	73	76	74	296	1,127.50
Bill Longmuir	72	75	75	74	296	1,127.50

Open Catalonia

Club de Golf Bonmont Terres Noves, Tarragona, Spain
Par 36-36—72; 7,050 yards

March 14-17
purse, £300,000

	SCORES				TOTAL	MONEY
Jose Maria Olazabal	66	68	64	73	271	£50,000
David Feherty	71	73	61	72	277	33,330
Michael McLean	68	69	68	73	278	18,780
Steven Richardson	72	67	69	71	279	13,850
Eduardo Romero	67	70	70	72	279	13,850
Malcolm Mackenzie	70	71	68	74	283	10,500
Anders Forsbrand	74	71	68	71	284	8,250
Giuseppe Cali	70	70	68	76	284	8,250

	SCORES				TOTAL	MONEY
Santiago Luna	66	71	73	75	285	6,345
Miguel Angel Jimenez	72	68	68	77	285	6,345
Manuel Moreno	71	73	70	72	286	5,520
Roger Chapman	70	75	71	71	287	4,357.50
Magnus Persson	72	73	73	69	287	4,357.50
Peter Teravainen	75	68	75	69	287	4,357.50
Costantino Rocca	68	72	73	74	287	4,357.50
Eoghan O'Connell	73	72	68	74	287	4,357.50
Ova Sellberg	68	73	71	75	287	4,357.50
Richard Boxall	69	69	73	76	287	4,357.50
Jean Van de Velde	69	71	71	76	287	4,357.50
Sam Torrance	70	73	73	72	288	3,465
Miguel Angel Martin	71	74	70	73	288	3,465
Mark Roe	74	70	71	73	288	3,465
Gordon Brand, Jr.	71	69	71	77	288	3,465
Mark James	70	72	72	75	289	3,195
Jesper Parnevik	69	68	74	78	289	3,195
Manuel Calero	71	73	72	74	290	2,748.75
Martin Poxon	74	72	70	74	290	2,748.75
Ronan Rafferty	71	74	70	75	290	2,748.75
Armando Saavedra	68	73	73	76	290	2,748.75
Peter Mitchell	72	73	69	76	290	2,748.75
Kenneth Trimble	73	67	73	77	290	2,748.75
Vijay Singh	67	73	72	78	290	2,748.75
Chris Cookson	67	74	71	78	290	2,748.75
Manuel Pinero	70	75	74	72	291	2,280
Ken Brown	76	70	74	71	291	2,280
Alberto Binaghi	76	70	75	70	291	2,280
Bernard Gallacher	71	70	73	77	291	2,280
Jose Rivero	66	74	72	79	291	2,280
David J. Russell	75	70	71	76	292	2,040
Josh Maria Canizares	73	72	72	75	292	2,040
Eamonn Darcy	69	72	72	79	292	2,040
Magnus Sunesson	72	70	74	77	293	1,830
Johan Rystrom	72	74	71	76	293	1,830
Mikael Hoegberg	71	71	75	76	293	1,830
Jose Carriles	70	72	76	75	293	1,830
Gavin Levenson	72	73	72	77	294	1,560
Ernie Els	70	76	72	76	294	1,560
Grant Turner	68	78	74	74	294	1,560
Alfonso Pinero	73	71	72	78	294	1,560
Jay Townsend	71	72	72	79	294	1,560

Portuguese Open

Estela Rio Alto, Oporto, Portugal
Par 36-36—72; 6,701 yards

March 21-24
purse, £275,000

	SCORES				TOTAL	MONEY
Steven Richardson	71	67	71	74	283	£45,825
Vicente Fernandez	73	70	76	67	286	30,530
Jimmy Heggarty	72	76	71	68	287	17,215
Roger Winchester	74	72	72	70	288	11,676.67
Martin Poxon	73	69	75	71	288	11,676.67
Brian Barnes	72	72	70	74	288	11,676.67
Per-Ulrik Johansson	71	69	70	79	289	8,250
Jean Van de Velde	74	67	79	70	290	6,517.50

	SCORES				TOTAL	MONEY
Wayne Riley	72	69	77	72	290	6,517.50
Ronan Rafferty	73	70	81	67	291	5,096.67
Chris Moody	72	76	70	73	291	5,096.67
Philip Parkin	75	72	70	74	291	5,096.67
Jose Maria Canizares	73	73	75	71	292	4,052
Jose Rivero	71	70	77	74	292	4,052
Michael McLean	72	71	74	75	292	4,052
Peter Teravainen	71	76	70	75	292	4,052
Des Smyth	68	75	72	77	292	4,052
Anders Sorensen	74	72	75	72	293	3,147.22
Costantino Rocca	75	73	77	68	293	3,147.22
Peter Mitchell	74	71	75	73	293	3,147.22
Eduardo Romero	73	73	74	73	293	3,147.22
Peter Lonard	75	72	73	73	293	3,147.22
Colin Montgomerie	75	66	75	77	293	3,147.22
Mike Clayton	71	75	70	77	293	3,147.22
Tony Johnstone	72	71	72	78	293	3,147.22
Jesper Parnevik	73	71	71	78	293	3,147.22
Malcolm Mackenzie	74	73	76	71	294	2,598.75
Manuel Pinero	75	72	76	71	294	2,598.75
Denis Durnian	71	73	75	75	294	2,598.75
Justin Hobday	74	73	70	77	294	2,598.75
Glenn Ralph	74	74	74	73	295	2,288.75
Brian Marchbank	70	72	80	73	295	2,288.75
Robert Lee	78	71	76	70	295	2,288.75
Miguel Fernandez	73	74	74	74	295	2,288.75
Jose Davila	72	73	75	76	296	2,117.50
Rick Hartmann	72	75	73	76	296	2,117.50
Wraith Grant	73	75	74	75	297	1,870
Ross Drummond	75	71	77	74	297	1,870
Ove Sellberg	76	70	77	74	297	1,870
Miguel Angel Jimenez	76	69	78	74	297	1,870
Ken Brown	79	70	75	73	297	1,870
David J. Russell	71	77	76	73	297	1,870
Derrick Cooper	71	76	74	76	297	1,870
Mark Roe	76	72	75	75	298	1,540
Jeff Pinsent	79	68	76	75	298	1,540
David Gilford	71	75	78	74	298	1,540
Jeremy Bennett	70	77	78	73	298	1,540
Howard Clark	73	73	74	78	298	1,540
Andrew Sherborne	73	75	75	76	299	1,320
John Hawksworth	75	73	76	75	299	1,320
Rob Huff	73	76	68	82	299	1,320

Volvo Open di Firenze

Ugolino Golf Club, Firenze, Italy
Par 36-36—72; 6,280 yards

March 28-31
purse, £200,000

	SCORES				TOTAL	MONEY
Anders Forsbrand	71	72	66	65	274	£33,330
Barry Lane	68	69	67	71	275	22,220
Mark Roe	70	73	68	66	277	11,260
Sam Torrance	69	68	69	71	277	11,260
Mats Lanner	70	65	70	73	278	8,470
Johan Rystrom	72	68	70	69	279	7,000
Phil Golding	71	69	71	69	280	5,500

	SCORES				TOTAL	MONEY
Mark James	77	68	66	69	280	5,500
Santiago Luna	72	71	70	68	281	3,760
Adam Hunter	69	67	73	72	281	3,760
Peter Smith	69	70	69	73	281	3,760
Paul Curry	67	71	69	74	281	3,760
Gordon Brand, Jr.	69	72	65	75	281	3,760
Justin Hobday	70	75	68	69	282	3,000
Peter Lonard	68	70	71	73	282	3,000
Patrick Hall	75	71	69	68	283	2,553.33
Alberto Binaghi	75	68	71	69	283	2,553.33
Wraith Grant	72	71	69	71	283	2,553.33
Miguel Angel Martin	69	69	73	72	283	2,553.33
David R. Jones	74	66	69	74	283	2,553.33
Andre Bossert	65	75	68	75	283	2,553.33
John Hawksworth	74	72	70	68	284	2,250
Jim Rutledge	68	75	70	71	284	2,250
Robert Lee	74	69	73	69	285	2,040
Neal Briggs	73	72	72	68	285	2,040
Brian Nelson	72	74	69	70	285	2,040
Giuseppe Cali	73	70	70	72	285	2,040
Vilhelm Forsbrand	67	68	73	77	285	2,040
Roger Winchester	72	72	71	71	286	1,610.91
Robert Karlsson	74	71	71	70	286	1,610.91
David Llewellyn	71	73	73	69	286	1,610.91
Armando Saavedra	71	73	73	69	286	1,610.91
Phillip Price	73	73	72	68	286	1,610.91
Russell Claydon	67	72	74	73	286	1,610.91
Glen Day	71	72	70	73	286	1,610.91
Stephen McAllister	70	73	70	73	286	1,610.91
Peter Mitchell	70	72	70	74	286	1,610.91
Glyn Krause	67	76	69	74	286	1,610.91
Paul Broadhurst	68	70	70	78	286	1,610.91
Andrew Sherborne	70	75	71	71	287	1,280
Jean Van de Velde	70	74	72	71	287	1,280
Martin Gates	72	73	74	68	287	1,280
David Gilford	66	80	69	72	287	1,280
John McHenry	69	71	73	74	287	1,280
Darren Clarke	74	68	73	73	288	1,040
Peter McWhinney	73	71	72	72	288	1,040
Steven Bowman	73	71	74	70	288	1,040
Miguel Fernandez	71	74	74	69	288	1,040
Ken Brown	70	72	72	74	288	1,040
Emmanuel Dussart	72	70	71	75	288	1,040
Andrea Canessa	70	72	70	76	288	1,040

Jersey European Airways Open

LaMoye Golf Club, Jersey
Par 36-36—72; 6,817 yards

April 11-14
purse, £200,000

	SCORES				TOTAL	MONEY
Sam Torrance	68	69	69	73	279	£33,330
Mark Davis	72	71	66	71	280	22,220
Mats Lanner	72	69	68	73	282	10,330
Anders Sorensen	70	67	70	75	282	10,330
Jeff Hawkes	70	65	73	74	282	10,330
Christy O'Connor, Jr.	75	68	68	73	284	5,615

	SCORES				TOTAL	MONEY
Colin Montgomerie	71	69	71	73	284	5,615
James Spence	67	73	69	75	284	5,615
Craig Parry	70	65	75	74	284	5,615
Phillip Price	73	71	68	73	285	3,480
Eamonn Darcy	74	68	66	77	285	3,480
Des Smyth	71	70	68	76	285	3,480
Ross Drummond	68	72	71	74	285	3,480
Denis Durnian	69	70	72	74	285	3,480
Glenn Ralph	73	69	69	75	286	2,608.57
Frank Nobilo	69	74	68	75	286	2,608.57
Paul Curry	68	73	70	75	286	2,608.57
Gordon Brand, Jr.	73	67	71	75	286	2,608.57
Steven Richardson	73	66	72	75	286	2,608.57
Roger Chapman	70	68	71	77	286	2,608.57
Brian Marchbank	67	70	75	74	286	2,608.57
Richard Boxall	71	71	70	75	287	2,250
Jim Rutledge	69	69	72	77	287	2,250
Keith Waters	70	72	74	72	288	1,980
Philip Walton	72	70	72	74	288	1,980
Darren Prosser	70	74	65	79	288	1,980
Barry Lane	73	72	70	73	288	1,980
Steven Bowman	72	70	73	73	288	1,980
Brian Barnes	71	70	71	76	288	1,980
Tony Charnley	69	71	73	75	288	1,980
Peter O'Malley	69	74	70	76	289	1,644
David Feherty	71	72	75	71	289	1,644
Wayne Stephens	73	71	69	76	289	1,644
Rodger Davis	71	71	75	72	289	1,644
David Gilford	69	73	71	76	289	1,644
Derrick Cooper	72	72	71	75	290	1,480
Anders Forsbrand	73	72	76	69	290	1,480
Andrew Hare	71	70	73	76	290	1,480
Martin Gates	72	71	70	78	291	1,320
Peter Baker	71	73	70	77	291	1,320
Patrick Hall	72	70	74	75	291	1,320
John Hawksworth	72	69	75	75	291	1,320
Michael McLean	72	69	78	72	291	1,320
Wayne Riley	73	72	75	72	292	1,100
Jeremy Bennett	75	70	71	76	292	1,100
Paul Way	70	71	73	78	292	1,100
Martin Poxon	71	69	77	75	292	1,100
Chris Moody	69	68	75	80	292	1,100
Bill Malley	69	68	74	81	292	1,100

Benson & Hedges International Open

St. Mellion Golf & Country Club, Saltash, Cornwall, England
Par 36-36—72; 7,054 yards

April 18-21
purse, £400,000

	SCORES				TOTAL	MONEY
Bernhard Langer	73	68	75	70	286	£66,660
Vijay Singh	74	75	69	70	288	44,440
Philip Walton	70	69	77	73	289	22,520
Jose Rivero	72	73	67	77	289	22,520
Mark Roe	74	72	73	71	290	13,235
Craig Parry	75	74	70	71	290	13,235
Gordon Brand, Jr.	72	74	69	75	290	13,235

	SCORES				TOTAL	MONEY
Steven Richardson	73	75	73	69	290	13,235
Costantino Rocca	75	74	73	73	295	8,920
David Feherty	77	73	74	72	296	6,960
Joakim Haeggman	76	75	78	67	296	6,960
Barry Lane	76	73	72	75	296	6,960
Peter Senior	75	76	73	72	296	6,960
Glen Day	75	76	71	74	296	6,960
Christy O'Connor, Jr.	71	76	77	73	297	5,640
Jose Maria Olazabal	72	77	71	77	297	5,640
Paul Curry	73	77	70	77	297	5,640
David Williams	75	78	75	70	298	4,766.67
Greg J. Turner	79	73	71	75	298	4,766.67
Mark McNulty	75	72	80	71	298	4,766.67
Sandy Lyle	74	82	70	72	298	4,766.67
Andrew Sherborne	75	74	75	74	298	4,766.67
Eduardo Romero	72	74	79	73	298	4,766.67
Peter Teravainen	74	76	78	71	299	4,140
Eamonn Darcy	74	73	75	77	299	4,140
Michael McLean	75	80	73	71	299	4,140
Wayne Riley	77	79	70	73	299	4,140
Ronan Rafferty	72	84	73	71	300	3,720
Gavin Levenson	74	81	71	74	300	3,720
Rodger Davis	72	76	79	73	300	3,720
Paul Broadhurst	72	74	82	73	301	3,330
Santiago Luna	73	79	74	75	301	3,330
Roger Chapman	75	81	72	73	301	3,330
Kenneth Trimble	83	71	76	71	301	3,330
James Spence	72	78	73	79	302	3,040
Patrick Hall	77	77	76	72	302	3,040
Steven Bottomley	75	79	74	74	302	3,040
Anders Sorensen	73	79	77	74	303	2,760
Peter Baker	76	75	75	77	303	2,760
Phillip Price	74	82	75	72	303	2,760
Des Smyth	72	83	74	74	303	2,760
Chris Williams	78	78	75	73	304	2,400
Frank Nobilo	75	77	78	74	304	2,400
Glenn Ralph	74	78	75	77	304	2,400
David Gilford	77	79	76	72	304	2,400
Steven Bowman	76	80	75	73	304	2,400
Ken Brown	73	78	78	76	305	2,000
Malcolm Mackenzie	73	76	81	75	305	2,000
Nick Faldo	70	80	82	73	305	2,000
Manuel Pinero	77	77	77	74	305	2,000
Stephen Hamill	75	80	80	70	305	2,000

Madrid Open

Real Club de la Puerta de Hierro, Madrid, Spain
Par 36-36—72; 6,941 yards

April 25-28
purse, £275,000

	SCORES				TOTAL	MONEY
Andrew Sherborne	70	67	69	66	272	£45,825
Miguel Angel Martin	69	67	67	70	273	30,530
Mark James	71	72	67	65	275	17,215
Vijay Singh	71	68	70	67	276	13,750
Mats Lanner	72	66	70	69	277	11,655
Des Smyth	72	69	70	67	278	9,625

	SCORES				TOTAL	MONEY
Santiago Luna	74	66	71	68	279	7,095
Paul Curry	70	67	74	68	279	7,095
David Feherty	70	68	73	68	279	7,095
Glenn Ralph	71	70	67	72	280	5,280
Darren Clarke	70	71	70	69	280	5,280
Eduardo Romero	73	66	72	70	281	4,255
Vicente Fernandez	74	70	68	69	281	4,255
Gavin Levenson	73	73	66	69	281	4,255
Martin Gates	72	70	71	68	281	4,255
Denis Durnian	74	71	68	68	281	4,255
Jose Carriles	70	74	68	70	282	3,632.50
Yago Beamonte	73	70	72	67	282	3,632.50
Eoghan O'Connell	69	73	71	70	283	3,263.75
Daniel Silva	71	69	71	72	283	3,263.75
Juan Quiros	74	71	70	68	283	3,263.75
Jay Townsend	74	70	72	67	283	3,263.75
*Luis Gabarda	74	70	70	69	283	
David Gilford	72	69	74	69	284	2,971.67
Sam Torrance	73	70	73	68	284	2,971.67
Eamonn Darcy	73	69	72	70	284	2,971.67
James Spence	73	71	72	69	285	2,598.33
Jose Rivero	70	73	69	73	285	2,598.33
Russell Claydon	66	72	74	73	285	2,598.33
Simon Hobday	73	71	71	70	285	2,598.33
Giuseppe Cali	73	71	70	71	285	2,598.33
Ronald Stelten	71	73	72	69	285	2,598.33
Steven Bowman	72	74	70	70	286	2,227.50
Robert Lee	72	74	68	72	286	2,227.50
John Bland	71	70	73	72	286	2,227.50
Philip Walton	76	67	75	68	286	2,227.50
Ignacio Gervas	73	70	74	70	287	1,925
Anders Forsbrand	77	67	72	71	287	1,925
Peter Fowler	72	71	73	71	287	1,925
Craig Parry	71	69	72	75	287	1,925
Paul Way	73	68	73	73	287	1,925
Manuel Pinero	75	70	72	70	287	1,925
Armando Saavedra	76	70	73	68	287	1,925
Tony Charnley	73	72	71	72	288	1,540
Peter Teravainen	71	72	72	73	288	1,540
David J. Russell	69	72	70	77	288	1,540
Juan Anglada	76	69	75	68	288	1,540
Christy O'Connor, Jr.	72	72	72	72	288	1,540
Derrick Cooper	75	71	70	72	288	1,540
Emilio Rodriguez	74	72	69	73	288	1,540
Grant Turner	73	72	73	71	289	1,265
Michael McLean	73	70	74	72	289	1,265
Robert Karlsson	74	70	73	72	289	1,265

Credit Lyonnais Cannes Open

Cannes Mougins Golf Club, Cannes
Par 36-36—72; 6,896 yards

May 2-5
purse, £350,000

	SCORES				TOTAL	MONEY
David Feherty	69	68	69	69	275	£58,330
Craig Parry	72	71	67	68	278	38,880
Mark McNulty	70	66	70	73	279	21,910

	SCORES				TOTAL	MONEY
Steven Richardson	72	70	66	72	280	17,500
Eamonn Darcy	70	70	70	71	281	13,540
Jean Ignace Mouhica	68	70	72	71	281	13,540
Costantino Rocca	68	75	68	71	282	9,625
Stephen Hamill	67	70	74	71	282	9,625
Mark Roe	71	69	71	72	283	7,086.67
Adam Hunter	77	67	70	69	283	7,086.67
Haydn Selby-Green	72	71	69	71	283	7,086.67
Vicente Fernandez	73	69	74	68	284	5,825
Anders Sorensen	70	69	76	69	284	5,825
Ken Brown	70	69	70	76	285	5,036.25
Malcolm Mackenzie	71	73	71	70	285	5,036.25
Brian Marchbank	70	71	77	67	285	5,036.25
John Hawksworth	71	71	73	70	285	5,036.25
Jimmy Heggarty	71	72	71	72	286	4,351.67
Joakim Haeggman	73	70	72	71	286	4,351.67
Peter Teravainen	71	73	73	69	286	4,351.67
Stephen McAllister	73	71	68	75	287	3,675
Andrew Sherborne	73	71	70	73	287	3,675
Howard Clark	70	73	70	74	287	3,675
Jean Francois Remesy	76	68	70	73	287	3,675
Brian Barnes	69	71	73	74	287	3,675
James Spence	71	73	71	72	287	3,675
Glenn Ralph	71	74	70	72	287	3,675
Phillip Price	71	70	74	72	287	3,675
David Williams	66	71	75	75	287	3,675
Barry Lane	70	72	74	72	288	2,885
David J. Russell	73	70	68	77	288	2,885
Laurent Lassalle	72	69	71	76	288	2,885
Marc Pendaries	72	73	73	70	288	2,885
Tim Planchin	74	70	71	73	288	2,885
Manuel Moreno	73	72	70	73	288	2,885
Mikael Hoegberg	76	69	71	72	288	2,885
Vijay Singh	72	73	71	73	289	2,520
Ronan Rafferty	71	71	72	75	289	2,520
Des Smyth	73	68	74	74	289	2,520
Michael McLean	78	67	74	71	290	2,135
John Bland	68	72	76	74	290	2,135
Miguel Angel Martin	72	70	75	73	290	2,135
Magnus Persson	76	68	71	75	290	2,135
Alberto Binaghi	72	72	74	72	290	2,135
Gavin Levenson	71	72	74	73	290	2,135
Jose Davila	75	69	74	72	290	2,135
Mike Clayton	70	71	73	76	290	2,135
Vilhelm Forsbrand	75	69	78	69	291	1,610
Patrice Barquez	74	67	71	79	291	1,610
Denis Durnian	66	74	76	75	291	1,610
Ross Drummond	75	69	74	73	291	1,610
Steven Bowman	72	73	72	74	291	1,610
Peter Lonard	72	73	76	70	291	1,610
Neal Briggs	71	73	72	75	291	1,610

Peugeot Spanish Open

Club de Campo, Madrid, Spain
Par 36-36—72; 6,966 yards

May 9-12
purse, £350,000

	SCORES				TOTAL	MONEY
Eduardo Romero	68	63	72	72	275	£58,330
Severiano Ballesteros	63	70	67	75	275	38,880
(Romero defeated Ballesteros on seventh extra hole.)						
Vijay Singh	68	71	71	70	280	21,910
Ross McFarlane	72	69	70	70	281	16,165
Bernhard Langer	69	73	68	71	281	16,165
Glen Day	70	67	76	70	283	12,250
Steven Richardson	75	69	70	70	284	10,500
Sam Torrance	74	67	70	74	285	8,750
Colin Montgomerie	73	68	71	74	286	7,820
Joakim Haeggman	77	66	70	74	287	5,930
Jose Davila	70	73	72	72	287	5,930
Robert Lee	74	69	74	70	287	5,930
Tony Johnstone	73	73	69	72	287	5,930
Michael McLean	73	71	71	72	287	5,930
Rodger Davis	70	75	72	70	287	5,930
Armando Saavedra	72	70	76	70	288	4,723.33
Vicente Fernandez	76	71	72	69	288	4,723.33
Paul Way	70	72	74	72	288	4,723.33
Mark Davis	71	69	73	76	289	4,102
Frank Nobilo	75	70	76	68	289	4,102
Sandy Lyle	74	70	73	72	289	4,102
David Williams	70	72	73	74	289	4,102
Santiago Luna	76	70	72	71	289	4,102
Peter Teravainen	75	68	71	76	290	3,622.50
Greg J. Turner	70	72	74	74	290	3,622.50
David Feherty	75	69	72	74	290	3,622.50
Thomas Levet	72	74	75	69	290	3,622.50
Chris Williams	73	72	73	73	291	2,940
John Hawksworth	74	73	72	72	291	2,940
Glenn Ralph	72	75	70	74	291	2,940
Andre Bossert	72	74	71	74	291	2,940
Manuel Calero	71	73	76	71	291	2,940
Jose Maria Olazabal	73	74	72	72	291	2,940
Mark Roe	74	71	70	76	291	2,940
Jesper Parnevik	72	73	76	70	291	2,940
Olivier Edmond	72	74	72	73	291	2,940
Jose Maria Canizares	73	71	73	74	291	2,940
Peter Hedblom	71	71	75	75	292	2,345
Jimmy Heggarty	73	74	72	73	292	2,345
Manuel Pinero	71	72	75	74	292	2,345
Des Smyth	73	70	76	73	292	2,345
Anders Forsbrand	73	73	72	74	292	2,345
John Bland	74	70	73	75	292	2,345
Marc Farry	71	75	75	72	293	1,855
Justin Hobday	76	67	76	74	293	1,855
Robert Karlsson	70	75	76	72	293	1,855
Mark McNulty	70	73	74	76	293	1,855
David Gilford	74	72	73	74	293	1,855
Torsten Giedeon	75	71	74	73	293	1,855
Manuel Moreno	75	70	72	76	293	1,855
Peter Fowler	75	71	70	77	293	1,855

Lancia Martini Italian Open

Castelconturbia Golf Club, Milan, Italy
Par 36-36—72; 6,852 yards

May 16-19
purse, £325,400

	SCORES				TOTAL	MONEY
Craig Parry	71	71	67	70	279	£54,212.77
Ian Woosnam	69	71	73	67	280	36,120.15
Costantino Rocca	69	73	74	66	282	20,370.46
Martin Gates	71	71	73	70	285	15,033.80
David Gilford	70	70	71	74	285	15,033.80
Stephen McAllister	72	70	73	71	286	10,575.72
Paul Way	68	73	75	70	286	10,575.72
Colin Montgomerie	71	72	72	72	287	8,135.17
Jose Maria Olazabal	70	79	73	66	288	6,898.63
Chris Cookson	72	73	68	75	288	6,898.63
Wayne Riley	68	75	77	69	289	5,987.48
Mark Davis	70	73	73	74	290	5,418.03
Adam Hunter	72	73	75	70	290	5,418.03
Anders Forsbrand	75	73	74	69	291	4,783.48
Jose Cantero	72	73	72	74	291	4,783.48
Robert Karlsson	72	74	71	74	291	4,783.48
David Williams	70	73	75	74	292	4,392.99
David J. Russell	73	76	74	70	293	4,045.89
Vijay Singh	73	75	75	70	293	4,045.89
Paolo Quirici	73	69	75	76	293	4,045.89
Sam Torrance	72	77	73	72	294	3,758.45
Kenneth Trimble	71	79	71	73	294	3,758.45
Jose Maria Canizares	74	75	77	69	295	3,612.02
Howard Clark	72	77	72	75	296	3,270.34
Peter Senior	74	72	77	73	296	3,270.34
Chris Platts	74	71	72	79	296	3,270.34
James Spence	74	74	73	75	296	3,270.34
Frank Nobilo	73	74	74	75	296	3,270.34
Glen Day	73	72	77	74	296	3,270.34
Mike Miller	72	78	71	76	297	2,717.15
Alessandro Rogato	74	70	77	76	297	2,717.15
Peter O'Malley	73	76	77	71	297	2,717.15
Baldovino Dassu	74	73	75	75	297	2,717.15
Tony Johnstone	73	73	79	72	297	2,717.15
Ken Brown	75	75	72	75	297	2,717.15
Jim Rutledge	73	74	76	75	298	2,375.47
Justin Hobday	72	78	74	74	298	2,375.47
Wraith Grant	73	74	77	74	298	2,375.47
Mikael Hoegberg	72	74	76	76	298	2,375.47
Anders Gillner	70	73	79	77	299	2,180.23
Quentin Dabson	72	73	76	78	299	2,180.23
Jose Davila	75	76	77	72	300	2,050.06
Peter Mitchell	72	74	81	73	300	2,050.06
Miguel Angel Jimenez	79	70	72	80	301	1,822.28
Ove Sellberg	71	80	79	71	301	1,822.28
Phillip Price	74	75	77	75	301	1,822.28
Andrew Sherborne	73	77	74	77	301	1,822.28
Jose Coceres	73	73	75	80	301	1,822.28
Peter Teravainen	76	75	72	79	302	1,399.25
Lee Vannet	73	72	77	80	302	1,399.25
Miguel Fernandez	74	73	81	74	302	1,399.25
Ross Drummond	73	78	75	76	302	1,399.25
Jose Rivero	75	74	80	73	302	1,399.25
Andrew Hare	72	78	75	77	302	1,399.25

	SCORES				TOTAL	MONEY
Neal Briggs	73	75	82	72	302	1,399.25
Roger Chapman	75	76	77	74	302	1,399.25

Volvo PGA Championship

Wentworth Club, West Course, Virginia Water, England
Par 35-37—72; 6,945 yards

May 24-27
purse, £500,000

	SCORES				TOTAL	MONEY
Severiano Ballesteros	67	69	65	70	271	£83,330
Colin Montgomerie	69	66	69	67	271	55,550
(Ballesteros defeated Montgomerie on first extra hole.)						
Eamonn Darcy	69	66	70	67	272	31,300
Bernhard Langer	67	67	69	70	273	25,000
Jesper Parnevik	73	67	65	69	274	19,350
Nick Faldo	69	70	65	70	274	19,350
Gordon Brand, Jr.	66	69	71	70	276	15,000
Rodger Davis	71	66	68	72	277	10,710
Jose Rivero	69	70	69	69	277	10,710
Johan Rystrom	68	69	68	72	277	10,710
Sandy Lyle	71	72	69	65	277	10,710
Ian Woosnam	70	70	66	72	278	8,590
Peter Teravainen	67	71	74	67	279	7,845
David Feherty	70	73	70	66	279	7,845
Anders Forsbrand	71	70	73	66	280	6,760
Wayne Riley	63	71	71	75	280	6,760
Stephen Field	69	68	71	72	280	6,760
Brian Barnes	68	70	68	74	280	6,760
Steven Richardson	69	66	74	71	280	6,760
Anders Sorensen	72	70	71	68	281	5,925
Mark James	67	68	77	69	281	5,925
Bryan Norton	68	70	74	70	282	5,250
Sam Torrance	70	73	70	69	282	5,250
Craig Parry	72	68	70	72	282	5,250
Gavin Levenson	70	69	73	70	282	5,250
John Bland	71	69	72	70	282	5,250
Eduardo Romero	71	68	70	73	282	5,250
Phillip Price	71	70	69	72	282	5,250
Richard Boxall	68	68	73	74	283	4,500
Peter Senior	72	70	72	69	283	4,500
Peter Mitchell	77	65	69	72	283	4,500
Mark Davis	69	70	71	74	284	4,150
Jose Davila	69	69	71	75	284	4,150
Peter Smith	68	70	71	76	285	3,800
David J. Russell	70	73	71	71	285	3,800
Magnus Sunesson	70	69	76	70	285	3,800
Mike Harwood	71	70	72	72	285	3,800
Glenn Ralph	69	70	74	72	285	3,800
Giuseppe Cali	71	68	74	73	286	3,400
Peter O'Malley	73	69	74	70	286	3,400
Russell Claydon	67	75	74	70	286	3,400
Malcolm Mackenzie	70	71	73	73	287	3,100
Mats Lanner	74	68	74	71	287	3,100
Frank Nobilo	69	71	74	73	287	3,100
David Gilford	72	67	78	71	288	2,650
Paul Broadhurst	75	67	70	76	288	2,650
Jim Rutledge	76	67	72	73	288	2,650

	SCORES				TOTAL	MONEY
Andrew Sherborne	71	71	72	74	288	2,650
Jose Maria Olazabal	70	72	72	74	288	2,650
Mike Miller	70	69	78	71	288	2,650

Dunhill British Masters

Woburn Golf and Country Club, Bucks, England
Par 34-38—72; 6,940 yards

May 30-June 2
purse, £450,000

	SCORES				TOTAL	MONEY
Severiano Ballesteros	66	66	68	75	275	£75,000
Tony Johnstone	67	75	68	68	278	27,096
Eamonn Darcy	69	67	71	71	278	27,096
Sam Torrance	70	68	71	69	278	27,096
Keith Waters	69	67	73	69	278	27,096
David Gilford	72	72	65	69	278	27,096
Ross McFarlane	72	69	72	67	280	13,500
Tony Charnley	73	70	66	72	281	11,250
Ian Woosnam	71	69	71	71	282	9,110
Peter O'Malley	70	69	73	70	282	9,110
Gordon Brand, Jr.	68	72	75	67	282	9,110
Brett Ogle	69	71	75	68	283	6,532.50
Philip Walton	69	70	73	71	283	6,532.50
Stephen McAllister	74	70	69	70	283	6,532.50
Brian Barnes	72	72	69	70	283	6,532.50
Costantino Rocca	70	71	69	73	283	6,532.50
Vijay Singh	71	70	72	70	283	6,532.50
Ronan Rafferty	75	67	72	69	283	6,532.50
Mark Calcavecchia	70	66	74	73	283	6,532.50
Hugh Baiocchi	68	73	71	72	284	5,197.50
John Bland	69	70	76	69	284	5,197.50
Mike Harwood	73	72	71	68	284	5,197.50
Jean Van de Velde	71	73	72	68	284	5,197.50
Paul Way	71	68	76	70	285	4,320
Rodger Davis	72	71	72	70	285	4,320
Mark James	70	68	73	74	285	4,320
Peter Fowler	70	75	69	71	285	4,320
Howard Clark	70	70	70	75	285	4,320
Martin Poxon	69	72	73	71	285	4,320
Steven Richardson	72	66	75	72	285	4,320
Miguel Angel Jimenez	70	72	73	70	285	4,320
Mats Lanner	73	71	68	73	285	4,320
Juan Quiros	73	71	70	72	286	3,600
Bryan Norton	71	74	71	70	286	3,600
Colin Montgomerie	66	73	77	70	286	3,600
Bernard Gallacher	72	72	73	70	287	3,150
Manuel Pinero	72	72	71	72	287	3,150
Jose Maria Canizares	72	70	69	76	287	3,150
Danny Mijovic	70	72	69	76	287	3,150
Robert Lee	74	67	73	73	287	3,150
Stephen Bennett	72	72	70	73	287	3,150
Peter Mitchell	68	70	77	72	287	3,150
David A. Russell	72	71	72	73	288	2,655
Derrick Cooper	70	70	75	73	288	2,655
Stephen Hamill	68	71	78	71	288	2,655
Philip Parkin	68	71	72	77	288	2,655
Peter McWhinney	69	73	72	75	289	2,160

	SCORES				TOTAL	MONEY
Peter Smith	70	73	70	76	289	2,160
David J. Russell	72	69	73	75	289	2,160
Barry Lane	73	70	74	72	289	2,160
Miguel Angel Martin	73	71	73	72	289	2,160
Rick Hartmann	73	69	77	70	289	2,160
Russell Claydon	71	74	73	71	289	2,160

Murphy's Cup

Fulford Golf Club, York, England
Par 36-36—72; 6,807 yards

June 6-9
purse, £350,000

	SCORES				TOTAL	MONEY
Tony Johnstone	10	9	9	12	40	£58,330
Eamonn Darcy	13	9	11	7	40	38,860
(Johnstone defeated Darcy on second extra hole.)						
Stephen Field	15	12	7	4	38	19,705
Peter O'Malley	10	6	8	14	38	19,705
Ross McFarlane	9	15	8	5	37	13,540
Peter Baker	5	12	10	10	37	13,540
Sam Torrance	8	10	3	14	35	10,500
Martin Poxon	6	6	8	14	34	8,765
Adam Hunter	4	11	8	9	32	7,071.67
Jay Townsend	2	10	12	8	32	7,071.67
Colin Montgomerie	7	9	9	7	32	7,071.67
Ian Woosnam	14	6	4	7	31	5,608.33
Mike Harwood	13	15	3	0	31	5,608.33
Jose Rivero	16	4	4	7	31	5,608.33
Des Smyth	11	4	9	6	30	4,615
Christy O'Connor, Jr.	10	10	9	1	30	4,615
Per-Ulrik Johansson	13	10	4	3	30	4,615
Ronan Rafferty	7	9	7	7	30	4,615
Mark James	8	7	8	7	30	4,615
Jean Van de Velde	11	8	5	5	29	3,892
James Spence	9	7	13	0	29	3,892
Barry Lane	14	5	5	5	29	3,892
Carl Mason	5	9	9	6	29	3,892
Russell Claydon	7	6	9	7	29	3,892
Jesper Parnevik	12	3	8	5	28	3,530
Paul Curry	7	6	8	7	28	3,530
Paul Way	4	10	6	7	27	3,151.67
Philip Walton	6	11	7	3	27	3,151.67
Manuel Moreno	10	12	7	-2	27	3,151.67
Manuel Pinero	9	3	10	5	27	3,151.67
Howard Clark	14	4	0	9	27	3,151.67
Peter Smith	8	6	9	4	27	3,151.67
Anders Forsbrand	11	6	6	3	26	2,800
David A. Russell	10	6	8	2	26	2,800
Gordon Brand, Jr.	8	7	8	3	26	2,800
Miguel Angel Martin	11	4	8	2	25	2,555
Mark Roe	10	6	7	2	25	2,555
Peter Teravainen	12	4	7	2	25	2,555
Mark Davis	8	6	11	0	25	2,555
Peter Senior	10	4	-1	11	24	2,275
Stephen McAllister	10	6	3	5	24	2,275
John Morse	9	4	7	4	24	2,275
Kenneth Trimble	5	9	9	1	24	2,275

	SCORES				TOTAL	MONEY
Mark Mouland	12	2	13	-4	23	2,065
Darren Clarke	5	6	5	7	23	2,065
Peter Mitchell	8	6	4	4	22	1,925
Sandy Lyle	6	11	4	1	22	1,925
Alberto Binaghi	6	10	1	4	21	1,820
Jose Maria Canizares	4	8	8	0	20	1,640
Emmanuel Dussart	6	7	5	2	20	1,640
Wayne Westner	16	1	3	0	20	1,640
Richard Boxall	9	4	6	1	20	1,640
Fredrik Lindgren	2	10	10	-2	20	1,640

Renault Belgian Open

Royal Waterloo Golf Club, Brussels, Belgium
Par 35-37—72; 6,803 yards

June 13-16
purse, £250,000

	SCORES				TOTAL	MONEY
Per-Ulrik Johansson	68	70	70	68	276	£41,660
Paul Broadhurst	67	71	69	69	276	27,770
(Johansson defeated Broadhurst on first extra hole.)						
Chris Williams	70	73	70	64	277	15,650
Jorge Berendt	70	71	70	67	278	12,500
Robert Karlsson	70	69	68	73	280	10,600
Daniel Silva	73	66	71	71	281	7,500
Mats Lanner	75	72	65	69	281	7,500
Bill Longmuir	71	69	72	69	281	7,500
Eoghan O'Connell	74	70	69	69	282	5,300
Costantino Rocca	70	72	70	70	282	5,300
Robert Lee	74	70	68	71	283	4,182.50
Jeremy Bennett	73	74	69	67	283	4,182.50
Barry Lane	70	71	72	70	283	4,182.50
David James	72	67	70	74	283	4,182.50
Paul Way	67	72	70	75	284	3,521.67
David Gilford	72	73	70	69	284	3,521.67
Alberto Binaghi	76	70	71	67	284	3,521.67
Luis Carbonetti	69	71	73	72	285	2,979.17
Juan Anglada	70	69	72	74	285	2,979.17
Mark James	72	71	75	67	285	2,979.17
Danny Mijovic	75	72	69	69	285	2,979.17
Jean Van de Velde	74	68	70	73	285	2,979.17
Gordon Brand, Jr.	73	71	69	72	285	2,979.17
David J. Russell	75	72	71	68	286	2,587.50
Michael McLean	71	68	74	73	286	2,587.50
James Spence	70	69	73	74	286	2,587.50
Paul Carrigill	69	76	70	71	286	2,587.50
Marc Farry	72	73	74	68	287	2,127.78
Patrick Hall	74	74	70	69	287	2,127.78
Santiago Luna	71	72	73	71	287	2,127.78
Mark Mouland	72	71	72	72	287	2,127.78
Roger Winchester	75	73	74	65	287	2,127.78
Chris Cookson	72	74	72	69	287	2,127.78
Hugh Baiocchi	73	71	71	72	287	2,127.78
Chris Patton	72	71	72	72	287	2,127.78
Carl Mason	74	72	68	73	287	2,127.78
Jeff Pinsent	74	69	74	71	288	1,750
David A. Russell	72	72	72	72	288	1,750
Stephen Bennett	73	75	67	73	288	1,750

	SCORES				TOTAL	MONEY
Jay Townsend	78	70	70	70	288	1,750
Paul Carman	75	73	70	70	288	1,750
Armando Saavedra	73	69	75	72	289	1,475
Paul Curry	74	74	69	72	289	1,475
Miguel Fernandez	77	69	75	68	289	1,475
Sven Struver	72	71	69	77	289	1,475
Lucien Tinkler	72	70	71	76	289	1,475
Ossie Moore	69	72	77	71	289	1,475
Mark Litton	74	74	71	71	290	1,175
Peter Baker	71	71	73	75	290	1,175
Fredrik Lindgren	75	73	72	70	290	1,175
Andrew Hare	72	72	72	74	290	1,175
Jim Rutledge	74	72	70	74	290	1,175
Anders Gillner	71	76	71	72	290	1,175

Carrolls Irish Open

Killarney Golf Club, County Kerry, Ireland
Par 35-37—72; 7,061 yards

June 20-23
purse, £365,800

	SCORES				TOTAL	MONEY
Nick Faldo	68	75	70	70	283	£60,960.22
Colin Montgomerie	68	72	76	70	286	40,640.15
Carl Mason	69	73	76	69	287	20,594.42
Frank Nobilo	72	70	74	71	287	20,594.42
Ross Drummond	75	75	69	69	288	14,147.24
Jose Maria Olazabal	71	70	75	72	288	14,147.24
Craig Parry	69	78	72	70	289	10,059.45
Philip Walton	74	72	72	71	289	10,059.45
Russell Claydon	69	75	72	74	290	7,123.91
Eduardo Romero	73	77	71	69	290	7,123.91
Howard Clark	74	73	75	68	290	7,123.91
David Feherty	77	73	75	65	290	7,123.91
Christy O'Connor, Jr.	76	70	77	68	291	5,889.35
Peter O'Malley	71	71	79	71	292	5,486.97
Mark Davis	69	76	76	71	292	5,486.97
Armando Saavedra	69	75	77	72	293	4,748.05
Vijay Singh	75	75	73	70	293	4,748.05
Payne Stewart	69	71	77	76	293	4,748.05
Bernhard Langer	75	73	72	73	293	4,748.05
David Williams	78	74	74	67	293	4,748.05
Grant Turner	78	73	70	73	294	4,224.97
Hugh Baiocchi	74	76	75	69	294	4,224.97
Malcolm Mackenzie	69	75	80	71	295	3,731.14
Mark Calcavecchia	74	73	78	70	295	3,731.14
Martin Gates	72	69	79	75	295	3,731.14
Steven Bowman	78	74	73	70	295	3,731.14
Peter Mitchell	73	73	77	72	295	3,731.14
Thomas Levet	76	74	76	69	295	3,731.14
Robert Karlsson	72	73	79	71	295	3,731.14
Jeff Hawkes	72	76	78	70	296	3,094.65
Tony Charnley	70	81	74	71	296	3,094.65
Darren Clarke	77	75	76	68	296	3,094.65
Richard Boxall	74	73	77	72	296	3,094.65
Derrick Cooper	79	73	76	68	296	3,094.65
Fredrik Lindgren	75	76	76	70	297	2,633.74
Magnus Persson	71	76	77	73	297	2,633.74

	SCORES				TOTAL	MONEY
Mark Roe	77	74	75	71	297	2,633.74
Mark Mouland	74	73	80	70	297	2,633.74
Gordon Brand, Jr.	69	73	83	72	297	2,633.74
Steven Richardson	73	76	74	74	297	2,633.74
Rick Hartmann	74	72	77	74	297	2,633.74
Bill Longmuir	74	72	78	74	298	2,194.79
Miguel Ángel Martin	75	77	71	75	298	2,194.79
Glenn Ralph	74	77	77	70	298	2,194.79
Wayne Westner	73	79	75	71	298	2,194.79
Roger Chapman	72	73	76	77	298	2,194.79
Miguel Fernandez	73	79	76	71	299	1,828.99
Sandy Stephen	75	75	77	72	299	1,828.99
Greg J. Turner	75	77	76	71	299	1,828.99
Mike Miller	74	73	81	71	299	1,828.99
James Spence	76	74	76	73	299	1,828.99

Peugeot French Open

National Golf Club, Paris, France
Par 36-36—72; 6,994 yards

June 27-30
purse, £400,000

	SCORES				TOTAL	MONEY
Eduardo Romero	69	69	67	76	281	£66,660
Jose Maria Olazabal	74	67	68	74	283	34,740
Sam Torrance	72	70	72	69	283	34,740
Nick Faldo	73	73	67	71	284	20,000
Robert Lee	70	74	74	67	285	16,940
Colin Montgomerie	75	68	73	70	286	11,230
Paul Broadhurst	72	68	74	72	286	11,230
Gordon Brand, Jr.	72	70	74	70	286	11,230
Vijay Singh	70	70	73	73	286	11,230
Mark James	79	70	72	66	287	7,170
Steven Richardson	73	72	70	72	287	7,170
Sandy Lyle	71	72	70	74	287	7,170
Santiago Luna	71	72	69	75	287	7,170
Barry Lane	73	72	68	75	288	5,422.86
Peter Mitchell	75	71	69	73	288	5,422.86
Carl Mason	72	71	73	72	288	5,422.86
Paul Way	72	70	74	72	288	5,422.86
John Bland	70	74	73	71	288	5,422.86
David Feherty	73	70	72	73	288	5,422.86
Frank Nobilo	69	69	78	72	288	5,422.86
Paul Curry	72	72	74	71	289	4,380
Mats Lanner	74	71	73	71	289	4,380
Martin Poxon	76	73	68	72	289	4,380
Ross Drummond	73	71	71	74	289	4,380
Chris Moody	76	66	71	76	289	4,380
Jose Rivero	77	71	72	69	289	4,380
Anders Sorensen	75	72	71	72	290	3,506.67
Miguel Angel Martin	74	71	74	71	290	3,506.67
Eric Giraud	73	72	73	72	290	3,506.67
Johan Rystrom	72	71	76	71	290	3,506.67
Marc Farry	78	68	69	75	290	3,506.67
Peter O'Malley	71	72	73	74	290	3,506.67
Ronald Stelten	78	69	70	73	290	3,506.67
Peter Senior	76	69	70	75	290	3,506.67
Stephen McAllister	71	71	77	71	290	3,506.67

	SCORES				TOTAL	MONEY
Jim Rutledge	78	69	76	68	291	2,920
Mark Roe	73	72	73	73	291	2,920
Kenneth Trimble	72	70	69	80	291	2,920
Peter Teravainen	77	72	72	70	291	2,920
Michael McLean	75	69	74	74	292	2,560
Brian Barnes	74	71	73	74	292	2,560
Glen Day	75	71	74	72	292	2,560
Daniel Silva	75	74	74	69	292	2,560
Peter Baker	75	70	73	74	292	2,560
Bernard Gallacher	73	75	73	72	293	2,080
Jeff Hawkes	70	75	77	71	293	2,080
Malcolm Mackenzie	79	65	70	79	293	2,080
Glenn Ralph	73	74	76	70	293	2,080
Stephen Hamill	76	71	73	73	293	2,080
David Gilford	73	76	75	69	293	2,080
Jose Coceres	76	67	78	72	293	2,080

Torras Monte Carlo Open

Mont Agel Golf Club, La Turbie, Monte Carlo
Par 34-35—69; 6,198 yards

July 3-6
purse, £400,000

	SCORES				TOTAL	MONEY
Ian Woosnam	67	66	61	67	261	£66,927.71
Anders Forsbrand	72	62	66	65	265	44,618.47
Mats Lanner	67	67	68	63	266	19,071.28
Peter Mitchell	67	67	65	67	266	19,071.28
Vijay Singh	68	69	67	62	266	19,071.28
Rodger Davis	68	62	67	69	266	19,071.28
Jeff Hawkes	66	65	71	65	267	11,044.18
Vicente Fernandez	71	66	63	67	267	11,044.18
Chris Williams	70	66	65	67	268	8,955.82
Jean Van de Velde	65	69	68	67	269	7,198.80
Sandy Stephen	65	62	71	71	269	7,198.80
Johan Rystrom	66	70	65	68	269	7,198.80
Severiano Ballesteros	62	69	69	69	269	7,198.80
Paul Curry	65	70	68	67	270	5,903.61
Darren Clark	67	67	66	70	270	5,903.61
Payne Stewart	69	68	67	66	270	5,903.61
Manuel Moreno	68	65	73	65	271	4,876.65
Ignacio Gervas	64	71	67	69	271	4,876.65
Neil Hansen	68	69	69	65	271	4,876.65
Hugh Baiocchi	63	69	68	71	271	4,876.65
Tim Planchin	69	70	66	66	271	4,876.65
Eduardo Romero	71	67	67	66	271	4,876.65
Silvio Grappasonni	66	68	67	70	271	4,876.65
Des Smyth	66	69	69	68	272	3,975.90
Robert Lee	72	65	67	68	272	3,975.90
John Bland	68	69	69	66	272	3,975.90
Magnus Sunesson	63	70	69	70	272	3,975.90
David Williams	67	69	65	71	272	3,975.90
Jim Rutledge	68	70	66	68	272	3,975.90
Peter Senior	71	68	66	67	272	3,975.90
Torsten Giedeon	65	67	72	69	273	3,343.37
Jose Rivero	64	67	68	74	273	3,343.37
James Spence	68	68	64	73	273	3,343.37
Per-Ulrik Johansson	67	72	67	67	273	3,343.37

	SCORES				TOTAL	MONEY
Richard Boxall	68	70	65	71	274	2,811.24
Ronald Stelten	67	69	68	70	274	2,811.24
David Ray	69	69	68	68	274	2,811.24
Philip Walton	68	71	67	68	274	2,811.24
Peter McWhinney	67	69	69	69	274	2,811.24
Grant Turner	68	66	66	74	274	2,811.24
Paul Carrigill	68	66	72	67	274	2,811.24
Santiago Luna	67	68	69	70	274	2,811.24
Bernhard Langer	70	67	66	71	274	2,811.24
Michel Besanceney	71	68	68	68	275	2,168.67
Costantino Rocca	70	66	72	67	275	2,168.67
Frederic Regard	72	66	65	72	275	2,168.67
Peter Lonard	67	70	72	66	275	2,168.67
Ian Mosey	70	69	69	67	275	2,168.67
Jose Davila	68	70	64	73	275	2,168.67
Miguel Fernandez	73	66	68	68	275	2,168.67

Bell's Scottish Open

Gleneagles Hotel, King's Course, Gleneagles, Scotland
Par 35-35—70; 6,789 yards

July 10-13
purse, £500,000

	SCORES				TOTAL	MONEY
Craig Parry	65	67	69	67	268	£83,330
Mark McNulty	65	68	70	66	269	55,550
David Gilford	68	67	71	65	271	31,300
Danny Mijovic	64	66	73	69	272	25,000
Jose Rivero	67	68	72	66	273	19,350
Mats Lanner	65	66	72	70	273	19,350
Colin Montgomerie	65	68	72	69	274	15,000
Severiano Ballesteros	63	68	71	73	275	11,825
Rodger Davis	69	69	67	70	275	11,825
Ian Woosnam	69	69	69	69	276	10,000
Mark James	65	70	74	68	277	8,606.67
David Feherty	69	63	73	72	277	8,606.67
Jean Van de Velde	69	70	69	69	277	8,606.67
Barry Lane	66	66	72	74	278	7,500
Nick Faldo	66	69	72	71	278	7,500
Steven Richardson	66	69	78	66	279	6,900
James Spence	69	70	70	70	279	6,900
Gordon Brand, Jr.	67	72	71	70	280	6,216.67
Peter O'Malley	66	71	72	71	280	6,216.67
Jay Don Blake	70	69	69	72	280	6,216.67
Paul Hoad	66	71	71	73	281	4,885.71
Rick Hartmann	66	69	74	72	281	4,885.71
Sam Torrance	67	70	71	73	281	4,885.71
Jose Maria Canizares	64	70	75	72	281	4,885.71
Costantino Rocca	66	72	71	72	281	4,885.71
Bernhard Langer	67	71	72	71	281	4,885.71
Masahiro Kuramoto	70	69	72	70	281	4,885.71
Donnie Hammond	69	64	75	73	281	4,885.71
Jeff Hawkes	71	66	68	76	281	4,885.71
Carl Mason	68	70	71	72	281	4,885.71
Stephen McAllister	68	68	71	74	281	4,885.71
Malcolm Mackenzie	71	68	72	70	281	4,885.71
Mike Clayton	69	64	77	71	281	4,885.71
Kenny Perry	69	68	71	73	281	4,885.71

	SCORES				TOTAL	MONEY
Robert Gamez	70	67	74	71	282	3,850
Chris Williams	68	71	72	71	282	3,850
*Rolf Muntz	68	69	70	75	282	
Des Smyth	69	70	68	76	283	3,450
Tom Weiskopf	71	64	72	76	283	3,450
Eamonn Darcy	66	67	75	75	283	3,450
Steve Martin	71	68	71	73	283	3,450
Mark Roe	63	71	75	74	283	3,450
Jesper Parnevik	70	67	74	72	283	3,450
Jose Maria Olazabal	69	69	72	74	284	3,100
Alberto Binaghi	69	68	72	76	285	2,850
John Huston	68	69	74	74	285	2,850
Kevin Stables	69	68	74	74	285	2,850
Philip Walton	67	67	74	77	285	2,850
Howard Clark	65	70	76	75	286	2,500
Juan Quiros	66	72	72	76	286	2,500
Tony Johnstone	67	69	75	75	286	2,500

British Open Championship

Royal Birkdale Golf Club, Southport, England
Par 34-36—70; 6,940 yards

July 18-21
purse, £994,200

	SCORES				TOTAL	MONEY
Ian Baker-Finch	71	71	64	66	272	£90,000
Mike Harwood	68	70	69	67	274	70,000
Mark O'Meara	71	68	67	69	275	55,000
Fred Couples	72	69	70	64	275	55,000
Jodie Mudd	72	70	72	63	277	34,166.67
Eamonn Darcy	73	68	66	70	277	34,166.67
Bob Tway	75	66	70	66	277	34,166.67
Craig Parry	71	70	69	68	278	27,500
Greg Norman	74	68	71	66	279	22,833.33
Bernhard Langer	71	71	70	67	279	22,833.33
Severiano Ballesteros	66	73	69	71	279	22,833.33
Magnus Sunesson	72	73	68	67	280	17,100
David Williams	74	71	68	67	280	17,100
Vijay Singh	71	69	69	71	280	17,100
Rodger Davis	70	71	73	66	280	17,100
Roger Chapman	74	66	71	69	280	17,100
Lee Trevino	71	72	71	67	281	10,055.56
Barry Lane	68	72	71	70	281	10,055.56
Nick Faldo	68	75	70	68	281	10,055.56
Chip Beck	67	78	70	66	281	10,055.56
Ian Woosnam	70	72	69	70	281	10,055.56
Paul Broadhurst	71	73	68	69	281	10,055.56
Mark Mouland	68	74	68	71	281	10,055.56
Andrew Sherborne	73	70	68	70	281	10,055.56
Peter Senior	74	67	71	69	281	10,055.56
Colin Montgomerie	71	69	71	71	282	6,750
Mike Reid	68	71	70	73	282	6,750
Wayne Grady	69	70	73	70	282	6,750
Tom Watson	69	72	72	69	282	6,750
Eduardo Romero	70	73	68	71	282	6,750
Mark James	72	68	70	72	282	6,750
Gary Hallberg	68	70	73	72	283	5,633.33
Payne Stewart	72	72	71	68	283	5,633.33

	SCORES				TOTAL	MONEY
Steven Richardson	74	70	72	67	283	5,633.33
Gordon Brand, Jr.	71	72	69	71	283	5,633.33
Mike Miller	73	74	67	69	283	5,633.33
Christy O'Connor, Jr.	72	71	71	69	283	5,633.33
Curtis Strange	70	73	69	72	284	4,980
Anders Forsbrand	71	72	73	68	284	4,980
Peter O'Malley	72	71	70	71	284	4,980
Nolan Henke	77	71	66	70	284	4,980
Martin Poxon	71	72	67	74	284	4,980
*Jim Payne	72	72	70	70	284	
Graham Marsh	69	73	72	71	285	4,234.62
Robert Gamez	71	72	72	70	285	4,234.62
Tom Kite	77	71	68	69	285	4,234.62
Steve Elkington	71	68	76	70	285	4,234.62
Fulton Allem	70	72	71	72	285	4,234.62
Sam Torrance	72	76	70	67	285	4,234.62
Costantino Rocca	68	73	70	74	285	4,234.62
Davis Love III	71	72	69	73	285	4,234.62
Des Smyth	71	73	73	68	285	4,234.62
James Spence	70	73	70	72	285	4,234.62
Jack Nicklaus	70	75	69	71	285	4,234.62
Nick Price	69	72	73	71	285	4,234.62
Donnie Hammond	70	75	67	73	285	4,234.62
Gavin Levenson	72	73	73	68	286	3,550
Andrew Magee	71	74	69	72	286	3,550
Hale Irwin	74	70	73	69	286	3,550
Scott Simpson	74	72	70	70	286	3,550
Tim Simpson	72	72	72	70	286	3,550
Jose Rivero	74	73	68	71	286	3,550
Gary Player	75	71	69	71	286	3,550
Miguel Angel Martin	71	75	71	70	287	3,155.56
Jay Don Blake	75	73	72	67	287	3,155.56
Michael McLean	71	75	72	69	287	3,155.56
Andrew Oldcorn	71	67	77	72	287	3,155.56
Mark McNulty	76	71	70	70	287	3,155.56
Steve Jones	70	77	71	69	287	3,155.56
Steve Pate	73	72	74	68	287	3,155.56
Gil Morgan	72	74	74	67	287	3,155.56
Darren Clarke	79	67	68	73	287	3,155.56
Martin Gates	67	75	73	73	288	3,000
Peter Jacobsen	75	72	68	73	288	3,000
Lanny Wadkins	71	75	71	71	288	3,000
Frank Nobilo	74	74	71	69	288	3,000
Tony Johnstone	69	74	71	74	288	3,000
Brett Ogle	73	75	66	74	288	3,000
*Phil Mickelson	77	67	73	71	288	
Daniel Silva	73	71	75	70	289	3,000
David Gilford	72	67	73	77	289	3,000
Danny Mijovic	70	72	74	73	289	3,000
Santiago Luna	67	77	72	73	289	3,000
Malcolm Mackenzie	71	73	74	71	289	3,000
Miguel Angel Jimenez	74	74	72	69	289	3,000
Ben Crenshaw	71	75	72	71	289	3,000
Fuzzy Zoeller	72	72	75	70	289	3,000
Mark Brooks	73	74	70	72	289	3,000
John Bland	71	76	71	71	289	3,000
Howard Clark	71	69	73	76	289	3,000
Jose Maria Olazabal	74	67	74	74	289	3,000
Peter Teravainen	71	72	72	75	290	3,000
Rick Gibson	73	75	70	72	290	3,000

	SCORES				TOTAL	MONEY
Brian Marchbank	72	73	75	70	290	3,000
Patrick Hall	77	71	72	71	291	3,000
Carl Suneson	69	77	69	77	292	3,000
Peter Allan	70	71	75	76	292	3,000
Alastair Webster	73	74	73	72	292	3,000
Peter Hedblom	74	74	73	71	292	3,000
John Hoskison	74	73	74	71	292	3,000
Chris Moody	74	71	78	71	294	3,000
Craig Stadler	77	71	74	72	294	3,000
Tom Weiskopf	74	74	73	73	294	3,000
Jeffrey Sluman	71	71	75	77	294	3,000
John Morse	73	71	77	73	294	3,000
Magnus Persson	77	71	74	72	294	3,000
Stephen McAllister	79	69	70	77	295	3,000
Eoghan O'Connell	74	74	74	75	297	3,000
Robin Mann	73	74	75	75	297	3,000
John Oates	77	71	76	75	299	3,000
Paul Mayo	71	74	71	83	299	3,000
Neal Briggs	73	74	77	76	300	3,000
Richard Boxall	71	69 WD				3,000

Out of Final 36 Holes

	SCORES		TOTAL
Kenny Perry	73	76	149
Corey Pavin	74	75	149
Tony Charnley	75	74	149
*Robert Allenby	73	76	149
David Frost	76	74	150
Mats Lanner	75	75	150
Simon Townend	78	72	150
Jim Rutledge	74	76	150
John Hawksworth	77	73	150
Jean Van de Velde	73	77	150
Marc Farry	75	75	150
Jimmy Heggarty	74	76	150
Philip Walton	74	76	150
Mark Calcavecchia	71	79	150
Adam Hunter	75	75	150
Jose Maria Canizares	77	73	150
Larry Mize	75	75	150
Masahiro Kuramoto	71	80	151
Rocco Mediate	76	75	151
*Henry Roblin	71	80	151
Ricky Kawagishi	71	81	152
Greg J. Turner	77	75	152
Peter Smith	78	74	152
Lucien Tinkler	75	77	152
David Feherty	79	74	153
Glyn Krause	75	78	153
Manuel Pinero	79	74	153
David Graham	75	78	153
Yago Beamonte	72	81	153
*Gary Evans	77	76	153
*Andrew J. Coltart	73	80	153
Miguel Fernandez	81	73	154
Sandy Stephen	75	79	154
Johnny Miller	74	80	154
*Rolf Muntz	75	79	154
Mark Roe	73	82	155
Fredrik Lindgren	79	76	155

	SCORES		TOTAL
*Jonathan Wilshire	76	79	155
Mikael Hoegberg	78	78	156
Craig Corrigan	76	82	158
Raymond Floyd	80	78	158
Ronald Gregan	79	87	166
Sandy Lyle	79	WD	

(Each professional who did not complete 72 holes received £600.)

Heineken Dutch Open

Noordwijkse Club, Randweg, Holland   July 25-28
Par 36-36—72; 6,826 yards   purse, £500,000

	SCORES				TOTAL	MONEY
Payne Stewart	67	68	62	70	267	£83,330
Per-Ulrik Johansson	78	67	62	69	276	43,425
Bernhard Langer	63	71	69	73	276	43,425
Peter Fowler	72	69	66	71	278	23,100
Peter Mitchell	65	71	70	72	278	23,100
Brett Ogle	72	68	65	74	279	12,556.67
Fred Couples	68	74	69	68	279	12,556.67
Steven Richardson	67	77	69	66	279	12,556.67
David Feherty	70	69	71	69	279	12,556.67
John Hawksworth	71	70	67	71	279	12,556.67
Danny Mijovic	67	67	70	75	279	12,556.67
Jose Rivero	69	71	68	72	280	8,315
Mike Harwood	69	68	72	71	280	8,315
Jose Maria Olazabal	67	72	71	71	281	7,500
Johan Rystrom	72	67	69	73	281	7,500
Wayne Grady	68	70	74	70	282	6,383.33
Tony Charnley	70	69	69	74	282	6,383.33
James Spence	66	69	72	75	282	6,383.33
Miguel Angel Jimenez	70	75	68	69	282	6,383.33
Vicente Fernandez	74	68	70	70	282	6,383.33
Paul Way	71	68	72	71	282	6,383.33
Keith Waters	75	70	69	69	283	5,400
Eamonn Darcy	65	77	69	72	283	5,400
Miguel Angel Martin	72	72	70	69	283	5,400
Joakim Haeggman	71	71	70	71	283	5,400
Marc Farry	74	70	70	69	283	5,400
Mike Clayton	67	76	70	71	284	4,800
Howard Clark	70	68	74	72	284	4,800
Andrew Murray	72	71	69	72	284	4,800
Phillip Price	68	75	70	72	285	4,175
Peter McWhinney	70	72	71	72	285	4,175
Nolan Henke	73	71	71	70	285	4,175
Michael McLean	71	71	69	74	285	4,175
Brian Marchbank	71	70	74	70	285	4,175
Jesper Parnevik	72	71	72	70	285	4,175
Ronald Stelten	70	74	68	74	286	3,650
Frank Nobilo	73	70	71	72	286	3,650
Anders Forsbrand	73	70	72	71	286	3,650
Ove Sellberg	74	71	70	71	286	3,650
Mark Roe	65	72	72	78	287	3,000
*Stephane Lovey	71	74	70	72	287	
David Williams	74	68	72	73	287	3,000

	SCORES				TOTAL	MONEY
Costantino Rocca	71	67	77	72	287	3,000
Gordon Brand, Jr.	70	70	72	75	287	3,000
Fredrik Lindgren	73	69	72	73	287	3,000
Justin Hobday	71	72	72	72	287	3,000
Jose Davila	71	72	71	73	287	3,000
Manuel Moreno	74	70	68	75	287	3,000
Glenn Ralph	68	73	74	72	287	3,000
Santiago Luna	70	69	74	75	288	2,400
Malcolm Mackenzie	74	70	72	72	288	2,400
David Gilford	75	69	70	74	288	2,400

Scandinavian Masters

Drottningholm Golf Club, Stockholm, Sweden
Par 36-36—72; 6,747 yards

August 1-4
purse, £600,000

	SCORES				TOTAL	MONEY
Colin Montgomerie	68	65	70	67	270	£100,000
Severiano Ballesteros	70	64	73	64	271	66,660
Robert Karlsson	71	65	68	68	272	33,780
Ian Woosnam	67	69	63	73	272	33,780
David Feherty	71	67	70	65	273	25,400
Brett Ogle	75	66	63	70	274	13,800
Steven Richardson	66	69	71	68	274	13,800
Per-Ulrik Johansson	70	66	71	67	274	13,800
Mark McNulty	71	65	69	69	274	13,800
David James	68	65	68	73	274	13,800
Russell Claydon	70	70	69	65	274	13,800
Fred Couples	74	61	71	68	274	13,800
Paul Broadhurst	65	69	71	69	274	13,800
*Klas Eriksson	72	68	66	68	274	
Peter Mitchell	70	67	69	69	275	9,000
Rodger Davis	71	68	69	67	275	9,000
Gary Hallberg	69	71	65	71	276	8,460
Peter Teravainen	72	67	68	70	277	7,086.67
David Williams	69	68	70	70	277	7,086.67
Jimmy Heggarty	71	69	69	68	277	7,086.67
Johan Rystrom	71	67	67	72	277	7,086.67
Michael McLean	71	66	71	69	277	7,086.67
Andrew Sherborne	67	67	70	73	277	7,086.67
Peter Fowler	70	67	72	68	277	7,086.67
Costantino Rocca	69	69	67	72	277	7,086.67
Peter Senior	69	68	73	67	277	7,086.67
Mike Clayton	69	69	70	70	278	5,670
Miguel Angel Martin	67	71	71	69	278	5,670
Joakim Haeggman	66	70	69	73	278	5,670
Martin Poxon	69	68	69	72	278	5,670
Barry Lane	72	69	69	68	278	5,670
Mark Roe	69	64	71	74	278	5,670
Paul Carrigill	69	69	68	73	279	4,500
Peter O'Malley	72	68	70	69	279	4,500
Vicente Fernandez	69	68	68	74	279	4,500
Craig Parry	69	72	67	71	279	4,500
Frank Nobilo	69	70	68	72	279	4,500
Danny Mijovic	69	69	71	70	279	4,500
Kenneth Trimble	68	70	71	70	279	4,500
Keith Waters	70	70	71	68	279	4,500

	SCORES				TOTAL	MONEY
Phillip Price	71	70	67	71	279	4,500
David J. Russell	71	70	70	68	279	4,500
Gordon Brand, Jr.	68	72	70	70	280	3,360
Mike Harwood	68	71	70	71	280	3,360
Paul Curry	71	68	72	69	280	3,360
Derrick Cooper	65	72	70	73	280	3,360
Paul Way	72	69	70	69	280	3,360
Mike Miller	71	69	69	71	280	3,360
Roger Chapman	74	65	72	69	280	3,360
Santiago Luna	71	63	72	74	280	3,360
Stephen Bennett	73	66	66	75	280	3,360

European Pro-Celebrity

Royal Liverpool Golf Club, Hoylake, England
Par 36-36—72; 7,069 yards

August 8-11
purse, £250,000

	SCORES				TOTAL	MONEY
Paul Broadhurst	67	70	69	66	272	£41,660
Ronan Rafferty	68	72	69	70	279	27,770
Keith Waters	70	70	71	69	280	14,075
Christy O'Connor, Jr.	70	67	72	71	280	14,075
Peter Smith	75	67	72	67	281	10,600
Steven Bowman	70	71	71	72	284	8,750
Peter Fowler	72	70	70	73	285	6,450
David A. Russell	70	72	75	68	285	6,450
Fredrik Lindgren	68	75	72	70	285	6,450
Justin Hobday	68	67	76	75	286	4,477.50
Peter McWhinney	68	70	74	74	286	4,477.50
Mike Clayton	71	73	69	73	286	4,477.50
Phillip Price	71	73	70	72	286	4,477.50
Darren Clarke	73	69	72	73	287	3,451.67
David J. Russell	72	74	68	73	287	3,451.67
Peter Mitchell	74	72	72	69	287	3,451.67
Stephen Hamill	72	72	72	71	287	3,451.67
Lee Vannet	73	76	70	68	287	3,451.67
Michael McLean	68	73	73	73	287	3,451.67
Eamonn Darcy	72	73	69	74	288	2,775
Thomas Levet	72	73	72	71	288	2,775
Brian Nelson	69	71	74	74	288	2,775
Neil Hansen	70	73	72	73	288	2,775
Kenneth Trimble	71	73	73	71	288	2,775
Brian Marchbank	74	70	70	74	288	2,775
Peter Teravainen	75	70	71	72	288	2,775
Mark Davis	79	68	71	71	289	2,362.50
Derrick Cooper	71	70	76	72	289	2,362.50
Paul Carrigill	66	71	77	75	289	2,362.50
Stephen Field	75	74	70	70	289	2,362.50
Donald Stirling	73	75	70	72	290	1,978.13
Grant Turner	72	77	70	71	290	1,978.13
Des Smyth	72	72	71	75	290	1,978.13
Andrew Oldcorn	77	69	71	73	290	1,978.13
Glen Day	71	74	72	73	290	1,978.13
Carl Mason	71	72	75	72	290	1,978.13
Robert Lee	71	74	68	77	290	1,978.13
Denis Durnian	76	72	68	74	290	1,978.13
Anders Forsbrand	74	73	71	73	291	1,675

	SCORES				TOTAL	MONEY
Alberto Binaghi	70	72	73	76	291	1,675
Philip Harrison	73	74	74	70	291	1,675
Ross Drummond	73	74	69	75	291	1,675
Jeremy Bennett	73	70	75	74	292	1,325
Paul Curry	73	74	69	76	292	1,325
George Ryall	71	76	70	75	292	1,325
Vilhelm Forsbrand	78	71	75	68	292	1,325
Hugh Baiocchi	75	71	74	72	292	1,325
Martin Gates	74	74	72	72	292	1,325
Noel Ratcliffe	72	74	74	72	292	1,325
Mike Miller	70	75	71	76	292	1,325
Peter Baker	72	74	74	72	292	1,325
Glenn Joyner	75	74	70	73	292	1,325

NM English Open

The Belfry, Sutton Coldfield, England
Par 36-36—72; 7,202 yards

August 15-18
purse, £450,000

	SCORES				TOTAL	MONEY
David Gilford	70	71	67	70	278	£75,000
Roger Chapman	69	66	74	71	280	50,000
Steven Richardson	71	70	68	73	282	25,335
Severiano Ballesteros	70	71	70	71	282	25,335
Per-Ulrik Johansson	69	73	69	73	284	17,405
Rodger Davis	71	73	71	69	284	17,405
Grant Turner	77	71	70	67	285	13,500
Peter Baker	73	73	69	71	286	9,264
Mark James	66	70	74	76	286	9,264
Craig Parry	74	73	74	65	286	9,264
Glenn Joyner	73	73	68	72	286	9,264
Peter Mitchell	75	69	71	71	286	9,264
Derrick Cooper	74	73	73	67	287	7,240
Jesper Parnevik	68	74	75	71	288	6,340
Magnus Persson	75	72	70	71	288	6,340
James McLean	76	71	72	69	288	6,340
James Spence	74	74	74	66	288	6,340
Ronan Rafferty	79	67	71	71	288	6,340
Costantino Rocca	68	73	75	73	289	5,274
Justin Hobday	74	71	72	72	289	5,274
Stephen Field	72	73	73	71	289	5,274
Russell Claydon	76	72	71	70	289	5,274
Vijay Singh	75	72	71	71	289	5,274
*Ricky Willison	74	72	72	71	289	
Glen Day	73	72	71	74	290	4,792
Peter O'Malley	75	71	70	74	290	4,792
Peter Fowler	73	71	72	75	291	4,320
Gavin Levenson	70	77	70	74	291	4,320
Barry Lane	71	75	70	75	291	4,320
Sam Torrance	72	73	72	74	291	4,320
Paul Broadhurst	69	74	76	72	291	4,320
Keith Waters	74	71	72	75	292	3,746
Eamonn Darcy	75	71	78	68	292	3,746
Carl Mason	76	70	72	74	292	3,746
Mikael Hoegberg	76	73	72	71	292	3,746
*Andrew J. Coltart	75	72	69	76	292	
Johan Rystrom	77	68	76	72	293	3,420

	SCORES				TOTAL	MONEY
Alberto Binaghi	73	72	72	76	293	3,420
Fredrik Lindgren	72	71	74	76	293	3,420
Brian Marchbank	70	72	76	76	294	3,105
Greg J. Turner	73	75	72	74	294	3,105
Ian Mosey	74	73	74	73	294	3,105
David J. Russell	79	68	74	73	294	3,105
Peter Smith	72	77	68	78	295	2,610
Mike Clayton	72	71	78	74	295	2,610
Hugh Baiocchi	72	73	76	74	295	2,610
Rob Huff	77	67	76	75	295	2,610
Lucien Tinkler	73	71	77	74	295	2,610
Jean Van de Velde	75	73	74	73	295	2,610
John Hawksworth	73	75	74	73	295	2,610
Patrick Hall	73	71	72	80	296	1,804.09
Ross Drummond	71	77	73	75	296	1,804.09
Howard Clark	77	72	73	74	296	1,804.09
Bill Longmuir	71	78	71	76	296	1,804.09
Andrew Sherborne	75	74	72	75	296	1,804.09
Brian Barnes	71	75	76	74	296	1,804.09
Neal Briggs	78	71	73	74	296	1,804.09
Juan Quiros	74	72	78	72	296	1,804.09
Antonio Garrido	72	75	78	71	296	1,804.09
David Llewellyn	71	76	73	76	296	1,804.09
Tony Charnley	73	76	75	72	296	1,804.09

Volvo German Open

Hubblerath Golf Club, Dusseldorf, Germany
Par 36-36—72; 6,788 yards

August 22-25
purse, £525, 000

	SCORES				TOTAL	MONEY
Mark McNulty	68	67	72	66	273	£87,500
Paul Broadhurst	73	67	68	65	273	58,275
(McNulty defeated Broadhurst on first extra hole.)						
Sam Torrance	69	67	69	72	277	29,550
David J. Russell	72	70	69	66	277	29,550
Ronan Rafferty	70	70	67	71	278	18,795
Barry Lane	71	66	73	68	278	18,795
Daniel Silva	72	72	67	67	278	18,795
Rick Hartmann	70	67	73	69	279	11,265
Rodger Davis	70	69	69	71	279	11,265
Costantino Rocca	73	70	69	67	279	11,265
Ross McFarlane	69	72	72	66	279	11,265
Vijay Singh	67	71	71	71	280	8,750
Mark James	70	73	67	70	280	8,750
Greg J. Turner	77	67	70	67	281	7,404
Glen Day	72	70	72	67	281	7,404
James Spence	72	70	69	70	281	7,404
John Bland	72	68	71	70	281	7,404
Michael McLean	70	70	73	68	281	7,404
Gordon Brand, Jr.	70	70	66	76	282	6,310
Tony Johnstone	70	72	71	69	282	6,310
Mark Roe	69	72	68	73	282	6,310
Jesper Parnevik	73	70	70	70	283	5,385
Mats Lanner	71	72	73	67	283	5,385
Jeff Hawkes	70	69	72	72	283	5,385
Bernhard Langer	73	71	73	66	283	5,385

	SCORES				TOTAL	MONEY
Jeff Pinsent	71	70	74	68	283	5,385
Quentin Dabson	69	68	71	75	283	5,385
Jose Rivero	72	67	70	74	283	5,385
Frank Nobilo	71	70	73	69	283	5,385
Mike Clayton	71	71	72	70	284	4,320
Colin Montgomerie	70	71	69	74	284	4,320
Ralf Berhorst	72	69	71	72	284	4,320
David Gilford	69	73	69	73	284	4,320
Philip Walton	71	72	67	74	284	4,320
Wayne Riley	71	73	74	66	284	4,320
Adam Hunter	69	71	74	70	284	4,320
Andrew Murray	67	73	77	67	284	4,320
Johan Rystrom	72	72	70	70	284	4,320
Antonio Garrido	70	69	74	72	285	3,540
Chris Williams	66	70	74	75	285	3,540
Ross Drummond	70	70	71	74	285	3,540
Peter Fowler	72	70	69	74	285	3,540
Russell Claydon	70	71	74	71	286	2,659.09
Martin Poxon	71	72	75	68	286	2,659.09
Anders Forsbrand	72	71	73	70	286	2,659.09
Christian Hardin	71	72	68	75	286	2,659.09
Jean Van de Velde	73	70	71	72	286	2,659.09
Sandy Lyle	67	69	74	76	286	2,659.09
Jose Coceres	72	72	74	68	286	2,659.09
Eoghan O'Connell	71	73	71	71	286	2,659.09
Per-Ulrik Johansson	74	69	73	70	286	2,659.09
Brian Barnes	71	71	69	75	286	2,659.09
Jim Rutledge	73	69	74	70	286	2,659.09

GA European Open

Walton Heath Golf Club, Tadworth, England
Par 36-36—72; 7,163 yards

August 29-September 1
purse, £500,000

	SCORES				TOTAL	MONEY
Mike Harwood	70	72	70	65	277	£83,330
Sandy Lyle	74	69	69	67	279	55,550
John Bland	69	74	70	67	280	25,833.33
Payne Stewart	73	69	70	68	280	25,833.33
Severiano Ballesteros	70	70	70	70	280	25,833.33
Brett Ogle	76	68	70	67	281	14,037.50
Paul Broadhurst	71	70	71	69	281	14,037.50
Craig Parry	70	69	71	71	281	14,037.50
Peter Fowler	69	69	72	71	281	14,037.50
Glen Day	70	72	74	66	282	9,595
Rick Hartmann	72	74	68	68	282	9,595
Des Smyth	71	77	68	67	283	7,736
Mark James	71	76	68	68	283	7,736
Martin Poxon	70	73	70	70	283	7,736
Stephen McAllister	70	69	72	72	283	7,736
Costantino Rocca	72	68	69	74	283	7,736
Frank Nobilo	72	74	72	66	284	6,466.67
Nick Faldo	74	71	70	69	284	6,466.67
Michael McLean	70	70	74	70	284	6,466.67
Mark McNulty	76	66	73	70	285	6,000
Peter Senior	72	74	72	68	286	5,550
Peter O'Malley	73	70	74	69	286	5,550

	SCORES			TOTAL	MONEY
Vicente Fernandez	71	75 71	69	286	5,550
Ian Woosnam	74	69 72	71	286	5,550
Jesper Parnevik	71	70 73	72	286	5,550
Santiago Luna	75	73 72	67	287	4,725
David Gilford	77	71 72	67	287	4,725
Keith Waters	71	76 73	67	287	4,725
Ross Drummond	75	72 71	69	287	4,725
Jose Rivero	76	68 73	70	287	4,725
Barry Lane	70	72 70	75	287	4,725
Greg J. Turner	73	72 74	69	288	4,200
Sam Torrance	72	73 73	71	289	3,800
Denis Durnian	73	71 74	71	289	3,800
Patrick Hall	74	71 76	68	289	3,800
Roger Chapman	72	74 77	66	289	3,800
Mark Roe	74	69 74	72	289	3,800
John Morse	72	74 71	72	289	3,800
Wayne Grady	73	74 68	74	289	3,800
Peter Mitchell	76	70 72	72	290	3,350
Philip Walton	73	74 71	72	290	3,350
Gordon Brand, Jr.	77	71 70	73	291	3,150
Mark Palmer	72	70 74	75	291	3,150
Kenneth Trimble	69	74 75	74	292	2,850
Stephen Field	70	76 74	72	292	2,850
Malcolm Mackenzie	75	71 75	71	292	2,850
Carl Mason	72	75 76	69	292	2,850
Stephen Bennett	74	73 72	74	293	2,450
Glenn Ralph	74	72 73	74	293	2,450
Peter Baker	73	72 76	72	293	2,450
James Spence	77	70 71	75	293	2,450

Canon European Masters-Swiss Open

Crans-sur-Sierre Golf Club, Crans-sur-Sierre, Switzerland
Par 36-36—72; 6,745 yards

September 5-8
purse, £444,015

	SCORES			TOTAL	MONEY
Jeff Hawkes	68	69 65	66	268	£73,972.37
Severiano Ballesteros	69	67 70	63	269	49,285.71
Peter Teravainen	71	68 64	67	270	27,795.37
Philip Walton	68	71 66	66	271	22,200.77
Paolo Quirici	72	67 66	67	272	15,895.75
Patrick Hall	69	67 68	68	272	15,895.75
Malcolm Mackenzie	69	69 66	68	272	15,895.75
Carl Mason	68	68 69	68	273	9,524.13
Jean Van de Velde	71	68 65	69	273	9,524.13
Mark McNulty	68	68 68	69	273	9,524.13
Steven Richardson	69	69 66	69	273	9,524.13
Vijay Singh	70	65 70	69	274	6,449.33
Lanny Wadkins	70	70 67	67	274	6,449.33
Howard Clark	67	72 68	67	274	6,449.33
Gordon Brand, Jr.	64	74 69	67	274	6,449.33
Mats Lanner	69	69 66	70	274	6,449.33
Glenn Ralph	65	71 72	66	274	6,449.33
Eduardo Romero	68	65 70	71	274	6,449.33
Marc Farry	73	65 66	70	274	6,449.33
Santiago Luna	66	70 68	71	275	5,261.58
Chris Moody	70	70 67	68	275	5,261.58

	SCORES				TOTAL	MONEY
Johan Rystrom	69	72	69	66	276	4,795.37
Manuel Pinero	65	71	70	70	276	4,795.37
Manuel Moreno	72	67	72	65	276	4,795.37
Joakim Haeggman	67	71	71	67	276	4,795.37
Andrew Murray	68	69	71	68	276	4,795.37
Sandy Lyle	68	73	74	62	277	4,195.95
Sandy Stephen	68	70	71	68	277	4,195.95
Peter O'Malley	71	68	72	66	277	4,195.95
Per-Ulrik Johansson	71	69	67	70	277	4,195.95
Jose Rivero	70	70	69	69	278	3,696.43
Sven Struver	67	71	72	68	278	3,696.43
Emmanuel Dussart	70	69	71	68	278	3,696.43
David Williams	71	68	71	68	278	3,696.43
Danny Mijovic	69	69	70	71	279	3,285.71
Greg J. Turner	71	68	70	70	279	3,285.71
Miguel Angel Martin	72	69	65	73	279	3,285.71
Juan Quiros	71	66	74	68	279	3,285.71
Martin Poxon	70	69	70	70	279	3,285.71
James Spence	68	67	72	73	280	2,841.70
Paul Curry	72	68	71	69	280	2,841.70
Vicente Fernandez	70	69	71	70	280	2,841.70
Brett Ogle	70	70	69	71	280	2,841.70
Giuseppe Cali	71	69	70	70	280	2,841.70
Armando Saavedra	67	70	70	74	281	2,397.68
Ross McFarlane	68	70	74	69	281	2,397.68
Jose Coceres	69	68	76	68	281	2,397.68
Robert Lee	68	71	71	71	281	2,397.68
Derrick Cooper	70	69	70	72	281	2,397.68
Stephen Bennett	72	67	72	71	282	2,086.87
David James	67	69	72	74	282	2,086.87

Lancome Trophy

St. Nom la Breteche, La Tuilerie, France
Par 35-35—70; 6,756 yards

September 12-15
purse, £450,000

	SCORES				TOTAL	MONEY
Frank Nobilo	65	68	69	65	267	£75,000
David Gilford	67	68	68	65	268	29,932.50
James Spence	68	68	64	68	268	29,932.50
Ian Baker-Finch	68	65	68	67	268	29,932.50
Peter Fowler	66	67	68	67	268	29,932.50
Colin Montgomerie	64	69	68	68	269	15,750
Ronan Rafferty	67	68	69	66	270	13,500
Jesper Parnevik	73	65	65	68	271	10,100
John Bland	67	68	67	69	271	10,100
Nick Faldo	67	67	68	69	271	10,100
Steven Richardson	68	72	63	69	272	7,676.67
John Morse	68	68	66	70	272	7,676.67
Rodger Davis	71	65	65	71	272	7,676.67
Mark Roe	67	70	68	68	273	6,335
Paul Way	67	67	68	71	273	6,335
Michael McLean	69	66	72	66	273	6,335
Craig Parry	68	69	68	68	273	6,335
Gordon Brand, Jr.	73	66	66	69	274	5,565
Severiano Ballesteros	71	70	69	64	274	5,565
Mats Lanner	73	70	67	65	275	5,032

	SCORES				TOTAL	MONEY
Eduardo Romero	73	67	67	68	275	5,032
Vijay Singh	72	69	69	65	275	5,032
Miguel Angel Martin	73	74	63	65	275	5,032
Ian Woosnam	65	73	68	69	275	5,032
Jose Rivero	66	69	72	69	276	4,380
Peter Mitchell	67	69	68	72	276	4,380
Bernhard Langer	68	72	69	67	276	4,380
Per-Ulrik Johansson	69	66	73	68	276	4,380
Jose Maria Olazabal	71	70	67	68	276	4,380
Mark Calcavecchia	69	69	71	68	277	3,796
Sam Torrance	71	70	68	68	277	3,796
David Williams	72	67	66	72	277	3,796
Johan Rystrom	69	74	66	68	277	3,796
Malcolm Mackenzie	70	73	68	66	277	3,796
Paul Broadhurst	67	69	72	70	278	3,430
Mike Harwood	70	73	66	69	278	3,430
Roger Chapman	73	67	68	70	278	3,430
Brian Marchbank	72	71	66	70	279	3,115
Tony Johnstone	77	67	68	67	279	3,115
Eamonn Darcy	68	67	76	68	279	3,115
Philip Walton	71	67	69	72	279	3,115
Brian Barnes	67	70	72	71	280	2,800
Peter Teravainen	70	71	67	72	280	2,800
Mark James	72	70	69	69	280	2,800
Robert Karlsson	68	73	73	67	281	2,620
Keith Waters	74	71	69	68	282	2,305
David J. Russell	68	71	70	73	282	2,305
Costantino Rocca	72	75	67	68	282	2,305
Gavin Levenson	68	71	72	71	282	2,305
Jean Van de Velde	73	69	72	68	282	2,305
Christy O'Connor, Jr.	66	70	75	71	282	2,305

Epson Grand Prix of Europe

St. Pierre Golf and Country Club, Chepstow, Wales
Par 35-36—71; 6,922 yards

September 19-22
purse, £450,000

	SCORES				TOTAL	MONEY
Jose Maria Olazabal	64	68	67	66	265	£75,000
Mark James	70	64	70	70	274	50,000
Miguel Angel Martin	69	68	68	72	277	28,180
Michael McLean	65	73	72	69	278	20,775
Tony Johnstone	71	70	67	70	278	20,775
Peter Teravainen	71	70	69	69	279	14,625
James Spence	67	70	71	71	279	14,625
Jose Rivero	70	68	69	73	280	9,270
Russell Claydon	71	68	71	70	280	9,270
Ronan Rafferty	70	69	68	73	280	9,270
Jesper Parnevik	72	71	68	69	280	9,270
Malcolm Mackenzie	71	74	67	68	280	9,270
Phillip Price	70	66	71	74	281	6,490
Gordon Brand, Jr.	70	66	71	74	281	6,490
Colin Montgomerie	66	69	73	73	281	6,490
Rodger Davis	66	70	76	69	281	6,490
Per-Ulrik Johansson	72	68	69	72	281	6,490
Vicente Fernandez	71	68	74	68	281	6,490
Anders Sorensen	68	74	69	71	282	5,413.33

	SCORES				TOTAL	MONEY
Frank Nobilo	69	69	72	72	282	5,413.33
David Feherty	74	67	67	74	282	5,413.33
Mark Roe	72	72	67	72	283	4,637.50
Anders Forsbrand	69	71	70	73	283	4,637.50
Vijay Singh	75	66	71	71	283	4,637.50
Eamonn Darcy	73	67	69	74	283	4,637.50
Craig Parry	71	71	70	71	283	4,637.50
Glen Day	74	70	70	69	283	4,637.50
Steven Richardson	68	70	73	72	283	4,637.50
Peter O'Malley	75	69	69	70	283	4,637.50
Santiago Luna	71	70	70	73	284	4,000
David Gilford	71	69	73	71	284	4,000
Peter Mitchell	70	70	73	72	285	3,700
Mike Harwood	73	70	69	73	285	3,700
Chris van der Velde	70	71	70	74	285	3,700
Peter Senior	75	67	72	72	286	3,042.50
Stephen McAllister	75	71	67	73	286	3,042.50
Eduardo Romero	70	68	75	73	286	3,042.50
David Williams	74	71	69	72	286	3,042.50
Johan Rystrom	73	68	70	75	286	3,042.50
Danny Mijovic	73	67	72	74	286	3,042.50
Mats Lanner	73	70	72	71	286	3,042.50
Brett Ogle	78	69	69	70	286	3,042.50
Peter Fowler	72	69	71	75	287	2,440
Barry Lane	73	71	70	73	287	2,440
Daniel Silva	68	73	73	73	287	2,440
Gavin Levenson	74	71	72	71	288	2,140
Alberto Binaghi	73	71	68	76	288	2,140
Philip Walton	72	70	71	75	288	2,140
Ove Sellberg	75	73	72	69	289	1,860
David J. Russell	72	67	71	79	289	1,860
Paul Way	73	72	67	77	289	1,860

Mitsubishi Austrian Open

Gut Altentann, Salzburg, Austria
Par 36-36—72; 6,806 yards

September 26-29
purse, £250,000

	SCORES				TOTAL	MONEY
Mark Davis	66	66	71	66	269	£41,660
Michael McLean	71	68	71	64	274	27,770
Russell Claydon	68	70	71	66	275	12,916.67
Marc Farry	66	70	73	66	275	12,916.67
Vijay Singh	66	68	73	68	275	12,916.67
Santiago Luna	69	72	70	66	277	8,125
Sandy Lyle	70	69	72	66	277	8,125
Greg J. Turner	67	71	70	70	278	5,925
Craig Parry	71	70	71	66	278	5,925
Tony Johnstone	70	69	72	68	279	5,000
Chris Moody	67	72	72	69	280	4,080
David J. Russell	71	72	70	67	280	4,080
Phillip Price	75	66	71	68	280	4,080
Andrew Sherborne	70	70	70	70	280	4,080
Peter Fowler	65	69	72	74	280	4,080
Gordon Manson	71	69	70	71	281	3,305
Des Smyth	70	70	71	70	281	3,305
Mike Clayton	73	70	69	69	281	3,305

	SCORES				TOTAL	MONEY
Peter Baker	69	71	73	68	281	3,305
Brian Barnes	66	72	76	68	282	2,812.50
Vicente Fernandez	69	71	73	69	282	2,812.50
Peter Mitchell	68	69	73	72	282	2,812.50
Joakim Haeggman	71	72	72	67	282	2,812.50
Eoghan O'Connell	71	71	68	72	282	2,812.50
Vilhelm Forsbrand	71	70	74	67	282	2,812.50
Jim Rutledge	73	67	73	70	283	2,550
Glenn Ralph	68	73	71	72	284	2,221.88
Paul Curry	71	71	70	72	284	2,221.88
Martin Gates	71	68	77	68	284	2,221.88
Hugh Baiocchi	71	70	72	71	284	2,221.88
Costantino Rocca	70	70	74	70	284	2,221.88
Peter Smith	70	74	69	71	284	2,221.88
Fredrik Lindgren	69	69	70	76	284	2,221.88
Chris Cookson	67	72	72	73	284	2,221.88
David Williams	75	66	68	76	285	1,900
Anders Sorensen	74	69	72	70	285	1,900
Neal Briggs	74	70	66	75	285	1,900
Ken Brown	75	69	70	72	286	1,650
David A. Russell	72	72	66	76	286	1,650
Mike Miller	66	71	71	78	286	1,650
David A. Jones	73	71	72	70	286	1,650
Adam Hunter	71	71	71	73	286	1,650
Roger Winchester	67	71	75	73	286	1,650
Juan Quiros	71	71	68	76	286	1,650
Paul Carman	69	75	73	70	287	1,425
Joss Maria Canizares	69	71	75	72	287	1,425
Armando Saavedra	71	73	71	73	288	1,250
Wraith Grant	73	71	74	70	288	1,250
Lucien Tinkler	69	71	75	73	288	1,250
Steven Bowman	73	71	73	71	288	1,250
Daniel Silva	69	70	75	74	288	1,250

Mercedes German Masters

Stuttgarter Golf Club, Monsheim, Germany
Par 36-36—72; 6,839 yards

October 3-6
purse, £500,000

	SCORES				TOTAL	MONEY
Bernhard Langer	68	72	67	68	275	£83,330
Rodger Davis	73	72	65	65	275	55,550
(Langer defeated Davis on first extra hole.)						
Nick Faldo	67	71	67	72	277	31,300
Mike Harwood	71	74	62	71	278	21,233.33
Jose Maria Olazabal	71	64	72	71	278	21,233.33
Jean Van de Velde	68	72	68	70	278	21,233.33
David Feherty	69	74	69	67	279	12,833.33
Malcolm Mackenzie	70	67	71	71	279	12,883.33
Peter Mitchell	70	71	67	71	279	12,883.33
Vicente Fernandez	67	71	72	70	280	10,000
Paul Way	72	71	68	70	281	8,164
Steven Richardson	67	71	69	74	281	8,164
Brett Ogle	75	70	67	69	281	8,164
Ronan Rafferty	76	71	69	65	281	8,164
Gordon Brand, Jr.	72	71	68	70	281	8,164
Mats Lanner	66	76	68	72	282	6,612.50

	SCORES				TOTAL	MONEY
Barry Lane	70	73	69	70	282	6,612.50
David A. Russell	70	72	72	68	282	6,612.50
Per-Ulrik Johansson	70	69	72	71	282	6,612.50
Peter Baker	70	73	70	70	283	5,850
Severiano Ballesteros	69	72	70	72	283	5,850
Craig Parry	74	72	68	69	283	5,850
Jose Rivero	67	74	72	72	285	5,400
Carl Mason	70	73	70	72	285	5,400
Miguel Angel Jimenez	70	75	66	74	285	5,400
James Spence	74	72	66	74	286	4,581.25
Danny Mijovic	72	70	72	72	286	4,581.25
Paul Curry	70	72	72	72	286	4,581.25
Sven Struver	73	71	73	69	286	4,581.25
Sandy Lyle	71	72	72	71	286	4,581.25
Steven Bowman	71	69	70	76	286	4,581.25
Jose Maria Canizares	73	72	69	72	286	4,581.25
Vijay Singh	74	72	71	69	286	4,581.25
Derrick Cooper	73	71	71	72	287	3,850
Hugh Baiocchi	75	71	69	72	287	3,850
Thomas Goegele	69	73	74	71	287	3,850
Hale Irwin	72	72	74	69	287	3,850
Stephen Bennett	73	71	74	70	288	3,400
Tom Watson	73	69	74	72	288	3,400
Paul Broadhurst	71	72	72	73	288	3,400
Johan Rystrom	72	75	70	71	288	3,400
Tony Charnley	72	70	73	73	288	3,400
Keith Waters	73	71	73	72	289	3,050
Frank Nobilo	72	74	70	73	289	3,050
Howard Clark	72	74	72	72	290	2,700
Anders Forsbrand	75	71	71	73	290	2,700
Mike Clayton	69	73	72	76	290	2,700
Andrew Sherborne	74	73	72	71	290	2,700
Dennis Durnian	72	70	74	74	290	2,700
Grant Turner	73	73	73	72	291	2,300
Peter Senior	68	75	74	74	291	2,300
David Williams	74	72	72	73	291	2,300

Dunhill Cup

The Old Course, St. Andrews, Scotland
Par 36-36—72; 6,933 yards

October 10-13
purse, £1,000,000

FIRST ROUND

CANADA DEFEATED AUSTRALIA, 2-1
Danny Mijovic (C) defeated Mike Harwood, 71-73; Craig Parry (A) defeated Dan Halldorson, 70-75; Dave Barr (C) defeated Wayne Grady, 70-71.

SOUTH AFRICA DEFEATED SWITZERLAND, 2-1
David Frost (SA) defeated Andre Bossert, 69-73; John Bland (SA) defeated Paolo Quirici, 74-74, 21st hole; Karim Baradie (S) defeated Gary Player, 75-76.

ENGLAND DEFEATED THAILAND, 3-0
Paul Broadhurst (E) defeated Sukree Onsham, 70-77; Nick Faldo (E) defeated Thaworn Wiratchant, 69-75; Steven Richardson (E) defeated Boonchu Ruangkit, 71-77.

IRELAND DEFEATED PARAGUAY, 3-0
Ronan Rafferty (I) defeated Carlos Franco, 70-74; David Feherty (I) defeated Pedro

Martinez, 75-77; Eamonn Darcy (I) defeated Angel Franco, 75-77.

SCOTLAND DEFEATED ITALY, 2-1
Costantino Rocca (I) defeated Sam Torrance, 72-74; Gordon Brand, Jr. (S) defeated Alberto Binaghi, 74-74, 23rd hole; Colin Montgomerie (S) defeated Giuseppe Cali, 67-71.

WALES DEFEATED SPAIN, 2-1
Ian Woosnam (W) defeated Santiago Luna, 70-70, 20th hole; Jose Rivero (S) defeated Philip Parkin, 71-74; Phillip Price (W) defeated Miguel Angel Martin, 73-74.

UNITED STATES DEFEATED KOREA, 2-1
Steve Pate (US) defeated Park Nam Sin, 70-71; Choi Sang Ho (K) defeated Curtis Strange, 72-74; Fred Couples (US) defeated Lee Kang Sun, 71-76.

SWEDEN DEFEATED CHINA (TAIWAN), 2-1
Wang Ter Chang (T) defeated Per-Ulrik Johansson, 72-74; Mats Lanner (S) defeated Chung Chun Hsing, 73-77; Anders Forsbrand (S) defeated Yu Chin Han, 72-82.

(Each member of losing teams received £7,500.)

SECOND ROUND

SOUTH AFRICAN DEFEATED UNITED STATES, 2-1
Bland (SA) defeated Strange, 68-69; Frost (SA) defeated Pate, 70-71; Couples (US) defeated Player, 67-74.

SCOTLAND DEFEATED IRELAND, 3-0
Torrance (S) defeated Rafferty, 68-72; Brand (S) defeated Darcy, 71-72; Montgomerie (S) defeated Feherty, 73-74.

SWEDEN DEFEATED ENGLAND, 2-0
Johansson (S) defeated Faldo, 73-74; Lanner (S) tied with Broadhurst, 70-70; Forsbrand (S) defeated Richardson, 69-70.

WALES DEFEATED CANADA, 2-1
Price (W) defeated Mijovic, 69-70; Barr (C) defeated Parkin, 68-69; Woosnam (W) defeated Halldorson, 67-70.

(Each member of losing teams received £15,000.)

SEMI-FINALS

SOUTH AFRICA DEFEATED SCOTLAND, 3-0
Frost (SA) defeated Torrance, 64-70; Player (SA) defeated Brand, 70-74; Bland (SA) defeated Montgomerie, 69-72.

SWEDEN DEFEATED WALES, 2-1
Woosnam (W) defeated Johansson, 65-68; Forsbrand (S) defeated Parkin, 68-68, 21st hole; Lanner (S) defeated Price, 71-71, 23rd hole.

PLAYOFF FOR THIRD/FOURTH PLACES

SCOTLAND DEFEATED WALES, 2-0
Torrance (S) defeated Woosnam, 70-71; Montgomerie (S) defeated Parkin, 69-70; Brand (S) tied with Price, 69-69.

(Each Scottish player received £36,666; each Welsh player received £26,666.)

FINAL

SWEDEN DEFEATED SOUTH AFRICA, 2-1
Forsbrand (S) defeated Bland, 68-69; Frost (SA) defeated Johansson, 68-74; Lanner (S) defeated Player, 74-74, 19th hole.

(Each Swedish player received £100,000; each South African player received £50,000.)

BMW International Open

Golfplatz Munchen Nord-Eichenried, Munich, Germany   October 10-13
Par 36-36—72; 6,910 yards   purse, £400,000

	SCORES				TOTAL	MONEY
Sandy Lyle	65	65	71	67	268	£66,660
Tony Johnstone	67	70	67	67	271	44,440
Peter Fowler	66	69	70	67	272	25,040
Paul Azinger	65	73	64	71	273	15,735
Mark Mouland	69	68	69	67	273	15,735
Tom Purtzer	69	68	68	68	273	15,735
Rodger Davis	67	69	68	69	273	15,735
Peter Baker	69	70	68	67	274	10,000
David Gilford	67	70	68	70	275	7,286.67
Joakim Haeggman	68	70	70	67	275	7,286.67
David J. Russell	66	68	70	71	275	7,286.67
Roger Chapman	68	69	71	67	275	7,286.67
Magnus Sunesson	65	70	68	72	275	7,286.67
Martin Gates	68	71	69	67	275	7,286.67
Eduardo Romero	68	70	68	70	276	5,520
Bernhard Langer	67	70	70	69	276	5,520
Derrick Cooper	69	73	68	66	276	5,520
Peter Senior	71	69	66	70	276	5,520
Peter Mitchell	71	71	67	68	277	4,688
Nolan Henke	69	71	69	68	277	4,688
Thomas Goegele	70	68	68	71	277	4,688
Jay Townsend	67	71	70	69	277	4,688
Mike Miller	68	72	68	69	277	4,688
Ronald Stelten	70	70	68	70	278	4,320
Ross Drummond	69	71	69	70	279	3,960
Carl Mason	70	69	70	70	279	3,960
Payne Stewart	67	70	68	74	279	3,960
Mark James	72	70	71	66	279	3,960
Des Smyth	71	69	70	69	279	3,960
Paul Curry	71	68	71	70	280	3,340
David A. Russell	66	70	73	71	280	3,340
Andrew Sherborne	69	73	69	69	280	3,340
Roger Winchester	70	68	74	68	280	3,340
Mark Roe	70	69	73	68	280	3,340
Glenn Ralph	69	71	73	67	280	3,340
Jean Van de Velde	68	72	71	70	281	2,840
Robert Lee	71	71	71	68	281	2,840
Brian Marchbank	70	72	69	70	281	2,840
Chris Williams	69	70	70	72	281	2,840
Frank Nobilo	73	68	71	69	281	2,840
Scott Simpson	71	68	71	71	281	2,840
Jesper Parnevik	72	69	72	69	282	2,320
Steven Bottomley	71	71	71	69	282	2,320
Mike Clayton	66	74	71	71	282	2,320
Ralf Berhorst	70	72	71	69	282	2,320

	SCORES				TOTAL	MONEY
Steven Bowman	71	69	75	67	282	2,320
Keith Waters	71	71	72	68	282	2,320
Philip Walton	70	69	68	75	282	2,320
Anders Sorensen	70	72	69	72	283	1,920
Bryan Norton	70	71	72	70	283	1,920
Wraith Grant	68	73	72	70	283	1,920

Toyota World Match Play

Wentworth Club, West Course, Virginia Water, England   October 17-20
Par 434 534 444—35; 345 434 455—37—72; 6,945 yards   £500,000

FIRST ROUND

Billy Andrade defeated Tom Purtzer, 3 and 2

| Purtzer | 5 3 5 | 4 3 4 | 5 3 4 | 36 | 3 5 5 | 5 3 4 | 5 4 4 | 38 | 74 |
| Andrade | 4 3 4 | 5 4 4 | 4 3 4 | 35 | 4 4 5 | 4 3 5 | 4 4 4 | 37 | 72 |

Andrade leads, 2 up

| Purtzer | 5 3 5 | 4 5 4 | 5 6 5 | 42 | 3 4 5 | 4 3 4 | 3 |
| Andrade | 5 3 4 | 5 2 3 | 4 4 4 | 34 | 3 5 5 | 5 4 5 | 3 |

Fred Couples defeated Joe Ozaki, 4 and 3

| Couples | 4 3 3 | 3 2 4 | 4 4 5 | 32 | 3 4 5 | 5 4 5 | 4 5 4 | 39 | 71 |
| Ozaki | 4 3 4 | 5 3 5 | 4 4 5 | 37 | 4 4 4 | 4 3 5 | 3 5 5 | 37 | 74 |

Couples leads, 2 up

| Couples | 5 3 5 | 4 4 4 | 4 4 4 | 37 | 3 3 5 | 5 3 3 |
| Ozaki | 5 3 5 | 6 2 4 | 4 4 6 | 39 | 3 4 5 | 4 3 4 |

Colin Montgomerie defeated Mark Calcavecchia, 5 and 4

| Calcavecchia | 5 2 5 | 4 3 5 | 4 4 5 | 37 | 3 4 4 | 4 4 5 | 3 4 5 | 36 | 73 |
| Montgomerie | 4 3 4 | 5 3 4 | 4 4 5 | 36 | 4 4 4 | 4 3 4 | 4 4 4 | 35 | 71 |

Montgomerie leads, 2 up

| Calcavecchia | 5 3 5 | 5 4 5 | 5 5 C | X | 3 3 4 | 4 3 |
| Montgomerie | 5 3 4 | 4 3 5 | 4 4 W | X | 3 4 5 | 6 3 |

Nick Price defeated Steven Richardson, 5 and 3

| Price | 4 3 5 | 4 3 4 | 4 4 4 | 35 | 3 4 4 | 4 3 5 | 4 5 4 | 36 | 71 |
| Richardson | 4 3 5 | 6 3 4 | 4 5 5 | 39 | 2 4 5 | 4 3 4 | 4 5 5 | 36 | 75 |

Price leads, 3 up

| Price | 4 3 4 | 3 3 4 | 4 4 4 | 33 | 3 4 4 | 4 3 4 |
| Richardson | 4 3 4 | 4 2 4 | 5 4 4 | 34 | 3 4 4 | 4 3 5 |

SECOND ROUND

Billy Andrade defeated Ian Woosnam, 7 and 6

| Woosnam | 5 3 4 | 5 4 4 | 4 5 4 | 38 | 4 4 4 | 4 3 3 | 4 4 5 | 35 | 73 |
| Andrade | 4 3 5 | 4 2 4 | 3 4 4 | 33 | 2 4 5 | 4 3 4 | 3 5 4 | 34 | 67 |

Andrade leads, 4 up

| Woosnam | 5 2 4 | 5 3 4 | 4 4 4 | 35 | 4 5 C |
| Andrade | 4 3 4 | 3 3 4 | 4 4 4 | 33 | 3 5 4 |

Seve Ballesteros defeated Fred Couples, 3 and 1

| Ballesteros | 4 2 5 | 4 3 3 | 4 4 4 | 33 | 2 5 4 | 4 2 5 | 4 5 4 | 35 | 68 |
| Couples | 3 3 5 | 4 3 4 | 4 3 5 | 34 | 3 4 5 | 5 3 4 | 4 5 4 | 37 | 71 |

Ballesteros leads, 3 up

Ballesteros	4 3 4	4 3 5	4 4 4	35	3 4 6	5 3 5	3 3		
Couples	5 3 4	4 3 5	3 3 4	34	4 4 4	5 3 4	4 4		

Nick Faldo defeated Colin Montgomerie at 38th hole

Faldo	4 3 4	W 3 4	3 4 4	X	3 4 4	4 3 5	3 6 4	36	X
Montgomerie	4 2 4	C 3 5	5 3 4	X	3 4 3	4 3 4	4 5 5	35	X
Match all-square									
Faldo	4 2 5	4 3 4	4 4 5	35	3 4 4	4 3 4	4 4 5	35	70
Montgomerie	6 4 4	4 3 3	4 4 5	37	3 4 4	4 3 4	4 6 4	36	73
Match all-square									
Faldo	4 3								
Montgomerie	4 4								

Nick Price defeated Ian Baker-Finch, 3 and 2

Baker-Finch	4 3 4	4 3 4	4 4 4	34	3 5 4	3 3 4	4 5 6	37	71
Price	4 2 3	4 5 4	5 4 4	35	3 4 4	3 3 4	5 4 4	34	69
Price leads, 2 up									
Baker-Finch	5 3 5	4 3 5	4 4 4	37	2 4 5	3 4 3	4		
Price	5 3 5	4 2 4	4 4 4	35	4 4 4	4 3 4	4		

SEMI-FINALS

Seve Ballesteros defeated Billy Andrade, 3 and 2

Andrade	3 3 5	5 3 5	4 4 4	36	4 4 4	3 3 5	5 5 4	37	73
Ballesteros	4 3 5	5 2 3	3 4 4	33	4 3 5	4 3 4	3 5 4	35	68
Ballesteros leads, 3 up									
Andrade	4 3 4	4 4 4	4 4 5	36	3 3 4	4 4 4	4		
Ballesteros	4 4 4	4 2 4	4 5 4	35	3 3 5	4 3 4	4		

Nick Price defeated Nick Faldo, 5 and 3

Price	4 3 4	4 3 4	3 4 4	33	3 4 5	5 3 4	5 5 4	38	71
Faldo	4 3 5	5 3 4	5 4 5	38	4 4 4	3 3 5	4 5 3	35	73
Price leads, 2 up									
Price	4 3 3	4 3 3	3 4 4	31	3 3 5	4 3 W			
Faldo	4 3 5	4 3 5	5 4 4	37	3 3 4	4 3 C			

FINAL

Seve Ballesteros defeated Nick Price, 3 and 2

Ballesteros	4 3 4	5 2 4	4 4 4	34	2 3 5	4 2 3	4 4 4	31	65
Price	4 2 3	4 3 4	3 4 4	31	3 4 4	4 3 5	4 4 4	35	66
Match all-square									
Ballesteros	4 3 4	4 2 4	4 4 4	33	3 4 4	4 3 4	4		
Price	4 4 5	4 3 4	4 3 5	36	3 4 4	4 3 4	4		

THIRD-PLACE PLAYOFF

Nick Faldo defeated Billy Andrade, 5 and 3

Andrade	5 2 5	4 3 4	5 4 4	36	4 4 4	4 4 5	
Faldo	4 C 4	5 3 3	3 3 4	X	3 5 4	4 3 4	

PRIZE MONEY: Ballesteros £150,000; Price £90,000; Faldo £45,000; Andrade £35,000; Woosnam, Couples, Montgomerie, Baker-Finch £25,000 each; Purtzer, Ozaki, Calcavecchia, Richardson £20,000 each.

LEGEND: C—conceded hole to opponent; W—won hole by concession without holing out; X—no total score.

Volvo Masters

Valderrama Golf Club, Sotogrande, Spain
Par 35-36—71; 6,951 yards

October 24-27
purse, £600,000

	SCORES				TOTAL	MONEY
Rodger Davis	68	73	68	71	280	£100,000
Nick Faldo	72	70	71	68	281	66,660
Bernhard Langer	70	69	70	74	283	37,560
Severiano Ballesteros	72	73	69	70	284	25,750
Steven Richardson	68	70	76	70	284	25,750
Mark James	67	72	72	73	284	25,750
Costantino Rocca	72	67	72	75	286	18,500
Mark McNulty	71	71	74	71	287	15,500
Craig Parry	71	69	73	75	288	12,560
Sandy Lyle	71	73	73	71	288	12,560
James Spence	70	74	73	71	288	12,560
Frank Nobilo	74	65	75	75	289	10,123.33
Jose Maria Olazabal	73	72	74	70	289	10,123.33
Barry Lane	71	72	72	74	289	10,123.33
Gordon Brand, Jr.	74	71	72	73	290	9,000
Colin Montgomerie	73	72	72	73	290	9,000
Mark Roe	74	70	72	75	291	8,093.33
David Gilford	73	73	77	68	291	8,093.33
Keith Waters	71	70	74	76	291	8,093.33
Peter O'Malley	74	75	69	74	292	7,220
Ronan Rafferty	74	70	74	74	292	7,220
Vicente Fernandez	74	69	74	75	292	7,220
Miguel Angel Jimenez	78	71	71	72	292	7,220
Peter Mitchell	69	73	72	78	292	7,220
Eamonn Darcy	74	70	71	78	293	6,382.50
Malcolm Mackenzie	75	72	71	75	293	6,382.50
Peter Teravainen	77	72	74	70	293	6,382.50
Mike Harwood	71	72	77	73	293	6,382.50
Jean Van de Velde	72	73	74	75	294	5,925
Jesper Parnevik	69	74	78	73	294	5,925
Philip Walton	74	73	69	79	295	5,257.14
Jose Rivero	75	71	75	74	295	5,257.14
David Feherty	75	74	74	72	295	5,257.14
Michael McLean	76	70	75	74	295	5,257.14
Sam Torrance	73	75	76	71	295	5,257.14
Russell Claydon	72	73	73	77	295	5,257.14
Per-Ulrik Johansson	72	70	80	73	295	5,257.14
David J. Russell	74	73	73	76	296	4,600
Vijay Singh	74	72	78	72	296	4,600
Tony Johnstone	70	73	79	74	296	4,600
Gavin Levenson	77	73	74	73	297	4,360
Jeff Hawkes	80	71	74	73	298	4,180
Roger Chapman	69	76	83	70	298	4,180
Paul Way	74	78	72	75	299	3,880
Eduardo Romero	76	72	78	73	299	3,880
Andrew Sherborne	71	75	77	76	299	3,880
Carl Mason	75	75	75	75	300	3,580
Anders Forsbrand	73	71	79	77	300	3,580
Miguel Angel Martin	74	76	77	74	301	3,280
Mats Lanner	75	75	78	73	301	3,280
Paul Broadhurst	78	77	77	69	301	3,280
Mark Davis	76	75	76	78	305	2,980
Peter Fowler	79	80	73	73	305	2,980
Howard Clark	81	77	75	82	315	2,800

World Cup

Le Querce Golf Club, Rome, Italy
Par 36-36—72; 7,030 yards

October 31-November 3
purse, $1,100,000

	INDIVIDUAL SCORES				TOTAL
SWEDEN (563)—$240,000					
Anders Forsbrand	73	73	65	68	279
Per-Ulrik Johansson	69	75	69	71	284
WALES (564)—$120,000					
Ian Woosnam	70	69	67	67	273
Phillip Price	72	75	72	72	291
SCOTLAND (567)—$88,000					
Sam Torrance	71	71	66	73	281
Colin Montgomerie	73	70	74	69	286
ENGLAND (570)—$57,000					
Steven Richardson	69	73	74	68	284
Nick Faldo	68	73	74	71	286
GERMANY (570)—$57,000					
Bernhard Langer	69	69	71	67	276
Torsten Giedeon	69	75	78	72	294
NEW ZEALAND (571)—$37,000					
Frank Nobilo	73	69	71	72	285
Greg J. Turner	73	71	70	72	286
SPAIN (571)—$37,000					
Severiano Ballesteros	68	69	71	72	280
Jose Rivero	73	69	72	77	291
IRELAND (574)—$19,333					
Ronan Rafferty	76	70	72	68	286
Eammon Darcy	71	69	74	74	288
JAPAN (574)—$19,333					
Satoshi Higashi	73	71	73	67	284
Nobuo Serizawa	69	74	72	75	290
CANADA (574)—$19,333					
Dave Barr	72	72	70	70	284
Dan Halldorson	72	75	69	74	290
SWITZERLAND (575)—$14,000					
Andre Bossert	71	71	70	68	280
Paolo Quirici	72	75	70	78	295
AUSTRALIA (578)—$10,000					
Rodger Davis	74	70	69	71	284
Mike Harwood	76	75	72	71	294
ITALY (578)—$10,000					
Costantino Rocca	72	70	74	70	286
Giuseppe Cali	78	73	67	74	292

	INDIVIDUAL SCORES				TOTAL

UNITED STATES (578)—$10,000
Wayne Levi	72	70	72	73	287
Joey Sindelar	75	73	70	73	291

FRANCE (579)—$10,000
Marc Farry	74	73	70	70	287
Jean Van de Velde	72	74	73	73	292

NORWAY (582)—$10,000
Gard Midtvage	76	73	70	71	290
Per Haugsrud	72	71	77	72	292

MEXICO (583)—$10,000
Rafael Alarcon	77	68	74	71	290
Carlos Espinosa	73	71	75	74	293

REPUBLIC OF KOREA (584)—$10,000
Sang Ho Choi	74	75	68	73	290
Nam Sin Park	69	80	72	73	294

DENMARK (584)—$10,000
Anders Sorensen	69	73	69	72	283
Jacob Rasmussen	73	78	73	77	301

ARGENTINA (585)—$10,000
Eduardo Romero	70	71	72	73	286
Rubin Alvarez	74	71	79	75	299

HOLLAND (585)—$10,000
Chris van der Velde	73	69	69	75	286
Willem Swart	74	75	76	74	299

PORTUGAL (592)—$10,000
Daniel Silva	75	71	68	71	285
David Silva	83	72	79	73	307

PHILIPPINES (594)—$10,000
Antolin Fernando	73	75	74	73	295
Mario Siodina	77	72	73	77	299

FINLAND (595)—$10,000
Mikael Piltz	74	71	75	73	293
Anssi Kankkonen	78	76	74	74	302

ZIMBABWE (603)—$10,000
William Koen	72	77	74	78	301
Tim Price	82	72	72	76	302

COLOMBIA (606)—$10,000
Ivan Rengifo	75	76	72	76	299
Eduardo Arevalo	79	75	77	76	307

BRAZIL (608)—$10,000
Joao Corteiz	80	74	69	75	298
Rafael Navarro	84	72	75	79	310

PARAGUAY (611)—$10,000
Jorge Murdoch	75	73	77	78	303
Angel Menez	76	78	77	77	308

	INDIVIDUAL SCORES				TOTAL
MALAYSIA (615)—$10,000					
Marimuthu Ramayah	78	68	76	76	298
Endera Mohd Yusof	77	81	82	77	317
AUSTRIA (618)—$10,000					
Marcos Burger	78	73	76	77	304
Ossie Gartenmaier	78	82	80	74	314
VENEZUELA (626)—$10,000					
Ramon Munoz	78	78	72	79	307
Francisco Alvarado	81	80	71	84	319
BELGIUM (647)—$10,000					
Olivier Buysse	78	80	73	83	314
Michel van Meerbeek	87	83	81	82	333

INTERNATIONAL TROPHY

WINNER: Woosnam - 273 - $75,000. RUNNER-UP: Langer - 276 - $50,000. ORDER OF FINISH: Forsbrand - 279 - $40,000; Bossert, Ballesteros - 280 - $25,000 each; Torrance - 281 - $15,000; Sorensen - 283; Davis, Higashi, Richardson, Barr, Johansson - 284; Daniel Silva, Nobilo - 285; Romero, van der Velde, Rocca, Rafferty, Faldo, Turner - 286.

Johnnie Walker World Championship

Tryall Resort, Montego Bay, Jamaica
Par 34-37—71; 6,848 yards

December 19-22
purse, $2,550,000

	SCORES				TOTAL	MONEY
Fred Couples	71	72	72	66	281	$525,000
Bernhard Langer	67	77	70	71	285	295,000
Paul Azinger	69	72	73	72	286	190,000
Craig Parry	68	77	71	71	287	112,500
Greg Norman	68	76	73	70	287	112,500
Nick Faldo	75	69	73	72	289	85,000
Severiano Ballesteros	70	75	73	71	289	85,000
Tom Purtzer	71	76	71	71	289	85,000
Steve Elkington	71	73	77	70	291	71,000
Larry Nelson	72	78	72	69	291	71,000
Rocco Mediate	71	78	74	68	291	71,000
Eduardo Romero	71	82	71	68	292	66,000
Andrew Magee	69	74	76	74	293	64,000
Frank Nobilo	69	79	74	74	296	61,000
Ian Woosnam	72	75	78	71	296	61,000
Kenny Perry	76	78	74	69	297	59,000
Corey Pavin	75	71	79	74	299	58,000
Craig Stadler	74	77	76	73	300	56,500
Davis Love III	73	82	74	71	300	56,500
Wayne Riley	74	76	76	76	302	55,000
Peter Senior	74	80	71	78	303	54,000
Payne Stewart	77	78	77	72	304	53,000
Rodger Davis	77	77	75	78	307	52,000
Ian Baker-Finch	75	76	78	80	309	51,000
Russ Cochran	73	86	77	75	311	50,000
John Daly	77	DQ				50,000

African Tours

Zimbabwe Open

Chapman Golf Club, Harare, Zimbabwe
Par 36-36—72; 7,173 yards

January 10-13
purse, £48,750

	SCORES				TOTAL	MONEY
Keith Waters	71	72	71	68	282	£8,028.92
Nick Price	70	72	66	74	282	4,183.13
Grant Turner	70	70	74	68	282	4,183.13
(Waters defeated Price and Turner on fifth extra hole.)						
Carl Magnus Stromberg	72	69	74	70	285	2,409.64
David Wood	70	72	68	77	287	1,725.30
Ramuncho Artola	75	73	68	71	287	1,725.30
Mark Litton	71	71	74	71	287	1,725.30
Darren Clarke	73	73	70	72	288	992.77
Roger Winchester	69	72	73	74	288	992.77
Patrick Hall	74	73	69	72	288	992.77
Tim Price	74	71	71	72	288	992.77
Ronald Gregan	71	76	71	70	288	992.77
Richard Fish	74	72	72	71	289	756.63
Joe Higgins	74	76	72	67	289	756.63
Paul Carrigill	74	68	76	72	290	708.43
David Jones	75	71	73	72	291	650.60
Philip Harrison	75	71	75	70	291	650.60
Mark Nichols	76	71	72	72	291	650.60
Peter Harrison	66	73	78	75	292	587.95
John Vingoe	74	77	71	70	292	587.95
Steven Richardson	75	71	71	76	293	534.94
Wayne Henry	68	75	75	75	293	534.94
Glyn Krause	72	72	73	76	293	534.94
Donald Stirling	73	72	80	68	293	534.94
Jeremy Robinson	71	73	77	72	293	534.94
Yngve Nilsson	72	73	74	75	294	477.11
Jonathan Sewell	75	74	75	70	294	477.11
Ian Spencer	73	72	69	80	294	477.11
Tony Stevens	73	76	73	73	295	414.46
Phil Golding	72	74	71	78	295	414.46
Mats Hallberg	74	75	73	73	295	414.46
Paul Eales	75	74	74	72	295	414.46
Andrew Hare	74	74	75	72	295	414.46
Craig Singleton	77	75	69	74	295	414.46

Zambia Open

Lusaka Golf Club, Lusaka, Zambia
Par 35-38—73; 7,252 yards

January 17-20
purse, £75,000

	SCORES				TOTAL	MONEY
David R. Jones	72	69	72	72	285	£12,500
Paul Carrigill	70	72	71	73	286	6,505
Phil Golding	71	72	71	72	286	6,505

	SCORES				TOTAL	MONEY
Ian Spencer	71	78	69	71	289	3,745
Darren Clarke	76	71	74	69	290	3,175
Sandy Stephen	76	72	70	73	291	2,106.25
Andrew Hare	74	73	74	70	291	2,106.25
Chris Platts	71	74	74	72	291	2,106.25
Steven Richardson	73	74	73	71	291	2,106.25
Craig Cassells	73	74	73	72	292	1,500
Patrick Hall	74	77	71	71	293	1,198.33
Jeremy Robinson	71	79	74	69	293	1,198.33
Paul Affleck	72	73	73	75	293	1,198.33
Keith Waters	74	74	70	75	293	1,198.33
John McHenry	75	74	71	73	293	1,198.33
Richard Fish	77	74	70	72	293	1,198.33
Paul Carman	76	75	71	72	294	990
Philip Talbot	75	77	69	73	294	990
Grant Turner	74	78	71	72	295	879
David Llewellyn	78	73	73	71	295	879
Glyn Krause	73	71	72	79	295	879
Paul Hurring	74	73	74	74	295	879
Tony Stevens	76	72	74	73	295	879
Jonathan Sewell	76	73	71	76	296	776.25
Glenn Ralph	72	76	75	73	296	776.25
Bill Longmuir	73	75	77	71	296	776.25
Philip Harrison	78	75	73	70	296	776.25
Ramuncho Artola	72	74	76	75	297	675
Anders Haglund	75	75	73	74	297	675
John Vingoe	74	76	74	73	297	675
Tim Price	71	81	73	72	297	675
Daniel Westermark	76	78	75	68	297	675

Standard Chartered Kenya Open

Muthaiga Golf Club, Nairobi, Kenya
Par 36-35—71; 6,765 yards

January 24-27
purse, £66,639

	SCORES				TOTAL	MONEY
Jeremy Robinson	68	62	69	70	269	£11,141.48
Sandy Stephen	69	69	69	67	274	4,624.76
Phil Golding	66	68	72	68	274	4,624.76
Paul Affleck	70	67	71	66	274	4,624.76
Andrew Hare	69	69	68	69	275	2,837.92
Jonathan Sewell	66	72	69	69	276	2,018.08
David Blakeman	70	65	70	71	276	2,018.08
Steven Richardson	65	70	67	74	276	2,018.08
Christy O'Connor, Jr.	71	65	76	65	277	1,225.91
John McHenry	75	67	70	65	277	1,225.91
Anders Haglund	67	71	71	68	277	1,225.91
Roger Winchester	67	74	67	69	277	1,225.91
James Mullen	70	67	71	69	277	1,225.91
Alan Saddington	69	65	72	71	277	1,225.91
*Andrew Rodgers	70	68	70	69	277	
Martin Poxon	74	65	66	73	278	893.20
Philip Harrison	71	68	73	66	278	893.20
Michael Brunton	70	68	73	67	278	893.20
Yngve Nilsson	69	68	71	70	278	893.20
Keith Waters	67	70	71	70	278	893.20
Carl Magnus Stromberg	70	69	69	70	278	893.20

	SCORES				TOTAL	MONEY
John Vingoe	68	70	73	68	279	767.29
John Morgan	70	68	72	69	279	767.29
Nick Godin	71	69	69	70	279	767.29
Roger Chapman	73	71	66	70	280	714.74
Richard Fish	71	70	71	68	280	714.74
Stephen McAllister	70	70	73	68	281	631.70
Jonathan Cheetham	70	70	71	70	281	631.70
Eamonn Darcy	68	67	72	74	281	631.70
Wayne Henry	70	72	71	68	281	631.70
Malcolm Gregson	71	67	73	70	281	631.70
Tim Price	70	69	69	73	281	631.70

Palabora Classic

Hans Merensky Golf Club, Phalaborwa, South Africa
Par 36-36—72; 6,727 yards

January 6-9
purse, R280,000

	SCORES				TOTAL	MONEY
John Bland	70	69	68	71	278	R43,988
Mark Wiltshire	72	70	67	70	279	31,612
Hugh Baiocchi	69	71	67	73	280	19,264
Chris Williams	70	69	69	73	281	13,748
Don Robertson	68	75	70	69	282	9,912
Fulton Allem	71	70	70	71	282	9,912
Ernie Els	73	68	67	74	282	9,912
Andre Cruse	74	69	72	68	283	6,468
John Fourie	68	72	73	70	283	6,468
Sean Pappas	68	72	71	74	285	5,488
David Feherty	72	74	67	74	287	5,012
Jeff Hawkes	73	74	71	70	288	4,396
Chris Davison	73	73	71	71	288	4,396
Bruce Vaughan	74	74	68	72	288	4,396
Gavin Levenson	72	70	74	73	289	3,920
Wayne Westner	69	74	72	74	289	3,920
Allan Henning	79	69	71	71	290	3,241.78
Robbie Stewart	73	74	71	72	290	3,241.78
A.P. Botes	72	72	73	73	290	3,241.78
Ashley Roestoff	69	74	73	74	290	3,241.78
Tony Johnstone	73	76	68	73	290	3,241.78
Justin Hobday	71	73	72	74	290	3,241.78
Desmond Terblanche	70	73	73	74	290	3,241.78
Retief Goosen	75	68	72	75	290	3,241.78
Craigen Pappas	70	73	72	75	290	3,241.78
De Wet Basson	72	73	74	72	291	2,688
Bobby Lincoln	70	75	69	77	291	2,688
Simon Hobday	72	73	70	76	291	2,688
Greg Reid	74	74	73	71	292	2,478
Teddy Webber	72	73	70	77	292	2,478

ICL International

Zwartkop Country Club, Verwoerdburg, South Africa
Par 36-36—72; 7,125 yards

January 16-19
purse, R280,000

	SCORES				TOTAL	MONEY
Fulton Allem	69	67	64	71	271	R43,988
Tony Johnstone	68	66	70	68	272	31,612
Gavin Levenson	71	68	67	68	274	14,858.67
Wayne Westner	67	71	67	69	274	14,858.67
Ashley Roestoff	68	64	68	74	274	14,858.67
Desmond Terblanche	71	69	66	69	275	9,912
Roger Wessels	70	69	70	67	276	6,339.20
Craigen Pappas	70	66	72	68	276	6,339.20
Hugh Baiocchi	68	69	69	70	276	6,339.20
Justin Hobday	69	71	67	69	276	6,339.20
Hugh Royer	70	70	66	70	276	6,339.20
Simon Hobday	69	71	68	69	277	4,536
Richard Kaplan	71	65	69	72	277	4,536
John Bland	70	72	69	67	278	4,116
Allan Henning	69	71	71	68	279	3,920
Steve Van Vuuren	71	69	69	70	279	3,920
John Fourie	68	70	72	70	280	3,340
Thomas L. Tolles, Jr.	68	73	69	70	280	3,340
Don Robertson	70	70	70	70	280	3,340
Wayne Bradley	69	68	71	72	280	3,340
Mark James	71	68	69	72	280	3,340
Rick Hartman	70	70	67	73	280	3,340
Scott Dunlap	69	71	67	73	280	3,340
De Wet Basson	73	71	70	68	282	2,730
Bruce Vaughan	71	72	71	68	282	2,730
Chris Davison	70	70	71	71	282	2,730
Phil Jonas	68	71	72	71	282	2,730
Andre Cruse	68	70	71	73	282	2,730
Wayne Player	71	68	69	74	282	2,730
Ernie Els	69	72	74	68	283	2,318.40
John Mashego	69	74	69	71	283	2,318.40
James Kingston	73	71	67	72	283	2,318.40
Jimmy Johnson	68	71	71	73	283	2,318.40
Teddy Webber	68	70	68	77	283	2,318.40

Lexington PGA Championship

Wanderers Golf Club, Johannesburg, South Africa
Par 35-35—70; 6,960 yards

January 23-26
purse, R350,000

	SCORES				TOTAL	MONEY
Roger Wessels	68	66	68	69	271	R55,200
Hugh Royer	63	69	67	72	271	31,912.50
Mark James	67	68	67	69	271	31,912.50
(Wessels defeated Royer on first, James on second extra hole.)						
Richard Kaplan	70	69	67	66	272	12,555
David Feherty	68	71	65	68	272	12,555
Ashley Roestoff	66	70	68	68	272	12,555
John Bland	69	68	66	69	272	12,555
Jeff Hawkes	62	73	68	69	272	12,555
Wayne Bradley	72	70	65	67	274	7,245
Bruce Vaughan	66	70	64	74	274	7,245

	SCORES				TOTAL	MONEY
Hugh Baiocchi	71	72	66	66	275	6,072.50
Justin Hobday	68	70	68	69	275	6,072.50
Mervyn Galant	70	69	68	69	276	5,520
Des Terblanche	75	64	71	67	277	4,745
De Wet Basson	70	69	70	68	277	4,745
Stuart Smith	71	71	67	68	277	4,745
Frank Verwey	70	70	68	69	277	4,745
Andre Bossert	70	69	68	70	277	4,745
Wayne Westner	69	67	70	71	277	4,745
Alan Pata	69	74	66	69	278	4,015
Wayne Player	71	68	70	69	278	4,015
Ernie Els	71	70	67	70	278	4,015
Trevor Dodds	71	68	69	71	279	3,693.33
Tony Johnstone	70	72	66	71	279	3,693.33
Andre Cruse	66	72	69	72	279	3,693.33
Scott Dunlap	68	70	76	66	280	3,383.33
Don Robertson	69	71	70	70	280	3,383.33
Chris Davison	66	71	70	73	280	3,383.33
Gavin Levenson	71	71	70	69	281	2,422.50
Jannie Le Grange	71	68	72	70	281	2,422.50
Dean Van Staden	67	72	70	72	281	2,422.50
Ian Dougan	71	67	70	73	281	2,422.50
Fulton Allem	68	73	66	74	281	2,422.50
Rick Hartman	70	70	66	75	281	2,422.50

Protea Assurance South African Open

Durban Country Club, Durban, South Africa
Par 36-36—72; 6,558 yards

January 30-February 2
purse, R400,000

	SCORES				TOTAL	MONEY
Wayne Westner	65	70	69	68	272	R64,000
Tony Johnstone	68	68	72	68	276	36,475
Mark James	70	66	69	71	276	36,475
John Bland	69	69	70	69	277	18,140
Hugh Baiocchi	71	69	67	70	277	18,140
Steve Van Vuuren	74	66	70	69	279	13,015
Jeff Hawkes	68	71	69	71	279	13,015
Justin Hobday	69	74	66	71	280	7,980
Trevor Dodds	72	67	69	72	280	7,980
Wilhelm Winsnes	69	67	71	73	280	7,980
Marty Schiene	73	68	66	73	280	7,980
Fulton Allem	69	66	69	76	280	7,980
Chris Williams	70	68	69	74	281	6,310
Ernie Els	74	65	71	73	283	5,820
Derek James	72	69	68	74	283	5,820
Bruce Vaughan	71	73	72	69	285	5,326.66
Gavin Levenson	71	68	75	71	285	5,326.66
Gary Gilchrist	71	70	72	72	285	5,326.66
Bobby Lincoln	69	76	68	73	286	4,746.66
Richard Kaplan	67	74	71	74	286	4,746.66
Stuart Smith	69	72	70	75	286	4,746.66
Phil Hatchett	75	69	74	69	287	4,165
Wayne Player	71	75	70	71	287	4,165
Tommy Tolles	71	71	73	72	287	4,165
Jay Townsend	71	74	70	72	287	4,165
Hugh Royer	77	70	65	75	287	4,165

	SCORES				TOTAL	MONEY
Teddy Webber	72	68	71	76	287	4,165
Alan Pate	73	73	71	71	288	3,633.33
Ashley Roestoff	74	71	71	72	288	3,633.33
Nico Van Rensburg	66	76	70	76	288	3,633.33

AECI Charity Classic

Rand Park Golf Club, Johannesburg, South Africa
Par 36-36—72; 7,320 yards

February 6-9
purse, R280,000

	SCORES				TOTAL	MONEY
Wayne Westner	69	69	70	65	273	R43,988
Thomas L. Tolles, Jr.	72	67	66	71	276	31,612
Bobby Lincoln	68	69	71	69	277	19,264
John Bland	72	71	66	69	278	12,656
Justin Hobday	69	69	70	70	278	12,656
Tony Johnstone	70	72	69	68	279	9,912
Desmond Terblanche	70	70	66	74	280	7,574
Nico Van Rensburg	70	69	71	70	280	7,574
Chris Williams	67	73	72	70	282	5,516
Jim Johnson	68	71	72	71	282	5,516
Chris Davison	69	67	73	73	282	5,516
Hendrik Buhrmann	69	65	72	77	283	4,676
David Feherty	72	72	71	69	284	4,162.67
Michael Green	70	73	72	69	284	4,162.67
Retief Goosen	71	68	72	73	284	4,162.67
Hugh Baiocchi	72	72	73	68	285	3,654
Allan Henning	74	70	73	68	285	3,654
Alan Pate	75	70	66	74	285	3,654
Richard Kaplan	70	71	73	71	285	3,654
Steve Van Vuuren	74	70	69	73	286	3,157
Peter Van Der Riet	70	72	71	73	286	3,157
Phillip Hatchett	72	70	73	71	286	3,157
Robin Freeman	69	71	74	72	286	3,157
Phil Simmons	72	72	74	69	287	2,772
Andre De Klerk	71	73	72	71	287	2,772
Gavin Levenson	72	73	71	71	287	2,772
Andre Cruse	73	73	72	69	287	2,772
Wayne Player	73	67	74	73	287	2,772
Ron McCann	74	70	71	73	288	2,408
De Wet Basson	71	70	74	73	288	2,408
Ernie Els	67	74	73	74	288	2,408
Bruce Vaughan	73	73	70	72	288	2,408

Hollard Insurance Swazi Spa Sun Classic

Royal Swazi Spa and Country Club, Swaziland
Par 36-36—72; 6,708 yards

February 13-16
purse, R280,000

	SCORES				TOTAL	MONEY
Hugh Royer	64	66	67	68	265	R43,988
Desmond Terblanche	68	67	67	67	269	25,438
Robin Freeman	65	65	68	71	269	25,438
Ian Palmer	66	66	73	67	272	13,748
John Fourie	66	67	73	67	273	9,912

	SCORES				TOTAL	MONEY
Bruce Vaughan	68	71	66	68	273	9,912
James Kingston	69	64	70	70	273	9,912
Roger Wessels	67	71	69	67	274	5,622
De Wet Basson	67	68	70	69	274	5,622
Alan Pate	69	70	66	69	274	5,622
Andre Bossert	69	69	64	72	274	5,622
Wayne Player	66	67	64	77	274	5,622
Marty Schiene	70	67	70	68	275	4,162
Gavin Levenson	69	73	64	69	275	4,162
Hendrik Buhrmann	67	68	66	74	275	4,162
Hugh Baiocchi	67	73	74	62	276	3,654
Retief Goosen	67	69	72	68	276	3,654
Dean Van Staden	69	70	68	69	276	3,654
John Bland	71	66	68	71	276	3,654
Nico Van Rensburg	69	68	73	67	277	3,113
Steve Van Vuuren	68	68	73	68	277	3,113
Andre Cruse	67	71	68	71	277	3,113
Greg Reid	73	66	67	71	277	3,113
David Carter	67	69	68	73	277	3,113
Frank Verwey	74	66	71	67	278	2,604
Schalk Van Der Merwe	67	72	71	68	278	2,604
Scott Dunlap	70	69	70	69	278	2,604
Jay Townsend	66	68	74	70	278	2,604
Stuart Smith	70	70	68	70	278	2,604
Craigen Pappas	70	68	70	70	278	2,604
Chris Davison	69	63	71	75	278	2,604

Bell's Cup Players Championship

Mowbray Golf Club, Cape Town, South Africa
Par 36-36—72; 6,664 yards

February 20-23
purse, R280,000

	SCORES				TOTAL	MONEY
John Bland	68	67	71	71	277	R43,988
Retief Goosen	72	68	73	65	278	31,612
Desmond Terblanche	71	71	67	70	279	16,506
Tony Johnstone	70	71	65	73	279	16,506
Bruce Vaughan	68	72	72	68	280	10,738
Hugh Royer	68	69	71	72	280	10,738
Thomas L. Tolles, Jr.	68	67	74	72	281	8,260
Richard Kaplan	74	72	68	68	282	6,468
Peter Van Der Riet	72	66	75	69	282	6,468
Gavin Levenson	72	72	69	70	283	4,893
Stuart Smith	72	68	71	72	283	4,893
Mark Wiltshire	68	69	73	73	283	4,893
Ernie Els	68	73	70	72	283	4,893
De Wet Basson	73	72	71	68	284	3,985.33
Robin Freeman	73	69	70	72	284	3,985.33
Phil Simmons	72	71	67	74	284	3,985.33
Hugh Baiocchi	69	72	74	70	285	3,654
Ben Fouchee	74	68	72	71	285	3,654
Hendrik Buhrmann	71	72	74	69	286	3,124
Scott Dunlap	71	69	76	70	286	3,124
Noel Maart	72	69	74	71	286	3,124
Dean Van Staden	71	70	72	73	286	3,124
Nico Van Rensburg	69	72	71	74	286	3,124
Brian Mahon	70	72	70	74	286	3,124

	SCORES				TOTAL	MONEY
Phillip Hatchett	70	72	68	76	286	3,124
Chris Davison	67	80	71	69	287	2,688
Ashley Roestoff	73	64	77	73	287	2,688
Ferdie Van Der Merwe	68	74	70	75	287	2,688
Ian Palmer	70	75	70	73	288	2,408
Bobby Lincoln	69	71	74	74	288	2,408
Steven Burnett	74	69	71	74	288	2,408
Wayne Bradley	70	68	75	75	288	2,408

Trust Bank Tournament of Champions

Kensington Golf Club, Johannesburg, South Africa
Par 35-37—72; 6,716 yards

February 27-March 2
purse, R280,000

	SCORES				TOTAL	MONEY
John Bland	62	71	70	66	269	R43,988
Justin Hobday	67	66	71	72	276	31,612
Hugh Baiocchi	69	69	70	70	278	14,858
Retief Goosen	68	68	72	70	278	14,858
Ernie Els	70	70	68	70	278	14,858
Bobby Lincoln	71	71	69	68	279	9,912
Jim Johnson	71	70	73	67	281	7,065
Richard Kaplan	68	74	70	69	281	7,065
Bruce Vaughan	67	71	72	71	281	7,065
Wayne Player	71	71	72	68	282	5,250
Chris Williams	72	69	70	71	282	5,250
De Wet Basson	73	69	71	70	283	4,536
Hendrik Buhrmann	73	68	71	71	283	4,536
Steven Burnett	75	70	72	67	284	4,046
Hugh Royer	72	67	71	74	284	4,046
Desmond Terblanche	73	67	73	72	285	3,864
Mark Wiltshire	71	73	73	69	286	3,584
Stuart Smith	73	68	75	70	286	3,584
Allan Henning	72	69	73	72	286	3,584
Gavin Levenson	74	70	70	73	287	3,248
Ashley Roestoff	69	74	71	73	287	3,248
Ron McCann	71	72	75	70	288	2,856
Tony Johnstone	70	72	74	72	288	2,856
Phillip Hatchett	73	73	70	72	288	2,856
Derek James	71	68	76	73	288	2,856
Graeme Whale	72	74	69	73	288	2,856
Teddy Webber	71	69	71	77	288	2,856
Jannie Le Grange	67	78	67	76	288	2,856
Steven Harris	72	73	74	70	289	2,296
Phil Simmons	69	73	75	72	289	2,296
John Mashego	71	69	76	73	289	2,296
Thomas L. Tolles, Jr.	71	73	72	73	289	2,296
Dean Van Staden	75	67	73	74	289	2,296
Craigen Pappas	72	75	69	73	289	2,296
Andre Cruse	73	70	71	75	289	2,296
Jeff Hawkes	67	69	76	77	289	2,296

Million Dollar Challenge

Gary Player Country Club, Sun City, Bophuthatswana
Par 36-36—72; 7,665 yards

December 5-8
purse, US$2,500,000

	SCORES				TOTAL	MONEY
Bernhard Langer	68	65	67	72	272	$1,000,000
Mark Calcavecchia	72	67	71	67	277	300,000
Mark McNulty	66	71	71	74	282	250,000
Nick Faldo	72	69	68	76	285	200,000
Fred Couples	71	71	74	71	287	145,000
John Bland	74	70	68	75	287	145,000
Ian Woosnam	73	68	78	74	293	130,000
John Daly	72	73	72	77	294	120,000
Steve Elkington	67	74	79	78	298	110,000
David Frost	72	75	77	76	300	100,000

Fancourt Hall of Fame Championship

Fancourt Country Club, George, South Africa
Par 36-36—72; 6,812 yards

December 12-15
purse, R450,000

	SCORES				TOTAL	MONEY
De Wet Basson	71	70	68	67	276	R70,695
Anders Forsbrand	69	72	69	68	278	50,805
Tony Johnstone	70	70	70	70	280	30,960
John Bland	74	69	66	74	283	22,095
Wayne Bradley	70	76	70	69	285	15,930
Wayne Westner	70	72	73	70	285	15,930
Justin Hobday	67	72	75	71	285	15,930
Ernie Els	75	68	73	70	286	11,070
Gary Evans	71	77	68	71	287	8,865
Mark Wiltshire	71	75	69	72	287	8,865
Chris Williams	67	77	69	74	287	8,865
Chris Moody	75	71	72	70	288	7,290
Clinton Whitelaw	72	73	71	72	288	7,290
Hugh Royer	75	72	71	71	289	6,405
Schalk Van Der Merwe	71	74	73	71	289	6,405
Mervyn Galant	75	74	69	71	289	6,405
Des Terblanche	75	73	74	68	290	5,452.50
Peter Van Der Riet	78	73	69	70	290	5,452.50
Chris Davison	73	73	71	73	290	5,452.50
Bobby Lincoln	73	71	73	73	290	5,452.50
Stephen McAllister	72	77	68	73	290	5,452.50
David Frost	70	76	69	75	290	5,452.50
Hugh Baiocchi	71	73	77	70	291	4,725
Jimmy Johnson	76	72	71	72	291	4,725
Ashley Roestoff	74	70	71	76	291	4,725
Tom Carr	72	72	76	72	292	4,252.50
Paul McGinley	74	74	72	72	292	4,252.50
Gary Gilchrist	74	74	69	75	292	4,252.50
Derek James	69	74	72	77	292	4,252.50
Greg Reid	74	73	72	74	293	3,847.50
Gavin Levenson	80	68	75	70	293	3,847.50

Goodyear Classic

Humewood Golf Club, Port Elizabeth, South Africa
Par 35-37—72; 6,454 yards

December 18-21
purse, R300,000

		SCORES			TOTAL	MONEY
Justin Hobday	71	71	69	69	280	R47,130
Hugh Royer	68	76	70	70	284	33,870
Malcolm McKenzie	70	71	73	71	285	20,640
Wayne Westner	67	76	74	70	287	14,730
Paul McGinley	72	73	75	68	288	12,390
Tony Johnstone	71	76	76	66	289	8,332.50
Stuart Little	73	74	75	67	289	8,332.50
John Bland	71	73	74	71	289	8,332.50
Craigen Pappas	71	72	74	72	289	8,332.50
Ian Palmer	70	73	79	68	290	5,420
Richard Kaplan	71	75	74	70	290	5,420
Bobby Lincoln	71	72	75	72	290	5,420
Alan Pate	73	71	77	70	291	4,460
Ian Mosey	76	70	74	71	291	4,460
Ashley Roestoff	71	74	72	74	291	4,460
Steve Van Vuuren	73	75	77	67	292	3,915
Ernie Els	72	77	76	67	292	3,915
Gary Gilchrist	73	76	74	69	292	3,915
Jack Ferenz	67	77	78	70	292	3,915
Hugh Baiocchi	72	71	78	72	293	3,430
Sammy Daniels	70	75	76	72	293	3,430
Stuart Smith	69	77	73	74	293	3,430
Nico Van Rensburg	70	77	76	71	294	3,060
Donald Gammon	73	76	74	71	294	3,060
Schalk Van Der Merwe	73	74	75	72	294	3,060
Mark Wiltshire	74	72	75	73	294	3,060
Trevor Dodds	76	70	75	73	294	3,060
Greg McMillan	72	75	80	68	295	2,590
Ian Hutchings	77	69	80	69	295	2,590
Steve Burnett	73	75	77	70	295	2,590
Paul Blaikie	72	77	76	70	295	2,590
De Wet Basson	77	71	76	71	295	2,590
Michael Gatenby	72	75	74	74	295	2,590

Hassan II Trophy

Royal Dar es Salam, Red Course, Rabat, Morocco
Par 36-37—73; 7,035 yards

November 21-24
purse, $500,000

		SCORES			TOTAL	MONEY
Vijay Singh	70	73	71	71	285	$100,000
Payne Stewart	76	70	70	69	285	60,000
(Singh defeated Stewart on first extra hole.)						
Nick Faldo	73	73	69	72	287	36,000
Brian Marchbank	77	69	70	72	288	26,500
Brian Claar	72	72	72	72	288	26,500
Dudley Hart	71	74	74	71	290	18,500
Anders Forsbrand	74	76	73	67	290	18,500
Jose Rivero	78	71	70	73	292	13,375
Paul Broadhurst	74	73	75	70	292	13,375
Manuel Pinero	75	73	72	72	292	13,375
Bernhard Langer	75	71	73	73	292	13,375

	SCORES				TOTAL	MONEY
Gary Player	71	78	74	72	295	11,500
Brian Barnes	76	74	73	73	296	10,750
Gery Watine	74	72	73	77	296	10,750
Jose Maria Canizares	74	72	78	73	297	9,800
Moussa Fatmi	78	74	70	75	297	9,800
Peter Baker	74	75	75	74	298	9,000
Eric Giraud	74	75	74	75	298	9,000
Peter Townsend	71	80	77	71	299	8,400
Butch Baird	76	77	71	76	300	8,000
Roger Chapman	78	75	75	73	301	7,700
Tommy Aaron	77	77	74	75	303	7,400
Bob Eastwood	77	76	75	76	304	7,100
Calvin Peete	78	79	74	74	305	6,650
Bob Toski	77	75	79	74	305	6,650
Billy Casper	79	77	75	75	306	6,050
Ove Sellberg	76	77	77	76	306	6,050
Bruce Devlin	75	78	77	77	307	5,600
Torsten Giedeon	77	76	81	75	309	5,300
Mohamed Makroune	77	74	79	81	311	5,000
Nobuhiro Sakata	80	79	78	82	319	5,000

Ivory Coast Open

President Golf Club, Yamoussoukro, Ivory Coast
Par 36-36—72; 6,677 yards

December 5-8
purse, £81,687

	SCORES				TOTAL	MONEY
Michael Besanceney	68	73	71	67	279	£13,605.72
Paul Carman	65	76	66	72	279	9,070.48
(Besanceney defeated Carman on first extra hole.)						
Mathias Gronberg	69	73	68	70	280	4,600.61
Lee Vannet	71	73	67	69	280	4,600.61
Frederic Regard	68	72	71	70	281	3,460.67
Wayne Stephens	66	72	71	73	282	2,860.06
Ian Spencer	71	74	68	70	283	1,810.02
Craig Cassells	72	71	72	68	283	1,810.02
Roger Sabarros	73	69	72	69	283	1,810.02
Quentin Dabson	70	71	70	72	283	1,810.02
Mark Nichols	76	67	69	71	283	1,810.02
Ek Korblah	77	67	70	69	283	1,810.02
Richard Fish	70	69	75	70	284	1,282.94
Jeff Pinsent	69	68	73	74	284	1,282.94
Adam Hunter	68	71	74	72	285	1,152.19
Paul Eales	72	71	71	71	285	1,152.19
Marc Pendaries	70	76	71	68	285	1,152.19
Laurent Lassalle	74	70	70	72	286	1,054.13
Mike Miller	73	75	70	69	287	996.93
Richard Foreman	71	69	73	74	287	996.93
James Mullen	68	72	75	73	288	931.56
Chris Platts	72	76	68	72	288	931.56
Campbell Elliott	76	73	68	71	288	931.56
J. Brave Mensah	72	74	72	71	289	858.01
David R. Jones	69	70	72	78	289	858.01
Philip Talbot	68	73	74	74	289	858.01
David Wood	68	72	72	78	290	784.47
Pascal Ferran	75	71	73	71	290	784.47
Peter Harrison	72	72	68	78	290	784.47

	SCORES				TOTAL	MONEY
Paul Lyons	76	72	69	74	291	691.31
Carl Sunesson	72	71	79	69	291	691.31
Frederic Anger	72	73	72	74	291	691.31
Anders Haglund	71	75	75	70	291	691.31
James Lebbie	75	69	72	75	291	691.31

Nigerian Open

Ikoyi Golf Club, Lagos, Nigeria
Par 36-35—71; 6,389 yards

December 12-15
purse, £105,027

	SCORES				TOTAL	MONEY
James Lebbie	67	66	66	71	270	£17,486.19
Paul Eales	70	69	69	66	274	11,651.93
Gordon J. Brand	68	70	68	69	275	6,571.82
David Llewellyn	70	69	65	72	276	5,248.62
Peter Akakasiaka	72	67	67	71	277	4,450.28
Philip Harrison	72	72	68	66	278	3,149.17
Paul Lyons	68	71	71	68	278	3,149.17
Mathias Gronberg	71	72	67	68	278	3,149.17
Glyn Krause	71	72	70	66	279	2,127.07
Marcel Soumaboro	69	73	69	68	279	2,127.07
J. Brave Mensah	74	65	67	73	279	2,127.07
Jeff Pinsent	68	75	69	68	280	1,661.60
Mike Miller	70	72	67	71	280	1,661.60
Philip Talbot	73	70	66	71	280	1,661.60
Garry Harvey	70	68	68	74	280	1,661.60
Amos Korblah	72	70	69	71	282	1,476.52
Anders Haglund	72	70	69	71	282	1,476.52
Mark Stokes	70	72	71	70	283	1,304.79
David Wood	70	71	70	72	283	1,304.79
Peter Harrison	70	70	69	74	283	1,304.79
Jonathan Cheetham	72	72	68	72	284	1,229.28
Richard Foreman	73	73	71	68	285	1,149.17
Sandy Stephen	72	74	68	71	285	1,149.17
Patrice Barquez	71	67	73	74	285	1,149.17
Salim Mwanyenza	71	73	67	74	285	1,149.17
Jeremy Bennett	71	76	71	68	286	1,007.73
Frederic Regard	72	71	73	70	286	1,007.73
Chris Platts	70	71	74	71	286	1,007.73
Phil Golding	73	72	69	72	286	1,007.73
Kenny Cross	70	69	71	76	286	1,007.73

Australasian Tour

Daikyo Palm Meadows Cup

Palm Meadows Golf Club, Gold Coast, Queensland
Par 36-36—72; 6,973 yards

January 10-13
purse, A$1,200,000

	SCORES				TOTAL	MONEY
Greg Turner	74	62	67	68	271	A$216,000
Greg Norman	66	70	70	69	275	129,600
Terry Price	72	67	69	68	276	71,280
Peter Lonard	70	70	66	70	276	71,280
Mark O'Meara	71	69	68	69	277	49,920
Yoshinori Mizumaki	67	73	71	67	278	40,880
Peter McWhinney	73	68	69	68	278	40,880
Hideki Kase	68	73	66	71	278	40,880
Glenn Joyner	72	68	69	70	279	26,700
John Clifford	67	73	68	71	279	26,700
Grant Waite	73	70	65	71	279	26,700
Brad Faxon	68	71	65	75	279	26,700
Roger Mackay	71	70	72	67	280	16,182.85
David De Long	73	71	69	67	280	16,182.85
Masahiro Kuramoto	70	70	71	69	280	16,182.85
Ed Pfister	67	72	70	71	280	16,182.85
Curtis Strange	70	66	72	72	280	16,182.85
Russell Swanson	67	69	72	72	280	16,182.85
John Morse	69	72	67	72	280	16,182.85
David Ecob	71	70	70	70	281	12,960
Brian Jones	72	69	70	70	281	12,960
Peter O'Malley	73	69	73	67	282	11,040
Craig Warren	74	68	71	69	282	11,040
Ken Trimble	68	72	71	71	282	11,040
Peter Fowler	69	72	69	72	282	11,040
Johan Rystrom	64	71	72	75	282	11,040
Chris Patton	67	71	66	78	282	11,040
Grant Kenny	73	69	72	69	283	8,700
Graham Marsh	70	70	72	71	283	8,700
Nobumitsu Yuhara	73	70	69	71	283	8,700
Koichi Suzuki	73	69	70	71	283	8,700

SXL Sanctuary Cove Classic

The Pines Course, Sanctuary Cove, Gold Coast, Queensland
Par 36-36—72; 7,308 yards

January 17-20
purse, A$700,000

	SCORES				TOTAL	MONEY
Rodger Davis	70	70	67	71	278	A$126,000
Frank Nobilo	69	65	70	75	279	75,600
Ian Baker-Finch	72	71	70	67	280	41,580
Mike Ferguson	71	67	71	71	280	41,580
Tod Power	70	68	67	76	281	29,120
Brad King	73	71	71	67	282	26,740
Glenn Joyner	69	69	76	69	283	20,055
Grant Waits	69	72	73	69	283	20,055
Futoshi Irino	71	69	73	70	283	20,055

	SCORES				TOTAL	MONEY
Bob Shearer	70	72	71	70	283	20,055
Richard Backwell	73	70	74	67	284	11,293.33
Brian Jones	72	68	73	71	284	11,293.33
David De Long	71	68	72	73	284	11,293.33
Wayne Grady	72	69	70	73	284	11,293.33
Hiroshi Makino	70	67	72	75	284	11,293.33
Anthony Gilligan	73	67	69	75	284	11,293.33
Simon Owen	72	69	76	68	285	8,225
Matthew Lane	70	70	75	70	285	8,225
Mike Clayton	69	75	69	72	285	8,225
Craig Parry	67	66	73	79	285	8,225
Terry Gale	71	70	74	71	286	7,140
Guy Boros	69	70	73	74	286	7,140
Mike Harwood	70	70	69	77	286	7,140
Mike Colandro	74	69	71	73	287	6,440
Brad Faxon	72	71	70	74	287	6,440
Brad Hughes	74	69	75	70	288	5,460
David Iwasaki-Smith	69	74	75	70	288	5,460
Stewart Ginn	73	71	72	72	288	5,460
Ken Kusumoto	72	69	74	73	288	5,460
Graham Marsh	71	71	70	76	288	5,460

The Vines Classic

The Vines Resort, Perth, Western Australia
Par 36-36—72; 7,111 yards

January 24-27
purse, A$700,000

	SCORES				TOTAL	MONEY
Blaine McCallister	68	70	70	70	278	A$126,000
Greg Turner	68	71	70	70	279	61,950
Wayne Grady	69	71	69	70	279	61,950
Graham Marsh	72	68	76	66	282	27,104
Zoran Zorkic	70	72	70	70	282	27,104
Peter McWhinney	69	71	72	70	282	27,104
Isao Aoki	69	73	70	70	282	27,104
Michael Bradley	66	72	70	74	282	27,104
Frank Nobilo	74	69	71	69	283	16,566.66
John Morse	71	73	69	70	283	16,566.66
Craig Warren	69	76	65	73	283	16,566.66
Koichi Suzuki	71	74	72	67	284	12,040
Mike Harwood	69	71	74	70	284	12,040
Danny Mijovic	69	70	70	76	285	10,360
Brett Ogle	71	71	70	74	286	9,800
Jeff Woodland	77	69	72	70	288	8,610
Nick Price	73	70	71	74	288	8,610
Ken Dukes	71	73	69	75	288	8,610
John Clifford	72	68	71	77	288	8,610
Roger Mackay	70	76	72	71	289	6,860
Tsukasa Watanabe	75	73	72	69	289	6,860
Ed Pfister	74	71	72	72	289	6,860
Mike Clayton	76	71	70	72	289	6,860
Anthony Gilligan	74	71	72	72	289	6,860
Scott Simpson	72	71	68	78	289	6,860
Lanny Wadkins	71	75	72	72	290	5,320
Terry Price	71	70	76	73	290	5,320
Bill Brask	72	71	73	74	290	5,320
Peter Lonard	74	73	77	66	290	5,320

	SCORES			TOTAL	MONEY
David De Long	77 70 72 72			291	4,480
Lyndsay Stephen	74 73 73 71			291	4,480
Stephen Bennett	70 75 76 70			291	4,480
Peter Fowler	74 74 72 71			291	4,480
Peter O'Malley	72 72 70 77			291	4,480

Mercedes-Benz Australian Match Play

Kingston Heath Golf Club, Melbourne, Victoria

Par 36-36—72; 6,814 yards

February 7-10

purse, A$200,000

FIRST ROUND

John Morse defeated Peter Jones, 1 up, 19 holes
Wayne Smith defeated Ian Stanley, 2 and 1
Ken Trimble defeated Paul Foley, 2 and 1
David De Long defeated Kyi Hla Han, 1 up, 19 holes
Mike Colandro defeated Peter Lonard, 3 and 1
Tod Power defeated Lee Carter, 5 and 4
Guy Boros defeated Peter O'Malley, 1 up, 19 holes
Ken Dukes defeated *Robert Allenby, 1 up, 19 holes
Wayne Riley defeated Chris Gray, 4 and 2
Brad King defeated *Stephen Leaney, 1 up, 21 holes
Peter Senior defeated Noel Ratcliffe, 5 and 3
Craig Mann defeated Terry Price, 2 up
Peter McWhinney defeated Mike Ferguson, 1 up
Bob Shearer defeated Lyndsay Stephen, 8 and 6
Danny Mijovic defeated George Serhan, 1 up
David Ecob defeated Stuart Hendley, 6 and 5
Brett Ogle defeated Steve Bann, 6 and 4
Ed Pfister defeated Gabriel Hjertstedt, 2 and 1
Brad Hughes defeated Ray Picker, 3 and 2
Glenn Joyner defeated Roger Mackay, 3 and 1
Anthony Painter defeated Mike Clayton, 1 up
Jack Kay, Jr. defeated Ossie Moore, 5 and 4
David Iwasaki-Smith defeated Russell Swanson, 1 up, 19 holes
Louis Brown defeated Michael Bradley, 1 up, 21 holes
Greg Hohnen defeated Greg Turner, 2 up
Stephen Bennett defeated Jeff Woodland, 2 and 1
Chris Patton defeated Anthony Gilligan, 4 and 3
John Clifford defeated Garry Merrick, 1 up
Wayne Case defeated Peter Fowler, 4 and 2
Stewart Ginn defeated Jon Evans, 4 and 2
Simon Owen defeated Paul Moloney, 1 up
Craig Warren defeated Sandy Armour, 1 up, 21 holes

(Each losing player received A$690.67.)

SECOND ROUND

Morse defeated Smith, 4 and 2
De Long defeated Trimble, 4 and 3
Power defeated Colandro, 4 and 3
Dukes defeated Boros, 4 and 2
Riley defeated King, 1 up
Senior defeated Mann, 3 and 2
McWhinney defeated Shearer, 1 up, 24 holes
Ecob defeated Mijovic, 1 up

Pfister defeated Ogle, 1 up
Hughes defeated Joyner, 3 and 2
Painter defeated Kay, 1 up
Brown defeated Iwasaki-Smith, 2 and 1
Bennett defeated Hohnen, 2 up
Patton defeated Clifford, 1 up
Ginn defeated Case, 3 and 1
Warren defeated Owen, 3 and 1

(Each losing player received A$1,855.)

THIRD ROUND

Morse defeated De Long, 1 up, 19 holes
Dukes defeated Power, 4 and 2
Senior defeated Riley, 4 and 3
McWhinney defeated Ecob, 1 up, 19 holes
Hughes defeated Pfister, 1 up
Brown defeated Painter, 4 and 3
Patton defeated Bennett, 4 and 3
Ginn defeated Warren, 5 and 3

(Each losing player received A$3,685.)

QUARTER-FINALS

Dukes defeated Morse, 4 and 3
Senior defeated McWhinney, 1 up
Hughes defeated Brown, 4 and 3
Patton defeated Ginn, 2 and 1

(Each losing player received A$7,190.)

SEMI-FINALS

Dukes defeated Senior, 2 and 1
Patton defeated Hughes, 1 up, 19 holes

THIRD-FOURTH PLACE PLAYOFF

Senior defeated Hughes, 4 and 3

FINAL

Patton defeated Dukes, 5 and 2

(Patton received A$36,000, Dukes A$21,600, Senior A$13,800, Hughes A$9,900.)

Pyramid Australian Masters

Huntingdale Golf Club, Melbourne, Victoria
Par 37-36—73; 6,955 yards

February 14-17
purse, A$500,000

	SCORES				TOTAL	MONEY
Peter Senior	68	71	69	70	278	A$90,000
Greg Norman	70	67	71	71	279	54,000
Mike Clayton	67	71	74	69	281	29,700
Peter O'Malley	72	68	71	70	281	29,700
David De Long	71	70	73	68	282	19,000

	SCORES				TOTAL	MONEY
Ian Baker-Finch	74	70	69	69	282	19,000
Rodger Davis	71	68	72	71	282	19,000
Jeff Woodland	71	67	73	72	283	14,900
John Morse	71	74	72	68	285	13,500
*Robert Allenby	74	70	70	71	285	
Tod Power	72	74	69	71	286	11,800
Wayne Riley	74	72	71	70	287	9,600
Frank Nobilo	73	68	71	75	287	9,600
Craig Parry	76	69	76	68	289	7,300
John Clifford	75	71	72	71	289	7,300
Peter Lonard	70	73	73	73	289	7,300
Stewart Ginn	72	71	70	76	289	7,300
Guy Boros	71	72	74	73	290	6,150
Terry Price	74	70	70	76	290	6,150
Greg Turner	73	74	74	70	291	5,300
Anthony Gilligan	71	74	75	71	291	5,300
Bob Shearer	68	74	75	74	291	5,300
Mike Ferguson	72	70	74	75	291	5,300
Roger Mackay	71	72	73	75	291	5,300
Hank Baran	76	72	74	70	292	4,600
Jeff Wagner	76	69	73	74	292	4,600
Brian Jones	73	73	76	71	293	4,200
Russell Swanson	72	72	73	76	293	4,200
Noel Ratcliffe	73	72	76	73	294	3,800
Graham Marsh	70	74	76	74	294	3,800

Tasmanian Open

Royal Hobart Golf Club, Tasmania
Par 36-36—72

February 21-24
purse, A$80,000

	SCORES				TOTAL	MONEY
Chris Gray	68	71	71	70	280	A$15,300
Brad Hughes	67	69	74	72	282	6,426
Robert Stephens	72	69	70	71	282	6,426
Jon Evans	70	70	70	72	282	6,426
John Clifford	71	70	71	71	283	3,536
Tim Elliott	71	71	76	68	286	2,898
Ian Stanley	68	70	71	77	286	2,898
Mike Collandro	65	75	78	68	286	2,898

AMP New Zealand Open

Paraparaumu Beach Golf Club, Wellington
Par 35-36—71; 6,492 yards

March 7-10
purse, NZ$200,000

	SCORES				TOTAL	MONEY
Rodger Davis	67	66	73	67	273	NZ$36,000
Frank Nobilo	66	69	72	68	275	21,600
John Morse	67	68	71	70	276	13,800
Glenn Joyner	68	68	70	71	277	9,960
Tod Power	67	67	73	72	279	8,320
Gabriel Hjertstedt	70	71	67	72	280	6,813.33
John Clifford	68	71	69	72	280	6,813.33
Jon Evans	71	72	64	73	280	6,813.33

	SCORES				TOTAL	MONEY
Cameron Howell	70	72	71	68	281	5,400
Jack Kay, Jr.	73	70	66	73	282	4,400
Mike Colandro	68	74	69	71	282	4,400
Brad Andrews	72	71	72	68	283	3,280
Simon Owen	71	71	71	70	283	3,280
Brad King	69	73	69	72	283	3,280
Ian Stanley	71	72	72	69	284	2,590
Noel Ratcliffe	71	70	73	70	284	2,590
Grant Waite	74	73	65	72	284	2,590
Terry Price	74	63	71	76	284	2,590
Anthony Painter	70	73	71	71	285	2,280
*Tony Christie	77	66	70	72	285	
Mark Allen	75	72	73	67	287	2,080
Ossie Moore	79	68	71	69	287	2,080
Jack Oliver	68	75	74	70	287	2,080
Matthew Lane	76	69	69	73	287	2,080
*Stuart Thompson	72	70	71	74	287	
Tim Elliott	73	74	69	72	288	1,840
Paul Maloney	71	73	71	73	288	1,840
*Michael Campbell	75	68	71	74	288	
Peter Giles	74	73	70	72	289	1,720
Paul Barnsley	75	72	73	70	290	1,520
Andre White	74	72	72	72	290	1,520
Russell Swanson	74	73	71	72	290	1,520
John Downs	75	68	73	74	290	1,520
*Steven Alker	70	72	74	74	290	
*David Smail	70	74	72	74	290	

Rothmans Malaysian Masters

Royal Selangor Golf Club, Kuala Lumpur
Par 36-36—72; 6,854 yards

October 3-6
purse, A$291,000

	SCORES				TOTAL	MONEY
Stewart Ginn	70	70	70	68	278	A$52,380
Nandasena Perera	67	71	74	69	281	31,428
Hank Baran	73	67	72	70	282	17,285.40
Anthony Painter	72	71	66	73	282	17,285.40
Boonchu Ruengkit	70	68	73	72	283	12,105.60
Lyndsay Stephen	73	65	75	71	284	9,913.40
Ray Picker	71	74	68	71	284	9,913.40
Marimuthu Ramayah	68	71	71	74	284	9,913.40
Terry Gale	68	74	72	71	285	6,134.28
Louis Brown	74	68	71	72	285	6,134.28
Tsao Chien Teng	70	71	72	72	285	6,134.28
Michael Long	72	70	71	72	285	6,134.28
Tony Maloney	70	69	70	76	285	6,134.28
John Clifford	75	69	71	71	286	4,308.80
Gabriel Hjertstedt	72	70	72	73	287	3,957.60
Jim Empey	72	70	71	74	287	3,957.60
Barie Bluah	69	73	75	71	288	3,288.30
Peter Lonard	75	72	69	72	288	3,288.30
Santi Sophon	72	72	72	72	288	3,288.30
Tod Power	70	72	72	74	288	3,288.30
Craig McLellan	69	76	69	74	288	3,288.30
Zaw Moe	71	70	71	76	288	3,288.30
Mikael Krantz	74	75	69	71	289	2,444.40

	SCORES				TOTAL	MONEY
Jeff Wagner	72	72	74	71	289	2,444.40
Stuart Thompson	70	72	75	72	289	2,444.40
Richard Backwell	73	73	70	73	289	2,444.40
Craig Mann	70	74	72	73	289	2,444.40
Ben Jackson	72	68	80	69	289	2,444.40
Chris Gray	71	72	76	70	289	2,444.40
Shane Robinson	69	71	70	79	289	2,444.40

Perak Masters

Royal Perak Golf Club, Ipoh
Par 36-36—72; 6,798 yards

October 10-13
purse, A$150,000

	SCORES				TOTAL	MONEY
Tod Power	69	73	66	67	275	A$27,000
Scott Taylor	70	70	72	68	280	13,275
Louis Brown	72	70	69	69	280	13,275
Jim Empey	71	70	73	67	281	6,855
Peter Lonard	71	66	71	73	281	6,855
Simon Owen	68	69	71	74	282	5,730
Sufian Tan	71	69	74	70	284	4,550
Robert Stephens	66	71	75	72	284	4,550
Mark Cato	72	71	70	71	284	4,550
Tony Maloney	70	74	71	70	285	2,580
Paul Moloney	77	70	72	66	285	2,580
Zaw Moe	76	69	69	71	285	2,580
Ian Stanley	70	68	75	72	285	2,580
Anthony Painter	70	71	72	72	285	2,580
Hank Baran	69	71	72	73	285	2,580
Ossie Moore	71	72	69	73	285	2,580
Nandasena Perera	74	71	71	70	286	1,890
Marimuthu Ramayah	72	69	74	72	287	1,755
Robert Farley	70	71	73	73	287	1,755
Tony Brigstock	71	74	72	71	288	1,530
Brad Wright	74	70	72	72	288	1,530
Krishna Singh	73	72	69	74	288	1,530
Craig Mann	69	68	76	75	288	1,530
Stewart Ginn	71	71	76	70	288	1,530
Gavin Stratfold	77	69	71	72	289	1,230
Kyi Hla Han	75	71	68	75	289	1,230
David Iwasaki-Smith	72	74	72	71	289	1,230
M. Murugiah	73	74	71	71	289	1,230
Barie Bluah	69	72	71	77	289	1,230
Mike Cunning	75	69	73	73	290	930
Craig McLellan	73	73	71	73	290	930
Mikael Krantz	72	74	74	70	290	930
Max Stevens	70	72	73	75	290	930
Michael Winfrey	72	70	78	70	290	930
Rishi Narain	73	73	73	71	290	930
Kevin Youngblood	74	73	72	71	290	930
Henrik Bergqvist	76	67	71	76	290	930
Leith Wastle	74	72	72	72	290	930

Pioneer Singapore PGA Championship

Singapore Country Club, Sime Course
Par 36-36—72; 6,564 yards

October 17-20
purse, A$150,000

	SCORES				TOTAL	MONEY
Peter Teravainen	67	69	67	71	274	A$27,000
Tony Maloney	66	71	68	70	275	16,200
Nandasena Perera	68	71	69	68	276	8,910
Robert Stephens	67	70	69	70	276	8,910
Richard Backwell	68	68	69	72	277	6,240
Paul Moloney	67	70	74	67	278	5,430
Samson Gimson	73	66	72	67	278	5,430
Scott Taylor	71	70	67	71	279	4,260
David Iwasaki-Smith	66	67	73	73	279	4,260
Magnus Rosenback	71	71	71	67	280	2,940
Kyi Hla Han	69	73	71	67	280	2,940
Donald Fardon	65	71	72	72	280	2,940
Craig Warren	70	69	65	76	280	2,940
Chua Guan Soon	68	69	76	68	281	1,998
Lim Swee Wah	71	71	69	70	281	1,998
Christian Post	73	68	70	70	281	1,998
Michael Winfrey	73	68	70	70	281	1,998
Ray Picker	70	69	70	72	281	1,998
Michael Long	71	73	66	72	282	1,650
Zaw Moe	74	67	68	73	282	1,650
Mike Clayton	72	65	71	74	282	1,650
Bill Fung Hee Kwan	69	71	73	70	283	1,410
Marimuthu Ramayah	72	68	71	72	283	1,410
Simon Owen	72	68	70	73	283	1,410
Craig Mann	71	69	74	69	283	1,410
Gavin Stratfold	72	71	71	69	283	1,410
Leith Wastle	72	72	69	71	284	1,116
Shane Robinson	73	71	71	69	284	1,116
Mikael Krantz	67	75	69	73	284	1,116
Bill Fua Tin Peau	70	71	73	70	284	1,116
Stuart Thompson	66	69	78	71	284	1,116

Air New Zealand Shell Open

Titirangi Golf Club, Auckland
Par 35-35—70; 6,311 yards

November 7-10
purse, NZ$250,000

	SCORES				TOTAL	MONEY
John Morse	67	67	66	73	273	NZ$45,000
Nandasena Perera	70	70	70	66	276	27,000
Martyn Roberts	71	68	70	69	278	17,250
Chip Beck	72	69	68	70	279	10,237.50
Anthony Maloney	66	69	73	71	279	10,237.50
Peter McWhinney	68	68	70	73	279	10,237.50
Stewart Ginn	68	65	71	75	279	10,237.50
*Michael Campbell	71	68	71	69	279	
Mikael Krantz	67	69	71	73	280	7,450
John Clifford	71	71	70	69	281	5,916.66
Simon Owen	72	67	70	72	281	5,916.66
Chris Gray	67	68	73	73	281	5,916.66
Jeff Woodland	72	70	72	68	282	3,820
Max Stevens	71	73	67	71	282	3,820

	SCORES				TOTAL	MONEY
Jeff Wagner	67	67	75	73	282	3,820
David De Long	66	75	68	73	282	3,820
Richard Backwell	68	68	70	76	282	3,820
*Tony Christie	69	74	70	70	283	
Matthew Lane	68	72	72	71	283	2,937.50
Gabriel Hjertstedt	68	71	71	73	283	2,937.50
Greg Carroll	71	71	68	73	283	2,937.50
Jim Kennedy	65	71	72	75	283	2,937.50
Paul Moloney	70	71	74	69	284	2,500
Jason Deep	74	68	72	70	284	2,500
Wayne Riley	69	70	73	72	284	2,500
Scott Taylor	69	74	68	73	284	2,500
Robert Farley	70	70	76	69	285	1,957.14
Anthony Painter	74	68	72	71	285	1,957.14
Bob Charles	75	67	71	72	285	1,957.14
Colin Hunt	70	71	71	73	285	1,957.14
George Serhan	72	72	69	72	285	1,957.14
Robert Stephens	73	71	69	72	285	1,957.14
Peter Fowler	73	69	69	74	285	1,957.14

Asahi Glass Four Tours Championship

Royal Adelaide Golf Club, Adelaide, Australia
Par 37-36—73; 7,000 yards

November 7-10
purse, US$1,150,000

FIRST ROUND

EUROPE 8, AUSTRALIA/NEW ZEALAND 4.
Ronan Rafferty (E) and Roger Mackay tied, 77-77.
Paul Broadhurst (E) defeated Craig Parry, 71-75.
Steven Richardson (E) and Graham Marsh tied, 76-76.
Sam Torrance (E) defeated Ian Baker-Finch, 73-79.
Mike Harwood (ANZ) defeated David Feherty, 75-78.
Colin Montgomerie (E) defeated Rodger Davis, 73-79.

UNITED STATES 8, JAPAN 4.
Jim Gallagher, Jr. (US) defeated Ricky Kawagishi, 74-77.
Tom Purtzer (US) defeated Tsukasa Watanabe, 73-74.
Yoshinori Kaneko (J) defeated Billy Mayfair, 76-79.
Lanny Wadkins (US) defeated Hideki Kase, 75-76.
Hiroshi Makino (J) defeated Bob Tway, 78-80.
Fred Couples (US) defeated Noboru Sugai, 73-76.

SECOND ROUND

EUROPE 6, JAPAN 6.
Rafferty (E) defeated Watanabe, 70-73.
Torrance (E) and Kawagishi tied, 72-72.
Kaneko (J) defeated Feherty, 71-73.
Richardson (E) and Kase tied, 74-74.
Broadhurst (E) defeated Makino, 72-74.
Sugai (J) defeated Montgomerie, 71-73.

AUSTRALIA/NEW ZEALAND 7, UNITED STATES 5.
Couples (US) defeated Baker-Finch, 70-76.
Marsh (ANZ) defeated Mayfair, 70-72.
Davis (ANZ) and Gallagher tied, 73-73.
Mackay (ANZ) defeated Tway, 71-78.

Parry (ANZ) defeated Purtzer, 71-72.
Wadkins (US) defeated Harwood, 70-77.

THIRD ROUND

EUROPE 6, UNITED STATES 6.
Tway (US) defeated Rafferty, 71-73.
Mayfair (US) defeated Richardson, 69-74.
Torrance (E) defeated Purtzer, 70-72.
Couples (US) defeated Feherty, 70-71.
Montgomerie (E) defeated Wadkins, 66-71.
Broadhurst (E) defeated Gallagher, 70-72.

AUSTRALIA/NEW ZEALAND 8, JAPAN 4.
Davis (ANZ) defeated Kawagishi, 73-74.
Watanabe (J) defeated Baker-Finch, 72-76.
Kaneko (J) defeated Harwood, 72-74.
Marsh (ANZ) defeated Kase, 71-74.
Mackay (ANZ) defeated Makino, 73-74.
Parry (ANZ) defeated Sugai, 68-78.

POINT STANDINGS AFTER 54 HOLES:
Europe 20, Australia/New Zealand and United States 19, Japan 14.

PLAYOFF FOR THIRD-FOURTH PLACES

UNITED STATES 6, JAPAN 6.
Tway (US) and Makino tied, 74-74.
Mayfair (US) defeated Sugai, 71-72.
Purtzer (US) defeated Kaneko, 70-72.
Watanabe (J) defeated Wadkins, 71-72.
Gallagher (US) and Kase tied, 73-73.
Kawagishi (J) defeated Couples, 72-75.

FINAL

EUROPE 8, AUSTRALIA/NEW ZEALAND 4.
Harwood (ANZ) defeated Montgomerie, 72-74.
Rafferty (E) defeated Davis, 65-70.
Feherty (E) defeated Marsh, 71-74.
Mackay (ANZ) defeated Richardson, 71-73.
Torrance (E) defeated Parry, 72-73.
Broadhurst (E) defeated Baker-Finch, 69-74.

MONEY BREAKDOWN:
Each European player received US$80,000; each Australia/New Zealand player US$45,000; each Japanese player US$35,000; each United States player $30,000.

West End South Australian Open

Royal Adelaide Golf Club, Adelaide, South Australia
Par 37-36—73; 7,000 yards

November 14-17
purse, A$200,000

	SCORES				TOTAL	MONEY
Brett Ogle	71	70	69	69	279	A$36,000
Mike Harwood	71	68	73	69	281	21,600
Colin Field	77	72	70	66	285	13,800
Stewart Ginn	76	73	69	68	286	9,140

	SCORES				TOTAL	MONEY
John Morse	71	72	72	71	286	9,140
Peter O'Malley	71	69	72	75	287	7,640
Brad Hughes	75	69	74	70	288	6,066.66
Shane Tait	74	73	69	72	288	6,066.66
Michael Long	75	69	70	74	288	6,066.66
Wayne Grady	76	73	68	72	289	4,400
Craig Warren	68	74	73	74	289	4,400
Russell Swanson	72	73	72	73	290	3,600
Paul Moloney	78	72	71	70	291	2,920
David De Long	75	73	72	71	291	2,920
Mark Cato	73	73	73	72	291	2,920
David Iwasaki-Smith	73	72	73	73	291	2,920
Stephen Bennett	72	75	74	71	292	2,520
Daniel Silva	75	72	75	71	293	2,250
Noel Ratcliffe	70	78	74	71	293	2,250
Mike Clayton	73	75	73	72	293	2,250
Ian Stanley	76	73	71	73	293	2,250
Wayne Riley	76	70	77	71	294	1,920
Hank Baran	77	74	71	72	294	1,920
Peter McWhinney	73	76	71	74	294	1,920
Greg Turner	77	71	68	78	294	1,920
Paul Foley	77	72	75	71	295	1,560
Robert Farley	75	75	73	72	295	1,560
Mats Lanner	79	71	73	72	295	1,560
Chris Gray	72	78	71	74	295	1,560
Paul Archbold	72	75	72	76	295	1,560

Ford Australian PGA Championship

Concord Golf Club, Sydney, New South Wales
Par 35-36—71; 6,067 yards

November 21-24
purse, A$250,000

	SCORES				TOTAL	MONEY
Wayne Grady	66	68	68	69	271	A$45,000
Brett Ogle	70	70	67	67	274	27,000
Neil Kerry	67	68	71	71	277	14,850
Steven Richardson	67	67	70	73	277	14,850
Wayne Smith	65	70	70	73	278	10,400
Jamie Spence	71	69	69	70	279	7,640
Simon Owen	73	68	69	69	279	7,640
Craig Parry	67	70	71	71	279	7,640
Craig Warren	69	71	69	70	279	7,640
Mike Clayton	69	72	67	71	279	7,640
Peter O'Malley	73	65	70	72	280	5,100
Peter Fowler	70	68	69	74	281	4,500
Jim Kennedy	70	73	72	67	282	4,100
Peter Lonard	75	68	70	71	284	3,412.50
David Ecob	75	70	71	68	284	3,412.50
Greg Turner	69	74	73	68	284	3,412.50
Lee Rinker	71	73	70	70	284	3,412.50
Mats Lanner	71	71	73	70	285	2,760
Paul Kent	72	73	71	69	285	2,760
Keith Valentine	74	69	70	72	285	2,760
Leith Wastle	73	72	70	70	285	2,760
Mark Cato	76	67	70	72	285	2,760
Shane Tait	73	72	72	69	286	2,400
Ken Dukes	68	71	73	74	286	2,400

	SCORES				TOTAL	MONEY
Glenn Joyner	71	72	75	69	287	1,918.75
Greg Carroll	70	75	74	68	287	1,918.75
Paul Foley	73	72	71	71	287	1,918.75
Robert Stephens	71	74	71	71	287	1,918.75
Craig Mann	73	72	68	74	287	1,918.75
David De Long	69	72	73	73	287	1,918.75
Jeff Woodland	69	72	73	73	287	1,918.75
Ken Trimble	66	77	72	72	287	1,918.75

Australian Open Championship

Royal Melbourne Composite Course, Melbourne, Victoria   November 28-December 1
Par 35-37—72; 6,959 yards   purse, A$700,000

	SCORES				TOTAL	MONEY
Wayne Riley	72	74	71	68	285	A$126,000
*Robert Allenby	70	78	70	68	286	
Rodger Davis	72	70	70	75	287	75,600
Brett Ogle	71	72	73	72	288	37,426.66
Steven Richardson	72	70	70	76	288	37,426.66
James Spence	70	72	72	74	288	37,426.66
Craig Parry	74	70	72	73	289	26,740
Mats Lanner	67	73	74	76	290	22,400
Hank Baran	72	68	74	76	290	22,400
Ronan Rafferty	75	73	74	69	291	14,023.33
Frank Nobilo	70	78	74	69	291	14,023.33
Michael Bradley	71	75	72	73	291	14,023.33
Grant Waite	68	78	71	74	291	14,023.33
Anders Forsbrand	72	74	71	74	291	14,023.33
Jack Kay, Jr.	72	76	68	75	291	14,023.33
Vijay Singh	78	72	73	69	292	9,286.66
Brad Andrews	73	75	72	72	292	9,286.66
Greg Norman	76	73	71	72	292	9,286.66
John Clifford	71	75	74	73	293	8,190
Glenn Joyner	75	72	71	75	293	8,190
Paul Moloney	75	73	73	73	294	7,420
Peter Fowler	75	77	69	73	294	7,420
Ian Baker-Finch	74	75	71	74	294	7,420
Martin Gates	77	73	75	70	295	6,440
Brad King	74	73	74	74	295	6,440
Matthew Lane	75	73	73	74	295	6,440
Anthony Painter	72	74	71	78	295	6,440
Jeff Wagner	72	74	77	73	296	5,600
Garry Merrick	74	73	73	76	296	5,600
Tod Power	74	78	75	70	297	4,788
Lyndsay Stephen	75	76	74	72	297	4,788
Danny Mijovic	72	77	73	75	297	4,788
Lee Rinker	67	77	77	76	297	4,788
Jon Evans	73	75	73	76	297	4,788
*Stuart Appleby	74	74	80	70	298	
Colin Montgomerie	76	75	75	72	298	4,200
Ken Trimble	72	76	73	77	298	4,200
Mike Harwood	72	75	73	78	298	4,200
Keith Valentine	73	76	76	74	299	3,710
Mike Ferguson	77	73	74	75	299	3,710
Daniel Silva	73	75	75	76	299	3,710
Mike Clayton	74	74	75	76	299	3,710

	SCORES				TOTAL	MONEY
Chris van der Velde	70	82	81	67	300	2,800
Scott Taylor	72	78	78	72	300	2,800
Anthony Edwards	76	76	76	72	300	2,800
Ken Dukes	71	80	76	73	300	2,800
Chris Gray	74	76	76	74	300	2,800
Ian Stanley	73	78	74	75	300	2,800
Bob Shearer	73	75	76	76	300	2,800
Jeff Maggert	73	79	72	76	300	2,800
Mike Colandro	74	78	71	77	300	2,800

Johnnie Walker Classic

The Lakes Golf Club, Sydney, New South Wales   December 5-8
Par 36-37—73; 6,866 yards   purse, A$1,000,000

	SCORES				TOTAL	MONEY
Peter Senior	66	71	72	73	282	A$180,000
Rodger Davis	69	70	70	74	283	88,500
Frank Nobilo	68	71	77	67	283	88,500
Wayne Grady	68	75	74	69	286	40,950
Peter Lonard	70	70	74	72	286	40,950
Robert Gamez	72	72	71	71	286	40,950
John Morse	72	69	71	74	286	40,950
Anders Forsbrand	70	71	74	72	287	26,800
Richard Backwell	68	74	72	73	287	26,800
Craig Parry	69	67	74	77	287	26,800
Brad Hughes	72	74	70	72	288	19,200
Steven Richardson	70	72	70	76	288	19,200
Brad King	69	68	80	72	289	15,066.66
Greg Turner	67	74	72	76	289	15,066.66
Colin Montgomerie	70	69	73	77	289	15,066.66
Ian Stanley	72	74	73	71	290	12,040
Ronan Rafferty	69	69	80	72	290	12,040
Brett Ogle	74	73	68	75	290	12,040
Greg Norman	74	72	69	75	290	12,040
Kyi Hla Han	70	69	71	80	290	12,040
Bob Shearer	70	73	74	74	291	10,000
Jamie Spence	72	75	72	72	291	10,000
Tod Power	69	75	75	72	291	10,000
Peter O'Malley	73	66	72	80	291	10,000
Tony Maloney	74	70	78	70	292	8,200
Gabriel Hjertstedt	69	73	79	71	292	8,200
Glenn Joyner	71	75	74	72	292	8,200
Martyn Roberts	73	72	72	75	292	8,200
Peter Fowler	68	69	76	79	292	8,200
Mike Colandro	70	76	75	72	293	6,300
Ken Trimble	71	71	75	76	293	6,300
Michael Bradley	72	74	74	73	293	6,300
Terry Gale	70	77	72	74	293	6,300
Grant Waite	70	73	74	76	293	6,300
Russell Swanson	74	71	69	79	293	6,300
Vijay Singh	73	71	72	77	293	6,300
Wayne Riley	70	70	74	79	293	6,300

Asia/Japan Tours

Hutchison Telecom Hong Kong Open

Royal Hong Kong Golf Club, Composite Course, Fanling
Par 71; 6,760 yards

February 7-10
purse, US$200,000

		SCORES			TOTAL	MONEY
Bernard Langer	65	72	69	63	269	US$33,320
Choi Sang Ho	65	73	70	68	276	17,370
Lu Wen Ter	67	71	70	68	276	17,370
Mike Cunning	67	68	73	70	278	10,000
Mike Harwood	69	72	68	70	279	6,192
Barry Lane	72	68	71	68	279	6,192
Mats Lanner	73	69	67	70	279	6,192
Craig Parry	68	71	74	66	279	6,192
Chen Tze Chung	68	71	68	72	279	6,192
Rafael Alarcon	69	73	69	69	280	3,733.33
Chen Liang Hsi	69	71	71	69	280	3,733.33
Chen Tze Ming	67	74	71	68	280	3,733.33
Robert Farley	67	70	73	71	281	3,320
Barry Conser	69	70	71	72	282	2,973.33
Ronan Rafferty	73	71	70	68	282	2,973.33
David Toms	69	71	71	71	283	2,492
Kuo Chi Hsing	70	72	69	72	283	2,492
Choi Kwang Soo	71	70	70	72	283	2,492
Brian Mogg	68	73	71	71	283	2,492
John O'Neill	67	73	71	72	283	2,492
Anders Sorensen	69	73	71	70	283	2,492
Steve Jurgensen	67	74	72	71	284	2,280
Carlos Espinosa	71	72	67	75	285	2,086.67
Rick Gibson	67	72	71	75	285	2,086.67
Gerry Norquist	70	73	74	68	285	2,086.67
Dennis Paulson	74	72	69	70	285	2,086.67
Bong Tae Ha	73	73	68	71	285	2,086.67
Wang Ter Chang	75	70	71	69	285	2,086.67
Bill Brask	72	74	68	72	286	1,795
Bill Israelson	71	71	73	71	286	1,795
Tray Tyner	70	74	70	72	286	1,795
Li Wen Sheng	69	74	72	71	286	1,795

San Miguel Philippine Open

Valley Golf Club, Manila, The Philippines
Par 72; 7,100 yards

February 14-17
purse, US$150,000

		SCORES			TOTAL	MONEY
Dennis Paulson	71	68	71	71	281	US$24,990
Chen Tze Ming	72	67	76	66	281	16,665
(Paulson defeated Chen on first extra hole.)						
Rick Gibson	70	71	69	73	283	9,390
Rodrigo Cuello	73	67	72	73	285	7,500
Tim Fleming	70	72	70	74	286	6,360

	SCORES				TOTAL	MONEY
Roger Antonio	73	70	71	73	287	5,250
Hsieh Chin Sheng	77	69	69	73	288	4,500
Hsieh Yu Shu	72	74	72	71	289	3,370
Lu Chien Soon	75	70	69	75	289	3,370
David Toms	77	72	68	72	289	3,370
Barry Conser	72	73	77	68	290	2,630
Brent Franklin	71	73	72	74	290	2,630
John O'Neill	74	72	73	71	290	2,630
Carlos Espinosa	72	73	72	74	291	2,124
Li Wen Sheng	75	71	72	73	291	2,124
Craig McClellan	80	69	68	74	291	2,124
Brian Mogg	75	69	71	76	291	2,124
Tray Tyner	77	73	70	71	291	2,124
Hung Wen Neng	76	72	74	70	292	1,830
Frankie Minoza	78	70	71	73	292	1,830
Michael Blewett	77	72	69	75	293	1,520
Chen Tze Ming	71	75	76	71	293	1,520
Choi Yoon Soo	74	69	76	74	293	1,520
Mike Cunning	74	73	71	75	293	1,520
Todd Hamilton	75	75	71	72	293	1,520
Dennis Harrington	74	74	76	69	293	1,520
Edward Kirby	72	75	76	70	293	1,520
Gregory Lesher	74	73	73	73	293	1,520
Casey Nakama	72	75	75	71	293	1,520
Robert Pactolerin	73	72	78	70	293	1,520
Marumuthu Ramayah	72	78	71	72	293	1,520
Don Walsworth	72	74	74	73	293	1,520

Epson Singapore Open

Tanah Merah Country Club, Garden Course, Singapore
Par 72; 7,102 yards

February 21-24
purse, US$400,000

	SCORES				TOTAL	MONEY
Jack Kay, Jr.	67	72	72	69	280	US$66,640
Wayne Riley	70	69	71	72	282	44,440
Chen Tze Chung	69	69	75	70	283	25,040
Remi Bouchard	72	73	70	70	285	18,480
Jean-Louis Lamarre	73	72	71	69	285	18,480
John Morse	71	73	72	70	286	11,240
Marumuthu Ramayah	74	72	72	68	286	11,240
Wayne Smith	72	71	72	71	286	11,240
Jim Strickland	74	71	67	74	286	11,240
Mike Cunning	74	73	70	70	287	7,064
Rick Gibson	68	71	73	75	287	7,064
Park Nam Sin	70	72	73	72	287	7,064
Tom Pernice	69	73	72	73	287	7,064
Peter Senior	77	68	72	70	287	7,064
Choi Yoon Soo	70	71	73	74	288	5,510
Harumitsu Hamano	71	74	71	72	288	5,510
Hsieh Yu Shu	72	75	69	72	288	5,510
Todd Power	74	72	73	69	288	5,510
Barry Conser	71	74	73	71	289	4,688
Edward Kirby	75	70	72	72	289	4,688
Craig McClellan	71	73	73	72	289	4,688
Masashi Shimoi	69	75	71	74	289	4,688
Don Walsworth	73	72	72	72	289	4,688

	SCORES				TOTAL	MONEY
Chris Baron	73	73	70	74	290	4,000
Chen Tze Ming	74	71	70	75	290	4,000
Robert Farley	72	73	72	73	290	4,000
Brent Franklin	73	72	72	73	290	4,000
Lin Chih Chen	72	69	76	73	290	4,000
Yuzo Oyama	73	67	73	77	290	4,000
E.J. Pfister	72	72	72	74	290	4,000

Benson & Hedges Malaysian Open

Kelab Golf Negara Subang Golf Club, Selangor, Malaysia
Par 72; 7,065 yards

February 28 - March 3
purse, US$200,000

	SCORES				TOTAL	MONEY
Rick Gibson	70	67	70	70	277	US$33,320
Chen Liang Hsi	72	68	69	69	278	22,220
John Morse	69	71	70	69	279	10,333
Gerry Norquist	71	69	67	72	279	10,333
Park Nam Sin	75	67	72	65	279	10,333
Hsieh Yu Shu	69	71	72	68	280	6,500
Tray Tyner	70	71	67	72	280	6,500
Tsutomu Higa	71	71	70	69	281	4,740
Tod Power	68	71	70	72	281	4,740
Remi Bouchard	67	74	71	70	282	3,733
Kyi Hla Han	72	69	69	72	282	3,733
Frankie Minoza	72	70	71	69	282	3,733
Samson Gimson	75	67	71	70	283	2,851
Ernie Gonzalez	72	69	72	70	283	2,851
Howie Johnson	72	70	71	70	283	2,851
Kim Jong Duk	68	68	73	74	283	2,851
Graham Marsh	68	74	69	72	283	2,851
E.J. Pfister	72	72	68	71	283	2,851
Dave Tentis	71	68	72	72	283	2,851
Jeff Bloom	76	69	69	72	284	2,257
Terry Gale	69	72	73	70	284	2,257
Robert Pactolerin	75	69	69	71	284	2,257
Tom Pernice	70	74	67	73	284	2,257
Mario Siodina	69	71	74	70	284	2,257
Wang Ter Chang	74	71	69	70	284	2,257
Carlos Espinosa	72	71	71	71	285	1,913
Antolin Fernando	68	73	71	73	285	1,913
Tim Fleming	73	71	69	72	285	1,913
Kuo Chi Hsiung	72	68	74	71	285	1,913
Aaron Meeks	70	73	70	72	285	1,913
Eric Meeks	70	70	71	74	285	1,913

Indonesian Open

Halim II Golf Course, Jakarta, Indonesia
Par 72; 7,208 yards

March 7-10
purse, US$150,000

	SCORES				TOTAL	MONEY
Chen Liang Hsi	69	70	66	72	277	US$24,990
Frankie Minoza	68	73	68	70	279	16,665
Kuo Chi Hsiung	66	69	74	72	281	7,125

	SCORES				TOTAL	MONEY
Li Wen Sheng	68	71	70	72	281	7,125
David Toms	71	70	72	68	281	7,125
Wang Ter Chang	70	71	67	73	281	7,125
Sumarno	70	71	69	72	282	4,500
Aaron Meeks	75	68	71	69	283	3,750
Christian Post	71	72	69	72	284	3,360
Kyi Hla Han	71	70	71	73	285	2,649
Eddie Kirby	69	70	73	73	285	2,649
M. Murugiah	69	75	70	71	285	2,649
Hatsuno Nakane	71	73	72	69	285	2,649
Gerry Norquist	69	74	69	73	285	2,649
Karim Baradie	72	71	72	71	286	1,869
Steve Chapman	75	69	73	69	286	1,869
Rick Gibson	69	74	71	72	286	1,869
Dennis Harrington	74	71	73	68	286	1,869
Hsieh Chin Sheng	75	71	73	67	286	1,869
Hsieh Yu Shu	72	72	69	73	286	1,869
Don Klenk	70	73	71	72	286	1,869
Tony Maloney	71	71	71	73	286	1,869
Eric Meeks	74	69	71	72	286	1,869
Rigoberto Velasquez	70	76	70	70	286	1,869
Mark Aebli	70	75	72	70	287	1,434
Buari	72	73	74	68	287	1,434
Robert Farley	69	74	74	70	287	1,434
Mikael Krantz	73	73	71	70	287	1,434
Eric Mercier	69	73	70	75	287	1,434
Robert Pactolerin	69	77	74	67	287	1,434
Tsao Chein Teng	73	73	73	68	287	1,434
Don Walsworth	68	74	74	71	287	1,434

Wills India Open

Delhi Golf Club, Delhi, India
Par 72; 6,860 yards

March 21-24
purse, US$150,000

	SCORES				TOTAL	MONEY
Ali Sher	71	67	74	71	283	US$24,990
Todd Hamilton	75	66	70	73	284	13,027
Wang Ter Chang	71	72	68	73	284	13,027
Basad Ali	73	69	71	74	287	6,370
Rick Gibson	70	72	71	74	287	6,370
Bill Israelson	74	75	69	69	287	6,370
Gregory Lesher	66	74	74	74	288	3,870
K. Nandasena Perera	69	74	69	76	288	3,870
Rigoberto Velasquez	69	70	78	71	288	3,870
John Jacobs	72	75	70	72	289	2,649
Danny Mijovic	74	71	71	73	289	2,649
Zoe Moe	76	72	71	70	289	2,649
Kumar Santosh	74	72	70	73	289	2,649
Jim Strickland	74	69	71	75	289	2,649
Mark Aebli	69	70	78	73	290	2,110
Antonio Barcellos	70	73	73	74	290	2,110
Tsao Chien Teng	71	74	71	74	290	2,110
Alex Espinosa	76	71	76	68	291	1,812
Carlos Espinosa	73	76	71	71	291	1,812
Jean-Louis Lamarre	76	73	68	74	291	1,812
Dennis Paulson	71	74	72	74	291	1,812

	SCORES				TOTAL	MONEY
Lee Porter	71	76	76	68	291	1,812
Paul Moloney	69	75	77	71	292	1,650
Kumar Vijay	71	77	71	73	292	1,650
Dennis Harrington	76	71	72	74	293	1,545
T. Nagraj	72	75	76	70	293	1,545
Rafael Ponce	69	78	73	73	293	1,545
Tracy Nakazaki	72	76	72	74	294	1,410
Tom Pernice	72	72	78	72	294	1,410
*Vikrajit Singh	77	72	72	73	294	
Scott Taylor	75	72	73	74	294	1,410

Thai International Thailand Open

Royal Thai Army Golf Course, Bangkok, Thailand
Par 72; 6,924 yards

March 28-31
purse, US$150,000

	SCORES				TOTAL	MONEY
Suthep Meesamasdi	67	70	65	70	272	US$25,000
Robert Pactolerin	70	69	72	62	273	16,665
Tony Maloney	66	67	70	71	274	9,390
Boonchu Ruengkit	65	69	72	69	275	7,500
Vijay Singh	69	71	71	65	276	5,805
Brian Mogg	69	70	70	67	276	5,805
Mark Aebli	64	71	70	74	279	4,500
Thamorn Wiratchant	69	70	71	70	280	3,750
Prayad Marksaeng	71	68	71	71	281	3,360
Danny Mijovic	72	72	70	69	283	2,722
Carlos Espinosa	72	67	70	74	283	2,722
Tim Fleming	70	71	73	69	283	2,722
Eddie Kirby	73	72	71	67	283	2,722
M. Murugiah	73	70	69	72	284	2,171.25
Poh Eing Chong	72	69	72	71	284	2,171.25
Dennis Harrington	75	71	67	71	284	2,171.25
Howie Johnson	72	70	72	70	284	2,171.25
Chen Liang Hsi	73	71	74	67	285	1,787.50
Lin Keng Chi	67	77	71	70	285	1,787.50
Lee Porter	74	70	72	69	285	1,787.50
Scott Taylor	74	69	71	71	285	1,787.50
Chamnien Chitprasong	65	72	75	73	285	1,787.50
Santi Sophon	73	71	69	72	285	1,787.50
Jean-Louis Lamarre	68	72	73	73	286	1,567.50
Kyi Hla Han	71	71	72	72	286	1,567.50
Gerry Norquist	70	70	73	73	286	1,567.50
Nares Navin	71	71	71	73	286	1,567.50
Mark Trauner	70	73	71	73	287	1,347.50
David Toms	71	73	71	72	287	1,347.50
Don Walsworth	74	69	74	70	287	1,347.50
Somyos Sukpinij	71	75	75	66	287	1,347.50
Sukree Onsham	71	72	67	77	287	1,347.50
Swan Kaewvises	70	73	71	73	287	1,347.50

Sanyang Republic of China Open

Taiwan Golf & Country Club, Tamsui Course, Taipei, Taiwan
Par 72; 7,161 yards

April 11-14
purse, US$300,000

	SCORES				TOTAL	MONEY
John Jacobs	73	67	70	75	285	US$50,000
Antolin Fernando	68	74	69	74	285	32,200
(Jacobs defeated Fernando on second extra hole.)						
Kuo Chi Hsiung	74	70	72	72	288	18,200
Aaron Meeks	72	75	72	70	289	12,333
Lin Chin Chen	77	73	70	69	289	12,333
Tom Pernice	72	71	71	75	289	12,333
Andrew Debusk	72	75	72	71	290	8,000
Rick Gibson	70	76	73	71	290	8,000
Brian Mogg	69	75	74	73	291	5,897
Scott Taylor	75	70	75	71	291	5,897
Hsieh Chin Sheng	72	72	71	76	291	5,897
Lee Wen Sheng	72	73	72	75	292	4,800
Lu Liang Huan	76	75	73	68	292	4,800
Chung Chun Hsing	70	77	74	71	292	4,800
Mark Aebli	72	77	74	70	293	3,716
Wang Ter Chung	72	73	75	73	293	3,716
Ho Ming Chung	74	72	73	74	293	3,716
Yung Ching Chi	72	74	72	75	293	3,716
Kelly Murray	78	70	73	72	293	3,716
Mike Cunning	74	74	71	74	293	3,716
Tim Fleming	73	73	71	76	293	3,716
Samson Gimson	74	76	74	69	293	3,716
Hsieh Yu Shu	71	73	75	75	294	2,935
Mark Trauner	72	75	74	73	294	2,935
Marumuthu Ramayah	80	68	74	72	294	2,935
Chen Tze Chung	78	70	73	73	294	2,935
Dennis Paulson	72	73	77	72	294	2,935
Carlos Espinosa	77	72	74	71	294	2,935
Chang Mu Chuan	74	74	73	73	294	2,935
Hsu Tien Lai	75	74	71	74	294	2,935

Maekyung (Korea) Open

Nam Seoul Country Club, Sungnam, Korea
Par 72; 6,901 yards

April 18-21
purse, US$300,000

	SCORES				TOTAL	MONEY
Choi Sang Ho	74	67	69	71	281	US$49,980
Hsieh Chin Hsing	72	72	69	70	283	26,055
Park Nam Sin	71	69	71	72	283	26,055
Choi Yoon Soo	75	73	68	69	285	15,000
Lin Chin Chen	75	74	69	68	286	11,610
Danny Mijovic	75	72	70	69	286	11,610
Lee Kang Sun	72	70	75	70	287	7,740
Lin Keng Chi	73	72	71	71	287	7,740
David Toms	74	72	72	69	287	7,740
Dennis Paulson	71	72	71	74	288	5,445
Tom Pernice	75	72	72	69	288	5,445
Aaron Meeks	76	71	70	71	288	5,445
Rick Gibson	76	72	69	71	288	5,445
Chen Tze Chung	72	74	75	68	289	4,400

	SCORES				TOTAL	MONEY
Chen Liang Hsi	73	73	73	70	289	4,400
Mike Cunning	76	67	74	72	289	4,400
Kuo Chi Hsiung	79	70	70	71	290	3,930
Gerry Norquist	75	71	75	69	290	3,930
Mark Aebli	74	72	72	73	291	3,562
Choi Kwang Soo	74	70	73	74	291	3,562
Kim Hak Suh	74	72	75	70	291	3,562
Park Jung Woong	69	73	73	76	291	3,562
Todd Hamilton	77	71	74	70	292	3,217
Tadao Nakamura	75	76	70	71	292	3,217
Liao Kuo Chi	74	73	71	74	292	3,217
Remi Bouchard	73	71	75	73	292	3,217
Brian Mogg	74	71	76	72	293	2,826
Antolin Fernando	74	72	73	74	293	2,826
Lee Myung Ha	74	71	78	70	293	2,826
Craig McClellan	72	73	75	73	293	2,826
Kim Jong Duk	71	77	74	71	293	2,826

Daiichi Fudosan Cup

Hibiscus Golf Club, Sadowaracho, Miyazaki
Par 72; 6,920 yards

March 7-10
purse, ¥100,000,000

	SCORES				TOTAL	MONEY
Saburo Fujiki	68	71	67	65	271	¥18,000,000
Brian Jones	68	68	68	68	272	10,000,000
Roger Mackay	71	66	72	69	278	5,800,000
Toru Nakamura	70	68	70	70	278	5,800,000
Masashi Ozaki	70	70	73	66	279	3,800,000
Yoshiyuki Isomura	69	73	71	66	279	3,800,000
Yoshinori Kaneko	69	75	68	68	280	3,200,000
Tsukasa Watanabe	71	69	72	69	281	2,450,000
Yutaka Hagawa	71	70	69	71	281	2,450,000
Yoshikazu Yokoshima	71	68	70	72	281	2,450,000
Kiyoshi Murota	69	68	70	74	281	2,450,000
Naomichi Ozaki	73	69	73	67	282	1,630,000
Hiroya Kamide	69	71	74	68	282	1,630,000
Tateo Ozaki	72	66	73	71	282	1,630,000
Yoshinori Mizumaki	68	72	69	73	282	1,630,000
Harumitsu Hamano	67	73	73	70	283	1,213,000
Chen Tze Ming	71	71	70	71	283	1,213,000
Seiichi Kanai	70	68	71	74	283	1,213,000
Kouki Idoki	71	73	73	67	284	960,000
Terry Gale	73	71	72	68	284	960,000
Akiyoshi Omachi	70	69	75	70	284	960,000
Haruo Yasuda	69	73	71	71	284	960,000
Ryoken Kawagishi	73	66	72	73	284	960,000
Yoichi Yamamoto	70	73	75	67	285	810,000
Joji Furuki	74	71	71	69	285	810,000
Shigeru Kawamata	75	69	70	71	285	810,000
Masahiro Shiota	72	72	70	71	285	810,000
Kiyoshi Maita	68	70	76	71	285	810,000
Katsuyoshi Tomori	70	71	71	73	285	810,000
Tadao Nakamura	71	74	72	69	286	740,000

Imperial Tournament

Seve Ballesteros Golf Club, Sakuragawamura, Ibaraki
Par 72; 6,909 yards

March 14-17
purse, ¥65,000,000

	SCORES				TOTAL	MONEY
Yutaka Hagawa	70	72	66	74	282	¥11,700,000
Naomichi Ozaki	70	68	70	75	283	6,500,000
Tsukasa Watanabe	73	75	72	67	287	4,420,000
Pete Izumikawa	73	73	71	71	288	3,120,000
Satoshi Higashi	72	75	73	69	289	2,226,000
Roger Mackay	75	70	71	73	289	2,226,000
Kikuo Arai	73	73	70	73	289	2,226,000
Tateo Ozaki	75	69	70	75	289	2,226,000
Chen Tze Ming	73	74	72	71	290	1,495,000
Yoshinori Mizumaki	77	70	70	73	290	1,495,000
Katsuyoshi Tomori	75	71	71	73	290	1,495,000
Kiyoshi Murota	72	69	77	73	291	1,196,000
Toru Nakamura	73	76	75	68	292	1,053,000
Harumitsu Hamano	75	71	71	75	292	1,053,000
Eiichi Itai	77	74	74	68	293	825,000
Akihito Yokoyama	78	74	70	71	293	825,000
Kazuhiro Takami	76	74	71	72	293	825,000
Chen Tze Chung	77	70	74	72	293	825,000
Masahiro Shiota	77	71	71	75	294	676,000
Hiroya Kamide	74	72	73	76	295	624,000
Akiyoshi Omachi	75	71	73	76	295	624,000
Yoshiyuki Isomura	73	73	71	78	295	624,000
Taisei Inagaki	75	71	76	74	296	552,000
Hiroshi Goda	73	75	73	75	296	552,000
Koichi Suzuki	73	75	73	75	296	552,000
Hiroshi Ueda	74	72	74	76	296	552,000
Anthony Gilligan	74	74	72	77	297	513,000
Toshiji Shirahama	72	75	72	78	297	513,000
Hideto Shigenobu	77	71	80	70	298	457,000
Hiroshi Makino	78	71	76	73	298	457,000
Haruhito Yamamoto	77	73	74	74	298	457,000
Toshimitsu Kai	76	73	74	75	298	457,000
Yoshinori Kaneko	72	74	76	76	298	457,000
Masanobu Kimura	78	73	71	76	298	457,000
Yutaka Suzuki	74	72	73	79	298	457,000

Daido Shizuoka Open

Shizuoka Country Club, Hamaoka, Shizuoka
Par 72; 6,930 yards

March 21-24
purse, ¥80,000,000

	SCORES				TOTAL	MONEY
Yutaka Hagawa	70	72	69	67	278	¥14,400,000
Noboru Sugai	72	76	68	63	279	8,000,000
Pete Izumikawa	71	75	66	68	280	5,440,000
Tomohiro Maruyama	73	73	69	66	281	3,120,000
Tsuneyuki Nakajima	67	76	71	67	281	3,120,000
Yoshinori Mizumaki	71	71	71	68	281	3,120,000
Yoshitaka Yamamoto	70	73	70	68	281	3,120,000
Hiroshi Makino	69	73	68	72	282	2,200,000
Isao Aoki	71	70	69	72	282	2,200,000
Katsuyoshi Tomori	72	74	71	66	283	1,637,000

	SCORES				TOTAL	MONEY
Yoichi Yamamoto	71	72	72	68	283	1,637,000
Yoshiyuki Isomura	71	73	69	70	283	1,637,000
Katsunari Takahashi	72	76	72	64	284	1,200,000
Masahiro Shiota	75	72	71	66	284	1,200,000
Eiichi Itai	71	74	73	66	284	1,200,000
Akiyoshi Omachi	68	75	70	71	284	1,200,000
Saburo Fujiki	73	74	70	68	285	972,000
Ryoken Kawagishi	72	76	69	68	285	972,000
Masayuki Kawamura	70	76	71	68	285	972,000
Masanobu Kimura	71	74	71	69	285	972,000
Chen Tze Ming	72	76	70	68	286	686,000
Yoshihisa Iwashita	74	73	71	68	286	686,000
Yoshikazu Yokoshima	73	72	72	69	286	686,000
Yutaka Suzuki	69	72	74	71	286	686,000
Shinji Ikeuchi	71	75	69	71	286	686,000
Hideki Kase	66	73	75	72	286	686,000
Chen Tze Chung	73	73	68	72	286	686,000
Nichito Hashimoto	74	71	69	72	286	686,000
Masahiro Kuramoto	75	71	72	69	287	569,000
Naomichi Ozaki	72	75	70	70	287	569,000
Tomoo Ozaki	72	75	69	71	287	569,000
Tetsu Nishikawa	71	73	72	71	287	569,000
Paul Hoad	68	72	75	72	287	569,000
Teruo Sugihara	71	72	70	74	287	569,000

Taylormade KSB Open

Shido Country Club, Shidocho, Kagawa
Par 72; 6,309 yards

March 28-31
purse, ¥60,000,000

	SCORES				TOTAL	MONEY
Masanobu Kimura	69	66	69	69	273	¥10,800,000
Teruo Sugihara	64	72	72	68	276	5,040,000
Nobuo Serizawa	66	66	74	70	276	5,040,000
Eduardo Herrera	71	71	72	64	278	2,880,000
Hiroshi Makino	70	68	72	69	279	2,280,000
Tsukasa Watanabe	70	69	70	70	279	2,280,000
Akiyoshi Omachi	71	68	74	67	280	1,830,000
Yoshinori Mizumaki	72	70	65	73	280	1,830,000
Tomohiro Maruyama	71	70	71	69	281	1,310,000
Hideyuki Sato	71	70	70	70	281	1,310,000
Noburo Sugai	68	67	74	72	281	1,310,000
Tadami Ueno	70	67	72	72	281	1,310,000
Kiyoshi Murota	69	71	72	70	282	1,008,000
Katsunari Takahashi	71	71	71	70	283	864,000
Katsuyoshi Tomori	68	72	71	72	283	864,000
Harumitsu Hamano	73	69	68	73	283	864,000
Seiki Okuda	71	72	71	70	284	654,000
Yoshinori Kaneko	73	67	73	71	284	654,000
Hideki Kase	70	71	72	71	284	654,000
Joji Furuki	68	71	73	72	284	654,000
Futoshi Irino	72	70	73	70	285	576,000
Yoshitaka Yamamoto	72	72	75	67	286	552,000
Takashi Hishinuma	70	75	73	69	287	516,000
Msayuki Kawamura	71	71	75	70	287	516,000
Wayne Smith	72	68	75	72	287	516,000
Naomichi Ozaki	71	73	76	68	288	486,000

	SCORES				TOTAL	MONEY
Yoichi Yamamoto	73	70	73	72	288	486,000
Yukio Noguchi	73	70	77	69	289	427,000
Toshimitsu Kai	73	72	73	71	289	427,000
Yutaka Hagawa	70	74	72	73	289	427,000
Kazushiro Nagao	70	72	74	73	289	427,000
Kenji Sogame	75	69	71	74	289	427,000
Eiichi Itai	70	71	73	75	289	427,000
Paul Hoad	69	72	73	75	289	427,000
Lyndsay Stephen	68	72	72	77	289	427,000

Pocari Sweat Open

Hakuryuko Country Club, Daiwacho, Hiroshima
Par 71; 6,780 yards

April 11-14
purse, ¥45,000,000

	SCORES			TOTAL	MONEY
Ryoken Kawagishi	67	66	66	199	¥8,100,000
Hiroshi Makino	70	66	67	203	4,500,000
Tsukasa Watanabe	68	68	68	204	2,016,000
Tomohiro Maruyama	67	69	68	204	2,016,000
Brian Jones	68	67	69	204	2,016,000
Kiyoshi Murota	69	66	69	204	2,016,000
Teruo Sugihara	69	64	71	204	2,016,000
Paul Hoad	69	71	65	205	1,237,000
Yoshinori Kaneko	67	68	70	205	1,237,000
Hideki Kase	71	70	65	206	921,000
Seiki Okuda	68	70	68	206	921,000
Tadami Ueno	69	66	71	206	921,000
Koichi Suzuki	71	70	67	208	648,000
Katsunari Takahashi	73	66	69	208	648,000
Shigeru Kawamata	68	71	69	208	648,000
Nobumitsu Yuhara	72	67	69	208	648,000
Toru Nakamura	72	66	70	208	648,000
Shinsaku Maeda	71	70	68	209	453,000
Tatsuo Fujima	71	70	68	209	453,000
Hiroshi Ueda	68	72	69	209	453,000
Kouki Idoki	74	66	69	209	453,000
Toshiaki Sudo	73	67	69	209	453,000
Yoshitaka Yamamoto	71	70	69	210	373,000
Hideyuki Sato	71	70	69	210	373,000
Hiroya Kamide	73	67	70	210	373,000
Tetsu Nishikawa	70	70	70	210	373,000
Noboru Sugai	69	70	71	210	373,000
Takashi Hishinuma	70	68	72	210	373,000
Hideto Shigenobu	73	69	69	211	324,000
Tatsuya Shiraishi	72	70	69	211	324,000
Masahiro Kuramoto	73	68	70	211	324,000
Toshio Ozaki	70	71	70	211	324,000
Katsuji Hasegawa	71	69	71	211	324,000

Bridgestone Aso Open

Aso Golf Club, Asomachi, Kumamoto
Par 72; 7,078 yards

April 18-21
purse, ¥50,000,000

	SCORES			TOTAL	MONEY
Kiyoshi Murota	68	72	68	208	¥6,750,000
Taisei Inagaki	71	70	69	210	3,750,000
Noboru Sugai	72	69	70	211	1,950,000
Isamu Sugita	72	68	71	211	1,950,000
Seiki Okuda	68	69	74	211	1,950,000
Yukio Noguchi	73	71	68	212	1,212,000
David Ishii	68	75	69	212	1,212,000
Kiyoshi Maita	71	70	71	212	1,212,000
Yoshinori Mizumaki	71	74	68	213	748,000
Yoshitaka Yamamoto	71	74	68	213	748,000
Paul Hoad	69	74	70	213	748,000
Sathoshi Higashi	73	69	71	213	748,000
Masanobu Kimura	69	72	72	213	748,000
Hideyuki Sato	70	71	72	213	748,000
Eiichi Itai	74	71	69	214	445,000
Saburo Fujiki	72	72	70	214	445,000
Teruo Sugihara	72	70	72	214	445,000
Futoshi Irino	73	69	72	214	445,000
Yoshinori Kaneko	70	68	76	214	445,000
Kinpachi Yoshimura	68	70	76	214	445,000
Toru Nakamura	73	71	71	215	352,000
Brian Jones	73	68	74	215	352,000
Harumitsu Hamano	71	75	70	216	307,000
Anthony Gilligan	72	72	72	216	307,000
Hikaru Emoto	72	72	72	216	307,000
Yoshikazu Yokoshima	73	70	73	216	307,000
Kouki Idoki	71	72	73	216	307,000
David Iwasaki-Smith	69	74	73	216	307,000
Joji Furuki	73	69	74	216	307,000
Yutaka Hagawa	77	69	71	217	266,000
Tsuyoshi Yoneyama	74	72	71	217	266,000
Shigeru Namiki	68	78	71	217	266,000
Shinji Iekuchi	71	74	72	217	266,000

Dunlop Open

Ibaraki Golf Club, West Course, Inamachi, Ibaraki
Par 72; 7,052 yards

April 25-28
purse, ¥100,000,000

	SCORES				TOTAL	MONEY
Roger Mackay	69	67	68	68	272	¥18,000,000
Teruo Sugihara	75	67	67	65	274	10,000,000
Seve Ballesteros	70	69	70	66	275	6,800,000
Hideki Kase	71	68	67	70	276	4,130,000
Naomichi Ozaki	71	65	68	72	276	4,130,000
Hideto Shigenobu	70	66	68	72	276	4,130,000
Ryoken Kawagishi	73	69	65	70	277	3,050,000
Masahiro Kuramoto	71	66	69	71	277	3,050,000
Chen Tze Chung	69	71	67	71	278	2,600,000
Rick Gibson	73	68	72	66	279	2,150,000
Masanobu Kimura	72	67	69	71	279	2,150,000
Chen Liang Sei	68	70	73	69	280	1,560,000

	SCORES				TOTAL	MONEY
Chen Tze Ming	74	70	66	70	280	1,560,000
Tsuneyuki Nakajima	71	69	68	72	280	1,560,000
Masashi Ozaki	70	71	66	73	280	1,560,000
Saburo Fujiki	69	69	68	74	280	1,560,000
Akiyoshi Omachi	68	72	72	69	281	1,120,000
Lee Porter	72	67	70	72	281	1,120,000
Frankie Minoza	68	69	70	74	281	1,120,000
Graham Marsh	69	72	72	69	282	940,000
Pete Izumikawa	69	69	74	70	282	940,000
Tod Power	73	67	72	70	282	940,000
Kyi Hla Han	71	67	73	71	282	940,000
Akihito Yokoyama	70	67	76	70	283	850,000
Nan Shin Pak	73	70	69	71	283	850,000
Brian Mogg	72	68	76	68	284	780,000
Hsieh Yu Shu	67	71	77	69	284	780,000
Yoshiyuki Isomura	70	69	75	70	284	780,000
David Ishii	72	70	71	71	284	780,000
Jim Strickland	71	67	74	72	284	780,000

Chunichi Crowns

Nagoya Golf Club, Wago Course, Togocho, Aichi
Par 70; 6,473 yards

May 2-5
purse, ¥120,000,000

	SCORES				TOTAL	MONEY
Severiano Ballesteros	67	75	64	69	275	¥21,600,000
Roger Mackay	70	72	69	65	276	12,000,000
Tatsuya Shiraishi	70	74	69	65	278	8,160,000
Naomichi Ozaki	69	70	73	68	280	5,280,000
Yoshikazu Yokoshima	69	71	67	73	280	5,280,000
Isao Aoki	68	70	71	72	281	4,320,000
Tsuneyuki Nakajima	70	70	68	74	282	3,840,000
Masahiro Kuramoto	75	71	69	68	283	3,300,000
Hideyuki Sato	73	74	65	71	283	3,300,000
David Ishii	74	70	70	70	284	2,760,000
Hajime Meshiai	73	74	69	69	285	2,400,000
Shinsaku Maeda	71	72	71	72	286	1,881,000
Katsunari Takahashi	70	71	72	73	286	1,881,000
Mike Reid	73	70	70	73	286	1,881,000
Mike Harwood	69	70	73	74	286	1,881,000
Ikuo Shirahama	70	70	70	76	286	1,881,000
Seiichi Kanai	74	73	71	69	287	1,276,000
Hiroshi Ueda	72	71	74	70	287	1,276,000
Tetsu Nishikawa	71	75	71	70	287	1,276,000
Brian Jones	72	70	74	71	287	1,276,000
Kiyoshi Muroda	72	70	72	73	287	1,276,000
Koichi Suzuki	72	75	72	69	288	1,036,000
Peter Senior	74	73	72	69	288	1,036,000
Tsukasa Watanabe	73	73	72	70	288	1,036,000
Hiroshi Makino	73	75	69	71	288	1,036,000
Graham Marsh	73	75	69	71	288	1,036,000
Chen Tze Ming	71	76	73	69	289	856,000
Teruo Sugihara	70	76	73	70	289	856,000
Taisei Inagaki	73	70	75	71	289	856,000
Shigeru Kawamata	74	74	69	72	289	856,000
Yoshimi Niizeki	66	78	73	72	289	856,000
*Shigeki Maruyama	77	72	68	72	289	

	SCORES				TOTAL	MONEY
Anthony Gilligan	76	69	71	73	289	856,000
Noboru Sugai	74	68	73	74	289	856,000
Akiyoshi Omachi	73	72	70	74	289	856,000
Masashi Ozaki	71	74	70	74	289	856,000
Kouki Idoki	69	73	72	75	289	856,000

Fuji Sankei Classic

Kawana Hotel Golf Club, Fuji Course, Ito, Shizuoka   May 9-12
Par 71; 6,694 yards   purse, ¥87,500,000

	SCORES				TOTAL	MONEY
Saburo Fujiki	69	68	72	70	279	¥15,750,000
Isao Aoki	72	68	75	64	279	6,300,000
Hideki Kase	69	71	72	67	279	6,300,000
Brian Jones	65	71	74	69	279	6,300,000
(Fujiki defeated Aoki, Kase and Jones on second extra hole.)						
Tateo Ozaki	74	71	71	64	280	3,150,000
Nobuo Serizawa	72	67	73	68	280	3,150,000
Koichi Suzuki	70	66	72	72	280	3,150,000
Frankie Minoza	71	66	73	72	282	2,537,000
Tsukasa Watanabe	70	69	75	70	284	2,012,000
Wayne Smith	71	68	75	70	284	2,012,000
Yoshitaka Yamamoto	74	70	68	72	284	2,012,000
Graham Marsh	66	71	73	75	285	1,610,000
Seiji Ebihara	68	74	74	70	286	1,365,000
Toru Nakayama	72	69	74	71	286	1,365,000
Hiroshi Ebihara	74	66	73	73	286	1,365,000
Chen Tze Ming	71	73	75	68	287	1,023,000
Yoshikazu Yokoshima	71	69	76	71	287	1,023,000
Kiyoshi Maita	74	69	73	71	287	1,023,000
Yoshinori Ichioka	73	71	71	72	287	1,023,000
Junji Hashizoe	73	73	76	66	288	785,000
Toshiji Shirahama	74	71	76	67	288	785,000
Pete Izumikawa	75	70	72	71	288	785,000
Yutaka Suzuki	70	73	74	71	288	785,000
Masahiro Kuramoto	73	69	74	72	288	785,000
Satoshi Higashi	74	70	71	73	288	785,000
Katsuji Hasegawa	71	70	73	74	288	785,000
Toshiaki Sudo	71	74	72	72	289	700,000
Hiroshi Makino	73	73	74	70	290	656,000
Masaru Amano	70	72	77	71	290	656,000
Tadami Ueno	70	71	75	74	290	656,000
Kinpachi Yoshimura	72	70	74	74	290	656,000

Japan Match Play Championship

Shinyo Country Club, Toki, Gifu   May 16-19
Par 72; 7,029 yards   purse, ¥50,000,000

FIRST ROUND

Tsuneyuki Nakajima defeated Tsuyoshi Yoneyama, 1 up, 19 holes
Shigeru Kawamata defeated Chen Tze Chung, 2 and 1
Masanobu Kimura defeated Yoshinori Kaneko, 4 and 3
Yoshitaka Yamamoto defeated David Ishii, 3 and 2

Katsuyoshi Tomori defeated Noboru Sugai, 1 up
Akihito Yokoyama defeated Tadao Nakamura, 2 and 1
Hideki Kase defeated Seiki Okuda, 1 up, 19 holes
Nobumitsu Yuhara defeated Katsunari Takahashi, 1 up
Naomichi Ozaki defeated Tateo Ozaki, 2 and 1
Satoshi Higashi defeated Seiichi Kanai, 1 up
Toru Nakamura defeated Katsuji Hasegawa, 1 up
Nobuo Serizawa defeated Kiyoshi Muroda, 1 up
Saburo Fujiki defeated Tadami Ueno, 1 up
Tsukasa Watanabe defeated Tomohiro Maruyama, 2 and 1
Yoshinori Mizumaki defeated Brian Jones, 4 and 3
Hiroshi Makino defeated Chen Tze Ming, 2 and 1

(Each losing player received ¥250,000.)

SECOND ROUND

Nakajima defeated Kawamata, 5 and 3
Kimura defeated Yamamoto, 2 and 1
Yokoyama defeated Tomori, 2 and 1
Kase defeated Yuhara, 6 and 5
Higashi defeated Naomichi Ozaki, 3 and 2
Serizawa defeated Toru Nakamura, 1 up
Watanabe defeated Fujiki, 6 and 4
Mizumaki defeated Makino, 1 up

(Each losing player received ¥500,000.)

QUARTER-FINALS

Nakajima defeated Kimura, 3 and 1
Kase defeated Yokoyama, 5 and 4
Higashi defeated Serizawa, 4 and 3
Watanabe defeated Mizumaki, 1 up

(Each losing player received ¥7,100,000.)

SEMI-FINALS

Nakajima defeated Kase, 8 and 7
Higashi defeated Watanabe, 3 and 2

THIRD-FOURTH PLACE PLAYOFF

Watanabe defeated Kase, 4 and 3

(Watanabe received ¥3,500,000; Kase ¥2,500,000.)

FINAL

Higashi defeated Nakajima, 2 up

(Higashi received ¥14,000,000; Nakajima ¥7,000,000.)

Pepsi Ube Kosan

Ube Country Club, West Course, Ajisu, Yamaguchi
Par 71; 6,853 yards

May 23-26
purse, ¥80,000,000

	SCORES				TOTAL	MONEY
Chen Tze Chung	69	74	66	65	274	¥14,400,000
Saburo Fujiki	73	69	61	73	276	8,000,000
Hikaru Emoto	67	72	69	69	277	5,440,000
Yoshinori Kaneko	71	68	70	69	278	3,520,000
Hiroshi Makino	69	66	71	72	278	3,520,000
Naomichi Ozaki	68	69	73	69	279	2,270,000
David Ishii	69	68	73	69	279	2,270,000
Yoshikazu Sakamoto	72	72	70	67	281	1,960,000
Tsukasa Watanabe	71	73	68	69	281	1,960,000
Kiyoshi Maita	65	75	69	72	281	1,960,000
Futoshi Irino	70	69	70	72	281	1,960,000
Yoshikazu Yokoshima	72	69	71	70	282	1,470,000
Teruo Sugihara	73	70	73	67	283	1,296,000
Kouki Idoki	71	68	73	71	283	1,296,000
Chen Tze Ming	72	72	73	67	284	923,000
Nozomu Kamatsu	70	74	71	69	284	923,000
Tsutomu Higa	70	69	75	70	284	923,000
Kiyoshi Muroda	70	71	72	71	284	923,000
Nichito Hashimoto	71	69	73	71	284	923,000
Motomasa Aoki	68	75	68	73	284	923,000
Masahiro Shiota	70	67	70	77	284	923,000
Tomohiro Maruyama	69	76	71	69	285	666,000
Yutaka Hagawa	67	73	75	70	285	666,000
Masaru Amano	70	74	70	71	285	666,000
Nobuo Serizawa	70	72	71	72	285	666,000
Shinji Ikeuchi	70	71	72	72	285	666,000
Akiyoshi Omachi	71	71	70	73	285	666,000
Tadami Ueno	65	72	75	73	285	666,000
Kazunari Matsunaga	70	72	69	74	285	666,000
Harumitsu Hamano	70	75	72	69	286	576,000
Osamu Watanabe	72	72	70	72	286	576,000
Gregory Meyer	70	71	71	74	286	576,000

Mitsubishi Galant

Noto Country Club, Oshimizumachi, Ishikawa
Par 72; 7,052 yards

May 30-June 2
purse, ¥85,000,000

	SCORES				TOTAL	MONEY
Koichi Suzuki	73	69	70	68	280	¥15,340,000
Isao Aoki	72	70	74	65	281	7,140,000
Tsuneyuki Nakajima	72	67	72	70	281	7,140,000
Tateo Ozaki	69	72	72	70	283	4,080,000
Tsukasa Watanabe	77	68	71	68	284	2,910,000
Rick Gibson	69	71	73	71	284	2,910,000
Katsunari Takahashi	73	69	70	72	284	2,910,000
Hiroshi Makino	69	75	67	73	284	2,910,000
Kiyoshi Maita	72	73	68	72	285	2,210,000
Tatsuya Shiraishi	72	71	74	69	286	1,470,000
Hideto Shigenobu	73	72	71	70	286	1,470,000
Graham Marsh	74	70	72	70	286	1,470,000
Seiki Okuda	70	71	73	72	286	1,470,000

	SCORES				TOTAL	MONEY
Harumitsu Hamano	74	70	70	72	286	1,470,000
Seiji Ebihara	72	71	70	73	286	1,470,000
Yoshinori Mizumaki	73	70	68	75	286	1,470,000
Taisei Inagaki	72	72	73	70	287	986,000
Nobuhiro Yoshino	73	72	69	73	287	986,000
Futoshi Irino	76	71	72	69	288	816,000
Hirofumi Miyase	72	73	72	71	288	816,000
Yutaka Hagawa	74	68	74	72	288	816,000
Yoshitaka Yamamoto	71	73	72	72	288	816,000
Shinji Ikeuchi	72	74	69	73	288	816,000
Frankie Minoza	75	71	74	69	289	697,000
Naomichi Ozaki	74	71	72	72	289	697,000
Ikuo Shirahama	74	71	72	72	289	697,000
Takenori Hiraishi	76	71	70	72	289	697,000
Nobumitsu Yuhara	74	73	68	74	289	697,000
Masahiko Akazawa	72	72	75	71	290	605,000
Noboru Sugai	77	69	72	72	290	605,000
Nobuo Serizawa	73	73	72	72	290	605,000
Roger Mackay	74	71	72	73	290	605,000
Joji Furuki	69	73	75	73	290	605,000
Toru Nakamura	76	71	69	74	290	605,000

JCB Sendai Classic

Zao Kokusai Golf Club, Shibatamachi, Miyagi
Par 71; 6,622 yards

June 6-9
purse, ¥70,000,000

	SCORES				TOTAL	MONEY
Tadami Ueno	66	72	66	67	271	¥12,600,000
Graham Marsh	69	68	67	68	272	7,000,000
Yutaka Hagawa	69	68	67	69	273	4,760,000
Koichi Suzuki	68	66	71	69	274	3,080,000
Tsuneyuki Nakajima	67	70	66	71	274	3,080,000
Hiroshi Makino	65	69	70	71	275	2,520,000
Masahiro Shioda	69	70	69	68	276	2,135,000
David Ishii	68	69	70	69	276	2,135,000
Toru Nakamura	68	71	71	67	277	1,458,000
Hideki Kase	67	71	71	68	277	1,458,000
Harumitsu Hamano	69	70	70	68	277	1,458,000
Satoshi Higashi	65	72	71	69	277	1,458,000
Takeru Shibata	68	71	69	69	277	1,458,000
Yoshitaka Yamamoto	69	68	76	65	278	966,000
Roger Mackay	72	69	70	67	278	966,000
Norikazu Kawakami	70	68	68	72	278	966,000
Isao Aoki	71	68	66	73	278	966,000
Nobuo Serizawa	70	71	71	67	279	705,000
Kiyoshi Maita	70	72	70	67	279	705,000
Hajime Meshiai	67	74	70	68	279	705,000
Brent Franklin	66	73	70	70	279	705,000
Yoshimi Nizeki	67	73	68	71	279	705,000
Yoshinori Mizumaki	69	69	74	68	280	567,000
Frankie Minoza	71	72	69	68	280	567,000
Yoshihiko Terakawa	69	74	69	68	280	567,000
Saburo Fujiki	70	72	69	69	280	567,000
Tomohiro Maruyama	72	69	70	69	280	567,000
Takashi Hishinuma	73	69	67	71	280	567,000
Yoshinori Kaneko	70	70	68	72	280	567,000
Akiyoshi Omachi	70	70	68	72	280	567,000

Sapporo Tokyu Open

Sapporo Kokusai Country Club, Shimamtsu Course, Sapporo
Par 72; 6,949 yards

June 13-16
purse, ¥60,000,000

	SCORES				TOTAL	MONEY
Rick Gibson	71	71	68	70	280	¥10,800,000
Masahiro Kuramoto	70	70	69	71	280	5,040,000
Shinsaku Maeda	69	70	70	71	280	5,040,000
(Gibson defeated Kuramoto and Maeda on first extra hole.)						
Chen Tze Ming	70	69	68	74	281	2,880,000
Tadami Ueno	68	72	69	73	282	2,280,000
Ikuo Shirahama	72	68	69	73	282	2,280,000
Nobuo Serizawa	70	77	69	67	283	1,740,000
Graham Marsh	70	75	70	68	283	1,740,000
Yutaka Hagawa	70	71	69	73	283	1,740,000
Akiyoshi Omachi	71	73	70	70	284	1,228,000
David Ishii	72	71	70	71	284	1,228,000
Yoshimi Nizeki	68	70	70	76	284	1,228,000
Koichi Suzuki	72	74	70	69	285	777,000
Yoshikazu Yokoshima	73	72	71	69	285	777,000
Yoshinori Ichioka	74	72	69	70	285	777,000
Haruhito Yamamoto	70	73	70	72	285	777,000
Tsuneyuki Nakajima	70	72	70	73	285	777,000
Shigeru Kawamata	71	69	72	73	285	777,000
Naomichi Ozaki	73	68	70	74	285	777,000
Futoshi Irino	69	72	70	74	285	777,000
Ryoken Kawagishi	74	73	70	69	286	521,000
Kouki Idoki	72	74	69	71	286	521,000
Hiroya Kamide	71	74	70	71	286	521,000
Tatsuya Shiraishi	73	70	71	72	286	521,000
Nobumitsu Yuhara	69	75	70	72	286	521,000
Yoshiyuki Isomura	72	68	71	75	286	521,000
Eiichi Itai	72	70	69	75	286	521,000
Masahiro Shioda	71	71	75	70	287	462,000
Tadao Nakamura	75	69	71	72	287	462,000
Seiki Okuda	73	72	73	70	288	411,000
Yukio Noguchi	71	75	71	71	288	411,000
Brian Jones	74	72	69	73	288	411,000
Yoichi Yamamoto	70	73	72	73	288	411,000
Hiromichi Namiki	73	72	70	73	288	411,000
Seiji Ebihara	69	73	72	74	288	411,000
Shigeru Namiki	70	72	72	74	288	411,000

Yomiuri Sapporo Beer Open

Yomiuri Country Club, Member Course, Nishinomiya, Hyogo
Par 72; 7,023 yards

June 20-23
purse, ¥80,000,000

	SCORES				TOTAL	MONEY
Tsuneyuki Nakajima	65	65	71	71	272	¥14,440,000
Rick Gibson	69	70	68	68	275	8,000,000
Hideyuki Sato	74	70	68	66	278	3,840,000
Yoshitaka Yamamoto	68	69	72	69	278	3,840,000
Katsunari Takahashi	69	70	69	70	278	3,840,000
Toru Nakamura	69	68	69	72	278	3,840,000
Tadami Ueno	69	71	71	68	279	2,080,000
Kouki Idoki	69	72	69	69	279	2,080,000

	SCORES				TOTAL	MONEY
Eiichi Itai	71	72	66	70	279	2,080,000
Koichi Suzuki	69	71	68	71	279	2,080,000
Naomichi Ozaki	69	67	70	73	279	2,080,000
Roger Mackay	69	69	74	68	280	1,304,000
Brian Jones	77	66	68	69	280	1,304,000
David Ishii	74	66	69	71	280	1,304,000
Graham Marsh	70	69	69	72	280	1,304,000
Yutaka Hagawa	71	69	75	66	281	908,000
Tomohiro Maruyama	69	72	72	68	281	908,000
Nobumitsu Yuhara	73	69	70	69	281	908,000
Tsuyoshi Yoneyama	73	68	71	69	281	908,000
Shigeru Kawamata	67	71	72	71	281	908,000
Akihito Yokoyama	70	73	71	68	282	686,000
Wayne Smith	71	72	70	69	282	686,000
Frankie Minoza	70	72	70	70	282	686,000
Terry Price	73	68	70	71	282	686,000
Isao Aoki	70	71	69	72	282	686,000
Tatsuya Shiraishi	69	70	71	72	282	686,000
Teruo Sugihara	73	68	68	73	282	686,000
Harumitsu Hamano	70	69	70	73	282	686,000
Tsukasa Watanabe	72	72	70	69	283	562,000
Toshimitsu Kai	74	68	72	69	283	562,000
Kinpachi Yoshimura	69	70	74	70	283	562,000
Seiki Okuda	74	67	71	71	283	562,000
Anthony Gilligan	69	75	68	71	283	562,000
Yoshikazu Yokoshima	71	73	67	72	283	562,000
Pete Izumikawa	69	68	70	75	283	562,000

Mizuno Open

Tokinodai Country Club, Hakui, Ishikawa
Par 72; 6,832 yards
(Third round cancelled; heavy rains.)

June 27-30
purse, ¥52,500,000

	SCORES			TOTAL	MONEY
Roger Mackay	66	70	71	207	¥9,450,000
Satoshi Higashi	71	68	68	207	5,250,000
(Mackay defeated Higashi on first extra hole.)					
Tatsuya Shiraishi	74	72	64	210	3,045,000
Noboru Sugai	70	73	67	210	3,045,000
Koichi Suzuki	72	68	71	211	1,995,000
Teruo Sugihara	70	70	71	211	1,995,000
David Ishii	72	72	68	212	1,522,000
Masanobu Kimura	71	71	70	212	1,522,000
Ikuo Shirahama	69	72	71	212	1,522,000
Yoshitaka Yamamoto	71	71	71	213	984,000
Futoshi Irino	74	68	71	213	984,000
Masaji Kusakabe	69	71	73	213	984,000
Masahiro Kuramoto	71	68	74	213	984,000
Nichito Hashimoto	71	67	75	213	984,000
Naomichi Ozaki	70	74	70	214	693,000
Yoshinori Ichioka	74	69	71	214	693,000
Yoshimi Niizeki	69	73	72	214	693,000
Akihito Yokoyama	73	72	70	215	567,000
Katsunari Takahashi	71	72	72	215	567,000
Tsuneyuki Nakajima	72	73	71	216	477,000
Kiyoshi Murota	74	71	71	216	477,000

	SCORES			TOTAL	MONEY
Frankie Minoza	73	72	71	216	477,000
Yukio Noguchi	73	72	71	216	477,000
Yutaka Hagawa	70	73	73	216	477,000
Paul Hoad	69	72	75	216	477,000
Tsukasa Watanabe	73	75	69	217	404,000
Seiji Ebihara	73	73	71	217	404,000
Brian Jones	72	73	72	217	404,000
Hideto Shigenobu	70	75	72	217	404,000
Yoshinori Mizumaki	69	75	73	217	404,000
Nobuo Serizawa	73	69	75	217	404,000

Takeda Cup

Gurenmoa Country Club, Sakaemachi, Chiba
Par 72; 6,679 yards

July 4-7
purse, ¥100,000,000

	SCORES				TOTAL	MONEY
Harumitsu Hamano	65	67	70	71	273	¥12,600,000
Masashi Ozaki	73	65	67	72	277	7,000,000
Yoshiyuki Isomura	66	71	67	75	279	4,760,000
Graham Marsh	70	73	70	67	280	3,080,000
Chen Tze Chung	70	69	70	71	280	3,080,000
Akihito Yokoyama	70	72	73	66	281	2,152,000
Nobuo Serizawa	66	75	72	68	281	2,152,000
David Ishii	73	70	69	69	281	2,152,000
Naomichi Ozaki	67	72	72	70	281	2,152,000
Hideyuki Sato	72	71	72	67	282	1,505,000
Hiroshi Makino	70	71	67	74	282	1,505,000
Yoshinori Mizumaki	70	74	71	68	283	1,097,000
Isao Aoki	72	74	68	69	283	1,097,000
Roger Mackay	70	73	70	70	283	1,097,000
Seiichi Kanai	71	70	69	73	283	1,097,000
Yoshinori Kaneko	66	70	71	76	283	1,097,000
Anthony Gilligan	70	72	74	68	284	763,000
Hiroshi Ueda	74	71	69	70	284	763,000
Hiromichi Namiki	69	75	70	70	284	763,000
Saburo Fujiki	69	68	68	79	284	763,000
Tsuneyuki Nakajima	67	74	72	72	285	672,000
Eiichi Itai	72	73	74	68	287	604,000
Chen Tze Ming	67	77	71	72	287	604,000
Nichito Hashimoto	70	75	69	73	287	604,000
Satoshi Ooide	74	70	70	73	287	604,000
Hideki Kase	71	70	72	74	287	604,000
Takeru Shibata	71	73	74	70	288	539,000
Taisei Inagaki	70	75	72	71	288	539,000
Shinichi Wakagi	68	80	69	71	288	539,000
Toshimitsu Kai	72	73	68	75	288	539,000

Yonex Open Hiroshima

Hiroshima Country Club, Higashi-Hiroshima
Par 71; 6,635 yards

July 11-14
purse, ¥70,000,000

	SCORES				TOTAL	MONEY
Eiichi Itai	67	69	71	65	272	¥12,600,000
Tsuyoshi Yoneyama	68	68	69	69	274	5,880,000
Yoshinori Mizumaki	68	66	69	71	274	5,880,000
Yoshitaka Yamamoto	71	70	69	67	277	3,360,000
Shinsaku Maeda	67	71	68	72	278	2,800,000
Ikuo Shirahama	67	71	72	69	279	2,263,000
Brent Franklin	72	67	71	69	279	2,263,000
Satoshi Higashi	68	72	68	71	279	2,263,000
Tsuneyuki Nakajima	72	72	72	65	281	1,458,000
Masashi Ozaki	73	72	68	68	281	1,458,000
Hiroshi Makino	70	73	69	69	281	1,458,000
Yoshikazu Yokoshima	68	77	66	70	281	1,458,000
Yukio Noguchi	65	68	74	74	281	1,458,000
Teruo Nakamura	73	68	73	68	282	1,050,000
Toru Nakamura	70	70	71	71	282	1,050,000
Teruo Sugihara	73	71	70	69	283	882,000
Haruhito Yamamoto	71	70	72	70	283	882,000
Norio Suzuki	75	71	72	66	284	705,000
Shigeru Kawamata	73	71	73	67	284	705,000
Junji Hashizoe	70	72	74	68	284	705,000
Yuzo Oyama	72	69	75	68	284	705,000
Katsunari Takahashi	71	75	68	70	284	705,000
Harumitsu Hamano	72	73	72	68	285	602,000
Kenji Nakamura	75	69	73	68	285	602,000
Tomishige Ikeda	72	71	71	71	285	602,000
Tadami Ueno	74	70	73	69	286	532,000
Tomohiro Maruyama	71	75	71	69	286	532,000
Hideto Shigenobu	74	71	72	69	286	532,000
Yoshihisa Iwashita	73	73	71	69	286	532,000
Anthony Gilligan	72	72	72	70	286	532,000
Nobumitsu Yuhara	70	73	72	71	286	532,000
Toshimitsu Kai	71	71	73	71	286	532,000

Nikkei Cup

Yasu Kogen Country Club, Yasu, Fukuoka
Par 70; 6,663 yards
(Third round cancelled; heavy rain.)

July 25-28
purse, ¥80,000,000

	SCORES			TOTAL	MONEY
Naomichi Ozaki	67	66	70	203	¥10,800,000
Eiichi Itai	70	65	68	203	6,000,000
(Ozaki defeated Itai on first extra hole.)					
Yoshinori Kaneko	68	70	66	204	3,480,000
Hiroshi Makino	68	66	70	204	3,480,000
Yoshinori Mizumaki	67	69	69	205	2,280,000
Shigenori Mori	69	67	69	205	2,280,000
Katsunari Takahashi	69	71	66	206	1,740,000
Teruo Nakamura	71	67	68	206	1,740,000
Motomasa Aoki	67	68	71	206	1,740,000
Brent Franklin	72	69	66	207	1,173,000
Seiki Okuda	70	67	70	207	1,173,000

	SCORES			TOTAL	MONEY
Masayuki Kawamura	68	69	70	207	1,173,000
Yoshitaka Yamamoto	64	69	74	207	1,173,000
Futoshi Irino	69	70	69	208	864,000
Yuji Takagi	71	68	69	208	864,000
Tadami Ueno	68	67	73	208	864,000
Kimpachi Toshimura	73	69	67	209	624,000
Haruo Yasuda	76	66	67	209	624,000
Teruo Sugihara	69	70	70	209	624,000
Noboru Sugai	72	67	70	209	624,000
Nobuo Serizawa	66	73	70	209	624,000
Yoshinori Ichioka	71	68	70	209	624,000
Satoshi Ogawa	70	72	68	210	492,000
Osamu Watanabe	72	69	69	210	492,000
Yuzo Oyama	73	68	69	210	492,000
Koichi Suzuki	69	70	71	210	492,000
Pete Izumikawa	68	71	71	210	492,000
Hiromichi Namiki	67	72	71	210	492,000
Toru Nakamura	69	69	72	210	492,000
Masashi Ozaki	72	69	70	211	421,000
Harumitsu Hamano	70	70	71	211	421,000
Masanobu Kimura	69	70	72	211	421,000
Tomohiro Maruyama	68	71	72	211	421,000
Tetsuya Tsuda	72	67	72	211	421,000

NST Niigata Open

Jyoetu Kokusai Country Club, Tokamachi, Niigata
Par 72; 6,971 yards

August 1-4
purse, ¥60,000,000

	SCORES				TOTAL	MONEY
Akihito Yokoyama	73	67	69	69	278	¥10,800,000
Hideki Kase	69	69	71	71	280	5,400,000
Koichi Suzuki	67	72	68	73	280	5,400,000
Noboru Sugai	74	70	68	69	281	2,880,000
Hiroshi Makino	72	73	68	69	282	2,055,000
Yukio Noguchi	67	72	74	69	282	2,055,000
Osamu Machino	72	70	69	71	282	2,055,000
Seiji Ebihara	70	68	71	73	282	2,055,000
Tomohiro Maruyama	68	73	70	72	283	1,380,000
Masayuki Kawamura	73	70	68	72	283	1,380,000
Eiichi Itai	73	73	64	73	283	1,380,000
Kimpachi Yoshimura	70	74	71	69	284	940,000
Teruo Sugihara	74	67	73	70	284	940,000
Toshio Shirahama	70	69	72	73	284	940,000
Haruhito Yamamoto	68	72	71	73	284	940,000
Shigenori Mori	71	68	72	73	284	940,000
Hideyuki Sato	72	69	73	71	285	638,000
Toshimitsu Kai	75	70	68	72	285	638,000
Keisuke Goi	72	74	67	72	285	638,000
Hideto Shigenobu	68	71	70	76	285	638,000
Katsuji Hasegawa	69	69	71	76	285	638,000
Kiyoshi Maita	71	73	73	69	286	518,000
Tsuyoshi Yoneyama	74	72	71	69	286	518,000
Teruo Nakamura	73	69	74	70	286	518,000
Shigeru Kawamata	76	69	69	72	286	518,000
Pete Izumikawa	71	69	69	77	286	518,000
Yasunori Ida	73	72	71	71	287	468,000

	SCORES				TOTAL	MONEY
Kunihiko Masuda	71	73	71	72	287	468,000
Katsunari Takahashi	72	71	71	73	287	468,000
Norikazu Kawakami	72	73	75	68	288	432,000
Tadao Nakamura	71	74	70	73	288	432,000
Saburo Hayashi	70	71	72	75	288	432,000

Japan PGA Championship

Prestige Country Club, Azusamachi, Tochigi
Par 72; 7,107 yards

August 15-18
purse, ¥100,000,000

	SCORES				TOTAL	MONEY
Masashi Ozaki	71	73	68	61	273	¥18,000,000
Tsukasa Watanabe	70	70	70	69	279	10,000,000
Tsuneyuki Nakajima	76	70	67	69	282	4,216,000
Masayuki Kawamura	69	75	69	69	282	4,216,000
Toshiaki Nakagawa	71	72	70	69	282	4,216,000
Masahiro Kuramoto	69	71	72	70	282	4,216,000
Nobumitsu Yuhara	71	68	72	71	282	4,216,000
Yoshikazu Yokoshima	68	70	72	72	282	4,216,000
Isao Aoki	72	70	76	65	283	2,084,00
Teruo Sugihara	72	71	73	67	283	2,084,00
Chen Tze Ming	73	72	71	67	283	2,084,00
Yukio Noguchi	70	75	68	70	283	2,084,00
Naomichi Ozaki	67	73	70	73	283	2,084,00
Brian Jones	75	69	69	71	284	1,500,000
Chen Tze Chung	68	75	68	73	284	1,500,000
Kiyoshi Muroda	72	71	73	69	285	1,320,000
Graham Marsh	72	73	71	70	286	1,017,000
Taisei Inagaki	73	70	73	70	286	1,017,000
Brent Franklin	72	75	69	70	286	1,017,000
Toshimitsu Kai	72	73	68	73	286	1,017,000
Hiromichi Namiki	74	69	70	73	286	1,017,000
Hiroshi Makino	71	69	71	75	286	1,017,000
Shigenori Mori	74	63	72	77	286	1,017,000
Tomohiro Maruyama	72	70	72	73	287	850,000
Tsuyoshi Yoneyama	74	70	70	73	287	850,000
Nobuhiro Yoshino	74	72	74	68	288	780,000
Akihito Yokoyama	73	73	70	72	288	780,000
Yoshitaka Yamamoto	72	70	73	73	288	780,000
Toru Nakamura	70	71	74	73	288	780,000
Yoshinori Mizumaki	69	74	71	74	288	780,000

Maruman Open

Hatoyama Country Club, Hatoyama, Saitama
Par 72; 7,068 yards

August 22-25
purse, ¥100,000,000

	SCORES				TOTAL	MONEY
Tetsu Nishikawa	68	70	66	70	274	¥18,000,000
Tateo Ozaki	74	66	66	68	274	10,000,000
(Nishikawa defeated Ozaki on third extra hole.)						
Yoshinori Kaneko	74	63	68	71	276	6,800,000
Masashi Ozaki	70	71	68	68	277	4,800,000
Brent Franklin	73	67	68	70	278	3,600,000

	SCORES				TOTAL	MONEY
Ian Woosnam	71	66	71	70	278	3,600,000
Hiroya Kamide	71	66	70	71	278	3,600,000
Roger Mackay	69	73	68	69	279	2,600,000
Tsuneyuki Nakajima	70	69	69	71	279	2,600,000
Kiyoshi Muroda	70	68	70	71	279	2,600,000
Chen Tze Chung	70	70	74	67	281	1,840,000
Masayuki Kawamura	73	69	69	70	281	1,840,000
Toshiaki Nakagawa	67	70	71	73	281	1,840,000
Tsuyoshi Yoneyama	71	69	73	69	282	1,440,000
Kouki Idoki	69	72	72	69	282	1,440,000
Hiroshi Makino	68	73	68	73	282	1,440,000
Nobuo Serizawa	71	73	70	69	283	1,160,000
Hirofumi Miyase	72	70	70	71	283	1,160,000
Frankie Minoza	70	72	72	70	284	960,000
Wayne Smith	77	65	71	71	284	960,000
Kouichi Uehara	71	71	71	71	284	960,000
Nobumitsu Yuhara	70	69	73	72	284	960,000
Graham Marsh	70	69	72	73	284	960,000
Tadashige Kusano	71	72	72	70	285	830,000
Chen Tze Ming	70	74	69	72	285	830,000
Shinsaku Maeda	68	74	71	72	285	830,000
Paul Hoad	71	68	74	72	285	830,000
Futoshi Irino	70	75	72	69	286	740,000
Tatsuya Shiraishi	72	70	74	70	286	740,000
Nobuhiro Yoshino	70	75	71	70	286	740,000
Seiichi Kanai	71	73	71	71	286	740,000
Toshimitsu Kai	73	69	71	73	286	740,000

Daiwa KBC Augusta Open

Kyushu Shima Country Club, Shima, Fukuoka
Par 72; 7,125 yards

August 29 - September 1
purse, ¥100,000,000

	SCORES				TOTAL	MONEY
Raymond Floyd	66	69	69	69	273	¥18,000,000
Frankie Minoza	66	70	71	67	274	10,000,000
Dan Forsman	70	66	69	72	277	6,800,000
Isao Aoki	70	69	73	67	279	4,800,000
Masashi Ozaki	70	72	70	68	280	3,420,000
Tadao Nakamura	72	73	67	68	280	3,420,000
Teruo Sugihara	70	71	69	70	280	3,420,000
Brent Franklin	68	67	74	71	280	3,420,000
Tsuneyuki Nakajima	70	73	71	67	281	2,300,000
Tetsu Nishikawa	71	69	74	67	281	2,300,000
Chen Tze Chung	73	68	68	72	281	2,300,000
Noboru Sugai	72	70	71	69	282	1,760,000
Saburo Fujiki	69	68	71	74	282	1,760,000
Seiki Okuda	73	72	71	67	283	1,440,000
Koichi Suzuki	72	71	69	71	283	1,440,000
Graham Marsh	68	69	73	73	283	1,440,000
Hiroshi Makino	71	70	73	70	284	1,160,000
Eiichi Itai	74	70	69	71	284	1,160,000
Tsukasa Watanabe	73	70	71	71	285	1,000,000
Nobumitsu Yuhara	73	70	71	71	285	1,000,000
Hajime Meshiai	71	71	69	74	285	1,000,000
Tateo Ozaki	74	71	72	69	286	886,000
Junji Hashizoe	71	73	72	70	286	886,000

	SCORES				TOTAL	MONEY
Yoshinori Mizumaki	69	72	71	74	286	886,000
Akiyoshi Omachi	70	70	79	68	287	780,000
Hiromichi Namiki	73	73	72	69	287	780,000
Masayuki Kawamura	67	76	74	70	287	780,000
Motomasa Aoki	70	72	75	70	287	780,000
Yoshimi Niizeki	71	71	72	73	287	780,000
Kiyoshi Muroda	68	74	71	74	287	780,000
Hideto Shigenobu	69	74	70	74	287	780,000

Kansai Open

Pinlake Golf Club
Par 72; 7,034 yards

September 5-8
purse, ¥20,000,000

	SCORES				TOTAL	MONEY
Toshikazu Sugihara	72	70	69	72	283	¥5,000,000
Teruo Sugihara	71	70	74	69	284	2,500,000
Takumi Horiuchi	70	72	72	73	287	1,300,000
Toshimitsu Kai	75	72	72	73	288	875,000
Koji Okuno	72	74	70	72	288	875,000
Hiroya Kamide	75	72	68	73	288	875,000
Toshiya Shibutani	70	72	72	74	288	875,000
Toru Nakamura	75	71	68	75	289	575,000
Yuzo Oyama	69	71	74	75	289	575,000
Yoshitaka Yamamoto	77	68	74	71	290	500,000

Kanto Open

Higashinomiya Country Club, Higashinomiya
Par 70; 6,774 yards
(Shortened to 54 holes, rain.)

September 5-8
purse, ¥22,500,000

	SCORES			TOTAL	MONEY
Yoshinori Kaneko	69	69	64	202	¥4,500,000
Eiichi Itai	66	71	70	207	2,250,000
Shigeru Kawamata	71	71	68	210	1,000,000
Mitsunobu Yuhara	71	70	69	210	1,000,000
Kiyoshi Maita	69	71	70	210	1,000,000
Masakazu Noritake	72	72	67	211	637,000
Masaji Kusakabe	70	69	72	211	637,000
Shigeru Namiki	71	71	70	212	525,000
Ryoken Kawagishi	69	71	72	212	525,000
Hajime Meshiai	70	70	71	212	525,000

Chubu Open

September 5-8
purse, ¥20,000,000

	SCORES				TOTAL	MONEY
Teruo Nakamura	73	69	68	69	279	¥5,000,000
Takeshi Shibata	75	73	67	71	286	2,050,000
Jun Hattori	70	74	69	73	286	2,050,000

	SCORES				TOTAL	MONEY
Masahiro Shioda	71	73	70	74	288	1,100,000
Yoshihiro Ito	70	73	75	71	289	900,000
Toshio Ozaki	69	77	74	70	290	700,000
Tatsuaki Nakamura	72	74	73	71	290	700,000
Saburo Hayashi	68	78	72	72	290	700,000
Yoshiaki Maruoka	75	74	73	70	292	475,000

Hokkaido Open

Noboribetsu Country Club
Par 72; 7,035 yards

September 5-8
purse, ¥10,000,000

	SCORES				TOTAL	MONEY
Katsunari Takahashi	69	66	76	70	281	¥3,000,000
Fumio Tanaka	71	71	75	67	284	1,500,000
Kazuhiro Takami	72	71	73	70	286	1,000,000
Satoshi Sudo	70	72	72	73	287	600,000
Koichi Uehara	75	70	75	70	290	450,000
Mamoru Takahashi	75	72	74	70	291	400,000
Mitsuyoshi Goto	72	71	79	71	293	235,000
Takayuki Shioya	74	70	77	72	293	235,000
Osamu Katakura	70	73	77	74	294	200,000

Chushikoku Open

Syunan Country Club
Par 72; 7,027 yards

September 5-8
purse, ¥20,000,000

	SCORES				TOTAL	MONEY
Kosei Miyata	69	70	68	77	284	¥5,000,000
Masahiro Kuramoto	72	72	73	70	287	2,000,000
Hideto Shigenobu	74	71	70	72	287	2,000,000
Norihiro Yoshino	71	74	74	71	290	1,000,000
Seiki Okuno	76	74	71	71	292	900,000
Masayuki Kawamura	75	73	71	75	294	800,000
Hiroshi Taninaka	69	76	80	71	296	562,000
Yoshikazu Sakamoto	74	74	73	75	296	562,000
Kunihiko Masuda	72	77	72	75	296	562,000

Kyushu Open

Dazaifu Golf Club
Par 72; 6,824 yards

September 5-8
purse, ¥20,000,000

	SCORES				TOTAL	MONEY
Kinpachi Yoshimura	76	69	73	72	290	¥5,000,000
Isamu Sugita	72	74	74	72	292	2,500,000
Norikazu Kawakami	71	74	76	72	293	1,500,000
Chikara Nagata	74	75	72	73	294	916,000
Keiji Tejima	73	71	75	75	294	916,000
Nobuyuki Ikeda	71	74	74	75	294	916,000
Tadashige Kusano	76	72	73	74	295	650,000
Takamasa Sakai	73	76	72	75	296	600,000

Suntory Open

Narashino Country Club, Inzai, Chiba
Par 36-36—72; 7,056 yards

September 12-15
purse, ¥100,000,000

	SCORES				TOTAL	MONEY
Naomichi Ozaki	67	69	72	68	276	¥18,000,000
Chen Tze Chung	69	68	70	71	278	10,000,000
Brent Franklin	70	68	69	73	280	6,800,000
Yoshinori Kaneko	71	72	70	69	282	4,400,000
Masahiro Kuramoto	72	66	73	71	282	4,400,000
Teruo Nakamura	70	74	68	71	283	3,600,000
Masashi Ozaki	72	71	70	71	284	2,750,000
Tateo Ozaki	69	71	73	71	284	2,750,000
Yoshinori Mizumaki	66	71	74	73	284	2,750,000
Toshimitsu Kai	70	68	72	74	284	2,750,000
Masahiro Shiota	73	73	70	69	285	2,000,000
Nobumitsu Yuhara	70	75	72	69	286	1,760,000
Isao Aoki	70	73	72	71	286	1,760,000
Frankie Minoza	73	72	70	72	287	1,560,000
Tsukasa Watanabe	72	70	77	69	288	1,074,000
Saburo Fujiki	72	70	76	70	288	1,074,000
Brian Jones	72	74	72	70	288	1,074,000
Mitsuyoshi Gotoh	72	73	72	71	288	1,074,000
Scott Simpson	71	74	72	71	288	1,074,000
Ryoken Kawagishi	74	71	71	72	288	1,074,000
Akiyoshi Omachi	66	73	75	74	288	1,074,000
Hirofumi Miyase	72	70	72	74	288	1,074,000
Hideto Shigenobu	70	76	67	75	288	1,074,000
Larry Nelson	68	68	75	77	288	1,074,000
Tadami Ueno	70	73	75	71	289	790,000
Eiichi Itai	68	75	74	72	289	790,000
Yoshitaka Yamamoto	70	75	72	72	289	790,000
Hideki Kase	70	71	75	73	289	790,000
Pete Izumikawa	71	75	70	73	289	790,000
Katsunari Takahashi	69	74	72	74	289	790,000

All Nippon Airways Open

Sapporo Golf Club, Wattsu Course, Sapporo
Par 72; 7,063 yards

September 19-22
purse, ¥100,000,000

	SCORES				TOTAL	MONEY
Akiyoshi Omachi	68	71	72	71	282	¥18,000,000
Ryoken Kawagishi	68	73	72	71	284	10,000,000
Tsuneyuki Nakajima	68	73	74	71	286	6,800,000
Yutaka Hagawa	70	75	73	70	288	4,133,000
Tsuyoshi Yoneyama	69	72	76	71	288	4,133,000
Masashi Ozaki	69	75	72	72	288	4,133,000
Chen Tze Ming	74	71	71	70	289	2,750,000
Bernhard Langer	71	72	74	72	289	2,750,000
Mark O'Meara	70	72	73	74	289	2,750,000
Pete Izumikawa	70	68	75	76	289	2,750,000
Seiji Ebihara	74	74	73	69	290	1,770,000
Katsuji Hasegawa	73	73	74	70	290	1,770,000
Hideki Kase	70	71	76	73	290	1,770,000
Tateo Ozaki	71	74	71	74	290	1,770,000
Anthony Gilligan	73	73	77	68	291	1,380,000

	SCORES				TOTAL	MONEY
Naomichi Ozaki	69	76	73	73	291	1,380,000
Isao Aoki	75	72	76	69	292	1,064,000
Nobumitsu Yuhara	70	74	76	72	292	1,064,000
Teruo Nakamura	74	72	74	72	292	1,064,000
Chen Tze Chung	73	70	76	73	292	1,064,000
Tadami Ueno	71	73	75	73	292	1,064,000
Roger Mackay	72	73	78	70	293	853,000
Eiichi Itai	74	71	78	70	293	853,000
Misao Yamamoto	69	75	78	71	293	853,000
Yoshinori Mizumaki	73	71	76	73	293	853,000
Teruo Sugihara	68	76	75	74	293	853,000
Toshiaki Sudo	69	76	72	76	293	853,000
David Ishii	73	74	76	71	294	740,000
Seiichi Kanai	75	73	73	73	294	740,000
Toshiji Shirahama	72	74	75	73	294	740,000
Akihito Yokoyama	70	74	76	74	294	740,000
Graham Marsh	71	72	75	76	294	740,000

Jun Classic

Rope Club, Shiotanimachi, Tochigi
Par 36-36—72; 6,992 yards

September 26-29
purse, ¥110,000,000

	SCORES				TOTAL	MONEY
Masahiro Ozaki	69	68	70	70	277	¥19,800,000
Ryoken Kawagishi	70	69	74	64	277	11,000,000
(Ozaki defeated Kawagishi on first extra hole.)						
Yoshinori Mizumaki	69	71	72	66	278	6,380,000
Chen Tze Chung	67	71	73	67	278	6,380,000
Yutaka Hagawa	67	68	69	75	279	4,400,000
Haruhito Yamamoto	68	74	70	68	280	3,382,000
Tadanori Kaneko	71	72	68	69	280	3,382,000
Minoru Hatsumi	71	72	68	69	280	3,382,000
Hideyuki Sato	72	67	71	70	280	3,382,000
Tomohiro Maruyama	73	69	70	69	281	2,063,000
Taisei Inagaki	69	67	73	72	281	2,063,000
Nobuhiro Yoshino	72	70	67	72	281	2,063,000
Hal Sutton	72	68	69	72	281	2,063,000
Toru Nakamura	70	70	68	73	281	2,063,000
Futoshi Irino	71	73	70	68	282	1,518,000
Shigeru Kawamata	69	69	72	72	282	1,518,000
Yukio Noguchi	73	71	72	67	283	1,170,000
Yoshinori Ichioka	72	71	73	67	283	1,170,000
Brian Jones	70	73	70	70	283	1,170,000
Isamu Sugita	70	72	69	72	283	1,170,000
Yukihiro Yamamoto	75	70	66	72	283	1,170,000
Katsunari Takahashi	71	72	72	69	284	962,000
Kimpachi Yoshimura	68	73	74	69	284	962,000
Nobumitsu Yuhara	73	71	69	71	284	962,000
Atsushi Murota	70	71	69	74	284	962,000
Toshimitsu Kai	72	73	72	68	285	880,000
Katsuji Hasegawa	72	68	72	73	285	880,000
Hideto Shigenobu	68	73	69	75	285	880,000
Ikuo Shirahama	73	70	73	70	286	825,000
Kenshi Ikeda	72	71	73	70	286	825,000

Tokai Classic

Miyoshi Country Club, Miyoshi, Aichi
Par 36-36—72; 7,089 yards

October 3-6
purse, ¥100,000,000

	SCORES				TOTAL	MONEY
Eiichi Itai	70	65	72	72	279	¥18,000,000
Nobumitsu Yuhara	74	70	68	71	283	10,000,000
Nobuo Serizawa	71	71	71	71	284	5,800,000
Yoshitaka Yamamoto	73	72	67	72	284	5,800,000
Larry Mize	70	72	71	72	285	3,800,000
Tateo Ozaki	69	73	70	73	285	3,800,000
Hideyuki Sato	71	73	73	69	286	3,050,000
Yuji Takagi	70	69	77	71	286	3,050,000
Toru Nakamura	74	71	71	71	287	2,450,000
Naomichi Ozaki	68	74	71	74	287	2,450,000
Hiromichi Namiki	71	71	75	71	288	1,920,000
Graham Marsh	69	71	74	74	288	1,920,000
Yoshinori Kaneko	77	72	77	63	289	1,500,000
Yutaka Hagawa	71	73	74	71	289	1,500,000
Toruo Nakamura	73	72	73	71	289	1,500,000
Chen Tze Ming	74	72	70	73	289	1,500,000
Seiki Okuda	76	71	74	70	291	1,064,000
Shinsaku Maeda	71	73	77	70	291	1,064,000
Yoshinori Mizumaki	71	75	74	71	291	1,064,000
Ikuo Shirahama	74	71	74	72	291	1,064,000
Kiyoshi Maita	70	76	72	73	291	1,064,000
Toshiaki Sudo	72	75	70	75	292	900,000
Hiroshi Makino	72	70	74	76	292	900,000
Shigenori Mori	77	72	74	70	293	820,000
Yoshikazu Sakamoto	71	75	75	72	293	820,000
Anthony Gilligan	79	71	70	73	293	820,000
Kouki Idoki	72	76	71	74	293	820,000
Kiminori Kato	73	74	72	74	293	820,000
Akihito Yokoyama	70	80	76	68	294	730,000
Hajime Meshiai	72	71	81	70	294	730,000
Takeru Shibata	76	74	71	73	294	730,000
Saburo Fujiki	70	73	73	78	294	730,000

Japan Open

Shimonoseki Golf Club, Toyoura, Yamaguchi
Par 36-36—72; 6,910 yards

October 10-13
purse, ¥100,000,000

	SCORES				TOTAL	MONEY
Tsuneyuki Nakajima	72	74	71	73	290	¥18,000,000
Noboru Sugai	74	70	76	70	290	10,000,000
(Nakajima defeated Sugai on first extra hole.)						
Isao Aoki	75	75	72	69	291	6,150,000
Tetsu Nishikawa	72	73	75	71	291	6,150,000
Masashi Ozaki	72	70	77	73	292	4,100,000
Hiroshi Makino	73	69	74	76	292	4,100,000
Graham Marsh	72	78	72	71	293	3,133,000
Katsunari Takahashi	74	75	73	71	293	3,133,000
Seiichi Kanai	74	73	73	73	293	3,133,000
Nobumitsu Yuhara	77	71	74	72	294	2,146,000
Hideto Shigenobu	75	75	72	72	294	2,146,000
Anthony Gilligan	71	72	79	72	294	2,146,000

	SCORES				TOTAL	MONEY
*Shigeki Maruyama	74	73	73	74	294	
*Kazuyoshi Yonekura	70	80	76	69	295	
Kinpachi Yoshimura	75	76	70	74	295	1,730,000
Tsukasa Watanabe	79	71	75	71	296	1,253,000
Shigeru Kawamata	73	72	78	73	296	1,253,000
Tateo Ozaki	78	74	70	74	296	1,253,000
Yoshitaka Yamamoto	71	77	73	75	296	1,253,000
Harumitsu Hamano	77	72	71	76	296	1,253,000
Brian Jones	74	71	73	78	296	1,253,000
Kiyoshi Muroda	70	70	76	80	296	1,253,000
Eiji Mizoguchi	72	73	71	80	296	1,253,000
Yoshinori Ichioka	74	74	77	72	297	909,000
Tsuyoshi Yoneyama	77	74	71	75	297	909,000
Hajime Meshiai	76	73	73	75	297	909,000
Frankie Minoza	75	71	74	77	297	909,000
Yukio Noguchi	74	76	78	70	298	772,000
Akihito Yokoyama	79	74	74	71	298	772,000
Kazuhiro Takami	73	76	78	71	298	772,000
Koichi Suzuki	74	74	77	73	298	772,000
Rick Gibson	73	77	75	73	298	772,000
Tadami Ueno	75	78	72	73	298	772,000
Toru Nakamura	76	75	74	73	298	772,000
Seiji Ebihara	70	76	76	76	298	772,000
Haruo Yasuda	75	72	75	76	298	772,000
Kikuo Arai	76	69	80	74	299	656,000
Peter McWhinney	78	72	74	75	299	656,000
Yoshinori Kaneko	73	79	70	77	299	656,000
Motomasa Aoki	75	71	75	78	299	656,000
John Morse	74	75	75	76	300	616,000
Tomohiro Maruyama	79	74	76	72	301	564,000
David Ishii	73	75	76	77	301	564,000
Naomichi Ozaki	75	78	70	78	301	564,000
Yutaka Hagawa	78	74	71	78	301	564,000
Eduardo Herrera	71	77	72	81	301	564,000
Shigenori Mori	76	75	77	74	302	476,000
Yuji Kato	74	79	75	74	302	476,000
Saburo Fujiki	77	72	78	75	302	476,000
Masahiro Kuramoto	71	80	75	76	302	476,000
Masanobu Kimura	72	75	78	77	302	476,000
Ikuo Shirahama	72	79	73	78	302	476,000
Masahiro Shioda	77	76	71	78	302	476,000
Dennis Paulson	77	72	74	79	302	476,000

Asahi Beer Golf Digest

Tomei Country Club, Susono, Shizuoka
Par 71; 6,801 yards

October 17-20
purse, ¥120,000,000

	SCORES				TOTAL	MONEY
Harumitsu Hamano	69	68	71	65	273	¥21,600,000
Masashi Ozaki	67	71	67	69	274	12,000,000
Nobumitsu Yuhara	71	65	66	74	276	8,100,000
Nobuo Serizawa	69	70	70	69	278	5,760,000
Rick Gibson	69	71	68	71	279	4,560,000
Haruo Yasuda	67	71	69	72	279	4,560,000
Shigeru Kawamata	72	68	73	67	280	3,120,000
Tsuneyuki Nakajima	71	71	68	70	280	3,120,000

	SCORES				TOTAL	MONEY
Akihito Yokoyama	65	73	70	72	280	3,120,000
Terry Gale	70	69	69	72	280	3,120,000
Tateo Ozaki	73	68	66	73	280	3,120,000
Tsukasa Watanabe	76	68	70	67	281	2,032,000
Hajime Meshiai	67	71	74	69	281	2,032,000
Noboru Sugai	69	72	68	72	281	2,032,000
Hiroshi Makino	71	71	72	68	282	1,468,000
Brian Jones	70	69	73	70	282	1,468,000
Joji Furuki	71	71	70	70	282	1,468,000
Tadami Ueno	67	71	73	71	282	1,468,000
Tsuyoshi Yoneyama	69	70	72	71	282	1,468,000
Frankie Minoza	69	71	73	70	283	1,076,000
Seiki Okuda	68	73	72	70	283	1,076,000
Nobuhiro Yoshino	67	76	70	70	283	1,076,000
Hale Irwin	73	72	68	70	283	1,076,000
Greg Norman	68	75	69	71	283	1,076,000
Kiyoshi Muroda	69	70	72	72	283	1,076,000
Roger Mackay	72	70	67	74	283	1,076,000
Yoshitaka Yamamoto	73	73	69	69	284	900,000
Ryoken Kawagishi	73	73	68	70	284	900,000
Masanobu Kimura	71	69	74	70	284	900,000
Eduardo Herrera	70	69	74	71	284	900,000
Saburo Fujiki	70	68	74	72	284	900,000
Yukio Noguchi	75	69	68	72	284	900,000

Bridgestone Open

Sodegaura Golf Club, Chiba
Par 36-36—72; 7,110 yards
(Friday, Sunday rounds rained out; tournament shortened to 36 holes.)

October 24-27
purse, ¥60,000,000

	SCORES		TOTAL	MONEY
Isao Aoki	71	63	134	¥10,800,000
Tsuyoshi Yoneyama	70	65	135	6,000,000
Hideki Kase	69	68	137	3,480,000
Andrew Magee	69	68	137	3,480,000
Yoshinori Mizumaki	72	66	138	2,160,000
Nobumitsu Yuhara	69	69	138	2,160,000
Chen Tze Ming	68	70	138	2,160,000
Chen Tze Chung	70	69	139	1,396,000
Nobuhiro Yoshino	70	69	139	1,396,000
Koichi Suzuki	69	70	139	1,396,000
Rick Gibson	69	70	139	1,396,000
Akiyoshi Omachi	67	72	139	1,396,000
Toshiji Shirahama	72	68	140	864,000
Brent Franklin	69	71	140	864,000
Seiki Okuda	68	72	140	864,000
Saburo Fujiki	67	73	140	864,000
Tsutomu Higa	67	73	140	864,000
Masashi Ozaki	73	68	141	604,000
Satoshi Higashi	73	68	141	604,000
Masayuki Kawamura	73	68	141	604,000
Brian Jones	72	69	141	604,000
Atsushi Muroda	71	70	141	604,000
Ikuo Shirahama	75	67	142	504,000
Toru Nakamura	73	69	142	504,000
Katsuji Hasegawa	71	71	142	504,000

	SCORES				TOTAL	MONEY
Kiminori Kato	69	73			142	504,000
Isamu Sugita	68	74			142	504,000
Tsukasa Watanabe	75	68			143	412,000
Satoshi Ogawa	74	69			143	412,000
Roger Mackay	73	70			143	412,000
Hideyuki Sato	73	70			143	412,000
Naomichi Ozaki	72	71			143	412,000
Tateo Ozaki	72	71			143	412,000
Teruo Nakamura	72	71			143	412,000
Yuichi Takano	72	71			143	412,000
Hiroya Kamide	71	72			143	412,000
Tsuneyuki Nakajima	70	73			143	412,000
Tomohiro Maruyama	69	74			143	412,000

Lark Cup

ABC Golf Club, Tojocho, Hyogo
Par 36-36—72; 7,176 yards

October 31 - November 3
purse, ¥190,000,000

	SCORES				TOTAL	MONEY
Yoshikazu Yokoshima	70	71	69	70	280	¥34,200,000
Roger Mackay	72	71	68	71	282	19,000,000
Koichi Suzuki	73	73	68	69	283	11,020,000
Naomichi Ozaki	73	73	67	70	283	11,020,000
Bob Gilder	70	74	73	67	284	6,194,000
Tsuneyuki Nakajima	73	71	69	71	284	6,194,000
Hideki Kase	67	74	69	74	284	6,194,000
Shigenori Mori	67	73	70	74	284	6,194,000
Barry Lane	71	70	68	75	284	6,194,000
Masashi Ozaki	70	72	73	70	285	3,714,000
Frankie Minoza	70	72	72	71	285	3,714,000
Peter Senior	71	68	75	71	285	3,714,000
Kazuhiro Takami	69	73	71	72	285	3,714,000
Yoshinori Kaneko	68	73	75	70	286	2,523,000
Jeff Maggert	70	73	73	70	286	2,523,000
Robert Gamez	73	69	74	70	286	2,523,000
Bill Glasson	73	71	70	72	286	2,523,000
Yutaka Hagawa	66	74	72	74	286	2,523,000
Ikuo Shirahama	74	70	73	70	287	1,824,000
Brian Jones	74	71	71	71	287	1,824,000
Brent Franklin	74	71	71	71	287	1,824,000
Katsuji Hasegawa	75	72	68	72	287	1,824,000
Chen Tze Ming	75	70	68	74	287	1,824,000
Nobumitsu Yuhara	71	73	75	69	288	1,482,000
Seiichi Kanai	71	74	74	69	288	1,482,000
Tateo Ozaki	73	71	74	70	288	1,482,000
Katsunari Takahashi	68	78	72	70	288	1,482,000
Kiyoshi Muroda	73	74	71	70	288	1,482,000
Toru Nakamura	72	72	74	70	288	1,482,000
Noboru Sugai	71	73	72	72	288	1,482,000
Chen Tze Chung	73	69	73	73	288	1,482,000
Kiminori Kato	73	69	73	73	288	1,482,000

Acom International

Narita Springs Country Club, Yamadacho, Chiba
Par 36-36—72; 7,122 yards

November 7-10
purse, ¥75,000,000

	POINTS	MONEY
Masahiro Kuramoto	32	¥13,500,000
Toru Nakamura	22	5,400,000
Yoshinori Mizumaki	22	5,400,000
Brent Franklin	22	5,400,000
Atsushi Muroda	21	3,000,000
Tomohiro Maruyama	20	2,550,000
Hideyuki Sato	20	2,550,000
Koichi Suzuki	19	2,175,000
Tateo Ozaki	18	1,950,000
Toshihiko Otsuka	17	1,725,000
Shinsaku Maeda	15	1,440,000
Ted Schulz	15	1,440,000
Seiichi Kanai	14	1,215,000
Taisei Inagaki	14	1,215,000
Hajime Meshiai	13	990,000
Shigenori Mori	13	990,000
Hiroya Kamide	13	990,000
Toshimitsu Kai	12	756,000
Yoshiyuki Isomura	12	756,000
Masaru Amano	12	756,000
Haruhito Yamamoto	12	756,000
Yoshinori Ichioka	12	756,000
Yutaka Hagawa	11	645,000
Ikuo Shirahama	11	645,000
Tsutomu Higa	11	645,000
Akira Funano	10	600,000
Norikazu Kawakami	10	600,000
Terry Gale	10	600,000
Nobumitsu Yuhara	9	540,000
Motomasa Aoki	9	540,000
Toru Nakayama	9	540,000
Hiromichi Namiki	9	540,000
Kiyoshi Maita	9	540,000

Visa Taiheiyo Club Masters

Taiheiyo Club, Gotemba Course, Gotemba, Shizuoka
Par 36-36—72; 7,072 yards

November 14-17
purse ¥150,000,000

	SCORES				TOTAL	MONEY
Roger Mackay	70	69	65	68	272	¥27,000,000
Yoshinori Kaneko	68	70	68	68	274	15,000,000
Tsuneyuki Nakajima	70	65	68	72	275	10,200,000
Jose Maria Olazabal	69	71	68	69	277	7,200,000
Jeff Sluman	71	72	70	66	279	6,000,000
Fred Couples	70	71	70	69	280	5,400,000
Brian Jones	73	73	67	68	281	4,350,000
Yutaka Hagawa	70	71	71	69	281	4,350,000
Peter Senior	71	69	71	70	281	4,350,000
Isao Aoki	71	71	74	66	282	3,450,000
Barry Lane	74	72	69	69	284	2,760,000
Katsunari Takahashi	74	72	68	70	284	2,760,000

	SCORES				TOTAL	MONEY
Tsukasa Watanabe	71	73	68	72	284	2,760,000
Saburo Fujiki	73	74	73	65	285	2,160,000
Masanobu Kimura	71	76	70	68	285	2,160,000
Nick Faldo	71	73	73	68	285	2,160,000
Philip Walton	68	78	71	69	286	1,680,000
Kinpachi Yoshimura	71	73	71	71	286	1,680,000
Chen Tze Ming	70	72	70	74	286	1,680,000
Chen Tze Chung	72	75	72	68	287	1,440,000
Mark Brooks	74	71	73	69	287	1,440,000
Rick Gibson	71	72	72	72	287	1,440,000
Nobuo Serizawa	76	70	71	71	288	1,290,000
Hajime Meshiai	72	72	72	72	288	1,290,000
Koichi Suzuki	71	72	70	75	288	1,290,000
Corey Pavin	75	73	70	71	289	1,200,000
Masahiro Kuramoto	74	74	69	72	289	1,200,000
Akihito Yokoyama	74	71	72	72	289	1,200,000
Naomichi Ozaki	74	70	77	69	290	1,081,000
Masashi Ozaki	74	72	74	70	290	1,081,000
Hideki Kase	69	76	73	72	290	1,081,000
Katsuji Hasegawa	75	73	70	72	290	1,081,000
Frankie Minoza	75	72	70	73	290	1,081,000

Dunlop Phoenix

Phoenix Country Club, Miyazaki
Par 72; 6,993 yards

November 21-24
purse, ¥200,000,000

	SCORES				TOTAL	MONEY
Larry Nelson	70	71	67	68	276	¥36,000,000
Isao Aoki	73	68	69	66	276	14,400,000
Jay Don Blake	69	71	68	68	276	14,400,000
Severiano Ballesteros	68	69	69	70	276	14,400,000

(Nelson won playoff, Blake eliminated on first, Ballesteros on third and Aoki on fourth extra hole.)

	SCORES				TOTAL	MONEY
Mike Reid	70	69	69	69	277	8,000,000
Nolan Henke	67	72	69	70	278	6,800,000
Mark Brooks	66	68	71	73	278	6,800,000
Craig Stadler	72	68	67	72	279	5,500,000
Roger Mackay	69	70	67	73	279	5,500,000
Sandy Lyle	68	74	72	66	280	4,300,000
Mike Harwood	71	70	71	68	280	4,300,000
Masashi Ozaki	71	76	66	68	281	3,386,000
Jeff Hawkes	71	69	72	69	281	3,386,000
Miguel Angel Martin	68	71	72	70	281	3,386,000
Graham Marsh	73	70	70	69	282	2,640,000
Katsuji Hasegawa	68	68	72	74	282	2,640,000
Jose Maria Olazabal	68	71	69	74	282	2,640,000
Naomichi Ozaki	73	73	67	70	283	2,240,000
Seiichi Kanai	71	71	69	73	284	2,040,000
Larry Mize	70	73	66	75	284	2,040,000
Terry Gale	72	69	73	71	285	1,715,000
Tadami Ueno	73	70	70	72	285	1,715,000
Akihito Yokoyama	69	75	69	72	285	1,715,000
Lanny Wadkins	71	67	75	72	285	1,715,000
Hiroshi Makino	70	72	70	73	285	1,715,000
Chen Tze Chung	70	71	70	74	285	1,715,000
Jeff Sluman	69	74	68	74	285	1,715,000
Akiyoshi Omachi	69	71	70	75	285	1,715,000

	SCORES				TOTAL	MONEY
Takayoshi Kaneko	73	72	71	70	286	1,500,000
Tsuneyuki Nakajima	72	70	71	73	286	1,500,000

Casio World Open

Ibusuki Golf Club, Kanmon Course, Ibusuki
Par 72; 7,014 yards

November 28 - December 1
purse, ¥140,000,000

	SCORES				TOTAL	MONEY
Naomichi Ozaki	71	67	64	68	270	¥25,200,000
Hajime Meshiai	69	67	70	66	272	14,000,000
Larry Nelson	70	64	69	70	273	9,520,000
Masahiro Kuramoto	65	71	74	65	275	6,160,000
Masashi Ozaki	68	68	71	68	275	6,160,000
Tsukasa Watanabe	74	65	70	67	276	4,760,000
Wayne Grady	68	71	70	67	276	4,760,000
Kimpachi Yoshimura	74	70	65	68	277	3,850,000
Nobumitsu Yuhara	70	67	70	70	277	3,850,000
Chen Tze Chung	73	69	70	66	278	2,737,000
Jerry Pate	73	66	70	69	278	2,737,000
Sandy Lyle	71	67	70	70	278	2,737,000
Taisei Inagaki	66	72	66	74	278	2,737,000
Tateo Ozaki	73	69	69	68	279	2,100,000
Mark Brooks	70	71	70	68	279	2,100,000
Roger Mackay	72	71	69	68	280	1,512,000
Tadayoshi Kaneko	71	71	70	68	280	1,512,000
Eiichi Itai	72	70	70	68	280	1,512,000
Akiyoshi Omachi	71	68	70	71	280	1,512,000
Tadami Ueno	70	70	69	71	280	1,512,000
Jeff Hawkes	69	69	71	71	280	1,512,000
Hiroya Kamide	70	70	65	75	280	1,512,000
Toru Nakamura	72	72	71	66	281	1,204,000
Per-Ulrik Johansson	69	70	70	72	281	1,204,000
Ken Green	73	66	68	74	281	1,204,000
Nobuo Serizawa	70	75	69	68	282	1,092,000
Noboru Sugai	69	70	74	69	282	1,092,000
Koichi Suzuki	70	69	73	70	282	1,092,000
Koki Idoki	71	73	66	72	282	1,092,000
Satoshi Higashi	70	69	69	74	282	1,092,000

Japan Series Hitachi Cup

Yomiuri Country Club, Tokyo
Par 72; 7,017 yards

December 5-8
purse, ¥60,000,000

	SCORES				TOTAL	MONEY
Naomichi Ozaki	71	65	66	66	268	¥15,000,000
Tsuneyuki Nakajima	70	69	67	70	276	6,650,000
Nobumitsu Yuhara	68	68	69	71	276	6,650,000
Kimpachi Yoshimura	66	73	72	67	278	3,800,000
Chen Tze Chung	71	71	70	67	279	2,666,000
Masahiro Kuramoto	66	71	73	69	279	2,666,000
Yuichi Yokoshima	68	68	71	72	279	2,666,000
Isao Aoki	71	70	70	69	280	1,725,000
Yoshinori Mizumaki	70	69	71	70	280	1,725,000
Harumitsu Hamano	70	69	70	71	280	1,725,000

	SCORES				TOTAL	MONEY
Roger Mackay	73	65	69	73	280	1,725,000
Tsukasa Watanabe	69	74	68	71	282	1,400,000
Koichi Suzuki	73	72	68	70	283	1,250,000
Yoshinori Kaneko	70	68	71	74	283	1,250,000
Hiroshi Makino	71	72	71	70	284	1,100,000
Ryoken Kawagishi	70	71	74	70	285	975,000
Atsushi Murota	73	70	70	72	285	975,000
Saburo Fujiki	67	71	74	75	287	850,000
Eiichi Itai	70	72	74	72	288	700,000
Akiyoshi Omachi	70	71	74	73	288	700,000
Tetu Nishikawa	74	74	71	71	290	590,000
Masanobu Kimura	73	71	75	73	292	540,000
Teruo Sugihara	75	74	72	72	293	490,000
Yutaka Hagawa	68	75	76	74	293	490,000
Tadami Ueno	76	70	76	72	294	460,000
Akihito Yokoyama	74	74	73	74	295	430,000
Satoshi Higashi	77	79	70	71	297	410,000
Rick Gibson	71	75	75	77	298	390,000

Daikyo Open

Daikyo Country Club, Okinawa
Par 71; 6,256 yards

December 12-15
purse, ¥120,000,000

	SCORES				TOTAL	MONEY
Yutaka Makino	69	70	67	70	276	¥21,600,000
Seiki Okuda	72	68	67	70	277	10,080,000
Brent Franklin	68	68	70	71	277	10,080,000
Koichi Suzuki	66	69	75	69	279	5,760,000
Yoshinori Kaneko	73	68	69	70	280	4,560,000
David Ishii	69	67	72	72	280	4,560,000
Tsuneyuki Nakajima	75	68	69	69	281	3,840,000
Kikuo Arai	74	65	69	74	282	3,480,000
Tetsu Nishikawa	77	70	67	69	283	3,120,000
Yutaka Hagawa	74	72	72	66	284	2,580,000
Yukihiro Yamamoto	72	67	68	77	284	2,580,000
Kiyoshi Maita	75	68	73	69	285	2,112,000
Motomasa Aoki	74	69	72	70	285	2,112,000
Futoshi Irino	72	71	73	70	286	1,800,000
Tomohiro Maruyama	74	68	70	74	286	1,800,000
Yoshinori Mizumaki	74	71	74	68	287	1,328,000
Takeru Shibata	73	74	71	69	287	1,328,000
Seiichi Kanai	73	73	68	73	287	1,328,000
Nobumitsu Yuhara	74	72	66	75	287	1,328,000
Hideki Kase	68	72	72	75	287	1,328,000
Teruo Sugihara	69	71	68	79	287	1,328,000
Toshimitsu Kai	69	72	78	69	288	1,024,000
Ryoken Kawagishi	74	71	73	70	288	1,024,000
Kiyoshi Murota	76	69	72	71	288	1,024,000
Yoshihisa Iwashita	76	70	71	71	288	1,024,000
Eiichi Itai	76	68	72	72	288	1,024,000
Kinpachi Yoshimura	76	69	71	72	288	1,024,000
Hiromichi Namiki	74	72	73	70	289	876,000
Hirofumi Miyase	76	69	74	70	289	876,000
Toshiaki Sudo	70	75	73	71	289	876,000
Noboru Sugai	75	69	73	72	289	876,000
Masanobu Kimura	74	70	71	74	289	876,000
Shigenori Mori	76	67	72	74	289	876,000

Women's Tours

Jamaica Classic

Tryall Club, Montego Bay, Jamaica
Par 34-37—71; 6,202 yards

January 18-20
purse, $500,000

	SCORES			TOTAL	MONEY
Jane Geddes	71	72	64	207	$75,000
Patty Sheehan	68	70	72	210	46,250
Ok Hee Ku	73	71	68	212	30,000
Dottie Mochrie	73	70	69	212	30,000
Shirley Furlong	72	70	72	214	17,834
Caroline Keggi	74	67	73	214	17,833
Judy Dickinson	72	68	74	214	17,833
Amy Benz	77	70	69	216	12,375
Colleen Walker	72	73	71	216	12,375
Dale Eggeling	73	72	72	217	10,000
Sarah McGuire	67	76	74	217	10,000
Tammie Green	75	73	70	218	8,250
Kathy Postlewait	70	78	70	218	8,250
Cindy Rarick	71	74	73	218	8,250
Cindy Schreyer	71	75	73	219	6,834
Michelle McGann	73	71	75	219	6,833
Cathy Johnston	72	71	76	219	6,833
Maggie Will	76	73	71	220	6,125
Hiromi Kobayashi	72	74	74	220	6,125
Joan Pitcock	78	70	73	221	5,500
Allison Finney	72	75	74	221	5,500
Penny Hammel	72	75	74	221	5,500
Tracy Kerdyk	76	75	71	222	4,554
Donna Andrews	72	78	72	222	4,554
Martha Nause	74	76	72	222	4,554
Elaine Crosby	77	72	73	222	4,554
Kim Shipman	74	75	73	222	4,553
Terry-Jo Myers	74	73	75	222	4,553
Deborah McHaffie	73	72	77	222	4,553
Jill Briles-Hinton	70	82	71	223	3,554
Lynn Connelly	78	73	72	223	3,554
Pamela Wright	73	78	72	223	3,554
Kate Rogerson	79	70	74	223	3,554
Deb Richard	73	74	76	223	3,553
Kris Tschetter	73	73	77	223	3,553
Stephanie Farwig	72	72	79	223	3,553

Oldsmobile Classic

Wycliffe Golf & Country Club, Lake Worth, Florida
Par 36-36—72; 6,324 yards

January 31-February 3
purse, $400,000

	SCORES				TOTAL	MONEY
Meg Mallon	66	70	69	71	276	$60,000
Dana Lofland	70	73	65	70	278	37,000
Tammie Green	71	68	71	70	280	21,667

	SCORES				TOTAL	MONEY
Laurel Kean	72	71	65	72	280	21,667
Dottie Mochrie	65	71	72	72	280	21,666
Pat Bradley	71	70	69	71	281	11,400
Amy Alcott	69	70	70	72	281	11,400
Kate Rogerson	68	71	69	73	281	11,400
Betsy King	71	67	69	74	281	11,400
Susan Sanders	66	74	70	72	282	8,000
Lenore Rittenhouse	72	68	69	73	282	8,000
Kristi Albers	71	71	72	69	283	6,200
Caroline Keggi	69	72	72	70	283	6,200
Ok Hee Ku	69	71	73	70	283	6,200
Hiromi Kobayashi	69	69	70	75	283	6,200
Donna Andrews	68	70	70	75	283	6,200
Jane Geddes	71	73	70	70	284	4,900
Cindy Rarick	68	71	74	71	284	4,900
Colleen Walker	68	68	77	71	284	4,900
Cathy Morse	70	71	71	72	284	4,900
Dawn Coe	72	72	73	68	285	3,984
Nancy Ramsbottom	70	73	71	71	285	3,984
Judy Dickinson	66	74	73	72	285	3,983
Bonnie Lauer	67	74	70	74	285	3,983
Jan Stephenson	69	70	72	74	285	3,983
Nancy Brown	69	71	70	75	285	3,983
Tina Barrett	73	72	73	68	286	3,340
Juli Inkster	72	74	70	70	286	3,340
Shirley Furlong	74	72	68	72	286	3,340
Cathy Marino	71	70	70	75	286	3,340

Phar-Mor at Inverrary

Inverrary Country Club & Resort, Lauderhill, Florida
Par 36-36—72; 6,286 yards

February 8-10
purse, $500,000

	SCORES			TOTAL	MONEY
Beth Daniel	67	73	69	209	$75,000
Nancy Lopez	73	69	69	211	46,250
Laura Baugh	75	68	69	212	33,750
Danielle Ammaccapane	71	72	70	213	23,750
Hiromi Kobayashi	68	73	72	213	23,750
Jane Geddes	77	72	65	214	11,310
Becky Pearson	74	73	67	214	11,310
Patty Sheehan	71	75	68	214	11,309
Lynn Connelly	73	72	69	214	11,309
Dottie Mochrie	71	74	69	214	11,309
Stephanie Lowe	69	76	69	214	11,309
Laurel Kean	71	73	70	214	11,309
Maggie Will	69	74	71	214	11,309
Colleen Walker	68	74	72	214	11,309
Cindy Rarick	71	76	68	215	6,842
Rosie Jones	73	72	70	215	6,841
Jennifer Wyatt	69	74	72	215	6,841
Diana Heinicke-Rauch	72	72	72	216	6,133
Cindy Figg-Currier	74	69	73	216	6,133
Betsy King	73	74	70	217	5,283
Dawn Coe	72	75	70	217	5,283
Donna White	72	75	70	217	5,283
Donna Andrews	73	73	71	217	5,283

	SCORES			TOTAL	MONEY
Chris Johnson	74	71	72	217	5,283
Kristi Albers	76	70	72	218	4,483
Cathy Marino	73	71	74	218	4,483
Alice Ritzman	71	73	74	218	4,483
Karen Davies	72	70	76	218	4,483
Pamela Wright	75	74	70	219	3,694
Ok Hee Ku	71	77	71	219	3,694
Judy Dickinson	73	74	72	219	3,694
Liselotte Neumann	72	75	72	219	3,694
Pat Bradley	73	73	73	219	3,694
Martha Nause	70	76	73	219	3,693
Deb Richard	72	71	76	219	3,693

Orix Hawaiian Open

Ko Olina Resort, Ewa Beach, Hawaii
Par 36-36—72; 6,241 yards

February 21-24
purse, $350,000

	SCORES			TOTAL	MONEY
Patty Sheehan	68	69	70	207	$52,500
Beth Daniel	69	70	71	210	32,375
Pat Bradley	71	71	71	213	23,625
Sherri Steinhauer	77	68	69	214	18,375
Amy Benz	73	72	70	215	11,638
Brandie Burton	73	70	72	215	11,638
Ok Hee Ku	69	73	73	215	11,637
Stephanie Maynor	72	68	75	215	11,637
Cindy Rarick	76	72	68	216	6,836
Tammie Green	72	73	71	216	6,836
Heather Drew	75	69	72	216	6,836
Dawn Coe	72	71	73	216	6,836
Val Skinner	70	72	74	216	6,835
Jane Geddes	75	73	69	217	4,848
Juli Inkster	74	73	70	217	4,848
Ayako Okamoto	73	73	71	217	4,848
Deb Richard	72	74	71	217	4,848
Sue Thomas	71	72	74	217	4,848
Amy Alcott	75	72	71	218	4,131
Chris Johnson	72	72	74	218	4,130
JoAnne Carner	73	70	76	219	3,868
Liselotte Neumann	77	73	70	220	3,431
Patti Rizzo	77	70	73	220	3,431
Kristi Albers	75	71	74	220	3,430
Dottie Mochrie	71	74	75	220	3,430
Lori Garbacz	76	68	76	220	3,430
Susan Sanders	72	78	71	221	2,888
Judy Dickinson	73	76	72	221	2,888
Cindy Scholefield	77	71	73	221	2,888
Rosie Jones	74	73	74	221	2,888
Barb Bunkowsky	72	73	76	221	2,888

Women's Kemper Open

Wailea Golf Club, Kihei, Maui, Hawaii
Par 35-36—71; 6,056 yards

February 27-March 2
purse, $500,000

	SCORES				TOTAL	MONEY
Deb Richard	68	70	67	70	275	$75,000
Cindy Rarick	66	68	69	72	275	46,250
(Richard defeated Rarick on second extra hole.)						
Dawn Coe	71	67	69	70	277	33,750
Ok Hee Ku	72	73	67	66	278	23,750
Patty Sheehan	72	71	66	69	278	23,750
Brandie Burton	67	70	73	69	279	16,125
Kris Tschetter	70	71	68	70	279	16,125
Betsy King	70	69	69	72	280	12,375
Jane Geddes	69	68	70	73	280	12,375
Pat Bradley	71	70	70	70	281	10,000
Lori Garbacz	72	66	73	70	281	10,000
Meg Mallon	72	70	70	70	282	8,250
Missie Berteotti	72	72	65	73	282	8,250
Joan Pitcock	73	68	68	73	282	8,250
Sally Little	72	69	71	71	283	6,833
Amy Alcott	72	69	71	71	283	6,833
Ayako Okamoto	73	69	69	72	283	6,833
Donna Andrews	71	73	72	68	284	6,125
Norimi Terazawa	74	70	71	69	284	6,125
Dottie Mochrie	71	74	68	72	285	5,003
Stephanie Maynor	70	72	70	73	285	5,003
Sue Ertl	70	72	70	73	285	5,003
Danielle Ammaccapane	69	70	73	73	285	5,003
Katie Peterson	70	68	74	73	285	5,003
Tammie Green	73	70	68	74	285	5,003
Cindy Figg-Currier	71	72	68	74	285	5,003
Karen Davies	67	70	73	75	285	5,003
Sherri Steinhauer	74	70	74	68	286	3,955
Donna White	71	71	75	69	286	3,955
Laura Davies	70	76	69	71	286	3,955
Chris Johnson	75	70	70	71	286	3,955
Beth Daniel	68	68	76	74	286	3,955

Inamori Classic

StoneRidge Country Club, Poway, California
Par 36-36—72; 6,197 yards

March 7-10
purse, $400,000

	SCORES				TOTAL	MONEY
Laura Davies	70	68	72	67	277	$60,000
Lynn Connelly	71	75	68	67	281	32,000
Judy Dickinson	70	74	68	69	281	32,000
Robin Walton	69	71	70	72	282	19,000
Tina Barrett	70	69	70	73	282	19,000
Patti Rizzo	75	72	70	66	283	14,000
Nicky LeRoux	72	70	72	70	284	10,533
Missie McGeorge	71	75	67	71	284	10,533
Lori Garbacz	74	70	69	71	284	10,533
Colleen Walker	73	76	68	68	285	8,000
Barb Mucha	75	72	69	69	285	8,000
Nancy Brown	75	68	75	68	286	7,000

	SCORES				TOTAL	MONEY
Lenore Rittenhouse	71	77	72	67	287	5,700
Donna Andrews	74	69	74	70	287	5,700
Betsy King	74	72	70	71	287	5,700
Jane Geddes	76	69	70	72	287	5,700
Dawn Coe	73	69	72	73	287	5,700
Missie Berteotti	73	72	67	75	287	5,700
Cindy Mackey	74	74	72	68	288	4,316
Cindy Figg-Currier	75	73	71	69	288	4,316
Caroline Pierce	76	71	71	70	288	4,316
Danielle Ammaccapane	71	72	75	70	288	4,316
Caroline Keggi	69	75	70	74	288	4,316
Martha Foyer	69	75	69	75	288	4,316
Ayako Okamoto	71	72	76	70	289	3,520
Penny Hammel	71	75	72	71	289	3,520
Martha Nause	75	71	71	72	289	3,520
Cindy Rarick	74	71	70	74	289	3,520
Penny Pulz	71	73	70	75	289	3,520
Liselotte Neumann	75	73	72	70	290	2,842
Michelle Mackall	79	70	70	71	290	2,842
Alison Munt	73	76	70	71	290	2,842
Ok Hee Ku	72	75	71	72	290	2,842
Terry-Jo Myers	71	71	75	73	290	2,842
Marta Figueras-Dotti	72	71	73	74	290	2,842
Kris Monaghan	76	69	70	75	290	2,842

Desert Inn International

Desert Inn Country Club, Las Vegas, Nevada
Par 36-36—72; 6,285 yards

March 15-17
purse, $400,000

	SCORES			TOTAL	MONEY
Penny Hammel	71	74	66	211	$60,000
Beth Daniel	72	71	69	212	37,000
Rosie Jones	75	73	66	214	27,000
Missie McGeorge	72	77	68	217	19,000
Patty Sheehan	72	72	73	217	19,000
Lori Garbacz	75	78	65	218	14,000
Cathy Gerring	76	75	68	219	10,000
Amy Benz	72	76	71	219	10,000
Michelle McGann	75	72	72	219	10,000
Kristi Albers	74	71	74	219	10,000
Laura Baugh	74	75	71	220	6,661
Dottie Mochrie	76	71	73	220	6,661
Jane Geddes	75	72	73	220	6,661
Danielle Ammaccapane	74	73	73	220	6,661
Cathy Johnston	76	70	74	220	6,661
Deborah McHaffie	75	77	69	221	4,547
Judy Dickinson	77	74	70	221	4,547
Nancy Lopez	75	76	70	221	4,547
Lynn Adams	79	71	71	221	4,547
Pamela Wright	77	73	71	221	4,547
Laura Davies	74	75	72	221	4,547
Nancy White	73	76	72	221	4,547
Deb Richard	76	72	73	221	4,547
Barb Thomas	75	73	73	221	4,547
Sally Little	74	72	75	221	4,547
Shelley Hamlin	74	77	71	222	3,421

	SCORES			TOTAL	MONEY
Cathy Reynolds	76	73	73	222	3,421
Jennifer Wyatt	73	76	73	222	3,421
Vicki Fergon	72	77	73	222	3,421
Nancy Brown	76	72	74	222	3,421

Standard Register Ping

Moon Valley Golf Club, Phoenix, Arizona   March 21-24
Par 36-37—73; 6,514 yards   purse, $550,000

	SCORES				TOTAL	MONEY
Danielle Ammaccapane	74	70	70	69	283	$82,500
Meg Mallon	73	75	70	67	285	44,000
Barb Bunkowsky	74	68	73	70	285	44,000
Colleen Walker	74	71	70	73	288	28,875
Alice Ritzman	75	74	70	70	289	17,215
Tina Barrett	75	73	70	71	289	17,215
Cathy Morse	75	70	73	71	289	17,215
Betsy King	72	72	72	73	289	17,215
Michelle McGann	77	70	68	74	289	17,215
Rosie Jones	78	72	73	67	290	11,550
Vicki Fergon	77	75	70	69	291	9,755
Cathy Gerring	70	74	76	71	291	9,755
Penny Hammel	76	71	72	72	291	9,755
Stephanie Maynor	76	71	73	72	292	7,807
Nina Foust	74	72	74	72	292	7,807
Chris Johnson	78	70	71	73	292	7,807
Karen Davies	74	71	72	75	292	7,807
Tracy Kerdyk	75	77	74	67	293	6,501
Missie McGeorge	76	75	73	69	293	6,501
Laura Davies	74	75	71	73	293	6,501
Kathy Guadagnino	76	71	72	74	293	6,501
Amy Alcott	74	75	74	71	294	5,401
Cindy Figg-Currier	73	76	73	72	294	5,401
Penny Pulz	75	75	70	74	294	5,401
Maggie Will	76	73	71	74	294	5,401
Jane Geddes	76	74	69	75	294	5,401
Beth Daniel	76	75	71	73	295	4,471
Gail Graham	76	75	71	73	295	4,471
Jenny Lidback	75	73	73	74	295	4,471
Laurel Kean	74	73	74	74	295	4,471
Elaine Crosby	75	70	76	74	295	4,471
Ok Hee Ku	73	74	72	76	295	4,471

Nabisco Dinah Shore

Mission Hills Country Club, Rancho Mirage, California   March 28-31
Par 36-36—72; 6,437 yards   purse, $600,000

	SCORES				TOTAL	MONEY
Amy Alcott	67	70	68	68	273	$90,000
Dottie Mochrie	70	71	71	69	281	55,500
Pat Bradley	70	72	73	67	282	36,000
Patty Sheehan	71	71	70	70	282	36,000
Lori Garbacz	73	71	70	70	284	25,500

	SCORES				TOTAL	MONEY
Caroline Keggi	72	70	73	70	285	17,100
Ayako Okamoto	72	68	74	71	285	17,100
Nancy Brown	74	69	70	72	285	17,100
Martha Nause	71	72	69	73	285	17,100
Ok Hee Ku	69	72	73	72	286	12,600
Betsy King	72	75	71	69	287	9,704
Danielle Ammaccapane	75	70	71	71	287	9,704
Amy Benz	73	70	73	71	287	9,704
Vicki Fergon	70	76	69	72	287	9,704
Judy Dickinson	71	75	67	74	287	9,704
Tammie Green	73	71	68	75	287	9,704
Tina Barrett	70	73	74	71	288	7,254
*Vicki Goetze	71	75	70	72	288	
Sherri Steinhauer	72	71	72	73	288	7,254
Jane Geddes	71	71	72	74	288	7,254
Laura Baugh	70	72	72	74	288	7,254
Elaine Crosby	72	70	71	75	288	7,254
Rosie Jones	73	75	70	71	289	5,715
Laura Davies	72	73	73	71	289	5,715
Laurel Kean	75	71	71	72	289	5,715
Chris Johnson	74	71	72	72	289	5,715
Dale Eggeling	71	74	72	72	289	5,715
Lynn Connelly	73	72	71	73	289	5,715
Alice Ritzman	72	71	70	76	289	5,715
Beth Daniel	74	70	76	70	290	4,172
Cathy Gerring	73	74	71	72	290	4,172
Jan Stephenson	74	70	74	72	290	4,172
Juli Inkster	72	69	77	72	290	4,172
Donna White	72	74	71	73	290	4,172
Liselotte Neumann	71	73	73	73	290	4,172
Nancy Lopez	75	72	69	74	290	4,172
Martha Foyer	73	71	72	74	290	4,172
Meg Mallon	70	70	76	74	290	4,172
Deb Richard	74	71	70	75	290	4,172
Shirley Furlong	71	68	74	77	290	4,172

Ping/Welch's Championship

Randolph Park North Golf Course, Tucson, Arizona
Par 35-37—72; 6,243 yards

April 4-7
purse, $350,000

	SCORES				TOTAL	MONEY
Chris Johnson	67	69	65	72	273	$52,500
Kris Tschetter	70	72	69	66	277	32,375
Kristi Albers	69	73	69	67	278	18,958
Betsy King	67	74	70	67	278	18,958
Jan Stephenson	69	70	65	74	278	18,958
Michelle McGann	69	68	72	70	279	11,287
Meg Mallon	72	67	69	71	279	11,287
Stephanie Maynor	72	71	68	70	281	8,662
Donna Andrews	70	71	67	73	281	8,662
Dale Eggeling	71	73	71	67	282	6,484
Colleen Walker	71	72	70	69	282	6,484
Patty Sheehan	68	73	70	71	282	6,484
Tracy Kerdyk	70	66	74	72	282	6,484
Karen Davies	68	74	71	70	283	5,262
Juli Inkster	72	71	67	73	283	5,262

	SCORES				TOTAL	MONEY
Pamela Wright	71	73	73	67	284	4,562
Kris Monaghan	71	73	70	70	284	4,562
Pat Bradley	71	74	68	71	284	4,562
Tammie Green	70	75	74	66	285	3,654
Becky Pearson	74	70	70	71	285	3,654
Elaine Crosby	70	74	69	72	285	3,654
Kathy Postlewait	70	73	70	72	285	3,654
Mitzi Edge	71	69	73	72	285	3,654
Cindy Rarick	70	74	68	73	285	3,654
Dottie Mochrie	70	70	70	75	285	3,654
Joan Pitcock	69	68	73	75	285	3,654
Brandie Burton	70	74	72	70	286	2,987
Sherri Steinhauer	74	72	66	74	286	2,987
Nancy Scranton Brown	68	72	72	74	286	2,987
Shelley Hamlin	73	72	73	69	287	2,543
Lynn Connelly	71	73	71	72	287	2,543
Janet Anderson	74	70	70	73	287	2,543
Allison Finney	68	73	73	73	287	2,543
Amy Alcott	72	73	68	74	287	2,543
Janice Gibson	72	71	69	75	287	2,543

Sara Lee Classic

Hermitage Golf Course, Old Hickory, Tennessee
Par 36-36—72; 6,242 yards

May 3-5
purse, $425,000

	SCORES			TOTAL	MONEY
Nancy Lopez	65	70	71	206	$63,750
Kris Monaghan	67	71	70	208	39,312
Sherri Steinhauer	68	68	73	209	28,687
Cindy Rarick	68	71	71	210	20,187
Marta Figueras-Dotti	69	69	72	210	20,187
Deb Richard	71	71	69	211	12,820
Cathy Marino	68	72	71	211	12,820
Missie McGeorge	70	68	73	211	12,820
Missie Berteotti	70	74	68	212	8,013
Ayako Okamoto	70	72	70	212	8,013
Colleen Walker	71	69	72	212	8,013
Pat Bradley	70	69	73	212	8,013
Cathy Morse	69	69	74	212	8,013
JoAnne Carner	69	68	75	212	8,013
Amy Benz	70	72	71	213	5,964
Tina Barrett	68	71	74	213	5,964
Tracy Kerdyk	72	73	69	214	4,720
Betsy King	71	74	69	214	4,720
Rosie Jones	72	71	71	214	4,720
Tammie Green	72	71	71	214	4,720
Heather Drew	70	73	71	214	4,720
Laura Baugh	74	68	72	214	4,720
Patty Sheehan	72	70	72	214	4,720
Dawn Coe	74	67	73	214	4,720
Kathy Postlewait	72	68	74	214	4,720
Patti Rizzo	70	75	70	215	3,443
Brandie Burton	73	71	71	215	3,443
Dottie Mochrie	71	73	71	215	3,443
Lauri Merten	73	70	72	215	3,443
Jerilyn Britz	70	73	72	215	3,443

	SCORES			TOTAL	MONEY
Kay Cockerill	70	72	73	215	3,443
Dale Eggeling	68	74	73	215	3,443
Meg Mallon	72	69	74	215	3,443

Crestar Farm-Fresh Classic

Greenbrier Country Club, Chesapeake, Virginia
Par 36-36—72; 6,412 yards

May 9-12
purse, $400,000

	SCORES				TOTAL	MONEY
Hollis Stacy	70	71	72	69	282	$60,000
Patty Sheehan	74	71	69	69	283	28,333
Tammie Green	71	66	73	73	283	28,333
Elaine Crosby	69	69	71	74	283	28,333
Tracy Kerdyk	73	72	70	69	284	17,000
Michelle McGann	70	72	75	68	285	12,900
Hiromi Kobayashi	71	71	71	72	285	12,900
Judy Dickinson	69	72	72	73	286	10,400
Cathy Morse	72	72	72	71	287	8,100
Val Skinner	72	72	70	74	287	8,100
Nina Foust	68	71	74	74	287	8,100
Rosie Jones	72	70	70	75	287	8,100
Donna Andrews	74	72	72	70	288	5,700
Susan Sanders	75	69	73	71	288	5,700
Shirley Furlong	77	70	69	72	288	5,700
Marta Figueras-Dotti	72	71	73	72	288	5,700
Cathy Marino	72	70	74	72	288	5,700
Sherri Steinhauer	70	71	74	73	288	5,700
Martha Foyer	72	71	76	70	289	4,500
Jane Crafter	73	72	73	71	289	4,500
Sally Little	70	70	76	73	289	4,500
Joan Pitcock	71	71	73	74	289	4,500
Lenore Rittenhouse	71	75	74	70	290	3,764
Amy Alcott	70	75	75	70	290	3,764
Jody Anschutz	70	76	73	71	290	3,764
Lisa Walters	77	68	73	72	290	3,764
Jan Stephenson	73	74	70	73	290	3,764
Penny Pulz	77	69	76	69	291	2,953
Muffin Spencer-Devlin	75	71	75	70	291	2,953
Joan Delk	74	74	72	71	291	2,953
Allison Finney	73	74	73	71	291	2,953
Heather Drew	70	77	73	71	291	2,953
Donna White	72	74	73	72	291	2,953
Vicki Fergon	70	71	77	73	291	2,953
Nancy Scranton	72	74	71	74	291	2,953
Kathy Guadagnino	72	74	71	74	291	2,953

Centel Classic

Killearn Country Club, Tallahassee, Florida
Par 36-36—72; 6,382 yards

May 16-19
purse, $1,100,000

	SCORES				TOTAL	MONEY
Pat Bradley	70	68	69	71	278	$165,000
Ayako Okamoto	69	68	72	70	279	101,750

		SCORES			TOTAL	MONEY
Dottie Mochrie	73	72	67	68	280	66,000
Judy Dickinson	69	69	70	72	280	66,000
Colleen Walker	70	72	70	69	281	46,750
Beth Daniel	69	73	71	69	282	35,475
Jody Anschutz	71	71	70	70	282	35,475
Hollis Stacy	70	74	69	70	283	25,850
Patty Sheehan	73	68	69	73	283	25,850
Laura Davies	69	70	71	73	283	25,850
Amy Alcott	72	71	75	67	285	15,407
Tina Barrett	71	70	74	70	285	15,407
Alice Ritzman	73	70	71	71	285	15,407
Trish Johnson	71	71	72	71	285	15,407
Lynn Connelly	73	70	70	72	285	15,407
Betsy King	70	70	73	72	285	15,407
Tammie Green	70	69	74	72	285	15,407
JoAnne Carner	68	71	74	72	285	15,407
Kristi Albers	68	71	74	72	285	15,407
Martha Nause	72	70	70	73	285	15,407
Danielle Ammaccapane	69	71	72	73	285	15,407
Juli Inkster	75	69	67	74	285	15,407
Laurel Kean	69	75	71	71	286	10,787
Jane Geddes	72	72	69	73	286	10,787
Allison Finney	71	71	71	73	286	10,787
Susan Sanders	74	69	73	71	287	9,449
Jenny Lidback	70	73	72	72	287	9,449
Dale Eggeling	70	73	72	72	287	9,449
Sally Little	74	68	73	72	287	9,449
Nina Foust	73	71	70	73	287	9,449

Corning Classic

Corning Country Club, Corning, New York
Par 36-36—72; 6,070 yards

May 23-26
purse, $400,000

		SCORES			TOTAL	MONEY
Betsy King	69	73	65	66	273	$60,000
Deb Richard	68	67	69	75	279	37,000
Val Skinner	72	69	74	65	280	21,666
Lynn Adams	70	70	73	67	280	21,666
Colleen Walker	69	71	69	71	280	21,666
Tammie Green	68	72	73	69	282	12,900
Ayako Okamoto	69	69	71	73	282	12,900
Kay Cockerill	70	73	74	66	283	8,560
Pat Bradley	72	70	71	70	283	8,560
Sherri Turner	72	68	73	70	283	8,560
Pearl Sinn	70	72	70	71	283	8,560
Danielle Ammaccapane	70	69	71	73	283	8,560
JoAnne Carner	72	73	71	68	284	5,840
Caroline Keggi	70	71	72	71	284	5,840
Vicki Fergon	70	71	71	72	284	5,840
Kris Tschetter	71	71	68	74	284	5,840
Cathy Morse	71	69	70	74	284	5,840
Cindy Figg-Currier	71	74	71	69	285	4,600
Donna White	73	71	72	69	285	4,600
Katie Peterson	72	70	72	71	285	4,600
Lauri Merten	70	70	70	75	285	4,600
Martha Foyer	66	72	72	75	285	4,600

	SCORES				TOTAL	MONEY
Anne-Marie Palli	76	69	73	68	286	3,764
Dana Lofland	72	73	71	70	286	3,764
Gina Hull	70	76	69	71	286	3,764
Lisa Walters	73	71	70	72	286	3,764
Carolyn Hill	73	71	69	73	286	3,764
Janet Anderson	72	72	74	69	287	3,110
Mary Beth Zimmerman	71	72	75	69	287	3,110
Amy Read	68	75	74	70	287	3,110
Dawn Coe	70	71	76	70	287	3,110
Lenore Rittenhouse	75	69	71	72	287	3,110
Donna Andrews	70	73	72	72	287	3,110

Rochester International

Locust Hill Country Club, Pittsford, New York
Par 35-37—72; 6,162 yards

May 30-June 2
purse, $400,000

	SCORES				TOTAL	MONEY
Rosie Jones	69	69	72	66	276	$60,000
Danielle Ammaccapane	68	73	71	66	278	32,000
Brandie Burton	73	68	69	68	278	32,000
Pat Bradley	69	71	69	70	279	21,000
Beth Daniel	68	69	71	72	280	15,500
Colleen Walker	68	69	69	74	280	15,500
Nancy Lopez	72	73	70	67	282	10,000
Donna White	72	72	71	67	282	10,000
Patty Sheehan	72	72	68	70	282	10,000
Dottie Mochrie	71	70	70	71	282	10,000
Cindy Rarick	68	70	75	70	283	7,300
Trish Johnson	68	70	71	74	283	7,300
Betsy King	73	73	68	70	284	6,200
JoAnne Carner	72	72	70	70	284	6,200
Sherri Steinhauer	72	73	67	72	284	6,200
Lynn Adams	70	74	73	68	285	5,100
Susie Redman	73	68	75	69	285	5,100
Lynn Connelly	73	70	71	71	285	5,100
Deb Richard	68	75	69	73	285	5,100
Sherri Turner	69	77	70	70	286	4,305
Vicki Fergon	74	71	67	74	286	4,305
Cathy Morse	69	71	72	74	286	4,305
Chris Johnson	67	70	75	74	286	4,305
Kris Monaghan	72	72	74	69	287	3,580
Laurie Rinker	72	72	73	70	287	3,580
Alice Miller	71	73	73	70	287	3,580
Janet Anderson	72	72	72	71	287	3,580
Ok Hee Ku	72	72	71	72	287	3,580
Barb Bunkowsky	72	72	70	73	287	3,580
Alice Ritzman	72	73	74	69	288	2,893
Kay Cockerill	70	74	75	69	288	2,893
Stephanie Maynor	71	73	72	72	288	2,893
Tracy Kerdyk	71	72	71	74	288	2,893
Patti Rizzo	71	70	73	74	288	2,893
Barb Mucha	72	71	70	75	288	2,893

Atlantic City Classic

Greate Bay Country Club, Somers Point, New Jersey
Par 36-35—71; 6,270 yards,

June 7-9
purse, $300,000

	SCORES			TOTAL	MONEY
Jane Geddes	71	68	69	208	$45,000
Cindy Schreyer	70	70	69	209	24,000
Amy Alcott	69	68	72	209	24,000
Robin Walton	75	66	69	210	15,750
Judy Dickinson	69	70	72	211	11,625
Jenny Lidback	68	70	73	211	11,625
Kate Hughes	73	69	71	213	8,325
Juli Inkster	71	71	71	213	8,325
Laurel Kean	75	69	70	214	6,350
Caroline Pierce	69	73	72	214	6,350
Joan Pitcock	72	68	74	214	6,350
Nancy White	76	73	66	215	4,312
Jayne Thobois	75	72	68	215	4,312
Pamela Wright	72	74	69	215	4,312
Susie Redman	73	70	72	215	4,312
Nancy Scranton	72	71	72	215	4,312
Patty Jordan	72	70	73	215	4,312
Janice Gibson	71	70	74	215	4,312
Melissa McNamara	75	65	75	215	4,312
Cindy Rarick	72	75	69	216	3,228
Barb Thomas	73	73	70	216	3,228
Ok Hee Ku	75	69	72	216	3,228
Laura Baugh	70	71	75	216	3,228
Tani Tatum	73	74	70	217	2,775
Martha Nause	73	71	73	217	2,775
Sandra Palmer	71	73	73	217	2,775
Caroline Keggi	71	71	75	217	2,775
Mitzi Edge	77	71	70	218	2,138
Dale Eggeling	75	73	70	218	2,138
Nancy Lopez	76	70	72	218	2,138
Terri Luckhurst	74	72	72	218	2,138
Anne Kelly	73	73	72	218	2,138
Kathy Whitworth	71	75	72	218	2,138
Gail Graham	74	71	73	218	2,138
Sherri Steinhauer	74	71	73	218	2,138
Nanci Bowen	72	73	73	218	2,138
Susie Berning	71	74	73	218	2,138
Caroline Gowan	72	70	76	218	2,138

Lady Keystone Open

Hershey Country Club, Hershey, Pennsylvania
Par 36-36—72; 6,348 yards

June 14-16
purse, $400,000

	SCORES			TOTAL	MONEY
Colleen Walker	70	70	67	207	$60,000
Kris Tschetter	71	70	68	209	32,000
Beth Daniel	68	71	70	209	32,000
Barb Bunkowsky	69	70	71	210	19,000
Barb Mucha	68	69	73	210	19,000
Nancy Lopez	75	68	68	211	11,400
Meg Mallon	72	68	71	211	11,400

	SCORES			TOTAL	MONEY
Michelle Estill	68	71	72	211	11,400
Jody Anschutz	68	69	74	211	11,400
Pat Bradley	70	72	71	213	8,007
Betsy King	75	66	72	213	8,007
Cathy Gerring	71	71	72	214	6,414
Sherri Steinhauer	70	70	74	214	6,414
Janet Anderson	67	73	74	214	6,414
Sandra Palmer	67	72	75	214	6,414
Brandie Burton	70	75	70	215	5,214
Nancy Scranton	72	72	71	215	5,214
Mitzi Edge	73	65	77	215	5,214
Rosie Jones	75	72	69	216	4,330
Shirley Furlong	74	71	71	216	4,330
Ann Walsh	73	71	72	216	4,330
Dawn Coe	72	70	74	216	4,330
Amy Benz	72	68	76	216	4,330
Juli Inkster	70	68	78	216	4,330
Peggy Kirsch	75	72	70	217	3,299
Jenny Lidback	73	73	71	217	3,299
Laurel Kean	73	73	71	217	3,299
Caroline Gowan	71	75	71	217	3,299
Nancy Ramsbottom	72	73	72	217	3,299
Lynn Adams	70	75	72	217	3,299
Kate Rogerson	72	72	73	217	3,299
Missie McGeorge	72	71	74	217	3,299
Jerilyn Britz	74	68	75	217	3,299

McDonald's Championship

Du Pont Country Club, Wilmington, Delaware
Par 35-36—71; 6,398 yards

June 20-23
purse, $750,000

	SCORES				TOTAL	MONEY
Beth Daniel	67	71	67	68	273	$112,500
Pat Bradley	69	67	70	71	277	60,000
Sally Little	67	69	67	74	277	60,000
Michelle McGann	70	66	72	70	278	35,625
Ayako Okamoto	70	65	73	70	278	35,625
Kristi Albers	68	70	72	69	279	24,187
Tammie Green	64	71	72	72	279	24,187
Dottie Mochrie	70	68	70	72	280	19,500
Dawn Coe	72	71	68	70	281	14,133
Trish Johnson	72	69	70	70	281	14,133
Vicki Fergon	70	70	71	70	281	14,133
Jane Geddes	71	69	70	71	281	14,133
Missie McGeorge	70	68	70	73	281	14,133
Sherri Steinhauer	70	68	69	74	281	14,133
Stephanie Maynor	70	69	70	73	282	10,888
Ok Hee Ku	73	68	71	71	283	9,763
Carolyn Hill	69	68	74	72	283	9,763
Betsy King	69	71	68	75	283	9,763
Caroline Keggi	68	74	69	73	284	8,825
Nancy Lopez	71	71	68	74	284	8,825
Laura Davies	68	69	75	73	285	7,899
Missie Berteotti	70	68	73	74	285	7,899
Cathy Gerring	69	68	73	75	285	7,899
Lisa Walters	73	71	74	68	286	6,949

	SCORES				TOTAL	MONEY
Nancy Harvey	72	71	72	71	286	6,949
Terry-Jo Myers	69	74	71	72	286	6,949
Deb Richard	67	72	74	73	286	6,949
Patty Sheehan	72	72	73	70	287	6,274
Cindy Figg-Currier	69	72	71	75	287	6,274
Meg Mallon	71	71	74	72	288	5,724
Barb Bunkowsky	71	70	73	74	288	5,724
Joan Pitcock	70	69	74	75	288	5,724

Mazda LPGA Championship

Bethesda Country Club, Bethesda, Maryland
Par 35-36—71; 6,246 yards

June 27-30
purse, $1,000,000

	SCORES				TOTAL	MONEY
Meg Mallon	68	68	71	67	274	$150,000
Pat Bradley	68	68	71	68	275	80,000
Ayako Okamoto	70	64	73	68	275	80,000
Beth Daniel	71	70	68	69	278	52,500
Deb Richard	67	70	72	70	279	38,750
Barb Bunkowsky	70	68	70	71	279	38,750
Betsy King	69	75	67	70	281	29,500
JoAnne Carner	71	70	70	71	282	26,000
Juli Inkster	72	70	71	70	283	23,500
Amy Alcott	69	70	71	74	284	21,000
Liselotte Neumann	72	73	71	69	285	17,158
Rosie Jones	69	69	75	72	285	17,158
Michelle Estill	69	75	67	74	285	17,158
Sherri Steinhauer	71	71	69	74	285	17,158
Nancy White	75	70	72	69	286	12,604
Lynn Adams	71	71	73	71	286	12,604
Pamela Wright	73	70	71	72	286	12,604
Jane Geddes	69	74	71	72	286	12,604
Colleen Walker	67	74	73	72	286	12,604
Judy Dickinson	69	73	71	73	286	12,604
Shirley Furlong	69	70	73	74	286	12,604
Danielle Ammaccapane	73	72	71	71	287	9,945
Dottie Mochrie	72	73	71	71	287	9,945
Val Skinner	74	70	70	73	287	9,945
Dawn Coe	70	73	71	73	287	9,945
Susie Redman	73	74	73	68	288	8,533
Cindy Figg-Currier	75	71	71	71	288	8,533
Nanci Bowen	74	71	72	71	288	8,533
Hollis Stacy	69	75	73	71	288	8,533
Nina Foust	68	75	72	73	288	8,533
Dana Lofland	72	74	71	72	289	7,008
Caroline Keggi	70	75	72	72	289	7,008
Laurie Rinker	70	73	74	72	289	7,008
Janet Anderson	74	70	72	73	289	7,008
Laurel Kean	71	73	72	73	289	7,008
Becky Pearson	76	70	68	75	289	7,008
Terry-Jo Myers	73	74	73	70	290	5,404
Kris Tschetter	76	69	73	72	290	5,404
Peggy Kirsch	71	74	72	73	290	5,404
Marta Figueras-Dotti	69	74	74	73	290	5,404
Martha Nause	73	72	71	74	290	5,404
Debbie Massey	70	71	75	74	290	5,404

	SCORES				TOTAL	MONEY
Katie Peterson	73	72	69	76	290	5,404
Mitzi Edge	71	73	74	73	291	4,333
Tina Barrett	70	74	73	74	291	4,333
Vicki Fergon	69	72	76	74	291	4,333
Hiromi Kobayashi	69	75	75	73	292	3,633
Trish Johnson	71	74	73	74	292	3,633
Kate Hughes	72	71	73	76	292	3,633
Chris Johnson	71	71	73	77	292	3,633

Jamie Farr Toledo Classic

Highland Meadows Golf Club, Sylvania, Ohio
Par 34-37—71; 6,270 yards

July 5-7
purse, $350,000

	SCORES			TOTAL	MONEY
Alice Miller	69	66	70	205	$52,500
Deb Richard	67	70	68	205	32,375
(Miller defeated Richard on third extra hole.)					
Lynn Connelly	71	66	71	208	23,625
Laurie Rinker	71	71	67	209	18,375
Chris Johnson	74	70	66	210	12,483
Kay Cockerill	71	68	71	210	12,483
*Vicki Goetze	68	71	71	210	
Dale Eggeling	70	68	72	210	12,483
Katie Peterson	72	72	67	211	7,502
Lynn Adams	72	70	69	211	7,502
Judy Dickinson	72	68	71	211	7,502
Nancy Rubin	68	72	71	211	7,502
Carolyn Hill	69	70	72	211	7,502
Donna Wilkins	73	71	68	212	4,907
Barb Bunkowsky	73	69	70	212	4,907
Dana Lofland	73	69	70	212	4,907
Diana Heinicke-Rauch	69	72	71	212	4,907
Sandra Palmer	70	70	72	212	4,907
Laurel Kean	71	68	73	212	4,907
Janice Gibson	70	69	73	212	4,907
Nancy White	74	69	70	213	3,969
Linda Hunt	71	70	72	213	3,969
Missie McGeorge	76	69	69	214	3,280
Martha Nause	72	73	69	214	3,280
Barb Thomas	72	72	70	214	3,280
Sandra Spuzich	70	74	70	214	3,280
Caroline Pierce	71	72	71	214	3,280
Cindy Schreyer	70	72	72	214	3,280
Brandie Burton	68	73	73	214	3,280
Elaine Crosby	68	72	74	214	3,280

U.S. Women's Open Championship

Colonial Country Club, Fort Worth, Texas
Par 36-35—71; 6,340 yards

July 11-14
purse, $600,000

	SCORES				TOTAL	MONEY
Meg Mallon	70	75	71	67	283	$110,000
Pat Bradley	69	73	72	71	285	55,000

	SCORES				TOTAL	MONEY
Amy Alcott	75	68	72	71	286	32,882
Laurel Kean	70	76	71	70	287	23,996
Dottie Mochrie	73	76	68	71	288	17,642
Chris Johnson	76	72	68	72	288	17,642
Joan Pitcock	70	72	72	75	289	14,623
Kristi Albers	76	70	71	73	290	12,252
Jody Anschutz	73	72	72	73	290	12,252
Brandie Burton	75	71	69	75	290	12,252
Beth Daniel	74	76	75	66	291	9,738
Tina Barrett	74	74	72	71	291	9,738
Debbie Massey	72	72	75	72	291	9,738
JoAnne Carner	73	72	73	73	291	9,738
Adele Lukken	75	76	70	71	292	7,665
Patty Sheehan	74	75	72	71	292	7,665
Liselotte Neumann	74	72	74	72	292	7,665
Alice Ritzman	72	71	77	72	292	7,665
Ayako Okamoto	76	72	71	73	292	7,665
Kris Tschetter	77	72	67	76	292	7,665
Colleen Walker	72	77	74	70	293	6,121
Mitzi Edge	75	76	71	71	293	6,121
*Tracy Hanson	75	76	71	71	293	
Cathy Gerring	76	70	76	71	293	6,121
Nancy Scranton	72	75	73	73	293	6,121
Judy Dickinson	72	74	74	73	293	6,121
Caroline Keggi	74	72	73	74	293	6,121
Betsy King	74	78	74	68	294	5,323
*Vicki Goetze	76	75	71	72	294	
Jane Geddes	71	74	76	73	294	5,323
Alison Nicholas	77	72	71	74	294	5,323
Dale Eggeling	77	72	75	71	295	4,882
Amy Benz	73	74	75	73	295	4,882
Gail Graham	77	72	69	77	295	4,882
Sandra Palmer	77	75	73	71	296	4,660
Vicki Fergon	77	75	73	72	297	4,330
Dana Lofland	72	77	75	73	297	4,330
Alice Miller	73	73	77	74	297	4,330
Barb Bunkowsky	81	68	73	75	297	4,330
Patti Rizzo	74	74	72	77	297	4,330
Hollis Stacy	73	76	78	71	298	3,946
*Sarah Lebrun Ingram	71	77	76	74	298	
Missie Berteotti	75	73	75	75	298	3,946
Kay Kennedy	77	75	73	74	299	3,563
Jan Stephenson	76	73	76	74	299	3,563
Alison Munt	78	72	74	75	299	3,563
Sally Little	72	74	76	77	299	3,563
Laura Davies	77	72	71	79	299	3,563
Caroline Pierce	79	72	75	74	300	3,125
Amy Read	82	70	72	76	300	3,125
Tammie Green	75	77	71	77	300	3,125

JAL Big Apple Classic

Wykagyl Country Club, New Rochelle, New York   July 18-21
Par 35-36—71; 6,109 yards   purse, $500,000

	SCORES				TOTAL	MONEY
Betsy King	73	66	67	73	279	$75,000
Ayako Okamoto	73	70	70	67	280	46,250
Caroline Keggi	75	70	70	68	283	27,083
Elaine Crosby	72	70	69	72	283	27,083
Cindy Figg-Currier	70	70	69	74	283	27,083
Vicki Fergon	75	72	69	68	284	16,125
Debbie Massey	70	71	73	70	284	16,125
Amy Alcott	71	71	75	68	285	13,000
Danielle Ammaccapane	76	68	72	72	286	11,125
Heather Drew	69	71	72	74	286	11,125
Sally Little	71	76	70	70	287	9,125
Rosie Jones	72	74	71	70	287	9,125
Lynn Connelly	76	73	71	68	288	7,300
Tammie Green	75	73	70	70	288	7,300
Martha Foyer	74	72	70	72	288	7,300
Beth Daniel	72	73	70	73	288	7,300
Gail Graham	73	72	69	74	288	7,300
Hiromi Kobayashi	72	75	73	69	289	5,875
Mitzi Edge	76	71	72	70	289	5,875
Amy Benz	74	72	71	72	289	5,875
Colleen Walker	67	77	73	72	289	5,875
Maggie Will	74	73	72	71	290	5,041
Missie Berteotti	78	69	71	72	290	5,041
Pamela Wright	74	74	69	73	290	5,041
Michelle Estill	75	72	74	70	291	4,250
Judy Dickinson	71	75	74	71	291	4,250
Nancy Scranton	75	74	69	73	291	4,250
Kay Cockerill	74	73	71	73	291	4,250
Jenny Lidback	72	72	74	73	291	4,250
Ok Hee Ku	73	72	72	74	291	4,250
Hollis Stacy	70	74	71	76	291	4,250

Bay State Classic

Blue Hill Country Club, Canton, Massachusetts   July 25-28
Par 36-36—72; 6,137 yards   purse, $400,000

	SCORES				TOTAL	MONEY
Juli Inkster	70	72	66	67	275	$60,000
Caroline Keggi	70	68	69	69	276	37,000
Meg Mallon	71	69	69	69	278	24,000
Kay Cockerill	70	68	69	71	278	24,000
Brandie Burton	71	68	69	71	279	17,000
Deb Richard	67	70	74	70	281	12,066
Pat Bradley	68	70	71	72	281	12,066
Nancy Scranton	69	68	72	72	281	12,066
Cindy Scholefield	70	73	66	73	282	8,900
Mitzi Edge	69	67	73	73	282	8,900
Jenny Lidback	74	65	74	71	284	7,636
Dana Lofland	71	73	72	69	285	6,069
Anne-Marie Palli	73	72	70	70	285	6,069
Nina Foust	72	72	71	70	285	6,069

	SCORES				TOTAL	MONEY
Betsy King	70	72	72	71	285	6,069
Laurie Rinker	72	70	70	73	285	6,069
Dawn Coe	76	68	67	74	285	6,069
Deborah McHaffie	72	74	71	69	286	4,636
Maggie Will	73	71	71	71	286	4,636
Michelle McGann	71	72	72	71	286	4,636
Laurel Kean	72	70	72	72	286	4,636
Deedee Lasker	74	68	71	73	286	4,636
Vicki Fergon	74	72	72	69	287	3,861
Colleen Walker	74	69	74	70	287	3,861
Tammie Green	73	68	76	70	287	3,861
Marta Figueras-Dotti	71	71	70	75	287	3,861
Melissa McNamara	74	71	73	70	288	3,204
Susie Redman	74	71	71	72	288	3,204
Nancy Ramsbottom	70	72	74	72	288	3,204
Caroline Pierce	74	69	72	73	288	3,204
Hiromi Kobayashi	73	71	70	74	288	3,204
Susie Berning	70	74	70	74	288	3,204
Terry-Jo Myers	70	70	70	78	288	3,204

Phar-Mor in Youngstown

Squaw Creek Country Club, Vienna, Ohio
Par 36-37—72; 6,297 yards

August 2-4
purse, $500,000

	SCORES			TOTAL	MONEY
Deb Richard	70	69	68	207	$75,000
Jane Geddes	69	70	68	207	46,250
(Richard defeated Geddes on first extra hole.)					
Tammie Green	71	68	69	208	33,750
Dottie Mochrie	69	70	70	209	23,750
Danielle Ammaccapane	66	72	71	209	23,750
Juli Inkster	70	65	75	210	17,500
Vicki Fergon	69	74	68	211	13,166
Shirley Furlong	68	75	68	211	13,166
Cindy Figg-Currier	69	71	71	211	13,166
Pamela Wright	67	76	69	212	9,250
Kathy Postlewait	73	68	71	212	9,250
Dawn Coe	71	70	71	212	9,250
Pat Bradley	69	69	74	212	9,250
Beth Daniel	73	73	67	213	6,750
Rosie Jones	73	70	70	213	6,750
Elaine Crosby	72	70	71	213	6,750
Martha Nause	73	68	72	213	6,750
Colleen Walker	71	70	72	213	6,750
Gail Graham	70	71	72	213	6,750
Ellie Gibson	74	72	68	214	4,919
Michelle Estill	73	73	68	214	4,919
Kim Shipman	74	70	70	214	4,919
Nina Foust	71	71	72	214	4,919
Marta Figueras-Dotti	68	74	72	214	4,919
Alice Miller	71	70	73	214	4,919
Missie McGeorge	71	69	74	214	4,919
Peggy Kirsch	67	73	74	214	4,919
Dale Eggeling	73	66	75	214	4,919
Amy Benz	72	73	70	215	3,881
Deedee Lasker	72	71	72	215	3,881

	SCORES	TOTAL	MONEY
Patty Sheehan	71 72 72	215	3,881
Sherri Steinhauer	71 70 74	215	3,881

Stratton Mountain Classic

Stratton Mountain Country Club, Stratton Mountain, Vermont   August 8-11
Par 36-36—72; 6,217 yards   purse, $450,000

	SCORES	TOTAL	MONEY
Melissa McNamara	71 70 67 70	278	$67,500
Patty Sheehan	71 67 70 72	280	41,625
Elaine Crosby	71 71 72 68	282	24,375
Pat Bradley	69 72 70 71	282	24,375
Deb Richard	68 70 72 72	282	24,375
Missie Berteotti	71 73 69 70	283	15,750
Cindy Figg-Currier	71 72 71 70	284	13,275
Rosie Jones	68 72 72 73	285	11,700
Sally Little	73 75 69 69	286	10,575
Dawn Coe	76 72 70 70	288	9,000
Laura Baugh	68 76 72 72	288	9,000
Mitzi Edge	70 77 73 69	289	6,976
Barb Bunkowsky	71 74 73 71	289	6,976
Alice Miller	74 70 73 72	289	6,976
Nina Foust	74 71 71 73	289	6,976
Nancy Scranton	69 73 73 74	289	6,976
Pearl Sinn	76 73 73 68	290	5,401
Michelle McGann	75 74 71 70	290	5,401
Martha Nause	73 74 72 71	290	5,401
Kris Monaghan	75 67 74 74	290	5,401
Sue Thomas	71 70 74 75	290	5,401
Sherri Steinhauer	72 74 72 73	291	4,623
Cindy Mackey	72 74 69 76	291	4,623
Donna Andrews	74 75 73 70	292	4,162
Karen Davies	75 72 74 71	292	4,162
Laurie Rinker	73 73 73 73	292	4,162
Chris Johnson	75 69 75 73	292	4,162
Ok Hee Ku	73 75 74 71	293	3,690
Michelle Estill	72 73 74 74	293	3,690
Missie McGeorge	76 71 71 75	293	3,690

Northgate Computer Classic

Edinburgh USA Golf Course, Brooklyn Park, Minnesota   August 16-18
Par 36-36—72; 6,153 yards   purse, $400,000

	SCORES	TOTAL	MONEY
Cindy Rarick	75 68 68	211	$60,000
Beth Daniel	72 68 71	211	32,000
Jody Anschutz	68 70 73	211	32,000
(Rarick defeated Anschutz on first extra hole, Daniel on third.)			
Alice Ritzman	71 72 69	212	19,000
Cindy Schreyer	69 73 70	212	19,000
Jane Geddes	71 71 71	213	12,900
Terry-Jo Myers	70 70 73	213	12,900
Carolyn Hill	76 70 68	214	9,400

	SCORES			TOTAL	MONEY
Caroline Gowan	73	70	71	214	9,400
Kathy Postlewait	73	70	71	214	9,400
Dottie Mochrie	73	73	69	215	5,955
Nina Foust	74	71	70	215	5,955
Nicky LeRoux	70	75	70	215	5,955
Pearl Sinn	73	71	71	215	5,955
Jan Stephenson	72	71	72	215	5,955
Missie McGeorge	71	71	73	215	5,955
Colleen Walker	70	72	73	215	5,955
Tina Barrett	68	74	73	215	5,955
Deedee Lasker	69	72	74	215	5,955
Joan Delk	75	72	69	216	4,600
Mitzi Edge	76	73	68	217	3,663
Myra Blackwelder	74	73	70	217	3,663
Kim Shipman	73	74	70	217	3,663
Sally Little	76	70	71	217	3,663
Kris Monaghan	71	75	71	217	3,663
Joan Pitcock	77	68	72	217	3,663
Robin Walton	75	70	72	217	3,663
Jenny Lidback	72	73	72	217	3,663
Page Dunlap	71	72	74	217	3,663
Gina Hull	72	70	75	217	3,663
Brandie Burton	67	72	78	217	3,663

Chicago Sun-Times Shoot-Out

Oak Brook Golf Club, Oak Brook, Illinois
Par 36-36—72; 6,231 yards

August 22-25
purse, $425,000

	SCORES				TOTAL	MONEY
Martha Nause	68	73	69	65	275	$63,750
Kris Monaghan	69	71	65	71	276	39,312
Tina Barrett	72	67	69	71	279	28,687
Elaine Crosby	69	72	72	67	280	20,187
Michelle Estill	69	71	70	70	280	20,187
Pat Bradley	75	71	68	67	281	13,706
Donna White	69	70	70	72	281	13,706
Patty Sheehan	71	76	69	66	282	9,987
Nancy Scranton	71	66	75	70	282	9,987
Colleen Walker	71	73	66	72	282	9,987
Kay Cockerill	71	74	70	68	283	6,843
Tani Tatum	74	70	70	69	283	6,843
Margaret Ward	70	72	72	69	283	6,843
Debbie Massey	70	69	74	70	283	6,843
Dottie Mochrie	73	71	68	71	283	6,843
Dawn Coe	73	69	69	72	283	6,843
Diana Heinicke-Rauch	75	72	70	67	284	5,001
Meg Mallon	70	73	73	68	284	5,001
Michelle Mackall	70	72	74	68	284	5,001
Anne-Marie Palli	70	73	71	70	284	5,001
Cindy Rarick	70	72	70	72	284	5,001
Liselotte Neumann	72	66	72	74	284	5,001
Janice Gibson	77	67	72	69	285	4,071
Deedee Lasker	71	71	74	69	285	4,071
Juli Inkster	71	71	72	71	285	4,071
Kate Rogerson	71	70	73	71	285	4,071
Vicki Fergon	73	68	77	68	286	3,431

	SCORES			TOTAL	MONEY
Alice Miller	75	72	70	69	286	3,431
Kathy Guadagnino	75	72	69	70	286	3,431
Marta Figueras-Dotti	72	72	71	71	286	3,431
Mitzi Edge	68	72	74	72	286	3,431
Danielle Ammaccapane	69	72	71	74	286	3,431

Rail Charity Classic

Rail Golf Club, Springfield, Illinois
Par 36-36—72; 6,403 yards

August 31-September 2
purse, $400,000

	SCORES			TOTAL	MONEY
Pat Bradley	67	65	65	197	$60,000
Danielle Ammaccapane	69	68	66	203	37,000
Meg Mallon	68	69	67	204	24,000
Laura Davies	62	70	72	204	24,000
Alice Miller	71	70	64	205	15,500
Dottie Mochrie	68	68	69	205	15,500
Michelle Mackall	68	69	69	206	11,800
Alice Ritzman	69	68	70	207	9,900
Laurel Kean	68	69	70	207	9,900
Barb Bunkowsky	72	68	68	208	8,400
Nina Foust	71	68	70	209	6,864
Ellie Gibson	69	70	70	209	6,864
Kim Shipman	68	71	70	209	6,864
Sherri Steinhauer	68	71	70	209	6,864
Dale Eggeling	72	72	66	210	5,147
Sandra Spuzich	71	71	68	210	5,147
Judy Dickinson	72	69	69	210	5,147
Brandie Burton	71	69	70	210	5,147
Kristi Albers	72	67	71	210	5,147
Kate Rogerson	71	68	71	210	5,147
Beth Daniel	74	70	67	211	3,865
Linda Hunt	70	74	67	211	3,865
Janet Anderson	72	70	69	211	3,865
Deedee Lasker	71	71	69	211	3,865
Susie McAllister	70	72	69	211	3,865
Vicki Fergon	69	73	69	211	3,865
Mitzi Edge	69	71	71	211	3,865
Page Dunlap	70	66	75	211	3,865
Nancy White	70	72	70	212	3,118
Joan Pitcock	72	68	72	212	3,118
Cindy Scholefield	69	71	72	212	3,118
Kathy Postlewait	70	69	73	212	3,118

Ping-Cellular One Championship

Columbia Edgewater Country Club, Portland, Oregon
Par 36-36—72; 6,261 yards

September 6-8
purse, $400,000

	SCORES			TOTAL	MONEY
Michelle Estill	69	69	70	208	$60,000
Rosie Jones	70	73	66	209	37,000
Marta Figueras-Dotti	69	73	68	210	21,666
Jennifer Wyatt	71	69	70	210	21,666

	SCORES			TOTAL	MONEY
Missie Berteotti	68	72	70	210	21,666
Pat Bradley	74	69	68	211	11,400
Meg Mallon	72	71	68	211	11,400
Karen Davies	69	70	72	211	11,400
Danielle Ammaccapane	68	71	72	211	11,400
Deb Richard	72	72	68	212	6,933
Nancy Scranton	72	71	69	212	6,933
Janet Anderson	70	73	69	212	6,933
Vicki Fergon	68	75	69	212	6,933
Sherri Steinhauer	71	70	71	212	6,933
Maggie Will	70	71	71	212	6,933
Laura Davies	74	72	67	213	4,900
Kristi Albers	76	68	69	213	4,900
Kris Monaghan	72	70	71	213	4,900
Beth Daniel	72	70	71	213	4,900
Tammie Green	70	71	72	213	4,900
Deedee Lasker	69	72	72	213	4,900
Caroline Pierce	75	70	69	214	3,965
Brandie Burton	73	71	70	214	3,965
Melissa McNamara	72	71	71	214	3,965
Kris Tschetter	69	70	75	214	3,965
Jane Geddes	73	73	69	215	3,460
Sally Little	72	73	70	215	3,460
Cindy Figg-Currier	76	67	72	215	3,460
Judy Dickinson	71	71	73	215	3,460
Kay Cockerill	74	74	68	216	2,893
Juli Inkster	74	71	71	216	2,893
Caroline Keggi	75	68	73	216	2,893
Laurel Kean	69	74	73	216	2,893
Nina Foust	73	69	74	216	2,893
Alice Miller	72	68	76	216	2,893

Du Maurier Ltd. Classic

Vancouver Golf Club, Coquitlam, British Columbia, Canada
Par 37-35—72; 6,421 yards

September 12-15
purse, $700,000

	SCORES				TOTAL	MONEY
Nancy Scranton	72	75	64	68	279	$105,000
Debbie Massey	67	70	72	73	282	64,750
Laura Davies	71	71	71	71	284	37,916
Trish Johnson	67	71	73	73	284	37,916
Pamela Wright	72	69	69	74	284	37,916
Dawn Coe	68	77	71	70	286	17,966
Vicki Fergon	72	72	72	70	286	17,966
Caroline Pierce	70	73	71	72	286	17,966
Betsy King	71	71	72	72	286	17,966
Dottie Mochrie	69	69	74	74	286	17,966
Rosie Jones	71	71	69	75	286	17,966
Deb Richard	72	71	74	70	287	11,550
Kristi Albers	69	74	73	71	287	11,550
Brandie Burton	71	71	72	73	287	11,550
Joan Pitcock	75	74	68	71	288	9,362
Marta Figueras-Dotti	71	74	72	71	288	9,362
Jane Geddes	69	77	70	72	288	9,362
Karen Davies	74	70	71	73	288	9,362
Stephanie Maynor	74	73	73	69	289	7,875

	SCORES				TOTAL	MONEY
Liselotte Neumann	72	72	75	70	289	7,875
Ellie Gibson	73	73	71	72	289	7,875
Deedee Lasker	74	70	70	75	289	7,875
Pat Bradley	76	72	72	70	290	6,587
Meg Mallon	71	73	75	71	290	6,587
Kate Rogerson	72	76	70	72	290	6,587
Tammie Green	75	72	71	72	290	6,587
Cindy Figg-Currier	70	73	73	74	290	6,587
Kathy Postlewait	69	76	78	68	291	5,537
Janet Anderson	74	73	72	72	291	5,537
Amy Benz	72	75	72	72	291	5,537
Sally Little	73	76	69	73	291	5,537
Hiromi Kobayashi	71	75	72	73	291	5,537

Safeco Classic

Meridian Valley Country Club, Kent, Washington
Par 36-36—72; 6,222 yards

September 19-22
purse, $400,000

	SCORES				TOTAL	MONEY
Pat Bradley	69	67	72	72	280	$60,000
Rosie Jones	68	72	71	69	280	37,000
(Bradley defeated Jones on second extra hole.)						
Danielle Ammaccapane	70	72	72	68	282	27,000
Brandie Burton	65	76	71	71	283	17,333
Dottie Mochrie	73	67	72	71	283	17,333
Mitzi Edge	68	69	73	73	283	17,333
Juli Inkster	74	71	73	66	284	10,000
Deedee Lasker	70	69	72	73	284	10,000
Kris Monaghan	72	71	67	74	284	10,000
Judy Dickinson	73	68	68	75	284	10,000
Marta Figueras-Dotti	70	73	73	69	285	7,300
Cindy Mackey	70	74	71	70	285	7,300
Nancy Scranton	75	70	71	70	286	6,400
Jody Anschutz	69	71	74	72	286	6,400
Laurie Rinker	72	71	75	69	287	5,800
Cindy Figg-Currier	70	72	74	72	288	5,400
Vicki Fergon	71	75	73	70	289	4,428
Pearl Sinn	74	72	72	71	289	4,428
Barb Mucha	71	74	72	72	289	4,428
Patty Sheehan	75	69	73	72	289	4,428
Donna White	74	70	73	72	289	4,428
Michelle McGann	75	68	74	72	289	4,428
Missie Berteotti	74	68	74	73	289	4,428
Anne-Marie Palli	71	73	71	74	289	4,428
Jane Crafter	75	67	73	74	289	4,428
Robin Hood	73	71	72	74	290	3,580
Michelle Estill	71	75	67	77	290	3,580
Colleen Walker	72	75	74	70	291	3,057
Myra Blackwelder	72	71	77	71	291	3,057
Kate Hughes	74	73	72	72	291	3,057
Tammie Green	71	74	73	73	291	3,057
Kate Rogerson	70	73	75	73	291	3,057
Deb Richard	71	74	72	74	291	3,057
Mary Murphy	72	71	72	76	291	3,057

MBS Classic

Los Coyotes Country Club, Buena Park, California
Par 36-36—72; 6,351 yards

September 26-29
purse, $350,000

	SCORES				TOTAL	MONEY
Pat Bradley	72	70	67	68	277	$52,500
Michelle Estill	71	70	71	66	278	32,375
Dottie Mochrie	68	73	69	70	280	23,625
Amy Alcott	71	72	68	70	281	12,985
Donna Andrews	69	70	71	71	281	12,985
Brandie Burton	71	70	68	72	281	12,985
Judy Dickinson	70	70	68	73	281	12,985
Meg Mallon	69	71	68	73	281	12,985
Dana Lofland	73	72	69	68	282	8,225
Betsy King	69	70	73	71	283	7,350
Sherri Steinhauer	72	72	71	69	284	5,654
Juli Inkster	71	73	71	69	284	5,654
Joan Pitcock	75	70	68	71	284	5,654
Robin Walton	73	71	67	73	284	5,654
Tina Barrett	70	69	71	74	284	5,654
Lisa Walters	71	65	71	77	284	5,654
Nancy Scranton	68	73	72	72	285	4,575
Anne-Marie Palli	71	72	73	70	286	4,137
Debbie Massey	72	73	70	71	286	4,137
Nancy Harvey	72	72	70	72	286	4,137
Danielle Ammaccapane	73	70	71	72	286	4,137
Karen Davies	74	70	74	69	287	3,382
Vicki Fergon	74	73	68	72	287	3,382
Alice Ritzman	74	72	69	72	287	3,382
Deedee Lasker	68	71	74	74	287	3,382
Elaine Crosby	71	70	71	75	287	3,382
Tracy Kerdyk	70	71	71	75	287	3,382
Cindy Rarick	70	71	72	75	288	3,000
Hollis Stacy	69	71	79	70	289	2,382
Jerilyn Britz	71	69	78	71	289	2,382
Jane Crafter	73	73	71	72	289	2,382
Colleen Walker	69	71	77	72	289	2,382
Caroline Pierce	72	74	70	73	289	2,382
Dawn Coe	72	73	71	73	289	2,382
Michelle Mackall	72	73	71	73	289	2,382
Lynn Adams	75	69	72	73	289	2,382
Kay Cockerill	68	74	74	73	289	2,382
Diana Heinicke-Rauch	77	68	70	74	289	2,382
Jan Stephenson	71	71	73	74	289	2,382
Dale Eggeling	71	73	70	75	289	2,382

Daikyo World Championship

Paradise Palms Golf Course, Cairns, Australia
Par 37-36—73; 6,358 yards

October 4-6
purse, $325,000

	SCORES			TOTAL	MONEY
Meg Mallon	73	72	71	216	$100,000
Dottie Mochrie	72	78	71	221	52,303.50
Juli Inkster	76	78	70	224	27,053.50
Danielle Ammaccapane	69	78	77	224	27,053.50
Jane Geddes	73	76	77	226	17,053.50

	SCORES			TOTAL	MONEY
Judy Dickinson	75	77	75	227	12,553.50
Ayako Okamoto	76	77	76	229	11,303.50
Corinne Dibnah	72	80	78	230	9,303.50
Tammie Green	73	78	79	230	9,303.50
Laura Davies	72	82	77	231	7,303.50
Deb Richard	78	77	78	233	6,803.50
Betsy King	81	77	76	234	6,053.50
Cathy Gerring	81	74	79	234	6,053.50
Caroline Keggi	79	77	79	235	5,303.50
Amy Alcott	81	82	79	242	4,803.50
*Akiko Fukushima	79	75	88	242	

Nichirei International

Tsukuba Country Club, Ina, Japan
Par 36-36—72; 6,268 yards

November 1-3
purse, $350,000

FINAL RESULT: United States 21-1/2, Japan 10-1/2.

FIRST ROUND
Better-Ball, Stroke Play

Deb Richard and Dottie Mochrie (US) defeated Ikue Ohta and Miyauki Shimabukuro, 68-73.
Ayako Okamoto and Tammie Green (US) defeated Aki Nakano and Kasumi Adachi, 68-70.
Colleen Walker and Sherri Steinhauer (US) defeated Fusako Nagata and Norimi Terasawa, 65-70.
Cindy Rarick and Elaine Crosby (US) defeated Ikuyo Shiotani and Junko Yasui, 70-71.
Laura Davies and Meg Mallon (US) defeated Miki Oda and Akane Ohshiro, 68-73.
Caroline Keggi and Kris Tschetter (US) defeated Aiko Takasu and Hiromi Takamura, 69-73.
Ai Yu Tu and Yueh Chyn Huang (Japan) defeated Jane Geddes and Barb Bunkowsky, 69-71.
Danielle Ammaccapane and Sally Little (US) defeated Yuko Moriguchi and Mayumi Hirase, 67-71.

United States leads, 7-1.

SECOND ROUND
Better-Ball, Stroke Play

Richard/Mochrie (US) defeated Takasu/Takamura, 67-72.
Okamoto/Green (US) and Oda/Hirase tied, 69-69.
Walker/Steinhauer (US) defeated Ohta/Shimabukuro, 66-68.
Rarick/Crosby (US) defeated Shiotani/Yasui, 64-69.
Davies/Mallon (US) defeated Adachi/Nakano, 65-68.
Terasawa/Nagata (Japan) defeated Keggi/Tschetter, 69-70.
Moriguchi/Ohshiro (Japan) defeated Geddes/Bunkowsky, 67-69.
Tu/Huang (Japan) defeated Ammaccapane/Little, 66-72.

United States leads, 11-1/2 - 4-1/2.

THIRD ROUND
Singles

Walker (US) defeated Takamura, 72-76.
Davies (US) and Ohta tied, 75-75.

Oda (US) defeated Bunkowsky, 74-77.
Mallon (US) defeated Shimabukuro, 71-77.
Green (US) defeated Nagata, 69-78.
Takasu (Japan) defeated Okamoto, 73-75.
Moriguchi (Japan) defeated Crosby, 73-79.
Hirase (Japan) defeated Little, 70-78.
Steinhauer (US) defeated Ohshiro, 75-79.
Tschetter (US) defeated Yasui, 73-76.
Huang (Japan) defeated Geddes, 76-82.
Ammaccapane (US) defeated Shiotani, 71-75.
Keggi (US) defeated Terasawa, 73-76.
Richard (US) defeated Nakano, 70-77.
Adachi (Japan) and Rarick tied, 72-72.
Mochrie (US) defeated Tu, 72-76.

(Each U.S. player received $14,000; each Japanese player $7,875.)

Mazda Japan Classic

Seta Golf Club, Shiga, Japan
Par 36-36—72; 6,524 yards

November 8-10
purse, $550,000

	SCORES			TOTAL	MONEY
Liselotte Neumann	70	72	69	211	$82,500
Caroline Keggi	73	70	70	213	44,000
Dottie Mochrie	71	71	71	213	44,000
Elaine Crosby	71	71	72	214	26,125
Meg Mallon	76	65	73	214	26,125
Tammie Green	74	70	71	215	16,591
Pat Bradley	73	69	73	215	16,591
Tatsuko Ohsako	70	71	74	215	16,591
Kaori Harada	74	70	72	216	11,651
Kris Monaghan	73	71	72	216	11,651
Brandie Burton	73	70	73	216	11,651
Cindy Rarick	73	74	70	217	9,104
Ayako Okamoto	73	73	71	217	9,104
Aki Nakano	72	70	75	217	9,104
Bie Shyun Huang	73	74	71	218	7,086
Danielle Ammaccapane	76	70	72	218	7,086
Ok He Ku	76	70	72	218	7,086
Laurel Kean	75	71	72	218	7,086
Vicki Fergon	74	71	73	218	7,086
Cindy Figg-Currier	72	72	74	218	7,086
Sherri Steinhauer	77	71	71	219	5,599
Missie Berteotti	75	73	71	219	5,599
Colleen Walker	70	78	71	219	5,599
Miki Oda	73	74	72	219	5,599
Mayumi Hirase	76	69	74	219	5,599
Kristi Albers	77	71	72	220	4,620
Dawn Coe	75	72	73	220	4,620
Nancy Scranton	74	72	74	220	4,620
Laura Davies	72	74	74	220	4,620
Amy Benz	75	70	75	220	4,620
Dana Lofland	72	73	75	220	4,620

JBP Cup Match Play Championship

Princeville Makai Golf Course, Princeville, Kauai, Hawaii
Par 36-36—72; 6,212 yards

December 12-15
purse, $500,000

FIRST ROUND

Kris Tschetter defeated Meg Mallon, 3 and 2
Elaine Crosby defeated Junko Yasui, 4 and 3
Martha Nause defeated Judy Dickinson, 4 and 3
Vicki Fergon defeated Tammie Green, 6 and 5
Betsy King defeated Sally Little, 1 up
Caroline Keggi defeated Sherri Steinhauer, 1 up
Rosie Jones defeated Chris Johnson, 2 and 1
Dawn Coe defeated Akio Takasu, 2 and 1
Deb Richard defeated Jennifer Sevil, 5 and 4
Laura Davies defeated Brandie Burton, 7 and 6
Kristi Albers defeated Amy Alcott, 2 up
Kasumi Adachi defeated Nancy Scranton, 5 and 4
Danielle Ammaccapane defeated Kris Monaghan, 2 and 1
Michelle Estill defeated Cindy Rarick, 3 and 1
Tina Barrett defeated Ikoyu Shiotani, 5 and 4
Juli Inkster defeated Barb Bunkowsky, 6 and 5

(Each losing player received $6,000.)

SECOND ROUND

Barrett defeated Inkster, 4 and 3
Estill defeated Ammaccapane, 3 and 1
Albers defeated Adachi, 3 and 1
Richard defeated Davies, 2 and 1
Coe defeated Jones, 2 and 1
King defeated Keggi, 4 and 3
Tschetter defeated Crosby, 4 and 3
Nause defeated Fergon, 1 up

(Each losing player received $8,500.)

THIRD ROUND

Richard defeated Albers, 3 and 2
Estill defeated Barrett, 4 and 3
King defeated Coe, 2 and 1
Tschetter defeated Nause, 1 up

(Each losing player received $17,500.)

SEMI-FINALS

Richard defeated Estill, 2 and 1
Tschetter defeated King, 3 and 1

PLAYOFF FOR THIRD-FOURTH PLACE

Estill defeated King, 3 and 2

(Estill received $56,000; King $41,000.)

FINAL

Richard defeated Tschetter, 2 and 1

(Richard received $100,000; Tschetter $70,000.)

Women's European Tour

Valextra Classic

Olgiata Golf Club, Rome, Italy
Par 35-37—72; 5,939 yards

April 18-21
purse, £80,000

	SCORES				TOTAL	MONEY
Laura Davies	71	71	70	69	281	£12,000
Tania Abitbol	71	76	70	68	285	8,120
Dale Reid	69	72	72	75	288	4,437.33
Corinne Soules	72	71	75	70	288	4,437.33
Catrin Nilsmark	70	74	75	69	288	4,437.33
Evelyn Orley	75	72	74	69	290	2,800
Corinne Dibnah	74	73	71	73	291	2,200
Li Wen-Lin	73	73	72	73	291	2,200
Regine Lautens	73	71	73	75	292	1,696
Helen Alfredsson	73	72	72	75	292	1,696
Anna Oxenstierna	73	70	76	74	293	1,344
Florence Descampe	73	71	74	75	293	1,344
Anne Marie Palli	77	72	71	73	293	1,344
Muffin Spencer-Devlin	73	72	75	73	293	1,344
Alison Nicholas	72	71	74	77	294	1,184
Sarah Nicklin	69	76	73	76	294	1,184
Maria Navarro Corbachio	74	75	73	73	295	1,120
Leslie A. Brown	75	72	77	71	295	1,120
Patricia Gonzalez	74	71	71	80	296	1,005.33
Sofia Gronberg	72	76	73	75	296	1,005.33
Susan Moon	70	75	70	81	296	1,005.33
Alicia Dibos	69	72	77	78	296	1,005.33
Jean Bartholomew	76	69	73	78	296	1,005.33
Lora Fairclough	72	74	74	76	296	1,005.33
Jane Connachan	78	72	74	73	297	884
Federica Dassu	74	71	74	78	297	884
Gillian Stewart	75	72	74	76	297	884
Lisa Hackney	71	75	73	78	297	884
Kitrina Douglas	72	79	71	76	298	788
Elisabeth Quelhas	72	78	76	72	298	788
Karyn Dallas	75	73	76	74	298	788
Julie Forbes	72	74	73	79	298	788

AGF Ladies Open de Paris

Racing Club de France, Paris, France
Par 36-36—72; 5,662 yards

April 25-28
purse, FF151,000

	SCORES				TOTAL	MONEY
Suzanne Strudwick	70	67	70	71	278	FF14,957.16
Laura Davies	69	71	70	71	281	7,727.20
Catherine Panton-Lewis	69	74	68	70	281	7,727.20
*Sandrine Mendiburu	69	73	73	67	282	
Alison Nicholas	69	73	73	68	283	5,483.63
Anna Oxenstierna	71	74	68	72	285	3,738.30
Corinne Soules	74	69	68	74	285	3,738.30
Gillian Stewart	68	71	74	72	285	3,738.30
Trish Johnson	68	70	72	76	286	2,367.88
Martha Nause	73	72	70	71	286	2,367.88
Tania Abitbol	68	75	72	72	287	1,838.77
Regine Lautens	74	69	72	72	287	1,838.77
Florence Descampe	76	72	70	69	287	1,838.77
Federica Dassu	75	72	68	73	288	1,495.21
Helen Alfredsson	69	72	71	76	288	1,495.21
Patricia Gonzalez	72	72	69	76	289	1,177.25
Sofia Gronberg	78	69	70	72	289	1,177.25
Jane Hill	72	75	72	70	289	1,177.25
Susan Moon	69	74	71	75	289	1,177.25
Muffin Spencer-Devlin	71	72	69	77	289	1,177.25
Jean Bartholomew	74	72	70	73	289	1,177.25
Joanne Furby	75	73	71	71	290	933.58
Maria Navarro Corbachio	71	71	74	74	290	933.58
Maureen Garner	73	74	70	74	291	865.73
Linda Percival	72	72	72	76	292	790.78
Anne Maria Palli	73	70	74	75	292	790.78
Evelyn Orley	73	72	71	76	292	790.78
Dale Reid	68	74	77	74	293	721.11
Xonia Wunsch-Ruiz	67	74	74	78	293	721.11
Kitrina Douglas	72	71	74	77	294	672.57
Sally Prosser	72	68	77	77	294	672.57

Ford Ladies' Classic

Woburn Golf and Country Club, Duchess Course, Woburn, England
Par 37-37—74; 6,079 yards

May 2-5
purse, £65,000

	SCORES				TOTAL	MONEY
Dale Reid	68	70	71	71	280	£9,750
Alison Nicholas	68	74	68	71	281	6,600
Janice Arnold	70	75	70	68	283	4,550
Stefania Croce	76	75	68	73	292	3,510
Alicia Dibos	74	72	73	74	293	2,756
Diane Barnard	76	73	74	71	294	1,950
Catherine Panton-Lewis	73	71	73	77	294	1,950
Florence Descampe	75	72	75	72	294	1,950
Federica Dassu	74	76	73	72	295	1,317.33
Li Wen-Lin	73	75	73	74	295	1,317.33
Helen Alfredsson	77	74	72	72	295	1,317.33
Rica Comstock	72	73	77	74	296	1,057
Corinne Soules	72	78	72	74	296	1,057
Jean Bartholomew	75	76	72	73	296	1,057

	SCORES				TOTAL	MONEY
Kitrina Douglas	75	74	76	72	297	936
Karen Lunn	72	75	77	73	297	936
Joanne Furby	72	72	76	77	297	936
Allison Shapcott	74	74	76	73	297	936
Corinne Dibnah	75	75	79	69	298	836.50
Barbara Helbig	71	72	78	77	298	836.50
Trish Johnson	71	79	79	69	298	836.50
Laurette Maritz-Atkins	71	73	77	77	298	836.50
Debbie Dowling	74	77	73	75	299	775
Sally Prosser	76	77	75	71	299	775
Peggy Conley	76	74	78	72	300	705
Gillian Stewart	80	71	72	77	300	705
Elisabeth Quelhas	74	74	75	77	300	705
Karyn Dallas	77	75	73	75	300	705
Liz Rogers	75	74	73	78	300	705
Claire Duffy	73	78	74	76	301	596.66
Regine Lautens	73	74	77	77	301	596.66
Janet Soulsby	75	77	77	72	301	596.66
Maria Navarro Corbachio	75	76	75	75	301	596.66
Helen Wadsworth	77	72	76	76	301	596.66
Evelyn Orley	72	78	76	75	301	596.66

BMW European Masters

Golf du Bercuit, Brussels, Belgium
Par 37-35—72; 6,002 yards

May 23-26
purse, £130,000

	SCORES				TOTAL	MONEY
Corinne Dibnah	70	71	71	72	284	£19,500
Florence Descampe	71	72	74	70	287	11,147.50
Catrin Nilsmark	69	73	74	71	287	11,147.50
Helen Alfredsson	72	71	72	74	289	7,020
Alison Nicholas	72	74	74	72	292	5,031
Julie Larsen	75	72	74	71	292	5,031
Janice Arnold	72	80	71	70	293	3,165.50
Rae Hast	71	73	73	76	293	3,165.50
Regine Lautens	73	77	71	72	293	3,165.50
Joanne Furby	75	72	73	73	293	3,165.50
Jane Hill	74	72	73	75	294	2,184
Dale Reid	76	74	75	69	294	2,184
Xonia Wunsch-Ruiz	76	74	71	73	294	2,184
Leslie A. Brown	73	72	76	73	294	2,184
Diane Barnard	79	74	71	71	295	1,898
Corinne Soules	74	78	70	73	295	1,898
Suzanne Strudwick	80	72	73	70	295	1,898
Laura Davies	76	72	73	75	296	1,742
Debbie Dowling	74	73	76	73	296	1,742
Shani Waugh	75	74	73	74	296	1,742
*Aline van der Haegen	78	76	73	69	296	
Claire Duffy	79	76	70	72	297	1,514.50
Patricia Gonzalez	74	76	74	73	297	1,514.50
Laurette Maritz-Atkins	77	72	74	74	297	1,514.50
Elisabeth Quelhas	77	78	73	69	297	1,514.50
Nicola Way	75	74	78	70	297	1,514.50
Stefania Croce	74	78	71	74	297	1,514.50
Jean Bartholomew	75	72	77	73	297	1,514.50
Helen Wadsworth	73	74	71	79	297	1,514.50

	SCORES				TOTAL	MONEY
Anna Oxenstierna	74	75	76	73	298	1,319.50
Helen Dobson	77	69	79	73	298	1,319.50

La Manga Classic

La Manga Golf Club, La Manga, Spain
Par 37-36—73; 6,065 yards

June 6-9
purse, £70,000

	SCORES				TOTAL	MONEY
Corinne Dibnah	72	77	69	68	286	£10,500
Laurette Maritz-Atkins	73	71	71	71	286	7,105
(Dibnah defeated Maritz-Atkins on first extra hole.)						
Dale Reid	73	72	73	70	288	4,900
Linda Percival	72	72	72	73	289	3,374
Florence Descampe	70	72	71	76	289	3,374
Catrin Nilsmark	74	71	75	70	290	2,450
Marie Laure de Lorenzi	74	78	69	70	291	1,704.50
Kitrina Douglas	68	75	76	72	291	1,704.50
Dennise Hutton	73	75	73	70	291	1,704.50
Kiernan Prechtl	67	74	79	71	291	1,704.50
Penny Grice-Whittaker	74	74	74	70	292	1,206.33
Alison Nicholas	71	79	70	72	292	1,206.33
Kristal Parker	70	74	75	73	292	1,206.33
Tania Abitbol	73	75	72	73	293	1,067.50
Susan Moon	69	73	76	75	293	1,067.50
Connie Baker	72	74	79	69	294	966
Maureen Garner	70	76	74	74	294	966
Karen Pearce	73	75	72	74	294	966
Helen Dobson	74	70	73	77	294	966
Helen Alfredsson	73	69	77	75	294	966
Julie Brown	79	71	75	70	295	847
Claire Duffy	73	78	72	72	295	847
Suzanne Strudwick	76	72	72	75	295	847
Judy Furst	70	80	73	72	295	847
Kim Saiki	70	76	76	73	295	847
Diane Barnard	69	78	75	74	296	763
Laura Davies	77	70	73	76	296	763
Allison Shapcott	74	72	72	78	296	763
Rica Comstock	71	73	81	72	297	605.50
Federica Dassu	72	78	70	77	297	605.50
Patricia Gonzalez	74	73	74	76	297	605.50
Sofia Gronberg	76	73	72	76	297	605.50
Jane Hill	71	77	75	74	297	605.50
Corinne Soules	71	79	70	77	297	605.50
Gillian Stewart	75	77	70	75	297	605.50
Alicia Dibos	73	76	75	73	297	605.50
Julie Larsen	73	75	72	77	297	605.50
Susan Elliott	71	74	76	76	297	605.50
Kimberly Kell	74	77	69	77	297	605.50
Jennny Germs	75	76	74	72	297	605.50

Hennessy Ladies' Cup

Golf und Landclub, Koln
Par 36-36—72; 5,913 yards

June 13-16
purse, £100,000

	SCORES				TOTAL	MONEY
Helen Alfredsson	70	71	71	68	280	£15,000
Marie Laure de Lorenzi	69	71	73	67	280	8,575
Corinne Dibnah	71	67	71	71	280	8,575

(Alfredsson defeated De Lorenzi on second, Dibnah on third extra hole.)

	SCORES				TOTAL	MONEY
Sharon Cranmer	70	74	75	67	286	4,820
Kiernan Prechtl	74	71	74	67	286	4,820
Laura Davies	70	72	77	68	287	2,648
Laurette Maritz-Atkins	74	74	69	70	287	2,648
Florence Descampe	70	77	68	72	287	2,648
Alicia Dibos	67	75	70	75	287	2,648
Amy Alcott	69	76	72	70	287	2,648
Kim Saiki	75	70	71	72	288	1,780
Helen Dobson	77	72	73	66	288	1,780
Patricia Gonzalez	70	75	72	72	289	1,553.33
Alison Nicholas	74	69	72	74	289	1,553.33
Gillian Stewart	71	76	71	71	289	1,553.33
Stefania Croce	72	69	75	74	290	1,440
Kristal Parker	74	70	75	71	290	1,440
Tania Abitbol	74	75	70	72	291	1,380
Janice Arnold	70	75	75	72	292	1,241.42
Federica Dassu	73	75	74	70	292	1,241.42
Alison Sheard	75	71	76	70	292	1,241.42
Suzanne Strudwick	73	74	74	71	292	1,241.42
Catrin Nilsmark	74	72	73	73	292	1,241.42
Julie Larsen	71	70	76	75	292	1,241.42
Leslie A. Brown	69	74	76	73	292	1,241.42
Beverley New	73	75	73	72	293	1,090
Corinne Soules	72	73	75	73	293	1,090
Li Wen-Lin	72	75	72	74	293	1,090
Allison Shapcott	73	74	74	73	294	1,000
Lora Fairclough	76	71	75	72	294	1,000
Helen Wadsworth	73	75	71	75	294	1,000

Trophee Coconut Skol

Golf de St. Germain, Paris, France
Par 35-37—72; 6,039 yards

June 20-23
purse, £100,000

	SCORES				TOTAL	MONEY
Helen Alfredsson	71	68	66	71	276	£15,000
Dale Reid	73	68	73	65	279	10,150
Kitrina Douglas	70	69	73	70	282	5,546.66
Alison Nicholas	70	69	73	70	282	5,546.66
Corinne Soules	72	71	70	69	282	5,546.66
Marie Laure de Lorenzi	71	70	69	75	285	3,250
Gillian Stewart	71	68	71	75	285	3,250
Federica Dassu	69	70	71	76	286	2,370
Maureen Garner	72	72	72	70	286	2,370
Janice Arnold	72	70	70	75	287	1,920
Corinne Dibnah	69	71	76	71	287	1,920
Jane Connachan	72	72	72	72	288	1,626.66
Alicia Dibos	70	76	70	72	288	1,626.66

	SCORES				TOTAL	MONEY
Kim Saiki	73	71	69	75	288	1,626.66
Ray Bell	73	74	71	71	289	1,460
Beverly Huke	76	72	72	69	289	1,460
Regine Lautens	70	72	74	73	289	1,460
Tania Abitbol	74	72	70	74	290	1,340
Diane Barnard	73	71	75	71	290	1,340
Helen Dobson	71	74	75	70	290	1,340
Catherine Panton-Lewis	75	70	74	72	291	1,240
Denise Baldwin	73	73	71	74	291	1,240
Kelly Crawford	74	74	71	72	291	1,240
Judy Furst	77	71	71	73	292	1,180
Elisabeth Quelhas	76	69	74	74	293	1,090
Jill Kinloch	77	73	74	69	293	1,090
Kiernan Prechtl	71	75	74	73	293	1,090
Karen Pearce	71	74	76	72	293	1,090
Julie Forbes	72	79	72	70	293	1,090
Beverley New	76	75	71	72	294	970
Maria Navarro Corbachio	71	76	73	74	294	970
Leigh Ann Mills	78	73	76	68	294	970

Bloor Homes Eastleigh Classic

Fleming Park Golf Club, Eastleigh, Herts, England
Par 31-34—65; 4,456 yards

July 4-7
purse, £70,000

	SCORES				TOTAL	MONEY
Dale Reid	63	64	64	58	249	£10,500
Diane Barnard	65	65	63	64	257	7,105
Claire Duffy	65	65	64	64	258	4,340
Li Wen-Lin	66	62	66	64	258	4,340
Xonia Wunsch-Ruiz	64	62	71	62	259	2,968
Tania Abitbol	66	68	59	67	260	1,759.33
Jane Connachan	58	70	65	67	260	1,759.33
Gillian Stewart	66	66	63	65	260	1,759.33
Suzanne Strudwick	65	67	64	64	260	1,759.33
Joanne Furby	68	66	63	63	260	1,759.33
Julie Forbes	66	65	62	67	260	1,759.33
Janice Arnold	69	64	65	63	261	1,064
Julie Brown	68	67	64	62	261	1,064
Rica Comstock	65	64	66	66	261	1,064
Corinne Dibnah	66	64	68	63	261	1,064
Regine Lautens	68	65	65	63	261	1,064
Alicia Dibos	67	69	64	61	261	1,064
Michelle Wooding	69	62	66	64	261	1,064
Kitrina Douglas	66	64	68	64	262	924
Corinne Soules	67	67	64	64	262	924
Debbie Dowling	63	67	66	67	263	878.50
Rae Hast	63	66	69	65	263	878.50
Nadene Hall	68	65	67	64	264	836.50
Helen Wadsworth	65	69	66	64	264	836.50
Maureen Garner	64	69	68	64	265	752.50
Tracy Hammond	68	63	67	67	265	752.50
Jennifer Lawrence	67	65	66	67	265	752.50
Beverley New	66	71	65	63	265	752.50
Helen Dobson	68	65	63	69	265	752.50
Lora Fairclough	67	69	68	61	265	752.50

Lufthansa Ladies' German Open

Worthsee Golf Club, Munich, Germany
Par 36-36—72; 6,180 yards

July 25-28
purse, £100,000

	SCORES				TOTAL	MONEY
Florence Descampe	66	71	71	64	272	£15,000
Liselotte Neumann	70	71	68	66	275	10,150
Mardi Lunn	70	66	70	70	276	6,200
Ayako Okamoto	67	74	70	65	276	6,200
Kelly Leadbetter	70	71	65	71	277	3,870
Dale Reid	68	69	68	72	277	3,870
Trish Johnson	69	71	68	70	278	3,000
Marie Laure de Lorenzi	69	75	69	66	279	2,370
Laurette Maritz-Atkins	69	69	73	68	279	2,370
Kitrina Douglas	71	70	66	73	280	1,853.33
Leigh Ann Mills	69	70	68	73	280	1,853.33
Li Wen-Lin	70	70	67	73	280	1,853.33
Karine Espinasse	70	73	68	71	282	1,508
Sofia Gronberg	72	73	69	68	282	1,508
Corinne Soules	69	73	69	71	282	1,508
Suzanne Strudwick	73	70	71	68	282	1,508
Jane Geddes	66	74	69	73	282	1,508
Diane Barnard	72	70	72	69	283	1,290
Karen Lunn	69	72	72	70	283	1,290
Alicia Dibos	71	72	70	70	283	1,290
Julie Larsen	73	72	69	69	283	1,290
Patti Rizzo	70	70	70	73	283	1,290
Helen Alfredsson	67	71	72	73	283	1,290
Muffin Spencer-Devlin	67	74	68	75	284	1,180
Alison Nicholas	73	73	71	68	285	1,120
Eva Dahllof	71	75	72	67	285	1,120
Kristal Parker	76	71	69	69	285	1,120
Tania Abitbol	72	70	71	73	286	985
Janice Arnold	70	69	73	74	286	985
Jane Hill	72	74	71	69	286	985
Sally Prosser	74	71	70	71	286	985
Kelly Crawford	71	71	71	73	286	985
Lisa Hackney	71	70	70	75	286	985

Weetabix Women's British Open

Woburn Golf and Country Club, Dukes Course, Woburn, England
Par 37-36—73; 6,224 yards

August 1-4
purse, £150,000

	SCORES				TOTAL	MONEY
Penny Grice-Whittaker	69	69	77	69	284	£25,000
Diane Barnard	73	72	71	71	287	13,250
Helen Alfredsson	73	69	76	69	287	13,250
Laura Davies	71	74	71	72	288	7,175
Stefania Croce	75	74	70	69	288	7,175
Helen Wadsworth	68	75	72	74	289	5,250
Marie Laure de Lorenzi	73	70	76	71	290	3,650
Trish Johnson	71	72	76	71	290	3,650
Kristal Parker	73	69	75	73	290	3,650
Evelyn Orley	75	71	72	72	290	3,650
Alison Nicholas	75	73	70	73	291	2,516.66
Kelley Markette	72	69	77	73	291	2,516.66

	SCORES				TOTAL	MONEY
Julie Forbes	74	73	71	73	291	2,516.66
Kitrina Douglas	73	75	71	73	292	2,280
Rica Comstock	71	75	76	71	293	2,120
Corinne Soules	74	77	72	70	293	2,120
Julie Larsen	77	72	72	72	293	2,120
Jan Stephenson	74	73	71	75	293	2,120
Suzanne Strudwick	69	75	74	76	294	1,970
Federica Dassu	73	70	75	77	295	1,887.50
Karen Pearce	76	70	74	75	295	1,887.50
Karine Espinasse	76	75	73	72	296	1,752.50
Patricia Gonzalez	73	79	72	72	296	1,752.50
Kim Gregg	71	75	74	76	296	1,752.50
*Akiko Fukushima	73	73	78	72	296	
Lora Fairclough	72	78	77	69	296	1,752.50
Debbie Dowling	72	78	76	71	297	1,572.50
Dennise Hutton	72	77	77	71	297	1,572.50
Beverley New	73	76	75	73	297	1,572.50
Sally Prosser	73	77	76	71	297	1,572.50

IBM Ladies Open

Haninge Golf Club, Stockholm, Sweden
Par 37-36—73; 6,058 yards

August 15-18
purse, £80,000

	SCORES				TOTAL	MONEY
Liselotte Neumann	69	70	69	74	282	£12,000
Marie Laure de Lorenzi	71	75	71	68	285	8,120
Laura Davies	73	73	71	69	286	5,600
Alison Nicholas	77	72	70	68	287	3,856
Helen Alfredsson	75	70	72	70	287	3,856
Corinne Dibnah	72	72	70	74	288	2,600
Lisa Hackney	70	70	73	75	288	2,600
Laurette Maritz-Atkins	72	75	70	74	291	1,797.33
Dale Reid	73	71	73	74	291	1,797.33
Catrin Nilsmark	72	75	73	71	291	1,797.33
Debbie Dowling	70	74	75	73	292	1,424
Karen Lunn	73	73	73	73	292	1,424
*Maria Bertiskold	73	73	73	73	292	
Alicia Dibos	74	75	71	73	293	1,288
Diane Barnard	75	74	71	74	294	1,137.14
Rica Comstock	70	77	71	76	294	1,137.14
Sofia Gronberg	74	74	75	71	294	1,137.14
Xonia Wunsch-Ruiz	72	74	75	73	294	1,137.14
Mardi Lunn	77	72	71	74	294	1,137.14
Helen Dobson	74	75	73	72	294	1,137.14
Lora Fairclough	75	73	77	69	294	1,137.14
Tania Abitbol	76	73	73	73	295	968
Trish Johnson	71	76	73	75	295	968
Corinne Soules	74	75	75	71	295	968
Nadene Hall	73	75	72	75	295	968
Frances Martin	71	76	71	77	295	968
Claire Duffy	75	75	72	75	297	872
Dennise Hutton	74	76	72	75	297	872
Suzanne Strudwick	75	75	71	76	297	872
Gillian Stewart	75	79	72	72	298	788
Tina Yarwood	74	78	77	69	298	788
Li Wen-Lin	72	75	78	73	298	788

		SCORES			TOTAL	MONEY
Sarah Nicklin	75	76	74	73	298	788
*Annika Sorenstam	74	77	75	72	298	

BMW Italian Ladies Open

Albarella Golf Club, Venice, Italy
Par 36-36—72; 6,012 yards

September 19-22
purse, £100,000

		SCORES			TOTAL	MONEY
Corinne Dibnah	71	65	69	67	272	£15,000
Florence Descampe	69	69	69	68	275	10,150
Marie Laure de Lorenzi	68	64	73	71	276	5,546.66
Mardi Lunn	70	68	68	70	276	5,546.66
Siobhan Keogh	69	68	67	72	276	5,546.66
Kitrina Douglas	73	69	65	70	277	3,250
Sandrine Mendiburu	75	64	72	66	277	3,250
Dale Reid	72	70	69	67	278	2,500
Karen Pearce	70	68	70	71	279	2,240
Tania Abitbol	68	71	68	73	280	1,637.50
Debbie Dowling	69	71	72	68	280	1,637.50
Sofia Gronberg	70	68	73	69	280	1,637.50
Laurette Maritz-Atkins	75	66	73	66	280	1,637.50
Alison Nicholas	69	71	70	70	280	1,637.50
Corinne Soules	70	69	70	71	280	1,637.50
Xonia Wunsch-Ruiz	72	71	70	67	280	1,637.50
Kelly Crawford	73	72	68	67	280	1,637.50
Laura Davies	71	70	68	72	281	1,340
Penny Grice-Whittaker	74	68	70	69	281	1,340
Evelyn Orley	69	71	70	71	281	1,340
Sally Prosser	72	69	71	70	282	1,270
Janice Arnold	72	70	70	71	283	1,210
Catherine Panton-Lewis	69	70	73	71	283	1,210
Alicia Dibos	70	72	70	71	283	1,210
Kelly Leadbetter	72	68	70	74	284	1,105
Catrin Nilsmark	72	70	70	72	284	1,105
Jill Kinloch	71	70	75	68	284	1,105
Allison Shapcott	69	74	70	71	284	1,105
*Anna Nistri	72	69	69	74	284	
Federica Dassu	75	72	68	70	285	1,015
Julie Forbes	71	75	70	69	285	1,015

English Open

The Tytherington Club, Cheshire, England
Par 36-36—72; 5,812 yards

September 26-29
purse, £75,000

		SCORES			TOTAL	MONEY
Kitrina Douglas	72	71	72	70	285	£11,250
Evelyn Orley	69	72	71	73	285	7,610
(Douglas defeated Orley on third extra hole.)						
Corinne Dibnah	70	71	78	70	289	4,650
Helen Alfredsson	76	69	72	72	289	4,650
Jane Hill	74	73	70	74	291	3,180
Suzanne Strudwick	76	71	73	72	292	2,437.50
Julie Forbes	71	74	69	78	292	2,437.50

	SCORES				TOTAL	MONEY
Stefania Croce	73	74	72	74	293	1,875
Laurette Maritz-Atkins	71	73	74	76	294	1,590
Catherine Panton-Lewis	73	73	74	74	294	1,590
Maureen Garner	75	72	74	74	295	1,232.80
Patricia Gonzalez	76	74	74	71	295	1,232.80
Sharon Cranmer	76	71	78	70	295	1,232.80
Eva Dahllof	75	69	76	75	295	1,232.80
Sandrine Mendiburu	73	74	74	74	295	1,232.80
Peggy Conley	77	74	71	74	296	1,050
Debbie Dowling	74	76	75	71	296	1,050
Catrin Nilsmark	80	69	73	74	296	1,050
Nadene Hall	76	71	75	74	296	1,050
Pamela Wright	72	74	77	74	297	963.50
Kristal Parker	77	73	75	72	297	963.50
Marie Laure de Lorenzi	73	73	77	75	298	894.50
Penny Grice-Whittaker	75	74	71	78	298	894.50
Anna Oxenstierna	77	71	73	77	298	894.50
Sally Prosser	74	72	76	76	298	894.50
Claire Duffy	75	72	75	77	299	802.50
Karine Espinasse	78	71	75	75	299	802.50
Regine Lautens	77	74	74	74	299	802.50
Joanne Furby	78	73	73	75	299	802.50
Susan Moon	72	75	77	77	301	722.33
Florence Descampe	77	75	71	78	301	722.33
Karen Pearce	78	75	71	77	301	722.33

Woolmark Ladies Match Play Championship

Crimate Golf Club, Milan, Italy
Par 36-36—72; 5,432 yards

October 17-20
purse, £80,000

SECOND ROUND

Federica Dassu defeated Corinne Dibnah, 4 and 3
Xonia Wunsch-Ruiz defeated Janice Arnold, 1 up
Patricia Gonzalez defeated Karine Espinasse, 1 up
Suzanne Strudwick defeated Julie Forbes, 2 and 1
Jenny Germs defeated Jill Kinloch, 1 up, 19 holes
Sofia Gronberg defeated Laurette Maritz-Atkins, 1 up, 19 holes
Trish Johnson defeated Alicia Dibos, 3 and 2
Helen Dobson defeated Lora Fairclough, 2 up
Maureen Garner defeated Maria Navarro, 1 up, 19 holes
Mardi Lunn defeated Anne Jones, 3 and 1
Claire Duffy defeated Catrin Nilsmark, 1 up, 21 holes
Patricia Wright defeated Kitrina Douglas, 2 and 1
Sarah Nicklin defeated Alison Sheard, 2 and 1
Kathryn Marshall defeated Li Wen-Lin, 1 up
Helen Wadsworth defeated Gillian Stewart, 1 up, 26 holes
Dale Reid defeated Kelly Leadbetter, 4 and 3

(Each losing player received £800.)

THIRD ROUND

Dassu defeated Wunsch-Ruiz, 2 and 1
Gonzalez defeated Strudwick, 1 up, 20 holes
Gronberg defeated Germs, 2 and 1
Johnson defeated Dobson, 3 and 2

Garner defeated Lunn, 4 and 3
Wright defeated Duffy, 3 and 1
Nicklin defeated Marshall, 2 and 1
Reid defeated Wadsworth, 7 and 6

(Each losing player received £1,300.)

QUARTER-FINALS

Dassu defeated Gonzalez, 5 and 4
Johnson defeated Gronberg, 2 and 1
Wright defeated Garner, 3 and 2
Reid defeated Nicklin, 1 up, 21 holes

(Each losing player received £2,600.)

SEMI-FINALS

Dassu defeated Johnson, 1 up
Reid defeated Wright, 1 up

(Johnson, Wright received £5,200.)

FINAL

Dassu defeated Reid, 5 and 4

(Dassu received £12,000, Reid £8,000.)

Longines Classic

Golf Club de Cannes Mandelieu
Par 35-36—71; 5,759 yards

October 24-27
purse, £110,000

	SCORES				TOTAL	MONEY
Penny Grice-Whittaker	71	63	71	72	277	£16,500
Laura Davies	68	66	69	75	278	9,412.50
Corinne Dibnah	72	71	66	69	278	9,412.50
Pamela Wright	73	71	68	68	280	5,302
Helen Wadsworth	69	71	69	71	280	5,302
Florence Descampe	69	69	72	71	281	3,850
Janice Arnold	73	72	65	72	282	3,300
Karine Espinasse	73	69	71	70	283	2,359.50
Anne Marie Palli	70	71	71	71	283	2,359.50
Pearl Sinn	73	70	70	70	283	2,359.50
Helen Alfredsson	73	71	70	69	283	2,359.50
Kitrina Douglas	73	69	68	74	284	1,754.50
Sofia Gronberg	74	70	70	70	284	1,754.50
Susan Moon	69	71	70	74	284	1,754.50
Corinne Soules	73	66	73	72	284	1,754.50
Trish Johnson	71	73	71	70	285	1,565.33
Helen Dobson	69	75	69	72	285	1,565.33
Sandrine Mendiburu	72	69	70	74	285	1,565.33
Debbie Dowling	74	71	69	72	286	1,433.66
Alison Nicholas	76	66	73	71	286	1,433.66
Muffin Spencer-Devlin	71	71	71	73	286	1,433.66
Rae Hast	76	69	74	68	287	1,331
Gillian Stewart	72	67	75	73	287	1,331
Stefania Croce	78	70	68	71	287	1,331

	SCORES				TOTAL	MONEY
Catherine Panton-Lewis	75	68	71	74	288	1,215.50
Jennifer Allmark	70	69	77	72	288	1,215.50
Veronique Palli	69	75	74	70	288	1,215.50
Lora Fairclough	73	72	75	68	288	1,215.50
Marie Laure de Lorenzi	70	75	74	70	289	1,034
Claire Duffy	71	76	71	71	289	1,034
Jane Hill	72	73	73	71	289	1,034
Regine Lautens	69	73	74	73	289	1,034
Kay Cornelius	72	70	73	74	289	1,034
Eva Dahllof	73	71	71	74	289	1,034
Lisa Hackney	73	72	70	74	289	1,034

Benson & Hedges Mixed Team Trophy

Las Brisas Golf Club, Marbella, Spain
Par 36-36—72

November 7-10
purse, £200,000

	SCORES				TOTAL	MONEY (Team)
Anders Forsbrand/Helen Alfredsson	73	66	68	68	275	£33,900
Malcolm Mackenzie/Penny Grice-Whittaker	70	70	68	69	277	22,075
Bryan Norton/Pearl Sinn	75	67	66	69	277	22,075
Per-Ulrik Johansson/Florence Descampe	69	71	71	67	278	15,000
Santiago Luna/Marie Carmen Navarro	69	73	70	67	279	11,700
Gordon Brand, Jr./Evelyn Orley	74	67	70	69	280	10,000
Phillip Price/Catrin Nilsmark	75	64	72	73	284	8,570
Jimmy Heggarty/Li Wen-Lin	71	77	69	68	285	6,960
Peter Mitchell/Helen Wadsworth	73	71	70	71	285	6,960
Manuel Pinero/Marta Figueras-Dotti	74	72	71	69	286	5,350
Andrew Sherborne/Kitrina Douglas	72	71	69	74	286	5,350
Derrick Cooper/Lorette Martitz-Adkins	71	73	76	67	287	4,505
Alberto Binaghi/Federica Dassu	76	72	66	73	287	4,505
Glenn Ralph/Corinne Dibnah	73	73	73	69	288	3,632.50
Carl Mason/Gillian Stewart	72	70	72	74	288	3,632.50
Roger Chapman/Diane Barnard	72	72	72	72	288	3,632.50
Keith Waters/Janice Arnold	75	72	66	75	288	3,632.50
David J. Russell/Suzanne Strudwick	74	71	74	70	289	2,890
Juan Quiros/Alicia Dibos	72	75	70	72	289	2,890
Peter Smith/Regine Lautens	77	73	71	69	290	2,503.33
Denis Durnian/Stefania Croce	77	69	72	72	290	2,503.33
Ross McFarlane/Mardi Lunn	66	72	75	77	290	2,503.33
Gordon J. Brand/Corinne Soules	76	73	69	73	291	2,270
*Diego Borrego/*Amaya Arruti	76	74	69	72	291	
Tony Charnley/Dale Reid	77	71	74	70	292	2,160
Jose Maria Canizares/Tania Abitbol	73	75	74	71	293	1,995
John Hawksworth/Marie Laure de Lorenzi	74	77	71	71	293	1,995
Mark Mouland/Alison Nicholas	81	74	69	71	295	1,780
Des Smyth/Maureen Garner	73	76	72	74	295	1,780
Brian Barnes/Jane Hill	74	77	73	73	297	1,650
David Jones/Cathy Panton-Lewis	80	73	72	73	298	1,600
Miguel Angel Jimenez/Xonia Wunsch-Ruiz	76	73	73	80	302	1,600